Osage Dictionary

Osage Dictionary

Carolyn Quintero

University of Oklahoma Press : Norman

Also by Carolyn Quintero

Osage Grammar (Lincoln, Nebr., 2004)

Library of Congress Cataloging-in-Publication Data

Qiuntero, Carolyn.
Osage dictionary / Carolyn Quintero.
p. cm.
Includes bibliographical references and index.
ISBN 978-0-8061-3844-2 (hardcover)
1. Osage language—Dictionaries—English. 2. English languge—Dictionaries—Osage. I. Title.
PM2081.Z5Q85 2010
497'.5254321—dc22

2009051459

The paper in this book meets the guidelines for permanence and durability of the Committee on Production Guidelines for Book Longevity of the Council on Library Resources, Inc. ∞

To Robert Bristow

Contents

Preface and Acknowledgments

In 1982, as a graduate student in linguistics at the University of Massachusetts, Amherst (UMA), I decided to look into the Osage language, spoken by the grandmothers of friends who grew up with me in Hominy, Oklahoma, in the 1950s and '60s. I knew nothing about Native American languages, but my training in linguistic research both in Venezuela and at UMA made me confident that such an exploration would be interesting, rewarding, and fun.

The Osages I spoke with about the language that summer of 1982 all mentioned a white man, Robert Bristow, who knew a lot about their language. Robert Bristow and I began interviewing Osage elders together in their homes, combining his sensitivities to protocol and my linguistic knowledge to explore crucial aspects of the language. When I returned to Amherst to continue work on Osage, Robert did follow-up interviewing. He expressed a wish that I publish his materials someday if I so chose.

When I first met Robert Bristow in 1982, after many Osages' recommendations, we spent hours discussing the language. Although not a linguist, he had a good understanding of Osage and a fascination with it, and that, coupled with my own interest, inspired us to work together. At that time, Robert had already been involved for many years in Osage traditional ceremonies, such as the annual *ilǫ́ǫška* ceremonial dances, and was an active member of the Native American Church. Most important, he was a natural language learner who had fond and strong relationships with many Osage elders in the last generation to speak the language. They admired his talent and willingness to assist, and he had for years been writing out words and sentences he heard from them and others while attending various Osage events and visiting in their homes.

Robert's practical skill in the language and my training in linguistics proved an excellent combination; we each complemented and respected the other's knowledge. We began gathering our own data. Ours was a close and rewarding relationship, and we continued it until his untimely death in 1988.

A few years later, after I had become active in my translation company, Inter Lingua, Inc., in Tulsa, Oklahoma, a call came concerning a two-year grant from the National Endowment for the Humanities, through David Rood at the University of Colorado. This grant allowed me in 1993–95 to begin compiling data for a grammar of the language. After years of analysis of the materials gathered, further supported for one more year in 2001–2002 by the NEH, I completed *Osage Grammar* (Quintero 2004).

Now, more than twenty years after Robert Bristow and I began working together, the fluent speakers who worked on this beautiful and complex language have passed on. Robert would have been thrilled to see this dictionary published, and I dedicate it to him. He had the interest, perseverance, and talent to gather a written record of a language that he could see would soon be gone. None of the speakers whose words and sentences Robert wrote down are with us today. Everyone who is interested in knowing more about Osage owes Robert Bristow a debt of gratitude for his careful work, which he generously shared with me and which served as the initial framework upon which this volume began. The only modern Osage dictionary that will ever be possible from a corpus gathered from the last generation of speakers came about in large part because of Robert Bristow. Thank you, Robert. We will always remember you.

Osage elder Frances Oberly Holding's dedication to the preservation of her tribal language is to be commended most especially. Mrs. Holding persisted in her efforts to remember her tribal language so that this record of it could be possible. Several other Osage speakers were involved, and grateful appreciation goes to all who are listed in the section on "Sources" below.

The National Endowment for the Humanities generously supported three and a half years (in 1993–95 and 2001–2002) of the twenty years or so of work that I have done on the Osage language. Nancy Pillsbury Shirley at the Pillsbury Foundation contributed significantly to this effort through a grant for a computer purchase and a generous subsidy that made publication of this book possible. Hominy Friends Meeting (an Osage Quaker church) was also supportive and helpful.

I would also like to thank attorney Robert Hart of Los Angeles (Northridge), California, for his assistance in sorting out copyright issues at the beginning of this endeavor. David Nagle was instrumental in raising funds for publication and in helping me obtain images of the Osage speakers. Mrs. Annette Oswald, Robert Bristow's mother, of Huntsville, Alabama, was lovingly supportive during all this time. Dorothy Manzer, a tribal member in Hominy, extended her gracious hospitality. Wallace Hooper at Indiana University was patient and helpful in dealing with software database problems for the years it took to organize this data after its conversion from Shoebox form. Siouan linguist Linda A. Cumberland shared helpful comments.

Special thanks go to eminent Siouanist Robert L. Rankin for his help in providing historical perspective on the phonology of Siouan languages, and especially for generously sharing his drafts of his Kaw and Quapaw lexicons, cited throughout, as well as consultation on other Siouan languages for comparison with Osage forms. Dr. Rankin's help as a consultant is deeply appreciated. Other contemporary Siouan linguists were helpful with data from related languages during the final stages of dictionary preparation, among them Ken Miner, whose Winnebago (Hochunk) Field Lexicon (1992) was useful for comparative purposes; Kathy Shea (Ponca language); Richard T. Carter (Lakota language); John Koontz (Omaha-Ponca language); Rory Larson (Omaha and Lakota languages); and Douglas R. Parks (Pawnee and Arikara languages).

Without the assistance of all those named above and below, the present dictionary would not exist, or would exist in a considerably less adequate form. Any remaining deficiencies or mistakes are my own.

Introduction

1. Sources for the Dictionary

1.1. Procedures

To collect the forms in this volume, I began by meeting with speakers and re-eliciting and retranscribing all of Robert Bristow's words and sentences, to the extent possible. In most cases, when speakers were willing, the sessions were recorded. In these interviews, a great deal more material was gathered, as speakers were stimulated by hearing the Bristow materials read to them by me, including many interesting and complex sentences. They corrected the pronunciation (and thus the orthography) and began to offer new sentences. Thus I was able to confirm or correct Osage forms, as well as to record certain phonological distinctions that had been overlooked in the Bristow materials. Robert's children, Robin L. Bristow and Michael T. Bristow, extended the legal right to use his original dictionary as a base for the dictionary work.

I organized all the re-elicited Bristow material and additional materials I gathered into a single database using Shoebox software, subsequently double-checking every form with a second speaker.

All of my analysis was done on my own recorded materials first, before consulting any historical sources such as La Flesche or Dorsey. This was in part due to challenges presented by the difficult nature of the historical sources for someone who did not yet know the language. The most important reason to delay work with the La Flesche and Dorsey materials was that Osage speakers were growing fewer each year, and their memories fading; thus the task of making as many audio recordings as possible as soon as possible was imperative. It seemed crucial to gather forms from actual speakers before resorting to historical records, which I had already determined were either faulty in some important ways (La Flesche) or quite difficult to decipher and of unknown (to me) reliability (Dorsey). Additionally, speakers were not inspired to work on word lists compiled from these two sources. Because all speakers were in fairly poor health and advanced in age, gathering of the data proceeded at a slow pace, the elders being at the time able or willing to work only an hour or so per day in most cases, and not every day of the week.

Despite dogged pursuit of forms, the dictionary was left with some large gaps, but still with a wealth of material gathered and double-checked. The majority of the entries were then enriched by direct excerpts from La Flesche's dictionary, which had to be updated and in some instances corrected. Some Dorsey materials were also added.

1.2. Speakers of Osage

The Osage speakers whom I interviewed (pictured on pages xlvii–lvi), and whenever possible recorded on audio tape, included the following (all residents of Oklahoma towns): Frances Oberly Holding (Hominy), Hazel Wahrisi Harper (Pawhuska), Mary Lookout Standing Bear (Pawhuska), Jo Ann Shunkamolah Alred (Hominy), Laura Shannon (Hominy), Myrtle Oberly Jones (Tulsa), Margaret Red Eagle Iron (Pawhuska), Preston Morrell (Hominy), Edward Red Eagle (Pawhuska), Leroy Logan (Hominy), and Gladys Shunkamolah Rouwalk (Hominy).

No Grayhorse district speakers were available to work on this volume.

Most sentences given as examples in dictionary entries are accompanied by an abbreviation indicating the speaker who is the source. Among those examples without a source identified, many are sentences that came from Bristow notebooks with no source noted. Others are sentences transferred directly from *Osage Grammar,* the publisher of which omitted the source identification due to considerations of text length. However, all the sentences are considered reliable, whether followed here by source information or not.

1.3. Other sources

After there were no longer fluent speakers available who could help clear up remaining doubts, I turned in the 1990s to the historical sources, such as Francis La Flesche's Osage dictionary (1932). In the La Flesche (LF) materials included here, I have in every instance added a modern transcription corresponding to La Flesche's own transcription, for readability's sake. I have also made many corrections, noted apparent errors, and offered contrasts with modern (late twentieth-century) forms, citing Modern Osage ("Mod. Os.") versions. Most of the LF entries offered here are complete, but some of his lengthier explanations are omitted.

Another valuable historical source is James Owen Dorsey's slip file and other manuscript material, transcribed into Modern Osage wherever it is cited. Dorsey's work is quite reliable in comparison with any other written records of Osage, including La Flesche. Aside from these two, no other reliable written source of Osage is available, because the orthography in other sources does not reflect the many distinctive Osage sounds. Even La Flesche and Bristow omitted several important distinctions; but after these omissions are corrected, both of these records are quite valuable and useful.

For detailed discussion of problems that arise in using La Flesche's and Dorsey's materials, see the section "Interpretation of Osage forms in older sources" below.

Contemporary community members and institutions who provided useful assistance from time to time include the following: Harry Red Eagle, Jr. (Hominy), Mongrain Lookout (Hominy), William Fletcher (Hominy), White Hair Memorial (Fairfax), Addie May Sells (Hominy), and David Nagle (Hominy). Thanks to all of them.

2. Organization of Dictionary Entries

The main component of this dictionary is the Osage-to-English section. A shorter English-to-Osage Index is also provided. The Index does not provide anything like full information about Osage words; rather, it merely lists the Osage words that are approximate equivalents of a given English word. Having found an Osage word in the Index, the reader should then always refer to the Osage-to-English entry, which provides full information about the word's meaning and grammatical properties, along with examples of its usage in sentences.

For each Osage word (or sometimes phrase) that heads an Osage-to-English entry (referred to below as the "headword" of the entry), the entry includes various kinds of information:

- Significant variants in pronunciation, if there are any, in parentheses after the headword. (See the section "Alphabet and pronunciation" for some of the processes responsible for such variation. That section also suggests alternate spellings under which a word may be looked for.) Occasionally it is noted that a variant seems to be attested for only a particular locality, speaker, or other source. (Variants also usually appear as brief separate entries, containing no definitions or grammatical information, but cross-referenced to the main entry. Entries for variants are omitted if they would be alphabetically adjacent to the main entry for the word.)
- The grammatical class of the word, as an abbreviation in small capitals (e.g., N 'noun', V 'verb', etc.; see the list of abbreviations). Some entries may have more than one grammatical class.
- Information about the inflection (conjugation) of the headword, in square brackets after the grammatical class. (Inflectional information is relevant primarily for verbs. For details about the types of inflection and the terms and abbreviations used to identify them, see the section on "Grammar" below, especially the subsection "Pronominal prefixes.")
- In many cases, derivational information is provided in another set of square brackets, indicating the components from which the word is formed.
- Verbs (and phrases based on verbs) are noted as transitive ("*(trans.)*") or intransitive ("*(intr.)*"), when it is clear which they are.
- Definitions. (See the section on "Grammar" below, especially the subsection on "Meaning and translations," for some of the complications involved here.) The source (speaker or written source) of a definition is sometimes noted when that definition appears not to be attested from other sources.
- In some cases, remarks on usage and other matters are added in square brackets after the definitions.
- Examples of use of the headword. Especially for verbs, examples are generally complete sentences (rather than infinitives, etc.), taken from Modern Osage sources; their English translations typically reproduce the English version offered by the original Osage speaker of the sentence. (When it seems helpful, a more literal translation is added in parentheses and noted as "lit.") Most examples are accompanied by abbreviations indicating their sources (including abbreviations for the speakers who produced them, and other information relating to fieldnote sources, in parentheses following the example translation; see the list of abbreviations) and

sometimes by other comments. Often rather large numbers of examples are provided. Although this policy has resulted in some lengthy entries, it seemed advisable given that not very much precisely transcribed Osage text material is available elsewhere for readers to consult.

In some entries, it seemed useful to separate definitions; in that case, examples follow the particular definition that they match best. When different definitions are associated with different grammatical classes or inflectional properties, grammatical class specifications and inflectional information accompany the definitions with which they are associated.

Some entries contain additional information as well:

- Information from earlier sources. Occasionally, a form from Robert Bristow's notes ("RB") is specially noted. More often, examples of the headword from historical sources are provided: from James Owen Dorsey's unpublished work ("JOD") or from Francis La Flesche's 1932 dictionary ("LFD"). These are presented in the source's original orthography (in angle brackets < >), accompanied by a modernized retranscription, translations provided in the source, and additional comments or corrections by myself (in square brackets [ ]) when these seem necessary. (See the section "Interpretation of Osage forms in older sources" below for full discussion of the problems that arise in dealing with these sources. Note, too, that the historical sources have not been completely sampled; thus, if no "LFD" forms are provided in a given entry, that does not mean that no relevant form may be found in La Flesche's dictionary. Definitions and translations have occasionally been lightly edited to remove idiosyncratic or old-fashioned punctuation and spellings; passages within quotation marks are verbatim quotes, however.)
- Comparative information. Sometimes related forms in other Siouan languages have seemed worth noting. Most often, these forms come from the closest relatives of Osage, the other Dhegiha languages—Omaha ("*OM*"), Ponca ("*PO*") (or both Omaha and Ponca, "*OP*"), Kansa or Kaw ("*KS*"), and Quapaw ("*QU*"). Occasionally they are drawn from further afield—Winnebago (Hochunk) ("*WI*") or Lakota ("*LAK*").
- Cross-references to other entries in the dictionary (these are marked by "Cf."). These include words or phrases grammatically related to the headword (and not mentioned elsewhere in the entry), as well as other words or phrases to which it seemed worth drawing attention for one reason or another.

3. Alphabet and Pronunciation

3.1. The alphabet

Osage has a number of sounds that are quite different from those found in English. Simply using the English alphabet would make it difficult to accurately represent the sounds of this beautiful language. Instead, this dictionary employs a version of the International Phonetic Alphabet (IPA) that has been adapted and widely used for Siouan languages. Osage language learners who accomplish the simple feat of learning the few special symbols in this alphabet will also find that much information from related languages becomes more accessible, and this in the long term can potentially add to the linguistic patrimony of Osage itself.

The alphabetical order of the symbols used is:

a ą b c cˀ č ð e ɣ h i į k kˀ l m n o ǫ p pˀ r s š t u w x y z ž ˀ

Certain sounds written with sequences of letters—in particular the long vowels *aa, ąą, ee*, etc., and the preaspirated stops *hc, hk, hp, ht*—can reasonably be regarded as units (see discussion below), but are alphabetized as sequences of letters; thus, *ee* follows *eð* and precedes *eɣ*, *hk* follows *hį* and precedes *ho*, and so on. Occasional occurrences of *ü* (see the discussion of vowels below) are alphabetized with *u*.

Pronunciation of the Osage symbols is explained below.

3.2. Vowels

3.2.1 Basic vowels

There are five plain vowels in Osage:

a	(open back vowel)	like English a in *father*
e	(half-open front vowel)	like English e in *pet*
i	(high front vowel)	like English i in *ski*
o	(mid-back rounded vowel)	like English o in *hotel*
u	(high nonback rounded vowel)	like English u in *tuba*

The vowel *u* is often pronounced as *ü* (a very front rounded vowel, like the German vowel *ü*), especially following *k*; sometimes it is even heard as *i*. Many forms are correct with either *u* or *i* (the same variation is found between the long vowels *uu* and *ii*). The common instrumental prefix *ðu-* ~ *ði-* ~ *ðuu-* ~ *ðii-* 'by hand; cause' is one prominent place where such variation is seen; it is often hard to decide whether to take the form with *u* as basic and the form with *i* as a variant or vice versa.

In fast speech, *e*, especially when in final position, often becomes *i*. For example, *nįkšé aape* is sometimes heard as *nįkší aape*.

3.2.2. Nasalized vowels

Osage also has three nasalized vowels (vowels during which air is allowed to flow out through the nose as well as the mouth); these are not closely equivalent to English sounds:

ą	(nasalized open back vowel)	similar to English o in *pond* (or French *an* in *langue*)
į	(nasalized high front vowel)	similar to English i in *marine*
ǫ	(nasalized rounded back vowel)	similar to English *cone* (or French *on* in *oncle*)

In certain words, such as *hą́hka* 'bald eagle', *ą* (or accented *ą́*) is given a more relaxed pronunciation [ə̨, ə̨́] (that is, similar to the vowel of English *hunh?* or *hunk*), but in every such case, the less relaxed pronunciation [ą, ą́] is also recognized as correct.

There is a great deal of fluctuation between nasalized *ą* and nasalized *ǫ*. It is also fairly common for nasalized vowels to be pronounced as ordinary nonnasalized vowels—*ą* as *a*, *ǫ* as *o*, *į* as *i*. Nonnasalized vowels may be heard as nasalized, too. (Thus, if one has difficulty locating a word in the dictionary that apparently contains *į*, one should check under *i*, and vice versa; if one has difficulty finding a word that apparently contains *ą*, one should check under *a* and *ǫ* as well, and vice versa; and if one has difficulty finding a word that apparently contains *ǫ*, one should check under *o* and *ą*, and vice versa.)

Each nasalized vowel is alphabetized immediately after the corresponding non-nasalized vowel.

3.2.3. Long vowels

Long vowels have a more prolonged pronunciation and are indicated by doubling the vowel letter: *aa, ąą, ee, ii, įį, oo, ǫǫ, uu*. When long vowels are accented, the accent is normally placed on the first vowel letter: *áa, ą́ą*, etc. (No rearticulation of the vowel is implied by this representation. Another way in which linguists commonly represent vowel length is to use a colon after the vowel—e.g., *ą:* instead of *ąą*. The representation of length by a doubled vowel has been chosen here because it is slightly easier to read, especially on computer screens.)

Although vowel length is certainly significant in Osage, it nonetheless can be tricky to perceive and is subject to a good deal of variation (at least to the linguist's ear). For example, it is quite common for long vowels to be reduced to short ones when they are not accented (see below for "Accent"; shortening of unaccented vowels happens also in Winnebago [Hochunk], the one language within Siouan where vowel length is most clearly and consistently transcribed). In cases of this kind of variation, I have generally continued to represent the vowel as long, since I take this to be the basic or underlying form.

Lengthening of otherwise short vowels often occurs in questions. This is especially frequent with *škǫ́šta* 'you want', which becomes *škǫ́ǫšta?* in the question form (with especially high pitch on the first part of *ǫ́ǫ* and falling pitch on the second half of *ǫ́ǫ*). Another way in which long vowels can arise is when *ð* is omitted between identical vowels (as it often optionally is). For example, *ðáalį škáaɣee* 'you've done well, you made that well' arises from *ðáalį škáaɣe ðe*, where *škáaɣe* is 'you make, you made' and *ðe* is the declarative sentence-final ending; the *ð* of *ðe* is often omitted after a vowel, and *e+e* results in a long vowel *ee*. Similarly, *ðakˀéwaða* 'be kind to them' may omit its second *ð*, becoming *ðakˀéwaa*.

Many monosyllabic nouns and verbs have long vowels, but not all do. More complete instrumental measurements are needed to determine the exact properties of long and short vowels and to track their occurrence, which will greatly contribute to specifying exactly how the accent system works in Osage.

Since a good deal of variation and uncertainty surrounds Osage vowel length, if one looks up an Osage form with a short vowel (*a, ą, e*, etc.) and fails to find it in the dictionary, it is worth checking whether the word appears with the corresponding long vowel (*aa, ąą, ee,* etc.), and vice versa.

3.3. Consonants

The inventory of Osage consonants is represented in table 1. Comments on their pronunciation and other matters follow.

Occasionally, other letters appear in non-Osage words cited at various points in dictionary entries; the most important such letter is *ǰ*, pronounced like English *j* in *judge*.

3.4. Alternations between sounds

Osage sounds undergo changes in various circumstances and contexts. This is too large a topic to cover in full here (see chapter 2 of *Osage Grammar* [Quintero 2004]), but a few types of change frequently seen in dictionary entries and examples are mentioned.

(1) An *e* or *ee* at the end of a verb is replaced by *a* or *aa* when the verb is followed by certain postverbal elements that begin with *a*. Such elements include the negative marker *aží* 'not', the imperative marker *a*, and the plural or completive marker *api* (which often contracts with a following declarative marker *ðe*, resulting in *ape*):

ðaaché 'eat'
ðaacháži 'don't eat, didn't eat' (negative)
ðaachá 'eat it!' (imperative)
ðaachápe 'they ate' (plural or completive, including declarative *ðe*)

pšé 'pound'
pšáži 'not pound it' (negative)
pšá 'pound it!' (imperative)
pšápe 'they pounded it' (plural, including declarative *ðe*)

After vowels other than *e(e)*, the *a* of these postverbal elements is typically lost:

waaðǫ́ 'sing'
waaðǫ́ži 'not sing' (negative) (sometimes also *waaðǫ́ǫzi*)
waaðǫ́ 'sing!' (imperative)
waaðǫ́pe 'they sang' (plural or completive, including declarative *ðe*)

Note that other postverbal elements beginning with *a* (e.g., *aha* 'whenever', *aape* 'reportative', and the 3rd person continuative markers *akxa* and *apa*) or *ą* (many 1st person dual or plural continuative markers) do not cause a preceding *e* or *ee* to be replaced by *a* or *aa*.

ąkóðuuxpaðe ąkatxái 'we're going to take it out'
mą́zeíe ohkíe áha ohkíhkie akxái 'they talked by phone whenever he called'
ǫkóðihkiepi áha ðakʔéwaðakie hta nįkšé áape 'they said you would pity us whenever we talk to you'

(2) When *e(e)* changes to *a(a)*, an immediately preceding *c* is (often, though not always) replaced by *t*:

TABLE 1. Consonants

Labial	Dental	Palato-alveolar	Velar	Glottal	
Glottalized stops	*pʔ*	*cʔ*		*kʔ*	(*ʔ*)
Lax voiceless stops	*p*	*t*	*č*	*k*	
	c				
Preaspirated/tense	*hp*	*ht*	*hč*	*hk*	
voiceless stops		*hc*			
Voiced stop	*b* (only in *br*)				
(Post)aspirated stops	*pš, px*	*ch, tx*		*kš, kx*	
Voiceless/tense fricatives		*s*	*š*	*x*	*h*
Voiced/lax fricatives		*z*	*ž*	*γ*	
Nasals	*m*	*n*			
Approximants	*w*	*l, ð, r* (only in *br*)			

ð: The most ubiquitous consonant in Osage is probably the one represented by the letter *ð* ("eth," alphabetized just before e). This is the sound of English *th* in *thee* or *though* (these words would be written simply as *ði* and *ðo* in Osage). A common sort of variation in Osage is for *ð* to be omitted between vowels.

c, č: The dental affricate *c* is pronounced like English *ts* in *hats* (and is written as *ts* in older Osage orthographies). The much rarer palato-alveolar affricate *č* is pronounced like English *ch* in *church.* See below for the substitution of *t* for *c* when the following vowel changes from *e* to *a.*

š, ž: The voiceless palato-alveolar fricative *š* is pronounced like English *sh* in *shut* (and is so written in some older Osage orthographies). Its voiced counterpart *ž* is pronounced like English *s* in *measure* (it is written as *zh* in some older Osage orthographies).

s, z: While these typically sound much like English *s* as in *saw* and *z* as in *zoo*, respectively, the difference between them was probably originally one of tenseness rather than voicing—*s* was tense, and *z* was lax. (Even in the 1980s and 1990s, Osage *s* and *š* occasionally sounded quite strident in comparison with English *s* and *sh*.)

γ: The voiced or lax velar fricative *γ* ("gamma," alphabetized just before *h*) has no equivalent in English. It sounds a bit like the English *g* in *go*, but without full closure.

x: The voiceless velar fricative *x* has approximately the sound of German *ch* in *Bach.* It is harsher or more turbulent than its voiced counterpart *γ*. The difference is or was probably more one of laxness and tenseness than of voicing; *γ* and *x* are often difficult to distinguish from each other auditorily, and as the language has declined, speakers do not always clearly differentiate the two. For example, *xúða* 'eagle' is sometimes heard as less tense *γúða* but without much voicing of the *γ*, if any; it may even be heard as *húða.* An underlying *γ* in some words may also soften almost to *h*; for example, *kåaγe* 'make' occasionally approaches *kåahe* in fast speech, though this pronunciation is not approved by speakers when it is drawn to their attention.

l: This is much like English *l.* In a few words, older variant pronunciations *hl* or *dl* can be heard; e.g., *áli̧i̧* 'sit upon' is sometimes heard as *ádli̧i̧.*

pʔ, cʔ, kʔ: The glottalized consonants have no equivalent in English. They are probably best learned by listening to an Osage speaker, but they can be roughly characterized as sounding like *p*, *c* (*c* = English *ts*), or *k*, respectively, followed immediately by a catch in the throat (like the catch that occurs between the syllables of English *uh-oh!*).

ʔ: The glottal stop *ʔ* is quite rare on its own (although it is common as part of one of the glottalized consonants *pʔ, cʔ, kʔ*). When it does occasionally occur (typically to separate vowels that would otherwise contract), it is similar to the break (or catch in the throat) between the syllables of the English interjection *uh-oh!* The glottal stop appears in parentheses in the table since it is best considered a phonetic device used occasionally at utterance level, rather than a true consonant of Osage.

(Notes to Table 1 continued)

***p, t, k*:** The lax (or plain) stops are somewhat different from English *p, t, k*. English *p, t, k* are typically aspirated (particularly at the beginning of words)—that is, they are followed by a small burst of air. Osage *p, t, k* are not aspirated; they are more lax than English *p, t, k* and are not followed by a burst of air. This sometimes causes them to sound like English *b, d, g* (and some earlier transcriptions wrote them as *b, d, g*), but they are not voiced as these English sounds are.

***hp, ht, hc, hk*:** The preaspirated (or "tense") stops have no close English equivalent. They sometimes are pronounced as *p, t, c, k* with a light *h* sound before them, and sometimes as long *p, t, c, k*. (In *Osage Grammar* [Quintero 2004], the preaspirated stops were consequently sometimes written as doubled [geminate] consonants: *pp, tt, cc, kk*. In the dictionary, however, it seemed best to write them consistently as *hp, ht, hc, hk*.) While *hp, ht, hc, hk* are best regarded as single sounds, they are alphabetized as *h+p*, etc. (that is, *hk* follows *hį* and precedes *hl, hp* follows *ho*, and so on). The distinction between plain *p, t, c, k* and preaspirated *hp, ht, hc, hk,* though sometimes hard for English-speaking learners of the language to hear, is a very important one in Osage; a system of transcription that did not represent this distinction would not do justice to the language.

***ch*:** The aspirated dental affricate *ch* is pronounced as *c* (i.e., English *ts*) followed by a puff of breath. Though best thought of as a single sound, it is alphabetized as *c+h* (that is, *ch* can be found between *ce* and *ci*.)

***px, pš, tx, kx, kš*:** What presumably were originally the aspirated (or postaspirated) stops *ph, th, kh* appear in Osage as *px, tx, kx* (before the back vowels *a, ą, o, ǫ*) or *pš, ch, kš* (usually before other vowels). These are alphabetized as *p+x*, *p+š*, etc.

océ 'look for, hunt for'
otáži 'don't look for it, didn't look for it' (negative)
otá 'look for it!' (imperative)

Some changes that involve pronominal prefixes and other prefixes to verbs are briefly discussed in the section on "Grammar" below.

3.5. Accent

Generally speaking, primary accent (higher pitch, greater prominence, or loudness) is found on the first or second syllable of the Osage word. It is marked by an acute accent over the vowel (*á é í ó ú ą́ į́ ǫ́*). When a long vowel is accented, the accent mark appears on the first letter, indicating accent on the entire long vowel (e.g., *ą́ą*). (In a few words, long vowels were heard with accent on their second component, and are so written: e.g., *ǫǫ́, šaáke*.) Secondary accent usually occurs on every second syllable thereafter, but is not marked in most forms here. For a more detailed explanation, see *Osage Grammar* (Quintero 2004).

Accent is generally ignored in the alphabetical order of this dictionary; that is, *a* and *á* are alphabetized in exactly the same place, as are *e* and *é*, *į* and *į́*, etc. In rare cases where two words are exactly the same except that one lacks an accent on its first syllable while the other has an accented first syllable, the word with the unaccented first syllable is placed before the word with the accented first syllable. Thus, *océ* 'look for (it)' is ordered before *óce* 'look for stuff'.

It is not always easy to predict which syllable of an Osage word will be accented. (It is also easy for the linguist or language learner to mishear a long vowel as accented, or vice versa.) In nouns, modifiers, and other nonverb elements, it is common to find first syllable accent. Verbs tend to have their accent on the second syllable (counting syllables from the beginning of the word, including any prefixes), though many factors produce exceptions to this rough generalization. Some specific points about accent placement are noted in the discussions of "Pronominal Prefixes" and "Other Prefixes of Verbs" below; for further details, see *Osage Grammar*.

One common situation in which first-syllable accent occurs in verbs is when an original initial syllable has been lost or reduced. For example, when the valence reducer prefix *wa-* (which can be translated as 'things', 'stuff', or 'people' and replaces the object of the verb) is added to a verb that begins with unaccented *o*, *wa-* does not appear, but the resulting verb begins with a stressed *ó*. For example, adding *wa-* to *oðáake* 'tell (it) (e.g., a story, news, etc.)' produces the valence-reduced verb *óðaake* 'tell things, tell stuff, recite a tale'. (Compare *wamą́ąðǫ* 'steal stuff', the valence-reduced form of *mąąðǫ́* 'steal [it]'.) Similarly, the prefix *kik-* (reflexive possessive ["suus" prefix], implying that the action is done to a possession of the subject's own or to the subject's own relative) contracts with a following *ð* to become *l*; accent then typically remains on the syllable following the *l*. For example, adding *kik-* to *ðuuzé* 'take' results in *lúuze* 'take one's own'. (Compare *kihtǫ́pe* 'look at one's own', the suus form of *tǫ́pe* 'look at (it)'.)

In another sort of two-syllable verb that has first-syllable accent, the causative element *ðe* is added to a one-syllable stem. For example, *cˀéðe* 'kill' (from *cˀé* 'die' + *ðe* 'cause') has accent on the first syllable.

Accent and vowel length can cause perceptual problems for the linguist or learner of Osage. Long vowels (unrecorded in all previous work on the language) can easily be heard as accented, and accented vowels can be heard as long. For example, the verb *hiiðá* 'bathe' is easily mistranscribed as *hiiðaa*.

3.6. Dialects

Some slight differences in lexical items are seen among speakers of the different districts (Hominy, Grayhorse [sometimes known as Fairfax], Pawhuska), but these items are so few that there is no reason for positing separate dialects for these districts. The most notable difference detected is that a number of speakers, including many of those in the Hominy district, shift *c* to *č* when it is preceded by *š*; i.e., *šc* becomes *šč* for these speakers. This is not to be confused with change of *t* or *c* to *č* when *š* does not precede, a change that signals a diminutive or endearment in all three districts (e.g., *wihcóšpa* 'my grandchild' becomes *wihčóšpa* 'my dear little grandchild'); see kinship terms especially for this phenomenon.

Another difference among speakers is seen with the sequence *tx*. For some speakers, this sequence is replaced by *tkx* or *kx*. Thus, one sometimes hears *ąkxą́he* or *ątkxą́he* instead of *ątxą́he* '1st person standing continuative'. The variants with *k* are heard in the speech of some Hominy speakers recorded in the corpus. Aside from these slight differences and a couple of kinship terms that are recognized as being Pawhuska District variants, no other major differences have been noted among the districts (despite claims to the contrary made mostly by nonspeakers).

3.7. Men's and women's speech

Although Osage speakers were fond of mentioning the difference between men's and women's speech, no general distinction could be reliably detected in the speech of modern Osages. One male speaker claimed that double conjugation of verbs was "woman's way." However, this double conjugation of verbs was attested on occasion exclusively in male speech in the 1980s, and female speakers flatly denied the suggested patterns; see *Osage Grammar* (section 1.3) for discussion. There are clear gender differences only with regard to lexical items in the kinship system and the word for 'yes'.

4. Remarks on Osage Grammar

This brief introduction is intended only to sketch some facts of Osage grammar that will be helpful to the reader for locating dictionary entries or for interpreting the information in entries. Fuller information on all the topics discussed here, and on many other topics as well, can be found in *Osage Grammar* (Quintero 2004).

4.1. Pronominal prefixes

Subject and object pronouns in Osage take the form of prefixes added to verbs (**pronominal prefixes**). These prefixes involve various complications that it is helpful for users of this dictionary to know about.

- Pronominal prefixes are not always the first element in a word. A great many verbs insert such prefixes at some later point. Thus the 2nd person singular form of *océ* 'look for it' is *o**ðá**ce* 'you look for it'. Since it is not always easy to predict where these prefixes go, the inflectional information in dictionary entries shows their position (the point of inflection) with an underscore: *o_cé*. (The 1st person agent prefix *ą-* or *ąk-* is sometimes placed earlier than the point of inflection.)

- Pronominal prefixes vary in form. In some cases, too, particular prefixes cause modifications to the stem to which they are added. The rest of this section reviews the various conjugations and prefix forms of Osage, presenting sample paradigms. (In these paradigms, pronominal prefixes are marked by bold type, as are changes in stem form that are induced by pronominal prefixes. Forms enclosed in square brackets in some of the paradigms are forms that happen not to be attested in dictionary examples for the verb in question.)

Like other Siouan languages, Osage distinguishes between **agent** and **patient** pronominal prefixes. Agent prefixes are used for the subjects of **active** verbs (these include verbs, especially ones referring to activities and processes, and nearly all transitive verbs); patient prefixes are used for the subjects of **stative** verbs (nearly all of these are intransitive) and for the objects of transitive verbs. (The terms "active," "stative," "agent," and "patient" are not always semantically accurate, but are used here since they are widely used in studies of Siouan languages.) Agent prefixes are more complex and are discussed first here.

4.1.1. Active verbs: regular

There are two primary types of active conjugation (i.e., with agent pronominal prefixes): **regular** (abbreviated in dictionary entries as "reg.") and **syncopating** (abbreviated as "sync."). To oversimplify somewhat, syncopating inflection is used for most active verbs in which the point of inflection is followed by *ð* or by *p*, *t*, *k*, or sometimes *h*, and regular inflection is used for other verbs (including verbs whose point of inflection is followed by glottalized *pʔ*, *cʔ*, *kʔ*, aspirated *pš*, *px*, *ch*, *tx*, *kš*, *kx*, or preaspirated *hp*, *ht*, *hc*, *hk*; also verbs with *ki* or *ka* after the point of inflection typically use regular inflection).

The basic paradigm of regular agent pronominals is:

a-	1st person singular ('I')
ða-	2nd person ('you')
(no prefix)	3rd person ('he, she, it, they')
ą- (*ąk-* before vowels)	1st person dual or plural ('we')

The 2nd person prefix *ða-* represents two or more persons when it is accompanied by the pluralizer suffix *api*; otherwise it is understood as singular, unless a plural continuative aspect marker follows the verb. The 1st person dual/plural prefix *ą-/ąk-* represents three or more people ('I and two or more others') when it is accompanied by the pluralizer suffix *api*; when not accompanied by *api*, it is interpreted as dual ('I and one other person'), unless a plural continuative aspect marker follows the verb. (For *api* and the continuative markers, see the section on "Postverbal markers" below. Paradigms are given here without *api*.) The paradigm is seen in its clearest form in verbs that do not begin with *i* or with *wa*.

reg.: *_lúuža* 'wash (one's own)'

***a**lúuža*	'I wash (something of my own)'
***ða**lúuža*	'you wash (something of your own)'
lúuža	'he/she washes (something of his/her own)'
***ą**lúuža*	'we wash (something of our own)'

Regular verbs that begin with *wa* or *waa* place the 2nd person prefix *ða-* after *wa(a)* (and this is marked as the point of inflection by an underscore in dictionary entries), but place 1st person singular *a-* before *wa(a)*. (The 1st person plural prefix *ą-* also precedes *wa(a)*.)

reg. [with initial *wa*]: *waa_chí* 'dance'

***á**waachi* ~ ***a**wáachi*	'I dance'
*wa**ðáa**chi*	'you dance'
waachí	'he/she dances'
***ą**wáachi*	'we dance'

Regular verbs of the *iða* subtype (abbreviated in entries as "reg.-*iða*") begin with *i* or *ii*, which is followed by the 1st sg. and 2nd person prefixes; *ð* is inserted between *i* and

1st sg. *a*-. First and 2nd person are differentiated by accent: on the agent prefix *a*- for 1st person, on initial *i(i)* for 2nd person. The 1st pl. prefix blends with *i(i)* to form *ąną*.

reg.-*iða*: *ii_chį́* 'hit with'

*iið**á**chį*	'I hit with it'
*íi**ða**chį*	'you hit with it'
iichį́	'he/she hit with it'
***ąną́**chį*	'we hit with it'

reg.-*iða*: *íi_ðe* 'see'

*iið**á**ðe*	'I see'
*íi**ða**ðe*	'you see'
íiðe	'he/she sees'
***ąną́**ðe*	'we see'

Verbs with initial *ki* or *ka* (or *kaa*) present further complexities. Many verbs in which *kaa* or *ka* follows the point of inflection (especially when *ka(a)* represents the instrumental prefix 'by striking') follow a pattern whereby *ka(a)* is deleted after the 1st sg. and 2nd person agent prefixes; accent typically then falls on these prefixes. These verbs are noted in entries as "reg. *kaa*-del." (or "reg. *ka*-del.").

reg. *kaa*-del.: *_(kaa)cí* 'wipe'

***áa**ci*	'I wipe'
***ðáa**ci*	'you wipe'
kaací	'he/she wipes'
***ą**káaci*	'we wipe'

Similarly, a few verbs in which *ki* follows the point of inflection (especially verbs in which *ki* represents the dative prefix) delete *ki* after inflectional prefixes. These verbs are noted in entries as "reg. *ki*-del." Thus, for example, the 1st person singular of *kíðahapa* 'divorce' is ***á**ðahapa* 'I divorce him', and the 2nd person singular is ***ðá**ðahapa* 'you divorce him'. (There appears to be variation as to whether *ki* deletes after the 1st person dual/plural prefix.) However, more *ki*-deleting verbs in the dictionary follow the syncopating paradigm or are stative, rather than following the regular paradigm; see below (under "Agent pronominal prefixes: syncopating" and "Stative verbs").

On the other hand, some verbs where *kaa*, *ka*, or *ki* follows the point of inflection (noted as "reg. *kaa*-ret.," "reg. *ka*-ret.," "reg. *ki*-ret."), retain *kaa*, *ka*, or *ki* in all persons.

reg. *kaa*-ret.: *_kaaží* 'drive'

***a**káaži*	'I drive'
***ða**káaži*	'you drive'
kaaží	'he/she drives'
[***ą**káaži*	'we drive' (expected 1st dual/plural form)]

reg. *ki*-ret.: *_kíhpą* ‘invite one’s relatives’

***a**kíhpą*	‘I invite him/her’
***ða**kíhpą*	‘you invite him/her’
kíhpą	‘he/she invites him/her’
***ą**kíhpą*	‘we invite him/her’

4.1.2. Agent pronominal prefixes: syncopating

Instead of the regular paradigm, some active verbs follow one or another version of the **syncopating** paradigm. In this paradigm of agent pronominals, 1st person plural is *ą*-, as in the regular paradigm, but 1st person singular and 2nd person prefixes have special forms (which differ somewhat in different subtypes of syncopating inflection), and moreover these prefixes in some cases modify the form of the stem.

The most common subtype of syncopating verb is that in which *ð* follows the point of inflection. In this type, 1st person singular is *b*- and modifies the *ð* of the stem to *r*, and 2nd person is *š*- and modifies the *ð* of the stem to *t* (to *c* before *e*, *i*, or *u*). Accent falls on the syllable that immediately follows the pronominal prefix. Syncopating verbs of this common type are noted in dictionary entries simply as “sync.” (Because their inflectional forms include *br*- and *š*-, such verbs are sometimes known as “brush” verbs.)

sync.: *_ðaaché* ‘eat’

***br**áache*	‘I eat it’
***št**áache*	‘you eat’
[*ðaaché*	‘he/she eats it’ (expected 3rd person form)]
***ą**ðáache*	‘we eat it’

sync.: *_ðuuléke* ‘shatter’

***br**úuleke*	‘I shatter it’
***šc**úuleke*	‘you shatter it’
ðuuléke	‘he/she shatters it’
***ą**ðúuleke*	‘we shatter it’

Also common is the fortisizing stop stem pattern (noted as “sync. fortisizing stop stem”). In these verbs, the point of inflection is followed by a simple unaspirated stop (*p*, *t*, or rarely *k*). The 1st person singular prefix is *h*- (i.e., it converts the simple stop to a preaspirated stop, sometimes called “fortis”); 2nd person is *š*-.

sync. fortisizing stop stem: *_tǫ́pe* ‘watch’

***h**tǫ́pe*	‘I watch it’
***š**tǫ́pe*	‘you watch it’
tǫ́pe	‘he/she watches it’
***ą**tǫ́pe*	‘we watch it’

sync. fortisizing stop stem: *í_pahǫ* 'know'

***íh**pahǫ*	'I know'
***íš**pahǫ*	'you know'
[*ípahǫ*	'he/she knows' (expected 3rd person form)]
***ąną́**pahǫ*	'we know'

(In the paradigm of *í_paho* 'know', stem-initial *i* combines with 1st person plural *ą-* to form *ąną*, as in a reg. *-iða* verb.) More verbs in which *k* follows the point of inflection belong to a subtype ("sync. *k>p*") in which the *k* of the stem is replaced by *p* after the 1st person prefix, though the other forms of the paradigm are like those of the fortisizing stop stem type.

sync. *k>p*: *_káaɣe* 'make'

***hp**áaɣe*	'I make'
***š**káaɣe*	'you make'
káaɣe	'she makes'
***ą**káaɣe*	'we make'

A few verbs belong to other subtypes of the syncopating pattern. Certain verbs in which the point of inflection is followed by a nasal vowel take *m-* for 1st person singular and *ž-* for 2nd person; the 1st person plural prefix takes the form *ąk-*, as it normally does before a vowel. These verbs are noted in entries as "sync. nasal vowel stem." (In writings on Siouan languages, these are sometimes also referred to as "glottal stop stems.")

sync. nasal vowel stem: *_į́* 'wear'

***m**į́*	'I wear'
***ž**į́*	'you wear'
į́	'he/she wears'
***ąk**į́*	'we wear'

A small number of verbs follow the h-stem pattern (noted as "sync. h-stem"). In these, the point of inflection presumably was earlier followed by *h*, though this has been lost or has contracted with the pronominal prefixes.

sync. h-stem: *é_(h)e* 'say':

*é**pš**e*	'I say'
*é**š**e*	'you say'
ée	'he/she says'

(1st person dual/plural of this verb is not used)

Syncopating verbs with a prefix *ki-* that is deleted after pronominal prefixes (the "*ki*-del." pattern) typically have both a regular pronominal prefix and a syncopating pronominal prefix in the singular. Such verbs are noted as "reg. *ki*-del.+sync."

reg. *ki*-del.+sync. stem: *_(kí)_ðuwį* 'buy it for (him/her)'

ábr_uwį_	'I bought it for him/her'
ðáš_cuwį_	'you bought it for him/her'
kíðuwį	'he/she bought it for him/her'
ą́_ðuwį_	'we bought it for him/her'

4.1.3. Stative verbs

The patient pronominal prefixes, used to inflect stative verbs, are as follows:

ą-	1st person singular ('I, me')
ði-	2nd person ('you')
(no prefix)	3rd person ('he, him; she, her; it; they, them')
wa-	1st person dual or plural ('we, us')
wa-	3rd person plural ('they, them') (sometimes omitted)

As with the agent paradigm, 1st person plural *wa-* is usually dual [two people] when not accompanied by the pluralizing suffix *api*, and plural [three or more people] when it is accompanied by *api*.

Various irregularities arise in the inflection of many stative verbs, particularly in 1st person dual/plural forms; these cannot be reviewed here (see *Osage Grammar* [pp. 120–26] for full discussion). Typical regular statives (noted as "stat." in dictionary entries) are shown below. (In these and other stative paradigms, 3rd person plural forms with prefix *wa-* are given; 1st person dual/plural forms are not given, since they will typically be identical to the 3rd person forms except that the suffix *api* is frequently present. The "expected" but unattested forms enclosed in square brackets should be regarded as especially uncertain in stative paradigms.)

stat.: *ní_hce* 'be (feel) cold'

*ní*___ą___*hce*	'I am cold'
*ní*___ði___*hce*	'you are cold'
níhce	'he/she is cold'
[*ní*___wa___*hce*	'they are cold' (expected 3rd plural form)]

stat.: *o_xpáðe* 'get lost'

*o(w)*___ą___*xpaðe*	'I get lost'
*o*___ðí___*xpaðe*	'you get lost'
oxpáðe	'he/she gets lost'
*o*___wá___*xpaðe*	'they get lost'

Stative verbs in which *ka* or *kaa* follows the point of inflection normally delete it after a pronominal prefix (*ka(a)* is retained in 3rd person forms, where there is no prefix).

stat. *kaa*-del.: *_káaskike* 'be tired'

ą́*skike*	'I am tired'
ðí*skike*	'you are tired'
káaskike	'he/she is tired'
[***wáa****skike*	'they are tired' (expected 3rd plural form)]

As with active verbs, some stative verbs delete *ki* after a pronominal prefix, while others retain *ki*.

stat. *ki*-del.: *_(kí)ðalį* 'be glad'

ą́ą*ðalį*	'I am glad'
ðíi*ðalį*	'you are glad'
kíðalį	'he/she is glad'
wáa*ðalį*	'they are glad'

stat. *ki*-ret.: *_kítąhe* 'get well'

ą*kítąhe*	'I get well'
ði*kítąhe*	'you got well'
kítąhe	'he/she gets well'
[***wa****kítąhe*	'they get well' (expected 3rd plural form)]

4.1.4. Objects

The objects of transitive verbs are also expressed by patient pronominal prefixes:

[***ði****ną́kˀǫ* 'he/she (no prefix) hears you' (expected form with prefix *ði-* '2nd person sg. patient' added to the stem *_nakˀǫ́* 'hear')]

ąðá*nąkˀǫ* 'you hear me' (*ą-* '1st person sg. patient', *ða-* '2nd person agent')

However, for the combination of 1st person singular subject with 2nd person object, a special prefix *wi-* 'I-you' is used:

wi*ną́kˀǫ*	'I hear you'

4.1.5. Inalienable possessive pronominals

One additional set of pronominal prefixes expresses **inalienable possession**. For the most part, these prefixes are found not in verbs, but in kinship terms such as ***wi****žǫ́ke* 'my daughter', ***ði****žǫ́ke* 'your daughter', ***i****žǫ́ke* 'his/her daughter'. In other Siouan languages, inalienable possession is sometimes used in domains other than that of kinship, but this does not occur in Osage. One verb that does inflect by means of the inalienable prefixes is *íhta* 'belong to; be his/hers/yours/mine/ours':

wí*hta*	'belong to me, be mine'
ðí*hta*	'belong to you, be yours'
í*hta*	'belong to him/her, be his/hers'
ąkó*hta*	'belong to us, be ours'

The 1st person plural inalienable prefix *ąko-* is used in verbs, but not in kinship terms. The few verbs that take the inalienable paradigm are noted as "inalien." in dictionary entries. (The possessed forms of kinship terms are listed as separate entries because they sometimes involve irregularities of form or require complicated and specific glossing. The English-to-Osage Index may be consulted to locate related forms of kinship terms.)

4.1.6. Uninflected verbs

Finally, some verbs—especially ones with adjective-like meanings—are **uninflected**. These are not found with pronominal prefixes in the corpus, but rather express the person and number of their subject only by means of continuative markers that follow the verb, or sometimes by an emphatic pronoun. (For more on continuative markers, see the section "Postverbal markers" below.) Such verbs are noted in dictionary entries as "uninfl."

uninfl.: *áachi* '(be) sick, feverish'

áachi nįkšé 'you are sick' (*nįkšé* 'continuative marker for 2nd person singular sitting subject')

uninfl.: *iišcéwai* (*iiščéwa(i)*, etc.) '(be) ashamed'

iiščéwa ąðįhe 'I am ashamed' (*ąðįhe* 'continuative marker for 1st person singular moving subject')

4.1.7. Irregularities in use of pronominal prefixes

Some verbs are **doubly inflected** (or even triply inflected)—that is, the subject is represented by two (or three) pronominal prefixes, which in some cases are at different positions in the verb (and may belong to different inflectional types). Each of the points of inflection is marked by an underscore in the inflectional information in dictionary entries, and the inflectional types of the points of inflection are separated by a plus sign.

sync. fortisizing stop stem+sync.: *_kǫ́_ða* 'want'

***h**kǫ́**br**a*	'I want'
***šk**ǫ́**št**a*	'you want'
kǫ́ða	'he, she wants'
***ą**kǫ́ða*	'we want'

A number of verbs of motion ('go', 'come', etc.) have an initial *a-* which appears in some forms of the verb but is omitted in others (typically in the presence of a pronominal prefix or in imperative forms). Thus, for example, the initial *a* of *aðée* 'go there' appears in the 3rd person form *aðée* 'he/she goes there', but is omitted in the 1st person singular and 2nd person forms *brée* 'I go there', *šcée* 'you go there' (these have the usual first person singular and second person prefixes for a syncopating verb in *ð*).

A few other verbs show differences from the patterns of inflection outlined in this survey. In general, when an inflected form of a verb diverges enough from normal patterns to cause difficulty for identification, the inflected form is given a separate entry in the dictionary, with a cross-reference to the verb's main entry.

4.2. Postverbal markers

A large number of grammatical elements may follow the verb in Osage. Full details can be found in *Osage Grammar* (chap. 5), but some brief remarks on some of the more important and frequent will be useful here.

4.2.1. Pluralizer and noncontinuative marker

The *a* of the pluralizer and noncontinuative marker *api* is normally lost, but causes a preceding *e* or *ee* to be replaced by *a* or *aa* (see "Alphabet and pronunciation: alternations between sounds," above). The declarative marker *ðe* frequently follows *(a)pi*, and the two elements normally contract to *(a)pe*. Similarly, *(a)pi* usually contracts with the negative marker *aží* 'not', producing *(a)paží*.

Postverbal *api* has two main functions. (1) It pluralizes 1st or 2nd person pronominal prefixes in the verb, when there is no continuative aspect marker. (Postverbal *api* is not used in conjunction with 1st person singular prefixes.)

> *hǫ́ǫpa háa**ž**ǫ**pe**?* 'what did you [two or more] do today?' (*ž-* '2nd sg. agent' *háaǫ* 'do how, what?' [sync. nasal vowel stem, *háa_ǫ*])
> *záani wa**wí**hǫį**pi*** 'I address you all as friends and relatives' (*wi-* 'I-you'; *wahǫ́į* 'address with respect, address as friends and relatives')

With the 1st person plural prefixes *ą(k)-* and *wa-*, *api* indicates that three or more people are involved. Without *api* and in the absence of a continuative aspect marker (see below), these prefixes indicate only two people ('I and one other person', the 'dual' meaning); *api* is not used with the first person singular prefixes. The suffix *api* can also pluralize inalienable possessive prefixes.

(2) For 3rd person verbs, *api* does not mark number; it merely indicates that the verb has noncontinuative aspect (often translated into English as past tense).

> *súhka záani ðaanį́**pe*** 'he ate [consumed] all the chicken' (*súhka* 'chicken', *záani* 'all', *ðaanį́* 'consume')

4.2.2. Imperative marker

The imperative marker *a* typically does not appear overtly, but causes change of preceding *e* or *ee* to *a* or *aa*. Much as in English, imperative verbs are understood as having a 2nd person subject, but no overt 2nd person prefix appears.

> *hką́ącezi ðiilóca* 'peel the orange' (*ðiilóce* 'peel')

4.2.3. Continuative aspect markers

There are a large number of continuative aspect markers; see the Osage-English Index entry "continuative aspect markers" for a full list. Besides indicating that the verb is continuative in aspect (which often, though not always, can be translated as an English present progressive with *be . . . -ing*), these postverbal elements also agree with the person and number of the subject, and convey information about the shape or position (sitting, standing, lying down), presence vs. absence, or moving vs. stationary status of the subject.

("Moving" here means "changing location"; motions or gestures that do not change the entity's location in horizontal space do not take "moving" continuative markers.)

kǫ́ða **apa** 'he's wanting it' (he is moving or absent)
ąžį́įhe ąðįkšé 'we two are sleeping' (we are sitting or lying down)
wabrílą ***mįkšé*** 'I'm thinking about it' (I am sitting or lying down; *waðílą* 'think')
pšú aðį̨he 'I'm coming' (*pšú* 'I come' is 1st person singular of *ahú* 'come here')

The suffix *api* is not used to mark plurality of a subject pronominal prefix when a dual or plural continuative aspect marker is present:

ąk*áku* ***ąkáðe*** 'we [three or more] are coming back' (*ąk-* '1st person dual/plural agent', *akú* 'come back here', *ąkáðe* '1st person plural moving continuative aspect marker')

4.2.4. Other postverbal markers
There are a good many other particles that follow the verb and mark mood, aspect, or other grammatical categories. Some of these are: the negator *aží* 'not' (with its special 1st person singular form *maží* 'I do/did/am/was not'); the potential (future tense, etc.) marker *hta*; injunctive *hce* 'may it be that'; suppositional *ska* 'I suppose that, I deduce that'; evidential *che* (indicating that the speaker did not witness the event, but acquired circumstantial or sensory evidence that it occurred); *ðąąché* 'possible'; declarative *ðe*; and reportatives such as *áape* or *áapa* 'they say, it is said'. (This is not an exhaustive list.)

4.3. Other prefixes of verbs

It will be useful to mention briefly here some other prefixes that are frequently seen in dictionary entries for verbs.

A very common one is the valence reducer *wa-* (not to be confused with the 1st person plural and 3rd person plural patient pronominal prefixes of the same form). The valence reducer eliminates the object of the verb to which it is added, implying instead an unspecified object. It is frequently convenient to translate it into English as 'stuff, things' (when the implied unspecified object is inanimate), or as 'folks, people' when the implied reference is human. Sometimes, too, valence reducer *wa-* need not be translated in English at all. (Note, by the way, that the expressions "s.o." [= "someone"] and "s.t." [= "something"] indicate an object and are not used when glossing the valence reducer in dictionary entries.) The valence reducer *wa-* contracts with a following *o* to form *ó-* (accented).

waðáahtą 'he/she drinks stuff; he/she drinks' (*ðaahtą́* 'he drinks it')
óce 'he/she searches for stuff; he/she searches' (*wa-* + *océ* 'he/she searches for it')

The prefix *hkik-* (*hkih-*, *hki-*) forms reflexive and reciprocal verbs. The prefix *kik-* (*kih-*, *ki-*), known as the "suus" prefix, indicates that the object of the verb is possessed by or related to the subject. The dative prefix *ki-* indicates that the action is done for someone or to someone's possession, or involves the transfer of something to someone.

hkihkúce 'shoot each other, shoot at each other' (reflexive/reciprocal; *hkik-* + *hkúce* 'shoot (at)')
kihtǫ́pe 'watch one's own things' (suus; *kik-* + *tǫ́pe* 'watch')
kíðuwį 'buy for someone' (dative; *ki-* + *ðuwį́* 'buy')

The reflexive/reciprocal prefix and the suus prefix can affect the form of the following stem. Notably, reflexive/reciprocal *hkik-* plus *ð* becomes *hkil*, and suus *kik-* plus *ð* becomes *l*.

hkilúušawa 'undress oneself' (*hkik-* + *ðuušáwa* 'undress')
lúuža 'wash one's own' (*kik-* + *ðuužá* 'wash')

A great many verb stems contain instrumental or locative prefixes. The locative prefixes (*á-*, *í-*, *ó-*, with variation between short and long vowels and between accented and unaccented forms) generally precede the point of inflection of the verb. Their meanings are often hard to pin down, although *í-* often means 'with, by means of'. ("Locative" is not an ideal term for this group of prefixes; it is used here mostly because it has some currency in studies of Siouan languages.) The instrumental prefixes, most of which follow the point of inflection, indicate the instrument or the kind of action by which an action is performed; e.g., *ðaa-* 'by mouth', *ðu-* (with variants *ði-*, *ðuu-*, *ðii-*) 'by hand; cause', *paa-* 'by pushing or pressing'. (See the index entry "instrumental prefixes" for a full list.)

4.4. Causatives

Osage causative markers include *ðe* 'make, have (someone do something), cause (something to happen' and the related *hkíðe* 'make oneself (do something)', *kíðe* 'allow (someone to do something), have (someone do something)', and *kšíðe* 'allow (someone to do something), have (someone do something)'. (The instrumental prefix *ðu-* 'by hand' can also be used with a more general causative meaning; so can the verbs *káaɣe* 'make' and *kšíɣe* 'make for someone'.) The causative markers *ðe*, *hkíðe*, *kíðe*, and *kšíðe* are like suffixes in that they follow the verb stem that they causativize, and that verb stem retains its accent. However, agent pronominal inflection (of the regular type, not the syncopating type) is inserted before the causative marker.

cˀéaðe 'I killed him' (*cˀé* 'die' + *a-* '1st sg. agent' + *ðe* 'cause')

The *ð* in causative forms (like *ð* elsewhere) is often elided in speech. Some verb stems end in *ðe* before which pronominal prefixes are inserted, but a causative meaning is no longer detectable.

4.5. Syntax

Osage is a verb-final language, with constituents of the clause generally following the order subject + object + verb. (However, since person and number of subject and object are coded in verb inflection, as outlined above, overt subject or object nouns are not required, and are often not present.) Adverbial modifiers likewise mostly precede the verb, and postpositions rather than prepositions are used. (That is, Osage conforms to the rigid subtype of Greenberg's [1966] word order type III.) Sentence-modifying adverbs typically precede the subject (if there is one). Yes-no questions are signaled prosodically, using added length and high-to-low pitch in the last accented syllable of the verb root. Question words ('who', 'what', where', etc.) are often at the beginning of the sentence, but may appear in situ. Subordinate clauses (including complement clauses, adverbial clauses, 'if'-clauses, volition and purpose clauses, relative clauses, etc.) precede the main clause.

Qualifying adjectives and numbers follow the nouns they modify; a possessor, however, precedes the possessed noun, with a possessive pronoun in turn following the possessed noun (*kšǫ́ka šǫ́ke íhta* [second.son dog his] 'second son's dog'). Singular or plural number is not directly expressed on nouns (e.g., *níhka* is both 'man' and 'men'). There is a system of positional articles that follow the noun (and modifying adjectives or numbers, if any) that indicate stance or position of the entity; these articles can also express plurality. Subject nouns are instead followed by special subject markers that code the moving vs. stationary (as with continuative markers, "moving" means changing location) and present vs. absent status of the entity. (See the index entries "positional articles" and "subject markers" for lists of these elements. When it is clear which positional article a noun requires, that is noted in the entry for the noun.)

Many Osage words are flexible as to their grammatical function. For example, a single form may function as noun, verb, adjective, and adverb. Grammatical categories are given for most entries, but should be viewed as more approximate than the same labels are for English. Use of nouns in predicate function (meaning 'be [noun]') is frequent; for instance, the noun *kašpéǫpa* 'quarter (twenty-five cents)' is so used in the sentence *kašpéǫpa hta akxai* 'it will be a quarter' (*hta* marks future tense; *akxai* is a continuative aspect marker *akxa* plus a reduced form of declarative *ðe*). Adjectives ('good', 'big', 'cold', etc.) can likewise be used as predicates on their own. (This can make it somewhat difficult to tell the difference between adjectives and stative verbs.) As in English, nouns are frequently used to modify other nouns; it seems better to take this kind of construction to be a compound noun than to regard modifying nouns as adjectives. Where it could be determined from the stress pattern, or other phonological adjustment, that two nouns have merged, they are written as one word, with no intervening space; otherwise, a space is written in noun-noun combinations (but they are still assigned the category label N ["noun"]). This policy is adopted for reasons of convenience and readability, and should not be interepreted as making a strong theoretical claim about the status of such combinations. Combinations of noun and verb, or of noun and adjective, are treated in a similar manner.

4.6. Meaning and translations

It should be clear even from the above brief discussion that English and Osage differ greatly in structure, and that word-for-word translation from either language to the other is usually not possible. Many words in English have no real one-word equivalent in Osage and vice-versa. As one example of dozens that could readily be cited, the conjunction 'and' is often not overtly expressed in Osage:

mihkákˀe skáha štáha 'the stars are bright and shiny' (literally, 'stars bright shiny')
hkáwa ðéeka mąðį́ káaɣa ščewai hta mįkšéa 'bring the horses here and I'll doctor them' (literally, 'make the horses walk here, I will doctor them')

Kinship is a domain of vocabulary where the lack of one-to-one matching between English and Osage terms is especially obvious; Osage distinguishes between various kinds of relatives that are lumped together in English, and vice versa. Consider the terms for 'niece' or 'brother' (see the English-to-Osage Index) as examples of the kind of complexities that arise.

The force of some postverbal particles (e.g., the reportatives, or modal particles such as *ska* or *ðąąché*) is not always easy to render into English (or to render without an effect of greater emphasis or awkwardness than is the case in Osage); speakers' English translations of Osage sentences sometimes omit glosses for these particles, or render them in indirect ways.

Given these and other complexities, the definitions offered in a dictionary entry are often to be understood, not as the "meaning" of the Osage term, but as less precise contextual equivalent. For example, the Osage modal marker *ðąąché* strictly speaking means something like 'be possible, be probable'. But an English sentence whose gloss includes 'look like' in the sense of 'it looks like rain' will likely contain *ðąąché*. Hence 'look like' is listed as one of the glosses for *ðąąché*, as an aid to users who wish to express the idea 'look like'; this policy is not intended to imply that 'look like' is really one of the meanings of *ðąąché*. In short, this dictionary includes some customary usages and links masquerading as definitions. We hope that linguists will forgive this informality and that other users will find such links helpful.

5. Interpretation of Osage Forms in Older Sources

A good deal of Osage material collected by Francis La Flesche (nearly all of it from La Flesche 1932) and from the unpublished data of J. O. Dorsey (1883a, 1883b) has been incorporated into the present dictionary. (Examples from La Flesche [1932] in dictionary entries are preceded by "LFD" plus a page number; examples from Dorsey's data are preceded by "JOD".) Interpretation of some of this older material can be problematic, and therefore requires discussion here.

The spellings used for Osage in these earlier sources present some difficulty for the present-day reader, partly because those transcriptions differ considerably from the transcription used here for Modern Osage, and partly because of deficiencies or inconsistencies in Dorsey's and, especially, La Flesche's practice. Examples taken from Dorsey's and La Flesche's materials are therefore given both in their original spellings (enclosed in angle brackets < >) and in a modernized retranscription (in italics) that is closer to the spelling used here for Modern Osage.

In the following discussion, "Modern Osage" refers to Osage data recorded by Robert Bristow or myself in the last decades of the twentieth century.

5.1. Dorsey

James Owen Dorsey provides the most reliable historical data on Osage. With few exceptions, he heard and recorded the phonological distinctions of the language. Dorsey's typical spellings and their modern equivalents are tabulated below.

Dorsey spelling	**Modern Osage equivalent**
a^{n}, añ, an	*ą*
c	*š*
ç$_{x}$	*ž*
¢	*ð*
ctc	*šc*
i^{n}, iñ, in	*į*
k	*hk* (and *kx*, *kš*?)
k$_{x}$	*k*
k'	*kʔ*
k$_{x}$¢	*l* (presumably historically *gð*)
kq	*kx*
p	*hp*, *px* (and *pš*?)
p$_{x}$	*p*
p'	*pʔ*
p$_{x}$¢	*br*
q	*x*
q¢	*l* (presumably historically *xð*)
qtc	*xc*
t	*ht* (and *tx*?)
t$_{x}$	*t*
s	*s*
s$_{x}$	*z*
ts	*ch*, *hc*
t$_{x}$s$_{x}$	*c*
ts'	*cʔ*
u	*o*
ü	*u*
u^{n}, uñ, un	*ǫ*
x	*ɣ*

In general, Dorsey reliably distinguishes the lax voiceless stops (*c*, *k*, *p*, *t*), which he writes with a small subscript <x>, from the preaspirated stops (*hc*, *hk*, *hp*, *ht*), which he writes as plain <ts, k, p, t>. (He also uses the plain symbols for stops when they are the second elements of consonant clusters such as *sk*, *št*, *xp*, etc. Note that the meaning of the subscript <x> in Dorsey's spelling is quite different from that of the subscript dot in La Flesche's spelling.) There is not much evidence on his treatment of the postaspirated stops (*ch*, *kx/kš*, *px/pš*, *tx*); as far as one can tell, he writes both *hc* and *ch* as

<ts>, and both *hp* and *px* as <p>; he at least occasionally writes *kx* as <kq> and *kš* as <kc> (distinct from *hk*, which he writes as <k>).

Occasional unexpected uses of symbols do occur in Dorsey's material; e.g., he sometimes writes *iihkó* 'his/her grandmother' as <ih´-$\underset{x}{\text{k}}$u>, whereas from his normal spelling practices one would expect <i-ku´>.

Dorsey's normal symbol for *ð* is <¢>. He writes <$\underset{x}{\text{p}}$¢, $\underset{x}{\text{k}}$¢, q¢> where Modern Osage has *br, l,* and *l*, respectively. Presumably this means that the change of historical *bð, gð,* and *xð* to *br, l,* and *l* had not yet taken place in Dorsey's day. (The earlier forms *bð, gð,* and *xð* are supported by comparison with other Dhegiha and other Siouan languages.) Modernized retranscription of Dorsey's examples with these combinations substitutes the Modern Osage sounds (*br, l, l*) in this case, since they are easier for present-day Osages to recognize.

Dorsey did not record length in vowels (unless his occasional use of a breve mark (<ŭ>, etc.) is intended to indicate that a vowel is short). Thus, for example, his <a> may represent either *a* or *aa* in Modern Osage. (La Flesche did not record vowel length either; see discussion below.) The modernized retranscription of Dorsey examples likewise usually does not indicate vowel length.

5.2. La Flesche

Although La Flesche's dictionary (1932) is a valuable resource, it is also beset by problems. To begin with, his spelling system differs in numerous respects from that used in the present dictionary. In certain cases, differences probably reflect genuine differences between the Osage of La Flesche's day and Modern Osage. There are more serious problems as well, however: some aspects of La Flesche's system of spelling fail to accurately represent the pronunciation of Osage of any period; La Flesche (or his publisher) sometimes fails to apply his spelling system consistently; and a certain number of the forms that La Flesche presents as Osage are in fact Omaha (La Flesche's native language).

Since the "Phonetic Key" prepared by W. David Baird (La Flesche 1932: 2) is inaccurate or misleading in a number of respects, the typical Modern Osage equivalents for those spellings in La Flesche's system that differ from the orthography used in the present dictionary are listed here. Variation and inconsistent usage are discussed following the table.

La Flesche spelling	**Typical Modern Osage equivalent**
(not all variant usages are listed here; see text)	
b	*p*
bth	*br*
ç	*s, z*
d	*t*
ds	*c*
g	*k*
gth	*l*
i	*i* (but sometimes appears where Modern Osage has *u*)

La Flesche spelling (*continued*)	**Typical Modern Osage equivalent** (not all variant usages are listed here; see text)
i^n	*į*
iu	*u*
k	*kx* (and *k* in a consonant cluster, e.g., *sk*, *šk*)
ksh	*kš*
k'	*kʔ*
ḳ	*hk* (but sometimes erroneously used for *kš*, *kx*)
ḳ'	*kʔ*
o^n	*ą*, *ǫ*
p	*px* (and *p* in a consonant cluster, e.g., *sp*, *šp*, *xp*)
psh	*pš*
p'	*pʔ*
p̣	*hp* (but sometimes erroneously used for *pš*, *px*)
p̣'	*pʔ*
sh	*š*
t	*tx* (and *t* in a consonant cluster, e.g., *st*, *št*, *xt*)
ṭ	*ht* (but sometimes erroneously used for *tx*)
ts	*ch* (and *c* in a consonant cluster, e.g., *sc*; sometimes erroneously used for *hc*)
ts'	*cʔ*
ṭs	*hc* (but sometimes erroneously used for *ch*)
ṭs'	*cʔ*
u	*u*, *o*
x	*ɣ*, *x*
xth	*l*
zh	*ž*

In the following discussion of problems in La Flesche's transcriptional practice, remarks are also offered on how these problems are dealt with in the modernized retranscription.[1]

La Flesche's spelling does not differentiate *s* from *z* (spelling both as <ç>), *x* from *ɣ* (spelling both as <x>), nor *ą* from *ǫ* (spelling both as <o^n>). Osage in La Flesche's day presumably distinguished these sounds just as Modern Osage does, but La Flesche failed to record the differences. The use of <ç>, rather than <s>, for both *s* and *z* was apparently a change made not by La Flesche but by his editor, who "found it necessary to change the original spelling of the words to conform to modern times: s has been changed to ç (as th in thin)" (La Flesche 1932: 2). This is a surprising remark, since Modern Osage *s* and *z* are never pronounced like English *th* in *thin*; nor is there any reason to think that earlier Osage had this pronunciation. In all these cases the modernized

1. A computer program devised by John Koontz was extremely helpful in producing the modernized retranscriptions of La Flesche examples. Naturally, some additional editing was required to deal with underdifferentiation, inconsistency, and variation in La Flesche's spellings.

retranscription of La Flesche's forms reintroduces the differentiation of *s* from *z*, *x* from *ɣ*, and *ą* from *ǫ*; thus, e.g., La Flesche's <ça-gi´> is modernized as ***sakí*** (cf. Mod. Os. *saakí* 'tight') and his <ça-ni´> is modernized as ***zaní*** (cf. Mod. Os. *zaaní* 'whole, all').

Like Dorsey, La Flesche did not differentiate short and long vowels; e.g., <a> in his spelling may represent either *a* or *aa* in Modern Osage. Probably a difference between short and long vowels did exist in La Flesche's and Dorsey's day, but they did not record it (or did not record it consistently, if Dorsey's breve marks short vowels). The modernized retranscription of La Flesche's forms does not distinguish vowel length either. Thus <tho^{n}-tse´> 'suitable' is modernized as ***ðąché***, although Modern Osage *ðąąché* 'suitable' shows that the first vowel was probably long.

La Flesche's <u> corresponds to both Modern Osage *o* (the most frequent value) and *u*; his <i>, though most often corresponding to Modern Osage *i*, also appears in some cases where Modern Osage has *u*. The modernized retranscription restores the difference between *o* and *u*, but retranscribes La Flesche's <i> as *i* regardless of whether Modern Osage has *i* or *u*.

Some other La Flesche spellings presumably represent real differences between the Osage of his day and Modern Osage. In particular, what he writes as <bth, gth, xth> probably were actually pronounced as *bð*, *gð*, and *xð* (Dorsey's recordings show comparable spellings, as noted above, and other Siouan languages have forms that are compatible with earlier Osage *bð*, *gð*, and *xð*); the change of these to Modern Osage *br*, *l*, and *l*, respectively, took place after La Flesche and Dorsey's recordings of Osage. The modernized retranscription of La Flesche examples uses the Modern Osage sounds *br* and *l* in these cases (as is also done in the modernized transcriptions of Dorsey examples), since they are easier for present-day Osages to recognize (although these spellings probably misrepresent the actual sounds of Osage in La Flesche's day).

In some cases, La Flesche is simply inconsistent in his use of symbols in ways that probably reflect errors. A frequent problem of this sort affects consonant symbols with a subscript dot <ḳ, p̣, ṭ, ṭs>. La Flesche evidently intended to use these symbols to represent the "preaspirated" (or "tense") stops (which are spelled *hk, hp, ht, hc* in the transcription of Modern Osage used in the present dictionary), while the corresponding letters without subscript dot are intended to represent the "postaspirated" stops (i.e., *kš/kx, pš/px, tx, ch*—though he typically represents *kš* by <ksh> and *pš* by <psh>). (As noted above, the meaning of the subscript dot in La Flesche's spelling is quite different from that of the subscript <x> in Dorsey's spelling.) However, it is quite common to find a dotted letter in La Flesche's transcription of words where Modern Osage has a postaspirated consonant (<ḳ> for *kš* or *kx*, etc.). In such cases, the Osage of La Flesche's day probably had a postaspirated consonant too, and La Flesche's use of a dotted symbol reflects some sort of error: either a mishearing of the Osage sound by La Flesche, or a typographical error by the publisher of his dictionary. In these cases, the modernized retranscription of La Flesche examples usually represents the dotted symbol by a preaspirated consonant, but accompanies it with a comment indicating that this is likely to be an error for a postaspirated sound.

In addition, La Flesche often uses <ts> (which ought to represent *ch*) where Modern Osage has *hc*. Occasional other interchanges of stop symbols, or of other symbols, occur in La Flesche's spellings. (For example, note his varying transcription of 'egg' as <ba´-ṭa> and <p̣a´-ṭa> [see entries *hpáata* and *hpáatazi*]; 'egg' in Modern Osage is *hpáata*.)

La Flesche's transcription of glottalized sounds (*cʔ, kʔ, pʔ*) fluctuates. Often he represents these by a combination of a dotted consonant plus an apostrophe (<ṭs', ḳ', p̣'>, respectively), but sometimes the dot is omitted (<ts', k', p'>, respectively). Both types of spelling are simply modernized as *cʔ, kʔ, pʔ*.

Another problem with La Flesche's examples is the intrusion of Omaha forms. Omaha was La Flesche's native language; it is related to, but by no means identical with, Osage. As a result, Omaha rather than Osage forms appear in some examples in his data. This problem is especially significant in the case of 2nd person forms of verbs of the syncopating type ("sync.") whose stem has *ð* immediately after the point of inflection. As was seen in the discussion of verb inflection above, the 2nd person form of such verbs in Osage has *št* (replacing *ð*), or *šc* when the following vowel is *e, i,* or *u*; thus, the 2nd person form of *ðaaštą́* 'finish eating, finish doing something with the mouth' is *štáaštą* 'you finish eating, you finish doing something with the mouth', that of *ðaahtą́* 'drink' is *štáahtą* 'you drink', and that of *ðiištą́* 'finish' is *šcíistą* 'you finish'. In La Flesche's data, however, 2nd person forms of such verbs often have <n> or <shn> instead: <na-shto^{n}> 'you stop crying' (modernized retranscription *naštą*), <shna´-ṭo^{n}> 'you drink' (modernized retranscription *šnáhtą*), <ni´-shto^{n}> 'you finished' (modernized retranscription *níštą*). These forms with <n> or <shn> are almost certainly Omaha forms, and do not represent correct Osage of any period. To somewhat reduce the confusion they can cause, such Omaha 2nd person forms have been removed from the La Flesche examples in entries in the present dictionary, and collected in a list of "Problematic forms in La Flesche's dictionary" (see following page).[2]

Clause-final particles are another problem area; several of the final particles that occur in La Flesche's examples do not match Modern Osage forms. One such particle is <i>, which occurs as a marker of 1st person plural in La Flesche's data where Modern Osage would usually have *pe* (contracted from the pluralizer *api* plus declarative *ðe*). The modernized retranscription substitutes *pe* for <i> in such examples. Full-sentence examples in La Flesche's data also sometimes end in what are apparently declarative particles <ha> or <o>—particles that are not used in Modern Osage. Modernized retranscription of such examples retains *ha* and *o*, though usually with a comment pointing out that the particle is not presently used.

6. Problematic Forms in La Flesche's Dictionary

Examples of 2nd person singular forms in La Flesche's Osage dictionary (1932) that appear not to be Osage and are probably Omaha are collected in the list below. Nearly all of these are verbs of the syncopating ("sync.") type in which *ð* follows the point of inflection and that have *n* <n> or *šn* <shn> instead of the expected Osage *št* or *šc*. The

2. La Flesche's 2nd person forms of syncopating verbs are not always Omaha. For *ðaacé* 'call by name', for example, he gives the 2nd person form as <shda´-dse> 'you call by name', which corresponds exactly to Modern Osage *štáace*.

list is arranged by the verb whose inflection is in question (accompanied by a brief gloss). The location of the example in the La Flesche dictionary is indicated by "LFD" plus a page number. As usual, La Flesche's forms are presented both in a modernized retranscription (in italics) and in his original orthography (in angle brackets <>). The expected Osage form (and other comments, when necessary) are noted in square brackets. In some entries below, for instance, it is pointed out that La Flesche presents both a problematic 2nd person form and the expected Osage one for the verb. ("Doubly inflected" indicates verbs that allow two subject pronominal prefixes at different positions; see "Irregularities in use of pronominal prefixes" in the section "Pronominal prefixes.") It should be recalled that there is a good deal of variation in Osage between *u* and *i* (see "Alphabet and pronunciation"), and that La Flesche regularly represents Modern Osage *u* or *uu* as <i>; this is seen in many entries in the list that contain the instrumental prefix *ðu(u)-* (2nd person *šcú(u)-*). Several other forms in LF's examples appear to be Omaha rather than Osage (and this is noted in relevant dictionary entries): e.g., non-Osage consonant clusters *sn* and *šn* appear in LF's forms *ðasni* 'eat', seen in the Osage entry *páðo* 'locust, insect' (cf. normal Osage *ðaaché* 'eat'); *snáðe* 'grease', seen in the Osage entry *stáðe* 'smear on, anoint' (*stáðe* is the normal Osage form); and *šna* 'in the habit of', seen in the Osage entry *sáhku* 'watermelon' (apparently an equivalent of normal Osage *štą* 'always, keep on'; LF also has *štą* <shto^{n}> 'in the habit of' [LFD 134]). Also probably Omaha is LF's form *mązé* <mo^{n}-çe´> 'woman's breast' (LFD 96); contrast normal Osage *paazé* 'breast, udder'.

áalǫðį 'forget'. [Expected Osage 2nd sg.: *áaðalǫšcį* (doubly inflected).] LFD 10: *áðalǫnį* <a´-tha-gtho^{n}-ni^{n}> you failed to remember.

aðée 'go'. [Expected Osage 2nd sg.: *šcée*.] LFD 143: *né į to* <ne´ i^{n} do> you are going. *néškǫsta ži a* <ne´-shko^{n}-sda zhi a> you do not want to go. LFD 13: *ámąši ne ha* <a´-mo^{n}-shi ne ha> you went upstairs. LFD 14: *ápše ne ha* <a´-pshe ne ha> you go. LFD 61: *hiðá ne ha* <hi-tha´ ne ha> you go to bathe. LFD 125: *hpahą́le šne ha* <p̣a-ho^{n}´-gthe shne ha> you precede. LFD 76: *ne htathe íðanąhį a* <ne ṭa-te i´-tha-no^{n}-hi^{n} a> [expected Mod. Os. form of this sentence: *scée che íiðanąhi*] you are willing to go. LFD 55: *lǫ́lǫ ne* <gtho^{n}´-gtho^{n} ne> you muttered. [It is not entirely clear that *ne* <ne> in this last example should be related to *aðée* 'go'. However, LF also provides a 1st sg. form *lǫ́lǫ bre* <gtho^{n}´-gtho^{n} bthe> 'I muttered' (LFD 55), which does appear to contain the expected 1st sg. form (*bré(e)* <bthe>) of *aðée* 'go'.] LFD 102: *moðį́ne*<mo-thi^{n}´-ne> you go afoot, walking. LFD 37: *totą́neha* <do-do^{n}´ne-ha> [expected Mod. Os. form of this sentence: *totą́ scée*] you go to war. • LF also cites something quite close to the expected Osage 2nd sg. form of *aðée*: *hkíhko sce* <ḳi´-ḳu stse> 'you go to a feast' (LFD 86) (expected Mod. Os. form of this sentence: *kíkxo šcée*).

áðiitą 'close by pulling'. [Expected Osage 2nd sg.: *ášciitą*.] LFD 15: *ášnitǫ* <a´-shni-do^{n}> you pulled it over.

áðikʔo 'cover with earth'. [Expected Osage 2nd sg.: *ášcikʔo*.] LFD15: *ášnikʔo* <a´-shni-ḳ'u> you pull earth over it.

aðį 'have'. [Expected Osage 2nd sg.: *ašcį*.] LFD 15: *anį́* <a-ni^{n}´> you have. LFD 54: *akahami lezé wį ani* <a-ga-ha-mi gthe-çe´ wi^{n} a-ni> you have a striped coat. LFD 177: *óðihtą ðalį xci ani* <u´-thi-ṭo^{n} tha-gthi^{n} xtsi a-ni> you have a good position (unconfirmed). LFD 171: *oíhni žįka wį ani* <u-i´-hni zhi^{n}-ga wi^{n} a-ni> [expected Mod. Os. form of this sentence: *oðinii wį ašcį*] you have a parasol.

aðįaðee 'carry, take away'. [Expected Osage 2nd sg.: *ašcį́šcee* (doubly inflected).] *ani sce* <a-ni stse> you took it away.

aðįalee 'take back'. [Expected Osage 2nd sg.: *ašcį́ðalee* (doubly inflected).] LFD 16: *aní ðale* <a-ni´ tha-gthe> you take something home.

aðįali 'bring back here'. [Expected Osage 2nd sg.: *ašcį́ðali* (doubly inflected).] LFD 16: *aní ðali* <a-ni´ tha-gthi> you brought something home.

áðubra 'spread upon'. [Expected Osage 2nd sg.: *áščubra* or *áščibra*.] LFD 15: *ánibra* <a´-ni-btha> you spread oilcloth.

áhkie 'talk for or against'. [Expected Osage 2nd sg.: *áðahkišta* (doubly inflected).] LFD 12: *áðahkina* <a´-tha-ḳi-na> you contend.

aláðį 'carry one's own, inherit'. [Expected Osage 2nd sg.: *aláščį*.] LFD 9: *mǫ́ze ska alani* <mo^{n}´-çe çka a-gtha-ni> you inherited money.

ámąši (a)ðée 'go upstairs': see under **aðée** in this list.

ápše (a)ðée 'go around': see under **aðée** in this list. **ðaahtą́** 'drink'. [Expected Osage 2nd sg.: *štáahtą*.] LFD 142: *šnáhtą* <shna´-ṭo^{n}> you drink.

ðaaštápe 'lick'. [Expected Osage 2nd sg.: *štáaštape*.] LFD 140: *šnástape<shna´-çta-be>* you tasted it.

ðaaštą́ 'stop an activity involving the mouth (eating, drinking, speaking, etc.)'. [Expected Osage 2nd sg.: *ščáaštą*.] LFD 141: *naštą* <na-shto^{n}> you stop crying.

ðiihą́ 'lift'. [Expected Osage 2nd sg.: *ščíihą*.] LFD 147: *níhą* <ni´-ho^{n}> you lift.

ðiðóhtą 'behave'. [Apparently not attested in Mod. Os., but cf. *oðóhtą* 'behave'; expected Osage 2nd sg. of *ðiðóhtą* would be *ščíðohtą*.] LFD 150: *niðóhtą* <ni-tho´-ṭo^{n}> you regulate.

ðiihíce 'play with, tease, persecute'. [Expected Osage 2nd sg.: *ščíihice*.] LFD 147: *níhice* <ni´-hi-dse> you persecuted him.

ðiimǫ́ 'sharpen'. [Expected Osage 2nd sg.: *ščíimǫ*.] LFD 148: *nímǫ* <ni´-mo^{n}> you whet.

ðiištą́ 'finish'. [Expected Osage 2nd sg.: *ščíištą*.] LFD 149: *níštą* <ni´-shto^{n}> you finished, you relinquish claim.

ðiiscúe 'pull open (?), milk (?)'. [Perhaps found only in the expression *paazénii ðiiscúe* 'milk'. Expected Osage 2nd sg.: *ščíiscue*.] LFD 19: *paséni hni, scue* <ba-çe´-ni hni, stsu-e> you milk.

ðiišúpe 'open'. [Expected Osage 2nd sg.: *ščíišupe*.] LFD 149: *níšipe* <ni´-shi-be> you opened the box. • LF also cites the expected Osage form: *hcíže scišupe* <ṭsi´-zhe stsi-shu-be> 'you opened the door' (LFD 149).

ðiitą́ 'pull, tug'. [Expected Osage 2nd sg.: *ščíitą* 'you tugged'.] LFD 145: *nítą waðašką* <ni´-do^{n} wa-tha-shko^{n}> you tugged hard.

ðiiwážįhpíižį 'make angry'. [Not attested in Mod. Os., but expected 2nd sg. would be *ščúuwažihpíiži* or *ščíiwažihpíiži*.] LFD 211: *níwažį hpiži* <ni´-wa-zhi^{n} ṗi-zhi> you angered him.

ðiixǫ́ 'break s.t. long'. [Expected Osage 2nd sg.: *ščíixǫ*.] LFD 151: *níxǫ* <ni´-xo^{n}> you broke the stick in half. • LF also cites the expected Osage form: *žą́xa kše scixǫ* <zho^{n}´-xa ke stsi-xo^{n}> 'you broke the stick in two' (LFD 151).

ðiižóži 'hurt, harm s.o.'. [Expected Osage 2nd sg.: *ščížoži*.] LFD 152: *nížoži* <ni´-zho-zhi> you suffered from humiliation. [LF's translation of this example is erroneous as well; expected Osage meaning is 'you caused suffering, you hurt another emotionally, you humiliated him'.]

ðikšį́ce 'miss, drop'. [Expected Osage 2nd sg.: *ščíkšįce*.] LFD 147: *níkšįce* <ni´-kshi^{n}-dse> you failed to grasp it.

ðikˀíðe 'scratch, tickle'. [Expected Osage 2nd sg.: *ščíkˀiðe*.] LFD 147: *níhkiða* <ni´-ḳi-tha> you tickled him.

ðílą 'flirt, woo'. [Expected Osage 2nd sg.: *ščílą*.] LFD 146: *šnílą* <shni´-gtho^{n}> you court.

ðiwáštake 'tame s.t.'. [Expected Osage 2nd sg.: *ščíwaštake* (doubly inflected).] LFD 150: *níwaštake* <ni´-wa-shta-ge> you tamed the horse.

ðuhpíiži 'harm, make bad'. [Expected Osage 2nd sg.: *ščíhpiži* or *ščúhpiži*.] LFD 148: *níhpiži* <ni´-ṗi-zhi> you ruined it by cutting.

ðupáxa 'pull apart'. [Expected Osage 2nd sg.: *ščípaxe*.] LFD 144: *šnipáxe* <shni-ba´-xe> you broke the string in two.

ðuuláwa 'spread s.t. out'. [Expected Osage 2nd sg.: *ščíilawa* or *ščúulawa*.] LFD 146: *šnílawa weðįkše* <shni´-gtha-wa we-thi^{n}-kshe> you stretched the rope. [*weðį kše* could also precede the verb in Mod. Os.]

ðuušáwa 'undress'. [Expected Osage 2nd sg.: *ščíišawa* or *ščúušawa*.] LFD 148: *níšae* <ni´-sha-e> you undress.

ðuuškáke 'untie'. [Expected Osage 2nd sg.: *ščíišk(ak)e* or *ščúušk(ak)e*.] LFD 149: *níške* <ni´-shke> you untied the knot.

ðuutáaži 'turn off, extinguish'. [Expected Osage 2nd sg.: *ščíitaaži* or *ščúutaaži*.] LFD 36–37: *hpéce nitaži ha* <ṗe´-dse ni-da-zhi ha> you extinguished the fire.

ðuuzáži ‘reject’. [Expected Osage 2nd sg.: *šcíizaži* or *šcúuzaži*.] LFD 145: *nísa ži* <ni´-ça zhi> you reject.
ðuuzé ‘take’. [Expected Osage 2nd sg.: *šcíize* or *šcúuze*.] LFD 154: *níse* <ni´-çe> you take.
ðuwį́ ‘buy’. [Expected Osage 2nd sg.: *šcíwį* or *šcúwį*.] LFD 151: *níwį* <ni´-wi^{n}> you purchase. LFD 34: *šni wį škǫšta ékǫ táatą ðe špaha* <shni wi^{n} shko^{n}-shda e-go^{n} da-do^{n} the-shpa ha> you made him a proposition (unconfirmed; LS/02/95/LS/pc:uk). [Expected Mod. Os. form of this sentence: *šcúwį škǫ́šta éekǫ táatą ðée špáahą* ‘as you wanted to buy, you made that one a proposition’.]
hiiðá (a)ðée ‘go to bathe’: see **aðée** in this list.
hpahą́le (a)ðée ‘go first’: see under **aðée** in this list.
iištáðe ðiitóže ‘wink, blink’. [Expected Osage 2nd sg.: *iištáðe šciitóže* ‘you wink’.] LFD 77: *į̨štáðe nitože* <i^{n}-shta´-the ni-do-zhe> you winked at her.
į́ ‘wear’. [Expected Osage 2nd sg.: *žį́* LFD 74: *oį htą šni*<u-i^{n}´ ṭo^{n} shni> you wear earrings.
lǫ́ðį ‘(be) drunk’. [Expected Osage 2nd sg.: *ðalǫ́šcį* (doubly inflected).] LFD 56: *ðalǫ́ni* <tha-gtho^{n}´-ni> you are drunk.
lǫ́ǫlǫǫ (a)ðée (?) ‘mutter(?)’: see under **aðée** in this list.
mąðį́ ‘walk, live’. [Expected Osage 2nd sg.: *mąšcį́*.] LFD 102: *mǫ́ni* <mo^{n}´-ni> you exist. LFD 14 *áška xci mǫni ha* <a´-shka xtsi mo^{n}-ni ha> you walked a short distance.
mąðį́ (a)ðée ‘go walking’: see under **aðée** in this list.
oðíitą ‘stop, halt’. [Expected Osage 2nd sg.: *ošcíitą*.] LFD 176: *hkáwa ðį ošnitą* <ḳa´-wa thi^{n} u-shni-do^{n}> you checked the horse.
oðíši ‘wrap’. [Expected Osage 2nd sg.: *ošcísį*.] LFD 177: *oníšį* <u-ni´-shi^{n}> you wrap it up.
oðį́įke ‘grasp, hold’. [Expected Osage 2nd sg.: *ošcį́įke*.] LFD 181: *óxta škaɣe ekǫ saki onike* <u´-xta shka-xe e-go^{n} ça-gi u-ni ge> you hold it precious [more exactly, ‘you made it precious, therefore you hold tightly to it’].
omą́ðį ‘walk in, live’. [Expected Osage 2nd sg.: *omą́šcį*.] LFD 179: *oðóšiha omąšni* <u-thu´-shi-ha u-mo^{n}-shni> you walked in advance.
paazénii ðiiscúe ‘milk’: see under **ðiiscúe** in this list.
totą́ha (a)ðée ‘go to war’: see under **aðée** in this list.
waðíhtą ‘do work’. [Expected Osage 2nd sg.: *wašcíhtą*.] LFD 202: *waníhtą* <wa-ni´-ṭo^{n}> you work.
waðíhtąštą ‘workaholic’. [Expected Osage 2nd sg.: *wašcíhtąštą*.] LFD 202: *wanihtąštą* <wa-ni-ṭo^{n}-shto^{n}> you are industrious.
waðíiški ‘do laundry’. [Expected Osage 2nd sg.: *wašcíiški*.] LFD 202: *waníški* <wa-ni´-shki> you wash clothes.
waðílą ‘think things’. [Expected Osage 2nd sg.: *wašcílą*.] LFD 201: *wašnílą* <wa-shni´-gtho^{n}> you meditate.
wáðuɣe ‘(female) be/get married’. [Expected Osage 2nd sg.: *wášcuɣe*.] LFD 152: *ðižį́ka xci tą waniɣe* <thi-zhi^{n}´-ga xtsi do^{n} wa-ni-xe> you married when you were very young (unconfirmed; 02/27/95/JS/pc:uk).
xíða ‘fall, topple’. [Expected Osage 2nd sg.: *ðaxíšta* (doubly inflected).] LFD 218: *ðaxíshna* <tha-xi´-shna> you fall.

7. Abbreviations

7.1. Symbols

* (single asterisk) Marks the following form as a reconstructed form of an earlier stage of the language.
** (double asterisk) Marks the following form as ungrammatical or unacceptable to speakers.
/ (forward slash) Separates alternative glosses or alternative grammatical properties.
~ (tilde) Separates alternative forms.

_ (underscore) Indicates where pronominal prefixes are placed (e.g., *_kʔú* ‘give’ places those prefixes initially; *o_cé* ‘look for’ inserts prefixes between *o* and *c*). See discussion of “Pronominal prefixes” in the “Remarks on Osage grammar.”

< (less-than sign) X < Y + Z signifies that X derives from Y combined with Z.

< > (angle brackets) These enclose the original transcription of examples from historical sources. See “Interpretation of Osage forms in older sources.”

7.2. Grammatical terms

Many of these terms are discussed in the section “Remarks on Osage grammar.”

1st, 2nd, 3rd	first person, second person, third person
ADJ	adjective
ADJP	adjective phrase
ADV	adverb
ADVP	adverb phrase
CAU	causative
CONJ	conjunction
conjug. unknown	conjugation unknown
CONT	continuative auxiliary
DAT	dative prefix
DECL	declarative marker
inalien.	inalienable possessor inflection
INDEF	indefinite
INSTR	instrumental prefix
INTERJ	interjection
INTERR	interrogative
intr.	intransitive
kaa-del.	*kaa*-deleting conjugation
kaa-ret.	*kaa*-retaining conjugation
ka-del.	*ka*-deleting conjugation
ka-ret.	*ka*-retaining conjugation
ki-del.	*ki*-deleting conjugation
ki-ret.	*ki*-retaining conjugation
LOC	locative prefix (*á*-, *í*-, *ó*-)
MODAL	modal marker following verb
N	noun
NEG	negative
NP	noun phrase
N ROOT	noun root
PL, pl.	plural
POSIT	positional article
PPN	postposition
PRNM	pronominal (prefixed element in verb)

PRON	pronoun (independent word)
PRONP	pronoun phrase
RECIP	reciprocal
REFL	reflexive
reg.	regular conjugation
reg.-*iða*	regular conjugation, *iða* subtype
sg.	singular
s.t.	something
s.o.	someone
SUU	suus (reflexive possessive; i.e., object is possessed by subject)
sync.	syncopating conjugation
sync. h-stem	syncopating conjugation, h-stem variant
sync. *k>p*	syncopating conjugation, fortisizing with *k* replaced by *p* in first person singular
trans.	transitive
uninfl.	uninflected (unconjugated)
V	verb
VAL	valence reducer prefix (*wa-*)
VP	verb phrase
V ROOT	verb root

7.3. Language names and comparative and historical sources

For discussion of historical sources, see "Interpretation of Osage forms in older sources." Abbreviations for names of languages other than Osage are in italic capitals.

Cf.	compare (refers to other Osage-English entries)
JOD	Dorsey 1883a, 1883b (James Owen Dorsey manuscript material; see References)[3]
KS	Kansa (Kaw)
LAK	Lakota
LF	Francis La Flesche
LFD	La Flesche 1932 (see References); numbers after "LFD" are page numbers in La Flesche 1932
Mod. Os.	Modern Osage (i.e., late-twentieth-century Osage)
OM	Omaha
OP	Omaha and Ponca
Osage Grammar	Quintero 2004 (see References)
PO	Ponca
QU	Quapaw
RB	Robert Bristow

3. *Eds.*: Carolyn Quintero had not clarified the point, but as far as we can determine, "JOD (slip file)" refers to Dorsey 1883b, while other JOD material is from Dorsey 1883a.

RR	Robert Rankin (normally refers to his draft dictionaries of Kansa and Quapaw [Rankin 1986, 1991])
WI	Winnebago (Hochunk)

7.4. Source codes for Modern Osage forms and examples

7.4.1. Speakers and linguists

AMS	Addie May Sells, of Hominy, Oklahoma
CQ	Carolyn Quintero (linguist)
DN	David Nagle, of Hominy, Oklahoma
ERE	Edward Red Eagle, of Pawhuska, Oklahoma
FH	Frances Oberly Holding, of Hominy, Oklahoma
GR	Gladys Shunkamolah Rouwalk, of Hominy, Oklahoma
HH	Hazel Wahrisi Harper, of Pawhuska, Oklahoma[4]
HHsk	Henry Haskell (written record by Robert Bristow)
HP	Henry Pratt
HRE	Harry Red Eagle, Jr., of Hominy, Oklahoma
HREsr	audiotape of speech at 1965 Osage ceremonial dances by Harry Red Eagle, Sr.
HW	Henry Walker
JK	personal communication from John Koontz (linguist working on Omaha-Ponca)
JS	Jo Ann Shunkamolah Alred, of Hominy, Oklahoma
JW&FW	Josephine and Fred Walker, of Hominy, Oklahoma (written record by Robert Bristow)
KDS	personal communication from Kathy Shea (linguist working on the Ponca language)
KM	Miner 1992 (see References)
LH	Lenora Hamilton (tapes and written record by Robert Bristow)
LL	Leroy Logan, of Hominy, Oklahoma
LS	Laura Shannon, of Hominy, Oklahoma
ML	Mongrain Lookout, of Hominy, Oklahoma
MOJ	Myrtle Oberly Jones, of Tulsa, Oklahoma
MREI	Margaret Red Eagle Iron, of Pawhuska, Oklahoma
MSB	Mary Lookout Standing Bear, of Pawhuska, Oklahoma
PM	Preston Morrell, of Hominy, Oklahoma
RB	Robert Bristow
RL	personal communication from Rory Larson
WF	William Fletcher, of Hominy, Oklahoma

4. *Eds.*: Carolyn Quintero had indicated that in some cases in forms and remarks derived from Robert Bristow's notes, "HH" instead of "HHsk" was inadvertently used for "Henry Haskell." Unfortunately we were unable to determine exactly where this had occurred.

WHM White Hair Memorial, Fairfax, Oklahoma
WM Walter Matin (as reported by Robert Bristow)

7.4.2. Other abbreviations in source codes

c corrected form (XYc = correction made by speaker or linguist XY)
ma expression tentatively approved by speaker ("maybe")
no not acceptable to speaker
ok confirmed as correct
okc "OK as corrected"; i.e., small changes have been made by the Osage speaker to the original example

8. References

For additional references relating to Osage and Siouan, see Quintero (2004:489–90).

Dorsey, James Owen. 1883a. Osage myths, letters, and phrases. Manuscript no. 4800/263. Dorsey Papers: National Anthropological Archives (NAA), Smithsonian Institution, Suitland, MD.

Dorsey, James Owen. 1883b. Osage-English vocabulary. Manuscript no. 4800/268. Dorsey Papers: NAA, Smithsonian Institution, Suitland, MD.

Greenberg, Joseph H. 1966. Some universals of grammar with particular reference to the order of meaningful units. In *Universals of Language*, edited by Joseph H. Greenberg, 73–113. Cambridge, MA: MIT Press.

Kindscher, Kelly. 1987. *Edible Wild Plants of the Prairie: An Ethnobotanical Guide*. Norman: University of Oklahoma Press.

La Flesche, Francis. 1932. *A Dictionary of the Osage Language*. Bureau of American Ethnology Bulletin 109. Washington, DC: Government Printing Office.

Larson, Rory M. 2005. Acculturation terms in Omaha. M.S. thesis, University of Nebraska. 2005.

Miner, Kenneth L., with Robinson Johnson, Lavina Thorud, and Dora Topping. 1992. Winnebago field lexicon. Incorporates most of Josephine P. White Eagle's published dictionary. Ms.

Quintero, Carolyn. 2004. *Osage Grammar*. Lincoln: University of Nebraska Press.

Rankin, Robert L. 1986. "Dictionary of the Kansa Language." Electronic MS. Based on fieldwork conducted between 1974 and 1978 with the last few speakers of the language and on unpublished MS materials from the NAA, Smithsonian Institution. Database program and data fields are similar to those used for Quapaw (Rankin 1991).

Rankin, Robert L. 1991. "Dictionary of the Quapaw Language." Electronic MS. (mk. II, 1991 version extensively edited). Based on salvage fieldwork conducted in 1973–74 and on philological analysis of MS lexical materials from the NAA, Smithsonian Institution.

Photographs of Native-Osage-Speaking Consultants

Photograph of Jo Ann Shunkamolah Alred (*enáetǫįpe*) unavailable.
Photograph of Gladys Shunkamolah Rouwalk (*iniopi*) unavailable.

Robert Bristow (*ðixípe*)

Frances Oberly Holding (*letǫ́wį*)

Hazel Harper

Leroy Logan (*mixóce*)

Mary Lookout Standing Bear (*xúðawį*, Sacred Eagle Woman)

Preston Morrell (*xúa wahkǫ́ta*, Good Eagle), with the author

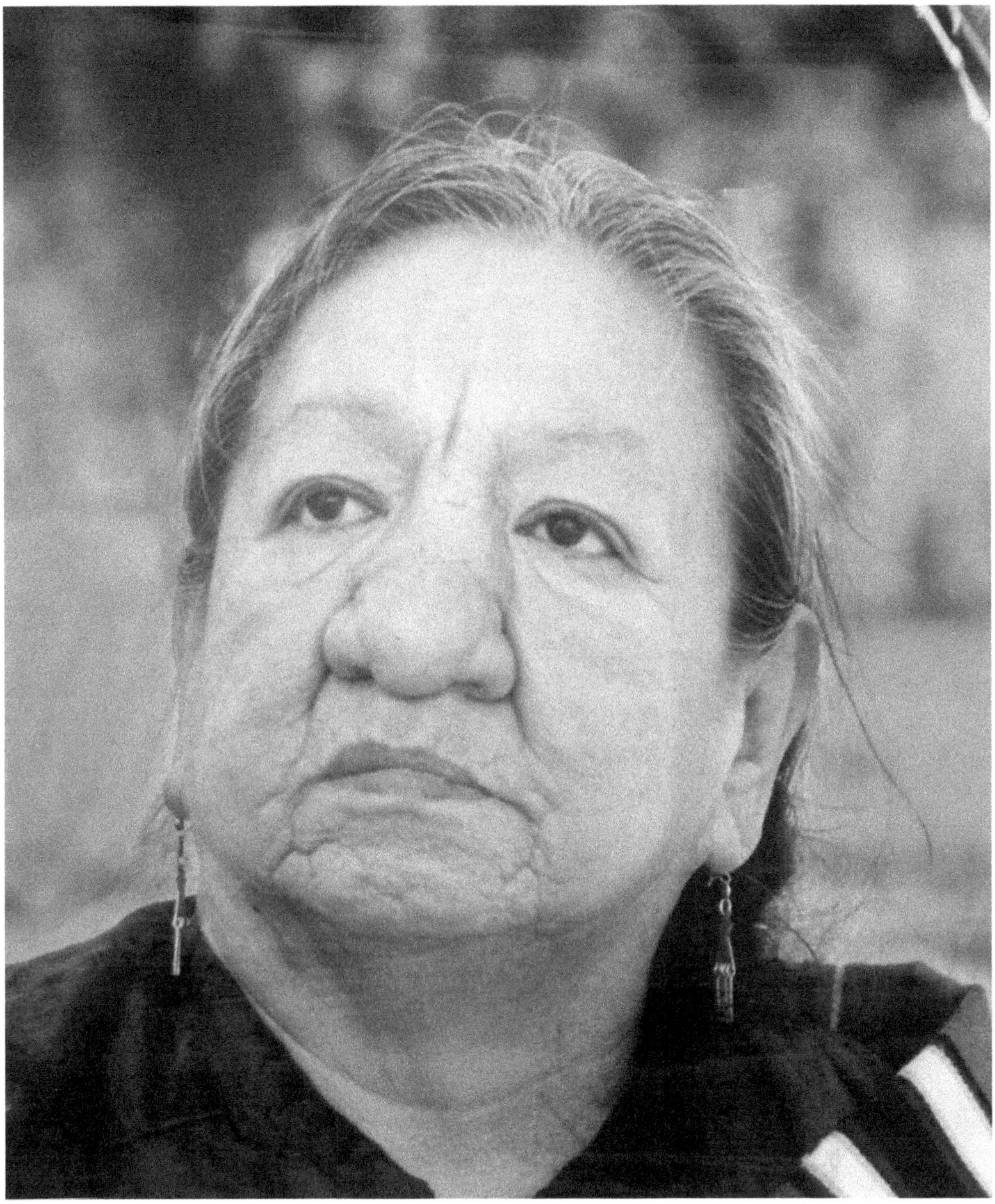

Myrtle Oberly Jones (*wažáxeį̨*)

Margaret Red Eagle Iron (*hį́kamǫke*)

Edward Red Eagle, Sr. (*wahkǫ́ta ohkíe*)

Laura Shannon (*xúða tǫ́į*)

Osage Dictionary

a, á

a. IMPERATIVE MARKER **imperative (particle appearing at the end of a command; replaces final e of verb).** *ąąkú ðaa* go get it for me [*a-ą-ku aðee-a*] (01/31/95/FH/pc:ok). *hápa púzeða!* dry that corn! (FH). *wižįke líi tą, húu hce éa* when Sonny gets back here, have him come over here. *kusúðe a* remember it [archaic; expected form is *kusúða*] (RBn10-5:JW). *óžį hpíiži ðįké, ókˀą ðáalįhkí[ð]a* don't get angry, have good ways (01/04/95/FH/pc). *hkáącezi ðiilóca* peel the orange [from *ðiilóce* 'peel'] (RBn10-20).

a-. PRNM **1st person sg. agent pronominal ('I', subject of regular verbs).**

á-. LOC **on, upon; for (locative prefix; sometimes has benefactive sense).** [Retains accent.] *níhkaši nąhka ški álįį íisipe, ínahižipe* he didn't like to carry people on his back, he didn't agree with it (RBn10-2:MOJ/79).

••• Cf. *álįį*.

áa. N **arm.** *áa ąðíxǫpe* they broke my arm (BE2.4; 01/19/95/FH/pc:ok).

•• LFD 5: *a* arm; that part of the shoulder to and including the hand.

áace. V [reg., *áa_ce*] *(trans.)* **climb, climb onto (by using the arms)** (01/09/95/FH/pc). *įpehi áace* climb back on the pallet (BE2.20; RBn10-6:JW). *įpehi áaca* get on the pillow (crawl onto it) (FH/11/19/01/pc:prod). *hpǫ́ye áace zį* yellow climbing squash. *žįkážį apa žą́ą áaci apai* the children are climbing a tree (RBn10-6:JW).

• *(trans.)* **embrace, wrap one's arms around.**

•• LFD 7: <a´-dse> to embrace; to clasp in the arms with affection; to climb a tree. *áace* <a´-a-dse> I clasped in my arms. *áðace* <a´-tha-dse> you clasped in your arms.

••• Cf. *walézeáace*.

áacexcį. V [reg., *á_cexcį*] *(intr.)* **feel sorry for (lit., 'embrace indeed').** *áacexcį* I feel sorry for you (spoken to someone in pitiful shape) (FH/pc).

áachi. V, ADJ [uninfl. or stat., *áa_chi*] *(intr.)* (be) **sick with fever; feverish, running a little fever** (RBn2-38; MREI/pc). *áachi* he's sick (MREI/pc). *áachi nįkšé?* do you have fever? are you sick? (MREI/pc).

•• LFD 268: *áchį* <a´-tsi^{n}> to be feverish. LFD 45: *ą́chį* <o^{n}´-tsi^{n}> I am feverish. *áðichį* <a´-thi-tsi^{n}> you are feverish. *wachį pe* <wa-tsi^{n} i> we are feverish.

••• *QU hátˀe* to be sick, ill (RR), *žóhkahte* fever, to have a fever (RR).

áadle (variant of **ále**).

áahkǫ. N **armband** (FH; HRE)**; muscle** (LS) (not 'muscle' 04/19/95/FH/pc; HRE/12/29/01/pc).

•• LFD 12: *áhkǫ* <a´-ḳo^{n}> muscle of the arm (04/20/95/LS/pc:ok). *áhką ąnie ha* <a´-ḳo^{n} o^{n}-ni-e ha> [sentence-final *ha* is not used in Mod. Os.] my muscle is sore.

áahkǫle (04/13/95/LS) (variant: **áahkǫla** (BE2.11). N **bracelet.**

•• RB: <áh-ko^{n}-lah> (lit., arm put inside).

•• LFD 13: *áhkǫhta* <a´-ḳo^{n}-ṭa> wrist band, wrist guard.

áahu. N **wing.** *áahu saakí* wing, the kind used in peyote meetings (lit., 'hard or firm wing'; in a peyote meeting, a wing is sent around after midnight so that everyone can fan off [RB]) (LS). *áahu saakí ðée hpaaɣé* I'm going to let the wing go; I'm sending the wing (05/01/95/LS/pc:ok). *áahu ðée hpáaɣe hta mįkšé* I'm going to send the wing (BE2.159; 05/01/95/LS/pc:okc).

• N **shoulder blade** (MREI).

•• LFD 10: *áhu* <a´-hiu> wings.

áahu htą. N **big wing** (LS); **one who possesses wings.**

•• LFD 11: *áhu htǫi* <a´-hiu-ṭo^{n}i> who possesses wings. A ritual term. [LF unconfirmed, 05/01/95/LS/pc: *áahu htǫ́* or *áahu htą́* does not state possession.]

áahu mą́ðį. N **turkey cock** (LF only).

•• LFD 10: *áhu mąðį* <a´-hiu mo^{n}-thi^{n}> wings walking; the turkey cock.

áahualįį. N **angel (lit., 'wings upon')** (01/04/95/FH/pc:ok; RBn2-moj/p3).

áahukˀoe. N **Holes in the Wings (personal name).** *áahukˀoe kikˀǫ́ kšíe hta apái* Henry [holes-in-the-wings] is going to paint him (for burial) (03/03/95/FH/pc:ok; RBn2-moj/p21).

áakxa. VP [*ée* 'say' + *akxa* CONT] **they say, he/she says; they were saying, he/she was saying; they/he/she said (postverbal singular or plural marker of reported information deriving from person[s] who is/are present and not moving).** ['Moving' here means 'changing location'; motions or gestures that do not change the entity's location in horizontal space do not take this affix.] *óohǫ akxa tooská ðįké áakxa* the cook says there are no potatoes (RRBn1-43).

áakxa (*continued*)

•• JOD (Devouring Mountain, p2, ln10): *wahǫ́ižįka bráanį na nąącé ąpastǫka ku káaɣape áakxa ska* <Wahŭ^{n}iç͓iñ´k͓a p¢a´hni^{n}-na´ năn´t͓ç͓e a^{n}p͓astŭñ´k͓a k͓ü k͓axap͓͓i, á akqa ska> the orphan that I devoured made my heart turn soft, he said.

áakxą (variant: **áatkxą**). v [uninfl.?] [possibly a contraction of *áðiikxą*] *(intr.)* **lie down, as to sleep or rest.** *áatkxą mįkšé* I'm lying down (FH). • *(trans.)* **lie against; lean up against** (FH). *áatkxa ážą* lie up against it, lie on (e.g., a divan) (FH/pc).

••• Cf. *áðiikxą.*

áalake. v [reg., *aa_lake*] *(trans.)* **be bothered or annoyed by, be irritated by; find bothersome** (dn/fh980930; FH/11/19/01/pc). [Not stative; ***ðílake* is unacceptable.] *áalake* it bothers me, it irritates me, it's bothersome (03/01/95/FH/pc:pc). *íixa štą áalake* her laughing all the time bothers me. *íixa štą áaðalake?* does her laughing all the time bother you? (lit., 'you are bothered by her laughing incessantly?') (FH/11/19/01/pc:prod). *íixa štą che wáali ąąlakape* her laughing all the time really bothers us (FH/11/19/01/pc:prod).

••• Cf. *waaláke, wáalake.*

áale (variant of **ále**).

áalįį. N **chair, seat** (01/09/95/FH/pc:ok). *áalįį táahpa* stool (lit., 'round chair'). *áalįį wahéhe tǫpéwai* the chair looks weak (BE2.152; 03/16/95/JS/pc:ok).

•• LFD 10: *álį tahpa* <a´-gthi^{n} da-p͓a> round chair; a stool. *álį sǫsǫða* <a´-gthi^{n} ço^{n}-ço^{n}-tha> a rocking. LFD 170: *aliche aðalį* <a-gthi-tse a-tha-gthi^{n}> you occupied the chair.

áalǫðį (variant: **áalǫði**). v [reg.+sync., *aa_lǫ_ðį* (first or second slot in verb may optionally remain unconjugated)] *(trans.)* **forget; leave behind** (01/30/95/FH/pc:prod; orig; FH/07/09/01/pc). *áawilǫbre ðąąché įké* I'll never forget you (01/12/95/FH/pc). *áalǫbrį* I forgot. *áalǫbri* I forget. *áðalǫšcį* you forget. *áaðalǫðį ðįké* you didn't forget it (01/30/95/FH/pc:okc; BE2.50). *tooská áaðalǫšcį ðalíe* you forgot to bring back potatoes. *áaðilǫðį* he forgot you (FH:5/02/96/prod). *John akxa áalǫðį akxai* John forgets. *ą́ąðilǫðį ðąąché įké* we'll never forget you (FH:5/02/96/prod). *ąkáalǫðį akátxa* we forget (RBnot-nd-1/10; 01/30/95/FH/pc:ok). *áalǫðį įká ðį* don't forget it [said to one person] (RBn10-7:JW). *áaðalǫðį ðįké!* don't forget it! (01/30/95/FH/pc:okc; BE2.50).

•• LFD 10: *álǫðį* <a´-gtho^{n}-thi^{n}> to forget; failure to remember; unable to recall something that is past. *áalǫbrį* <a´-a-gtho^{n}-bthi^{n}> I failed to remember. *ąkálǫ ðį pe* <o^{n}-ga´-gtho^{n} thi^{n} i> we forgot.

áalǫ́ðį (variant of **álǫðį**).

áapa. REPORTATIVE [*ée* 'say' + *apa* CONT] **they say or are saying or were saying; he/she says or is saying or was saying (indicates that information in the sentence is or was reported by another or others).** *níhkaši apa wálį ók?ą hpíiži brį́ aapái* people say I'm hard to get along with (RBn17-p02). *níhkašie tówa apa pą́ apa áapa* those people coming there are just hollering, they're saying (01/04/95/FH/pc:okc; FH/11/19/01/pc:prod). *Carolyn apa wéðuɣe aðeé hta apa áapai* Carolyn is going to a wedding [they say] (02/27/95/JS/pc). *wižį́ke akxa wažážeíe ípahǫ áapai* Sonny knows Osage, that's what they're saying. *mąxpúmęį apa oðíchįpe aapai* lightning and thunder are getting you [pl.], they are saying (line from a children's song) (FH).

áape (variants: **áapie** [archaic], **áap, éepe**). REPORTATIVE [*ée* 'say' + *api* + *ðe*] **he/she/they said, it is said, known by hearsay (indicates that information in the sentence was reported by another or others; often used in ceremonial speech and in storytelling).** *žįkážį ški c?éðe apa áape* it is said that they are also killing children (RBn3-03). *wahkǫ́taki nį́ áapie* they said you were a doctor [expected Mod. Os. form of *áapie* is *áape*] (BE2.33). *ąkóðihkíepi áha, ðak?éwaðakíðe hta nįkšé áap* when we talk to you, they said you would pity us. *áwanǫbre ðiištą́pe, štǫ́pe škǫ́šta, ónǫbre ški ážupi áape, waskúe ški ážupe* they got the tables finished, do you want to look at them?; and they've even put the food on, they said, they've got fruit on the table, too (FH:prod). *hcí hcéka ðiištą́pi áape wahǫ́e* [i.e., *wahǫ́i*] *hta akxai* they said that the new house is finished so she's going to move in (FH/06/20/95). *hkiistó panáapi áape* he adjourned the meeting, they said. *tówa apa waachípi áape* they said those men danced. *taaké ðaašé áape* they said you were fighting (RBn22-19). *wišį́ke íe akxa áape* they said he talked; they said he was talking. *táatą ðáalį waðakšíe hta ðíe nįkši áape* they said you're the one that's going to make everything good for us (RBn22-02). *íe ohkípše nįkší áape* they said you keep your word. • **as it is or was told or said (e.g., in a story or in the Bible).** *įhtáci wahkǫ́ta, mą́žą ðáalį įkši ðaníhkaši nįkší eepe* our father, who art in heaven. *hcí káaɣi che éži ípahǫži apa áape* no one would ever know where she made her nest (RBn19-03).

••• Cf. *áapa.*

áapiolą. N **armband** (HRE/12/29/01/pc:ok; RBn).

áatkxą (variant of **áakxą**).

ábro N **shoulder** (BE2.120; 03/09/95/MREI/pc:ok).

•• LFD 6: *ábro* <a´-btho> shoulder or shoulder blade; upper arm. [The gloss 'upper arm' is unconfirmed (MREI).]

••• Cf. *áahu.*

áceðe. v [reg., *á_ceðe*] *(trans.)* **build a fire on.**

•• LFD 7: *áceðe* <a´-dse-the> to build a fire on some place or object. *áaceðe* <a´-a-dse-the> I built a fire on (a stone). *áðaceðe* <a´-tha-dse-the> you built a fire on (a stone). *ǫkáceða pe* <o^{n}-ga´-dse-thape> we built a fire on (a stone).

••• Cf. *océðe.*

achí v [reg., *_achí*] [initial *a* is sometimes omitted in 3rd person forms and normally omitted in imperatives] *(intr.)* **arrive here, come here (motion accomplished), reach as a location or place.** *achíe* I've arrived. *mąðí ðachíe?* did you come afoot? *hą́ąhkaži, oðíhta olį́į achíe* no, I came in a car (BE2.22). *mį́įoðaake šáhpe tą achíe* I got here at six o'clock (RBn10-22/JW&FW). *ðáalį wažǫ́, waðákitǫpe ðachí che* it's good, what you have done, to come and see us (01/06/95/FH/pc:ok). *ðáalį wažǫ́, waðákitǫ ðachí che* it's good, what you have done, to come and see us (01/06/95/FH/pc:ok). *ðachíe* you [sg.] have arrived. *hcéka ðachíe?* did you just get here? (01/06/95/FH/pc:ok). *háatxąta waðákištǫpaapi ðachí hta nąkxáaše?* when are you all going to come see us? [to more than one, seated]. *ðachípe* you have come; you've arrived [to more than one] (01/06/95/FH/pc:ok). *ðachíe ska* you have been here before; you must have come here before (01/06/95/FH/pc:ok). *níhkašíe achípe* some people came. *chí hta ðé?* is he coming? will he arrive here? (RBn12-06). *níhkašíe tóe achípe* some people came (01/06/95/FH/pc). *achípe* they've arrived; they have come. *wažážeíe ąkáchipe* we've come here to speak Osage (RBn23-01). *ąkáchipe* we [three or more] arrived; we've arrived; we've come (RBn3-47; 01/06/95/FH/pc:ok; BE2.4). *ąkáchie* we [two] arrived; we [two] have come. *miðóhtą tą wanǫ́bre chí pai* at noon, come here to dine [pl. addressee]. *miðóhtą tą wanǫ́bre chí ði* at noon, come here to dine [sg. addressee]. *chípi tą íinǫǫhpapai íðaapi tą* when they come be careful when you [pl.] speak (FH/11/19/01/pc:prod).

•• LFD 16: *achíį to* <a-tsi´i^{n} do> I have come. *achínąžį* <a-tsi´-no^{n}-zhi^{n}> came and stood. LFD 162: *hci* <ṭsi> [expected Mod. Os. form: *chi*] to come. *achi* <a-tsi> I have come. *ðachi* <tha-tsi> you have come. *ąkachi* <o^{n}-ga-tsi> we have come. *ðihtą́ke chi a(?)* <thi-ṭo^{n}´-ge tsi a(?)> has your sister come?

áðaace. v [sync., *á_ðaace*] *(trans.)* **repeat or say again, call upon again, name again.** [Unattested in modern Osage.]

•• JOD (Raccoons and Crawfish p24, ln9): *wížįðé, waaðǫ́ che áðaata ðį hau* <Wíçi^{n}¢é, wa¢ŭ^{n}´ tsĕ á¢atá-¢i^{n} haú> Elder Brother, that song, repeat it.

áðahtaha. N **(location) on the other side** (FH:4/18/96/tape). *áðahtaha ípšape ąži owáhkie apažíe* they went right past us [on the other side] but didn't speak to us (RB-MSB 4/7/83; FH:4/18/96/tape:okc). *áðahtaha íðapše* you passed right by (FH:4/18/96/tape:prod).

áðasta (variant of **ásta**).

aðée (variants: **aðíi, ðée, ðíi**). v [sync., *(a)_ðée*] [initial *a* is often omitted, regularly so with 1st singular and 2nd person subject; this verb is rarely used in imperatives (*mąðį́* is preferred)] *(intr.)* **go there (motion underway), set out for there, be on the way to there** (RBn23-17). *hpǫ́hka htą́wą įkši brée* I'm going to Ponca City (01/31/95/FH/pc:prod). *htáabre brée* I'm going [big game] hunting (FH:ok). *waachí abrée* [initial *a* is unexpected] I'm going to dance (PM). *žą́ą akubrée na* I'm going to get wood. *ówehci ce brée hkǫ́bra* I want to go to the grocery store (02/01/95/FH/pc:okc). *hową́įki šcée?* where are you going? *hową́įki štáape?* where are you [pl.] going? *waachí watǫ́a šcée hta ðąįšé?* are you going to the dance? *šcée hta paašé?* are you [pl.] going? *ilǫ́įhpa hową́įki ðée?* where did Sonny go? (02/01/95/FH/pc:ok). *ilǫįhpa akxa htą́wą ki aðáape* Sonny went to town (02/01/95/FH/pc:ok; BE2.56-57). *hkáwa alį́į aðée iche* he's gone horseback riding (01/31/95/FH/pc:ok). *šǫ́ke akxa htą́wą kši aðée apai* the dog is on his way to town. *hkáwa alį́į aðáapi che* they went horseback riding (01/31/95/FH/pc:plural). *šį́toži apa aðée įké hta apai* the boys aren't going to go (RBn10-2). *oðíhtą olį́į aðáape* they got in the car and went (01/31/95/FH/pc:ok). *kahíke, mą́hi htąą, éðǫǫpa nímąse aðáapi áape* the chief and superintendent went abroad [it is said] (02/01/95/FH/pc:okc). *hcí hta aðáape* they went into the house (05/01/95/FH:pd). *mą́ąye ðáalį tą,*

aðée (*continued*)
hóolą ąkái hta ąkái if the weather is good, we are going to go fishing (02/01/95/FH/pc:ok). *hkiistóhci ci ąkái hce* let's [two persons] go to the courthouse. *sį́ka ąkóce ąkái hce* let's [two persons] go squirrel hunting. *húhekahci ci ąkáðe ðálį* we ought to go to the hospital. *hǫpái wanǫ́bre ąkáðape* we're going to the dinner today (01/31/95/FH/pc:ok). *hǫpái wanǫ́bre ąkái htai* let's [three or more persons] go to the dinner today. *opáwįye ąkái htai* let's [three or more persons] go for a ride. *ðíi įká, wáaspa ði!* [for *ðée ðįįká . . .*] don't go anywhere, stay there! (FH). *ąąkú ðaa* go get it for me (01/31/95/FH/pc:ok). *pée ðaažį́ hta apai* nobody is going (MSB02583). • **leave, be leaving.** *šǫðeðe brée hta mįkšé* I'm going to leave for good (02/15/95/FH/pc:ok). *ščée ðáalį!* leave! go on! (lit., 'you should leave') (02/15/95/FH/pc:ok; BE2.78). *šǫðéðe aaðáape* he left for good (e.g., when a husband leaves a wife, not to come back) (02/15/95/FH/pc:okc). • **go forward, set out, start off.** *kaðǫ tǫ́pe aðáape* he started off to see what he could see (lit., 'and he immediately went looking') (RBn15-03).

•• LFD 143: *bréį to* <bthe´-i^{n} do> [expected Mod. Os. form: *brée*] I am going. *ąka ða į to* <o^{n}-ga tha i^{n} do> [expected Mod. Os. form: *ąkáðape*] we are going. *ðée* <the´-e> he went. *ðekǫ́ðaži* <the-go^{n}´-tha-zhi> no desire to go. *bréhkǫbra mąži* <bthe´-ḳo^{n}-btha mo^{n}-zhi> I do not want to go.

áðibra (variant of **áðubra**).

áðihta. v [sync., *á_ðihta*] *(trans.)* **go or be contrary to.** *wahkílaace áðihtą* he violates the law (02/15/95/FH/pc:okc).

•• LFD 192: *wáhkilace aðihta* <wa´-ḳi-gtha-dse a-thi-ṭa> to violate [the law]. *wahkilace aðihta* <wa-ḳi-gtha-dse; a-thi-ṭa> goes-contrary-to-rule; to violate.

aðíi (variant of **aðée**).

áðiihtą (variants: **áðihta, álihtą**). v [sync., *á_ðihtą*] [*á-* LOC + *ðiihtą́*] *(trans.)* **close by grasping.** [Contrasts with *áðiitą* 'close by pulling'.] *okáhǫpa áðiihta* close the window (04/28/95/LS/pc:okc). *okáhąpa áðiihta, níižu akxai* close the window, it's raining.

••• *QU ádihtą* aim at something (RR).

••• Cf. *waðíhtą.*

áðiikxą (variant: **áðįįkxa**). v [uninfl.] *(intr.)* **lie down against; lean up against, recline, rest** (FH:4/25/96/tape). *kaatxá aðįįkxa ažį́įhe hce* let me just lie down and sleep a while. *áðįįkxa ažį́įhe hta mįkšé* I'm going to go lie down and sleep. *aðįįkxa! aðįįkxa mąðį́!* lie down and rest! go lie down! (e.g., to a child) (FH:6/25/01). *áðįįkxa žį́įhe mąðį́* you'd better go lie down and sleep.

•• LFD 315: *áðihkǫ* <a´-thi-ḳo^{n}> to recline as when attacking.

••• *QU ádikhą ithéde* pull over [a sg. standing object]; make an upright object lean by pulling it (RR).

••• Cf. *áakxą.*

áðiikxą žąą. VP [reg., *áðiikxą _žąą*] **recline.**

•• LFD 15: *áðihką žą* <a´-thi-ḳo^{n} zho^{n}> to recline. *áðihką́ ažą* <a´-thi-ḳo^{n} a-zho^{n}> I recline. *áðihką́ ðažą* <a´-thi-ḳo^{n} tha-zho^{n}> you recline. *áðihką́ ąžą pe* <a´-thi-ḳo^{n} o^{n}-zho^{n} i> we recline.

áðiitą. v [sync., *á_ðiitą*] [*á-* LOC + *ðiitą́*] *(trans.)* **close by pulling; pull to; shut** (RBn1-25). [Contrasts with *áðiihtą* 'close by grasping'.] *hcižé áðiita níwahce akxa* close the door, it's cold (01/09/95/FH/pc: ok; BE2.20).

•• LFD 15: *áðitǫ* <a´-thi-do^{n}> to pull over one, as a blanket; to shut, as a door. *ábritǫ* <a´-bthi-do^{n}> I pulled it over me. *ąkaðitǫ pe* <o^{n}´-ga-thi-do^{n} i> we pulled it over.

••• *KS áyaidą* (MR) pull on (RR).

áðikˀo. v [sync., *á_ðikˀo*] *(trans.)* **cover with earth; pull dirt over.**

•• LFD 15: *áðikˀo* <a´thi-ḳ'u> to pull earth over some object. *ábrikˀo* <a´-bthi-ḳ'u> I pull earth over it. *ǫ́kaðikˀo pe* <o^{n}´-ga-thi-ḳ'u i> we pull earth over it.

••• *OM* same as Osage (LFD 15).

aðímą. v [sync., *a_ðimą*] *(trans.)* **fasten.** *saakí aščíma* you fastened it [tightly] (FH).

áðixope. v [sync.?, *á_ðixope*?] *(trans.)* **honor.** *hǫ́ǫpa ðé wéeną akxai ðe níhkaši tóa áðixopape, hpáðį wéhkili íweeehkili į kšíγape* she's grateful today because they honored her, they dressed her [lit., 'made her clothe herself'] in Kiowa clothes (RBn23-17; cqc).

••• Cf. *ðixópe.*

áðižą. v [reg., *á_ðižą*] *(trans.)* **put s.o. to bed; make s.o. lie upon a bed; have s.o. in bed.** *John akxa Mary áðiižą hį́ðokižį* John has Mary in bed naked (RB).

aðį́. v [sync., *a_ðį́*] *(trans.)* **have, own, possess** (01/04/95/FH/pc:prod; BE2.64). *mą́zeska tóa ascį nįkšé?* do you [sitting] have any money? *mą́zeska tóa ascį́ ðaįšé?* do you [moving] have any money? (01/04/95/FH/pc). *mą́zeska háaną ascį ðatxą́še?* how much money do you [standing] have? (01/04/95/FH/pc:ok). *mą́zeska aðį́ ðe?* does he have money? *mą́zeska aðį́ akxai* he has money. *mą́zeska húuwaalį apai* he has a lot of money. *hį́įce húu aðį́ akxai* they have a lot of dishes. *wahóohta ašcį́ paašé?* do you [pl.] have guns? *howé, ąkáðį ąkáe* yes, we have them [guns]. *níhkaši apa hkáwa záani aðį́ apai* all of them own a horse.

•• LFD 15: *aðį́* <a-thi^{n}´> to have. *abrį́* <a-bthi^{n}´> I have. *ąkáðį́ pe* <o^{n}-ga´-thi^{n}´ i> we have.

••• *OM* same as Osage (LFD 15).

aðįachi. v [sync.+reg., *a_ðį(a)_chi*] [*aðį́* + *achí*] [initial *a* of *achí* is sometimes omitted in 3rd person forms] *(trans.)* **bring here; arrive here with (motion accomplished).** *žąąnížį awíbrįachíe* I brought you some candy. *óŋǫbre tóe ašcį́ðachi hta ðaašé?* are you going to bring some food? (01/09/95/FH/pc:ok). *haxį́ wį ašcį́ðachie?* did you bring a blanket? (01/09/95/FH/pc:ok). *hą́ąhkaži, haaskámi abrį́achie* no, I brought a shawl (01/09/95/FH/pc:ok). *óŋǫbre háachi ąðįchí apai* they keep on bringing food. *óðaake waléze aðįchípe?* did they bring the newspaper? (01/09/95/FH/pc:ok). *táatą ąšcį́ðachíe?* what did you bring me? *ąkáðįąkáchie* we [two] brought it. *ąkáðįąkáchipe* we [three or more] brought it.

aðįaðee. v [sync.+sync., *a_ðį́(a)_ðee*] [*aðį́* + *aðée*] [initial *a* of *aðée* is often omitted, regularly so with 1st singular and 2nd person subject and in imperative] *(trans.)* **carry.** *ábrįbree hta mįkšé* I will take it (JS, 03/15/95/PM/pc:ok). *haxį́ wį́ abrį́bree mįkšé* I'm taking a blanket [there]. *mą́zeska aðį́ðee?* is he taking any money [with him as he leaves]? (RB). *ópoce ášihta aðį́ðaa* take the trash outside (03/23/95/FH/pc:okc). • **take there (motion underway); take away** (03/15/95/PM/pc:ok). *wak?óžį wį mąhką́ aðįðíi aape iiðáahpapi* wait for little white woman carrying medicine (translation of the Cree name of woman who married into the Kaw tribe) (FH).

•• LFD 16: *aðį́ðe* <a-thi^{n}´-the> to take away an object. *abrį́bre* <a-bthi^{n}´-bthe> I took it away. *ǫkáðį ǫkaða pe* <o^{n}-ga´-thi^{n} o^{n}-ga-tha i> we took it away (03/15/95/PM/pc:ok).

••• *OM* same as Osage (LFD 16).

aðįahi. v [sync.+sync. h-stem, *a_ðį́(a)_hi*] [*aðį́* + *ahí*] [initial *a* of *ahí* is often omitted, regularly so with 1st singular and 2nd person subject] *(trans.)* **take there; bring there (motion accomplished), deliver.** *ówe che hcí ąkóhtapi aðįhi* bring those groceries [there] to our house (FH). *táatą aðįhi* take something there, deliver things to someone (04/04/95/FH/pc:ok). *wižį́ke akxa haxį́ wį aðįahípe* my son took a blanket over there.

•• LFD 16: *aðįhi* <a-thi^{n}´hi> to reach a place with some object. LFD 34: *tátą aðį hi* <da´-do^{n} a-thi^{n} hi> delivery of gifts.

••• *OM* same as Osage (LFD 16).

aðįahu. v [sync.+reg., *a_ðį(a)_hu*] [*aðį́* + *ahú*] [initial *a* of *ahú* is often omitted, regularly so with 1st singular and 2nd person subject] *(trans.)* **bring here (motion underway).** *wižį́ke akxa haxį́ wį́ aðįahu akxai* my son is bringing a blanket here. *abrį́pšu mįkšé* I'm bringing it there. *žą́ąxe wį aðįhú hta apai* they're going to bring a board [for the baby] (FH:prod).

aðįakši. v [sync.+reg., *a_ðį(a)_kši*] [*aðį́* + *akší*] [initial *a* of *akší* is sometimes omitted with 3rd person subject] *(trans.)* **take back there; take home; bring back there; bring home (motion accomplished).** *wižį́ke akxa haxį́ wį́ aðįakšipe* my son took a blanket home, got home with it.

aðįaku. v [sync.+reg., *a_ðį(a)_ku*] [*aðį́* + *akú*] [initial *a* of *akú* is sometimes omitted with 3rd person subject and in imperative forms] *(trans.)* **bring back here.** *hcí hta ówe aðįku* bring the groceries in the house. *ðéekaa áðįku* bring it here (01/09/95/FH/pc:ok). *ówe che hcí hta áðįku* bring those groceries sitting there inside (01/09/95/FH/pc:ok). *áðįku* bring it back (01/09/95/FH/pc:ok; BE2.12).

aðįalee. v [sync.+reg., *a_ðį(a)_lee*] [*aðį́* + *alée*] [initial a of *alée* often omitted with 3rd person and in imperative forms] *(trans.)* **take back, take home (motion underway); set out to take s.t. home, back (only in sentences showing completed action).** *aðįalaape* they set out to take it home. *abrį́alee* I took it back/home (03/15/95/PM/pc:okc). *aðį́ðalee* you take something back/home [*aðį́* is unexpectedly unconjugated in this example] (03/15/95/PM/pc:okc). *ąkáðįąkálaape* we took something back/home (03/15/95/PM/pc:ok). *wáaðįlaa* take this [back home] to them (2/3/84/080).

•• LFD 16: *aðį́le* <a-thi^{n}´-gthe> to take something home. *abrįale* <a-bthi^{n}-a-gthe> I took something home. *ąkáðį ąkala pe* <o^{n}-ga´-thi^{n} o^{n}-ga-gtha i> we took something home.

••• *OM* same as Osage (LFD 16).

aðįali. v [sync.+reg., *a_ðį(a)_li*] [*aðį́* + *alí*] [initial *a* of *alí* is often omitted in 3rd person forms and in imperative] *(trans.)* **bring back here, bring back home (motion accomplished).** *žą́ą toa abrį́alie* I'm back with wood. *ówe toe aðį́įli* bring some groceries back (01/06/95/FH/pc: prod).

aðįali (*continued*)

•• LFD 16: *aðįli* <a-thi^{n}-gthi> to bring something home. *abrį ali* <a-bthi^{n} a-gthi> I brought something home. *ąkáðį ąkali pe* <o^{n}-ga´-thi^{n} o^{n}-ga-gthi i> we brought something home.

••• *OM* same as Osage (LFD 16).

aðįažą. v [sync.+reg., *a_ðįa_žą*] [*aðį* + *ážą*] *(trans.)* **copulate with, screw, lay, have intercourse with.** *óžąke paskúha abrįažą hta akxai* I could screw her beside the road (RB).

••• *KS áažą* lie on, to "lay," have sex (RR).

áðįchi (see **áðįachi**).

aðíðee (see **aðįaðée**).

aðįhé, áðįhé (variants of **ąðįhé**).

aðíhi (see **aðįahi**).

aðįhú (see **aðįahu**).

áðįįkxa (variant of **áðiikxą**).

aðíkši (see **aðįakši**).

áðįku (see **aðíaku**).

aðįlee (see **aðíalee**).

áðįli (see **aðíali**).

aðímąðį. v [sync.- reg., *a_ðímą_ðį*] *(trans.)* **take away.** *káache aðímąðį* take away this thing here.

aðóoha ADV **again** (RB, unconfirmed).

•• LFD 16 (unconfirmed): *aðóha* <a-thu´-ha> again.

áðubra (variant: **áðibra**). v [sync., *á_ðubra*] *(trans.)* **spread upon; spread over** (04/26/95/FH/pc:okc).

•• LFD 15: *áðibra* <a´-thi-btha> to spread oilcloth. [This verb does not actually imply 'oilcloth'.] *ábribra* <a´-bthi-btha> I spread oilcloth. *ą́kaðibra* <o^{n}´-ga-thi-btha> we spread oilcloth.

••• *KS blá* spread out, as dishes on the table (RR).

áðuɣe. v [sync., *á_ðuɣe*] *(trans.)* **marry, get married to, take as a husband (gender-specific term).** *howaðéeški áðuɣe hkǫ́bra įké* I don't want to marry anybody (RBn17-p02). *wášcuɣe?* did you marry? (FH:4/25/96/tape). *Davea áščuɣe?* did you marry Dave? (FH:4/25/96/tape:prod). *Johna wáščuɣe hta ðaįší aape* they said you were going to get married to John. *Dave áðuɣe akxai* she married Dave (02/24/95/FH/pc:ok). *wáðuɣe* they're married (02/24/95/FH/pc:ok).

•• JOD (slip file): *waðúɣe* <wa-¢ú-xĕ> to take a husband, to marry.

•• LFD 204: *wáðuɣe* <*wa´-thu-xe*> to marry; to take a husband.

••• *QU ádiɣe* marry a man, take a man for a husband (RR); *KS áayüɣe* marry a man, take a husband (RR).

••• Cf. *wáðuɣaži, wáðuɣe, wéðuɣe.*

áðuuhta. PPN **across.** *níi htą́ą áðuuhta brée hta mįkšé* I'm going to go across the ocean (FH/04/08/01/pc). *áðuuhta ðée* go across.

••• *QU dihté* cross a stream (RR).

áðuuhta ðée. VP [sync., *áðuuhta _ðee*] *(trans.)* **cross.**

áðuwį. v [sync., *á_ðuwį*] [*á-* LOC (benefactive sense) + *ðuwį́*] *(trans.)* **buy for another.** [Not used when the person benefiting from the purchase is present at the time of speaking; in that case *kíðuwį* (dative) is used.] *ábruwį* I bought it for him. *áščuwį* you bought it for him. *áðuwį* she bought it for him. *ą́ąðuwį* we bought it for him. *áðuwį* they bought it for him.

••• Cf. *áwaðuwį.*

áðuzu. v [sync.?, *á_ðuzi?*] *(trans.)* **pull over to cover; tug s.t. over in order to cover s.t. or s.o.** (RBn3-23; cqc). *omíži áðuzu* cover him with a blanket (as a person sleeping) (RBn3-23).

•• JOD (slip file): *áðuzúpe* <a´-¢ü-şǘ-pe> to pull the edge of a blanket, etc., over one, to cover him.

••• *KS áayüzübe* pull the edge over one, as a blanket (JOD, RR).

áɣaake. v [reg., *á_ɣaake*] [*á-* LOC (benefactive sense)+ *ɣaaké*] *(trans.)* **cry for.** *áðiɣaakí apai* they're crying for you (MSB). *áɣaake apai* they're crying for her.

áha (variants: **aha, ahá**). ADV, CONJ **whenever.** *mą́zeíe ohkíe áha ohkíhkie akxái* they talked [by phone] whenever he called (FH:prod; MSB). *íiwiði áha owíhkie mąží hta mįkšé* whenever I see you I'm not going to talk to you (FH/02/17/96/pc:prod). *ǫkóðihkiepi áha ðakˀéwaðakie hta nįkšé áape* they said you would pity us whenever we talk to you (RBn22-01). *ąną́ðapi áha awáhkie ðíląpe* whenever they saw me they wanted to talk (MSB). • **as soon as, immediately when; whereupon.** *šímižį apa aną́ðapi aha óhką apái* just as soon as the girls saw me, they helped her. *ąną́ðapi áha taaké apai* when they saw me, they started fighting (lit., 'they saw me, whereupon they were fighting') (3/2/753/MSB). *ąną́ðapi áha ąwą́hkie kǫ́ðape* when he saw me, he [immediately] wanted to talk with me.

•• JOD (slip file): *áha* immediately after; thereupon.

ahcí (variant: **hci**). v [reg., *_hci*] *(intr.)* **camp, make camp.** *ąąhcí htai* let's camp [more than two people] (01/09/95/FH/pc:ma). *ahcí apáiðe /hcí apáiðe* they are camping

(01/09/95/FH/pc:ma). *ðéekaa ðahcí ðaįšé?* are you [one person] camping here? (01/09/95/FH/pc:ok; RBn3-28). *ðéekaa ðahcí paašé?* are you [more than one person] camping here? (BE2.16).

áhcihtą. N **arbor; dance arbor; brush arbor** (HH/pc). *áhcihtą kši ąkái hce* let's go to the arbor (04/19/95/FH/pc:ok; BE2.4). **dance**

ahí. V [sync. h-stem, *(a)_hi*] [initial *a* is often omitted, regularly so with 1st singular and 2nd person subject] *(intr.)* **go there (motion accomplished), come there, arrive there** (03/20/95/FH/pc:prod). *wahkǫ́taki ci pšíe* I went to see the doctor (and he was standing up) (RB). *wahkǫ́taki įkšé pšíe* I went to see the doctor (and he was sitting down) (RB). *pšíe ðe* I went over there (01/31/95/FH/pc:prod). *haaská óce pšíe* I went to look for a shirt (01/31/95/FH/pc:ok). *htą́wą kši haakǫ́tą šíe?* what did you go to town for? *hcí wíhta ci ší hkǫ́bra* I want you to come to my house (T#14b- p2; (04/07/95/LS/pc:ok; BE2.23). *hǫǫpái hówaįki šíe?* where did you all go today? (02/01/95/FH/pc:ok). *wanǫ́bre ahípe* he came over and ate (FH:4/22/96/tape). *tookétą hípe* it's summer (lit., 'summer arrived') (BE2.129). *šímįžį okúla kǫ́ða apa, éehtana htą́wą įkši pšíe* the girls want some clothes, that's why I went to town (01/31/95/FH/pc:with *éehtana*, okc). *wižǫ́a éðǫǫpa ąkáhi* sister and I went over there (01/31/95/FH/pc:prod) orig). *miðóhta tą wanǫ́bre híi ði* come over and eat at noon [one person] (01/11/95/FH/pc:ok). *wanǫ́bre hí ði* you [sg.] must come eat over there (RBn3-39). *hcí ahí* come to the house [implied: 'my house'] *wanǫ́bre hí paði* you [pl.] must come eat over there RBn3-39). • **be there; be in attendance; stop in, go by, come by.** *ąkáhi hta ąkái* we'll be there (03/20/95/FH/pc:okc; BE2.137). *ąkáhi* we've been over there (RBn1-25). *ðáalį, pší hta mįkšé* yes, I'll be there (said in accepting an invitation) (RB). *ąkáhi hta che* we'll be there (said when accepting an invitation) (RB). *pée na ahí hta ðé?* who is going to be there? (MSB:02583). *ahí hta apai* they'll be there. *táatą ščíitą tą, hcí ci híðį* when you get through with what you're doing, come by the house. • **get (e.g., 'get old'), become (suddenly?).** [Perhaps to be understood as 'arrive at (a state or condition)'.] *wáali oðúucˀake šíe* you have really gotten lazy (lit., 'indeed you arrived at laziness') (02/15/95/FH/pc:ok; BE2.77). *nǫ́ǫ ąkáhipe* we've gotten old. *hpáze ahíi tą* when it gets evening (FH:4/17/96/tape). *íšpaðo ahíipe* all of a sudden, he became a Mexican (FH:08/05/99/DNpc; FH:okc). *wáli oðúucˀake šie* you really got tired (e.g., responding to an invitation) (RB). • **begin to, start to; suddenly start to.** *ɣaaké ahíipe* he started to cry. *awą́hkie šǫ́ akxa kaðǫ ɣaaké ahíipe* he was talking to me, then suddenly he started to cry (FH/8/30/94,prod).

•• LFD 10: *ahí* <a-hi´> he has been to. *ahílį* <a-hi´-gthi^{n}> having arrived there I sit (a ritual expression).

••• Cf. *híðe*.

ahíce (variant of **híce**).

áhkiasąci. V [conjug. unknown] [*hkik-* RECIP + *ásąci*] *(intr.)* **put each other to a test.** *ahkíasącí aðįkšé* we're putting each other to a test (RB, unconfirmed; (04/26/95/FH/pc:uk; PM: uk).

áhkie. V [reg., *á_hkie*] *(trans.)* **talk for or against; talk up or talk down, as when expressing one's emotions with respect to some topic; take up for, argue on behalf of; take s.o.'s side (as an attorney at law argues on behalf of a client)** (9/17/94/PM/pc; 01/09/95/FH/pc:prod; BE2.4). *áwihkie* I'm taking up for you (FH:prod).

•• LFD 12: *áhkiða* <a´-ḳi-tha> to contend as in a fight. *áahkibra* <a´-a-ḳi-btha> I contend. *ǫ́kahkiða pe* <o^{n}´-ga-ḳi-tha i> we contend. *áhkiða hce* <a´-ḳi-tha ṭse> defiance; to defy.

••• *OM* same as Osage (LFD 12).

••• Cf. *íe áhkie, wáhkie.*

áhkiha. ADV **beyond another thing** (05/01/95/LS/pc/prod)**; afterward; following, next.** *áhkihą ši škǫ́šta* if you want to, come afterward (FH:prod).

••• Cf. *ihcóšpa áhkiha, žįká owáhkihą.*

áhkihkaaspe. V [reg., *á_hkihkaaspe*] [*hkik-* REFL + *ákaaspe*] **cover oneself up.** *áahkihkaaspe* I'm covering myself (04/26/95/LS/pc; BE2.26).

áhkihkie. V [reg., *á_hkihkie*] [*hkik-* RECIP + *áhkie* 'talk for or against' (also used as transitive)] *(intr.)* **contend with or compete with one another** (01/11/95/FH/pc:ok). *áhkihkie apái* they're competing with each other. • *(trans.)* **compete with.** *áhkihkie hkǫ́bra įké* I won't compete with you (lit., 'I don't want to compete with you') (01/11/95/FH/pc:prodorig; BE2.23).

•• LFD 12: *áhkiða* <a´-ḳi-tha> to contend as in a fight.

••• *OM* same as Osage (LFD 12).

áhkihpa. V [reg., *á_hkihpa*] *(trans.)* **encounter, meet** (JOD; LF).

•• JOD (Wolf and Fawn p1 ln1): *hcaléže ozó ki áhkihpape ska* <Tca-ḳ͓¢eç͓e uṣ͓ú ḳ͓i ákipáp͓e ska> he met Fawn on the lowland.

áhkihpa (*continued*)

•• LFD 12: *áhkihpa* <a´-ḳi-pa> to meet another.

••• *OM* same as Osage (LFD 12).

áhkihtǫpe. v [reg.+sync. fortisizing stop stem, *á_hkih_tǫpe*] [*hkik-* REFL/RECIP + *átǫpe* (sometimes used as transitive with suus semantics)] *(intr.)* **watch over oneself; watch oneself; look at oneself; look after oneself** (02/22/95/FH/pc:okc). *áhkihtǫpai* watch out for yourself (MSB t2s2). *áhkihtǫpa* look out for yourself. *áhkihtǫpape* he looked at himself (MSB t2s2; 02/22/95/FH/pc:okc). *íe áhkihtǫpá ðíe* watch your talk (BE2.151; 03/16/95/JS/pc:okc). *áhkihtǫpa ðíe* watch yourself (admonition to a person who did something wrong). *waðiląekǫįkí apai, dekǫ́ǫci áhkihtǫ́pa ðį* there are crazies out there, watch out for yourself (FH:98/pc). *taapóska ščée hta ðąįšé tą áhkihtǫ́pa ði* when you're going off to school, take care of yourself. • **watch over each other.** *áhkihtǫpapai* you all watch each other, take care of each other (FH/07/09/01/pc). • *(trans.)* **watch over things for oneself; watch over one's own things.** *wacúe skú ahkíhtoį hcé* let me go look at my cake (e.g., while it's baking) (03/16/95/JS/pc:okc).

áhkiisto (variant: **ahkíisto**). N **trial, hearing; legal proceeding** (03/23/95/FH/pc:ok; BE2.144).

••• Cf. *hkiistó.*

ahkílaðį (variant: **hkílaðį**). v [reg.+(sync.), *_ahkila(_)ðį* (optionally doubly inflecting in 1st sg., single inflection in 2nd person)] [*hkik-* REFL + *aláðį*] *(intr.)* **carry oneself, conduct oneself, hold oneself or carry on in a certain way.** *ahkílaðį ~ ahkílabrį* I will carry myself. *ðahkílaðį* you will carry yourself. *waxpáðį ahkílabrį mǫ́žǫ ðéka* I'll carry myself pitiful here on earth. *wáli ahkíluhpíiži ąži óðąži ahkílabrį hta mįkšé* I made a bad mistake, but I'll carry myself on anyway (RBn 5/3/79). *wahkǫ́ta akxa eená hta akxa na, hpahą́le mą́į, ahkílaðį pai* soon it will be only God, put him first, carry yourself that way (04/04/99/FH/pc). *waxpáðį ną ahkílaipi* carry yourself humbly [to two or more persons] (RB). *wáðohtą ahkílae* I behave myself (lit., 'carry my body good') (MF 11-19-83). *wáðohtą męę ikʔúca* try to make me behave myself (MF 11-19-83).

ahkílį. v [reg., *a_hkilį*] [*hkik-* REFL + *aðį́* (sometimes used with suus semantics)] *(trans.)* **have for oneself; have as one's own.** *ahkílįaláape* he took it home to have it for himself.

ahkílįalée. v [reg.+reg., *a_hkilį(a)_lee*] [*hkik-* REFL +*aðį́* + *alée* (has suus semantics)] *(trans.)* **take home for oneself, take home as one's own.** *wižį́ke akxa haxį́ wį́ ahkí[į]laaláape* my son took a blanket home as his own.

ahkíliiški (variant of **hkilíiški**).

áhkiǫðe. v [reg.?, *á_hkiǫðe*] [apparently contains *hkik-* REFL/RECIP] *(trans.)* **meet; encounter; happen upon.** *áwihkiǫðe* I happened upon you in my life (9/4/94/FH/p.c.).

áhkita. N [shortened form of *áhkihtǫpe* 'look after each other' (FH)] **law enforcement; police; army, armed forces; soldier, armed person; officer, grenadier** (03/02/95/FH/pc:ok). *áhkita wahtǫ́ka* a soldier with authority (BE2.97; FH). *áhkita apa ahú apai* here come the police (BE2.105). *áhkitamąį* armed man (RB; PM/7/7/94; 03/10/95/FH/pc:ok).

•• LFD 11: *áhkita* <a´-ḳi-da> officer or soldier; grenadier; policeman. *áhkita hci* <a´-ḳi-da-ṭsi> officer's house. *áhkita žį́ka* <a´-ḳi-da zhi^{n}-ga> a private (soldier). *áhkita wahtǫka* <a´-ḳi-da wa-ṭo^{n}-ga> officers. *áhkita wahtǫka* <a´-ḳi-da wa-ṭo^{n}-ga> an officer of high rank, a general.

áhkita nąą́žį (variant: **áhkita náažį**). N **soldier** (03/13/95/FH/pc:ok).

áhkita okʔą. v [reg.?, *áhkita o_kʔą?*] *(intr.)* **conduct a drill; hold military maneuvers.**

•• LFD 11: *áhkita okʔą* <a´-ḳi-da u-ḳ'o^{n}> to drill; to engage in military exercises.

áhkita omą́ðį (variant: **áhkita omáį**). N **armed forces; army, navy, marines** (BE2.125; 01/06/95/FH; 03/13/95; 08/22/96).

••• Cf. *áhkita nąą́žį.*

áhkita onąą́žį waachí (variant of **áhkitanąą́žį waachí**).

áhkita totą́hąka. N **officer.**

•• LFD 11: *áhkita totąhąka* <a´-ḳi-da do-do^{n}-ho^{n}-ga> an army officer of rank.

áhkitanąą́žį waachí (variant: **áhkita onąą́žį waachí**). N **soldier dance.** *áhkitanáažį waaðǫ́* soldier dance song (03/13/95/FH/pc:ok; BE2.125). *ahkíhta onąą́žį waachí* soldier dance. *áhkita onąą́žį waaðǫ́* soldier dance song (lit., 'soldier song').

ahkížąmie v [1st sg. of *hkížį* 'be angry'] **I am angry.**

áhkižį. v [reg.?, *á_hkižį?*] [reflexive (*hkik-*) possibly from *ažį́*] *(intr.)* **think or feel oneself to be a certain way (?).** *líe ðáha óžo áhkižį ðí aape* when she came back she was proud of herself (RBn19-03).

••• Cf. *óžo áhkižį.*

áhkoopše. v [reg., *á_hkoopše*] [*á-* LOC + *hkóopše*] *(trans.)* **meet; encounter, run into.** *áwihkoopše* I met you (LS/prod: *áwehkoopše*). *áðahkoopše?* did you meet him? (05/01/95/LS/pc).

ahú. v [sync. h-stem, *a_hu*] [initial *a* is often omitted, regularly so with 1st singular and 2nd person subject] *(intr.)* **come here (motion underway).** *pšú mį́kše* I'm coming [sitting]. *pšú ąhé* I'm coming [moving, shortened form]. *pšú aðį́he* I'm coming [moving, full form]. *hcíhta pšú hkǫ́bra* I want to come inside (FH/prod). *ðekáha ðahų́?* [unconfirmed irregular form; *šú* is expected instead of *ðahų́*] are you coming over here? (7/8/94/PM/#98b). *hǫ́ǫpa hú akxai* morning's coming. *ahú apai* they're coming (RBn14-06). *šíi toe ahú apa* some people of those are coming here (7/8/94/PM/#98b).

aįpaxo. N **copperhead** (RBn HW13, unconfirmed); **Arapaho (lit., 'over the mountain')** (RBn HW13, unconfirmed).

ákaaɣace. v [reg. *kaa*-ret., *á_kaaɣace*] *(trans.)* **cover over by spreading some material upon.**

•• LFD 8: *ákaɣace* <a´-ga-xa-dse> to cover up something. *áakaɣace* <a´-a-ga-xa-dse> I cover it up. *áðakaɣace* <a´-tha-ga-xa-dse> you cover it up. *ą́kakaɣaca pe* <o^n´-ga-ga-xa-dsa i> we cover it up.

••• Cf. *paaɣáce.*

ákaahtami (variant of **íikaahtamą**).

ákaasįce. v [reg. *kaa*-ret., *á_kaasįce*; secondary accent on *sį́* in inflected forms] [*á-* LOC + *kaasį́ce*] *(trans.)* **close on; slam on.** *hcižé áðakaasį́ce* you closed/slammed the door on it (FH; MSB).

akáaspe. N **shade, blind, covering.** *okáhąpa akáaspe ðuumą́ši* raise the window shade.

ákaaspe. v [reg. *kaa*-ret., *á_kaaspe*] *(trans.)* **put over, put upon.** *žįkážį haxį́ ákaaspa* put a blanket on the child (RBn10-12:JW). • **cover (as with cloth or blanket), cover with dirt (as a grave), cover over, cover up** (04/26/95/LS/pc:ok; 01/13/95/FH/pc:ok). *áakaaspe* I covered it up (01/13/95/FH/pc). *áahkihkaaspe* I'm covering myself (04/26/95/LS/pc; BE2.26). *áðakaaspe hta ðáįše?* are you going to cover it up? (01/13/95/FH/pc). *ą́ąðakaaspe hta ðáįse?* are you going to cover me up [with a blanket]? (01/13/95/FH/pc). *haxį́ ákaaspa* cover him or her with a blanket (e.g., when someone is sleeping) (01/07/95/FH/pc:ok). *níi ákaaspa* cover the water (RBn HW). *ónǫbre ákaaspa* cover the food (RBn HW).

•• LFD 8: *ákaspe* <a´-ga-çpe> to cover up an object. *áakaspe* <a´-a-ga-çpe> I cover up an object. *áðakaspe* <a´tha-ga-çpe> you cover up an object. *ǫ́kakaspa pe* <o^n´-ga-ga-çpa i> we cover up an object. *ákaspe* <a´-ga-çpe> the falling of something heavy on a person or thing. *žǫ aðikaspe a* <zho^n a-thi-ga-çpe a> did a tree fall on you? *žǫ ąkaspe* <zho^n o^n-ga-çpe> a tree fell on me. *žǫ wakaspa pe* <zho^n wa-ga-çpa i> a tree fell on us.

••• *KS ágaspe* cover completely (RR).

ákaaži. v [reg. *kaa*-ret.?, *á_kaaži*] [*á-* LOC + *kaaží*] *(trans.)* **force over or through s.t.; order, command, or force s.o. to do a task, make s.o. do s.t.** *Mary iihǫ́ akxa ákaažipe* Mary's mother made her do that.

ákabra. v [reg. *kaa*-ret., *á_kabra*] *(trans.)* **open, as one's eyes or arms.** *įįštá ákabra* open your eyes (RBn17-p04). *hóšechíepi tą, įįštá ápisąi koe áa ákabra nąąke htaacéžį oðįįke ahú apai* he was excited, with his eyes closed and his arms open he came running to catch Whirlwind (RBn17-p; cqc).

•• LFD 7: *ákabra* <a´-ga-btha> to open the eyes on something. *įštá aakabra* <i^n-shta´ a-a-ga-btha> I opened my eyes on it. *įštá aðakabra* <i^n-shta´ a-tha-ga-btha> you opened your eyes on it. *įštá ǫkakabra pe* <i^n-shta´ o^n-ga-ga-btha i> we opened our eyes on it. LFD 77: *įštákabra* <i^n-shta´ ga-btha> to open the eyes. *įštá abra* <i^nshta´ a-btha> I open my eyes. *įštá ðabra* <i^n-shta´ tha-btha> you open your eyes.

ákaha. PPN **on top.** *ákaha álą* put it on top [of it]. *ákaha oolą́ąka* put it on top [of it] (PM; BE2.143; 03/23/95/FH/pc:ok; 03/22/95/PM/pc:ok). • N **top, summit.** *paaxó ákaha* the top of the hill or mountain.

•• LFD 5: *ákaha* <a´-ga-ha> on top of, on the outside. *ápahta akaha aažu į ta* <a´-ba-ṭa- a-ga-ha a-a-zhu i^n da> I put them on the fence. *ápahta akaha aðažu į ta* <a´-ba-ṭa a-ga-ha a-tha-zhu i^n da> you put them on the fence. *ápahta akaha ǫkažu į ta* <a´-ba-ṭa- a-ga-ha o^n-ga-zhu i^n da> [*į ta* is not used in Mod. Os.] we put them on the fence (01/24/95/FH/pc:uk). LFD 8: *ákaha* <a´-ga-ha> upon the brow of.

••• *OM* same as Osage (LFD 8).

ákahahpa. N **vest** (04/26/95/FH/pc:ok).

•• LFD 8: *ákahahpa* <a´-ga-ha-pa> vest. *ákahapa aki ǫbra achi mįkše o* <a´-ga-ha-pa a-gi o^n-btha a-tsi mi^n-kshe o> [sentence-final *o* is not used in Mod. Os.] I left my vest home.

ákahahta. ADV **outside of a certain area; on the outskirts of, in the surroundings of; on the other side (of a perimeter)** (03/03/95/FH/pc:ok).

ákahahta (*continued*)
hcí che ákahahta anáąžį akxąhé I'm standing outside of this/that house (03/23/95/FH/pc). *hcí che ákahahta ðanáąžį* you are [standing] outside of the house (03/23/95/FH/pc:okc). • ADV **afterward, after the present event; off the record, outside of the main events or activity and in secret; isolated from, socially distant from.** *ákahahta ahkílaðį ðíape* he's keeping himself on the outside (03/23/95/FH/pc).

•• LFD 8: *ákahahta* <a´-ga-ha-ṭa> on the outskirts. *ákahahta mąðį* <a´-ga-ha-ṭa mo^{n}-thi^{n}> a recluse. *ákaha* <a´-ga-ha> on top of, on the outside. *hci che akaha hta anǫ ži* <ṭsi tse a-ga-ha ṭa a-no^{n} zhi> I am outside of the house. *hci che akaha hta ðǫnǫ ži* <ṭsi tse a-ga-ha ṭa tho^{n}-no^{n} zhi> you are outside of the house.

ákahamį (Hominy form; variant: **ákahami**). N [*ákaha* + *mį́* 'blanket, robe'] **coat** (01/09/95/FH/pc:prod; BE2.21)**; cape.**

•• LFD 8: *ákahami* <a´-ga-ha-mi> a coat; a long cape; a mantle.

ákaške. V [reg. *kaa*-ret., *á_kaške*] *(trans.)* **tie to s.t.; tie up (as a horse)** (04/26/95/FH/pc:ok). *hkáwa ákaška!* tie up the horse! (04/26/95/FH/pc). *hǫ́ǫpa ókaayeįke híe ðáha, oðíhtą ákaškape* when Saturday came, they tied him to the wagon (RBn10-2:MOJ/79). • *(intr.)* **tie a knot** (04/26/95/FH/pc:ok). *ąkákaškape* we tied a knot (04/26/95/FH/pc:ok).

•• LFD 8: *ákaške* <a´-ga-shke> to tie a knot; to tie a scalp lock on a pole. *áakaške* <a´-a-ga-shke> I tie a knot. *áðakaške* <a´-tha-ga-shke> you tie a knot. *ǫ́kakaška pe* <o^{n}´-ga-ga-shka i> we tied a knot.

ákazo. V [reg. *kaa*-ret.?, *á_kazo*] *(trans.)* **inquire into, examine, inspect, probe, test by questions.**

•• LFD 263: *ákazo* <a´-ga-çu> to examine. LFD 8: *ákazo wahtǫka* <a´-ga-çu wa-ṭo^{n}-ga> to judge, the judge; one who inquires into.

••• Cf. *wákazo.*

ákiẙe. V [uninfl.?] *(trans.)* **move around, be all around, encircle a place or a person (especially in an annoying way)** (RRBn1-31; 12/30/94/FH/pc/ok). *níhka ákiẙe ðí áape* that man is all around [bothering] her [they said] (FH/09/22/01/pc). • *(intr.)* **be around, especially in a bothersome way.** *ákiẙe ðąįšé* you're bothering around (FH/09/22/01/pc). • *(trans., intr.)*, **pass by; circle around (as in a tipi meeting: 'go clear around', avoiding the center);** *(intr.)* **go table-hopping; table-hop; hang around, be around close; be arrayed around, as when making a path around; skirting the edge (such as cows around a pond).** *ákiẙe apái* they're around close; he's around the edges (12/30/94/FH/pc:ok; BE2.41; FH:4/22/96/tape:prod). *hcí ákiẙe akxái* he is passing by [or circling around] the house [but now he is motionless and present as this sentence is spoken] (RBn10-7:JW, unconfirmed). *hcí ákiẙe apai* they are hanging around the house, circling around the house (RBn10-7:JW; FH). • PPN **around (e.g., the edge of a pond); skirting the edge of s.t.** (HRE/12/29/01/pc:ẙ). *hlaaskážį ákiẙe kįįkįįežį huuhtą́ą íiðape* he saw many butterflies around the flowers (RBn15-03).

••• Cf. *opáwįẙe.*

ákihtǫpe. V [reg.(+sync.), *á_kih(_)tǫpe*] [*kik-* SUU + *átǫpe*] *(trans.)* **watch over, look after, look at (one's own things or people).** *žįkážį ákihtǫpe* watch that child [hearer's own child, or a relative's child], watch your child. • *(intr.)* **watch over, look after, look at one's own.** *ákihtǫpa ði* you look at your own (MSB t2-s2; 02/22/95/FH/pc:okc).

ákitǫpe. V [reg., *á_kitǫpe*] [*ki-* DAT + *átǫpe*] *(trans.)* **watch over, tend (s.o. who is not a family member or not close).**

•• LFD 354: *ákitǫpe* <a´-gi-do^{n}-be> watch over someone.

ákǫze. V [reg.?, *á_kǫze*] [*á-* LOC + *kǫ́ze*] *(trans.)* **examine.** *hcéka ðiníe che ákǫze hta akxa ska* I guess he will examine you now (04/13/95/LS/pc:ok; BE2.42).

akší. V [reg., *_(a)kši*] [initial *a* is often omitted with 3rd person subject] *(intr.)* **arrive back there; arrive home, return there.** *ksí hta ðe?* is he coming back? *šeeðo akší hta apai* they're going to come back there [where you are] (PM/7/8/94; 01/06/95/FH/pc:ok).

•• LFD 11: *akšíe ðaha* <a-ki´-e tha-ha> when I get home. LFD 141: *ðakšíe ðaha* <tha-ki´e tha-ha> when you get home.

akú. V [reg., *_(a)kú*] [initial *a* is often omitted with 3rd person subject and in imperative] *(intr.)* **come back here (motion underway).** *nǘžu apa akǘ apai* the rain is coming (RBn10-21/JW&FW/77). *htaacé hpíiži apa akǘ apai* a tornado is coming. *ąkáku ąkáðe* we're coming back (MSB 04-83-2). *ðeekáaha kǘ* come this way. *kü ðíe, ąkái hce* come on [you], let's [us two] go. *kǘpi, ąkái htai* come on, let's [three or more persons] go (01/11/95/FH/pc:ok; all).

óðaake waléze akų́ mąðį́ go get the newspaper (01/10/95/FH/pc:okc, with *kiu*). *ðékaa kų́* come here (01/10/95/FH/pc: *kyu, kiu* diphthong). *hcíhta kų́* come in the house. • *(trans.)* **get, fetch, bring, come here with.** *níi tóe akų́ mą́ðį* go get some water [and bring it here]. *óðaake waléze akų́ mąðį́* get the newspaper [and come here] (*akü* here contrasts with *ðuuzé* 'get [from a specific place; take it]') (01/10/95/FH/pc). *ną́ɣe toa ðuuzá* get [take] some ice (01/31/95/FH/pc:okc). *ną́ɣe toa akų́ mąðí* get some ice (01/31/95/FH/pc:okc). *ąąkų́ ðaa* go get it for me (01/31/95/FH/pc:ok). *ąąkų́ mąðį́* go get it for me (this expression is preferred over *ąąkų́ ðaa:* FH) (01/31/95/FH/pc:ok; BE2.54).

•• LFD 51: *kiu* <gi-o> to come.

••• Cf. ***akší.***

akxa. CONT [often appears as *akxai* (from *akxa* + *ðe* DECL; *ðe* earlier characterized female speech)] **continuative aspect postverbal marker (indicating ongoing action or state in present, past, or future time) for 3rd person sg. or pl. nonmoving subject that is present with speaker (contrast *apa*).** ['Moving' here means 'changing location'; motions or gestures that do not change the entity's location in horizontal space do not take this affix.] *íxope akxai* he's telling a lie, they're telling a lie. *kǫ́ða akxa* he's wanting it. *wapúška tóe nǫ́pʔį akxai* they've got beads around their neck (RBn12-08). *iisėwai, žeká akxa ą́nąkʔǫži akxái* the hateful thing is that my legs won't listen to me (01/09/95/FH/pc:prod; HRE:ok). *íiðaži akxá* they couldn't see (04/06/95/LS/pc:ok/prod). *ðe hpáata akxa hǫ́ǫžį akxai* those eggs are bad (FH:4/22/96/tape:prod, HP). *níhce akxa* he was cold. *įhtáci wahkǫ́ta akxa óxiða káaɣi akxái* God created this death (said at a peyote meeting). *hǫpái mą́ąɣe ðáalį akxai* today the weather is good (FH, PM). *hkáwa akxa cʔé akxai* that horse is dead. *kasį́xci hóolą bree hkǫ́bra ązi nuužúžu akxai* I wanted to go fishing this morning but it was sprinkling (01/30/95/FH/pc:prod. orig.). *mąɣíwaapi akxai* they're lying to us now. *mąɣíąðe/mąɣíąðape* we lied to him (MSB 3-83). *waachí akxai* he's dancing in place (MREI 1-14-82). *tąhį́ akxai* they are well [lying down or sitting or standing still and present]. *ahí hta akxai* he'll be there. • **he/she/it is characterized by, they are characterized by [the immediately preceding word or phrase, which may be a noun phrase].** *hį́į hpíiži akxa* he has bad teeth. *waðílą hpíiži akxa* they have a bad temper. *iitáipi ókikxą akxai* he's got a birthday.

akxa. SUBJECT MARKER **(follows a subject [sg. or pl.] that is not moving, including dead nonhuman animates [*apa* is used for dead humans] and is present with speaker or is an abstract entity; contrast *apa*).** ['Moving' here means 'changing location'; motions or gestures that do not change the entity's location in horizontal space do not take this affix.] *sitǫ́į mą́ąɣe akxa wálį hpíiži aape* the weather was very bad yesterday (RBn3-18). *ðée akxa íihǫ hą́ąpa ókʔą hta apai* they're going to have something on Mother's Day. *Christine akxa hóxpe ǫǫ́ į́kšé?* does Christine have a cold? (RBn3-55). *kaxé akxa okúhpu akxai* the creek is full (flooded) (RB; 04/26/95/LS/pc:ok; FH/09/21/01/pc:ok). • **generic noun subject marker.** *hpéecenii akxa žúoka ðíðuuhpíiži hta akxai* whiskey is bad for your health (lit., 'whiskey will make your body bad') (JS). *níi akxa opʔą́ðe nąpé* water steams (2-2-670). *iihǫ́ akxa* the mother [subject of sentence, if sitting or not moving].

•• LFD 7: *šǫke akxa hci che atǫ́pe pe ha* <sho^{n}´-ge a-ka ṭsi tse a-do^{n}-be pe ha> [sentence-final *ha* is not used in Mod. Os.] the dog guards the house. LFD 143: *ðe akxa* <the a-ka> this [person] sitting.

akxái (see **akxa** CONT).

ákʔahúe. N **south wind** (BE2.125, unconfirmed).

•• LFD 11: *ákʔa* <a´-ķ'a> the south wind. LFD 136: *htáce akʔa che* <ṭa´-dse a-k'a tse> south wind; south.

aláðį. V [reg.+sync., *a_lá_ðį*] *(trans.)* **carry one's items; carry along one's items; carry or take one's own, have or take as one's own, inherit** (02/27/95/JS/pc:okc). *šímižį apa haaskámi aláðį hta apai* the girls are going to take their shawls (02/27/95/JS/pc:ok). *alabrį hta mįkšé* I will take it.

•• RB: <áh-lah-thi^{n}> have as one's own, inherit.

•• LFD 9: *aláðį* <a-gtha-thi^{n}> to have or to keep one's own; to inherit. *mǫ́ze ska alabrį* <mo^{n}´-çe çka a-gtha-bthi^{n}> I inherited money. *mǫ́ze ska che ąkálaðį pe* <mo^{n}´-çe çka te o^{n}-ga´-gtha-thi^{n} i> we inherited money. LFD 34: *tátą alaðį* <da´-do^{n} a-gtha-thi^{n}> inheritance.

•• *KS aláyį* to have or keep one's own (RR); *OM* same as Osage (LFD 9).

aláðįðee. V [reg.+reg., *ala_ðį_ðee*] [apparently contains *kik-* SUU (perhaps irregular suus of *aðį́aðee*; by phonological rule would be *alį́aðee*

aláðįðee (*continued*) or *alį́ðee*)] *(trans.)* **take one's own.** *wióohǫžį alábrįbree hta ąhé* I'm going to take my little cooking utensils (02/27/95/JS/pc:ok). *žįkážį apa kasį́xcižį páahą nąpé, taahpóska wábrįbree nai* the children get up early, I take them to school (02/27/95/JS/pc:okc; BE2.131).

aláðįku (variant: **aláįku**). v [sync.+reg.?, *ala_ðį_ku*?] [apparently contains *kik-* SUU] **bring back s.t. that belongs to oneself, or come back with s.t. that belongs to oneself.** *mą́ą aláįku* bring the arrow back [where he belongs (*sic*)] (RBn23-17c).

álaha. v [reg., *á_laha*] **wear one's own; put on (as clothes, shoes, coats)** (04/06/95/PM/pc:ok).

•• LFD 9: *álaha* <a´-gtha-ha> to wear one's own clothing. *áalaha* <a´-a-gtha-ha> I wear my own. *áðalaha* <a´-tha-gtha-ha> you wear your own. *ǫ́kalaha pe* <o^{n}´-ga-gtha-ha i> we wear our own.

••• *OM* same as Osage (LFD 9).

álą. v [reg., *á_lą*] *(trans.)* **place vertically against (e.g., stick s.t. up against a fence); place on, put on** (2-2-849).

ále (variant: **áale**). v [reg., *á_le*] *(trans.)* **place an item upright on another item, set on (e.g., set a kettle on a fire).** [In this verb, *l* is sometimes pronounced *dl* (*áadle*).] *hpéece ále* set it on the fire (BE2.119; 03/09/95/MREI/pc:okc).

•• RB: <áh-d-?-leh>.

•• LFD 9: *ále* <a´-gthe> to place on top of another in an upright position. *áale* <a´-a-gthe> I placed on top. *áðale* <a´-tha-gthe> you placed on top. *ąkála pe* <o^{n}-ga´-gtha i> we placed on top.

alée. v [reg., *a_lee*] [initial *a* is often omitted in 3rd person and in imperative] *(intr.)* **go back there, return there, go home (motion under way).** *hcí ce alée* I am going back to the house (02/01/95/FH/pc:okc). *a[a]lée* I return there. *ðalée* you return there. *alée* he returns there. *ąkále[e]* we return there. *šį́tožį akxa achípe ąži aláape, ší achíži hta akxai* the boy who came here left [just now] and he won't be coming back again. *hcí ci ąkále* we are going back to the house. *oðíhtą ci ąkále hce* let's go back to the car. *aláape* they went back. *hcí ci ąkále htai* let's go home (02/01/95/FH/pc:okc; BE2.58). *haakǫ́ta Johna lée?* why did John go home? *alée hta apai* they're going home [going to go home] (5-83-2). *alée apai* they're on their way home (5-83-2).

•• LFD 53: *le* <gthe> to go home. *ále* <a´-gthe> I go home. *ðále* <tha´-gthe> you go home. *ąkála pe* <o^{n}-ga´-gtha pe> we go home.

alí. v [reg., *_(a)li*] [initial *a* is often omitted in 3rd person and in imperative] *(intr.)* **arrive back here; arrive home here; return here, come back, get back (motion accomplished)** (01/06/95/FH/pc:prod). *wąkǫ alí hta mįkšé* I'll come back quickly (FH). *sitǫ́į alí* I got home yesterday. *žą́ą toa abrį́alie* I'm back with the wood (RBn23-16). *mį́įoðaake sáhta ci alíe* I got back at five o'clock (02/01/95/FH/pc:okc). *ðalí tą hiiðáa* take a bath when you come back (01/06/95/FH/pc:okc; BE2.23). *tooská áaðalǫšcį ðalíe* you forgot to bring back potatoes. *háatxące ðalíe?* when did you get back? (02/01/95/FH/pc:ok). *háatkxąta ðalíe?* when are you coming back? (a line in the turtle song [FH]). *háatxą ðalí hta ðąąšé?* when will you come back? (T#14b-p7; 04/07/95/LS/pc:ok). *záani ši lí apai* you all came back (again) (RBn10-13). *ðáalį huukǫ́į ðalípe* it's good a lot of you came back (01/06/95/FH/pc:ok). *ðáalįe huukǫ́į lí apa che* it's good a lot of you have come back (as I see) (01/06/95/FH/pc:prod). *ną háakxąci líie?* when did she get back? (02/01/95/FH/pc:prod). *ną háakxątą líie?* but when is she coming back? (02/01/95/FH/pc:ok). *wižį́ke líi tą hú hce éa* she asks you to send Sonny to her when he gets here. *ðée lípi che ški wéewinai* I'm thankful, too, for these who have come here (FH/10/13/96). *alí apai* they're back. *alípe* they came back. *kasį́ta ąkáli hta ąkátxa* we'll come back tomorrow (01/06/95/FH/pc:ok; *kaasį́*). *ąkálipe* we came home. *hpázewanǫ́bre lí ði* come back for supper. *wižį́ke nahkǫ́į mį́įake šáhpe tą lí hcea* tell those two boys to come back at six o'clock. *Homer mį́įake šáhpe tą lí hcea* tell Homer to come back at six.

•• LFD 9: *alí* <a-gthi´> returning. "This expression is found frequently when referring to the return of one who has been searching for some particular thing. It is a ritual expression."

••• Cf. *akú*.

áliha, álįha (variant of **álįįha**).

álihtą (variant of **áðiihtą**).

álįį (variants: **álį, áli, álii**). v [reg., *á_lįį*] *(trans.)* **sit upon.** [In this verb, *l* is sometimes pronounced *dl* (*ádlįi*).] *ðéeka áðalįį škǫ́ǫšta?* do you want to sit in one of these? • **ride on.** *níhkaši nąhka ški álįį íisipe, iinąhižipe* he didn't like to carry people on his back, he didn't agree with it (RBn10-2:MOJ/79; RBn16-01). *hkáwa álįį/hkáwaalįį* ride a horse. • **place upon (e.g., put a suitcase on a table).** *áwanǫbre ádlįį* put it [the suitcase] on the table (FH:5/02/96/prod). *hpahą́le níi che ádlį̨į hta apai* they're going to set the water on the table (in a bucket or pitcher) (FH:5/02/96/prod). PPN **upon (used in numbers).** *lébrą álį̨į hce wį́ike* nineteen (lit., 'nine upon ten'). N **chair.** [Takes 'standing' positional article *che*.]

•• LFD 170: *aliche aalį* <a-gthi-tse a-a-gthi^n> expected Mod. Os. form: *álį̨įche oálį̨į*] I occupied the chair. *aliche aðalį* <a-gthi-tse a-tha-gthi^n> [expected Mod. Os. form: *álį̨įche oðálį̨į*] you occupied the chair.

••• Cf. *olį́į*.

álį̨į (variant of **lébrą álį̨į** in numbers between 'eleven' and 'nineteen').

álį̨įha (variants: **álį̨ha, áliha, álį̨įhai**). V [reg., *á_lį̨įha*] *(intr.)* **excel; be above others, outstanding, excellent, as in making good grades in school.** *áalį̨įha* I excel (03/06/95/FH/pc:ok). *ąkálį̨įhape* we excel (03/06/95/FH/pc:ok). • PPN **after, past** (RBn19-01). *hpéðǫǫpa álį̨įha akxa* it's past seven o'clock; it's after seven (RBn1-17). *mį́įoðaake lébrą álį̨įha tą brée hkǫ́bra* I want to go after ten o'clock (RRBn1-49). *mį́įoðaake lébrą álį̨įha akxái/mį́įake lébrą áliha akxai* it's past ten o'clock (03/06/95/FH/pc:okc; BE2.101). • ADV **afterward.** *áliiha ékimą etxa eškítą aha, ðíe ðáalį waðakšíe hkǫ́bra* afterward when I am done, also, I want you to make it good for them (RBn/FHok).

•• LFD 10: *álį ha* <a´-gthi^n ha> to exceed; to excel. *áalį ha* <a´-a-gthi^n ha> I excel (03/06/95/FH/pc:ok). *áðalį ha* <a´-tha-gthi^n ha> you excel (03/06/95/FH/pc:ok). *wǫkálį ha pe* <wo^n-ga´-gthi^n ha i> [expected Mod. Os. form: *ąkálį̨įhape*] we excel. *álį ha* <a´-gthi^n ha> excellent; excess.

álį̨įhceðe. N **wheelchair.** *álį̨įhceðe oðáha oðíhta owíbraha* hang the wheelchair on and I'll follow your car (RBn; MREI/01/11/93).

álį̨įscee. N [*álį̨į* + *scéce*] **divan, sofa, couch, chaise longue (lit., 'long chair')** (01/20/95/FH/pc:prod; BE2.32).

•• LFD 10: *alį́ scece* <a-gthi^n´ stse-dse> long chair—a settee.

álǫðį (variant: **áalǫ́ðį**). V [reg.+sync., *_álǫ_ðį*] [*á-* LOC + *lǫ́ðį*] *(intr.)* **get drunk.** *kaakǫ́ šǫ́ ðaašé, ðáalǫšči nana* keep on until you get drunk (RBn2-moj/p28). *áalǫbrį hta mįkšé* I am going to get drunk (RBn1-MOJ/p40; RBn2-MOJ/p27). *áðalǫšcį́* you got drunk.

áma (variant of **ą́mą**).

ámaxa. V [reg.?, *á_maxa*?] *(trans.)* **skin, as an animal; remove the hide from anything** (RBn10-16). • N **Omaha tribe or person** (RB, unconfirmed).

amą́ (variant of **ą́mą**).

ámąðį. V [(reg.+)sync., *á(_)mą_ðį*] *(trans.)* **walk on.** *níi ški ámaščį áape* they said you [even] walked on water (RBn23-17). • N **water-strider bug.**

•• LFD 105: *niámąðį* <ni-a´-mo^n-thi^n> walks on water (04/06/95/PM/pc:ok).

ámąhta (variant: **émąhta**). ADV **other way (lit., toward the other)** (RB, FH). *ámahta na hkilíihkoįya* turn yourself the other way. • N **the other side** (RB; BE2.146).

ámąhta hkilíikoįye. VP **turn around the other way; turn oneself the other way or to the other side; (metaphorically) begin to do right, mend your ways** (RB). *ámahta na hkilíikoįya* turn yourself around (BE2.146; FH:ok).

ámąhtaha (variant: **ámahtaha**). ADV **in the other direction, the other way, the other side.**

ámąši (variant: **ámaši**). V [conjug. unknown] [*á-* LOC + *mą́ši*] *(trans.)* **be on top of or above s.t. else.** *ámaši akxái* he or she is upstairs (02/27/95/JS/pc:ok; BE2.147). • **place s.t. up or above.** *ámaši hta mįkšé* I'm going to put it up above (HRE/01/17/02/pc). • ADV **up or up above, upstairs, in the upper part.** *paaxó ámaši ki mąðį́* go up into the mountains. *ámaši aðáape* she went upstairs (RB; 02/27/95/JS/pc:ok).

•• LFD 13: *ámąši* <a´-mo^n-shi> upstairs. *ámąši bre ha* <a´-mo^n-shi bthe ha> [sentence-final *ha* is not used in Mod. Os.] I went upstairs. *ámąši ąkaða pe ha* <a´-mo^{n}shi o^n-ga tha pe ha> [sentence-final *ha* is not used in Mod. Os.] we went upstairs. *ámąšiahta* <a´-mo^n-shi-a-ṭa> above; up there.

••• *QU mąší* upper, upward; heaven (RR), *mąšíde* go up, ascend (RR), *mą́ši hí* high, high up; incommunicative (RR).

ámąhta (variant of **émąhta**).

ámįce. V [reg., *á_mįce*] *(trans.)* **crawl on, crawl upon.** *hpáažį akxa ánaahkoe ámįci akxai* the baby is crawling on the floor.

•• LFD 92: *mįcé* <mi^n-dse´> to creep; to crawl on the hands and knees. *žą hkilé kše ci amįce bre ha* <zho^n ḳi-gthe´ ke dsi a-mi^n-dse bthe ha> [sentence-final *ha* is not used in Mod. Os.] I crawled under the log.

ámǫ (variant: **ámǫį**). V [1st sg. of *ǫ́ǫ* 'wear'] *(trans.)* **I wear.**

ánaašile (variants: **ánašįle, ánažįle**). N **stairs** (BE2.126; 04/06/95/LS/pc:okc; 03/14/95/FH/pc:uk).

ánaaži (variant of **ánąąžį**).

ánąąhkoe (variants: **ánahkoe, ánąhkǫ**). N **floor** (T#38a-p2/38HH10). *hpáažį akxa ánaahkoe ámįce akxái* the baby is crawling on the floor (RBn13-01). • **porch** *ą́nąąhkoe kši ąlį́į htai* let's sit on the porch (T#38a-p2/38HH12; 05/02/95/LS/pc:okc). *ánąąhkoe ci ąkái hce* let's [the two of us] go on back to the porch (RBn10-18; CQc).

•• LFD 13: *ánǫhkoke* <a´-no^{n}-ḳo-ge> floor; porch. *ánǫ́hkoke ðalį wį abrį* <a´-no^{n}-ḳu-ge tha-gthi^{n} wi^{n} a-bthi^{n}> I have a nice porch.

ánąąžį (variants: **ánaaži, ánąąži**). V [reg., *á_nąąžį*] [*á-* LOC + *nąąžį́*] *(trans.)* **stand on top of, be superior to in some quality (used in comparative and superlative constructions)** (MSB). *scécape, záani ánąąžį* he's taller than everyone else (lit., 'he is tall, he stands atop others [in tallness]'). • **step on, step in.** *áðanąąžį* you stepped in it. *mastósto áðanaažį́* you stepped in mud (FH:4/24/96/prod). *táatą hpíiži wį áðanąąžį́ ska táabrą ðąįšé* you must have stepped on something bad, because you're smelling bad (FH:prod). *į́į wį áanąąžį* I stepped on a rock (BE2.127; 03/14/95/FH/pc:ok).

ánąhkǫ (variant of **ánąąhkoe**).

ánąkʔǫ. V [reg., *á_nąkʔǫ*] [*á-* LOC + *nąkʔǫ́*] *(trans.)* **listen to, heed** (RBn10-6:JW). *ánąkʔǫ ðį́* [expected form: *ą́ąnąkʔǫ* (from *á-ą-nąkʔǫ*)] listen to me [sg. addressee] (02/16/95/FH/pc:okc; RBn2-moj/p23). *ánąkʔǫ pi* [expected form: *ą́ąnąkʔǫ pi*] listen to me [pl. addressee] (01/04/95/FH/pc:ok). *iiðánahįmaží mįkšé ąžį ą́ðanakʔǫžíe* I objected to it, but you didn't listen to me. *waaðáta tą áðinąkʔǫ́ hta akxái* pray and he will hear [listen to] you. • *(intr.)* **listen.** *áðanąkʔǫ, owíhkie aðįhé* are you listening, I'm talking to you (RBn19-05). *ánąkʔǫpi, íe tóa ékipše hkǫ́bra* listen [pl. addressee], I want to say a few words (RBn23-17). *ánąkʔǫǫ!* listen! (05/01/95/LS/pc).

apa. CONT [often appears as *apai* (from *apa* + *ðe* DECL; *ðe* earlier characterized female speech)] **continuative aspect postverbal marker (indicating ongoing action or state in present, past, or future time) for 3rd person sg. or pl. moving or absent subject (contrast *akxa*).** ['Moving' here means 'changing location'; motions or gestures that do not change the entity's location in horizontal space do not take this affix.] *ée ékiǫ apai* he's doing it himself (RBn10-21/JW&FW/77). *kǫ́ða apa* he's wanting it. *óxpa apái* he has just lost it (02/13/95/FH/pc:okc; 04/14/95/FH/pc; RBnOT 2/10/83/p3). *Meg apa šímižį ðáalį apai* Meg is a pretty girl (MSB 2/24/83). *mąðį́ alí a apai* she's walking home (MSB 2-24-83). *kahúužą mą́žą ðéka omą́įpe* he lived on this earth a long time (RBn10-13:JW): completed event, compare with: *kaahúužą mą́žą ðéka omą́į apai* he lived [was living and moving] on this earth a long time ago (RBn10-13:FH). *mąðį́ alí apai* she's walking home. *ðiskíke káaɣe apai?* are they making you tired? *iihǫ́ apa óohǫ apai* mother is cooking. *óxpa apái ðe* he lost something (04/11/95/LS/pc). *hóšechíepi tą, iištá ápisąi koe áa ákabra ną́ąke htaacéžį oðį́įke ahú apai* he was excited, with his eyes closed and his arms open he came running to catch Whirlwind (RBn17-p). *ðikʔú apa* he gave it to you as he was moving along (MSB 9-3-82). *waachí apai* he's dancing [moving through space, traveling horizontally]. *háakǫta wacúe skúe špáase ðikǫ́ða apai?* why did they want you to cut the cake? *háaną óožu apái?* how many people have put in? (e.g., cans of food, as a contribution) (03/09/95/FH/pc). *tąhí apa* they [absent and moving] are well. • **(following future/potential *hta*).** *áahukʔoe akxa kikʔǫ́ kšíe hta apái* Henry [holes-in-the-wings] is going to paint him for burial (03/03/95/FH/pc:ok; BE2.101, RBn2-moj/p21). *ahí hta apai* they'll be there. • **he/she/it is characterized by, they are characterized by [the immediately preceding word or phrase, which may be a noun phrase].** *hį́į hpíiži apa* he has bad teeth. *waðílą hpíiži apa* they have a bad temper.

apa. SUBJECT MARKER **(follows a subject [sg. or pl.] that is moving or is not present with speaker; contrast *akxa*).** ['Moving' here means 'changing location'; motions or gestures that do not change the entity's location in horizontal space do not take this affix.] *į́į apa skíke apai* that rock is heavy; those rocks are heavy (the rocks are being carried in this instance, therefore are moving) (FH/07/31/01/pc). *hą́ąkǫta šǫ́ke apa šką́kąða?* why is this dog moving around so much? *huuhtą́ka ohkíhkie apai, hcíle apa hípe* a whole bunch of them were talking when the family came over (3/2/89/MSB). *hkáwa apa okaxpápe* he got thrown off the horse (lit., 'the horse threw him') (RBn19-01). *iihǫ́ apa* the mother [subject of sentence, if "up and around"] (2-1-50-2). *wižį́ke apa mą́zeska ðįkí apai* Sonny doesn't have any money [Sonny is absent]. • **used for respect with deceased persons even if**

present (*akxa* is used with animals). *šíi apa c?ápe* that man died (RBn22-17).

•• LFD 39: *hkąace xoce apa cuuta pe o* <k̦o^n´-dse xo-dse a-ba dsiu-da bi o> [sentence-final *o* is not used in Mod. Os.] the plum is ripe.

ápahta N **fence** (BE2.46; 04/26/95/LS/pc:ok).

•• LFD 5: *ápahta* <a´-ba-ța> a fence; a stockade.

••• Cf. *mą́ze ápahta.*

apai (see **apa** CONT).

ápazo. V [sync., fortisizing stop stem, *á_pazo*] *(trans.)* **point at, point to.** *ápazo!* point at it! (RBn10-9:JW). *šáake ąwą́pazo ðįká* don't point the finger at me (said to the children by FH's mother) (01/24/95/FH/pc:prod). • **select by pointing to.**

•• LFD 5: *ápazo* <a´-ba-çu> to indicate, to point at; to select. *áhpazo* <a´-p̣a-çu> I select. *ášpazo* <a´-shpa-çu> you select. *ą́kapazope* <o^n´-ga-ba-çu i> [expected Mod. Os. form: *ąkápazope*] we select. *žą́che áhpazo* <zho^n´-tse a´-p̣a-çu> I point at the tree.

••• *OM* same as Osage (LFD 5).

••• Cf. *wéapazo.*

apaži. [*apa* CONT + *aží* NEG; contrast *paží*].

ápe. N **leaf** (?).

•• LFD 288: ápe <a´-be> leaf or leaves. LFD 57: *házi ape štaha* <ha´-çi a-be shta-ha> large wild grapes, with smooth leaves (02/03/95/FH/pc:uk, unconfirmed).

••• Cf. *žąąpé.*

ápetxa (variants: **ápetxą, ápetkxą**). PPN **around (e.g., house, tree, tipi, drum).** • N **wrapping; wrapper, covering wrapped around s.t.** (LS/pc). V [conjug. unknown] *(trans.)* **wrap or tie up.** *ápetxa!* tie that up! (RBn1-25).

••• Cf. *ópetxą.*

api (variant: **pi**). SUFFIX [*api* + *ðe* DECL contracts to *(a)pe*; *api* + *aží* NEG contracts to *(a)paží*] **pluralizer of 1st or 2nd persons ('we', 'us', 'you').** *žą́ąxe ąną́chįpe* we hit him with a stick. *ónǫbre wak?úpi apai* we were fed, food was given to us (lit., 'they fed us'). *žį́ihe ðáalį škáaɣapi?* did you sleep well? (03/10/95/MREI/pc:ok). *waðímǫpi akxai* he stole from you [pl.]. *hǫ́ǫpa háažǫpe?* what did you [pl.] do today? (03/22/95/FH/pc:ok). *záani wanǫ́bre hi pi* you all come over and eat (01/04/95/FH/pc:ok). *wéeðinąąpi akxai* he's grateful to you all, he's thanking you all. *záani wawíhǫįpi* I address you all as friends and relatives. *waachí hí žiišǫ́ ðée ðe hpahą́le hą́nahpaze oolą́ąpi wáhkǫ́bra* before the dances start, first I want you all [lit., 'them'] to put him in jail (FH/09/22/01/pc). *John apa íiðiðe kǫ́ðapí apa ną, šoðée hpaaɣé hta mįkšé* John wants to see you [pl.], so I'm going to send him to see you (FH:5/01/96/tape119a). *waðímǫpi akxai* he stole from you [pl.]. *oohǫ́ ðiištą́pe, ąwą́nǫ́bre htai* the cooking is finished [lit., 'they finished cooking'], let us [three or more] eat. *waachí ki štáapáži na* you [pl.] never go to dances [*štáapáži* from *šcée* + *api* + *aží* NEG]. *íiðiðapaži akxai* he doesn't see you [pl.]. *áðahtaha ípšape ąži owáhkiapažíe* they went right past us but didn't speak to us (RB-MSB 4/7/83; FH:4/18/96/tape:okc). *mą́ąhį wahúhka ą́kažupaží, mą́zehcuka na ąkážupe* we didn't put a knife or fork on, we just put spoons on (RBn3-49). *táatą záani šcíištąpe?* have you got everything all prepared? (lit., 'all things did you [pl.] finish?') (04/13/95/LS/pc:pl). *špáasape?* did you all cut it off? (FH/11/17/01/pc). *ąwámaðǫpe* we [pl.] stole things (contrast *ąwámaðǫ* 'we two stole things'). *ši záani ðalípi hkǫ́bra* I want you all to come back again (RBn10-21). • **pluralizer of imperative.** *škáace mąðį́pi!* you all go on and play!

• **pluralizer of 3rd person.** *wéenąpi* they're thankful (02/03/95/FH/pc:prod) orig). *pée kípąpažíe* he didn't invite anybody (FH:ok, reconf; 5/12/83/rbnot D). • **noncontinuative marker for 3rd person (sg. or pl.).** *žą́ąɣe ąną́chįpe* he hit me with a stick. *tówa apa aðáapažíe* he/they [moving] didn't go [*paží* < *api* + *aží*] (2-10-83-p2). *nąnióąpaži wį kǫ́ðape* he had wanted that "awhile back" (3-2-42[2]). • **marker of predicative noun-plus-adjective phrases.** *hkáwa ðáalįpi ną* he continues to be a good horse (RBn12-03p5). *hkáwa ðáalįpe* he's a good horse. *níhkaši wawį́kšapažíe* she's an untruthful person (RB:MSB). *kóe htáa htóhožį wį pe* once there was a little blue deer (RBn15-01). *waachí hpíǫpe* he is a good dancer (lit., 'he knows how to dance'). *níi akxa op?ą́ðe nąpé* water steams (2-2-670). *ošpéžį nąlǫ́ǫha apái ðée apa ahú apai óceštąpe* they're hiding their things because the people coming are snoops (or are always snooping).

•• LFD 17: *ą́kaxopapaži pe* <o^n´-ga-xo-ba-ba-zhi i> we desecrated it.

apíaapé [*api* + *áape* REPORTATIVE]. **plural or 3rd person plus reportative: e.g., 'it was said of him/her/it/them/us/you (pl.)'.**

ápisą. V [uninfl.? (sync. 1st sg. ***áhpisą* and reg. or sync. 2nd sg. ***áðapisą*, ***ášpisą* are all unacceptable)] *(trans.)* **hold down (e.g., a lid or**

ápisą (*continued*) **a person); mash, push down on; shut, close (e.g., one's eyes)** (02/24/95/FH/pc:ok). *ápisą nįkšé* you're holding it down (02/24/95/FH/pc). *hóšechíepi tą, iištá ápisąi koe áa ákabra nąąke htaacéžį oðįįke ahú apai* he was excited, with his eyes closed and his arms open he came running to catch Whirlwind (RBn17-p). *ápise hta mįkšé tą aðáaapia* I was going to hold him down, but he's gone (RBn10-5:JW, FH:okc).

••• *QU ábisąhte* [sync. fortisizing] catch by pressing on; hold down (e.g., on his back); lie on s.t. (RR).

ápše. ADV **around (e.g., pass around, give around, walk around).** *níi ápše wákˀue* pass the water around (lit., 'give the water to them around') (03/16/95/JS/pc:prod; BE2.151).

• V [reg.?, *á_pše*?] *(intr.)* **go around, circulate.** *húheka hpíiži wį ápše apai* there's a bad sickness going around (RBn22-09).

•• LFD 14: *ápše* <a´-pshe> to walk on, or to go from house to house [a more exact translation is probably 'go around']. *ápše bre ha* <a´-pshe bthe ha> [expected Mod. Os. form: *ápše brée*; sentence-final *ha* is not used in Mod. Os.] I go [probably better 'I go around']. *ápše ǫka ða pe* <a´-pshe o^{n}-ga tha i> [expected Mod. Os. form: *ápše ąkáðape*] we go [probably better 'we go around'].

••• Cf. *ípše.*

ápuɣe. V [uninfl.?] *(intr.)* **boil, as food boils when cooking, foam up** (01/07/95/FH/pc:ok; BE2.10). *níi ápuɣe* beer (lit., 'boiling or foaming liquid'; meaning 'beer' not confirmed) (RBn10-15).

•• JOD (slip file): *ápuɣe* to boil, as water; to foam.

•• LFD 6: *ápiɣe* <a´-bi-xe> the boiling of water.

ápuštai. V [reg., *á_puštai*] [*á-* LOC + *pu-* INSTR + *šta* (= *štáha*)] *(trans.)* **spread on (as shoe polish)** (RBn23-05). *wéli hǫǫpé ápuštai* polish your shoes (lit., 'spread grease on (your) shoes') (RBn23-05).

ásąci. V [conjug. unknown] *(trans.)* **put to the test, test s.o.** (RB). *ásąci apai* they're putting each other to a test (MSB, RB; 04/26/95/FH/pc:uk).

••• *KS áanąsąǰe* to stamp on something (JOD).

••• Cf. *áhkiasąci, kasǫ́ci, opásące.*

asíhpa. N **baby sister (anyone's; can be used as vocative); baby daughter (anyone's; used vocatively by father and mother)** (FH). [Does not use the inalienable possessive prefixes.]

asížį. N **fourth daughter (and subsequent daughters).**

•• LFD 6: *áçį žįka* <a´-çi^{n} zhi^{n}-ga> special kinship term for the fourth daughter.

asįka (variant: **ašįka**). N **third daughter** (04/07/95/LS/pc:okc; 02/27/95/FH/pc).

•• LFD 6: *asįka* <a-çi^{n}´-ga> same as <çi´-ge>. *asįka akxa įce luža pe* <a-çi^{n}´-ga a-ka i^{n}-dse gthu-zha bi a> little sister washed her face.

ásta (variant: **áðasta**). V [sync.?, *á_sta*?] *(trans.)* **stick to, adhere to.** *ónǫbre akxa áwanǫbre kši ásta akxai* the food is sticking to the table. *áwanǫbre áðasta akxai* the food is stuck to the table (MSB 2-25-83). *áwanǫbre ásta akxai* it's stuck to the table.

••• Cf. *stáðe.*

ášihta (variants: **áši, asíhta**). ADV **outside, outdoors.** *áši tǫ́pa* look outside (RBn10-21/JW&FW/77; 03/03/95/FH/pc:ok; RBn1-moj/p31). *ášihta alįį mįkšé* I was sitting outside (RBn22-09). *áši brée hkǫ́bra* I want to go outside (03/03/95/FH/pc:ok). *áši ąkáðe* we are going outside (03/03/95/FH/pc:okc). *áši ðée!* go outside! *ášihta mąðįpi* you all go outside (as to children) (03/03/95/FH/pc:ok; BE2.99; 03/03/95/FH/pc:ok).

•• LFD 14: *ášihta* <a´-shi-ṭa> outside.

ášihta wanǫ́bre VP [reg.-*awa*, *ášihta wa_nǫbre*] *(intr.)* **picnic, dine outdoors.** *ónǫbre ąkáðį tą ášihta ąwánǫbre škí ǫ́ǫ htai* we have food, so we will have a picnic (too) (BE2.102; 03/07/95/FH/pc:okc).

ašįka (variant of **asįka**).

áška. ADV **nearby, close, a short distance away** (01/09/95/FH/pc:ok). *áškažį lįįka* sit right here by me (BE2.20). *áška ku* come close. *áška mąįpai ąži oðáxpae hta ðaašé* [*mąįpai* < *mąðį* + *pai*] stay close or you'll get lost.

áška ci. PPN **close to or near s.t. or s.o.** *tóosku káxa kše áška ci alįį* I live near Spring River [Sweet Potato Creek].

•• LFD 14: *áška* <a´-shka> near; close by; short distance. *áška xci mǫbrį* <a´-shka xtsi mo^{n}-bthi^{n}> I walked a short distance.

••• *OM* same as Osage (LFD 14).

átaa. V [reg., *á_taa*] *(trans.)* **freeze to; freeze sticking to s.t.**

•• LFD 117: *nąɣe ata* <no^{n}´-xe a-da> iciness; icy.

••• Cf. *ótaa.*

átahką (variant: **átahkaį**). N **lamp, light.** *átahkaį ðuutáaži* turn off the light (02/14/95/FH/pc:ok). *átahkáį káaɣa* turn on the light (02/14/95/FH/pc:ok; BE2.75).

•• LFD 7: *átahkǫ* <a´-da-ḳo^{n}> a light; artificial light. *átahkǫðe* <a´-da-ḳo^{n}-the> a lantern [meaning unconfirmed].

••• *OM* <a-na-ḳo^{n}> (LF).

átahką wéli níini. N **oil well (lit., 'lamp' + 'oil' + 'spring, well').**

•• LFD 7: *átahkǫ weli nihni* <a´-da-ḳo^{n} we-gthi ni-hni> oil well. *átǫhkǫ weli̜ nihni wi̜ mǫžǫ ðǫti abri̜ ha* <a´-do^{n}-ḳo^{n} we-gthi^{n} ni-hni wi^{n} mo^{n}-zho^{n} tho^{n}-di a-bthi^{n} ha> [expected Mod. Os. form: *átahką wéli níini wi̜ mą́žą ci abrí̜*; *ðǫti* is not recognized in Mod. Os.; sentence-final *ha* is not used in Mod. Os.] an oil well is on my land.

átǫpe. V [sync., fortisizing stop stem, *á_tǫpe*] *(trans.)* **watch over; watch, tend, take care of (e.g., some entity, such as a baby or a purse, or some process, such as cooking)** (03/16/95/JS/pc:ok). *wacúe šku áhtǫ́pe brée hce* I'm gonna go see about the cake; let me just go see about the cake (0109/95/FH/pc:prod). *wacúe šku áhtǫ́pe hce* I'm gonna watch the cake (01/09/95/FH/pc:prod). *átǫpa!* you watch! (03/16/95/FH/pc:ok). *átǫpai* watch it; look out for it (e.g., baby, purse) (MSB t2s2; FH; same as *átǫpe*). *níhkaši ðe átǫpa* watch that man; take care of that man. *níhkaši pa wáatǫpa* take care of those men [standing or sitting]; look after those people. *waátǫpa!* watch over them! [sg. or pl. addressee] (FH/08/01/01/pc [not 'us']). *waátǫpapi* watch over us (FH/08/01/01/pc). *oohǫ́ átǫpe* tend cooking (03/16/95/JS/pc:ok).

•• LFD 38: *áhtǫpe* <a´-ṭo^{n}-be> I watched over him. *áštǫpe* <a´-shto^{n}-be> you watched over him. *ą́katǫpa pe* <o^{n}´-ga-do^{n}-ba i> we watched over him.

átxą (variant: **átkxą**). V [reg.?, *á_txą*?] **climb (by wrapping around?).** *hǫbrí̜ke átkxą ecí áape* they said that there were beans climbing (FH/09/09/01/pc).

••• Cf. *ápetxa*.

áwaachi. V [reg., *á_waachi*] [*á-* LOC (in benefactive sense) + *waachí*] *(trans.)* **dance for.** *áwawaachi* I danced for them. *ą́ąwaachi ðíe* dance for me. *áwaachi!* dance for him! *áwiwaachi ątxą́hé* I'll dance for you.

áwaðilą. V [sync., *áwa_ðilą*] [*á-* LOC + *waðílą*] *(trans.)* **meditate on, deliberate over, consider.** *áwabrilą* I'll meditate on it (when one is asked for a favor, this is a more tentative answer than *íbrilą*).

•• LFD 17: *áwaðilą* <a´-wa-thi-gtho^{n}> deliberate, consider. *áwabrilą* <a´-wa-bthi-gtho^{n}> I considered it (03/20/95/FH/pc:ok). *áwaštilą* <a´-wa-shti-gtho^{n}> [expected Mod. Os. form: *áwašcilą*; *áwaštilą* is archaic] you considered it. *ą́kawaðilą* <o^{n}´-ga-wa-thi-gtho^{n}> we considered it.

••• *OM* same as Osage (LFD 17).

••• Cf. *íðilą*.

áwaðuwi̜ V [sync., *áwa_ðuwi̜*] [*wa-* VAL + *áðuwi̜*] **buy stuff for s.o.**

áwahkie (variant of **wáhkie**).

áwanǫbre. N **table** (RB). *Íi̜ka áwanǫbre kší* be seated at the table (02/27/95/JS/pc:ok). *áwanǫbre hí̜ice ážu* put the dishes on the table (02/27/95/JS/pc; RBn1-43; BE2.131; 02/27/95/JS/pc:ok).

áwanǫbre aðibra (variant: **áwanǫbre haa**). N **tablecloth, any covering to spread on the table (e.g., oilcloth)** (05/02/95/LS/pc:ok; FH).

•• LFD 17: *áwanǫbre aðibra* <a´-wa-no^{n}-bthe a-thi-btha> oilcloth for table use, as a tablecloth [strictly speaking, 'oilcloth' is not part of the meaning].

áwaši. V [reg., *á_wasi*] [*á-* LOC + *waší*] *(trans.)* **work for, accomplish a task or tasks for s.o. (especially drumming for s.o. else's singing in a peyote meeting)** (RBn1-12). *áwawaši hkǫ́bra* I want to ask someone to work. **meeting**

áwawaši. V [reg., *á_wawasi* or *áwawa_si*?] [*á-* LOC + *wawáši*] *(trans.)* **ask folks to work for one; hire people to work for oneself.**

áwaži̜ka nąąke (variant of **éwaži̜ nąąke**).

áwisi. V [reg.? *á_wisi*?] [*á-* LOC + *wísi*] *(trans.)* **jump over** (02/13/95/FH/pc:okc; BE2.72).

áxa. V *(trans.)* **beat s.o., as in a race.**

••• Cf. *káaxa*.

áxopaži. V [*áxope* + *aží* NEG] *(trans.)* **desecrate, show dishonor to.**

•• LFD 17: *áxopaži* <a´-xo-ba-zhi> to desecrate. *ą́kaxopapažipe* <o^{n}´-ga-xo-ba-ba-zhi i> we desecrated it.

áxope. V [reg., *á_xope*] *(trans.)* **honor.** *ąkáxope ąkatxą́i* we honor that (RBn HW13; FH:okc).

•• LFD 17: *áxope* <a´-xo-be> deference; respect. *áaxope* <a´-a-xo-be> I respected it. *áðaxope* <a´-tha-xo-be> you respected it. *ąkáxopape* <o^{n}-ga´-xo-ba i> we respected it.

••• Cf. *ðixópe*.

ážami̜ (variants: **žaamí, žamí, žamí̜, žámi̜**). V [1st sg. of *aží̜* 'think'] **I think.**

ažáži̜ (variants: **ðažáži̜, žáʔaži**). V [2nd sg. of *aží̜* 'think'] **you think.**

ážą. V [reg., *á_žą*] [*á-* LOC + *žą́ą*] *(intr.)* **lie down.** *áažą* I'm lying down (02/15/95/FH/pc:okc;conf

áž̨ą *(continued)* *áaža* I lie down ok). *ážą áažą pšíe* I went to [lie down on the] bed (BE2.7; 04/11/95/LS/pc:ok; 01/07/95/FH/pc:ma 108-b/FH/200). *áðažą nįkšé?* are you lying down? (FH/pc). • N **bed.** *ážą kíkáaγa* make up your bed (01/07/95/FH/pc:). *ážą brée ðe* I went to bed (01/07/95/FH/pc). *ážąmąze* an iron bed (04/11/95/LS/pc:ok).

ážą žįka. N **divan** (LF).

•• LFD 17: *ážą žįka* <a´-zhoⁿ zhiⁿ-ga> a divan.

ážąį ðuuc?áke (variants: **ážąkį ðuuc?áke** [RB]; **ážaį ðuuc?áke**). VP [presumably from *ažį́* 'think', originally *ážą?į*; *?* has been replaced by *k* in RB variant] **(be) confused.** *ðée táatą ážąki brúuc?ake mįkšé* I'm confused, I'm mixed up, I can't make head nor tails out of it (lit., 'I am unable to think something about that') (RBn10-21/JW).

ážąžį. N **small cot** (PM).

aží (variant: **ži**). NEG [initial *a* replaces final *e(e)* of preceding verb; pl. negator *paží*; 1st sg. negator *maží*] **not (negative, negator).** *bráamąžíe* I didn't go [from *brée*]. *pée ðaaží hta apai* nobody is going (MSB). *tówa akxa aðáapažie* he didn't go, they didn't go (2-10-83-p2). *tówa apa aðáapažíe* he or they [moving] didn't go (2-10-83-p2). *kasį́ wanǫ́bre aðį́žipe* he didn't have breakfast. *waaðǫ́aži/waaðǫ́ǫži* they don't sing; not singing, don't sing! *mą́ąhį wahúhka ą́kažu apaží, mą́zehcuka na ąkážupe* we didn't put a knife or fork on, we just put spoons on (RBn3-49). *waachí ki štáapáži na* you [pl.] never go to dances [*štáapáži* from *šcée* + *api* + *aží* NEG]. *íiðiðapaži akxai* he doesn't see you [pl.]. *áðahtaha ípšape ąži owáhkiapažíe* they went right past us but didn't speak to us (RB-MSB 4/7/83; FH:4/18/96/tape:okc). *níhkaši wawį́kšapažíe* she's an untruthful person [*wawį́kšapažíe* from *wawį́kše* + *api* + *aží* NEG + *ðe* DECL] (RB:MSB).

•• LFD 17: *ą́kaxopapaži pe* <oⁿ´-ga-xo-ba-ba-zhi i> we desecrated it.

••• Cf. *ðįké.*

aži hta. [*aží* NEG + *hta* POTENTIAL MARKER] **never will be, never will, will not.** [No Osage word means simply 'never'.] *ékǫǫži hta akxái* [*ékǫ* + *aží* + *hta* + *akxa* + *ðe*] it will never be like that; it's never going to happen (02/27/95/FH/pc; BE2.92).

aži ną. [*aží* NEG + *ną* ITER] **never.** [No Osage expression means exactly the same thing as English 'never'. For the Osage equivalent of 'never' in future-time contexts, cf. *aži hta.*] *žįkážį wíhta wažážeíe awákšuįze maží ną* I never taught my kids the Osage language (RBn10-16).

ažį́ (variant: **ažákį** [RB only]). V [reg.+sync. nasal vowel stem, *(_)(a)ža_į* (object pronominals in first slot, subject pronominals in second slot; underlying stem *ažáį* becomes *ažį́* when no subject prefix precedes the *į*)] *(trans.)* **think or believe regarding s.o., hold an opinion of s.t.** *ážamį/ažamį́/žamį́* I think. *ažážį/ðažážį* you think. *ažį́* he thinks. *ąkážį* we think. *ožo ážį* admire or think something or someone is pretty (RBn HW; cqc). *ožo ážamį* I think she's pretty (RBn HW;cqc). *hpíiži ažį́* hate someone (lit., 'think badly of'). *c?éka wižamį́* I think you're crazy (RBn23-20). *ékǫ žamí įké* I don't believe it (RBn22-05). *ðáalį ážamíe, ðážažie?* I myself think that's good, do you think so? (FH/06/27/01/pc). *ðáalį ékǫ žámį* I think that's right (03/20/95/FH/pc). *ąkítąhé xci hta mįkšé ážamí* I'm sure enough going to get better, I think (03/20/95/FH/pc:okc). *ą́ðihice akxai žaamí/ážamí* he's teasing me, I think (03/20/95/FH/pc, both ok; BE2.138). *háakǫ žá?aži* [*?* is unexpected] what do you think of it? (03/20/95/FH/pc). *ékǫ žá?aži* do you think that's right? (03/20/95/FH/pc:okc). *wáali ohtáza ažį́pe* he thought they were very beautiful (RBn15-01). *ðáalį ąažį ðįkí apái* he doesn't think well of me. *níi táahpa įkší žįka nǫ́ǫðe ðáalį, ecíe ska ąąžį́ ąkátxa* the pond is a good place to raise children, we think it's there (RBn19-04). *hóo ðáalį ašcį́ ažį́ ąži ohláaži ašč́įe* they think you have a good voice, but it isn't right.

•• LFD 129: *hpíiži ažį* <pi̧´-zhi a-zhiⁿ> to have a bad opinion of a person.

••• Cf. *ážąį ðuuc?áke.*

ážǫ (variant: **ážǫe**). V [2nd sg. of *ǫ́ǫ* 'wear'] *(trans.)* **you wear.**

ážu (variant: **áažu**). V [reg., *á_žu*] *(trans.)* **put out, set out (multiple items); place, array, display (multiple items) on top of s.t. else** (01/20/95/FH/pc:ok, 03/09/95/FH/pc:ok; BE2.31). *áðažu?* did you put [s.t.] on top of [s.t.]? (MSB). *wižį́ke mą́zeska tóa céγenii ážu áwakšie hta mįkšé* I'm going to have my son put some money on the drum (RBn10-3:MOJ/79). *hįįcéžį ážu hta apai* they're going to set out their crafts (as for sale). (FH:5/02/96/prod). *hį́ice ážu ąðį́įštąpe* we finished setting the table (RB, 03/09/95/FH/pc:okc). *mą́ąhį, wahúhka ąkážupáži* we didn't put a knife or fork on (for each place setting) (03/09/95/FH/pc:okc). *mą́ze hcúka éena ąkážupe* we just put spoons on (03/09/95/FH/pc:okc; BE2.109). *hlaaská óxe ážu* put flowers on the grave • **pour s.t. on or over another surface; put a pourable substance on s.t. else** (FH:). *paašcéka žaaní (toa) ážu* put some sugar on the strawberries (03/14/95/MREI/pc:ok). *pąąšcéka žąąníe tóa ážu bríištą* I already put some sugar on top of the strawberries (RBnB1-52). *ážu* he's pouring it on there (e.g., on a grave) (PM).

•• LFD 17: *ážu* <a´-zhu> to put a number of articles on a rack [actually, on top of anything, not just a rack].

••• Cf. *hcíwažu.*

ą, ą́

ą-. PRNM **1st person sg. patient pronominal, used as object of active verbs ('me', 'for me', 'to me', 'from me', etc.).** *waléze wį ąkšíɣa* write a letter for me; write me a letter; write a letter to me (HHtape; 18a). *ąkísue ði* remember me. *íixa ąškáaɣe* you make me laugh. *ðą́ące oą́lįį* he lives within my heart (04/04/99/FH/pc). *óðohta ąškáaɣe ščuuc?áke* you can't make me behave (MJ 1-19-83). *nąnią́pažį ąkǫ́ða apai* a whole bunch of them wanted/want cigarettes from me (3-2-140). • **1st person sg. patient pronominal prefix, used as subject of stative verbs ('I').** *ą́skike* I'm tired. *žąąníe ą́hǫǫ* I like candy

ą- (see **ąk-**). PRNM **1st person dual or pl. agent pronominal ('we', subject).** [This is the form taken by this prefix before consonants. It contracts with verb-initial *i* to form *ąną.*]

ą́ą (variant of **ąhą́į**?). INTERJ **yes (female speaking).** *ą́ą, ékiǫ ðée hta ché* okay, we'll do it [verb lacks 1st pl. inflection] (RBn17-p03).

ąąðįhé (variant of **ąðįhé**).

ąąhé (variant of **ąhé**).

ąðé. CONT **continuative aspect postverbal marker for moving 1st dual subject 'we two' (indicating ongoing action or state in present or past time).** ['Moving' here means 'changing location'; motions or gestures that do not change the entity's location in horizontal space do not take this affix.] *wanáše é[ð]ǫǫpa ąkále hta ąðé* Wanáše and I are going home [the two of us]. • **(indicating action or state continuing from past to present, corresponding to English perfect 'have been' or 'had been').** *ą́ðihkihtǫpe ąðé* we've been looking after you. *táatą wį ąmą́ðǫe ąðé* we two stole [have stolen] something. • **we two are characterized by [the immediately preceding word or phrase, which may be a noun phrase].** *wawéeðe hǫ́ǫži ąðé* we see poorly (lit., 'we are of bad sight') (RB). *hową́įki ąðé* wherever we [two] are (04/28/95/LS/pc).

ąðįhé (variants: **aðįhé, áðįhé, ąąðįhé**). CONT **continuative aspect postverbal marker (indicating ongoing action or state in present or past time) for moving 1st sg. subject (more emphatic than *ąhé*).** ['Moving' here means 'changing location'; motions or gestures that do not change the entity's location in horizontal space do not take this affix.] *pšú aðį́he* I'm coming. *owíhkie ąąðįhé* I'm telling you [as I'm going along]. *iiną́, áðįhe* mother, here I am (RBn18-01). *óðohta ąhé* I'm behaving, I've been behaving (FH). *tóoska ak?é hta aðįhé* I'm going to dig potatoes (BE2.31; FH:ok). *owíhkie áðįhé* I'm going as I'm talking to you (MJ).

••• Cf. *ąhé.*

ąðįkšé (variants: **ąðį́kše, ąįkšé**). CONT **continuative aspect postverbal marker (indicating ongoing action or state in present or past time) for sitting or lying down 1st dual subject ('we two').** *ónǫǫ ąðįkšé* we [two, sitting/lying down] are old (FH). *ą́ðihkihtǫpe hta ąðįkšé* we [two, sitting/lying down] are going to look after you *ąžį́įhe ąðįkšé* we [two] are sleeping [while lying down] (02/15/95/FH/pc). *žįkáži wáaščįka ąðįkšé* we kissed our children (02/14/95/FH/pc; BE2.73).

ąhą́į (variants: **ąhái(?), ąhą́, ą́ą**). INTERJ **yes (female speaking)** (03/24/95/PM/pc:okc: į). *oðíhta hcéka wį ščúwį?* did you buy a new car? *ąhái, wį brúwį* yes, I bought one [woman speaking] (BE2.162).

ąhé (variant: **ąąhé**). CONT **continuative aspect postverbal marker (indicating ongoing action or state in present or past time) for moving 1st sg. subject (less emphatic than *ąðįhé*; action or state may continue from past to present, corresponding to English perfect ['have/had been']).** ['Moving' here means 'changing location'; motions or gestures that do not change the entity's location in horizontal space do not take this affix.] *kóoci aškąą ąąhé* I've been going on for a long time (MOJ). *awápuštaha ąhé* I've been ironing. *pšú ąhé* I'm coming [unemphatic]. • **I am characterized by [the immediately preceding word or phrase, which may be a noun phrase].** *hį́į hpíiži ąhé* I have bad teeth (03/23/95/FH/pc:okc). *waðílą hpíiži ąhe* I've got a bad temper (03/16/95/FH/pc:ok; (MREI/#95).

ąįkšé (variant of **ąðįkšé**).

ąk- (before *a, ą, o, ǫ* [and perhaps *u*?]), **ą-** (elsewhere). PRNM **1st person dual or pl. agent pronominal ('we', subject of regular or syncopating verbs).**

ąkáðe (variants: **ąkáe, ąkái**). CONT **continuative aspect postverbal marker (indicating ongoing action or state in present or past time) for moving, sitting, or lying 1st pl. subject.** ['Moving' here means 'changing location'; motions or gestures that do not change the entity's location in horizontal space do not take this affix.] *ékǫ ąkái* we're like that (RBn17-p03). *ąkáku ąkáðe* we're coming back. • **(action or state may continue from past to present, corresponding to English perfect ['have/had been']).** *ąwą́puštaha ąkái* we've been ironing. *žįkážį háachi ąką́ązą ąkái* we bawl the children out every time. • **we are characterized by [the immediately preceding word or phrase, which may be a noun phrase].** *hį́į hpíiži ąkáðe* we have bad teeth. *waðílą hpíiži ąhe* we've got a bad temper.

ąkatxą́ (variants: **ąkakxą́, ąkatkxą́, ąkatxá, ąkakxá, ąkatkxá**). CONT **continuative aspect postverbal marker (indicating ongoing action or state in present or past time) for standing (sometimes lying down) 1st pl. subject.** (RBn10-3:MOJ/79). *waachí wáazo ąkakxai* we're enjoying watching the dances. *ąníe ąkatxa* we're all living (MREI/6/7/94/#94; 01/06/95/FH/pc:ok). *ąžį́ihe ąkakxái* we [three or more] are sleeping [lying] (02/15/95/FH/pc). • **imminent future action or state, regardless of whether subject is standing.** *kasį́ta ąkáli hta ąkátxa* we'll come back tomorrow (01/06/95/FH/pc:ok). *mįðóhta wanǫ́bre táatą ąðáache hta ąkátxą?* what are we going to eat for lunch? (RBn12-07). *záani ąðáahtą hta ąkatxą́* we're all going to drink it (RBn10-21). *ąkóðuuxpaðe ąkatxái* we're going to take it out (FH/09/23/01/pc). *omą́įhka hcéka ðóha anǫ́ðe ąkatxá* we're about to see a new year (RB; cqc).

••• Cf. *ątxą́, ątxą́hé.*

ąkó (variant of **ąkóta**).

ąkóe (variant of **ąkóta**).

ąkóhta. PRON **ours; our (belonging to two or more of us).** *mą́žą akóhta* our land (RBn22-08). *hci ąkóhta* our house. • **we ourselves (emphatic).**

•• RB: <ó^{n}-ko-tah> (03/03/95/FH/pc:ok; BE2.99).

ąkóhtapi. PRON **ours; our (belonging to three or more of us)** (FHt#128a). *hcí ąkóhtapi* our house, the house belonging to us [three or more].

ąkóną (variant: **ąkóna**). V, PRON [*ąkó(ta) + na* 'only'] [1st person pl. of *eeną́* 'be the only one'] *(intr.)* **(be) only we.** *ąkóną* it is only we.

••• Cf. *ðíną, eeną́, wíną.*

ąkóški. PRON **we also.**

ąkóta (variants: **ąkóe, ąkó**) PRON **we (emphatic), us (emphatic).** *ąkóe ékiðaapažíe* [as for us] we don't think so (RBn15-01). *ąkóe ąhpáahą ąkái* we're getting up; we're waking up (LS). *ąkóta ški* we also. *ąkó ški* we also.

•• LFD 132: *ąkoški pe* <o^{n}-gu-shki i> we also.

ąkxąhé, ąkxą́he (variants of **ątxąhé**).

ą́mą (variants: **áma, amą́**). PRON **one of several; one to be chosen among many** (FH). *škǫ́šta tą ą́mą ðúuza* if you want it, choose one (04/18/95/FH/pc). • **other (one of two).** *áma htáha* the other way, the other side (MREI, LS).

•• LFD 122: *ą́mą* <o^{n}′-mo^{n}> one of two things.

ąnįkšé (variant of **ąðįkšé**).

ątxą́. CONT **continuative aspect postverbal marker (indicating ongoing action or state in present or past time) for standing 1st dual subject ('we two'); may also be used for imminent future action or state, regardless of whether subject is standing** (RBn10-3:MOJ/79; 1-1-65).

••• Cf. *ąkatxą́, ątxąhé.*

ątxąhé (variants: **ąkxąhé, ątkxąhé, ątxą́he, ąkxą́he, ątkxą́he**). CONT **continuative aspect postverbal marker (indicating ongoing action or state in present or past time) for standing 1st sg. subject** (MSB:t9). *mą́ąye akxa hpíiži akxái, waaspé hta atxąhé* the weather is bad, I'm going to stay (RBn12-06). *brúhcepe hta atxą́he* I can handle it (RBn; MREI/01/11/83; FH:okc). *súhka* *tóopa oowáhą ątxą́he* I'm [going to be] cooking four chickens. *šǫ́ ątxą́he* I'm still standing. *scéce akxą́he* I'm standing here tall. *íe ąðánąkˀǫ škǫ́šta įké paašé ąži iðáe ątxąhé* you all don't want to hear me talk, but I'm talking (RBn10-16). • **imminent future action or state, regardless of whether subject is standing.** *oðíhtą wį ąðúwį ątxą́he* we're about to buy a car [said while sitting] (MREI). *mį́įðohta wanǫ́bre táatą ąðáache hta akátxa?* what are we having for noon meal?

•• LFD 133: *šǫ́ahtąhe aðo* <sho^{n}´-a-ṭo^{n}-he a-tho> [expected Mod. Os.: *tx* rather than *ht*] I am still standing. *šǫ́ðahtąše* <sho^{n}´-tha-ṭo^{n}-she> [expected Mod. Os.: *tx* rather than *ht*] you are still standing.

••• Cf. *ąkatxą́, átxą.*

áwahkie. N **lawyer, attorney (lit., 'taking up for a person').**

••• Cf. *wáhkie.*

áwažįka nąąke (variant of **éwažį nąąke**).

ąži. CONJ **but.** *íe ąðánąkˀǫ škǫ́šta įké paašé ąži iðáe ątxąhé* you all don't want to hear me talk, but I'm talking (RBn10-16). *ékǫ brįe ąži ékǫ hkǫ́bra mąží* that's the way I am, but I don't want to be that way (FH). *íhkihkawi hpáaɣe ąži mą́zeska brúuze mįkšé* I exchanged it, but I took money (1/20/83/631; 04/13/95/FH/pc:ok). *mǫ́žǫ ðáalį ðékše mǫ́žǫ ðékše ðįké hta aži íe wíhta šǫǫšǫ́ðe aðée hta akxai* heaven and earth shall pass away, but my word shall endure (FH:02/07/96/pc). • **or.** *waaspé hta nįkšé ąži ščée hta nįkšé?* are you going to stay or are you going to go? (BE2.127). *ą́ška mą́įpai ąži oðáxpae hta ðaašé* [*oðáxpae* is unexpected (rather than *oðíxpae*, from *oxpáðe*)] stay close or you'll get lost.

ą́žǫ ðįké. INTERJ **goodness; my goodness!; I don't have the mind or nerve!** (FH/pc).

b

brá (variant of **brą́**).

bráaða (variant: **bráaðe** [FH]). ADJ **broad; wide and smooth, as a prairie; smoothed out (e.g., icing on a cake, a fabric or tablecloth lying flat on a surface, but not a blanket on a bed or pallet)** (04/19/95/FH/prod).

•• LFD 28: *bráða* <btha´-tha> broad; wide.

bráaɣe. N **edge, edging (e.g., a fabric or ribbon sewn around the edges of a blanket or garment).** *haaská háabrehka bráaɣe kaaɣá* put ribbon around the edges of the shirt [on the neck opening and/or on the lower edges and sleeves] (lit., 'make a ribbon edge on the shirt') (FH:4/22/96/tape: prod).

bráaska. ADJ **flat** (01/26/95/FH/pc:ok). *wéeli bráaska* a person with a flat head; a flat fish (perch) (lit., 'head' + 'flat') (01/26/95/FH/pc:okc; (BE2.49).

••• Cf. *wacúe ðubráaska.*

brákˀa. ADJ **flat** (FH).

•• LFD 28: *brákˀa* <btha´-ḳ'a> flat board.

brápxąąke. N **mosquito.** [Pawhuska usage (RB).]

•• RB: <bráh-pxáh-i^{n}-keh, bráh-pxah^{n}-keh> (BE2.89, unconfirmed).

••• *KS yáphǫįge* mosquito (JOD, RR).

••• Cf. *lápxąąke.*

bráze. ADJ **torn** (FH).

••• *KS bláablaze* torn in several places, torn up, chapped (RR), *blaze* torn (RR).

••• Cf. *hcéze bráze, įcé bráze, kaabráze.*

brą́ (variant: **bra**). V [uninfl.?] *(intr.)* **smell, emanate an odor, give off a fragrance.** *bra hpíiži* [it] smells bad (04/06/95/LS/pc:ok). *bra éži* it smells odd (04/06/95/LS/pc:ok; BE2.124). *wabrą́lį brą́ akxai* he/she smells like perfume (RBn10-20). *brą ðáalį* it smells good. *brą hpíiži* it smells bad. • N **smell, odor, scent** (03/02/95/FH/pc). *brąðáalį* a pleasing smell, a fragrance. *brąhpíiži* a bad odor.

•• LFD 28: *brą* <btho^{n}> odor; scent. *brą́ hpiži* <btho^{n}´ pi-zhi> an offensive smell. *brąðálį* <btho^{n}-tha´-gthi^{n}> fragrance; pleasing odor.

bréhka. ADJ **lean, thin.** *wacúe bréhka* pancakes, thin bread (03/20/95/FH/pc:ok).

•• LFD 28: *bréhka* <bthe´-ḳa> thin. LF 187: *wacúe brekxa* <wa-dsiu´-e bthe-ka> [expected Mod. Os. form: *wacúe bréhka*] thin bread. *wacúe brehka hkǫbre* <wa-dsiu´-e bthe-ka ḳo^{n}-bthe> [expected Mod. Os. form: *wacúe bréhka hkǫ́bra*] I want pancakes.

••• Cf. *háabrehka.*

brį (variant: **brįe**). V [1st sg. of *ðį́*] *(intr.)* **I am, I was.** *ékǫ brįe ąžį ékǫ hkǫ́bra įké* that's the way I

brį (*continued*) am, but I don't want to be that way (FH:08/22/96). *wažáže brį́* I'm Osage (RBn12-03). *níhce brį́e* I'm cold. *hą́ąpa záani wapúštaha brį́e* I ironed all day (FH:prod). *íkaski ąhé* I'm out of breath. *íkaski bríe* I'm out of breath [synonymous with preceding example] (FH). **• I am characterized by (e.g., I have a certain condition).** *wawéeðe hǫ́ǫži brį́* I see poorly (lit., 'I am of bad sight') (RB). **• I am present, I was present.** *hową́įki ðǫǫpá ðáabrį náški ecíe akxa tą, wíe ée brį́ hta mįkšé ną ée ešíe* wherever two or three only are, I will always be [even] there, you said (Matt.18:20; FH:prayer). *brį́e* I'm present (FH).

bróka. ADV **in bulk (e.g., a purchase of fruit, coffee, or kerosene); wholesale, in large quantities, overall, undivided; by the yard (fabrics); in large pieces, not merely pieces of some item but the entire item (cooking); in its entirety, fully, whole, entire, complete** (FH/pc). *bróka brúwį hta mįkšé* I'm going to buy it [fabric] by the yard (rather than made up into articles such as shawls and blankets). *watkxą́ bróka oowáha hta mikše* I'm going to cook some squash (by cutting whole squash up in big squares, laying skin side of each piece on bottom of pot for first layer, then skin upward for remaining layers, and cooking it outside on a fire with maple syrup and margarine). *hką́ące bróka brúwį hta mįkšé* I'm going to buy the fruit in large quantities [not piece by piece]. *bróka óðaake įká!* don't tell it all! (FH/09/23/01/prod). *súhka bróka oohǫ́!* cook a chicken whole! (03/16/95/MREI/pc:okc; BE2.157). • N **dollar.** *bróka sáhta* five dollars (FH:ok; BE2.33).

•• LFD 28: *bróka* <btho´-ga> entire; a whole thing, a whole; a dollar; firm; solid; strong; hard.

brúbruɣe (variant of **ðibrúbruɣe**).

brúuska. ADJ **flat, wadded up (crushed?).** *niikáapxokeoožu štáaštą tą, ðibrúuska* when you are through with the pop can, wad it up (02/24/95/FH/pc).

••• Cf. *bráaska*.

C

ce (variant: **ci**). ADJ **last; the most recent (used of units of time).** *wíe, hą́ąci ówatǫe pšíe* myself, I went to a show last night (RBn3-25). *htǫǫtą́ce htáabre šíe?* did you go hunting last fall? (RBn11-02/JW&FW; HH/14-a/274ff). *ómaįhka háaši ecí* the same place last year (RB).

••• *KS dogéǰi* last summer (RR).

ce (variant of **ci**).

céɣe (variant: **hcéɣe**). N **bucket, pail; kettle; pot** (01/09/95/FH/pc:ok; BE2.13).

•• JOD (slip file): *céɣe* <ṭṣe´-xe> a pot or kettle.

•• LFD 161: *hcéɣe* <ṭse´-xe> kettle, a pot for cooking; a tin pail.

•• *KS ǰéeɣe* kettle (RR).

céɣenii (variant: **hcéɣenii**). N **drum.** [Takes 'sitting' positional article *įkšé*.] *céɣenii ochį́ ðáalį škáaɣe* you hit the drum good (01/20/95/PM/pc:ok). *céɣenii ochį́ ðáalį káaɣape* he hit good drum for him (01/20/95/PM/pc:ok). *céɣenii ochį́ ðáalį įkší áape* he hit good drum for him (01/20/95/PM/pc:ok). *céɣenii ochį́ ooláaži káaɣape* he didn't hit drum quite right [not up to par] (01/20/95/PM/pc:ok). *céɣenii okˀóce ahí akxa* the drum has a hole in it (04/25/95/PM/pc:okc). *ilǫ́ǫška céɣenii* war dance drum (04/25/95/PM/pc). *céɣenii kaaðéšpa hta apai* they're going to give the drum away; they're pressing or pushing the drum over there [to another person] (BE2.36; 04/25/95/PM/pc:ok). *hǫ́ǫpa ðe céɣenii kašúpe hta apai* they're paying for the drum today (FH:prod) 8/96). *hǫ́ǫpa ðe céɣenii ðée káaɣe hta apa?* are they going to pass the drum today? (FH:prod) 8/96). *céɣenii ochį́ waašką́pi aha ðáalį ché aha, ahú ókašeįke céɣenii ðée įkše* whenever they're doing their best hitting the drum, when it's good, it's an untroubled, peaceful drum (RB; gloss by cq; *céɣenii* non-preaspirated; BF/12/30/01).

•• JOD (slip file): *céɣenį* <ṭṣe-xe-ni^{n}> a drum.

•• LFD 161, 259: *hcéɣeni* <ṭse´-xe-ni> tomtom; drum.

••• *KS ǰéeɣeyį* drum (RR).

céɣenii aðį́ (variants: **céɣenii waðį́, waðį́**). N **drumkeeper (lit., 'he has the drum')** (BE2.36).

•• RB: <tséh-xeh-ni ah^{n}-thí^{n}> (01/20/95/PM/pc:okc).

céɣenii ðée káaɣe. VP [sync. *k>p, _kaaɣe*] **pass the drum (lit., 'make the drum go').** *hǫ́ǫpa ðe céɣenii ðée káaɣe hta apa?* are they going to pass the drum today? (FH:prod; 8/96).

céɣenii káaɣe. VP [sync. *k>p, _kaaɣe*] **tie the drum (lit., 'make the drum'; involves wrapping the drum up and tying it).** *céɣenii káaɣa* tie the drum (04/25/95/PM/pc:ok). *céɣenii saakí káaɣa* tie the drum tight (RB).

céɣenii ochį́. N **drum boss; drumstick (lit., 'he strikes the drum')** (01/20/95/PM/pc:prod; BE2.36).
•• RB: <tséh-xeh-nó^{n}-tsi> (sits to the right of the roadman in a peyote meeting).

céɣenii ochį́ scée. N **drumstick (lit., 'drum beating long')** (RBn12-07; BE2.36; 01/20/95/PM/pc:ok). [Less preferred in this meaning than *céɣenii ochį́* (PM).]
••• Cf. *žą́ąxe céɣenii.*

céɣenii waðį́ (variant of **céɣenii aðį́**).

céɣeska (variant of **hcéheska**).

céɣežį. N **small kettle.**

céže. V [reg., *_céže*] *(intr.)* **urinate.** *acéže hkǫ́bra* I want to pee (RBn10-7:JW; 02/27/95/JS/pc:ok; FH:5/01/96/tape). *(trans.)* **urinate upon.** *ą́ðaceže* you peed on me.
•• JOD (slip file): *céže* <tşe-ce> v. to urinate. 1st sg. <¢atşece>, 2nd sg. <atşeçe>, 1st pl. <a^{n}tşecapi au>.
•• LFD 350: *hcéže* <ţse´-zhe> urinate.
••• *KS jéeže* urinate (RR).
••• Cf. *čéže, océže.*

céženii. N **urine** (RB; 02/27/95/JS/pc).
••• Cf. *hkáwaceženii.*

céženiioožú. N **bladder.**
•• JOD (slip file): *céženiožú* <tşe´-çe-ni-u-çú> a bladder.
•• LF162: *ccéženiožį* <ţse´-zhe-ni-u-zhi> urine pouch; the bladder.
••• Cf. *žé.*

che. POSIT **positional article for standing inanimate sg. nonsubject (also used for intangible entities: e.g., heart attack, song, pain).** *níe che húukaaɣa* pass the water. *mąhkásai ché* this coffee sitting [standing] here. *hcéka ðiníe che ákǫze hta akxa ska* I guess he will examine you now (lit., 'just now they'll examine your hurt, I suppose') (04/13/95/LS/pc:ok). *mǫ́šǫ che káaɣa* let the feather touch it (lit., 'make the feather stand upright [and thereby touch it]'). *wacúe che ípasąį* turn that bread over (FH). *óohǫ che átǫpa* look after the cooking (RBn3-26). *mį́įihuðe che?* is the sun coming up? (04/13/95/FH/pc:prod; FH:4/25/96/tape *káache táatą waaðǫ́?* what kind of song is that?
• **positional article for pl. sitting nonsubjects (those that would take *įkšé* when sg.).** *hǫbrį́ke che hpahíke* I sorted the beans (FH:ok). *ówe che hcíhta áðįku* bring those groceries sitting there inside (01/09/95/FH/pc:ok). *kachéðe* there's something sitting there; there it [pile or stack of sitting/round items] sits (lit., 'that standing there') (FH). *haxį́ hcéka che haaská wasúhu opétkxą* wrap up those new blankets in a clean cloth (03/22/95/FH/pc). *tooská che hkǫ́bra* I want the potatoes (RBn3-43). *haxį́ che paaxcé* tie those blankets up (FH). *haxį́ kóoche opétkxą* tie those old blankets up (FH). *hcéhežį hówąįki che?* where are the dishes [sitting]?
•• JOD (slip file) *žą ðuhtą́le che* <ça^{n} ¢u-tañ´-k¢e (tsĕ)> an upright tree, a tree that still stands [not a log].
•• LFD 48: *káche* <ga´tse> this; this pile of things before us (03/20/95/FH/pc:okc). LFD 170: *aliche aðalį* <a-gthi-tse a-tha-gthi^{n}> you occupied the chair. LFD 175: *aliche aalį* <a-gthi-tse a-a-gthi^{n}> I occupied the chair. *oscé che* <u-stse´ tse> the rest that has been gathered and stands in a pile; the remainder; part of a number left over.

che. COMPLEMENTIZER **that, whatever, until (links a preceding subordinate clause to the following main clause).** *táatą záani škáaɣe che žaažį?* do you think you can do all of it? (lit., 'do you think that you'll do everything?'). *ðáalį tą́he níkšé che, tą́he níkšé che ðáalį* it's good [that] you are keeping well (05/01/95/LS/pc:okc). *ðetkxą́ha haakǫ́ éepše che ékǫ hkǫ́bra* from now on, I want it to be like [that which] I've said (03/22/95/FH/pc). *wižį́ke hą́ąpaska híi che? káaną ahí akxa* Sonny, has daylight come? just a little bit (lit., 'like this [showing with hand]') (FH/09/24/01/prod). *ðáalį ðachí che* it is good that you [sg.] came. *ðée lípi che ški wéewinai* I'm thankful, too, for these who have come here (lit., 'I am also grateful that these ones have come back here') (FH/10/13/96). *lą́ aðée che iiðáahpe hta mįkšé* I will wait until he goes away mad. *taaké óhesaži hi chí aapé* the war is getting worse (lit., 'fighting fiercely has arrived there, they said') (01/24/95/FH/pc:ok).

che. EVIDENTIAL **evidential marker indicating that speaker or addressee has circumstantial or sensory evidence (rather than witnessing) that the situation reported in the sentence**

che (*continued*)
occurred (can often be approximately translated as 'have/has/had already'). *aalée che híe ðáha* I had already left by the time he got there. *wakˀó akxa táakapi che* that woman has fought; that woman did fight (FH:05/06/94). *káaɣapi che bráache mįkšé* they had prepared it, and I'm eating it. *alée che híe ðáha* I had left when he got there. *oðíhtą šką́ą ché?* is the car started? (FH:prod). *okáhąpa kaaléke ché* someone broke a window, that's the way it is (FH:01/07/95; LS:ok). *ooðáhą che bráache mįksé* you had cooked it and I'm eating it. *owáhką bríištą che achípe* I had already finished helping her when they got there (FH:prod). *aðée che híe ðáha* you [sg.] had already left when he got there (FH/07/27/95/pc:ok). *táatą záani ecí che?* is everything there? (RBn12-11). *óhką ecí che?* is there room over there? *wižį́ke hą́ąpaska híi che?* Sonny, has daylight come? (FH/09/24/01/prod). *táatą záani ée ecí che?* is everything there [ready]? (04/26/95/LS/pc:okc; BE2.42). *Jacka háakǫ eekíe che iiðáštą* I agree with what Jack said (contrast with *jacka háakǫ ékie tą iiðáštą* 'I agree with what Jack says') (FH/09/25/01/pc). *íiðaapi ché* they have seen it (RBn22-0). *háakǫpi ché?* how did they do?; what happened to them? (RBn22-01). *hašíhta apa ékiapi ché* the ones before me said that (RBn22-01). *hkáwa alį́į aðáapi che* they went horseback riding (01/31/95/FH/pc:plural). *žįkážį apa omíže wasúhuži káaɣapi ché* the children have dirtied the rug (BE2.31). *žįkážį apa hcéhežį ðuulékepi che* the children broke a dish, they've done it, and they've left it, and it's there (FH/07/27/95prod). *nąniópaži kǫ́ðapi che* she found out that he had wanted a cigarette. *súhka htą́ą oohǫ́ ðáalį káaɣapi ché* the turkey was well prepared RBn2-moj?/p2). *káaɣapi che bráache mįkšé* they had prepared it, I'm eating it. *hkáwalįį aðéei che/hkáwalįį aðáapi ché* they have gone on horseback.

chí (see **achí**).

chúe (variant: **chú**). v [reg., *_chu*] *(trans.)* **copulate with, have intercourse with, screw.** *ðalǫ́ščį tą, šį́tožį apa ðichú hta apai* when you get drunk, the boys will screw you (RB). *ną́ąke wachú* screwing while running (Buffalo clan personal name).
••• Cf. *wachú.*

ci (variant: **ce**). PPN **in.** *Johna táatą íiðe ðe watǫ́ehci ce?* what did John see in the store? *ecí akxa* he's in there (RBn10-21/JW&FW/77). *žą́ą cí olįįpe* he lived in the forest (RB/16-02). *Johna táatą íiðe ðe watǫ́ehci ce?* what did John see in the store? *súhka mą́zeoohǫ ce oowáhą* I baked a chicken (lit., 'I cooked a chicken in the oven') (FH/09/21/01/pc). • **to (s.t. upright or vertical, sg.).** *oðíhtą ci ąkále hce* let's go back to the car (RBnB1-41). *hkiistóhci ci ąkái hce* let's go to the courthouse (RBnB1-41). *waachí ci ąkái hta ąkái* we're going to the dance (RBn3-18). • **at.** *mį́oðaake sáhta ci alíe* I got back at five o'clock (RBnB1-46; cqc: *į*). *mįðóhta ci súhka taazíhi ąðáachape* at noon we ate fried chicken (RBn3-02; cqc: *į*). *mį́ðohta ci súhka taazíhi ąðáachape* we ate fried chicken at noon.
••• Cf. *ecí, ki* 'in', *kši* 'in'.

ci txą. PPN **from.**

cúða (variant of **cúuða**).

cúuce. ADJ **done (e.g., in cooking); cooked** (FH/07/09/01/pc). *htáa cúuce káaɣa* cook the meat well done (lit., 'make the meat be well done') (01/11/95/FH/pc; BE2.24). • **ripe, mellow, mature (e.g., fruit and grain)** (01/11/95/FH/pc:okc). *hką́ące xóce apa cúutape* the plum is ripe, the plums are ripe (01/11/95/FH/pc:ok). • v [conjug. unknown] *(trans.)* **cook well done** (01/11/95/FH/pc:ok).
•• LFD 39: *cúce* <dsiu´-dse> cook done (well done). *hką́ce xoce apa cuuta pe o* <ḳo^{n}´-dse xo-dse a-ba dsiu-da bi o> [sentence-final *o* is not used in Mod. Os.] the plum is ripe. *cúce* <dsu'-dse> mellow; softened with ripeness.
••• *KS ǰúüǰe* cooked, burned, blistered (RR), *waǰúüǰe* mush (RR); *QU títe(?)* [transcription of original source is ambiguous] ripe, cooked (RR), *watíhte* mush, "boiled until done" (RR).
••• Cf. *cúutaži.*

cúuða (variant: **cúða**). ADJ **ragged, torn, ripped** (PM/03/10/95/pc)**; worn out, worn, insufficient (said of clothing)** (RBn22-17). *áhkahamį wíhta akxa cúuða akxai* my coat is ragged (RBn22-17). *įléha wáli htąą akxai, híðaxa ðíhta akxa cúðažipe* his bottom is really large, your diaper is insufficient (BE2.14; 01/09/95/FH/pc:prod).
•• *KS ǰúüya* worn, of clothing, torn, ripped (RR).

cúutaži. ADJ [*cúuce + aží* NEG; *c>t* before *aží*] **unripe, green (e.g., unripe fruit); raw, uncooked, undercooked.**
•• LFD 39: *cutaži* <dsu-da-zhi> unripe or uncooked; applied to fruit.

cúxe (variant of **kaacúxe**).

cˀ

cˀá htą́ą. N **devil, Satan.** [Possibly a contraction of *wécˀa* 'snake' + *htą́ą, htą́ka* 'big'; perhaps borrowed from English *Satan.*]

•• RB: <ts'áh-tah> (lit., 'big snake' [RB]) (01/20/95/FH/pc:ok; RBn10-5:JW).

•• LFD 157: *cˀáhtąka* <ṭs'a´-ṭo^{n}-ga> Satan. "The Osage did not know the name of Satan till the missionaries came."

cˀáaðe. ADJ **sour (taste).** *paazénii cˀáaðe* sour milk.

•• JOD (slip file): *cˀuxe* <ṭ'u-qĕ> acrid, synonym of *cˀáðe* <ts'á¢e> (03/13/95/FH/pc:ok; BE2.125).

•• LFD 157: *cˀáðe* <ṭs'a´-the> sour; like the taste of green gooseberries. LFD 19: *paséni cˀaðe* <ba-çe´-ni ts'a-the> sour milk.

cˀáaži. N [*cˀé* + *aží* NEG] **cross; crucifix** (RBn2-moj/p30; 01/14/95/FH/pc:ok); **clubs (suit in a deck of cards) (lit., 'dies not')** (RBn10-21/JW).

•• LFD 157: *cˀáži* <ṭs'a´-zhi> the cross, crucifix; clubs in playing cards.

cˀáižį. N **husband (typically used by an older woman speaking to or referring to her elderly husband).** *cˀáižį wíhta* my husband. *cˀáižį ðíhta* your husband. *cˀáižį íhta* her husband. • **elderly man (used by anyone referring to an elderly man).**

•• LFD 157: *cˀáke žį̨ka* <ṭs'a´-ge zhi^{n}-ga> an old man.

cˀáke. N **my father-in-law (used by a man addressing or referring to his wife's father; used by anyone referring to a man's father-in-law).** *cˀáke ðíhta* your father-in-law.

cˀé. V [reg., *_cˀe*] *(intr.)* **die** (04/11/95/FH/pc:ok). *hǫpai hašíhta hóni acˀé* some days back I almost died (2/3/83/1/330; 01/20/95/FH/pc:okc). *hóni ącˀée* we died (01/20/95/FH/pc:prod). *hóni ðacˀé* you almost died (FH). *hkáwa akxa cˀé akxai* that horse is dead (RBn22-17). *šíi apa cˀápe* that man died [subject is present but deceased, hence subject marker *apa* is used] (RBn22-17). • N **death; the dead, dead person.** *cˀé ški šǫ́ įkše šcúhpaahą nįkšé aapai* they said you raised the dead [pl. dead; lying down pl. positional article *įkšé*] (RBn23-17).

•• LFD 157: *cˀe* <ṭs'e> to faint, to swoon; to die; decease; demise; defunct. *ahcé* <a-ṭse´> I faint. *ðahcé* <tha-ṭse´> you faint. *ą́hca pe* <o^{n}´-ṭsa pe> we faint.

cˀéðe. V [reg., *cˀé_ðe*] [*cˀé* + *ðe* CAU] *(trans.)* **kill, slay, assassinate, murder; make die** (02/14/95/FH/pc:ok). *cˀéða* kill it (02/14/95/FH/pc:ok). *hcéska wį ącˀéðe htai* let's kill a beef (02/14/95/FH/pc:okc). *žįkážį ški cˀéðe apá aape* they're also killing children [they said] (02/14/95/FH/pc:okc; BE2.73). *hcéska wį cˀéðe htai* let's kill a beef (RBn2-moj/p6b; 02/14/95/FH/pc:ok). *nąníǫpaži apa cˀéði[ð]e hta apai* cigarettes will kill you (RBn HW).

••• Cf. *wacˀéðe* (sometimes with non-valence-reduced meaning).

cˀéhkiðe (variant: **cˀéhkie**). V [reg., *cˀe_hkie*] [*hkik-* REFL + *cˀéðe*] *(intr.)* **kill oneself, commit suicide** (BE2.73; 02/14/95/FH/pc:okc).

•• LFD 159: *cˀéhkiðe* <ṭs'e´-ḳi-the> suicide; the killing of one's self.

cˀéka. V, ADJ [stat., *_cˀéka*] *(intr.)* (be) **crazy; insane; demented; mentally retarded; mentally unstable** (01/14/95/FH/pc:ok). *cˀéka ókˀą ée įká* don't try any funny stuff; don't act the fool (BE2.27, unconfirmed; 03/16/95/JS/pc:uk). *cˀéka okˀą́ ékiǫ ðįkápi* don't do crazy things; don't take crazy actions (RBn10-7:JW). *cˀéka wižamí* I think you're crazy (RBn23-20). *záani ðicˀéka paašé* you're all crazy (RBn23-20). *cˀéka nǫ́ǫ* grown but no sense. *cˀéka ókˀą įká* don't act the fool; don't try any funny stuff; don't act crazy (12/30/94/FH/pc/ok).

•• LFD 158: *cˀéka* <ṭs'e´-ga> to be crazy, insane, mentally unsound, demented; a dolt, a dunce, a crank.

cˀéka ókˀą. NP **funny stuff, foolish acts.** *cˀéka ókˀą ée įká* don't try any funny stuff, don't act the fool.

cˀélǫðį (variant: **cˀelǫ́ðe**) [*cˀé* + *lǫ́ðį*] ADJ **giddy; running here and there, not satisfied anywhere** (RBn10-2:MOJ/79); **dead drunk, excited, out of one's mind** (FH/3/19/00).

••• Cf. *páalǫðį.*

cˀéokˀa (variant of **hcéokˀa**).

cˀį́ða (variants: **cˀíða, cˀí** [LS]). N **wrinkle** (04/17/95/LS/pc).

••• *KS cˀį́ya* frown, wrinkle the forehead (RR).

••• Cf. *paacˀį́.*

cˀį̨ša (variant: **cˀį́že[?]**). ADJ **crooked, curved; bent over (as a person, a tree, or a hooked**

cˀįša (*continued*) **staff**) (RBn10-5:JW; 01/14/95/FH/pc:ok; 04/13/95/LS/pc:ok; BE2.27).

•• LFD 209: *wahléle cˀíša* <wa-xthe´-xthe-ts'-i^n sha> the standard made with a crook by the Osage and Omaha.

••• Cf. *paacˀį.*

cˀíxa (variant: **cˀįxe**). ADJ **crooked, bent over (referring to a human body)** (FH/12/16/94/pc; (04/13/95/LS/pc:uk).

••• *KS cˀíxa* bent (may be long) (RR).

••• Cf. *paacˀį.*

cˀóka ADJ **droopy** (FH/05/13/94).

••• Cf. *įįštáhaa cˀóka.*

cˀóxe. N **hunchback** (04/06/95/FH). *cˀóxe žį* little hunchback (personal name) [Gentnor Drummond's Indian name] (FH).

č

čáahpa. ADJ [diminutive of *táahpa*] **short; rounded and somewhat squat; short and small.** *čáahpa brįe* I'm short. *čáahpa nįe* you're short. *ðičáahpa* you're short (FH; RBn10-5:MOJ/79). *waaché wíhta čáahpa* my skirt is short (03/10/95/PM/pc; FH:4/24/96/pc). *iðáce akxa . . . čáahpape* his father . . . is short (2-2-259).

čáahpažį. ADJ [*čáahpa* + *-žį* 'little'] **short and small.**

čéže. V [diminutive of *céže*] **pee-pee.**

čóopa ADJ, N [diminutive of *tóopa*] **little, few; a small amount or number, a little bit.** (01/04/95/FH/pc:ok). *mǫhkása čóopa ąwážu* pour me a little coffee (RBnB1-36). *čóopa nąðe káaɣe* do/make a little at a time (FH/05/08/01:ok).

•• LFD 39: *čópa* <dsu´-ba> few; scant; not sufficient. *čópanąðe káɣe* <dso´-ba-no^n-the ga-xe> to do or make a little at a time.

čóopa ekǫ́ káaɣe (variant: **čóopa káaɣe**). VP [sync. *k>p, _kaaɣe*] **lessen, reduce, decrease (lit., 'make small-like')** (FH:prod).

•• LFD 39: *čópa ekǫ kaɣe* <dsu´-ba e-go^n-ga-xe> to reduce the amount; to lessen.

čóopažį. ADJ, N [diminutive of *čóopa*] **a very small amount; very little; a few** (BE2.3). *háazu čóopažį che* there are very few grapes. *nii čóopažį ąkˀú* give me a little bit of water (02/16/95/FH/pc:prod orig; 02/16/95/FH/pc:okc).

ð

ða-. PRNM **2nd sg. agent pronominal ('you', subject of regular verbs).**

ðaa-. INSTR **by mouth.**

ðáabrį. ADJ, N **three** (03/22/95/FH/pc:ok; BE2.140). *ðáabrį paašé?* are there three of you? *hį́ice ðáabrį akxa* there are three dishes.

•• LFD 140: *ðábrį* <tha´-bthi^n> three. *ðábrį ą* <tha´-bthi^n o^n> three times; thrice. *ðábrį ą eci pši e ðo* <tha´-bthi^n o^n e-dsi pshi e tho> [expected Mod. Os. form: *ðáabrį ecí pšíe*] I have been there [better 'I went there'] three times.

ðaacé. V [sync., *_ðaacé*] *(trans.)* **call on s.o.'s name; say the name of s.t. or s.o.** *wíbraacé* I call on your name. • **call, define as; assign a name to s.t. or s.o., use a name for s.t. or s.o.; say; pronounce** (03/22/95/FH/pc:okt). *"dog" táatą ðaatápe?* what do they call a dog? *šǫ́ke ðaatápe* they call it "šǫ́ke" (RBn19-02). *'telephone' akxa táatą ðaatápe?* how do you say 'telephone'? (lit., 'telephone, what did they name it?') (RBn10-9:JW; cq ok). *ékǫ ðaacé!* say it right! *pée ðaacé hta ðé?* who is going to name them? (2/25/83; PM/07/14/94). *pée žáže wáðaace hta ðé?* who is going to give them names? (MSB02/25/83; PM/07/14/94). *táatą ðaatáape?* what does one call it? (lit., 'what did they name it?') • **read.** *waléze ðaacápe* they read the book (FH/09/11/01/pc; not *ch*). *bráace* I read it (FH/09/11/01/pc).

•• LFD 140: *ðacé* <tha-dse´> to call as by name; to pronounce. *bráce* <btha´-dse> I call by name. *štáce* <shda´-dse> you call by name. *ąðáca pe* <o^{n}-tha´-dsa i> we call by name.

••• Cf. *láace.*

ðaaché. V [sync., *_ðaache*] *(trans.)* **eat** (03/22/95/FH/pc:okt). *bráache* I ate it (BE2.39). *ðáacha!* eat it! *toa štáache?* did you eat some? *tóa štáache ðalį* you ought to eat some. *štáace hkǫ́bra* I want you to eat it. *mį́įðohta ci súhka taazíhi ąðáachape* we ate fried chicken at noon. *sinǫ́bre štáache nąpe?* do you eat kidney? *káache ðaachá* eat this.

•• LFD 142: *ðaché ðalį* <tha-tse´ tha-gthi^{n}> delicious; good to eat. *ðaché* <tha-tse´> to eat. *bráche* <btha´-tse> I eat. *stáche* <sta´-tse> you eat. *ąðácha pe* <o^{n}-tha´-tsa i> we eat.

ðaacˀáke. ADJ, N **leftover; uneaten; items one was unable to eat, leftovers** (RBn22-18).

••• Cf. *ðuucˀáke.*

ðáahlį (variant of **ðáalį**).

ðaahtą́. V [sync., *_ðaahtą*] *(trans.)* **drink** (03/06/95/FH/pc:okc; 03/22/95/FH/pc:tape; MREI). *níi huuhtą́ bráahtą* I'm drinking a lot of water (03/22/95/FH/pc). *mąhkása bráahtą* I drank coffee. *mąhkása ðé bráahtą hce* I'll just drink coffee. *táatą štáahtape?* what did you all drink? *waðáahtą ąkái hta ąkái* we are going drinking [boozing]. *hkáwaceženíi tóa ąðáahta ąkái hce* let's [two people] go drink some beer. *hkáwaceženíi tóa ąðáahta ąkái htai* let's [more than two people] go drink some beer (BE2.35). *ąðáahtą ąðįkšé* we [two] drank [it]. • **puff, puff on, smoke.** *ðaahtą́* puff on it (RBn10-21). *nąníǫpažį tóopa ðaahtą́ą* smoke [lit., 'drink'] four cigarettes (RBn10-3:MOJ/79, unconfirmed).

•• LFD 142: *ðahtą́* <tha-ṭo^{n}´> to drink. *bráhtą* <btha´-ṭo^{n}> I drink. *hpéže mąhką sae brahtą* <pe´-zhe mo^{n}-ķo^{n} ça-e btha-ṭo^{n}> I drink tea.

••• Cf. *waðáahtą.*

ðaakˀį́ (variant: **ðaakˀí**). V [sync., *_ðaakˀį*] *(intr.)* **spit.** *ąðáakˀįpe* we spit. • *(trans.)* **spit on, spit out** (MSB 5/83/p1). *ąðáakˀį įká ði* don't spit on me.

•• LFD 334: *ðakˀi* <tha-ķ'i> to spit.

ðáalį (variant: **ðáahlį, ðą́ąlį**). ADJ, V [stat., *_ðaalį*] **(be) good.** *ðáalį húukǫ́į ðalípe* it's good a lot of you came back (said at War Dances to welcome public and dancers). • **feel good about s.t., be glad; thank you.** *ąðáalį* I feel good; I'm glad; I like it; thank you (02/01/95/FH/pc:ok; BE2.59). • ADJ **fine, splendid, pretty, beautiful, handsome; good (e.g., the weather).** *žį́kážį ðáalį* beautiful children. *šímižį ðáalį* a pretty girl. *hci ðáalį* a fine house. *hą́ąpa ðé akxa ðáalįži akxai* it's not a pretty day today (lit., 'this day is not good'; i.e., the weather is not good today) (FH/10/13/96). • ADV **well, finely, skillfully.** *súhkahtąą oohǫ́ ðáalį káaɣapi ché* the turkey was well-prepared (lit., 'they did well the cooking of the turkey, apparently').

•• JOD (slip file): *ðálį* <¢a´-k¢i^{n}> good, to be good.

••• Cf. *ðálį.*

ðáalį (variant of **ðálį**).

ðáalį káaɣe (variant: **ðą́ąlį káaɣe**). VP [sync. *k>p*, *ðáalį _kaaɣe*] *(intr.)* **be successful; do good works, do good (lit., 'do well').** *háakǫ ówǫe che ðą́ąlį škáaɣe* you were successful with what you set out to do (lit., 'whatever you undertook, that you did well') (FH/pc). *wahkǫ́ta iižį́ke íe oðáha ší aha, ðáalį škaaɣé* whenever you follow Jesus' teachings, you will do good works.

ðáalį kšíðe (variant: **ðą́ąlį kšíðe**). VP [reg., *ðáalį _kšíðe*] **achieve success for s.o., make s.o. successful.** *háakǫ ówǫe ší che, ðáalį ðikší[ð]aáape* they did for you what you set out to accomplish; you were successful due to their efforts (lit., 'whatever you went there to undertake, they did it well for you') (FH/pc).

ðáalįhkiðe. V [reg., *ðáalįhki_ðe*] **make oneself good (e.g., with respect to one's behavior).** *óžį hpíiži ðįké, ókˀą ðáalįhkí[ð]a* don't get angry, have good ways (01/04/95/FH/pc).

ðaanį́į (variant: **ðaaníi, nį́į**). V [sync., *_ðaanįį*] *(trans.)* **consume; eat up or drink up, devour.** *súhka záani ðaanį́įpe* he ate [consumed] all the chicken (FH07/31/01:ok). *ðaanį́į ði* drink it up (RBn22-09). *mąhkása ąðáanįpé* we drank all the coffee (RBn23-17). *mąhkása štáanie* you drank all the coffee up (RBn23-17). *súhka záani abráanįį* I ate all the chicken (FH). *mąhkása bráanie* I drank all the coffee up (RBn23-17). *hpáze wanǫ́bre nį́įpe?* did you all eat supper?

ðaašcúe. V [sync., *_ðaašcúe*] *(trans.)* **swallow (food or drink).** *bráašcue hta mįkšé* I'm going to swallow it (03/14/95/MREI/pc:ok; BE2.130).

ðaašé (variant of **ðaįšé**).

ðaaškíke. V [sync., *_ðaaškíke*] *(trans.)* **chew.** *mį́įihtǫ́ili bráaškike* I'm chewing this gum (RB; 01/24/95/FH/pc:prod).

ðaašóe. V [sync., *_ðaašóe*] [*ðaa-* INSTR + *šócc*] *(trans.)* **smoke (e.g., tobacco); suck.** *nąníǫpa ðaašóe tą* if he smokes tobacco.

ðaaštápe. V [sync., *_ðaaštape*] *(trans.)* **lick.** *šǫ́ke akxa hį́ice ðaaštápe akxái* the dog is licking the plate (02/15/95/FH/pc:okc; RBn2-moj/p22).

•• LFD 140: *ðastápe* <tha-çta´-be> to taste; to lick, as sugar off a cookie. *brástape* <btha´-çta-

ðaaštápe (*continued*)
be> I tasted it. *ąðástapa pe* <o^{n}-tha´-çta-ba i> we tasted it.

ðaaštą́. v [sync., *_ðaaštą́*] *(trans., intr.)* **finish eating or drinking (from).** [Appropriate for men or women, but more likely to be used by women than by men; according to some sources men are more likely to use *ðiištą́* (RB, HRE, FH).] *bráaštą* I'm finished (eating). *niikáapxokeoožu štáaštą tą, ðibrúuska* when you are through with the pop can, wad it up (02/24/95/FH/pc, HRE/12/29/01/pc). • *(trans.)* **end or stop an activity involving the mouth** (LS). *ɣaaké ðaaštą́ą!* stop crying! (HH; LS).

•• LFD 141: *ðaštą́* <tha-shto^{n}´> to stop whatever one is doing; used as a command. *braštą́* <btha-shto^{n}´> I stopped crying. *ąðáštą pe* <o^{n}-tha´-shto^{n} i> we stop crying.

ðaawá. v [sync., *_ðaawá*] *(intr.)* **count** (LS, FH). *ðaawá!* count, say the numbers! (FH). • *(trans.)* **count out; measure.** *ðaawá* count it out (or measure it) (01/13/95/FH/pc:ok). *ðaawáða hkǫ́bra* I want you to count it/them out (e.g., coins, beads). (01/13/95/FH/pc). *wáðaawa* count them (01/13/95/FH/pc:ok; BE2.26). *wažį́kake wáðaawa* count the birds.

••• Cf. *waðáawa, žą́ą wéðaawa.*

ðaaxǫ́. v [sync., *_ðaaxǫ́*] *(trans.)* **break by mouth; break by biting or with the mouth.** *ðaaxǫ́pe* he bit it and broke it.

••• Cf. *ðaaxǫ́ke.*

ðaaxǫ́ke. v [sync., *_ðaaxǫ́ke*] *(trans.)* **break into pieces by mouth; chew; chew into pieces, bite into small pieces.** *ną́ɣe ðaaxǫ́ke šǫ akxái, hi ðixǫ́kape* while he was chewing ice, he broke his tooth.

ðaaxtáke v [sync., *_ðaaxtáke*] *(trans.)* **bite** (01/07/95/FH/pc:ok; RBn10-2). *wécʔa akxa ðíðaaxtake hta akxai* a snake is going to bite you (in a generic sense: e.g., 'snakes bite' or 'what snakes do is bite') (FH/09/25/01/prod).

•• LFD 142: *ðaxtáke* <tha-xta´-ge> to bite. *bráxtake* <btha´-xta-ge> I bite. *štáxtake* <shta´-xta-ge> you bite. *ąðáxtaka pe* <o^{n}-tha´-xta-ga i> we bite.

••• Cf. *waðáaxtake.*

ðaazó (variant: **ðaazáį** [unconfirmed]). v [sync./uninfl., *_ðaazó*] *(intr.)* **whoop, lulu, ululate** (RBn12-06; FH/11/17/01/pc). *ðaazópi!* lulu, you all! (FH/11/17/01/pc:prod).

••• Cf. *oðáaze, oðáazo.*

ðaazúpe. v [sync., *_ðaazúpe*] *(trans.?)* **drink soup** (RBn12-07).

ðaažóce. v [sync., *_ðaažóce*] *(trans.)* **blow, blow on** (RBn22-08; PM/109).

•• LFD 354: *žóce* <zho´-dse> whistle.

••• *KS mąsóǰe* whistle, flute (RR), *wabóšoǰe* flute, a type of whistle (MR, RR).

ðaažóži (variant: **ðaažǫ́ži**). v [sync., *_ðaažóži*] *(trans.)* **insult by word, speak ill of, slander, malign, belittle.**

••• Cf. *hkiláažoži.*

ðáha. CONJ **when, upon a certain event.** *íiwiðe ðáha owíhkie mąží* when I saw you, I didn't talk to you (FH/02/17/96/pc:prod). *hąą káaši ðáha achípe* they came late at night (lit., 'when it had been night for a long time, they arrived here').

•• JOD (slip file): *ðáha* <ȼa´-ha> soon after, as soon as.

ðáhta. ADV **left; leftward; lefthand** (ERE; not recognized by FH). *hkilíhkǫįɣa, ðáhta ki* turn to your left (RBn10-21). *ðáhta ha* toward the left (RB). *ðáhta ci ha* to the left (RB). down a path to the left (02/15/95/FH/pc:uk, all).

•• LFD 112: *ðáhta* <tha´-ṭa> the left; on the left; lefthanded. *nąpe ðahta che* <no^{n}´-be tha-ṭa tse> the left hand. LFD 142: *ðáhta hta opahe* <tha´-ṭa ṭa u-ba-he> toward the left side; the left side. *ðahtáci* <tha-ṭa´-dsi> at the left side.

ðąįšé (variants: **ðąįšé, ðąąšé, ðaašé**). CONT **continuative aspect postverbal marker (indicating ongoing action or state in present or past time) for moving 2nd sg. subject (action or state may continue from past to present, corresponding to English perfect ['have/had been']).** ['Moving' here means 'changing location'; motions or gestures that do not change the entity's location in horizontal space do not take this affix.] *óce ðąįšé?* are you [moving, sg.] looking for things? *ą́špaɣo ðąįšé* you're pushing me. *wacúe skúe paðášce hta ðąįšé?* are you [moving, sg.] going to cut the cake? *ðihúheka ðąąše áape anąkʔǫ* I heard you [moving, sg.] were sick (03/09/95/MREI/pc:ok). *kasį́e ówǫ hta ðąįšé?* are you [moving, sg.] going to be busy tomorrow? (01/09/95/FH/pc:prod). *ðúuhpeece wį ašcį́ ðąįšé?* do you [moving, sg.] have a match? • **you are characterized by [the immediately preceding word or phrase, which may be a noun phrase].** *hį́į hpíiži ðąįšé* you have bad teeth. *waðílą hpíiži ðąįšé* you've got a bad temper.

ðakxą́še (variant of **ðatxą́še**).

ðakʔéðe (variants: **ðakʔée, ðakʔéi**). v [reg., *ðakʔé_ðe*] *(trans.)* **feel sorry for; pity**

(03/09/95/FH/pc:ok). *ðakˀéwai* be good to them; have pity on them (FH:prod). *ðakˀéwaðapi* have pity on us; be good to us (03/09/95/FH/pc:ok). *ðakˀéwie* I pity you; I feel sorry for you. *ðakˀéawaðe* I pity them (03/09/95/FH/pc:ok). *ðakˀéwaðáðe* you pity them (03/09/95/FH/pc:ok). *ðakˀéąwaðape* we pity them. *ðakˀéwiðe ðekǫ́ce óxi ðe ną* I am sorry for you now for this death. *ðakˀéwaðe hkǫ́bra* I want you to pity them. *ðakˀéwaðaðe, xíða ðéche íinǫǫhpe ðįké* you pity us, and we don't fear death. *wį́ðakše nįkšé ahá, wahkǫ́ta akxa ðakˀéðiðe hta akxai* if you are in earnest, God will pity you. *waðákˀeðíðe nįkšé aape, ðe etą, ðakˀéwaðapi* they said you were kind, so pity us. *ðakˀéwaðapi* have pity on us, be good to us [who are not your own] (03/09/95/FH/pc:ok). • **be good to, be merciful to.** *ðakˀéąðape* we were good to him; they were good to me; he was good to me. • **take care of.** *pée ðakˀéðie ðįké hta akxa? wahkǫ́ta akxa éeną* who will take care of you when everything is gone? only God (FH). • **bless** (BE2.23).

•• LFD 141: *ðakˀéðe* <tha-ḳ'e´the> pity; to be tender, gentle, and sympathetic to one who suffers with grief or is in great trouble; tenderness; kind-heartedness. *ðakˀé waðe* <tha-ḳ'e´ wa-the> to have pity for others. *ðakˀé awaðe* <tha-ḳ'e´ a-wa-the> I pity them. *ðakˀé waðaðe* <tha-ḳ'e´ wa-tha-the> you pity them. (03/09/95/FH/pc:ok).

••• Cf. *ðakˀékiðe, waðákˀeðe.*

ðakˀéhkiðe (variant: **ðakˀéhkie**). v [reg., *ðakˀé _hkiðe*] [*hkik-* RECIP/REFL + *ðakˀéðe*] *(intr.)* **be good to each other; be kind to each other; pity each other (reciprocal sense).** *ðakˀéhkiðe* be good to each other. *ðakˀéhkie pái* you all be good to each other [*pai* commands continuing future behavior]. *ðakˀéhkiepi* be good to each other; be kind to one another [now] (03/09/95/FH/pc:okc; BE2.104). • **pity oneself, feel sorry for oneself (reflexive sense).**

•• LFD 140 (unconfirmed, not accepted by modern speakers): *ðakˀéhkiðe* <tha-ḳ'e´-ḳi-the> self-pity; inward hurt. [FH: has nothing to do with pitying oneself or being hurt.] *ðahkeahkiðe* <tha-ḳe-a-ḳi-the> I was inwardly hurt (feelings). *ðahkeðahkiðe* <tha-ḳe-tha-ḳi-the> you pitied yourself. *ðahkeąhkiða pe* <tha-ḳe-o^{n}-ḳi-tha i> we were hurt inwardly (feelings).

ðakˀéi (variant of **ðakˀéðe**).

ðakˀékiðe. v [reg., *ðakˀé_kiðe*] [*kik-* SUU or *ki-* DAT+ *ðakˀéðe*] *(trans.)* **be good or kind to one's own** [SUU] **or to s.o. close** [DAT]**; pity or feel sorry for one's own** [SUU] **or s.o. close** [DAT]**.** *ðakˀéwikiðe* I feel sorry for you, I pity you, I sympathize with you (FH). *ðakˀéwikíe achíe* I came because I'm sorry for you. *ðakˀéwikíðe, ðiðáce ðíližóži* I pity you, your father hurt you [when he died]. *ąkóðihkíepi áha, ðakˀéwaðakíðe hta nįkšé aap* when we talk to you, they said you would pity us. *ðakˀékiðapai* be kind to one another, pity one another [understood in reciprocal sense]. *ðakˀéąðakíe* have pity on me [addressed to a close friend or relative] (03/09/95/FH/pc:okc). *ðakˀéąkíe nąpé* you've always been good to me (RBn10-6:JW). *ðakˀéąkiðe nąpe* you're always good to me. *ðakˀéwaðakíe* be good to us; be good to your own.

ðálį (variant: **ðáalį**). MODAL **should, ought to.** *táatą éekǫke ąwą́štaakaaži ðálį* you shouldn't tell me things like that.

••• Cf. *ðáalį,*

ðatxą́še (variants: **ðakxą́še, ðatkxą́še, ðątxą́še**). CONT **continuative aspect postverbal marker (indicating ongoing action or state in present or past time) for standing 2nd sg. or 2nd pl. subject; may also be used for imminent future action or state.** *wažáže nį́e ðatxą́še* you're an Osage [to someone standing]. *haakxą́ta waðákištǫ́papi ðachí hta ðąkxą́še?* when are you all going to come see us? (04/28/95/LS/pc:okc). *súhka háaną ooðáhą hta ðatxą́še?* how many chickens are you going to cook? *tąhé ðatxą́še?* are you [standing] well? *ðahkílǫ ðatkxą́še* you [standing] are calling yourself a name (01/09/95/FH/pc:ok).

•• LFD 142: *ðatxąše* <tha-to^{n}-she> standing (from a ritual).

ðažážį (variant of **ažážį**).

ðą. ADJ **round.** [Obsolete, unattested in Mod. Os.]

•• LFD 125: *hpahéðǫ* <p̣a-he´-tho^{n}> a round hill.

ðą́ące (variant: **ną́ące**). N **heart** (03/22/95/FH/pc:tape). *ðą́ące ðuusáaki akxái* he [has] had a heart attack. *ðą́ące ðuusáaki akxái* he has a broken heart, a disturbed heart (02/09/95/FH/pc:okc; BE2.66). *ðą́ące saakí káaɣapi ée nąpé* make your hearts strong, he used to say (RBn HW-MREI). • **hearts (suit in a deck of cards)** (RBn12-10/MOJ, 02/09/95/FH/pc:ok).

•• LFD 153: *ðą́ce* <tho^{n}´-dse> heart.

ðą́ące ðuusáaki. N **heart attack** (04/13/95/FH/pc:ok). *ðą́ące ðuusáaki akxái* he

ðą́ące ðuusáaki (*continued*)
had a heart attack (FH:5/02/96/prod; ok; RBn2-moj/p26). • **broken heart** *ðą́ące ðuusáaki akxái* he has a broken heart, a disturbed heart (02/09/95/FH/pc:okc; BE2.66).

ðą́ące óðisąha. VP, ADJ [uninfl.] *(intr.)* **(be) afraid (lit., 'heart fluttering')** (RBn23-14). • N **scare, fright.**
•• LFD 113: *nǫ́ce oðisąha* <no^{n}´-dse u-thi-ço^{n}-ha> a shock to the heart; a scare; a fright; heart palpitates quickly. LFD 203: *waðǫ́ce oðisąha* <wa-tho^{n}´-dse u-thi-ço^{n}-ha> to excite; excitement; his heart is fluttering with excitement.

ðą́ące ósai (variant: **ðą́ące ózai** [RB]). VP, ADJ [conjug. unknown] **(be) afraid (lit., 'heart burning, heart set on fire')** (RB, unconfirmed).
••• Cf. *osái*.

ðą́ące skúðe. N **sweetheart.** (MREI/t116, 03/14/95/MREI/pc:ok; BE2.130). [Slang, calque of English.]

ðą́ące xǫ́. N **broken heart** (MSB: 2-24-83).

ðą́ąceíki. V [reg. *iða?, ðą́ącei_ki] (trans.)* **love.** *ðą́ąceíwiki* I love you (RBn HW, unconfirmed). *ðą́ąceíwikipe* I love you all (RBn HW, unconfirmed).

ðą́ącenie. V [stat., *ðą́ące_níe*] [*ðą́ące* + *níe*] **suffer from heartache, have a pain in the heart.** N **heartache.**
•• LFD 153: *ðą́ce nie* <tho^{n}´-dse ni-e> heartache. *ðą́ce anie* <tho^{n}´-dse a-ni-e> I have a pain in my heart. *ðą́ce ðinie* <tho^{n}´-dse thi-ni-e> you have a pain in your heart.

ðąącháži. ADV [*ðąąché* + *aží* NEG] **improbably, against all odds.** *ðąącháži, wažážeíe šǫǫšǫ́we ðée hkǫ́bra* I want this Osage language to go on forever [against all odds] (FH:pc). • ADJ **impossible, unable.** *brúwį ðą́ąchažį* I am unable to buy it (02/27/95/JS/pc:okc; 04/06/95/FH/pc:ma).
•• LFD 281: *ðą́hta ži* <tho^{n}´-ṭa zhi> impossible. [The unnegated form <tho^{n}-tse´> (LFD 153) would lead one to expect a negative form <tho^{n}-tsa zhi> or <tho^{n}-ta zhi> rather than <tho^{n}´-ṭa zhi>.]

ðąąché. MODAL [uninfl. or impersonal form] **possible; suitable, appropriate.** *htáwą kši brée ðąąché hta mįkšé* I might go to town (MOJ/11/30/84). *ščíhtą ðąącháži e* you shouldn't touch it (lit., 'your touching it is not suitable'). *ékižǫ ðąąché nįkšé?* is it possible for you to do that? *ą́ąðilǫðį ðąąché įké* we'll never forget you (lit., 'it is not possible that we forget you') (FH:5/02/96/prod). • **could, would.** *oðíhtą wíhta akxa wasúhuži akxa hąðé ščúuža ðąąché?* my car is dirty, could you wash it this evening/tonight? (FH/06/16/01/pc). • **probable; look like; be at the point of happening.** *níižu ðąąché akxa* it might rain (lit., 'rain is probable/possible') (RBnB1-41). *níižu ðąąché hta akxai* it might rain (MOJ/11/30/84). *ónalįpi, pahúðe ðąąchí akxái* hurry up you all, it's about to snow (02/13/95/FH/pc:prod. orig; FH:4/25/96/tape; BE2.70).
•• LFD 153: *ðąché* <tho^{n}-tse´> suitable; appropriate; convenient. LFD 308: *ékǫ ðąché* <e-go^{n} tho^{n}-ṭse> possible.

ðą́ąlį (variant of **ðáalį**).

ðąąšé, ðąįšé (variants of **ðaįšé**).

ðe. CAU [reg., *_ðe*] **make; have or make s.o. do s.t.; cause s.t. to happen to s.o. or s.t.** *taazíhiðe* make it brown, as in cooking.

ðe (variant: **e**). DECL **indeed; sentence-final declarative marker ("oral period"; probably once limited to female speech but now optionally used by males as well).** [May be the same as LF's *he* 'female(?) declarative marker', not found in Mod. Os.] *ážą brée ðe* I went to bed [I did indeed] (01/07/95/FH/pc). *wéhice pši* I went far away (03/02/95/FH/pc:ok). *wéhice pšíeðe* I went far away (01/23/95/FH/pc:prod).
••• QU *į* female speech, oral period (RR).

ðe. POSIT **positional article for a sg. moving entity.** *tówa ðe táatą ohkíhce?* what tribe is he [that unfamiliar person moving]? **that, the aforesaid.** *Jacka háakǫ eekíe ðe tą iiðáštą* I agree with what Jack says (FH/09/25/01/pc; 03/23/95/FH/pc:okc).
••• Cf. *pa* POSIT.

ðe áape (variant of **ði aape**).

ðée (see **aðée**).

ðée (variants: **ðí, ðíi** [especially when followed by accented vowel]). PRON **that; this; those; these; they.** *líe ðáha óžo áhkiži ðíi aape* when she came back she was proud of herself [they said] (RBn19-03). *níhka ákiye ðí aape* that man is all around [bothering] her [they said] (FH/09/22/01/pc). *ókˀǫ éži ðíi eepe* he's confused [they said] (FH/09/24/01/pc/prod). *ðée akxa íihǫ hą́ąpa ókˀą hta apai* they [that group] are going to have something on Mother's Day. *hkóða ðíi áape* they were friends [they said of them] (RBn18-01). *[hkóða ðée áape] ðée che akű húe* come and get these [a group of stacked round objects: e.g., groceries]. *ðée lípi che ški wéewinai* I'm thankful, too, for these who have come here (FH/10/13/96). *haxį́ ðe, ðée apa kíða aðį́ hkǫ́bra* I want each of them to have this blanket for his/her own (i.e., they can all call it theirs, each one has a part in this blanket) (01/20/95/PM/pc:prod. orig; BE2.38). *ðée apa* these people, this group of people (BE2.137; RBn1-moj/p52b; 03/20/95/FH/pc:not sg). *ðée akxa* the whole bunch of them (RB; 03/20/95/FH/pc:ok).

•• LFD 143: *ðéapa* <the´-a-ba> these; with reference to people or animals. *ðékše* <the´-kshe> this that lies here; this gun, this pipe (03/20/95/FH/pc:ok; sg only). LFD 145: *ðéche* <the´-tse> this; as referring to the object close at hand. *hci ðeche* <ṭsi the-tse> this house standing. *hcížepe ðeche* <ṭsi´-zhe-be the-tse> this door hanging.

ðée áape (variant of **ði aape**).

ðée ekǫ́. ADV **this way, that way, thus, like this, like that.** *ðée ekǫ́ akxa ékiše nąną* you said it would be like this.

••• Cf. *haakǫ́, kaakǫ́.*

ðée hta ché. VP **(expresses certainty of a future event: 'that is how it will be').** *ą́ą, ékiǫ ðée hta ché* okay, we'll do it (lit., 'yes, done like that, that it will be') (RBn17-p03).

ðée įkšé. PRON **that one sitting.** *ðée įkšé ohkíhce hǫ́ǫxce ðįkšé?* that one sitting over there, what kind of tribe is he? (03/23/95/FH/pc).

ðée káaγe. VP *(trans.)* **send; dispatch; make s.t. go there.** *áhu ðée káaγe hta mįkšé* I'm going to send this wing around. *waléze ðée kaaγe* to send a letter (RBn2-moj/p13; 03/09/95/MREI/pc:ok). *mą́ze k?ą́saaki ðée káaγa!* send a wire! (RBn3-58). *wáleze ðée káaγa!* send a letter! (02/15/95/FH/pc:okc). • **mail** (MREI). *wáleze ðée káaγa* mail a letter (02/15/95/FH/pc:okc). • **let go.** *ši mǫ́šǫ ðée hpáaγe* I'm going to let that arrow go again (lit., 'again I make the feather go'). • **lead (in a card game such as pitch); play a card (in a card game).** *ðée hpáaγe* I send this (uttered when leading a card in a pitch game) (RB). *ðée hpáaγe* I play this (RBn12-10/mj).

•• LFD 143: *ðékaγe* <the´-ga-xe> to send. *ðéhpaγe* <the´-p̣a-xe> I sent it. *ðéškaγe* <the´-shka-xe> you sent it.

ðéeðe. V [reg., *ðée_ðe*] [*(a)ðée* 'go there' + *ðe* CAU] *(trans.)* **make go, cause to go; send; mail.**

•• LFD 143–44: *ðéðe* <the´-the> to send. *ðeáðe* <the-a´-the> I send. *ðeðáðe* <the-tha´-the> you send. *ðeą́ða pe* <the-o^n-tha i> we send. *John waleze wį ðeðeahkiðe Henry ðįkše ci* <John wa-gthe-çe-wi^n the-the a-ḳi-the Henry thi^n-ke dsi> [expected verb form: *ðéeðeakšíðe* 'I had him cause it to go'] I had John send a letter to Henry.

ðéeðekšíðe. V [reg., *ðéeðe_kšíðe*] [*ðéeðe* + *kšíðe*] *(trans.)* **have s.o. send or mail s.t.**

ðeeká (variants: **ðéka, ðéeka, ðeká, ðéekaa**). ADV, N **there, here, these.** *ok?ą́ hta apai ðeeká* they're going to have something there; they're going to hold an event there (FH/06/25/01/pc). • V [uninfl] *(intr.)* **be here.** *ðéekaa mįkšé* I'm here (FH:ee,aa).

ðeeká ci. VP, ADVP **(be) over here** (FH).

ðéeka wį. PRONP **one of these.** *ðéeka wį́ škǫ́šta?* do you want one of these? (e.g., when offering a cigarette from a pack) (03/16/95/JS/pc:ok).

ðeekáha. ADV **this way.** *ðekáha kú* come this way, in this direction, along this path. *ðekáha kše* this way, on this lying path [with positional *kše*] (RBn1-23).

•• LFD 143: *ðekáha* <the-ga´-ha> here; in this region; in this neighborhood; local.

••• *KS yegáha* those from here; Dhegiha (RR).

••• Cf. *ðeekíha.*

ðeekáiha. ADV **around this way, round about this way** (FH: prod). *žą́ą lą́ąðe kaasé, ðeekáiha ðiitą́* that big tree that was cut, around this way pull it (04/18/95/FH/pc).

••• *KS yegáha* Dhegiha (RR).

ðéeke. PRON [*ðée* 'that, this' + *ke*] **these scattered.** *táatą ðéeke hǫ́ǫžike* these bad things around.

ðéeke ci. ADV, PRON **sometimes, now and then; s.t. scattered** (RBn10-5:JW). *ðéeke cí ðé* anything over there (03/13/95/FH/pc:ma; LS:ma; PM:ma; RBn10-5:JW).

ðeekíha (variant: **ðekíha**). N **those from around here; Dhegiha.** *ðeekíha* those from here (said to be source of the name of the Dhegiha subfamily of Siouan languages, which includes Osage, Omaha-Ponca, Kansa-Kaw, and Quapaw).

•• LFD 143: *ðekáha* <the-ga´-ha> here; in this region; in this neighborhood; local.

•• *KS yegáha* those here, the people of this land (JOD), Dhegiha (RR); *OM dhégiha* those from around here (RR); *QU deká* those from around here (RR).

••• Cf. *ðeekáha, ðeekáiha.*

ðeekšíðe. V [reg., *ðee_kšíðe*] [*(a)ðée* 'go there' + *kšíðe*] *(trans.)* **send, mail or make s.t. go to another person.** *mą́zeohkihki ðeekšíe* telephone him/her (RBn3-58). *mą́zeohkíhkie ðeekšíe* call

ðeekšíðe (*continued*) him/her on the phone (03/16/95/FH/pc:ok). *mą́zeohkíhkie ðekší aape* they said they talked on the phone (03/16/95/FH/pc). *wáleze ðeekšíe* mail this letter to her (02/15/95/FH/pc:okc).

••• Cf. *ðée káaɣe, hukšíðe.*

ðéepa. N **chin; jaw** (04/07/95/LS/pc:ok; 01/09/95/FH/pc:okc).

•• LFD 143: *ðépa* <the´-ba> the jaw; the underjaw.

ðéeze. N **tongue** (03/23/95/FH/pc:okc). *ðéeze íhtaxe* the tip of the tongue (t118/03/23/95/FH/pc). *ðéeze xáka* thorny tongue (03/23/95/FH/pc:prod, BE2.142).

•• LFD 143: *ðése* <the´-çe> tongue (03/23/95/FH/pc: *ðéeze*; not ***ðéese*). *ðése ihtaxe* <the´-çe i-ṭa-xe> tip of the tongue. *ðésexaka* <The´-çe-xa-ga> Rough-tongue (personal name; refers to the rough tongue of the buffalo).

ðéeze opásike. VP [stat., *ðéeze o_pasike*] **stutter, be tongue-tied; tongue splayed or split, tongue-tied** (03/23/95/FH/pc:okc).

•• LFD 143: *ðéze opasike* <the´-çe u-ba-çi-ge> to stutter; to stammer; tongue-tied. *ðese ąwąpasike* <the-çe o^n-wo^n-ba-çi-ge> I stutter. *ðese oðipasike* <the-çe u-thi-ba-çi-ge> you stutter. *šį́hto žįka htą ðese opasike* <shi^n´-ṭo zhi^n-ga ṭo^n the-çe u-ba-çi-ge> the boy is tongue-tied [probably should be *šį́tožį txą ðéeze opasike* 'the boy standing there is tongue-tied'].

••• Cf. *paasíke.*

ðeká, ðéka (variants of **ðeeká**).

ðekáhtą. ADV **therefore.**

•• JOD (Wasápežįka ltr, p1 ln2): *ðekáhtą waléze šoðée hpáaɣe wihcížoe* <ȼeḳáta^n waḳȼéșe cuȼé páxi au, witsíçŭ^n é> therefore I'm sending this letter to you, niece [sister's daughter]. JOD (slip file): *ðekáhtą* <ȼe-ḳá-ta^n> from this place.

ðekíha (variant of **ðeekíha**).

ðekǫ́ǫce (variant: **ðekǫ́ǫci**). ADV [possibly *ðée* 'that, this' + *kaakǫ́* + *ci* PPN] **now; at this moment.** *ðekǫ́ǫci* from now on (FH). *ðekǫ́ǫci áha waxpáðe níhkašika, háaną įįksé ški ówašta apatąha* at the present time we are a pitiful people, and there are even very few of us left. *kóoci wažáže apa ðée ékiǫpe ążi ðekǫ́ǫci ðįkápi wihtáeži akxa íkʔuci akxai* long ago Osages used to do that but now they are gone and sister is trying her best (gloss by CQ; PM/7/7/94). *waðílą ekǫ́įkí apai, ðekǫ́ǫci áhkihtǫpa ðį* there are crazies around, now watch out for yourself.

••• *KS gagóoǰi* now, just now (RR).

ðékše. ADJ [*ðée* 'that, this' + *kše*] **this (lying); that (lying).** *mǫ́žǫ ðáalį ðékše mǫ́žǫ ðékše ðįké hta aaži íe wíhta šǫǫšǫ́we aðée hta akxai* heaven and earth shall pass away, but my word will endure (FH: from Matthew 24:35).

ðéskali. N **boil; sore.** *ðéskali šǫ́cheða!* let that boil alone! (RBn11-01/JW&FW&HHsk/c.1976; FH/11/19/01/pc:uk).

•• *QU déskakde* boil, sore (RR).

ðetkxą́ci (variant of **ðetxą́ci**).

ðetkxą́ha (variant of **ðetxą́ha**).

ðetkxą́tą (variant of **ðetxą́tą**).

ðétxą. (variant: **ðétxa**). ADV **this time.** *hǫ́ǫpa ðétxa híe ðáha ši owíhkie* at this time of the day I'm going to talk to you again (lit., 'when this time of the day arrives, again I speak to you'). **meeting**

ðetxą́ce (variant: **ðetxaci**). ADV **from now on.**

••• Cf. *ðetxą́tą.*

ðetxą́ci (variant: **ðetkxą́ci**). ADV **at this time.** *hą́ąci ðetkxą́ci wacúe bráache mįkšé ska* last night at this time I must have been eating this bread (FH/09/06/95/pc).

ðetxą́ha (variant: **ðetkxą́ha**). ADV **from now on; from this time on, henceforth** (03/22/95/FH/pc). *ðetxą́ha háakǫ éepše che ékǫ hkǫ́bra* from now on, I want it to be like I've said (03/22/95/FH/pc:ok). *ðetką́ąha, ðe haxį́ įkšé mį́ hta mįkšé* from now on, I'm going to wear that blanket (FH/09/06/95).

•• LFD 144: *ðetxą́ha ðeðe* <the-to^n´-ha the-the> henceforth. *ðetxą́ha ðeðe ece pše che ekǫ hkǫbra ha* <the-to^n´-ha the-the e-de pshe tse e-go^n ḳo^n-btha ha> [expected Mod. Os. form: *ðetxą́ha ðée ðe épše che éekǫ hkǫ́bra*; sentence-final *ha* is not used in Mod. Os.] from now on do as I say (lit., 'from now on I want those things to be the way that I say').

ðetxą́tą (variants: **ðetxą́ta, ðetkxą́tą**). ADV **from this time.** (FH/07/09/01/pc). *ðetkxą́tą awáachi hta mįkšé* I'm going to dance from now on (FH/07/09/01/pc). *ðetkxą́tą waðílą ðáalį íbrilą hta mįkšé* from now on I'm going to think good thoughts (FH/07/09/01/pc).

••• Cf. *haatxą́ta.*

ði (variants: **ðį, ni, nį**). IMPERATIVE MARKER **sentence-final marker for command to sg. addressee.** *šée nįkšé óhkie ni* you're just sitting there, speak to me (RBn10-6:JW; RR/pc). *ášihta brée ążį ðíe hcíhta wéðaahpa ði* I'm going outside but you stay inside and wait [for people] (FH:prod). *waxpáðį ną ąhkílai ði* carry yourself humble [to one person] (RB).

ðí (variant of **ðíe**).

ði-. PRNM **2nd person inalienable possessive pronominal ('your', used with some kin terms, e.g., *ðihcíko* 'your grandfather').**
••• Cf. *wi-* 'my'.

ði-. PRNM **2nd person patient pronominal ('you'), used as subject of stative verbs and as object of active verbs.**

ði- (variant of **ðu-**).

ðí (variant of **ðée**).

ðí aape (variants: **ði áape, ðée áape, ðe áape**). REPORTATIVE [possibly *ðe* POSIT + *áape*] **they said (that) of him/her (moving?).** *súhka htą́ą mį́ka wį hcí káaɣe ðí aape* the turkey went out to make a nest (RBn19-03). *wéeli ðumą́ða ðí aape* she held her head high (RBn19-05).

ðíbra (variant: **ðúbra**). V [sync., *_ðíbra*] *(trans.)* **spread, spread out, as a cloth.**
•• LFD 334: *haxį́ ðą bríbra* <ha-xi^{n}´, tho^{n} bthi-btha> [expected Mod. Os. form: *haxį́ bríbra*; *ðą* (or *ðǫ*) is an archaic form, not used in Mod. Os.] I spread my blanket.
••• Cf. *áðubra.*

ðíbrą. V [sync., *_ðíbrą*] *(trans.)* **smell.** *bríbrą* I smell it (e.g., cedar).

ðibrį́ɣa. V [sync., *_ðibrį́ɣa*] *(intr.)* **fart loudly, make a loud fart; break wind noisily** (01/23/95/FH/pc:ok; BE2.44).
•• *KS yübíɣą* to fart (JOD, RR).

ðibrúbruɣe (variant: **brúbruɣe**). V [sync., *_ðicíze*] *(intr.)* **shake; quiver; tremble** (MREI 11/1/83/7). *žą́ą akxa ðibrúbruɣe akxa* the tree is shaking.
••• Cf. *waskúe ðibrúbruɣe.*

ðibrúuska. V [sync., *_ðibrúuska*] *(trans.)* **wad up; flatten.** *niikáapxokeoožu štáaštą tą, ðibruuska* when you are through with the pop can, wad it up (02/24/95/FH/pc).

ðicíze. V [sync., *_ðicíze*] *(trans.)* **dust or clean (e.g., the house).** *mąšóšoce che, ðicíza* it's dusty, dust it (FH:4/22/96/tape;prod). • **move, remove, take away.** *áalįį ðihcíze* move that chair. *áalįį ąðíhcize* we [two] moved the chair. *hǫ́bre hpíiži ðéke ąðicize hkǫ́bra, waðílą hpíiži ðéke ški, waðílą wasúhu* I want you to take away these bad dreams, these bad thoughts, too, cleanse my mind (RBn10-14; cqc). *áwanǫbre akxa mąšóšoce akxai, ðicíza* the table is dusty, dust it (FH:4/22/96/tape:prod). *waðílą wákalą ą́ðiicíza* take this dirty mind away (RBn10-3:MOJ/79).
•• LFD 318: *ðicíze* <thi-dsi´-çe> remove from office [strictly speaking means 'remove' only; no mention of 'office'].
••• *QU íttize* [reg.-*iða*] clean out the house (RR), *kdittíze* pull one's own (RR), *dizé* get, take, receive (RR).

ðiðáce. N **your father.** *ðiðáce hową́įke ðe?* where is your father? (FH). • **your paternal uncle, your father's brother** (BE2.45).

ðiðácežį (variant: **ðiðácižį**). N **your paternal uncle, your father's brother (used when speaking to a man or a woman about his/her relative).**

ðíe (variant: **ði**). PRON **you (emphatic).** *ðíe mąðí!* you go! (emphatic and contrastive, as in 'I don't want to go, *you* go'). • **your turn.** *ðíe hta nįkšé* your turn (04/04/95/FH/pc:ok). *ðíe ðinį́e, ðíe níe* your turn (lit., 'it's you, you are it') (BE2.162). *waðíhta ðíe* it's your turn (e.g., to hit drum) (lit., 'handle it, you') (RBn3-22). *waðíðihta ði nį́e* it's your turn to take over (RBn23-16).

ðíɣe (variant of **ðúɣe**).

ðihą́ka. N **your sister-in-law (used only when speaking to a man, referring to his brother's wife or his wife's sister).**

ðihcíceðe (variant: **ðihcíciðe**). V [conjug. unknown] [perhaps *ðu-/ði-* INSTR + *hcíce* + *ðe* CAU?] **prance (lit., 'make s.t. produce a rhythmic sound'?)** (RB, unconfirmed). *ðihcíceðe aðáape, žúoka nǫ́ǫ ékǫ* he pranced along, with a grownup's stance (lit., '. . . as if his body were an adult's') (RBn15-03).

ðihcíko. N **your grandfather (paternal or maternal); your grandparents; your father-in-law (used by anyone speaking to a man or a woman about the father of his/her spouse).**

ðihcími. N **your father's sister (younger or older), your paternal aunt** (FH/09/22/01/pc).

ðihcíni. (variant: **ðihcínį**). N **your daughter-in-law, your son's wife.**

ðihcióžąke. N (variant: **ðihcóžąke**). N **your brother's daughter (used only when speaking to a woman; more precise than English 'niece').**

ðihcížo. N (variants: **ðihcížǫ, ðihcížoe**). N **your sister's daughter (used only when speaking to a man; more precise than English 'niece'); your father's sister's daughter (used when speaking to a man or a woman; more precise than English 'cousin').**

ðihcį́to. N **your older brother (used only when speaking to a woman)** (FH/09/24/01/ok).

ðihcóška. N **your wife's brother's son, your sister's son (used when speaking to a man); your brother's son (used when speaking to a**

ðihcóška (*continued*)
woman); your grandchild (used when speaking to a man or a woman); more precise than English 'nephew'). [Use as 'grandchild' is unexpected; cf. *ðihcóšpa.*]

ðihcóšpa. N **your grandchild** (RB, FH/09/24/01/ok).

ðihcóžą̨ke (variant of **ðihcióžą̨ke**).

ðíhota (variant: **ðíhotą, ðihótą**). V [sync. _*ðihota*] *(trans.)* **play a joke on, fool, trick.** *ščíhotąpe* you all played a joke on him (RBn HW). *ðíðihotape* they played a joke on you (RBn HW). *bríhota* I played a joke (on him/her) (RBn HW). *wábrihotą íðilą ðí apé* I have fooled them, she thought (RBn19-03). *wíbrihotai* I fooled you (RBn19-03). *súhkahtą́ą mį́įka éži pa wáðihota įkše ípahǫ įkši áape* turkey hen knew she had done everything she could to fool the others [them] (RBn19-05).
••• Cf. *wahóta.*

ðihpóe. N **match (for lighting fires)** (LF only).
•• LFD 148: *ðihpóe* <thi-po̩´-e> a match.

ðíhta (variant: **ðíihta**). PRON **yours, your (sg. or pl. 'you')** (RB, 04/27/95/FH/pc). • V [inalien.] **be yours.**
•• LFD 149: *ðíhta* <thi´-ṭa> (sometimes spoken as <thi-thi-ṭa>) yours. *hkáwa ðihta* <ḳa´-wa thi-ṭa> your horse. *hci ðíhta* <ṭsi thi´-ṭa> your house. *žį́ka žį́ka ðihta* <zhi^n-ga zhi^n-ga thi-ṭa> your child.

ðíhtaapi. PRON **your (two or more of you).** [*ðíhta* may also be used instead of *ðíhtaapi.*] *hci ðíhtaapi akxa žúucape* your [pl.] house is red. *ákahamį ðíhtaapi akxa šcúuce?* are your [pl.] coats warm?

ðihtáežį (variant of **ðihtéžį**).

ðihtą́ha. N **your father's sister's husband, your paternal uncle by marriage (used when speaking to a man or a woman); your wife's brother, your sister's husband (used only when speaking to a man; more precise than English 'brother-in-law').** (FH/09/24/01/ok).
•• LFD 238: *ihtáhą* <i-ṭa´-ho^n> a man's brother-in-law.

ðihtą́ke. N **your older sister (used by anyone speaking to a man or a woman, referring both to a sister older than the addressee and to the oldest of the addressee's sisters [who may not be older than the addressee]).**

ðihtéžį. N (variant: **ðihtáežį**). **your younger sister (used by anyone speaking to a man or a woman about a sister younger than the addressee)** (03/09/95/MREI/pc:ok; FH/09/22/01/pc).

ðihtǫ́ce. N **your son-in-law (used by anyone speaking to a man or a woman).**
•• LFD 150: *ðihtǫ́ce* <thi-ṭo^n´-dse> your son-in-law.

ðíhuuce (variant of **ðuuhúuce**).

ðíi (variants of **aðée, ðée** PRON).

ðii- (variant of **ðu-**).

ðiiɣó (variant: **ðiiɣóe, ðiiɣówe**). V [reg., _*ðiiɣo*] *(trans.)* **drag.**
•• JOD (Raccoons and Crawfish p24, ln13): *ðixówe* <¢iqúwe> drag along.
•• LFD 258: *ðíɣoe* <thi´xu-e> to drag on the ground.
••• *QU diɣówe* drag something along (RR).

ðiiɣóɣo (variant: **ðiiɣóɣoe**). V [reduplicated form of *ðiiɣó*] *(trans.)* **keep dragging.** *Brian akxa mą̨ą̨žą́ɣe tóa ðiiɣóɣo ną oðíhtą ci ehtáha* Brian keeps dragging those onions to put them in the car (RBn10-2:MOJ/79).

ðiiɣówe (variant of **ðiiɣó**).

ðiihą́ (variant: **ðíihą, ðíiha**). V [sync., _ *ðiihą́*] *(trans.)* **lift, pick up, hold up, or raise s.o. or s.t.** (02/15/95/FH/pc:okc). *bríiha* I lift him/it. *šcíiha* you lift him/it. *ą̨ðíiha* we lift him/it. *į́į šé įkšé ðiihą́* pick up that rock (RBn HW11; cq:okc). *ðiihą́ ðuuc?áke akxai* he can't lift it (02/22/95/FH/pc:ok). *wíbriihą* I lift you up (02/14/95/FH/pc; (BE2.79).
•• LFD 147: *ðihą́* <thi-ho^n´> to lift. *bríhą* <bthi´-ho^n> I lift.

ðiihcé (variants: **iihcé, ðíihce**). V [sync.?, _ *ðiihcé*?] *(trans.)* **touch softly, as with a feather fan; barely touch.** *mǫšǫ́ iihcé káaɣa* let the feather touch it (1/20/83/676; 03/23/95/FH/pc). *mą́šą ą̨ðíihce káaɣa* let the feather touch me (03/23/95/FH/pc:ok). *žą́ąxe ą̨ðíihce* the stick is touching me (03/23/95/FH/pc).

ðiihíce. V [sync., _ *ðiihíce*] *(trans.)* **play with s.t., fiddle with s.t.** *hcižé ðiihíce įká* don't play with the door (RBn12-07). *ðiihítaži apai* he's not playing with them (LS/07/19/95). *ðiihítaži apai* they won't play with them [with those things] (2/24/83). *ðiihíce hta apaží* they won't play with them (LS:prod). *žįkáži apa níi ðiihíce apái* the children are playing with the water (03/09/95/FH/pc:ok). • **fool, tease; be mischievous or deceitful toward; play slyly or meanly with; deceive, mistreat, persecute (an animal or person).** *wíbriihice ąhé* I was teasing you. *ą́ðiihice akxa ážamie* I think he's teasing me (03/05/95/JS/pc:okc). *ą́ðiihice štą* he just keeps on teasing me (03/16/95/FH/pc:okc). *wáðiihice* *akxai* he's teasing us (03/16/95/FH/pc). *ą́ðiihice į̨ká* stop teasing me (03/16/95/FH/pc). *ą́šciihíce ðatxą́še* you are toying with me (MSB/01/27/83).

•• JOD: *mą́ɣe* <ma^{n}-xe>.

•• LFD 147: *ðihíce* <thi-hi´-dse> to treat unkindly; maltreat. *bríhice* <bthi´-hi-dse> I persecuted him. *ąðíhica pe* <o^{n}-thi´-hi-dsa i> we persecuted him. LFD 103: *mąxe ðihice* <mo^{n}-xe, thi-hi-dse> conjuring the sky.

ðiihkó. N **your grandmother (paternal or maternal)** (02/03/95/FH/pc:ok)**; your mother-in-law (used only when speaking to a woman).** (02/03/95/FH/pc:ok). *ðiihkó akxa ðípą akxa, íiðikiðe kǫ́ða pátą* your grandmother is calling you, as she wishes to find you.

•• JOD (slip file): *ðihkó* <¢ihk̦ú> [your grandmother].

ðiihkóį̨ɣe. V [conjug. unknown] *(trans.)* **turn s.o./s.t. around.** *ðihkóįɣa!* turn it around! (04/04/95/FH/pc). *oðíhta ðihkǫ́įɣe* turn the car around (04/04/95/FH/pc/okc; BE2.146).

•• LFD 348: *nǫ́hkowįɣe* <no^{n}´-k̦u-wi^{n}-xe> to turn with the foot. *páhkowįɣe* <ba´-k̦u-wi^{n}-xe> to turn by pushing.

••• *KS yükkómįɣe* (reg.) to turn something around and around, crank (RR).

••• Cf. *hkilíihkǫįɣe*

ðiihkówa N **your friend** (01/20/95 /FH/pd:ok; BE2.51). **your grandparents (pl. only).** *ðiihkówa tąhé ðe?* how are your grandparents? (9T#14b-p3; 05/01/95/LS/pc).

ðiihǫ́. N **your mother (used by anyone speaking to a man or a woman)** (02/25/95/FH/pc:ok). *įcé waléze wį abrįe, ðiihǫ́ ðíhta* I have a picture of your mother (02/25/95/FH/pc:ok; BE2.90). *ðiihǫ́ akxa watáažoe oohǫ́ akxai* your mother is cooking hominy. *ðiihǫ́ kše tąhé akxai?* how is your [bedridden] mother?

ðiihǫ́ ðitáce. N **your parents (lit., 'your mother, your father').** *ðiihǫ́, ðitáce, tąhé apa?* how are your parents? (lit., 'your mother, your father, are they well?') (T#14b-p2; 04/17/95/LS/pc:ok).

ðiihǫ́htą. N **your mother's older sister (used by anyone speaking to a man or a woman; more precise than English 'maternal aunt').**

ðiihǫ́žį. N **your mother's younger sister (used by anyone speaking to a man or a woman; more precise than English 'maternal aunt').**

ðíihta (variant of **ðíhta**).

ðiihtą́ (variant: **ðiihtą́ą**). V [sync., *_ðiihtą́*] *(trans.)* **handle, knead, work s.t. with the hand (e.g., when cutting up squash and removing seeds to get it ready to cook or when getting dance clothes ready to be used by hanging them out to air)** (FH/09/24/01/prod). *hǫ́ǫpa ðé htáa ðiihtą́ hta apai* they're going to work the meat today (FH/09/24/01/prod). • **grasp; touch with the hand; feel s.o. or s.t.** (03/23/95/FH/pc; 04/06/95/LS/pc; very low *ą́* or *ą́ą*). *šcíihtą ðąąch// áažie* you shouldn't touch it (BE2.143; 1/20/83/693). *bríihtą* I touched it; I felt it (1/20/83/693). *ónǫbre ðiihtą́ į̨ká* don't touch the food (03/23/95/FH/pc). *ðiihtá į̨ká* don't touch it (1/20/83/693).

•• LFD 150: *ðihtą́* <thi-ṭo^{n}´> to touch with the hand; to feel. *bríhtą* <bthi´-ṭo^{n}> I touched it. *scíhtą* <stsi´-ṭo^{n}> you touched it.

••• *KS yüttą́* touch, feel with the hands (RR).

••• Cf. *áðiihtą, htaaðíihtą, oðíhtą.* **dance**

ðiilóce. V [sync.?, *_ðiilóce*?] *(trans.)* **peel.** *hką́ącezi ðiilóca* peel the orange (RBn10-20).

••• *KS yüxlóǰe (yüxlódabe)* peel something (RR).

ðiimǫ́. V [sync., *_ ðiimǫ́*] [perhaps *ðu-/ði-* INSTR + *mą́ą/mǫ́ǫ* 'arrow'] *(trans.)* **sharpen.** *mą́ąhį ðiimǫ́* sharpen the knife (RBn10-2). *mą́ąhį bríimǫ hta mįkšé* (RBn10-2).

•• LFD 148: *ðimǫ* <thi-mo^{n}> to whet. *brimǫ* <bthi-mo^{n}> I whet. *ąðímǫ* <o^{n}-thi´-mo^{n}> we whet.

••• *KS mą́hį iyű̃ma* whetstone, knife sharpener (RR).

ðiipíɣą (variant: **ðiipíɣa**). V [sync., *_ðiipíɣa*] [*ðu-/ði-* INSTR + *píɣą*] *(intr.)* **fart, pass air or gas; break wind.** (01/23/95/FH/pc:ok).

••• *KS yübíɣą* to fart (JOD, RR).

••• Cf. *opíɣą.*

ðiisą́ða (variant: **ðiisǫ́ða**). V [sync., *_ðiisą́ða*] *(trans.)* **turn, turn over; invert, reverse.** *oðíhtą ðiisą́ðape* he turned the car over (04/06/95/FH/pc:ok; BE2.146). *briisą́ða* I turned it over (FH).

•• LFD 145: *ðisą́ða* <thi-ço^{n}´-tha> to reverse.

••• Cf. *liisą́ða.*

ðiiskí. V [sync., *_ ðiiskí*] *(trans.)* **grab; grasp s.o. by the scruff of the neck** (FH:4/18/96:pc). *ðiiskí oðį́ka, lį́įðįka* grab a person by the neck and shake them up and set them down hard [shoving them]. • **wad up or wad together (e.g., clothing at the back of the neck).**

••• Cf. *hkilíiski, kaaskí, waðíiski.*

ðiiskíke. V [sync., *_ðiiskíke*] [apparently *ðu-/ði-* INSTR + *skíke*] *(trans.)* **wad up, bring the parts of a whole together with pressure; bring**

ðiiskíke (*continued*) **components into contact (e.g., parts of a blanket); make a fist; grind together (e.g., the teeth); gather.** *šáake ðiiskíke* make a fist. *šáake šcíiskike* you've got your fist doubled up. *hí ški ðiiskíke akxai* he's even grinding his teeth.

••LFD 269: *nǫpé ðiskike iðáchį ha* <no^{n}-be´ thi-çki-ge i-tha´-tsi^{n} ha> [sentence-final *ha* is not used in Mod. Os.] I struck him with the fist [FH: correct without the *ha* (01/26/95/FH/pc:ok)].

••• Cf. *hkilíiski.*

ðiisǫ́ða (variant of **ðiisą́ða**).

ðiistą́. v [sync., *_ðiistą́*] *(trans.)* **turn off.** *oðíhtą ðiistą́pe* he turned the car off (RBn10-12:JW, unconfirmed).

ðiišką́ (variant of **ðuušką́**).

ðiiškí (variant: **ðuuškí**). v [sync., *_ðiiškí*] *(trans.)* **wash (e.g., clothes, one's own or another's hair); launder.** (FH/06/26/01/pc).

••• Cf. *hkilíiški, líiški, waðíiški.*

ðiišǫ́ (variant of **ðuušǫ́**).

ðiištą́. v [sync., *_ðiištą*] *(trans.)* **finish.** *oohǫ́ ðiištą́pe, ąwą́nǫ́bre htai* the cooking is finished, let us [three or more] eat (lit., 'they finished cooking, . . .') (01/25/95/FH/pc:okc). *oohǫ́ ðiištą́ apai, ąwą́nǫ́bre htai* the cooking is finished, let us [three or more] eat (lit., 'they are finished cooking, . . .') (01/25/95/FH/pc:okc). *oohǫ́ ðiištą́pi che, ąwą́nǫ́bre htai* the cooking is finished [lit., 'they have evidently finished cooking'], let us [three or more] eat (01/25/95/FH/pc:okc). *oohǫ́ ąðíištąpe* we are finished cooking (01/25/95/FH/pc:ok). *wanǫ́bre ðóho ðíištape* dinner will be ready soon (WHM980326). • **stop (e.g., the weather stops doing s.t.).** *niižú ðiištą́ akxá* it stopped raining (03/14/95/MREI/pc:okc). • **already (did s.t.), be just finished (doing s.t.) [approximate translation].** *pąąšcéka žaníe tóa áažu bríištą* I already put some sugar on top of the strawberries (lit., 'I finished putting sugar on top') (RBnB1-52). • *(intr.)* **be finished, be through.** *ðiištą́ káaye* stop. *oážu bríištą* I'm finished planting (RBn14-01/LH). *bríištą* I'm finished (doing something) (01/25/95/FH/pc:prod). *ðóha bríištą* well, I'm just about through (FH). *šcíišta?* are you finished? (01/25/95/FH/pc:ok;[a]; BE2.47). *iðée bríištą tą, htą́wą įkši brée hta mįkšé* when I finish here, I'm going to town (01/25/95/FH/pc:ok; RBn HW8). *ąwą́ðiištą* we're through (02/03/95/FH/pc:prod orig). • **stop; finish, end.** *hóni bríišta* I almost finished (but did not) (01/25/95/FH/pc:ok). *tąąké šǫ́ apa, ąną́ðapi iaha ðiištą́pe* they were fighting, but they stopped when they saw me (lit., 'while they were fighting, when they saw me they stopped immediately'). *katxą́ ąðíištą htai* let's stop a while (RBn14-09; 03/14/95/MREI/pc:okc). *káaši wáli ąwáachipe, ąðíištą htái* we've danced a long time, let's stop (02/22/95/FH/pc:ok; BE2.81). *mį́įake hcewį́įke ąðíištą htai* let's stop at nine o'clock (03/14/95/MREI/pc:okc; BE2.128). *hkihtǫ́pe ðiištą!* quit looking at yourself! • **be ready.** *šcíištą?* are you ready? (RB).

•• LFD 149: *ðištą́* <thi-shto^{n}´> to stop, to finish, to make further claim to property in controversy; to relinquish the claim or right. *bríštą* <bthi´-shto^{n}> I finished, I relinquish claim. *ąðíštą pe* <o^{n}-thi´-shto^{n} i> we finished, we relinquish claim.

••• Cf. *ðaaštą́, kaaštą́, nǫ́ǫ ðiištą́.*

ðiištą́ káaye. VP *(trans.)* **stop; make it end; make s.o. end s.t.** *súhka mį́ka žį ðiištą́ káaye ðílą nąpé* sometimes the little hen tried to stop him (RBn18-01).

ðiištówe (variants: **ðištó, ðiištóe, ðiištówi**). v [sync., *_ðiištówe*] *(trans.)* **take off or remove a garment; undress.** *briištówe* I'm taking it off (FH). *húįke ðiištóa* take your leggings off (MREI). • **remove or take off by pulling, pull off (e.g., a shoe or boot).** *ðiitą́ ðiištópe* he pulled and broke it off [removed it] (RBn16-02; FH:ok). *hǫǫpé sí aníe étana hǫǫpé bríišto* my shoe was hurting me, so I took it off (FH/11/19/01/pc:prod). *sí ąðíxǫ étana hǫǫpé bríištoe* I broke my foot, so I took my shoe off (FH/11/19/01/pc). • **pull (e.g., a tooth) to remove it** (04/18/95/FH/pc:okc). *híi ðíištoe* pull your tooth (RB, 04/18/95/FH/pc:okc). *hii ą́ðiištoe* pull my tooth (04/18/95/FH/pc:okc; BE2.108).

ðiišúpe (variant: **ðuušúpe**). v [sync., *_ðiišúpe*] *(trans.)* **open (e.g., a can); unlock and open (e.g., a door, a box)** (RBn12-05). *niikáapxoke tóa ðuušúpa* open some pop (RBn12-05). *hci brúušupe* I opened the house (MREI 11-01-83). *hcižé ðiišúpa* [unlock and] open the door (FH). *hcižé ą́ðiišupe* we opened the door (03/02/95/FH/pc:okc). *hcižé bríišupe* I opened the door (03/02/95/FH/pc:okc). *hciže šcíišupe* you opened the door. *hcižé ą́ðiišupape* they opened the door (03/02/95/FH/pc:okc).

•• LFD 148: *ðišípe* <thi-shi´-be> to open anything that has a lid or a door. *bríšipe* <bthi´-shi-be> I opened the box. LFD 149: *ðišúpe* <thi-

shu´-be> to open or unfasten a door; to open. *hcíže brišupe* <ṭsi´-zhe bthi-shu-be> I opened the door. *hcíže scišupe* <ṭsi´-zhe stsi-shu-be> you opened the door.

••• *KS gašų́we* knock open a door or box (RR).

••• Cf. *wéðušupe.*

ðiitáaži (variant of **ðuutáaži**).

ðiitą́. v [sync., *_ðiitą́*] *(trans.)* **pull; drag; tug.** *oðíhtą ðiitą́* he pulled the car (04/18/95/FH/pc:okc). *ðiitą́!* pull it! (04/18/95/FH/pc:okc). *oðíhtą ški ðiitą́ kǫ́ða įkápe* he didn't want to pull the wagon either (RBn16-01). *oðíhtą ðiitą́* pull the car (04/18/95/FH/pc:okc). *žą́ą lą́ąðe kaasé, ðekáiha ðiitą́* that big tree that was cut, around this way pull it (04/18/95/FH/pc). *žą́ą wáli lą́ąðe ðiitą́pi* drag that big tree [speaking to a group] (04/18/95/FH/pc). *ðiitą́ waškáape* he pulled harder (lit.,'pulling, he did his best').

•• LFD 145: *ðitą́* <thi-do^{n}´> to tug, pull (something); to pull with the hands. *brítą awašką* <bthi´-do^{n} a-wa-shko^{n}> I tugged hard. *ąðítą pe ha* <o^{n}-thi´-do^{n} pe ha> [sentence-final *ha* is not used in Mod. Os.] he or they pulled me. LFD 214: *wéðį ðitą* <we´-thi^{n}-thi-do^{n}> to pull anything taut (e.g., rope, tent cover) or spread a blanket tight.

••• *KS oyų́ųdą, oyídą* pull on, rein in, restrain (RR).

••• Cf. *ðiihtą́, oðíitą.*

ðiixǫ́ (variant: **ðuuxǫ́**). v [sync., *_ðiixǫ́*] *(trans.)* **break by hand, break s.t. long** (MSB:02/03/83). *bríixǫ* I break it. *šcíixǫ* you break it. *ąðíixǫ* we break it. *ðiixǫ/ðiixǫ́* he/they break it. *hcižé šcíixǫ* you broke the door (04/19/95/FH/pc). *aa ąðíixǫpe* they broke my arm. • **break off a long item (e.g., a limb, sofa, car antenna) by using the hands; snap in two, break into two parts** (01/07/95/FH/pc:ok). *ščíixǫpe* you [two or more] broke it (FH/09/22/01/pc). *žą́ąxežį tóa ðiixǫ́* break off some little sticks (01/09/95/FH/pc:ok). *žą́ąxežį tóa ðiixǫ́pi* break off some little sticks [to two or more addressees] (01/09/95/FH/pc:ok). *álįįscee ðiixǫ́pe* they have broken the divan (01/09/95/FH/pc:ok).

•• LFD 151: *ðixǫ́* <thi-xo^{n}´> to break; to break a stick in half. *bríxǫ* <bthi´-xo^{n}> I broke the stick in half. *ąðíxǫpe* <o^{n}-thi´-xo^{n} i> we broke the stick in half. LFD 25: *žą́xa kše brixǫ* <zho^{n}´-xa ke bthi-xo^{n}> I broke the stick in two. *žą́xa kše scixǫ* <zho^{n}´-xa ke stsi-xo^{n}> you broke the stick in two. [LFD 219 also erroneously lists *bríxǫ* <bthi´-xo^{n}> 'I break (s.t.)' and *ąðíxǫpe* <o^{n}-thi´-xo^{n} i> 'we break (s.t.)' as if they were forms of *xǫ́* <xo^{n}> 'break' (intr.).]

ðiizíðe. v [sync., *_ðiizíðe*] *(trans.)* **stretch** (FH).

•• LFD 337: *ðisíða* <thi-çi´-tha> to stretch, as distend.

••• *KS áayüzübe* to pull the edge over one, as a blanket (RR); *OM* same as Osage (LFD 337).

••• Cf. *hkilíiziðe.*

ðiizó (variant: **ðiizóka**). v [sync., *_ðiizó*] *(trans.)* **make bend (e.g., bend a tree branch over with the hands).** *mį́ce bríizoke* I bent the bow (02-10-83-p4). *mį́ce šciizóke* you bent the bow. *mį́ce ðiizókape* they bent the bow. *mį́ce ąðíizokape* they bend my bow. *mį́ce ąlíizoke ąkátxai* we bend our bows.

••• *KS zóoge* lean, bend as a tree in the wind (RR).

ðiižóži (variants: **ðuužóži, ðižóži, ðužóži**). v [sync., *_ðiižóži*] *(trans.)* **hurt or harm another physically, mistreat.** *wáli ðiižóžipi kšé áape* he [lying down] has really been hurt, they said (RB; FH). *iwáli ðiižóžipi įkšé áape* he [sitting] is hurt [all beat up] (RB; FH). *ščížoži* you caused suffering, you hurt him (FH). • **harm another mentally, emotionally (e.g., by humiliating another or by dying).** *ðakʔéwikíe, ðiðáce ðíðižoži* I pity you, your father hurt you [when he died] (uttered at a funeral) (RB). *bríižoži* I caused suffering to him (e.g., by saying something harmful) (02/13/95/FH/pc:okc; BE2.70).

•• LFD 152: *ðižóži* <thi-zho´-zhi> to cause suffering by humiliating. *brížoži* <bthi´-zho-zhi> I suffered from humiliation [rather, 'I caused suffering to somebody']. *ðižoáži* <thi-zhu-a´zhi> to injure; hurt; to do bodily harm. *brížomąži* <bthi'-zhu mo^{n}-zhi> I hurt him.

••• Cf. *ðaažóži, hkilíižoži.*

ðikšį́ce. v [sync., *_ðikšį́ce*] *(trans.)* **miss; fail at; be incorrect at, not get right (e.g., an action).** *íe brikšį́ce* I didn't tell it right (lit., 'telling it, I failed') (RBn23-17). • **drop (e.g., an object or a comment into a conversation).** *brikšį́ce* I dropped it. *šcikšį́ce* you dropped it (01/20/95/PM/pc:ok; BE2.35). • **let slip (as a comment); let slip away (as when one takes one's eyes off a person for a minute and he/she is gone).**

•• LFD 147: *ðikšį́ce* <thi-kshi^{n}´-dse> failure to get a good grasp or hold. *bríkšįce* <bthi´-kshi^{n}-dse> I failed to grasp it.

••• Cf. *kakšį́ce.*

ðikʔíðe (variant: **ðikʔíe**). v [sync., *_ðikʔíðe*] *(trans.)* **scratch; tickle.** *nąhka ą́ðikʔíe* scratch my

ðikˀíðe (*continued*) back (03/08/95/MREI/pc:okc; 05/02/95/LS/pc:ok; BE2.117; RBn HW11). *wéeli ðikˀíði apa* he scratched his head (RBn19-02). *wéeli ðikˀíði e kší aape* he [lying down] scratched his head [they said] (RBn19-02).

•• LFD 147: *ðikˀíða* <thi-ķ'i´-tha> to tickle. *bríhkiða* <bthi´-ķi-tha> I tickled him. *ąðíhkiða pe* <o^{n}-thi´-ķi-tha i> we tickled them [expected translation: 'him'].

ðílą. ADJ, N, V [sync., *_ðílą*] *(trans.)* **flirt (perhaps of flirting with a woman only [RB]); court, woo.** *John akxa wakˀó ðílą štąpe* John flirts with women all the time (FH/11/27/01/pc:prod; BE2.49; 01/26/95/FH/pc:ok).

•• LFD 146: *ðilą́* <thi-gtho^{n}´> to court; to woo. *brílą* <bthi´-gtho^{n}> I court. *ąðílą pe* <o^{n}-thi´-gtho^{n} i> we court.

ðiléleze. N [reduplicated form] **forked lightning (lit., 'making repeated stripes').**

•• LFD 146: *ðiléleze* <thi-gthe´-gthe-çe> the lightning that breaks into branches (forked lightning) (04/14/95/PM/pc:ok).

ðilǫ́ke (variant: **ðilóke**). V [sync., *_ðilǫ́ke*] *(trans.)* **pinch** (04/17/95/LS/pc:okc; 01/19/95/FH/pc:prod). *ą́ðilokape* he pinched me (RBn23-07). *wíbriloke hta mįkšé* I'm going to pinch you (RBn23-07).

ðilǫ́že (variant: **ðilože**). V [sync., *_ðilǫ́že*] *(trans.)* **grind; grind up; chop.** *htáa che ðilǫ́ža, htóožu ąkáaye htai* grind up this meat, let's make meat pies (FH/09/24/01/prod). *nąye ðilǫ́že* chopped or chipped ice (RBn; MREI/01/11/83; FH:ok).

ðíną (variants: **ðína, ðiną́, ðį́ną**). V, PRON [*ðí(e)* + *na* 'only'] *(intr.)* **(be) only you.** *ðiną́* it is only you.

••• Cf. *ąkóną, eeną́, wíną.*

ðiníhka. N **your husband** (FHt#128a).

••• Cf. *níhka ðíhta.*

ðipúze. V [sync., *_ðipúze*] *(trans.)* **dry.** *iištábrį ðipúze hta akxai* he'll dry your tears (04/04/99/FH/pc:prod).

•• LFD 144: *ðipúze* <thi-biu´çe> to make dry by wringing the water out of clothing (03/02/95/FH/pc:ok); the drying of a marshy place by draining.

ðisíkxą. N **your sister-in-law (probably used only when speaking to a woman about her sister-in-law).**

ðisǫ́ežį (variant: **ðisǫ́ažį**). N **your younger brother (used when speaking to a woman)** (BE2.12; 01/09/95/FH/pc:prod; 04/13/95/LS/pc:ok).

ðisǫ́ka. N **your younger brother (used when speaking to a man)** (04/13/95/LS/pc:ok).

ðistópe. V [sync., *_ðištópe*] *(trans.)* **bless or give a blessing to with the hand (by touching a person's head or entire body: head, hands, heart, legs, feet)** (RBn10-2; FH:ok). *wihcíko ðistópe mąðį́* grandfather, go ahead and bless him. *wisǫ́ka akxa ðíðistope hta akxa* brother is going to give you a blessing (FH/09/25/01/pc). *wíbristope hta mįkšé* I'm going to give you a blessing (FH/09/25/01/pc; RBn).

ðišíkxą. N **your sister-in-law (used when speaking to a woman about her brother's wife, her husband's sister, or her husband's brother's wife)** (RBn14-10; (03/10/95/PM/pc:ok; FH/09/22/01/pc; BE2.122).

••• Cf. *šíkxą ðíhta.*

ðišíkˀe. N **your brother-in-law (used when speaking to a woman about her sister's husband, her husband's brother, or her husband's sister's husband)** (FH/09/24/01/rod).

ðiškítą (variants: **ðiškíta, ðiškí**). PRON [contains *ški* 'also'] **you too.**

•• LFD 132: *ðiški* <thi-shki> you also.

••• Cf. *eeškítą.*

ðišǫ́ži (variant: **ðižóži**). V [sync., *_ðišǫ́ži*] *(trans.)* **trouble or mistreat s.o.** *níhkašie apa wáli hkilížoži apai* the people are mistreating each other (RBn 3/3/77).

•• JOD (Wasápežįka ltr, ln5): *háahta ðíšǫži hkǫ́bra ðįké* <Háta ¢i´cŭ^{n}çi kŭ^{n}´p¢a ¢iñķe´> I want you not to be troubled at any time.

•• LFD 152: *ðižóži* <thi-zho´-zhi> to cause suffering by humiliating. *ðižuáži* <thi-zhu-a´zhi> to injure; hurt; to do bodily harm.

••• Cf. *hkilíižoži.*

ðištó (variant of **ðiištówe**).

ðiwákˀo. N **your wife** (04/27/95/FH/pc).

••• Cf. *wakˀó.*

ðíwakˀóžį. N **your mother-in-law (considered by some to refer only to a male's wife's mother; considered by others to refer to either a male's or a female's mother-in-law).**

••• Cf. *wakˀóžį.*

ðiwáštake (variant: **ðuwáštake** [FH]). V [sync., *_ðiwáštake*] *(trans.)* **tame (e.g., a horse)** (03/23/95/FH/pc).

•• LFD 150: *ðiwáštake* <thi-wa´-shta-ge> tame a horse, make a horse gentle; domesticate a horse or other animal. *bríwaštake* <bthi´-wa-shta-ge> I tamed the horse. *ąðíwaštakape* <o^{n}-thi´-wa-shta-ga i> we tamed the horses.

ðixí (variant: **ðuxí**). v [sync., *_ðixí*] [*ðu-/ði-* INSTR + *-xi* 'become awake'] *(trans.)* **wake.** *ðixí!* wake him up! wake her up! (FH:prod). *wáðixi!* wake them up! (FH:prod). *ą́ðixi akxai* he's waking me up (FH:prod; HRE/12/29/01/pc:ok). *ąwáðixíe* we [two] woke them up (1-20-83-p4).

ðixípe (variants: **ðihípe, ðihipi**). N **personal name of Robert Bristow, name in the Deer clan (lit., 'it caused to awaken', alluding to s.t. that awakens or arouses the sleeping deer).**

ðixópe. v [sync.? *_ðixópe*] [*ðu-/ði-* INSTR + *xópe*] *(trans.)* **revere; hold sacred.** *ąðíðixope* we honor you (FH/09/21/01/pc). *žáže ąðíðixope ąkatxą́* hallowed be thy name (lit., 'we stand honoring your name') • **honor; respect** (MSB 05-12-83).

ðixtą́. v [sync., *_ðixtą*] *(trans.)* **draw water or run water (e.g., into a bathtub); pour.** *hiiðánii tóe ąðíxta* run me some bathwater (RBn10-20). *mąhkása toe ą́ðixtą* pour me some coffee (04/17/95/LS/pc:ok).

ðižáža (variant: **ðižą́žą**). v [sync.?, *_ðižáža*?] *(trans.)* **shake (a person, an object, or one's own body part, such as shaking the head; human agent only, not nonhuman agents such as wind)** (FH:prod; MREI 11/1/83; 3/10/83/C). *wéehli ðižą́žą* he shakes his head [as one with palsy] (03/09/95/MREI/pc:okc; BE2.119). *žą́ą ðižážai* shake the tree (RBn, MREI/01/11/83). *wéehli brížažái* I shook my head [refusing] (03-10-93-C).

•• LFD 152: *ðižą́žą* <thi-zho^{n}´-zho^{n}> to arouse; to arouse a person from a sound sleep [definition unconfirmed]. *brížąžą* <bthi´-zho^{n}-zho^{n}> I aroused him by shaking him.

••• Cf. *ližážai.*

ðižíce. v [sync., *_ðižíce*] *(intr.)* **break wind, fart (with a small noise, by letting the air out slowly)** (FH).

••• *QU ákkiži* fart, break wind (RR); *KS áayüžįje* fart (with noise) (JOD, RR).

ðižį́ðe (variants: **ðižį́, ðižįe**). N **your older brother (used only when speaking to a man)** (01/09/95/FH/pc:ok).

ðižį́ke. N **your son; your brother's son (in both senses used when speaking to a man or to a woman, but its use for speaking to a woman may be more recent).** (02/27/95/FH/pc:ok) (03/13/95/FH/pc:ok; BE2.125).

••• Cf. *ðihcóška.*

ðižóži (variant of **ðišǫ́ži, ðiižóži**).

ðižǫ́ą. N **your older sister (used only when speaking to a woman)** (03/09/95/MREI/pc:ok).

ðižǫ́ke. N **your daughter (used when speaking to a man or woman); your sister's daughter (used only when speaking to a woman; more precise than English 'niece'); your brother's daughter (used only when speaking to a man; more precise than English 'niece')** (02/27/95/FH/pc:ok).

ðį (variant of **ði**).

ðį́. v [sync., *_ðį*; 2nd sg. usually *nį́*, occasionally *šcį́* or *ðanį́*; 1st sg. usually *brį́*, occasionally *mį́* or *anį́*; 1st pl. *waðį́*.] *(intr.)* **be (a certain way).** *ną́ąke kˀą́saaki brįe* I'm a fast runner (01/23/95/FH/pc:prod orig). *íe waská brį́ hta mįkšé* I'll be the interpreter (RB; MSB/02/17/83). *mǫ́pše anį́* I'm the elder (7/7/94/PM; 01/06/95/FH/pc:uk) *wahóšce brį́e* I'm small (FH:08/05/99). *scéce nį́* you're tall (02/25/83). *íe waská ðáalį nįe* you are a good interpreter (RB; MSB). *ðóðo nį́* you're greasy (02/25/83). *wažáže nį́pe?* are you all Osage? *wažáže nįe ðatxą́še* you're an Osage [standing]. *ðíe nąą́ke kˀą́saaki nįe* you're a fast runner (01/23/95/FH/pc:prod. orig.). *mǫ́pše ðanį́* you're the elder (7/7/94/PM; 01/06/95/FH/pc:uk). *wisǫ́ka akxa nąą́ke kˀą́saakipe* brother is a fast runner (01/23/95/FH/pc:prod. orig). *scéce waðį́pe* we're tall. *wahóšce ąkai* we're small (FH:08/05/99). • **live as, exist as.** *hǫ́ǫpa wį́xci nąą́ški níhkaši mį́ hkǫ́bra* I want to live [be a human] one day at a time (RBn10-21). • **be characterized by [the immediately preceding word or phrase, which may be a noun phrase].** *wawéeðe hǫ́ǫži ðį́* he sees poorly (lit., 'he is characterized by bad sight')

ðįcéki. N **your mother's brother, your maternal uncle (used by anyone speaking to a man or a woman)** (02/27/95/JS/pc).

•• LFD 70: *icéki* <i-dse´-gi> uncle; father's or mother's brother (LFD 349: "on mother's side").

•• *KS ijégi* uncle, man's mother's brother.

ðįįké (variant: **įįké**). v [stat., *_ðįįké*] [possibly from *aðį́* 'have'+ *ðįké* NEG] *(trans.)* **lack a thing, be devoid of, be lacking, not have s.t. any longer; have nothing.** *ąðį́įke* I lack it. *ðiðį́įke* you lack it. *waðį́įke* we lack it. *waðį́įke* we [two or more] don't have any (#90/FH). *ąðį́įke* I have none (RBn3-39). *mą́zeska ąðį́įke* I don't have any money. *wéðuwį ðįké atxą́he* I have nothing to buy with (RBnB1-58). *ðiðį́įke* you have none. *mą́zeska ąðį́įke* I have no money (CQ ok; BE2.94). *waðį́įke apa* there isn't any more (7/8/94/PM/#98b).

ðįįké (*continued*)

•• LFD 148: *ðíke* <thi^{n}´-ge> to have none, nothing. *tátą ąðįke* <da´-do^{n} o^{n}-thi^{n}-ge> I have nothing. *tátą ðiðįke* <da´-do^{n} thi-thi^{n}-ge> you have nothing. *tátą waðįka pe* <da´-do^{n} wa-thi^{n}-ga i> we have nothing; to have none.

••• *WI hįįké.*

••• Cf. *ðįké.*

ðįká (variant: **įká**). NEG [*ðįké* NEG + *a* IMPERATIVE MARKER] **don't!** *ékiǫ ðįká* don't do that (04/13/95/LS/pc:ok). *ékie ðįká* don't say that (04/13/95/LS/pc:pl; RBn1-26). *íixa ðįká* don't laugh (04/13/95/LS/pc:ok [ɣ]). *ðúwį įká* don't buy it (04/26/95/LS/pc:ok). *wéðuwį įká* don't sell it (04/26/95/LS/pc:ok). *íe ðįká* don't talk (04/26/95/LS/pc). *įįštáxį íe ðįká* don't talk English. *šką́ įká* don't move (01/20/95/ERE/pc:ok; 04/26/95/LS/pc:okc). *ɣaaké įká* don't cry (01/20/95/ERE/pc:ok). *kaakǫná kaaɣái* don't do that any more ('knock it off') (04/26/95/LS/pc:ok; BE2.33).

ðįké (variant: **įké**). V [conjug. unknown] *(intr.)* **be none; be gone, absent, extinct, nonexistent, lacking.** *hcí wį́ pšíe, pée ðįké* I went to the house, no one was there (BE2.157). *wawéðe mąžíe, įįštóolą ðįké* I can't see without my glasses (RB). *Mary apa ðįkápi che, pšíe ðáha* Mary was gone when I got there (FH/07/27/95/pc:prod). *ðįkápi che, achíe ðáha* it was already gone when he came in (MSB). *záani ðįkée* it's all gone (01/04/95/FH/pc). *wažážeíe ðįké ée ahípe* the Osage language is all gone (01/06/95/FH/pc). *hcí akxa ðįkí akxa* that house doesn't exist any more. *óohǫ akxa tooská ðįké áakxa* the cook says there are no potatoes (RBnB1-43). • **pass away, vanish.** *mǫ́žǫ ðáalį ðékše mǫ́žǫ ðékše ðįké hta aaži íe wíhta šǫǫšǫ́we aðée hta akxai* heaven and earth shall pass away but my word will endure (FH: from Matthew 24:35).• NEG **not, not at all.** *wacʔéąðe ðįké* we don't kill at all.

•• LFD 148: *ðįka pi a* <thi^{n}´-ga bi a> there were none.

••• Cf. *ðįįké.*

ðįké hta. NEG + POTENTIAL MARKER **won't.** *óxpaðe [ð]įké hta apái* he won't lose it (lit., 'he will not be losing stuff'). *aðáaži hta apai* she won't go.

••• Cf. ***aži*** *hta.*

ðįkšé, ðįkší (variants of **įkšé** CONT, POSIT).

ðóðo. ADJ **greasy.** *íhaa ðóðo* greasy mouth (BE2.61). *ðóðo nį́* you're greasy (02/03/95/FH/pc:ok). • N **stain** (LF only).

•• LFD 154: *ðóðo* <tho´-tho> oily, greasy; a stain. *waché ðą ðóðo aðaha akihpaɣe* <wa-tse tho^{n} tho´-tho a-tha-ha a-gi-p̣a-xe> I made my dress greasy (02/03/95/FH/pc:uk; LF sentence unconfirmed).

ðóha (variants: **ðǫ́ha, ðǫ́hą**). ADV **almost, nearly, about (to) (implies that the event is likely to occur).** *ðóha niižú akxai* it's about to rain (RBn3-52). *ðóha ąžį́įhe* I'm about asleep (MREI/04/27/94). *ðóha ąžį́įhe aðįkše* we two are about asleep (MREI/04/27/94). *ðǫ́ha mį́įoke sáhta ahí akxái* it's almost five o'clock (01/04/95/FH/pc). *ðǫ́ha nüžű́pé* it's about to rain; it's almost raining (RBn10-21/JW&FW/77; FH:okc). *ðóha aðáape* they're about ready to go (RBn22-10). *ðóha aalépe* I'm about to vomit (FH/06/27/01/pc). *ðǫ́ha étxąpe* it's almost time (01/04/95/FH/pc:okc:étkxą). *oohǫ́ ðǫ́ha étxąpé* it's almost time to cook (RBn3-moj/p21). *ðǫha oohǫ́ étxą akxái* it's almost time to cook (01/04/95/FH/pc:prod). *waachí ðǫ́hą éetkxą ahí akxai* it's almost time for the dance (FH/t116b).

•• LFD 153: *ðóha* <tho´-ha> almost. *ðóha alipe* <tho´-ha a-gthi bi a> it is almost time for them to come home.

ðótaðe. V [reg., *ðóta_ðe*] *(trans.)* **regard as a friend.**

•• LFD 152, 271: *ðótaðe* <tho´-da-the> (be) friendly; be on friendly terms with another person; peaceful relationship between two tribes; reciprocity.

ðótahkiðe (variant: **ðótahkie**). V [reg., *ðota_hkiðe*] [*hkik-* RECIP + *ðótaðe*] *(intr.)* **become acquainted with each other; make friends with each other, regard each other as friends, hold each other dear.** *ðótahkiðe* they made friends, got acquainted (01/30/95/FH/pc:okc; BE2.51: *thó-tah-ki-eh, thó-tah-ki-théh*). *ðótahkie ąðé* we [two] made friends. *ðótahkiape* you all made friends. • **take or regard each other as relatives, be related.** *Smokey, Eddie apa ðotahkie apai* Smokey and Eddie are related (RBn22-17).

•• LFD 152: *ðótahkie* <tho´-da-ḳi-e> reconcile, reconciliation [meaning unconfirmed, not accepted].

••• Cf. *iiðótahkiðe.*

ðóxe. N **buffalo; Buffalo clan.** *ðóxe kahíke* buffalo chief (BE2.13; 01/09/95/FH/pc:ok).

•• JOD (slip file): *ðóxe* <¢u´-qe> buffalo with reddish-yellow hair and long legs.

•• LFD 154: *ðóxe* <tho´-xe> archaic name for buffalo bull.

••• *QU toxe* reddish yellow buffalo (RR); *KS yoxe* [no stress marked] reddish yellow buffalo (JOD, RR).

ðóxe kahíke. N **Buffalo Chief (personal name).** [Russell Koshehe Mashunkashey's name.]

ðǫ́γu. N **lung, lungs.**

••• *KS yáaγü* lungs (RR); *QU dáγi/dáγį* lungs (RR).

ðǫ́ha, ðǫ́hą (variants of **ðóha**).

ðǫǫpá (variant: **ðǫǫpái** [JS]). ADJ, N **two; the two of them, both of them.** *waanáše é[ð]ǫǫpa ąkále hta ąðé* Waanáše and I are going home [the two of us]. • ADV **twice.** *hǫpái ðǫǫpá awáŋǫbre* I ate twice today (02/27/95/JS/pc:ok; BE2.146). *hkáwa ðǫǫpá* two horses.

•• LFD 153: *ðǫpá* <tho^n-ba´> two. *ðǫpá ha* <tho^n-ba´ ha> in two parts. *ðǫpá nąðe* <tho^n-ba´ no^n-the> two at a time; two to each person; two by two.

ðǫǫpáha káaγe. VP *(trans.)* **divide in two, halve (lit., make into two)** (04/11/95/FH/pc:ok). LF153: *ðǫpáha kaxe* <tho^n-ba´-ha ga-xe> to halve; to divide equally in two parts.

ðǫǫpái (variant of **ðǫǫpá** [JS]).

ðǫǫpátą. N **twin, twins.** (04/06/95/FH/pc:okc).

•• LFD 153: *ðǫpáta* <tho^n-ba´-da> two-born, twins. LFD 112: *nǫpáta* <no^n-ba´-da> born two.

ðu- (variants: **ðuu-, ði-, ðii-**). INSTR **action by hand; cause, make (not necessarily by hand).** *ðúuhpeece* lighter (lit., 'make fire'). *ðúulą* make angry. *ðuuštáko* make neat, straighten.

ðuatáaže (variant of **ðuutáaži**).

ðúbra (variant of **ðíbra**).

ðuðáalį. V [sync., _*ðuðáalį*] [*ðu-/ði-* INSTR + *ðáalį*] *(trans.)* **make good; fix, remedy; bless.** *óŋǫbre che šcuðáalį* bless this food.

ðúeži. V [sync., _*ðúeži*] [*ðu-/ði-* INSTR + *éži*] *(trans.)* **change (lit., 'make different').** *waðílą ðúežipe* he changed his mind (FH:prod). *ážą ščúeži* you changed the bed (FH:prod).

ðúγe (variant: **ðíγe**). V [sync., _*ðúγe*] *(trans.)* **mate, take as a sexual partner.** *htáa kiðíγepi* deer mating moon; October.

••• Cf. *wáðuγe.*

ðuháašįðe. V [sync., _*ðuháašįðe*] [*ðu-/ði-* INSTR + *háašįðe*] *(trans.)* **make inside out, turn wrong side out** (RBn10-15).

ðuhcépe. V [sync., _*ðuhcépe*] *(trans.)* **lift.** *įį htą kootáha wáli lą́ąðe, ðuhcépe įká* that big rock over there is really big, don't lift it (FH/09/25/01/pc). *tǫ́pa įį htą, ščúhcepe ðą́ąché įké* watch out with that big rock, you can't lift it (FH/09/25/01/pc). • **handle, deal with, manage.** *brúhcepe hta atxą́he* I can handle it (9RBn, MREI/01/11/83; FH:okc). *wakˀó wį oðáhkie ščúhcepe ðą́ąché?* is there a chance that you can handle it with that woman you talked to? (FH/09/25/01/pc).

ðuhkį́ki (variant of **ðuuhkíhkį**).

ðuhpáahą. V [sync., _*ðuhpáða*] [*ðu-/ði-* INSTR + *hpaahą́*] *(trans.)* **raise.** *cˀé ški šǫ́ įkše šcúhpaahą nįkšé aapai* they said you raised the dead.

ðuhpíiži. V [sync., _*ðuhpíiži*] *(trans.)* **harm, do harm to; make s.t. bad; ruin.** *hpéecenii akxa žúoka ðíðuhpíiži hta akxái* whiskey is bad for your health (01/04/95/FH/pc:ok; reprod; RBnot 5/3/79/p3; BE2.30). *omíže ðuhpíižipi įkše* they have ruined the rug. *žįkážį apa taðúhpiižipé, omíži ðuhpíižipi įkšé* children are destructive, they have ruined the rug (RBn24).

•• LFD 148: *ðihpíži* <thi-p̣i´-zhi> to ruin; damage; defilement (01/20/95/FH/pc:ok); to spoil; to ruin by tearing, cutting, or burning [the word actually does not imply any specific sort of causation such as cutting, burning, or tearing]. *bríhpiži* <bthi´-p̣i-zhi> I ruined it by cutting. *ąðíhpipaži* <o^n-thi´-p̣i-ba-zhi> we ruined it by cutting.

ðuhtáža. V [sync., _*ðuhtáža*] *(intr.)* **protrude or stick out in a round shape (e.g., have one's rear end sticking out)** (RB; 2-10-83-p1).

••• *KS ttáγe (ttáaγe?)* protrude (RR).

ðuhúce, ðúhuuce, ðuhúuce (variants of **ðuuhúuce**).

ðuléke (variant of **ðuuléke**).

ðumáða. V [sync., _*ðumáða*] *(trans.)* **lift, hold high, raise up, turn up** (RBn19-05). *wéeli ðumą́ða ðíape* she held her head high.

ðupáxa. V [sync., _*ðupáxa*] *(trans.)* **pull apart; tear apart (e.g., a tree limb from the trunk)** (01/19/95/FH/pc:okc).

•• LFD 144: *ðipáxe* <thi-ba´-xe> to break a string in half. *bripáxe* <bthi-ba´-xe> I broke the string in two. *ąðípaxa pe* <o^n-thi´-ba-xa i> we broke the string in two.

ðupˀį́pˀįze. V [sync., _*ðupˀį́pˀįze*] [reduplicated form of *ðupˀį́ze*] *(intr.)* **blink repeatedly** (FH).

ðupˀį́ze. V [sync., _*ðupˀį́ze*] *(intr.)* **close one's eyes, blink.**

ðusáaki. V [sync., _*ðusáaki*] [*ðu-/ði-* INSTR + *saakí*] *(trans.)* **shock, stun, instill fear in** (01/26/95/FH/pc:prod orig). *ðą́ące ðusáaki kšíape* it [e.g., a fire in which his home or car burned up] instilled fear in him; it stunned him; it shocked him (03/09/95/MREI/pc:ok; FH).

••• Cf. *ðą́ące ðuusáaki.*

ðusą́sąwį. v [sync.?, *_ðusą́sąwį*] *(trans.)* **twist, twist around (e.g., a crepe paper streamer); shake; turn over and over.**

ðuškápa. v [sync., *_ðuškápa*] *(trans.)* **carry s.o. who has his/her arms around one from the back, carry piggyback; swim supporting a child in the water.**

ðušpú. v [sync., *_ðušpú*] **shell, as corn.** *hápa brúšpu* I shelled the corn. • ADJ **shelled, as of corn.** *hápa ðušpú che ápše* I pounded the shelled corn.

•• LFD 149: *ðišpí* <thi-shpi´> to shell corn.

••• *QU dišpí* shell corn (RR); *dišpé* pull off something adhering (RR).

••• Cf. *páašpue.*

ðutáahpa v [sync., *_ðutaahpa*] [*ðu-/ði-* INSTR + *táahpa*] *(trans.)* **make round.** *hpáxį ðutáahpa* a bun [woman's hairdo] (lit., 'hair made round') [also recorded as *hpáxį ðuutáahpa*]. *wacúe ðutáahpa* biscuits (lit., 'bread made round').

ðuu- (variant of **ðu-**).

ðuuáze. v [sync., *_ðuuáze*] *(trans.)* **open (e.g., a door, a window, the lid on a box).** *hcižé ðuuáza* open the door (BE2.98). *okáhąpa záani ðuuáza* open all the windows (04/28/95/LS/pc:okc; RBnB1-52; BE2.159).

••• *QU diáze* pull open (RR).

ðuuc?áke. v [sync., _ *ðuuc?áke*] *(trans.)* **be unable to do, fail at** (FH/07/02/01/pc). *ðíihą ðuuc?áki akxái* he is unable to lift it (02/27/95/JS/pc:ok; 04/06/95/FH/pc:okc; BE2.147). *brúuc?ake* I can't (FH/06/16/01/pc). *ąðúuc?ake* we can't (FH/06/16/01/pc). *ðiihą́ ðuuc?áke akxai* they can't lift it (RBn10-12:JW). *wáali óchiže škáaye, ąkóhkihkie ąðúuc?ake* you're making too much noise, we can't even converse (02/27/95/FH/pc; BE2.94). *waxpéį ąkái, ók?u ąðúuc?ake še nąąhtą́htąą oðúuc?ake wį* we're too poor to feed that lazy donkey (lit., 'we are poor, that donkey who was lazy, we are unable to feed him') (RBn10-2:MOJ/79). *íe ðuuc?áki apai* he is unable to speak. *hpéece škáaye ščuuc?ake tą, opíyą* if you can't start the fire, blow on it (FH/11/19/01/pc). *hpéece ščúuc?ake tą ópiyą ík?uca* if you can't start the fire, try blowing on it (FH/11/19/01/pc:prod). • **go set, as in a card game** (RBn10-21/JW). *brúuc?ake mąží* I didn't go set (RBn10-21/JW).

••• Cf. *óðuuc?ake.*

ðuuhépe. v [sync., *_ðuuhépe*] [*ðu-/ði-* INSTR + *hépe*] *(trans.)* **lighten, make lighter or smaller.**

••• Cf. *hkilúuhepe.*

ðuuhkáamą (variant: **ðuuhką́ąmą**). v [sync., *_ðuuhkáamą*] *(trans.)* **ring; ring the bell; press the doorbell.**

•• JOD (slip file): *ðuhkámą* <¢ü-ka´-ma^{n}> v. of *kamą*; to ring, as a bell, by pulling a rope. *íikahtamą brúhkamą hta mįkšé* <íḳatama^{n} p̣¢ukama^{n} ta-miñ´kci au> I will ring the bell. [Sentence-final <au> is not used in Modern Osage.]

ðuuhkíhkį (variant: **ðu(u)hkį́ki**). v [sync., _ *ðuuhkíhkį*] [possibly *ðu-/ði-* INSTR + *hkíhkįnį* (borrowed from English *kinky*?)] *(trans.)* **curl (as a person's hair); make curly.** *hpaxį́ ðuuhkíhkį apai* they're curling their hair (FH/4/17/96/tape,4/22/96/tape).

ðuuhpéece. N [*ðu-/ði-* INSTR + *hpéece*] **lighter, flashlight, match.** *htáwą ki ščée tą ðúuhpeece tóe aðį́li* when you go to town, bring back some matches (RBn12-07; BE2.85; 04/17/95/LS/pc:ok).

•• LFD 148: *ðihpece* <thi-pe-dse> a match (localism).

ðuuhúuce (variants: **ðuhúuce, ðúhuuce, ðíhuuce, ðuhúce**). v [sync., *_ðuhúuce*] [*ðu-/ði-* INSTR + *húuce*] *(trans.)* **pull down; lower by pulling (e.g., a window shade); take down, remove (from a high place such as a shelf or from the wall, such as pictures).** *oðókinąąžį́ ðuuhúuce* pull your pants down. *brúuhuuce* I took it down (FH/06/16/01/pc).

ðuuláwa. v [sync., *_ðuuláwa*] *(trans.)* **spread, spread out (e.g., a tarpaulin, a blanket, corn to be dried).** *ðuuláwa* spread it out (BE2.126; 03/14/95/FH/pc:ok).

•• LFD 146: *ðiláwa* <thi-gtha´-wa> to stretch a rope; to stretch. *brílawa weðįkše* <bthi´-gtha-wa we-thi^{n}-kshe> I stretched the rope. *ąðílawa pe weðįkše* <o^{n}-thi´-gtha-wa pe we-thi^{n}-kshe> [expected Mod. Os. form: *wéðį kše ąðúulawape*] we stretched the rope [lying there].

ðúulą. v [sync., *_ðúulą*] [*ðu-/ði-* INSTR + *ólą*] *(trans.)* **make angry** (FH: prod).

ðuuléke (variant: **ðuléke**). v [sync., *_ðuuléke*] [*ðu-/ði-* INSTR + *léke*] *(trans.)* **cause to break, cause to shatter; break or shatter with the hands (e.g., a dish, an egg, a lightbulb, a window)** (RBn22-03). *brúulekei* I shatter it. *ščúuleke* you shatter it. *ðuuléke* she shatters it. *ąðúuleke* we shatter it. *hįįcé ðuuléke che* someone broke a dish [and it's there to see] (01/07/95/FH/pc:ok). *okáhąpa ðuuléke chí áape* they said that that window is broken (01/07/95/FH/pc). *hcéhežį ðúuleke* they broke the dishes (FH/11/19/01/pc:prod). *aa* *ščúuleke* you broke your arm (04/19/95/FH/pc). *axíða áha, aa brúuleke* when I fell down, I broke my arm (04/19/95/FH/pc). *ðuuléka* break it in two (01/09/95/FH/pc:ok). *hpáata tóa ðuuléka* break some eggs (to cook) (01/09/95/FH/pc:ok; BE2.11).

ðuumą́ši (variant: **ðuumáši**). v [sync., *_ðuumą́ši*] [*ðu-/ði-* INSTR + *mą́ši*] *(trans.)* **pull up; hold up, raise, lift** (04/18/95/FH/pc:okc). *įché waléze ščúumaši hta nįkše* you'll hold up the picture. *okáhąpa ðuumáši!* raise the window! (BE2.79; (02/15/95/FH/pc:okc). *okáhąpa akáspe ðuumą́ši* raise the window shade.

ðuupxáðe. v [sync., *_ðuupxáðe*] *(trans.)* **find out (e.g., about s.o.'s activities); investigate (e.g., by questioning)** (FH:prod).

••• Cf. *waðúupxai, wáopxá.*

ðuusé. v [sync., _ *ðuusé*] [*ðu-/ði-* INSTR + *se* (root not found as an independent word)] *(trans.)* **cut (e.g., with scissors).** *hpáxį brúuse* I cut my hair (FH/07/09/01/pc).

ðuustáko. v [sync., _ *ðuustáko*] *(trans.)* **straighten; straighten out, arrange, tidy, tidy up; smooth out (e.g., one's clothes, icing on a cake, one's hair with a hand, comb, or brush, or the soil after planting seeds); straighten up (e.g., the rows when planting a garden)** (03/14/95/MREI/pc:ok; 02/27/95/FH/pc:ok). *wéhkilį ðuustáko* straighten up your clothes (BE2.92; 01/14/95/FH/pc:ok; 03/14/95/MREI/pc:ok; RBn2-moj/p20). *hci ðuustáko* straighten up the house (WHM981119; FH:ok). *hci ščúustako* you straightened up your house. *íe ðuustáko* straighten that word out (FH/11/19/01/pc:prod). *hpáxį ðuustáko* comb your hair (FH).

ðuušáake. v [sync., _ *ðuušáake*] *(trans.)* **pull out multiple (long?) pieces from or of s.t. (e.g., yank out all of one's hair); husk (corn), pick or pluck (a chicken), peel (a banana); strip, denude.** *hpáxį ðuušáake* pulling someone's hair out. *súhka ðuušáaka* pick/pluck the chicken! *htóžąke ðuušáaka* peel the bananas!

ðuušáwa. v [sync., *_ðuušáwa*] *(trans.)* **undress, take clothes off (another person or oneself)** (FH). [Despite its apparent meaning, the verb is not reflexive or suus in form.] *brúušawa hta mįkšé* I'm going to undress him. *brúušawa* I'm going to take these clothes off [myself].

•• LFD 148: *ðišáe* <thi-sha´-e> to divest, to undress. *bríšae* <bthi´-sha-e> I undress. *ąðišaape* <o^{n}-thi´-sha-a i> we undress. [If the LF forms are essentially correct, then *ðuušáwa* and *ðuušáwį* probably developed from *ðuušá-e* with epenthetic *w*.]

ðuušáwį. v [sync., *_ðuušáwį*] *(trans.)* **tie up; restrain by tying (e.g., a belligerent or uncontrollable person)** (RB, unconfirmed; FH rejects the translation 'tie up'); **take off a person's clothes (e.g., a child's clothing before a bath); undress s.o.; denude** (FH). *ðuušáwį* take off his clothes (FH/t116b).

ðuuškáke (variants: **ðuušká, ðúuška**). v [sync., _ *ðuuškáke*] *(trans.)* **untie (e.g., a horse).**

•• LFD 350: *ðušké* <thu-shke´> to untie a knot. LFD 28: *brúške į to* <bthu´-shke i^{n} do> [sentence-final *į to* is not used in Mod. Os.] I untie the knot. LFD 149: *ðiške* <thi-shke> to untie a knot. *bríške* <bthi´-shke> I untied the knot. *ąðíška pe* <o^{n}-thi´-shka i> we untied the knot.

ðuušką́ (variant: **ðiišką́**). v [sync., *_ðuušką́*] [*ðu-/ði-* INSTR + *šką́*] *(trans.)* **start (e.g., a car motor); place in operation.** *oðíhtą ðuušką́?* did he start the car? *oðíhtą ðuušką́ ðuuc?áki apai* he can't get his car started (FH/09/24/01/pc).

ðuuškí (variant of **ðiiškí**).

ðuušǫ́ (variant: **ðiišǫ́**). v [sync., *_ðuušǫ́*] *(trans.)* **bend one's limb or body part (e.g., leg or arm).** *žeká bríišǫ* I bend my leg (021083). *áa ą́ðiišǫpé* they bend my arm (021083). *šáake ðiisǫ́!* bend your hand! (021083 p4).

••• Cf. *ðiizó.*

ðuuštá. v [sync., *_ðuuštá*] [*ðu-/ði-* INSTR + *štáha*] *(trans.)* **make bald or bare, jerk s.o.'s hair out; denude.**

•• LFD 148: *ðistą́* <thi-sda´> to pull the grass until the ground becomes bare, to pluck the beard and eyebrows until the skin becomes bare.

••• Cf. *ðuuštáštai, hpeeštá.*

ðuuštáha. v [sync., *_ðuuštáha*] [*ðu-* INSTR + *štáha*] *(trans.)* **iron.** *hą́ąpa záani wabrúuštaha* I ironed all day.

••• Cf. *waðúuštaha.*

ðuuštáka. v [sync., *_ðuuštáka*] [presumably *ðu-/ði-* + *štáke*] *(trans.)* **calm** (FH:4/22/96/tape:ok).

ðuuštáke. v [sync., *ðuuštáke*] *(trans.)* **undress, relieve s.o. of clothing.** *ą́ðuštake* she undressed me. *ákahamį žúuce ðée pée ðuuštáke hta ðe?* who is going to undress that one with the red coat on? (refers to receiving a wedding coat when the drum is being paid for).

••• Cf. *ðuuštá, hkilúuštake.*

ðuuštáštai. v [sync., *_ðuuštaštai*] [reduplicated form, probably of *ðuuštá*] *(trans.)* **jerk hair out with repeated motion; make bald by plucking out hair over and over** (RB).

ðuušúpe (variant of **ðiišúpe**).

ðuutáaži (variants: **ðiitáaži, ðuatáaže** [HRE]). V [sync., _ *ðuutáaži*] [*ðu-/ði-* INSTR + *táaži*] *(trans.)* **turn off, switch off; extinguish.** *hpéece ðuutáaži, átahkai ðuutáaži* put out the fire and turn off the light (RBn HW).

•• LFD 36–37: *hpéce britaži ha* <pe´-dse bthi-da-zhi ha> [sentence-final *ha* is not used in Mod. Os.] I extinguished the fire. *hpéce ąðitaži pe* <pe´-dse oⁿ-thi-da-zhi i> we extinguished the fire.

ðuuwásu (variants: **ðuuwási, ðuuwássu**). V [sync., _*ðuuwásu*] *(trans.)* **clean up; cleanse; clean, disinfect (e.g., a buffalo hide)** (01/09/95/FH/pc:ok). *hcí ðuuwásu ðí* clean the house [sg. addressee] (BE2.19). *ðáące, waðílą, wašcúuwasupi tą* as you cleanse our hearts and minds. *haxį kóoci ščúuwasu tą wíe pašǫ́we* if you'll clean that oldtime blanket, I'll bind it (FH/11/19/01/pc:prod). *brúuwasu tą ðíe pašǫ́wa* if I clean it, you bind it (FH/11/19/01/pc:prod).

••• Cf. *hkilúuwasu, wasúhu.*

ðuuxǫ́ (variant of **ðiixǫ́**).

ðuuxpáðe (variant: **ðuuxpáði**). V [sync., _*ðuuxpáðe*] *(trans.)* **lose s.t.**

••• Cf. *lúuxpaðe, oxpáðe.*

ðuuxpáwį (variant of **ðuxpáwį**).

ðuuzáži. V [sync., _*ðuuzáži*] [*ðuuzé* + *aží* NEG] *(trans.)* **reject (lit., 'not take')** (01/31/95/FH/pc:okc).

•• LFD 145: *ðíza ži* <thi´-ça zhi> to reject. *brísa mąži* <bthi´-ça moⁿ-zhi> I reject. *ąðisa paži pe* <oⁿ-thi-ça ba-zhi i> we reject.

ðuuzé (variants: **ðúuze, ðuuzí**). V [sync., _*ðuuzé*] *(trans.)* **select, choose; take; get; draw (water), gather or pick (e.g., fruit).** *brúuze hta mįkše* I'm going to take it (03/07/95/FH/pc). *hkáące hį́šče tóe ðuuzá* help yourself to the peaches, take some peaches (03/07/95/FH/pc). *wį́xci ðuuzá* choose one (03/07/95/FH/pc; BE2.102). *ną́ye toa ðuuzá* get [take] some ice (01/31/95/FH/pc:okc). *íhkihkawi hpáaye ąži mązeska brúuze mįkšé* I exchanged it, but I took money (1/20/83/631; 04/13/95/FH/pc:ok). *hkáącezi záani ðuuzí akxái wáli wawálį akxai* she took all the oranges, she's really stingy (04/26/95/FH/pc). *níi ðúuza* draw water (FH; ok). *íe ðíhta wíbruuze hta mįkšé* I'll take your word for it (FH). *ðuuzá* take it away (FH/09/23/01/pc:prod). *žą́axe žį ðuuzái cʔéða xci* take a stick and just almost kill someone (FH:prod).

•• LFD 154: *ðuzé* <thu-çe´> to take; to receive or accept. *brúze* <bthu´-çe> I take. *ąðúza pe* <oⁿ-thu´-ça i> we take.

••• Cf. *kiðúuze, kilúuze, lúuze.*

ðuužá (variants: **ðužáawa, ðuužą́**). V [sync., _*ðuužá*] *(trans.)* **wash (e.g., dishes, parts of the body, food items, a car)** (03/16/95/JS/pc; FH:3/21/96). *šáake ðuužá hkǫ́bra* I want to wash my hands (03/16/95/JS/pc:okc). *hǫpái ðǫǫpái hį́ice wábruuža* I washed dishes twice today (03/16/95/JS/pc:ok). *hį́ice ški wábruuža* I washed dishes, too (RBn3-15). *oðíhtą wíhta akxa wasúhuži akxa hąðé ščúuža ðąąché?* my car is dirty, could you wash it this evening? (FH/06/26/01/pc). *ée ðuužá* wash this (RBnB1-50). *hǫbrį́ke ðuužá* wash those green beans (FH/06/16/01/pc). *sí ąðúuža* wash my feet (RB; 03/16/95/JS/pc:ok). *hkáące ðuužą́* wash the apples.

••• *KS yüžá* wash something (RR).

ðuužóži (variant of **ðiižóži**).

ðuwáštake (variant of **ðiwáštake**).

ðúwe. N **waist; diaphragm; rib cage** (BE2.150; 03/16/95/JS/pc:ok; WF).

•• LFD 150: *ðúwe* <thiu´-we> the waist; the body, from the armpits down to the hips (03/10/95/FH/pc:ok).

ðúwenie. N [*ðúwe* + *níe*] **pneumonia (lit., 'diaphragm hurt')** (BE2.105; 03/10/95/FH/pc:ok; BF/12/30/01).

ðuwį́ (variant: **ðúwį**). V [sync., _*ðuwį́*] *(trans.)* **buy.** *brúwį atxąhé* I am buying it. *brúwį hkǫ́bra ðį́ke* I don't want to buy it (01/09/95/FH/pc:ok). *brúwį ðąąché įké, mą́zeska éeną abrį mąží* I am unable to buy it, I don't have enough money (01/09/95/FH/pc:okc). *owé ðúwį brée* I'm going to buy groceries. *žį́káži hkáące wábruwį brée* I'm going to buy the kids some apples. *brúwį* I bought it. *brúwį hce* let me buy. *brúwį ðálį* I ought to buy. *wį́ ąðúwi ðáalį* we ought to buy one (108-b/FH/322). *brúwį hkǫ́bra ðį́ke* I don't want to buy it (01/09/95/FH/pc:ok). *hówaiki ščúwuį* where did you buy it? (BE2.15). *šcúwį?* did you buy it? *hkáące záani ąðúwį hce* let's buy all the apples. *waskú tóa ąðúwi ðáalį* we ought to buy some fruit. *sáhku wį ąðúwį hcé* let's buy a watermelon. *ðúwį* you buy it. *ðúwį įká* don't you buy it. *ðúwį ðį́ įká!* don't you buy it! (01/09/95/FH/pc:prod; FH/07/02/01/pc). *hpáze wanǫ́bre ówe brúwį ókxąži ąhé* I was slow buying groceries for supper (04/19/95/FH/pc:okc). *hpáze wanǫ́bre ówe ðuwį́ ókxąži ąhé* I was slow buying groceries for supper (04/19/95/FH/pc:okc).

•• LFD 151: *ðiwį* <thi-wi^n´> to purchase; to buy; to get by exchange of money for article. *bríwį* <bthi´-wi^n> I purchase. *hcíche brįwį hta ahtą hi o* <ṭsi´-tse bthi^n-wi^n ṭa a-ṭo^n hi o> [expected Mod. Os. form: *hcí che brúwį hta ątxáhe*; sentence-final *o* is not used in Mod. Os.] I will purchase a house. *hcíche scįwį hta ðahtą ši a?* <ṭsi´-tse stsi^n-wi^n ṭa tha-ṭo^n shi a?> [expected Mod. Os. form: *hcí che ščúwį hta ðatxáše?*] will you purchase the house?

••• Cf. *kíðuwį, lúwį, waðúwį.*

ðuxí. v [sync., *_ðuxí*] *(trans.)* **chase.** *šǫ́ke apa mąščį́ka ðuxí apai* the dogs were chasing the rabbits.

ðuxí (variant of **ðixí**).

ðuxpáwį (variant: **ðuuxpáwį**). v [sync., *_ðuxpáwį*] *(trans.)* **lift off; remove, take down (e.g., from a shelf or the back of a truck); unload** (FH/pc).

••• Cf. *oxpáðe.*

ðužáawa (variant of **ðuužá**).

ðužóži (variant of **ðiižóži**).

e, é

é (variant of **ðe** DECL, **ée**).

éąkiǫ. v [1st pl. of *ékiǫ*] *(trans.)* **we do.**

ecí. v [uninfl.] *(intr.)* **be present here/there, exist here/there; be at that time** (RBn12-10/MJ). *hową́ąiki ðǫǫpá ðáabrį náški ecíe akxa tą, wíe ée brį́ hta mįkšé na ée ešíe* wherever two or three only are, I will always be there, you said (citing a verse of the Christian Bible) (FH:prayer). *ecíke* the things that are there, these things [around] here. *táatą hǫ́ǫži ecíkie tą ékiǫ ðįkápai* if there's anything bad around, don't do that. *níi ecí hta* in the water there (RBn10-10:JW). *mǫ́žǫ ðáalį kši ðakši tą, níhkaši lą́ąðe tóa ecí akxai* when you get to that good land, there are some great men there [spoken to the deceased]. *táatą záani ecí che?* is everything there? (RBn12-11). *táatą záani ée ecí che?* is everything there [ready]? (04/26/95/LS/pc:okc). *óhką ecí che?* is there room over there? *omą́įhka haašíhta ecí che* same place as last year (03/20/95/FH/pc:okc). *ecí tą* if it's there. *ecíkie* they are around. *táatą hǫ́ǫžį ecíkie* there are bad things around; there is evil around. *ecí hta nįkšé?* will you be there? (1/2/132).

•• *ecí mąðį* <e-dsi´ mo^n-thi^n> go there. *ecí ži ðe ðįke* <e-dsi´ zhi the thi^n-ge> one who is never absent. *ecíhi* <e-dsi´-hi> when that happens, when I get there. *ecítxą* <e-dsi´-to^n> thence, from that place. *ecí txą ðeðe* <e-dsi´ to^n the-the> thenceforth. *eci, ha* <e-dsi, ha> thither.

éci. CONJ **and (in numbers only), plus.** *lébrą huužį́ ðǫǫpá éci wį́xci* two hundred and one (04/11/95/LS/pc:ok). *lébrą ðǫǫpá éci wį́xci* twenty-one (lit., 'twenty and one') (05/02/95/LS/pc). *éci wį́xci* plus one.

ecí che. VP [uninfl.] *(intr.)* **be definitely decided.** *žóąhkile ecí che* it's final that we're to be married. *ą́, ékiǫ ðe hta ché* okay, we'll do it (RBn17-p03).

••• Cf. *ðée hta ché.*

ecí mįkšé. VP **there where I am, my home (similar to French *chez moi*).** *ecí mįkšé ecí žówaðale ðalíe ðe* you brought them [people] home to me.

ecí pa. PRNP, ADVP **them, those who are there/here; there where they are, the place where they are/were, at their place or their home (similar to French *chez eux*).** *ecí pa žóąðale šíe ðe* you went with me to them, you brought me to them, to where they were, to their place.

ecíke (variant: **ecíkie**). v [uninfl.] **there are, there exist scattered around or dispersed.**

éðe (variant: **ée**). v [sync., *é_ðe*] *(trans.)* **think about, consider, believe** (RBn12-10mj). *mǫ́žǫ ðáalį kši, ecí ðakší ébre hta mįkšé* to that good land, I'm going to think that's where you went (back to). *súhka mį́ka čáahpažį, mąhį́ apa ohcíle ðáalįpe, ecíe ska ébre mįkšé* the little hen [said], hay is good for a nest, I'm thinking it's there (RBn19-04). *iihǫ akxa htážį ohtáza mǫ́žǫ záani éwa[ð]e* his mother thought that he was the most beautiful little deer in the world.

••• Cf. *ékiðe.*

éðǫǫpa (variant of **éeðǫǫpa**).

ée (variant: **é**). PRON **3rd person emphatic or contrastive pronoun (that one, that person, she/her, he/him; those persons, them; this [pragmatically obvious] person or thing; the**

ée *(continued)*
foregoing; she herself, he himself, they themselves). *ée kípą káaɣa* make her invite him. *ée wáapą káaɣa* make her invite them. *wihtéžį akxa ée akxai* this is my younger sister (RBn12-03p2). *ée ékimą* I did this (RBn22-06). *hową́įki wašcíhtą ðą́įše? ówehci ée é* where are you working? the grocery store, that's it (03/24/95/PM/pc:ok). *Maggie ée htá įkšé* it's Maggie's turn (lit., 'Maggie, *she's* going to be it'). *ée ékiǫ hta apai* he'll do it himself (RBn10-21/JW&FW/77). *ée ékiǫ apai* he's doing it himself (RBn10-21/JW&FW/77).
••• Cf. *tówa.*

ée. V [sync. h-stem, *é_(h)e*] *(trans.)* **say.** *šį́tožį íhkimąį híðe, iiðáðe hta mįkšé ée ðí áape* I will find it, said the boy who had come to visit (RBn19-05;CQ:okc). *ée eší áape* they said you said (FH 8/8/94/pc). *ðíe éwie mįkšé* I mean you [pointing at the person] (RBn10-18). *ešéše* you keep saying. *ékǫ ékipše mįkšé?* am I saying that right? (RB). *háakǫ įkšé ékipše škǫ́šta?* what is it you want me to say? (RB). *ékǫ ékiše* you said it right (RB). *háakǫta šée éše?* why did you say that? (RB). *wažážeíe šée ékia* say that in Osage (RBn11-02/JW&FW&HHsk/c.1976). *íiðaxopeži éše* you said that you didn't lie (RB). *našo "ąhái" áaapi* at least you all could say "yes" [speaking to women] (lit., 'leastways say "yes"!') (RB). *kóoci wažáži ée ékia nąpe* that's what old-time Osages used to say (RB). *Dave akxa íe ðįkí ape* Dave didn't say anything (RB). *ékie ðįká* don't say that (RB; CQc). *ší ékia* say that again (RB). *lúže íe* say it slow (RB). *wažážeíe háakǫ ešé nąpe?* how do you say that in Osage? (RB, CQ/okc/02). *haakǫ́ épše?* how do I say? (HH/14-a/172ff&pc). *haakǫ́ éeše?* how do you say? (HH/14-a/172ff&pc). *ðą́ące saakí káaɣapi ée nąpé* make your hearts strong, he used to say (RBn HW-MREI). *ée háakǫ ešé nąpé?* how do you say that? *įhtáci wahkǫ́ta, mą́žą ðáalį įkši ðaníhkaši nįkší eepe* our father, who art in heaven. • **ask or tell s.o. to do s.t.** *wižį́ke oðíhka hce épše* I asked Sonny to help you.
•• LF 40: *e* <e> to say. *epše* <e-pshe> I say. *eše* <e-she> you say. *eąkiðą pe* <e-o^{n}-gi-tho^{n} i> we said.
••• Cf. *ékie, hce ée.*

ée htáha. ADV **in the direction of, toward that direction, over there, along that way.** *Brian akxa mąąžą́ɣe tóa ðiiɣóɣo ną oðíhtą ci ée htáha* Brian keeps dragging those onions to put them in the car (RBn10-2:MOJ/79). • **toward that time, in that time, near that time.** *hǫ́ǫpa wį́ páðe ée htáha* one day toward winter, one winter day (RBn16-02).

ée htáhaži. ADJ, ADV **wrong, out of reason, unlikely, unsuitably, unreasonable, unreasonably; off the subject, pointlessly (lit., 'not toward there')** (RBn1-56). *ée htáhaži ékie* they are talking way off the subject (05/02/95/LS/pc). *í[e] htahaži íape* he talked wrong (LS: prod; BE2.143; 03/23/95/FH/pc:uk; RBn1-MOJ/p56; 03/23/95/FH/pc:uk). *ée htáha aži ékia* they're talking out of reason, way off the subject.

ée kše. PRONP [*ée* 'that one' + *kše* POSIT] **that one lying down (animate or inanimate).**

éeðǫǫpa (variant: **éðǫǫpa**). ADJ, PRON **group including just-mentioned individual(s) (can sometimes be translated as 'both', 'all', 'and another', 'and others', or as 'and I' when followed by a verb with 1st pl. inflection).** *wižǫ́a éeðǫǫpa ąkáhi* sister and I went over there (lit., 'sister and another we went there') (01/31/95/FH/pc:prod orig). *háachi wižį́ke wisǫ́ka éeðǫǫpa ąkaazą ąkai* wisǫ́ka [my younger brother] and I are always bawling out Sonny [*wižį́ke*]. *Stephanie, David, éeǫǫpa ąkále hta ąkáðe* Stephanie, David, and I are going home. *Jane, Ann éðǫǫpa mąžą́ hta íihkimai ahíe ðí áape* Jane and Ann had come to visit the farm (FH). *šǫ́ke wíhta akxa hkáwa, hceeská éðǫǫpa owákaša nąpé* my dog takes care of horses and cows (RBn12-03). *kį́įkįįežį hlaaskážį éeðǫǫpa ǫ́ǫðe aðáape* he went leaving [both] the flowers and butterflies behind (RBn15-03). *hkóða éeðǫǫpa ąkáðe ąðįkšé* my friend and I are going.
•• LFD 89: *hkóða eðǫpa* <ķo´-tha e-tho^{n}-pa> my friend and I [rather, '(my) friend and another (not necessarily I)'].

éehna (variant of **eená**).

éehtaną (variant of **éetana** [possibly future form]).

eekǫ́ (variant of **ékǫ**).

eekǫ́ ðįké. ADJ **unsound; not right; wayward.** *waðílą eekǫ́ įkí apai* his mind isn't right; he's wayward (FH/pc). *ókʔą eekǫ́ įké* wayward deeds, acts that are not right or suitable.
••• Cf. *waðílą eekǫ́ įké.*

éekxą (variant of **éetxą**).

eená (variants: **éena, éhna, éehna, eeną́**). V [inalien.] *(intr.)* **be the only (one).** *wahkǫ́ta akxa eená hta akxa ną, hpahą́le mę́į, ahkílaðįpai* soon it will be only God, put him first, carry yourself that way (04/04/99/FH/pc). *ðée eeną́ aape* they said it's the only way (lit., 'that is the only one, they said') (RBn10-21/JW&FW/77). *winą́* it is only I. *ðiną́* it is only you. *eená/eeną́* it is only she. *ąkóną* it is only we. • PRONP **therefore, that's why** (RBn3-02). *hąącí opáwįye pšíe, éena įštáha cˀóka* I went riding last night, that's why I'm sleepy. *šímižį ókülą kǫ́ða tą, éena htą́wąkši pšíe* the girls want some clothes, that's why I went to town. *céepe hpíiži kšíape waðáahtą štą éhna* he has a bad liver because he's always drinking. *šímižį apá įcé káaye éena wáli wascúutape* the girls put on their makeup, that's why they're very slow (BE2.137). • **that only.** *éena ą́tąhe mįkšé* that's the only thing that pleases/satisfies me. • ADJ **enough.** *brúwį ðąąché įké, mą́zeska éeną abrį́ mąží* that's enough, I am unable to buy it, I don't have enough money (12/30/94/FH/pc:ok; 01/09/95/FH/pc:okc).

eeną́tǫįpe (variant: **eeną́ˀtǫ́įpi**). N **Looking Only at Her, Look Only at Her (name for a second daughter in *hcížo* clan)** (HRE/pc/12/02). [Name of Jo Ann Shunkamolah Alred.]

eeną́ži. ADJ [*eená* + *aží* NEG] **insufficient, not enough.** *mą́zeska éenąži akxai* there's not enough money (FH/09/23/01/pc). *mą́zeska sáhta ąkˀú kǫ́ða akxai, ąži éenąąžį́ akxai* he wanted to give me five [dollars] but he didn't have enough (lit., '. . . but it was insufficient') (FH/09/23/01/pc). *mą́zeska ąkáaye ąkóða akakxái ąži htóožu éenąąžį́ káayi akxai* we wanted to make some money, but he didn't make enough meat pies (FH/09/23/01/pc).

eeną́ˀtǫ́įpi (variant of **eeną́tǫįpe**).

éepe (variant of **áape**). REPORTATIVE **they/he or she said, it is said, known by hearsay.**

éeše. INTERJ **golly (slang)** (04/06/95/FH/pc:ok; RBn2-MOJ/p5).

eeškí (variant of **éški**).

eeškítą (variants: **eeškíta, eeškí, éeški**). PRON **he/she too, it too, they too** (02/09/95/FH/pc:okc; BE2.67). *nǫ́ǫ apa eeškíta íixa apa* the grownups laughed too (lit., 'the grownups, they too laughed') (RBn10-2:MOJ/79). *wihé oáhką eeškítą ąwą́hką nąpé* when I help second daughter, she helps me (2-1-G).

•• RB: <eh-shkí>.

•• LFD 41, 132: *eški* <e-shki>, *eškí* <e-shki´> he, she, or it too.

••• Cf. *ški.*

éetana (variants: **éetąną, éehtaną**). CONJ **that is why, therefore, thus, so** (FHt#128). *opáwįye pšíe éetana ą́škike* I went riding and that is why I'm tired (LH 07/18/96:tape). *hką́ącezi ánǫbre ážu nąpé éetana brúwį* they usually put oranges on the table, that's the reason I bought some (FHt#128). *éwahkikˀǫ akxai, éetana ðakˀéðe įká* don't pity him because he did it himself (FHt#128). *hobrį́ke oowáhą hta mįkšé kasį́, éehtaną hą́ðe brúuwasú hta nį́ oowážu hta* I'm going to cook beans tomorrow, therefore tonight I'll clean them and put them in water.

éetxą (variants: **éetxa, éetkxą, éekxą**). V [uninfl.] *(intr.)* **it is time.** *ðǫ́ha éetkxąpe* it's almost time (03/22/95/FH/pc:ok). *waachí ðǫ́hą éetkxąpe* it's almost time to dance (03/22/95/FH/pc:ok). *hápa óožu éetkxą akxái* it's time to plant corn (03/22/95/FH/pc:okc; BE2.141). • N **time, the moment for s.t.** *ónalį, étkxą akxa ahí akxai* hurry up, it is time (lit., 'hurry, the time has arrived') (03/22/95/FH/pc:ok; 03/22/95/FH/pc). • ADV **when (lit., 'at the time that').** • PRON **that (standing animate).**

•• LFD 40: *etxą* <e-do^{n}> when. (Frequently found in rituals.)

éewǫ (variant: **éewą**). V [3rd sg. of *éǫ*] *(trans.)* **he does (it), he did (it)** (FHt#128:prod).

éeži (variant: **éži**). ADJ **odd, unusual, of a different kind, inappropriate, unsuitable** (03/02/95/FH/pc:okc); **different, other, otherwise, strange.** *tówa níhka hpá éeži apái* that man has an odd-looking nose (lit., 'that one man is characterized by an odd nose') (03/02/95/FH/pc:okc; BE2.97). *bra éži* smells odd (04/06/95/LS/pc:ok; BE2.124). *kį́kįežį hį́į éži kíhǫpe* he liked the different colors of the butterflies (RBn15-02). *brą́ éeži* [he/she/it] smells strange (03/02/95/FH/pc). *súhkahtą́ą mį́įka éžipa wáðihota įkše ípahǫ įkši aape* turkey hen knew she had done everything she could to fool the others (RBn19-05). *éžiški húheka* the others [also] who are sick.

•• LFD 42: *éži* <e´-zhi> not that kind. *éži kaye* <e´-zhi ga-xe> to make different. *éži hpaye* <e´-zhi p̣a-xe> I made different. *éži škaye* <e´-zhi shka-xe> you made different. *éži ąkaya pe* <e´-zhi o^{n}-ga-xa i> we made different. *éži hkihkaye* <e´-zhi ḳi-ḳa-xe> to disguise one's self. *éži ahkihpaye ha* <e´-zhi a-ḳi-p̣a-xe ha> [sentence-final *ha* is not used in Mod. Os.] I disguised myself. *éži ðahkiškaye ha* <e´-zhi tha-ḳi-shka-xe ha> [sentence-final *ha* is not used in Mod. Os.] you disguised yourself. *eži ohką́ci* <e-zhi o-ḳo^{n}´-dsi> separate, distinct, belonging to another class.

éhkiǫ. V [sync. nasal vowel stem, *éhki_ǫ*] [*hkik-* REFL + *éǫ*] **do to oneself, do s.t. without listening to advice, "go overboard," doing s.t. to excess while paying no heed to others** (FHt#128). *éehkižǫe, éetana ðakʔéðe océ į̨ká* you did it yourself so don't look for pity (FHt#128).

••• Cf. *éwahkikʔǫ.*

éhna (variant of **eená**).

éhtaha. PPN **toward** (FH:t119a).

ehtą́. INTERJ **well.** *ehtą́, ówǫ hta mįkšé* well, I'll be busy (RBn2-MOJ/p20). *éhtą, ąkáaži hta mįkšé* well, I'll drive (RBn10-12:JW).

ékene. N **Aiken (surname).** *ékene akxa hkáwa žúuce níðape* Aiken gave the red horse away (words to Aiken song) (BE2.55).

ékiðe. V [sync., *éki_ðe*; inflection may be absent in 1st pl. form] [possibly *ki-* DAT or INCEPTIVE + *éðe*] **think about, consider, think so.** *ékibra mąžíe* I don't care to, I don't want to (lit., 'I don't think that'). *ąkóe ékiðaapažíe* we don't think so (RBn15-01). *ékiðe ąkáðe* we [three or more] are thinking about doing it. *ékibre įké* I don't care to, I don't want to. *ékištaži nįkšé* you don't think so.

ékie. V [sync. h-stem, *éki_(h)e*] [*ki-* DAT + *ée* 'say'] *(trans.)* **say.** *šee ékia ąkái* that's what we said (LS:prod). *ékie ée ðe* they said he's saying that (FH:prod). *ekíape* they said. *ékie ðįká!* don't say that! *ée ékiapi ó* [archaic form; Mod. Os. would have final *ape* rather than *api ó*] he said it [man's way of speaking] (RBn22-06). *éąkie* we say (FH/09/11/01/pc). *íe tóa ékipše hta, ówaštake hkǫ́bra* I'm going to say something, I want you to tell them (RBn10-15). *óohǫ akxa toská ðįké ée ée akxa* the cook says there are no potatoes (03/05/95/JS/pc:ok). *éekiða! wažážeíe haakǫ éše nąpé?* say it! how do you say that in Osage? [*éekiða* = *ékie* + *a* IMPERATIVE MARKER; *ð* is epenthetic] (RBn12-11; 03/05/95/JS/pc:ma). *wažážeíe šée ékia!* say that in Osage! • *(intr., trans.)* **talk for another, talk in the presence of others.** *wihtáeži akxa íe tóa ékipše kǫ́ða akxai* my little sister wants me to say a few words [for her] (RBn23-17). *íiǫǫška záani íe tóa ékipše hta atxą́he* all you *ilǫ́ǫška* [drumkeeper and committee], I'm going to say a few words (BE2.132). *ékipše* I said (03/15/95/PM/pc:ok; 03/16/95/JS/pc:ok). *ékiše* you said (03/15/95/PM/pc:ok; 03/16/95/JS/pc:ok). *éki[e] akxá* he's saying it (03/15/95/PM/pc). *ékie ðįká* don't say that (03/15/95/PM/pc:okc; 03/16/95/JS/pc:uk). *ši ékia* say it again (03/15/95/PM/pc:ok; 03/16/95/JS/pc:ok). *kóoci wažáže ékie nąpé* old-time Osages used to say (FH:5/01/96/tape: *óo;* 03/05/95/JS/pc:ok). *íe tóe ékipše hkǫ́bra* I want to say something [a few words] (03/05/95/JS/pc:ok).

ékimą. V [1st sg. of *ékiǫ*] **I do.**

ékiǫ. V [sync. nasal vowel stem, *éki_ǫ*] [apparently *ki-* DAT + *éǫ* (but pronominal prefixes unexpectedly follow *ki-*)] *(trans.)* **do s.t. (in the presence of others or for others), proceed or go ahead with s.t. (in the presence of others or for others).** *ékimǫ/ékimą* I do it. *ékižǫ/ékižą* you do it. *ékiǫ/ékią* she does it. *éąkiǫ/eą́kiǫ/éąkią/eą́kią* we do it. *ékiǫpe* he did it (RBn10-2). *ši ékiǫ* do it again (RBn10-2). *haakǫ́ta ékižǫ?* why did you do that? (RBn; HW). *ekiǫ́!* go ahead and do it! *ékimą na* I do that/I do it that way (04/11/95/FH/pc). *ðée ékižǫ na?* did you do this? (04/11/95/FH/pc:okc). *ékimą* I did this (04/11/95/FH/pc:ok). *ékiǫ ðįká* don't do it (04/11/95/FH/pc:okc). *ékiǫpi* go ahead and do it [pl. addressee]. • **can, be able to.** *ékimą* I can do it (lit., 'I do').

•• LFD 40: *ékiǫ*<e´-gi-o^n> to do so. *ékiwaǫ* <e´-gi wa-o^n> he does so to them (unconfirmed; 04/11/95/FH/pc:incorrect)).

ékitxą. MODAL [*ki-* INCEPTIVE + *etxą́*] **it's time again.**

••• Cf. *mį́įǫpa wahkǫ́ta ižį́ke iitáe ékitxą* December (lit., 'it's time again for the month when God's son was born').

ékižǫ. V [2nd sg. of *ékiǫ*] **you do.**

ékǫ (variant: **eekǫ́**). ADV, ADJ **like, similar to; like that; likewise, similarly.** *kį́į ékǫ wáli hkǫ́brai, htáažį akxa ékiape* "if only I could fly like that," the little deer said (RBn15-02). *wiškítą šée ékǫ brį́e* me too, I'm just like that (RBn17-p03). *ékǫži žą akxai* he doesn't believe it; he believes it's otherwise (lit., 'not like that he believes') (RBn17-p03). *ékǫ káaye* make it like that (FH:prod). *mą́žą ðekáha táatą́ ékǫ ðįkí akxai* there's nothing like it here on earth (RBn10-2). *haxį́ kóoci ščuuwasu tą wíe pašǫ́wį, hcéka ée ékǫ hta akxai* if you will clean that old [striped] blanket, I'll bind it and it will be like new (FH/11/19/01/pc:prod). *hǫ́ǫe ékǫ* somebody like her (RBn17-p03). *žáže ðíhta akxa ðáalįe, žúoka ékǫ aščíe* your name is pretty and your body is likewise (RBn17-p01). *ékǫ kǫ́ða apa, ékǫ waðákšiye hkǫ́bra* whatever they want, fix it for them (lit., 'like that they want it, like that you make it for them, that I want') (RBn22-10). *eekǫ́ kǫ́ða tą* what he wants to do

(04/11/95/FH/pc:prod). • **somewhat, kind of, rather, slightly, a bit.** *ooláaži ékǫ kíe* he is somewhat lacking. • **right, correctly, correct, appropriate, appropriately, that is right, true! correct!, that's the way!** (RBn1:40). *ekǫ́xci* just right, exactly right. *ékǫ žaamí* I think it's right (PM). *ékǫ žaaži* you think it's right (PM; RBn1-40). *ékǫ ékiše* you said it right (RBn10-2:MOJ/79). • CONJ **thus, therefore.** *brúwį hkǫ́bra ekǫ táatą éhpaahą* I made him a proposition (lit., 'I wanted to buy it, therefore I raised something'). • V [uninfl.] *(intr.)* **mean, signify.** *éčoǰi mǫškó nihkáši íe 'htáažį' ékǫ akxai* Echogee in the Creek language means 'little deer'. • **happen, be so.** *óðąži ékǫ ží hta akxái* anyway it's never going to happen (lit., 'anyway, it will not be so') (04/17/95/LS/pc:okc; RBn1-MOJ/p28). • **(be) as . . . as.** *mą́ąɣe htóho ékǫpe* he was as blue as the sky (RBn15-01).

••• Cf. *ékǫži, waðílą eekǫ́ įké.*

ékǫ ðaacé. VP [sync., *ékǫ _ðaacé*] **say s.t. right or correctly.** *ékǫ štáace* you said it right; you named it right (RBn10-6:JW).

ékǫ kǫ́ðaaži. VP [sync. fortisizing stop stem + sync., *ékǫ _kǫ́_ðaaži*] [*ékǫ* + *kǫ́ða* + *ažíNEG*] **be sorry about being a certain way, not want to be a certain way.** *ékǫ bríe ąži ékǫ hkǫ́bra mąži* that's the way I am but I don't want to be that way (this phrase is the closest Osage equivalent to "I'm sorry" [FH]).

ékǫ ska. VP [uninfl.] **I guess that's right.**

••• *KS šéeyǫska* that size, it was that big (RR).

ekǫ́įke. ADJ, ADV [*ékǫ* 'appropriate'+ *ðįké* NEG] **crazy, crazily, inappropriately, unsuitably.** *John akxa íe ekǫ́įke étana nǫ́ǫahpe* John talks crazy so I'm afraid [of him] (FH). *waðílą ekǫ́įkí apai, ðekǫ́ǫci áhkihtǫpa ðį* there are crazies around, now watch out for yourself. • ADV **off, not where or how it is supposed to be, off target, out of line, incorrectly** (108-b/fh/078; 04/17/95/LS/pc). *ekǫ́įke íðae nįkšé* you're talking off the subject.

••• Cf. *ekǫ́xci.*

ékǫska ha. ADJ, N **make-believe** (RBn23-22, unconfirmed).

ekǫ́xci. ADJ, ADV [*ékǫ* + *xci*] **correct, correctly.**

•• LFD 40: *ekǫ́xci* <e-go^{n}´-xtsi> exact, precise, downright, real, in reality (03/02/95/FH/pc:ok; 04/17/95/LS/pc:ok).

ékǫži (variant: **ekǫ́ži**). V [uninfl.] [*ékǫ* + *aží* NEG] *(intr.)* **not be like this or that, be not thus, be otherwise** (RBn17-p03). *šée ékǫžie* it's not that way (RBn3-22). *ékǫži [a]žą́ą akxai* he doesn't believe it (lit., 'he believes it's otherwise') (RBn17-p03). • ADJ **unseemly, inappropriate, not right, unsuitable, unfitting, ill-advised, wrong** (RBn10-21/JW; FW/77). *ekǫ́ži mįkšé* I'm not right (RBn10-21/JW&FW/77). *šíi akxa ekǫ́ži akxai* he's not right (RBn10-21/JW&FW/77). *hǫ́ǫpa wį súhka tóoka ókˀą ékǫži káaɣe nąpe* sometimes the rooster did things he shouldn't do (lit., '. . . things that were unsuitable') (RBn18-01).

ékǫžie ska. ADJP **improbable (lit., 'not thus I suppose').**

•• LFD 40 (unconfirmed): *ékǫ aži eską* <e´go^{n} a-zhi e-çko^{n}> improbable.

émą. V [1st sg. of *éǫ*] **I do.**

émąhta (variant: **ámąhta**). ADV **that way, that direction (lit., 'toward the other').**

émąhtaži. ADV [*émąhta* + *aží* NEG] **the other way.**

émąhtažíha. ADV [*émąhtaži* + *ha* PPN] **not toward that way.** *émąhtaži ha!* not toward that way! toward the other way! (implying 'turn this way instead'; expression used while getting everybody sitting in the correct way in a peyote meeting [RB]) (BE2.146; CQokc; 04/04/95/FH/pc:okc).

••• Cf. *ímąhtaha.*

éǫ. V [sync. nasal vowel stem, *é_ǫ*] *(trans.)* **do (not in the presence of others or for others).** *éwǫ iiðáðe* I saw them do it (RBn22-06). *éwǫpe* he did this (RB: <éh-wo^{n} pí-ah>, with archaic *pía* instead of Mod. Os. *pe*) (04/11/95/FH/pc:okc). *émą/émǫ* I do. *éžą/éžǫ* you do. *éǫ/éwǫ* he does, they do. *ðíe éwažǫ* you did that [*ðie é-wa-žǫ*]. *pée éwǫ?* who did that? [*pee é-wa-ǫ*]. *wí wamǫ́e* I did that.

••• Cf. *éhkiǫ, ékiǫ.*

ešéše. V [2nd sg. of *ée* 'say', reduplicated] **you keep (on) saying.** *ešéše* you keep saying it. *ée ešéše* you keep saying that (FH).

éški. ADV, ADJ **else; also, otherwise.**

•• LFD 41: *eškí* <e-shki´> he, she, or it too.

••• Cf. *ðiškítą, eeškítą, howachéeški, howaðéeški, péeški, ški.*

étą. CONJ **therefore.** *étą ąkále htai* we should go home now (lit., 'therefore we go, let's us') (RBn10-12:JW).

•• LFD 40: *etǫ́* <e-do^{n}´> therefore.

etxą́. ADV **still.** *įtíla ąðįkšé hta akxai mą́žą įké etxą́* we will still be gossiping when the world ends. • V [uninfl.] *(intr.)* **it is time** (MSB).

••• Cf. *ékitxą.*

éwahkikˀǫ. V [reg., *éwa_hkikˀǫ́*] [*wa-* VAL + *hkik-* REFL + *éǫ*] **do to oneself** (RB; FHt128a,b).

éwahkikˀǫ́ akxai he did it to himself (RBn10-4:MOJ/79; FH/11/17/01/pc; FHt#128). *éwaahkikˀǫ́* I did it to myself (FH/11/17/01/pc). *éwaðahkikˀǫ́* you did it to yourself (FH/11/17/01/pc).

••• Cf. *wéhkikˀǫ.*

éwahkiǫ́ðe. V [uninfl./reg.+sync., *éwa_hkiǫ́_ðe*] [contains *hkik-* REFL] *(intr.)* **get oneself into s.t. by oneself.** *éwahkiǫ́ðe* we did it to ourselves (02/01/95/FH/pc:prod orig; 03/09/95/MREI/pc:ok/ma). *éwaðahkiǫšce* you got your own self into something.

••• Cf. *ohkíǫðe.*

éwažį. ADV **alone, by oneself, on one's own** (HRE/12/29/01/pc:ok).

éwažį nąąke (variants: **éwaži nąąke, áwažįka nąąke**) N **automobile, car (lit., 'it runs by itself')** (FH/09/21/01/pc; HRE/12/29/01/pc:ok). [An archaic expression.] *éwažį nąąki akxai* the car is running by itself (RBn1-40; FH/09/21/01/pc).

• ADV **by car.**

éži (variant of **éeži**).

éži wį. PRON **another one, a different one.** *hǫ́ǫpa ókaayeįki tą htą́wą ki abrį́bree hta akxai ší éži wį waðíhta hpíǫ ke wį íhkihkawi hta mįkšé?* on Saturday, what if I take him to town and trade him for another one that knows how to work? (RBn10-2:MOJ/79; CQ: okc).

éžixci. ADJ [*éži + xci*] **unique (lit., 'different indeed'), odd-looking, funny-looking, appearing different or abnormal (e.g., a person who has fever)** (04/26/95/FH/pc:ok)**; changeable** (04/06/95/PM/pc). *tówa akxa éžixci akxái, lǫ́ði akxa ska* he looks funny [different] so he must be drunk (04/26/95/FH/pc). *áa éžixci, žeká ški éžixci, hóo ški éžixci, íhį įįcé ohkáska éžixcį aščį́e* you have funny arms and funny legs and a funny voice and a funny-looking moustache in the middle of your face (RBn17-p01).

•• LFD 42: *éži xci* <e´-zhi xtsi> singular, unlike.

éžǫ. V [2nd sg. of *éǫ*] **you do.**

ɣ

ɣaaké. V [reg., *_ɣaaké*] *(intr.)* **cry** (01/14/95/FH/pc). *ɣaaké wáhpaaɣe* I made them cry (RBn2-MOJ/p24; 01/14/95/FH/pc:okc). *ɣaaké įká* don't cry. *ɣaaké akxa* he/she is crying. *ɣaaké ą́škáaɣe* you made me cry. *ɣaaké wihpáaɣe* I made you cry. *ɣaaké ðikáaɣe* he/they made you cry. *ɣaaké kaašéną* enough crying, stop crying (HH). *awáata šǫ́ mįkšé, záani ɣaaké wáhpáaɣe* while I was praying, I made them all cry (01/14/95/FH/pc:ok; BE2.28).

•• JOD (slip file): *ɣake* <xa-ḳe> to cry or weep.

•• LFD 217: *ɣaké* <xa-ge´> to weep, to cry, lamentation. *áɣake* <a´-xa-ge> I weep. *ðáɣake* <tha´-xa-ge> you weep. *ąɣáka pe* <o^{n}-xa´-ga i> we cry or weep.

••• *OP ɣagé* cry.

ɣáɣaka. ADJ **rough (e.g., chapped hands or any rough surface).**

•• JOD: *ɣáɣaka* <xa´-xa-ḳa> rough, as a file, chapped hands.

ɣį (variant: **xį́**). ADJ **light in color** (BE2.88). *įįštáxį/įįštáɣį* white person (lit., 'light eyes') [*įįštá + xį́*] (FH/09/25/01/pc).

••• *DAK ɣi* dark brown.

ɣépe (variant of **xépe**)

ɣoį́ (variants: **ɣowį́, xoį́**). V, ADJ [stat., *_ɣoį*] **stink, (be) stinky, it stinks!, phew!, malodorous, have a fetid odor or offensive smell (worse than *žą́xta*); vocative derogatory exclamation (e.g., to an offensive drunk person).** *si ąɣoį́* my feet stink (RBn12-08; WF/12/30/01, 03/14/95/MREI/pc:okc).

•• LFD 22: *ɣwį* <xwi^{n}> fetid, offensive smell.

ɣówe. N **noise** (PM).

ɣǫ́ǫce. ADJ **sloppy, slouchy, unkempt, messed up** (9/4/94/FH/p.c.). *wéhkilį ɣǫ́ǫci* his clothes are all messed up (wrinkly, etc.) (FH/11/19/01/pc:prod). *ɣǫǫce tǫ́pewai* you look sloppy, something makes you look sloppy (FH:prod). *ɣǫ́ǫce ðiká* don't be sloppy (FH:prod). *žįkážį ɣǫ́ǫce hcí ci achípi wahkǫ́bra įké* I don't want sloppy children to come to my home (BE2.123).

h

ha. PPN **through (direction), along a path, in a direction, by way of.** *howaįkíha bree?* how do I get there? (lit., 'through where do I go?') (t#14b-p4; 04/26/95/FH/pc:uk). *háakǫ kšíha brée?* how will I get there? (04/26/95/FH/pc). *šeðóha* that way. *okahą́ąpa cí ecíha óhpepi áape* the house has been broken into (lit., 'through the window the house had been entered, they said') (05/01/95/FH/pc). *owé che ðáabrį ha káaɣa* make three piles of groceries (lit., 'make the groceries into three piles'). • **from.** *ðetkxą́ha haakǫ́ éepše che ékǫ hkǫ́bra* from now on, I want it to be like I've said (03/22/95/FH/pc). *ðetkxą́ha ~ ðetxą́ha* from here on, from now on.

ha. DECL **declarative.** [Archaic or incorrect, not heard in Modern Osage.]

•• LF 80: *nąpé ðiskike íðachį ha* <no^{n}-be´ thi-çki-ge i´-tha-tsi^{n} ha> [sentence-final *ha* is not used in Mod. Os.] you struck him with the fist. [This sentence-final *ha* may be Omaha (FH).]

há. INTERJ **well (often precedes a statement or command).** *há wanǫ́brepi* well, go ahead and eat (RBn11-02/JW&FW; HH/pc/c.1976).

••• Cf. *hą́ą* (possibly the same word).

háa. N **hide, skin of an animal, rind, fabric, cloth.** *céɣenii háa* drum hide. *htáahaa* hide, skin, deerskin (WHM981022; CQokc). • **surface(?).** *niiháa htóho ékǫ* blue [as distinct from green] [*niiháa* = *níi* 'water' + *háa* 'surface'?] (RB, unconfirmed; 01/07/95/FH/pc:uk).

•• LFD 56: *ha* <ha> skin of any animal; the bark of a tree; shell of nuts; cuticle.

••• Cf. *ópxąhaa, walúška háa šooká, wašį́haa.*

háa šooká. NP **thick skin, exoskeleton.**

••• Cf. *walúška háa šooká.*

háabrehka. N [*háa* + *bréhka*] **ribbon (lit., 'thin cloth')** (RBn1-44; FH).

háachi (variant: **háchi**). ADV **all the time, every time, continually, repeatedly, always.** *ónǫbre háachi ąðįchí apai* they keep on bringing food. *žįkážį háachi ąkązą ąkai* we boss the kids around every time. *háachi wižį́ke wisǫ́ka éeðǫǫpa ąkáazą ąkai* we're always bawling out Sonny and my brother. *háachi wižį́ke wisǫ́ka éðǫpa ąkáazą ąkái* we're always bawling out Sonny and younger brother.

háaðaską. INTERR/INDEF ADV **how big, how small.** *háaðaską́ įkšé?* how big/small is it?

haakǫ́ (variant: **háakǫ**). INTERR/INDEF ADV **how much.** *haakǫ́ wažáže?* how much Osage are you? • **whatever.** *haakǫ́ kǫ́ða tą* whatever he wants to do (04/11/95/FH/pc:prod). *haakǫ́ háažǫ* whatever you do (FH/06/25/01/pc, length and stress confirmed). *ðíe, haakǫ́ éše škǫ́šta tą ékia!* just say whatever you want to! • **how.** *haakǫ́hce* how [in the future] (02/09/95/FH/pc:okc). *háakǫ kǫ́ða apa, ékǫ ékima hta mįkšé* however they want it, that's how I'm going to do it (RBn10-21/JW&FW/77). *šé, háakǫ [e]šé nǫpe?* how do you say this? [regarding something near hearer] (RBn12-11) *ée háakǫ ešé nąpé?* how do you say that? • **which way.** *háakǫ ðée?* which way did they go? where did they go? (RBn1-23). • INTERR/INDEF V [uninfl.] **be how.** *haakǫ́ įkšé?* how are they? [of people sitting] (FH). *háakǫ nįkše?* how are you? (02/09/95/FH/pc:ok). *háakǫ žą́kšé?* how are you? [to someone lying down] (02/09/95/FH/pc:ok). *háakǫ ðatkxąšé?* how are you? [to someone standing] (02/09/95/FH/pc:okc; BE2.69). *mą́ąɣe háakǫ che áši?* what's it [the weather] like outside? (03/22/95/PM/pc:prod). • INTERR/INDEF PRON **what.** *háakǫ?* what do you want? (RBn1-23; 04/28/95/LS/pc:ok). *háakǫ?* what is it? (RBn1-23; 04/28/95/LS/pc:ok). *háakǫ che?* what is it? (04/28/95/LS/pc:ma). *hą́akǫ?* what's the matter? (04/28/95/LS/pc:ma). *háakǫpe?* what's the matter? (RB, unconfirmed). *háakǫ įkše ékipše škǫ́šta?* what is it you want me to say? (RBn10-22/JW&FW). • **what is wrong with.** *háakǫ nįkšé, táatą nįkšé?* what's wrong with you, what are you doing? (RBn12-11).

•• LFD 58: *hákoe* <ha´-go-e> what has happened?

háakǫta. INTERR/INDEF ADV **why.** *háakǫta íišcewai ðąįšé?* why are you dressed up? *haakǫ́ta Jóhna haxį́ wakʔú ðe?* why did John give the blankets away?

haakxą́, háakxą (variants of **háatxą**).

haakxą́ci (variant of **haatxą́ci**).

haakxą́ta, haakxǫ́ta (variants of **haatxą́ta**).

haaléžowaake. N [*háa* + *léže* + *óðaake*] **handkerchief, scarf, neckerchief (lit., 'spotted cloth for telling folks things', but not necessarily actually spotted).** *haaléžowáake ąwą́xpaðe mįkše* I have lost my handkerchief (04/11/95/LS/pc:ok; BE2.63).

haaléžowaake (*continued*)

•• RB: <hah-léh-zho-áh-keh>.

•• LFD 58: *haléže waðake* <ha-gthe´-zhe wa-tha-ge> handkerchief. *haaléže waðáake ąwą́xpaðe mįkše o* <ha-gthe´-zhe wa-tha-ge o^{n}-wo^{n}-xpa-the mi^{n}-kshe o> I lost my handkerchief.

háamą (variant: **haamą́**). INTERR/INDEF VP [1st sg. of *háaǫ*] **what I do, whatever I do, what did I do.**

háaną (variants: **háana, hą́ąną**). INTERR/INDEF ADJ **how many, how much** (02/13/95/FH/pc:ok). *mą́zeska háaną ašcį́ nįkšé?* how much money do you have? *háaną che?* how many are there? how much is there? (02/09/95/FH/pc:okc). *háaną pa?* how many [people or things] are there? *mį́į oðaake háaną che?* what time is it? (02/09/95/FH/pc:okc). *mį́į oðaake háaną pa?* how many clocks are there? (02/09/95/FH/pc:prod orig). *omą́įhka háaną ðaašé?* how old are you? (02/09/95/FH/pc:ok). *kiistómaį háaną híipe?* how many councilmen were there (at that place)? (lit., 'how many councilmen went there?') (02/09/95/FH/pc:okc: *híi*; BE2.69). *mą́zeska háaną ašcį́ ðaįšé?* how much money do you have? (02/25/95/FH/pc:ok).

•• LFD 58: *háną* <ha´-no^{n}> how much, how many?

háaǫ (variant: **hǫ́ǫ**). INTERR/INDEF V [sync. nasal vowel stem, *háa_ǫ*] *(trans.)* **do how, do however, do in whatever way.** *háamą hta che?* how am I going to do this? (04/11/95/FH/pc). *háamą hta che?* how shall I do this? (04/11/95/FH/pc). *háamą škǫ́šta tą . . .* however you want me to do it . . . (FH/04/11/95/pc). *súhka hǫ́ǫ che?* how's the chicken doing [cooking]? (RBn2-MOJ/p19b). *mǫšǫ́ oðį́įke háažǫ hta nįkšé?* how are you going to vote? *háažǫ?* how are you doing it? (BE2.32; 04/11/95/FH/pc). *háažǫ ðaįšé?* how are you doing it? (04/28/95/LS/pc). *háamą škǫ́šta tą?* how do you want me to do it? (04/11/95/FH/pc). • **do what.** *hą́ąpa ðe háažǫ?* what did you [sg.] do today? (03/16/95/MREI/pc:okc). *hǫpa ðe háažǫpe?* what did you [pl.] do today? (03/16/95/MREI/pc:okc). *hą́ąci háažǫ?* what did you do last night? (03/16/95/MREI/pc:ok). *táatą haažǫ́?* what did you do? *háamą hce?* what am I going to do? what shall I do? [calls for hearer's opinion] (FH/06/27/01/pc). *Johna háaǫ hce?* what will John do? (FH/06/27/01/pc). *háa ąkǫ́ hce?* what shall we do? *háaǫ ðe?* what did he do? • **do what with, do what about.** *šǫ́ke ékše háažǫ?* what are you going to do with that dog lying there? (FH). *háažǫ?* what did you do with it? (03/16/95/MREI/pc:ok). *hcúka háažǫ?* what did you do with the spoons? (RBn1-53; 03/16/95/MREI/pc:ok). *óðaake waléze háažǫ?* what did you do with the newspaper? (BE2.154). *haxį́ hǫ́ǫ ðe?* what did he do with the blanket? (MSB). *háažǫ?* what did you do about it? (03/16/95/MREI/pc:ok). • **do whatever with, do whatever.** *háamą hkǫ́bra ékimą hta mįkšé* whatever I want to do, I'll do it. *háamą* whatever I do. *háažǫ* whatever you do. *háaǫ ~ hǫ́ǫ* whatever she does (MSB).

•• LFD 59: *hážǫ* <ha´-zho^{n}> what are you doing? what did you do?

••• Cf. *ékiǫ, éǫ.*

haaská (variant: **haašká**). N **dress, buckskin dress; shirt** (LS); **clothes, clothing; fabric, cloth, material.** [Speaker comment: both variants are correct (LS, ERE).] *háaska žíhi íðahkie?* did you find your brown dress/shirt? (04/07/95/LS/pc:okc). *haaská océ pšíe* I went [shopping] to look for a dress (04/07/95/LS/pc:ok; BE2.34). *haaská ská káaɣa* make the buckskin dress white (FH/10/09/01/pc). *haaská ðé žį́ hkǫ́bra* I want you to wear this shirt (RBn1-44). *Mary akxa haaská wį kikáaɣape* Mary made over a shirt. *haaská wasúhužike paahípai, ščúuwasu htai* be sorting the [scattered] dirty clothes, let's you wash them (FH/11/17/01/pc, BE2.120; 03/09/95/MREI/pc:ok; 04/07/95/LS/pc:ok).

•• LFD 57: *haská* <ha-çka´> calico, gingham, canvas, or any cotton goods; gingham or calico shirt, a woman's jacket.

••• Cf. *háa.*

haaská wanǫ́pʔį. NP **handkerchief, neckerchief (lit., 'cloth worn on neck')** (RBn).

haaskáhci (variants: **haaskáihci, haaskíhci**). N [*haaská* + *hcí* 'house'] **tent, long arbor house (lit., 'cloth house')** (03/16/95/FH/pc:okc; BE2.136).

•• LFD 57: *háská hci* <ha´çka´ ṭsi> a canvas tent.

haaskámį (variant: **haaskámi**). N [*haaská* + *mį́* 'blanket'] **shawl** (BE2.120; 03/09/95/MREI/pc:ok).

•• LFD 57: *haskámi* <ha-çka´-mi> shawl, skin-white-robe. *haskámi wihta ðą sape* <ha-çka´-mi wi-ṭa tho^{n} ça-be> [expected Mod. Os. form: *haaskámį wíhta sápe;* the form *ðǫ* is not recognizable in Mod. Os.] my shawl is black.

haaskíhci (variant of **haaskáhci**).

haaší (variant: **háaši**). ADJ **last.** [Speaker comment: both variants are correct (FH).] *ómaįhka háaši* *ecí* it was [in the] the same place last year (RB). *hą́ąpa wahkǫ́taki haaší che* last week (BE2.75). *mį́įǫpa haašíhta* last month (HH/09/10/93). • PPN **in the back of, behind.**

•• LFD 58: *háši* <ha´-shi> the last one, the end of things, Omega.

haašíhta (variants: **hašíhta, haašį́hta**). ADV **before, earlier, in the past.** • PRON **those long ago, those old ones.** *haašíhta apa ékiapi ché* the ones before me said that (RBn22-01). • ADJ **last, past, back in time, ago.** *omą́įhka haašíhta ecí ce* [in the] same place as last year (03/20/95/FH/pc:okc). *hǫpái haašíhta hóni ącʔé* some days back I almost died. *hǫ́ǫpa ðáabrį haašíhta* three days ago (FH:01/05/01/pc).

háašįðe. ADJ, ADV **inside out** (RBn10-15).

haašį́hta (variant of **haašíhta**).

haašká (variant of **haaská**).

háaški (variant**: hą́ąški, hǫ́ǫški**). N **everywhere, wherever, all over, all paths and directions (e.g., children running, s.t. spilled)** (03/23/95/FH/pc). *háaški ípahǫ apai* everybody knows him (lit., 'everywhere they know him') (FH:prod). *Mary apa iižį́ke óxpaða apa ná háaški okíci apái* Mary's son is lost and she's looking everywhere for him (03/23/95/FH/pc). *háaški otápe* they looked all over for it.

•• LFD 58: *ha ški* <ha shki> in every direction, in any place.

haaštáha. N [*háa* + *štáha*] **broadcloth** (03/03/95/FH/pc:ok; RBn HW).

•• LFD 58: *hášta ha* <ha´-shda ha> broadcloth.

haatkxą́ci (variant of **haatxą́ci**).

haatkxą́ta (variant of **haatxą́ta**).

háatxą (variants: **haatxą́, háakxą, háatkxą, haakxą́**). INTERR/INDEF ADV **how far, what distance, (for) how long** (04/06/95/LS/pc). *háatxą brée hta ąhé?* how far do I have to go? (t#14v-p5). *hátxą ąkái htą akatxa?* how far do we have to go? (t#14b-p5). *háatkxą ščée?* how far are you going? (FH/06/26/01/pc; 04/06/95/LS/pc). *háatkxą ščée?* how long are you going? (FH/06/26/01/pc).

•• LFD 58: *hatxą́* <ha-to^{n}´> how far, what distance.

haatxą́ci (variants: **haakxą́ci, haatkxą́ci, hátxąci**). INTERR/INDEF ADV **when in the past, at what time in the past** (04/28/95/LS/pc:ok). *háatxąci ðalį́e?/haakxą́ci ðalíe?* when did you return? what time did you get back? (1/2/335; 03/16/95/MREI/pc:prod; BE2.154). *haakxą́ci ðalípe?* when or what time did you all get back? (04/28/95/LS/pc; BE2.155).

haatxą́ta (variants: **háatxąta, haatkxą́ta, haakxą́ta, haakxǫ́ta**). INTERR/INDEF ADV **when in the future, what time in the future** (04/28/95/LS/pc:okc; FH:6/25/01/pc). *kasį́e, haakxą́ta htą́wąįkši ščée hta ðáiše?* tomorrow, when are you going to town? (04/28/95/LS/pc:okc). *ðíe haakxą́ta ščée škǫ́ǫšta?* when do you want to go? (04/28/95/LS/pc:ok). *haatxą́ta ðalíe?* when will you be back? *haakxą́ta ðalí hta ðaįše?* when are you coming back? (04/28/95/LS/pc:ok). *haakxą́ta awánǫbre hta ąkakxą́i?* when are we going to eat? (04/28/95/LS/pc:okc). *haakxą́ta waðákištǫ́papi ðachí hta ðąkxą́še?* [expected form: . . . *nąkxą́še*] when are you all going to come see us? (04/28/95/LS/pc:okc). *haakxą́ta ðahkíhkǫ́ze hta paašé?* when are you all going to have a peyote meeting? (04/28/95/LS/pc:ok). *haakxą́ta hci oðáhpe?* when are you going in [entering] the house? (04/28/95/LS/pc:okc). *haakxą́ta htáa paasé hta apai?* when are they going to cut up the meat?

•• LFD 58: *hatxątą ðale hta che a(?)* <ha-ṭo^{n}-do^{n} tha-gthe ṭa -tse a(?)> [sentence-final *a* is not used in Modern Osage] when will you go home?

haawálele. N [*háa* + *waléle*] **flag, American flag, banner, standard (when flaglike), staff with feathers** (BE2.48).

•• LFD 189: *haská walele* <ha-çka´ wa-xthe-xthe> ensign, flag, banner, symbolic standard. [In LF's day, *waléle* <wa-xthe-xthe> evidently meant specifically the feathered standard of the Osages, and *haaská* 'cloth' was added to distinguish the American flag. In Mod. Os., *waléle* and *haawálele* signify both 'flag' and 'feathered standard'.]

háaweáze (variant: **háawüüze** [FH]). N **thread.** *háawüüze sápe tóa ąkʔú* give me some black thread (03/22/95/FH/pc, BE2.140).

•• LFD 58: *háweaze* <ha´-we-a-çe> thread, skin, with which to lace. *háweaze sápe hépe ąkʔú a* <ha-we-a-çe ça-be he-be o^{n}-ki a> [sentence-final *a* is not used in Modern Osage] give me some black thread.

háazu. N **grape.** *háazu íiðuspa ðǫǫpá brúwį* I bought two pounds of grapes (05/01/95/LS/pc:ok; BE2.60). *háazu žúuce ą́ðalį* I like red grapes (02/03/95/FH/pc:okc).

•• LFD 57: *házi* <ha´-çi> grapes. *hási žuce ąðalį ha* <ha´-çi zhu-dse o^{n}-tha-gthi^{n} ha> [sentence-final *ha* is not used in Mod. Os.] I like red grapes. *háasu ape štaha* <ha´-çi a-be shta-ha> large wild grapes, with smooth leaves (unconfirmed; 02/03/95/FH/pc:uk).

••• *WI: haapsį́č* (KM).

háazunii. N [*háazu* + *níi*] **grape juice** (RB; 02/03/95/FH/pc:ok; BE2.60).

•• LFD 57: *házini* <ha´-çi-ni> juice of grapes, wine.

háažǫ. INTERR/INDEF V [2nd sg. of *háaǫ*] **do why, do what for.** *htą́wą įkší háažǫ šíe?* what did you go to town for? (FHt#128b).

haažúuce. N [*háa* + *žúuce*] **shroud (lit., 'red cloth')** (HRE); **stroud (a coarse woolen cloth, blanket, or garment formerly used by the British in bartering with the North American Indians in the late 1600s).**

•• LFD 59: *hážuce* <ha´ zhu-dse> red strouding.

háchi (variant of **háachi**).

háha. ADJ **ready.** *ðée che háha nįkšé?* are you ready to go? (RBn10-5:JW).

•• LFD 289: *háha* <ha´-ha> light weight. [Translation unconfirmed.]

háhahkie. V [reg., *háha_hkie*] [*háha* + *hkik-* REFL + *ðe* CAU] *(intr.)* **get ready, make oneself ready, make yourself ready.** *háhaðahkíe* you got ready.

hahkíe. V [stat., *_hahkíe*] *(trans./intr.)* **be unable to understand, be unsure (of s.t.), not quite get the idea.** *ą́hahkie* I don't quite get it (02/27/95/JS/pc:ok; RBn10-5:JW). *ðihahkíe* you don't understand (02/27/95/JS/pc; BE2.147).

hámąsi. N **spade, spades (suit in a deck of cards)** (FH).

hápa. N **corn, fresh corn** (FH/t116b). *hápa ákalįekǫžį́* Osage corn (speckled corn) (01/13/95/FH/pc:uk; BE2.25). *hápa óožu éetkxą akxai* it's time to plant corn (FH/t116b).

•• LFD 57: *hápažuce* <Ha´-ba-zhu-dse> Red-corn (personal name; refers to a life symbol). LFD 58: *hápa* <ha´-ba> corn on the cob (03/07/95/FH/pc:ok). *hápaleze* <ha´-ba-gthe-çe> [expected Mod. Os. form: *hápaleže* (*léže* 'spotted')] spotted corn (03/07/95/FH/pc:ok).

hápa wacúe. N **cornbread.** [Not commonly used.]

hápa wacʔéka (variant: **hápa wahcéka** [LR]). N **fresh (lit., 'gentle') corn.** [Speaker's comment: "squaw corn" is the white man's term (LR).]

hápa waléke. N **cracked corn** (FH/09/22/01/prod).

hápa wasúta (variant: **hápa wasutą**). N **corn when it first gets ripe, "just right" corn (when it is just ready to be picked for drying); "fresh" corn** (FH). [This newly ripe corn was called "fresh corn" by some Osage speakers.]

hašíhta (variant of **haašíhta**).

hátxąci (variant of **haatxą́ci**).

hawé (variants: **havé, havéu**). INTERJ **hello** (02/09/95/FH/pc:okc; BE2.66). [Female speakers may say either *hawé* or *havé/havéu* (where *v* is a sound between English *v* and a semivoiced *w;* this word is the only place such a sound occurs in Osage).]

•• LFD 58: *hawé* <ha-we´>, female <ha-ve´> to greet.

haxį́. N **blanket (bed blanket or Pendleton-type wool blanket for wearing).** *haxį́ į́ kšie* put a blanket on him (lit., 'have him wear the blanket') (01/07/95/FH/pc:prod). *haxį́ke opétkxą* wrap up those blankets [lying around haphazardly, not stacked] (03/22/95/FH/pc).

•• LFD 59: *haxį́* <ha-xi^n´> a woolen blanket. *haxį́ ðįkše brehka* <ha-xi^n´ thi^n-kshe bthe-ķa> [Mod. Os. would normally use *įkšé* rather than *ðįkšé*] the blanket is thin. *haxį́ wį aðį akxa ha ohtaza xci* <ha-xi^n´ wi^n a-thi^n a-ka ha u-ţa-ça xtsi> [Mod. Os. would have *akxa* rather than *akxa ha*] he has a showy blanket.

haxį́ležekáaye. N [*haxį́* + *léže* + *káaye*] **Navajo (tribe or tribal member) (lit., 'one who makes spotted/speckled/stippled [*léže*] blankets').**

•• LFD 59: *haxį́ležekaye* <Ha-xi^n´-gthe-zhe-ga-xe> Navajo.

-hą. V ROOT [uninfl.] **rise.**

••• Cf. *paahą́, watáahą.*

hą́ą (variant: **hą́**). INTERJ **so! (an exclamation used especially in storytelling).** *hą́ą wanǫ́brapi* come on now and eat (MOJ). *hą́ą ékǫ* well, so, that's the way it was. • **how about, so (interrogative)** (PM). *hą́ą ðí, mą́šǫ oðį́ike škǫ́šta?* how about you? do you want to vote right now? (PM/7/7/94). *hą́ą ði?* so? how about you? (PM071494). *hą́ą ðí apa?* how about you all? (PM071494)

••• Cf. *há* 'well' (possibly the same word).

hą́ą. N **night, nighttime.** • ADV **during the night, at night.** *hą́ini ðáha ahípe* they came late at night (FH:108-b; BE2.93). *hą́ą ðe achí hta apai* they'll arrive during the night [tonight] (02/27/95/FH/pc:prod). • ADJ **nocturnal.**

•• LFD 65: *hą́tą* <ho^n´-do^n> during the night.

••• Cf. *hą́įnį.*

hąą káaši. ADVP **late at night, already night for a long time** (RB; 02/24/95/FH/pc:okc). *hąą káaši ðáha achípe* they came late at night (lit., 'when it had been night for a long time, they arrived here').

hą́ą kootáha ce (variant of **hą́ące kootáha ce**).

hą́ą ohkáska (variants: **hą́ą ohkáske, hą́ąhkaska**). N **midnight.** *hą́ą ohkáske akxai* it's midnight (02/24/95/FH/pc:ske). *hą́ą ohkáske* *ahípe* midnight is here (02/24/95/FH/pc:ske; BE2.87). *háą ohkáske ahí akxa* midnight has arrived, it's midnight (02/24/95/FH/pc: ske; BE2.87).

háą ohtą́ka. N **midnight.**

•• LFD 66: *hą ohtąka* <hoⁿ u-ṭoⁿ-ga> night at its greatest strength, middle of the night, midnight (03/01/95/FH/pc:ok).

háą tą wakˀó. N **woman of the night (lit., 'when night, the woman'; possibly a clan name).**

•• LFD 65: *hą́tąwákˀo* <Hoⁿ´-doⁿ-wa´-ḳ'u> female personal name, Woman-of-the-night.

háą wakˀó. N **night woman.**

•• LFD 66: *hą́wakˀo* <Hoⁿ´-wa-ḳ'u> Night-woman, female personal name (02/27/95/FH/pc:ok, ma).

háące (variant: **háąci**). N, ADV **last night** (03/23/95/FH/pc; FH:5/01/96/tape:prod). *háące háažǫ?* what did you do last night? (02/14/95/FH/pc:okc; BE2.75). *wižį́, waaðǫ́ ðáalį škáaye háąci* older brother, you sang good last night (02/24/95/FH/pc:ok; 03/09/95/MREI/pc:okc: *háąci*).

•• RB: <hahⁿ-tsí>.

•• LFD 63: *hą* <hoⁿ> night. *hǫ aci* <hoⁿ a-di> [expected Mod. Os. form: *hą́ące*] last night.

háące kootáha ce (variant: **háą kootáha ce**). ADVP, NP **night before last** (02/24/95/FH/pc).

•• RB: <háhⁿ-gó-tah-háh-tsi>.

••• Cf. *háąpa kootáha ce.*

hąąðé. N **tonight.** *hąąðé wižį́ke akxa wažážeíe hpíǫ kǫ́ða akxa* tonight son wants to learn the Osage language (BE2.143).

hąąé. INTERJ **yes (response when listening to a story).**

háąekǫ́žį. N [*hą́ą* 'night' + *ékǫ* + *-žį* 'little'] **early morning (lit., 'a little like night')** (BE2.89, unconfirmed; 02/25/95/FH/pc:uk).

háąhkaska (variant of **háą ohkáska**).

háąhkaži. INTERJ **no** (02/27/95/FH/pc; BE2.94).

•• LFD 66: *hą́hkaži* <hoⁿ´-ḳa-zhi> no, not so.

háąhpazé (variant of **háąnahpazé**).

háąmąðį (variants: **háąmąį, hąąmǫ́į**). N **Hominy (place name); Night Walker (personal name).** [Osage name of Frances Holding's maternal grandfather, after whom the town of Hominy (Osage County, Oklahoma) was named.]

háąnahpazé (variant: **háąnąhpazé, háąnąhpáze, háąhpazé**). ADJ, V [uninfl.] *(intr.)* **dark, darken, become/get dark.** *wáli hą́ąnąhpáze akxai* it's really dark (RBn12-06). • N **jail, guardhouse, prison.** *hą́ąhpaze olį́į akxái* he's in jail. • **dark night, darkness of night** (BE2.29; 01/19/95/FH/pc:okc; t#14a-p2).

•• LFD 66: *hą́ąnąhpaze* <hoⁿ´-noⁿ-p̣a-çe> jail, night-darkness (refers to the gloomy aspect of the prison). *hą́nąhpaze olį* <hoⁿ´-noⁿ-p̣a-çe u-gthiⁿ> a jail sentence. *hąnąhpaze omąðį pe* <hoⁿ-noⁿ´-p̣a-çe u-moⁿ-thiⁿ bi o> they walked in darkness.

••• Cf. *hą́ąnahpazéhci.*

háąnahpazé oolą́. VP [reg., *oo_lą́*] *(trans.)* **arrest, put s.o. in jail (lit., 'place into darkness').** *waachí hí žiišǫ́ ðée ðe hpahą́le hą́ąnahpazé oolą́ąpi wáhkǫ́bra* before the dances start, first I want you all [lit., 'them'] to put him in jail (FH/09/22/01/pc).

•• LFD 66: *hą́nąhpaze olą* <hoⁿ´-noⁿ-p̣a-çe u-gthoⁿ> to arrest one, to place in jail (04/19/95/FH/pc:ok). *hą́nąhpaze ąwąlą pe* <hoⁿ´-noⁿ-p̣a-çe oⁿ-woⁿ gthoⁿ i> they put me in jail. *hą́pehpaze oðilą pe* <hoⁿ´-be-p̣a-çe u-thi-gthoⁿ i> [expected Mod. Os. form: *hą́ąnahpaze ooðíląpe*; LF's syllable <-be-> is perhaps a typographical error] they put you in jail (unconfirmed, 04/19/95/FH/pc).

háąnahpazéhci. N [*hą́ąnąhpazé* + *hcí*] **jailhouse, jail (lit., 'night house', 'darkness house')** (02/13/95/FH/pc:ok). *hą́ąnąhpazéhci olį́į akxái* he's in jail (RBn10-12:JW; BE2.72, (02/13/95/FH/pc:ok).

•• LFD 66: *hą́nąhpaze hci* <hoⁿ´-noⁿ-p̣a-çe ṭsi> guardhouse, prison. *hą́ąnąhpazehci che olįį aðaa pe* <hoⁿ´-noⁿ-p̣a-çe ṭsi tse u-gthiⁿ a-tha bi a> he went to prison.

háąną (variant of **háaną**).

háąnąhpazé, háąnąhpáze (variants of **háąnahpazé**).

háąni, háąnį (variants of **háįnį**).

háąpa (variants: **hǫ́ǫpa, hąąpái, hąąpáe, hǫǫpái**). N **day; today.** *hą́ąpa ðé* today. *hą́ąpa háažǫ́?* what did you do today? (01/19/95/FH/pc:ok; BE2.290). *hǫǫpái haašíhta hóni acˀé* some days back I almost died (2/3/83/1/330; 01/20/95/FH/pc:okc). *hą́ąpa ðé akxa ðáalįži akxai* it's not a pretty day today, the weather is not good today (FH/10/13/96).

•• LFD 63: *hą́pa* <hoⁿ´-ba> day.

háąpa hpahą́le. N **Monday (lit., 'first day')** (02/25/95/FH/pc:ok; BE2.88). [Names of days were historically not used in Osage and sound unnatural to Osage speakers (HH).]

•• LFD 64: *hą́pa hpahąle* <Hoⁿ´-ba p̣a-hoⁿ-gthe> first day: Monday.

hą́ąpa htaaðáachaži (variants: **htaaðáachaži hą́ąpa, htaaðáachaži**; perhaps also **htáa[ð]aachaži** [RB, unconfirmed]). N [*hą́ąpa* + *htáa* + *ðaaché* + *aží*] **Friday (lit., 'day of no meat-eating')** (BE2.50, 01/30/95/FH/pc:ok, all). [Names of days were historically not used in Osage and sound unnatural to Osage speakers (HH).]

•• LFD 139: *htaðátxaži hąpa* <ṭa-tha´-ta-zhi ho^{n}-ba> meat eat not day: Friday. [LF's <tha´-ta-zhi> is probably a typographical error for *ðáchaži* <tha´-tsa-zhi>; LF has <o^{n}-tha´-tsa i i> for *ąðácha pe* elsewhere.]

hą́ąpa ihtóį ðeha. ADVP, NP **(in the) future, in days to come** (01/30/95/FH/pc:ok). *hą́ąpa ihtúį ðeha, ókašéįke žóawahkíe hkǫ́bra* I want to be with them from now on with nothing to bother (01/30/95/FH/pc:okc; BE2.52). *hą́ąpe ihtóį ðehá įkše* in future days (FH).

hą́ąpa ke záani. ADVP, NP **every day.**

••• Cf. *hą́ąpa záani.*

hą́ąpa kootáha ce. NP **day before yesterday** (FH: prod).

hą́ąpa oðóhake (variant: **hą́ąpa oðáhike**). N **last day; final day of the** ***ilǫ́ǫška*** **dance, giveaway day** (04/06/95/FH:ok:both variants).

•• RB: <hó^{n}-pah o-tháh-hi-keh>, <o-thó-hah-keh> (04/06/95/FH:ok; BE2.75).

hą́ąpa ohkíeche. ADVP, NP **every day** (BE2.42; MJ).

hą́ąpa ohkísce. N **March (lit., 'half a day', days so called because they could be warm or cold between morning and afternoon, unpredictable days)** (t#38a-p1-HH1; 04/28/95/LS/pc:ok). [Names of months were historically not used in Osage and sound unnatural to Osage speakers (HH).] **hą́ąpa ókaayéįke.** N **Saturday (lit., 'day on which nothing is done')** (BE2.116; 03/08/95/MREI/pc:ok). [Names of days were historically not used in Osage and sound unnatural to Osage speakers (HH).]

•• LFD 64: *hą́pa okayeðįke* <Ho^{n}´-ba u-ga-xe-thi^{n}-ge> Saturday.

hą́ąpa wahkǫtáki (variant: **hǫ́ǫpa wáhkǫtáki**) N **week, Sunday.** [Names of days were historically not used in Osage and sound unnatural to Osage speakers (HH).] *hǫ́ǫpawáhkǫhtaki ðé niižúepe* this week it rained (BE2.153; RBn1-MOJ/p41).

•• RB: <hóm-pah-wáh-ko^{n}-dáh-gi>.

•• LFD 64: *hą́pa wahkǫtaki* <ho^{n}´-ba wa-ḳo^{n}-da-gi> a week (04/06/95/PM/pc:ok).

hą́ąpa wahkǫ́taki (variants: **hǫ́ǫpa wahkǫ́taki, hą́ąpa wahkǫ́ta**) N **Sunday (lit., 'sacred day')** (03/14/95/MREI/pc:ok; BE2.129). [Names of days were historically not used in Osage and sound unnatural to Osage speakers (HH).]

•• LFD 64: *hą́pa wahkǫtaki* <Ho^{n}´-ba Wa-ḳo^{n}-da-gi> Sunday, sacred day.

hą́ąpa wéðaabrį. N **Wednesday (lit., 'third day')** (05/01/95/LS/pc:ok; BE2.153; 04/06/95/PM/pc:ma). [Names of days were historically not used in Osage and sound unnatural to Osage speakers (HH).]

•• LFD 64: *hą́pa weðabrį* <ho^{n}´-ba we-tha-bthi^{n}> third day: Wednesday.

hą́ąpa wéðǫǫpa. N **Tuesday (lit., 'second day')** (RB; 04/04/95/FH/pc:ok; BE2.145). [Names of days were historically not used in Osage and sound unnatural to Osage speakers (HH).]

•• LFD 64: *hą́pa weðǫpa* <Ho^{n}´-ba we-tho^{n}-ba> the second day: Thursday.

hą́ąpa wétoopa. N **Thursday (lit., 'fourth day')** (03/22/95/FH/pc; BE2.140). [Names of days were historically not used in Osage and sound unnatural to Osage speakers (HH).]

•• LFD 64: *hą́pa wetopa* <Ho^{n}´-ba we-do-ba> the fourth day: Thursday.

hą́ąpa záani. ADVP, NP **every day.**

•• LFD 63: *hǫ́pa zani* <ho^{n}´-ba ça-ni> daily; from day to day.

••• Cf. *hą́ąpa ke záani.*

hąąpáe, hąąpái (variants of **hą́ąpa**).

hą́ąpascee. N [*hą́ąpa* + *scéce*] **January (lit., 'days long' or 'days lengthen')** (WHM981022, unconfirmed; FH/11/17/01/pc:uk). [Names of months were historically not used in Osage and sound unnatural to Osage speakers (HH).]

hą́ąpaska, hą́ąpaskaha (variants of **hǫ́ǫpaskaha**).

hą́hceka. N **fly, housefly** (01/26/95/FH/pc:prod orig; BE2.49).

•• LFD 66: *hą́hceka* <ho^{n}´-tse-ga> common house fly. *hą́hceka htoho* <ho^{n}´-ṭse-ga ṭo-ho> blue fly, the blowfly [unconfirmed 'blue fly' and 'blowfly' (01/26/95/FH/pc:uk)].

hą́iną (variants: **hą́ini, hą́ąną, hą́ąni**). N **dark, darkness.** *hą́iną žiišǫ́ ąkále* we'll go home before dark (RBn10-7:JW). *hą́ini hí tą* when it gets dark (FH/11/17/01/pc:prod). *hą́ąni hí žiišǫ, lípai* get back here before dark (FH/11/17/01/pc). *hą́ini ahí akxa* it's dark (FH/11/17/01/pc:prod).

•• LFD 66: *hą́iðįtą* <ho^{n}´-i-thi^{n}-do^{n}> [expected Mod. Os. form: *hą́iną tą*] pertaining to the night, nocturnal [rather, 'when it is night'] (02/27/95/FH/pc:uk).

••• Cf. *hą́ą* 'night'.

hą́ka. N, ADJ **sacred, holy.** • N **bald eagle** (HRE/pc/2002); **dark-plumed eagle; earth division (of the Osage tribe); innocence emblem in peace ceremony (a child).**

•• JOD (slip file): *hą́ka* <Hañ´-ķa> the name of the gentes on the right side of the Osage tribal circle.

•• LFD 65: *hą́ka/hǫ́ka* <Hoⁿ´-ga> "The name of one of the two great tribal divisions of the Osage Tribe, the division representing the earth with its water and dry land. The word signifies sacred or holy, an object that is venerated. It is also the name of a subdivision representing the dry land of the earth. The dark-plumed eagle is spoken of by this term, because of its symbolic use; a child chosen as an emblem of innocence in a peace ceremony is called Hoⁿ´-ga. The origin of the word, being obscure, can not be analyzed."

••• Cf. *hcížo, hpáðįhǫka.*

hą́ka léže. N **golden eagle when young, spotted eagle** (HRE). [Harry Red Eagle, Jr., whose adult name is *hcížo hą́ka,* contrasts *hą́ka* [hą̃ka] 'bald eagle' with *hcížo* 'golden eagle'.]

•• JOD (slip file): *xúða léže* <qü-¢á ķ¢e-çe> the spotted eagle, syn. *hą́ka ópe léže* <hañķa üpe ķ¢eçe> spotted tail eagle.

•• LFD 65: *hą́ka léže* <hoⁿ'-ga gthe-zhe> the mottled sacred one, the immature golden eagle.

hąpái (variant of **hǫ́ǫpa ðé**).

hce. INJUNCTIVE **may it be that (often translated as 'let, allow, have, tell (s.o. to); let's [speaker and one other person]')** (03/15/95/PM/pc:ok; 03/16/95/JS/pc:ok; FH/06/26/01/pc). *brúwį hce* let me buy it, I'll just buy it (LS). *mąhkása ðé bráahtą hce* I'll just drink this coffee; let me just drink this coffee. *žówile brée hce* let me accompany you (RBn1-30). *šáake owíbrįįke hce* let me shake your hand (RBn22-08). *Įįį žówile hce* let me sit with you (RBn10-4:MOJ/79). *hkáące záani brúwį hce* let me buy all the apples. *ðekáiha kų̃, áwitǫpe hce* come over here and let me look at you; come over this way so that I can watch you. *John akxa Mogri Mary óhką hce éeakxai* John told Mogri to help Mary (FH). *hkáące záani ą́ðuwį hce* let's [us two] buy all the apples (RBn1-45). *óʔie che kašǫ́e hce* [let's] leave the problem alone (04/26/95/FH/pc). *mą́ąhispe ðuuzaa, žą́ą toe ąkáase ąkái hce* get the axe and let's go cut some wood (RBn2-MOJ/p20; 01/06/95/FH/pc: okc). *hkáwacežeņį tóa ąðáahtą ąkái hce* let's [us two] go drink some beer.

••• Cf. *htai.*

hce ée. [*hce* INJUNCTIVE + *ée* 'say'] **(sequence often translated as 'request [that s.o. do s.t.]', 'ask [s.o. to do s.t.]', 'propose [that s.o. do s.t.]', 'instruct/tell [s.o. to do s.t.]', 'have s.o. do s.t.').** [Pronounced with no interruption, as *hcée.*] *íe tóa ékipše hce ée apa* they've asked me to say a few words. *iðái hce ée apa* they've asked me to speak (03/15/95/PM/pc:ok; 03/16/95/JS/pc:ok). *iðáe hce ée akxa* he wants me to talk, he proposes that I talk (RBn10-21). *owáhǫį įhtáce épše hce ée apa* they told me to call you father (RBn10-21/JW&FW/77). *wižį́ke oðíhką hce épše* I asked Sonny to help you. *šéeðǫ nąąžį́ txa hú hce éa* tell the person standing there to come here. *šéetxa kų̃ hce éa* tell him [standing] to be coming back here. *mąlį́ hce éa* tell him to go home. *hiiðá hce éa* have him take a bath (FH/06/26/01/pc). *mį́įake šáhpe tą, lí hce éa* have them come back at six o'clock.

hcé xópe (variant of **hcéxope**).

hcéðe (variant: **hcéða** [FH]). N **automobile wheel, tire.** *hcéðe mąąstósto* a muddy tire (03/22/95/FH/pc). *hcéðe akxa tóže akxái* the tire is flat (03/22/95/FH/pc:okc; BE2.141). *hcéðe mąąðǫ́ hta mįksé* I'm going to steal a tire (RBn12-07).

hcéðe álįį. N **bicycle.**

•• LFD 160: *hceðéalį* <ṭse-the´-a-gthiⁿ> a cycle, bicycle.

••• Cf. *hcelį́ álįį.*

hcée. N **buffalo.**

•• LFD 157: *hce* <ṭse> bison.

••• Cf. *hceemį́įka, hceetóe, hceetóoka.*

hceehį́į. N [*hcée* + *hį́į*] **woman's yarn belt (lit., 'buffalo hair')** (BE2.162; 01/07/95/FH/pc:prod).

•• LFD 159: *hcehį́* <ṭse-hiⁿ´> buffalo hair, woven for belts and armlets, for straps for tying bundles, and for sacred articles.

hceemį́įka. N **buffalo cow** (04/25/95/PM/pc:okc; BE2.13).

•• LFD 159: *hce míka* <ṭse mi´-ga> female buffalo, a cow.

hceeníxaxa (variant: **hceeníxąxą**). N **tripe.** [One speaker claimed that this form means 'the ruffly leafed layers of a buffalo'; cf. *xáxa.*] *hceeníxąxą ðaaché ą́zo štą* I like tripe (03/23/95/FH/pc:okc; BE2.144).

•• LFD 159: *hceníxąxą* <ṭse-ni´-xoⁿ-xoⁿ> tripe (03/23/95/FH/pc:ok). *hceníxąxą ðache azo šna aða* <ṭse-ni´-xoⁿ-xoⁿ tha-tse a-çu shna a-tha> [expected Mod. Os. form: *hceeníxaxa ðaaché ą́zo štą* (*šna* appears to be Omaha rather than Osage)] I like tripe.

hcéeska (variant: **hceeská**). N **beef (lit., 'white buffalo'); head of cattle, cow (not necessarily female).** *hcéska wį c?éðe htai* let's kill a beef (RBn11-02/JW&FW&HHsk/c.1976).

•• LFD 157: *hcéska* <ṭse´-çka> white buffalo, domesticated cattle. *hceská apa kizo pi a niskiðe saki* <ṭse-çka´ a-ba gi-çu bi a ni-çki-the ça-gi> [preferable Mod. Os. word order is: *hceeská apa niskúðe saakí kízope*] cattle like rock salt. *hceskác?eðe* <ṭse-çka´-ṭs'e-the> the slaughter of beeves.

••• *OM* same as Osage (LFD 157).

••• Cf. *hceeskátooka.*

hceeská mįįka (variant: **hceeská mįe**). N **cow, heifer** (01/14/95/FH/pc:prod; 01/14/95/FH/pc:ok).

•• LFD 157: *hceská mika* <ṭse-çka´ mi-ga> domestic cow, white buffalo female. *hceskámika žįka* <ṭse-çka´-mi-ga zhi^n-ga> a heifer.

••• *OM* same as Osage (LFD 157).

hceeskátooka (variants: **hceeská tóe, hceeská tooká**). N [*hcéeska* + *tooká*] **bull, steer** (01/14/95/FH/pc:prod; ok).

•• LFD 157: *hceskátoka* <ṭse-çka´-do-ga> bull, steer.

hceetóe (variant of **hceetóoka**).

hceetóežįká. N **young or small male buffalo.**

•• LFD 158: *hce tóe žįká* <ṭse-do´ zhi^n-ga> a young buffalo bull, bladder [the translation 'bladder' is dubious] (04/25/95/PM/pc:okc: young buff. bull, not bladder).

hceetóoka (variant: **hceetóe**). N **buffalo bull** (01/09/95/FH/pc:ok; 04/25/95/PM/pc:okc).

•• LFD 158: *hcetóka* <ṭse-do´-ga> buffalo bull (also a personal name) (04/25/95/PM/pc:ok). *hcetóka akxa nóhpewaða pe* <ṭse-do´-ga a-ka no^n´-pe-wa-tha bi a> the buffalo was dreadful (04/25/95/PM/pc:ok).

hceetóoka kišipi. N [*kišipi* apparently contains *ki-* INCEPTIVE + *wašį́* + *api*] **June, hunting time (lit., 'the buffalo bull is fat anew')** (04/25/95/PM/pc:ok). [Names of months were historically not used in Osage and sound unnatural to Osage speakers (HH).]

•• LFD 158: *hcetóka kišipi* <ṭse-do´-ga gi-shi-bi> Moon when the buffalo bulls regain fat, June (04/25/95/PM/pc:ok).

hceetóoka mąąnáɣape. N **June (lit., 'buffalo bull is rutting').** [Names of months were historically not used in Osage and sound unnatural to Osage speakers (HH).]

•• LFD 158: *hcetóka mąnąɣapi* <ṭse-do´-ga mo^n-no^n-xa bi> when the buffalo bulls rut, the month of June (04/25/95/PM/pc: *ɣápe* 'ready for the female').

••• *KS mąnáɣe* to be in rut, to paw the ground (RR).

hceežį́. N **small buffalo, unborn buffalo calf, any unborn calf** (04/25/95/PM/pc:ok). [A valued food, especially for older people without good teeth. At peyote church the older ones get the unborn calf as the best part of the beef at breakfast, along with corn, fruit, and water; these are the four things allowed (PM).]

•• LFD 162: *hcé žį́ka* <ṭse zhi^n-ga> little buffalo, unborn calf.

hcéɣe (variant of **céɣe**).

hcéɣenii (variant of **céɣenii**).

hcéhapa. N **spoon** (FH).

•• LFD 158: *hcéhapa* <ṭse´-ha-ba> shell spoons.

hcehé. N **buffalo horn(s).**

•• LFD 159: *hcehéhko* <ṭse-he´-ḳu> a buffalo-horn spoon.

hcéheska (variant: **céɣeska**). N **cup (identical with *mąhkásai oožú*)** (BE2.28; 01/14/95/FH/pc:ok).

•• JOD (slip file): *mąðįk?a céɣe* <ma^n-¢iñk'ă ṭṣĕ´xĕ>, <ma^n-%oiñk'ă ṭṣĕ´xĕ> pottery.

•• LFD 159: *hcehé žįa* <ṭse-he´ zhi^n-a> a cup.

hcéhežį. N **dish, dishes (e.g., a set of plates, cups, and bowls)** (FH:6/25/01/pc:*h* not *ɣ*); **cup.**

•• LFD 159: *hcehé žįa* <ṭse-he´ zhi^n-a> a cup.

hcehpé (variants: **hcéhpe, hcehpú**). N **liver.** *waðáahtą štą éhtana hcéhpe hpííži kší aape* he has a bad liver from always drinking (02/16/95/FH/pc:okc). *hcéhpe kihúheka áape* he had liver trouble (02/16/95/FH/pc:ok; BE2.80). *hcée hcéhpe* buffalo liver.

•• RB: <tséh-pú> (02/16/95/FH/pc:okc).

•• JOD (slip file): *hcehpú* <tse-pű> a liver.

•• LFD 159: *hcehpíscece* <ṭse-pi´-stse-dse> the long liver, spleen.

••• *KSččeppű* liver (RR).

hcéka. ADJ **new, fresh, recent.** *oðíhtą hcéka wį ščúwį?* did you buy a new car? *wahcéka owákihce* I'm looking for new things (FH/09/24/01/prod). *hcéka xci* brand new, as a new car (02/27/95/FH/pc:okc; BE2.93). *hcéka žį* really new, very new. • ADV **just now, newly, recently, just a while ago** (RBn23-17; MREI/#94). *hcéka ðachíe?* did you just get here? *hcéka ðahpáahą tǫpéwai* you look like you just got up (RBn14-12). *hcéka ðiníe che ákǫze hta akxa ska?* are you just [now] going to be examined? (02/13/95/FH/pc:ok; RBn3-MOJ/p17;

04/11/95/LS/pc:ma). *hcéka alíipe* he just got back (02/13/95/FH/pc:prod orig; 04/11/95/LS/pc:ok). *hcéka ðanǫ́e ðe* you are young (lit., 'recently you grew up') (02/27/95/FH/pc:okc).

•• LFD 158: *hcéka* <ṭse´-ga> recently, anew, early, new (e.g., a new blanket, a new robe). *hcéka ali pe* <ṭse´-ga a-gthi bi a> he has come recently. *hcéka xci ce* <ṭse´-ga-xtsi-dse> inchoate, incipient (unconfirmed, 02/13/95/FH/pc:uk). *hcékaxci* <ṭse´-ga-xtsi> fresh, new. *hcékamą̨į* <ṭse´-ga-mo^{n}-i^{n}> Goes-in-new-plumage (personal name; refers to the young eagle) (02/27/95/FH/pc:name ok, but unfamiliar, possibly weather clan?). *hcéka nǫ* <ṭse´-ga no^{n}> newly grown, just grown to maturity.

••• Cf. *wahcéka.*

hcéka nǫ́ǫ. N **teenager, young person or young people, children in their teens (lit., 'recently grown-up' or 'recently adult')** (03/24/95/PM/pc:ok, FH: children in their teens). *hcéka nǫ́ǫ šǫ ąhé, wábruye hkǫ́bra įké* I'm still young, I don't want to get married (BE2.162; RBn17-p02). *níhka žúuce hcéka nǫ́ǫ ohkíhpache apa hąðé waachí hta apai* Indian Youth Council are having a dance tonight (lit., 'man red newly grown council . . .') (RBn23-14).

•• LFD 158: *hcéka nǫ* <ṭse´-ga no^{n}> newly grown, just grown to maturity (02/13/95/FH/pc:ok).

hcékažį. ADV **just now, just barely.** *hcékažį alípe* she had just got back here.

hcelį́. N [presumably contracted from *hcéðe + álįį*] **wheel** (FH:5/01/96/tape).

hcelį́ álįį. N **bicycle (lit., 'sit upon a wheel')** (FH:4/22/96/tape:okc). *hcéðe álįį achípe* he came on a bicycle (RBn12-06).

••• Cf. *hcéðe álįį.*

hcéokʔa (variants: **hcúekʔa, cʔéokʔa** [MOJ]). N **frog** (01/30/95/FH/pc:prod; MOJt#150a).

•• LFD 271 (unconfirmed): *hcépiukʔa* <ṭse´-biu-ḳ'a> a frog.

hcéwa. N **yonkapin** (RBn11-02/JW&FW&HHsk/c.1976).

•• LFD 160: *hcéwaðe* <ṭse´-wa-the> *Nelumbo lutea:* "The root of this plant is gathered and used for food. . . . The seeds are also eaten (raw). In taste the meat of this seed is not unlike the chestnut. . . . Its common name is water chinquapin."

hcewį́įke (variant of **lébrą hce wį́įke**).

hcéxi. ADJ **sacred, precious, difficult.**

••• Cf. *hkáwa wahcéxi, mįįhcéxi.*

hcéxope (variant: **hcé xópe**). N **spider.** *hci hcé xópe ochíe* the house has a lot of spiders (03/14/95/FH/pc:ok; BE2.125).

•• LFD 161: *hcéxope* <ṭse´-xo-be> a spider. *hcéxope sape* <ṭse´-xo-be ça-be> black spider. *hcéxope žeka* <ṭse´-xo-be zhe-ga> spider legs.

hcéxopehuuscee. N **tarantula (lit., 'spider of long legs').**

•• LFD 162: *hcéxopehuscee* <ṭse´-xu-be hiu stse e> long leg spider: tarantula.

hcéze (variant: **htéze** [RB, archaic]). N **stomach, abdomen, belly.** *išíkʔą hcéze íhuheka kší aape* my sister-in-law is sick with her stomach, they say (FH/09/23/01/pc:prod). *hcéze íhuheka kší áape* he [lying down] is sick of his stomach (FH/09/23/01/pc).

•• RB: <téh-zeh> [older form *htéze* also accepted, possibly heard as *hcéze*] (03/14/95/MREI/pc:ok; BE2.128 & RBn1-MOJ/p26b).

•• JOD (slip file): *hcéze* <tse´-ṣe> the abdomen, belly.

•• LFD 157: *hcéze* <ṭse´-çe> abdomen, the belly.

hcéze bráze. N **hernia (lit., 'torn [in the] stomach or abdomen')** (03/14/95/MREI/pc:okc).

•• LFD 157: *hcéze bráze* <ṭse´-çe btha-çe> hernia, rupture.

hcí. N **house** (02/09/95/FH/pc:ok; BE2.68). [Takes 'standing' positional article *che.*] *hcí ðuuwásu ðí* clean the house (RBn10-12:JW). *hcí che wébruwį bríištą* I concluded the selling of the house; I sold the house. • **nest.** *súhka htą́ą mį́ka wį hcí káaye ðí aape* the turkey went out to make a nest (RBn19-03). *hcí káayi che éži ípahǫži apá aape* no one would ever know where she made her nest (RBn19-03). *miʔíðǫpeįkše htaha, mįhiðéįkše htaha, aðápe ški hǫ́waį hcí wíhta íiðaži htape* they may go to the east, they may go to the west, but they'll never find where I built my nest (RBn19-03). *súhka htą́ą mį́ka hcí nalǫ́hkile ðáalį káaye che ožoáhkiži ðe áape* turkey hen was proud because she could hide her nest so well (RBn19-05). • V [reg., *_hci*] *(intr.)* **camp, make camp.**

•• LFD 133: *šǫ́ke hci* <sho^{n}´-ge ṭsi> dog-house, a kennel. LFD 162: *hci* <ṭsi> house, dwelling, hovel. *hci wihta* <ṭsi wi-ṭa> my house. *hcí ðihta* <ṭsi´ thi-ṭa> your house.

••• Cf. *ahcí.*

hcí hpííži. N **shack (lit., 'bad house').** *hci hpííži wį paaxó ki* a shack in the hills (RBn10-2:MOJ/79).

hcí tóopa. N **(personal name)** [Name of Charlie Pasetopah (?)] (FH).

hcíce (variant: **hcíci**). N **drumbeat, beat of a drum, beating or thumping sound (e.g., footsteps)** (RB). *céɣenii hcíci ðáalį škáaɣe* you hit drum well (RBn1-40).

•• LFD 155: *hticé* <ṭi-dse´> the sound of a drum or the thud of many feet.

••• Cf. *ðihcíceðe.*

hcíhta. ADV [*hcí* + *hta* 'toward'] **inside, in (motion into rather than position within, as in 'come in, come inside'; lit., 'into house')** (02/13/95/FH/pc:okc). *niižúe tą hcíhta kų́a* come inside when it rains (02/13/95/FH/pc:okc; BE2.71; RBn1-41). *hcíhta ówe aðį́ku* bring the groceries in the house (FH:prod). *ówe hcíhta aðį́ku* bring the groceries in the house. *áših ta brée ąžį ðíe hcíhta wéðaahpa ði* I'm going outside, but you stay inside and wait [for people] (FH:prod). *hcíhta pšú hkóbra* I want to come inside (FH/prod).

hcíi (variant of **hcį́į**).

hcíko. N **my grandfather (shortened form, used informally or as an endearment).**

••• Cf. *wihcíko.*

hcíle. V [reg., *hcí_le*] *(intr.)* **live, reside; make a home, set up a household, set up housekeeping** (FH). *paaxó ki nąhtą́htąžį žíhi wį hcílepe* in the hills lived a little brown donkey (RBn15-0). *ní áška hcíle tą ée ðáalį* it's good to live near water. *wakˀó hta apa ðéka hcíle apái* that's where eldest daughter lives. • N **house, home, household** (FH; 04/11/95/LS/pc). *hówaiki ąhcíle ąkáðe tą* wherever we're living (02/09/95/FH/pc:okc; BE2.67). *hcíle ąkóhta škaškáða ąkái* we are happy in our home (RBn12-03p5). *wakˀóhtą hcí ðe ée aðį́ apa, hcílepa ðée káaɣe* my daughter has this house, she's making a home in it (PM/7/7/94; 02/03/95/FH/pc:ok). • **family** (HRE/12/29/01/pc; BE2.43; 04/13/95/FH/pc:ok). *ðé hcíle ðáalį škáaɣe [w]aawíta, waxpáðį hta akxai* I pray you make it good for this family, when they're pitiful (RBn10-6:JW). *huuhtą́ka ohkíhkie apai, hcíle apa hípe* a whole bunch of them were talking when the family came over (3/2/89/MSB). *ðe hcíle akxa tooká ðįké* that family has all girls (01/14/95/FH/pc).

•• LFD 163: *hcíle* <ṭsi´-gthe> to keep house, to reside, to dwell, to set up house. *hci ále* <ṭsi a´-gthe> I keep house. *hci ðale* <ṭsi tha-gthe> you keep house. *hci ąla* <ṭsi o^{n}-gtha> we keep house.

hcíohka. N [*hcí* + *óhką́*] **room.** *hcíohka wį ðáalį ówakˀupe* they lent us a nice room (RBn23-14).

hcióška. (variant **hcióška** possibly used only by women) N **my/your/his/her father's sister's son (used when speaker is male or female; more precise than English 'my/your/his/her cousin').** [Does not use inalienable forms.]

hcipóɣa. N **Native American Church house.**

•• LFD 162: *hcípoɣe* <ṭsi´-bo-xe> a conical tent, a tipi.

••• *KS ččíiboɣa* tipi, tent with poles tied at the top (RR).

hcíwažu. N [*hcí* + *wa-* VAL + *ážu* (or *hci* + *wa-* VAL + *oožú*?)] **headright (lit., 'they put in the house')** (01/04/95/FH/pc:prod, BE2.65).

•• LFD 164: *hcíwažu* <ṭsi´-wa-zhu> household, family.

hcižé (variant: **hcíže**). N **door.** *hcižé ðuuáza* open the door (01/20/95/ERE/pc:ok). *hcižé áðįįtą* close the door (01/20/95/ERE/pc; BE2.34).

•• LFD 164: *hcíže oðakacˀį* <ṭsi´-zhe u-tha-ga-ṭs'i^{n}> you peeped in the door.

hcižépe. N **doorway, threshold (formal, used especially for "God's doorway" at funerals [RB])** (HH/09/10/93; 04/13/95/FH/pc:ok; BE2.34). [Takes 'standing' positional article *che.*]

•• LFD 168 *htížepeche oðakáhcį* <ṭi´-zhe-be-te u-tha-ga´-ṭs'i^{n}> [expected Mod. Os. form: *hcižépe che oðákacˀį*] you peeped in the door.

hcížepe áhkita. N **porter (lit., 'doorway soldier').**

•• LFD 164: *hcížepe ahkita* <ṭsi´-zhe-be a-ḳi-da> a porter, door-servant.

hcížo. N **golden eagle** (HRE/pc/Dec.2002)**; Hcížo, an important Osage tribal division.**

•• LFD 165: *hcížo waštake* <Ṭsi´-zhu Wa-shta-ge> the Gentle Tsí-zhu (refers to its office as Peacemaker).

••• Cf. *hą́ka, xúða.*

hcį́į (variants: **hcíi, hcíe; htį́e** [archaic], **htį́į** [archaic]). V [reg.?, *_hcį́į*] *(intr.)* **appear, show.** *žé wahtį́e apái* his penis is showing [to them, to others] (anonymous source). *wakáahcįe* appears to them suddenly (personal name, referring to deer aroused by something that suddenly appears; George Shannon's Osage name).

•• JOD (Raccoons and Crawfish p24 ln6): *áhci aðápe* <átciaȼápe> he suddenly charged.

•• LFD 119: *nąžį́hcie* <No^{n}-zhi^{n}´-tsi-e> [expected Mod. Os. form: *nąąžį́hcįe* or *nąąžį́hcįį*] Rises-suddenly (personal name; refers to the alertness of the buffalo).

hcošpá. N [shortened form of *wihcóšpa*] **pal, friend, buddy; my grandchild.** *hcošpá wíhta* my friend, my pal.

•• LFD 165: *hcošpaðǫ* <ṭsu-shpa-thoⁿ o> grandchild (unconfirmed; 05/01/95/LS/pc:uk with *ðǫ*).

••• Cf. *wihčóšpa*.

hcú hápa. N **ladle.**

••• Cf. *níiðaahtą*.

hcúekˀa (variant of **hcéokˀa**).

hcúɣe. ADJ **dried up.** *wakáaži wihta hcúɣeži̧* that's my driver, he's a little dried up guy (PM).

•• LFD 165: *cˀóɣe* <ṭs'o-xe> tart; Astringent (personal name; refers to the taste of the root of the blazing star). *še cˀoɣe* <she ts'o-xe> [<ts'> is presumably a typographical error for <ṭs'>] the apple is tart.

••• Cf. *hcúxe* (possibly related or a variant).

hcúke (variant: **hcúka**). N **spoon (Osage spoons were originally clamshells from creeks, used only for scraping corn, with little ones for children, larger ones for adults; this term is now used for spoons of other materials such as metal, plastic, or wood)** (03/14/95/FH/pc:ok; BE2.126)**; abalone shell; shovel** (03/09/95/FH/pc; unconfirmed as 'shovel'). *ðée hcúke* that spoon (03/14/95/FH/pc:hc). *mą́ze hcúke* metal spoon. *htaaníi hcúke íðaachapi* eat soup with a spoon [to pl. addressee].

•• LFD 163: *hciuke* <ṭsiu´-ge> a spoon, a shell spoon.

••• *QU htíke* cup, ladle made of horn (refers to clamshell spoon etymologically) (RR).

••• Cf. *žą́ąhcuke*.

hcúkˀa. ADJ **decayed, rotten.**

••• Cf. *žąąhcúkˀa*.

hcúxe. ADJ **mangy.** *šǫ́ hcúxe* mangy dog (PM/7/7/94; 02/24/95/FH/pc:ok; BE2.84).

•• JOD (slip file): *cˀuxe* <ts'u-qe> mangy.

he. DECL **sentence-final declarative marker used by female speakers (recorded by LF only; not found in Mod. Os.).**

•• LFD 129: *hápa ðišpi che apše he* <ha´-ba thi-shpi tse a-pshe he> I pounded the corn [woman speaking]. *hápa ðišpi che ðapše he* <ha´-ba thi-shpi tse tha-pshe he> you pounded the corn [woman speaking].

hé. N **horn (e.g., of cow or buffalo).** *htaahékaaɣe* deer-making-horns (personal name) (RBn22-04). *hé ðúška* crooked horns (02/09/95/FH/pc:ok; BE2.67).

•• LFD 59: *he* <he> horn. LFD 159: *hcehéxoce* <ṭse-he´-xo-dse> a young buffalo with gray horns (not yet turned black with age).

hé ðúška. N **name of a dance (lit., 'crooked horns') received by Poncas before they had horses, when dogs carried their loads.** [The dance was given by the Poncas to the Kaws; subsequently the Kaws gave their drum to Pawhuska and Hominy Osages; the drum was given by Poncas to Grayhorse Osages (RBn11-01/JW&FW; HHsk/c.1977).]

hé káaɣe. N **roached hair, little boy's roached hair with a tail (lit., 'make horn')** (RBn11-01/JW&FW; HHaskell/c.1976, unconfirmed).

••• *KS hegáɣe* scalp lock (LF The Omaha Tribe) (RR).

héchi̧. V [reg., *_héchi̧*] [onomatopoeic] *(intr.)* **sneeze** (RBn19-01). *ahéchie* I sneezed (021083p4). *ðahéchie* you sneezed (021083p4). *héchi̧pé* he sneezed. *ąhéchi̧pe* we sneezed.

héðǫǫpa. N [*hé* + *ðǫǫpá*] **braids (lit., 'two horns'); ponytails (two sections of hair, one gathered from left and one from right side of the head, bound close to the scalp, and hanging loosely).** *héðǫǫpa i̧* wearing braids (lit., 'wearing two horns'). *héðǫǫpa káaɣe akxái* he's wearing braids (01/07/95/FH/pc:ok; BE2.11). *héðǫǫpa* wearing braids (FH; 04/13/95/LS/pc).

hée. N **lice, louse** (BE2.79, RBn2-MOJ; HH; 02/15/95/FH/pc:ok).

•• LFD 59: *he* <he> louse.

••• *OM* same as Osage (LFD 59).

heehé (variant of **hehé**).

héeoce (variant: **hióce**). N [*hée* + *océ*] **monkey (lit., 'looks for lice').**

hehúha (variant: **hehúhai**) V [reg.?, *_hehúha*] [reduplicated?] *(intr.)* **breathe hard, pant** (01/09/95/FH/pc:ok; BE2.12).

hehé (variant: **heehé**). V [reg.?, *_hehé*] *(intr.)* **short of breath.** *heehé apai* he's shortwinded (RBn HW; FH:okc).

•• LFD 59: *hehé* <he-he´> rapid breathing, to pant, respiration. *áhehe* <a´-he-he> I pant. *ðahéhe* <tha-he´-he> you pant. *ąhéha pe* <oⁿ-he´-ha i> we pant.

••• Cf. *hehúha*.

héka. N **buzzard** (RBn23-08, unconfirmed [01/04/95/FH/pc:uk; 04/17/95/LS/pc:uk])**; hawk.** *héka mǫ́šǫ* hawk feathers (unconfirmed; 01/24/95/FH/pc:uk).

•• LFD 59: *heká* <he-ga´> turkey buzzard.

••• *QU héga* buzzard (RR); *OM* same as Osage (LFD 59).

hépe. ADJ, N **a small amount, approximately half a container; piece, part, some, a bit.** *níi hépe*

hépe (*continued*)
ąkʔú give me a little water [about half a glass]. *hépe žį ąkʔú* give me some, not very much. *hépe ąkʔú* give me a piece (of paper towel or napkin, etc.). *súhka hépe abráache* I ate some of the chicken (PM).

•• LFD 59: *hépe* <he´be> the half of (ritual expression). *hépeną* <he´-be-no^{n}> partly, not whole, partial [*na* 'only'] (03/08/95/FH/pc:ok). *hépeðąðą* <he´-be-tho^{n}-tho^{n}> piece by piece (unconfirmed).

••• *QU hébe* piece, part (RR).

••• Cf. *ohépe.*

hépežį. N **a little piece, a small amount, a little bit (used with both count nouns and mass nouns).** • ADV **a little.** *wažážeíe hépežį hpímą* I know how to talk Osage a little bit (2/2/MSB/504).

héxpa. ADJ, N [stat., *_héxpa*] **bushy head, frowzy, unkempt** (BE2.14; 01/19/95/FH/pc:ok)**; fuzzy; disheveled (e.g., having mussed or messed-up hair).** *šǫ́žį héxpa žį́* little fuzzy dog (RBn22-08).

•• LFD 59: *hpáhįhexpa* <p̣a´-hi^{n}-he-xpa> disheveled. *héxpa* <he´-xpa> frowzy, unkempt. *wakʔo akxa htaxpi ðǫ héxpa pi a* <wa-ḳ'u a-ka ṭa-xpi tho^{n} he´-xpa bi a> [*htaxpi ðǫ* is unconfirmed] the woman has a frowzy head. *níhka akxa héxpa pe* <ni´-ḳa a-ka he´-xpa bi a> the man is unkempt. LFD 125: *hpáhį ąhexpa* <p̣a´-hi^{n} tho^{n} o^{n}-he-xpa> I am disheveled. *hpáhį ðǫ ðihexpa* <p̣a´-hi^{n} tho^{n} thi-he-xpa> [Mod. Os. omits *ðǫ* <tho^{n}>] you are disheveled. *hpáhį wahexpa pe* <p̣a´-hi^{n} tho^{n} wa-he-xpa i> we are disheveled, unkempt. LFD 126: *hpáxį hexpa* <p̣a´-xi^{n} he-xpa> disheveled, hair disarranged.

hi (variant of **hú** 'trunk').

hí (see **ahí** 'arrive there').

híce (variants: **ahíce, hícewae**). V [reg., *_híce*] *(trans.)* **hurry.** *áhice* I hurry s.o. along (108-b/FH/400). *íhice apái* they're hurrying s.o. along (108-b/FH/416). • **encourage** (PM; RBn23-12). *tówe pa awáhihce* I'm trying to encourage these people (PM/7/7/94). *wažáže apa ahice apa* Osages encourage one another (PM; LS).

••• Cf. *íhice, wáhice.*

híceðe. V [reg., *híce_ðe*] [*híce* + *ðe* CAU] *(trans.)* **hurry s.o., cause to hurry.** *híceąðe akxai* they're hurrying me (RB: HHaskell). *hícewaðe* tell them to hurry (lit., 'make them hurry') (RB:HHaskell).

•• LFD 59: *híceðe* <hi´-dse-the> hurry, hasten. *híceaðe* <hi´-dse-a-the> I hurried him. *híceðaðe* <hi´-dse-tha-the> you hurried him. *híceąwąða pe* <hi´-dse-o^{n}-wo^{n}-tha i> we hurried him.

hícewae (variant of **híce**).

híðaxa (variant: **hį́ðaxai**). N **breechcloth, loincloth, diaper** (01/09/95/FH/pc:prod). *híðaxa oxpáði akxai* he [has] lost his breechcloth (RBn23-13). *híðaxa éži wį kšiɣa* change his diaper (lit., 'make him up another diaper') (RBn23-13; ok).

•• LFD 62: *híðaxa* <hi´-tha-xa> loin cloth, diaper, breechcloth (BE2.12) (RB note: also baby's diaper).

híðe. V [reg., *hí_ðe*] [*ahí* + *ðe* CAU] *(trans.)* **send there (lit., 'cause to arrive there').** *ihtéžį akxa mázeíe híðape* his sister called (lit., 'his sister made a phone call arrive there').

•• LFD 62: *hiðé* <hi-the´> to have gone, to have departed, cause to reach there, send thither [all meanings except 'send thither' unconfirmed (03/06/95/FH/pc:uk)].

híðǫkxeį (variant of **hį́ðohkižį**).

híeną (variants: **híenąi, híną**). VP [uninfl.] **happen.** *híenąi* it happens (FH/pc). *híną* when it gets to be that time (lit., 'just as it arrives').

•• LFD 93: *míǫpa ohkiste hi e ną* <mi´-o^{n}-ba u-ḳi-çte hi e no^{n}> semimonthly. (02/25/95/FH/pc:ok). LFD 61: *hí ną* <hi´ no^{n}> come to.

hii (variant of **íhį**).

híi (variant: **hį́į**). N **tooth, teeth** (03/23/95/FH/pc:ok). [Originally *híi* 'tooth' had a non-nasal vowel, while *hį́į* 'hair, fur' had a nasal vowel, but currently both forms are used for both meanings.] *hį́į ðáalį šǫ́ ðąįšé* your teeth are still good (03/23/95/FH/pc:okc). *hį́į hpíiži ąhé* I have bad teeth (03/23/95/FH/pc:okc). *hį́į lúuža* brush your teeth [imperative] (03/23/95/FH/pc:ok; BE2.143). *híi ški ðiiskíke akxai* he's even grinding his teeth.

•• LFD 59: *hi* <hi> tooth, teeth.

••• *OM* same as Osage (LFD 59).

híi (variant of **hú** 'trunk, leg' and of **hį́į** 'hair').

híi įke. ADJP [*híi* 'tooth' + *ðįké* NEG] **toothless, without teeth** (BE2.143; 03/23/95/FH/pc:ok).

hiiðá. V [reg.+sync., *_hii_ðá*] *(intr.)* **bathe** (01/06/95/FH/pc:prod). *hąpái ahíibra* I took a bath today (01/06/95/FH/pc:ok). *ahíibra hkǿbra* I want to take a bath (01/06/95/FH/pc:prod). *ahíibra hta ąhé* I'm going to take a bath. *ðahíiða ðáalį* you ought to take a bath [unexpected form of the verb] (01/06/95/FH/pc:ok; BE2.7). *ðahíišta nįkšé* you are bathing (FH:prod). *hiiðáape* he bathed (FH:prod: *aa*). *hiiðá akxa* he's taking a bath (FH/06/16/01/pc). *hiiðá wikí[ð]e* I'm giving you a bath (lit., 'I am causing you, my own, to bathe') (MREI 1-01-93-8). • **swim.** *ąhíiða ški hta ąkái* we are also going to swim (05/02/95/LS/pc:ok; BE2.130).

•• LFD 61: *hiðá* <hi-tha´> to bathe in a stream. *hiðá bre ha* <hi-tha´ bthe ha> [sentence-final *ha* is not used in Mod. Os.] I go to bathe. *hiðá ąkaða pe ha* <hi-tha´ oⁿ-ga-tha pe ha> [sentence-final *ha* is not used in Mod. Os.] we go to bathe.

híihką (variant: **híihka**). N **ankle** (01/04/95/FH/pc:prod). *híihką wasúhuži* dirty ankles (01/04/95/FH/pc:prod; BE2.3). *híihka wákalą akxái* your ankles are dirty (RBn10-3:MOJ/79).

•• LFD 60: *híhką* <hi´-ḳoⁿ> ankles. *híhką wihta žįka* <hi´-ḳoⁿ wi-ṭa zhiⁿ-ga ha> my ankles are small. *híhką ižįka* <hi´-ḳoⁿ i-zhiⁿ-ga> small of the leg, the ankle.

híinąąži (variant of **hínąąžį**).

híiˀį (variant of **hį́į**). N [*hį́į* 'hair, whiskers' (with unexpected denasalization) + *į́* 'wear'] **whiskers** (FH).

híko. N **fable; learning(?)** (RB, unconfirmed, FH: not 'learning'). [Fables are the Osage children's stories in which animals are the main characters, told especially during winter. Some modern speakers (LS) say that snakes will come out if these stories are told at other times of the year; others (FH) disagree that there is danger of snakes, but all agree that winter or when it is snowing is the time for telling a *híko*.] *híko wį obráake hta mįkšé* I'm going to tell you a story (JS) (BE2.77).

•• LFD 60: *híko* <hi´-go> a fable, a myth, a story not to be taken literally.

híną (variant of **híeną**).

hínąąžį (variant: **híinąąži**). V [sync.+reg.?, *_hí_nąąžį?*] *(intr.)* **become.** *ókaayeįke akxa ðée nąkˀǫ́pi áha wáli kíhpiiži hínąąžįpe* when Useless heard that, he really got sad (RBn10-2:MOJ/79). *John akxa ðée nąkˀǫ́pi áha, wálį kíhpiiži hínąąžįpe* when John heard that, he got very sad. • **begin, start.** *oðíhtą ðiitą́ šǫ́ apa, waachí hínąąžį nąpé* when he would pull the wagon, he'd start in dancing (RBn10-2:MOJ/79). [The 2nd sg. form parallel to this example would presumably be *waachí šíðanąąžį* (?) 'you would start in dancing'.]

•• LFD 61: *hínąžį* <hi´-noⁿ-zhiⁿ> having arrived there and stood (from a ritual).

hióce (variant of **héeoce**).

híǫ (variant: **húį**). V [conjug. unknown] **move to another location.**

••• Cf. *wahúį*.

híǫnįį (variants: **hṹũni** [FH], **hįúni**). N **garter (as for Osage dance costume)** (BE2.53). (01/31/95/FH/pc:ok: *hṹũni*).

hípše. V [reg., *_hípše*] *(intr.)* **stumble and fall.** *ahípše* I stumbled and fell (RBn10-2). *hípšape* he stumbled and fell (RBn10-2). *hípša įká!* don't stumble and fall! (RBn10-2).

hiú (variant of **hú**).

hiúšce (variant of **húuscee**).

hį́. INTERJ **isn't it so (expression inserted between phrases, marking pauses, in certain speeches of early to mid-1900s, somewhat like French "n'est-ce pas?" or use of "you know?" by some English speakers).**

••• *KS hį́e* question-marking particle (JOD, RR).

hį́ (variant of **hį́į**).

hį́ðaxai (variant of **híðaxa**).

hį́ðohkižį (variant: **híðǫkxeį**). ADJ **naked, nude** (RBn22-08, unconfirmed). *John akxa Mary áðiižą hiðohkižį* John has Mary in bed naked (RB, unconfirmed).

•• LFD 338: *ðohkáðį* <tho-ḳa´-thiⁿ> stripped to the waist.

••• *KS yokkáyį* naked or stripped to the waist (MR, RR); *QU ðokką́nį, tokką́nį* naked to the waist (RR), *žó ðokkánį hí* naked, nude (RR).

hį́į (variant: **hį́**). N **color, colors, bright colors.** *hį́į ke wáli ohtázape* their colors [of the flowers] were very beautiful.

••• *QU hįhtazí* brown, oak colored (RR); *KS óphą hį ekǫ́* elk colored, dun [may be *hį́į*] (JOD, RR).

hį́į (variants: **híi, híiˀį**). N **hair, whiskers, fur, fuzz as on a peach** (03/23/95/FH/pc:ok)**; slivers or small strips of anything.** [Originally *hį́į* 'hair, fur' had a nasal vowel, while *híi* 'tooth' had a non-nasal vowel, but currently both forms are used for both meanings.]

••• Cf. *hceehį́į, hpahį́į, hpaxį́į, įįštáhįį, mąąhį́.*

hį́į (variant of **híi** 'tooth').

hį́į (variant of **į́hį**).

hį́įce (variant: **hįįcé**). N **dish, plate** (FH/8/30/94; prod; PMt#97A; 02/27/95/JS/pc)**; crockery, bowl; bark (of a tree)** (BE2.6; 01/20/95/FH/pc:ok). *hį́įce huuwáli* a lot of dishes. *hį́įce žį ąðíištąpe* we're through with these dishes (FH:prod). *áwanǫbre hį́įce ážu* set the dishes on the table (BE2.31). *hį́įce húu aðį́ akxai* they have a lot of plates (RBn14-10). *hį́įce huuhtą́ka* a lot of dishes (FH:4/17/96/tape). *hį́įce wíbrulekc* I broke your dish.

•• LFD 60: *hįce* <hiⁿ-dse> the linden tree and its bark. "The inner bark of this tree was often

hį́ce (*continued*)
used in making twine and for rough weaving. The inner bark of the following trees was also used: hi^n-dse xo-dse, gray linden (saplings). hi^n-dse zhu-dse, red linden. hi^n-dse sha-be, dark linden. hi^n-dse wa-xtha, the papaw." *hį́ce xci hi chece oða nąžį* <hi^n´-dse xtsi hi tse-dse u-tha no^n-zhi^n> [expected Mod. Os. form: *hį́cehi che ce oðánąąžį́*] you stood under the linden tree. *hį́ce braða* <hi^n´-dse btha-tha> bowls made of basswood, widened. *hį́ce braxe* <hi^n´-dse btha-xe> china plate. LFD 61: *hį́cehpe* <hi^n´-dse-pe> a wooden tray or bowl for bread or meat. LFD 101 (unconfirmed): *mǫ ǫ́hka hįce* <mo^n-o^n´-ka hi^n-dse> [expected Mod. Os. form: *mǫ́įhka hį́ce* 'earth plate'] crockery. [Modern speaker's comment: Both 'plate' and 'crockery' are *hį́ce*, but *mǫ́įhka hį́ce* is unknown (LF) (04/17/95/LS/pc).] LFD 225: *žą́hįce* <zho^n´-hi^n-dse> a wooden bowl. LFD 233: *hį́ce* <hi^n´-dse> inner bark of a tree.
••• *KS hį́įǰebe* dish, plate, tray, bowl (RR).

hį́ce apakˀą́. N **platter** (t#14b-p1; 04/17/95/LS/pc:uk).

hį́ce braaka. N **platter** (HHtL3-B-p1)**; dish that is flat and wide** (HH).
•• LFD 61: *hį́ce brakˀa* <hi^n´-dse btha-k'a> a plate.

hį́ce hu. N **pawpaw (the plant, not the fruit).**
•• LFD 60–61 (unconfirmed): *hį́ce hu* <hi^n´-dse hiu> the papaw (*Asimina triloba*).

hį́ce íðuuža wépukxa. N [*hį́ce* + *í-* LOC + *ðuužá* + *wépukxa*] **dish soap, dish detergent (lit., 'soap for washing dishes with')** (01/20/95/FH/pc:ok; BE2.32).
••• JOD (slip file): *wépuka* <we´-püi-ka> soap.

hį́ce ípukxa (variant: **hį́ce ípuxa**). N **dish towel** (04/07/95/LS/pc:ok; BE2.32).

hį́cecˀohu. N **fire-drill stick, stick used to rub fire-making wood (*žą́ąhpeece*).**
••• JOD (slip file): *hį́ tsetˀoho* <hi^n´ tse-t'uhu> stick . . . used to revolve on the [*žą́ąhpeece*] as a fire-drill.

hįcéžį. N [*hį́ce* + *-žį* 'little'] **small crafts (lit., 'small bark', 'small plate').** *hįcéžį ážu hta apai* they're going to put out [set out] their crafts [for sale] (FH:5/02/96/prod).

hį́įhkiąpi. N [presumably *hį́į* 'colors' + *hkik-* REFL + *ǫ́ǫ* 'wear' + *api*] **Wearing Bright Colors (personal name)** (FH: prod). [Name of FH's relative Martha.]

hį́įǫke (variants: **húuįke, hų́ųįke, hų́ųke**). N [perhaps from *hį́į* 'color'] **hosiery, stockings, socks, leggings.** *hų́įke xó* gray leggings; gray stockings (02/09/95/FH/pc:okc; RB). *hų́ųįke ðiištóe* take off one's stockings (02/15/95/FH/pc:prod orig). *húuįke bríištoe* I took off my stockings (MREI). *húuįke ąðíištoe* we took off our stockings (03/14/95/MREI/pc:ok).
•• LFD 62: *húįke* <hiu´-i^n-ge> leggings (man's).

hį́įǫke xóe (variant: **hų́ųke xóe**). N **socks (lit., 'gray hosiery').** *hų́ųke xóe ðiiškí* wash the socks.

hį́įska. N **beads** (01/06/95/FH/pc:prod).
•• LFD 60: *hįská wanǫpˀį* <hi^n-çka´ wa-no^n-p'i^n> bead necklace. *hįská žįka* <hi^n-çka´ zhi^n-ga> small beads.
••• *KS hįská* beads (RR).

hį́įska káaɣe. VP [sync. *k>p*, *hį́įska _káaɣe*] **do beadwork** (04/19/95/FH/pc). • N **beadwork.**

hįįská wekáaɣe. VP [sync. *k>p*, *hįįská we_káaɣe*] **do beadwork** (RB). • N **beadwork.**

hį́įskawáata. N [*hį́įska* + *waatá*] **rosary (lit., 'beads for prayer/praying').**

hįįšá. N **Caddo (tribe or tribal member)** [tribe near Kingfisher or Anadarko, Oklahoma, of which Stanley Edge and John Wilson were members] (01/20/95/FH/pc:prod orig; 03/08/95/PM).
•• LFD 61: *hįšá* <Hi^n-sha´> Caddo Indian Tribe.

hį́įšce (variants: **hį́įšce, hį́įšcece, hį́įščece**). ADJ **fuzzy.** *šǫ́ke akxa hį́įščece akxai* the dog is shaggy, the dog is fuzzy (BE2.52; 01/30/95/FH/pc:okc).
•• LFD 61: *hį́scece* <hi^n´-stse-dse> shaggy or long haired. *šǫ́ke akxa hį́sceca pe* <sho^n´-ge a-ka hi^n´-stse-dsa bi a> the dog is shaggy.

hį́įščežį (variant: **hį́įšče žį** [Hominy version]). N **fuzzy balls (especially the small fuzzy balls on yarn garters or on a woman's belt), "pill" (as on a sweater when loose fibers form tufts or balls)** (01/30/95/FH/pc:okc).

hį́įščece (variant of **hį́įšce**).

hį́įzįį. N [possibly *hį́į* 'hair' + *zízi* 'brown' (PM)] **mink** (BE2.88, RBn1-MOJ/p22, RBn1-24).
•• LFD 60: *hįzį́mąį* <Hi^n-çi^n´-mo^{n}i^n> Brown-hair-walker (personal name; refers to the color of the buffalo calf).

hį́še. ADJ, V [uninfl.] **fat (said of a person).** *wáli hį́še ąhé* I'm really fat (BE2.45; RBn2/p17, unconfirmed; 01/23/95/FH/pc:no).

hįúni (variant of **hį́ǫnįį**).

hkaamą́. V [uninfl.] *(intr.)* **ring** (FH).
•• JOD (slip file) *hkámą* <ka´-ma^{n}> vb. root: ring, as a bell. *íikaahtamą hcéska nǫpʔį́ kšíðe, hkaamą́ mąðį́ apá* <íḳatama^{n} tséska nŭ^{n}´p'i^{n} kcí¢ĕ, kama^{n}´ ma^{n}´¢i^{n} apa´> the cow being made to wear a bell on the neck, it rings as she walks.
•• LFD 82: *hkamą́* <ḳa-mo^{n}´> the sound produced by the striking of a bell.
••• Cf. *ðuuhkáamą* (and perhaps *íikaahtamą*).

-hkace (variant: **-hkaci**). V ROOT **heat, hot.**
••• Cf. *óhkace, táahkace.*

hkáɣe. N **crow** (BE2.27; FH:4/22/96/tape:ok).
•• JOD (slip file): *hkáɣe* <k'a´-xĕ> crow.
•• LFD 83: *hkáɣe* <ḳa´-xe> crow. LFD 84: *hkáɣe htąka* <ḳa´-xe ṭo^{n}-ga> big crow, a raven.
••• *OP kkáɣe* crow.

hkáɣe htą́ka. N **raven.**

hkáwa. N **horse, pony.** *hkáwa ðé kxa* that horse standing (02/09/95/FH/pc:prod orig; BE2.68).
•• LFD 82: *hkáwa* <ḳa´-wa> horse, nag, pony (corruption of the Spanish word for horse).

hkáwa hkipáną. N **horserace** (04/13/95/FH/pc:ok; BE2.68).

hkáwa óʔku (variant: **hkáwaakʔu**). N **Horse Feeder (personal name).** [May be an error for *hkáwa ókʔu.*]

hkáwa wahcéxi. NP **wild horse (lit., 'difficult horse'), untamed horse** (RBn HW13; RBn22-06).

hkáwa wakʔú. N **Horse Giver (personal name).**

hkáwa xóe (variant: **hkáwa xóce**). N **gray horse.**
••• Cf. *hkáwaxoce.*

hkáwaakʔu (variant of **hkáwa óʔku**).

hkáwaalį̨. V [reg., *hkáwaa_lį̨*] [*hkáwa* + *álį̨*] *(intr.)* **ride horseback** (02/09/95/FH/pc:ok). • ADV **horseback, mounted on a horse.** *hkáwaalį̨ aðáapi che* they have gone horseback riding (02/09/95/FH/pc:ok; BE2.68).
•• LFD 82: *hkáwaalį* <ḳa´-wa-a-gthi^{n}> to ride horseback. *hkáwa aalį* <ḳa´-wa a-a-gthi^{n}> I ride horseback. *hkáwa aðalį* <ḳa´-wa a-tha-gthi^{n}> you ride horseback. *hkáwa ąkalį pe* <ḳa´-wa o^{n}-ga-gthi^{n} i> we ride horseback.

hkáwaalį̨ aðée. VP [sync., *hkáwaalį̨ a_ðée*] *(intr.)* **go on horseback.** *hkáwalį̨ aðéei ché* he has gone on horseback (RBn3-05; FH/11/19/01/pc:ok). *hkáwalį̨ aðáapi ché* they have gone on horseback (RBn3-05).

hkáwaceženii. N [*hkáwa* + *céženii*] **beer (lit., 'horse urine').** *hkáwaceženii tóa ąðáahtą ąkái hce* let's go drink some beer [said to one person] (01/07/95/FH/pc:ok).
••• *QU téže* urinate (RR); *KS jéže* urinate (RR).

hkáwatǫpa. N [*hkáwa* + *tǫ́pe*] **horse herder, horse watcher** (WHM981022, unconfirmed).

hkáwaxoce. N **Grayhorse camp (near Fairfax, Oklahoma)** (02/03/95/FH/pc:ok: use *hkáwaxoce* for the town name).

hkáwažį htą́wą. N [*hkáwa* + *-žį* 'little' +*htą́wą*] **Bartlesville, Oklahoma (lit., 'little-horse town')** (RBn2-MOJ/p32; HRE/01/17/02/pc:ok).
•• LFD 83: *hkáwažįka* <ḳa´-wa-zhi^{n}-ga> name given to the town of Bartlesville, Kansas [*sic*], by the Osage.

hk̨ą́ (variant: **hkǫ́**). N **vein, artery, blood vessel.**.
•• JOD (Devouring Mountain p2 ln10): *ną́ące ką pápaaye akxa ska* <nănṭṣe-k'ă^{n} p̣ăp̣axe akqá ska> he cut off a heart vein or artery.
•• LFD 351: *hkǫ* <ḳo^{n}> vein.

hk̨ą́ące. N **apple; fruit.** *hk̨ą́ące áazo* I like apples (BE2.3; FH/09/09/01/pc). *hk̨ą́ące wį hą́ąpa záani štáache tą, ðáalį aapé* an apple a day is good, they say (equivalent of "an apple a day keeps the doctor away") (FH/09/09/01/pc).

hk̨ą́ące hį́įsce (variant: **hk̨ą́ące hį́įšče**). N **peach** (03/07/95/PM/pc:ok; BE2.102).
•• LFD 89: *hką́ce hį scee* <ḳo^{n}´-dse hi^{n} stse-e> hairy plums, peaches. *hką́ce hį scee che zi* <ḳo^{n}´-dse hi^{n} stse-e tse çi> [expected Mod. Os. form: *hk̨ą́ące hį́isce zi*, without *che*] yellow peaches.

hk̨ą́ące hpá álą. N **pear (lit., 'apple with a nose placed upon it')** (BE2.102; 03/06/95/FH/pc:okc).

hk̨ą́ące oolą́ (variant of **hk̨ąącóolą**).

hk̨ą́ące púze. N **dried fruit.**

hk̨ą́ące sápe. N **prune.**
•• LFD 89: *hką́cesape* <ḳo^{n}´ dse-ça-be> black plums dried, prunes.

hk̨ą́ące xóce. N **plum.** *hk̨ą́ące xoce apa cuuta pe* the plum is ripe (LFD 39; FH; 01/11/95/FH/pc:ok).
•• LFD 89: *hką́ce xoce* <ḳo^{n}´-dse xo-dse> the wild plum.

hk̨ą́ące zi. N **orange** (BE2.99; 03/02/95/FH/pc:ok).
•• LFD 89: *hką́cezi* <ḳo^{n}´-dse-çi> an orange. *hką́ce si wį hkǫbra* <ḳo^{n}´-dse çi wi^{n} ḳo^{n}-btha> I want an orange. *hką́ce si wį škǫšta* <ḳo^{n}´-dse çi wi^{n} shko^{n}-shda> you want an orange. *hką́cezi hi* <ḳo^{n}´-dse-çi hi> an orange tree (unconfirmed, 03/03/95/FH/pc:uk).

hk̨ą́ące zi cʔáaðe. N **lemon** (02/15/95/FH/pc:ok; BE2.78).
•• LFD 89: *hkącési cʔaðe* <ḳo^{n}-dse´-çi ṭs'a-the> sour orange, lemon.

hk̨ą́ące zi žį́. N **apricot** (01/06/95/FH/pc:ok, ok; BE2.3).

hką́ące žąą. N **burial stick, red stick put into coffin at head or foot, made of special wood** (FH/11/19/01/pc).

hką́ące žúe (variant: **hką́ące žúuce**). N **tomato** (BE2.142; 04/26/95/FH/pc:okc).

hką́ącenii. N [*hką́ące* + *níi*] **fruit juice** (t#14a-p5; 04/14/95/FH/pc).

hkąącóolą (variant: **hką́ące oolą́**). N [*hką́ące* + *oolą́*] **pie of any sort (fruit, cream, etc.) (lit., 'place fruit into it')** (03/08/95/MREI/pc:ok). *watxą́ hkąącóolą* pumpkin pie.

•• RB: <káhⁿ-tseh o-d-?-láhⁿ>.

•• LFD 89: *hką́ce olą* <ķoⁿ´-dse u-gthoⁿ> pie.

hką́ąze. N **Kaw, Kansa (tribe or tribal member)** (02/13/95/FH/pc:ok, PM ok; BE2.73).

•• LFD 88: *hką́ze* <ķoⁿ´-çe> Kaw Indian.

••• *KS kką́ąze* Kansa tribe, gens, the Kaws (RR).

hkéðo. N **clear sky, as after a storm.**

•• LFD 85: *hkéða* <ķe´-tha> the sky, the unclouded or clear sky. *hkéðamąį* <ķe´-tha-moⁿ-iⁿ> Clear-day-approaching (personal name).

hkée. N **turtle, tortoise, terrapin** (04/06/95/FH/pc:ok; BE2.145).

•• LFD 84: *hké* <ķe´> turtle, tortoise, terrapin. *hke táhpa žį́ka* <ķe da´-p̣a zhiⁿ-ga> little round turtle.

••• *WI: kee* turtle (KM).

hkeetáxe. N **shadow** (BE2.119; 03/09/95/MREI:ma). [Archaic.]

•• LFD 84: *hkétaxe* <ķe´-da-xe> shadow. *hkétaxe wį hpaxe* <ķe´-da-xe wiⁿ p̣a-xe> I cast a shadow. *hkétaxe wį nǫhpa pe šį́htožį́ka akxa* <ķe´-da-xe wiⁿ noⁿ-p̣a bi a shiⁿ-ṭo zhiⁿ-ga a-ka> [expected Mod. Os. form: *hkéetaxe wį nǫ́ǫhpape šį́htožį akxa*] the boy was afraid of the shadow.

••• *KS kkédaɣe* (JOD), *kkédaxe* (MR) shadow, shade (RR).

hkéetaxewatǫ́e. N [*hkeetáxe* + *watǫ́e*] **movies (lit., 'watch shadows')** (RB, unconfirmed).

hki- (form of the reflexive prefix *hkik-* except before *c, k, p, t, ?* [where it is *hkih-*]; see **hkik-**).

hkíaci. V [reg., *_hkíaci*] [*hkik-* REFL + *kaací*] *(intr.)* **wipe oneself (in the bathroom, after using the toilet)** (RB; LS). *ðahkíaci?* did you wipe yourself? (in the bathroom only) (05/01/95/LS/pc; BE2.159). *žįkáži apa hkíaci apai* the children are wiping themselves (05/01/95/LS/pc). *hkiácipi* wipe yourselves (05/01/95/LS/pc).

hkícheðe (variants: **hkíicheðe**). V [reg., *hkíche_ðe*] [perhaps *hkik-* REFL + *che* POSIT + *ðe* CAU] *(trans.)* **put down, set down, or place a standing item on a surface (e.g., a bowl of soup or basket of rolls)** (FH:04/24/96/t-s2). *hkíicheðaa!* set it down! (FH).

•• LFD 80: *hkíicheðe* <ķi´-i-tse-the> to put down a thing that can stand, as a filled bag, a pole, or a gun. LFD 86: *hkíicheaðe* <ķi´-i-tse-a-the> I put it down. *hkíicheðaðe* <ķi´-i-tse-tha-the> you put it down. *hkíicheąða pe* <ķi´-i-tse-oⁿ-tha i> we put it down.

••• *KS kkiičhégiye* put down his [standing inanimate] object before its owner (RR).

••• Cf. *kícheðe, ohkíicheðe.*

hkiðé. ADV [contains *hkik-* RECIP] **beside each other** (12/30/94/FH/pc:prod). *hki[ð]etóopa* eight (lit., 'two fours beside each other').

hkíðe CAU [reg., *_hkíðe*] [*hkik-* REFL + *ðe* CAU] *(intr.)* **make oneself (to do or be).** *óžį hpíiži ðįké, ók?ą ðáalį hkí[ð]a* don't get angry, have good ways (lit., '. . . make yourself be of good ways') (01/04/95/FH/pc).

hkietóopa (variant: **hkiðétoopa**). ADJ, N [*hkiðé* 'beside each other' + *tóopa*] **eight (lit., '[two] fours beside each other')** (12/30/94/FH/pc:prod). *hkíðetóopa oožú nąpé* they [used to, always] put in eight (BE2.41; 04/18/95/FH/pc:ok).

•• LFD 85: *hkíetopa* <ķi´-e-do-ba> eight; the archaic word for eight is <p̣e-tha-bthiⁿ>. [Unconfirmed as 'eight' by Mod. Os. speakers.]

••• *OM* same as Osage (LFD 85).

hkih- (form of the reflexive prefix *hkik-* before *c, k, p, t*; see **hkik-**).

hkihkáaɣe. V [reg.+sync. *k>p*, *_hkih_kaaɣe*] [*hkik-* REFL + *káaɣe*] *(trans.)* **make, build, or make up for oneself (e.g., one's bed), do for oneself.** [The expected (but perhaps not attested?) 1st sg. form of this verb is *áhkihpáaɣe* or *ahkíhpaaɣe* 'I built it for myself'; the expected 2nd sg. form is *ðáhkiškáaɣe* or *ðahkíškaaɣe* 'you built it for yourself'.] *ážą hkíhkáaɣa* make your bed up (02/24/95/FH/pc; RBn2-MOJ/p33). *ðíe hkihkáaɣa* do it for yourself.

••• Cf. *waðílą hkihkáaɣe.*

hkíhkįnį. ADJ **curly, kinky, tangled** (FH:okc,08/96). [Borrowed from English *kinky.*] *hpaxį́į hkíhkįnį* curly hair, black (African) hair, tangled hair.

hkihkǫ́ða. V [reg.+sync. fortisizing stop stem, *_hkih_kǫ́ða*] [*hkik-* REFL + *kǫ́ða*] *(trans.)* **want as one's own, want for oneself.** *ðáhkiškǫsta* you want it as your own.

hkihkǫ́ze. v [reg., *_hkihkǫ́ze*] [*hkik-* REFL/RECIP + *kǫ́ze*] *(intr.)* **hold a Native American Church meeting, have or put on a peyote meeting (lit., 'teach oneself, teach each other').** *haakxą́ta ðahkíhkǫ́ze hta paašé?* when are you all going to have a peyote meeting? (04/28/95/LS/pc:ok). *haatxą́ta ðahkíhkǫze hta paašé?* when are you all going to have a meeting? (RBn14-06). *iiną́žį akxa hkihkǫ́ze hta akxái* my aunt is going to have a meeting (03/16/95/FH/pc:ok; 03/05/95/JS/pc:ok). • N **Native American Church (the religion also known as peyote religion, brought to the Osages by John Wilson [known as Moonhead]); peyote meeting, Native American Church meeting.**

•• LFD 86: *hkihkǫ́ze* <ḳi-ḳo^{n}´-çe> the act of religious devotion.

hkihkǫ́ze waaðǫ́. N **peyote song, song sung in peyote meeting.**

hkihkúce. v [reg., *_hkihkúce*] [*hkik-* RECIP + *hkúce*] **shoot each other, shoot at each other.**

hkíhpaahi v [reg.+sync. fortisizing stop stem, *_hkíh_paahi*] [*hkik-* REFL + *paahí*] *(trans.)* **pick, pick up, choose, select for oneself.** *tanákˀa hkíhpaahi!* pick up your papers [yourself]! (03/07/95/FH/pc:ok; BE2.102). *ðahkíšpaahi* you chose it for yourself.

•• LFD 87: *hkihpáhi* <ḳi-p̣a´-hi> to choose a man or woman from their own number, as in a ball game.

hkihpíǫ (variant: **hkíhpiǫ**). v [reg.+sync.+sync. nasal vowel stem, *_hki_hpí_ǫ*] [*hkik-* REFL + *hpíǫ*] *(trans.)* **know or learn for oneself** (RB; 04/14/95/PM/pc:ok). *ðahkíšpížǫ škǫ́šta* it's yours and you want to learn it [speaking of Indian ways] (lit., 'you learn it yourself; you learn it for yourself') (RB: PM:ok). *ahkíhpimą* I learn for myself. *ðahkíhšpižǫ* you learn for yourself. *hkihpíǫ* she learns for herself. *ąhkíhpiǫ* we learn for ourselves.

hkíhtǫpe (variant: **hkihtǫ́pe**). v [reg.+sync. fortisizing stop stem, *_hkíh_tǫpe*] [*hkik-* REFL + *tǫ́pe*] *(intr.)* **look at oneself.** *hkíhtǫpa!* look at yourself! *hkihtǫ́pe ðiištą!* quit looking at yourself! *ąhkíhtǫpe* we're looking at ourselves. • *(trans.)* **look at one's own.** [Reflexive used as suus.] *waáhkihtǫ́papi húða* come and look down upon us.

hkíicheðe (variant of **hkícheðe**).

hkiistó. N **council meeting, tribal council session meeting; conference.** *hkiistó panáape* he adjourned the council meeting.

•• LFD 85: *hkistó* <ḳi-çto´> a council, assemblage, meeting, U.S. Congress, the Senate, court, session.

••• *KS kkistó čʰí* council house or church (RR); *QU kistó* council of a gens, *kkistó htą́ka* tribal council (RR).

••• Cf. *kiistó.*

hkiistó omąðį (variant: **hkiistómąį**). N **council member, senator, congressional representative, lawmaker, legislator (lit., 'walks to council')** (BE2.26; 01/13/95/FH/pc:ok). *hkiistómaį háaną hípe?* how many councilmen were present? (lit., '. . . arrived there') (RBn3-01).

•• LFD 85: *hkistó omąðį* <ḳi-çtu´ u-mo^{n}-thi^{n}> a member of the United States Congress, a Senator or Representative.

hkiistóhci. N [*hkiistó* + *hcí*] **courthouse** (01/13/95/FH/pc:okc; BE2.26), **council house.**

•• LFD 85, 245: *hkistóhci* <ḳi-çtu´ṭsi> council house, council house at the agency.

hkiistómąį (variant of **hkiistó omąðį**).

hkik-. PREFIX [*hkih-* before *c, k, p, t*; contracts with following *ð* to form *hkil-*; *hki-* elsewhere, but possibly *hkik-* before *ˀ*] **reflexive prefix: oneself, myself, yourself, himself, herself, itself, ourselves, yourselves, themselves.** *éwaahkikˀǫ́* I did it to myself (FH/11/17/01/pc). *owáhkihkie* I'm talking to myself (RBn10-21; FH/11/17/01/pc). *áhkihtǫ́pa ðį* watch out for yourself. *éwaðahkikˀǫ́* you did it to yourself (FH/11/17/01/pc). *éwahkikˀǫ́* he did it to himself (RBn10-4:MOJ/79; FH/11/17/01/pc). *hkikˀą́zehkíe* make oneself comfortable (RBn2-MOJ/p31). • **reflexive prefix with benefactive interpretation: for oneself, for myself, for yourself, for himself, for herself, for itself, for ourselves, for yourselves, for themselves.** • **with reflexive possessive (suus) interpretation (object is possessed by subject): my, your, his, her, our, their.** *wacúe skúe áhkihtǫį hce* let me look at my cake. • **reciprocal prefix: each other, one another.** *ðakˀéąhkiðe* we are kind to each other (FH/pc). *žóhkile* with each other (RBn15-01). *níhka wakˀó hkíoxta akxai* the man and woman love each other (FH:t142). *óxtahki[ð]api* cherish each other, regard each other as great. *óxtahkiapi* cherish one another, cherish each other (FH/12/95 prod). • **reciprocal prefix with indirect interpretation (dative, benefactive, etc.): for each other, to each other, with each other.** *haxį́ hkíkˀu pe* they gave each other blankets. *waahkíhta paahá* pray for each other, raise it up (RBn10-15).

hkikʔą́ze. v, ADJ [stat.?, *_hkikʔą́ze?*] [perhaps contains *hkik-* REFL] *(intr.)* **(be) comfortable.**

hkikʔą́zehkiðe. v [reg., *hkikʔą́ze_hkiðe*] [*hkikʔą́ze* + *hkíðe* 'make oneself'] *(intr.)* **rest (lit., 'make oneself comfortable')** (RBn10-5:MOJ/79). *hkikʔą́zehkíe* making oneself comfortable (RBn2-MOJ/p31).

••• *KS kʔą́zegile* (JOD) to rest (intr.) (RR).

hkikʔú (variant: **hkíkʔu**). v [reg., *_hkikʔú*] [*hkik-* REFL + *kʔú*] *(trans.)* **give each other.** *haxį́ hkikʔúpe* they gave each other blankets (01/31/95/FH/pc:ok).

hkiláawa. v [reg., *_hkiláawa*] [*hkik-* REFL + *ðaawá*] *(intr.)* **count oneself.** *táatą níðaepi tą ðáalį ée ną aape ąži hkiláawa ée įkápi* they say it is good to give but not to count yourself (lit., 'when you [pl.] give something at giveaway, it's always good, they said, but as for counting yourselves, don't do that') (RBn23-17; CQ:okc).

hkilaaxǫ́. v [reg., *_hkilaaxǫ́*] [*hkik-* REFL + *ðaaxǫ́*] *(intr.)* **bite oneself.**

hkiláažoži v [reg., *_hkiláažoži*] [*hkik-* RECIP + *ðaažóži* (lit., 'hurt each other by mouth'), but with simple transitive interpretation] *(trans.)* **curse a person; say bad things about s.o., "down" s.o. by slandering, maligning or belittling** (RBn2-MOJ/p12; 01/14/95/FH/pc:ok; 04/25/95/PM/pc:ok).

••• Cf. *ðiižóži, hkilíižoži.*

hkilázo. v [reg., *_hkilázo*] [contains *hkik-* REFL] *(intr.)* **relax, recover, come to, after being unconscious.** *ðahkílazo?* did you get relaxed? (RBn23-15, unconfirmed). *ą́skike ąązį́ ðekǫ́ǫci ahkílazo* I was tired but now I'm recovered (FH:t#128). *žúoka ahkílazo mįkšé* my body is recovering (FHt#128). *hkilázo akxai* he's waking up (as after surgery) (FHt#128).

hkilą́ke. v [reg., *_hkilą́ke*] [*hkik-* RECIP + *lą́ke*] *(intr.)* **marry each other.**

•• LFD 86: *hkilą́ke* <ḳi-gtho^{n}´-ge> intermarrying into another tribe [JS: *hkilą́ke* is 'marry', not 'intermarry'.]

••• Cf. *mį́įląke.*

hkilíihkǫįye. v [reg., *_hkilíihkǫįye*] [*hkik-* REFL + *ðiihkóįye*] *(intr.)* **turn oneself around.** *ámahta na hkilíihkoįya* turn yourself the other way.

••• Cf. *-hkóįye, -wįye.*

hkilíisą (variants: **hkíliisąðe, hkilíisąðe**). v [reg., *_hkilíisą(ðe)*] [*hkik-* REFL + *ðiisą́ða*] *(intr.)* **turn oneself around.** *níhka akxa hkilíisąpi iáha ǫǫwíbre tą wakʔą́ hta mįkšé áape* the man turned around and said, "I'll sure be glad when I get rid of you" (RBn79/p4). • **change one's ways.**

hkilíiski. v [reg., *_hkilíiski*] [*hkik-* REFL/RECIP + *ðiiskí*] *(trans.)* **gather up for oneself, gather together for oneself.** *táatąžį ðahkíliiski hta nįkšé?* those little things that you've got, small items, are you going to gather them up? (JS) • *(intr.)* **(with reciprocal interpretation) gather with each other, gather together.** *ðahkíliiski hta pąąšé?* are you all going to gather [together with each other]? (FH:5/02/96/pc). *ąhkíliiski* we gather together (FH). *hǫ́ǫpa hpahą́le che hkilíiski hta apai* the first day of the week, they're going to gather together (FH:4/24/96/tape). *ąhkiliiski ąkatxą́* we are gathered together; we are gathering together. • N **(with reciprocal interpretation) gathering of people, meeting, people gathering with each other.**

hkilíiša. v [reg. *_hkilíiša*] [contains *hkik-* REFL] *(intr.)* **undress oneself, get undressed.**

•• LFD 85: *hkilíša* <ḳi-gthi´-sha> to disrobe, to undress, to remove one's clothes. *ahkíliša* <a-ḳi´-gthi-sha> I undressed. *ðahkíliša* <tha-ḳi´-gthi-sha> you undressed. *ąhkíliša pe* <o^{n}-ḳi´-gthi-sha i> we undressed.

hkilíiški (variants: **hkíliiški, ahkíliiški**). v [reg., *_hkilíiški*] [*hkik-* REFL + *ðiiškí*] *(intr.)* **do laundry for oneself, wash clothes for oneself.** *ahkííliški* I did laundry for myself (FH/08/01/01/pc). *hkíliiški akxa* she washed [clothes] for herself (FH/08/01/01/pc). *ahkíliiški* she washed for herself (FH/01/08/01/pc).

hkíliištą. v [reg., *_hkíliišta*] [*hkik-* REFL + *ðiištą́*] *(intr.)* **ready oneself, get oneself ready.** *ahkíliištą ąkái hce* I've got myself ready, let's go (RBn14-07; FH:okc). *ahkíliištą* I'm ready (RBn14-07&FH: *a* not *ą*). *hkíliišta akxai* he's ready (RBn14-07).

hkilíiziðe. v [reg.?, *_hkilíiziðe?*] [*hkik-* REFL + *ðiizíðe*] *(intr.)* **stretch oneself** (FH).

hkilíižoži. v [reg., *_hkilíižoži*] [*hkik-* RECIP + *ðiižóži*] *(intr.)* **mistreat one another, hurt one another physically or emotionally.** *níhkašie apa wáli hkilíižoži apai* the people are mistreating each other (RBn 3/3/77).

hkilǫ́ǫyemąį. N **honey** (FH:4/22/96/tape, ok).

•• JOD (slip file): *hkilǫ́ǫyemąðį* <ki-ḳ¢ŭ^{n}'-xe ma^{n}'-¢i^{n}> a bee, bees.

hkílǫ(lǫ). v [reg., *_hkílǫ(lǫ)*] [contains *hkik-* RECIP; reduplicated] *(intr.)* **call each other names.** *ðahkílǫ ðaašé* you [moving] are calling yourself a name (01/09/95/FH/pc:ok). *hkílǫlǫ apái* they are calling each other names; they called each other names (01/09/95/FH/pc:ok; RBn10-7:JW). *hkílǫlǫpe* they called each other names (01/09/95/FH/pc:ok).

hkilúhpiiži. v [reg., *_hkilúhpiiži*] [*hkik-* REFL + *ðuhpíiži*] *(intr.)* **make a mistake causing dishonor to oneself, do or cause oneself ill or harm, harm oneself by making a serious mistake.** *wáli ahkíluhpíiži ąži óðąži ahkílabrį hta mįkšé* I made a bad mistake but I'll carry myself on anyway (RBn 5/3/79).

hkilúuhepe. v [reg.?/uninfl., *_hkilúuhepe*] [*hkik-* REFL + *ðuuhépe*] *(intr.)* **urinate (lit., 'make oneself lighter'; euphemism used principally by men rather than women).** *hkilúuhepe hta mįkšé* I'm going to urinate.

hkilúušawa. v [reg., *_hkilúušawa*] [*hkik-* REFL + *ðuušáwa*] *(intr.)* **undress oneself.**

•• LFD 85: *hkilíša* <ḳi-gthi´-sha> to disrobe, to undress, to remove one's clothes. *ahkíliša* <a-ḳi´-gthi-sha> I undressed. *ðahkíliša* <tha-ḳi´-gthi-sha> you undressed. *ąhkíliša pe* <o^{n}-ḳi´-gthi-sha i> we undressed.

hkilúuštake (variant: **hkíluuštake**). v [reg., *_hkilúuštake*] [*hkik-* REFL + *ðuuštáke*] *(intr.)* **undress oneself.** *hkíluuštake* he's undressing himself.

hkilúuwasu. v [reg., *_hkilúuwasu*] [*hkik-* REFL + *ðuuwásu*] *(intr.)* **clean oneself.** *hkilúuwasu!* clean yourself up! (RBn12-08).

hkíluwį. v [reg., *_hkíluwį*] [*hkik-* REFL + *ðuwį́*] *(trans.)* **buy for oneself.** *ahkíluwį* I bought it for myself (04/06/95/FH/pc). *oðíhtą wį ahkíluwį* I bought a car for myself. *wíe ahkíluwį akxą́he* I'm buying it for myself. *ðahkíluwį* you're buying it for yourself. *wahkíluwį apai* he bought stuff for himself. *hkilúwį akxai* she's buying it for herself. *ðée hkilúwį apai* she bought that for herself. *hkilúwį apai* they bought it for themselves.

hkíǫðe. v [reg.+sync., *_hkíǫ_ðe*] [*hkik-* RECIP + *ǫ́ǫðe*] *(intr.)* **divorce, throw each other away (usually used for the process of divorce).** [Once the divorce is accomplished, *ohkóǫðe* is more likely to be used.] *hkíǫðe apai* they are getting a divorce, they're separated, they are throwing each other away (04/06/95/PM/pc:ok; BE2.32). *ohkíǫðape* they divorced each other.

•• LFD 87: *hkiǫ́ða* <ḳi-o^{n}´-tha> to throw each other away; divorce. *ąhkíǫða* <o^{n}-ḳi´-o^{n}-tha> I am divorced. *ðahkíǫšta* <tha-ḳi´-o^{n}-shta> you are divorced.

hkipáną. v [reg., *_hkipáną*] [perhaps contains *hkik-* REFL] *(intr.)* **run in a competition (perhaps lit., 'place oneself first')** (FH). *hkáwa hkipáną* the horse races (FH). • N **race.**

•• JOD (slip file): *hkipaną* <ki-p̣a-na^{n}> [no definition given; no accent mark visible].

•• LFD 85: *hkípaną* <ḳi´-ba-no^{n}> to run a race. *ahkípaną* <a-ḳi´-ba-no^{n}> I run a race. *ðahkípaną* <tha-ḳi´-ba-no^{n}> you ran a race. *ąhkípaną pe* <o^{n}-ḳi´-ba-no^{n} i> we ran a race.

••• Cf. *hkáwa hkipáną, níhkahkipáną.*

hkíxiða v [reg.+sync., *_hkíxi_ða*] [probably *hkik-* REFL + *xí_ða*] *(intr.)* **despair, mistrust oneself, not trust oneself, doubt oneself, give up.** *ahkíxibrai* I give up, I can't; I don't think I can do that, I'm not sure of myself (e.g., about driving a car) (FH/11/19/01/pc:ok). *ahkíxibrai* I don't trust myself (RBn22-05). *hkixíðaaži* self-confident, undismayed, not doubting (personal name). *hkíxiðape* he gave up (FH/11/19/01/pc).

•• LFD 88: *hkixíða* <ḳi-xi´-tha> to despair, to become hopeless, disheartened. *ahkíxibra* <a-ḳi´-xi-btha> I am in despair. *ðahkíxista* <tha-ḳi´-xi-sda> [expected Mod. Os. form: *ðahkíxišta*] you are in despair. *ąhkíxiða pe* <o^{n}-ḳi´-xi-tha i> we are in despair. *kkixíðapaži* <ḳi-xi´-tha-ba-zhi> Self-confident (personal name, refers to the warlike spirit of the gens). *hkixíðaži* <ḳi-xi´-tha-zhi> undismayed.

hkížį (variant: **hkížaį**). v [reg. (+sync. nasal vowel stem), *_hkíža(_)į* (the second inflectional position is only optionally used)] [contains *hkik-* RECIP] *(intr.)* **be angry at each other, feel quarrelsome;** *(trans.)* **be angry at s.o., feel mad at s.o.** *ahkížąmie* I'm mad at him (RBn10-5:JW). *ąhkíži apái* she is mad [angry] at me (02/24/95/FH/pc:ok). *wíe ahkíži ąhé* I'm mad at him (02/24/95/FH/pc:ok). *ąhkížį ðįká* don't be mad at me (02/24/95/FH/pc:ok). *awáhkižį mįkšé* I'm mad at them (MSB mar83). *ąðáhkiži* you're mad at me (2/3/83/p2; PM/7/7/94; 01/04/95/FH/pc:ok). *ąhkíži apa* he's mad at me (RBn10-5:JW).

•• LFD 88: *hkižį* <ḳi-zhi^{n}> to quarrel. *ðahkížį* <tha-ḳi´-zhi^{n}> you quarrel.

••• Cf. *ažį́, ihkížį, ohkížį.*

hkóða. N **friend** (01/30/95/FH/pc:prod orig). *hkóða ðí áape* they were friends (lit., 'he was a friend, they said') (RBn18-01; CQc). *hkóða akxa hkáwa ðǫpá kǫzéhkihkǫ waaðįpe* my friend has two horses just alike.

•• LFD 90: *hkóða* <ḳu´-tha> a friend.

hkohkóma. N **pickle, cucumber** (03/07/95/FH/pc:ma; BE2.102). [Possibly borrowed from English *cucumber.*]

hkohkóma (*continued*)

•• LFD 88: *hkohkóma* <ḳo-ḳo´-ma> cucumbers. *hkohkóma ðizo a(?)* <ḳo-ḳo´-ma thi-çu a(?)> [sentence-final *a* is not used in Mod. Os.] do you like cucumbers? *hkohkóma cˀaðe* <ḳo-ḳo´-ma ts'a-the> pickles. *hkohkóma skuðe* <ḳo-ḳo´-ma çku-the> sweet pickles.

hkóhkosa (variant: **hkohkósa**). N **pig, hog, shoat, pork** (t#14a-p4). [Possibly borrowed from French *cochon.*] *hkóhkosa léze* [expected form: . . . *léže*] spotted pig. *hkóhkosa htáa* pork (03/08/95/FH/pc:okc).

•• LFD 88: *hkohkósa žįka* <ḳo-ḳo´-çi zhi^{n}-ga> a young pig, a shoat. *hkohkósi hta* <ḳo-ḳo´-çi ṭa> pork; pig meat. *hkóhkosa hta ðízo na?* <ḳo-ḳo´çi ṭa thi-çu a(?)> do you like pork?

hkohkósa ékǫ. ADJ **hoggish.**

•• LFD 88: *hkohkósa ékǫ* <ḳo-ḳo´-ça e-go^{n}> like a hog, hoggish (03/08/95/FH/pc:ok).

hkohkósa wéli. N **lard, pork fat** (03/08/95/FH/pc:ok).

•• LFD 88: *hkohkosa weli* <ḳo-ḳo-ça we-gthi> hog grease, lard.

-hkóįye. V [root, conjug. unknown] *(intr.)* **turn, turn around.**

•• LFD 348: *nǫ́hkowįye* <no^{n}´-ḳu-wi^{n}-xe> to turn with the foot. *páhkowįye* <ba´-ḳu-wi^{n}-xe> to turn by pushing.

••• Cf. *ðiihkóįye, hkilíihkǫįye, opáwįye, -wįye.*

hkóopše (variant: **hkóopši**). V [reg., *_hkóopše*] *(intr.)* **sneak off, flee, run away** (FH/02/17/96/pc:prod). *ahkóopšeštą aapé* she says I'm always sneaking off (RBnot 5/3/79/p4). *šį́htožį wį iiðáðe hkóopši apai* the boy that I saw was running away (3-2-163).

•• LFD 88: *hkóipše* <ḳo´-i-pshe> fear, misgiving [definition not acceptable in Mod. Os.]. *ahkoipše* <a-ḳo-i-pshe> I had misgivings.

••• Cf. *kíhkoopše.*

hkǫ́ (variant of **hką́**).

hkǫ́ha. N **edge.**

•• LFD 127 (unconfirmed): *hpéce hkǫha* <pe´-dse ḳo^{n}-ha> edge of the fire.

••• *KS ištáxüha kką́ha* edge of the eyelids (RR).

hkúce. V [reg., *_hkúce*] *(intr.)* **fire a gun, shoot a bow and arrow** (03/09/95/MREI/pc:ok). *ahkúce* I shoot (03/09/95/MREI/pc:ok; FH:4/24/96/tape:ok). *ðahkúce* you shoot (03/09/95/MREI/pc:ok; FH:4/24/96/tape:ok). *ée hkúcape* he shot (FH:4/24/96/tape). • *(trans.)* **shoot s.o., shoot at s.o.** *ąhkútapé* they shot me (RB). *ąhkúcape* they shot me (FH:4/24/96/tape). *ahkúce ąži akšįįce* I shot at it but I missed it (FH:4/24/96/tape,ok; RBnot-nd-1).

•• LFD 90: *hkúce* <ḳu´-dse> to shoot. *ðahkúce* <tha-ḳu´-dse> you shoot.

••• Cf. *hkihkúce.*

hlaaská (variant of **laaská**).

hlaazípe (variant: **hlaazípepí**). N [*laaská + zi + pe* POSIT] **August, sunflowers in bloom (lit., 'there are yellow flowers')** (HRE/01/17/02/pc:ok; RBn12-05). [One of the very few words in which an initial *hl* is preserved in Mod. Os. Names of months were historically not used in Osage and sound unnatural to Osage speakers (HH).]

hléke (variant of **léke**).

hlį́į (variant of **lį́įže**).

hlúže, hlúži (variants of **lúži**).

hó. N **fish.**

hó bráaska (variant: **hobráaska**). N **perch (lit., 'flat fish')** (03/07/95/FH/pc:ok; RBn3-MOJ/p5).

•• LFD 63: *hobráska* <ho-btha´-çka> flat fish, perch. *hobráaska apa ðaaché ðáalį pe* <ho-btha´-çka a-ba tha-tse tha-gthi^{n} bi a> perch is good to eat.

hóhkihpaache (variant of **óhkihpaache**).

hóhtąka. N **Winnebago (Hochunk) (tribe or tribal member)** (unconfirmed; 03/08/95/PM/pc:uk; 04/06/95/LS/pc:uk).

•• LFD 68 (unconfirmed): *hóhtąka* <Hu´-ṭo^{n}-ga> Big Fish, the name given to the Winnebago by the Osage. [It is not certain that LF's etymological explanation of this name as 'Big Fish' is correct.]

hóhtąka íe. N **Winnebago language.**

•• LFD 68 (unconfirmed): *hóhtąka ie* <Hu´-ṭo^{n}-ga i-e> Winnebago language (05/01/95/LS/pc:uk).

hóize (variant: **hóízi**). N **line, fishing line, hook and line** (RBn3-MOJ/p4; ERE:ok; 02/16/95/FH/pc:uk; 04/14/95/PM/pc:uk).

•• LFD 63: *hóizi* <ho´-i-çi> fishhook.

hóize žą́ąxe. N **fishing pole** (RBn3-MOJ/p5).

hóni (variant: **hǫ́ni**). ADV **almost, nearly (can be used to express 'fail to').** *hóni wažážeíe akxai* he can almost talk Osage (01/04/95/FH/pc:prod; BE2.2). *hóni brį́įštą* I'm almost finished (RBn3-MOJ/p15; LH tape; 01/04/95/FH/pc:ok). *hóni axíbra* I almost fell. *šǫ́ke akxa hǫ́ni ą́ðaxtake* the dog almost bit me (RBn22-10). *hóni ðacˀé* you almost died (FH:prod). *hóni ąwą́chįpe* they almost whipped me (04/28/95/LS/pc:okc).

hóo. N **voice.** • V *(intr.)* **bark, moo, quack, etc., make an animal noise.** *šǫ́ke apa hóo apái ðe* the dogs are howling (01/04/95/FH/pc:ok).

••• *WI hóo* voice (KM).
••• Cf. *óhoo*.

hooðáalį. N [*hóo* + *ðáalį*] **Good Voice (personal name)** (WF/02/pc). [Name of William Fletcher's paternal grandfather.]

hóohtą. V [reg.?, *_hóohtą*?] *(intr.)* **yell, holler, shout (lit., 'loud voice')** (RBn1-11); **sing or sound out, make a loud sound; make animal sounds (e.g., sing like a bird, moo, bark, howl)** (FH). *hóohtąmąį* [*hóohtą* + *mąðį*] Goes Around Hollering (personal name of John Stink) (FH/01/10/99). *kasįexcį wažįka apa hóohtą nąąpé* the birds sing early in the morning (02/25/95/FH/pc:okc). *lǫ́ǫ hóohtą wáliįpe* the thunder was really loud (03/22/95/FH/pc:ok). *wažįka apa hóohtą apái* the birds are singing (01/04/95/FH/pc:ok). *hceeská apa hóohta apái* the cows are mooing. *šǫmįhkási apa hóo apái* the coyotes are howling (RB).
•• LFD 67: *hóhtą* <ho´ṭo^{n}> the cry or call of animals or birds. LFD 68: *hohtąmąį* <Hu-ṭo^{n}-mo^{n}-i^{n}> Roars-as-he-comes (personal name).

hóolą. N [*hó* + *oolą́*] **fishing.** *hóolą brée* I'm going fishing (01/25/95/FH/pc:okc). *kasį́xci hóolą bree hkǫ́bra ązi nuužúžu akxai* I wanted to go fishing this morning, but it was sprinking (01/30/95/FH/pc:prod orig). *hóolą aðée* they went fishing (01/25/95/FH/pc:ok; BE2.48). *iiną́ akxa žįkážį hóolą ížoši nąpe* mother used to tell the children not to go fishing (FH:4/18/96/tape:okc). *hóolą ąkái hce* let's go fishing [speaking to one person]. *hóolą ąkái htai* let's go fishing [speaking to more than one].
•• LFD 67: *hóolą* <ho´-o-gtho^{n}> to fish, to go fishing (01/25/95/FH/pc:ok). *hóolą ąðahpe* <ho´-o-gtho^{n} o^{n}-tha-pe> [expected Mod. Os. form: *hóolą ąðáhpape*] you invited me to go fishing. *hóolą bre a ðo* <ho´-o-gtho^{n} bthe a tho> [expected Mod. Os. form: *hóolą brée*; the ending *a ðǫ* is not used in Mod. Os.] I am going fishing.

hóosaaki. V [reg., *_hóosaaki*] [*hóo* + *saakí*] *(intr.)* **whoop, call loudly (lit., 'hard voice').** *hóosaaki* he whoops.
•• LFD 28: *pą hósaki* <bo^{n} hu´-ça-gi> to call or shout loudly. *ahósaki* <a-hu´-ça-gi> I call loudly. *ðahósaki* <tha-hu´-ça-gi> you call loudly. *ąhósaki pe* <o^{n}-hu´-ça-gi i> we call loudly.

hooxcį́ (variant of **hǫ́ǫxcį**).

hóoxpe (variant of **hóxpe**).

hóšechie (variants: **óošechia, óošechie**). V [conjug. unknown] *(trans.)* **startle or shock s.o.** (RB); *(intr.)* **be excited, startled, shocked.** *hóšechíepi tą, įįštá ápisąi koe áa ákabra ną́ąke htaacéžį oðį́įke ahú apai* he was excited, with his eyes closed and his arms open he came running to catch Whirlwind (RBn17-p). • *(intr.)* **jump, as when startled** (RBn23-14, unconfirmed). • N **shocking news, startling report.** • ADJ **shocking, overwhelming, startling.**
•• LFD 67: *hóšachiðe* <ho´sha-tsi-the> to startle. *hóšachiðe ąðikaaγa pe* <ho´-sha-tsi-the o^{n}-thi-ga-xa i> we startled you. [This example seems to be a double causative, having both *-ðe* and *káaγe*.]
••• *QU óža* dance (RR).

hówa. INTERR/INDEF ADJ, INTERR/INDEF PRON **which, which one.** *hówa įkše škǫ́šta?* which one do you want? (04/28/95/LS/pc:ok, BE2.156). *hówaxcį txá?* exactly which one [standing person]? LS/07/27/95/pc:prod). *hówaxcį ché?* exactly which one [standing object]? (LS/07/27/95/pc:prod). *hówa ðe?* where?/which one? (04/28/95/LS/pc).
•• LFD 67: *hówaðe* <ho´-wa-the> where, which one. *hówaðįkše* <ho´-wa-thi^{n}-ke> which one (sitting).
••• Cf. *hówaįkše, hówaxcį*.

howachéeški. INTERR/INDEF ADJ, INTERR/INDEF PRON **whichever one (inanimate), whatever (thing), anything, everything.** *howachéeški íiðaðe?* did you see anything?

howaðéeški. INTERR/INDEF PRON **whichever one (animate), whatever one (person or animate being); anybody; everybody.** *howaðéeški ohkíe nąpé* he talks to just anybody (RBn10-4:MOJ/79). *howaðéeški áðuγe hkǫ́bra įké* I don't want to marry anybody (RBn17-p02). *howaðéeški ðak?éða[ð]e* you're good to everybody (FH prayer). • **whoever.** *howaðéeški chí tą, hcíhta hu hce éa* whoever comes, tell them to come in the house (RBn10-4: MOJ/79).
••• Cf. *háaški*.

howáįki (variants: **hówaįki, hówaįkice, howáike, hówai**). INTERR/INDEF ADV **where, wherein, where at, where to; be where.** *howáįki šcée?* where are you going? (03/16/95/MREI/pc:okc). *hową́įki štáape?* where are you [pl.] going? (03/16/95/MREI/pc:prod). *hówaįki oálįį škǫ́šta?* where do you want me to sit? (RBn10-4:MOJ/79; BE2.156). *howáįki apai?* where are they? (04/28/95/LS/pc). *howáįki paašé?* where are you all? (04/28/95/LS/pc:ok). *howáįkí ðaįšé?* where are you? • **wherever, be wherever.** *howáįki apa* wherever they're at (7/8/94/PM/t#98b). *hową́įki*

howáįki (*continued*)
ðǫǫpá ðáabrį náški ecíe akxa tą, wíe ée brį́ hta mįkšé na ée ešie wherever only just two or three are, I will always be there, you said (from a verse of the Christian Bible) (FH:prayer). *howáįki apa ðée* wherever they're at (04/28/95/LS/pc). *howáįki ąðé* wherever we [two] are (04/28/95/LS/pc). *hǫ́wai íiðai hce* you'll never find it (lit., 'wherever will you find it?') (03/16/95/MREI/pc:okc).
•• LFD 67: *howaįkíhtąche* <ho-wa-i^n-gi´-ṭo^n-tse> [expected Mod. Os. form: *howaįkí hta che*] from what source, what direction. LFD 67 (unconfirmed): *hówake ðįke* <ho´-wa-ge thi^n-ge> nowhere. *hówaki htą ðachi a?* <ho´-wa-gi ṭo^n tha-tsi a(?)> [expected Mod. Os. form: *hówaįkí hta ðachíe?*] where did you come from? *hówaįke* <ho´-wa-i^n-ge> where, in what place. LFD 68 (unconfirmed): *hówake* <hu´-wa-ge> where.

howaįkíha. INTERR/INDEF ADV **through where, by what pathway, which way.** *howaįkíha brée?* through where should I go? which way should I go?

hówaįkše (variants: **hówąįkše, hówąąkše).** INTERR/INDEF PRON [*hówa + įkšé* POSIT] **which one (round, sitting).** *hówąįkše?/hówąąkše?* which one [round or sitting thing or sitting person]? (04/28/95/LS/pc).

hówaxcį (variant: **hówaxci**). INTERR/INDEF PRON [*hówa + xci*] **exactly which one** (LS/07/27/95/pc:prod). *hówaxcį txá* exactly which one [person]? *hówaxcį ché?* exactly which one [inanimate]?

hówąąkše, hówąįkše (variants of **hówaįkše).**

howé (variant: **hówe** [PM]). ADV **yes (men's speech only).** *oðíhta hcéka wį šcúwį?* did you buy a new car? *howé, wį brúwį* yes, I bought one [man speaking].
•• LFD 67: *howé* <ho-we´> yes. *hówe eci ahi pi o* <ho´-we e-dsi a-hi bi o> [expected Mod. Os. form: *howé ecí ahípe*; sentence-final *o* is not used in Mod. Os.] yes, he arrived there.
••• *KS howé* yes (male speech) (RR).

hówe. N **mortar, grinder, mill** (RBn23-07).
•• LFD 67: *hówe* <ho´-we> mortar coffee mill, gristmill.

hóxpe (variant: **hóoxpe**). V [reg., *_hóxpe*] **cough** (01/13/95/FH/pc:prod; FH: 6-30-94). *ée hóxpape* they coughed (BE2.25; 2/10/83/p4). *ðahóxpe* you cough. *ahóxpe* I cough (2-10-83-p4). • N **cough; cold with sniffles and fever** (RB, FH). *hóxpe hpíiži* bad cold; bad cough (01/19/95/FH/pc:ok). *wéeli hóxpe záani ąwážu mįksé* I have a head cold (BE2.21; 01/19/95/FH/pc:uk).
•• LFD 68: *hóxpe lili* <hu´-xpe xthi-xthi> to cough mucus, to expectorate. *hóxpe li íðatxo* <hu´-xpe xthi i´-tha-to> [*íðatxo* unconfirmed] you expectorate.

hóxpe hpíiži. N **whooping cough (or tuberculosis?), influenza, flu, bad cough, bad cold** (FH). *hóxpe hpíiži ǫ́ǫ akxái* she has whooping cough(?) (BE2.157; FH:08/22/96).
•• LFD 67: *hóxpe hpiiži* <hu´-xpe-p̣i-zhi> bad cough, grippe, influenza.

hóxpe léle (variant: **hóxpe líli**). N **phlegm** (WF/12/30/01:prod).
•• LFD 67: *hóxpelíli* <ho´-xpe-xthi-xthi> phlegm.

hóxpe ǫ́ǫ. VP [sync. nasal vowel stem, *hǫ́xpe _ǫ́ǫ*] *(intr.)* **be suffering from a cold, cough, whooping cough** (01/19/95/FH/pc:ok). *hóxpe mǫ́ę mįkšé* I have a cold (FH/11/19/01/pc:ok). *hóxpe hpíiži [m]ǫ́ǫ mįkšé* I have a bad cold (RB; 01/19/95/FH/pc:ma). *hóxpe žǫ́ę?* do you have a cold? *hóxpe ǫǫ́ įkší aape* I heard he has a cold (RBn19-01). *Smokey akxa hóxpe ǫǫ́ akxai* Smokey has a cold (RBn19-01). *hóxpe ǫǫ́ ąkxai* she has a cold. *Christine akxa hóxpe ǫǫ́ įkšé?* does Christine have a cold? (RBn3-55).
•• LFD 68: *hóxpeǫ* <hu´-xpe-o^n> croup, a hard cough.
••• *KS hóxpe* cough (RR).

hóxpe zúpe. N **whooping cough** (FH); **tuberculosis(?)** (FH, 04/28/95;LS/pc:ok). *hóxpe hpíiži ǫ́ǫ akxái* she has whooping cough (BE2.157; FH:08/22/96).

hǫ́bre. V [reg.?, *_hǫ́bre* (LF reports *hǫ́_bre*)] *(intr.)* **dream, have a dream.** *hą́ące ahǫ́bre* last night I dreamed (FH/5/2/95). *wáli áhǫbre* I really dreamed [if this verb is actually stative, the expected form would be *ąhǫ́bre*] (RBn10-3:MOJ/79). • N **dream, dreaming.** *hǫ́bre oðíhpazái?* did you have a nightmare? (lit., 'dreaming, did it startle you?').
•• LFD 65: *hǫ́bre* <ho^n´-bthe> to dream. *hǫábre* <ho^n-a´-bthe> I dream. *hǫðábre* <ho^n-tha´-bthe> you dream. *hǫąbra pe* <ho^n´-o^n-btha i> we dream. [Verb forms unconfirmed.]

hǫbrį́ hi. N **bean vine.**
•• LFD 65 (unconfirmed): *hǫbrį́ hi* <ho^n-bthi^n´ hi> the wild-bean vine.

hǫ́brį htóho (variant of **hǫbrį́ke htóho**).

hǫbrį́ke. N **beans; green beans** (01/06/95/FH/pc:prod). *hkohkósi htáa hǫbrį́ke oðóhkihą ą́zo* I like beans cooked with pork meat

(FH/09/21/01/pc). *hǫbrį́ke che hpaahíke* I sorted the beans (FH:ok).

•• LFD 65: *hǫbrį́ke* <hoⁿ-bthiⁿ´-ge> beans.

hǫbrį́ke htóho (variant: **hǫ́brį htóho**). N **green beans.** *hǫbrį́ke htóho tóa ooðáhą hkǫ́bra* I want you to cook some green beans (BE2.7; RBn1-52).

hǫ́brįke htóho žį. N **peas; green beans** (03/07/95/PM/pc:both; BE2.102).

hǫ́ǫ (variant of **háaǫ**).

hǫ́ǫche. INTERR/INDEF ADV [perhaps contains *che* POSIT] **how; however.** *mą́ąɣe hǫ́ǫche?* how's the weather? (RBn12-09).

hǫ́ǫe wį (variant: **hǫ́ǫe**). PRON **nobody.** *hǫ́ǫe wį ahú apa ðakˀéðie hta ðe* nobody will be coming to take care of you (lit., 'nobody is coming here that will have pity on you' [FH's father used to say this often]). *waðílą hkihkáaɣipe, koe šómįhkasi hǫ́ǫe éekǫ ší íiðe htai* [expected form: *waðílą hkihkáaɣape koe šómįhkasi hǫ́ǫe éekǫži íiðe hta ðe*] she made up her mind, the coyote would never see anybody like her again (lit., 'her mind she made up thus: the coyote will see nobody like her') (RBn17-p03).

hǫ́ǫpa (variant of **hą́ąpa**).

hǫ́ǫpa ðé (variants: **hą́ąpa ðé, hǫpái, hąpái, hǫpá, hǫ́ǫpa, hą́ąpa**). N, ADV **today (lit., 'this day')** (03/22/95/FH/pc:okc). *hǫ́ǫpa háažǫ?, hą́ąpa háažǫ?* what did you [sg.] do today? (01/19/95/FH/pc:ok; BE2.29). *hǫ́ǫpa htáwą įkši pšíe* I went to town today (03/22/95/FH/pc:ok; BE2.142). *hą́ąpa ðé akxa ðáalįži akxai* it's not a pretty day today (the weather is not good today; lit., 'today is not good') (FH/10/13/96). *hǫpái* today [not formal]. *hǫ́ǫpa ðé* this day [somewhat formal] (03/22/95/FH/pc:ok). *hǫǫpá waðíhtą pšíe* I went to work today (03/24/95/PM/pc:ok).

•• LFD 64: *hǫ́pa ðéka* <hoⁿ´-ba the-ga> this day, today (03/22/95/FH/pc:ok).

hǫ́ǫpa hú (variant of **hǫ́ǫpahu**).

hǫ́ǫpa huuwáli. ADVP, NP **(for) a long time (lit., 'many days').** *hǫ́ǫpa huuwáli žówaðale hkǫ́bra* I want you to be with us a long time (RBn12-10/mj).

hǫ́ǫpa scée. N **February (lit., 'long days')** (RBn12-05). [Names of months were historically not used in Osage and sound unnatural to Osage speakers (HH).]

hǫ́ǫpa wį (variant: **hą́ąpa wį**). NP, ADVP **day, one day, sometimes, some days** (RBn10-3:MOJ/79); **sometime, some day.** *hǫ́ǫpa wį súhka tóoka ókˀą ékǫži káaɣe nąpe* sometimes the rooster did things he shouldn't do (RBn18-01). *hǫ́ǫpa wį́ ątǫ́į hí ði* come over and see me sometime (RBn10-3:MOJ/79).

hǫ́ǫpa wį́xci ðǫǫpá hta ški. NP, ADVP **a day or two, for a day or so** (RBn18-02).

hǫ́ǫpahu (variant: **hǫ́ǫpa hú**). V [uninfl.] **be daylight, (day) break.** *hǫ́ǫpahu akxai, íikiðapi* it's daylight, wake up (RBn23-17). *hą́ąpa hú, hpáahą* it's daylight, get up (e.g., out of the chair or out of bed) (FH:prod) • ADV, N **(at) daybreak, dawn, daylight.** *hą́ąpahu žišǫ́* before daylight (04/25/95/PM/pc:ok). *hǫ́ǫpahu ðáalį* daylight came good (said at morning light after a peyote meeting, talking to creator) (04/25/95/PM/pc:ok). • **daylight approaches, it's coming daylight (personal name).** [Name of Herman Petsemoie, Frances Holding's maternal uncle.]

hǫǫpái (variant of **hą́ąpa**).

hǫ́ǫpaskaha (variants: **hǫ́ǫpaska, hą́ąpaskaha, hą́ąpaska**). V [uninfl.] [*hǫ́ǫpa* + *skáha*] **be daylight (when the sky is all light or white).** *hą́ąpaskaha akxai, hpáahą* get up, it's daylight (FH:prod) *hǫ́ǫpaskaha akxai* it's daylight (04/25/95/PM/pc:ok; BE2.29). • N, ADV **(at) daylight** (PM). *wižį́ke hą́ąpaska híi che? káaną ahí akxa* Sonny, has daylight come? just a little bit [like this, showing with hand] (FH/09/24/01/prod).

•• LFD 63: *hǫ́pa ska* <hoⁿ´-ba çka> daylight (04/25/95/PM/pc:ok). LFD 64: *hǫ́pa íhtaxe* <hoⁿ´-ba i´-ṭa-xe> the tip or beginning of day (04/25/95/PM/pc:uk; unconfirmed, *íhtaxe* unknown).

hǫǫpé. N **moccasins; shoes.** *hǫǫpé tóohka* wet moccasins (a female personal name, probably referring to dew on moccasins). *hǫ́ǫpekaaɣe* shoemaker (BE2.120; 03/09/95/MREI/pc:ok; HRE).

•• LFD 64: *hǫpé* <hoⁿ-be´> moccasins.

hǫǫpé okáwįɣe. N **socks (lit., 'go-around shoes', 'go-around moccasins')** (03/13/95/FH/pc:ok; RBn2-MOJ/p2).

•• LFD 64: *hǫpé okawįɣe* <hoⁿ-be´u-ga-wiⁿ-xe> socks, moccasins, in which a winding is made. *hąpe okawįɣe htoho* <hoⁿ-be u-ga-wiⁿ-xe ṭo-ho> blue socks.

••• *OM hįbé gáwįxe* <hiⁿ bé gá wiⁿxe> stockings (originally referred to either hair from buffalo's head or red grass, which was wrapped around the feet before putting on moccasins) (Larson 2005: 263).

hǫǫpé scéce (variant of **hǫǫpésce**).

hǫ́ǫpekaaɣe. N [*hǫǫpé* + *káaɣe*] **shoemaker, cobbler** (BE2.120; 03/09/95/MREI/pc:ok; HRE).

hǫǫpésce (variant: **hǫǫpé scéce**). N **boot (lit., 'tall shoe')** (BE2.10; 01/07/95/FH/pc:ok).

•• LFD 64: *hǫpe stehce/steche* <hoⁿ-be ste-ṭse> tall moccasins: boots. [LF normally writes 'long, tall' as <stse-dse>; see, e.g., LFD 134.]

hǫ́ǫški (variant of **háaški**).

hǫ́ǫxcį. (variants: **hooxcį́, hǫ́ǫxce, hǫ́ǫxci**). INTERR/INDEF PRON **what kind.** *oðíhtą hǫǫxcį́ ðáažį nįkšé?* what kind of car are you driving? (RBn10-18). *nąníǫpažį hooxcį́ štáašoe ną?* what kind of cigarettes do you regularly smoke? (RBn23-15). *kóota įkšé ohkíhce hǫ́ǫxce ðįkšé?* that one sitting over there, what kind of tribe is he? (03/23/95/FH/pc).

hǫ́ǫži (variants: **hǫ́ǫžį, hǫ́žį**). ADJ **bad, evil, wicked.** *táatą ðéke hǫ́ǫžike* these bad things [scattered around]. *táatą ðeke hǫ́ǫžįke ékiǫ įká* don't do these bad things (RBn10-18). • **spoiled, ruined; inefficient, inferior, of poor quality, poor.** *ðe hpáata akxa, hǫ́ǫžį akxai* those eggs are bad (FH:4/22/96/tape:prod, HP). *į́išta hǫ́ǫzi apai* she has bad eyes (RBn3-49:CQc: *į*). *wawéeðe hǫ́ǫži nį́* you see poorly (lit., 'you are of bad sight') (RB).

hǫpá, hǫpái (variants of **hǫ́ǫpa ðé**).

hǫpái hašíhta. N, ADVP **this day some time back, this day back in time.** *hǫpái haašíhta hóni ąc?é* some days back I almost died; some days ago I almost died.

hpá. N **nose, snout** (03/01/95/FH/pc:ok; 04/17/95/LS/pc:ok). *ðe hpá* that nose (FH:4/25/96/tape). *hpá piɣǫ́* blow your nose. *hpá oc?į́ze* stuffed-up or stopped-up nose (03/01/95/FH/pc:ok; 04/17/95/LS/pc:ok). *hpahlíxtoe* a runny nose (FH). *hpá lį́stowe* your nose is running (03/01/95/FH/pc:ok). *hpá lį́xtowe* [his/her] nose is running (RB). *hpa lį́stowe nįkšé* your nose is running (RBn12-08). *hpá káaži* blow your nose (03/01/95/FH/pc:ma; BE2.95; unconfirmed; 04/17/95/LS/pc:uk). • **head, protuberance, bulge, mound** (FH:4/25/96/tape:HP). • ADJ **bitter** (FH/09/25/01/prod). *mąhkáhpa* pepper (lit., 'bitter medicine') (02/24/95/FH/pc:okc).

•• LFD 125: *hpa* <p̣a> snout, the projecting nose of an animal, the head; bitter. *hpa kísceke* <p̣a gi´-stse-ge> The Nose Splitting [taboo word; refers to a ceremony in which the tip of the nose of a captive is scratched with the tip of the sacred knife].

hpá tóohka. N **Comanche (tribe or tribal member), Kiowa (tribe or tribal memeber) (lit., 'wet noses' [RB, PM], 'dew on the head' [PM])** (RBnote: rare usage) (BE2.21; PM:ok; 01/14/95/FH/pc:uk).

•• LFD 125, 243: *hpátǫhka* <p̣a´-doⁿ-ḳa> the Osage name for the Comanche Tribe, Comanche Indian.

hpaahą́. V [reg. or sync. fortisizing stop stem, *_hpaahą́*] *(intr.)* **arise or get up from a bed or chair, get up, wake up.** *ahpáahą* I get up. *ðahpáahą* you get up. *ąhpáahą* she gets up. *kaasį́xcįžį ahpáahą* I got up very early (01/31/95/FH/pc:okc). *hcéka žį ðahpáahą tǫpéwai* you look like you just got up (FH/11/19/01/pc:ok). *hą́ąhkaži kóoci ahpáahą* no, I got up a long time ago (01/31/95/FH/pc:okc; BE2.53). *mį́ǫke šáhpe tą ahpáahą ną* I get up at six o'clock (RBn22-09). *kaasį́xcį žįkáži apa hpaahą́ nąpé* the children [usually] get up early (01/31/95/FH/pc:okc). *kaasį́xcį žįkáži apa hpaahą́pe* the children got up early (01/31/95/FH/pc:okc). *hą́ąpaskaha akxai, hpaahą́* get up, it's daylight (FH:prod). *hą́ąpa hú, hpaahą́* it's daylight, get up [e.g., out of the chair or out of bed] (FH:prod). *hpaahą́pi* get up [pl.]! (FH01/31/95; FH/11/19/01/pc:HP). *špáahą* [expected form: *ðahpáahą*] you got up (LS). *ąkóe ąhpáahą ąkái* we're getting up; we're waking up (LS).

•• LFD 125: *hpahą* <p̣a-hoⁿ> to rise. *akíhpahą* <a-gi´-p̣a-hoⁿ> [Mod. Os. omits *kí-*] I rise. *ðakíšpahą* <tha-gi´-shpa-hoⁿ> [Mod. Os. omits *kí-*] you rise. *ąkíhpahą pe* <oⁿ-gi´-p̣a-hoⁿ i> [Mod. Os. omits *kí-*] we rise.

••• Cf. *paahą́.*

hpaahíži (variant of **hpaahį́ži**).

hpaahį́ (variant: **páahi** [JOD]). ADJ, V [uninfl.] *(intr.)* **(be) sharp.** *mą́ąhi hpaahí* sharp knife (BE2.119; 03/09/95/MREI/pc:ma).

•• LFD 125: *hpahí* <p̣a-hi´> sharp. *mąhį hpahi* <moⁿ-hiⁿ p̣a-hi> the knife is sharp.

hpaahį́ži (variant: **hpaahíži**). ADJ, V [reg., *hpaa_hį́ži*] [*hpaahį́* + *aží* NEG] *(intr.)* **(be) dull (perhaps originally 'be unable to cut s.t. into small pieces').** *mą́ąhį akxa hpaahíži* the knife is dull (BE2.37; 01/20/95/PM/pc:ok).

••• Cf. *pahį́įži.*

hpáata. N **egg.** *hpáata léže káaɣe akxai* he's coloring eggs (e.g., for Easter; lit., 'he's making eggs spotted, speckled') (12/30/94/FH/pc/prod, HP; BE2.41). *ðe hpáata akxa hǫ́ǫžį akxai* those eggs are bad (FH:4/22/96/tape:prod, HP).

•• JOD (slip file): *hpáta* <pa´-ṭa> an egg (of any sort).

•• LFD 125: *páhta* <ba´-ṭa> an egg. [LF's transcription of *hpáata* 'egg' varies considerably; compare <ba´-ṭa> here with <p̣a´-ṭa> in the entry *hpáatazi* and <p̣a-da> and <p̣a´-ṭa> in the entry *hpáažį*.]

••• *KS ittá* egg (RR).

hpáata xúha. N **eggshell (the shell of an egg of any kind).**

hpáataska. N [*hpáata* + *ská* 'white'] **egg white (lit., 'white of egg').**

hpáatazi. N [*hpáata* + *zí*] **egg yolk (lit., 'yellow of egg').**

•• LFD 126 (unconfirmed): *hpáhta zi ðįkše* <p̣a-ṭa çi thi^{n}-kshe> [expected Mod. Os. form: *hpáata zi ðįkšé* (*ðįkšé* POSIT)] the yolk of an egg. [LF's transcription of *hpáata* 'egg' varies considerably; see the entry *hpáata*.]

hpáažį (variants: **hpáatažįka** [archaic], **hpáatažį**). N [*hpáata* + *-žį* 'little'] **baby, infant, babyhood, infancy** (BE2.6; 01/06/95/FH/pc:ok). *hpáažį paamáši akxái* he's holding up the baby (e.g., for people to see it).

•• LFD 125: *hpata žįka* <p̣a-da zhi^{n}-ga> infancy, babyhood. LFD 126: *hpáhta žįka* <p̣a´-ṭa zhi^{n}-ga> baby; an infant, infancy. [LF's transcription of *hpáata* 'egg' varies considerably, as in these two examples; see the entry *hpáata*.]

••• *KS ittá* egg (RR).

hpáažį okˀǫ́he. VP [reg.?, *hpáažį o_kˀǫ́he*] **place a baby on a baby board, put a baby inside.**

hpáce (variant: **hpáci**). V [reg., *_hpáce*] *(trans.)* **operate on, perform surgery on, butcher, dissect.** *hpátapi įkší aape* he was operated on; they operated on him [they said] (03/02/95/FH/pc:okc). *wahkǫ́taki akxa ðihpáce kǫ́ða hta akxái* the doctor might want to operate on you (03/02/95/FH/pc:okc; BE2.98). • N **surgery** (03/02/95/FH/pc:ok, FH:4/22/96/tape).

•• RB: <páh-tah>.

•• LFD 125, 239: *hpáce* <p̣a´-dse> to butcher, to dissect (also *hpáhce* <p̣a´-ṭse> butcher [LFD 126, 239]). *ahpáce* <a-p̣a´-dse> I butcher. *ðáhpace* <tha´-p̣a-dse> you butcher. *ąhpáca pe* <o^{n}-p̣a´-dsa i> we butcher. LFD 125: *hpátapi* <p̣a´-da-bi> operation, surgical operation.

••• *KS ppáaǰe* butcher an animal (RR).

••• Cf. *wahpáce.*

hpaðímaha (variants: **hpáįmaha, hpáimąhą**). N **Pawnee Indians** (RB; PM; 03/06/95/FH/pc:ok; BE2.101).

•• LFD 126: *hpáðįmąhą* <p̣a´-thi^{n}-mo^{n}-ho^{n}> the Osage name for the Pawnee Indians. *hpaį mąhą* <p̣a-i^{n} mo^{n}-ho^{n}> the Osage name for a band of the Pawnees known as <Shki-thi>.

hpáðį (variant: **hpáį**). N **Kiowa (tribe or tribal member)** (RBn23-17). *hǫ́ǫpa ðé wéena akxai ðe níhkaši tóa áðixǫpape, hpáðį wéhkili íwehkili į kšíɣape* she's grateful today because they honored her, they dressed her [lit., 'made her clothe herself'] in Kiowa clothes (RBn23-17; CQc). • **Pawnee (tribe or tribal member).** *hpáðį apa achípe* the Pawnees have arrived (BE2.144; 01/09/95/FH/pc:ok; BE2.18). • **western tribe or tribal member (refers to any tribe from the western United States)** (03/08/95/PM/pc; 03/23/95/FH/pc:ok).

•• LFD 126: *hpáðį* <p̣a´-thi^{n}> a general term for tribes not related to the Osage. LFD 126: *hpaį* <p̣a-i^{n}> the Osage name for the Pawnee Tribe.

hpáðįhǫka. N **stranger.**

•• LFD 126 (unconfirmed): *hpáðįhǫka* <p̣a´-thi^{n}-ho^{n}-ga> sacred stranger (personal name).

hpaɣáce (variant of **hpaxáce**).

hpahą́le. ADJ, ADV **first, first in line, at the outset, from the beginning.** *wahkǫ́ta akxa eená hta akxa na, hpahą́le mą́į, ahkílaðį pai* soon it will be only God, put him first, carry yourself that way (04/04/99/FH/pc). *hpahą́le wihtéžį iðáe škǫ́šta che wéewinai* first, younger sister, I am grateful for your wanting me to speak. *hpahą́le che* from the beginning (BE2.48; 01/25/95/FH/pc:ok; 04/26/95/LS/pc:ok).

•• LFD 125: *hpahą́le* <p̣a-ho^{n}´-gthe> in advance of the storm, in the first order of time, original, primary. *hpahą́le che* <p̣a-ho^{n}´-gthe tse> at the outset, from the beginning. [Example contains *che* POSIT.]

hpahą́le ákaaleke. N **First Striker (personal name)** (WHM980326; CQc).

hpahą́le ðée. VP [sync., *hpahą́le _ðée*] **precede (lit., 'go first').**

•• LFD 125: *hpahą́le ðe* <p̣a-ho^{n}´-gthe the> to precede. *hpahą́le bre ha* <p̣a-ho^{n}´-gthe bthe ha> [expected Mod. Os. form: *hpahą́le brée;* sentence-final *ha* is not used in Mod. Os.] I precede.

hpahą́le mąðį́. VP [sync., *hpahą́le mą_ðį́*] **place s.t. or s.o. first.** *wahkǫ́ta hpahą́le mąðį ée ekǫ ahkílaði šǫǫšǫ́we* place God first and keep yourself in that way forever (FH/pc).

hpahą́le mąðį́ ąðíðaace (variant: **hpahą́le mąį́ ąðį́ðaace**). N **God, God's name as "we'll-call-you-first-in-our-lives" (lit., 'placed first we call you').** [FH, quoting her father's term for 'God'.]

hpáhiihto. N [*hpá + hį́į +htóho*] **mallard duck (lit., 'green head feathers').**
•• LFD 125 (unconfirmed): *hpáhihto* <p̣a´-hi-ṭu> the mallard duck. "The skin of the neck and breast of this bird are put upon the sacred pipes of the Osage, Omaha, and Pawnee Tribes."

hpahíke. V [conjug. unknown] *(trans.)* **sort, classify, categorize.** *hǫbrį́ke che hpahíke* I sorted the beans (FH:ok).

hpáhį. N **porcupine.**
•• LFD 125: *hpáhį* <p̣a´-hi^{n}> porcupine [LF form unconfirmed]. "This animal was useful . . . for its quills, which were used for decorating moccasins, leggings, and other articles of clothing. The quills were colored with native dyes and flattened before using."

hpahį́į (variant of **hpaxį́į**).

hpahį́įska. N [*hpá + hį́į + ská*] **Pawhuska (the seat of Osage County, Oklahoma; lit., 'white head hair'); white hair (of the head).**
•• LFD 125: *hpahúska* <p̣a-hiu´-çka> White-hair (personal name; refers to the sacred white buffalo). LFD 126: *hpáxįska* <p̣a´-xi^{n}-çka> a white mane (of horse).
••• Cf. *hpaxį́į.*

hpahlíxtoe. N **mucus, runny nose** (FH).
••• Cf. *hpalį́.*

hpahlį (variant of **hpalį́**).

hpáhtąą. N **hickory nut** (02/09/95/FH/pc:okc; BE2.66).
•• LFD 129: *hpą́htąa hi* <p̣o^{n}´-ṭo^{n}-a hi> large hickory tree, *Hicoria. hpą́htąka* <p̣o^{n}´-ṭo^{n}-ga> nut of the hickory, hickory nut.

hpahúuse (variants: **hpahúase, hpahúese**). N **scissors** (RB; 03/08/95/MREI/pc:okc; BE2.117). *hpahį́ðuusé* haircutters, scissors.
•• LFD 125: *hpahuðise* <p̣a-hiu thi-çe> hair + cutter: scissors. *hpahúðise htąka* <p̣a-hiu´-thi-çe ṭo^{n}-ga> large scissors, shears.

hpahúusehtąą. N [*hpahúuse + htą́ą*] **shears (lit., 'large scissors').**

hpahúze. N **comb** (BE 2:21: unconfirmed; 01/09/95/FH/pc:uk; 04/20/95/LS/pc:uk).
••• *KS hélüze* [may be *hée-*] fine tooth comb (RR).

hpáimąhą (variant of **hpaðímaha**).

hpáį (variant of **hpáðį**).

hpáįmaha (variant of **hpaðímaha**).

hpalį́. (variant: **hpahlį, hpalí**). N **mucus from the nose, runny nose, snot** (FH/09/11/01/pc; FH/t128). *hpalį́stowe* runny nose (FH/t128, (BE2.124; 03/13/95/FH/pc:ok).
•• LFD 126: *hpaxðį́* <p̣a-xthi^{n}´> mucus from the nose.
••• Cf. *hpá.*

hpánąąke. V [reg., *_hpánąąke*] *(trans.)* **push s.o. onward.** *ðée ðe hpánąąke* this one here, push him [making him walk, run] (FH/09/21/01/pc).
••• Cf. *hpahą́le.*

hpápaxǫ (variant: **hpą́paxǫ**). N [*hpá + paaxǫ́* 'break'] **Sioux (tribe or tribal member), cutthroats (lit., 'nose cutter', 'head cutter')** (RBnHW13) (unconfirmed, 03/08/95/PM/pc:uk; 04/19/95/FH/pc:uk as a tribe name). *šée hpápaxǫ ihtá* this belongs to *hpápaxǫ* (FH/09/22/01/pc) • **Nose Cutter (personal name for a second son)** (04/19/95/FH/pc). [Alfred Oberly, Frances Holding's brother, and Louis Red Eagle both were named *hpą́paxǫ.*]
•• LFD 124: *hpápawaxǫ* <P̣a´-ba-wa-xo^{n}> Head-cutter (personal name). *pxápawaxǫ* <Pa´-ba-wa-xo^{n}> [LF's form is presumably a typographical error for the expected *hpápawaxǫ* <P̣a´-ba-wa-xo^{n}>] Head-cutters, the Osage name for the Sioux Tribe of Indians (unconfirmed; FH:4/24/96/tape:uk as tribe name).

hpasiólįį (variant of **hpasú olį́į**).

hpásitoopa. N **Four Cliffs (personal name referring to buffalo descending in four lines from the hills); Pahsetopa (family name among the Osages).**
•• LFD 124: *hpasitopa* <p̣a-çi-do-ba> Four-hills (personal name; refers to the descent of a herd of buffalo from a hill in four lines).

hpasólįį (variant of **hpasú olį́į**).

hpasú. N **tip or point of an object.**
•• LFD 124: *hpasí* <p̣a-çi´> the top of a tree, the top of a pole, a peak. LFD 19: *pasíke* <ba-çi´-ge> spiked.

hpasú olį́į (variants: **hpasólįį, hpasiólįį, hpasúlį**). N **living on the end, dwelling on the cliffs** (02/03/95/FH/pc:ok; BE2.61)**; Fairfax or Grayhorse group of Osages (lit., 'living on the end', referring to the west end of the allotment)** (FH; PM; RB; RBn2-MOJ/p16; 01/19/95/FH/pc:ok).
•• JOD (slip file): *hpasü'* <pa-sü´> the tip or point of an object.
•• LFD 124: *hpasiólį* <p̣a-çiu´-gthi^{n}> Dwellers-upon-the-hill-top. "When the river (Mississippi) overflowed its banks, a group of Osage Indians fled from their village and sought the high hills and there established a camp. They were known by the name of <p̣a-çiu' -gthi^{n}> and settled in Grayhorse."

hpasúkoša. N [*hpasú* + *koša*] **paisley, paisley patterned cloth, said to be the first cloth that Osages saw (lit., 'curved points')** (MSB 3/3/83).

hpaxáce (variant: **hpaɣáce**). N **roach haircut, roached hair** (RBn11/JW&FW&HHaskell/c.1976).
•• JOD (slip file): *hpaxace* <pa-qá-ṭṣe> roach(?).
•• LFD 126: *hpaxáce* <p̣a-xa´-dse> a peculiar style of hair cut among the Osage Indians and also in other tribes.

hpáxį (variant of **hpaxį́į**).

hpáxį ðutáahpa (variant of **hpáxį ðuutáahpa**).

hpáxį ðuusé. N **haircut.**

hpáxį ðuutáahpa (variant: **hpáxį ðutáahpa**). N **woman's bun hairdo (lit., 'hair made round')** (FH:conf).

hpaxį́į (variants: **hpáxįį, hpahį́į, hpáxį**). N [probably *hpá* + *hį́į*] **hair of the head or neck of a human or an animal, mane** (JS/pc; FH 4/17/96). *hpáxįį brúuse íbrilą* I'm thinking about cutting my hair (FH/06/16/01/pc). *wahkǫ́ta ižį́ke iihǫ́ hpaxį́į įkše xǫ́ǫce íkǫce káaɣi apai* they're making the cedar like Mary's hair (FH).
•• LFD 125: *hpahú, hpahí* <p̣a-hiu´> the hair of a man's head. *hpáhį ðihta akši šoká* <p̣a´-hi^{n} thi-ṭa a-ki sho-ga´> your hair is thick. LFD 126: *hpaxį́* <p̣a-xi^{n}´> hair of the head.
••• Cf. *hpahį́įska.*

hpáxįįsą (variant: **hpáxįįsa**). N **braid** (RBn, unconfirmed).
•• LFD 237: *wéðįsą* <we´-thi^{n}-ço^{n}> braided lariat.
••• *KS wabésą sábe* rope made of buffalo mane (RR).

hpáze. ADJ, ADV, N **evening, in the evening time, not quite dark yet, night** (02/24/95/FH/pc:prod). *hą́ąną hpáze* night, at night (FH:prod). *hpáze ðe* this evening. *hpáze íhtą* when it gets evening (FH:4/17/96/tape). *ðé hpáze* that evening (FH). *hpáze waachí watǫ́į ąkái hta akái* we are going for the night dance [to observe the dance].
•• LFD 124: *hpáze* <p̣a´-çe> evening, close of the day.

hpáze waachí. N **night dance.** *hpáze waachí watǫ́e ąkái hta ąkái* we're going for the night dance [to watch] (RBn3-12).

hpáze wanǫ́bre. N **supper, evening meal.** *hpáze wanǫ́bre nį́įpe?* did you all eat supper? (BE2.130). *hpáze wanǫ́bre ónǫbre ðúwį ókxąži ąhé* I was slow buying groceries for supper (03/10/95/MREI/pc:okc; BE2.123; 03/14/95/MREI/pc:ok).
•• LFD 124: *hpáze wanǫbre* <p̣a´-çe wa-no^{n}-bthe> an evening meal.

hpázece. N, ADV **last evening.** *hpázece súhka záani ąðáachape* we ate all the chicken up last night (MSB).

hpą́paxǫ (variant of **hpápaxǫ**).

hpée. N **forehead, brow, head** (01/30/95/FH/pc:prod; 04/26/95/LS/pc; BE2.50).
•• LFD 126: *hpé* <p̣e´> the forehead. LFD 127: *hpéotxą* <p̣e´-o-to^{n}> the forehead.

hpéece. N **fire (e.g., cooking fire, meeting fire, cooking stove gas fire).** *hpéece ðé íištope* use this fire to bless yourself (RB). *hpéece ðuutáaži* turn the fire off [imperative] (03/14/95/MREI/pc). *hpéece ístope* they used the fire to bless themselves (04/25/95/PM/pc:ok:sto; 01/25/95/FH/pc:okc, BE2.47).
•• LFD 127: *hpéce* <p̣e´-dse> fire.
••• *OM* <p̣e´-de>fire (LFD 127).

hpéece íhta. N **fireman (a position in Native American Church meetings; lit., 'his fire').** *hpéece íhta hpahą́le* first fireman (04/25/95/PM/pc:ok). *hpéece íhta wéðǫǫpa, hpéece íhta wáðǫǫpa* second fireman (04/25/95/PM/pc:ok). *hpéece íhta wéðabrį, hpéece íhta wáðabrį* third fireman (04/25/95/PM/pc:okc). *hpéece wéðabrį hpáaɣe* I worked as third fireman (04/25/95/PM/pc:okc; BE2.47). *hpéece íhta wéðabrį che olį́į a* you sit in third [fireman] place (RBn10-21/JW&FW/77; 04/25/95/PM/pc:okc).

hpéece íiška. N **heating stove, wood-burning stove (for heat, not cooking; lit., 'fire to warm oneself')** (MSBt#9RB; 3).

hpéece mąðį́ (variant: **hpéece mǫ́į**). N **Fire-Walker (personal name); family name Petsemoie.** [*hpéece mǫį́* was Frances Holding's ancestor on her mother's side. The city park in Hominy is named after *hpéece mǫ́į*.]
•• LFD 127: *hpécemǫį* <p̣e´-dse-mo^{n}-i^{n}> Fire-walker (personal name; refers to the finding of the red bear walking in the night, a light like a fire shone from his breast).

hpéece océðe. N **fire (cooking fire, meeting fire, fire of gas stove).**

hpéece žą́ą. N **firewood** (RB).

hpéecenii. N [*hpéece* + *níi*] **liquor (lit., 'fire-water')** (RB; 03/16/95/MREI/pc/ok). *níhka akxa wáli lǫ́ði akxai, hpéecenii huuwáli waðáahtąpe* that man is really drunk, he's drunk a lot of liquor (RBn12-06).

hpéecenii (*continued*)

•• LFD 127: *péce ni* <pe´-de ni> fire water, intoxicant.

••• Cf. *hpéeceniihci.*

hpéecenii ðaahtą́ hci. N **bar, saloon.**

hpéeceniihci. N [*hpéecenii + hcí*] **liquor store (lit., 'fire-water house')** (FH)**; bar, saloon (archaic meaning).**

•• LFD 127: *hpéceni hci* <p̣e´-dse-ni-ṭsi> fire-water house, a saloon, whisky house.

hpéeðǫǫpa (variant: **hpéeǫpa**). ADJ, N **seven (lit., 'two foreheads')** (BE2.119; 03/09/95/MREI/pc:ok; FH:4/24/96/tape).

•• LFD 127: *hpéðǫpa* <p̣e´-tho^{n}-ba> seven.

hpéeleke. N [*hpée + léke*] **Shattered Forehead (nickname; refers to scar from an injury to the head).** [George Treadway's nickname in the mid-1900s (FH).]

hpéeǫpa (variant of **hpéeðǫǫpa**).

hpeeštá. N [*hpée + štáha*] **bald head, smooth forehead or brow (lit., 'clear, smooth or bald of brow')** (04/07/95/PM/pc). [Nickname used by Osages for a man in a store where they traded.]

hpéɣe. N **gourd; gourd rattle (used in peyote meeting** [RB]**).** *hpéɣe ðé ą́wali mįkšé* I'm really stingy with this gourd (RBn2-MOJ/p37; 02/03/95/FH/pc:okc). *Arthur akxa Mongrain hpéɣe wį́ káaɣape* Arthur made Mongrain a gourd (RBn10-10:JW).

•• LFD 128: *hpéɣe* <p̣e´-xe> gourd rattle. *hpéɣe ðuzapi waðǫ* <p̣e´-xe thu-ça-bi wa-tho^{n}> Songs of Taking up the Rattle. *hpéɣe ipa* <p̣e´-xe i-ba> rattle handle. *hpéɣe su* <p̣e´-xe çu> rattle seeds. *hpéɣe ðuze waðǫ* <p̣e´-xe thu-çe wa-tho^{n}> Songs of Taking up the Rattle.

••• *OM* same as Osage (LFD 128).

hpéže. N **weed** (RBn HW13)**; sage, sage bush, sagebrush** (RBn HW13). [Takes 'lying down' positional article *kše*.]

•• LFD 128: *hpéže* <p̣e´-zhe> grass, hay, weeds. *hpéže kše aši aǫbra ha* <p̣e´-zhe ke a-shi a-o^{n}-btha ha> [expected Mod. Os. form: *hpéže kše áši aǫ́ǫbra* 'I tossed the weeds outside'; sentence-final *ha* is not used in Mod. Os.] I took the weeds out.

hpéže brąðáalį. N **sweet-smelling grass.**

•• LFD 128: *hpéže brąðalį* <p̣e´-zhe btho^{n}-tha-gthi^{n}> sweet-smelling grass.

hpéže htóho. N **green tea (lit., 'green/blue weed')** (WHM98102; FH/09/23/01/pc:ok).

••• Cf. *hpéžehtoho.*

hpéže mą́hka (variant: **hpéže mąhkása, hpéže mąhkásae**). N **tea (lit., 'weed medicine')** (03/15/95/PM/pc:ok; 03/05/95/JS/pc:ok; 03/16/95/FH/pc:ok, *hpéže níi* preferred).

•• LFD 128: *hpeže mąhka sae* <p̣e´-zhe mo^{n}-ḳo^{n} ça-e> weed coffee. *hpéže mąhką sae štahtą* <p̣e´-zhe mo^{n}-ḳo^{n} ça-e shta-ṭo^{n}> you drink tea.

hpéže xóhtą (variants: **hpéže xóhta**). N **sage** (03/23/95/FH/pc:ok; 03/23/95/FH/pc:ok; RBn10-21/JW; BE2.116) (RB note: refers to sage employed in peyote meeting).

•• LFD 128: *hpéžexohta* <p̣e´-zhe-xu-ṭa> wild sage, *Artemisia.*

••• *KS péeže xóttą* wild sage, used in flute dance against mosquitos (RR).

hpéžehtoho. N **lettuce** (02/15/95/FH/pc:prod; BE2.78).

•• LFD 128: *hpéžetxoho* <p̣e´-zhe-tu-hu> [LF's *-txo-* <-tu-> is presumably a typographical error for *-hto-* <-ṭu->] pennyroyal (*Hedeoma pulegioides*). *ðáhpąke apa hpéžehtoho isi pi a* <tha´-p̣o^{n}-ge a-ba p̣e´-zhe-ṭu-hu i-çi bi a> [expected Mod. Os. form: *lápxąąke apa hpéžehtóho íisipe*] mosquitos do not like pennyroyal.

hpéženíi. N **tea (lit., 'weed-water').**

hpéženii ną́ɣe oolą́. N **iced tea (lit., 'weed-water with ice put in').**

hpíiži. ADJ, V [uninfl./stat., *_hpíiži*] *(intr.)* **(be) bad, awful, evil, wicked.** *óðaake wálį hpíiži* the news was very bad (01/06/95/FH/pc:okc). *hpíižie* that's bad [as to a child] (01/06/95/FH/pc:okc; BE2.6). *wálį hpíižie óhesažį alįį ðáha níi hpáasike* it's awful that I sat down real quick and splattered water (04/19/95/FH/pc). *táatą hpíižį ecíke tą . . .* if there are bad things around . . .

•• LFD 129: *hpíži* <p̣i´-zhi> bad, evil.

hpíiži ažį́. V [sync. nasal vowel stem, *a_žį́*] [*hpíiži + ažį́*] *(trans.)* **hate a person, think ill of s.o., hold s.o. in contempt.**

hpióka. N **part in the hair.** *hpióka káaɣa* part your hair (lit., 'make a part') (BE2.101; 03/06/95/FH/pc:okc; RBn2-MOJ/p35).

•• LFD 127–28: *hpeókasą* <p̣e-u´-ga-ço^{n}> the parting of the hair, the part of the hair (colored red to symbolize the path of the sun).

hpíǫ. V [sync.+sync. nasal vowel stem, *_hpí_ǫ*] *(trans.)* **know how to do s.t.; learn** (02/14/95/FH/pc)**; be skilled at or expert in.** *hpímą/hpímǫ* I have learned; I know how (02/14/95/FH/pc:ok; 04/14/95/PM/pc:ok). *špížǫ* you know how (02/14/95/FH/pc:ok; BE2.74). *špížǫ?* did you learn? do you know how? *wažážeíe špíižǫ?* do you know how to talk

Osage? (RBn1-58). *óohǫ hpíǫpe* she is a good cook (lit., 'she knows how to cook') (BE2.23; 02/14/95/FH/pc:ok). *wažážeíe špížǫ?* can you speak Osage? *hpímą hkǫ́bra* I want to learn (04/14/95/PM/pc:ok). *wažážeíe hpíǫ wáhkǫ́bra* I want them to learn the Osage language (04/14/95/PM/pc). *hpíǫ áhkǫ́bra* I want him to learn it (04/14/95/PM/pc). *wažážeíe hpíǫ ðihkǫ́bra* I want you to learn the Osage language (04/14/95/PM/pc). *Bob akxa wáli wažážeíe hpíǫ akxai* Bob sure has learned the Osage language (BE2.77). *hąðé wižį́ke akxa wažážeíe hpíǫ kǫ́ða akxa* tonight son wants to learn the Osage language (RBn22-02). *waachí hpíǫpe* he's a skilled dancer (RBn3-42). *waaðǫ́ hpíǫpe* he's a skilled singer (RBn3-42).

•• LFD 129: *hpiǫ́* <p̣i-o^n´> expert. *hpímą* <p̣i´-mo^n> I am expert. *špi žǫ* <shpi zho^n> you are expert. *ąhpiǫ pe* <o^n-p̣i-o^n i> we are expert, skillful. LFD 70: *ié hpiǫ* <i-e´ p̣i-o^n> skilled in the use of language.

••• Cf. *hkihpíǫ*.

hpisúhu. N **oak (lit., 'acorn tree')** (RBn HW13; FH/09/22/01/pc:uk).

•• LFD 128: *hpisí hi* <p̣i-çi´ hi> red oak tree. LFD 299: *hpisi* <pi-çi> acorn.

hposú. N **acorn** (RBn HW, unconfirmed; FH:uk).

••• *KS ppüsü̃* acorn (RR).

hpǫ́ɣe. N **artichoke, radish, squash.** *hpǫ́ɣe áace zį* yellow climbing squash (BE2.126, unconfirmed).

•• JOD (slip file): *hpą́xe* <pa^n´-qe> artichoke.

•• LFD 129: *hpǫ́ɣe* <p̣o^n´-xe> the artichoke (*Cynara scolymus*), an edible plant.

••• *KS ppą́ąɣe* small white gourd (RR); *OP ppą́ɣe ~ ppą́xi* Jerusalem artichoke, radish (JK).

hpǫ́ɣe áace žį. N **yellow climbing squash (small squash that the Osages used to cultivate, now extinct; lit., 'little climbing squash')** (RB).

•• JOD (slip file): *$_x$póɣiðacˀį́* <$_x$p̣o´-xi-¢a-ts'i^n> a small spotted squash ("Some are dark or greenish, others white").

hpǫ́hka. N **Ponca (tribe or tribal member).** *hpǫ́hka ąkítaake* we fight the Poncas (BE2.46; BE2.105; 03/10/95/FH/pc:ok; 03/08/95/PM/pc:ok; 04/17/95/LS/pc:ok).

•• LFD 129: *hpǫ́hka* <p̣o^n´-ḳa> the Ponca Tribe.

hpuzá. N **sand.**

•• LFD 128: *hpizá* <p̣i-ça´> sand, silt. *hpizá katace* <p̣i-ça´ ga-da-dse> quicksand, loose sand in the bed of a river in which there is danger of sinking. *hpizáole kaxa* <p̣i-ça´-u-gthe ga-xa> Sand Creek, Okla. *hpizáska* <p̣i-ça´-çka> white sand.

••• *KS ppüzá* sand (RR); *OM* same as Osage (LFD 128).

hta. PPN **toward, in the direction of, from, into.** *níi ecí hta* in the water [toward] there (RBn10-10:JW). *hci hta* into the house (contrasts with *hcí htaha* 'to the house'). *ówe che hcí hta áðįku* bring the groceries in the house.

•• LFD 135: *hta* <ṭa> in that direction (term used in ceremonial ritual). LFD 67: *howąįkíhtąche* <ho-wa-i^n-gi´-ṭo^n-tse> [expected Mod. Os. form: *howąįkí hta che*] from what source, what direction? *hóbwaki htą ðachi a(?)* <ho´-wa-gi ṭo^n tha-tsi a(?)> [expected Mod. Os. form: *hówąįkí hta ðachíe*] where did you come from? LFD 91: *mi hiekéhta* <mi hi-e-ge´-ṭa> [expected Mod. Os. form: *mį́įhiðe kše hta*; LF's *-ké-* <-ge´-> may be a typographical error] toward the setting of the sun (03/23/95/FH/pc:uk).

hta. POTENTIAL MARKER **future tense marker: will, be going to.** *íe tóa ékipše hta, ówaštaake hkǫ́bra* I'm going to say something, I want you to tell them (RBn10-15). *háamą hta che?* how am I going to do this? (04/11/95/FH/pc). *ákahamį žúuce ðée pée ðuuštáke hta ðe?* who is going to undress that one with the red coat on? [refers to receiving a wedding coat when the drum is being paid for]. • **irrealis marker: could, so that it could/might be; what if, were it the case that, would be.** *kį́į iðákˀuce hta mįkše* I will try to fly [circumlocution for 'if I could fly'] (04/13/95/FH/pc:prod). *iiðáðe hta* if I could see (FH:4/25/96/tape). *haaská ną ščihtą tą ðikítąhe hta* if you just touch his garment you could get well (FH/pc). *šímižį wé[ð]uɣekí[ð]e akxai, wáðohta hta ną* they were marrying their girl off so she would be proper, respectable (RBn22-17).

•• JOD (Devouring Mountain p2 ln13–14): *wakˀó ðáalį xci šímįžįka ðáalį xci tóopa kˀúpe ska, wahǫ́įžįka walą́ke hta* <Wak'u´ ¢áḳ¢i^n-qtsi, cími^{n}çiñ´ka ¢áḳ¢i^n-qtsi ṭúp̣a k'üp̣e ska, Wahŭ^n´ çiñ´ka waḳ¢añ´ke ta> they gave him four very pretty women, four very pretty girls so that he, the orphan, could take them as wives.

hta (variant of **íhta**).

hta akxa. POTENTIAL MARKER+CONT **irrealis or potential: be it (the case that), if (it is the case that), it will be the case that, in the event that, it may be that; would that.** [Note that 3rd person continuative *akxa* is used even with 1st or 2nd person subjects in clauses of this type.] *ąži*

hta akxa (*continued*)
brée tą, oániži mąží hta akxai [but] if I go I won't be afraid. *iðák?ue šo ąhé wažážeíe íhpahǫ hta akxai* I'm going to keep on [trying] until I learn the Osage language (RBn10-10:JW). *brúwį hta akxa, wik?ú hta mįkše* if I buy it, I'll give it to you. *waachíe watǫ́į scée ną hta akxai* you're always going to go to dances (MSB-9-3-82). *hǫ́ǫpa ókaaɣeįki tą htą́wą ki abrį́bree hta akxai ší éži wį waðíhta hpíǫ ke wį íhkihkawi hta mįkšé* on Saturday what if I take him to town and trade him for another one that knows how to work (cf. *abrį́bree hta akxai* 'what if I take him') (RBn10-2:MOJ/79; CQ: okc). *wáščuɣe tą Mary íščuɣe hta akxai* if you get married, Mary will be your bridesmaid (lit., 'if you marry, you would have Mary as bridesmaid'). *ší íiwikie hta akxai* we'll see each other again (lit., 'would that I [might] see you again'). *íinǫǫhpa, ðaxíšta hta akxai* be careful, you might fall (04/26/95/LS/pc:ok; BE2.43). *įtį́la ąðįkšé hta akxai mą́žą įké etxą́* we will still be gossiping when the world ends (MSB). *kį́į ékimą hta akxai, kóe mǫ́žǫ záani iiðáðe hta akxai* if I could fly, then I could see the whole world (RBn15-02, FH:prod). *ehta wábruɣe mąží hta akxai* maybe I better not get married (RBn17-p02).

hta apa tą (or **hta pa tą**?). **may.**
•• LF 135: *hta patą* <ṭa ba-do^{n}> that they may.

htáa. N **deer, doe, fawn, buck** (02/24/95/FH/pc:okc). *htáa léže žį* fawn (lit., 'small spotted deer') (01/20/95/FH/pc:ok; BE2.30). • **meat.** *htáa hépe* piece of meat (02/24/95/FH/pc:ok). *htáa zíhi* fried meat. *htáa che táazihi* fry the meat [imperative] (FH:4/25/96/tape; 02/24/95/FH/pc). *htáa okášą* take care of the meat [imperative] (02/24/95/FH/pc:okc; 04/11/95/FH/pc:ok). *hkóhkosa htáa* pork (lit., 'pig meat') (03/08/95/FH/pc:okc).
•• LFD 135: *hta* <ṭa> deer; meat of any kind.

htáa htą́ka. N **buck, male deer (lit., 'large deer').**

htáa kiðíɣepi. N [*ki-* INCEPTIVE + *ðúɣe* + *api*] **deer mating moon, October.** [Names of months were historically not used in Osage and sound unnatural to Osage speakers (HH).]
••• *KS ttáa kkṹyüɣabe* month when the deer mate in late autumn (RR).

htáa lįkó. N **gravy.**

htáa mį́įka. N **doe, female deer.**

htáa nihkaši. N **Deer clan.**
••• Cf. *htáanihkáši.*

htáa púze. N **dried meat** (FH:4/22/96/tape:prod).

htáa štǫ́ka. N **meatball, meat candy (lit., 'softened meat').**

htáa taazíhi. N **steak (lit., 'browned meat').** *htáa taazíhi* fried meat (01/30/95/FH/pc:okc).

htáabre. V, N **hunting for big game or small game.** [Probably from an original Osage form *tábre*, cognate with KS *dáble* and QU *tápde*, but reinterpreted as containing *htáa* 'deer'.] *htáabre brée* I'm going hunting (02/13/95/FH/pc:ok). *htáabre aðée iché* he has gone hunting (RB). *kasį́xci htáabre pšíe* this morning I went hunting.
•• LFD 135: *htábre* <ṭa´-bthe> to hunt deer, deer hunting.

htáabre aðée. VP [sync., *htáabre (a)_ðée*] *(trans./intr.)* **go hunting (for).** *htáabre brée* I'm going hunting (RBn3-05).

htaacé. N **wind, air** (03/16/95/MREI/pc:ok). *htaacé lą́ąðį* (lit., 'big wind') a tempest (03/23/95/FH/pc).
•• LFD 136: *htacé* <ṭa-dse´> the winds, the four quarters of the earth; air. *htaacé lǫǫðe* <ṭa-dse´ gtho^{n}-the> great windstorm, a tempest.

htaacé hpíiži. N **tornado, tempest, windstorm.** *htaacé hpíiži apa hṹ ðí apai* a tornado is coming (BE2.143; 03/23/95/FH/pc:ok).
•• LFD 136: *htace hpíiži* <ṭa-dse pi´-zhi> a bad wind, blustery.

htaacé oðį́ike. N **radio (lit., 'catching the wind')** (04/20/95/LS/pc:prod).

htaacé óhesaži. N **cyclone, tornado, storm with strong winds, gale.** *htaacé óhesaži wį húðí apai* a cyclone is coming (03/07/95/FH/pc:prod orig). *htaacé óhesaži húði eepé* they said strong winds are coming (FH:4/24/96/prod).

htaacé saakí. VP **be windy.** *htaacé saakí akxa* it is a strong wind; the wind is strong; it's windy (03/16/95/MREI/pc:ma). *htaacé saakípe* the wind was strong. • N **strong or violent wind, windstorm, gale.**
•• LFD 136: *htacé saki pi a* <ṭa-dse´ ça-gi bi a> the wind was strong. *htacé sakí* <ṭa-dse´-ça-gi> violent wind, windstorm, a gale. LFD 356: *htaacé sasaki* <ṭa-dse´-ça-ça-gi> windy. [The probable Mod. Os. pronunciation of LF's reduplicated form <ça-ça-gi> is *saasáaki* (from *saakí* 'strong').]

htáaceomą́i. N **Cheyenne (tribe or tribal member)** (RB; FH:ok? 'walking in the wind'?).

htaacéxowe. N **electric fan (lit., 'wind roaring').** *htaacéxowe káaɣa* turn the fan on [imperative] (04/25/95/PM/pc:okc; BE2.43; FH:4/18/96/tape,ok).

htaacéžį. N **Whirlwind (name in an Osage fable).**

htaaðáachaži, htaaðáachaži hą́ąpa (variants of **hą́ąpa htaaðáachaži**).

htaaðíihtą. V [sync., *htaa_ðiihtą*] [*htáa* + *ðiihtą́*] **handle, knead, or work meat with the hand (as in cutting meat up)** (FH/09/24/01/prod). *htaaðíihtą* handle the meat, take care of the meat [imperative] (01/14/95/FH/pc:ok; RBn1-MOJ/p50). *htaabríihtą hta mįkšé* I'm going to take care of the meat (01/14/95/FH/pc:ok).

htaaháa. N [*htáa* + *háa*] **buckskin, deerskin.**
•• LFD 137: *htaha* <ṭa-ha> deerskin.

htaahékaaɣe. N [*htáa* + *hé* + *káaɣe*] **Deer making horns (personal name)** (RBn22-04).

htaaníe céɣe. N **soup kettle.** [A term reportedly connected with the district of Grayhorse (DN-WHM; unconfirmed).]

htáanieoožú. N **bowl** (FH:4/22/96/tape:okc).

htáanihkáši. N [*htáa* + *nihkáši*] **Deer clan** (BE2.30; 01/20/95/FH/pc:ok).
•• LFD 137: *htáinihkašika* <ṭa´i-ni-ḳa-shi-ga> Deer People.

htaaníi. N [*htáa* + *níi*] **soup, broth, consommé.** *htaaníi káaɣe* to make soup (03/13/95/FH/pc:ok; BE2.125). *htaaníi oohǫ́!* make soup! (RBn1-50; FH). *súhka htą htaaníi káaɣa* make soup with the turkey [imperative] (FH/11/17/01/pc). *htaaníi žúe* vegetable soup (lit., 'red soup') (FH:4/24/96/ok: ht). *súhkahtą htaaníi oohǫ́ ðáalį káaɣapi ché* they cooked the turkey soup well (01/12/95/FH/pc:okc). *htaaníi hcúke íðaachapi* eat soup with a spoon [to pl. addressees].
•• LFD 138: *htaní* <ṭa-ni´> soup, broth.
••• *KS htaanį́* soup (RR).

htáaoolą (variant of **htóolą**).

htaapé. N **ball (used in a game)** (BE2.6; 01/06/95/FH/pc:prod). *htaapé kˀǫ aðáape* they went to play ball (RBn2-MOJ/p20; 01/06/95/FH/pc:ok).
•• LFD 135: *htapé* <ṭa-be´> ball. "The Osage usually make their balls of the root of a plant called <ṭa-be´ hi> 'ball tree', sometimes of the root of the grapevine." *htapésu* <ṭa-be´-çu> ball stick [unconfirmed]. *htapésu ipastace* <ṭa-be´-çu i-ba-sta-dse> [expected Mod. Os. form: *htaapésu* (?) *ípaastace*] a curved stick covered with a net (used by the Chippewas in a certain kind of ball game, also used by the Osage, Iowa, Kansas, and Winnebago Tribes).

htaapéskažįkˀǫ́. V [reg., *htaapéskažį_kˀǫ́*] [*htaapé* + *ská* + *-žį* 'little' + *kˀǫ́*] **play golf (lit., 'play with little white ball').** • N **golf.**

htáapše (variant: **htaapšé**). N [*htáa* + *pšé*] **pounded meat, pounded dry meat** (FH/09/25/01/pc; (02/24/95/FH/pc:ok)**; meat candy.** [Barbecued meat is dried in cotton sacks or in a container or hung on a line then pounded with a mallet in a wooden pounder or ground up in a grinder; honey is added, and the mixture is rolled into small balls. Contrast *tǫ́ǫpše* 'frankfurter, sausage'.]
•• LFD 138: *htápše* <ṭa´-pshe> pemmican. "Both the Osage and the Omaha prepare this from jerked lean meat of any kind, roasted and pounded, then mixed with marrow grease."

htaasíilee htáwą. N **Tulsa, Oklahoma (lit., 'deer crossing town').**

htaasį́įce. N [*htáa* + *sį́įce*] **headdress (lit., 'deer tail').**

htaasį́įce wahú. N **spreader for Osage headdress, roach bone (lit., 'deer-tail bone')** (RB; 03/14/95/FH/pc:ok).

htaaská. N [*htáa* + *ská*] **sheep (lit., 'white deer')** (MOJt#150).

htáaweli. N **meat grease, known as Indian butter.** [The grease coming from beef when cracklings were made was poured or spread over pounded meat and corn to make "platter corn" (FH).]

htachí. N **muskrat.**
•• LFD 136 (unconfirmed): *htachí* <ṭa-ci´> muskrat.

htáha. ADV, PPN **toward; on the way or path to a certain point; in the direction of** (MREI, LS). *hcí htaha, hcíhtaha* toward the house. *ecíhtaha* toward there. *éhtaha* toward that way, in that direction (RBn1-56; 03/23/95/FH/pc:ok). *ehtáha ąkái htái* let's get over that way (04/04/95/FH/pc). *mąchéhtaha* toward the center, inward (03/23/95/FH/pc). *hcíhtaha aðáape* he went direct[ly] to the house. *wasúhuži kšíhtaha* into temptation (lit., 'toward that lying uncleanliness') (HH's Lord's Prayer). *Preston apa htą́wa kši éhtaha maðį́ apai* Preston was walking toward town (03/23/95/FH/pc; 05/02/95/LS/pc:ok). *mį́įhiiðé éhtaha* toward the setting sun (03/23/95/FH/pc; 05/02/95/LS/pc:ok). *mį́į éhtaha* toward the sun (03/23/95/FH/pc). *ámąhtáha* toward the other side. *šéehtaha* over that way [toward you], go that way (01/31/95/FH/pc:prod). *émąhtaži* not that other way.
•• LFD 137: *hta ha* <ṭa ha> toward. *ni kše hta ha* <ni kshe ṭa ha> toward the water or river (03/23/95/FH/pc:ok).
••• Cf. *hta* 'toward'.

htáha, htáhą (variants of **htą́hą**).

htáhtaze (variants: **htáhtáaze, htáhtáeze**). v [uninfl., or reg.? _*htáhtaze*?] [onomatopoeic] *(intr.)* **tick (e.g., clock or insect making noise); clatter (e.g., typewriter keys)** (04/06/95/FH:ok). • n **grasshopper, cricket (lit., 'makes a whizzing noise')** (FH); **ticking, tapping, whizzing, or clicking sound.** *htáhtaze huuhtą́ka* a lot of grasshoppers (BE2.60; 02/03/95/FH/pc:okc). *htáhtáze óochižape* grasshoppers are noisy (RBn3-55; 02/27/95/FH/pc:ok).

•• RB: <táh-táh-áh-zeh>, <tah-táh-eh-zeh> (02/03/95/FH/pc:ok both).

•• LFD 34: *tatáze* <da-da´-çe> grasshopper. *tatáze ho htąka* <da-da´-çe ho ṭo^{n}-ga> great green grasshopper. *tatáze sape* <da-da´-çe ça-be> cricket, black grasshopper. LFD 97: *htahtaze* <ṭa-ṭa-çe> clicking, ticking. [Note that LF has both <ṭa-ṭa-çe> and <da-da´-çe> forms. The latter are erroneous.]

••• Cf. *į́įštáxį htáhtaze, mą́ze htáhtaze, žą́ą káahtahta.*

htáhu. n **neck** (02/27/95/FH/pc).

•• LFD 137: *htáhu* <ṭa´-hiu> the neck, the nape of the neck.

htai. injunctive **clause-final element conveying an exhortation or suggestion for a group including the speaker and at least two other persons: let's.** [Contrast *hce* injunctive 'let's (speaker and one other person)'.] *hkáwaceženi̜ tóa ąðáahtą́ ąkái htai* let's [three or more people] go drink some beer (RBn10-12:JW). *haaská wasúhužike hpaahípai, ščúuwasu htai* be sorting the dirty clothes, let's you wash them (i.e., 'how about you wash them?') (FH/11/17/01/pc). *ónalį žįkážį šáake lúuže htai hpáxįį ški káapše htai* hurry up and tell the children to wash their hands and comb their hair. *hką́ące záani ąðúwi htái* let's buy all the apples (01/04/95/FH/pc:ok).

htákue. n **walnut, black walnut.**

•• LFD 137: *htákehu* <ṭa´-ge-hiu> the black walnut (*Juglans nigra*). "The Osage use the nut of this tree for food. The bark and leaves are used for enticing fish to the hook when one is fishing."

••• *KS ttágü* black walnut (RR).

htamá. n **worm** (2/2/1237/MSB/p8; 03/24/95/PM/pc:okc).

•• LFD 138: *htamą́* <ṭa-mo^{n}´> an angleworm, earthworm.

htanąkʔa (variant: **htanákʔa** [FH]). n **deed, legal document, document** (04/11/95/FH/pc:ok; RBn1-MOJ/p28); **paper, paper money, bills** (02/25/95/FH/pc:ok); **playing cards** (03/06/95/FH/pc:ok; BE2.101); **blank paper, stationery**.

•• LFD 138: *htanąkʔa* <ṭa-no^{n}´-ḳ'a> paper of any kind.

••• *KS ttanąkʔa* paper, playing cards (RR).

htanąkʔa ðiihíce. n **playing cards, deck of cards (lit., 'paper for playing')** (BE2.105; 03/10/95/FH/pc:ok).

htanąkʔa ípukxa. n **paper napkin, paper towel** (FH).

htanąkʔa kʔǫ́. vp [reg., *htanąkʔa _kʔǫ́*] **play cards (lit., 'play/gamble [with] paper').** *htanąkʔakʔǫ́ hta apai* they're going to play cards (FH; RBn12-06). • n **deck of cards, card game** (RB, unconfirmed; FH: verb only).

•• LFD 138: *htanąkʔakʔǫ* <ṭa-no^{n}´-ḳ'a-ḳ'o> playing cards.

htanąkʔa mą́zeska. n **paper money, bills of currency.**

htanąkʔa waléze. n **newsprint (the material), newspaper (the publication)** (03/10/95/FH/pc).

htáška hí. n **buckeye tea (used in the sweat lodge before a peyote meeting to induce vomiting)** (BE2.13). [Most expressions for various kinds of teas contain *níi* 'water' rather than *hí*. LF's translation (see below) implies that *hí* here is a variant of *hú* 'trunk' and that the use of *htáška hí* to mean 'buckeye tea' is an extension from an earlier meaning, 'buckeye tree'.]

•• RB:<táh-shkah-hu> (04/25/95/PM/pc:okc ht).

•• LFD 138: *htáška hi* <ṭa´-shka hi> buckeye (*Aesculus*). "A kind of tea is made from this tree and taken just before a sweat bath to bring up bile. This is also the name given to the white oak tree." *htašká skue* <ṭa-shka´ çkiu-e> sweet acorn. *htaškáskue hi* <ṭa-shka´-çkiu-e hi> sweet acorn tree, the oak family (*Quercus alba*).

htą́ą (variants: **htǫ́ǫ, htǫ́, htą́**). v, adj [uninfl.] *(intr.)* **big, full size; become big, grow, increase in size, enlarge.** [This form is said to imply a smaller size than does the form *htą́ka*.] *waðílą htǫ́ hta apai* their minds are going to grow. • **oldest, eldest.** *ilǫ́ǫhtą(ą)* eldest son.

htą́ąða. v, adj [conjug. unknown] *(intr.)* **roll; rolling.** *oðíhtąą[ða]hcí oðáha* a trailer house [*ó-* loc + *ði-* instr + *htąąða* + *hcí oðáha*, lit., 'whereby a house is made to roll and follow'] (04/13/95/FH/pc:okc).

•• LFD 321: *htąða* <ṭo^{n}-tha> rolling. *poáhtąða* <bu-a´-ṭo^{n}-tha> I shot it and sent it rolling. LFD 177: *oðíhtąða hcioðaha* <u-thi´-ṭo^{n}-tha ṭsi-u-tha-

ha> little-wagon-with-a-house-attached-to-it; action by pulling + to roll or to make run: a buggy.

••• *QU odíhtąhtąda* to roll something over and over (RR), *oyúhtąya* wagon, cart (RR).

htą́ąðį. v [conjug. unknown] *(intr.)* **run, hurry along, walk fast, move fast** (RBn1-47, unconfirmed). *htą́ąðįðį́* hurrying, walking fast (RBn10-7:JW).

••• *KS ttą́ąyį* to run two-legged (RR).

htąątą́ (variants: **htǫ́ǫtą, htǫǫtá**). ADV, N [perhaps *htą́ą* + *tą* 'if, when'] **(in the) fall, autumn.** *htǫǫtáce htáabre šíe?* did you go hunting last fall? (RBn11-02/JW&FW; HH/14-a/274ff).

••• *KS ttą́dą* midwinter; 'when things abound' (probably 'autumn' rather than 'winter') (RR).

htą́hą (variants: **htáhą, htą́ha, htáha**). N [shortened form of *wihtą́ha*] **my father's sister's husband (i.e., my paternal uncle by marriage; speaker may be either male or female; more precise than English 'uncle'); my wife's brother; my sister's husband (used when speaker is male).**

htą́ka (variants: **htą́ke, htǫ́ka**). ADJ **big, large** (01/07/95/FH/pc:ok); **great, grand.** [This form is said to imply a larger size than does the form *htą́ą*.] *wak^{ʔ}ó htąą* big woman; first daughter (BE2.8). *ǫ́pe htą́ke* big hips (02/09/95/FH/pc:ok; BE2.67).

•• LFD 155: *htąká* <ṭo^{n}-ga´> big. *hta htąka* <ṭa ṭo^{n}-ga> large deer.

••• *OM* same as Osage (LFD 155).

htą́wą. N **town** (03/23/95/FH/pc:ok). *htą́wą ki* in town [as opposed to in the country] (03/23/95/FH/pc:ok). *htą́wą ki oálį́* I live in town (03/23/95/FH/pc:ok). *htą́wą kši* to town (03/23/95/FH/pc:ok). *htą́wa kši brée* I'm going to town (03/23/95/FH/pc:ok; BE2.143).

•• LFD 156: *htąwą* <ṭo^{n}-wo^{n}> a town or city. *htą́wą ki bre* <ṭo^{n}´-wo^{n} gi bthe> I am going to town. *txą́wą ki sce* <to^{n}´-wo^{n} gi stse> [expected Mod. Os. form: *htą́wą ki ščée*; <to^{n}´-wo^{n}> is presumably a typographical error for <ṭo^{n}´-wo^{n}>, and <stse> is perhaps an error for <shtse>] you are going to town. *htą́wą ki ąkaða pe* <ṭo^{n}´-wo^{n} gi o^{n}-ga-tha i> we are going to town. *htą́wą žį́ka* <Ṭo^{n}´-wo^{n} Zhi^{n}-ga> Little Village, an old village of the Osage on the Neosho River (03/23/95/FH/pc:ok).

htą́wąkáaɣe (variant: **htą́wakáaɣe**). N [*htą́wą* + *káaɣe*] **Town Builder (personal name).**

htą́wąla. N **clan.** *táatą htą́wąla nį́e?* what clan are you? (01/09/95/FH/pc:ok; 04/25/95/PM/pc:ok).

•• LFD 156: *htą́wąlą* <ṭo^{n}´-wo^{n}-gtho^{n}> the common name for the gens. *htą́wąlą hkiðitxǫka* [or *hkiðitǫka*] *hkilą́ke* <ṭo^{n}´-wo^{n}-gtho^{n} ḳi-thi-to^{n}-ga ḳi-gtho^{n}-ge> to intermarry, marriage of people from two villages ('marriage' expression unconfirmed; 04/25/95/PM/pc:uk).

htéze (variant of **hcéze**).

htį́e, htį́į (variants of **hcį́į**).

htó nąke, htohną́ke (variants of **htónąke**).

htóho (variant: **htóhu** [rare]). ADJ **blue** (RBn10-5:MOJ/79). *htóho* blue (vs. *htóhohoe* 'some kind of blue or green') (01/07/95/FH/pc). *htóho šápe* dark blue (01/07/95/FH/pc:ok; BE2.9; FH/8/30/94).

•• LFD 155: *htóho* <ṭo´-ho> green or blue. LFD 236: *htósape* <ṭo´-ça-be> blue (color). *htóho ekǫ* <ṭo´-ho e-go^{n}> like blue; similar to blue or green (01/19/95/FH/pc:ok).

••• *KS ttóho* blue or bluish black (RR).

htóho sápe. ADJ, N **purple (lit., 'blue black')** (RBn12-07; ERE, BE2.108).

•• LFD 155: *htóhosape* <ṭo´-ho-ça-be> blue, blue-black. LFD 236: *htósape* <ṭo´-ça-be> blue (color).

htóhohoe. N **personal name for a young man in the Deer clan** (FH/3/19/00). [Harriett Shadlow's oldest brother's name.]

htóhu (variant of **htóho**).

htónąke (variants: **htó nąke, htohną́ke**). N **otter; otter skin, otter hide (e.g., in Osage dance clothes)** (RBn1-24; FH/03/03/95).

•• LFD 155: *htohnǫ́ke* <ṭo-hno^{n}´-ge> otter.

htoníle. N **rainbow.**

•• LFD 165 (unconfirmed): *htohníle* <ṭu-hni´-gthe> rainbow.

htóolą (variant: **htáaoolą**). N [*htáa* + *oolą́*] **sandwich** (BE2.116; 03/08/95/MREI/pc:okc); **meat pie (original meaning)** (03/08/95/MREI/pc:okc). [*htáaoolą* now means 'sandwich' only, and not 'meat pie' (02/24/95/FH/pc).]

•• LFD 187: *htáolą* <ṭa´-u-gtho^{n}> meat pie. LFD 139: *wacúe hta olą* <wa-dsiu´-e ṭa u-gtho^{n}> meat pie, bread, meat, put inside.

htóožu. N [*htáa* + *oožú*] **meat pie.** [Pawhuska and Hominy term (RB).] *htóožu ąkóohǫ hta ąkái* we're going to cook some meat pies (02/24/95/FH/pc:ok; BE2.86).

htóze. N **catfish** (BE2.17).

•• LFD 165: *htóze* <ṭu´-çe> catfish.

htóžąke. N **banana, pawpaw (archaic meaning)** (01/06/95/FH/pc:ok; BE2.6).

htóžąke (*continued*)
•• LFD 156: *htóžąke* <ṭo´-zhoⁿ-ge> the fruit of the papaw tree, much liked by the Osage Indians.
htóžąke eekǫ́. N **pawpaw** (FH:prod).
htǫ́ (variant of **htą́ą**).
htǫ́ka (variant of **htą́ka**).
htǫ́ǫ (variant of **htą́ą**).
htǫǫtá, htǫ́ǫtą (variants of **htąątą́**).
hú (variants: **hi, híi, hiú, húu**). N **trunk, stalk; leg (e.g., of spider).**
•• LFD 59: *hi* <hi> stalk, trunk of a tree or vine, legs (04/03/95/PM/pc:okt). LFD 162: *hu* <hiu> a leg, trunk of a tree, vines, stalks of plants.
••• Cf. *huuscée.*
hú (see **ahú** 'come here').
hú hce (variant **húu hce**). VP [sync. h-stem, *(a)_hú hce*] [*(a)hú* + *hce*] **send here, have come here.** *wižį́ke líi tą hú hce éa* have Sonny come to her when he gets here, she asks you to send Sonny to her when he gets here.
húðe (variant: **húuðe**). V [reg., *hú_ðe*] [*(a)hú* + *ðe* CAU] *(trans.)* **cause to come here, send here** (01/19/95/FH/pc:ok). *húða* send it here. • **hand over, hand to, pass to by hand or other means (e.g., food at the table).** *húða* pass it (to me) (03/06/95/FH/pc:ok, short form). *žąąníe huðá* pass the sugar (RBn2-MOJ/p5; 03/06/95/FH/pc:ok). *ąkʔú huðá* pass it to me (lit., 'pass it here giving it to me'). *húða* hand it to me; hand it here. *haxį́ che ąkʔú huðá* give me those blankets [and make them come here]. • *(intr.)* **come here.** *waachí ki ši tą hąðé húða ði* when you arrive at the dances tonight I want you to come over to me. *waðákištǫ́papi húðe hkǫ́bra* I want you to [come and] look down upon us (MSB/t2, side 2). *pá húðe* snow falling.
•• JOD (*Wasápežį̨ka* letter p26 ln3): *wíe waléze wį huðáðe tą, ðéka húða ðį* <Wíe wak̜¢é̜ṣe wiⁿ hü¢á¢a-ṭaⁿ, ¢ek̜á hü´¢a-yiⁿhaú!> [sentence-final <hau> is not used in Modern Osage, and the final <a> in <hü¢á¢a> is likely a typo for e] if you send me a letter, send it here.
•• LFD 62: *húðe* <hiu´-the> to cause to come (ritual expression).
húheka. V (see **kihúheka**). • N **illness, sickness** (03/09/95/MREI/pc:ok).
•• LFD 62: *húheka* <hiu´-he-ga> sick, ill, sickness.
húheka káaɣe. VP [sync. *k>p*, *húheka _káaɣe*] *(trans.)* **sicken, make sick.**
•• LFD 62: *húheka kaɣe* <hiu´-he-ga ga-xe> to sicken.
húheka okášą. VP [reg., *húheka o_kášą*] **nurse or care for the sick.** • N **nurse** (03/01/95/FH/pc:ok; BE2.96).
húhekahci. N [*húheka* + *hcí*] **hospital (lit., 'sickness house')** (02/09/95/FH/pc:ok; BE2.68). *húhekahci ožą́ akxai* he's lying in the hospital (RBn12-06).
•• LFD 62: *húheka hci* <hiu´-he-ga ṭsi> sick house, hospital. *húhekahci ce hta ąkáðįąkáhi pe* <hiu´-he-ga ṭsi tse ṭa oⁿ-ga-thiⁿ oⁿ-ga hi bi a> we took him to the hospital.
húhka (variant: **hṹhke**). V [reg.?, *_húhka*?] *(trans.)* **hook s.t. (e.g., clothing or a tree, by using a thrown line)** (02/09/95/FH/pc:okc; RBn3-MOJ/p4). • N **hook of any kind.**
••• Cf. *wahúhka.*
húį (variant of **híǫ**).
húkaaɣe. V [sync. *k>p*, *hú_kaaɣe*] [*(a)hú* + *káaɣe*] *(trans.)* **pass (lit., 'cause to come here')** (LS). *htáaliko che húkaaɣa, wacúe ški* pass the meat gravy and also the bread. (BE2.101,03/06/95/FH/pc:ok).
hukšíðe. V [reg., *hu_kšíðe*] [*(a)hú* + *kšíðe* CAU] *(trans.)* **send here.** *mą́zeohkíhkie hukší[ð]a ði* have him call here on the phone (RB; CQ gloss).
húu. ADJ, PRON [shortened form of *huuhtą́ka, huuwáli*] **many, lots (of), large amount (of).** *ónǫbre húu ážu iché* there is lots of food prepared, on the table (lit., 'there is a lot of food set out', 'there are many foods set out') (RBn3-14).
••• Cf. *huuhtą́ka.*
húu (see **ahú** 'come here').
húu (variant of **hú** 'trunk').
húu hce (variant of **hú hce**).
húuce (variant: **huucéha**). ADV **down, downward** (BE2.34). [Used to direct someone who is looking for something; opposite of *ámaši* (RB).]
•• LFD 168: *húce hta* <hiu´dse ṭa> down below. LFD 62: *okáhuce* <u-ga´-hu-dse> steep, a steep hill, a steep bank.
••• Cf. *ðuuhúuce.*
húuðe (variant of **húðe**).
huuhtą́ka (variant: **huuhtą́ą**). ADJ, PRON **many, a large number (of), a whole bunch (of), lots (of), a lot (of), a large amount (of).** *huuhtą́ka ohkíhkie apai, hcíle apa hípe* a whole bunch of them were talking when the family came over (3/2/89/MSB). *hį́ce huuhtą́ka* a lot of dishes (FH:4/17/96/tape). *mą́zeska huuhtą́ka waðákʔupe* you gave them lots of money.
•• LFD 62: *huhtąka* <hiu-ṭoⁿ-ga> a great many, a multitude.
••• Cf. *húu* 'many'.

húuįke (variant of **hį́įǫke**).
huukǫ́ða (variant: **huukǫ́į**). PRON **many people, a lot of people, everybody, everyone.** *huukǫ́ða waachí apai* everybody is dancing (FH). *huukǫ́ða achípe* a lot of people came (FH/06/26/01/pc).
hų́ų̈ni (variant of **híǫnįį**).
húuscee (variants: **huuscé, hiúšce**). ADJ [*hú* 'trunk, leg' + *scé(c)e*] **tall, long (e.g., a tree, a piece of lumber), having long legs** (FH); **taller** (03/15/95/PM/pc:okc; 03/05/95/JS/pc:ok; BE2.133).
••• Cf. *hcéxopehuuscee.*
huuwáli (variants: **huuwáhli, huuwáalį**). ADJ **many, a lot of, a large number of.** *níhkašika huuwáli* a lot of people. *mą́zeska húuwaalį apai* he has a lot of money. *nąnįǫ́pažį huuwáli apai húheka ąkáaɣe nąpé* a lot of cigarettes make me sick (MSB 3-2-29).
••• Cf. *húu* 'many'.
huužį. ADJ, N **a bit (of), a small amount (of), a swallow or two (of a liquid), a little bit (of a liquid or other mass noun, such as ground coffee)** (FH); **a few, a small number (of a countable noun, such as people).** *mąhkásai huužį ąkʔú hu* give me a swallow or two of coffee [more than *hépežį*; "approximately half a cup"]. *wakʔó huužį* a few women.
hų́ųįke, hų́ųke (variants of **hį́įǫke**).
hų́ųke xóe (variant of **hį́įǫke xóe**).

---

i, í

i. SUFFIX **3rd sg. or 3rd pl. noncontinuative postverbal marker.** [A rare or archaic equivalent of *api;* precedes the evidential *che.*] *htáabre aðée i ché* he has gone hunting. *hóolą aðée i ché* he went fishing, he's gone fishing. *okáhąpa kaaléka i ché* they broke the window, the window is broken. *ónǫbre oohǫ́ ðáalį káaɣa i ché* the food was cooked good (01/20/95/FH/pc:ok; BE2.30). *ónǫbre húu ážu i ché* there is a lot of food set out, there are many foods set out (lit., 'food in large amounts they set out, it is apparent') (RBn3-14). *hkáwa alį́į aðée i che* he's gone horseback riding (01/31/95/FH/pc:ok). *hkáwalįį aðée i ché, hkáwalįį aðáapi ché* they have gone on horseback.
í- (variants: **íi-, i-, ii-**). LOC **with, using, as a means of or to, through (an action represented by the verb stem), from, due to.** *šúpe iihúheka kši áape* he [lying down] has intestinal trouble, they said (12/30/94/FH/pc; BE2.1). *ðekǫ́ǫci ðíe íðakʔewaðakie, táatą ówaðakihką hkǫ́bra* now through your kindness to us, I want you to help us with things (RB).
•• LFD 100: *mąįhka iði štǫka* <mo^{n}-i^{n}´-ḳa i-thi shto^{n}-ga> harrow (lit., 'with which to make soil soft').
••• Cf. *íðaache, níiðaahtą.*
iáha. ADV **immediately when, as soon as.** *ąnáðapi iáha ðíištąpe* as soon as they saw me, they stopped. *achí nápi iáha mą́zeohkíhkie akxa kaamą́ąpe* they were just arriving when the phone rang.
ichóhtąka (variant of **įchóhtąą**).
íðaache. V [conjug. unknown] *(trans.)* **eat with.** *htaaníi hcúke íðaachapi!* eat soup with a spoon!
iðáce (variants: **iðáci**). N **his/her father.** *iðáce akxa čáahpape* his father is short (2-2-259). • **his/her paternal uncle, his/her father's brother.**
•• LFD 78: *iðaci* <i-tha´-dsi> his or her father. *iðaci akxa huheka pe* <i-tha-dsi a-ka hiu-he-ga bi a> his father is ill. *iðáci ie okihpa akxa o* <i-tha´-dsi i-e u-gi-p̣a a-ka o> [expected Mod. Os. 'obey' is *okípše* rather than *okihpa;* sentence-final *o* is not used in Mod. Os.] he obeyed his father's words.
••• *OM* same as Osage (LFD 78).
••• Cf. *iðácežį.*
íðace įké. ADJP, N **fatherless, illegitimate (lit., 'father lacking')** (RBn10-3:MOJ/79); **illegitimate child.**
iðácežį. N [*iðáce* + *-žį* 'little'] **his/her father; his/her father's brother (his/her paternal uncle).** [A diminutive form of *iðáce,* possibly an endearment.]
iðáci (variant of **iðáce**).
iðáhpe. V [reg., *iðá_hpe;* sometimes uninfl.] *(trans., intr.)* **wait, wait for.** [*Osage Grammar* erroneously treated this as a reg.-*iða* verb. Its 2nd person form has sometimes been influenced by the reg.-*iða* pattern, however, as noted for some examples below.] *iðáhpi akxai* he's waiting.

iðáhpe (*continued*)
iðáahpe I am waiting for him. *iðáahpe ąkxąhé* I'm waiting (04/27/95/FH/pc). *íðaahpe* you are waiting for him [2nd person form remodeled on the analogy of reg.-*iða* verbs]. *íðaahpe škǫ́šta tą, šeðó nąąžį́* if you want to wait for someone, just stand there [2nd person form remodeled on the analogy of reg.-*iða* verbs] (04/27/95/FH/pc; RBn2-MOJ/p32; 03/16/95/JS/pc:ok). *iðáhpe ąkátxą, iðáahpe ąkátxą* we've been waiting [uninfl.]. *hą́ąpa záani ąná[ð]aðihpape* we waited for you all day (FH:5/01/96/tape). *wáli niižúpe ąžį ąná[ð]aðihpape* it really rained but we waited for you (FH:8/15/95; FH:5/01/96/tape).

•• LFD 79: *iðáhpe* <i-tha´-pe> to wait for someone. *iðáahpe* <i-tha´-a-pe> I wait for someone. *iðáðahpe* <i-tha´-tha-pe> you wait for someone. [Contrast the modern 2nd sg. form *íðaahpe* (remodeled on the analogy of reg.-*iða* verbs) in examples above.]

••• Cf. *wéðahpe.*

iðákihpe. V [reg., *iðá_kihpe*] [*kik-* SUU + *iðáhpe*] **wait for one's own family or close persons.** *aną́ðikihpe* we're waiting for you [our own relative] (MSB:2/25/83).

•• LFD 79: *ąðąakihpa pe* <o^{n}-tho^{n}-a-gi-pa i> we wait for someone. [A more accurate translation would be 'wait for someone of one's own'.]

íðakˀeðe. V [reg., *íðakˀe_ðe*] *(trans.)* **show pity with, be kind with, use kindness or pity with.** *ónǫbre waatái ški íðakˀewaðakíapí* [you] pity us with this food and these prayers. *ðekǫ́ǫci ðíe íðakˀéwaðákie, táatą ówaðakihką hkǫ́bra* now through your kindness to us, I want you to help us with things (RB).

íðiištą. V, ADJ [uninfl.] *(intr.)* **(be) ready.** *íðiištą ðaašé?* are you ready? (RBn14-03, unconfirmed).

••• Cf. *íkiðiištą.*

íðilą (variant: **íðila**). V [sync., *í_ðilą*] *(trans.)* **have on one's mind.** *íbrilą* I have it on my mind. *íšcilą, íščilą* you have it on your mind. *íðilą* she has it on her mind. *ąną́ðilą, ąąðílą* we have it on our minds. *táatą íbrila* I have something on my mind (RBn10-5:JW). *táatą íšcila?* what do you have on your mind? what's on your mind? (RBn10-5:JW, CQc). • **want, wish.** *ąwą́ðahkie íšcilą* you wanted to talk to me (FH:5/01/96/tape). *owíhkie íbrilą* I wanted to talk to you (FH:5/01/96/tape). • **think about.** *íbrilą* I'll think about it (when asked for a favor). *íbrilą hta mįkšé* I'm going to think about it (03/20/95/FH/pc:ok; RBn2-MOJ/p8). *íwibrilą (mįkšé)* I'm thinking about you (FH:prod). *wabrílą mįkšé, íbrilą mįkšé* I'm thinking about it. *íščilą?* are you thinking about it? have you thought about it? (FH). *íbrilą hta mįkšé* I'll think about it, I'm going to be thinking about it. *waðílą ðáalį na íbrilą hkǫ́bra* I want to think good thoughts all the time (a sentence used to ask for guidance when praying) (FH/8/30/94). *háakǫ íščilą ðáįše?* what are you thinking about? what's on your mind? (03/20/95/FH/pc:prod). *ąðílą ąkákxai* we're thinking about it (FH). *íðilą!* you think about it! (FH: prod). *táatą íšcilą?* do you have something on your mind?

•• LFD 79: *íðilą* <i´-thi-gtho^{n}> to think; to consider; to study; to contemplate. *ąðą́ðilą pe* <o^{n}-tho^{n}´-thi-gtho^{n} i> [expected Mod. Os. form: *ąną́ðilą pe*] we consider. *hįta íbrilą hte ha* <hi^{n}-da i´-bthi-gtho^{n} te ha> [expected Mod. Os. form: *íbrilą hce; hįta is* unknown and sentence-final *ha* is not used in Mod. Os.] let me think. [LF's forms <a´-wa-bthi-gtho^{n}> 'I consider' and <a´-wa-shti-gtho^{n}> 'you consider' are actually 1st sg. and 2nd sg. forms of a different verb: see *áwaðilą* 'meditate on, consider'.]

••• Cf. *waðílą.*

íðilą ðįké. ADVP **thoughtlessly, in an offhand manner (lit., 'not thinking').** *íðilą ðįke íðae* you spoke without thinking.

•• LFD 79: *íðilą ðįke íe* <i´-thi-gtho^{n} thi^{n}-ge i-e> offhand; said without preparation (03/20/95/FH/pc:ok). *íðilą ðįke* <i´-thi-gtho^{n} thi^{n}-ge> reckless; recklessness. *íðilą ðįké hpaγé* <i´-thi-gtho^{n} thi^{n}-ge pa-xe> I am reckless [lit., 'I did it without thinking'] (03/20/95/FH/pc:ok). *iðílą ðįke škaγé* <i-thi´-gtho^{n} thi^{n}-ge shka-xe> you are reckless.

íðišąha. V [sync., *í_ðišąha*] *(trans.)* **detour around, go around, avoid** (02/27/95/FH/pc). *íšcišąha* you go/are going around (02/09/95/FH/pc:ok).

•• LFD 79: *íðišąha* <i´-thi-sho^{n}-ha> to detour; to go around. *íbrišą ha* <i´-bthi-sho^{n} ha> I go around. *ístišą ha* <i´-sti-sho^{n} ha> [expected Mod. Os. form: *íšcišąha*] you go around. *ąðą́ðišą pe* <o^{n}-tho^{n}´-thi-sho^{n} i> [expected Mod. Os. form: *ąną́ðišąha pe*] we go around.

••• Cf. *ihkílašą.*

íðoce (variant: **íðoci**). V, ADJ [conjug. unknown] *(intr.)* **(be) open (e.g., a door).** *hcižé akxa íðoci akxai* the door is open (RBn10-20).

••• *KS íyų́je* open, as a door (RR).

íðohtą. ADJ **straight, in a straight line.**
•• LFD 80: *íðohtą* <i´-thu-ṭoⁿ> in a straight line, or to cut across (04/13/95/FH/pc:ok).
••• Cf. *óðohtą, wáðohtą.*

iðǫ́eðįhé. v [uninfl.] *(intr.)* **be in the way, be in the middle** (FH 8/8/94/pc). *ąkáe hce, iðǫ́eðįhé ąkái* let's go, we're in the way (04/13/95/FH/pc:ok). *iðǫ́eðįhé* you're in the way (04/13/95/FH/pc:ok).

íðǫye. v [sync., *í_ðǫye*] *(trans.)* **ask a question of s.o., interrogate or question s.o.;** *(intr.)* **ask questions about a certain topic** (FH:5/02/96/prod; 01/06/95/FH/pc:prod orig). *táatą wį íwibrǫye* I want to ask you something (01/06/95/FH/pc:ok). *íðǫya* ask him (01/06/95/FH/pc:ok; BE2.5). *Carolyn akxa šíną wažážeíe iðǫ́ye akxa* Carolyn keeps asking about Osage words (01/13/95/FH/pc). *áši šcée škǫ́šta tą iðǫ́ya* if you want to go outside, ask the question (i.e., ask if you may go) (FH/8/8/94/pc). *ékǫ škǫ́šta tą ąnáðǫya* if that's what you want, ask me (FH/07/09/01/pc). *íbrǫye hta mįkšé* I'm going to ask a question (FH:5/01/96/tape:prod).
•• JOD (slip file): *íðǫye* <í-¢ŭⁿ-xe> to ask a question.
•• LFD 80: *íðǫye* <i´-thoⁿ-xe> to ask a question; to question. *šįhtožįka ðe íbrǫye ha* <shiⁿ-ṭo-zhiⁿ-ga the i´-bthoⁿ-xe ha> [sentence-final *ha* is not used in Mod. Os.] I questioned the boy. *íštǫye?* <i´-shtoⁿ-xe a(?)> did you question him? LFD 283: *ímǫye* <i´-moⁿ-xe> to inquire [Omaha usage, unconfirmed in Osage].
••• *OP ímąye* to question.
••• Cf. *ilǫ́ye.*

íðǫpe. v [conjug. unknown] *(intr.)* **appear.** *óðąži wéc?a apa íðǫpe hta apai* the snakes will come out [appear] anyway (RBn23-21). *mį́į akxa íðǫpi akxai* the sun is coming up (RB; BE2.38, unconfirmed).
•• LFD 80: *íðǫpe* <i´-thoⁿ-be> to appear; come into sight. *mi akxa íðǫpa pe* <mi a-ka i´-thoⁿ-ba bi a> the sun has appeared. LFD 90: *míiðǫpe* <mi´-i-thoⁿ-be> the sun appears; sunrise.
••• Cf. *mį́į íðǫpe įkšé.*

íðuye. v [sync., *í_ðuye*] *(trans.)* **have as a bridesmaid.** *wáščuye tą Mary íščuye hta akxai* if you get married, Mary will be your bridesmaid (lit., 'if you marry, you would have Mary as bridesmaid').
••• Cf. *wáðuye.*

íðuspa (variant: **iðúspa**). N **pound (measure of weight).** *tooská íðuspa lébrą hkǫ́bra* I want ten pounds of potatoes (BE2.106: 04/17/95/LS/pc:ok; with 2nd syll. accent *iðúspa*).
•• RB: <i-thú-spah>.
•• LFD 79: *íðispą* <i´-thi-çpoⁿ> scales for weighing.

íðuwį. v [sync., *í_ðuwį*] *(trans.)* **buy with, acquire in trade for, sell or trade for.** *mą́zeska íbruwį* I bought it with money.
••• Cf. *wéðuwį.*

íe. v [reg.-*iða, í_e*] *(trans.)* **talk about, discuss, speak of.** *íðae, íðai* you speak of it. *iðáe, iðái* I speak of it. *íe, ée* she speaks of it. *pée íðai ðaašé?* who are you talking about? (RBn10-18). • *(intr.)* **talk, say, speak, make a speech or talk.** *iðáe* I speak. *įðáe htai* let's talk (lit., 'let's all let me talk') (FH/pc). *iðáe mįkšé* I am speaking (03/15/95/PM/pc:ok; 03/16/95/JS/pc:ok). *iðái hce* let me say something, let me speak (03/15/95/PM/pc:ok; 03/16/95/JS/pc:ok). *iðáe atxąhé* I'm speaking [standing] (03/15/95/PM/pc:okc; 03/16/95/JS/pc:ok). *iðái hta mįkšé* I'm going to make a talk (03/15/95/PM/pc:ok; 03/16/95/JS/pc:ok; RBn2-MOJ/p12). *háakǫ iðáe mįkšé Jack akxa íištą akxai* Jack agrees with what I say (lit., 'Jack agrees with how I speak') (FH/11/18/01/pc; RBn1-26). *háakǫ iðáe tą Jack akxa íištą akxai* Jack agrees with what I said (FH/11/18/01/pc). *óweną iðáe hkǫ́bra* I want to say something in appreciation (03/05/95/JS/pc:ok). *iðáiži tą* if I say nothing (03/15/95/PM/pc:ok; 03/16/95/JS/pc:uk). *iðái hce ée apa* they've asked me to speak (03/15/95/PM/pc:ok; 03/16/95/JS/pc:ok). *íðaiži tą* if you say nothing (03/15/95/PM/pc:ok; 03/16/95/JS/pc:uk). *íe hta akxái* he's going to speak (03/14/95/FH/pc). *íe akxai* she is talking, she is saying it (03/15/95/PM/pc:ok; 03/16/95/JS/pc:ok). *wáli íiži akxai* he sure won't talk [*íiži* from *íe aží*] (RBn10-2). *íeži akxa* he/she is not talking, he/she is not saying anything (03/15/95/PM/pc:ok; 03/16/95/JS/pc:uk). *íe óhesaži* to talk hatefully (RBn10-14). *íaži* to say nothing (03/15/95/PM/pc:okc; 03/16/95/JS/pc:uk). *íhtaháaži íape* he talked wrong, inappropriately (LS: prod; BE2.143; RBn1-MOJ/p56). • *(trans.)* **speak a language**. *wažáže íe!* talk Osage! *wažáže ía!* talk Osage! (03/15/95/PM/pc:okc, both ok; 03/16/95/JS/pc:ok). *wažážeíe įðák?uce htai* [expected Mod. Os. form of verb: *ąnąk?uce*] let's try to speak Osage (03/14/95/FH/pc). • N **word, words; language; teachings, one's word; speech; prayer.** *íe ðíhta ąkóðaha ąkǫ́ða ąkái ški* even though we want to follow your word (part

íe (*continued*)
of a prayer) (02/14/95/FH/pc:ok; BE2.75).
wahkǫ́ta ižį́ke íe Jesus' teachings. *íe ðáalį
káaɣape* he made a good speech. *íe ðuustáko*
straighten that word out (FH/11/19/01/pc:prod).
wažážeíe Osage language. *íe kaašéną ékipše* this
prayer ends now, I have spoken (JS: prayer).
•• LFD 70: *íe* <i´-e> to speak. *íe ðáalį káaɣa
pe* <i´-e tha-gthiⁿ ga-xa bi a> he delivered a fine
oration. *íe* <i´-e> a language. *íe ðáalį škáaɣe o*
<i´e tha-gthiⁿ shka-xe o> [sentence-final *o* is not
used in Mod. Os.] your oration was good.
••• Cf. *ékie, wíkie*.

íe áhkie. VP (*trans.*) **talk for or against s.o.**
••• Cf. *áhkie*.

íe ðaaéži. VP [sync., *íe _ðaaéži*] (*trans.*) **misconstrue** (lit., 'mouth different words') (LF).
•• LFD 70 (unconfirmed): *íe ðaeži* <i´-e tha-e-
zhi> repeating falsely: to misconstrue.

íe ðáalį žį. N **greeting card, gift card** (lit., 'good
little words') (MREI).

íe ðáawaska. VP (*intr.*) **speak clearly.** *íe štáawaska
nǫpe* you speak clearly (RBn HW).

íe ðuuzé. VP **tape, make a recording with an
audio device** (lit., 'take the words'). *mázeíe
akxa íe ą́ðuuzi akxái* the tape recorder is taping
my talk (RBn12-06).

íe hpíiži. N **curse, bad words** (BE2.28; RBn2-
MOJ/p16; 01/19/95/FH/pc:ok).

íe kipšé (variant of **íe okípše**).

íe okaaɣéįke. N **curses** (considered as scattered
useless words), **things people say maliciously
that are untrue, malicious false gossip** (FH:prod).

íe okípše (variant: **íe kipšé**). VP [reg., *íe o_kípše*]
[*kik*- SUU + *íe opšé*] **keep one's own word**
(RBn10-21/JW&FW/77). *ðíe, íe oðákipše ðąą́šé*
you're a person who keeps his word (RBn10-14).
íe ðakípše you keep your word (RBn10-22/JW).
• N **promise-keeper.** *íeokípše* a person who
keeps his/her word.

íe opšé. VP [reg. *íe o_pšé*] (*trans.*) **obey, follow, or
keep true to s.o.'s word.** *íe oðápše* you're going
to do what their word said (03/02/95/FH/pc:ok).
Mary íe owápše hta mįkše I'm going to obey
Mary (03/02/95/FH/pc:ok). *íe oðípše hta akxai*
he's going to make your word true (RBn10-
3:MOJ/79; BE2.97). *íe opšáape aap* they said
they obeyed the word (MGreen tape).
••• KS *ophé* follow (RR).

íe scece (variant: **íe scee**). VP **talk too long.** • N
talker, person who talks too long (BE2.133;
03/15/95/PM/pc:okc; 03/05/95/JS/pc:ok).

íe wáðohta. VP **speak truthfully, talk straight**
(FH/pc).

íe waská. N **clear words, interpreter.** *íe waská brį́
hta mįkšé* I'll be the interpreter
(RB:MSB/02/17/83). *íe waská ðáalį nįe* you are a
good interpreter (RB:MSB). *íe waska íkihpáaɣe
hkǫ́bra* I want to interpret for you (BE2.157;
03/16/95/MREI/pc:ok).

íe waská íkikaaɣe. VP [sync., k>p, *íe waská
íki_kaaɣe*] [*íe* + *wa*- VAL + *ská* 'white, clear' +
ki- DAT + *íkaaɣe*] **interpret for another.** *íe
waska íkihpáaɣe hkǫ́bra* I want to interpret for
you (RB).

íe wasúhu. N **clean talk, clear speaking.** *íe
wasúhu!* speak clearly! (01/09/95/FH/pc:ok).

íekie. N **crier, town crier.** [Archaic.]

íeska (variant: **íewaská**). V [*íe* + *ská*] (*intr.*) **speak
clearly.** • N **clear words, clear language.**

íeštą. N [*íe* + *štą*] **talker** (one who talks too much,
is mouthy, or interrupts [RB]; lit., 'talk
constantly') (RB; 03/15/95/PM/pc:ok;
03/05/95/JS/pc:ok).
•• LFD 70: *íeštą* <i´-e-shtoⁿ> a talkative
person.

íewaská (variant of **íeska**).

íeži. V [reg.-*iða, í_eži*] [*íe* + *aží* NEG] (*intr.*) **say
nothing; refuse to talk.** *íeži akxá* she is saying
nothing, she is not talking (RBn1-26). *iðáeži tą* if
I say nothing (RBn1-26). *íðaeži tą* if you say
nothing (RBn1-26). *wáli íiži akxai* he sure won't
talk (RBn10-2).

íhaa. N **mouth** (02/27/95/FH/pc:okc). [Takes
'standing' positional article *che*.] *íhaa che ąníe*
my mouth is sore (BE2.90; 02/27/95/FH/pc:ok).
•• LFD 72: *íha* <i´-ha> mouth. *íha che ąníe ha*
<i´-ha te oⁿ-ni´-e ha> [sentence-final *ha* is not
used in Mod. Os.] my mouth is sore.

íhaa ípukxa (variant: **íhaa ápukxa**). N **napkin**
(lit., 'with which to wipe the mouth')
(02/27/95/FH/pc:ok).
•• LFD 72: *íha ipihka* <i´-ha i-bi-ka> a napkin.

íhaa žáhta. N **broken or split lip, harelip.**
•• LFD 72: <i´-ha zha-ṭa> broken lip; harelip.
šį́hto žįka akxa íhažahta pe ha <shiⁿ´-ṭo zhiⁿ-ga
a-ka i´-ha-zha-ṭa pe ha> [expected Mod. Os.
form: *šį́tožį akxa íhaa žáhtape*; sentence-final *ha*
is not used in Mod. Os.] the boy has a broken lip.

iháka. N **his brother's wife or his wife's sister**
(more precise than English 'his sister-in-law')
(FH/09/22/01/pc).

ihcíko. N **his/her grandfather; his/her father-in-
law** (01/23/95/FH/pc:ok; BE2.45).

••• LFD 80: *ihcíko* <i-ṭsi´-go> grandfather.
••• Cf. *wihcíko.*

ihcíkoapí. N [*ihcíko+ api*] **president (e.g., of the United States; lit., 'grandfather of all')** (04/17/95/LS/pc:ok; BE2.107).

ihcími. N **his/her father's sister (his/her paternal aunt; more precise than English 'his aunt' or 'her aunt').** *Johna ihcími* John's aunt (FH/09/22/01/pc).
•• LFD 80: *ihcími* <i-ṭsi´-mi> aunt, his or her father's sister (04/13/95/LS/pc:ok).
••• Cf. *wihcími.*

ihcíni (variant: **ihcínį**). N **his/her daughter-in-law.**
•• LFD 81: <i-ṭsi´-ni>.
••• Cf. *wihcíni.*

ihcióšpa (variant of **ihcóšpa**).

ihcióžąke (variant of **ihcóžąke**).

ihcížo (variants: **ihcížǫ, ihcížoe**). N **his sister's daughter (more precise than English 'his niece'); his father's sister's daughter (more precise than English 'his cousin').**
•• RB: <i-tsí-zho>his niece
•• LFD 81: *ihcížǫ* <i-ṭsi´-zho^n> niece, daughter of a sister or a father's sister [should be 'niece, daughter of a *man's* sister or a *man's* father's sister'].
••• *QU ihtížǫ* man's sister's daughter, niece (RR); *KS iččížo* aunt; man's sister's daughter, niece (RR); *OM ihtížą* sister's daughter (RR).

ihcįto. N **her older brother (i.e., any of her brothers who is older than she is).**
•• LFD 80: *ichį́to* <i-tsi^n´-do> her elder brother, ritual term.

ihcóška. N **his wife's brother's son, his sister's son, her brother's son (more precise than English 'his/her nephew'); his/her father's sister's son (his/her paternal aunt's son; more precise than English 'his/her cousin')** [meaning 'his/her father's sister's son [male cousin]' is attested in LF only, unconfirmed; modern term for 'his/her father's sister's son' is *hcióška* 'father's sister's son']; **his/her grandchild** [use of term to mean 'grandchild' is unexpected].
•• LFD 81: *ihcóška* <i-ṭsu´-shka> nephew, son of a sister or a father's sister.
••• *KS iččóškayą* woman's sister's son (RR).

ihcóšpa (variant: **ihcióšpa**). N **his/her grandchild.** *ihcióšpa háaną waaščį?* how many grandchildren do you have? (FH/09/24/01/prod).
•• LFD 81: *ihcóšpa* <i-ṭsu´-shpa> to issue; to bring forth (05/01/95/LS/pc:ma); his or her grandchild.

ihcóšpa áhkiha. NP **his/her great-grandchild** (05/01/95/LS/pc:prod).

ihcóžąke (variant: **ihcióžąke**). N **her brother's daughter (more precise than English 'her niece').**
•• LFD 81: *ihcóžąke* <i-ṭsu´-zho^n-ge> a niece, her brother's daughter.

íhcuke. N **big mouth (lit., 'spoon with')** (RBn23-17, unconfirmed).

íhice. V [stat., *í_hice*] [1st and 3rd persons appear in examples without stative pronominal] *(trans.)* **be anxious for, be eager that s.t. take place** (01/06/95/FH/pc:ok). *iðą́hice, įðą́hice, ąðą́hice, ąną́hice* I am anxious to do it, I am anxious for it. *ðée hta ąną́hice mįkšé* I'm anxious to go (MREI 2-1-82). *alée che ąną́hice* I was anxious to go home (01/06/95/FH/pc:okc). *waachí ke brée che iðą́hice mįkšé* I was anxious to go to the dances (FH:prod). *ðalée che įðą́hice* I'm anxious for you to go [back/home] (FH:prod). *brée hta mįkšé įðą́hice hta mįkšé* I'm anxious to go (01/06/95/FH/pc:prod). *ðalí che iðą́hice* I'm anxious for you to come home (01/06/95/FH/pc:ok; LS; RB; FH:4/25/96/tape). *hǫ́ǫpa štáke iðą́hice* I'm anxious for warm weather (FH:4/25/96/tape). *ðalí che íðihice?* are you anxious to come home? (FH:prod). *alí che íðihice?* are you anxious for me to come home? (FH:prod). *wanǫ́bre íhice apai* they're anxious to eat (FH:4/25/96/tape:prod). *waachí ke ðée che íhice apái* they were really anxious to go to the dances (FH:prod; no *wa*). *aðée hce íhice apai* they were anxious to go (FH:prod). *ąną́hice ąðįkšé ~ íhice ąðįkšé* we [two] are anxious to do it (MREI 22-1-82). *ąną́hice apai* they're anxious for me (MREI 22-11-82). *íwihice* I'm anxious for you (MREI-22-11-82). *íðihice apai* they're anxious for you (MREI 22-11-82). • *(intr.)* **be impatient.** *ąðą́hice* I am impatient (02/13/95/FH/pc:prod). *íðihice* you are impatient (02/13/95/FH/pc:prod). • *(trans.)* **hurry s.o. along.** *íhice apái* they're hurrying someone along (108-b/FH/416). • *(intr.)* **be ready.** *wí, ąðáhice, ąną́hice, ąðą́hice* as for me, I'm ready to go (RBn10-5:JW).
•• LFD 281: *íhice* <i´-hi-dse> impatience; earnest, eager, impatient. LFD 73: *ąðą́hice* <o^n-tho^n´-hi-dse> I am impatient. *iðíhice* <i-thi´-hi-dse> [expected Mod. Os. form: *íðihice*] you are impatient (LF accent unconfirmed).
••• Cf. *híceðe.*

íhkihkawį. N [presumably *hkik-* RECIP + *íkawį* (otherwise unattested)] **exchange, trade, swap, change (money, coins)** (1/20/83/631; 04/13/95/FH/pc:ok). *íhkihkawį ąkʔú pe* they gave me back change (after a purchase) (1/20/83/631). *íhkihkáwį hpaaɣé ąži mą́zeska brúuze* I exchanged it, but I took money.

íhkihkawį káaɣe. VP [sync. *k*>*p*, *íhkikawį _káaɣe*] *(trans.)* **exchange one item for another, trade, swap.** *hkáwa íhkihkawį ąkáaɣape* we traded horses (1/20/83/631). *íhkihkawi hpáaɣe ąži mą́zeska brúuze mįkšé* I exchanged it, but I took money (1/20/83/631; 04/13/95/FH/pc:ok). • *(intr.)* **change, make change, make a change.**

•• LFD 73: *íhkihkawįðe* <i´-ḳi-ḳa-wi^n-the> to exchange; to trade; to barter [LF forms all unconfirmed]. *íhkiwawį aðe* <i´-ḳi-wa-wi^n a-the> I exchange. *íhkihkawį ðaðe* <i´-ḳi-ḳa-wi^n tha-the> you exchange. *íhkihkawį ąða pe* <i´-ḳi-ḳa-wi^n o^n-tha i> we exchange.

íhkihkie. V [reg.-*iða*, *í_hkihkie*] [evidently reduplicated form of *hkik-* RECIP + *íe*] *(trans.)* **talk or speak to each other using (a certain language or the hands).** *wažážeíe ąną́hkihkíe hce* let's talk Osage to each other [two persons] (9-6-82). *wažážeíe ąną́hkihkíe htai* let's talk Osage to each other [three or more persons].

íhkihpahǫ. V [reg.-*iða*, *í_hkihpahǫ*] [*hkik-* REFL + *ípahǫ*] *(trans.)* **recognize oneself as.** *íxopeštą íhkihpahǫpe* he knows he always lies (lit., 'he knows himself a liar') (RBn23-17c).

íhkilai (variant: **íhkilaį**). V [reg.-*iða*?, *í_hkilai*?] [presumably *í-* LOC + *hkik-* REFL + *aðį*] *(trans.)* **ration, apportion, divide, give out in portions.** [Giving out food is a custom among the Osages, especially at the annual ceremonial dances.] *wéhkili íhkilai hta apai.* they're going to divide clothes (RBn22-17). *ónǫbre íhkilai tą, káache wihta óščeche* when they divide up the groceries, put mine here (03/06/95/FH/pc:prod all; BE2.101). *ówe óščeche ąnáhkilai htai, ówe oščeche ąðáhkilai htai* let's all of us divide these leftover groceries (03/06/95/FH/pc). *ówe óščeche íhkilaiapi* divide the leftover groceries into piles [pl. addressee]. *ónǫbre íhkilaipi* give out food [pl. addressee] (03/06/95/FH/pc:okc).

•• RB: <í-ki-lai^n>.

ihkílašą (variant: **ihkílaša**). V [reg.-*iða*?, *i_hkílašą*?] **pass or go back and forth** (RBn23-07; HRE/01/17/02/pc:okc).

••• Cf. *íðišąha.*

íhkiluuža. V [reg.-*iða*?, *í_hkiluuža*?] [*í-* LOC + *hkik-* REFL + *ðuužá*] *(trans.)* **wash oneself with.** *wépukxa íhkiluužaa* wash yourself with soap (03/16/95/JS/pc:okc).

íhkišike. V [reg.-*iða*, *í_hkišike*] [presumably *hkik-* RECIP + *íšike* (unattested elsewhere)] *(intr.)* **miss each other.** *ąną́hkišike ąðįkše* we [two] miss each other (MSB 3-3-83).

íhkišoce. N **fog, misting rain, drizzle, mist** (01/26/95/FH/pc:okc).

•• RB: <í-keh-shó-tseh>.

•• LFD 74: *ihkišoce* <i-ḳi-sho-dse> haze; mist; fog. *páce apa oxpáða pe ha, íkišoce kše* <ba-dse a-ba u-xpa´-tha pe ha, i´-ḳi-sho-dse ke> the boat was lost in the fog.

••• Cf. *šóce.*

ihkížį (variant: **ihkíži**). V [reg., *i_hkiži*] [*í-* LOC + *hkížį* (possibly from *ažį* 'think'); evidently contains *hkik-* RECIP/REFL, but is used as simple transitive] *(trans.)* **be angry with.**

ihkówa (variant: **iihkówa**). N **friend.** *hawé ihkówa* hello, my friend (RB). *ihkówa wíhta* my friend. *ðihkówa* your friend (01/30/95/FH/pc:ok; BE2.51).

•• RB: <gó-lah, gó-wah, kó-wah, kó-weh>.

•• LFD 74: *ihkóða* <i-ḳu´-tha> crony. *ihkóða* <i-ḳo´-tha> fellow, a friend. *ihkóða owakihkie* <i-ḳo´-tha u-wa-gi-ḳi-e> I spoke to a friend. *ihkóðą hkihkaxe* <i-ḳo´tho^n ḳi-ḳa-xe> making friends. LFD 90: *ihkóða wihta* <i-ḳu´-tha wi-ṭa> he is a friend of mine. LFD 147: *ðihkóða* <thi-ḳu´-tha> your friend.

íhkowa (variant of **íhkǫe**?). V [conjug. unknown] *(intr.)* **catch on s.t., get caught on s.t.** *haaská íhkowa akxai* my shirt caught on something (and is caught) (3-3-83-p1).

íhkǫe. N **hook, fishhook, hook and line** (RBn3-MOJ/p5, unconfirmed; 02/09/95/FH/pc:uk). *hóize íhkowa* hook and line (RB; 01/25/95/FH/pc:uk).

•• LFD 74 (unconfirmed): *íhkǫðe* <i´-ḳo^n-the> the pot hanger. LFD 68: *hoíhkǫðe* <hu-i´-ḳo^n-the> fishline. *ho; ihkǫðe* <hu; i-ḳo^n-the> fish; line. LFD 74 (unconfirmed): *íhkǫðe* <i´-ḳo^n-the> the pot hanger.

íhkuáci (variant: **íhkuéci**). N **fan made of tail feathers.** *xúða íkueci* eagle tail fan (RBn13-01).

•• RB: <í-ku-éh-tseh> <í-kyu-áh-tsi> (04/13/95/FH/pc:ok; 01/23/95/PM/pc:uk; BE2.43).

•• JOD (slip file): *íhkiðacú* <i´-ki-¢a-ts̱ü´> a fan.

•• LFD 73: *íhkiacį* <i´-ḳi-a-dsi^n> a fan. *mąšą íhkiacį wį abrį ha* <mo^n-sho^n i´-ḳi-a-dsi^n wi^n a-

bthi^n ha> [sentence-final *ha* is not used in Mod. Os.] I have a feather fan (LF, unconfirmed; 01/23/95/PM/pc:uk).

íhpią (variants: **íhpie, íhpia**). N **belt worn by men with dance clothes or outside a blanket to hold it up** (BE2.8); **any belt** (FH).

•• JOD (slip file): *úhpuða* <ü´-pü-¢a> a belt or girdle.

•• LFD 78: *íhpiða* <i´-p̣i-tha> belt; sash; girdle.

íhpiiži. V [stat., *_(í)hpiiži*] [1st person form: *ą́hpiiži, ąhpíiži*, or *ąną́hpiiži*] *(intr.)* **be sick with, be very troubled by (e.g., an illness, an ailing body part), have health problems due to, be in bad shape because of, be distraught about.** *šáake wáli ąhpíiži síi ški* my hands really hurt and my feet too. *brée brúucʔáke ą́hpiiži ąhé* I'm sick about not being able to go (RBn10-3:MOJ/79). *wáli níhka kǫ́ða, íhpiiži akxai, ąžą́ą htai* she really wants a man, she's bad off, let's have her stay all night (lit., 'she's sick from wanting a man so much, let's all go to bed'). • **be sick or unwell, be near death, be gravely ill.** *ą́hpiiži ąhé* I haven't been feeling well (05/01/95/LS/pc:okc). *ąną́hpiiži mįkšé* I'm really sick (2/3/83/1/311).

íhta (variants: **ihtá, hta**). V, PRON [inalien.] *(intr.)* **(be) his/hers, theirs; belong to (him/her, them).** *kšǫ́ka šǫ́ke íhta apa zípe* second son's dog is yellow (lit., 'second son his dog is yellow') (2-1-F). *íhtaaži* it's not theirs (03/20/95/FH/pc:ok; 03/20/95/FH/pc:ok; BE2.137). *pée íhta?* who does this belong to? *ihtá na* [this] belongs to each one, one for each one (01/07/95/FH/pc:ok). • V **fit, be suitable or appropriate.** *ihtáaži* it's not his/her way of life, it doesn't fit him/her/them (01/19/95/FH/pc:ok; RBn1-MOJ/p56).

•• LFD 78: *ihtá* <i-ṭa´> his or hers.

ihtá na. VP [inalien.] *(intr.)* **belong to each person; there is/was one or part of s.t. for each person.** *ihtá na* [this] belongs to each one, one for each one. (01/07/95/FH/pc:ok).

••• Cf. *ną* 'always'.

íhtaapi. PRON [inalien.] **their.** *Mary Johna hci íhtaapi* Mary and John's house.

ihtáežį (variant of **ihtéžį**).

ihtáɣe. N **tip.** *ðéeze ihtáɣe* tip of the tongue (03/23/95/FH/pc).

•• JOD (slip file): *ihtáɣe* <i-ta´-xe> an end or tip of an obj[ect].

•• LFD 143: *ðéze ihtaɣe* <the´-çe i-ṭa-xe> tip of the tongue.

íhtahááži. ADJ, ADV **wrong, unsuitable/unsuitably, inappropriately.** *íhtahááži íape* he talked wrong (LS: prod; BE2.143; RBn1-MOJ/p56).

íhtą. PPN **from.** *ecí íhtą* from here (04/13/95/FH/pc).

•• LFD 80: *ihtą* <i-ṭo^n> whence.

••• Cf. *ihtǫ́į hta įkšé.*

íhtąą. V [stat.?, *_íhtąą*?] [*í-* LOC + *htą́ka* 'big'] *(trans.)* **feel good about.** *íhtąą akxai* he feels big over it (RBn23-15; WF).

ihtą́ha (variants: **ihtą́hą, ihtáhąi**). N **his/her father's sister's husband (his/her paternal uncle by marriage; more precise than English 'his/her uncle'); his brother-in-law (his wife's brother or his sister's husband)** (FH/09/23/01/pc:ok).

••• Cf. *ðihtą́ha.*

ihtą́ke. N **his/her older sister (i.e., the oldest among a group of sisters; not necessarily older than the person referred to by "his" or "her").**

•• LFD 80: *ihtą́ke* <i-ṭo^n´-ge> his elder sister.

ihtéžį (variant: **ihtáežį**). N **his/her younger sister.** *óhkie šǫ́ įkšé ihtéžį akxa mą́zeíe híðape* he was talking to someone on the telephone when his little sister called.

•• LFD 80: *ihtą́e žį́ka* <i-ṭo^n´-'e zhi^n-ga> his or her younger sister.

ihtǫ́ce. N **his/her son-in-law.**

•• LFD 80: *ihtǫ́ce* <i-ṭo^n´dse> son-in-law.

ihtǫ́į. ADV **the future, the days to come, onward in time.**

•• LFD 80 (unconfirmed): *ihtǫ́ðį hkiðe* <i-ṭo^n´-thi^n ḳi-the> to go first; to go ahead. *ihtǫðį hkiðe bre* <i-ṭo^n-thi^n ḳi-the bthe> I go ahead. *ihtǫ́ðį hkiðe mą́ðį o* <i-ṭo^n´-thi^n ḳi-the mo^n-thi^n o> [sentence-final *o* is not used in Mod. Os.] you go ahead.

ihtǫ́į ðéha (įkšé) (variant: **ihtų́į ðéha**). ADVP [optionally includes 'sitting, round' positional article *įkšé*] **in the days to come, from now on, meantime** (FH/09/21/01/pc). *wažážeíe mąðí ihtų́į ðeha ðée ąkǫðape* we want the Osage language to endure (04/06/95/FH/pc; BE2.71). *hǫ́ǫpa ihtǫ́į ðéha įkšé* from this day on into the future. *wažážeíe mąðí ihtų́į ðeha ðée ąkǫðape* we want the Osage language to endure (04/06/95/FH/pc; RBn23-17).

•• RB: <i-twí-theh-hah> going a long time; into the future (FH).

ihtǫ́į ðihé (variant: **ihtúį ðihé**) [possibly *ihtǫ́į*+ *aðįhé*] ADVP **in the future.** *ihtúį ðihé ąkáðapi tą* as we go along in the future (FH/pc/98; RBn23-17).

ihtǫ́į hta įkšé. ADVP **from now on.**
•• JOD (slip file): *ihtų́įhta* <i-tu^{n}´-i^{n}´ta>in the future.
••• Cf. *ihtǫ́į ðéha.*

ihtúį ðihé (variant of **ihtǫ́į ðihé**).

ihtų́į ðéha (variant of **ihtǫ́į ðéha [įkšé]**).

íhuheka (variant: **ihúheka**). V [uninfl.] *(trans.?)* **be sick or have health trouble with (an ailing part of the body or some other condition).** *išík?ą hcéze íhuheka kší aape* my sister-in-law is sick with her stomach, they say (FH/09/23/01/pc:prod). *hcéze íhuheka kší áape* he [lying down] is sick of [i.e., 'to, in'] his stomach (FH/09/23/01/pc). *šúpe ihúheka kší áape* he [lying down] has intestinal trouble, they said (12/30/94/FH/pc: lying down; FH/09/23/01/pc; BE2.1). *šúpe ihúheka ąhé* I've had intestinal trouble.
••• Cf. *húheka.*

ii-, íi- (variants of **í-** LOC).

íibrą (variant: **íibra**). V [stat., *íi_brą*] [doubly stative (semantic subject and object both use patient pronominals); 2nd person either stative or active] *(trans.)* **have enough of, get enough of, have one's fill of, be sated with (either a positive or negative thing); be satiated with; be tired of, be negatively affected by too much of s.t.** (02/03/95/FH/pc:ok). *ąną́bra* I've had enough of it. *íðibra* you've had enough of it. *ąną́bra* we've have enough of it. *waxpéį įįðą́brą, waxpáðį įįną́bra* I've had enough of being pitiful (12/30/94/FH/pc). *íiðabrą, íiðibrą* you've had enough. *wawéebrąpe* we're tired of them; we've had enough of them (FH:10/12/95; RBn1-MOJ/p56). *íiwinąbra* I've had enough of you [from *íi-wi-ą-brą*]. *wéebrą įkšé* we [two] had enough (MSB). *íbra xcį* have more than one's fill (especially more than one's share of pain and suffering) (03/08/95/FH/pc:ok). *waxpáðį įðą́bra* I'm pitiful with suffering [*įðą́brą* from *i-ą-brą*] (RBn1-56; (FH/09/23/01/pc: prod). *waxpáðį ąną́bra xcį* I'm pitiful with suffering (RBn1-56; FH/09/23/01/pc: ok).
••• Cf. *íibrąži.*

íibrąxcį. V [stat., *íi_brąxcį*] *(trans.)* **have more than enough of, have more than one's fill or share of (e.g., sorrow to the point of being pitiful, excessive woe).** *íibraxci* to have had more than one's share [e.g., of pain] or more than one can bear (RBn1-MOJ/p56; BE2.61; 12/30/94/FH/pc/ok). *waxpáðį íibraxci* pitiful with suffering (RBn1-MOJ/p56).

íibrąži. V, ADJ [stat., *íi_brąžį*] *(intr.)* **(be) greedy, not (be) satisfied, can't get enough.** *įįną́brą mąží* I'm greedy, I can't get enough (RB). *íibraži* she's greedy, unsatisfied (RBn1-MOJ/p56; 12/30/94/FH/pc/ok). • N **greed** (02/03/95/FH/pc:okc; BE2.61).

iichį́. V [reg.-*iða*, *ii_chį*] *(trans.)* **hit with, strike with** (04/13/95/FH/pc:ok; 2/10/83/p5-2/24-5/83; MSB; FH/09/22/01/pc). *iiðáchi* I hit with it. *íiðachį* you hit with it. *iichį́* he hit with it. *ąnąchįpe* we hit with it. *šáake iiðáchįe* I hit him with my hand (05/02/95/LS/pc). *žą́ąxe wį iiðáchį* I hit him with a stick (03/14/95/FH/pc:no). *kxážį žą́ą wį íiðachį* you hit *kxažį* with a stick (LS). *íį íiðachį íiwie ðe* I saw you hit him with a rock (LS/07/27/95/pc:okc). *šáake íiðachį?* did you hit him with the hand? (03/14/95/FH/pc). *wéeðachįpe* you hit us [with it] (LS). *wékaaži ąną́chįpe* he hit me with a stick [a whip] (05/02/95/LS/pc; 11/14/82/MREI; 05/02/95/LS/pc:ok). *weáchįe* I hit him with them.
•• LFD 80: *íchį* <i´-tsi^{n}>club (hatchet). *nǫpé ðiskike iðáchį ha* <no^{n}-be´ thi-çki-ge i-tha´-tsi^{n} ha> [sentence-final *ha* is not used in Mod. Os.] I struck him with the fist (01/26/95/FH/pc:ok; correct without the *ha*).

íiðe. V [reg.-*iða*, *íi_ðe*] *(trans.)* **see.** *iiðáðe* I saw (04/06/95/LS/pc:ok). *iiðá[ð]a mąží* I did not see (04/06/95/LS/pc:ok). *íiwiðe hta mįkšé* I'll be seeing you (RB). *kahúuža íiwiðe mąži* I haven't seen you for a long time (RB). *weeáðe* I saw them/I saw [indeterminate] him. *iiðáðe* I saw him/her/it (2/24-5/83; MSB). *iiðáði áha* if I see him (MSB). *íiðaðe* you saw him (MSB). *wée[ð]aðe* you saw them. *šáakeoolą́k?ǫ pée íiðaðe?* who did you see at the hand game? (RB). *íiðaðe nįkšé?* do you see? (04/06/95/LS/pc:ok). *íiðape* he saw (04/06/95/LS/pc:prod). *íiðaži akxá* he can't see (04/06/95/LS/pc:ok). *še níhka íiði apái?* does he see those men? (RBn12-10; CQc). *níhka akxa íiði apái?* did the man see him? (RBn12-10; BE2.118; CQc). *wéeðape* he saw them; he saw us; they saw them; they saw us (MSB). *mįhkása ðéeðe, hpahą́le iiðápi che* this black man, the first one they had ever seen (RB). *íiðaži* they didn't see (04/06/95/LS/pc:ok). *íiðaži akxá* they couldn't see (04/06/95/LS/pc:ok/prod). *íiðape* they saw (04/06/95/LS/pc:ok). *ąną́ðapi áha* when they saw me (MSB). *ąną́ðe ðáha* if we see them (MSB). *omáįhka hcéka ðóha ąną́ðe ąkátxa* we're about to [lit., 'we almost'] see a new year (RB). *ší íiwiki[ð]e hta akxai* we'll see each other again. • **find.** *mą́ąhį hpaahí íiðaðe?* did you find the sharp knife? (02/14/95/FH/pc:okc; BE2.74). *iiðáðe* I found him/her/it (2/24-5/83; MSB). • *(intr., trans.)* **understand.** *iiðáðe ðée ðaną́kʔǫ nąkxą́še* those of you that understand are listening.

LFD 79: *íðe* <i´-the> to see; to find; to discern; to discover. *iðáðe* <i-tha´-the> I discern; I discovered. *íðaðe* <i´-tha-the> you discern; you discovered. *ąðą́ða pe* <oⁿ-thoⁿ´-tha i> we discern; we discover.

iiðée. v [stat., *ii_ðée*] *(trans.)* **go by using, travel on (e.g., certain funds).** *wažáže mą́zeska iiðáapi áape* they went on Osage money (lit., 'with Osage money they went, it is said') (02/01/95/FH/pc:ok). *wažáže mą́zeska iibrée* I went on Osage money (FH).

íiðį. v [sync., *íi_ðį*] *(intr.)* **win, go out (in a card game)** (1-27-83). *hóni íibrį* I almost won. *íišcį* you won. *ðóha íiðį akxai* he's about to win.

iiðótahkiðe. v [reg.?, *iiðóta_hkiðe*?] [*í-* LOC + *hkik-* REFL + *ðótaðe*] *(trans.)* **make a friend of.** • N **person who is made into a friend.** *iiðótahkie káaγi akxai* he's making a friend of him (lit., 'he is making him be a person made a friend of oneself') (RBn10-13).

••• Cf. *ðótahkiðe.*

iihcé (variant of **ðiihcé**).

iihkíðe. v [reg.*-iða, ii_hkíðe*] [*hkik-* + REFL + *íiðe*] *(intr.)* **come to one's senses, come to, regain consciousness.** *iihkíðe akxai* he came to his senses (RBn10-2). • **wake up, awaken (lit., 'see oneself').** *íihkiða! mąhkása akxa íihkiðe ðikáaγe hta akxai* wake up! the coffee will make you wake up (03/16/95/JS/pc:okc; BE2.150; 1/20/83/p4; RBn10-2). • *(trans.)* **find for oneself, find one's own.**

•• LFD 74: *íhkiðe* <i´-ḳi-the> to be awake. *iðáhkiðe* <i-tha´-ḳi-the> I am awake. *íðahkiðe* <i´-tha-ḳi-the> you are awake. *íhkiðe* <i´-ḳi-the> to find that which is lost. [For the inceptive meaning 'find what was lost, find anew', the expected LF form would be <i´-ki-the> (Mod. Os. has plain *k*: see *íikiðe* with plain *k*).]

íihkiðemąðį (variants: **íihkimąį, íihkimą́ą**). ADV [evidently contains *hkik-* RECIP, but is also used as transitive] **visiting, on a visit (lit., 'going to see each other')** (HRE/12/29/01/pc:ok). *šį́tožį íhkimąį híðe, iiðáðe hta mįkšé ée ðí áape* I will find it, said the boy who had come to visit (RBn19-05; CQ:okc). *Smokey įkší íihkimai brée* I'm going visiting to Smokey's (RBn19-05).

íihkihkiðe. v [reg.*-iða*?, *íi_hkihkiðe*?] [evidently contains two instances of *hkik-* RECIP, but is also used as transitive] *(intr.)* **meet each other;** *(trans.)* **meet s.o.** *wasái akxa šómįhkasi íihkihkiðapé* the bear met the coyote (RBn16-02, unconfirmed).

••• Cf. *íikiðe.*

íihkimą́ą, íihkimąį (variants of **íihkiðemąðį**).

iihkó. N **my/his/her grandmother (father's mother or mother's mother)** (02/03/95/FH/pc); **my husband's mother (my mother-in-law; used only by a woman addressing or referring to this relative)** (DN-WHM; FH/09/25/01/okc). *iihkó lǫ́ǫ* grandmother thunder (02/03/95/FH/pc:okc; BE2.59). *iihkó apa okíhce achípe ska* his grandmother, seeking her own, came (JOD, CQc).

•• RB: <í-ko> (RB note: paternal or maternal grandmother).

•• JOD (slip file): *íko* <ih´-ķu> his or her grandmother, including a mother's mother's sister [transcription contains an unusual mistake for JOD; expected form is *iihkó* (<iku´> in JOD's transcription); it is likely that his <h> here reflects length of the *i*, and it is possible that <x> under <k> is an error]; [Additional meanings given by JOD are:] mother's mother's brother's daughter, and any other ihuñķa of SELF's mother's father; a father's mother's sister, father's mother's brother's daughter, and any other ihúñķa (in her gens) of the father's father of SELF. *íkoé* <íhķué> voc. masc.; *íkoéi* <íhķué-i> voc. fem.; *ikó* <ihķú> [my grandmother]. JOD (How Naq¢e-cape Was Eaten by His Grandmother ln3): *ikó* <Iķu´> [expected form is *ihkó* <iku´>]. JOD (slip file): *igó* <i-ķu´> a grandmother, his or her grandmother.

•• LFD 74: *ihkǫ́* <i-ḳo´> a man's mother-in-law, his wife's mother [in Mod. Os. 'a woman's mother-in law, her husband's mother'; not applied to a man's mother-in-law]. *ihkó* <i-ḳo´> grandmother.

••• *KS ikkǫ́* his/her grandmother (RR).

••• Cf. *ðiihkó, ihkówa.*

iihkó ąkóhta. NP **our grandmother** (02/03/95/FH/pc:prod orig).

iihkó lǫ́ǫ. N **grandmother lightning** (02/15/95/FH/pc:ok, but more 'thunder'; BE2.79); **grandmother thunder** (FH). [For some speakers, *lǫǫ* is only 'thunder' and does not include 'lightning'.]

•• RB: <í-ko lóⁿ> thunder.

íihkoáhkiha. N **grandchild, grandchildren, descendants, those who follow** (MREI; 02/03/95/FH/pc:uk; BE2.59, unconfirmed).
•• RB: <í-ko-ah-kí-hah>.
••• *WI hakogíʃa* grandchild (KM); *KS owákkihą́he* succession of, one after another, descendants (RR).
••• Cf. *wihcóšpa.*

iihkówa (variant of **ihkówa**).

iihóe, iihóo (variants of **íihǫ**).

iihǫ́. N **his/her mother, the mother, a mother** (02/25/95/FH/pc:ok). *wahkǫ́ta ižį́ke iihǫ́* mother of God's son (Mary, mother of Jesus) (02/25/95/FH/pc:okc). • **his/her mother's older sister (his/her maternal aunt; more precise than English 'his/her aunt')** (02/25/95/FH/pc:ok). [Shortened version of *iihǫ́htą.*] • **wife, in the expression [name of son] *iihǫ́.*** [E.g., if Sam's son is John, Sam may use the expression *John iihǫ́* 'John's mother' in speaking to or about Sam's wife.]
•• LFD 77: *inǫ́hǫ* <i-no^{n}'-ho^{n}> my mother.

íihǫ (variants: **iihǫ́ǫ, iihóo, iihóe**). V [reg.-*iða, íi_hǫ*] *(trans.)* **ask permission from s.o. for s.t., ask or request s.o. to do s.t.** *ąną́hoa, áši šcée škǫ́šta tą* ask me if you want to go outside (01/06/95/FH/pc:ok). *Mary ðée hce iiðáhǫǫ* I asked Mary to go (MOJ; FH:hce).

íihǫhą́ąpa. N [*iihǫ́ + hą́ąpa*] **Mother's Day.** *ðée akxa íihǫhą́ąpa ók?ą hta apai* they're going to have something [an event] on Mother's Day.

iihǫ́htą. N **his/her mother's older sister (more precise than English 'his/her maternal aunt')** (04/13/95/LS/pc:ok).
••• Cf. *iihǫ́.*

iihǫ́ǫ (variant if **íihǫ**).

iihǫ́žį. N **his/her mother's younger sister (more precise than English 'his/her maternal aunt').**

íikaahtamą (variant: **ákaahtami**). N [*í-* LOC + *kaahtáama*] **bell, large bell (e.g., the big bell rung before a dance), dinner bell, church bell** (01/07/95/FH/pc:prod; 04/07/95/PM/pc:okt). *iikaahtámą ðuuhkáamą* ring the bell (01/07/95/FH/pc:okc; BE2.8). *íikaahtámą ðuuhką́ąmą* ring the bell (RBn10-12:JW; RBn14-033; FH). *wíkiehcižį ci ákaahtamį ðuuhkáamą hta akxai hąðé* they're going to ring the little church bell this evening (FH/06/26/01/pc).
•• JOD (slip file): *íkatamą* <i´-ḳa-ta-ma^{n}> [noun derived from] ḳatama^{n}; a bell. *íkaahtamą hcéska nǫ́p?į kšíðe, hkaamą́ mą́ðį apá* <iḳatama^{n} tséska nŭ^{n}´p'i^{n} kcí¢ĕ, kama^{n}´ ma^{n}´¢i^{n} apa´> the cow being made to wear a bell on the neck, it rings as she walks (under <ka´-ma^{n}>).
•• LFD 71: *íkahtamą* <i´-ga-ṭa-mo^{n}> ringing sound as of metal: a bell.
••• *KS mą́ązettąmą* bell (RR); *QU dikáda* ring a bell [by] pulling a rope (RR).

íikiðe. V [reg.-*iða, íi_kiðe*] [*ki-* INCEPTIVE + *íiðe*] *(trans.)* **find, discover or discern s.t.** *íiðakie?* did you find it? (01/24/95/FH/pc:prod orig). *íiki[ð]ape* it is found; they found it (01/24/95/FH/pc:ok). • [*kik-* SUU + *íiðe*] *(trans.)* **find one's own relative or possession.** *iiðáki[ð]e* I found it (01/24/95/FH/pc:prod orig). *ohkúlą wii[ð]áki[ð]e mąžíe* I can't find my clothes (BE2.46; CQc). *háatxąci ákahami ðé íiðakie?* when did you find this [your own] coat? (RBn1-36). *óoląke íiðakie?* did you find your hat? (01/24/95/FH/pc:ok). *ðiihkó akxa ðípą akxa, íiðikiðe kǫ́ða pátą* your grandmother is calling you, as she wishes to find you. *hkáwa ąną́ki[ð]ape* we found our horses (RB).

íikiščįka (variant: **íikiščįka**). V [reg. *ki*-del., *íi_(ki)ščįka*] [*kik-* SUU + *íiščįka*] *(trans.)* **kiss or caress one's own.** *wéakiščįka* I caressed them, my children (2/1/813). *íiwiščįka* I'm going to kiss you (RBn12-07). *žįkáži wáaščįka ąðįkšé* we [two] kissed our children (02/14/95/FH/pc; BE2.73).

íikitaðe V [*ki-* INCEP + *iitáðe*] **be born again (i.e., have a recurring birth date).** *wahkǫ́ta ižį́ke íikitaðe* Christmas (lit., 'God's son is born again').

iilána (variant of **ílaną**).

iináhi (variant of **iiną́hi**).

iinážį (variant of **iiną́žį**).

iiną́. N **my mother** (01/06/95/FH/pc:prod; 02/25/95/FH/pc:ok). *įįną́ ðe htóožu che ąk?ú wakáaya* mother, make them give those meat pies to me. *iiną́ akxa žįkážį hóolą ížoši nąpe* mother used to tell the children not to go fishing (FH:4/18/96/tape:okc). • **my mother's sister (my maternal aunt, either younger or older than my mother; more precise than English 'my aunt')** (BE2.5; 04/13/95/LS/pc:ok).
•• LFD 77 (unconfirmed): *inǫ́hǫ* <i-no^{n}´-ho^{n}> my mother (02/25/95/FH/pc:no, incorrect).
••• Cf. *iiną́htą, iiną́žį.*

iiną́hi (variant: **iináhi**), V [reg.-*iða, ii_ną́hi*] *(intr.)* **agree.** *íinahi akxai* he agrees (RBn10-3; (FH/09/25/01/pc). *záani ąną́hipe* we all agree (RBn10-3; FH:ok). • *(trans.)* **agree with, be willing to** (FH:01/05/01/pc). *iiðánahiži íhpahǫ* I

know you don't agree with me (RBn10-3).
• **accept; approve of.** *iináhiži akxai* he doesn't accept it (RBn17-p03; RBn23-05). *htanąk?ak?ǫ́ hta apai, kaðǫ́ hcí tóopa akxa iinąhiži akxai* they're going to play cards, but Charley [Indian name *hcí tóopa*] doesn't approve of it.
•• LFD 76: *ínąhį* <í-no^{n}-hi^{n}> to be willing. *bre hta che iiðánąhį ha* <bthe ṭa-te i-tha´-no^{n}-hi^{n} ha> [expected Mod. Os. form: *brée che iiðánąhi;* sentence-final *ha* is not used in Mod. Os.] I am willing to go.

iinąhiži (variant: **iinąhįži**). v [*iinąhi* + *aží* NEG] *(trans.)* **disagree with, be unwilling to, object to.** *iiðánahįmaží mįkšé ąžį ąðanak?ǫžíe* I objected to it, but you didn't listen to me.
•• LFD 77: *inąhį aži* <i-no^{n}-hi^{n} a-zhi>to loathe; to dislike.

iinąhtą. N [*iiną* + *htąą*] **my mother's older sister (more precise than English 'my aunt')** (04/13/95/LS/pc:ok).
•• Cf. *iiną.*

iinąžį (variants: **iinážį, iiną**). N [*iiną* + *-žį* 'little'] **my mother's younger sister (more precise than English 'my aunt')** (BE2.5; 04/13/95/LS/pc:ok). *iinąžį akxa ðikǫ́ze hta akxái* my aunt is going to teach you (03/16/95/FH/pc:prod; 03/05/95/JS/pc:ok; BE2.133).
•• Cf. *iiną.*

iiníhka. N **her husband.**
•• LFD 76: *iníhka* <i-ni´-ḳa> her man, her husband (04/27/95/FH/pc).

íinǫǫhpaži (variant: **iinǫ́ǫhpaži**). V, ADJ [reg., *íinǫǫ_hpaži*] [*íinǫǫhpe* + *aží* NEG] *(trans.)* **(be) reckless with, unafraid of, not careful of, wayward** (12/30/94/FH/pc:ok).

íinǫǫhpe. V [reg., *íinǫǫ_hpe*] *(trans.)* **be careful with, be wary of, watch out for, have a care with regard to, be afraid of, be scared of.** [3rd person pl. patient prefix *wa-* is not possible with 1st pl. agent in this verb; note that ***ąnąnǫǫwahpe*, ***ąwanǫǫhpe*, and ***wéeąnǫǫhpe* are ungrammatical.] *wec?á iinǫ́ǫðahpe?* are you watching out for snakes? *wéc?a iinǫ́ǫhpapái* be careful of snakes; be afraid of snakes [pl. addressee] (12/30/94/FH/pc:ok). *íinǫǫhpapai, íe áhkihtǫ́papaðí* be careful with him/her, watch your talk [pl. addressee] (01/04/95/FH:pc; FH/11/19/01/pc:okc: *ahkihtǫpapaðí*). *ąnąnǫǫhpe ąkáðe* we're afraid of them. *wéenǫǫhpa ðí!* be careful of them [sg. addressee]! *wéenǫǫhpaaži apai* they're not wary of them. *íiwinǫǫhpe* I'm afraid of you. • *(intr.)* **be careful or wary, watch out, have a care, not be reckless.** *chípi tą íinǫǫhpapai íðaapi tą* when they come be careful when you [pl.] speak (FH/11/19/01/pc:prod). *iinǫ́ǫhpa ði* be careful [sg. addressee] (01/04/95/FH:pc; 12/30/94/FH/pc:ok; BE2.1). *íinǫǫhpapi* be careful [pl. addressee] (LS; BE2.17). *iinǫ́ǫhpapái* be careful [now and into the future; pl. addressee] (01/09/95/FH/pc). *íinǫǫhpaaží apai* he's reckless.
••• Cf. *nǫ́ǫhpe.*

íipuukxa (variant of **ípukxa**).

íisa. N **cane, walking stick, crutch** (BE2.17; RBn1-MOJ/p42; 04/25/95/PM/pc:okc).
•• LFD 239: *ísale* <i´-ça-gthe> a cane. LFD 69: *ísae* <i´-ça-e> ridgepole (unconfirmed; 04/25/95/PM/pc:uk).
••• *KS íisale* cane, crutch (RR).

iiscéwai. V, ADJ [uninfl.] *(intr.)* **(be) mischievous** (FH/06/28/01/pc). *tówa apa iiscéwai apai* that one, he's doing something wrong, he is into things (FH/06/28/01/pc). *iiscéwai níe* you're being mischievous, you're being awful (FH/06/28/01/pc).
•• LFD 70: *ísie waðe* <i´-çi-e wa-the> a knave; a tricky, deceitful person.

íise (variant of **íisi**).

iiséwaðe (variants: **iiséwai, iisíwai, iisíwae, íisiwaðe**). V, ADJ [reg.?, *iiséwa_ðe*?] *(intr.)* [*íisi* + *wa-* VAL + *ðe* CAU] **(be) mean, hateful, disliked, detestible, contemptible, despicable, base, vile, infamous, spiteful (lit., 'cause folks to hate him/her')** (01/04/95/FH/pc:prod). *šǫ́ke iiséwai wį aščįe* you have a mean dog (BE2.33). *iiséwai, žeká akxa ąnąk?ǫži akxái* the thing [that's] hateful is that my legs won't listen to me (01/09/95/FH/pc:prod; HRE:ok). *iiséwai!* he's hateful! (RB). *iiséwai!* that's mean! (an admonishment to children) (BE2.64; RBn2-MOJ/p12ff).
•• LFD 70: *ísiwaðe* <i´-çi-wa-the> contemptible; despicable; base; vile; infamous.

íisi (variant: **íise**). V [reg.*-iða, íi_si*] *(trans.)* **hate, dislike, detest, abhor, despise.** *iiðási* I don't like it (02/15/95/FH/pc:okc). *íiwisi* I don't like you. *íiðasi* you don't like it. *ąąnąðasi nįkšé* you dislike me (RB: MREI 1-14-82). *íisi akxai* he doesn't like him. *íisipe* he didn't like it; he didn't like him. *ąąnąsi apai* he dislikes me. *íisi akxai* he doesn't like it (02/16/95/FH/pc:ok).
•• LFD 70: *ísi* <i´-çi> to dislike; to hate; to abhor; repugnance. *iðási* <i-tha´-çi> I hate. *íðasi* <i´-tha-çi> you hate. *ąðási pe* <o^{n}-tho^{n}´-çi i> we

íisi *(continued)*
hate. *ísiwalį* <i´-çi-wa-gthi^{n}> to detest; great contempt. *iðásiwalį* <i-tha´-çi-wa-gthi^{n}> I detest. *íðasiwalį* <i´-tha-çi-wa-gthi^{n}> you detest. *ąðą́siwalį pe* <o^{n}-tho^{n}´-çi-wa-gthi^{n} i> we detest. LFD 190: *wálįisi* <wa´-gthi^{n}i-çi> to detest; to despise; to hate. *walį iðási* <wa-gthi^{n} i-tha´-çi> I detest. *walį íðasi* <wa-gthi^{n} i´-tha-çi> you detest. *walį ąðą́si pe* <wa-gthi^{n} o^{n}-tho^{n}´-çi i> [expected Mod. Os. form: *walį ąną́sipe*] we detest.

íisiwaðe, iisíwae, iisíwai (variants of **iiséwaðe**).

íista (variant: **íišta**). V [reg.-*iða?, íi_sta?*] *(trans.)* **bless with.** *mį́į íista* bless [him/her/it] with the sun [imperative] (02/27/95/JS/pc:okc; BE2.147).
••• Cf. *íištope.*

íistahkiðe (variants: **íistahkie, íištahkie, íištahki**). V [conjug. unknown] *(trans.)* **use (e.g., cedar smoke or words of a prayer) to bless oneself.** [At meals after peyote meetings, birthday dinners, etc., the one praying would say *šáake paahápi* 'raise your hands' before praying to capture the good of the prayer and after praying would say *íistahkiepi* 'bless yourselves with it', whereupon the supplicants pass that hand or those hands over their body lightly, including mind and heart. The same procedure was used in the cedar smoking ceremony (04/07/95/PM).] *íistahkiepi, íištahkiepi* bless yourselves with it (01/25/95/FH/pc:okc:*š* [*s* ~ *š* variation]). *íistahkiapai* use it on yourselves (to bless yourselves). *kaakǫ́naa, šáake paahą́pi, iíštahkíapai* that's all, raise your hand, use it on yourselves (ending for a prayer). *Johna akxa žįkážį waatá apa íistahkiepi* John is praying for the children and the children are asking God for a blessing (lit., '. . . and they are blessing themselves with it'). *hpéece íištahkipa* use the fire to bless yourselves (PM:04/07/95 pc).

iistó (variant: **į́štǫwą** [LS]). N **elbow** (12/30/94/FH/pc:prod; 04/07/95/LS/pc:okc).
•• LFD 70: *istóhi* <i-çtu´-hi> elbow.
••• *KS áastohü* elbow (RR); *QU istóhi* elbow (RR).

iiscéwai (variants: **iišcéwa, iišcé, iiščéwai**). V, ADJ [uninfl.] *(intr.)* **(be) ashamed, feel ashamed** (04/20/95/LS/pc). *iiščé mįkšé* I'm ashamed (04/20/95/LS/pc). *iiščéwa ąðį́he* I'm ashamed. *iiščéwai ðąįše* you're shameful (9/17/94/FH/pc). *iišcéwai ðé* you should be ashamed (lit., 'that makes one feel ashamed') (RBn10-21/JW&FW/77; CQc). *šíi apa iišcéwai apa* he's ashamed of himself (RBn10-21/JW&FW/77).
•• LFD 78: *íšce waðe* <i´shtse wa-the> shameful.
••• *QU íšte* be ashamed (RR).

íišcewai (variants: **íiščewa, íišcewa, íšcewa;** [Hominy dialect] **íiščewai, iiščéwai**). V, ADJ [reg.-*iða, íi_šcewai* (often uninfl.)] *(intr.)* **dress up in one's best attire, get dolled up or dressed up; (be) dolled up or dressed up** (04/26/95/LS/pc:okc). [Usually uninflected when used with adjectival meaning ('be dressed up').] *iiðáščewa mįkšé* I'm all dressed up (RBn12-12). *iiðášcewa mįkšé, íišcewa mįkšé* I'm all dressed up (01/20/95/ERE/pc:ok; 04/26/95/LS/pc:ok; BE2.34). *wáli íiščewai ðąįšé* you are really all dressed up (04/26/95/LS/pc:okc; 9/4/94/FH/p.c.; FH/06/28/01/pc). *háakǫta íišcewai ðąįšé?* why are you dressed up? *íiščewa akxa* she's making herself pretty, she's dolled up (04/25/95/PM/pc). *íišcewa apai* they're all dressed up (RBn10-21/JW&FW/77).

íišcįka. V [reg.-*iða, íi_šcįka*] *(trans.)* **kiss, caress** (02/14/95/FH/pc:ok).
••• Cf. *íikišcįka.*

íiščewa, íiščewai (variants of **íišcewai**).

iiščéwai (variant of **iišcéwai** '(be) ashamed').

iištá (variant of **įįštá**).

íišta (variant of **íista**).

iištáa cʔóka (variant of **įįštáhaa cʔóka**).

iištábri (variant of **įįštábri**).

iištáðe ahkíliitože. VP [reg.?, *iištáðe a_hkíliitože?*] [presumably *hkik-* RECIP + *ðu-/ði-* INSTR + *tóže*] *(intr.)* **wink at each other, blink at each other** (LS). *iištáðe ahkíliitóže* they are winking at each other (RBn2-MOJ/p11; 05/01/95/LS/pc:ma).

iištáðe ðiitóže (variant: **iištáði ðiitóže**). VP [sync., *iištáðe _ðiitóže*] *(intr.)* **wink or blink the eyes (lit., 'mash the eyelid[s]')** (05/01/95/LS/pc). *iištáðe ðiitóže akxái* he/she is winking (05/01/95/LS/pc:ok; BE2.159). • *(trans.)* **wink at, blink the eyes at.** *iištáðe ąðíitože akxai* he's winking at me.
•• LFD 77: *įštá ðitože* <i^{n}-shta´ thi-do-zhe> to wink; to nictitate. *įštá ebritože* <i^{n}-shta´ e-bthi-do-zhe> I winked at her.

iištáhaa cʔóka (variant of **įįštáhaa cʔóka**).

iištáhii (variant of **įįštáhįį**).

íištahki, íištahkie (variants of **íistahkiðe**).

iištáxį (variant of **įįštáxį**).

íištą. V [reg.-*iða, íi_štą*] *(trans.)* **agree with s.t.** *Jacka háakǫ eekíe ðe tą iiðáštą* I agree with what Jack says (FH/09/25/01/pc). *Jacka háakǫ ékie che iiðáštą* I agree with what Jack said

(FH/09/25/01/pc). *háakǫ iðáe tą Jack akxa íištą akxai* Jack agrees with what I said (FH/11/18/01/pc). • *(intr.)* **agree.** *záani íištąpe* they all agreed (FH/09/25/01/pc).

íištope (variant: **íštope**). v [reg.-*iða?*, *íi_štope?*] *(trans.)* **bless with, use to bless** (PM). *hpéece ðé íištope* use this fire to bless yourselves/yourself (said to person[s] standing in the altar [concrete floor by the fire] in a Native American Church meeting) (04/07/95/PM/pc:okc; JS:uk).

•• RB: <péh-tseh théh í-shto-peh>.

••• Cf. *ðistópe, íista.*

íišupe. N **men's dance belt worn outside the blanket to hold it up** (01/07/95/FH/pc:prod; RBn14-03/LH).

iitáðape ékitxą (variants: **iitáipi ékikxą, iitáipi ékxą, iitáekietxą**). VP [*iitáðe + api + ðe* DECL + *ékitxą*] *(intr.)* **have a birthday (lit., 'again be the time that one is born').** *iitáipi ékikxą; íiðitáðape ékitxą* it's your birthday (either expression may be used for 'happy birthday') (01/07/95/FH/pc:prod). *iitáðape ékitxą akxái* it's his birthday (BE2.8). *iitáipi ékikxą akxai* he's got a birthday (lit., 'he is characterized by a birthday') (01/07/95/FH/pc:prod).

iitáðe (variants: **íitaðe, iitáe, iitái**). v [reg.-*iða*, *ii_táðe*] *(trans.)* **give birth to.** *eeškí iiðátai na* [*iiðáta(ð)e na*] I gave birth to him, too (RBn HW7). *weeátaðe* I gave birth to them. *iitáðape* she gave birth to him/her; he/she was born. *šímižįka iitáaðe* I gave birth to a girl (04/19/95/FH/pc:ok). *ąnáta[ð]ape* she gave birth to me; I was born. *íiðita[ð]a pe* she gave birth to you; you were born. *hpáažį wį íita[ð]ape* she had a baby. *íitaðaðe* you gave birth to a child (04/19/95/FH/pc:ok). *hą́ąpa íiðitaðape wéewinai* happy birthday (lit., 'I'm grateful for you being born today') (FH). *wéeana akxąhé íiðitáipe ska* I'm glad you were born; happy birthday! (lit., 'I'm standing here grateful as it seems that this is the day you were born') (9/13/94/FH/470). *íiðitaepe, wéeąną ąkai, wisǫ́ežį* we wish you a happy birthday, younger brother [of a woman] (this phrase was used to decorate a cake) (FH). • *(intr.)* **give birth.** *íitaaðe* I gave birth (FH).

•• LFD 70: *ítaðe* <i´-da-the> to bear a child; to give birth to an offspring. *ítaaðe he* <i´-da-a-the he> I gave birth to a child. *ítaðaðe he* <i´-da-tha-the he> you gave birth to a child. LFD 131: *šímižįka itaaðe he* <shi´-mi-zhi^{n}-ga i-da-a-the he> I gave birth to a girl.

••• *KS íidaye* bear a child, have a baby (RR).

••• Cf. *wasápe iitáipi, wéetaðe.*

iitáekietxą, iitáipi ékikxą, iitáipi ékxą (variants of **iitáðape ékitxą**).

iitái (variant of **iitáðe**).

iiwákˀo (variant of **iwákˀo**).

íixa. v [reg.-*iða*, *íi_xa*] *(intr.)* **laugh.** *íixa leléze* laugh big; [be] laughing a lot (02/14/95/FH/pc:ok). *íixa léleze* [be] laughing over and over (03/22/95/FH/pc). *íixa íkaski* he's running out of breath from laughing (FH). *íixa akxa* she's laughing (02/14/95/FH/pc:ok). *nǫ́ǫ apa eeškítą íixa apa* the grownups laughed too (lit., 'the grownups, they too, laughed') (RBn10-2:MOJ/79). *íixa ðįká!* don't laugh! (02/14/95/FH/pc:ok). • *(trans.)* **laugh at.** *wisǫ́ežį iiðáxa nái* I always laugh at my little brother (RB; MREI/01/11/83). *íiðixa akxa* he's laughing at you (BE2.76; 01/11/95/FH/pc:x). *ąnáxa akxai* she's laughing at me (02/14/95/FH/pc:ok). *íiwixa mįkšé* I'm laughing at you. *ąnáðaxa nįkšé?* are you laughing at me? (MREI).

•• LFD 81: *íxa* <i´-xa> to laugh; to titter. *iðáxa* <i-tha´-xa> I laugh. *íðaxa* <i´-tha-xa> you laugh. *íxa íkaski* <i´-xa i-ga-çki> a hearty laugh; a laugh that makes the sides ache.

íixaéewaðe (variant: **íixaéewai**). v [reg., *íixaéewa_ðe*] [*íixa + ée* 'say' (?) + *wa-* VAL + *ðe* CAU] *(intr.)* **be funny or laughable, cause folks to laugh at s.o. else's expense.** (04/26/95/FH/pc:ok; 02/13/95/FH/pc:okc). • N **laughing stock.** *íixaéewaðae waškaaɣé* you made us laughable, you made a joke out of us (lit., 'you caused folks to laugh and you did it to us') (04/26/95/FH/pc:ok).

•• LFD 81: *íixaewaðe* <i´-xa-e-wa-the> humorous; ludicrous. *íxaewaða pi a níhkašika* <i´-xa-e-wa-tha bi a ni´-ķa-shi-ga> [expected Mod. Os. form: *níhka íixaéewaðape*] he is very humorous.

íixažį. v [reg., *íi_xažį*] [*íixa + -žį* 'little'] *(intr.)* **snicker (lit., 'laugh a little').** *íixažį akxai* they're snickering (BE2.124; 03/10/95/MREI/pc:ok). • N **smile, grin.** • ADV **with a grin, grinningly.** *íixažį tǫ́pe* to look at with a grin. *íixažį ąkǫ́įpe akxai* he's grinning at me (RBn12-06).

•• LFD 81: *íxa žįka* <i´-xa zhi^{n}-ga> a grin; a smile.

iizíke. v [uninfl.] *(intr.)* **be or become embarrassed by making mistakes in front of a crowd** (RBn12-12). *iizíke ąškáaɣe* you shamed my face, you embarrassed me (lit., 'you caused me to be embarrassed'). *iizíke apai* they're embarrassed (RBn10-21/JW&FW/77). • *(intr.?)*

iizíke (*continued*)
be embarrassing. *iizíki akxai* it's embarrassing (RBn12-12).

íizizike (variant of **ízizike**).

iižį́ke (variant of **ižį́ke**).

íižoši (variant of **ížoši**).

íkaaɣe. v [sync. *k>p, í_kaaɣe*] *(trans.)* **make out of.** *žą́ąxe íkaaɣe akxai íiðaðe?* did you see the thing he made out of wood? did you see the thing he made with wood? (lit., 'he was making it with wood, did you see it?'). *kaalíže wéškaaɣe nae* you used to make them with flint.

íkaahǫǫpa (see **íkǫpa**).

íkaase. v [reg. *kaa*-ret. or *kaa*-del., *í_(kaa)se*] *(trans.)* **cut with, sever or chop by striking with.** *mą́hispe íkaase* cut it with the axe (RBn10-16).

íkahci (variant: **íkiahci**). N (05/02/95/LS/pc:okc; BE2.142). **toilet paper** (RB, unconfirmed; 03/23/95/FH/pc:uk). *íkahci wį́ aðį́li* bring some toilet paper back (RBn12-06, unconfirmed).
•• JOD (slip file): *kahcé* or *kaché* <k͓a-tsĕ´> skim off grease from the surface of water in a kettle.
•• LFD 71: *íkahce* <i´-ga-ṭse> an implement for skimming grease from food that is cooking.
••• *KS gaccé* to skim a liquid, skim grease (RR).

íkaske (variant: **íkaski**). v, ADJ [conjug. unknown] *(intr.)* **(be) out of breath.** *íkaski ąhé* I'm out of breath. *íkaski bríe* I'm out of breath (FH). *íkaske nį́e* he's out of breath, choking, as when having a heart attack (FH). • v *(trans.)* **run out of breath from, become breathless from, choke from (some activity).** *ną́ąke íkaske* he's out of breath from running (FH). *íixa íkaski* she is running out of breath from laughing (02/14/95/FH/pc). *šómįhkasi mąąšóšoce íkaski* the coyote was choking in [from] the dust (RBn17-p05, unconfirmed).
•• LFD 81: *íxa íkaski* <i´-xa i-ga-çki> a hearty laugh; a laugh that makes the sides ache.

íkaskike. v [conjug. unknown] *(trans.)* **smother with smoke or dust** (RBn23-14, unconfirmed).

íkiahci (variant of **íkahci**).

íkiðiištą. v, ADJ [uninfl.] [*ki-* INCEPTIVE + *íðiištą*] *(intr.)* **(be) ready.** *íkiðiištą ątxąhé* I'm ready (RBn14-03, unconfirmed).

íkie. v [reg.-*iða, í_kie*] [presumably *ki-* DAT + *íe*] *(trans.)* **talk for or against s.o., speak positively or negatively of s.o., take sides with respect to s.o.** [An expected 3rd person form (not actually attested) would be *íkie akxa* 'he's talking against s.o.'] *íðikía apái* they're talking against you (LS:okc; FH:okc).

íkiha. ADV **always, repeatedly.** *Preston apa oðíhta íkiiha íihpiži apai* Preston's car is always going bad on him (01/04/95/FH/pc:prod orig).
•• JOD (Wasápežįka letter p26 ln4): *ókaše ðįké ðaįšé ðáha wikínakˀǫ ąðą́kiha hkǫ́bra* <úk͓acé ¢iñk͓e´ ¢á¢iⁿcé u¢áha wik͓ínak'ŭⁿ aⁿ¢añ´k͓iha kŭⁿp͓¢au´> I always want to hear that you are fine. [The form *ąðą́kiha* in this example (*ąðą́kiha hkǫ́bra* 'I always want') suggests that *íkiha* inflects (stat., *í_kiha*). No such inflected examples were found in Mod. Os.]
•• LFD 71: *íkiha* <i´-gi-ha> always; ever; often; frequent; incessant. LFD 56: *lǫ́ðį ikiha* <gthoⁿ´-thiⁿ i-gi-ha> habitual drunkard; a sot.

íkihtǫpe (variant: **íkihtǫe**). v [reg.-*iða* or sync. fortisizing stop stem, *í_kihtǫpe* or *í_kih(_)tǫpe?*] [presumably *í-* LOC + *kihtǫ́pe*] *(trans.)* **visit a relative or one's own (family).** *wíikihtǫe achíe* I have come to see you [expected Mod. Os. form: *íwikihtóe achíe*] (t#14-b-p3; 05/02/95/LS/pc:ok).

íkikaaɣe. v [sync. *k>p, íki_kaaɣe*] [*ki-* DAT + *íkaaɣe*] *(trans.)* **make for s.o., cause to be for s.o.** *íe waska íkihpáaɣe hkǫ́bra* I want to interpret for you (RB).

íkinaaži. v [reg.-*iða, ki*-ret., *í_kinaaži*] [*í-* LOC + *ki-* DAT + *nąąžį́*] *(trans.)* **depend on, count on, rely on (lit., 'stand with another')** (RBn10-2:MOJ/79; CQ:okc). *íwikinaaži įké hta akxa* I won't depend on you. *iðákinaaži hta akxa* you can depend on it (RBn12-06).

íkišike. v [reg.-*iða, ki*-ret., *í_kišike*] [presumably *ki-* DAT + an unattested stem *íšike*] *(trans.)* **be lonesome for s.o.** (3-10-83-D). *iðákišike mįkšé* I'm lonesome for him (3-10-83-D). *íðakišike nįkšé* you're lonesome for him (3-10-83-D). *ąną́kišike ąðįkše* we're lonesome for him (3-10-83-D). *weákišike mįkšé* [from *wa-i-ðá-kišike*] I'm lonesome for them (3-10-83-D). *wéðakišike nįkše* you're lonesome for them (3-10-83-D). *íwikišíke mįkše* I'm lonesome for you (3-10-83-D). *ąną́kisike apai* they're lonesome for me (3-10-83-D).

íkǫpa. N [probably *í-* LOC + *ka-* INSTR + *hą́ąpa*] **glass (lit., 'whereby day strikes').**
•• RB: <í-koⁿ-pah> glass for drinking (BE2.55, unconfirmed; 01/31/95/FH/pc:uk; 05/01/95/LS/pc:uk).
••• *KS ogáhǫba* window, window glass, glass generally (RR), *óožü kˀǫ́yǫba* lamp, a glass (JOD, RR), *kˀǫ́yǫba* transparent? (JOD [uncertain], RR).
••• Cf. *okáhąpa, okáhǫpa.*

íkǫska (variant: **íkǫske**). ADJ, V [conjug. unknown] *(trans.)* **resemble (visually), (be) equal or similar in appearance to, look like (e.g., s.t. carved to resemble another thing).** *íkǫske káaɣi akxai* he's making it like that (FH:prod). *Mary akxa iihǫ́ íkǫske* Mary looks just like her mother (FH:4/24/96/tape:prod). *wacúe skue mą̨ščį́ka íkǫske káaɣa* make the cake like a rabbit (FH:4/24/96/tape:prod). *níhkaši íkǫske* scarecrow (FH).

•• LFD 53 (unconfirmed): *kǫzé hkikǫ* <go^{n}-çe´ ḳi-go^{n}> alike; resembling.

••• Cf. *ékǫ, kǫzékǫ.*

íkǫskahkíðe. V [reg., *íkǫska_hkíðe*] [*íkǫska* + *hkik-* REFL + *ðe* CAU] *(trans.)* **imitate, act like, make oneself equal to.** *įįštáxį íkǫskahkíe apai* he's making himself equal to that white man.

íkǫske (variant of **íkǫska**).

íkuspe. V [reg.-*iða*?, *í_kuspe*?] *(intr.)* **sign with a thumbprint, make a thumbprint on a document in lieu of a signature** (HRE/12/29/01/pc, unconfirmed). *íkuspa* make your print there (HRE/12/29/01/pc).

íkˀo. N **belch, burp.** *íkˀo akxa* it's a belch; it's a burp (RBn10-21/JW&FW/77).

••• Cf. *wawékˀo.*

íkˀuce (variants: **ikˀúci, íkˀue**). V [reg.-*iða*, *í_kˀuce*] *(trans.)* **try to, strive to, risk, test, taste, try on, attempt.** *pší iðákˀuce hta mįkšé* I'm going to try to go there (RBn23-21). *mą̨scį́ iðakˀuce ąžį ðaxíða* you tried to walk but you fell down (PM). *nąąžį́ íkˀucapé* he tried to get up (RB: Coyote fable). *wažážeíe anąkˀuce* we're trying to talk Osage. *íkˀüta!* try! (Osage First Book). *íkˀuca* try it on (RBn10-16). *íkˀuca!* try it! (01/06/95/FH/pc:ok;108/FH/170). *mąðį́ íkˀuca* try to walk (PM). • **study.** *hǫ́ǫpaðe wažáže žį́ toa ohkíeche žóąhkile ąkái, wažážeíe íkˀuce ąkáli* today a bunch of Osage young people, we're gathered together, we've come back to study Osage (RBn10-13; FH/11/19/01/pc:okc). • *(intr.)* **try, make an effort, do one's best, try one's best, make one's best effort** (RBn22-20; 04/25/95/PM/pc:ok). *iðákˀuce hta mįkše* I'm going to try (04/03/95/PM/pc:ok; BE2.145). *iðákˀue šo ąhé wažážeíe íhpahǫ hta akxai* I'm going to keep on [trying] until I learn the Osage language [note reduction of *ce* to *e*] (RBn10-10:JW). *kóoci wažáže apa ðée ékiǫpé ąži ðekǫ́ci ðįkápi wihtáeži akxa íkˀuci akxai* long ago Osages used to do that, but now they are gone and sister is trying her best (gloss by CQ; PM/7/7/94). *záani íkˀucapí áape* they all did their best (RBn19-04). • N **class, practice, practice session, workshop.** *wažážeíe íkˀuca* Osage language class [unexpected form ending in -a] (01/09/95/FH/pc:ok; RBn1-36).

•• LFD 74: *ikˀuche, ikˀuhce?* <i-ḳ'u-tse> [expected Mod. Os. form: *íkˀuce*] to risk. *iðáhkuche* <i-tha´-ḳu-tse> I risk. *íkˀuche* <i´-ḳ'u-tse> to test the taste.

••• *QU ikkíhte* to scramble for something (RR).

••• Cf. *íkˀuce.*

ílaną (variants: **ílana, iilána**). V [reg.-*iða*, *í_laną*] *(intr.)* **damage or hurt one's reputation or standing by doing s.t. inappropriate, make a mistake or commit an error that brings attention to oneself (e.g., dropping s.t. at a dance, thereby causing a commotion), goof, goof up, use bad judgment (e.g., choosing to confide s.t. private to a gossipy person).** *iðálanai* I made a mistake (02/25/95/FH/pc:ok). *íðalanai* you made a mistake (02/25/95/FH/pc:okc). *íðalaną* you made a mistake. *ílanąpe* someone made a mistake (and they hurt somebody) (BE2.88; RBn1-51). *ąną́lanąpé* we made a mistake/had an accident (RB notes). • **be in disgrace because of having made a mistake.** *ílanąpi che kíhǫǫžipe* he's unhappy because he is in disgrace (02/25/95/FH/pc:okc).

•• LFD 255: *ílanǫ* <i´-gtha-no^{n}> disgrace. LFD 79: *íðalaną hta khį to* <i´-tha-gtha-no^{n} ṭa ki^{n} do> [expected Mod. Os. form: *íðalaną hta nikšé* 'you will damage your standing'] you will hurt yourself.

ilánąðįké. V, ADJ [reg.-*iða*, *i_lánąðįké*] [*ílaną* + *ðįké*] **(be) innocent, having made no mistakes or blunders to disgrace oneself.**

•• LFD 72: *ílaną ðįke* <i´-gtha-no^{n} thi^{n}-ge> guiltless; blameless; innocence.

ilánąhkistó. N [*ílaną* + *hkiistó*] **court (lit., 'meeting or assemblage for mistakes or offenses').**

•• LFD 72: *ilanąhkisto* <i-gtha-no^{n}-ḳi-çtu> court.

ílanąwakíšupe. N [*ílaną* + *wakíšupe*] **fine, penalty (lit., 'pay folks for a mistake').**

•• LFD 72: *ílaną wakišipe* <i´-gtha-no^{n} wa-gi-shi-be> a fine; the payment of money for some offense.

íli. N **phlegm, saliva** (RBn HW12; RBn10-15). *íli ðaakˀí!* spit out the phlegm! (RBn HW12).

•• LFD 305: *hóxpe lili* <ho´-xpe-xthi-xthi> phlegm.

íliðáak?i (variant of **íluek?í**).
ilǫ́ahpa iihǫ́ (variant of **ilǫ́ǫhpa iihǫ́**).
ilǫ́ąhpa (variant of **ilǫ́ǫhpa**).
ilǫ́eži (variants: **ilǫ́eži̧, ilǫ́eže**). N **cat, puma** (01/09/95/FH/pc:prod; FH/pc). *ðé ilǫ́eži̧ akxa Jane ihtápe* this is Jane's cat (BE2.17; RBn12-03p2).
•• LFD 75: *i̧lǫ́ka* <iⁿ-gthoⁿ´-ga> puma; also the name given to the domesticated cat when it was first introduced.
ilǫ́eži iisáwai. N **hellcat** (RBn22-08).
••• Cf. *iiséwaðe.*
ilǫ́eži̧ (variant of **ilǫ́eži**).
ilǫ́ɣe. V [reg.-*iða, i_lǫ́ɣe*] [*kik-* SUU + *íðǫɣe*] *(intr.)* **ask or inquire concerning one's own people or things** (04/19/95/FH/pc:ma; WF/12/30/01:ɣ). • N **devil, Satan, ghost, spirit** (01/20/95/FH/pc:prod orig; BE2.30; RBn2-MOJ/p3).
•• JOD (slip file): *ilǫ́ɣe* <i-k-¢uⁿ´-xe> to ask a question about his or her own.
•• LFD 72: *ílǫɣe* <i´-gthoⁿ-xe> to make inquiry concerning a relative or some personal belonging. *iðálǫɣe* <i-tha´-gthoⁿ-xe> I made an inquiry about a relative. *íðalǫɣe* <i´-tha-gthoⁿ-xe> you made an inquiry about a relative. *ąðą́lǫɣa pe* <oⁿ-thoⁿ´-gthoⁿ-xa i> we made an inquiry about relatives. LFD 272: *waną́ɣe i̧lǫ́ɣe* <wa-noⁿ´-xe iⁿ-gthoⁿ´-xe> ghost.
ilǫ́ǫ (variant of **ilǫ́ǫhtą**).
ilǫ́ǫhpa (variants: **ilǫ́i̧hpa, ilǫ́ąhpa**). N **first son in any clan (probably a baby name)** (FH/11/17/01/pc). [Kinship terms with *-hpa* may be baby names; at any rate their use beyond 1st and 2nd person (e.g., for 'my first son' and 'your first son') seems limited.] *ilǫ́i̧hpa akxa htą́wą ki aðáape* Sonny went to town (02/01/95/FH/pc:ok; BE2.56–57). *ži̧kážį nakxą́še wéewina akxą́he, ilǫ́i̧hpa waachí štǫ́pape* I want to thank you children for watching my son dance.
••• *KS ilóappa* first son (RR); *PO šéppahąga* eldest child (male or female) (KDS).
••• Cf. *ilǫ́ǫhtą.*
ilǫ́ǫhpa iðáce. N **husband (lit., 'eldest son's father'), my/your/her husband (vocative and referent)** (02/13/95/FH/pc:okc; RBn2-MOJ/p5b).
ilǫ́ǫhpa iihǫ́ (variant: **ilǫ́ahpa iihǫ́**). N **wife (lit., 'eldest son's mother')** (RBn2-MOJ/p5b; 03/16/95/MREI/pc:okc), **my/your/his wife (vocative and referent).**
ilǫ́ǫhtą (variants: **ilǫ́ǫ, i̧lǫ́ǫ**). N **eldest son** (RBn2-MOJ/p9; CQ:ok; 03/13/95/FH/pc:okc).
•• LFD 75: *i̧lǫ́* <iⁿ-gthoⁿ´> special kinship term for the first son.
••• Cf. *htą́ą, ilǫ́ǫhpa.*
ilǫ́ǫka. N **wildcat** (RBn1-24; DN-WHM; FH/10/09/01/pc:uk).
•• LFD 75: *i̧lǫ́ka* <iⁿ-gthoⁿ´-ga> puma; also the name given to the domesticated cat when it was first introduced by the early settlers.
••• Cf. *ilǫ́eži.*
ilǫ́ǫška (variant: **i̧lǫǫška**). N ***ilǫ́ǫška*** **dances (the war dances or ceremonial dances of the Osages)** (RBn1-25; HRE/12/29/01/pc). [By folk etymology, 'playground of the eldest son' (cf. *ilǫ́ǫhpa* 'eldest son', *škáce* 'play').]
•• RB: <i-lóⁿ-shkah> (03/16/95/JS/pc:okc).
•• LFD 76: *i̧loška* <iⁿ´-gthu-shka> the name of a dance which originated with the Omaha and Ponca (04/13/95/FH/pc:ok).
ilǫ́ǫška záani (variant: **ilǫ́ǫška zaaní**). NP **drumkeeper and committee** (RB). *ilǫ́ǫška záani, íe tóa ékipše hta ąkxą́he* the drumkeeper and all you committeemen, I am going to say a few words (RB).
íluek?í (variant: **íliðáak?i**). N **spittoon.** *íluek?i húða* hand me the spittoon (03/14/95/FH/pc:ok; BE2.125).
•• RB: <í-lu-eh-k'í>.
•• LFD 34: *ðak?í* <tha-k'i´> spit.
••• Cf. *ðaak?í̧, íli.*
ímahtaha (variant of **ímąhtaha**).
ímą. INTERR/INDEF ADJ, INTERR/INDEF PRON **which.** *ímą Johna íiðe?* which of these did John see? (MSB). • **other.** [Sometimes used with two nouns to imply a choice between alternatives, much like English 'or'; see *ímąðe.*]
•• LFD 74: *ímą* <i´-moⁿ> the other one (03/02/95/FH/pc:ok).
••• Cf. *hówa.*
ímąche. PRON, ADJ [*ímą* + *che* POSIT] **next (one)** (RBn10-8:JW, unconfirmed; FH/11/17/01/pc:uk). • **other (one).**
••• Cf. *ą́mą.*
ímąðe. PRON, ADJ **one or the other.** [Often used to convey the equivalent of English 'or'.] *ímąðe hǫbrį́ke watkxą́ hpáaɣe hta mįkšé* I'll fix either beans or squash (03/02/95/FH/pc:ok).
••• Cf. *ímąkše.*
ímąhtaha (variant: **ímahtaha**). ADV, N **the other way** (RBn19-02). *ímahtaha mąðį́* go the other way (RBn19-02)
••• Cf. *émąhtažíha.*

ímąkše. ADJ [*ímą* + *kše* POSIT] **other.**
•• LFD 192: *wahóhtąðe ímąkše* <wa-ho´-ṭo^{n}-the i-mo^{n}-kshe> [expected Mod. Os. form: *wahóohtą ímąkše* 'the other (lying or long) gun'] the other of the two guns (03/02/95/FH/pc:ok).
••• Cf. *amą́*.

ínihkašie (variant: **nihkáši**). V [reg., *í_nihkašie*] *(intr.)* **become a person, live as a person (lit., 'by which means one becomes a person').** • N **clan (lit., 'folks you were born with')** (01/09/95/FH/pc:ma). *táata iðáníhkaši nįe?* what clan are you? (01/09/95/FH/pc:ma; 04/25/95/PM/pc:ok; BE2.19).
••• *KS: níkkašį-ŋ-a* person, people, men, gens, or clan (RR).

íniiðaahtą. N [*í-* LOC + *níi* + *ðaahtą́*] **dipper, ladle (lit., 'with which to drink water').**
•• JOD (slip file): *žą́ íniiðáhtą* <ça^{n} i´-ni-i-¢a´-ta^{n}> "wood for drinking water," a wooden cup or dipper.
••• Cf. *níiðaahtą*.

íopˀąðą. N **steam.**
•• LFD 81: *iópˀoðą* <i-u´-p'u-tho^{n}> vapor issuing from the mouth (e.g., of a deer or any other animal) (04/07/95/PM/pc:okc).
••• Cf. *opˀą́ða*.

ípaase. V [sync., fortisizing stop stem, *í_paase*] [*í-* LOC + *paasé*] *(trans.)* **cut (s.t.) with (s.t. else) by pushing down on the item being cut** (02/13/95-/FH/pc; 04/25/95/PM/pc:ok). *íhpaase* I cut it with it. *íšpaase* you cut it with it. *ąną́paase* we cut it with it. *mą́ąhį ípaasa* cut it with a knife (RBn22-03; CQc).
•• LFD 68: *ípase* <i´-ba-çe> to cut with a knife. ['With a knife' in glosses of this and the other LFD forms is probably not strictly part of the meaning of the Osage term (FH).] *ihpase* <i-p̣a-çe> I cut with a knife. *íšpase* <i´-shpa-çe> you cut with a knife. *ąðą́pasa pe* <o^{n}-tho-^{n}´-ba-ça i> we cut with a knife.

ípaašąha. N **turnaround place, U-turn, return point, turn in the road (lit., 'by which to make a turn').** *ípaašąha šíe, ókašeįke ðalíe ðe, awáata mįkšé* I pray for you to have a safe trip (lit., 'you go to the turnaround, you return safely, I'm praying').
•• LFD 348: *opášǫ* <u-ba´-sho^{n}> turn (in a road).

ípaaxce. V [sync. fortisizing stop stem, *í_paaxce*] [*í-* 'with' + *paaxcé*] *(trans.)* **tie down using, tie down with, bind, handcuff, or manacle using, tie into a bundle or bundles using.** *wéðį íhpaaxce* I tied it [down] using rope. *wéðį íšpaaxce* you tied it [down] using rope. *wéðį ąną́xpaacape* we tied it [down] using rope (FH).
•• LFD 69: *ípaxce* <i´-ba-xtse> to tie with a cord [expected Mod. Os. gloss 'to tie with', no mention of 'cord']. *wéðį žįka íhpaxce ha* <we´-thi^{n} zhi^{n}-ga i´-p̣a-xtse ha> [sentence-final *ha* is not used in Mod. Os.] I tied it with a cord. *wéðį žįka išpaxce ha* <we´-thi^{n} zhi^{n}-ga i-shpa-xtse ha> [sentence-final *ha* is not used in Mod. Os.] you tied it with a cord. *wéðį žįka ąðą paxca pe* <we´-thi^{n} zhi^{n}-ga o^{n}-tho^{n} ba-xtsa i> we tied it with a cord.

ípahǫ (variant: **ípaho**). V [sync. fortisizing stop stem, *í_pahǫ*] *(trans.)* **know (e.g., a fact, the answer to a question).** *ðíoxta íhpahǫ mįkšé* I know you love him/her. *iiðánąhíži íhpahǫ* I know you don't agree with me (RBn10-3:MOJ/79). *íhpahǫ mąží* I don't know. *íšpahǫ* you know. *íšpahǫži* you don't know. *ąną́pahǫpe* we know that (RBn10-15). • **understand.** *wažáže íšpahǫ?* do you understand Osage? [contrasts with *wažáži špíižǫ́?* 'do you know how to talk Osage?'] (RBn1-MOJ/p58). • **know as a person, be acquainted with, recognize, know s.o. as (being a certain way or a certain type of person).** *wažáže huuwáli íhpahǫ* I know a lot of Osages (RBn10-2). *wíihpahǫ* I know you [unexpected variant of *iwíhpahǫ*] (02/14/95/FH/pc:ok). *ąną́špahǫ* you know me (RBn10-18). *ąðą́špahǫ́* [variant of *ąną́špahǫ*] you know me (FH). *wéšpahǫ* you know them (MSB 5-12-83). *omáįhka tóe šímižį íšpahǫ?* have you known this girl for some years? (RBn; MREI/01/11/93). *níhkašika íšpahǫ?* do you know that man? (02/14/95/FH/pc:ok; BE2.74). *íšpahǫpe* [expected Mod. Os. form: *wéšpahǫpe*] you [pl.] know them; you [pl.] know him (MSB 5-12-83). *ąną́pahǫ akxai* he knows me (RBnotes). *íðipahǫ* he knows you. *ðíipahǫ* [unexpected variant of *íðipahǫ*] he knows you. *wépahǫpe* they know us (MSB 5-12-83). *weą́paho a[ð]įkše* we [two] know them (MSB 2-24-83). *ąną́pahǫ ąðįkše* we [two] know him (RBnotes). *ąną́pahǫpe* we know him, we know them (MSB 2-12-83). *weą́pahǫpe* we know them (MSB 5-12-83). • *(trans.)* **guess.** *ąžį howáįki súhkahtą́ą mį́įka hcí káaye che ípahǫži akxa áape* but they could not guess where turkey hen made her nest (RBn19-05; 02/14/95/FH/pc:ok).
•• LFD 69: *ípahǫ* <i´-ba-ho^{n}> to know. *íhpahǫ* <i´-p̣a-ho^{n}> I know. *íšpahǫ* <i´-shpa-ho^{n}> you know. *ąðą́pahǫ pe* <o^{n}-tho^{n}´-ba-ho^{n} i> we know.

ípahǫ (*continued*)
íhpahǫ mąži <i´-pa-ho^n mo^n-zhi> I do not know. *íšpahǫ aži* <i´-shpa-ho^n a-zhi> you do not know. *ąðą́pahǫ paži pe* <o^n-tho^n´-ba-ho^n ba-zhi i> we do not know.

ípasą. v [conjug. unknown] *(trans.)* **turn over.** *wacúe che ípasą [ð]į* turn that bread over (FH).
••• Cf. *ípaašąha.*

ípehi, ípehį (variants of **į́pehi**).

ípihį oðíši. N **pillowcase** (RBn1-54).
••• *QU ípahį* pillow (RR).
••• Cf. *į́pehi.*

ípše. v [reg.-*iða, í_pše*] *(intr.)* **pass by, come by, go by, go past** (FH:prod). *íðapše įhtáci ðak?éwai* when you pass by, father, remember [i.e., be kind to] us (FH/09/11/01/pc). *áðahtaha íðapše* [on the other side] you passed right by (FH:4/18/96/tape:prod). *mąðį́ šǫ apa kį́įkįįežį toa kį́į ípšape* while they were walking some butterflies came flying by (RBn15-01). *áðahtaha ípšape ąži owáhkiapažíe* they went right past us [on the other side] but didn't speak to us (RB-MSB 4/7/83; FH:4/18/96/tape:okc).
••• Cf. *ápše.*

ípukxa (variants: **ípuutkxa, íipuukxa**). v [conjug. unknown] *(trans.)* **wipe with, dry with (by wiping).** *haaská ípuutkxa* wipe it with the shirt (BE2.159; FH:4/24/96/prod).
••• Cf. *htaną́k?a ípukxa.*

ípuze. v [stat., *í_puze*] *(trans.)* **be thirsty for.** [Expected Mod. Os. verb forms: *íðipuze* 'you are thirsty', *ípuze* 'she is thirsty', *wépuze* 'we are thirsty'.] *níi ǫðápuzé* [expected Mod. Os. form: *níi ąðą́puze* or *níi ąną́puze*] I'm thirsty (03/20/95/FH/pc:ok; BE2.139). *níi ąną́puze* I'm thirsty (HH). *ðíe, nį́e ąnų́puze?* are you thirsty [for water]? (RBn10-21/JW&FW/77).
•• LFD 69: *ípize* <i´-bi-çe> thirsty. *ąðąpize* <o^n-tho^n-bi-çe> I am thirsty. *íðipize* <i´-thi-bi-çe> you are thirsty. *weápizape* <we-a´-bi-ça i> we are thirsty.

isǫ́ežį (variant: **isǫ́ažį**). N **her younger brother (more precise than English 'her brother').**

isǫ́ka. N **his younger brother (more precise than English 'his brother').** *Mogri akxa isǫ́ka hcí íhta ci aðáape* Mogri went to his brother's house.
•• LFD 70: *isǫ́ka* <i-ço^n´-ga> a younger brother.

íšcewa (variant of **íišcewai**).

išíkxą. N **her husband's sister, her husband's brother's wife, her brother's wife (more precise than English 'her sister-in-law').** *Mary išíkxą* Mary's sister-in-law (BE2.122; FH/pc).
•• RB: <shi-kxáh^n>.
•• LFD 78: *išíkxą* <i-shi´-ko^n> a woman's sister-in-law; her brother's wife or her husband's sister. LFD 329: sister-in-law (a woman's).
••• Cf. *šíkxą.*

išík?e. N **her sister's husband, her husband's brother, or her husband's sister's husband (more precise than English 'her brother-in-law')** (BE2.12; 01/09/95/FH/pc:prod orig).
•• LFD 78: *išík?e* <i-shi´-k'e> a woman's brother-in-law; her sister's husband or her husband's brother.

íšpaðǫ (variants: **íšpaðo, į́špaðǫ**). ADJ **Spanish, Mexican, French** (2/24/95/FH/pc:okc; BE2.87).
• N **Spaniard, any native Spanish-speaking person (especially a Mexican), French person; Spanish language, French language.** [Borrowed from Spanish *español.*]

íštope (variant of **íištope**).

íštǫka. ADV **right, on the right, rightward, to the right** (RBn23-07, unconfirmed). *íštǫka ci ha* on the right, rightward, to the right (RBn23-07, unconfirmed).
•• LFD 112: *nǫ́pe istoke che* <no^n´-be i-sdo-ge tse> the right hand.

ítaasuhu. N [*í-* LOC + *taasúhu*] **sweat lodge (lit., 'cleanse with heat').**
•• LFD 70 (unconfirmed): *ítasihi* <i´-da-çi-hi> sweat lodge.

íto. INTERJ **expressing surprise (said to be a woman's exclamation).**

iwák?o (variant: **iiwák?o**). N **his wife** (FH: t#128). *šée nąhtą́htą wéąðuwį hta ąkatxą́, níhka iiwák?o ékiepe* we're going to sell that donkey, the man's wife said (RBn10-2:MOJ/79; FH/10/09/01/pc:ii).

íwak?óžį. N **his/her mother-in-law.**

íwehkilį v [conjug. unknown] *(intr.)* **clothe oneself with, dress in.** *hǫ́ǫpa ðé wéeną akxai ðe níhkaši tóa áðixǫpape, hpáðį wéhkili íwehkili į kšíyape* she's grateful today because they honored her, they dressed her [lit, 'had her clothe herself'] in Kiowa clothes (RBn23-17; CQc).

íwihe. ADJ **mixed in, mixed among.** *šíi akxa htáa wį íwihe hcéská toa žǫ́[w]ale akxai* look, there's a deer mixed in with all those cows (lit., 'that near you is a deer mixed in with some cows') (RBn17-p04).

íwili. ADJ? **burning.** *íwili, iiwili* (fragment collected by CQ).
••• Cf. *táalį.*

íxope. v [reg.-*iða*, *í_xope* (2nd person is inflected as either reg. or stat.)] *(intr.)* **lie, tell untruths.** *íðaxopaží* you [sg.] didn't lie. *íðixope ðą́ąché į́ké* you wouldn't lie (FH/05/02/95). *íðixope apažíe, íðaxope apažíe* you [pl.] didn't lie (02/15/95/FH/pc:prod). *íxope štą́* he is always lying (02/15/95/FH/pc:ok). *íxope apa* they're lying (FH:90). *ąną́ąxopapé* we [more than two] lied. *íxope įká* don't lie! (02/15/95/FH/pc:prod; BE2.79). • n **lie, fib, untruth, falsehood.** *íxope ąwą́štaake* you told me a lie (02/15/95/FH/pc:ok). *íxope!* liar! (lit., 'a lie!') (FH 2-24-83; MSB). *íxopeštą* one who always lies; a liar (02/15/95/FH/pc:prod).

•• LFD 81: *íxope* <i´-xo-be> to fib; to tell a falsehood; to perjure oneself. *ąðą́ xopa mąži* <o^{n}-tho^{n}´ xo-ba mo^{n}-zhi> [expected Mod. Os. form: *iðáxopa mąží*] I did not perjure myself. *iðixope* <i-thi-xo-be> you perjured [*sic*].

íxopeštą́. n [*íxope + štą*] **liar (lit., 'one who always lies')** (RB; 02/15/95/FH/pc:ok).

•• LFD 81: *íxope štą* <i´-xo-be shto^{n}> a liar ('habitually lying'). *níhkašika ixope štą ðe iðási ha* <ni´-ḳa-shi-ga i-xo-be shto^{n} the i-tha´-çi ha> [expected Mod. Os. form: *níhkašika íxopeštą ðée iiðási;* sentence-final *ha* is not used in Mod. Os.] I hate a liar.

ízizike (variant: **íizizike**). n **bad things, evil** (FH). • adj **unclean, sick, dirty, evil** (FH/07/09/01/pc). [Apparently a reduplicated form of *iizíke* 'embarrassed' (but note short *i* and difference in meaning).] *táatą ízizike ecíke tą, ékiǫ ðįkápi* if there is anything unclean, don't do it (FH: Hǫopétóohka). *ízizike įké akxai* it's not dirty.

••• *KS šíge* bad, evil, injury [not cognate] (RR).

ízizike káaɣe. vp [sync. *k>p*, *ízizike _káaɣe*] *(trans.)* **contaminate or pollute (e.g., water or air), dirty or spoil s.t.** *níi ízizike škáaɣape* you all polluted the water.

•• LFD 107: *níizizike kaɣe* <ni´-i-çi-çi-ge ga-xe> to make water unclean; to make water unfit for use by pollution. *níizizike ąkaɣa pe* <ni´-i-çi-çi-ge o^{n}-ga-xa i> we made the water unclean.

iž́įðe (variants: **iž́į, iž́įe**). n **his older brother (more precise than English 'his brother')** (01/09/95/FH/pc:ok).

iž́įke (variant: **iiž́įke**). n **his/her son (any son).** *Yvonnea iž́įke akxa húheka akxa* Yvonne's son is sick/has a sickness (FH). *wahkǫ́ta iž́įke íikitaðe* Christmas (lit., 'God's son is born again') (FH; RB) • **his brother's son, her sister's son (more precise than English 'his nephew' or 'her nephew')** (02/27/95/FH/pc:ok). [The corresponding 1st person form *wiž́įke* 'my son' can be used also by a woman speaking to or about her brother's son (perhaps a recent usage or one confined to certain dialects or families).]

•• LFD 82: *iž́įke* <i-zhi^{n}´-ge> his or her son. (02/27/95/FH/pc:ok).

iž́įke iihǫ́. n **Virgin Mary (lit., 'his son's mother' or 'mother of his son')** (HRE/12/29/01/pc:ok).

••• Cf. *wahkǫ́ta iž́įke iihǫ́.*

ížoši (variant: **íižoši**). v [reg.-*iða*, *í_žoši*] *(trans.)* **prohibit, forbid, order or tell s.o. not to, disallow.** *iðážoši ąži óðąži akxai* I said no, but he's going to have his way (lit., 'I disallowed it, but [he's doing it] anyway') (FH/11/19/01/pc:prod). *žįkáži žąąníežį ðaaché iðážoši* I told the children not to eat candy (FH:4/18/96/tape:prod). *žįkážį hóolą iðážoši ną* I always used to tell the children not to go fishing (FH:prod). *žąąníežį ðaaché iðážoši* you told me not to eat candy (lit., 'you forbid eating candy'). *iiną́ akxa žįkážį hóolą ížoši nąpe* mother used to tell the children not to go fishing (FH:4/18/96/tape:okc). *žąąníežį ðaaché ížoši apai* they said not to eat candy (FH:4/18/96/tape:prod). • **be against doing or refuse or be reluctant to do s.t., say no when asked to do s.t.** (t#14a-ps; 04/19/95/FH/pc:ok). *waachí iiðážoši* I refuse to dance (FH/11/18/01/pc:prod). *waachí iižoši akxai* he doesn't want to dance (FH/11/18/01/pc:prod).

iž́ǫą. n **her older sister (more precise than English 'her sister').**

•• LFD 82: *iž́ǫðe* <i-zho^{n}´-the> her elder sister.

iž́ǫke. n **his/her daughter; his brother's daughter, her sister's daughter (more precise than English 'his/her niece')** (02/27/95/FH/pc:ok).

•• LFD 82: *iž́ǫke* <i-zho^{n}´-ge> his or her daughter.

į, į́

į. v [sync., nasal vowel stem, _į́] *(trans.)* **wear (e.g., earrings, warm clothes, a coat, a shawl)** (5/12/83/4). *mį* I wear; I am wearing (03/16/95/JS/pc:ok). *mį́ hkǫ́bra* I want to wear it (03/16/95/JS/pc:ok). *haaskámį brį́ ąąhé* [with unexpected variant *brį́* of 1st sg. *mį́*] I'm wearing my shawl (FH). *žį́* you wear; you are wearing (03/16/95/JS/pc:ok). *žį́ wihkǫ́bra* I want you to wear it (03/16/95/JS/pc:okc). *haaská ðé žį́ hkǫ́bra* I want you to wear this shirt (RBn1-44). *ąkį́ ąąðé* we [two] are wearing [it] (5/12/83/1). *haaská ščúuce ąkį́* we're wearing warm clothing. *haaskámį į́ ąkái* we're wearing our shawls (FH:5/01/96/tape:prod). *haxį́ šooká į́ ðįké* don't wear that thick blanket (FH/09/24/01/prod). *ákahamį į́* put on [wear] your coat (02/15/95/JS/pc:ok; RBn10-12:JW). *haxį́ į kší[ð]e* let him wear a blanket, cover him with a blanket (lit., 'make him wear a blanket'). • **carry** (PM). *wáįį akxa, šį́mįžį* those girls, he's carrying them (04/25/95/PM/pc). • **have s.t. positioned so that it surrounds part of the body (such as the head or arm).** *ípehį ípéhį į kší[ð]a* put a pillow under his or her head (lit., 'have him wear/use a pillow under his head') (BE2.103; RBn2-MOJ/p20; FH: *ípehį*). *ípehį áa kše į́ kšíe* put a pillow under his arm.

•• LFD 74: *į* <i^{n}> to wear, as a robe or a blanket. LFD 171 (unconfirmed): *oį* <u-i^{n}> to wear earrings. *oį́ htą brį* <u-i^{n}´ ṭo^{n} bthi^{n}> [expected Mod. Os. form *mį* 'I wear', not *brį*] I wear earrings. *oį htą ąðį pe* <u-i^{n} ṭo^{n} o^{n}-thi^{n} i> we wear earrings. LFD 192: *wáį ɣake* <Wa´-i^{n} Xa-ge> Carrying (a pipe) and Wailing. "This is the first act in the initiatory ceremony of a candidate." [*wa-* VAL + *į́*] (04/25/95/PM/pc:ok: *wáį ɣaake*).

įcé. n **face.** *táata ą́hǫǫ íhpahǫ, įcé ðuuhpííži ą́hǫǫ* I know what I like, I like to make [bad] faces (RBn22-20). *įcé xúɣa* wrinkly face (a comical and metaphorical usage).

•• RB: <í^{n}-tseh, i^{n}-tséh> (04/26/95/LS/pc:ok; BE2.43).

•• LFD 75: *įcé* <i^{n}-dse´> face.

įcé bráaska. n **slap.**

įcé bráze. n **slap.**

įcé ðuuhpííži. vp [sync., *įcé _ðuuhpííži*] *(intr., trans.?)* **make faces (at), grimace (at) (lit., 'make a bad face').** *táata ą́hǫǫ íhpahǫ, įcé ðuuhpííži ą́hǫǫ.* I know what I like, I like to make faces (RBn22-20).

įcé hpáze. vp, adjp [stat., *įcé _hpáze*] **(be) dizzy** (01/20/95/ERE/pc:ok; FH: ok). *įcé ąhpáze* I am dizzy (FH:6/25/01/pc). *įcé ðihpáze nįkšé* you are dizzy. *įcé ąhpáze ąkakxái* we're dizzy [expected Mod. Os. 1st pl. form: *wahpáze*] (FH:6/25/01/pc). *įcé wahpáze* we're dizzy (FH). *įcé wahpáze apai* they are dizzy (BE2.32; FH: 4/17/96/tape). *htǫ́pe tą įcé ąhpáze ną* when I look at it, it makes me dizzy (RBn10-7:JW; FH:ok).

įcé káaɣe vp [sync. *k>p*, *įcé _káaɣe*] **put on makeup (lit., 'make a face').** *šímižį apa įcé káaɣe éena wáli wascútape* the girls put on their makeup, which makes them very slow (RBn3-19).

įcé waléze. n **picture of anything, photograph, portrait.** [Takes 'sitting' positional article *įkšé*.] *įcé waléze įkšé ą́hǫǫ* I like that picture (speaking of a picture on the wall). *įcé waléze hpaamáši hta mįkše* I'll hold the picture up (02/15/95/FH/pc:prod). *icé waléze íiðaðe?* do you see the picture? (RBn1-44).

įcéki. n **his/her mother's brother (his/her maternal uncle; more precise than English 'his/her uncle')** (02/27/95/JS/pc:ok).

įchóhtąą (variant: **ichóhtąka**). n **muskrat** (BE2.91; 04/17/95/LS/pc:prod); **rat.**

•• RB: <i-tsó-tu^{n}-kah> big rat.

•• LFD 75 (unconfirmed): *įchǫ́ htąka* <i^{n}-cho^{n}´ ṭo^{n}-ga> a rat. *įchǫ́htąka oðįįke* <i^{n}-cho^{n}´-ṭon-ga u-thi^{n}-ge> the butcher bird; a shrike [lit., 'rat grabber'].

įchóka. n **mouse** (04/17/95/LS/pc:prod).

•• LFD 296: *įchǫ́ka žįka* <i^{n}-cho^{n}´-ga zhi^{n}-ga> a mouse.

įcóolą. n [*įcé + oolą́*] **sleep-matter-in-eyes, sand-in-eyes, sleepy-in-eyes (lit., 'put in the face').**

-íɣe (variant of **-wįɣe**).

íhį (variants: **hii, hį́į, į́į**). n **beard** (BE2.7; 01/07/95/FH/pc:ok; 03/23/95/FH/pc:hii). *į́į htǫ́ ǫ́ǫ akxa* he is wearing a beard (04/25/95/PM/pc).

•• LFD 76: *íhį* <i^{n}´-hi^{n}> beard.

íhįhkicéže (variant: **íhį áhkiceže**). n **goat** (05/01/95/LS/pc:ok:hk; BE2.59, RBn2-MOJ/p2; FH/11/19/01/pc:ma). [By folk etymology, 'urinates upon his whiskers'.]

•• LFD 73: *íhį akiceže žįka* <i´-hi^{n} a-gi-dse-zhe zhi^{n}-ga> a kid; a young goat.

įhtáci. N **my father; my father's brother (my paternal uncle; more precise than English 'my uncle')** (02/27/95/JS/pc:ok (BE2.147).

••• *QU įttátte* my father (RR).

įhtácižį. N [*įhtáci* + *-žį* 'little'] **my father's brother (my paternal uncle; more precise than English 'my uncle').**

íį. N **rock.** *íį htą kootáha wáli lą́ąðe, ðuhcépe įká* that big rock [yonder] is really heavy, don't lift it (FH/09/25/01/pc). *tǫ́pa íį htą, ščúhcepe ðąąché įké* watch out with that big rock, you can't lift it (FH/09/25/01/pc). *íį kootáha skíke* that rock over there is heavy (FH/07/31/01). *íį šé įkše ðíhą* pick up that rock (RBn HW11).

íį (variant of **íhį**).

íį olíį. VP [reg., *íį o_líį*] **sweat** (03/14/95/MREI/pc:ok). *íį olíį hta akxai* they're going to sweat (RBn2-MOJ/p8; 03/14/95/MREI/pc:ok). *íį olíį ší hkǫ́bra* I want you to come sweat.

íįhtǫ. N [*íį* + *í* + *htą́ka*] **earring(s).** *íhįhtǫ ðíhta škáaye?* did you make your earrings? (RBn; MREI/01/11/93). *íįhtǫ ǫǫ akxai* he/she has on earrings (RB).

•• RB: <í^{n}-to^{n}>.

•• LFD 76: *íįhtǫ* <i^{n}´-i^{n}-ṭo^{n}> earrings. LFD 73: *íįhtǫ* <i´-i^{n}-ṭo^{n}> an earring.

••• *KS ččíhoba ska óį tto* shell earrings, 3 or 4 in. long (RR).

įįké (variant of **ðįįké**).

íįolįįhci. N [*íį olíį* + *hcí*] **sweat house, sweat lodge** (05/02/95/LS/pc; 03/14/95/MREI/pc; MOJt#150).

įįštá (variant: **iištá**). N **eye.** *įįštá hǫ́ǫži apai* she has bad eyes (lit., '[her] eyes are bad') (BE2.42; 12/30/94/FH/pc:prod).

•• JOD (slip file): *ištá* <i-cta´> an eye, eyes.

•• LFD 77: *įštá* <i^{n}-shta´> eye; eyes. *įštá ni ąwąkihpi* <i^{n}-shta´ ni o^{n}-wo^{n}-gi-pi> [expected Mod. Os. form: *įįštá níi ąwą́kuhpu*] my eyes are full of tears.

••• *OM* same as Osage (LFD 77).

••• Cf. *mą́ze įįštóolą*.

įįštá wawéeðeži (variant: **iištá wawéeðeži**). VP [uninfl.] [*įįštá* + *wawéeðe* + *aží* NEG] *(intr.)* **be blind, have eyes that don't see things.** *iištá wawéeðe mąži* I can't see [contrasts with *iiðáðe mąži* 'I can't see it'] (FH/08/22/96; FH:prod). *iištá wawéeðeži apai* he can't see.

••• Cf. *íiðe*.

įįštáa cˀóka (variant of **įįštáhaa cˀóka**).

įįštábri (variant: **iištábri**). N **tear, teardrop.**

•• LFD 77: *įštábri* <i^{n}-shta´-bthi> tears (04/04/95/FH/pc:okc).

įįštáhaa. N [*įįštá* + *háa*] **eyelid.**

įįštáhaa cˀóka (variants: **įįštáa cˀóka, iištáhaa cˀóka, iištáa cˀóka**). VP [stat., *įįštáhaa _cˀóka*] **be sleepy (lit., 'eyelids droop').** *opáwįye pšíe, étana įįštáhaa ącˀóka mįkše* I went riding and that is why I'm sleepy (03/10/95/MREI/pc:ok; BE2.123). *kaaskíke įįštáhaa cˀóka ški akxai* he was tired and sleepy (MREI: *įįštá cˀóka* or *įįštáhaa cˀóka*, same).

•• LFD 77: *įštá ocˀoxe* <i^{n}-shta´ u-ṭs'u-xe> drowsy; lethargic; sleepiness. *įštá ąhcoxe* <i^{n}-shta´o^{n}-ṭsu-xe> [expected Mod. Os. form: *įįštá ącˀóka*] my eyes are sleepy.

įįštáhįį (variant: **iištáhii**). N [*įįštá* + *hį́į*] **eyebrows.** JOD (slip file): *ištáhi* the eyebrows.

••• *LAK ištáxe* the ridge above the eyebrows (Buechel), *ištáxe hį́* the eyebrows (Buechel).

įįštáxį (variant: **iištáxį**). N [evidently *įįštá* + *ɣį*] **white person, French person, Canadian or English person** (BE2.157; 03/16/95/MREI/pc:prod) **(lit., 'light eyes, gray, brown, or yellow eyes').** *įįštáxį šímižį wasúhuži wahókˀa* a dirty little white girl (FH/04/14/94, 76b). *įįštáxį žáže táatą ašcíe?* what is your English name? (02/27/95/FH/pc:ok).

•• JOD (slip file): *ištáxį hcí* <ictaqi^{n} tsi> a white man's house. *ištáxį* <i-cta´-qi^{n}> a Frenchman, a Canadian; a white man; white men in general as distinguished from Indians.

•• LFD 77: *įštáxį* <i^{n}-shta´-xi^{n}> yellow eyes, a white man.

įįštáxį htáhtaze. N [reduplicated form, onomatopoeic] **grasshopper.**

•• LFD 77: *įštáxį tatase* <i^{n}-shta´-xi^{n} da-da-çe> [expected Mod. Os. form: *įštáxį htahtaze*] the white man's grasshopper. "This refers to the red-winged grasshopper believed to have been introduced by the white people. It makes a crackling noise as it flies up and down in the air."

įįštáxį íe (variant: **iištáxį íe**). N **English, white man's language.** *įįštáxį íe ðįká* don't talk English. *įįštáxi íe ékie ðįká ði, oðíchį hta apai, háakǫ ékiše che íšpahǫži* don't speak English, they're going to whip you, you don't know what you are saying (FH/09/24/01/prod [FH's mother said this to FH's father, who spoke only a few words of English]).

į̨štáxį sáhku (variant: **iištáxį sáhku**). N **cantaloupe (lit., 'white man's melon')** (01/09/95/FH/pc:ma).

•• LFD 77: *į̨štáxį sahku* <i^{n}-shta´-xi^{n} ça-ķiu> white man's melon; a cantaloupe. *į̨štáxį sahku ðache ą̨ða lį* <i^{n}-shta´-xi^{n} ça-ķiu tha-tse o^{n}-tha gthi^{n}> I like cantaloupe.

į̨štáxįžį. N [*į̨štáxį* + *-žį* 'little'] **person of mixed blood (white and Osage; lit., 'a little white')** (04/17/95/LS/pc:ok; FH/09/25/01; BE2.88).

įká (variant of **ðįká**).

įké (variant of **ðįké**).

įkšé (variants: **įkší, ðįkší, ðįkšé**). CONT **3rd person sitting continuative aspect marker.** *lį́į šǫ́ įkšé* while he was sitting (04/28/95/LS/pc:prod). *wáli ðižóžipi įkšé áape* he [sitting] is hurt or all beat up. *ðihkówa lǫ́ði įkšé?* is your friend [sitting] drunk? (RBn3-54). *wak?ó tąhé įkšé?* is your wife well? (BE2.5). *haakǫ́ įkšé?* how are they? (FH). *howáįki įkšé?* where is it? (03/16/95/MREI/pc:ok). *óoląke wíhta hówaįki įkšé?* where is my hat? *kóota įkšé ohkíhce hǫ́ǫxce ðįkšé?* that one sitting over there, what kind of tribe is he? (03/23/95/FH/pc). *waníe ikší aape* she is having birth pains, they said; she is in the hospital having her baby, they said (FH prod orig). *waníe ðįkší aape* they said she's in labor (FH/pc). *mihkák?e hą́ą tą ðįkšé* the evening star (lit., 'when evening, the star sitting'). *óoląke wíhta hówaįki įkšé?* where is my hat? *lį́į šǫ́ įkšé* while he was sitting (04/28/95/LS/pc:prod). *ée įksí áape* they said it was he/she [sitting]. *Christine akxa hóxpe ǫǫ́ íkšé?* does Christine have a cold? (RBn3-55)

įkšé (variant: **ðįkšé**). POSIT **sitting sg. animate or inanimate positional article (follows a noun or pronoun [usually not the subject of a sentence] that represents a singular sitting entity or singular round entity).** *ðée įkšé* this one [man] here. *šée įkše kú hcea* tell him [sitting down] to come here (RBn23-17). *kóota įkšé* the one sitting over there. *háakǫ įkše ékipše škǫ́šta?* what is it you want me to say? (RBn10-22/JW&FW). *tówa įkše tǫ́pa* look at him/her/that. *ðée įkše awáši hkǫ́bra* I want that person [sitting] to help me (e.g., one of the other firemen in a meeting) (01/06/95/FH/pc:prod). *hpǫ́hka htą́wą įkšé mąhką́ ðaaché šcée hta ðaįšé?* are you going to the meeting over at Ponca? (02/24/95/FH/pc:okc). *táatą ohkíhce kóota įkšé?* (RBn:87) what tribe is that guy [sitting] over there? (03/23/95/FH/pc). *šǫ́ke ðįkše áanąąžį* I stepped on the dog (RB; 01/20/95/ERE/pc:ok). *šǫ́ke ðįkše aðánąąžį* you stepped on the dog (RB; 01/20/95/ERE/pc:ok; 02/22/95/FH/pc:ok). • **lying down or horizontal inanimate plural positional article (follows an inanimate noun or pronoun [usually not the subject of a sentence] that would normally take the positional article *kšé* 'lying down, long' to show plurality of that noun or pronoun).** *c?é ški šǫ́ įkše šcúhpaahą nįkšé aapai* they said you [even] raised the dead [pl. of the presumably 'lying down' dead person(s) expressed with 'sitting' positional] (RBn23-17).

įkší. PPN **to s.t. sitting or round.** *hǫ́ǫpa htáwą įkši pšíe* I went to town today (03/22/95/FH/pc:ok; BE2.142). *Smokey įkší íihkimai brée* [*íihkimai* from *íihkiðe mąðį́ bree*] I'm going visiting to Smokey's (RBn19-05). *niitáahpa įkší ąkáipe* we are going to that pond (RBn3-09). • **in that (sitting or round) place.** *įhtáci wahkǫ́ta, mą́žą ðáalį įkší ðaníhkaši nįkší eepe* our father, who art in heaven [they said].

įkší (variant of **įkšé** CONT).

įkšíðe (variant: **įkšíe**). V [reg.?, *į_kšíðe*?] [presumably *į́* + *kšíðe*] *(trans.)* **have s.o. wear, cause s.o. to put on an article of clothing.** *haxį́ įkšį́[ð]e* put a blanket on him (lit., 'have him wear a blanket') (RBn10-12:JW).

įkšítxą (variant: **įkšítxa**). PPN **off (s.t. round or sitting).** *paaxó [į]kšitxa okáxpape* he threw him off the hill (RBn19-02). *paaxó įkšítxa ąkókaxpai* we threw him off the hill (RBn19-02).

įlé. N **excrement, feces, dung, ordure, excretory function, bowels.**

•• JOD (slip file): *įle* <iñ-ķ¢ĕ> dung, ordure, faeces.

•• LFD 75: *įlé* <i^{n}-gthe´> dung; excrement.

įléha. N **buttocks, ass, bottom, anus, rectum, asshole.** *įléha wáli htąą akxai, híðaxa ðíhta akxa cúðažipe* his bottom is really large, your diaper is insufficient (BE2.14; 01/09/95/FH/pc:prod).

•• RB: <įgléha> (RBn12-08).

•• JOD (slip file): *įléha* <iñ-ķ¢é-ha> the anus.

įlǫ́ǫ (variant of **ilǫ́ǫhtą**).

ílǫǫška (variant of **ilǫ́ǫška**).

ípehi (variant: **ípehi, ípehį, ípehį**). N **pillow** (RBn1-MOJ/p54; 03/08/95/FH/pc:ok). *ípehį sí kše ǫǫ kšíe* put a pillow under his foot (03/08/95/FH/pc). *ípehį áa kše į kšíe* put a pillow under his arm. *ípehį štǫ́ke* a soft pillow (FH). • ADV **under the head** (RBn1-MOJ/p54; 03/08/95/FH/pc:ok). *ípehį ípéhį į kší[ð]a* put a pillow under his/her head (lit., 'have him/her use a pillow under his/her head') (BE2.103; RBn2-MOJ/p20; FH: *ípehį*).

•• RB: <í-pi-hi^{n}, í^{n}-peh-hi>.

•• LFD 74: *į́pehį* <i^{n}´-be-hi^{n}> a pillow. *į́pehį štǫka xta aðe ha* <i^{n}´-be-hi^{n} shto^{n}-ga xta a-the ha> [sentence-final *ha* is not used in Mod. Os.] I like a soft pillow (unconfirmed; 03/08/95/FH/pc:uk verb *xta*). *į́pehį sakí* <i^{n}´-be-hi^{n} ça-gi> a hard pillow (03/08/95/FH/pc:ok: *saakí*). *į́pehį htąka* <i^{n}´-be-hi^{n} ţo^{n}-ga> a large pillow (03/08/95/FH/pc:ok).

••• Cf. *ípihį oðíši*.

į́špaðǫ (variant of **íšpaðǫ**).

į́štǫwą (variant of **iistó**).

įžį́akika. N **bobcat** (ML, unconfirmed; FH:4/22/96/tape:uk).

---

k

ká (variant of **káa**).

kaa- (variant: **ka-**). INSTR **by striking, by sudden application of force or sudden movement.**

káa (variant: **ká**). PRON, ADJ **these, this, this one (animate or inanimate [may apply to abstract entities], emphatic or expressing certainty or immediacy).** *húheka ški ǫ́ðe apai, káa pa ški įhtáci, na íšpahǫ háakǫ ðáalį che* there are also the sick, these ones too, father, only you know how to heal them (FH/08/01/01/pc). *wéewinai káa che įhtáci* I am grateful for this, father (FH/08/01/01/pc). *íhtáežį ški húheka kšíepe, káa ðe įhtaci, ðakˀéðai ði* younger sister, too, has been made sick, that one, father, bless her (FH/08/01/01/pc). *káa che* here it is; this is it (e.g., referring to a cup of coffee or a pile of blankets). *káa įkšé* here it is (e.g., a blanket or a pie or a plate of food). (02/09/95/FH/pc:ok). *káa įkšé, mį́įhtoeli hkilúwį* here [e.g., handing over money], buy yourself some gum. *káa ðįkšé* this person [sitting] (PM071494). *káa íe txą pée txą?* who is that who is talking? (RB note: *káa íe txą* sounds harsh, as by an older person). *káa níhka íe txą pée txą?* who is that who is talking (RB note: sounds more polite, as usage characteristic of a younger person) • ADV **here, in this place** (02/09/95/FH/pc:ok). *ðéekaa ąwą́nǫbre htai* let's eat here (FH:prod). *ðéekaa kü̃e* come here; come over here. *ðéekaa aðį́kü.* bring it here (02/09/95/FH/pc:okc; BE2.66; 02/09/95/FH/pc:ok).

káa che PRONP [*káa* PRON + *che* POSIT] **this (standing; a default combination of demonstrative and positional article used for both concrete and abstract items).** *káa che táatą waaðǫ́?* what kind of song is that? (RB). *howaðéeški ðakˀéðai, įhtáci káa che wéewinai* you're good to everyone, father, for which we're grateful (FH: prayer). *káa che ðaachá* eat this (RBn12-11). *káa che aðį́mąðį* take away this thing here. • **those inanimate sitting/round things in the surrounding area (referring to a group of sitting items that would be considered 'standing' when gathered together).** *káa che ǫ́bre hta mįkšé* I'm going to throw away that stuff sitting there (e.g., a stack of trash). *htóožu tóe káa che* here's some meat pies for you. *káa che!* here! (when handing a person multiple things that normally sit, such as meat pies or blankets). *haxį́ che húða* give me those blankets (FH).

•• LFD 48: *káche* <ga´tse> this; this pile of things before us.

kaa ché ðe. PRONP [*káa* PRON + *che* POSIT + *ðée* PRON] **group of inanimate items sitting there.** ['Standing' positional article *che* pluralizes 'sitting' entities.] *kaa ché ðe* there's something sitting there; there it sits (FH).

káa įkše. PRONP [*káa* PRON + *įkšé* POSIT] **this one (sitting)** (03/15/95/PM/pc:ok). *káa įkše oochíže* this one [a person] talks too much; this is too loud (e.g., speaking of the television) (RBn11-02; 03/15/95/PM/pc:ok; BE2.133). • **these (lying down or horizontal things gathered into a bundle or a sack that sits).** *káa įkšé* these things tied into a bundle.

kaabráze. V [reg. *kaa*-del., _*(kaa)bráze*] [*kaa-* INSTR + *bráze*] *(trans.)* **hit or punch (e.g., hit s.o. on the side of the head)** (03/07/95/FH/pc:prod orig); **tear.** *oðókanąąžį anąkaabrazé* I tore my pants (04/03/95/PM/pc:prod).

•• LFD 43: *kabráze* <ga-btha´-çe> to burst, or cause to rip open by falling, a sack of anything.

kaabráze (*continued*)
kabrázeaðe ha, ožuhake <ga-btha´-çe a-the ha, u-zhi ha ke> [expected Mod. Os. form: *oožuhaa kaabráze hpáaɣe*] I burst the sack.

kaací. v [reg. *kaa*-del., _*(kaa)cí*] *(trans.)* **wipe (any surface); remove some substance from a surface by wiping, raking, or shoveling; wipe clean (after using the toilet)** (RB; 05/01/95/LS/pc). *kaací!* wipe yourself! *áaci* I wipe. *ðáaci* you wipe. *kaací* he wipes. *ąkáaci* we wipe.

•• JOD (slip file): *kacü* <ḳaṭṣü> to wipe clean (under <ḳi´-ṭṣü> 'to wipe clean for another, to perform this act for a child, who can not do it himself').

•• LFD 44: *kací* <ga-dsi´> to hoe snow away from around the house. *áci* <a´-dsi> I hoed away the snow. *ðáci* <tha´-dsi> you hoed the snow. *ąkáci pe* <oⁿ-ga´-dsi i> we hoed the snow.

kaacíže. v [reg. *kaa*-del., _*(kaa)cíže*] *(trans.)* **scrape or push aside.** *niixoce kaacíža* push all the ashes aside (as in a peyote meeting) [imperative].

•• JOD (slip file): *kacíze* <ḳa-ṭṣi´-ṣe>.

kaacúxe (variant: **cúxe**). v [reg. *kaa*-del., _*(kaa)cúxe*] *(trans.)* **sweep** (01/09/95/FH/pc:prod). *hcíoka kaacúxe* sweep the room (BE2.130).

•• LFD 45: *kacúxe* <ga-dsu´-xe> to sweep with a broom; swept. *ácuxe* <a´-dsu-xe> I sweep. *ðácuxe* <tha´-dsu-xe> you sweep. *ąkácuxa pe* <oⁿ-ga´-dsu-xa i> we sweep. *hci che acuxe* <ṭsi tse a-dsu-xe> I swept the house.

kaacʔó. v [reg. *kaa*-del.?, _*(kaa)cʔó?*] *(intr.?)* **shave the head.**

•• LFD 48: *kacʔú* <ga tsʔu´> to shave the head; to make shavings from a stick.

kaaðée. v [conjug. unknown] *(trans.)* **pass or give away (e.g., the drum at *ilǫ́ǫ̱ška* dances).** *céɣenii kaaðée hta apai* they're going to pass the drum (RBn2-MOJ/p5; 01/31/95/FH/pc:ok).

kaaðéešpa. v [conjug. unknown] *(trans.)* **give away by pressing or pushing away (e.g., the *ilǫ́ǫ̱ška* drum).** *céɣenii kaaðéešpa hta apai* they're going to give the drum away; they're pressing or pushing the drum over there (to another person) (BE2.36; 04/25/95/PM/pc:ok).

kaaðó. ADV **over there.** *kaaðó hkíiche[ð]a* put it down over there (RBn10-15, unconfirmed).

káaɣe. v [sync. k>p, _*káaɣe*] *(trans.)* **make, fix, prepare, bake.** *hpáaɣe* I make. *škáaɣe* you make. *káaɣe* she makes. *ąkáaɣe* we make. *ónǫbre káaɣe* to fix food, fixing food. *mąhkása*

hpáaɣe I made coffee (02/24/95/FH/pc:ok). *háazunii tóe káaɣa* make some grape juice (02/24/95/FH/pc:ok). *wacúeskue wį káaɣa* go bake a cake (RBn10-12:JW). *óohǫ ðáalį káaɣapi ché* it was well prepared [cooked well] (RBn3-02). *xǫǫcéhu káaɣe hǫ́ǫpa* Christmas (lit., 'cedar tree preparation day'). *Arthur akxa Mongrain hpéɣe wį káaɣape* Arthur made Mongrain a gourd (RBn10-10:JW; LFD 128). • **build.** *hci káaɣe apai* they're building a house. *htą́wakáaɣe* Townbuilder (personal name). • **make or force s.o. (to do s.t.).** *Mary iihǫ́ akxa ðihípe htóožu toa oohǫ́ che Johna kʔú káaɣape* Mary's mother made her give John the meat pies that *ðixípe* [Robert Bristow] made (RBn; MREI/01/11/83). *óðohta káaɣa* make him behave (RBn22-19).

• **cause s.t. to be a certain way.** *hkihkǫ́ze ðáalį škáaɣe hącé* you made the peyote meeting [be] good last night (02/24/95/FH/pc:okc). *wižį́, waaðǫ́ ðáalį škáaɣe hącé* older brother, you made good songs last night (lit., 'you made the songs be good') (RBn1-40). *hci stáko škáaɣe* you straightened up your house (lit., 'you made the house neat'). • **turn on.** *káaɣa* turn it on (FH:bnbw-MOJ). *htaacéxowe káaɣa* turn the fan on (04/25/95/PM/pc:okc; BE2.43). • **do, perform, engage in.** *hǫ́ǫpa wį súhka tóoka ókʔą́ ékǫži káaɣe nąpe* sometimes the rooster did things he shouldn't do [unseemly things] (RBn18-01). • *(intr.)* **make it (in a card game).** *hpáaɣe mažíe* I didn't make it (RBn10-21/JW).

••• Cf. *kikáaɣe, kšíɣe.*

kaaɣú. v [conjug. unknown] *(trans.)* **brush.** *hpáxį kaaɣú* brush your hair [imperative] (FH).

kaahtáama. v [conjug. unknown] *(intr.)* **ring, make a ringing noise, ring like a bell** (RBn10-2:MOJ/79).

•• JOD (slip file): *kahtamą* <ḳa-ta-maⁿ> 'ring' (under <í-ḳa-ta-maⁿ>). *íkaahtamą hcéska nǫpʔį́ kšíðe, hkaamá mąðį́ apá* <iḳatamaⁿ tséska nŭⁿ´pʼiⁿ kcíȼĕ, kamaⁿ´ maⁿ´ȼiⁿ apa´> the cow being made to wear a bell on the neck, it rings as she walks (under <ka´-maⁿ> 'ring').

••• QU *dikáda* ring a bell [by] pulling the rope (RR); KS *mą́ązettąmą* bell (RR).

••• Cf. *íikaahtamą.*

kaahúuža (variants: **kahúža, kahúžą, kahúuža**). ADV, N **(for a) long time, for quite a while.** *kaahúuža aðáape* he's been gone a long time (02/22/95/FH/pc:prod orig; BE2.81). *kaahúuža íiwiðe mąži* I haven't seen you for a long time. *kaahúužą mą́žą ðéka omą́įpe* he lived on this earth a long time (RBn10-13:JW). • **a long time ago, long ago** (FH/8/30/94). *kaahúužą mą́žą ðéka omą́į apai* he lived on this earth a long time ago (RBn10-13:FH).

kaakǫ́ (variant: **káakǫ**). ADV **that way, thus with certainty, in this manner.** *kaakǫ́ kǫ́ða tą* that's the way he's going to do it; since he wants it this way; that's the way he wants it [contrast *haakǫ́ kóða tą* 'whatever he wants to do', *eekǫ́ kǫ́ða tą* 'what he wants to do'] (04/11/95/FH/pc:prod).
•• LFD 45: *kákǫ* <ga´-go^{n}> in this manner.
••• *KS gaagǫ́* thus, in that manner (RR).
••• Cf. *ékǫ, haakǫ́.*

káakǫ tą. ADVP **therefore, so, and then, whereupon** (RBn22-01), **when thus, when at last, when at that time.**
•• JOD (slip file): *káhkǫta* <ḳa´-kŭ^{n}-ṭa>.
•• LFD 45: *kákǫtą* <ga´-go^{n}-do^{n}> when this was done, or being done; therefore; then: from a ritual.
••• *KS gaagó(o)ǰedą* then, during that time, at last (RR).

kaakǫ́ną (variant: **kaakǫ́nąą** [HH]). N [*kaakǫ́* + *na* 'only'] **plenty, sufficient, enough (lit., 'only like this')** (108-b/FH/001). *kaakǫną́ą* that's plenty (e.g., of coffee) (FH). *kaakǫną́ą* that's enough (of an activity, such as making s.t.). • **end of an activity, final part of s.t.** *kaakǫ́ną ée ðe* that's all (RBn10-5:JW). *kaakǫną́e?* is that all? is that everybody? (01/04/95/FH/pc:prod). *kaakǫną́e ðe* that's all (the end of a story). *kaakǫną́ą* there's no more (e.g., food) (HH/t#38b-p3). *htaaníi kaakǫ́ną* the soup is gone, that's all there is (HH:prod). *htaaníi kaakǫ́ną* soup's all gone (04/26/95/LS/pc:ok). *kaakǫ́ną ée ðe* that's all (RBn10-5:JW).
•• LFD 45 (unconfirmed): *kakǫ́ ną škitą* <ga-go^{n}´ no^{n} shki-do^{n}> sufficient. *kakǫ́eðo* <ga-go^{n}´-e-tho> that is all (unconfirmed; 04/26/95/LS/pc:uk).
••• *KS gaago hną́* enough, that is all (RR).

kaakǫ́ną káaye. VP [sync. *k>p*, *kaakǫ́ną _káaye*] *(intr., trans.)* **make no more (of), do no more, stop there, cease an unnamed activity.** *htaaníi kaakǫ́ną káaya* don't make any more soup (04/26/95/LS/pc; t#38b-p4; HH). *kaakǫ́ną káaya* don't do that any more; put a stop to that (e.g., said to children if they are fighting) (04/26/95/LS/pc:ok; t#38b-pHH). *kaakǫną́ kaayá* don't do that anymore, make that the end, do it to there only (BE2.2).

kaalą́ðe (variant of **kaalǫ́ðe**).

kaaléke. V [reg. *kaa*-del, *_(kaa)léke* (1st sg. *aaléke*, 2nd sg. *ðaaléke*, 3rd sg. *kaaléke*, 1st pl. *ąkáaleke*); also conjugated as sync. *k>p*, *_kaaléke* (1st sg. *hpáaleke*, 2nd sg. *špáaleke*, 3rd sg. *kaaléke*)] *(trans.)* **shatter or break (e.g., glass), shatter by striking or by sudden movement, fracture (e.g., one's skull).** [Historically probably *kaaxléke*; modern speakers use *l* or occasionally slightly preaspirated [hl] in all forms based on *-léke*. Compare the LFD examples below.] *okáhąpa kaaléke ché* someone broke a window, that's the way it is (01/07/95/FH/pc:ok). *pée kaaléke?* who broke it? *šį́tožį apa okáhąpa kalékape* the boys broke the window (04/28/95/LS/pc:okc). *áa ðíhta kaaléke* they broke your arm (FH/pc). *hįįcé ąkáalekapé* we broke the dishes (MSB 02-24/25-83). *hįįcéžį wibriileke* I broke your dish (MREI 11-01-83-8). • *(intr.)* **shatter, fracture, crack, break, be broken.** *kaaléke* it breaks [as an eggshell does]. *kaalékepe* it's broken (RBn22-03; 01/07/95/FH/pc:ok).
•• LFD 49: *kaléke* <ga-xthe´ge> to crack something brittle like glass, china, or stone. *į́ xe che aléke ha* <i^{n}´ xe tse a-xthe´-ge ha> [expected modern Os. form: *įį che aaléke;* sentence-final *ha* is not used in Mod. Os.] I cracked the stones. *į́ xe ąkáleka pe* <i^{n}´ xe o^{n}-ga´-xthe-ga i> we cracked the stones.
••• Cf. *ðuuléke, kíleke, paaléke.*

kaalíiže (variant of **kaalįįže**).

kaalį́. V [uninfl.] *(trans.)* **lightning strikes.** *žą́ą kaalį́* the lightning struck a tree (RBn1-12, unconfirmed; 02/15/95/FH/pc:uk). • N **lightning strike.**
•• LFD 225: *žą́kali* <Zho^{n}´-ga-xthi> Tree-killer; personal name (refers to the lightning that strikes and kills the tree).

kaalįįže (variant: **kaalíiže**). N [*kaa-* INSTR + *lį́įže*] **sparks that are struck (as by hitting the "iron" against the flint to create sparks to make the sponge-like material from a tree catch fire)** (BE2.49; 01/26/95/FH/pc:prod). • N **flint used to make flint fire (for peyote meetings or sweat lodge)** (RB).

kaalǫ́ðe (variant: **kaalą́ðe**). V [conjug. unknown] *(intr.)* **travel, migrate, go on a hunting expedition** (FH:5/01/96/tape:uk).
•• JOD (slip file): *kalą́ðe* <ḳa-q¢a^{n}´ ¢e> to migrate, to go on a hunting expedition with many or all of the tribe, to go with a large party, each man taking his household.
•• LFD 49: *kalǫ́ðe* <ga-xtho^{n}´-the> to migrate; to go on a hunting expedition.

kaalǫ́ðį. v [reg. *kaa*-del., *_(kaa)lǫ́ðį*] [*kaa-* INSTR + *lǫ́ðį*] *(trans.)* **knock s.o. out.**

•• LFD 45: *kalǫ́ðį* <ga-gthoⁿ´-thiⁿ> to knock a person senseless. *álǫðį* <a´-gthoⁿ-thiⁿ> I knocked him senseless. *ðálǫðį* <tha´-gthoⁿ-thiⁿ> you knocked him senseless. *ąkálǫðį pe* <oⁿ-ga´-gthoⁿ-thiⁿ i> we knocked him senseless.

kaamą́šąšie (variants: **kaamáši, kaamášiši**). v, ADJ [conjug. unknown] *(intr.)* **bounce up, (be) bouncy (as in a rough ride in a car or wagon)** (BE2.10; 01/07/95/FH/pc:prod).

•• LFD 46: *kamą́* <ga-moⁿ´> feathery (down).

káaną. ADV, PPN **this much, just right, just the right amount, only this much.** *káaną ahí akxai* just a little bit [showing with hand] and it'll be here (referring to sunup) (FH/09/24/01/prod).

••• Cf. *éena, háaną.*

kaaníeži. v [reg. *kaa*-del., *_(kaa)níeži*] [*kaa-* INSTR + *ónie* 'breathe' +*aží* NEG] *(trans.)* **knock s.o. out, hit s.o. in a way that shakes him/her up badly** (02/14/95/FH/pc:okc; RBnot 5/3/79/p2,corr'd). [Implies a less strong impact than *káasaaki.*] *ðáanieži* you knocked him out (02/14/95/FH/pc). *áanieži* I knocked him out (02/14/95/FH/pc). *ą́kaanieži* we knocked him out (02/14/95/FH/pc).

kaapáacʔį v [reg.? *kaa*-del.?, *_(kaa)páacʔį*] *(intr.)* **bend over (as when placing one's hands on the floor from a standing position or bending over a table for a medical examination)** (PM, unconfirmed). [PM's intransitive gloss is unexpected; a more expected meaning would be 'cause s.o. to bend over by pushing suddenly'.]

•• LFD 42: *kapácʔį* <ga-ba´-ts´iⁿ> to strike a blow and cause one to bow his head.

káapše (variant: **kaapšé**). v [reg. *kaa*-del.?, *_(káa)pše*?] *(trans.)* **brush or comb (one's hair), curry (an animal's coat)** (04/20/95/LS/pc:okc). *hpáxį kaapšé* brush or dress one's hair (01/09/95/FH/pc:prod: aa). *hkáwa káapše* brush the horse. *hpáxį káapša!* brush your hair! (01/09/95/FH/pc:ok) *hpáxį kaapšé* comb your hair (FH:04/17/96). *káapša!* brush it/comb it! (FH/11/19/01/pc:prod).

••• Cf. *kípše, wékaapše.*

kaapxóhke. v [reg. *kaa*-del., *_(kaa)pxóhke*] *(trans.)* **burst, explode, pop (e.g., a balloon); hit s.o. on the back, knocking the wind out; stun, crash** (03/10/95/FH/pc:okc). *áapxohke* I burst it (03/10/95/FH/pc).

•• LFD 46: *kapxóhkiąhe* <ga-po´-ḳi-oⁿ-he> to crash with a blow. *ápxohkiąhe* <a´-po-ḳi-oⁿ-he> I crashed it with a blow. LFD 129: *hpohkié* <p̣o-ḳi-e´> [possibly erroneous for *pxohkie* or *pxohke*] a sound like the report of a gun or a popgun.

••• Cf. *niikáapxohke.*

káasaaki. v [reg. *kaa*-del., *_(káa)saaki*] *(trans.)* **knock out, hit hard, hit with a stunning blow, stun** (FH/pc). *ásaaki* I give a stunning blow. *ðásaaki* you give a stunning blow. *ąkáasai* we give a stunning blow. *káasaakipe* he knocked him out (BE2.74; 02/14/95/FH/pc:okc).

•• LFD 43: *kasáki* <ga-ça´-gi> to give a stunning blow; to knock down; to thrash or kill; to stun.

kaascú. v [reg. *kaa*-del.?, *_(kaa)scú?*] *(trans.)* **slice, slit, punch through.**

••• Cf. *wacúe kaascú.*

kaasé (variant: **káase**). v [reg. *kaa*-ret., *_kaasé*; or reg. *kaa*-del., *_(kaa)sé*] [*kaa-* INSTR + *-se*] *(trans.)* **chop or cut with a striking blow (e.g., from a blade, such as an axe or knife); cut with a lawnmower, chop up (e.g., long, thin sticks of wood for a fire); chop down (not by sawing).** [It is not clear that all translations are equally appropriate for both the *kaa*-ret. and *kaa*-del. conjugations of this verb. 'Cut with a lawnmower' and 'chop up' seem to be attested only for the *kaa*-ret. variant, 'chop down' only for the *kaa*-del. variant.] Examples of *kaa*-ret. forms: *ákaase* I chop. *ðákaase* you chop. *káase* she chops. *ąkáase* we chop. *mąąhí kaasé hta apai* they're going to cut grass (FH/11/17/01/pc:prod). *žą́ą kaasé brée hta mįkšé* I'm going to go cut wood (01/14/95/FH/pc:okc). *wéewinai, mąąhí wíhta ðákaase* thank you for cutting my grass (01/14/95/FH/pc:prod; BE2.28). *žą́ą ðákaase hta ðąįšé?* are you going to cut down the trees [with an axe]? (FH/06/16/01/pc). *mąąhíįspe ðuuzái žą́a tóe ąkáase ąkái hce* get the axe and let's [us two] go cut some wood (01/14/95/FH/pc:prod). *ąkáase hta ąkatxą́i* we're going to chop/cut (FH/06/16/01/pc). *žąąkáase* cut wood, engage in woodcutting (RBn10-16; 03/02/95/FH/pc:ok). *htáa ðákaase hta ðąįšé?* are you going to chop the meat? (FH/06/16/01/pc). Examples of *kaa*-del. forms: *áase, aasé* I chop. *ðáase, ðaasé* you chop. *kaasé* he chops. *ąkáase* we chop (01/09/95/FH/pc:prod). *žą́ą áase* I chop wood (03/02/95/FH/pc:okc). *žą́ą ðáase* you chop wood (03/02/95/FH/pc:okc). *žą́ą káase* chopping wood (MSB:t9).

•• RB: <káh-séh>.

•• LFD 248: *kasé* <ga-çe´> to cut with a striking blow. *žą áse* <zhoⁿ a´-çe> I chop wood.

žą ðáse <zho^{n} tha´-çe> you chop wood. LFD 225: *žąkáse* <zho^{n}-ga´-çe> to chop wood. *žą ąkása pe* <zho^{n} o^{n}-ga´-ça i> we chop wood. LFD 43: *kase* <ga-çe> to cut by a striking blow ['by sudden action' (as in haircutting, mowing grass) rather than 'by a striking blow' (01/14/95/FH/pc: not with a striking blow)]. *įcé ðą ðase le ha* <i^{n}-dse´ tho^{n} tha-çe gthe ha> [sentence-final *ha* is not used in Mod. Os.] you cut his face [*ðǫ* is not used in Mod. Os.; *le he* is unknown; and *kaasé* is not used for cutting someone's face (01/14/95/FH/pc:uk: not someone's face)].

kaasį́ (variants: **kaasį́e, kaasį́ta, kaasį́tą**). ADV, N **tomorrow.** *kasį́ táatą hta paašé?* what are you [pl.] doing tomorrow? (03/23/95/FH/pc:okc; BE2.142).

•• RB: <kah-sí^{n}-eh> (03/23/95/FH/pc:ok).

•• LFD 441: *kasą́į tą* <ga-ço^{n}´-i^{n} do^{n}> [expected Mod. Os. form: *kasį́, kasį́tą*] tomorrow; some time; the morrow; dawn of another day (unconfirmed; 03/23/95/FH/pc:no).

kaasį́ kootáha (variant: **kaasį́ kootáha ce**). ADVP, N **day after tomorrow** (BE2.30; 01/09/95/FH/pc:prod:ok with or without *ce*).

kaasį́ wanǫ́bre (variant of **kaasį́exci wanǫ́bre**).

kaasį́ce. V [reg. *kaa*-ret., _ *kaasį́ce*] *(trans.)* **close, slam, close suddenly or by striking** (HRE/12/29/01/pc: *į* not *įį*). *ákasįce* I slam. *ðákasįce* you slam. *ąkasįce* we slam.

••• Cf. *ákaasįce.*

kaasį́e (variant of **kaasį́**).

kaasį́exci (variants: **kaasį́excį, kaasį́xci**). ADV, N **(in the) early morning, morning, this morning.** (RBn3-MOJ/p12, LH tape). *kasį́excį wažį́ka apa hóohtą nąpé* the birds sing early in the morning (02/25/95/FH/pc:ok). *kasį́excį mį́į ątǫ́pe htái* let's go see the morning sun coming up (as in a meeting) (BE2.129; 01/14/95/FH/pc). *kasį́xci htáabre pšíe* this morning I went hunting (FH).

•• LFD 44: *kasǫ́įxci* <ga-ço^{n}´-i^{n}-xtsi> early morning.

••• Cf. *kasį́excįžį.*

kaasį́exci ónǫbre. N **cereal, breakfast food** (01/09/95/FH/pc:ok). [A new coinage.]

kaasį́exci wanǫ́bre (variant: **kaasį́ wanǫ́bre**). N **breakfast** (01/14/95/FH/pc:ok). *kasį́ wanǫ́bre aðį́žipe* he didn't have breakfast [to offer us] (BE2.12).

•• LFD 44: *kasąį xci wanǫbre* <ga-ço^{n}-i^{n} xtsi wa-no^{n}-bthc> carly morning meal; breakfast.

kaasį́excį (variant of **kaasį́exci**).

kaasį́excįžį. N, ADV [*kaasį́exci* + *-žį* 'little'] **(in the) very early morning, very early in the morning** (RBn3-MOJ/p12, LH tape; BE2.38; 12/30/94/FH/pc:prod). *kasį́excižį* very early in the morning (BE2.38; 12/30/94/FH/pc:prod).

•• LFD 44: *kasǫ́į xci žį́ka* <ga-ço^{n}´-i^{n} xtsi zhi^{n}-ga> early in the morning; when the morning is young or little. *kasą́į xci wažį́ka apa hothą šna pi a* <ga-ço^{n}´-i^{n} xtsi wa-zhi^{n}-ga a-ba hu-to^{n} shna bi a> [*shna* is probably Omaha (expected Mod. Os. form is *štą*); Mod. Os. form of *pi a* is *pe*] the birds sing early in the morning.

kaasį́ta, kaasį́tą (variants of **kaasį́**).

kaasį́xci (variant of **kaasį́exci**).

kaaskí. V [reg. *kaa*-del., _*(kaa)skí*] *(trans.)* **compress, gather up or wad together with a sudden movement, pinch off (as in making balls out of cornmeal for cornmeal dumplings), grab** (FH:4/18/96:pc).

•• LFD 47: *kaðíski* <ga-thi´-çki> gathering together corn or wheat.

••• Cf. *ðiiskí, hkilíiski, pahúkaaski.*

kaaskíke (variant: **kaaškíke**). V, ADJ [stat. *kaa*-del, _*(kaa)skíke*, some variation between *ði-* and *ða-* for 2nd person] [*kaa-* INSTR + *skíke*] **(be) tired, worn out, exhausted.** *ą́skike* I'm tired. *ðískike* you're tired. *káaskike* he's tired. *wáaskike* we're tired. *wálį ą́skike mįkšé* I'm really tired (03/22/95/FH/pc:ok). *ą́škike* I'm tired, I'm worn out (FH/tape 108-b; 04/26/95/FH/pc; RBn1-40). *ą́skike ąškáaɣape* you [pl.] make me tired. *aðískike nįkšé?* are you tired? [*a-* is unexpected in 2nd person; may be a false start] (FH). *kaaskíke tǫ́pewai nįkše* you look tired. *kaaskíke ðą́įše?* are you tired? *Johna akxa kaaskíke akxái* John is tired (03/22/95/FH/pc:prod). *kaaškíke akxái* he's tired (04/26/95/FH/pc). *kaaskíke akxa* he's tired (BE2.141; CQc). *waaskíke apái, kaaskíke apái* they're tired (04/26/95/FH/pc:ok both). *wáaskike ąðįkše* we [two] are tired (03/22/95/FH/pc:ok). *ą́ąskike ąðįkšé* we [sitting] are tired [unexpected 1st dual form; the expected 1st dual or 1st pl. verb form is stative *wáskike* or *wáaskike*].

•• LFD 43: *kaaskíke* <ga-çki´-ge> tedious; wearisome; lassitude; fatigue; to be weary; exhausted (03/22/95/FH/pc:ok). *ąáskike* <o^{n}-a´-çki-ge> I am weary (from running). *ðiáskike* <thi-a´-çki-ge> you are weary (from running). *waskika pe* <wa-çki-ga i> we are weary (from running).

kaašéną. V, ADJ [reg. *kaa*-del., _*(kaa)šéną*] *(intr.)* **(be) ended, finished, that's all, s.t. (e.g., soup, coffee) is finished (i.e., ready)** (HH). *aašéna na*

kaašéną (*continued*) that's enough, I'm through (HRE/12/29/01/pc). *γaaké kaašéna* don't cry (ERE prod: CQc). *mą́hkasa kaašénąą* don't make any more coffee (T38b-p4; HH, T38b-p3; 04/26/95/LS/pc:ok). *mą́hkasa kaašéną káaγa* don't make any more coffee (HH:prod). *wacúe kaašéną káaγa* don't make any more bread (HH/t38b-p3). • N **closing of a prayer, amen.** *kaašéna* amen, the end (of a prayer) (FH). *íe kaašéną ékipše* this prayer ends now, I have spoken (JS prayer).

•• LFD 46: *kašé* <ga-she´> to force one to abandon his property [unconfirmed]. *áše* <a´-she> I forced him to abandon his property.

••• Cf. *kaakǫ́ną.*

káaši. V [uninfl.] *(intr.)* **be long.** *hǫpa akxa káaši akxái* the days are longer now (RBn2-MOJ/p40; 02/22/95/FH/pc:uk). *hąą káaši ðáha achípe* they came late at night (lit., 'the night was long when they arrived here'). • ADV **for a long time.** *káaši lį́įpe* he sat a long time. *wéhice hí áape hcí káaγe káaši ðí áape* she went a long way and took a long time to build her nest [they said] (RBn19-03). *káaši wáli ąwáachipe, ąðíištą htái* we've danced a long time, let's stop (02/22/95/FH/pc:ok; BE2.81). • N **a long time (which has passed).** *káaši ðachíe* here you are already! (lit., 'so long a time has passed!') (FH/pc; BE2.75).

•• LFD 230: *hkáši* <ḳa´-shi> [expected Mod. Os. form: <ka´-shi>, with plain *k*] long ago.

••• *KS gaší* long time ago; for a long time (RR), *gašídą* long time ago [may have long *aa*] (RR).

••• Cf. *kaahúuža, kaašǫ́ka.*

káaškíke (variant of **kaaskíke**).

kaašǫ́ (variants: **kaašǫ́e, kaašǫ́we**). N **enough (of some activity), final point, end (e.g., of one's earthly existence)** (HH; 04/26/95/LS/pc). *kaašǫ́ káaγe* make that the end, stop! put an end to something, stop some activity (04/26/95/LS/pc:okc).

•• LFD 47: *kašǫ́* <ga-sho^{n}´> it is enough; sufficient.

kaašǫ́ káaγe. VP [sync. *k*>*p*, *kaašǫ́ _káaγe*] *(intr.)* **cease, stop (lit., 'make it the final point').** *kaašǫ́ waðíhtą škáaγe* you stopped work; you made the work stop (04/26/95/LS/pc). • **reach a point of sufficiency, produce enough of s.t.** (04/26/95/LS/pc).

•• LFD 47: *kašǫ́ hpaγe* <ga-sho^{n}´ p̣a-xe> I stopped work. *kašǫ́ ą́kaγa pe* <ga-sho^{n}´ o^{n}´-ga-xa i> we stopped work [definition makes no specific mention of 'work'].

kaašǫ́e. ADV **always.** *kaašó ðáalį* good for all time (RBn10-15).

kaašǫ́e (variant of **kaašǫ́** and **kaašǫ́eðe**).

kaašǫ́e che. VP [uninfl.] **leave it alone, let it alone, just let it sit, let it be (standing sg. item or construct)** (04/26/95/FH/pc:okc). *ó?ie che kaašǫ́e che* [let's] leave the problem alone (04/26/95/FH/pc).

kaašǫ́eðe (variants: **kaašǫ́iðe, kaašǫ́e**). INTERJ **good-bye, farewell (more literally, 'that's all', 'it's over with'; to a dead person)** (BE2.59; FH/11/19/01/tape); **exclamation acknowledging the end of earthly living, the final event in life** (HH; BE2.59). [Some speakers only use this expression in bidding farewell to a dead person; others use it in other circumstances, e.g., saying good-bye at the airport (RB).] *kaašǫe, wihtą́ke, kaašǫeðe* good-bye, sister, good-bye (02/15/95/FH/pc:ok) *há, kaašǫ́įðé* well now, this is it.

•• RB: <háh-káh-shó^{n}-i-théh> (02/03/95/FH/pc:okc).

••• Cf. *kaašéną, kaašǫ́ka.*

kaašǫ́įke. INTERJ **good-bye, the end, the final event, nothing more** (HH). *kaašǫ́įke* that's all, the end, this is it, final event; good-bye; that's the end of earthly living, it's over (HH).

••• Cf. *kaašǫ́.*

kaašǫ́ka. INTERJ **(it's) sufficient, basta, (it's) enough.**

kaašǫ́we (variant of **kaašǫ́**).

kaaštá. V [reg. *kaa*-del *_(kaaštá)*] *(trans.)* **hammer, hit or beat (e.g., a drum), flatten by striking.**

•• LFD 44: *kastá* <ga-çta´> to beat or hammer metal.

kaaštą́. V [conjug. unknown] *(trans.)* **end, stop an activity, put an end to s.t., cease** (LS). *wacúe káaγe kaaštą́* don't make any more bread (04/07/95/LS/pc:okc). *wacúe káaγa kaaštá* stop, don't make any more bread (HH:prod). • INTERJ **stop, that's the end, there is no more** (HH).

••• *KS büštą́* stop, cease rubbing, pressing (RR).

••• Cf. *ðaaštą́, ðiištą́.*

káataace. V [reg.? *kaa*-del.?, *_(káa)taace?*] *(intr.)* **stick, get stuck** (RB). *oðíhtą akxa káataace akxai* the car is stuck (RBn23-14).

••• *KS dáǰe* stuck in the mud, mired (RR), *gadáǰe* stuck in the mud, to get mired (RR).

kaatxá, kaatxą́ (variants of **katxą́**).

káawįye. v *(intr.)* **soar, as an eagle.** *xúða apa káawįye nąpe* the eagle soars (LFD 218; CQc).

káaxa. v [reg. *kaa*-del., *_(káa)xa* (inflection is irregular in that *ka* seems to be retained in 3rd pl. *káaxa*)] *(trans.)* **beat s.o. in a race** (RBnotes). *ą́xape* he beat me (in a race). *ðiáxape* he beat you (in a race). *wiáxae* I beat you (in a race). *ðáaxae* you beat him (in a race). *aawáxae* I beat them (in a race). *ąąwą́xa ąðe* we [two] beat them (in a race) (2-10-83-p5). *áaxa* I beat him. *ðáaxa* you beat him. *áxa* ~ *xa* he beat him. *káaxa* they beat him.

•• LFD 48: *kaxá* <ga-xa´> to excel; outrun; outstrip; to outdistance. *áxa* <a´-xa> I excel. *ðáxa* <tha´-xa> you outstripped him. *ąkáxape* <o^{n}-ga´-xa i> we outran him.

••• *KS wáxa* [from *wa* + *gaxa*] 'beat, surpass them' (JOD, RR).

••• Cf. *wakáaxa.*

kaaxíye (variant of **kaaxúye**).

kaaxǫ́. v [reg. *kaa*-del., *_(kaa)xǫ́*] [*kaa*- INSTR + *xǫ́*] *(trans.)* **break off, break by striking (a long object, such as a stick).** *oðópše kaaxǫ́pe* he broke the cradle board (04/19/95/FH/pc; 04/19/95/FH/pc). *htáhu kaaxǫ́ áape* they said he broke his neck (01/09/95/FH/pc:ok; CQ:okc). *áaxǫ* I break it (e.g., the leg from a small horse statue). *ðáaxǫ* you break it. *ąkáaxǫpe* we break it. • *(intr.)* **be broken (when used with continuative auxiliary *akxa* or *apa*).** *hų́üni wíhta akxa kaaxǫ́ akxai* my garter is broken (RBn12-05).

•• JOD (slip file): *kaxǫ́* <ķa-qü^{n}´> to break, as a nail, ear of corn, stick, etc., without breaking it entirely in two; to break or be broken by falling.

kaaxúye (variants: **kaaxúya, kaaxíye**). v [conjug. unknown] *(trans.)* **split, split open, crack or splinter by sudden impact** (RBn; HRE at WHM981022).

•• JOD (slip file): *kaxúye* <ķa-qŭ-xe> to break, as any small or thin object, requiring little force.

•• LFD 48 (unconfirmed): *kaxíye* <ga-xi´-xe> to break or crack hard substance like corn, nuts, etc., by striking.

kaazą́ (variants: **káazą**). v [reg. *kaa*-del., *_(kaa)zą́*] *(trans.)* **scold, reprimand, chastise, censure, bawl out** (RBn12-06; 03/08/95/MREI/pc:ok). *áazą* I scold. *ðáazą* you scold. *kaazą́* she scolds. *ąkáažą* we scold. *záani awáazą* I scolded them all (RB). *wiizą́ hta mįkšé* I'm going to bawl you out (RBn HW). *kaazą́pi okíce apai* she is looking for a scolding (03/08/95/MREI/pc:ok; 01/06/95/FH/pc:okc; RBn2-MOJ/p6). *ą́ąząpe* they scolded me (RB). *ðíizą hta apai* they're going to bawl you out, they're going to scold you (RBn HW; CQc). *wáli wáaząpe* they bawled us out, they really scolded us (RBn HW). *kóoci wáaząpe* a long time ago they bawled us out. *kaazą́ži nǫ́ąðape* I was raised without being scolded (i.e., was given favored treatment) (RB). *žįkáži ąkáazą štą* we boss the kids around all the time (FH:prod). *kaazą́ ði* scold him, bawl him out (03/08/95/MREI/pc:okc; BE2.117). *oðáhkie tą káazą, taašéða!* when you tell him, bawl him out, get after him! (FH:98/pc). *ą́ązą įká* don't scold me (FH).

•• LFD 43: *kazą́* <ga-ço^{n}´> censure; abuse; reprimand; to scold. *ázą* <a´-ço^{n}> I scold or censure. *ðázą* <tha´-ço^{n}> you scold or censure. *ąkázą pe* <o^{n}ga´-ço^{n} i> we scold or abuse.

kaazą́zą. v [reg. *kaa*-del., *_(kaa)zą́zą*] [reduplicated form of *kaazą́*] **scold over and over, keep on scolding.**

kaaží (variant: **kaažį́**). v [reg. *kaa*-ret., *_kaaží*] *(trans.)* **drive (a vehicle), herd (animals)** (01/20/95/PM/pc:ok). *oðíhtą akáaži hta mįkšé* I'll drive the car. *ðíe kaaží!* you drive! *ðákaaži* [contrastive accent on *ða*-; expected form would be *ðakáaži*] you're driving. *oðíhtą ąkáaži* drive the car for me. *hkáwa wakáaži* driving horses. • **make or force s.o. to do s.t., command s.o. to do s.t.** *šáake lúuže wákaaži* [*wakáaži* 'make them' would be expected rather than *wákaaži*; accent shift due to imperative?] make them wash their hands (RBn3-13). • **blow with force (as in blowing one's nose).** *hpá kaažį́* blow your nose (RBn12-09).

•• LFD 49: *kažį́* <ga-zhi^{n}´> to drive a team of horses or an automobile. *hkawa ðąkxa awakažį alį hta mįkše ha* <ķa-wa tho^{n}-ka a-wa-ga-zhi^{n} a-gthi^{n} ţa mi^{n}-ke ha> [Mod. Osage: *hkáwa pa áwakaaži alí hta mįkšé* 'I'll return home driving the horses'; sentence-final *ha* is not used in Mod. Os.] I can drive the horses home. *hkawa ðąkxa waðakažį ðalį htathe ha* <ķa-wa tho^{n}-ka wa-tha-ga-zhi^{n} tha-gthi^{n} ţa-te ha> [Mod. Osage: *hkáwa pa waðákaaži ðalí hta ðaįšé* 'you will return home driving the horses'; sentence-final *ha* is not used in Mod. Os.] you can drive the horses home.

••• Cf. *ákaaži, kíži, wakáaži.*

kaðǫ́. CONJ **then, and then, and next, and then immediately, and right away.** *kaðǫ háakǫ?* and then what happened? (RBn19-04). * oąhkie šǫ́ akxa kaðǫ waðílą ðúeži hįį naažípe* he was

kaðǫ́ (*continued*) talking to me, then all of a sudden he changed his mind. *awą́hkie šǫ́ akxa kaðǫ ɣaaké ahípe* he was talking to me, then suddenly he started to cry. • **and.** *táatą žáži aščį́e kaðǫ hówaįkiha ðachíe?* what is your name and where did you come from? (RBn17-p1; HRE/01/17/02/pc/okc; w/*ha*). *įlǫ́aže kaðó šǫ́ke niižú akxai* it's raining cats and dogs (RBn). • ADV **here next to.** *žúuce, ska kaðǫ́ htóho* red, white, and blue.

••• *KS ga* and (introduces a sentence) (RR), *gayó, gayǫ́* and (RR).

••• Cf. *kóe.*

kahą́naže. ADV **for several days.** *kahą́naže owíce ąhé* I've been looking for you [for] several days (03/09/95/MREI/pc:okc; BE2.119).

•• RB: <kah-háh-nah-zhah^n>.

kahíke (variant: **kahíka**). N **chief.** *kahíke owátxą* assistant chief (01/14/95/FH/pc). *kahíke okxą́* assistant [lit., 'next'] chief (01/09/95/FH/pc:ok; BE2.18). *áhkita kahíke* chief of the soldiers (03/02/95/FH/pc:ok). *šǫmį́hka kahíke mą́ze wanǫ́pʔį wį kʔúpi áape* they gave the Pope [lit., 'Catholic chief'] a medal, they say (02/01/95/FH/pc:ok).

•• LFD 11: *kahíke* <ga-hi´-ge> the great one; the chief. *áhkita kahike* <a´-ḳi-da ga-hi-ge> captain. Also used as a personal name by the Osage and Omaha tribes. LFD 45: *kahíkenąžį* <Ga-hi´-ge-no^n-zhi^n> Standing-chief (personal name; so named on account of position of the chief, permanent, chosen to represent a division). *kahíkexci* <Ga-hi´-ge-xtsi> Real-chief (personal name). *kahikežįka* <Ga-hi-ge-zhi^n-ga> Young-chief (personal name). *kahíketxą* <Ga-hi´-ge-to^n> Standing-chief (personal name).

kahíke okxą́ (variant of **kahíke otxą́**).

kahíke ókʔą. N **assistant chief** (FH).

kahíke otxą́ (variants: **kahíke okxą́, kahíke otkxą́**). N **assistant chief** (01/06/95/FH/pc:ok; HRE/01/17/02/pc:ok; RBn2-MOJ/p19).

•• LFD 45: *kakíke owátxą* <ga-gi´-ge u-wa´-to^n> the second chief.

••• Cf. *ótxątxą.*

kahką́. V [reg. *ka*-ret.?, *_kahką́*] *(trans.)* **fan or fan off s.o.** *ą́kahkąpi* you [pl.] fan me off (PM).

•• LFD 46: *kahką́* <ga-ḳo^n´> to shake a rug or blanket.

••• *QU ákakxą* powder, sprinkle on (RR); *KS gakhą́* to shake something, to shake off something (RR). [RR claims that the QU and KS forms are not cognate with the Mod. Os. form.]

••• Cf. *kíhką.*

kahúuža, kahúža, kahúžą (variants of **kaahúuža**).

kakšį́ce (variant: **kakšį́ze**) V [reg. *ka*-del., *_(ka)kšį́ce*] *(trans.)* **miss (a target), miss out on (e.g., a dinner) by arriving late.** *akšį́ce* I miss it. *ðakšį́ce* you miss it. *kakšį́ce* she misses it. *ąkšį́ce* we [two] miss it [expected Mod. Os. 1st dual form is *ąkákšįce*] (FH:05/03/95). *ákšįce* I missed it (MSB-3-10-83-D). *ðákšįce* you missed it (MSB-3-10-83-D). *kakšį́tape* he missed it (MSB-3-10-83-D). *ąkákšįce* we [two] missed it (MSB-3-10-83-D).

••• Cf. *ðikšį́ce.*

kalǫ́eže. N **horned toad.** [Old-time Osages used to make 'woman catchers' from the skin stuffed with medicine (RB).]

•• RB: <káh-ló^n-eh-zhi^n> (02/09/95/FH/pc:okc; BE2.67).

kasǫ́ci. V [reg. *kaa*-del., *_(ka)sǫ́ci*] *(trans.)* **test s.o., try s.o. out** (3-3-83-p1). *ásǫci ąhé* I'm testing her out. *ðásǫci ðaašé* you're testing her out. *kasǫ́ci akxai* he's testing him out.

••• Cf. *áhkiasąci, ásąci, opásące.*

kašíni. N **shinny (a team ballgame played on a field with a buckskin ball, sticks, and goals at the opposite ends of the field).**

••• Cf. *ohkíce.*

kašké. V [reg. *ka*-del., *_(ka)šké*] *(trans.)* **tie up or together (e.g., shoelaces).** [Expected but unattested inflectional forms: 1st sg. *áaške* 'I tied his shoe', 2nd sg. *ðáaške* 'you tied his shoe', 3rd sg. *kašké* 'he tied her shoe', 1st pl. *ąkáške* 'we tied his shoe'.] *hpáažį akxai hǫǫpé kaškí akxai* the baby ties his shoes (FH:5/01/96/tape:prod). *hǫǫpé ą́ąške* tie my shoe! (03/22/95/FH/pc:ok). *hǫǫpé ąðáške škǫ́šta?* do you want to tie my shoe? (FH/t116b). *káške* tie it (FH: prod).

••• Cf. *ákaške, oðáške, okáške.*

kašpé. N **bit, portion (of any item); twelve and a half cents.**

kašpéǫpa (variant: **kašpé ðǫǫpá**). N [*kašpé* + *ðǫǫpá*] **quarter (25-cent coin; lit., 'two bits')** (04/11/95/LS/pc:okc; t14a-p1b/14, t44). *kašpéǫpa hta akxai* it will be a quarter (lit., 'it will be two bits' [noun is used as verb]; a phrase said by seller to ask for his money) (BE2.110). *kašpéǫpa oolą́* put your 25 cents in.

•• LFD 47: *kašpé ðǫpa* <ga-shpe´ tho^n-ba> two bits; 25 cents.

kašúpe. V [reg. *ka*-del., *_(ka)šúpe*] *(trans.)* **pay (a debt), pay for (a purchase).** [Used to describe the ceremony of paying for the drum at the Osage

War Dances.] *ášupe* I paid for it. *ðášupe* you paid for it. *kašúpape* she paid for it. *ąkášupape* we [pl.] paid for it. *ášupe* I'll pay for it (FH:prod, 2/97). *weúuze htą ášupe hta míkše* I'm going to pay this big debt (03/06/95/FH/pc:prod). *ąkašupepi na* he paid me for it (MSB). *ąðášupe na* you paid me for it. *kašúpapi!* pay for it [pl. addressee]!

•• LFD 46 (unconfirmed): *kašípe* <ga-shi´-be> to pay a debt [not ***kašípe*, but *kašúpe* (FH)].

••• Cf. *kíšupe*.

katxą́ (variants: **katxá, kaatxá, kaatxą́**). ADV, N **while, meanwhile, awhile, for a while, after a while, a little while.** *katxá*! stop! wait! [i.e., 'pause or suspend an activity']. *katxá ąpánaa htai* let's stop for a while (RBn3-27) *katxá, íe akxa* wait, he is speaking; wait, they are speaking (03/16/95/JS/pc:ok; also3p; BE2.150).

•• JOD (slip file): *kaḳxą́* <ḳa-kqaⁿ´> that far; awhile (subdialect).

••• *KS gakhą́* awhile, for a time (RR).

káxa (variants: **káxe, kaxé**). N **creek, branch (e.g., of a stream or brook)** (RBn1-MOJ/p13; 04/07/95/LS/pc:ok). [This term was used for 'creek' by some older Osage speakers in Oklahoma in the 1990s. The variant forms with final *e* are unexpected.] *káxa akxa okű́hpu akxa* the creek is full (RBn10-6:JW). *kaxé akxa okű́hpü akxai* the creek is full (flooded) (RB; 04/26/95/LS/pc:ok; FH/09/21/01/pc:ok). • **branch of a tree, limb.**

•• JOD: *kaxá* <ḳa-qa´> a limb, bough, or branch of a tree; a branch of a stream, a stream of water, a creek or river.

••• *KS gaxáhį ga* creek, small, branch, fork (RR).

••• Cf. *žą́ą káxa*.

káxa žį (variants: **kaxáži, kaxážį, káxe žį**). NP **branch, small creek or stream** (03/14/95/MREI/pc:ok; FH:ok; RBn1-MOJ/p13; RBn10-21/JW&FW/77). [This term was used for 'creek' by some older Osage speakers in Oklahoma in the 1990s.]

•• LFD 48: *kaxá žįka* <ga-xa´ zhiⁿ-ga> small limbs of a tree; a little branch or runlet. *kaxá* <ga-xa´> a branch; a creek. *kaxa žįka kše žoáhe* <ga-xa zhiⁿ-ga ke zhu-a´-he> [expected Mod. Os. form: *káxa žį kše žóapše*] I waded across the creek. *kaxáhtąka* <Ga-xa´-ṭoⁿ-ga> Big Branch; Big Pawnee, Oklahoma.

kaxé, káxe (variants of **káxa**).

kažą́si. N **unmarried person, maiden** (JOD). [It is not clear whether this word was used only of women, or of either men or women.]

••• *KS gažą́si* virgin, unmarried person (RR).

ke. POSIT **positional article for dispersed, scattered, or randomly located entities (modifies noun or noun phrase).** *haaská wasúhužike paahípai, ščúuwasu htai* be sorting the [scattered] dirty clothes, let's you wash them (i.e., 'how about you [pl.] wash them?') (FH/11/17/01/pc). *táatą ðéke hǫ́ǫžike* these bad things [scattered around]. *ošcéke* remainders or leftovers that are scattered around. *haxį́ke opétkxą* wrap up those blankets [lying around haphazardly, not stacked neatly] (03/22/95/FH/pc). *waažį́kake wáðaawa* count the [scattered] birds. *hǫ́ǫžįke* these bad things around. *haxį́ hkǫ́bra ke ðíe ðikˀu apai* the blankets [lying around] that I want are the ones she gave you (3-2-209). • SUFFIX **around, in dispersed locations or with dispersing action.** *táatą hpíižį ecíke tą* if there are bad things around. *ecíke* be around, exist around. *ną́ye ðaaxǫ́ke šǫ akxai hii ðiixǫ́kape* while he was chewing ice, he broke his tooth. *hǫbrį́ke che hpaahíke* I sorted the beans (FH).

•• LFD 175: *oscéke* <u-stse´-ge> [expected Mod. Os. form: *ošcé* 'remainder' + *ke* 'scattered'] the rest that are scattered about.

ki. PPN **in, into, at, on.** *htaacé ki waachí eeškítą kíhǫǫpe* he also liked the way they danced in the wind (RBn15-02). *waachí ki* to the dance. *htą́wą ki oálįį* I live in town (03/23/95/FH/pc:ok). • **to s.t. pl. or multiple.** *paaγó ámaši ki* up into the mountains. *paaγó ki aðáape* they went to the mountains (RBn10-12:JW). *waachí ki pšíe ðe* I went to the dances (04/26/95/FH/pc). *htáwą ki ščée tą ðúhpeece tóe aðį́li* when you go to town [viewed as a collection of buildings], bring back some matches (RBn12-07).

ki-. PREFIX **(dative prefix, indicating that an action is done in the presence of s.o. [e.g., *ékie* 'speak in the presence of s.o.'], for the benefit of s.o. ["benefactive"], in place of s.o., or to s.o. else's possession; can also indicate action transferring s.t. to s.o.).** [Dative *ki-* is omitted after pronominal prefixes (*ki*-del.) in most but not all verbs. Verbs where dative *ki-* is retained include *ékie* 'talk for another, talk in the presence of others' (*ki-* precedes the pronominal subject) and *kípše* 'brush s.o.'s hair'.] *kíðuwį apai* they're buying it for him, they are buying it from him,

ki- (*continued*)
they are buying what is his. *wižį́ke kípą* she's calling *wižį́ke* [Sonny] [to appear before others] (FH). *šǫ́ke kíðuwį* buy the dog for him. *ąkísupa* pay for it for me. *ékipše* I spoke [before others]. *akípše* I brushed her hair.

ki-. PREFIX **(inceptive prefix) anew, again, in reaction, in return, back.** [Inceptive *ki-* is retained after pronominal prefixes (*ki*-ret.) in most but not all verbs.] *okíce* search for an item again [*ki-* + *océ*]. *kiðíiški* rewash. *wahkǫ́ta ižį́ke iikitáðe* Christmas, birthday of the son of God (lit., 'God's son is born again' [implying that the day recurs]). *kišúpe* to pay back, repay. *kiðúwį* to buy back (an item that one had before or sold).

ki- (variant of **kik-**).

kícheðe (variant: **kíche**). v [reg.?, *kíche_ðe*?] *(trans.)* **keep, set aside, put away, save as a memento or treasure.** *kícheðaa patą́hą* they set it [the date, the occasion] aside (HREsr#68).
•• JOD (slip file): *kíicheðe* <ḵi´-i-tse´-¢ĕ> to put a standing object back in its place (?).

kiðá (variant: **kíða**). ADJ **each.** *hóxpe níhkašie kiðá áðįpe* each person, everyone has this sickness (01/20/95/PM/pc). *haxį ðé, ðée apa kiðá aðį́ hkǫ́bra* I want each of them to have this blanket for his/her own; they can all call it theirs, as each one has a part in this blanket (01/20/95/PM/pc:prod orig; BE2.38; RBn1-MOJ/p52b).
•• RB: <kí-tháh>.

kíðahapa (variant: **kíðaha**). v [reg. *ki*-del., *_(kí)ðahapa*] *(intr.)* **be apart, separated, divorced, divided, distant, or estranged from each other (e.g., an estranged married couple, egg yolks separated from whites).** *kíðahapáe* they're separated [by physical distance] (02/22/95/FH/pc:prod orig; 04/14/95/PM/pc:ok). *kiðáhapa ną* they are separated from one another [as in a divorce], they're divided (01/20/95/PM/pc:ok). • *(trans.)* **divide or separate the parts of s.t.; separate from, divorce, or become estranged from.** *hpáata ðe kíðahapa ąhé* I'm dividing the egg yolk from the white (lit., 'I'm separating the egg') (04/14/95/PM/pc:ok). *aðahapa hta mįkšé* I'm going to quit him/jump from him (04/14/95/PM/pc:prod). *áðahapa* I divorce him. *ðáðahapa* you divorce him. *kíðahpa* he divorces her. *ąkíðahapa* we divorce.
•• RB: <ki-tháh-hah pah-nah>.

kiðálį (variant: **kíðalį**). v [stat. *ki*-del., *_ðálį*] *(intr.)* **be glad, feel good (also used as an equivalent of 'thank you').** *ą́ąðalį* I'm glad. *ðíiðalį* you're glad. *kíðalį* she's glad. *wáaðalį(?)* we're glad. *ąðálį* I feel good, I'm glad, I like it, thank you (02/01/95/FH/pc:ok; BE2.59).
• *(trans.)* **like, love, enjoy, be happy about, be pleased with.** *ooðáha tą ą́ðalį* when you cook, I like it (RBn; MREI/01/11/93). *háazu žúuce ą́ðalį* I like red grapes (02/03/95/FH/pc:okc). *žąąníe kíðalį* he likes candy (02/16/95/FH/pc:ok; BE2.79). *htáa ðaaché kíðalįpe* she likes to eat meat (FH). *waðáahtą kíðalįpe* he likes to drink (02/16/95/FH/pc:ok). *žįkážį pa kíðalį nąpé* the children enjoy it. *žąąníi ðaaché ąąðálį* I enjoy eating candy (3-10-83-A; 01/04/95/FH/pc:ok; BE2.64).
•• LFD 52: *kíðalį* <gi´-tha-gthi^{n}> he is pleased. LFD 57: *házu žúuce ąðalį ha* <ha´-çi zhu-dse o^{n}-tha-gthi^{n} ha> [sentence-final *ha* is not used in Mod. Os.] I like red grapes. LFD 104: *mąžą́xe ą́ðalį* <mo^{n}-zho^{n}´-xe o^{n}-tha-gthi^{n}> I like onions. *mąžą́xe ðiðalį* <mo^{n}-zho^{n}´-xe thi-tha-gthi^{n} a> do you like onions? LFD 135: *htáabre kiðalį* <ta´-bthe gi-tha-gthi^{n}> one who loves to hunt, a sportsman.

kíðe (variant: **kíe**). CAU [reg. *ki*-ret., *_kíðe*] [*ki-* DAT or *kik-* SUU + *ðe* CAU] *(trans.)* **make or have s.o. engage voluntarily in some act; let or allow s.o. to do s.t.** *žįkážį haxį́ į kíðape* he had his children wear their blankets. *įįhǫ́ akxa šį́tožį hiiðá kí[ð]ape* the mother had the child take a bath.

kíðiixǫ. v [stat. *ki*-del., *_(kí)ðixǫ*] [*ki-* DAT + *ðiixǫ́*] *(trans.)* **break off or break s.o.'s (e.g., body part).** *áa ðíiðiixǫpe* they broke your arm. *áa kíðiixǫpe* they broke his arm. *ą́ąðiixǫ* they broke my. *ðíiðiixǫ* they broke your. *kíðiixǫ* they broke his. *wáaðiixǫpe* they broke our. *wáaðiixǫ* they broke their.

kiðúuze. v [sync. *ki*-del., *(ki)_ðúuze*] [*ki-* DAT + *ðuuzé*] **take away from s.o.** *kiðúuza mąðį́* go take it away from him (03/16/95/JS/pc). *wáawažį ą́šcuuze hta níkšé?* are you going to take pennies/change away from me? (03/15/95/PM/pc:okc; LS ok; BE2.131). *wahkǫ́ta táatą hpíiži ą́ðuuze* God takes away bad things from me (03/15/95/PM/pc:ok). *wahkǫ́ta akxa táatą hpíiži wáðuuze* God takes away bad things [from us, from them] (FH/09/23/01/pc). *wahéhe mįkšé ąži sisí nįkšé, wahkǫ́ta táatą hpíiži ąðúuzai* I am weak but thou art strong, Jesus keep me from all wrong (MJ partial version of the

Christian hymn "I Am Weak But Thou Art Strong"). *ðíðuuze* they took something away from you (03/16/95/JS/pc:ok). *wáawažį ðíðuuze hta apai* they are going to take pennies away from you (03/15/95/PM/pc:ok; 03/16/95/JS/pc:ok).

kíðuwį. v [reg. *ki*-del.+sync., *_(kí)_ðuwį*] [*ki-* DAT + *ðuwį́*] *(trans.)* **buy for s.o., buy in s.o.'s place for the benefit of a third person.** *ábruwį* I bought it for him. *ðášcuwį* you bought it for him. *kíðuwį* she bought it for him. *hkáące tóa kíðuwį* she's buying him some apples. *kíðuwį* they bought it for him. *ą́ðuwį* we bought it for him. *hkáące tóa ą́ðuwį* buy me some apples [for him or her].

kíðuwį. v [sync. *ki*-ret., *kí_ðuwį*] *(trans.)* **buy from s.o. (s.t. that belongs to that person).** *kíbrúwį* I'm buying it from him.

kíe (variant of **kíðe**).

kiɣúhke(?). N **comfort** (HHt9b-p2, unconfirmed).

kih- (variant of **kik-**).

kíhike. v [reg. *ki*-ret., *_kíhike*] *(trans.)* **be chief over.**

•• JOD: *wikíhikape eðaú* [Mod. Os. omits *eðaú*] I have been chief over you.

kihkápo. N **Kickapoo Indians.**

•• RB: <ki-káh-po> (04/11/95/LS/pc:uk; BE2.73, unconfirmed; 02/14/95/FH/pc:uk, but *kihkápo* pron. corrected).

kíhką (variants: **kihką́, kíhkǫ**). v [reg. *ki*-ret., *_kíhką*] *(trans.)* **fan off, as at a peyote meeting** (RB; 04/13/95/FH/pc:ok). *há, kihką́pi* you [pl.] fan them off (PM/7/7/94; RBn11-02). *ðikíhką hta apai* they're going to fan you off. *ðikíhkǫ ðée pa, ðe* these people want to fan you off (01/23/95/PM/pc:prod). *ąkíhką* fan me off (BE2.43). *kíhką káaɣa* fan him, fan him off (PM 7/7/94; 7/8/94). *há, kíhkąpi* [you pl.] fan them off [possibly colloquial use of 'them' for 'him/her']. *wákíhką* fan them off (PM/pc). • N **fan, fanning** (RB).

••• Cf. *kahką́*.

kíhkoopše. v [reg.? (not known whether *ki*-del. or *ki*-ret.), *_kíhkoopše?*] [*ki-* SUU (or DAT or both?) + *hkóopše*] **run off (on s.o.), abandon, leave (s.o.).** *wakˀó apa kíhkoopše apai* his wife ran off on him.

kíhkǫ (variant of **kíhką**).

kíhleke (variant of **kíleke**).

kíhǫǫ. v [stat. *ki*-del., *_(kí)hǫǫ*] *(trans.)* **like, love.** [Synonymous with *kiðálį*.] *wažáže óŋbre ą́hǫǫ* I like Osage food (02/16/95/FH/pc:okc). *ooðáhą tą ą́hǫǫ* when you cook I like it (RBn; MREI/01/11/93). *waaðáštǫ tą ą́hǫǫ* when you sing I like it (RBn (MREI/01/11/93). *waskúe táatą ðíhǫǫ?* what kind of candy do you like? (RBn10-18; CQc). *táata ðíhǫǫ íšpahǫ?* do you know what you like? (RBn22-20). *táata ą́hǫǫ íhpahǫ, įcé ðuuhpíiži ą́hǫǫ* I know what I like, I like to make faces (RBn22-20). *htáa ðaaché kíhǫǫpe* she likes to eat meat (FH). *waðáahtą kíhǫǫpe* he likes to drink, he loves to drink (RBn2-MOJ/p22; 02/16/95/FH/pc:ok). *htaacé ki waachí eeškítą kíhǫǫpe* he also liked the way they danced in the wind (RBn15-02). *žįkážį watxą́ kíhǫǫ* those kids like squash.

•• LFD 51: *kíhǫ aži* <gi´-ho^{n} a-zhi> he does not like it.

••• Cf. *hǫ́ǫži*.

kihǫ́ǫži. v [stat. *ki*-del. *_(ki)hǫ́ǫži*] [*kíhǫǫ* + *aží* NEG] *(trans.)* **dislike s.t.** (FH); *(intr.)* **grieve, be unhappy.** *kihǫ́ǫži hpáaɣe* I made him grieve (03/02/95/FH/pc:okc). *kihǫ́ǫži ąkáaɣape* we made him grieve (03/02/95/FH/pc:okc). *kihǫ́ǫži škáaɣe* you made him grieve (03/02/95/FH/pc:okc). *ílanąpi che kíhǫǫžipe* he's unhappy because he is in disgrace (02/25/95/FH/pc:okc). • N **grief, anything one doesn't like** (03/02/95/FH/pc:ok).

•• LFD 51: *kihǫ́aži* <gi-ho^{n}´-a-zhi> grief; sorrow. *kíhǫaži kaɣe* <gi´-ho^{n} a-zhi ga-xe> made to grieve. *kíhǫ aži* <gi´-ho^{n} a-zhi> he does not like it. *kíhǫ aži* <gi´-ho^{n} a-zhi> to displease; to give dissatisfaction; to repine; to resent. *ą́hǫ mąži* <o^{n}´-ho^{n} mo^{n}-zhi> I am displeased. *ðíhǫ aži* <thi´-ho^{n} a-zhi> you are displeased. *wáhǫ paži pe* <wa´-ho^{n} ba-zhi i> we are displeased.

kíhpaahi. v [reg.? *ki*-ret.?, *_kíhpaahi?*] [*kik-* SUU + *paahí*] *(trans.)* **select from one's own people or items.**

•• JOD (Devouring Mountain, p1 ln2): *šímižįka ðáalį kíhpaahi páta žóle ahípe ska* <Címiçiñka ¢ák¢i^{n} kípahi-páta^{n} çúk¢e ahípe ska> they would select good [or pretty] girls and take them there.

kíhpą. v [reg. *ki*-ret., *_kíhpą*] [*kik-* SUU + *pą́*] *(trans.)* **call, invite one's relative(s).** *akíhpą* I invite him. *ðakíhpą* you invite him. *ąkíhpą* we invite him. *wakíhpą hkǫ́bra* I want to invite my relatives (01/09/95/FH/pc:prod). *wihtáežį akíhpą hkǫ́bra* I want to invite my sister (01/09/95/FH/pc:prod). *waachípitą akíhpą hta mįkšé* if they dance, I'm going to call him [my relative]. *ðakíhpą paašé?* are you [pl.] inviting your relatives? (FH/11/19/01/pc:prod). *wihkípą*

kíhpą (*continued*) *achíe* I have come to invite you [my relative] (HH/14-a/172ff&pc). *wakíhpą akxai* he's inviting his relatives (01/09/95/FH/pc:prod). *wihcíko apa wa(a)kíhpąpe* Grandpa called us [his own grandchildren], Grandpa asked us to come (01/09/95/FH/pc:prod). *Carolyna ihcíko akxa kíhpą akxai* Carolyn's grandpa is asking Carolyn to come (01/09/95/FH/pc:prod).

kíhpiiži. v, ADJ [stat. *ki*-del., *_(kí)hpiiži*] **(be) sad.** *ą́hpiiži* I am sad. *ðíhpiiži* you're sad. *wáhpiiži* we're sad. *John akxa ðée nąkʔǫ́pi áha, wáli̜ kíhpiiži hínąąži̜pe* when John heard that, he got very sad.

kihtǫ́pe. v [reg. *ki*-ret., *_kihtǫ́pe*] [*kik-* SUU + *tǫ́pe*] *(trans.)* **watch one's own things, look at one's own things.** *wacúe skúe áhkihtǫi̜ hce* let me look at my cake.

kihúheka. v [stat., *ki*-del., *_(ki)húheka* (1st dual and 1st pl. subject can be either *ą-* or *wa-; ki-* is sometimes omitted in 3rd person subject forms as well)] *(intr.)* **be sick, suffer from an illness.** *hą́ąpa tóa ąhúheka* I was sick for a few days (lit., 'for some days I was sick') (03/09/95/MREI/pc:ok). *ðihúheka ðąąšé áape anąkʔǫ* I heard you [moving, sg.] were sick (03/09/95/MREI/pc:ok). *ðihúheka žąkší aape* I heard you [lying down, sg.] were sick (03/09/95/MREI/pc:ok). *húheka akxái* she is sick (03/09/95/MREI/pc:ok, he's sick). *wahúheka ąkái* we were sick; we are sick. *ąhúheka ąkái* we were sick; we are sick. *ąhúheka ąði̜kšé* we two are sick (FH). *wahúheka ąði̜kšé* we two are sick. *nąniǫ́pažį huuwáli apai húheka ąkáaɣe nąpé* a lot of cigarettes make me sick (MSB 3-2-29). *ðihúheka* you're sick (02/13/95/FH/pc). *ąhúheka* I am sick (02/13/95/FH/pc:ok). *hcéhpe kihúheka áape* he had liver trouble [they said] (02/16/95/FH/pc:ok; BE2.80). *iihǫ́ kihúheka akxái* his mother has a sickness (BE2.121; 03/09/95/MREI/pc:ok).

•• LFD 62: *húheka* <hiu´-he-ga> sick, ill, sickness. *ąhúheka* <on-hiu´-he-ga> I am sick (02/13/95/FH/pc:ok). *ðahúheka* <tha-hiu´-he-ga> you are sick. *wahúheka pe* <wa-hiu´-he-ga i> we are sick (02/13/95/FH/pc:ok).

••• Cf. *húheka*.

kiistó. v [reg.? *ki*-ret.?, *_kiistó?*] *(intr.)* **assemble (as for a council), gather for council, meet and talk things over.** *kiistó apa ska* I guess they are counciling (said upon seeing many cars around a building) (01/13/95/FH/pc:ok). *kiistó apa áape* I heard they are counciling (01/13/95/FH/pc; BE2.26). *kiistó omąi̜ apai, kiistó mąði̜ apai* they're in the tribal council (MSBt#9a).

•• JOD (slip file): *kistó* <ķi-stu´> to assemble in council.

••• *KS gistó* to gather or assemble (RR), *kkistó* council (RR).

••• Cf. *hkiistó*.

kiixǫ́. v [stat. *ki*-del. *_(kii)xǫ́*] *(intr.?)* **break one's own (e.g., a body part).** *aa ąąxǫ́pe* my arm broke. *aa ðiixǫ́pe* your arm broke. *aa kiixǫ́pe* his arm broke. *žéka ąąxǫ́pe* my leg broke (FH).

••• Cf. *ðiixǫ́, kíðiixǫ*.

kik- (variants: **kih-, ki-**). PREFIX **one's own (suus prefix: object belongs to or is related to the subject).** [*kik-* becomes *kih-* before *c, k, p, t;* while *kik-ð* simplifies to *kð* and becomes *l* (e.g., *kik-* + *ðuužá* 'wash' becomes *lúuža* 'wash one's own'); otherwise, *kik-* becomes simple *ki-*.] *žóðakile ðaišé* you are with him [family]. *ži̜kówahkihą óxtawakíe akxai grandchildren* he's making his grandchildren special.

kikáaɣe. VP [reg. *ki*-ret.+sync. *k>p*, *_ki_káaɣe*] [*ki-* DAT + *káaɣe*] *(trans.)* **make or produce for s.o.** *žáže kikáaɣe.* to sign (as a document), subscribe, undersign, affix one's signature (05/02/95/LS/pc:prod, non-preasp; HRE/12/29/01/ok).

kikáaɣe. v [reg. *ki*-ret.+sync. *k>p*, *_ki_káaɣe*] [*ki-* INCEPTIVE + *káaɣe*] *(trans.)* **make over, do over, repair or fix s.t. (belonging to oneself or to another person; e.g., repair a torn place in a dress), redo, reform** (FH/98/pc; PM/10/13/96/pc). *ákihpáaɣe* I make it over. *ðákiškáaɣe* you make it over. *ą́kikáaɣe* we make it over. *ži̜káži̜ wíhta wáðohta níhkašika waðákiškaaɣe hkǫ́bra* I want you to make my children proper people (RBn19-06). *ðakíškaaɣe?* did you fix it? (01/26/95/FH/pc:ok; BE2.48). *Mary akxa haaská wi̜ kikáaɣape* Mary made over a shirt. *hpéece kikáaɣa* fix that fire (02/24/95/FH/pc:ok; BE2.84).

kíkǫða. v [sync. fortisizing stop stem+sync., *kí_kǫ_ða*] [*ki-* DAT + *kǫ́ða*] *(trans.)* **want s.t. that is another's.** *oðíhtą ðíhta kíkǫða akxai* he's wishing for your car, he wants a car like yours.

kíkxą. v [reg. *ki*-ret., *_kíkxą*] *(trans.)* **mourn** (RBn22-12).

•• LFD 296: *kíkxǫ* <gie´-kon> to mourn. *akíkxą* I mourn him. *ðakíkxą* you mourn him. *ąkíkxąpe* we mourn him.

kíkxo (variant: **kikxó**). v [reg.? *ki*-ret.? *_kíkxo?*]

(trans.) **put on or prepare a feast for another or others, invite others to feast** (04/25/95/PM/pc:okc; PM:2001:ok). *wikíkxopi achíe* I have come to invite you all to eat (04/14/95/FH/pc:okc; 04/25/95/PM/pc:ok; t14b-p3/170/HH; HRE/12). • N **feast.** *wažáže kikxó* an Osage feast or dinner (FH).

•• LFD 284 (unconfirmed): *kihkó* <gi-ḳo´> [<ḳ> may be a typographical error for <k>, Mod. Os. *kx*] invitation (formal). LFD 86 (unconfirmed): *hkíhko* <ḳi´-ḳu> [expected Mod. Os. form: *kíkxo* (<ki´-kxu> in LF's transcription)] a feast. *hkíhko sce* <ḳi´-ḳu stse> [expected Mod. Os. form: *kíkxo šcée*] you go to a feast [unconfirmed; 04/25/95/PM/pc:no].

••• *OM gíkhu* invite another to a feast, *ðíkhui* you are invited (JOD, RR).

kikʔǫ́. v [reg.? *ki*-ret.?, *_kikʔǫ́?*] *(trans.)* **paint the face of a deceased person, apply face paint** (RBn12-07, unconfirmed). *kikʔǫ́ hta pa?* are they going to paint him [in the religious Indian way for burial]? (FH#128), *áahukʔoe kikʔǫ́ kšíe hta apái* Henry [*áahukʔoe*] is going to [have someone] paint him [for burial] (03/03/95/FH/pc:ok; BE2.101, RBn2-MOJ/p21). • N **makeup, cosmetics, face paint.**

•• RB: <kí-k'ó> face paint; also makeup, cosmetics (03/03/95/FH/pc:ok).

•• LFD 73: *íhkikʔǫ* <i´-ḳi-ḳ'o^{n}> to put upon the face as a symbol: from a ritual.

kíkʔu. v [reg. *ki*-ret., *_kíkʔu*] [*ki-* INCEPTIVE + *kʔú*] *(trans.)* **give back** (01/31/95/FH/pc:ok). *ąkíkʔu* give it back to me (BE2.55).

kíkʔu. v [reg. *ki*-ret., *_kíkʔu*] [*kik-* SUU + *kʔú*] *(trans.)* **give to one's own, give away to one's own people.** *haaskámi wį akíkʔu hkǫ́bra* I want to give you [my relative] a shawl (RBn10-6:JW). *hpáažį iihǫ́ akxa kíkʔupe* the mother gave it to her baby. *haxį́ waðákikʔu* you gave them [your own people] blankets. *haxį́ ąðakíkʔu* you gave me [your relative] a blanket. *ónǫbre hį́į, waðákikʔu pi* you gave us groceries (lit., 'groceries you gave us').

••• Cf. *wakíkʔu.*

kíleke (variant: **kíhleke**). v [reg.+reg.?, *_kí_leke*] [*kik-* SUU + *kaaléke*] *(trans., intr.)* **break s.t. of one's own by shattering, shatter one's own.** [Expected but unattested Mod. Os. forms are as follows: *akíaléke* 'I shatter my own', *ðakíðaléke* 'you shatter your own', *kíhleke* she shatters her own', *ąkíhléke* 'we shatter our own'.] *mą́ze ištola akíąleke* I broke my glasses (lit., 'I broke my own glasses unto myself').

••• Cf. *ðuuléke, paaléke.*

kilǫ́že. v [reg. *ki*-del.?, *_(ki)lǫ́že?*] [apparently contains *ki-* DAT] *(trans.)* **curse, bewitch or "witch" s.o., cast a spell on a person** (04/25/95/PM/pc:prod; FH/ok). [The form *kilǫ́ɣe* would have been expected instead, judging from Mod. Os. *íðǫɣe* and *ilǫ́ɣe*, LFD's *hkilǫ́ɣe*, and related forms in KS.]

•• LFD 86: *hkilǫ́ɣe* <ḳi-gtho^{n}´-xe> to practice magic upon each other. [A reciprocal form; no dative form of this stem is found in LFD.]

••• *KS lóɣe* to bewitch, to practice sorcery, to shoot projectiles (RR).

kilúuze. v [reg. *ki*-ret., *_kilúuze*] [*ki-* DAT + *lúuze*] *(trans.)* **take s.t. of s.o.'s own away, take s.o.'s own from him/her.** *kíluuza!* take it away from him! *kíluuze mąðį!* go take it [something that is his] away from him! (03/15/95/PM/pc:okc; RBn14-06).

kínąkʔǫ (variant: **kínakʔǫ**). v [reg. *ki*-ret., *_kínąkʔǫ*] [*kik-* SUU + *nąkʔǫ́*] *(trans.)* **hear s.t. about s.o. or s.t. belonging to or connected with oneself.**

•• JOD (letter from Wasap͓e-ç͓iñk͓a to Prudy Eagle-feather, Carlisle, Pennsylvania, p1 ln4): *ókaše ðįké ðaįšé oðáha wikínakʔǫ ąðą́kiha hkǫ́bra* <úk͓acé ¢iñk͓é ¢á¢i^{n}cé u¢áha wik͓ínak'ŭ^{n} a ¢añ´k͓iha kŭ^{n}p͓¢au´> I always want to hear that you are fine.

kiní (variant: **kiníe**). v [stat. *ki*-ret. (2nd person), reg. *ki*-ret. (1st sg.), *_kiní*] [*ki-* INCEPTIVE + *ní* 'be well, live'] *(intr.)* **heal, recuperate, recover from illness (lit., 'be alive anew').** *kiní akxai* it's healing (e.g., a sore) (01/04/95/FH/pc:prod; RBn1-MOJ/p40). *kóota akxa kiní akxai* that one over there is recovered (FH/09/25/01/prod). *ðikínie?* are you recovered? (FH/09/25/01/prod). *akínie* I'm recovered (FH/09/25/01/prod). • [*ki-* DAT + *ní* 'be well, live'] *(trans.)* **live for another or others.** *akínie* I live for him. *ðikínie* you live for him. *ąkínie* we live for him.

•• LFD 51: *kiní* <gi-ni´> to recover from sickness. *ą kíni bre ha* <o^{n} gi´-ni bthe ha> [sentence-final *ha* is not used in Mod. Os.] I am getting well.

••• Cf. *kitą́he.*

kiní káaɣe. VP [sync. *k*>*p*, *kiní _káaɣe*] [contains variant of *kiníe*] *(trans.)* **heal (lit., 'make to recover').**

•• LFD 51: *kiníkaɣe* <gi-ni´-ga-xe> to heal; restore to health.

kiníe (variant of **kiní**).

kíopxa. v [stat. *ki*-del., *_(kí)opxa] (intr., trans.)* **understand, be able to understand.** *ą́opxa* I understand it. *ðíopxa* you understand it. *kíopxa* he understands it. *wáopxa (?)* we understand it. *íiðai ðíopxái nąkxą́še* those of you who can understand (said when addressing a crowd, some of whom do not understand Osage) (04/06/95/FH/pc:okc; BE2.147).

••• Cf. *wáopxa.*

kíopxaži (variant: **kiópxaži**). v [stat. *ki*-del., *_(kí)opxaži*] [*kíopxa* + *aží* NEG] N *(trans., intr.)* **be ignorant (of s.t.), be vague about, not understand, be unable to understand** (RBn1-23; 04/06/95/PM/pc:ok). *ą́opxaži* I didn't understand. *ðíoxpaži* you didn't understand (04/26/95/FH/pc). *kíoxpaži* she didn't understand. *ą́opxaži ąðikše* we [two] didn't understand (04/26/95/FH/pc). *waléze tóa bráace ąži ą́opxaži* I read some letters but I was vague [didn't understand] (02/27/95/JS/pc:okc; 04/26/95/FH/pc:ok). *ą́opxaži* I don't understand (HH/14-a/172&pc). *kíopxaži* they don't understand it (RBn19-05

••• Cf. *pxáðaži.*

kíoxta. v [stat. *ki*-del., *_(kí)oxta* (transitive with stative object and stative subject pronominal prefixes; object pronominal prefixes precede subject pronominal prefixes)] [*ki-* DAT + *óxta*] *(trans.)* **cherish, love, like, treasure or honor s.o.** [In 3rd person form, this verb is indistinguishable from suus *kíoxta.*] *wíoxta* I love you (RB). *ą́ðioxta* you love me (FH/10/12/95/prod). *žįkážį wáðioxta ðąąšé* you are honoring the children (FH/10/12/95). *žįkážį wað[i]óxta ðąąšé* you love the children. *wað[i]óxta* you love them. *ą́oxta* I love him. *ðíoxta* you love him. *níhka wakʔó kíoxta* the man loves the woman (FH:4/25/96/tape:prod). *šį́tožį akxa šǫ́žį kíoxta akxai* the boy likes/treasures the little dog (FH:4/25/96/tape). *ée ą́oxtape* he/she/it loves me. *ðíoxtape* he loves you. *ąkóe ą́oxtape* we love him. *ąkóe waóxtape* they like us.

kíoxta. v [reg. *ki*-ret., *_kíoxta*] [*kik-* SUU + *óxta*] *(trans.)* **love one's own (relative[s] or s.o. else close)** (7/8/94/PM/#98b). [In 3rd person form, this verb is indistinguishable from dative *kíoxta.*] *wíkióxta* I love you (02/22/95/FH/pc:ok). *awákióxta* I love them all (02/22/95/FH/pc:ok: not *ąwą*). *žį́ka owáhkihą awákióxta* I love my grandchildren (02/22/95/FH/pc:okc; BE2.82).

kíǫǫða. v [reg.+sync., *_kíǫǫ_ða*] [*kik-* SUU + *ǫ́ǫða*] *(trans.)* **leave behind one's own.**

•• LFD 8: *ákahahpa akiǫǫbra achi mįkše o* <a´-ga-ha-pa a-gi o^{n}-btha a-tsi mi^{n}-kshe o> [sentence-final *o* is not used in Mod. Os.] I left my vest home.

kípą. v [reg. *ki*-del., *(kí)_pą*; sometimes reg. *ki*-del. +sync. fortisizing stop stem, *_(kí)_pą* (*ki-* may appear in forms without full inflection)] [*ki-* DAT + *pą́*] *(trans.)* **call or visit to ask or summon s.o. to attend or appear before others** (01/09/95/FH/pc:prod). *ą́ąpą* he calls me. *ðíipą* he calls you. *kípą* he calls her. *wáapą* he calls us. *wáapą* he calls them. *áapą* I call him. *ðáašpą* you call him. *kípą* she calls him. *ą́ąpą* we call him. *wíhpą achíe* I came to invite you (RBn10-20). *Carolyna kípą apai* they're asking Carolyn to come (01/09/95/FH/pc:prod). *wáapąpee* they called us (to appear) (PM, pc; 01/09/95/FH/pc:ok). *šée txą kípą* call him [standing]. *kípą ðíe!* call him over here! *John-a ðáašpą* you invited John (MSB051283; PM). *ą́pą įkšé* we're inviting him (5-12-83-2). *wáhpąi* I'm inviting them (5-12-83-2). *ðíipą akxai* he's calling you (2-10-8). *ą́ąpą apai* they're calling me, inviting me. • **invite s.o. (not a relative).** *ðíipąpi?* did they invite you? (04/11/95/LS/pc:okc; BE2.71). *wanǫ́bre ą́ąpąpi* I am invited to eat (04/11/95/LS/pc:okc). *kípą apai* they invited him [*kípą* is reportedly for sg. object 'him/her' only, not pl. object 'them' (PM)]. *miðǫ́hta tą wanǫ́bre wáapąpi* they invited us to [the] noon meal (04/11/95/LS/pc:okc). *záani wáapąpi* we are all invited (04/11/95/LS/pc:okc). *ą́pą įkšé* we're inviting him (MSB). *wíihpa mįkšé* I'm inviting you (MSB051283). *wáhpai* [expected form: *áhpai*] I'm inviting him (5-12-83-p2).

•• LFD 50: *kípą* <gi´-bo^{n}> to summon; to call to appear. *ðípą pe ha* <thi´-bo^{n} i ha> [sentence-final *ha* is not used in Mod. Os.] you were called to appear. *ą́pą pe ha* <o^{n}´-bo^{n} i ha> [sentence-final *ha* is not used in Mod. Os.] I was summoned.

••• Cf. *kíhpą.*

kípše. v [reg. *ki*-ret. *_kípše*] [*ki-* DAT + *káapše*] *(trans.)* **brush or curry the mane or coat of an animal** (RBn2-MOJ/p6; 04/13/95/LS/pc:ok). *hkáwa kípše akxa* they're brushing the horse's mane. • **brush or comb s.o.'s hair.** *ąkípše* they're brushing my hair, they're combing my hair (04/13/95/LS/pc; FH:4/22/96/tape: not *hk*). *ąkípša* brush my hair (01/09/95/FH/pc:ok; BE2.13). *akípše* I brushed her hair, I combed her hair (FH).

kíse. v [reg. *ki*-ret., *_kíse*] [*ki-* DAT + *kaasé*] *(trans.)* **cut s.t. for s.o.**

•• JOD (slip file, under k͓í-sĕ 'to cut wood, etc., for another'): *ąkísa* <Añk͓ísa> cut (them) for me. [The expected Mod. Os. meaning of this form would be 'cut it for me'.]

•• LFD 50: *kíse* <gi´-çe> to cut wood for someone. *akíse* <a-gi´-çe> I cut wood for him. *ðakíse* <tha-gi´-çe> you cut wood for him. *ąkísa pe* <o^{n}-gi´-ça i> we cut wood for him.

kisúðaži (variants: **kisúaži, kusúaži**). v [reg. *ki*-ret., *_kisúðaži*] [*kisúðe* + *aží* NEG] *(trans., intr.)* **forget.** *awákisue mąží* I forgot them (3/3/83/MSB; FH). *akísue mąžį* I forgot (01/30/95/FH/pc:okc). *ðakísuaži* did you forget? (01/30/95/FH/pc:okc). *küsúažį* he forgot. *ąkísuaži apá* they forgot about me (RBnot-nd-1/p10; 01/30/95/FH/pc:okc). *kisúaži ðįké!* don't forget!

•• LFD 50: *kisúðaži* <gi-çi´-tha-zhi> to forget. *akísiðamąži* <a-gi´-çi-tha-mo^{n}-zhi> I forgot. *ðakísiða ži* <tha-gi´-çi-tha zhi> you forgot. *ąkísiði paži pe* <o^{n}-gi´-çi-thi ba-zhi i> we forgot.

kisúðe (variants: **kisúe, kusúe**). v [reg. *ki*-ret., *_kisúðe*] *(trans.)* **remember.** *wikísue* I remember you (RBn14-06). *ąkísue ąkái įhtáci ðakʔéða ðį* we're remembering her, father, bless her (FH:prayer). *küsúðe a* remember it (RBn10-5:JW). *ðée ékiǫpai [ðe] ąðákisuðe šk̇ǫ́štapi tą* do this in remembrance of me (lit., 'do this when you want to remember me') (FH/09/11/01/pc). *wahkǫ́ta oðáhkiepi tą ąkísuepai* when you talk to your God, remember me (FH/09/24/01/pc/prod). *akísu[ð]e maží* I don't remember. *ðakísu[ð]eži* you don't remember. *ąkísu[ð]e ąðįkšé* we [two] don't remember. *kisú[ð]apé* he remembered.

kíškace. v [reg. *ki*-del., *_(kí)škace*] [*ki-* DAT + *škáce*] *(trans.)* **play with s.o. (i.e., with any animate being).** *šǫ́žį áškace ą́hǫǫ* I like to play with the puppy [someone else's].

kíškace. v [reg. *ki*-ret., *_kíškace*] [*kik-* SUU + *škáce*] **play with s.o. related to oneself, or with animate being of one's own.** *šǫ́žį akíškace ą́hǫǫ* I like to play with the puppy [mine].

kíšupe. v [reg. *ki*-ret., *_kíšupe*] [*ki-* DAT + *kašúpe*] *(trans.)* **pay s.o., pay for s.o.** *awánǫ́bre tą ąkíšupa ði* if I eat, you pay for it (FH). *ąkíšupapé* he paid me [back] for it (MREI). *ąðíkišupé* we paid you [back] for it (MREI). *ąðákišupe* you paid me [back] for it (MREI). *ą́kišupa* pay me, pay it for me, pay for it (03/06/95/FH/pc:prod; BE2.101). *ąðikišupe na* we paid you for it. *ąšúpa ðíe* pay me for it. *ehtą, ą́kíšupai* well, pay me [for what I did] (RB). • [*ki-* INCEPTIVE + *kašúpe*] *(trans.)* **pay back, repay, reimburse.** *ákišupe* I repaid him. *ðákišupe* you repaid him. *ðakíšupe?* did you pay them back? (FH/12/1/9ʔpc).

•• JOD (slip file, under <k͓i-cü-´p͓e>): *íðakíðe tą, wikíšupe hta mįkšé* <I´¢ak͓í¢ĕ-ṯa^{n}´, wik͓ícüp͓e ta-miñkci au> if you find it, I will pay you.

•• LFD 189: *akíšipe* <a-gi´-shi-be> I repaid him. *ðakíšipe* <tha-gi´-shi-be> you repaid him. *ąkíšipa pe* <o^{n}-gi'-shi-ba i> we repaid him. [The form *wakíšipe* <wa-gi´-shi-be> (LFD 189) is a valence-reduced form; see *wakíšupe.*]

kítaake. v [reg.? *ki*-ret., *_kítaake*] [*ki-* DAT + *taaké*] *(trans.)* **fight, fight against.** *hpǫ́hka ąkítaake* we fight the Poncas (BE2.46).

kitą́he. v [reg. *ki*-ret., *_kitą́he*] [*ki-* INCEPTIVE + *tąhé*] *(intr.)* **improve (with regard to an illness), get better** (02/13/95/FH/pc:ok; RBn1-MOJ/p39). *ðakítąhe hkǫ́bra* I want you to get better (02/13/95/FH/pc:prod orig). *mą́hka žóika mą́į akxai, kitą́he hta akxa hǫ́ǫpa hu* he's haywire with peyote but he'll be all right at daylight (01/06/95/FH/pc:prod; BE2.102; RBn HW). *kitą́he hkǫ́bra* I want him/her to get better (03/09/95/MREI/pc:ok; 02/13/95/FH/pc:ok). *haaská ną ąðíðihtapi tą ąkítąhe nąpe* just a touch of your garment makes us well (lit., 'if we touch only your garment, we get well') (FH/09/11/01/pc). *ąkítąhe ąkǫ́ða* we want to get better (02/13/95/FH/pc:prod orig; BE2.71; ok).

•• LFD 50: *kitą́he* <gi-do^{n}´-he> he is better.

••• Cf. *kiní.*

kítąhe. v [stat. *ki*-ret., *_kítąhe*] [*ki-* INCEPTIVE + *tąhé*] *(intr.)* **heal fully, get well.** [Contrast *kitą́he* (reg.).] *ąkítąhe* I got well. *ðikítąhe* you got well. *kítąhe* he got well. *wakítąhe* we got well. *ðikítąhę hkǫ́bra* I want you to get/be well (a wish for one's friend or family) (03/09/95/MREI/pc; prod). *haaská ną ščihtą tą ðikítąhe hta* if you just touch his garment you could get well (FH/pc). *kítąhe* it makes him well (FH/09/25/01/prod). *wakítąhe* it makes us well (FH/09/25/01/prod).

kitǫ́pe (variant: **kitǫ́**). v [reg. *ki*-ret. + sync. fortisizing stop stem, *_ki(_)tǫ́pe*; object pronominals appear only in the first slot] [*ki-* DAT + *tǫ́pe*] *(trans.)* **see s.o.; look with regard to s.o., look down on (benevolently), watch over.** *ðáalį ąðákištǫ ðachí che* it's good you came to see me (RBn10-15). *ðáalį wažǫ́ waðákitǫ ðachí che* it is good what you've done, to come and see us (RBn1-2). *waðákištǫ́papi hų́ðe hkǫbra* I want

kitǫ́pe (*continued*) you to [come and] look down upon us (MSB t2-s2). *wakítǫpapi hų́ða* look down upon us (MSB/t2-s2; 02/22/95/FH/pc:ok).

kítǫpe (variant: **kítǫ**). v [reg.+sync., *_kí_tǫpe*] [*ki-* DAT + *tǫ́pe*] **look at s.t. that belongs to s.o.** *kítǫpa ði* look at what he's got (as when one looks in someone's sack to see if something is all there or see if it's what it is supposed to be) (FH:prod).

kíwaata. v [reg. *ki*-del. *_(kí)waata*] [*ki-* DAT + *waatá*] *(trans.)* **pray for** (RBn10-15, unconfirmed). [Expected forms are as follows: *áawaata* 'I pray for him', *ąðáawaata* 'you pray for me', *ąkíwaata* 'we pray for him', *awáawaata* 'I pray for them', *ą́ąwaata* 'pray for me', *ðíiwaata* 'he prayed for you', *kíwaata* 'pray for him', *wáawaata* 'pray for us', *wáawaata* 'pray for them'.]

kíwalį (variants: **kíwahlį, kíwali**). v, ADJ [stat. *ki*-del., *_(kí)walį*] [*ki-* DAT + *wálį* 'selfish'] [Mod. Os. *kíwalį* 'stingy' was earlier *ki-* + *wáxlį* and is not related to *wáli* 'lots, much, very' (although the final vowel of both words now varies between nasal *į* and nonnasal *i*).] *(trans.)* **(be) stingy or selfish with, reluctant to share s.t. of one's own because of valuing it so highly** (03/14/95/MREI/pc:prod). *ą́ąwalį* I'm stingy with it. *ðíiwalį* you're stingy with it. *kíwalį* he's stingy with it. *wáawalį* we're stingy with it. *hpéɣe ðe ą́ąwalį mįkšé* I'm really stingy with this gourd (03/14/95/MREI/pc:okc: [sitting]; RBn2-MOJ/p37; 02/03/95/FH/pc:okc, not *ki*). *oðíhtą kíwali akxái* he's stingy with his car (03/14/95/MREI/pc:okc; BE2.128; RBn2-MOJ/p36). • **value, prize, or treasure s.t.** *hci ðíiwali?* do you value your home? (03/14/95/MREI/pc) *hcí ą́ąwalį* I value my home (03/14/95/MREI/pc:okc). *kíwali* he values it. *hci ąkóhta wáawali* we value our home (MREI).

•• LFD 52: *kíwali* <gi´-wa xthi> to value highly some particular property. *kíwali* <gi´-wa-xthi> to prize very highly that which is one's own. *hcíche wawali pe* <ṭsi´-tse wa-wa-xthi i> we value our home. *hcíche ąwali ha* <ṭsi´-tse oⁿ-wa-xthi ha> [sentence-final *ha* is not used in Mod. Os.] I value my home. *hcíche ðiwali* <ṭsi´-tse thi-wa-xthi> you value your home. *mi óðaake ðą ąwacheli ha* <mi u´-tha-ge thoⁿ oⁿ-wa-tse-xthi ha> [verb appears garbled (should be *ą́ąwali* rather than *ąwacheli*); sentence-final *ha* is not used in Mod. Os.] I prize my watch. *nąpe oðíla ðą ąwacheli ha* <noⁿ-be u-thi´-xtha thoⁿ oⁿ-wa-tse-xthi ha> [verb appears garbled (should be *ðíiwali* rather than *ąwacheli*); sentence-final *ha* is not used in Mod. Os.] you prize your ring (unconfirmed; 03/14/95/MREI/pc:uk). LFD 53: *kiwáliži* <Gi-wa´-xthi-zhi> Not-stingy, personal name.

••• *KS gíwaxlį* stingy (RR).

kíxope. v [conjug. unknown] [perhaps *ki-* DAT + *xópe*] *(trans.)* **respect** (RBn1-41).

kixǫ́. v [stat. *ki*-del., *_(ki)xǫ́*] [*ki-* DAT + *xǫ́*] **s.t. belonging to one breaks.** [Possessor of the broken thing is expressed by patient pronominal prefixes.] *ąxǫ́pe* something of mine broke (MRB 2-24-83). *ðixǫ́pe* something of yours broke. *kixǫ́pe* something of his broke.

kízo. v, ADJ [stat. *ki*-del., *_(kí)zo*] *(trans.)* **enjoy, like, (be) happy or glad about s.t.** (12/30/94/FH/pc). *ą́ązo* I enjoy it. *ðíizo* you enjoy it. *kízo* she enjoys it. *wáazo, waazǫ́* we enjoy it. *kízo, wáazo, waazǫ́* they enjoy it [all three forms are correct and synonymous]. *oðáha tą ą́ązo* when you cook I enjoy it (RBn; MREI/01/11/93?). *ðíizoži xci nįkšé, háakǫ?* you look very unhappy, what is it? (04/26/95/LS/pc:ma). *kízo akxai* he's enjoying it (1/20/83/p5; 2/1/902). *waachí kízo apa* they are enjoying the dance (RBn1-25). *waachí kízo apa* they like to dance (12/30/94/dl:ok; 04/26/95/LS/pc:ok). *kízope* they enjoyed it. *wáazope* we enjoyed it (1/20/83/p5). *wáazo* we like (it). *kízo káaɣe* gladden (or 'he/she gladdens him/her') (04/26/95/LS/pc:ok). *waðíihice wáazope* he likes to tease (03/05/95/JS/pc). *waðíihice kízope* he likes to tease (03/16/95/FH/pc:okc; MREI/t116a). *waazó žįkážį tóa kíðalį wakáaɣape* it was fun to make the children happy. *hceeská apa niskų́ðe saakí kízope* cattle like rock salt. • *(intr.)* **have fun; feel enjoyment, be happy, have a good time.** *kízo ðaašé* you were having fun (RBn14-11). *kízo apái* he's having fun (RBn14-11). *waazó ąkái* [expected form: *wáazo*] we were having fun (BE2.52; RBn14-11). *kízo apai* we had fun, we are having fun (04/26/95/LS/pc:ok). *waazóe ąkšíe hta ąkái* we are going to make them have a good time (e.g., someone returning after being gone will be feted) (FH/07/09/01/pc). *waazó apa* they are having a good time (t108-b/FH/438). *ą́ązo mįkšé* I'm really having a good time (04/26/95/LS/pc:ok). *hą́ce kízo ðąįšé* you were having a good time last night

(BE2.41;04/26/95/LS/pc:ok). *kizó paašé?* [expected accent pattern: *kízo*] are you [pl.] having a good time? (FH). *kízo apai* he is having a good time, they are having a good time (04/26/95/LS/pc:ok, both). *wáazi apa* [expected form: *wáazo apa;* synonyomous with *kízo apai*] they are having a good time (04/26/95/LS/pc:ok with *-zi* or *-zo*). *ékiǫ ðįká, wáazi ąkatxą́i!* [expected form: . . . *wáazo ąkatxą́*] don't do that, we're having a good time! (e.g., admonishment to a woman who is jealous of another and therefore would want to make trouble at an event). *kízo apai* we're happy (04/26/95/LS/pc:ok). *kízo ðįke* he's unhappy (04/26/95/LS/pc). *kízoži* she's sad (04/26/95/LS/pc:ok). *ą́zo maží mįkšé* I'm sad (MSB).

•• LFD 50: *kízo* <gi´-çu> to be happy. *ą́zo* <o^{n}´-çu> I am happy. *ðízo* <thi´-çu> you are happy. *wázo pe* <wa´-çu i> we are happy. *kízo káaye* <gi´-çu-ga-xe> gladden; to make glad. *ðą́ące wihta kizo škáaye ha* <tho^{n}´-dse wi-ṭa gi-çu-shka-xe ha> [sentence-final *ha* is not used in Mod. Os.] it gladdened my heart. *kízo ðįke* <gi´-çu thi^{n}-ge> without mirth; unhappy. *ðizo ži xci nikše hakǫ?* <thi-çu zhi xtsi ni-ke ha-go^{n}> you look very unhappy, what is it? LFD 138: *htáapše ązo* <ṭa´-pshe o^{n}-çu> I like pemmican. *htáapše ðizo* <ṭa´-pshe thi-çu> you like pemmican.

kízoži. V, ADJ [stat. *ki*-del. *_(kí)zoži*] [*kízo* + *aží* NEG] *(intr.)* **(be) lonesome, unhappy, sad, disconsolate.** *ą́ązo mąžie* I'm lonesome (RBn HW10). *ą́ązo mąži mįkšé* I'm sad, I'm lonesome.

•• JOD (slip file): *kíšǫži* <ḳi´-cŭ^{n}-çi> to dislike; to disagree with; to disapprove of. *kízo ži* <gi´-çu-zhi> crestfallen; despondent; disconsolate; dispirited; downcast.

•• LFD 50: *kízo aži* <gi´-çu a-zhi> disconsolate; he is not happy over it. *ązo mąži* <o^{n}-çu mo^{n}-zhi> I am downcast; I am disconsolate. *ðizo aži* <thi-çu a-zhi> you are downcast; you are disconsolate. *wazo paži pe* <wa-çu ba-zhi i> we are downcast; we are disconsolate.

kíža. V [conjug. unknown] **doubt(?).**

•• LFD 53: *kíža* <gi´-zha> to doubt another's word.

••• *KS gíža* (JOD) doubt someone's word (RR), *wagíža* (JOD), *wagíža ~ waagíža* doubt one's own (child, etc.) (RR).

••• Cf. *wažá.*

kíži. V [reg. *ki*-ret., *_kíži*] [*ki-* DAT + *kaaží*] *(trans.)* **drive for s.o.** *oðíhtą ą́kiži* drive the car for me (RBn2-MOJ/p5, FH:okc, not ***ą́ka[a]žį*). *oðíhtą kíži* drive for him (BE2.35; FH:prod.).

kį́į. V [reg.?, *_kį́į*] *(intr.)* **fly (as birds do), ride in an airplane.** *wažį́ka akxa kį́į akxa* birds fly (01/26/95/FH/pc:ok; BE2.49). *kį́į ékimą hta akxai, kóe mǫ́žǫ záani iiðáðe hta akxai* if I could fly, then I could see the whole world (RBn15-02). *kį́į akxai* he's flying (FH:prod). *kįį ékiǫ* fly (lit., 'do flying'). *kį́į aðée* fly (lit., 'go by flying' or 'go by airplane'). • N **airplane.** *kį́į ðée hta apai* they're going to fly (lit., 'they are going to go in an airplane') (FH/11/18/01/pc:prod; BE2.2). *kį́į olį́į* ride in a plane (lit., 'sit in an airplane') (FH).

•• JOD (slip file): *kią́* <ḳi-a^{n}´> v. to fly.

•• LFD 51: *kią́* <gi-o^{n}´> to fly (unconfirmed; 01/26/95/FH/pc:uk).

kį́įðe. V [reg. *kį́į_ðe*] [*kį́į* + *ðe* CAU] *(trans.)* **throw (lit., 'cause to fly')** (01/10/95/FH/pc:prod).

kį́įkįįežį. N [reduplicated form] **butterfly.** *mąðí šǫ apa kį́įkįįežį toa kį́į ípšape* while they were walking some butterflies came flying by (RBn15-01).

kóe. CONJ **and then, and.** *níhkašie kíhǫǫpe kóe mąžą́ki olį́į kíhǫǫpe* he liked the people and he liked living on the farm (RBn10-2:MOJ/79). *koe ónǫǫ žišǫ ší tą šį́ tą koe hpíiži žišǫ ší tą koe péeški ðikǫ́ða htai wáščuye ðáalį* [and] before you get old and before you get fat and ugly and nobody wants you, you should get married. • **but, rather.** *táatą[e]žiški káaye íisipe kóe wanǫ́bre, hóo saakí, waachí kíhǫpe* he didn't like to do anything but eat, holler, and dance (RBn10-2:MOJ/79; RBn16-01).

kóoce (variant of **kóoci**).

kóoche (variant: **kóochi**). ADJ + POSIT (?) [perhaps *kóoci* + *che* POSIT] **old and stacked or piled.** *haxį́ kóoche* those old blankets that are stacked up there (FH/t116b).

kóoci (variant: **kóoce**). ADJ **old-fashioned, old-time, antique, old, from far back in time, ancient** (LS/04/26/95:prod). *haxį́ kóoci ščúuwasu tą wíe paašǫ́we* if you'll clean that old-time blanket, I'll bind it (FH/11/19/01/pc:prod). *haxį́ kóoci* old blankets (03/22/95/FH/pc). • ADV **long ago, once upon a time.** *kóoci wažáže apa ðée ékiǫpe ąži ðekǫ́ǫci ðįkápi wihtáeži akxa íkʔuci akxai* long ago Osages used to do that, but now they are gone and sister is trying her best (gloss by CQ; PM/7/7/94). *kóoci, hci hpíiži wį, paaxó ki, nąhtą́htą žíhi wį hcílipe* once upon a time, in a little shack in the hills, lived a little brown donkey (RBn10-2:MOJ/79). *kóoci ékiape*

kóoci (*continued*) they said that a long time ago (02/22/95/FH/pc:ok). *kóoci wáaząpe* a long time ago they bawled us out. *kóoce wažáži apa ée ékiapé* a long time ago Osages used to say that. • **for a long time.** *kóoci aškáą ąąhé* I've been going on for a long time (MOJ). • N **those who lived long ago.** *kóoci apa* those who lived long ago (03/02/95/FH/pc:okc). *kóoci apa ékie nąpe* the ones that lived a long time ago used to say (02/22/95/FH/pc:ok; BE2.81). *kóoci apa ée ékiapé* old-time people used to say.

•• LFD 56: *kóci* <gu´-dsi> in times past; a long time ago (primitive), farther into the house.

kootá. ADV **farther over there, beyond, on the other side of s.t.** (04/19/95/FH/pc:okc). *žáą akxa ápahta kootá ecí* the tree is on the other side of the fence (04/19/95/FH/pc).

kóota. ADJ **that yonder, that (person or thing) over there (beyond speaker and hearer).** *kóota níhka akxa óðuucˀakape* that man is lazy (RBn3-39). *kóota wakˀó akxa óðuucˀakape* that woman is lazy (02/15/95/FH/pc:ok). *kóota okála!* face the other way! (RBn19-02). • PRON **the farther one, in space or time.** *kóota įkšé ohkíhce hǫ́ǫxce ðįkšé?* that one sitting over there, what kind of tribe is he? (03/23/95/FH/pc).

•• LFD 53: *kótaðišǫ* <go´-da thi-sho^n> on the other side (unconfirmed; 04/06/95/LS/pc:uk). *kóta txą* <go´-da to^n> that person standing yonder (unconfirmed; 04/26/95/LS/pc:uk).

kóota che. PRONP **those farther over there (pl., inanimate only, beyond speaker and hearer).** [Contains *che*, the positional article for pl. sitting nonsubjects (those that would take *įkšé* when sg.).]

kóota ðe. PRONP **that one over there (beyond speaker and hearer).** *kóota ðe níhka tǫ́pa* look at that man farther over there.

kóota ðée. ADVP **(in the) future, future months (refers to traveling or going along in age, traveling down the road moving into the future)** (04/13/95/FH/pc:ok; HH#38a-p1).

kóota įkšé. PRONP **that one sitting over there or yonder (beyond speaker and hearer).** *kóota įkšé ohkíhce hǫ́ǫxce ðįkšé?* that one sitting over there, what kind of tribe is he? (03/23/95/FH/pc).

kóota kše (variant: **kootá kše**). PRONP **that one lying over there (beyond speaker and hearer).** *kootá kše pée ée kše?* that [one] lying over there, who is it?

kootáha. ADV [*kóota* + *ha* PPN] **(to/from) farther away (in space); farther back, farther ahead (in time or space)** (02/14/95/FH/pc:ok; 04/26/95/LS/pc:ok; FH/07/09/01/pc). [Contrasts with *kootáįke* 'over there'.] *kootáha nąąží* stand farther over (FH). *kootáha!* move over! (e.g., said to a person taking up too much room in bed) (FH). *kootáha alíį hkǫ́bra* move over because I want to sit down (FH). *kootáha, kóotaha* farther back in time (04/06/95/FH/pc:ok). • PPN **beyond.** *níižuuce kootáha* beyond the Arkansas River (04/11/95/LS/pc:prod). • ADJ, PRON **the next-to-last, the one before last.** *míįǫpa kootáha* next-to-last month; the month before last. • **the one after next, the one past the next.**

•• RB: <gó-tah-hah>.

•• LFD 53: *kotáha mąðí o* <go-da´-ha mo^n-thi^n o> [sentence-final *o* is not used in Mod. Os.] go farther away (04/05/95/MREI/pc:ok). *kotáha* <go-da´-ha> go away; depart.

••• Cf. *háąpa kootáha ce, kaasí kootáha, sitǫ́į kootáha ce.*

kootáįke (variant: **kootáįki**). ADV **over there, yonder, farther than another thing, way over there, way back in time or distance** (04/06/95/FH/pc:ok). [Contrasts with *kootáha* 'farther away'.] *kootáįke líįpi* you all sit over there (BE2.44; 04/06/95/FH/pc). *kootáįke alíį hkǫ́bra* I want to sit over there. *kootáįke nąąží* go stand over there (03/14/95/FH/pc:ok; BE2.126).

•• RB: <gó-tai^n-ki>.

koša. N [accent perceived as equal in both syllables; possibly *koošá*?] **curve.**

••• Cf. *hpasúkoša.*

kǫ́ða. V [sync. fortisizing stop stem+sync., *_kǫ́_ða*; infrequently with triple conjugation, reg.+sync. fortisizing stop stem+sync., *_ _kǫ́_ða*] *(trans.)* **want, desire.** [2nd person form customarily lengthens the *ǫ́* in interrogatives, though this is not normally indicated in writing: *škǫ́ǫšta* 'do you want?'.] *hkǫ́bra* I want (03/16/95/JS/pc:ok). *hkǫ́bra įké* I don't want to (do something). *šée wihkǫ́bra* I want that for you (03/16/95/JS/pc:ok). *ðée ka wį škǫ́šta?* do you want one of these? *háakǫ škǫ́šta tą ékiǫ* do whatever you want to do (03/16/95/JS/pc:ok). *ðée škǫ́šta?* do you want this? (03/16/95/JS/pc:ok). *škǫ́šta?* do you want [it]? (03/16/95/JS/pc:ok). *kǫ́ða įkí akxai* he/she doesn't want to (do something) (03/16/95/JS/pc:ok; BE2.150). *mázeska háąna kǫ́ða akxa?* how much money does he want? (03/16/95/JS/pc:okc). *kǫ́ða* he/she wants [it], they want [it] (03/16/95/JS/pc:ok). *ąkǫ́ða* we want [it] (03/16/95/JS/pc:ok). *kǫ́ða wáli* to really want something; to crave it. *wažážeíe hpíǫ áhkǫ́bra* I want him to learn Osage [*áhkǫ́bra*: triple conjugation] (RBn10-7:JW). *hpíǫ áhkǫ́bra* I want him to learn, I want him to learn it [*áhkǫ́bra*: triple conjugation] (04/14/95/PM/pc:ok; RB).

•• LFD 53: *kǫ́ða walį* <go^n´ tha wa-gthi^n> to crave; a longing (03/16/95/JS/pc:ok). *khokhóma hkǫbra walį* <ku-ku´-ma k͓o^n-btha wa-gthi^n> [expected Mod. Os. form: *hkohkóma* rather than *khokhóma*] I have a longing for cucumbers. *žąąnii škǫšta walį* <zho^n-ni shko^n-shda wa-gthi^n> you crave sugar.

kǫ́ðawaðe (variant: **kǫ́ðaéewaðe**). v [reg., *kǫ́ðawa_ðe*] [*kǫ́ða* + *wa-* VAL + *ðe* CAU] *(trans.)* **make folks want to, make one want to.** *óohǫ kǫ́ðawai* it makes one want to cook. *hǫpái mą́ąɣe akxa ðáalį akxái, opáwįɣe kǫ́ðaéewae* today the weather is good, it makes one want to go riding (03/16/95/JS/pc:ok).

kǫ́kǫe. v [conjug. unknown] [reduplicated form] *(intr.)* **go around.** *kǫ́kǫe nąpé* he would go around and around (FH/11/19/01/pc:uk). *ší kǫ́kǫe apai, žįkážį apa páskuha nąąkí apai* he went round and round, children ran beside him (RBn10-2:MOJ/79). • N **merry-go-round, carousel.**

kǫpé. N **hackberry, hackberries.**

•• JOD (Raccoons and Crawfish p21 ln6): *kǫpé* <k͓u^{n}p͓é>.

kǫzé. v [sync. *k>p, _kǫzé*] *(trans.)* **pretend, feign, make believe.** [Unconfirmed by modern speakers.]

•• JOD (slip file): *kǫzé* <ko^n-s͓e´> pretend [but:] <k͓ŭ^n´-s͓e é-k͓ŭ^n>. *kǫ́ze ékǫ* alike, resembling something else referred to.

•• LFD 53: *kǫzé* <go^n-çe´> to feign; to make believe. *hpǫze* <p͓o^n-çe> I pretend. *ąkǫza pe* <o^n-go^n-ça i> we pretend.

kǫ́ze. v [sync. *k> p, _kǫ́ze*] *(trans.)* **teach s.t. to s.o.; show s.o. how to do s.t.** *iinąžį akxa kǫ́ze hta akxái* my aunt is going to teach him (03/16/95/FH/pc:ok; 03/05/95/JS/pc:ok; not *kikǫ́ze*). *iinąžį akxa ðikǫ́ze hta akxái* my aunt is going to teach you (JS/pc:ok; BE2.133). *wikǫ́ze hta mįkšé* I'm going to show you (03/09/95/MREI/pc:ok).

••• Cf. *hkihkǫ́ze, kšíǫze, wakǫ́ze.*

kǫzéhkihkǫ. ADJ [*hkik-* REFL + *kǫzékǫ*] **similar to or like each other, resembling each other.** *hkóða akxa hkáwa ðǫǫpá kǫzéhkihkǫ waaðį́pe* my friend has two horses just alike.

•• LFD 53: *kǫzé hkikǫ* <go^n-çe´ k͓i-go^n> alike; resembling.

kǫzékǫ. ADJ, v [conjug. unknown, uninfl.?] *(trans.?)* **(be) the same as or like another, like, similar to or identical to.** *hpǫ́hkaíe wažážeíe hǫ́ni kǫzékǫ* Ponca and Osage language are almost the same (FH:4/24/96/tape ; BE2.116) *wacúe skue mąščįka kǫzékǫ káaɣa* make the cake like a rabbit (FH:4/24/96/tape:prod). *Mary akxa iihǫ́ kǫzékǫ akxai* Mary is just like her mother [acts like, looks like, or both]. *hkąącezi akxa watkxą́ kǫzékǫ akxai* the orange is just like the pumpkin (FH:4/24/96/tape:prod). *kǫzékǫ káaɣi akxai* he's making it like that (FH:prod). *éhta, ðáalį kǫzékǫ ąkái* well, it's good we're just alike (RBn17-p02). *htóožu akxa nahkoį kǫzékǫ akxai* both those meat pies are just alike (FH:prod). *kǫzékǫ káaɣi akxai* he's making it like that (FH:prod). *hpǫ́hka íe wažáže íe kǫzéko* Poncas and Osages talk the same (03/08/95/MREI/pc:okc; MREI)

•• JOD (slip file): *kǫ́ze ékǫ* <k͓ŭ^n´-s͓e é-k͓ŭ^n> alike, resembling something else referred to.

•• LFD 53: *kǫzékǫ* <go^n-çe´-go^n> alike in appearance; similar; uniform. LFD 38: *tǫ́pe kǫzékǫ* <do^n´-be go^n-çe´-go^n> alike; look alike; similar. *tǫ́pe kǫzekǫ pe, wakˀo nǫpa akxa* <do^n´-be go^n-çe-go^n bi a, wa-u no^n-ba a-ka> [expected Mod. Os. form: *ðǫǫpá* rather than *nǫpa*] the women look alike [rather, 'the two women (here) look alike'].

kǫ́žįka. v [sync. *k>p, _kǫ́žįka*] *(trans., intr.)* **be unskilled (at), not know how (to).** *wahǫ́ǫ hpážika* I don't know how to address folks. *škǫ́žįka* you don't know how; do you know how? [either a statement or a question] (02/14/95/FH/pc:ok; 02/14/95/FH/pc:ok). *kǫ́žįka akxai* he doesn't know how.

•• LFD 53: *kǫ́žįka* <go^n´-zhi^n-ga> failure to do a thing for lack of skill; unskilled. *hpǫ́žįka* <p͓o^n´-zhi^n-ga> I am unskilled. *škǫ́žįka* <shko^n´-zhi^n-ga> you are unskilled. *ąkǫ́žįka pe* <o^n-go^n´-zhi^n-ga i> we are unskilled.

kšąka (variant of **kšǫka**).

kše (variant: **kši**). POSIT **positional article for an entity that is lying down or long, used after a noun or pronoun that is not an active subject.** *mą́ąhisi wakˀó kše abrį́* I have the queen of spades. *iihǫ́ kše tąhé įkšé?* is his or her mother [who is bedridden or lying down] all right? *ðiihǫ́ kše tąhé akxai?* how is your [bedridden] mother? *mǫ́žǫ ðáalį ðé kše mǫ́žǫ ðé kše ðįké hta aaži íe wíhta šǫǫšǫ́we aðée hta akxai* heaven and earth shall pass away but my word will endure (lit.,

kše (*continued*)
'that good land lying there and this land lying here will be nothing but my word always will go on') (FH: from the Bible, Matthew 24:35) *kóota kše pée ée kše?* that [one] lying over there, who is it? *šée kše k^{ʔ}į alípe* they hauled him back, they hauled back that one near you lying down (RBn23-17). *hkáwa kše húheka kše?* is that horse lying there sick? *šǫ́ke ékše háažǫ?* what are you going to do with that dog lying there? *žą́ą kše* the one sleeping over there (03/24/95/PM/pc). *ípehį sí kše ǫ́ǫ kšíe* put a pillow under his foot (03/08/95/FH/pc). *ípehį áa kše į kšíe* put a pillow under his arm. *tówa kše šcéða!* doctor that one lying there, doctor him! • POSIT **positional article that indicates plurality of an inanimate entity that takes *che* 'standing' positional in the singular.** [No examples available in Mod. Os. data.]
•• LFD 224: *žą́ kše* <zho^{n}´ kshe> term used in speaking of a log lying on the ground. LFD 192: *wahóhtąðe ímąkše* <wa-ho´-ṭo^{n}-the i-mo^{n}-kshe> the other of the two guns [the other lying down or long gun] (03/02/95/FH/pc:ok). LFD 37 (unconfirmed): *tóosku káxa kše áška ci alį́į* <Do´-çkiu ga-xa ke a-shka dsi a-gthi^{n}> I live near Spring River [Sweet Potato Creek]. LFD 92: *žąą hkilé kše ci amįce bree ha* <zho^{n} ḳi-gthe´ ke dsi a-mi^{n}-dse bthe ha> [sentence-final *ha* is not used in Mod. Os.] I crawled under the log.

kše (variant: **kši**). CONT **lying down or long (used clause-finally; often followed by *áape*, denoting reported information).** *šúpe kíhúheka kší áape* he [lying down] has stomach trouble, they said (RBn3-49). *wáli húheka kší áapa ążį nąąyeska kší áape* she [lying down] is awfully sick, but her mind is all right [they said] (FH/6/16/95). *waðáahtą štą éhtana céepe hpíiži kší aape* he [lying down] has a bad liver from always drinking [they said] (02/16/95/FH/pc:okc). *céepe hpíiži kší aape waðáahtą štą éhna* he [lying down] has a bad liver [they said] because he's always drinking (RBn3-55). *wáli ðiižóžipi kší áape* he [lying down] has really been hurt, they said (02/13/95/FH/pc:okc; BE2.70). *žą́ą kší áape* that person's lying down, they said (02/15/95/FH/pc:prod orig). *ée kší áape* [it is] she lying there, they said (RBn11-02). *pée ée kše?* who is that over there lying down? *šúpe iihúheka kší áape* he [lying down] has intestinal trouble, they said (12/30/94/FH/pc; FH/09/23/01/pc). *išík^{ʔ}ą hcéze íihuheka kší áape* my sister-in-law [lying down] is sick with her stomach, they say (FH/09/23/01/pc:prod). *ąwą́xpaðe, íkišoce kše* I was lost in the [overlying] fog (01/26/95/FH/pc:okc).

kše áape (variant of **kší áape**).

kši. PPN **to, at, on, in that (something lying down or spread out lengthwise).** *wahkǫ́taki kši pšíe ðe* I went to the doctor [*kši* is optional in this sentence; reference to the office of the doctor is implied] (04/26/95/FH/pc:okc). *níižuuce kši mąðį́* go to the river [imperative] (RBn16-02). *lį́įka áwanǫbre kší* be seated at the table [imperative] (RBn1-3, 17). *ą́nąkoe kši lį́įka* sit on the porch [imperative] (HH/t38-sA-p2). *htą́wą kši* in town (contrasts with 'in the country' [RB]) (03/23/95/FH/pc:ok).

kši (variant of **kše**).

kší (see **akší**).

kší áape (variant: **kše áape, kšíaape**). REPORTATIVE [*kše* CONT + *áape*] **it is said of him/her lying down.** *šúpe kihúheka kší áape* they said he [lying down] has intestinal trouble (RB).

kšíðe (variant: **kšíe**). CAU [reg. _*kšíðe*] [*ki-* DAT + *kíðe*] *(trans.)* **let or allow s.o. to do s.t.** *ée óhką kšíe* let her help (FH). *íe ðée ochíchachae káaye kšiðé įká* don't let him go on and on [talking] (MSB:t9). • **have s.o. do s.t. for his/her own benefit.** *haxį́ į kšíe* have him wear a blanket. *hiiðá ąðákšie* you had me bathe (MREI). *wáleze ðée kšíe* mail this letter to her ['to her' implied by *kšíe*] (02/15/95/FH/pc:okc). *waazóe ąkšíe hta ąkái* we're going to show them a good time.
•• LFD 116: *nǫ́p^{ʔ}į kšiðe* <no^{n}´-p̣'i^{n} kshi-the> to cause one to wear something around the neck. *wak^{ʔ}o ðe wánǫp^{ʔ}į htą akšiðe ha* <wa-ḳ'u the wa´-no^{n}-p̣'i^{n} ṭo^{n} a-kshi-the ha> [sentence-final *ha* is not used in Mod. Os.] I caused the woman to wear a necklace.

kšíye. V [reg. _*kšíye*] [presumably *ki-* DAT + *káaye*] *(trans.)* **make or prepare for s.o. (e.g., prepare a bed, clothing, or food).** *htáaoolą toa ąkšíya* make me some sandwiches (RBn10-2). *síekǫ wikšíye* I made a meat pie for you (MREI 11-1-83-8). *Mary akxa haaská wį kšíyape* Mary made a shirt for him. • **fix (prepare or repair) for s.o.** *ąkšíya* fix it for me (02/13/95/FH/pc:prod orig). *wíe na ąkšíyape* they did it just for me. *ážą ąkšíya* fix my bed for me (02/13/95/FH/pc:prod orig). *ónǫ́bre akšíye* I'm fixing the food for her. *ǫnǫ́bre ąwákšíye ąðikše* we're fixing it for them (02/13/95/FH/pc:prod orig). *ǫnǫ́bre awákšiye hta mįkšé* I'm going to fix food for them. *wisǫ́ka súhka wį óohǫ kšíyape* they cooked a chicken for

Sonny (lit., 'they made a cooked chicken for Sonny'). *ékǫ kǫ́ða apa, ékǫ waðákšiɣe hkǫ́bra* whatever they want, [I want you to] fix it for them (RBn22-10). *táatą howachéeški waðákšiɣe hkǫ́bra* whatever [it is], I want you to fix it for them. *haaská íikšiɣa* fix his shirt/their shirts (FH/09/21/01/pc). *haaská ą́kšiɣa* fix my shirt (FH/09/24/01/prod). *haaská wikšíɣe hce* let me fix your shirt. • **have or make s.t. or s.o. be a certain way, have or make s.o. do s.t.** *íe káache ðáalį waðakšíɣe* make these words good for us (JS prayer). *óðohta wakšíɣa* make him behave (RBn22-19). *wižį́ke mą́zeska tóa céɣenii ážu áwakšie hta mįkšé* I'm going to have my son put some money on the drum (RBn10-3:MOJ/79; CQc).

•• LFD 90: *kšíɣe* <kshi´-xe> to make or do something for another. *šį́hto žį́ka ðe mą wį akčiɣe aða* <shi^{n}´-ṭo zhi^{n}-ga the mo^{n} wi^{n} a-kchi xe a-tha> [expected Mod. Os. form: *šį́tožį ðe mą́ą wį akšį́ɣe ąhé*] I am making an arrow for the boy. *akšiɣe* <a-kshi-xe> I made something for him. *ðakšiɣe* <tha-kshi-xe> you made something for him. *ąkšiɣa pe* <o^{n}-kshi-xa i> we make something for him. LFD 131: *šį́hto žį́ka ðe mą wį ðakčiɣe aðo* <shi^{n}´-ṭo zhi^{n}-ga the mo^{n} wi^{n} tha-kchi xe a-tho> [expected Mod. Os. form: *šį́tožį ðe mą́ą wį ðakšį́ɣe ðąįšé*] you are making an arrow for the boy.

kšíǫze (variants: **kšúįze, kšíǫ́ze**). v [reg.+(sync. vowel initial stem), *_kší(_)ǫze* (optionally doubly inflected in 1st sg. as *akšímǫze* or *akšíǫze* 'I teach him'; but singly inflected in other forms, e.g., 2nd person *ðakšíǫze* 'you teach him')] [*ki-* DAT + *kǫ́ze*] *(trans.)* **teach s.t. to s.o.** *wažážeíe akšíǫze* I teach [the] Osage language (03/23/95/FH/pc). *awákšuįze* I teach them (my kids) (2/2/p7). *táatą íšpahǫ škǫ́šta tą, wikšímǫze hta mįkšé* what you want to know, I will teach you (RBn10-16). *kxážį mą́ą ðíhtą akšímąze* I taught *kxážį* how to draw the bow (03/23/95/FH/pc). *žį́kážį wíhta wažážeíe awákšuįze maží na* I never taught my kids the Osage language. *ðakšíǫze* you teach [him]. *wažážeíe šée ąkšíǫza* teach me that in Osage, teach me that Osage (03/16/95/FH/pc:ok). *wacúe káaɣe ąkšúįze* teach me how to make bread (RBn23-14). • **show s.o. how to do s.t.** *hpímǫ wikšíǫ́zc* I know how so I'm going to show you how (FH/8/30/94: or *wikšímǫze* as second preference). *awákšiǫ́ze* I showed them how (FH/8/30/94; 03/05/95/JS/pc: *ąwą́kšiǫze*). *wikšímǫ́ze hta mįkšé* I'll show you how (03/09/95/MREI/pc:ok). *ąkšíǫ́zape* he showed me how (03/09/95/MREI/pc:ok). *įhtáci akxa kšíǫ́zapc* my father showed him how (03/09/95/MREI/pc:ok). *pee ðikšíǫ́ze?* who showed you how? (03/09/95/MREI/pc:ok). *ąðíkšiǫ́ze* we'll show you how (03/09/95/MREI/pc:ok). *ąkšíǫ́za* show me how (03/09/95/MREI/pc:okc). *wakšíǫza* show them how! (FH/8/30/94: *ǫ́za* has strong secondary stress).

•• LFD 90, 283: *kčiǫze* <kchi´-o^{n}-çe> [expected Mod. Os. form: *kšíǫze*] to instruct, to teach another (05/02/95/LS/pc:okc). LFD 84: *hkážįka mąðitą ahkčimąze aðo* <ḳa´-zhi^{n}-ga mo^{n}-thi-do^{n} a-ḳchi-mo^{n}-çe a-tho> [expected Mod. Os. form: *kxážį mą́ą ðiitą́ ðakšíǫze* (05/02/95/LS/pc:okc)] I taught *kxážį* to draw the bow. *hkážįka mąðitą ðakčiǫze aðo* <ḳa´-zhi^{n}-ga mo^{n}-thi-do^{n} tha-kchi-o^{n}-çe a-tho> [expected Mod. Os form: *kxážį mǫ́ǫ ðiitą́ ðakšíǫze*] you taught *kxážį* to draw the bow. LFD 84 (unconfirmed): *číǫze* <chi´-o^{n}-çe> [expected Mod. Os. form: *kšíǫze*] to teach, to instruct. *akčíǫze* <a-kchi´-o^{n}-çe> I teach. *ðakčíǫze* <tha-kchi´-o^{n}-çe> [expected modern Os. form: *ðakšíǫze*] you teach.

••• Cf. *wakšíǫze.*

kšǫ́ka (variant: **kšą́ka**). N **second son (in any clan)** (FH/11/17/01/pc). *kšǫ́ka šǫ́ke íhta apa zípe* second son's dog is yellow (2-1-F).

kšúįze (variant of **kšíǫze**).

kú (see **akú**).

kusúe (variant of **kisúðe**).

kxáhpą (variant: **kxahpái**). N **baby son; baby brother (said to be used by a woman to refer to her youngest brother or to her youngest son if she has at least two older sons).**

••• *KS khâge ppahą́le* son, third born (JOD) (RR), *khága* son, fourth born (JOD), third born (RR).

kxáke. N **third son or subsequent son** (FH/pc). [Synonymous with *kxážį.*]

kxážį (variant: **kxážįka**). N **third son or subsequent son (in any clan)** (FH/11/17/01/pc; 04/26/95/FH/pc:ok). [Synonymous with *kxáke.*]

•• LFD 84: *hkážįka* <ḳa´-zhi^{n}-ga> the third son, a special kinship term. *hkážįka akxa wae nihkašika pi a* <ḳa´-zhi^{n}-ga a-ka wa e ni-ḳa-shi-ga bi a> [probable expected Mod. Os. form: *kxážį akxa ówe níhkašikape*] my third son is a farmer [unconfirmed sentence].

kxą (variant of **txą** CONT and POSIT).

kxą́ha (variant of **txą́ha**).

kˀ

kˀą́saaki. ADJ, V [reg. *_kˀą́saaki*] *(intr.)* **(be) fast in movement, fleet (as a runner).** *wisǫ́ka akxa kˀą́saakipe* brother is fast, speedy (BE2.45), *wisǫ́ka akxa ną́ąke kˀą́saakipe* brother is a fast runner (01/23/95/FH/pc:prod orig), *ną́ąke kˀą́saaki brį́e* I'm a fast runner (01/23/95/FH/pc:prod orig), *ðíe ną́ąke kˀą́saaki nį́e* you're a fast runner (01/23/95/FH/pc:prod orig). • ADV **quickly, fast, rapidly, swiftly.**

•• LFD 88: *kˀą́saaki* <ḳ'o^{n}´-ça-gi> fleet; swift; very fast. *ahką́saki* <a-ḳo^{n}´-ça-gi> [expected Mod. Os. form: *akˀą́saaki*] I am swift of foot. *ðahką́saki* <tha-ḳo^{n}´-ça-gi> [expected Mod. Os. form: *ðakˀą́saaki*] you are swift of foot (01/23/95/FH/pc:no). *ąhkąsaki pe* <o^{n}-ḳo^{n}-ça-gi i> [expected Mod. Os. form: *ąkˀą́saakipe*] we are swift of foot.

••• Cf. *mą́zekˀąsaaki.*

kˀé. V [reg. *_kˀé*] *(trans.)* **dig, dig up.** *tóoska akˀé hta aðįhé* I'm going to dig potatoes (BE2.31; FH:ok). *tóoska ąkˀé hta ąkái* we're going to dig potatoes (01/20/95/FH/pc:ok).

•• LFD 84: *kˀe* <ḳ'e>to dig. *to hke bre į to* <do ḳe bthe i^{n} do> [expected Mod. Os. form: *tooská kˀé brée*] I go to dig potatoes. *ahke* <a-ḳe> [expected Mod. Os. form: *akˀé*] I dig. *ðahké* <tha-ḳe´> [expected Mod. Os. form: *ðakˀé*] you dig. *ąhka pe* <o^{n}-ḳa i> [expected Mod. Os. form: *ąkˀápe*] we dig.

••• *KS kˀé* dig (RR); *QU kˀe* dig (RR).

kˀíe (variant of **kˀúe**).

kˀį́. V [reg. *_kˀį́*] *(trans.)* **carry, carry on the back.** *ną́hka wíhta áalįį hta wikíkˀį hta mįkše áapa* I'll carry you on my back, he said (t#24a-p4; 04/11/95/FH/pc:ok). *kˀį́ ðée* they are carrying them on their back (FH:prod). *kˀį́ðaape* they are carrying them [i.e., *kˀį́ aðée api ðe*]. *kˀį́pe* they carried them. *mą́zeska kˀį́ apai* they're carrying money (FH:prod).

•• JOD (slip file): *kˀį́* <k'i^{n}> to carry a load on the back.

•• LFD 86–87 (unconfirmed): *kˀį* <ḳ'i^{n}> to carry. *ahkį́* <a-ḳi^{n}´> [expected Mod. Os. form: *akˀį́*] I carry. *ąhkį́ pe* <o^{n}-ḳi^{n}´ i> [expected Mod. Os. form: *ąkˀį́*] we carry.

kˀį́ahi. V [sync. h-stem, *kˀį́a_hi*] [*kˀį́ + ahí*] *(trans.)* **take, transport, carry (lit., 'carrying arrive there').** *Billie akxa ąkˀį́ahi hta akxai* Billie is going to bring [take] me [there] [the object pronominal *ą-* 'me' precedes *kˀį́*].

kˀó. N **hole.**

••• Cf. *okˀó.*

kˀǫ́. V [reg., *_kˀǫ́*] *(trans.)* **play;** *(intr.)* **gamble.**

kˀǫ́he. V [reg., *_kˀǫ́he*] *(trans.)* **lay into.**

••• Cf. *ohkíkˀǫhe.*

kˀǫ́su (variant: **kˀǫ́se** [FH]). N **dice, Osage dice** (RB, 01/20/95/FH/pc:prod orig). *kˀǫ́su kˀǫ́ aðáape ska* I guess they went to play dice (BE2.31; RBn2-MOJ/p18; 01/20/95/FH/pc:ok).

kˀǫ́sukˀǫ́. V [reg., *kˀǫ́su_kˀǫ́*] [*kˀǫ́su + kˀǫ́*] *(intr.)* **play dice.** • N **Osage dice game** (01/20/95/FH/pc:ok; BE2.31).

kˀú. V [reg., *_kˀú*] *(trans.)* **give.** *wikˀú* I give it to you (01/31/95/FH/pc:okc). *Bob akxa Joe haxį́ wį kˀúpe* Bob gave Joe a blanket. *mį́įǫpa šáhpe ną kˀú apai, wahkǫ́taki* the doctors gave him only six months (RBn10-2). *haxį́ wį ðikˀúpe* he gave you a blanket. *haxį́ wį ąkˀúpe* he gave me a blanket (01/31/95/FH/pc:ok). *ąkˀúpe* it was given to me (lit., 'they gave it to me') (01/31/95/FH/pc:okc; RBn1-23). *ónǫbre wakˀúpi apai* we were fed (lit., 'they gave us some food'). *ąkˀúži* they did not give [it] to me (01/31/95/FH/pc:okc). *ąkˀú!* give [it to] me! (01/31/95/FH/pc:okc). *žáže kˀú* give him/her an Indian name [imperative] (02/27/95/FH/pc:ok). *hǫ́ǫpa hpahą́leche žáže kˀú hkilíiski hta apai* the first day of the week, they're going to gather together for a naming (i.e., to give [him/her] an Osage name). • **pass s.t. to s.o. (e.g., at the table).** *níi toa ąkˀú* pass the water (lit., 'give me some water') (03/06/95/FH/pc:ok).

•• LFD 85 (unconfirmed): *kˀi* <ḳ'i> to give; to present to another. *akˀí* <a-ḳ'i´> I give. *ðakˀí* <tha-ḳ'i´> you give. *ąkˀí pe* <o^{n}-ḳ'i´ i> we give.

••• *KS kˀű* give (RR).

kˀú huu (variant: **kˀú huðe**). VP *(trans.)* **pass by hand.** *ąkˀú huu* hand it to me (RBn1-7). *hcúke ðǫǫpá ąkˀú huu* hand me two spoons (RBn1-52).

kˀúe (variant: **kˀíe**). V [reg., *_kˀúe*] *(intr.)* **scratch an itch.** *ną́hka akˀíe* I scratch on my back (spoken by a person whose back itches) (RBn10-6:JW, unconfirmed; CQ:okc).

••• *QU daxˀíxˀíke* itch one (RR).

---

l

láace (variant: **laacé**). v [reg., *_láace*] [*kik-* SUU + *ðaacé*] **name one's own, call one's own by name.** *táatą laatáape?* what did they name him [their relative]?

laaská (variant: **hlaaská**). N **flower** (01/26/95/FH/pc). [This is virtually the only word in which an initial *hl* is commonly preserved in Mod. Os.] *kį́įkįįežį hlaaskážį éðǫǫpa ǫ́ǫðe aðáape* he went leaving [both] the flowers and butterflies behind (RBn15-03; BE2.49).

•• RB: <hláh-skah, xláh-shkah, kláh-skah>.

láaxǫ. v [reg., *_láaxǫ*] [*kik-* SUU + *ðaaxǫ́*] **break s.t. of one's own by mouth.** *híi laaxǫ́pe* he broke a tooth.

laazípe (see **hlaazípe**).

lápxąąke (variant: **lapxą́įke**). N **mosquito** (02/25/95/FH/pc:ok). [Hominy usage.]

•• RB: <láh-pxáh-i^{n}-keh>.

•• JOD (slip file): *lápąke* <k¢a´-pañ-k͓e> the musquito; musquitoes [*sic*].

lažį́į. ADJ **skinny (e.g., a person or a tree), slim, slender, thin; lean (describes a person or an animal, not meat); poor, pitiful, gaunt, haggard.** *wálį lažį́į ðaįšé* you're really skinny (BE2.122; FH:prod; 03/10/95/PM/pc:ok).

•• RB: <láh-zhí^{n}>.

•• LFD 220: *lažį́ ka* <xtha-zhi^{n}´ ga> lean; gaunt; haggard; slender; slim; thin; lean.

lą́ (variant: **lǫ́**). ADJ **mad, angry.** *lą́ aðée che iiðáahpe hta mįkšé* I will wait until he goes away mad [angry] (FH:prod).

•• LFD 220: *alǫ bre* <a-xtho^{n} bthe> [expected Mod. Os. form: *ólą brée*] I went away in a sulk.

••• Cf. *ólą.*

lą́ą (variant of **lǫ́ǫ**).

lą́ąðe (variant: **lą́ąði**). ADJ, V [uninfl.] *(intr.)* **(be) big, large, broad, wide** (01/07/95/FH/pc:ok); **great, stupendous; important; fat, overweight.** *wáli íhaa lą́ąðape* she has a big mouth (RBnote). *lą́ąðe htą́* very large (02/14/95/FH/pc:ok; BE2.75). *lą́ąðe wáli* enormous, huge. *nihkáži lą́ąðipe* he's a big man (2-2-259). *htaacé lą́ąðį* a tempest (03/23/95/FH/pc). *táatą wį́xce lą́ąðe* a great thing (RBn23-09). *lą́ąðe brį́e* I'm fat (FH). *táatą haamáį che lą́ąði ekxai* what I did was important (02/14/95/FH/pc:ok).

•• LFD 56: *lą́ðe* <gtho^{n}´-the> magnitude; greatness; broad; wide; stupendous; prodigious. LFD 136: *htacé lą́ðe* <t̯a-dse´ gtho^{n}-the> great windstorm, a tempest.

lą́ąðe wálį. ADJP **huge, enormous, exceedingly large.**

•• LFD 56: *lą́ąðe walį* <gtho^{n}´-the wa-gthi^{n}> enormous; exceedingly large; huge. *lape lą́ðe walį htǫpe ha* <xtha-be gtho^{n}´-the wa-gthi^{n} t̯o^{n}-be ha> [expected Mod. Os. form: *žą́ą lą́ąðe wálį htǫ́pe*; *lape* 'tree' unconfirmed; *lape* and sentence-final *ha* not used in Mod. Os.] I saw huge trees.

lą́ąðehtą. ADJ **chubby, very large** (RBn1-MOJ/p22; 01/09/95/FH/pc:ok).

lą́ąði (variant of **lą́ąðe**).

lą́ke. v [reg., *_lą́ke*] *(trans.)* **marry a woman, take as a wife.** *šómįhkasi akxa htaacéžį lą́ke kǫ́ðape* the coyote wanted to marry the whirlwind (RBn17-p; 02/27/95/JS/pc).

•• JOD (Devouring Mountain p2 ln13–14): *wak?ó ðáalį xci šímįžįka ðáalį xci tóopa k?úpe ska, wahǫ́įžįka walą́ke hta* <Wak'u´ ¢ák͓¢i^{n}-qtsi, cími^{n}çiñ´k͓a ¢ák͓¢i^{n}-qtsi t̯úpa k'üpe ska, Wahŭ^{n}´içiñ´k͓a wak͓¢añk͓e ta> they gave him four very pretty girls so that he, the orphan, might take them as wives.

•• LFD 55: *lą́ke* <gtho^{n}´-ge> to take a wife; to marry.

••• Cf. *hkilą́ke, mį́įląke.*

lébrą (variant: **lébra**). ADJ, N **ten, tenth.**

•• RB: <léh-brah> (03/16/95/FH/pc; BE2.136).

•• LFD 54: *lébrą* <gthe´-btho^{n}> [final *a* or *ą* is quite short] ten.

lébrą álįį ðáabrį (variant: **álįį ðáabrį**). ADJ, N **thirteen, thirteenth.**

lébrą álįį ðǫǫpá (variants: **álįį ðǫǫpá, álįį ðǫ́ǫpa**). ADJ, N **twelve, twelfth** (BE2.146; 02/27/95/JS/pc:okc).

•• RB: <áh-li-thó^{n}-pah> [JS: full form or shortened form equally correct].

•• LFD 10: *alį ðǫpa* <a-gthi^{n} tho^{n}-ba> two sixes; twelve; a dozen. *súhka žįka alįį ðǫǫpa waškǫsta* <çiu´-k͓a zhi^{n}-ga a-gthi^{n} tho^{n}-ba wa-shko^{n}-sda> you want twelve chickens.

lébrą álįį hce wį́įke (variant: **álįį hce wį́įke**). ADJ, N **nineteen, nineteenth.** [Full form would be *lébrą álįį lébrą hce wį́įke*, which is rarely if ever used but clearly understood.]

lébrą álį̨ hkietóopa (variant: **álį̨ hkietóopa**). ADJ, N **eighteen, eighteenth.**
lébrą álį̨ hpéǫǫpa (variant: **álį̨ hpéǫǫpa**). ADJ, N **seventeen, seventeenth.**
lébrą álį̨ sáhtą (variant: **álį̨ sáhtą**). ADJ, N **fifteen, fifteenth.**
lébrą álį̨ šáhpe (variant: **álį̨ šahpe**). ADJ, N **sixteen, sixteenth.**
lébrą álį̨ tóopa (variant: **álį̨ tóopa**). ADJ, N **fourteen, fourteenth.**
lébrą álį̨ wį́xce (variant: **álį̨ wį́xce**). ADJ, N **eleven, eleventh.**
lébrą ðáabrį. ADJ, N **thirty, thirtieth.**
lébrą ðǫǫpá (variant: **lébrąðǫ́ǫpa**). ADJ, N **twenty, twentieth.**
lébrą ðǫǫpá álį̨ wį́xci (variants: **lébraðǫ́ǫpa áliwį́xci, lébraðǫ́ǫpa éci wį́xci**). ADJ, N **twenty-one, twenty-first** (RB; 05/02/95/LS/pc: ok). [The version with *éci* possibly sounds old-fashioned (LF).]
lébrą hce wį́įke (variant: **hcewį́įke**). ADJ, N **nine, ninth** (BE2.94; 02/27/95/FH/pc:ok).
lébrą hkietóopa. ADJ, N **eighty, eightieth.**
lébrą hpéðǫǫpa (variant: **lébrą hpéǫǫpa**). ADJ, N **seventy, seventieth.**
lébrą huužį́. ADJ, N **hundred, hundredth.** *lébrą huužį́ ðǫǫpá* two hundred (04/11/95/LS/pc:ok). *lébra huužį́ ðǫǫpá éci wį́xci* two hundred and one (04/11/95/LS/pc:ok; BE2.69).
lébrą lébrą hce wį́įke. ADJ, N **ninety, ninetieth.**
lébrą sáhtą. ADJ, N **fifty, fiftieth.**
lébrą šáhpe. ADJ, N **sixty, sixtieth.**
lébrą tóopa. ADJ, N **forty, fortieth.**
lébrąðǫ́ǫpa (variant of **lébrą ðǫǫpá**).
léepa, léepe (variants of **lépe**).
léke (variant: **hléke**) V [reg., *_léke*] *(intr.)* **shatter.** *lékape* it's broken; it broke.
••• Cf. *ðuuléke, kaaléke.*
lépe (variants: **léepe, léepa** [JS]), **lélepe** (reduplicated; variant: **lélepa**). V [reg., *_lépe*] **vomit.** *alépe* I'm vomiting (FH). *ðóha alépe* I'm about to vomit (FH/06/27/01/pc). *lelépe akxai* he/she is vomiting (04/26/95/FH/pc:ok; BE2.149; RBn2-MOJ/p22; 02/27/95/JS/pc:uk; FH/06/27/01/pc).
•• RB: <léh-leh-pah> (04/26/95/FH/pc:ok; 02/27/95/JS/pc: *léepa;* 04/26/95/FH/pc:ok).
•• LFD 54 (unconfirmed): *lépe mąkhą* <gthe´-be mo^{n}-ko^{n}> an emetic (04/26/95/FH/pc:uk).
••• *QU kdéwe* vomit [reg. conj.] (RR).
letą́ (variant of **letǫ́**).
letą́ ǫ́pe žúuce. N **redtailed hawk** (04/20/95/LS/pc:prod).
letą́mąze. N [*letą́* + *mą́ze* 'metal'] **Iron Hawk** (BE2.65; FH). [A *hcížo* clan name referring to the metal color of the eagle; Frances Holding's father's name.]
•• LFD 54: *letą́mąze* <Gthe-do^{n}´-mo^{n}-çe> Iron-hawk, personal name.
letǫ́ (variant: **letą́**). N **hawk** (01/04/95/FH/pc:ok). *žekáxǫ letǫ́* crippled hawk.
•• LFD 54: *letǫ́* <gthe-do^{n}´> hawk, falcon, used also as a personal name in the Osage Tribe. *letǫ́ htąka* <gthe-do^{n}´ ṭo^{n}-ga> the large hawk, Cooper's hawk. *letǫ́ žį̨ka* <gthe-do^{n}´ zhi^{n}-ga> the little hawk. *letąaɣe* <Gthe-do^{n}-a-xe> [expected Mod. Os. form: *letǫ́kaaɣe*] Hawk-maker, personal name. *letąhce* <Gthe-do^{n}-ṭse> New-hawk, personal name. *letǫ́chie* <Gthe-do^{n}´-tsi-e> Hawk-passing-by, personal name, refers to the hawk attacking prey. *letǫ́mihcexi* <Gthe-do^{n}´-mi-ṭse-xi> New-hawk-woman, female personal name. *letǫ́sąwį* <Gthe-do^{n}´-ço^{n}-wi^{n}> White-hawk-woman, female personal name. *letǫ́scece* <Gthe-do^{n}´-stse-dse> Long-hawk, personal name, refers to the long scalp locks attached to the sacred hawk. *letǫ́ska* <Gthe-do^{n}´-çka> White-hawk, personal name. *letǫ́wahką* <Gthe-do^{n}´-wa-ḳo^{n}> Mystery-hawk, personal name. *letǫ́wahkǫða* <Gthe-do^{n}´-wa-ḳo^{n}-tha> Attacking-hawk, personal name. *letǫ́xoce* <gthe-do^{n}´-xo-dse> brown hawk [expected Mod. Os. translation 'gray hawk'].
••• Cf. *letą́ ǫ́pe žúuce, letǫ́wį.*
letǫ́sape. N [*letǫ́* + *sápe*] **black hawk.**
•• LFD 54: *letǫ́ sape* <gthe-do^{n}´ ça-be> black hawk; "symbolizes the courage of the warriors, . . . also represents night."
letǫ́wį. N **hawk woman.** [Frances Oberly Holding's name.]
•• LFD 54: *letǫ́wį* <Gthe-do^{n}´-wi^{n}> Hawk-woman, female personal name, refers to the sacred hawk. *letǫ́wįžį̨ka* <Gthe-do^{n}´-wi^{n}-zhi^{n}-ga> Little-hawk-woman, female personal name, refers to the smallest of hawks.
léze. V, ADJ [stat.?] *(intr.)* **(be) striped, lined (having lines).** *súhka léze* guinea hen (striped fowl). *sį́ka hpaléze* striped-nosed squirrel, a square dance call in Osage in imitation of "swing your partners" (RBn19-06).
•• LFD 54: *lezé* <gthe-çe´> striped. *waché leze wį abrį* <wa-tse´ gthe-çe wi^{n} a-bthi^{n}> [expected Mod. Os. form: *haaská léze wį abrį́*] I have a striped dress. *akahami lezé wį ani* <a-ga-ha-mi gthe-çe´ wi^{n} a-ni> [expected Mod. Os. form:

ákahamį léze wį aščį; LF's <a-ni> 'you have' is probably an Omaha form, not used in Osage] you have a striped coat.

••• Cf. *páaleze, waléze.*

léže (variant: **léži**). ADJ **spotted, speckled, stippled** (05/02/95/LS/pc). *hpáata léže káaɣe akxai* he's coloring eggs (as for Easter) (12/30/94/FH/pc/prod). *hápa léže* spotted corn, like Osage corn (although this name not used for Osage corn) (FH). *hpáata léže* decorated Easter eggs (FH). *xúða léže* the spotted eagle.

•• JOD (Wolf and Fawn, p1 ln3): *ha wisǫ́ka háažǫtą ðiléže aape ska šǫ́mihkase akxa* <Há, wisŭñ´ka, ha´çuⁿ-ṭaⁿ´ ¢ik¢éçĕ, áp̧e ska Cŭⁿmikáse akqa> ho, younger brother, what did you do to get spotted, asked the wolf.

•• LFD 55: *ležé* <gthe-zhe´> spotted. *ležáža* <gthe-zha´-zha> spotted in different parts of the body. LFD 54 (unconfirmed): *míɣa žįka ðįkše ležé* <mi´-xa zhiⁿ-ga thiⁿ-kshe gthe-zhe´> [expected Mod. Os. form: *míɣažį įkše léže*] the duck is spotted.

••• Cf. *haxį́ležekáaɣe.*

lí (see **alí**).

líi (variant of **lį́į**).

liisą́ða. V [reg., *_liisą́ða*] [*kik-* SUU + *ðiisą́ða*] *(trans.)* **turn, turn over, reverse or invert one's own** (04/06/95/FH/pc:ok). *haxį́ alíisąða* I turned over my blanket (FH).

•• LFD 145: *haxį ðą alisąða ha* <ha-xiⁿ thoⁿ a-gthi-çoⁿ-tha ha> [*ðą* and *ha* are unconfirmed; sentence-final *ha* is not used in Mod. Os.] I reversed my blanket. *haxį ðą ðalisąða ha* <ha-xiⁿ thoⁿ tha-gthi-çoⁿ-tha ha> [*ðą* and *ha* are unconfirmed; sentence-final *ha* is not used in Mod. Os.] you reversed your blanket; to turn.

líiški (variant: **lúuški**). V [reg., *_líiški*] [*kik-* SUU + *ðiiškí*] *(intr.)* **do one's own laundry, wash one's own clothing or hair.** *líiški akxa* she did her laundry (FH/08/01/01/pc). *alíiški* I did my laundry (FH/08/01/01/pc). *hpaxį́į alíiški hta mįkšé* I'm going to wash my hair (RBn23-15). *ðíe haaská líiški!* wash your clothes yourself! (CQnotes). *haaská líiški akxai* he washes his clothes himself. *wéhkilai ąlíiškipe* we washed our clothes. *alúuški* I did my laundry (FH/01/08/01/pc). *lúuški akxa* she did her laundry (FH/01/08/01/pc). *hpaxį́į alíiški hta mįkšé* I'm going to wash my hair (RBn23-15).

líixǫ. V [reg., *_líixǫ*] [*kik-* SUU + *ðiixǫ́*] *(trans.)* **break one's own (body part or possession).** *alíixǫ* I broke my own (RBn22-03).

líizoke (variant: **líizoka**). V [reg., *_líizoke*] [*kik-* SUU + *ðiizó* (it is not known what the final *ke* is here)] *(intr.)* **bend oneself;** *(trans.)* **bend one's own (body part or possession).** *mį́ce ąlíizoke ąkátxai* we bend our bows.

ližážai. V [reg., *_ližážai*] [reduplicated form] [*kik-* SUU + *ðižáža*] *(trans.)* **shake one's own (body part or possession).** *žą́ą ližážai* shake your tree (MREI/01/11/83). *áa ližážai* shake your arm (MREI/01/11/83). *ližážai* shake him (your own) (MJ).

lį́į (variant: **líi**). V [reg., *_lį́į*] *(intr.)* **sit.** *líipi* you all sit down. *šeðó lį́į* sit down over there (RBn10-3:MOJ/79).

•• LFD 55: *lį* <gthiⁿ> to sit. *alį* <a-gthiⁿ> I sit. *ðalį* <tha-gthiⁿ> you sit. *ąlį pe* <oⁿ-gthiⁿ i> we sit.

••• Cf. *álįį.*

lį́į (variant of **lį́įže**).

lį́įðįke (variant of **lį́įke**).

lį́įka. V [*lį́įke* + *a* IMPERATIVE MARKER] *(intr.)* **sit!**

lį́įke (variants: **lį́įðįke**). V [reg., *_lį́įke*] *(intr.)* **sit down, sit suddenly** (PM). *howąįki ðalį́įke nįkšé?* where are you going to sit? where are you sitting down? (1/13/83/434; 03/10/95/PM/pc). *lį́į žówile hce* let me sit with you (RBn10-4:MOJ/79). *lį́įka* be seated, sit down (03/08/95/MREI/pc:okc). *lį́į žóąle* sit with me (03/10/95/PM/pc:okc). *aškážį lį́įka* sit right here by me, sit close to me (03/10/95/PM/pc). *lįįðikápi* you all sit down. *lį́įkapi* be seated; sit down [pl. addressee] (03/10/95/PM/pc; 03/08/95/MREI/pc:okc; BE2.117).

•• LFD 55: *lį́įka* <gthiⁿ´-iⁿ-ga o-u> [sentence-final <o-u> is not used in Mod. Os.] sit down.

lį́įže (variants: **hlį́į, lį́į**). N **sparks that fly from a fire.**

•• LFD 220 (unconfirmed): *lįžá* <xthiⁿ-zha´> sparks of a fire; sparks that fly upward from the sticks or fire drills used for starting a fire. [FH: wrong pronunciation, should be *lį́įže.*]

••• Cf. *kaalį́įže.*

lįkó. N **gravy** (03/07/95/FH/pc:ok). *súhka lįkó wiksíɣe hta mįkšé* I'm going to make you some chicken gravy (FH/09/21/01/pc). *htáa lįkó* meat gravy (FH/09/21/01/pc; BE2.60).

lįlį́įe. V [conjug. unknown] *(intr.)* **sleep sitting up** (RB, unconfirmed).

lį́xa. N **bobcat** (RBn HW10; unconfirmed; FH:uk).

lóce. V [reg., *_lóce*; accent seems to be variable in 1st sg. and 2nd sg.] *(intr.)* **snore.** *ðáloce? ðalóce?* do you snore? (04/26/95/FH/pc). *áloce* I snore (04/26/95/FH/pc). *ąžį́ihe ta wáalį ðalóce nąį,*

lóce (*continued*)
ášihta ðiną́kʔǫ apai when we go to sleep, you snore loud and they even hear you outside (04/26/95/FH/pc).

•• LFD 227: *žą́loce* <zho^{n}´-xtho-dse> to snore. *žąáloce* <zho^{n}-a´-xtho-dse> I snore. *žą́ðaloce* <zho^{n}´-tha-xtho-dse> you snore.

lǫ́ (variant of **lą́**).

lǫ́ðį (variants: **lǫ́ðe, lǫ́ði**). v, adj [reg.+sync., *_lǫ́_ðį* or *_alǫ́_ðį;* vowels of 1st sg. *a-* and 2nd person *ða-* are normally lengthened before the *l* of this verb (*aalǫ́brį, ðaalǫ́šcį*)] **(be) drunk, inebriated, intoxicated.** *ðihkówe akxa lǫ́ðį akxa žaamí* I think your friend [sitting] is drunk (01/20/95/PM/pc:ok, ma; FH:5/02/96/tape). *lǫ́ði ąpa žaamí* I think he [moving] is drunk (01/20/95/PM/pc:prod; FH:5/02/96/tape). *ðihkówa lǫ́ðį txa?* is your friend [standing] drunk? (01/20/95/PM/pc:ok). *aalǫ́brį hta mįkšé* I'm going to get drunk, I'm going to get angry or frustrated (04/25/95/PM/pc:okc; FH:4/22/96/tape:okc). *ðaalǫ́šcį hta ðąįšé?* are you going to get drunk? (FH:4/22/96/tape:prod). *lǫ́ði hta mįkšé* I'm going to get drunk (01/20/95/ERE/pc). *kaakǫ́ šǫ́ ðąįše, ðaalǫ́šči nana* keep on until you get drunk (spoken sarcastically) (RB:MOJ). *lǫ́ðištą štą éhtana hcéhpe hpíiži kší aape* he has a bad liver from always being drunk (02/22/95/FH/pc:okc).

•• LFD 56: *lǫ́ðį* <gtho^{n}´-thi^{n}> to be drunk. *alǫ́brį* <a-gtho^{n}´-bthi^{n}> I am drunk. *walǫ́ðį pe* <wa-gtho^{n}´-thi^{n} i> we are drunk. *lǫ́ðį ikiha* <gtho^{n}´-thi^{n} i-gi-ha> habitual drunkard; a sot. *lǫ́ðį kaye* <gtho^{n}´-thi^{n} ga-xe> to make drunk; to intoxicate. *lǫ́ðįštą* <gtho^{n}´-thi^{n}-shto^{n}> intemperance; drunkenness.

••• Cf. *cʔélǫðį, kaalǫ́ðį.*

lǫ́ǫ (variant: **lą́ą**). v [reg., *_lǫ́ǫ*] *(trans.)* **call s.o. a bad name, revile s.o., "blast" s.o. in an argument.** *ðilǫ́ǫpe* they called you names (RBn; MREI/01/11/83; CQc). *ðilǫ́ǫ* he called you names. *ąlǫ́ǫpe* they called me names. *ðilǫ́ǫ apai* they called you names. *ąlǫ́ǫlǫǫpe* they called me names (3-3-83 [not *hl*]). • *(intr.)* **say bad words, curse; sulk, be angry, mutter in complaint.** *lǫ́ǫ ðée che iðáahpe hta mįkšé* I'll wait until he goes away mad [angry]. *óðąąceši įká, olą́ą akxa* don't pay any attention to him, he's mad (RBn11-01/JW&FW&HHaskell).

•• JOD (slip file): *lǫ́ðį* <k̯¢u^{n}´-¢i^{n}> foolish, silly, beside himself with anger, etc.

•• LFD 55: *lǫ* <gtho^{n}> to call one bad names; to revile. *ðálǫ* <tha´-gtho^{n}> you reviled him.

••• *KS lą* (JOD), *lą́le, lǫ́* curse, revile (RR), *yalǫ́ya* (JOD), *yalą́ye* deceive, call names, snap at (RR).

••• Cf. *lǫ́ǫlǫǫ, walǫ́ǫ.*

lǫ́ǫ (variant of **lǫǫhǫ́**).

lǫǫ ðúleze. n **thunder with lightning** (BE2.140; RB, unconfirmed; 02/15/95/FH/pc:uk)

lǫǫ húu. n **large amount of thunder, lots of thunder** (02/15/95/FH/pc:prod).

lǫ́ǫ iníhkašika. n **Thunder clan, person of the Thunder clan.**

•• LFD 56: *lǫ́inihkašika* <Gtho^{n}´i-ni-ķa-shi-ga> People of the Thunder, the name of a gens in the Osage tribe (unconfirmed; 03/22/95/FH/pc:ma).

lǫ́ǫ níhkašika. n **thunder people** (FH/t116b).

lǫ́ǫ waléze. n **lightning. (lit., 'stripes from thunder'?)**

•• LFD 56: *lǫ́ waleze* <gtho^{n}´ wa-gthe-çe> lightning (zigzag).

lǫǫhóohtą. n, v [uninfl.] [*lǫǫhǫ́* + *hóohtą*] *(intr.)* **thunder** (RB; HH/pc).

•• RB: <ló-ho-tah>.

•• JOD (slip file): *lǫ hohtą* <k̯¢ŭ^{n} hu^{n}ta^{n}> "the thunderbird roars," thunder, it thunders.

•• LFD 56: *lǫhóhtą* <gtho^{n}-ho´-ţo^{n}> thunder. *lǫǫhóohtą walį pe* <gtho^{n}-ho´-ţo^{n} wa-gthi^{n} bi a> the thunder was loud.

••• *KS gló ~ ló* thunder (n) (RR), *lo hóhta* to thunder (RR).

lǫǫhǫ́ (variant: **lǫ́ǫ**). n **thunder** (RBn1-1). *iihkó lǫǫ* grandmother thunder (02/03/95/FH/pc:okc; BE2.59).

•• RB: <lo^{n}>.

•• LFD 55 (unconfirmed): *lǫ* <Gtho^{n}> Thunder deity. LFD 56: *lǫ́į* <Gtho^{n}´-i^{n}> the Thunder deity (unconfirmed; 03/22/95/FH/pc:uk).

lǫǫhúu (variants: **lǫǫhúa, lǫǫhúe**). n **Osage wedding hat (top hat with colorful plumes that may be worn by the bride in an Osage wedding)** (MREI/6/7/94/num94; 01/04/95/FH/pc:ok; FH/8/30/94).

•• RB: <ló^{n}-hyú>.

•• LFD 56: *lǫhi* <gtho^{n}-hi> a hat with ornaments worn by a bride at a wedding.

lǫ́ǫlǫǫ. v [reg., *_lǫ́ǫlǫǫ*] [reduplicated form of *lǫ́ǫ*] *(trans.)* **call names, revile, or curse over and over.** *ną lǫ́ǫlǫǫ apa áape* they said that they were saying bad words, they said they were calling names. *ą́lǫǫlǫǫ apa áape* they called me names, they said.

•• LFD 55: *lǫlǫ* <gtho^{n}´-gtho^{n}> repeated mutterings, as when one is angry.

lúðaalį. v [reg., *_lúðaalį*] [*kik-* SUU + *ðuðáalį*] *(trans.)* **fix one's own, fix up s.t. of one's own.**
lušúpe. N [presumably *ki-* SUU + *ðiišúpe/ðuušúpe*] **vein in the body** (FH: prod).
lúuški (variant of **líiški**).
lúuwasu. v [reg., *_lúuwasu*] [*kik-* SUU + *ðuuwásu*] *(trans.)* **wash your own (body part or possession).** *nąąɣúce lúuwasü!* wash your ears! (12/30/94/FH/pc:prod; 04/26/95/LS/pc:ok).
••• Cf. *hkilúuwasu.*
lúuxpaðe. v [reg., *_lúuxpaðe*] [*kik-* SUU + *ðuuxpáðe*] *(trans.)* **lose one's own.** *wéleze ąlúuxpaðe* we lost our pencils.
lúuze. v [reg., *_lúuze*] [*kik-* SUU + *ðuuzé*] **get, take, or take away one's own.** *wáleze ðalúuze?* did you get your letter? (02/15/95/FH/pc:ok; BE2.78).
lúuža. v [reg., *_lúuža*] [*kik-* SUU + *ðuužá*] *(trans.)* **wash one's own (body parts or possessions)** (1-20-83-p1). *šáake alúuža hkǫ́bra* I want to wash my hands (RBn1-50). *oðíhtą hąðé ðalúuža?* are you washing your car tonight? (FH/06/16/01/pc). *Preston akxa oðíhtą hąðé lúuža akxa* Preston is washing his car tonight. *šáake ąlúuža* we wash our hands. *įįcé luužá, šáake ški* wash your face, also your hands (03/16/95/JS/pc:okc; BE2.151). *síi luužá* wash your feet (03/16/95/JS/pc:ok). *nąhta luužá* wash your ears (RBn11-02/JW&FW; RB:HHsk,c.1976). *híi luužá* brush your teeth (03/16/95/JS/pc). *hį́į luužá* wash your mustache (JS). *hpáxį luužá* wash your hair (03/16/95/JS/pc:okc). *įcé alúužamazí* I didn't wash my face.
•• LFD 56: *lúža* <gthu´-zha> to wash (one's face).
lúwį. v [reg., *_lúwį*] [*kik-* SUU + *ðuwį́*] *(trans.)* **buy s.t. of one's own (buy back)** (1/2/147-190). *áluwį* I bought it back and it belonged to me (lit., 'I bought my own'). • **buy for one's own (people, family).**
lúži (variants: **hlúži, hlúže, lúže**). ADV **slow, slowly, slower** (JS; 03/10/95/MREI/pc:ok). *lúže ía, lúže íe* say it slow (03/15/95/PM/pc:ok; 03/16/95/JS/pc:ok: *hlúže ía*). *lúži íe* say it slowly (03/10/95/MREI/pc:okc; BE2.123). *lúžį káaɣa* do it slower, go slowly. *lúži ekǫ!* slow down, ease up! (RBn3-MOJ?/p3; 03/10/95/MREI/pc:ok).
lúži káaɣe (variant: **hlúži káaɣe**). VP [sync. *k>p*, *lúži _káaɣe*] *(trans.)* **make slower, slow down** (RBn10-5:MOJ/79).
lúžihkiðe (variant: **lúžihkie**). v [reg., *lúži_hki(ð)e*] [*lúži* + *hkik-* REFL + *ðe* CAU] *(intr.)* **slow down, take it slow (lit., 'make oneself slow').**

---

m

máihka (variant of **mąįhka**).
mašcúce. v [conjug. unknown] *(intr.)* **slide (e.g., on ice).**
máši (variant of **mąši**).
mašká. N **crawfish.**
•• JOD (Raccoons and Crawfish p20 ln6): *máškąą* <mácka^{n}>. JOD (Raccoons and Crawfish p24 ln7): *máška* <mácka>.
maží (variant: **mąží**). NEG **not (negator for 1st sg. only: 'I am/was not', 'I do/did not', etc.; follows the verb).** *puštáha mąží* I don't iron (FH/12/11/94). *įįcé alúuža mąží* I didn't wash my face.
mą́ą (variants: **mǫ́ǫ, mą́, mǫ́**). N **arrow.** *ší mą́ą šó ðée hpáaɣe* I'm going to let the arrow go again (BE2.4, expression used at peyote meetings; 01/06/95/FH/pc:okc). *céɣenii mą́ą nąąží* the drum and arrow stop/stand (RBn10-22/JW&FW). *mǫ́ǫ xǫ́* broken arrow (RBn10-6:JW). *mą́ą xǫ́* a broken arrow (MSB 2-24-83). • **staff used at peyote meetings** (RB).
•• LFD 95: *mǫ* <mo^{n}> an arrow. "The Osage made their arrows out of a wood they call <mo^{n}´-çahi>, arrow wood (*Cornus asperi folia*). When this wood is not obtainable they use the ash. Two arrows, ceremonially made, are used in some of the Osage tribal rites, one painted black and the other red, to represent night and day, they being symbols of everlasting life."
mąą-. N ROOT **related to the ground or the earth.**
mąąðǫ́ (variant: **mǫ́ǫ**). v [sync., *mąą_ðǫ́*] *(trans.)* **steal.** *mąąbrǫ́e* I stole it. *wámąąbrǫðe* I stole them. *mąąðǫ́pe* she was stolen (lit., 'they stole her'). *táatą wį ą́mąąðǫe ąðé* we [two] stole something (05/12/83/3). *ðimǫ́ǫ štą akxa* he's [always] stealing from you (5-12-83-3). *táatą wį*

mąąðǫ́ (*continued*)
ąmą́ąðǫpe we stole something (2-10-83-p4). • **rape.** *ðímąąðǫ́pe* you're being raped (lit., 'they raped you'). *mąąðǫ́pe* she was raped (lit., 'they raped her').
••• *PO mąną́ðiwaðe* little people [fairies] (lit., 'they take folks off, steal them') (KDS); *KS gímǫyǫ* steal something from someone (RR).
••• Cf. *mąąlǫ́, wakˀó mąąðǫ́štą, wamą́ąðǫ.*

mą́ąɣe (variant: **mǫ́ǫɣe**). n **sky** (BE2.122); **weather** (03/10/95/PM/pc:not sky). [Takes 'sitting' positional article *įkšé* or 'standing inanimate' positional article *che*.] *mą́ąɣe háakǫ che áši?* what's it [the weather] like outside? (03/22/95/PM/pc:prod). *háakǫ įkšé ášihta?* what is it [the weather] like outside? (RBn3-51). *hą́ąpa mą́ąɣe ðáalį akxa* today the weather is good (03/22/95/PM/pc:ok; BE2.153). *mą́aɣe ðáalį tą hóolą ąkái hta ąkái* if the weather is good, we're going fishing (03/22/95/PM/pc:ok). *mą́ąɣe ðáalį* good weather (03/22/95/PM/pc:ok). *mą́ąɣe akxa ðáalįži akxa* the weather is not good (FH:1998/pc). *mą́ąɣe hpííži* bad weather (03/22/95/PM/pc:ok). *mą́ąɣe hǫ́ǫche?* how's the weather? (RBn12-09). *mą́ąɣe hǫ́įche?* how is the weather? (03/22/95/PM/pc:ok). • **the upper world.**
•• JOD (slip file): *máɣe* <ma´-xe> sky, upper world, weather.
•• LFD 103: *mą́ɣe* <mo^{n}´-xe> the sky. *mą́ɣe ðálį* <mo^{n}´-xe tha-gthi^{n}> a good sky; a clear day. *mąɣe ðihice* <mo^{n}-xe thi-hi-dse> conjuring the sky.

mąąhí (variant of **mąąhį́** 'grass, hay').

mą́ąhi (variant of **mą́ąhį** 'knife').

mą́ąhisi wakˀó (variant of **mą́ąhįsu wakˀó**).

mą́ąhispe (variant of **mą́ąhįspe**).

mąąhį́ (variants: **mąąhį́į, mąąhí**). n [possibly *mąą-* 'earth' + *hį́į* 'hair'] **grass, hay** (02/03/95/FH/pc:okc; BE2.60). *súhka mį́įka čáahpažį, mąąhį́ apa ohcíle ðáalįpe, ecíe ska ébre mįkšé* the little hen [said], hay is good for a nest, I'm thinking it's there (RBn19-04).
•• LFD 98: *mąhį́* <mo^{n}-hi^{n}´> grass.
••• KS *mąąhį́, mahį́* (JOD) grass, weeds (RR).

mąąhį́ htóho (variant: **mąąhí htóho**). adjp, n **green (lit., 'blue/green grass')** (MSB:t9).

mąąhį́ htóho éekǫ. adjp **green (lit., 'like blue/green grass').**

mąąhį́ kaasé (variant: **mąąhí kaasé**). vp [reg. *kaa*-del., *mąąhį́ _(kaa)sé*] **cut the grass.** *mąąhí áase hta mįkšé* I'm going to cut the grass (FH/11/17/01/pc:prod). *mąąhį́ kaasé mąðį́* go cut the grass (01/14/95/FH/pc:ok).

mąąhį́ paasé (variant: **mąąhí paasé**). vp [sync. fortisizing stop stem, *mąąhį́ _paasé*] **cut the grass.** *mąąhí špáase hta ðaįšé?* are you going to cut the grass? (FH/11/17/01/pc:prod). *mąąhí špáasape?* did you all cut the grass? (FH/11/17/01/pc:prod). *ąą mąąhí ąpáasape* yes, we cut grass [female speaking] (FH/11/17/01/pc:prod). *ąą mąąhí hpáasa* yes, I cut the grass [female speaking] (FH/11/17/01/pc:prod).
••• Cf. *paa-, -se.*

mą́ąhį (variant: **mą́ąhi**) n **knife.**
•• LFD 286: *mą́hį* <mo^{n}´-hi^{n}>.

mą́ąhį htą́ą (variant: **mą́ąhį htą́ka**). n **superintendent (as of the Osage Agency), officer or other white person of rank, the government (lit., 'big knife')** (PM/7/7/94; 02/03/95/FH/pc:ok; 03/14/95/MREI/pc:ok; BE2.130); **white person (archaic or rare)** (RBn HW13).
•• RB: <mó^{n}-hi^{n}-tah^{n}, máh^{n}-hi-táh^{n}>.
•• LFD 99: *mą́hįhtąka kahike* <Mo^{n}´-hi^{n}-ṭo^{n}-ga ga-hi-ge> Indian agent. *mąhį, htąka, kahike* <mo^{n}-hi^{n}, ṭo^{n}-ga, ga-hi-ge> knife, big, chief, big-chief-knife. *mąhį htąka* <mo^{n}-hi^{n} ṭo^{n}-ga> knife, big, lit., 'big-knife'. The Osage name for an Englishman.

mąąhį́hpa. n **ragweed (lit., 'bitter grass')** (RB).
•• LFD 99: *mąhį́hpa* <mo^{n}-hi^{n}´-p̣a> bitter-weed, ragweed, or hogweed (*Artemisiae folia*).

mąąhį́į (variant of **mąąhį́**).

mą́ąhįsi wakˀó (variant of **mą́ąhįsu wakˀó**).

mą́ąhįska. n **axe** (RBn10-12:JW, unconfirmed) [Presumed error in RB records for *mą́ąhįspe* (?).]

mą́ąhįspe (variants: **mą́ąhiispe, mą́ąhispe**). n **axe** (01/06/95/FH/pc:ok). *mą́ąhispe ną́ɣe kaaxǫ́* he broke the ice with his axe (BE2.5 RBn2-MOJ/p20; FH/09/22/01/pc). *mą́ąhispe ðuuzá, žą́ą toe ąkáase ąkái hce* get the axe and let's go cut some wood (RBn2-MOJ/p20; 01/06/95/FH/pc;okc). • **Strike Axe** [name of the band that the Oberlys (FH's father's family) belonged to] (FH). • **spade (e.g., for gardening); spades (suit in a deck of cards)** (RBn12-10/MOJ; FH/09/22/01/pc). [The image of an axe appears only on the king of diamonds and the jack of hearts, however.]
•• JOD (slip file): *mąhįspe* <ma^{n}-hi^{n}-spe> axe.
•• LFD 98: *mą́hįspe* <mo^{n}´-hi^{n}-çpe> ax. *mą́hįspewechį* <Mo^{n}´-hi^{n}-çpe-we-tsi^{n}> Battle-ax

(personal name) [*mą́ąhispe* + *wa-* VAL + *iichį́*, lit., 'axe with which to strike persons or things'].
••• Cf. *hámąsi, mą́ąhįsu, mą́ąhįsu wak?ó.*

mą́ąhįspežį. N **hatchet** (FH).
•• LFD 99: *mą́hįspe žįka* <moⁿ´-hiⁿ-çpe zhiⁿ-ga> a tomahawk, a battle-ax or a hatchet.

mą́ąhįsu (variants: **mą́ąhusa, mą́ąhusi, mǫ́ǫhisu, mǫ́ǫhisi**). N **spade (e.g., gardening tool); spades (suit in a deck of cards)** (03/06/95/FH/pc:ok; RBn10-21/JW; FH/11/17/01/pc).

mą́ąhįsu wak?ó (variants: **mą́ąhįsi wak?ó, mą́ąhisi wak?ó**). N **queen of spades in a deck of cards (lit., 'spade woman')** (04/18/95/FH/pc:okc). [Takes 'lying' positional article *kše*.] *mą́ąhisi wak?ó kše abrį́* I have the queen of spades (RB, FH).
•• LFD 98: *mą́hisi wak?o kše abrį* <moⁿ´-hi-çi wa-ḳ´u kshe a-bthiⁿ> I have the queen of spades.

mą́ąhpiiži N [*mą́ą* + *hpíiži*] **slave** (RB, unconfirmed); **worthless thing, s.t. of no value (lit., 'bad arrow')** (RB); **bad weather** (03/10/95/PM/pc); **bad shaft of an arrow** (PM).
•• RB:<móⁿ-pi-zhiⁿ>.

mą́ąhusa, mą́ąhusi (variants of **mą́ąhįsu**).

mą́ąke (variant: **mǫ́ǫke**). N **chest** (01/09/95/FH/pc:prod; RBn1-MOJ/p27).
•• LFD 97: *mą́ke* <moⁿ´-ge> breast or chest of a human being.
••• *KS mą́ąge* chest of a man (RR); *WI mąąk* chest (of the body) (KM).

mą́ąke ní. N **tuberculosis, consumption (lit., 'chest hurts').**
•• LFD 97: *mą́ke nie* <moⁿ´-ge ni-e> consumption, breast-ache, chest-ache.

mą́ąke púze. N **tuberculosis, consumption** (BE2.145; RBn2-MOJ/p14; 04/04/95/FH/pc:okc).

mąąlǫ́. V [reg.?, *_maalǫ́?*] [*kik-* SUU + *mąąðǫ́*] *(trans.)* **steal s.t. of one's own, steal back.**

mąąnáγe. V [conjug. unknown] [presumably contains *mąą-* and *nąą-*] **paw the ground when in rut (said of a male animal ready to breed with a female animal)** (04/25/95/PM/pc). *hceetóoka mąąnáγape* buffalo bull is rutting (PM).
•• LFD 158: *hcetóka mąnąγapi* <ṭse-do´-ga moⁿ-noⁿ-xa bi> when the buffalo bulls rut, the month of June [unconfirmed as name of month].
••• *KS mąnáγe* to be in rut, to paw the ground (RR).

mąąpíaza (variant: **mą́ąpeza** [RB]) N **wasp** (03/16/95/JS/pc:ok; BE2.151). [JS prefers *mąąpíaza* to *wapázike*, which she considers archaic.]
•• RB: <máhⁿ-peh-zah>.

mą́ąsase (variant: **mǫ́ǫsase**). N [*mą́ą* + *sase*] **sauerkraut (lit., 'arrow cuttings')** (RB, unconfirmed; 03/08/95/MREI/pc:uk; 04/19/95/FH/pc:uk).

mą́ąse, mą́ąsi (variants of **mǫ́ǫse**).

mą́ąsihcexi (variant: **mą́ąsihcexį**). N [*mǫ́ǫse* + *hcéxi*] **Sacred Arrow Shaft (female personal name).** [Dora Lookout's name.]
•• LFD 97: *mǫ́šihcexi* <Moⁿ´-çi-ṭse-xi> Sacred-arrow-shaft (female personal name).
••• Cf. *hcéxi, mǫ́ǫse.*

mąąstósto. ADJ, N **muddy, mud** (02/27/95/FH/pc:okc; FH:4/22/96/tape:prod; BE2.91). *ožąke kše mąąstósto* the road is muddy (02/27/95/FH/pc:ok). *hcéðe mąąstósto* a muddy tire (03/22/95/FH/pc).
•• RB: <mahⁿ-stó-sto> ~ <máhⁿ-sto-sto>.
•• LFD 97: *mąstósto* <moⁿ-çto´-çto> soft mud, a muddy road. *ožąke kše mąstósto* <u-zhoⁿ-ge ke moⁿ-çto´-çto> the road is muddy.

mąąšcé. V, N [uninfl.] **(be) warm weather** (JS prod), **hot weather, sunny weather** (02/09/95/FH/pc:okc; RBn2-MOJ/p19; 03/22/95/PM/pc:ok). *mąąšcé akxa* the weather is hot (03/22/95/PM/pc:ok). *mąąštáži akxái* it's not hot (weather) (BE2.68).
•• LFD 102: *mą́sce* <moⁿ´-stse> hot weather, a hot day.

mąąšcé kšíhtaha (variant: **mąąščé kši ehtáha**). N, ADJP, ADVP **south (lit., 'in/to the direction of warm weather').** *mąąščé kši ehtáha koe mįįáðee ehtáha tookétą táahkace ci achíe* I come from the south and the west in the heat of summer (RBn17-p01; 03/13/95/FH/pc:okc; BE2.125).

mąąšcį́ka (variant of **mąšcį́ka**).

mąąšóce (FH). V, ADJ [uninfl.] [*mąą-* + *šóce*] *(intr.)* **(be) dusty (as of a table top).** *áwanǫbre akxa mąąšóce akxai, ðiicíza* the table is dusty, dust it (FH:4/22/96/tape138b).
•• LFD 101: *mąšóce* <moⁿ-sho´-dse> dust blown or carried by the wind.

mąąšóšoce (FH) (variants: **mą́ąšošo** [PM], **mą́ąšošóce** [FH]). V, ADJ [uninfl.] [reduplicated form of *mąąšóce*] **(be) dusty.** *mą́ąšošóce* it [the air] is dusty/smoky (01/20/95/PM/pc:prod; BE2.37). *áwanǫbre akxa mąąšóšoce akxai, ðiicíza* the table is dusty, dust it (FH:4/22/96/tape138b).
•• LFD 102: *mąšóšoce* <moⁿ-sho´-sho-dse> dust, dusty, soft mud along the edges of a stream [reduplicated form; unconfirmed as any sort of

mą̨ą̨šóšoce (*continued*) 'mud']. *mą̨šóšoce ðaða pi a* <mo^{n}-sho´-sho-dse tha-tha bi a> [expected Mod. Os. form: *mą̨ą̨šóšoce škáaɣe; ðaða* unconfirmed by Mod. Os. speakers] you are raising the dust.

mą̨ą̨štáha (variant: **mą̨štáha**). ADJ [*mą̨ą̨-* + *štáha*] **slippery (as of a surface).**

•• LFD 102: *mą̨štáha* <mo^{n}-shta´-ha> slippery ground, wet ground.

mą̨ą̨tóohka. ADJ [*mą̨ą̨-* + *toohká*] **moist.**

•• LFD 97 (unconfirmed): *mą̨tóhka* <mo^{n}-do´ḳa> moist.

mą́ą̨žą̨xe (variant: **mą̨ą̨žą́xe**). N **garlic, onion** (03/02/95/FH/pc; BE2.98).

•• JOD (slip file): *mą́žą̨xe* <ma´-ça^{n}-q^{a}ĕ> an onion, onions.

•• LFD 104: *mą̨žą́xe* <mo^{n}-zho^{n}´-xe> onions, garlic. *mą̨ą̨žą́xe ðiðalį a* <mo^{n}-zho^{n}´-xe thi-tha-gthi^{n} a> [expected Mod. Os. form: *mą́ą̨žą̨xe ðihǫ́ǫ?*] do you like onions? "Garlic was plentiful on the prairies, but until the Indians saw white men using it for food they did not use it because its odor was offensive."

••• *KS mǫ́žǫxe*, *mážą-* (JOD) onion (RR).

mą̨ą̨žą́xe htóho. N **green onion** (05/01/95/LS/pc:okc; RBn1-MOJ/p14; FH/09/21/01/pc).

mą̨ché. ADV **in the center of s.t. (centrally located), within, underneath (03/23/95/FH/pc).**

•• LFD 103: *mą́che/mą́hce* <mo^{n}´-tse> in the deepest of secret places.

••• *QU mą́the* inside, in, within, under (RR); *KS mą́čhe* [vowel may be long: *ą́ą*] (JOD) underneath, within (RR).

mą̨ché éhtaha (variant of **mą̨chéhtaha**).

mą́che oðúxa (variant: **mą́che oðúɣa**?). N **underwear, undergarment (for men or women)** (02/27/95/JS/pc; BE2.147). [Likely a direct loan-translation from English 'under' + 'wear', although *oðúxa* is otherwise unattested in Mod. Os.]

•• LFD 180: *oðúxa* <u-thu´xtha> to pull on, as leggings.

mą̨chéhta. ADV, N **other side, on/to the other side, underneath, inner one or innermost one.**

•• JOD (Devouring Mountain p2 ln9): *mą̨hcéhta* <Ma^{n}tse´ta> inside.

•• LFD 103: *mą̨hcéhta* <mo^{n}-ṭse´-ṭa> inside, interior of anything. *mą̨chéhta xci* <mo^{n}-tse´-ṭa xtsi> inmost, innermost.

mą̨chéhtaha (variant: **mą̨ché éhtaha**). ADJ, ADV **inward, toward the center** (03/23/95/FH/pc:prod; FH:t119a).

•• LFD 103: *mą̨chéhtaha/mą̨hcéhtaha* <mo^{n}-tse´-ṭa-ha> inward, toward the center.

mą̨ðį́ (variants: **méį, mą́į, mée, mę́į**). V (reg.+sync., *(_)mą_ðį́*] *(intr.)* **walk, go by walking, go by foot.** *mą̨ðį́ alí apai* she's walking home (03/16/95/JS/pc:ok). *áwanǫbre ápetxa mą̨ðį́* walk around the table (03/16/95/JS/pc:ok). *mą̨ðį́ íkˀuca* try to walk (03/16/95/JS/pc:ok; BE2.150). *mą̨ðašcį́ hta ðaašé?* are you going to walk? are you going to go afoot? *mą̨ðį alí apai* she's walking home (03/16/95/JS/pc:ok). *mą̨ðį́ ðachíe?* did you come afoot? (03/16/95/JS/pc:ok). • **go away.** *mą̨ðį́pi* go away [pl. addressee]; go! go on! [pl. addressee]. • **go, go on, walk, get moving.** *óðaake waléze akų́ mą̨ðį́* go get the newspaper (02/01/95/FH/pc:ok). *puuspé mą̨ðį́* go hide (RBn22-06). *ðíe mą̨ðį́!* you [sg.] go! [contrastive: e.g., 'I don't want to go, so *you* go']. • **go ahead.** *mą̨ðį́pi* go ahead and do it [pl. addressee]. • **approach, move in closer.** *hkéðo mą́į* clear weather traveling, approaching (FH). • **stay.** *šée mą̨ðį́* stay where you are (PM/109-a). • **act or live a certain way, go around a certain way** (JS, PM). *oáðohta ą̨mą́brį ą̨škáaɣe íkˀuca* try to make me behave (MOJ 1/19/83).

•• RB: <mah^{n}-thí, mo^{n}-thí^{n}> (01/31/95/FH/pc:ok).

•• LFD 85: *mą̨ðį́ðe* <mo^{n}-thi^{n}´-the> [expected Mod. Os. form: *mą̨ðí ðée*] to go afoot, walking. *hkéðamąį* <ḳe´-tha-mo^{n}-i^{n}> Clear-day-approaching, refers to the clearing of the sky after a storm. LFD 102: *mą̨ðį* <mo^{n}-thi^{n}> to exist, to walk [unconfirmed as 'to exist']. *mą̨ðį́bre* <mo^{n}-thi^{n}´-bthe> [expected Mod. Os. form: *mą̨ðį́ brée*] I go afoot. *mǫ́ni* <mo^{n}´-ni> [expected Mod. Os. form: *mą̨šcį́*] you exist. *mą̨ðį́ðe* <mo^{n}-thi^{n}´-the> onward.

••• Cf. *hpahą́le mą̨ðį́, hpéece mą̨ðį́, oðóšimą, ómą̨ðį, šée mą̨ðį́.*

mą̨ðį́ aðée. VP **go for a walk, go walking.** *mą̨ðį́ ą̨káðe* let's go for a walk.

mą̨ðį́ ðíe. VP *(intr.)* **go on, get moving (a command to one person).** [Used only as imperative.]

mą̨ðį́ káaye. VP [sync. *k*>*p*, *mą̨ðį́ _káaɣe*] *(trans.)* **herd, drive (lit., 'force to walk').** *hkáwa ðéeka mą̨ðį́ káaɣa ščewai hta mįkšé a* [sentence-final *a* is not used in Mod. Os.] bring the horses here and I'll doctor them (lit., 'make the horses walk here, I will doctor them') (RBn HW).

mą̨ðį́hka (variant of **mą́įhka**).

mą̨ɣíðe (variant: **mǫxíðe**). V [reg., *mą̨ɣí_ðe*] *(trans.)* **deceive, trick, lie, swindle, defraud, fool**

(MSB: t9). *mąɣíawai mįkšé* I lied [to folks]; I lied to them [*mąɣíawai < mąɣí-a-wa-ðe*]. *mąɣíðai nįkšé* you lied to him [*mąɣíðai < mąɣí-ða-ðe*]. *mąɣíąðae* you lied to me [< *mąɣí-ą-ða-ðe*]. *mąɣíwaðaape* you [sg./pl.] lied to us [< *mąɣí-wa-ða-ðe-api-ðe*]. *mąɣíąðape* he lied to me (02/15/95/FH/pc:okc). *mǫxįąða api a* [expected form in Mod. Osage: *mąɣíąðape*] he lied to me (RBn10-5:JW). *mąɣíðiðe apai* he's lying to you. *mąɣíwaðape* he lied to us. *mąɣíwaapi akxai [mąɣí-wa-ðe-api akxa-ðe]* they're lying to us now. *mąɣíwaape* they fooled us (3-1-326ff).

•• LFD 103: *mǫɣéðe* <mo^{n}-xe´-the> to deceive, swindle, hoodwink, delude or defraud. *mǫɣéaðe* <mo^{n}-xe´-a-the> I deceived him. *mǫɣéðaðe* <mo^{n}-xe´-tha-the> you deceived him. *mǫɣe óða pe ha* <mo^{n}-xe o´-tha i ha> [expected Mod. Os. form: *mąɣíąða pe;* sentence-final *ha* is not used in Mod. Os.] he swindled me.

••• *KS mąɣíye* fool someone, deceive, tease (RR).

mąɣíhkiðe. V [reg., *mąɣí_hkiðe*] [*hkik-* REFL + *mąɣíðe*] *(intr.)* **deceive oneself, be mistaken.**

mąhká (variant: **mąhką́**). N **peyote, aspirin, or any other kind of medicine** (02/24/95/FH/pc:okc). *mąhkánii* peyote tea (lit., 'medicine water') (02/24/95/FH/pc; BE2.86; RBn1-MOJ/p40). *mą́hkažóika mą́į akxai, kitą́he hta akxa hǫ́ǫpahu* he's haywire with peyote, but he'll be all right at daylight (lit., 'peyote is moving throughout his body, but he will recover at/by dawn') (01/06/95/FH/pc:prod; BE2.102; RBn HW). *mą́hkaštǫ́ka* pounded peyote (lit., 'soft medicine').

•• LFD 100: *mąhką́* <mo^{n}-ḳo^{n}´> drugs, any kind of medicine except poisons. LFD 193: *wahkío mąhką* <wa-ḳi´o mo^{n}-ḳo^{n}> [expected Mod. Os. form *wakʔó mąhká* (lit., 'woman medicine')] love potion.

••• *WI mąąká* medicine (KM).

••• Cf. *mąhkáhpa, mąhkása.*

mąhká aðį́ (variant: **mąhką́ aðį́**). N **pharmacist, druggist, one who has medicine** (04/17/95/LS/pc:ok).

•• LF 100: *mąhką́ aðį* <mo^{n}-ḳo^{n}´a-thi^{n}> a druggist, one who sells drugs.

mąhká hpíiži (variant: **mą́hkąhpíiži**). N **poison, bad medicine.** *hcéxopehuuscee apa waðáaxtake che mąhką hpíižipe* the bite of a tarantula is poison (lit., 'tarantulas biting folks is poison').

•• LFD 162: *hcéxope huuscee apa waðaxtake che mąhką́ hpiižipe* <ṭse´-xu-be hiu stse-e a-ba wa-tha-xta-ge te mo^{n}-ḳo^{n} p̣i-a-zhi bi a> the bite of a tarantula is poison.

mąhká oðáahtą eeną́. N **liquid medicine, medicine that comes in liquid form only** (FH).

•• LFD 101 (unconfirmed): *mąhką́ oðahtą eną* <mo^{n}-ḳo^{n}´ u-tha-ṭo^{n} e-no^{n}> strong; forcible; potent; said of a drug (02/24/95/FH/pc:uk). "Used also to represent a dose." [Unconfirmed as 'strong, forcible, potent' or as 'dose'; FH: expected form and gloss: *oðahtą* 'drink' + *eną* 'only', lit., 'only comes in liquid form'.]

mąhká oðíkʔe (variant: **mąhką́ oðíkʔe**). VP [sync., *mąhká o_ðíkʔe*] *(trans., intr.)* **administer a shot or inoculation.** *mąhká owíbrikʔe* I gave you a shot (FH:4/25/96/t141, prod).

•• LFD 101: *mąhką́ oðikʔe* <mo^{n}-ḳo^{n}´ u-thi-ḳ'e> to inoculate.

mąhká saakí. N ***Liatris punctata,* gayfeather, blazing star, dotted gay feather, Kansas gayfeather, dotted button-snake-root, starwort (lit., 'hard/strong medicine'; roots were stored to be used for their sweetness)** (Kindscher 1987:142).

mąhkáðaaché (variants: **mąhką́ðaaché, mąhkáaaché, mąhkáaache**) N [*mąhká + ðaaché*] **Native American Church meeting, peyote meeting (lit., 'eat medicine')** (02/24/95/FH/pc:okc). *hpǫ́hka htą́wą įkše mąhką́ðaaché šcée hta ðajšé?* are you going to the meeting over at Ponca? (02/24/95/FH/pc:okc; BE2.87).

mąhkáhpa (variant: **mąhką́hpa**). N [*mąhká + hpá*] **pepper (lit., 'bitter medicine')** (02/24/95/FH/pc:okc).

•• LFD 100: *mąhkąhpa* <mo^{n}-ḳo^{n}-p̣a> bitter medicine, pepper.

mąhkáhpa sápe. N **black pepper (lit., 'black medicine')** (03/07/95/FH/pc:ok).

•• LFD 100: *mąhką́hpa sape* <mo^{n}-ḳo^{n}´-p̣a ça-be> black pepper.

mąhkáhpa žúuce (variant: **mąhką́hpa žúuce**). N **red pepper** (03/07/95/FH/pc:ok).

•• LFD 100: *mąhką́hpa žuce* <mo^{n}-ḳo^{n}´-p̣a zhu-dse> red pepper.

mąhkáhpaóožu (variant: **mąhką́hpaóožu**). N [*mąhkáhpa + oožú*] **pepper shaker** (RBn1-7).

mąhkása (variants: **mąhkásai, mǫhkásai**). N [*mąhká + sápe*] **coffee (lit., 'black medicine')** (BE2.21; 01/19/95/FH/pc:ok).

•• LFD 100: *mąhką́ sape* <mo^{n}-ḳo^{n}´ ça-be> coffee. *mąhką́ sape hkǫbra* <mo^{n}-ḳo^{n}´ ça-be ḳo^{n}-btha> I want some coffee. *mąhką́ sape che skiðe*

mąhkása (*continued*) *walį* <mo^{n}-ḳo^{n}´ ça-be tse çki-the wa-gthi^{n}> the coffee is too sweet. *mąhką́sape oðahtą* <mo^{n}-ḳo^{n}´-ça-be u-tha-ṭo^{n}> coffee cup (lit., 'wherein coffee is drunk').

mąhkásaioožú. N **cup (lit., 'wherein coffee is put', coffee cup: refers to any cup)** (01/14/95/FH/pc:prod).
  •• RB: <mó^{n}-kah-sah-o-zhú>.

mąhkáxope. N [*mąhká* + *xópe*] **sacred medicine** (RB).

mą́hkažóika. V, ADJ [uninfl.] [*mąhká* + *žúoka*] *(intr.)* **(be) haywire or crazed with medicine, have one's body affected by peyote.** *mą́hkažóika mą́į akxai, kitą́he hta akxa hǫ́ǫpahu* he's haywire with peyote, but he'll be all right at daylight (01/06/95/FH/pc:prod; BE2.102; RBn HW).

mąhką́ (variant of **mąhká**).

mąhką́hpa (variant of **mąhkáhpa**).

mąhką́hpaóožu (variant of **mąhkáhpaóožu**).

mą́hki. V [conjug. unknown] *(intr.)* **take hold of one another, similar to wrestling** (PM:prod; LS:uk, unconfirmed).

mą́hkisǫce (variant: **mą́hkiesi**?). V [conjug. unknown] [presumably *hkik-* REFL/RECIP + *mą́sǫce* (unattested)] *(intr.)* **wrestle one another** (BE2.161; 04/06/95/LS/pc:okc). *mą́hkiesi apai* they are wrestling (BE2.161; 03/24/95/PM/pc:prod).
  •• LFD 100: *mą́hkisǫce* <mo^{n}´-ḳi-ço^{n}-dse> to wrestle (03/24/95/PM/pc:uk, unconfirmed). *mą́hkisǫce ąkiðali pia nihkašika aka* <mo^{n}´-ḳi-ço^{n}-dse o^{n}-gi-tha-gthi bi a, ni-ḳa-shi-ga a-ka> [expected Mod. Os. form: *mą́hkiesi kiðálį pe, níhkašika akxa*] the man likes to wrestle.
  ••• Cf. *ásąci.*

mą́į (variant of **mąðį́**).

mą́įhka (variants: **mǫ́įhka, máihka, mǫðį́hka, mąðį́hka**). N **soil, ground, earth, clay, mud, dirt** (BE2.125; 03/13/95/FH/pc:okc: non-nasal *i*); **Earth (name for a second son)** (FH:prod). [*mą́įhka* was the personal name of FH's cousin, whose English name was Joe Kemohah.]
  •• RB: <mó-i^{n}-kah, mo^{n}-thí^{n}-kah>.
  •• LFD 100: *mǫį́hka* <mo^{n}-i^{n}´-ḳa> ground, earth, soil, clay, mud. *mǫį́hka aðiðaha e ðo* <mo^{n}-i^{n}´-ḳa a-thi-tha-ha e tho> [expected Mod. Os. form: *mą́įhka akxa áðista akxa*] the mud sticks to you. *mǫį́hka ąðaha e ðo* <mo^{n}-i^{n}´-ḳa o^{n}-tha-ha e tho> [expected Mod. Os. form: *mą́ihka akxa ą́ąsta akxa*] the mud sticks to me. *mǫ́įhka kaxe* <Mo^{n}´ i^{n}-ḳa ga-xe> Maker-of-the-Earth, the name of a gens, also found among the Omahas. *mǫį́hka ska* <mo^{n}-i^{n}´-ḳa çka> white clay, gypsum. "Lime made from this kind of stone was used by both the Osage and Omaha for whitening the sinew used in making arrows; a variety of selenite, calcium sulphate." *mǫį́hkažįka* <Mo^{n}-i^{n}´-ḳa-zhi^{n}-ga> Little-clay (personal name) refers to the four different colors of clay, given by the crawfish.
  ••• Cf. *omą́įhka.*

mą́įhka íðištǫka. N **hoe (lit., 'with which to make the earth soft').**
  •• LFD 100: *mǫįhka iði štǫka* <mo^{n}-i^{n}-ḳa i-thi shto^{n}-ga> a harrow.

mą́įhkaši. N **cellar, basement** (HH tape 8Ap4).

mą́ka (variant: **mǫ́ka**). N **skunk** (03/10/95/PM/pc:ok; BE2.122). [During the early twentieth century, some Osages enjoyed eating skunk and would have white hunters kill and clean skunks to deliver to them at their houses. Mr. George Sells often did so for *hǫǫpé tóohka* (AMS:pc).]
  •• RB: <mó^{n}-kah>.
  •• LFD 97: *mą́ka* <mo^{n}´-ga> skunk.
  ••• *KS mǫ́ǫga, mą́ga* (JOD) skunk (RR).

mą́le. ADV **down.** *hpée mą́le* forehead down.
  •• LFD 127 (unconfirmed): *hpemą́le* <pe-mo^{n}´-gthe> head bowed down.

mąlį́ V [reg.?, *_mąlį́*?] [*ki-* VERTITIVE + *mąðį́*] *(intr.)* **go home.** *mąlį́e!* go on home! (RBn HW10) *mąlį́ hce éa* tell him to go home.

mąsį́ha. ADV **to or on the other side, opposite** (RBn, unconfirmed). *mǫsį́ha káaya* go on the other side, referring to a mud hole.
  •• RB: <mo^{n}-shí-ha>.
  •• LFD 97 (unconfirmed): *mǫsǫ́ ðį́htaapaasta* <mo^{n}-ço^{n}´ thi^{n}-ṭa-a-ba-sda> shave-on-one-side-of-the-head: penitentiary, <mo^{n}-ço^{n}´ thi^{n}-ṭa> on one side (of the head), <a-ba-sda> shave. *mąsǫíhta* <mo^{n}-ço^{n}-i´-ṭa> at the other side.

mą́šą (variants: **mąšą́, mą́šǫ, mǫ́šǫ** [RB]). N **feathers of certain kinds of birds (such as eagle, hawk, and macaw)** (01/24/95/FH/pc). [Not used for more ordinary feathers such as chicken feathers (*súhka hį́į*) (HRE).] *xúða mą́šą* eagle feathers (01/24/95/FH/pc:ok). *xuðámąšǫ* eagle-feather. *úpežą́hta mǫ́šǫ* scissortail feathers (01/24/95/FH/pc:uk). *wažį́kaíe mǫ́šǫ* parrot feathers (01/24/95/FH/pc:ma; BE2.45). *súhkatąą mǫ́šǫ* turkey feathers. • **fan made of feathers or loose feathers (as used in peyote meeting)** (RB).

xúða mǫ́šǫ eagle feather fan (RB). *wažį́kaíe mǫ́šǫ* parrot feather fan (RB).

•• RB: <mó^{n}-sho^{n}>.

•• LFD 101: *mǫšǫ* <mo^{n}-sho^{n}> feather, plume, plumage.

mą́šą oðį́įke (variants: **mǫ́šǫ oðį́įke, mǫšǫ́ oðį́įke**). VP [sync., *mą́šą _oðį́įke*] *(intr.)* **vote (lit., 'grasp the feather'); *(trans.)* vote for** (PM/7/7/94). *kahíke mą́šǫ obrį́įke hta mįkšé* I'm going to vote for the chief (04/26/95/FH/pc; BE2.149). *mǫšǫ́ oðį́įke háažǫ hta nį́kše?* how are you going to vote? (RBn2-MOJ/p19; PM). *hąą ði, mą́šǫ oðį́įke škǫ́šta?* how about you, do you want to vote right now? (PM/7/7/94). *pée mǫšǫ́ oščį́įke?* who did you vote for? • *(trans.)* **endorse, as a check** (04/26/95/FH/pc:ok; 02/27/95/JS/pc:ma; RBn2-MOJ/p19).

•• LFD 102: *mą́šą oðįke* <mo^{n}´-sho^{n}-u-thi^{n}-ge> voting; indorsing a check. *mą́šą obrįke* <mo^{n}´-sho^{n} u-bthi^{n}-ge> I indorsed it. *mą́šą oscįke* <mo^{n}´-sho^{n} u-stsi^{n}-ge> you indorsed it. *mą́šą ąkiðįka pe* <mo^{n}´-sho^{n} o^{n}-gi-thi^{n}-ga i> we indorsed it.

••• Cf. *súhkahtąą mą́šǫ oðį́įke.*

mąšcį́ka (variants: **mąąšcį́ka, mą́šcįka**). N **rabbit** (BE2.111; JS:ok), **hare.**

•• RB: <mó^{n}-shtsi^{n}-kah>.

•• LFD 102: *mǫšcį́ke* <mo^{n}-shti^{n}´-ge> the cottontail rabbit.

mą́ši (variant: **máši**). V [reg., *_mą́ši*] *(intr.)* **be upward or upright.** *mą́šį ce škǫ́šta?* do you want to be pulled up [to a sitting position in the bed]? (BE2.107; RBn10-7:JW, unconfirmed),

•• LFD 101: *mǫ́ši* <mo^{n}´-shi> up above, the arch of heaven, zenith.

••• Cf. *ámąši, ðuumą́ši.*

mąšíhta. ADV, V [reg.?, *_mąšíhta?*] *(intr.)* **(be) above.** *mąšíhtamąį* walking-above (personal name) (RBn22-04). • *(trans.)* **place above.** *ámašihta mįkšé* I'm going to put it up above (HRE/01/17/02/pc).

••• Cf. *ámąši.*

mą́šǫ (variant of **mą́šą**).

mąštáha (variant of **mąąštáha**).

mą́xpu (variant: **mǫ́xpu**). N, ADJ **cloud, cloudy.** *mąxpúmęį apa oðíchįpe aapai* lightning and thunder are getting you (line from a children's song) [*mą́xpu-mąðį́* (lit., 'clouds moving') alludes to lightning and thunder] (FH). *mǫ́xpu akxá* it's cloudy (BE2.20; 01/19/95/FH/pc:ok).

•• LFD 103: *mąxpí* <mo^{n}-xpi´> cloud, cloudy. *mąxpímąį* <Mo^{n}-xpi´-mo^{n}-i^{n}> Traveling-cloud (personal name).

mą́ze. N **metal of any kind, lead or iron (metal); wire, cable.** *mą́ze hcúke* metal spoon. *hkáwa apa mą́ze ohkíǫðe apái* the horses are tangled up in the wire (RBnot-nd-1/p18; FH:ok).

mą́ze ápahta (variant: **mą́ze ápahtą**). N **wire or metal fence** (04/06/95/LS/pc:ok; 03/16/95/MREI/pc:uk).

•• LFD 96: *mą́ze apahta* <mo^{n}´-çe a-ba-ṭa> wire fence.

mą́ze hcúke. N **metal spoon.**

mą́ze htáhtaze. N **typewriter** (04/06/95/FH:ok); **ticking, tapping, or clicking noise against metal (as made by a typewriter)** (FH/10/09/01/pc:ok).

•• LFD 97: *mą́ze htahtaze* <mo^{n}´-çe ṭa-ṭa-çe> ticking iron: typewriter. *mą́ze htahtaze hceka wį abrį* <mo^{n}´-çe ṭa-ṭa-çe tse-ga wi^{n} a-bthi^{n}> I have a new typewriter.

mą́ze íe ówatǫe. N **television (lit., 'speaking metal item wherein one watches things').**

mą́ze įįštóolą N [*mą́ze + įįštá + oolą́*] **glasses, eyeglasses, spectacles, lorgnette, any device worn over the eye or eyes (lit., 'metal to place on the eyes')** (BE2.55; 05/01/95/LS/pc:ok, 04/26/95/LS/pc:ok).

•• LFD 96: *mą́ze įstolą wihta ðą mąšošoce įða ha* <mo^{n}´-çe i^{n}-stu-gtho^{n} wi-ṭa tho^{n} mo^{n}-sho-sho-dse i^{n}-tha ha> [expected Mod. Os. form: *mą́ze įįštóolą wíhta mąšóšoce;* sentence-final *ha* is not used in Mod. Os. and *ðą* is not used in this context] my spectacles are dirty.

mą́ze įįštóolą sápe. N **sunglasses (lit., 'black metal to place on the eyes').**

mą́ze níi táahkace káaye. N **hot water heater (lit., 'metal for making water hot')** (01/23/95/FH/pc:prod orig). [New coinage by FH.]

mą́ze nǫp?į́ (variant of **mą́ze wanǫ́p?į**).

mą́ze oðóbrįįke. N [*mą́ze + í-* LOC + *obrį́įke* (1st sg. of *oðį́įke*); *i + o* regularly becomes *oðo*] **trap (lit., 'I catch it with metal')** (FH/09/09/01/pc).

•• LFD 222: *žápe wį obrį́įke, mą́ze oðóbrįįke* <zha´-be wi^{n} u-bthi^{n}-ge, mo^{n}-çe u-thu bthi^{n}-ge> I caught a beaver in a steel trap.

mą́ze ohkíe. VP [reg., *mą́ze o_hkíe*] *(trans., intr.)* **call by phone.**

mą́ze oohǫ́ (variant: **mą́zeóohǫ**). N **oven.**

mą́ze wanǫ́p?į (variant: **mą́ze nǫp?į́**). N **necklace of iron or other metal; iron necklace (personal name)** (BE2:87; 02/24/95/FH/pc:ok).

mą́ze wépaache. N [*mą́ze + wa-* VAL + *í-* LOC + *paaché*] **sewing machine (lit., 'metal with which to sew stuff').**

mą́zehtahiži̧ (variant: **mą́zehtaiži̧**). N **bells, little bells (as on a cradleboard)** (RB; 01/07/95/FH/pc:uk).

••• Cf. *htáhtaze, mą́zeštahiži̧.*

mą́zeie. N [*mą́ze* + *íe*] **radio** (RBn12-06); **recording device, tape recorder, tape player, phone, phone call (lit., '[something] metal [that] talks').**

mą́zeie híðe. VP [reg., *mą́zeie hí_ðe*] *(intr.)* **make a call by phone (lit., 'cause a phone call to arrive there').** *óhkie šo̧ i̧kšé ihtézi̧ akxa mą́zeie híðape* he was sitting and talking to someone when his younger sister called.

mą́zeie ohkíe. VP [reg., *mą́zeie o_hkíe*] *(intr.)* **converse by phone, talk on the phone.** • N **conversation by phone, phone call.**

mą́zeie ohkíe híðe. VP [reg., *mą́zeie ohkíe hí_ðe*] *(intr.)* **make an outgoing phone call, call s.o. to converse on the phone (lit., 'cause a phone call to arrive there').**

mą́zekʔąsaaki. N [*mą́ze* + *kʔą́saaki*] **telegraph, telegraph wire, message sent by wire (lit., 'fast metal').** *mą́ze kʔą́saki ðée hpaaɣé* I sent it by wire (03/16/95/FH/pc; BE2.134). *mą́ze kʔą́saaki ðée káaɣa* send a wire (RBn3-58).

•• LFD 96: *mą́ze kʔąsaki* <mo^{n}´-çe ḳ'o^{n}-ça-gi> telegraph.

mą́zekʔąsaaki ðée káaɣe. VP *(trans.)* **send by wire, send there by telegraph** (RBn10-12:JW).

mą́zeohkíhkie. N [*mą́ze* + *ohkíhkie*] **telephone (lit., 'talk to each other over a wire')** (03/16/95/FH/pc:ok). *mą́zeohkíhkie o̧wą́hkie* call me on the phone (03/16/95/FH/pc). *mą́zeohkíhkie ðée kší[ð]e* call him/her on the phone (03/16/95/FH/pc:ok). *mą́zeohkíhkie ðeekší[ðe]áape* they said they talked on the phone (03/16/95/FH/pc). *mą́zeohkíhkie akxa hkáamaa akxái* the telephone is ringing (03/16/95/FH/pc:ok; BE2.134).

•• LFD 97: *mą́ze ohkihkie* <mo´n´-çe u-ḳi-ḳi-e> telephone.

mą́zeohkíhkie hükšíe. VP [*mą́zeohkíhkie* + *hukšíðe*] *(trans.)* **have s.o. call by phone.** *mą́zeohkíhkie hükší[ð]e!* have her call me on the phone! call me on the phone! (RB; 03/16/95/FH/pc:ma).

mą́zeóohǫ (variant of **mą́ze oohǫ́**).

mą́zeǫ́ohǫ oohǫ́. VP [reg., *mą́zeóohǫ oo_hǫ́*] *(trans.)* **bake in an oven** (BE2.6; FH/09/21/01/pc/okc). *súhka mą́zeoohǫ ce oowáhą* I baked a chicken (FH/09/21/01/pc).

mą́zeska (variant: **mązéske**). N **money, coin, silver (lit., 'white metal')** (02/25/95/FH/pc:ok; 03/09/95/MREI/pc:ok; BE2.121; MOJ). *oðóota mą́zeska* interest money (02/25/95/FH/pc:okc). *mą́žą oota mą́zeska* lease money (02/25/95/FH/pc:okc). *mą́zeska huuhtą́ą waðákʔupe* you gave them a lot of money (02/25/95/FH/pc:okc). *mą́zeska huuhtą́ą waðákʔupe* you gave us a lot of money (02/25/95/FH/pc:okc). *mą́zeska háanąą ašcí̧ ðaašé?* how much money do you have? (02/25/95/FH/pc:ok: [ðai̧še]). *mą́zeska tóa ąkʔú* give me some money (02/25/95/FH/pc:ok). *mą́zeska tóe ową́kʔu* loan me some money (02/25/95/FH/pc:ok).

•• LFD 96: *mą́zeska* <mo^{n}´-çe-çka> white metal (money). *mą́zeska ąði̧ke* <mo^{n}´-çe-çka o^{n}-thi^{n}-ge> [expected Mod. Os. form: *mą́zeska ąðí̧ke*] I have no money. *mą́zeska ðiði̧ke* <mo^{n}´-çe-çka thi-thi^{n}-ge> [expected Mod. Os. form: *mą́zeska ðiðí̧ke*] you have no money. *mą́zeska waði̧ka pe* <mo^{n}´-çe-çka wa-thi^{n}-ga i> we have no money (02/25/95/FH/pc:all okc).

mą́zeska oðótą (variants: **mą́zeska oðóta, mą́zeska óotą, mą́zeska óota**). N **interest money (lit., 'usage of money').**

mą́zeska ootá waléze. N **note, document of borrowed money, loan.**

•• LFD 96: *mą́zeska ootá waleze* <mo^{n}´-çe-çka u-da wa-gthe-çe> paper or writing for borrowing money, a note.

mą́zeska wanǫ́pʔi̧. N **medal, medallion (lit., 'coin worn around the neck').**

•• LFD 96: *mą́zeska wanǫpʔi̧* <mo^{n}´-çe-çka wa-no^{n}-p'i^{n}> silver medal, peace medal (02/24/95/FH/pc:ok).

mą́zeska zí. N **gold (metal), coins (lit., 'yellow money')** (05/01/95/LS/pc:ok; BE2.59).

•• LFD 96: *mą́zeska zi* <mo^{n}´-çe-çka çi> gold.

mą́zeska zí ékǫ. ADJP **gold (in color), golden, goldlike** (05/01/95/LS/pc:ok; RBn10-5:MOJ/79).

mą́zeskahci. N [*mą́zeska* + *hcí*] **bank (lit., 'money house')** (BE2.6; 01/06/95/FH/pc:prod).

•• LFD 96: *mą́zeska hci* <mo^{n}´-çe-çka ṭsi> bank.

mą́zeskaoožú (variant: **mą́zeskožu** [LS]). N [*mą́zeska* + *oožú*] **purse, wallet, pocketbook, money bag, handbag, billfold** (BE2.108; 04/17/95/LS/pc:ok).

•• LFD 96: *mą́zeska ožu* <mo^{n}´-çe-çka u-zhu> purse, pocketbook, wallet. *mą́zeska ožo ąwą xpaðe ha* <mo^{n}´-çe-çka u-zhu o^{n}-wo^{n} xpa-the ha> [expected Mod. Os. form: *mą́zeskaoožú ą́wąxpaðe;* sentence-final *ha* is not used in Mod. Os.] I lost my wallet.

mązéske (variant of **mą́zeska**).
mą́zeskožu (variant of **mą́zeskaoožú**).
mą́zeštahiži̧. N **bells (such as the ones dancers tie around their legs)** (04/19/95/FH/pc:prod).
mą́zewéoohǫ (variant: **mą́zewíoohǫ**). N [*mą́ze* + *wéoohǫ́*] **cookstove, metal stove (lit., 'metal to cook things with')** (BE2.25; 01/12/95/FH/pc:ok; MSBt9; 04/06/95/LS/pc:okc; 03/14/95/MREI/pc:ma). [In RB's time, a cookstove that used wood, though its usage may have been extended since then to include any stove used for cooking.]
mąžáhku. N **medicine bundle** (RBnote-nd-1/p20, unconfirmed; 02/24/95/FH/pc:uk).
•• LFD 101: *mą́šahkǫ* <mo^{n}´-sha-ḳo^{n}> burden strap. "The burden strap was the holiest of the sacred symbols, surpassing even the hawk, the symbol of the warrior's courage. When a husband wishes to honor his wife he has one made for her ceremonially. This was one of the first ceremonies to die out when new religious ideas were introduced by missionaries."
mą́žą (variants: **mǫ́žǫ, mąžą́**). N **allotment** (04/17/95/LS/pc:ok), **farm** (RB; FH). [Takes 'lying' positional article *kše*.] *níhkašie kíhǫǫpe kóe mąžą́ki olį́i̧ kíhǫǫpe* he liked the people and he liked living on the farm (RBn10-2:MOJ/79). *Jane, Ann éðǫǫpa mąžą́ hta íihkimai ahíe ðí áape* Jane and Ann had come to visit the farm (FH). *mą́žą olį́i̧ aláape* they went back to live on the farm (01/13/95/FH/pc:ok; BE2.26). • **earth** (12/30/94/FH/pc/pron), **world.** *mǫ́žǫ ðáali̧ mǫ́žǫ ðéka ški ði̧kápi tą, íe wíhta akxa šǫǫšǫ́we hta akxai* heaven and earth shall pass away, but my word shall endure (BE2.38; FH:4/22/96/tape:prod). *mǫ́žǫ ðáali̧ ðékše mǫ́žǫ ðékše ði̧ké hta aži íe wíhta šǫǫšǫ́ðe aðée hta akxai* heaven and earth shall pass away, but my word shall endure (FH:02/07/96/pc: from the Bible, Matthew 24:35). *mǫ́žǫ ðáali̧ ðékše* heaven. • **land, country, countryside.** *mą́žą htąą* big country (LS). *mǫ́žǫ ðíhta ée ðáali̧* your country is good (RBn12-11). *níi žópše pšíe ðáha, táatą wi̧ mąžą́ olį́i̧ iiðáðe* when I would go to wade in the river, I saw something that was in the woods (lit., 'when I went to wade in the water, I saw a thing that lived in the countryside') (t24b-p17/num24CQ119; 04/27/95/FH/pc:okc, added *iiðáðe*). • **personal name in the Eagle clan (only the variant *mǫ́žǫ* is used in this sense)** (HRE:pc).
•• LFD 103: *mąžą́/mǫžǫ́* <mo^{n}-zho^{n}´> earth, country, farm, world, land.
••• *OM* same as Osage (LFD 103).
mą́žą ðáali̧ (variants: **mą́žą ðáali̧ ðékše, mǫ́žǫ ðáali̧ ðé**). N **heaven.** [Takes 'lying' positional article *kše*.] *i̧htáci wahkǫ́ta, mą́žą ðáali̧ i̧kši ðaníhkaši ni̧kší eepe* our father, who art in heaven. *mǫ́žǫ ðáali̧ ðékše mǫ́žǫ ðékše ði̧ké hta aži íe wíhta šǫǫšǫ́we aðée hta akxai* heaven and earth shall pass away, but my word will endure (FH: from the Bible, Matthew 24:35).
mą́žą ðé ómąði̧ (variant: **mǫ́žǫ ðé ómąði̧**). VP [reg.+sync., *mą́žą ðé ó_mą_ði̧*] *(intr.)* **live this life (lit., 'walk on this earth').** *wéewina mǫ́žǫ ðé škaškáða oámąbri̧* I want to thank you for this good life (lit., 'I am grateful, I walk on this earth peacefully') (RBn10-10:JW).
mą́žą óota (variants: **mą́žą óotą, mą́žą óðootą, mą́žą óðoota**). N **leasing of land (lit., 'land use')** (02/15/95/FH/pc:okc).
•• RB: <mó^{n}-zho^{n}-o-táh>.
•• LFD 318: *mąžą́ ota wakašupe* <mo^{n}-zho^{n}´ u-da wa-ga-shi-pe> rent (money paid).
mą́žą šką́. N **earthquake (lit., 'earth move')** (04/07/95/LS/pc:okc).
mą́žą záani. NP **world, whole world, universe (lit., 'all the land')** (01/04/95/FH/pc:prod).
mąžą́htą. N [*mą́žą* + *htą́ą*] **countryside.**
mąžą́waleze. N [*mą́žą* + *wáleze*] **map, chart of land, plat (lit., 'earth letter')** (04/17/95/LS/pc:ok).
mąží (variant of **maží**).
mée, méi̧, mȩ́i̧ (variants of **mąðí̧**).
mí (variant of **mí̧i̧**).
miáðuyeží̧ka. N **his wife's brother's wife (more precise than English 'his sister-in-law')** (JOD).
•• JOD (slip file): *miáðuyeži̧ka* <mi-a´-¢ü-xĕ-çiñ´-ḳa> his wife's brother's wife.
míaye (variant: **mí̧aye**). N **daughter-in-law** (04/07/95/LS/pc; BE2.29, RBn2-MOJ/p9; 01/19/95/FH/pc:ok). [Vocative and referent, more familiar than *wihcíni* 'daughter-in-law' (RB); no difference between *wihcíni* and *míaye* (FH).]
•• JOD (slip file): *miáðuye* <mi-a´-¢ü-xĕ> his wife's brother's wife.
••• *PO míwaðiye* daughter-in-law (KDS); *KS mi̧wayű́ye* sister-in-law, man's wife's brother's wife (RR).
miáke (variant of **mí̧ioðaake**).
míalǫška (variant: **milǫ́ška**). N **little people** (04/17/95/LS/pc:ok), **elf, sprite, brownie, leprechaun, fairy.** [Strictly speaking, the Osage "little people" are not fairies, but rather a scarier sort of being, not so small and dainty, and rather more ominous.]

míalǫška (*continued*)

•• LFD 93: *míwaluška* <mi´-wa-gthu-shka> fay, an elf, a fairy. LFD 90: *míaloška* <mi´-a-gthu-shka> elf, sprite.

miása (variant of **mįįása**).

míaxoke (variant of **miixóke**).

míąɣe (variant of **míaɣe**).

mią́ke (variant of **mį́įoðaake**).

michó. N **lion** (BE2.80, RBn2-MOJ/p2; 02/16/95/FH/pc:ok). [Perhaps originally 'grizzly bear'?]

•• LFD 92: *mįhcó* <mi^n-ṭsu´> grizzly bear. *michúžįka* <Mi-tsiu´-zhi^n-ga> Little-grizzly-bear (personal name).

míe (variant of **mį́įka**).

míɣa. N **duck** (PM); **goose** (PM); **game bird or other large bird** (01/20/95/PM/pc; BE2.37). [Takes 'sitting' positional article *įkšé*.]

•• JOD (slip file): *míɣa* <mí-xa>.

•• LFD 94: *míɣa žįka* <mi´-xa zhi^n-ga> a teal duck. LFD 95: *míɣa žįka xoce* <mi´-xa zhi^n-ga xo-dse> teal duck. *míɣa šape žįka* <mi´-xa sha-be zhi^n-ga> a gosling. *míɣašape* <mi´-xa-sha-be> dark goose. LFD 93: *míɣahpahtoho* <mi´-xa-p̣a-ṭo-ho> mallard duck [*míɣa* + *hpá* 'head' + *htóho*] (01/20/95/PM/pc:ok, all above okc). *míɣatoka* <mi´-xa-do-ga> a drake. LFD 54 (unconfirmed): *míɣa žįka ðįkše ležé* <mi´-xa zhi^n-ga thi^n-kshe gthe-zhe´> [expected Mod. Os. form: *míɣažį įkše léže*] the duck is spotted.

míɣa htą́ka (variant: **mį́ɣa htą́ke**). N **goose, big goose or big duck (lit., 'big duck')** (RBn1-24; FH/09/21/01/pc; BE2.59; 02/03/95/FH/pc:ok).

míɣa ska. N **swan (lit., 'white duck')** (FH/09/21/01/pc).

•• LFD 93: *míɣaska* <mi´-xa çka> the white swan.

mihkákˀe. N **star; mushroom** (04/17/95/LS/pc:uk; 04/18/95/FH/pc:ok, 03/14/95/FH/pc:pl; BE2.127).

•• LFD 91: *mihkákˀe* <mi-ḳa´-k'e> mushroom; star.

mihkákˀe hą tą ðįkšé. N **evening star (lit., 'the star when it's evening, sitting').** [Takes 'sitting' positional article *įkšé*.]

mihkákˀe hą́ąpa tą ðįkše. N **morning star.** [Takes 'sitting' positional article *įkšé*.]

•• LFD 91: *mikákˀe hǫ́ǫpatą ðįkše* <mi-ḳa´-ḳ'e ho^n´-ba-do^n thi^n-kshe> the morning star, used in rituals.

mihkákˀe hą́ąpaska tą. N **morning star (lit., 'star when it is daylight')** (FH/09/24/01/prod).

mihkákˀe oxpáðe. N **falling star, meteor** (FH/09/24/01).

•• LFD 91: *mihkákˀe oxpaðe* <mi-ḳa´-ḳ'e u-xpa-the> meteor, falling star.

mihkákˀe óžąke. N **orbit of star (lit., 'star path').**

•• LFD 91: *mihkákˀe ožąke* <mi-ḳa´-ḳ'e u-zho^n-ge> the path of a star, orbit.

mihkákˀehtąą. N **morning star (lit., 'great star').**

mihkákˀežįka. N [*mihkákˀe* + *žįká*] **little star.**

•• LFD 91: *mihkákˀežįka* <Mi-ḳa´-ḳ'e-zhi^n-ga> Little-star (personal name).

míi (variant of **mį́į** and **mį́įka**).

miiáðee (variant of **mįįáðee ehtáha**).

míihtoili (variant of **mį́įhtǫeli**).

míika (variant of **mį́įka**).

míina. N **eldest daughter** (01/09/95/FH/pc:prod). [Pawhuska district usage.]

•• LFD 92: *mína* <mi´-na> the first daughter; "this is a special kinship term. This term is used by a father and mother for their first daughter. The term is also used by other members of the family. It is not a personal name, it is, however, a gentile name, by which she may be addressed by anybody."

••• *KS mínaga* daughter (RR).

míiǫpa (variant of **mį́įǫpa**).

miitáašcuuce (variant of **mįįtáašcuuce**).

miixóke (variant: **míaxoke** [FH]). ADJ, N **homosexual, lesbian, gay person (for some, this term refers only to males)** (BE2.67; FH).

•• RB: <mí-ho-keh, mí-ah-xó-keh> (02/09/95/FH/pc:okc).

milǫ́ška (variant of **míalǫška**).

míwaapaache (variant of **mį́waapaache**).

míwatą (variant: **míwata**). V, ADJ [reg.?, *míwa_tą?*] *(intr.?)* **(be) jealous (the jealous person is male)** (RBn10-19). *míwata štą* he's jealous all the time (02/13/95/FH/pc:ok) (RB note: jealous, applies to men's jealousy). N **man who is jealous of [about] his wife** (RB).

•• LFD 93 (unconfirmed) : *míwata* <mi´-wa-da> to be jealous, As a man of a woman. *waó wį miaata ha* <wa-u´ wi^n mi-a-a-da ha> [sentence-final *ha* is not used in Mod. Os.] I am jealous of a woman. *waó wį miaðata ha* <wa-u´ wi^n mi-a-tha-da ha> [sentence-final *ha* is not used in Mod. Os.] you are jealous (02/13/95/FH/pc:uk). [*waú* or *waó* in the last two examples is probably Omaha; Mod. Os. instead uses *wakˀó* 'wife, woman'.]

mį́. N **blanket, robe, garment, any item worn like a blanket or robe.**

•• JOD (slip file): *mį* <mi^n> a robe.

mį́. v [alternate form of 1st sg. of *ðį́*; cf. *brį́*] *(intr.)* **I am, I was, I live, I exist as.** *níhkaši mį́* I live, I am a person, I live as a human. • [1st sg. of *į́* 'wear'] **I wear.**

mį́ce. N **bow** (BE2.10; 04/13/95/LS/pc:ok). [Takes 'lying' positional article *kše*.] *žą́ąmį́ce* a wooden bow, an ordinary bow to shoot arrows.
•• JOD (slip file): *mį́ce* <mi^{n}´-ṭṣe> a bow.
•• LFD 92: *mį́ce* <mi^{n}´-dse> bow. "The Osage made their bows of the Osage orange saplings. When this wood is not obtainable, they use the hickory or the ash sapling." *mį́ce kše aluze* <mi^{n}´-dse ke a-gthu-çe> I recovered my bow. *mį́ce kaɣe hpimą* <mi^{n}´-dse ga-xe p̣i-mo^{n}> I am skilled in bow making.

mį́cehką. N [*mį́ce* + *hką́*] **bowstring** (LF, unconfirmed; 04/07/95/PM/pc:uk; 04/19/95/FH/pc:uk); **trigger.**
•• LFD 92 (unconfirmed): *mį́cehką* <mi^{n}´-dse-ḳo^{n}> the trigger of a gun. *wahóhtąðe mį́cehką che brítą ha* <wa-hu´-ṭo^{n}-the mi^{n}´-dse-ḳo^{n} tse bthi´-do^{n} ha> [expected Mod. Os. form: *wahóohtą mį́cehką bríitą;* sentence-final *ha* is not used in Mod. Os.] I pulled the trigger. *mį́cehką* <Mi^{n}´-dse-ḳo^{n}> Bow-string (personal name).

mį́ceštá hu. N **Osage orange tree, bois d'arc** (RBn22-01).
•• LFD 301: *mį́ceštahi* <mi^{n}´-dse-shta hi> Osage orange.

mį́e (variant of **mį́įka**).

mį́ɣa htą́ke (variant of **míɣa htą́ka**).

mį́hkaa (variants: **mįhká, mįhkáa**). N **raccoon** (MOJt150; BE2.111; 04/20/95/LS/pc:ok).
•• JOD (slip file): *mikʔá* <mi´k'ă´>, *mįhká* <mi^{n}hká> the raccoon.
•• LFD 91: *mihká* <mi-ḳa´> raccoon. "The raccoon was used for food by both the Osage and the Omaha."
••• *KS mikká* raccoon (RR).

mįhkása. N **black person** (01/07/95/FH/pc:prod). [Slang; a corruption, blending *mįįása* 'black person' (lit., 'blackened by the sun') with *mį́hkaa, mįhká(a)* 'raccoon'; influenced by the English derogatory expression *coon,* which applied to a useless person of any race.] *kóoci įhtáci akxa íiną éðǫǫpa óðaake ðée, oą́ðaake ðée: mįhkása ðée ðe, hpahą́le iiðápi che* a long time ago my father and mother, they told things, they told me this: that that black person was the first one they ever saw (RBn23-10; translation by CQ).
•• JOD (slip file): *mihká sápe* <Mi-ka´ sa´-p̣e> a Negro.

mį́į (variants: **míi, mí**). N **sun.** *kasį́excį mį́į ątǫ́pe htái* let's go see the morning sun coming up (as in a peyote meeting) (BE2.129; 01/14/95/FH/pc). *mį́į íistahkie* bless yourself with the sun (RBn2-26). *mį́į akxa íðǫpi akxai* the sun is coming up (RB; BE2.38). • **moon (used in phrases such as "east door, west moon" [a way of running peyote meetings]** [PM]). *mį́įohką́ce* February, the solitary moon.
•• JOD (slip file): *mį́* <mi^{n}> the sun.
•• LFD 90: *mi* <mi> sun.
••• *OM* same as Osage (LFD 90).
••• Cf. *mį́įǫpa.*

mį́į. N, ADJ **female.**
••• Cf. *mį́įka, wį́į.*

mį́į íðǫpe. N **sunrise, the emergence of the sun (lit., 'sun appears').** [Takes 'sitting' positional article *įkšé*.] (RB; BE2.38).

mį́į íðǫpe įkšé (variant: **mį́į íðǫpa įkšé**). ADV, N **east (lit., 'sun appears, sitting').**
•• RB <mí-í-tho^{n}-pah-i^{n}-kshéh>.

mį́į okʔą́įke. N [*mį́į* 'month' + *okʔą́* + *ðįké*] **March (the month when the sun is just teasing: e.g., sun in the morning but blizzard in the afternoon) (lit., 'month of no events')** (RBn12-05).

mįįáðee ehtáha (variants: **mįįáðee ehtá, miiáðee**). N **west (lit., 'toward where the sun goes', i.e., 'where the sun sets'** [RB]). *mąąščékši ehtáha koe miáðee ehtáha tokétą taakáce ci achíe* I come from the south and the west in the heat of summer (RBn17-p01). • ADVP **toward sundown (as a time of day)** (04/06/95/PM/pc).
•• RB: <mi-áh-theh-eh-táh>.

mį́įake, mį́įąke (variants of **mį́įoðaake).**

mįįása (variants: **mį́įasa, mį́įasai, miása**). N **black person (lit., 'sun-blackened')** (HH-T8a-p5; 01/07/95/FH/pc:ok:all).
•• RB: <mi^{n}-áh-sah>.
••• Cf. *mįhkása.*

mįįðóhta (variants: **mį́įðohtą, mį́įðohta**). ADV, N **(at) noon, midday, high noon, sun seen straight overhead** (03/01/95/FH/pc:okc). *mį́įðohta ahí akxa* it's straight up noon (lit., 'it's arrived at sun straight up') (PM). *ónalįpi, mį́įðohta ahíe akxái* hurry up you all, it's [noon]time (02/13/95/FH/pc:prod orig).
•• RB: <mí-tho^{n}-tah>.

mįįðóhta ðiištą́ (variant: **mįįðóhtą ðiištą́**). ADV, N **(in the) afternoon (lit., 'noon finished')** (12/30/94/FH/pc:prod).

mįįðóhta waaðǫ́. N **midday songs, noontime songs.**

mįįðóhta waaðǫ́ (*continued*)

•• LFD 93: *miðóhtą waðǫ* <Mi-tho´-ṭo[n] Wa-tho[n]> Mid-day Songs.

mįįðóhta wanǫ́bre (variant: **mį́įðohtáwanǫ́bre**). N **lunch, noon meal, dinner eaten at midday** (03/01/95/FH/pc:ok; 04/17/95/LS/pc:ok). *mį́įðohta wanǫ́bre táatą ąðáache hta akátxa?* what are we having for noon meal? (BE2.83).

•• LFD 103: *miðóhtą wanǫbre* <mi-tho´-ṭo[n] wa-no[n]-bthe> dinner. *miðóhtą áwanǫbre* <mi-tho´-ṭo[n] a-wa-no[n]-bthe> I had dinner [expected gloss: 'I ate at noon']. *miðóhtą waðánǫbre* <mi-tho´-ṭo[n] wa-tha-no[n]-bthe> you had dinner [expected gloss: 'you ate at noon'].

mįįðóhta žišǫ́. ADV, N **(in the) forenoon, late morning** (CQnote80; RBn1-10).

mį́įðohta, mį́įðohtą (variants of **mįįðóhta**).

mį́įðohtáwanǫ́bre (variant of **mįįðóhta wanǫ́bre**).

mįįhcéxi (variant: **mį́įhcéxį**). N [*mį́į* 'sun' or 'female'? + *hcéxi*] **personal name for a first daughter (perhaps 'precious female', 'difficult female', 'stout daughter', 'sacred sun')** (FH).

•• LFD 92: *mį́hcexi* <Mi[n]´-ṭse-xi> Sacred Robe. LFD 54: *letǫ́mihcexi* <Gthe-do[n]´-mi-ṭse-xi> New-hawk-woman (female personal name).

••• Cf. *wažážemį́įhcéxį.*

mį́įhiðe (variant: **mį́įhįðe**). N **sundown, evening** (BE2.129; MREI; 04/05/95/LS/pc:ok). *brée aðįhe mį́įhiðe kši hta ąhé* I go onward toward the west (BE2.154).

•• LFD 28: *bre aðį heða mihiðe kše htahe* <bthe a-thi[n] he-tha mi-hi-the kshe ṭa-he> [expected Mod. Os. form: *brée aðįhé, mį́įhiðe kšehta*] I go onward toward the west. LFD 91: *mį́įhiekšéhta* <mi hi-e-ge´-ṭa> [LF's <ge> is presumably an error for <ke>, modern *kše*] toward the setting of the sun.

mį́įhpapo. N [*mį́į* 'sun' + *hpapó* 'going down' (not otherwise attested in the Mod. Os. data, but presumably related to *papó*)] **late afternoon, but not close to dark** (HRE/01/17/02/pc:RBn1-10; WF:ok: 12/30/94/FH/pc/uk). [Synonymous with *mį́įhiðe* (HRE).]

•• LFD 124: *hpapó* <p̣a-bu>down hill, a steep incline.

mį́įhtǫeli (variant: **mííhtoili).** N [*mį́į* + *tǫ́pe* + *alí*] **sunflower; gum, chewing gum.** [Secondary accent recorded on *-htǫ-*.] *mį́įhtoeli oolą́ akxa* he's chewing gum (lit., 'he has put gum in [his mouth]') (RBn14-03; HRE/12/29/01/pc:ok). *mį́įhtǫili bráaškike* I'm chewing this gum (01/24/95/FH/pc:prod). *mį́įhtoili wį ąk?ú* give me a piece of gum. *káa įkšé, mį́įhtoeli hkilúwį* here, buy yourself some gum (BE2.62).

•• RB: <mí-to-eh-li>.

•• LFD 92: *míhtoole* <mi´-ṭo-o-xthe> sunflower, looks always to the sun. "The compass weed, from this weed there is a gum that exudes from the stalk."

mį́įhuðe. N **daybreak, dawn, morning, moment when the sun is coming up.** *mį́įhuðe che?* is the sun coming up? (04/13/95/FH/pc:prod; FH:4/25/96/tape).

mį́įka (variant: **míika**). ADJ **female.** *ąžį howáįki súhkahtą́ą mį́įka hcí káaye che ípahǫži akxa áape* but they could not guess where turkey hen made her nest [they said] (RBn19-05).

•• LFD 90: *miká* <mi-ga´> female. *hce míka* <ṭse mi´-ga> female buffalo. *hkáwa mika* <ḳa´-wa mi-ga> female horse (mare). [All LF forms should have nasal *į* or *įį*.]

••• *KS mįgá* ~ *mį́ga* female, female animal, female of any species (RR).

••• Cf. *šǫmį́įka.*

mįįká ðįké. ADJP, VP [uninfl.] *(intr.)* **(be) without females (said of a family with all daughters and no sons).**

mį́įląke. V [reg., *mį́į_ląke*] [*mį́į* + *lą́ke*] *(intr.)* **marry a woman, take a wife, marry** (MREI/6/7/94/num94; 02/24/95/FH/pc:okc). *mį́įðaląke?* are you getting married? *haakxą́ta mį́įðaląke hta ðaįšé?* when are you going to get married? (RBn10-18). *John mįįlą́kiape* John got married (RBn14-08). *Johna mį́įląki áape* John got married [they said] (RBn). *mį́įląke aðáape* they went to get married (02/24/95/FH/pc; BE2.85). *mį́įląke ąkáðe* we went to get married (02/24/95/FH/pc:okc). • ADJ **married (referring to a man).** *John akxa mį́įląki akxai* John's married (02/24/95/FH/pc). *mį́įðaląke ðaįšé* you're married (02/24/95/FH/pc:okc). • N **wedding, marriage (used by friend or family of groom)** (02/24/95/FH/pc:ok; MREI/6/7/94/num94). *mį́įląke brée ðe* I'm going to a wedding (spoken by family or friend of the groom) (02/27/95/JS/pc; 02/24/95/FH/pc:ok).

•• JOD (slip file): *mįląke* <mi[n]-ḳ¢añ-ḳe>.

•• LFD 93: *míða ląke į to* <mi´-tha gtho[n]-ge i[n] do> [*į to* is not used in Mod. Os.] you are married.

mį́įoðaake (variants: **mį́įake, mį́įąke, mią́ke, miáke, mį́įǫke**). N [*mį́į* 'sun' + *oðáake*] **clock, o'clock, time, time of day (lit., 'sun tells it')** (FH). *mį́įoðaake háaną che?* what time is it?

(BE2.20; 01/07/95/FH/pc). *mį́įoðáake háatkxą hí che?* what time has it gotten to be? (FH:prod). *mį́įake háaną įkšé?* what time is it? (RBn3-35). *mį́įǫke lébrą tą alí hta mįkšé* I'll be back at ten o'clock.

•• LFD 93: *míoðake* <mi´-u-tha-ge> a clock. *míoðake wihta ðą wahosca* <mi´-u-tha-ge wi-ṭa tho^{n} wa-hu-stsa> my clock is small.

mį́įoðaake háaną (variant: **mį́įǫke háaną**). NP **what time? (lit., 'how much on the clock?').** *mį́įoke háaną che?* what time is it? (03/16/95/MREI/pc:ok). *mį́įoðaake háaną ci ðalíe?* at what time did you get back? (RBn1-46).

mį́įoðaake ohtáną. N **hour.**

mį́įohkące. N [*mį́į* + *óhkace*] **January (lit., 'moon alone')** (RBn12-05; FH/11/17/01/pc:ok); **February, the solitary moon** (LF).

•• LFD 93: *míohkąci* <Mi´-u-ḳo^{n}-dsi> the solitary moon, month of February. "This is the version of Black Dog, while Chief Look-out says it is the month of January."

mį́įǫke (variant of **mį́įoðaake**).

mį́įǫkˀaįke. N [*mį́į* + *ókˀą* + *ðįké*] **February (lit., 'month of inaction')** (RBn10-19, unconfirmed). [Reported by RB as 'half days good, half not good'.]

•• LFD 93: *mi ókˀǫ ðįke* <Mi´ u-ḳ'o^{n} thi^{n}-ge> Moon of the Idle days, March.

mį́įǫpa (variant: **míįǫpa**). N **moon, month, month's time** (PM:pc,02/25/95/FH/pc:ok; BE2.89). [Names of months and days were not used in Osage and are not natural for Osage speakers (HH).]

•• LFD 92: *míǫpa* <mi´-o^{n}-ba> the moon. *míǫpa kikˀape kile* <mi´-o^{n}-ba gi-k'a-be gi-gthe> the waning of the moon (unconfirmed; 02/25/95/FH/pc:uk).

••• Cf. *mį́į* 'sun, moon'.

mį́įǫpa aðikeže. N **crescent moon** (02/25/95/FH/pc:ma). [*aðikeže* is not otherwise attested in the Mod. Os. data.]

•• LFD 92 (unconfirmed): *míǫpa aðikeže* <mi´-o^{n}-ba a-thi-ge-zhe> a half moon, a crescent.

mį́įǫpa álįį ðǫǫpá. N **December (lit., 'month twelve')** (HH/14-a/305ff; HH/pc).

mį́įǫpa álįį wį́xci. N **November (lit., 'month eleven')** (HH/14-a/249ff; HH/pc).

mį́įǫpa hkíetoopa. N **August (lit., 'month eight')** (HH/14-a/274ff).

mį́įǫpa hpąhą́le. N **January (lit., 'first month to arrive')** (04/28/95/LS/pc; HH/14-a/249ff).

mį́įǫpa hpeðǿǫpa (variant: **mį́įǫpa hpéǫǫpa**). N **July (lit., 'month seven')** (HH/pc).

mį́įǫpa kootáha. N **month before last (lit., 'the month beyond', 'that month farther away')** (HH/t38a-p1).

mį́įǫpa lébrą. N **October (lit., 'month ten')** (HH/14-a/305ff; HH/pc).

mį́įǫpa lébrą hce wį́įke. N **September (lit., 'month nine')** (HH/14-a/305ff; HH/pc).

mį́įǫpa šápe. N **April (lit., 'shaded moon' or 'dark moon')** (RBn12-05, unconfirmed).

mį́įǫpa táahpa. N **full moon (lit., 'round moon')** (02/25/95/FH/pc).

•• LFD 92: *míǫpa ðǫ tahpa* <mi´-o^{n}-ba tho^{n} da-pa> the moon is round.

mį́įǫpa wahkǿta ižį́ke iitáe ékitxą. N **December (lit., 'the month when God's son was born, it's that time again')** (HH/14-a/347; HH/pc).

mį́įǫpa weðáabrį. N **March (lit., 'third month')** (HH/14-a/249ff).

mį́įǫpa weðǿǫpa (variant: **mį́įǫpa wéðǫǫpa**). N **February (lit., 'second month')** (HH/14-a/249ff).

mį́įǫpa wesáhtą. N **May (lit., 'fifth month')** (HH/14-a/449ff).

mį́įǫpa wešáhpe. N **June (lit., 'sixth month')** (HH/pc).

mį́įǫpa wetóopa. N **April (lit., 'fourth month')** (HH/14-a/449ff).

mį́įšechie. N **Follows-the-Sun, an Eagle clan name** (03/13/95/FH/pc:ok; BE2.171). [Smokey Lookout's name.]

•• RB: <mí-sheh-tseh>.

••• *KS mį́čhiyé-khe* (JOD) south, the course the sun passes (RR).

mįįtáašcuuce (variant: **miitáašcuuce**). N [*mį́į* + *táa-* + *šcúuce*] **sunbeam (lit., 'warm by heat from the sun')** (FH/09/23/01/pc).

•• LFD 90: *mi táscuce* <mi da´-stsu-dse> sunbeam.

mįįwáaðǫžį. N [*mį́į* + *waaðǿ* + *-žį* 'little'] **sun songs** (based on LF).

•• LFD 93 (unconfirmed): *mi wáǫ žįka* <mi wa´-o^{n} zhi^{n}-ga> little songs of the sun. "These songs are the ṭsi´zhu [*hcížo*] version and are appeals for aid from that heavenly body for success in defeating the enemies of the tribe. In these songs the Sun is referred to as Grandfather, reference is made to its rising—first, its outspreading rays, second, its appearance above the horizon visible to the supplicant, third, the appearance of plumelike shafts, and, fourth, when it has fully arisen."

mįkšé. CONT **continuative aspect postverbal marker (indicating ongoing action or state in**

mįkšé (*continued*)
present, past, or future time) for 1st sg. sitting or lying down subject. [*mįkšé* is sometimes used for 1st sg. subjects that are not lying down; hence it can be regarded as the default 1st sg. continuative marker.] *ðéekaa mįkšé* I'm here (FH). *brée hta mįkšé* I'm going; I will go. *oáhą mįkšé* I was cooking; I am cooking. *šée mįkšé* I'm just sitting here [near you]. *haaléžowaáke ąwą́xpaðe mįkše* I have lost my handkerchief (04/11/95/LS/pc:ok; BE2.63; 04/11/95/LS/pc:okc) [contrast this example with *haaléžowaáke ąwą́xpaðe* 'I lost my handkerchief' (04/11/95/LS/pc:ok)]. *žéka xǫ́ mįkšé* my leg is broken (FH). *wébruwį mįkšé* I'm selling it [contrast this example with *wébruwį* 'I sold it'].

mį́waapaache (variant: **míwaapaache**). N [*mį́* 'blanket' + *wáapaache* 'ribbon work, sewing'] **woman's broadcloth blanket** (RB; 01/07/95/FH/pc:ok; FH/09/10/01/pc:ok).

mǫ́. V [1st sg. form of *ǫ́* 'do'] **I do (rare usage).**

mǫ́ (variant of **mǫ́ǫ** 'I wear').

mǫ́, mǫ́ǫ (variants of **mą́ą**).

mǫðį́hka (variant of **mą́įhka**).

mǫhkásai (variant of **mąhkása**).

mǫ́įhka (variant of **mą́įhka**).

mǫ́ka (variant of **mą́ka**).

mǫkápo. N **coat** (BE2.21, unconfirmed; 01/09/95/FH/pc: *mǫ́kápxo?*; 04/13/95/LS/pc:uk; PM/uk; BE2.21). [Pawhuska usage; borrowed from French (RB).]
•• LFD 97: *mąkápo* <mo^n-ga´-bu> "same as a-ga-ha-mi [i.e., *ákahamį* 'coat, cape']."

mǫ́nǫį (variant: **mǫ́noi**). N **prairie chicken** (BE2.107; 04/17/95/LS/pc:ok). *žǫhpazi mǫnoį océ pšíe* I went to look for quail and prairie chicken (RBn3-MOJ/p1).
•• LFD 101: *mǫ́nǫį* <mo^n´-no^n-i^n> prairie chicken.

mǫ́ǫ (variants: **mǫ́, mǫ́į, mǫ́ę**). V [1st sg. form of *ǫ́ǫ*] *(trans.)* **I wear.**

mǫ́ǫ (variant of **mąąðǫ́**).

mǫ́ǫɣe (variant of **mą́ąɣe**).

mǫ́ǫha. N **cliff, bank, escarpment, mountain** (RB; 04/06/95/PM/pc:ok).
•• LFD 98: *mǫ́ha* <mo^n´-ha> a cliff.

mǫ́ǫhahtáhu. N [presumably *mǫ́ǫha* + *htaacé* + *ahú*] **west wind.** *mǫ́ǫ htahú* weather, coming toward us (04/06/95/PM/pc:okc; BE2.154).
•• LFD 98: *mǫ́ha hto iðe* <mo^n´-ha ṭu i-the> wind from the west (unconfirmed; 04/06/95/PM/pc:uk).

mǫ́ǫhisi, mǫ́ǫhisu (variants of **mą́ąhįsu**).

mǫ́ǫke (variant of **mą́ąke**).

mǫ́ǫke zí htą́ą. N **meadowlark (lit., 'large yellow chest')** (RBn18-01, unconfirmed).

mǫ́ǫsa (variant of **mǫ́ǫse**).

mǫ́ǫsa hu. N **dogwood** (RBn HW13), **arrow shaft tree** (RBn22-01).
••• *QU mą́sa hí* dogwood bush or tree, *Cornus* (RR).

mǫ́ǫsase (variant of **mą́ąsase**).

mǫ́ǫse (variants: **mą́ąse, mą́ąsi, mǫ́ǫsa**). N **arrow shaft** (RB10:15, unconfirmed). *mǫ́ǫse hcéxi* sacred arrow shaft (RBn10-15, unconfirmed). *mą́ąsihcexi* Sacred Arrow Shaft (female personal name).
•• JOD (slip file): *mą́sa* <ma^n´-sa> an arrow-shaft.
•• LFD 232: *mǫ́sa* <mo^n´-ça> arrow shaft.

mǫ́ǫsi céɣe. N **willow** (RBn10-21/JW&FW/77, unconfirmed).

mǫ́pše. N **older generation.** *mǫ́pše ðanį* you're the elder (7/7/94/PM). *mǫ́pše anį* I'm the elder (7/7/94/PM; 01/06/95/FH/pc:uk). • **forebears, ancestors** (05/01/95/LS/pc:ok).
•• LFD 101: *mǫ́pše* <mo^n´-pshe> birth, the beginning of a family, the start of a generation.

mǫ́šǫ (variant of **mą́šą**).

mǫxíðe (variant of **mąɣíðe**).

mǫ́xpu (variant of **mą́xpu**).

mǫ́žǫ (variant of **mą́žą** 'land, country').

muskóke. N **Creek Indians** (04/07/95/LS/pc:ok).
•• LFD 246: *mǫškóke* <Mo^n-shko´-ge> Creek Indians.

n

na (variant: **ną**). ADV **only, just, solely, not anything else than, not anything but.** *wahkǫ́ta akxa eená hta akxa na, hpahą́le mę́į, ahkílaðįpai* soon it will be only God, put him first, carry yourself that way (04/04/99/FH/pc). *mą́ąhį wahúhka ą́kažupaží, mą́zehcuka na ąkážupe* we didn't put a knife or fork on, we just put spoons on (RBn3-49). *wálį toocéehape waachí ną apái* he eats too much and he doesn't do anything but dance (lit., 'indeed he is an over-eater, he only dances') (RBn10-2:MOJ/79). *éenąįtǫ́įpi* looking-only-at-her (personal name). *wína, wíną* I only. *ðína, ðíną* you only. *éena, éeną* he/she/it only, that only. *ąkóna, ąkóną* we only. *mąhką́ oðáahtą éeną* a liquid medicine to drink only, a dose of medicine.

••• *KS hną́* only (RR).

na (variant of **ną** 'always').

na-, naa- (variants of **nąą-**).

naa (variant of **nąðé**).

naaɣúce níe (variant of **nąąɣúce níe**).

naaɣúhaše (variant of **nąąɣúhaše**).

naahléke, naaléke (variants of **nąąléke**).

naastą́ (variant of **nąąstá**).

naaxí (variant of **nąąxí**).

naaxǫ́ (variant of **nąąxǫ́**).

nahkǫį́ (variants: **nąhkówį, nąhkųį́**). PRON **both** (BE2.10; 01/07/95/FH/pc:prod; 03/02/95/FH/pc:prod hk); **pair, couple, the two of them.**

•• LFD 115: *ną́hkowį* <no^{n}´-ķu-wi^{n}> the two, both.

nakxáše, nakxą́še (variants of **nąkxáše**).

nalǫ́ǫha (variant of **nąlǫ́ǫha**).

nana (variant of **nąną**).

náški (variant of **ną́ški**).

našǫ (variant: **našo**). ADV **at least, leastways.** *našo "ąhái" áaapi!* at least you all [women] could say "yes"! (lit., 'leastways say "yes"!').

náwaze (variant of **ną́wązi**).

ną (variant of **na** 'only').

ną (variants: **na, nǫ**). ITERATIVE MARKER **always, repeatedly, habitually, customarily, usually, recurringly, continually, continue to, used to.** [Placed after verbs.] *ékie nąpe* they always said. *mįxa htąą, hą́ wíe ní kši áška brée nai* well, I always go near water, said the goose (RBn19-04). *ąwáðahtą ną* we drink (MREI 11/01/83). *wamą́ąðǫ nąpe* he steals all the time. *wį́[e] áoxta tą táata éžiški ékimą ną* when I like somebody, I'll do anything for them (RBn17-p03; HRE/01/17/02/pc:okc). *waachíe watǫ́į ščée ną hta akxai* you're always going to go to dances (MSB-9-3-82). *wį́[e] áoxta tą táata éžiški ékimą ną* when I like somebody, I'll do anything for them (RBn17-p03; HRE/01/17/02/pc:okc). *kalíže wéškaaɣe ną[ð]e* you used to make them with flint. *žįkážį hóolą iðážoši ną* I always used to tell the children not to go fishing (FH:prod). *hkáwa ðáalįpi ną* he continues to be a good horse (RBn12-03p5). • ADJ(?) **distributed to each.** *ihtá na* it belongs to each of them.

••• Cf. *šíną, štą.*

ną. INTERJ **now, but, well.** *ną haakxą́ta líie?* but when is she coming back? well, when is she coming back? (02/01/95/FH/pc:ok: well). *ną haakxą́ci líie?* [now,] when did she get back? (02/01/95/FH/pc:prod orig). • **I wonder.** [Used at the beginning of the sentence, *ną* adds a speculative tone to an otherwise simple question and is often glossed as 'wonder'.] *ną háakxąhta lí?* I wonder when she's coming back? (lit., 'now, when in the future does she return?') (RBn2-MOJ/p10, FH:ok).

•• LFD 112: *ną* <no^{n}> look you; lo!

nąą (variant of **nąðé**).

nąą- (variants: **na-, ną-, naa-**). INSTR **on or with one's foot or feet, by foot.** *nąąžį* he is standing. *naaxǫ́* break with the foot (LS:prod: *nąąɣǫ́*).

•• LFD 117: *nąɣáke(?)* <no^{n}-xa´-ge> to make one cry out by kicking him. *ðanąɣake(?)* <tha-no^{n}´-xa-ge> you made him cry out by kicking him.

nąą́ce (variant of **ðą́ące**).

nąąɣe. N **spirit.**

nąąɣeska. V, ADJ [uninfl.] [*nąąɣe* 'spirit' + *ská* 'clear'] *(intr.)* **(be) sober, not drunk, clear-minded, in one's right mind (lit., 'spirit clear').** *nąąɣeskažį mįkšé* I'm sober, in my right mind (03/13/95/FH/pc:ok; 03/13/95/FH/pc:ok; 03/13/95/FH/pc:ok; FH:prod). *nąąɣeska įkšé?* is he sober? (FH). *nąąɣeska nįkšé?* are you sober? (FH). *wáli húheka kši apa ąžį nąąɣeska kší ape* she's awfully sick, but her mind is all right

ną́ąɣeska (*continued*) (FH/6/16/95). *ną́ąɣeskažį* very sober, not drunk at all (RB). *ną́ąɣeská ðą́ąšé?* are you sober?

•• LFD 117: *nąɣeska* <no^{n}´-xe-çka> sober. *nąɣeąska* <no^{n}´-xe-o^{n}-çka> I am sober. *nąɣe ði ska* <no^{n}´-xe thi çka> you are sober. *nąɣe ska pi a* <no^{n}´-xe çka bi a> he is sober, staid, dignified, spirit, white, clearness of mind, return to consciousness, sane, sober. [Stative conjugation is used for this verb in LF's examples.]

ną́ąɣeskahkiðe (variant: **ną́ąɣeskahki[ð]e**). V [*ną́ąɣeska* + *hkik-* REFL + *ðe* CAU] [conjug. unknown] *(intr.)* **sober up.** *ną́ąɣeskahkíe!* sober up!

nąąɣúce. N **ear, inner ear.** *nąąɣų́ce lų́uwasü!* wash your ears! (12/30/94/FH/pc:prod; 04/26/95/LS/pc:ok). • **act of hearing, understanding, paying attention, heeding advice** (RB; 01/20/95/PM/pc:prod).

•• LFD 119: *nąɣuce* <no^{n}-xu´-dse> the internal ear, that which holds the hearing orifice.

nąąɣúce ðįké (variants: **nąąɣúuce ðįké, nąąɣúce įké**). N **no ears (refers to a person who won't listen and is doing things wrong)** (FH/09/22/01/pc:okc) [Not a clan name.] *nąąɣúce įké* doesn't listen to advice (RBn2-MOJ/p5;12/30/94/FH/pc:ok; 01/20/95/PM/pc:prod).

•• LFD 119: *nąɣúceðįke* <No^{n}-xu´-dse-thi^{n}-ge> No-ears (personal name). [May refer to not hearing or heeding warnings of danger, thus 'brave' (KDS). Unknown as a name to Mod. Os. speakers.]

nąąɣúce níe (variant: **naaɣúce níe**). VP [reg., *nąąɣúce _níe*] **have an earache** (04/17/95/LS/pc:ok). • N **earache.**

•• LFD 119: *nąɣúce nie* <no^{n}-xu´-dse ni-e> earache.

nąąɣúce oðipxokši. N **ear pop** (WF/12/30/01).

•• LFD 119: *nǫɣúceoðipxokši* <no^{n}-xu´-dse-u-thi-po-ki> ear pop, oak gall. "Children gather the oak gall and pop them in each other's ears; hence the name."

nąąɣúce xéka. V, ADJ [stat., *nąąɣúce _xéka*] *(intr.)* **(be) deaf.** *nąɣúce xékapi na* he's deaf (RBn23-15). [Expected Mod. Os. forms: *nąąɣúce ąxeka* 'I'm deaf', *nąąɣúce ðixeka* 'you're deaf'.]

•• LFD 249: *nąɣúce xeka* <no^{n}-xu´-dse xe-ga> deaf.

nąąɣúhaše (variant: **naaɣúhaše**). N **ear wax** (WF). *naaɣúhaše akxa* he has ear wax (WF/12/30/01).

nąąɣúuce ðįké (variant of **nąąɣúce ðįké**).

nąąhtą́ (variant: **ną́ąhta** [FH]). N **ear (of a person or animal), outer part of ear, earlobe** (12/30/94/FH/pc:prod: short final *a;* 01/20/95/PM/pc:ok both). *ną́ąhtą lúuža* wash your ears (12/30/94/FH/pc:ok; BE2.38). *ną́ąhtą ąðúuža* wash my ears.

•• RB: <na^{n}-táh>.

•• LFD 117: *nąhtá* <no^{n}-ṭa´> the lobe of the ear.

nąąhtą́htąą (variant: **nąąhtą́htąka**). N [*nąąhtą́* + *htą́ka*] **mule, jack mule, donkey, burro, ass (lit., 'big ears')** (02/27/95/FH/pc:ok, prod; 01/20/95/PM/pc:prod). *waxpéį ąkái, ókʔu ąðúucʔake še nąąhtąhtąą oðúucʔake wį́* we're too poor to feed that lazy donkey (lit., 'we are poor, that donkey who was lazy, we couldn't feed him') (RBn10-2:MOJ/79).

•• LFD 117: *nąhtá htąka* <no^{n}-ṭa´ ṭo^{n}-ga> a mule.

ną́ąke. V [reg., *_ną́ąke*] *(intr.)* **run** (RBn12-07). *ší hkǫ́hkǫe apai, žįkážį apa páskuha nąąkí apai* he went round and round, as children ran beside him (RBn10-2:MOJ/79). *wisǫ́ka akxa ną́ąke kʔą́sakipe* brother is a fast runner (01/23/95/FH/pc:prod orig).

•• LFD 114: *nąke* <no^{n}´-ge> to gallop. *anąke* <a-no^{n}´-ge> I galloped. *ðanąke* <tha-no^{n}´-ge> you galloped. *ǫnąka pe* <o^{n}-no^{n}´-ga i> we galloped, to run, the running of a four-legged animal.

••• *KS nąge* to run four-legged (RR).

nąąkʔǫ́ (variant of **nąkʔǫ́**).

nąąléke (variants: **naaléke, naahléke**). V [reg.?, *_nąąléke?*] [*nąą-* INSTR + *léke*] *(trans.)* **shatter by foot or with the foot.**

nąąstá (variant: **naastą́**). V [reg., *_nąąstá?*] [*nąą-* INSTR + *stá*] *(trans.)* **kick** (RB-MOJ); *(intr.)* **stomp the ground, trampling or flattening it (lit., 'make bare by foot').** *hpahą́le nąąstą́ apa ną kówe įlǫ́ǫška waachípe* first he kicked, then he war-danced (RBn10-2:MOJ/79; CQ:okc: *ąą*). *hkáwa apa nąąstá apai* the horses are kicking (RBn23-14, unconfirmed).

•• LFD 113: *nąstáke* <no^{n}-çta´-ge> trample down, crush the grass: *áną stake* <a´-no^{n}-çta-ge> I trampled it down. *ðáną stake* <tha´-no^{n}-çta-ge> you trampled it down. *ąnąstakape* <o^{n}-no^{n}-çta-ga i> we trampled it down.

••• Cf. *kaaštá, ostá* .

nąąxí (variant: **naaxí**). V [reg., *_nąąxí*] [*nąą-* INSTR + *-xi*] *(trans.)* **wake or awaken by (nudging someone with the) foot.**

•• LFD 117: *nąxí* <no^{n}-xi´> to awaken a sleeping person. *aną́xi* <a-no^{n}´-xi> I awoke him by heavy walking. *ðaną́xi* <tha-no^{n}´-xi> you awoke him by heavy walking, by walking heavily or by dancing around him ['by heavy walking/dancing' unconfirmed].

••• Cf. *ðixí.*

nąąxǫ́ (variant: **naaxǫ́**). V [reg., *_nąąxǫ́*] [*nąą-* INSTR + *xǫ́*] *(trans.)* **break by foot, break with the foot** (FH:4/16/96/ok; 04/07/95/LS/pc: *nąąγǫ́*). *níitahpa ną́γe nąąxǫ́* he broke the pond ice (FH/09/22/01/pc/prod).

•• LFD 117–18: *nąxǫ́* <no^{n}-xo^{n}´> to hurt oneself [expected Mod. Os. gloss 'to break with the foot'). *aną́xǫ* <a-no^{n}´-xo^{n}> I hurt myself by breaking the board in the floor [expected Mod. Os. gloss: 'I broke it with my foot']. *ðaną́xǫ* <tha-no^{n}´-xo^{n}> you hurt yourself by breaking the board in the floor [expected Mod. Os. gloss: 'you broke it with your foot']. *ąną́xǫ pe* <o^{n}-no^{n}´-xo^{n} i> we hurt ourselves by breaking the board in the floor [expected Mod. Os. gloss: 'we broke it with our feet'].

nąąží́ (variant: **nąąží**). V [reg., *_nąąží́*] *(intr.)* **stand, be standing.** *hįį nąąží́* he stood there (FH:prod). *šée nąąží́!* wait! (lit., 'there where you are, stand!'). *hįį ną́ąžį ðįká, mąðí* don't just stand there, get going (FH:prod). *kahíkeną́ąžį* standing chief (personal name) (03/14/95/FH/pc:ok). *kootáįke nąąží́* go stand over there (03/14/95/FH/pc:ok; BE2.126). *kootáha nąąží́* stand farther over (FH). *hkáwa akxa nąąží́ akxai* that horse is standing there. *aną́ąži šǫ́ ąkxą́he* I'm still standing here (04/26/95/FH/pc). *šéðǫ nąąží́ txa hú hce éa* tell the person standing there to come here. • **stand up, get up; terminate ongoing activity preparatory to departing.** *žįkážį apa nǫhpéhi apai ąną́ąžį hta ąkatxái* the children are hungry so we're going to [get up to] leave (FH). *nąąží́e* stand up (RBn10-5:JW). *aną́ąžį ąkxą́he* I'm getting ready to leave (lit., 'I'm going to stand up') (04/26/95/FH/pc). *ąkále hta ąkai éhtą ąną́žį hta ąkái* we're going to leave (said after sitting and talking a while, to indicate that we're going leave now, spoken while still sitting, indicating that we are going to get up from our sitting position) (FH). *háakǫ óʔie ąkǫ́ða tą ąðíištą nai ehtą ąną́ąžįe* what we had to talk about we finished so I'm going to get up (i.e., 'I'm going to go now') (04/26/95/FH/pc). *aną́ąži ąkatkxai* I'm leaving (FH). *nąąží́ íkʔucapé* he tried to get up (RB: Coyote fable). • **(come to a) stop.** *céγenii mą́ą nąąží́* the drum and arrow stop (RBn10-22/JW&FW). *wálį ohtáza tą nąąží́ che ðíitą tǫ́pape* she was so pretty he stopped in his tracks to look at her (RBn17-p1;CQc; RBn1-MOJ/p40). *ąwą́lǫǫ nąąží́ apai* we [two] never call people names (lit., 'our calling people names stopped', i.e., 'we have stopped calling people names') (FH:prod). • *(trans.)* **stop, cause to stop (e.g., a motor or s.o. engaged in an activity), halt, detain s.o. who is passing by** (03/14/95/MREI/pc; MREI: *nąąží́*). *wacʔéðe ąną́ąžį* we don't kill (lit., 'we stopped killing folks') (FH:prod).

•• LFD 119: *nąží* <no^{n}-zhi^{n}> to rise or stand. *aną́žį* <a-no^{n}´-zhi^{n}> I rise. *ðáną́žį* <tha´-no^{n}-zhi^{n}> you rise. *ąną́žį pe* <o^{n}-no^{n}´-zhi^{n} i> we rise. *nąžį oo!* <no^{n}-zhi^{n} o-u> get up, arise! *nąží́waðe* <No^{n}-zhi^{n}´-wa-the> Causes-them-to-stand (personal name). *ną́žįžį* <no^{n}´-zhi^{n}-zhi^{n}> repeatedly to stand, from a ritual. LFD 131: *šénąžį o* <she´-no^{n}-zhi^{n} o> [sentence-final *o* is not used in Mod. Os.] stand there a while.

••• Cf. *oðókiną́ąžį, okínąąžį.*

nąąží́le. V [reg.?, *_nąąží́le?*] *(trans.)* **stop** (RBn1-40). *nąąží́la!* you stop him or her! (RBn1-40; FH/09/23/01/pc).

ną́ce káaye. V [sync. *k>p*, *ną́ce _káaye*] *(intr.)* **trench.** *ną́ce hpáaye* I'm trenching (around the tipi) (RBn12-09).

•• LFD 13: *ną́ce* <no^{n}´-dse> the back of the house, the walls or sides.

••• *KS ną́je ke ogádą* to peg the walls of a tent or tipi (JOD) (RR).

ną́ceaha (variant: **ną́ceahe**). N **trench, small ditch around tipi for drainage** (BE2-32; 04/25/95/PM/t124/pc:ok; 12/30/94/FH/pc:prod; 04/26/95/LS/pc:ok).

nąðé (variants: **nąą, naa**). ADV **a certain number or amount at a time, a certain number or amount per person (e.g., 'a bit at a time', 'two at a time', 'two each').** *čóopa nąðe káaye* do or make a little at a time (FH/05/08/01:ok). *ihtá na* belongs to each one, one for each one (01/07/95/FH/pc:ok).

ną́γe. N **ice.** *ną́γe ðilǫ́že* chopped ice (RBn, MREI/01/11/83,FH:ok). *ną́γe toa ðuuzá!* get some ice! (lit., 'take some ice!') (01/31/95/FH/pc:okc). *ną́γe akxa táaskąpe* the ice has melted (02/13/95/FH/pc:okc). *ną́γe átaa* iced over, iced (e.g., referring to an iced road or river) (02/13/95/FH/pc:okc). *ną́γe ðaaxǫ́ke šǫ*

ną́ɣe (*continued*)
akxai híi ðiixǫ́kape while he was chewing ice, he broke his tooth.
•• RB: <náh-xeh, núh^{n}-xeh> (02/13/95/FH/pc:ok).
•• JOD (slip file): *náɣe* <náxĕ> ice.
•• LFD 117: *ną́ɣe* <no^{n}´-xe> ice. *ną́ɣe akxa táskąpi a* <no^{n}´-xe a-ka da´-çko^{n} bi a> [expected Mod. Os. form: *nąɣe akxa táaskąpe*] the ice has melted. *ną́ɣe ata* <no^{n}´-xe a-da> iciness, icy.

ną́ɣe kípše. N **ice cream (lit., 'ground up ice')** (RB, unconfirmed).
•• RB: <núh^{n}-xeh kí-psheh> (02/13/95/FH/pc:uk; 04/17/95/LS/pc:uk).
••• Cf. *pšé.*

ną́ɣe paazénii. N **ice cream (lit., 'ice milk')** (02/13/95/FH/pc:ok; 04/17/95/LS/pc:ok; BE2.71).

ną́ɣehci. N [*ną́ɣe* + *hcí*] **refrigerator, icebox, cooler, ice chest (lit., 'ice house').** *ną́ɣehci obrúxpaðe hta mįkšé* I'm going to take it out of the refrigerator (FH/09/23/01/pc).

ną́ɣenii. N **ice water** (02/13/95/FH/pc:ok; BE2.71).

ną́ɣeoožú. N [*ną́ɣe* + *oožú*] **refrigerator, icebox, cooler, ice chest.** *ną́ɣe oožú tǫ́pa mąðí* go look in the icebox.

ną́ɣežį. N [*ną́ɣe* + *-žį* 'little'] **sleet (lit., 'small ice')** (03/10/95/MREI/pc:ok; FH:4/24/96/ok; MREI). *ną́ɣežį húði akxái* it's sleeting (RBn12-10). • V [uninfl.] *(intr.)* **sleet.** *ną́ɣežį akxa* it's sleeting (FH:okc).

ną́hka. N **back (of a human or animal's body)** (12/30/94/FH/pc:ok). *ną́hka aníe* my back hurts (01/06/95/FH/pc:prod). *ną́hka lúuža* wash your back [imperative]. *ną́hka ąðúuža!* wash my back! (BE2.6). *ną́hka wíhta áalįį hta wikíkˀį hta mįkše áapa* I'll carry you on my back, he said (t24a-p4/num24CQ25; 04/11/95/FH/pc:ok).
•• LFD 114: *ną́hka* <no^{n}´-ķa> the back, the part of the body from the shoulders to the hips.

ną́hkai (variant: **ną́hkale**). N **saddle** (03/23/95/FH/pc:ok; BE2.116; 03/23/95/FH/pc:prod).
•• RB: <nó^{n}-kai>.
•• LFD 114: *nąhkale* <no^{n}-ķa-gthe> a saddle (03/23/95/FH/pc:ok). LFD 115: *ną́hkale kaɣe* <no^{n}´-ķa-gthe ga-xe> a saddler. *ną́hkale, kaɣe* <no^{n}´-ķa-gthe, ga-xe> a saddle, to make, or the art of making: one skilled in making saddles (03/23/95/FH/pc:ok: *ną́hkale káaɣe*). *ną́hkalehpa* <no^{n}´-ķa-gthe-p̧a> [expected Mod. Os. form: *ną́hkale hpá*] saddle head, the pommel.

nąhkówį, nąhkųį́ (variants of **nahkǫį́**).

ną́htą. ADV **what if, what would you think if.** *ną́htą pá húðe tą mąąščé?* what if it snows in summer? (lit., 'what if when it snows it is warm weather?') (04/14/95/FH/pc).

nąka (variant: **nąką**). ADV **maybe** (DN:FH, unconfirmed). *kasį́į nąką pší hta mįkšé* maybe I'll go tomorrow. *nąka ną́ąke hta akxa* maybe he'll run.

nąkxáše (variants: **nąkxą́še, nakxą́še, nakxáše**). CONT **continuative aspect postverbal marker (indicating ongoing action or state in present, past, or future time) for 2nd pl. (i.e., pl. addressee) sitting subject.** [Often heard in the greeting to the participants and the audience at the *ilǫ́ǫška* (war dance) gathering, as most are seated.] *xóhka nąkxą́še* you singers (singers are addressed as a group in this manner by a person making a speech at the war dances) (03/09/95/MREI/pc:okc; BE2.121). *hátxąta waðákištǫpaapi ðachí hta nąkxáaše?* when are you all going to come see us? *íiðai ðí opxái nąkxą́še* those of you who can understand (said when addressing a crowd, some of whom do not understand Osage) (RB: 04/06/95/FH/pc:okc). *žįkážį nakxą́še, wéewina akxą́he, ilǫ́įhpa waachí štǫ́pape* I want to thank you children for watching my son dance (lit., 'you children sitting here, I stand here grateful, you watched my eldest son dance').
•• LFD 115: *ną́hkaše* <no^{n}´-ķa-she> [should be *ną́kxaše* <no^{n}´-ka-she>] you who are sitting there.

nąkˀǫ́ (variants: **nǫkˀǫ́, nąąkˀǫ́**). V [reg., *_nąkˀǫ́*] *(trans.)* **hear, hear about, understand** (RBn10-5:MOJ/79). *ánąkˀǫ, aną́kˀǫ* I heard it. *ðánąkˀǫ, ðaną́kˀǫ* you heard it. *ąną́kˀǫpé* we heard it. *áanąkˀǫ* I heard it myself (01/04/95/FH/pc). *áanąkˀǫ* I hear it [with contrastive emphasis on "I"] (05/01/95/LS/pc). *ðaną́kˀǫ?* have you heard about it? did you hear about it? (05/01/95/LS/pc:ok). *waachí pa ðánąkˀǫ?* do you hear the dances? did you hear about the dances? (05/01/95/LS/pc). *Tony ðaną́kˀǫ?* did you hear about Tony? (01/04/95/FH/pc; 05/01/95/LS/pc:ok). *íe ąðánąkˀǫ škǫ́šta įké paašé ąži iðáe ątxąhé* you all don't want to hear me talk, but I'm talking (RBn10-16).
•• LFD 115: *nąkˀǫ́* <no^{n}-ķ'o^{n}´> to hear. *aną́kˀǫ* <a-no^{n}´-ķ'o^{n}> I hear. *ðaną́kˀǫ* <tha-no^{n}´-ķ'o^{n}> you hear. *ąnąhkǫ pe* <o^{n}-no^{n}´-ķo^{n} i> [presumably a typographical error for *ąną́kˀǫ pe* <o^{n}-no^{n}´-ķ'o^{n} i>] we hear.
••• Cf. *ánąkˀǫ, ónąkˀǫ.*

nąlǫ́ǫha (variant: **nalǫ́ǫha**). ADJ, V [reg., *_nąlǫ́ǫha*] *(intr.)* **(be) sneaky, hide, be sly, secretly scheme against s.o., go behind s.o.'s back, be cunning (as Coyote is in stories);** *(trans.)* **hide, conceal.** *táatą wíbruwį, ánąlǫǫha* I bought something for you and I've hidden it (FH). *ðánąlǫǫha* did you hide it? (FH). *ðé šǫ́mhįkasi akxa nąlǫ́ǫhape* this coyote was sneaky (RBn16-02). *ošpéžį nąlǫ́ǫha apái ðée apa ahú apai óceštąpe* they're hiding their things because the people coming are snoops. *ą́nąlǫǫhape* we hid it (FH). *mą́zeska ðíhta nąlǫ́ǫha* hide your money (RBn10-2; BE2.124; 03/13/95/FH/pc:ok). • ADV **on the sly, covertly.**
•• LFD 119: *nąlǫ́ha* <no^{n}-xtho^{n}´-ha> underhand, privacy, retirement, secrecy. *nąlǫ́ha owahkie* <no^{n}-xtho^{n}´-ha u-wa-ḳi-e> I am underhanded [expected Mod. Os. gloss: 'I spoke to him on the sly']. *nąlǫ́ha oðahkie* <no^{n}-xtho^{n}´-ha u-tha-ḳi-e> you are underhanded [expected Mod. Os. gloss: 'you spoke to him on the sly']. *nąlǫ́ha owahkie hkǫbra ha* <no^{n}-xtho^{n}´-ha u-wa-ḳi-e ḳo^{n}-btha ha> [sentence-final *ha* is not used in Mod. Os.] I want a private consultation with him. *nąlǫha wanąkˀǫ* <no^{n}-xtho^{n}´-ha wa-no^{n}-ḳ'o^{n}> an eavesdropper.

nąlǫ́ǫha átǫpe. VP [sync. fortisizing stop stem, *nąlǫ́ǫha á_tǫpe*] *(trans., intr.)* **conduct espionage, spy, have under surveillance (lit., 'on the sly, watch over').**
•• LFD 119: *nąlǫ́ha atǫpe* <no^{n}-xtho^{n}´-ha a-do^{n}-be> espionage.

nąlǫ́ǫha wanąkˀǫ. VP [reg., *nąlǫ́ǫha wa_nąkˀǫ*] [*nąlǫ́ǫha* + *wa-* VAL + *nąkˀǫ́*] **eavesdrop (lit., 'listen to things on the sly').**

nąlǫ́ǫhkile. N [presumably contains *nąlǫ́ǫha* and *hkik-* REFL] **hidden item, hiding place, cache.** *súhkahtą́ą mį́ka hcí nąlǫ́ǫhkile ðáalį káaɣe che ožoáhkiži ðe áape* turkey hen was proud because she could hide her nest so well (RBn19-05).

nąną (variant: **nana**). ITERATIVE MARKER [reduplicated form of *ną* 'repeatedly'] **on and on, continually, keep on with the action of the verb.** [Placed after verbs. May be pronounced with very relaxed vowels, as (nənə).] *kaakǫ́ šǫ́ ðaašé, ðáalǫščį naná* keep on until you get drunk (RBn2-MOJ/p28).

nąniókioožu (variant of **nąnįǫ́kužu**).

nąnióožuhaa (variant of **nąnúhuoožúhaa**).

nąníǫpaži (variant of **nąnį́ǫpažį**).

nąnįǫ́kužu (variant: **nąnlókioožu**) N [*nąnúhu* + *ó-* LOC + *kik-* SUU + *oožú*] **tobacco pouch, tobacco bag (a long bag for carrying or storing tobacco, usually beaded)** (04/07/95/PM/pc:okc; 03/22/95/FH/pc; 03/22/95/FH/pc:okc; BE2.142). • **giveaway, the event of giving items away (archaic)** (RB). *nąnįókŭžu* it's giveaway time (FH:prod).
•• RB: <nah-nyó^{n}-kyu-zhu>.

nąnį́ǫpa. N **pipe, smoke.**
•• LFD 16: *nánįǫpa* <no^{n}´-ni-o^{n}- ba> a pipe.

nąnį́ǫpa káaɣe. VP **make a smoke, roll a cigarette** (04/25/95/PM/pc:prod). *nąnį́opa káaɣe hkǫ́bra* I want to make a smoke, as in a peyote meeting (PM:pc).

nąnįǫ́pa olį́į. N **tobacco boss (who sits to the left of the roadman in a peyote meeting).** (04/07/95/PM/pc:ok; RB).
•• RB: <nah-ni-óm-pah-o-lí^{n}>.

nąnį́ǫpažį (variant: **nąníǫpaži**). N [*nąnį́ǫpa* + *-žį* 'little'] **cigarette (lit., 'little pipe' or 'little tobacco')** (4/17/96/FH). *nąníǫpažį káaɣe hkǫ́bra mįkšé* I want to make a cigarette (as at a peyote meeting, for prayer). *nąníǫpaži hpáaɣe hkǫ́bra mįkšé* I want to make a cigarette (as at a peyote meeting, for prayer) (01/09/95/FH/pc:prod; BE2.19).
•• LFD 116 (unconfirmed): *nąníǫpažįka* <no^{n}-ni´-o^{n}-ba-zhi^{n}-ga> a little sacred pipe, a symbol of the Wa-zha´-zhe gens.

nąnúhu. N **tobacco.**
•• RB: <nah-niú-hu, nah-nú-hu> (03/22/95/FH/pc:ok; BE2.142).
•• LFD 115: *nąníhi* <no^{n}-ni´-hi> tobacco, white man's tobacco, trade tobacco, archaic Osage name for plants used for smoking (03/22/95/FH/pc: not archaic for 'tobacco').

nąnúhu íkiahį. N **plant to mix with tobacco (a small, sweet-smelling plant with yellow flowers that is mixed with tobacco; apparently lit., 'mix into tobacco')** (RBn10-18, unconfirmed).
••• *KS ígahi* ~ *íigahi* mix together, as tobacco and sumac (RR).

nąnúhuoožúhaa (variant: **nąnióožuhaa**). N [*nąnúhu* + *oožú* + *háa*] **tobacco bag (lit., 'skin for putting tobacco inside')** (03/22/95/FH/pc).
•• LFD 116: *nąnúžiha* <no^{n}-nu´-zhi-ha> a tobacco pouch.

nąpe (variant: *nǫpe*). ITERATIVE MARKER [*ną* 'habitually' + *api* + *ðe* 'declarative'] **always did, used to do; usually, normally.** [Used after verbs with 1st pl., 2nd pl., and 3rd person (sg. or pl.) subjects, especially in generic statements.] *kóoci ékie nąpé* that's what they used to say [contrasts

nąpe (*continued*)
with *kóoci ékiape* 'they said that a long time ago'] (02/22/95/FH/pc:ok). *iiną́ akxa žįkážį hóolą ížoši nąpe* mother used to tell the children not to go fishing (FH:4/18/96/tape:okc). *kasį́excį wažį́ka apa hóohtą nąpé* the birds sing early in the morning (02/25/95/FH/pc:okc). *pée tą nuužú nąpé* when it becomes spring, it usually rains (RBn3-52). *hkiistómąį háaną oožú nąpe?* how many councilmen do they usually put in? *níi akxa op?ą́ðe nąpé* water steams (MSB 2-2-670).

nąsą́sąwa. v [reg.?, *_nąsą́sąwa?*] *(trans.)* **clap (e.g., the hands).** *íixa apa šáake nasą́sąwa škí apai* they laughed and clapped their hands (RBn10-2:MOJ/79, unconfirmed).

•• LFD 31: *sǫsǫ́* <ço^{n}-ço^{n}´> to tremble. *ðasǫ́sǫ* <tha-ço^{n}-ço^{n}´> you tremble.

nąški (variant: **náški**). ADV [*na* 'only' + *ški*] **only, just, even only, merely, solely.** *hǫ́ǫpa wį́xci nąški níhkaši aní hkǫ́bra* I want to live [just] one day at a time (RBn10-21). *hǫ́ǫpa nąški ðáalį* only one good day (RBn10-21, gloss by CQ). *hową́įki ðǫǫpá ðáabrį náški ecíe akxa tą, wíe ée brį́ hta mįkšé na ée ešie* wherever only just two or three are, I will always be there, you said (from the Bible, Matthew 18:20; FH:prayer).

nąwązi (variant: **náwaze**). v [reg., *_nąwązi*] *(trans.)* **be jealous about s.o. in regard to the opposite sex (the jealous person is usually female)** (04/14/95/FH/pc:okc). *ánawazé* I'm jealous (about him) (BE2.72; HH/pc; 04/14/95/FH/pc:ok; RBn1-MOJ/p22). *ą́nąwazé apa* they're jealous of me [PM: a man speaking of a woman's or women's jealousy] (PM/96b; 02/13/95/FH/pc:okc). *ą́nawazé akxai* she's jealous of me (RBn12-10). *ánawazí* I'm jealous of [about] him (said by a woman whose boyfriend is talking to another woman). • N **woman who is jealous (e.g., about her spouse or boyfriend)** (LH; 02/13/95/FH/pc:ok).

•• RB: <náh-wah-zi> (04/14/95/FH/pc:okc).

•• LFD 117: *ną́wązi* <no^{n}´-wo^{n}-çi> jealousy by a woman. *aną́wązi he* <a-no^{n}´-wo^{n}-çi he> I am jealous. *ðaną́wązi he* <tha-no^{n}´-wo^{n}-çi he> you are jealous.

ni (variant of **ði** IMPERATIVE MARKER).

ni (variant of **ðíe** 'you').

ní (variant: **níe**). v [reg., *_ní*] *(intr.)* **be well or all right, be in good health** (FH/09/25/01/prod). *aní, aníe, anį́* I'm well. *ðaní, ðaníe* you're well. *ąníe* we're well. *ní* he's well (01/06/95/FH/pc). *aníe* I'm well (FH/09/25/01/prod). *ðaníe?* are you well? (FH/09/25/01/prod). *ní akxai* he's well (FH/09/25/01/prod). • **live, be alive, be living.** *wawépahǫ aní šǫ́ ąhé* I'm a witness and I'm still living (RBnot 5/8/79/p2). *hǫ́ǫpa wį́xci ną́ški níhkaši aní hkǫ́bra* I want to live one day at a time (RBn10-21). *aníe mįkšé* I'm alive (FH 01/06/95/pc:prod). *níe mįkše* I'm living, I'm alive (MREI/num94; 01/06/95/FH/pc:ma). *ní aži akxai* he's not living, he's not alive (RBn12-10/MJ). *íkaske níe* he's out of breath, I'm choking (as when having a heart attack) (FH). *ní akxai* he's alive. *ní šǫ́ ðe?* is he living still? (RBn12-10/MJ). *ní šǫ́ apai* he's still living (RBn12-10/MJ). *ąníe ąkatxa* we're all living (MREI/6/7/94/num94; 01/06/95/FH/pc:ok). *hą́ąpa ihtǫ́į ókašeįke ną́ace nąąžį́ káakǫ ðaníhkašika [ð]aní ąkǫ́ða* in future days, standing with untroubled hearts is how we want you to live.

•• LFD 105: *ni* <ni> to exist, to live. *aníe ðo* <a-ni´e tho> [expected Mod. Os. form; *aní* or *aníe; ðo* is not used in Mod. Os.] I live. *ðaní e ðo* <tha-ni´ e tho> [expected Mod. Os. form *ðaní* or *ðaníe*] you live. *ąní pi a ðo* <o^{n}-ni´ bi a tho> [expected Mod. Os. form: *ąní pe*] we live.

••• Cf. *ðį́, ónie.*

ní (variant of **nį́** 'you are').

níaǫhta záani (variant of **níǫhta záani?**).

níažį. ADJ, N **quiet** (RBn10-5:MOJ/79).

••• *KS nią́ži* silent, quiet, still (stative) (RR).

níðe. v [reg.?, *ní_ðe?*] [*ní* 'live' + *ðe* CAU] *(trans.)* **allow to live.**

•• LFD 110: *níðe* <ni´-the> to permit to live. "When captives are brought in, it is the ṭsi-zhu Wa-shta-ge gens that makes the decision as to which one may live."

••• Cf. *toníðe, waníðe.*

níðe. v [reg., *ní_ðe*] *(trans.)* **give away, divest oneself of.** *táatą ðáalį toa níða!* give some good things away! *haxį́ ðé niáðe atxąhé* I'm giving this blanket away (RBnotes). *ékene akxa hkáwa žúuce níðape* Aiken gave the red horse away (words to "Aiken song") (BE2.55; 01/31/95/FH/pc:ok). *haxį́ ðéche ée ðe níðape* these are the blankets that they gave away. *wihtáežį akxa ékipše kǫ́ða akxa, hǫ́ǫpa ðé wéeðina akxai, mą́zeskažį níðe kǫ́ða akxa* Sister wants me to say something, she's grateful today and wants to give away a little money (RBn23-17). • **be out of, be lacking.** *níi níðe akxai* he's out of water (FH:prod). *ónǫbre níðe akxai* he's out of food (FH:prod). *mą́zeska ąníðe* we [two] are out of money (FH:prod).

•• LFD 110: *níðe* <ni´-the> to exterminate, to destroy utterly, annihilate. *níðe* <ni´-the> to spend money, to give away one's own possessions, till all are gone. *níakiðe* <ni´-a-gi-the> [expected Mod. Os. form: *niáðe*] I spend. *níðakiðe* <ni´-tha-gi-the> [expected Mod. Os. form: *niðáðe*] you spend. *níąkiða pe* <ni´-o^n-gi-tha i> [expected Mod. Os. form: *ąníðape*] we spend.

••• Cf. *waníðe.*

níe. v [reg./stat., *_níe* (reg. for 1st sg. subject, reg. or stat. for 1st pl. or 2nd person subject)] **hurt, experience pain.** *aníe* it hurts me, I feel pain. *ðiníe, ðaníe* it hurts you, you feel pain. *ąníe* [expected 1st pl. form: *ąníe* or *waníe*] it hurts us, we feel pain. *žeká aníe* my leg hurts (02/13/95/FH/pc:ok). *šáake aníe* my hand hurts (02/13/95/FH/pc:ok; MREI/6/7/94/num94). *aníe* it hurts me. *šų́pe aníe* my stomach hurts (02/13/95/FH/pc:ok; BE2.70). *wéehli aníe* my head aches (RBn3-39). *nąąyúce aníe* I have an earache. *tóoce ąníe* I have a sore throat [the pronominal prefix form *ą-* in this example is probably not the stative prefix, but rather is due to leftward spread of nasality to *a-*] (FH/t116b). *tóoce ðiníe?* do you have a sore throat? (FH/t116b). *táatą ðiníe?* what hurts you? (02/13/95/FH/pc:ok). *šáake ðaníe* your hand hurts (MREI/6/7/94/num94). *táatą ðiníe?* what was hurting you? (RBn3-16). *wéehli ðiníe, wéehli ðaníe* your head aches. *hcéka ðiníe che ákǫze hta akxa ska* I guess he will examine you now (lit., 'just now, he will examine your hurting, it seems') (04/13/95/LS/pc:ok; BE2.42). *hówąįki ðiníe?* where do you hurt? (02/13/95/FH/pc:ok). *waníe ðįkší aape* they said she's in labor (FH/pc). *íkaske níe* he's out of breath, choking (as when having a heart attack) (FH).

•• LFD 107: *níe* <ni´-e> an ache. *wéðili ąnie ha* <we´-thi-xthi o^n-ni-e ha> [expected Mod. Os. form: *wéeli aníe;* sentence-final *ha* is not used in Mod. Os.] my head aches. *wéðili ðinie ha* <we´-thi-xthi thi-ni-e ha> [expected Mod. Os. form: *wéeli ðiníe;* sentence-final *ha* is not used in Mod. Os.] your head aches. *ąníe* <o^n-ni´-e> I have pain. *ðinie* <thi-ni-e> you have pain. LFD 72: *íha che ąníe ha* <i´-ha te o^n-ni´-e ha> [expected Mod. Os. form: *íhaa che aníe;* sentence-final *ha* is not used in Mod. Os.] my mouth is sore. LFD 228: *žóika nie* <zhu´-ga ni-e> ache; pain in any part of the body. *žóika anie* <zhu´-i-ga a-ni-e> I have a pain. *žóika ðinie* <zhu´-i-ga thi-ni-e> you have a pain.

••• Cf. *waníe.*

níe (variant of **ní** 'be well').

níe (variant of **nį́** 'you are').

níhce (variant: **níhci**). v [stat. *ní_hce*] *(intr.)* **be cold, feel cold (animate subject).** [Replacement of final *e* by *a* before the completed action marker *(a)pi* and the negative marker *(a)ží* is especially variable with this verb.] *níąhce* I'm cold (01/19/95/FH/pc:ok). *níðihce* you're cold (BE2.21). *níhce ški akxai* he was cold, too (RBn16-02). *níąhtamažíe* I'm not cold (1-20-83-p2). *níhcipe* he's cold (1-20-83-p2).

níhka. n **man, person.** *níhka wį achípe* a man came (01/06/95/FH/pc:prod). *níhkašie wį́ cʔéðape* they killed a man (RBn10-20). *níhkaši pa wátǫpa* look after those men. • **husband.** [Either alienable possessive pronouns or inalienable possessive prefixes are used for 2nd and 3rd person possessor; only alienable pronouns are used for 1st person possessor (***winíhka* for 'my husband' does not exist).] *níhka* my husband. *níhka wíhta* my husband (04/27/95/FH/pc; 02/24/95/FH/pc:ok; BE2.84). *níhka ðíhta* your husband [*níhka ðíhta* is preferred over *ðiníhka* (FH)] (04/27/95/FH/pc). *níhka íhta* her husband.

•• LFD 107: *níhka* <ni´-ķa> man. LFD 109: *níhkaðǫpa* <Ni´-ķa-tho^n-ba> Two-men (personal name) [*níhka* 'man' + *ðǫpá* 'two'].

••• Cf. *iiníhka, níhkašie.*

níhka sápe. n **black person, African American** (01/07/95/FH/pc:prod; BE2.9).

•• LFD 107: *nihká sape* <ni-ķa´ ça-be> negro.

••• Cf. *sáežį.*

níhka watą́įke. n **Gentle Man (personal name)** [Antoine Pryor's name] (FH).

•• LFD 186: *watáįka* <wa-da´-i^n-ga> a lover of jests, a joker, one who is fond of fun or a frolic.

níhka wažį́htąą. adj, n **determined, strong-willed (person)** (RBn1-29).

•• LFD 21: *wažį́ htąka* <wa-zhi^n´- ţo^n-ga> great courage, very brave.

••• *KS wažį́ lą́ąye* brave(?) (RR).

níhka žúuce. n **Indian, Indians (lit., 'red man', 'red people')** (BE2.71).

•• LFD 109: *níhka žuce* <Ni´-ķa zhu-dse> Red man, Indian.

níhkahkipáną. n [*níhka* + *hkipáną*] **Running Man (personal name)** [Name of the father of Weuɣaake, who was the father of John Oberly; Níhkahkipáną was Frances Holding's paternal great-grandfather (FH:pc).]

nihkáši (variant of **ínihkašie**).

nihkáši, níhkaši (variants of **níhkašie**).

níhkaši íkǫske. N **scarecrow (lit., 'similar to a person').**

níhkašie (variant: **níhkaši**). N **human, person, individual, man** (FH/09/22/01/pc:prod). *wažáže níhkaši* an Osage person. *níhkašíe wį achípe* a person came (01/06/95/FH/pc). *hǫ́ǫpa wį́xci nį́ški níhkaši mį́ hkǫ́bra* I want to live [be a human] one day at a time (RBn10-21). • **persons, people.** *níhkašie ąnį́si ecíke* there are people around that don't like me. *níhkašíe achípe* some people came (01/06/95/FH/pc:okl 03/07/95/PM/pc: same as *níhka apa ahí*). *níhkašika čóopažį* just a few people (BE2.102).
 ••• Cf. *níhka.*

níhkašika. N **the people, a people** (03/07/95/PM/pc:ok). *níhkašika apa waxpáðįpe* the people are poverty-stricken (FH/pc).
 •• LFD 108: *nihkašika ekǫ* <ni-ķa-shi-ga e-go^{n}> human, mankind. *níhkašika* <ni´-ķa-shi-ga> a people, a ritual term. *níhkašika hu pi a* <ni´-ķa-shi-ga hiu bi a> many people.

níhkašika. V [reg., _*níhkašika*] *(intr.)* **live, exist.** *ðaníhkašika* you're living. *aníhkašika* I'm living. *hą́ąpa ihtǫ́į ókašeįke nąace nąąžį́ káakǫ ðaníhkašika (ð)aní ąkǫ́ða* in future days, standing with untroubled hearts is how we want you to live (RB). *mǫ́žǫ ðáalį įksé ðaníhkašika nįkšé, éebré hta mįkšé* you'll be living in heaven, I'll be thinking. *hǫ́ǫpa húu aníhkašie hkǫ́bra* I want to live a long time (RBn12-10/MJ).
 •• LFD 13: *aníhkašika* <a-ni´ķa-shi-ga> I am a person having that power (an expression from a ritual) ['having that power' unconfirmed] .

níhkašika ochí. N **country (lit., 'people plentiful').**
 •• LFD 108 (unconfirmed): *níhkašika ohci* <ni´-ķa-shi-ga u-ţsi> a village or country full of people, a populous country.

níhkašikažį. N **little people (small beings in Osage mythology)** (PM).

níi (variant: **nį́į**). N **water, any fluid, liquid** (03/16/95/JS/pc:prod; BE2.151). *níi che huukáaya* pass the water (03/06/95/FH/pc:ok). *nį́ye níi* ice water (03/16/95/JS/pc:ok). *níi ápše wákˀue* pass the water around. *níi níni* cold water (HH;t15a-p1).
 •• LFD 105: *ni* <ni> water, river, rivulet, creek.
 ••• *OM* same as Osage (LFD 105).

níi ápuye. N **beer (lit., 'boiling or foaming water or liquid') (archaic)** (01/07/95/FH/pc:ok; BE2.10).

níi cˀáaðe. N **vinegar (lit., 'sour water')** (FH).
 •• LFD 110: *nícˀaðe* <ni´-ts'a-the> sour water, vinegar.

níi htą́ka (variant: **níi htą́ą**). N **Mississippi River (lit., 'big water'), ocean, sea.** *níi htą́ą áðuuhta brée hta mįkšé* I'm going to go across the ocean (FH/04/08/01/pc).

níi wécˀa. N **water moccasin** (RBn HW13).
 •• LFD 215 (unconfirmed): *wécˀa niki* <we´-ţs'a ni-gi> water snake, water moccasin.

niiámąðį. N [*níi* + *ámąðį*] **water-strider bug.**

niiámąsa, niiámąse (variants of **níimąse**).

níiðaahtą (variant: **níiiðaahtą**). N [*níi* + *í*- LOC + *ðaahtą́*] **dipper, ladle (lit., 'with which to drink water')** (T14b-p1; 04/07/95/LS/pc:ok).
 ••• Cf. *íniiðaahtą.*

niiháa. N [*níi* + *háa*] **algae (lit., 'water's skin/surface'); surface of water (perhaps 'superficial appearance of a body of water').** *niiháa htóho ékǫ* blue (as distinct from green) (RB, unconfirmed; 01/07/95/FH/pc:uk). [The proper meaning of this term is perhaps 'water's surface' rather than 'algae'; that is implied by the fact that *niiháa htóhoekǫ* means 'blue' rather than 'green'.]
 •• LFD 107: *níha* <ni´-ha> algae, a green, red, and brown plant found in both sea and fresh water, commonly called kelp or seaweed.

niiháa htóhoékǫ. ADJP [*niiháa* + *htóho* + *ékǫ*] **blue (as distinct from green) (lit., 'green/blue like the surface of water')** (RB, unconfirmed; 01/07/95/FH/pc:uk).

niikáapxohke. N [*níi* + *kaapxóhke*] **soda pop, soft drink (lit., 'liquid explodes')** (BE2.106).

niikáapxokeoožú. N [*niikáapxohke* + *oožú*] **can, bottle, or other container for soda pop.** *niikáapxokeoožu štáaštą tą, ðibrúuska* when you are through with the pop can, wad it up (02/24/95/FH/pc).
 ••• Cf. *mą́zeskaoožú.*

níimąse (variants: **niiámąse, niiámąsa**). ADV **abroad, overseas.** *kahíke mą́ąhihtą éðǫǫpa níimąse aðáaapi áape* the chief and superintendent went abroad (lit., 'chief, superintendent, both abroad went, they said') (02/01/95/FH/pc:okc). *Sara akxa niiámąsa ahípe* Sara went abroad (03/02/95/FH/pc). • N **ocean.** *niiámąsa aðáapi áape* they went across the water (the ocean) (03/02/95/FH/pc; BE2.97).
 •• RB: <ní-mo^{n}-sí^{n}-tah>.

níini N [*níi* + *níni*] **spring, well (sources of water)** (04/07/95/LS/pc:ok).

•• LFD 107: *niní* <ni-hni´> water cold, a spring or well.

niióhkiacʔį. N [*níi* + *hkik-* REFL + *okácʔį*] **mirror (lit., 'peer at oneself in the water')** (PM) (BE2.88; 03/01/95/FH/pc).

•• RB: <níu-kiah-ts'í^{n}>.

•• LFD 110: *nióhkilacʔį* <ni-u´ḳi-gtha-ṭs'i^{n}> a mirror. LFD 168: *okáhąpa nuhkila sį* <u-ga´ ho^{n}-ba niu-ḳi-gtha çi^{n}> a looking-glass.

níioožú. N [*níi* + *oožú*] **pitcher (lit., 'pour water into it')** (t14b-p1; 04/17/95/LS/pc:ok).

niióšo. N **Neosho (town in Oklahoma)** (FH). [Possibly from *níi* + *oožú* 'pour water into it', i.e., 'main river'.]

níipxaðe. V [conjug. unknown] *(intr.)* **drown.**

•• LFD 109: *nihpáhaiðe* <ni-pa´-ha-i-the> [expected Mod. Os. form: *niipxáðe* or *níipxaðe*] drown (to), drowned. *nihpáhaibre* <ni-pa´-ha i-bthe> I drowned. *nihpáha ąka i aðápe* <ni-pa´-ha o^{n}-ga i a-tha i> we drowned. [LF forms all unconfirmed; all should have *-pxa*.]

níiskue (variants: **niiskúðe, níiskuðe, níisku**) N [*níi* + *skúðe*] **salt (lit., 'sweet water').** *níiskueoožú* salt shaker (lit., 'put salt in it') (03/23/95/FH/pc:ok; BE2.116; 03/23/95/FH/pc:ok).

•• RB: <ní-skyu-theh>.

•• LFD 105: *niskíðe saki* <ni-çki´-the ça-gi> hard salt, rock (03/23/95/FH/pc:ok). *niskíðe* <ni-çki´-the> salt (03/23/95/FH/pc:ok). "The Osage knew salt and the use of it long before the coming of the white man. They knew the salt springs and the places where rock salt could be obtained."

níiskueoožú. N [*níiskue* + *oožú*] **salt shaker.**

níišoce. N [*níi* + *šóce*] **drizzle, mist, gray rain, haze** (FH: prod).

níita (variant: **níitą**). N **flooding water, running water that is flooding (as over a spillway).** *níitą akxái* water is running over (e.g., a spillway) (FH). • **elephant** (12/30/94/FH/pc:prod).

•• LFD 106: *níta* <ni´-da> elephant. "The bones of great animals were frequently found in banks by . . . the Osage, which they indiscriminately called by this name. When they saw the elephant in a circus they applied this name to it."

niitáahpa (variant: **níi táahpa**). N **pond (lit., 'round water').** [Takes 'sitting' positional article *įkšé*.] *níi táahpa įkší žįka nǫ́ǫðe ðáalį, ecíe ska ąąžį ąkátxa* the pond is a good place to raise children, we think it's there (RBn19-04; CQ:okc; BE2.105; 03/10/95/FH/pc:ok).

•• RB: <ní-tah´-pah>.

•• LFD 106: *nítahpa* <ni´-da-pa> round water, a pond.

níitą (variant of **níita**).

níixoce. N **ashes** (BE2.4; 01/06/95/FH/pc:prod).

•• LFD 111: *nixóce* <ni-xo´-dse> ashes.

••• Cf. *xóce.*

níixoce weoožu. N [*níixoce* + *wa-* VAL + *í-* LOC + *oožú*] **flask for gunpowder.**

•• LFD 111: *nixóce weoži* <ni-xo´-dse we-u-zhi> flask, powder flask.

niixócoožu. N [*níixoce* + *óožu*] **ashtray** (FH).

níižu (variants: **núužu, niižú, nuužú**). V [uninfl.] *(trans., intr.)* **rain** (01/24/95/FH/pc:ok). *níižu akxa* it is raining (04/17/95/LS/pc:ok). *įlǫ́aže kaðó šǫ́ke niižú akxai* it's raining cats and dogs (RBn). *níižuži akxa* it's not raining (04/17/95/LS/pc:ok). *níižu ðiištą́ akxa* it's stopped raining (04/17/95/LS/pc:ok). *kasįe níižu hta akxa* tomorrow it will rain (04/17/95/LS/pc:ok). *níižu ðąąché akxa* it looks like rain. *pée tą nuužú štą* in the spring, it rains a lot (03/14/95/FH/okc; BE2.126; 04/17/95/LS/pc:ok). • N **rain.**

níižu oxáke. N **toad** (FH:5/01/96/tape:ok).

niižú xóce. N **drizzle, mist (lit., 'gray rain')** (FH:prod).

•• LFD 111: *nižú xoce* <ni-zhiu´ xo-dse> gray rain, drizzle (04/13/95/FH/pc:ok).

níižu xóhtą. N **drizzle, mist, fine raindrops (lit., 'small rain')** (FH).

níižue (variant of **níižuuce**).

níižue hkąące (variants: **núužue hkąące, níižuuce hkąące**) (03/10/95/FH/pc:ok). N **plum (lit., 'river apple')** (BE2.105).

•• LFD 111: *nížuce hkące* <ni´-zhu-dse ḳo^{n}-dse> the sand plum.

niižúpa. N [*níižu* + *pá*] **sleet (lit., 'rainy snow').**

•• LFD 111 (unconfirmed): *nižú pa itape* <ni-zhiu´ ba i-da-be> sleet, rain and snow mixed.

níižuuce (variant: **níižue**). N [*níi* + *žúuce*] **river (lit., 'red water').**

níižuuce hkąące (variant of **níižue hkąące**).

níižužį. N [*níižu* + *-žį* 'little'] **a rain shower (lit., 'small rain').**

•• LFD 111: *nižú žįka* <ni-zhiu´ zhi^{n}-ga> a small rain, a shower.

niižúžu (variant: **nuužúžue**). N [reduplicated form of *níižu*] **light rain, sprinkle** (FH/06/27/01/pc).

nílǫze. ADJ **scrambled.** *hpáata nilǫ́ze bráache hta mįkšé* I'm going to eat scrambled eggs (FH:4/24/96/tape:prod).

níni. V, ADJ [uninfl.] *(intr.)* **(be) cold (used for inanimates only), cool to the touch, cool, as weather** (RB). *nínie* it's cold (BE2.21; 01/19/95/FH/pc:uk, unconfirmed). *htóožu níni wį* a cold meat pie (FH). *htóožu akxa níni akxai* the meat pie is cold (FH/07/21/95:prod; 04/13/95/LS/pc:ok). *níi níni* cold water (HH;t15a-p1). *níni mą́ąɣe ðéche, níni ahí akxa* this weather is cold, it's cold now (lit., 'it's cold, this weather, cold has arrived here') (PM071494). *mą́ąɣe níni ahí akxa* it's cold here (lit., 'cold weather has arrived here') (PM). • N **cool weather.**

••• Cf. *níwahce.*

níǫhta. V [conjug. unknown] *(intr.)* **be frustrated (?), become frustrated (?).** [This form was recorded on an early tape (speaker: Henry Pratt, whose Indian name was Nǫ́ǫhpewaðe or Nonpewalla) but is unfamiliar to three Mod. Os. speakers. Probably it is influenced by Omaha.]

•• LFD 111 (unconfirmed): *ni óhta ðį* <ni u´-ṭa thi^{n}> shall become exhausted (from a ritual).

••• *QU oníǫkdázi* breathe (RR).

níǫhta záani (variant: **níaǫhta záani**?). N **world, universe, all the universe, all the world** (RBn1-MOJ/p13, unconfirmed) [Rejected by some (03/24/95/PM/pc:no), but accepted by others as a borrowing from Omaha, according to HH (01/04/95/FH/pc:ok).]

•• RB: <ni-ao^{n}-tah záh-ni> (BE2.1610).

•• LFD 109: *niǫ́* <ni-o^{n}´> breath. *niǫ́ akxa* <ni-o^{n}´ a-ka> he breathes.

níǫhta žį́ka. N **island** (WHM981022, unconfirmed).

níǫpapa (variants: **níǫpapai, nįǫ́papai**). N **lightning** (RB; 02/15/95 /FH; HH/pc).

níwahce [*wa-* VAL + *níhce*]. V, ADJ [uninfl.] *(intr.)* **(be) cold (an impersonal weather expression, not used for people).** *wáli níwahci akxái* it's very cold weather (01/19/95/FH/pc:ok).

•• LFD 111: *níwahce* <ni´-wa-tse> it is cold. *níwahce ikiha* <ni´-wa-tse i-gi-ha> cold, rigors of the winter weather, severity of the weather.

níwahcekši htáha (variant: **níwahcikši ehtáha**). ADV, N [*níwahce* + *kši* + *htáha/éhtaha*] **north (lit., 'in the direction of the cold', 'toward the cold')** (BE2.94; 03/01/95/FH/pc:okc).

nį (variant of **ði** IMPERATIVE MARKER).

nį́ (variants: **nį́e, níe, ní**). V [2nd person form of *ðį́*] *(intr.)* **you are/were, you are/were a certain way or a certain thing, you live(d) or exist(ed) as, you are/were characterized by a quality.** *wažáže nį́pe* you [who are] Osages. *wahkǫ́taki nį́ áapie* [expected Mod. Os. ending: *áape*] they said you were a doctor (BE2.33). *ðóðo nį́* you're greasy. *šcéce nį́* you're tall. *čáahpa nį́e* you're short (FH). *wascúuce nį́e* you're late! (you have arrived late!) (FH:08/22/96). *ðíe nárąkc kʔą́saaki níe* you're a fast runner (FH/pc:prod orig). *waðíðihta ði nį́e* it's your work (lit., 'you are characterized by your work') (RBn23-16). *wawéeðe hǫ́ǫžį nį* you have bad eyesight. *wascúuce nį́e* you're late! (you've arrived late; you're always late) (FH:08/22/96). *hą́ąpa záani wapúštaha nį́e?* were you ironing iron all day? (FH:prod). *iiscéwai níe* you're being mischievous, you're being awful (FH/06/28/01/pc). *wahkǫ́taki nį́ áapie* they said you were a doctor (BE2.33).

nį́ ké hta huðe. N **north wind** (RB, unconfirmed, RB2-94; 03/01/95/FH/pc:uk; 04/17/95/LS/pc:uk). [Probably *nii įkšé ée hta húðe* 'water (sitting or round), from there it comes'.]

•• RB: <ní^{n}-kéh-táh-hu-theh>

•• LFD 109: *nikšéci* <ni´-ke-dsi> [expected Mod. Os. form: *níi įkše ci*] at the river or the water.

nį́cekʔa. N **hearts (suit in a deck of cards)** (RBn10-21/JW, unconfirmed).

nį́e (variant of **nį́** 'you are').

nį́į (variant of **ðaanį́į**).

nį́į (variant of **níi**).

nįkšé (variant: **nįkší**). CONT **continuative aspect postverbal marker (indicating ongoing action or state in present, past, or future time) for 2nd sg. sitting subject.** [*nįkšé* is sometimes used for 2nd sg. subjects that are not sitting; hence it can be regarded as the default 2nd sg. continuative marker.] *wažáže nįkšé* you're Osage [to one sitting]. *háakǫ nį́kše?* how are you? (02/09/95/FH/pc:ok). *šée nįkšé óhkie ðį* you're just sitting there, speak to me (RBn10-6:JW). *hpa lį́stowe nįkšé* your nose is running (RBn12-08). *ðúuhpeece wį ašcį́ nįkšé?* do you [sitting] have a match? *kasį́e ówǫ hta nįkšé?* are you [sitting] going to be busy tomorrow? (01/09/95/FH/pc:prod). *táatą ðáalį waðakšíe hta ðíe nįkši áape* they said you're the one that's going to make everything good for us (RBn22-02). *íe ohkípše nįkší áape* they said you keep your word. • **you are characterized by [the preceding expression, which may be a noun phrase].** *žéka xǫ́ nįkšé* your legs are broken (lit., 'you are characterized by broken legs') (FH). *haakǫ́ nįkšé*? what's wrong with you? (HH).

nį́ǫpapai (variant of **níǫpapa**).
nǫ (variant of **ną** 'always').
nǫ ahí (variant of **nǫ́ǫ ahí**).
nǫ́e (variant of **nǫ́ǫ**).
nǫhǫǫ. ADJ **wayward (said of females only, not applicable to a male).** *wak?ó nǫhǫ* woman of bad reputation, wayward woman (03/16/95/JS/pc:ok).
nǫ́hǫžį (variant: **nǫ́ǫžį**). N [*nǫ́hǫ* (Mod. Os. *nǫ́ǫ*) + *-žį* 'little'] **secret society (religious society of men who conducted ceremonies)** (RB; 04/07/95/PM/pc:ok; 03/08/95/MREI/pc:uk; BE2.117; 04/07/95/PM/pc:ok); **young men** (PM only) (04/07/95/PM/pc).
•• LFD 114: *nǫ́hǫžįka* <no^n´-ho^n-zhi^n-ga> old men (04/07/95/PM/pc:ok: *nǫ́hǫžį* or *nǫ́ǫžį*). "The title of a man who has been initiated into the mysteries of the tribal rites."
nǫhpéhi. V, ADJ, ADV [uninfl. or stat., *nǫhpé_hi*; commonly appears uninflected and followed by a continuative, e.g., *nǫhpéhi ąhé* 'I'm hungry'] *(intr.)* **(be) hungry** (12/30/94/FH/pc). *nǫhpéhi ąhé* I'm hungry [moving]. *nǫhpéhi akxai* he's hungry (FH; BE2.69). *wasái akxa nǫhpéhipe* the bear was hungry (RBn16-02). *hą́ąhkaži nǫhpéąhi* no, I'm hungry (04/13/95/FH/pc:ok; t14b-p30).
•• LFD 116: *nǫhpéhi* <no^n-pe´-hi> to be hungry. *nǫ́hpeąhi* <no^n´-pe-o^n-hi> I am hungry. *nǫ́hpeawahi pe* <no^n´-pe-a-wa-hi i> [expected Mod. Os. form: *nǫhpéwahipe*] we are hungry.
nǫhpéhic?e. V [reg.?, *nǫhpéhi_c?e?*] [*nǫhpéhi* + *c?é*] *(intr.)* **be famished, starving, dying from hunger.**
•• LFD 116: *nǫhpéhic?e* <no^n-pe´-hi-ts'e> to be famished, to suffer for want of food, to starve. *nǫhpéhi ahce* <no^n-pe´-hi a-tse> [expected Mod. Os. form: *nǫhpéhi ac?é*] I am famished. *nǫhpéhi ąhca pe* <no^n-pe´-hi o^n-tsa i> [expected Mod. Os. form: *nǫhpéhiąc?á pe*] we are famished.
nǫk?ǫ́ (variant of **nąk?ǫ́**).
nǫ́ǫ (variant: **nǫ́e**). V [reg., *_nǫ́ǫ*] *(intr.)* **be old, grow up to adulthood, mature** (03/02/95/FH/pc:okc). *anǫ́ǫ mįkšé, ánǫǫ mįkšé* I'm old. *ðanǫ́ǫ nįkšé, ðánǫǫ nįkšé* you're old (MSB). *nǫ́ǫ akxa/ónǫǫ akxai* she's old. *ą́nǫǫ ąkatxái* we [pl.] are old (FH). *ónǫǫ ąðįksé* we [two] are old. *hcéka ðanǫ́e ðe* you are young (lit., 'recently you grew up/matured/became an adult') (FH). *nǫ́ǫ kǫ́ða akxai* he is old (lit., 'he wants to be old') (03/02/95/FH/pc:okc; BE2.98). • N **adulthood, grownups, adults** (03/02/95/FH/pc:okc). *nǫ́ǫ žáže* adult name. *nǫ́ǫ apa eeškítą íixa apa* the grownups laughed, too (RBn10-2:MOJ/79). • **old folks, elders in times past, old ones.** *nǫ́ǫ apa tąhí apai* the old folks are well (FH/07/11/01/pc). • **advanced age, old age.**
•• LFD 112: *nǫ* <no^n> to grow, to age, to mature. *anǫ́ aða* <a-no^n´ a-tha> [Mod. Os. omits *aða*] I have grown to maturity. *ðanǫ́ aða* <tha-no^n´ a-tha> [Mod. Os. omits *aða*] you have grown to maturity. *ǫnǫ pi a ða pe* <o^n-no^n bi a tha i> [expected Mod. Os. form: *ąnǫ́ǫpe*] we have grown to maturity. *nǫ* <no^n> an adult (03/02/95/FH/pc:ok: *nǫ́ǫ*). LFD 117: *nǫ wálį* <non^n wa´-gthi^n> superannuate, very old age. LFD 114: *nǫ́hǫ* <no^n´-ho^n> older person (03/02/95/FH/pc: not with *h*, should be *nǫ́ǫ*).
••• Cf. *hcéka nǫ́ǫ, ónǫ.*
nǫ́ǫ ahí (variants: **nǫ ahí, nǫǫhí**). VP [sync. H-stem, *nǫ́ǫ _(a)hí*] **grow up (lit., 'arrive at adulthood').** *níhkašika ð[e]įkše nǫ́ǫ ahípe* the person [sitting] has grown to be an adult (03/02/95/FH/pc:okc). *nǫ́ǫ ąhí tą* when I get old (lit., 'when I arrive at old age') (RBn HW12).
•• LFD 112: *šémi žįka htą nǫ ahǫ* <she´-mi zhi^n-ga to^n no^n a-ho^n> [expected Mod. Os. form: *šį́mįžį txą nǫ́ǫ ahípe*] the girl has grown up. *níhkašika ðįkše nǫ hiahǫ* <ni´-ka-shi-ga thi^n-ke no^n hi-a-ho^n> [expected Mod. Os. form: *níhkaši įkšé nǫ́ǫ ahípe*] the person has grown to be an adult.
nǫ́ǫ ðiištą́. VP. **grow up, reach maturity (lit., 'finish growing up')** (03/02/95/FH/pc:ok). *George akxa nǫ́e ðiištą́* George has reached maturity (03/02/95/FH/pc).
•• LFD 117: *nǫ ðíštą* <no^n thi´-shto^n> mature, maturity.
nǫ́ǫðe. V [reg., *nǫ́ǫ_ðe*] [*nǫ́ǫ* + *ðe* CAU] *(trans.)* **raise, rear, bring up.** *nǫ́ǫðape* they raised him. *nǫ́ǫwiðe* I raised you (RBn; MREI/01/11/93?). *níi táahpa įkší žįka nǫ́ǫðe ðáalį, ecíe ska ąąžį ąkátxa* the pond is a good place to raise children, we think it's there (RBn19-04; CQ:okc). *kaazą́ži nǫ́ǫąðape* I was raised without being scolded (given favored treatment).
••• Cf. *nǫ́ǫwaapi.*
nǫǫhí (variant of **nǫ́ǫ ahí**).
nǫ́ǫhiži. ADJ [*nǫ́ǫ* + *ahí* + *aží* NEG] **immature.**
•• LFD 114: *nǫhíži* <no^n-hi´-zhi> immature, not fully grown (03/02/95/FH/pc:okc).
nǫ́ǫhpaži. V [reg., *nǫ́ǫ_hpaži*] [*nǫ́ǫhpe* + *aží* NEG] **unafraid, fearless.**
•• LFD 116: *nǫ́hpaži* <no^n´-pa-zhi> not afraid, not afraid to face danger. *nǫáhpamąži* <no^n-a´-

nǫ́ǫhpaži (*continued*) p̣a-mo^{n}-zhi> I am not afraid. *nǫðáhpaži* <no^{n}-tha´-p̣a-zhi> you are not afraid. *nąą́hpapaži pe* <no^{n}´-o^{n}-p̣a-ba-zhi i> we are not afraid.

nǫ́ǫhpe (variant: **nǫ́ǫhpi**). V [reg., *nǫ́ǫ_hpe*] [*w* is sporadically heard in 1st sg. (*nǫ́ǫwahpe*)] *(intr.)* **be afraid or scared.** *nǫ́ǫahpe* I am afraid, I'm dreading to do that (12/30/94/FH/pc:prod). *nǫ́ǫ[w]ahpe* I'm afraid (12/30/94/FH/pc:ok). *nǫ́ǫðahpe?* are you afraid? (FH). *nǫ́ǫahpe įké mįkšé* I'm not afraid. *nǫ́ǫahpa mąží hkǫ́bra* I don't want to be afraid (FH:prod). *nǫ́ǫhpa!* be careful! have a care! (an admonishment to someone who exaggerates when speaking, to tell the person to hold himself or herself back) (FH). *nǫ́ǫhpaži* [be] unafraid (12/30/94/FH/pc) (FH). *nǫ́ǫhpe įkápi* don't be afraid [pl. addressee] (12/30/94/FH/pc:prod). *nǫǫhpé įká!* be unafraid! (12/30/94/FH/pc:prod; FH/11/18/01/pc:prod; LR:6/25/01/pc). • *(trans.)* **be afraid of, be scared of, fear** (12/30/94/FH/pc:ok; LR). *nǫ́ǫwihpe* I'm afraid of you (12/30/94/FH/pc:ok). *nǫ́ǫawahpe ąhé* I'm afraid of them (12/30/94/FH/pc:ok). *John akxa íe ekǫ́įke étana nǫ́ǫahpe* John talks crazy so I'm afraid [of him]. *nǫ́ǫawahpe ðįké, ðiškítą nǫ́ǫwihpe įké* I'm not afraid of them or you either (12/30/94/FH/pc:ok). *howaðéeški nǫ́ǫwahpe ðįké* I'm not afraid of anybody at all (RBnot-nd-1/p17; 12/30/94/FH/pc:ok). *níhka ðe nǫ́ǫðahpe?* are you afraid of that man? (12/30/94/FH/pc/ok). *šǫ́ke kšé nǫ́ǫðahpe?* are you afraid of that dog [lying down]? (12/30/94/FH/pc:prod orig; LR:6/25/01/pc). *nǫ́ǫðahpe?* are you afraid of that? (e.g., indicating a dog nearby). *htáace hpíiži nǫ́ǫhpi akxai* he's afraid of storms (FH/11/18/01/pc:prod). *nǫ́ǫąwahpe* we're afraid of them. *íe hpíiži nǫ́ǫąhpape* we're afraid of his bad words (FH/11/18/01/pc:prod).

•• LFD 116: *nǫ́hpe* <no^{n}´-p̣e> to be timid, to fear, to dread, to have a horror, to be afraid. *nǫ́ahpe* <no^{n}´-a-p̣e> I am timid. *nǫ́ðahpe* <no^{n}´-tha-p̣e> you are timid. *nǫą́hpa pe* <no^{n}-o^{n}´-p̣a i> we are timid. *nǫ́hpe ðįke* <no^{n}´-p̣e thi^{n}-ge> fearless. *ną́hpe ąðįke* <no^{n}´-p̣e o^{n}-thi^{n}-ge> I am fearless. *ną́hpe ðiðįke* <no^{n}´-p̣e thi-thi^{n}-ge> you are fearless. *nǫ́hpe ewaðe* <no^{n}´-p̣e e-wa-the> hideous, makes one afraid, scary. *nǫ́hpewaðe* <No^{n}´-p̣e-wa-the> Fear-inspiring (personal name). *nǫ́hpewaðe* <no^{n}´-p̣e-wa-the> dangerous, formidable, hideous, horrible, terrible, frightful, dreadful.

••• *WI: nąąkéwe* be afraid of, fear (KM).

••• Cf. *íinǫǫhpe.*

nǫ́ǫhpewaðe (variants: **nǫ́ǫhpewae, nǫ́ǫhpewai, nǫ́ǫhpewe**). ADJ, V [reg.?, *nǫ́ǫhpewa_ðe?*] [*nǫ́ǫhpe* + *wa-* VAL + *ðe* CAU] **(be) scary, make folks fearful (lit., 'make folks be afraid').** • N **fearful thing, s.t. to be afraid of** (12/30/94/FH/pc:ok); **Fearful One (personal name)** [with variant pronunciation *nǫ́ǫhpewali,* Henry Pratt's name].

nǫ́ǫhpi (variant of **nǫ́ǫhpe**).

nǫǫpé (variant: **nǫ́pe**). N **palm of the hand** (BE2.101; 03/03/95/FH/pc:ok); **fist** (04/17/95/LS/pc:ok). ['Hand' is an archaic meaning, not found in Mod. Os. (contrary to frequent claims).]

•• LFD 112: *nǫpé* <no^{n}-be´> the hand [unconfirmed; translation perhaps should be 'fist']. *nǫpé hi wihta nǫpe hi ða pi ðą ški* <no^{n}-be´ hi wi-ṭa no^{n}-be hi tha bi tho^{n} shki> [expected Mod. Os. form: *nǫǫpé wíhta nǫǫpé ihtáapi tą* 'when my hands are their hands'] and when they make my hands their hands (04/17/95/LS/pc: fist; use as 'hand' archaic).

nǫǫpé aski (variant: **nǫǫpé askíke**). N **fist** (BE2.48). [Possibly *askíke* implies a harder fist than *aski* (FH).] *nǫǫpé askíke* a very hard fist (01/26/95/FH/pc:prod orig).

•• LFD 112: *nǫpé ðiskike* <no^{n}-be´ thi-çki-ge> hand folded, the fist.

nǫǫpióolą. N [*nǫǫpé* + *oolą́*] **ring (for wearing on the finger) (lit., 'put it on the fist').**

nǫ́ǫwaapi. N [*wa-* 'us' + *nǫ́ǫðe* + *api*] **those who raised us, our forebears, all our parents, the old ones, somebody older than us** (03/02/95/FH/pc:ok). *nǫ́ǫwaapi apa* the people that raised us (BE2.98).

nǫ́ǫžį (variant of **nǫ́hǫžį**).

nǫpe (variant of **nąpe**).

nǫ́pe (variant of **nǫǫpé**).

nǫ́pxata (variant: **nǫ́pxahta).** N **clan subdivision (of the Deer clan; meaning unknown, may refer to a deer's coloring).** [According to Walter Maten, *nó^{n}-pxah-tah* is the clan to which the Pitts and Whitehorn families belong (RB).]

••• *OM nápąta* deer (possibly from 'thundering hooves'), name of a group (sub-gens) (RL/pc). **cultural object, society**

nǫpʔį́ (variant: **nǫ́pʔį**). V [reg.?, *_nǫpʔį́?*] *(trans.)* **wear around the neck** (02/27/95/FH/pc:ok). *wapúuska nǫ́pʔį akxái* she's wearing beads around her neck (RBn2-MOJ/p30;

02/27/95/FH/pc:okc; BE2.92). *wapúuška tóe nǫ́pʔį akxai* they've got beads around their neck (RBn12-08).

•• LFD 116: *nǫ́pʔį* <no^{n}´-p̣'i^{n}> to wear around the neck. *nǫ́pʔį kšiðe* <no^{n}´-p̣'i^{n} kshi-the> to cause one to wear something around the neck, as a necklace. LFD 96: *mą́zenǫpʔį* <Mo^{n}´-çe-no^{n}-p'i^{n}> Iron-necklace (personal name).

••• Cf. *wanǫ́pʔį.*

nuužú, núužu (variants of **níížú**).

núužue hką́ące (variant of **níížue hką́ące**).

nuužúžu. v [uninfl.] *(intr.)* **sprinkle, rain lightly.** *kasį́xci hóolą bree hkǫ́bra ązi nuužúžu akxai* I wanted to go fishing this morning, but it was sprinkling (01/30/95/FH/pc:prod orig).

••• Cf. *níížúžu.*

nuužúžue (variant of **niižúžu**).

o, ó

ó- (variant: **o-**). LOC **place at which, culmination of (a certain action or state), wherein (a certain thing takes place).** *huukǫ́ða ðalípe nąą, ðe ówaachi ilǫ́ǫška* many of you have come back to this place of the *ilǫ́ǫška* dances.

oážu (variant: **wážu**). N [*ó-* + *ážu*] **rack, barbecue rack (lit., 'place for setting things upon').**

océ. v [reg., *o_cé*] *(trans.)* **look for or search for s.t. or s.o. (for one's own purposes, not because it or he/she was previously lost)** (2/22/95/FH). [Contrast *okíce* 'find again that which was lost'.] *oáce, owáce* I look for. *oðáce* you look for. *ąkóce* we look for. *otá* look for it! *haaská océ pšíe* I went to look for a shirt (02/22/95/FH/pc). *Bill owáce pšíe* I went to look for Bill (02/22/95/FH/pc). *owíce ąhé* I've been looking for you (02/22/95/FH/pc:ok; BE2.81). *táatą oðáce ðaįšé?* what are you looking for? (02/22/95/FH/pc:okc, with *ðaįše*; 02/22/95/FH/pc:prod). *otá* look for it (02/22/95/FH/pc:ok). • **hunt for, go hunting for (small game)** (108-b/FH/9-13-94) *sį́ka ąkóce ąkái hce* let's go squirrel hunting [sg. addressee] (02/22/95/FH/pc:ok). *žǫ́hpazi mǫ́nǫį océ pšíe* I went to look for quail and prairie chickens (BE2.70; 02/22/95/FH/pc:ok).

•• LFD 167: *océ* <u-dse´> to seek, to hunt for something missing. *owáce* <u-wa´-dse> I seek. *oðáce* <u-tha´-dse> you seek. *ąkóca pe* <o^{n}-gu´-dsa i> we seek. LFD 180 (unconfirmed): *ohcé* <u-ṭse´> [expected Mod. Os. form: *océ*] to hunt, to search for. *owahcé* <u-wa-ṭse´> [expected Mod. Os. form: *owáce*] I hunt. *oðahcé* <u-tha-ṭse´> [expected Mod. Os. form: *oðáce*] you hunt. *ąkóhca pe* <o^{n}-gu´-ṭsa i> [expected Mod. Os. form: *ąkóca pe*] we hunt.

••• *KS ojé* look for (RR).

••• Cf. *óce, océštą, okíce, sįkóce.*

óce. v [uninfl. or reg., *ó_ce*] [*wa-* VAL + *océ*] *(intr.)* **search, search for stuff, look for things.** *óce ðaįšé?* are you looking for things?

••• Cf. *ócеštą.*

océðe. v [reg.?, *océ_ðe?*] (*intr.* [perhaps *trans.?*]) **build a fireplace or fire.** *súhka ooðáhą škǫ́štapi tą, hpéece océðapi, oohǫ́pi* if you want to cook a chicken, build a fire and cook it (FH/09/21/01/pc). • N **fireplace or fire for cooking or warming oneself, place to build a fire, stove.**

•• LFD 167: *océðe* <u-dse´-the> hearth, fireplace, a place hollowed out in the ground in which to place or kindle a fire.

••• *KS jéeye* kindle a fire, set fire to (*je_ye*, reg. conjugation) (RR).

••• Cf. *áceðe.*

océhci. N [presumably *océðe* + *hcí*] **fireplace in a home or in a place used for religious purposes, including the ceremonial fireplace used in the peyote times** (BE2.47; FH/09/21/01/pc; 02/27/95/FH/pc:okc; FH:4/18/96/tape,ma).

océštą. v [reg., *o_céštą*] [*océ* + *štą*] **snoop or look for constantly (lit., 'searches constantly').**

ócеštą. ADJ, v [reg., *ó_ceštą*] [*óce* + *štą*] **(be) snoopy.** *ošpéžį nąlǫ́ǫha apái ðée apa ahú apai óceštąpe* they're hiding their things because the people coming are snoops (or 'are always snooping'). • N **snoop, s.o. who looks for things constantly, s.o. who likes to get into another's things.**

océže. N [*ó-* LOC + *céže*] **urinal** (04/26/95/FH/pc).

•• LFD 167: *océže* <u-dse´-zhe> urinal.

••• Cf. *ožéhci.*

océžehci (variant of **ožéhci**).

ochí (variants: **oochí, ochíe**). ADJ, V [stat., *o_chí*] **(be) plentiful, many, abound, exist in large quantity, (be) a lot of, (be) full of (e.g., worms).** *huuwáli ǫ́wǫ ǫ́ąchi* I've got a lot to do (lit., 'many chores abound for me') (RBn12-07; FH/11/19/01/pc: okc). *wáali ówǫ oðíchi* you're really busy (04/25/95/PM/pc:prod). *ówǫ oðíchi ðaašé íhpahǫ* I know you have had a lot to do (RBn10-4:MOJ/79). *mǫ́žǫ ðékše táatą ðáalį ochíe tą, iiðáðe brée ðáalį* if there are such beautiful things [abounding] in the world, I ought to go see them. *wéc?a ochíe* there are lots of snakes (RBn3-09). *watástoe ochí* there are a lot of pecans (RBn10-2; LS:ok). *žįkážį oochí* a lot of kids (LS). *ónǫbre oochí* a lot of food (04/17/95/LS/pc:ok). *haxį́ oochí* a lot of blankets (LS). *waðílą ochíe* smart (lit., 'mind plentiful') (04/17/95/LS/pc:ok; MJ/11/19/83). *waðílą ochí akxai* he has a lot on his mind (EREsr). *walúška ochí* wormy, full of worms. • **(be) excessive or the most extreme, worst or best (above all others in a certain aspect).** *íxopeštą ochí akxa* he's standing on top of all the liars; he's the worst of the liars (lit., 'he is extreme in lying constantly') (RBn12-10/MJ; CQc).

•• LFD 180: *ohcí* <u-ṭsi´> [expected Mod. Os. form: *ochí*] plenty, plentiful. LFD 185: *wasápe ochi* <Wa-ça´-be u-tsi> where bears are plentiful, Bear Creek.

••• Cf. *óochiže*.

ochíchacha. V, ADV [conjug. unknown] *(intr.)* **(be) excessive.** *íe ðée ochíchachae káaɣe kšiðé įká* don't let him go on and on [talking] (MSB:t9).

ochíe (variant of **ochí**).

ochį́. V [reg., *o_chį́*] *(trans.)* **whip strongly, beat up, spank or "get" s.o, drub, thrash.** *owíchį hta mįkšé, owíchį mįkšé* I'm going to whip you (04/28/95/LS/pc:prod). *oáchį hta ąhé* I'm going to whip him (04/28/95/LS/pc:ok; RBn10-7:JW). *tówa įkše owáchį hta mįkšé* I'm going to whip that one [sitting there, male or female] (04/28/95/LS/pc:ok). *hóni ąwą́chįpe, hóni ową́chįpe* they almost whipped me (04/28/95/LS/pc:okc; BE2.156). *mąxpúmęį apa oðíchįpe aapai* lightning and thunder [lit., 'clouds moving'] are getting you (line from a children's song) (FH). • **hit or strike (e.g., a drum or a person).** *céɣenii ochį́ brée* I'm going [to attend] to hit drum (02/09/95/FH/pc:ok). *céɣenii ochį́ ðáalį škáaɣe* you hit drum good (02/09/95/FH/pc:ok). *céɣenii ochį́ ðáalį įkšiape* he hit drum good for him (BE2.67). *įįštáxi íe ékie ðįká ði, oðíchį hta apai, háakǫ ékiše che íšpahǫži* don't speak English, they're going to whip you, you don't know what you are saying (said by the speaker's mother to the speaker's father, who didn't speak English well) (FH/09/24/01/prod). *žą́ąxe abrįe áwachį* I hit him with a stick (lit., 'I had a stick, I hit him') (04/28/95/LS/pc:ok).

•• LFD 180: *óchį* <u´-tsi^{n}> to strike. *owáchį* <u-wa´-tsi^{n}> I struck him. *oðáchį* <u-tha´-tsi^{n}> you struck him. *ąkóchį pe* <o^{n}-gu´-tsi^{n} i> we struck him, to maul, to beat, to pound; to give a drubbing, to thrash.

óchį. V [reg., *ó_chį*] [*wa-* VAL + *ochį́*] *(intr.)* **hit or beat things (such as a drum).** *óchį ðáalį káaɣį aha wíkie* whenever he hits [drum] well, there's a prayer (RBn10-18; gloss by CQ).

••• Cf. *ochį́*.

oc?į́ze. V, ADJ [stat.?, *o_c?į́ze?*] **(be) stopped up, stuffed up, congested.** *hpooc?į́ze akxai* he has a stopped up nose [i.e., *hpa oc?į́ze akxai*].

ódla (rare variant of **ólą**).

oðáake. V [sync., *o_ðáake*] *(trans.)* **tell (e.g., news, stories), relate, narrate, recite, state, proclaim, inform, say so** (03/16/95/FH/pc:ok). *táatą záani owíbraake* I've told you everything (03/16/95/FH/pc). *owíbraake ná* I told you so (lit., 'I used to tell you it') (03/16/95/FH/pc:ok). *híko wį owíbraake šką́šta* you want me to tell a story (03/16/95/FH/pc). *pée oðíðaake?* who told you that? (FH:prod). *táatą oðíðaake?* what did he tell you? (03/16/95/FH/pc). *ową́ðaakape* he told me [it] (03/16/95/FH/pc). *ąwą́ðaakape* he told me (03/16/95/FH/pc:ok). *ǫwą́ðaake nąpé* they used to tell me (03/16/95/FH/pc:ok). *oðáake įká* don't tell it (03/16/95/FH/pc:okc). *ąwą́ąðaki apai* they're telling me something (MSB Mar 83). *ąwą́ðaaka* tell it to me (RBnot-nd-1/p9; 03/16/95/FH/pc:ok). *oą́štaake ðálį* you ought to tell me. *táatą éekǫke ąwą́štaakaaži ðálį* you shouldn't tell me things like that. *íxope ąwą́štaake* you told me a lie (MSB-03-83). • *(intr.)* **bid.** *pée oðáake hta įkšé?* whose bid is it? (in a card game; lit., 'whose bid will it be?') (RBn12-11).

•• LFD 175–76: *oðáke* <u-tha´-ge> to make a statement, to tell a tale or a story. *obráke* <u-btha´-ge> I made a statement. *oštáke* <u-shta´-ge> you made a statement. *ąkóðaka pe* <o^{n}-gu´-tha-ga i> we made a statement (02/27/95/FH/pc:ok). LFD 123: *oðáke* <o-tha´-

ge> to relate. *obráke* <o-btha´-ge> I relate. *óštake* <o´-shta-ge> you relate, to tell, recite, narrate.
••• Cf. *óðaake, ohkílaake.*

oðáake kʔǫ. N **pitch (a card game: lit., 'telling it game'; this phrase may also refer to other card games)** (FH; BE2.103; 03/08/95/FH/pc:ok).

óðaake. V [sync., *ó_ðaake*] [*wa-* VAL + *oðáake*] *(intr.)* **tell things, inform.** *owíbraake* I'll tell you (03/16/95/FH/pc:ok). *ówabraake* I tell them (things, stuff). *ą́waðaakape* they told me (RBn19-02). *ówaðaakapi* tell us (03/16/95/FH/pc:okc). • N **story, tale, legend, narrative, telling of s.t., reporting of news.**

óðaake waléze. N **newspaper, letter, magazine (lit., 'document with writing that tells things')** (02/27/95/FH/pc:ok; BE2.93).
•• RB: <ó-thah-keh wáh-leh-zeh>.
•• LFD 123: *óðake waleze* <o´ tha-ge wa-gthe-çe> newspaper.

oðáašce. [sync., *o_ðáašce*] [*ðaa-* INSTR + *ošcé*] *(trans.)* **leave by mouth (e.g., remaining food).**
•• JOD (Raccoons and Crawfish p24 ln7): *wížįðé, wį oðáašta ðį hau* <wíci^{n}¢é, wi^{n} u^{n}¢ácta-¢i^{n} haú> Elder Brother, leave one.

óðaašce. N **lunch, food taken home from a feast** (02/24/95/FH/pc:okc; BE2.83) . • V [sync., *ó_ðaašce*] [*wa-* VAL + *oðáašce*] *(intr.)* **leave some as a remainder by mouth.**
•• RB: <ó-thah^{n}-shtseh>.
•• JOD (Raccoons and Crawfish p24 ln9): *ówaðaaštá ðį haú, íihkitaðe htape* <úwa¢actá-¢i^{n} haú, íki-xtá¢ĕ tápe> leave some [of them, the crawfish], they will breed among themselves.

oðáaze. N [*ó-* LOC + *ðaazó*] **whoop, ululation (applies only to the noise that women make)** (RBn22-08).

oðáazo. N [*ó-* + *ðaazó*] **female singers** (FH: HH/t10-B-p1).

oðáha (variant: **oláha**). V [sync., *o_ðáha*] *(trans.)* **follow (e.g., a path, a person, God's word, a car, or a horse)** (01/26/95/FH/pc; PM). *ąwą́šipe oláha brée* he hired me so I'm going [to follow him?] (03/24/95/PM/pc). *ékǫ anąkʔǫe ékǫ obráhai* I heard it like that, I'm going to follow it like that [woman speaking] (RBn10-21/JW&FW/77). *hkáwa obráha* I followed the horse (FH:prod; BE2.49). *ékǫ anąkʔǫ įtó ékǫ obráha įtó* I heard it like that, I'm going to follow it like that [man speaking] [*įtó* is unfamiliar and not used in Mod. Os. (FH)] (RBn10-21/JW&FW/77). *óžąke obráhą įtó* I'll follow that road [*įtó* is unfamiliar and not used in Mod. Os. (FH)] (RBn10-21/JW&FW/77). *ožą́ke obrą́ha ąhé* I'm following the road (RBn22-05). *kį́įkįįežį ówaðáha apa, kóe watǫ́pe che* he followed the butterflies so that he could watch them (RBn15-02; FH:ok). *íe ðíhta ąkóðaha ąkǫða ąkái* we want to follow your word (01/26/95/FH/pc:okc). *ąkóðiðaha ihtóį ðéha įkšé* we will follow you in the days to come (JS prayer). • *(intr.)* **be behind, be attached to the back, be hanging (on the back of or behind s.t. else).** *álįįhceðe oðáha oðíhta owíbraha* hang the wheelchair on and I'll follow your car (lit., 'wheelchair attached, I'll follow the car') (RBn; MREI/01/11/93). *oðíhtąhci oðáha* a trailer house (lit., 'house following car') (04/13/95/FH/pc:okc).
•• LFD 122: *oðáha* <o-tha´-ha> to follow. *óbraha* <o´-btha-ha> I follow. *ostáha* <o-sda´-ha> you follow. *ąkóðaha* <o^{n}-gu´-tha-ha> we follow.

oðáhaaðee. V [reg.+sync., *o_ðáha_(a)ðee* (object inflection and reg. subject inflection in first slot, sync. subject inflection in second slot)] [*oðáha* + *aðée*] *(trans.)* **go with, go following.** *ówaðahašcée?* are you going with them? (RBn11-02/JW&FW&HHsk/c.1976).

oðáške (variant: **oðą́ške**). V [sync., *o_ðáške*] *(trans.)* **tie (as a shoe).** *hǫǫpé obráške škǫ́šta?* do you want me to tie your shoe? (FH/t116b). *hǫǫpé oðáške škǫ́šta?* do you want me to tie your shoe? *hǫǫpé ǫðáške škǫ́šta? [hǫǫpé o-ą-ðáške škǫ́šta]* do you want to tie my shoe? (lit., 'do you want to tie for me the shoe?') (03/22/95/FH/pc).
••• Cf. *okáške.*

óðaži (variant of **óðąži**).

óðąąceši (variant: **óðąąše**). V [uninfl./reg., *óðąące_ši*] *(trans.)* **worry about, feel concern over, be concerned about** (05/01/95/LS/pc:ok; FH:4/24/96/prod). *óðąąceši mįkšé* I'm worried (BE2.161, unconfirmed). *mą́zeska oðą́ąceši mįkšé* I'm worried about money (RBn HW). *Mary akxa óðąąceši* Mary is worried about something. *oðíhtą óðąąceši akxai* he's worried about his car. *žékažį apa óðąącewaší apai* Little-legs is worried about us (RBn23-17). *óðąąceąiši ąkai* we're anxious [note unexpected *i* before *ši* in *óðąąceąiši*] (LS:prod). • **focus on, pay attention to, look into, attend to, think about** (FH:5/01/96/tape; 03/24/95/PM/pc:okc). *óðąącaži mįkšé ha* I haven't thought about it [expected Mod. Os. form: *óðąąceši(a)ži mį́kše* (*ha* is not usually used in Mod. Os.)] (03/24/95/PM/pc:prod). *žįkážį óðąąceši* pay attention to the children (05/01/95/LS/pc;

óðąąceši (*continued*) 01/04/95/FH/pc/ok). *žįkážį óðąącewaší* pay attention to the children (FH/09/25/01/prod; BE2.2; 03/24/95/PM/pc:ok). *óðąąceši įká, olą́ą akxa* don't pay any attention to him, he's mad (RBn11-01/JW&FW&HHask).

•• JOD (Raccoons and Crawfish p23 ln5): *ónąhceži* <u^{n}´nantseçi´> hearts . . . not easy.

•• LFD178: *óðąceši* <u´-tho^{n}-dse-shi> anxiety, to be anxious, deeply concerned, solicitous. *óðące ąši* <u´-tho^{n}-dse o^{n}-shi> I am anxious. *óðące ði ši* <u´-tho^{n}-dse thi shi> you are anxious. *óðące ąši pe* <u´-tho^{n}-dse o^{n}-shi bi a> he was solicitous for me.

óðąąceši ðįké (variant: **óðąąceši įké**). VP [conjug. unknown (presumably stat., *óðąąceši _ðįké*)] *(trans.)* **disuse, be unconcerned with, disregard, not pay attention to (lit., 'not worried about')** (05/01/95/LS/pc:ok: disregard). *óðąąceši įká* don't pay any attention to him (RBn11-01/JW&FW&HHsk/c.1976). • *(intr.)* **be unobserved, as a custom** (FH/09/25/01/ok).

•• LFD 178: *óðąceši ðįke* <u´-tho^{n}-dse-shi thi^{n}-ge> disuse, out of use.

óðąąše (variant of **óðąąceši**).

oðą́ške (variant of **oðáške**).

óðąži (variants: **ǫ́ðąži, ólaži, óoðąąži, óðaži**). ADV **in spite of everything, inevitably, contrarily, anyhow, anyway, even so, regardless, notwithstanding everything, however, nevertheless, at any rate** (RBn1-MOJ/p28b; 02/01/95/FH/pc:okc; 05/01/95/LS/pc:ok). *óðaži ékǫ kíe* it's that way anyway (FH). *óðąži niižú akxa* in spite of everything it's raining (05/01/95/LS/pc). *óðąži waachí apai* in spite of it, they're dancing (05/01/95/LS/pc). *óðąži niižú che waachí apai* in spite of the fact it's raining, they're dancing (05/01/95/LS/pc). *ókaayeįki akxa óðąži waachípe* Useless couldn't help but dance (lit., 'Useless danced anyway') (RBn10-2:MOJ/79). • V *(intr.)* [uninfl.] **get it, do it or make it despite s.t., have one's way.** *iðážoši ąži óðąži akxai* I said no, but he's going to have his way (FH/11/19/01/pc:prod).

•• JOD (Wasápežįka letter, lines 2–3): *ǫ́ðaži, wihcížoe, waðíhǫįki* <ŭ^{n}´¢açi, witsíçŭ^{n}é, wa¢íhŭ^{n}'-iñki au.> at any rate, niece, you are an orphan.

•• LFD 178: *óðąži* <u´-tho^{n}-zhi> inevitable. *óðąži ekǫ* <u´-tho^{n}-zhi e-go^{n}> infallible, unerring, unfailing.

oðíbrą. V [sync., *o_ðíbrą*] [*ó-* LOC + *ðíbrą*] *(trans.)* **smoke, cause to smell, as in making cedar smoke for a cleansing or a blessing (lit., 'wherein one causes there to emanate an odor').**

••• Cf. *xǫǫcóðibrą.*

oðíhtą (variants: **oðíhta, owíhta**). N **car, wagon** (BE2.150; 03/16/95/JS/pc:ok). [Describes a rolling motion (RB).] *oðíhtą olį́į hta mįkšé* I'm going in a car (01/09/95/FH/pc:ok). *oðíhtą olį́į hta apái* they're going in a car (01/09/95/FH/pc:ok). *oðíhtą šką́ káaya* start the car (01/09/95/FH/pc:ok). *oðíhta akxa šką́ži akxái* the car won't start (01/09/95/FH/pc:ok; BE2.17). *owíhta žúuce žį wíht[a] olį́į hu* come ride in my little red wagon.

•• LFD 177: *oðíhtąða* <u-thi´-ţo^{n}-tha> anything propelled by rolling, a wagon, buggy, a carriage.

••• *QU odíhtąhtąda* to roll something over and over (RR).

••• Cf. *oðíhtąhci.*

oðíhtą. N **work, occupation, position** (LF).

•• LFD 177: *oðihtą* <u´-thi-ţo^{n}> an occupation. *óðihtą ðalį xci owanąži* <u´-thi-ţo^{n} tha-gthi^{n} xtsi u-wa-no^{n}-zhi> I have a good position. *óhihtą thi wihta theti bre* <u´-hi-ţo^{n} ti wi-ţa te-di bthe> [expected Mod. Os. form: *oðíhtąhci wíhta che ci brée*] I went to my office. *óðihtą thi ðihta theti šni a(?)* <u´-thi-ţo^{n} ti thi-ţa te-di shni a(?)> [*šni* was never an Osage word, likely Omaha, should be *šcée*] are you going to your office?

••• Cf. *waðíhtą.*

oðíhtą hcí oðáha. N **trailer (lit., 'rolling house following')** (04/13/95/FH/pc:okc).

•• LFD 177: *oðíhtąða hcioðaha* <u-thi´-ţo^{n}-tha ţsi-u-tha-ha> little-wagon-with-a-house-attached-to it: a buggy.

oðíhtą hcižé. N **car door.**

oðíhtą kˀą́saaki. N **train (lit., 'pulls fast'), locomotive** (03/23/95/FH/pc:ok; BE2.144; RB).

oðíhtą olį́į. ADVP **by car.** *oðihtą olį́į achíe* I came by car.

oðíhtąhci. N [*oðíhtą + hcí*] **garage (lit., 'car house')** (01/31/95/FH/pc:ok; BE2.53).

•• RB: <o-thí-tah´-tsi>.

•• LFD 177 (unconfirmed): *oðíhtąða onąžį* <u-thi´-ţo^{n}-tha u-no^{n}-zhi^{n}> a garage (01/31/95/FH/pc:uk with *onąžį*).

oðíhtąhci hcíže. N **garage door.** *oðíhtą hci hcíže áðiitą* close the garage door (RBn1-MOJ/p45; FH/08/15/95/pc:okc).

oðíiną (variant: **oðíina**). V [sync.?, *o_ðíiną?*] *(trans.)* **fasten, button (e.g., an old-fashioned shoe with buttons or a sweater with buttons),**

zip, tie up, rope (e.g., a calf). *hcižé akxa oðíina akxái* the door is locked (fastened) (02/16/95/FH/pc:okc; BE2.80; RBn2-MOJ/p21). *oðíkinąą̨ži oðíina* zip up your fly (fasten your pants) (RBn2-MOJ/p21; 03/03/95/FH/pc:ok). *šǫ́ke oðíiną* go tie the dog up (03/22/95/FH/pc:ok). *hcéska oðíina akxai* he's roping a cow (RBn23-13). *hceeská oðíiną aðáape* they went to rope calves (RBn11-02; 3/22/95/FH/pc:ok).

oðíitą. v [sync., *o_ðíitą*] *(trans.)* **stop, halt (e.g., the horse pulling a buggy, the motion of a car), curb motion, check a horse's forward movement** (03/14/95/MREI/pc; BE2.128; RBn1-MOJ/p40; HH/14-a/172ff&pc: *ooðíitą*).

•• RB: <o-thí-dah^{n}>.

•• LFD 176: *oðítą* <u-thi´-do^{n}> check. *hkawa ðį obritą* <ķa-wa thi^{n} o-bthi-do^{n}> I checked the horse.

oðíkinąą̨žį (variant: **oðíkinąą̨ži**) (03/03/95/FH/pc:ok both *oðó-* and *oðí-*). n **pants, trousers, underwear** (03/03/95/FH/pc:ok; RBn2-MOJ/p2; MOJt150; FH/t116b). *oðíkinąą̨ži oðíina* zip up your fly (fasten your pants) (RBn2-MOJ/p21; 03/03/95/FH/pc:ok). *oðíkinąą̨žį okíkxą* put your underwear/trousers/pants on (03/22/95/PM/pc).

••• Cf. *oðókinąą̨žį.*

oðíkˀe. v [conjug. unknown] *(trans.)* **drop s.t. into (e.g., eyedrops into eyes)** (04/13/95/FH/pc:ok). *įįštá oðíkˀe* put some into your eyes.

•• LFD 77: *įštá oðikˀe* <i^{n}-shta´ u-thi-ķ'e> to drop anything into the eye, as an eyewash.

oðínii. n **umbrella** (04/06/95/FH/pc:ok). *oðínii žįka* a parasol (FH/pc).

•• LFD 171 (unconfirmed): *oíhnižįka* <u-i´-hni-zhi^{n}-ga> a parasol. *oíhni žįka wį abrį* <u-i´-hni zhi^{n}-ga wi^{n} a-bthi^{n}> I have a parasol. [The sequence of vowels *oi* <u-i>, <o-i> in LF's data often corresponds to *oði* in Mod. Os.]

óðisąha. v [conjug. unknown] *(intr.)* **flutter**. *ðą́ące óðisąha* a fright, a scare (lit., 'heart flutters') (RBn23-14).

•• LFD 113: *nǫ́ce oðisąha* <no^{n}´-dse u-thi-ço^{n}-ha> a shock to the heart, a scare, a fright: heart palpitates quickly. LFD 203: *waðǫ́ce oðisąha* <wa-tho^{n}´-dse u-thi-ço^{n}-ha> to excite, excitement. His heart is fluttering with excitement.

oðíši (variant: **oðíšį**). v [sync., *o_ðíši*] *(trans.)* **wrap** (01/14/95/FH/pc:prod). *obríši* I wrap it. *ošciši* you wrap it. *oðíši* she wraps it. *ąkóðiši* we wrap it. • n **cover (for a tipi, sweat house, pillow, etc.).** *ípihį oðíši* pillow cover, pillowcase (RBn1-54; BE2.26;01/13/95/FH/pc:ok).

•• LFD 177: *oðíšį* <u-thi´-shi^{n}> to wrap anything up. *obríšį* <u-bthi´-shi^{n}> I wrap it up. *ąkóðišį pe* <o^{n}-gu´-thi-shi^{n} i> we wrap it up. *oðíšįle* <u-thi´-shi^{n}-gthe> to surround an enemy as in an attack.

••• Cf. *wacúexǫ oðiši.*

oðízą (variants: **óðiząha, óðižąhe**) v [sync., *o_ðízą*] *(trans.)* **be among others in, be a member of (e.g., a club), belong to, be a part of, be among** (HRE/01/17/02/pc:ok). *hlaaskážį obrízą mįkšé* I'm a member of the *hlaaskážį* club (HRE/01/17/02/pc). *óðizą nįkšé* you're part of it; you belong; you're a member (LS05/08/01; BE2.3; 01/04/95/FH/pc:ok). *oðízą apai* they are among them (01/14/95/FH/pc). *ecí ąkóðizą́hape* we belong there (MSB 03-83).

•• RB: <ó-thi-záh^{n}-hah>.

oðį́į (variant of **oðį́įke**).

oðį́įðe (variant of **oðį́įmą**).

oðį́įke (variant: **oðį́į**). v [sync., *o_ðį́įke* (variant *oðįį* is sometimes uninfl.)] *(trans.)* **take hold of s.o.'s body part, take or have hold of, grasp, hug, embrace, catch (a person or an animal).** *owíbrįį* I hugged you. *oðíðįįke* catching you, to have a hold of you (01/09/95/FH/pc:prod). *oðíðįį* I caught you, I have hold of you (9/17/94/FH/pc; 9/17/94/PM/pc). *tóoce oscį́įke* you took him by the throat (03/22/95/FH/pc:ok). *wamąąðǫ́štą ošcį́įke* you caught the thief. • **hold, hold on to, embrace as tradition.** *mą́ša owíbrįįke* I voted (lit., 'I grasped the feather'). *mą́ša oščįįke?* did you vote? (8/8/94,FH, pc). *oðį́įke apai* they held on to it. *ąkǫðįįke* we're holding on to something. *saakí oðį́įka* hold on tight; hold it tight (FH/pc; BE2.67). *oðį́įkapi!* hold on to it! [pl.].

••• Cf. *mą́šą oðį́įke, mą́ze oðóbrįįke.*

oðį́įmą (variant: **oðį́įðe**). v [sync., *o_ðį́įmą*] *(trans.)* **lock (e.g., a house door, a trunk, a car door).** *saakí oðį́įmą* lock it tight; fasten it (03/22/95/FH/pc:ok). *oðíhtą oðį́įmą!* lock the car! (FH/t116b). *oðíhtą oðį́įma akxai* the car door is locked (FH). *saakí aščį́įmą* [*a-* prefix is unexpected; expected Mod. Os. form: *oscį́įmą* or *oščį́įma*] you fastened it (FH:ok).

•• LFD 29: *sakí oðimą* <ça-gi´ u-thi-mo^{n}> to make fast, to secure, to fasten. *sakí obrimą* <ça-gi´ u-bthi-mo^{n}> I made secure. *saki oscimą* <ça-gi u-stsi-mo^{n}> you fastened it. *sakí ąkoðimą pe* <ça-gi´ o^{n}-gu-thi-mo^{n} i> we fastened it.

oðóðe. v [reg., *oðó_ðe*] *(trans.)* **be in charge of, supervise, boss (e.g., an event), manage.** *oðo[w]aðe* I am in charge of it. *oðóðaðe* you are in charge of it. *ónǫbre oðóaðe hta mįkše* I'm going to be bossing [taking care of] the food. *ónǫbre che oðó[w]a[ð]i kǫ́ða* they want me to oversee this dinner (FH:prod). *htóožu wéðuwį kǫ́ða apai ąžį oðóða[ð]i hce ée apai* they want to sell meat pies, but they want you to oversee it (FH:prod). *oðówaapi akxai* he's bossing us around [*oðówaapi* from *oðo-wa-ðe-api*] (FH:prod).

••• Cf. *oðówaðe.*

oðóhake. ADJ **more, last, final.** *htáalįko oðóhake hkǫ́bra* I want more meat gravy (04/11/95/LS/pc:okc; t14-b-p2).

•• LFD 179: *oðóhake* <u-thu´-ha-ge> the last time. *oðóhake che* <u-thu´-ha-ge tse> final, the final act, the last. *hcížo oðohake* <Ṭsi´-zhu u-thu-ha-ge> the last in the line of the Ṭsi-zhu gens.

••• Cf. *hą́ąpa oðóhake.*

oðóhake íðilą. VP [sync., *oðóhake í_ðilą*] *(trans.)* **reconsider, think about again, rethink** (LF).

•• LFD 123 (unconfirmed): *oðóhake ílilą* <o-tho´-ha-ge i-gthi-gtho^{n}> [expected Mod. Os. form: *oðóhake íðilą*] to reconsider. *oðóhake iðálilą* <o-tho´-ha-ge i-tha´-gthi-gtho^{n}> I reconsidered. *oðóhake íðalilą* <o-tho´-ha-ge i´-tha-gthi-gtho^{n}> you reconsidered. *oðóhake ąðąliląpe* <o-tho´-ha-ge o^{n}-tho^{n}-gthi-gtho^{n} i> we reconsidered.

oðóhkiðe. v [reg.?, *oðó_hkiðe*] [presumably *hkik-* RECIP + *oðóðe*] *(trans.)* **intermingle, mix, blend, place together (as when cooking two or more items together).** *htáa ðé oðóhkiðaa* cook this meat with it (04/06/95/LS/pc:okc; RBn1-MOJ/p49b).

oðóhkihą. v [presumably *ó-* LOC + *hkik-* RECIP + *oohą́*] *(trans.)* **add in cooking.** *hǫbrį́ke owáha hta mįkšé, wašį́ ški oðóhkihą* when I'm going to cook beans, I [also] add salt meat (01/12/95/FH/pc:hk; BE2.24).

•• LFD 179: *oðóhkihą* <u-thu´-ḳi-ho^{n}> two kinds of food boiled or cooked together.

oðóhta (variant: **oðóhtą**). ADJ **straight up.**

óðohtą (variant: **óðohta**). v [reg., *ó_ðohtą*] *(intr.)* **behave.** *óðohta ąhé* I'm behaving (108-b/FH/152). *oáðohta ąmą́brį ąškáaye ík?uca* try to make me behave (MOJ 1/19/83). *óðohta ðaįšé* you're behaving (108-b/Fh/152). *óðohta káaya* make him behave. *óðohta ði!* behave yourself! (said when scolding someone for not living right) (RBn 3/3/77). *óðohtą mą́į!* behave! (lit., 'go on and behave', as an admonishment to children who are laughing too much). • ADJ **straight, virtuous.** *waðílą óðohta káaya* think straight (lit., 'make your mind straight'). • N **behavior, good behavior, acting with rectitude (may refer to conduct of the moment or to long-term behavior).**

•• LFD 124: *óðohtą* <o´-tho-ṭo^{n}> recititude, moral integrity, good behavior. *óðohtą aži* <o´-tho-ṭo^{n} a-zhi> depraved. *níhkašika wį óðohtą aži ha* <ni´-ḳa-shi-ga wi^{n} o´-tho-ṭo^{n} a-zhi ha> [sentence-final *ha* is not used in Mod. Os.] a depraved man, corrupt, wicked. *óðohtą ahkila ðį* <o´-tho-ṭo^{n} a-ḳi-gtha thi^{n}> demeanor, deportment, behavior [expected Mod. Os. gloss: 'to carry oneself with rectitude']. LFD 178: *oðóhtą* <u-tho´-ṭo^{n}> a virtuous woman [expected gloss for Mod. Os. form: 'virtuous', not necessarily a woman]. LFD 180: *oðóhtą aži* <u-thu´-ṭo^{n} a-zhi> not true, not straight, dishonest, not accurate, not upright. LFD 150 (unconfirmed): *ðiðóhtą* <thi-tho´-ṭo^{n}> to regulate [make straight], to make straight that which is crooked, reparation of a wrong; to regulate, to make a rule by which to guide or to be guided. *briðóhtą* <bthi-tho´-ṭo^{n}> I regulate. *ąðíhtohtąpe* <o^{n}-thi´-ṭho-ṭo^{n} i> [<-ṭho-> is a typographical error for <-tho->] we regulate.

••• Cf. *wáðohtą.*

óðohtąhkiðe. v [reg., *óðohtą_hkiðe*] [*óðohtą* + *hkik-* REFL + *ðe* CAU] *(intr.)* **behave oneself, make oneself straight by acting with rectitude (lit., 'cause oneself to act straight').** *óðohtąhkíe!* behave yourself! (lit., 'make yourself straight, properly behaving') (01/07/95/FH/pc; BE2.8). • N **good behavior.** *óðohtahkíe* good behavior (FH prod).

oðókahi. v [reg., *oðó_kahi*] *(trans.)* **stir (e.g., food when cooking).** (03/14/95/MREI/pc:ma; 04/06/95/LS/pc:ok). *oðóakahi* I'm stirring it. *oðóðakahi* you're stirring it. *ónǫbre ąkóðokahipe* we're stirring the food (RBn1-MOJ/p50; FH:ok).

•• LFD 178: *oðókahi* <u-thu´-ga-hi> to stir up. *oðówakahi* <u-thu´-wa-ga-hi> I am stirring what is in the pot cooking. [Strictly speaking, 'in the pot cooking' is not part of the meaning of the Os. form.] *oðóðakahi* <u-thu´-tha-ga-hi> you are stirring what is in the pot cooking, to stir up what is cooking or boiling. [Strictly speaking, 'in the pot' and 'cooking or boiling' are not part of the meaning of the Os. form.]

oðókanáaži, oðókanąąži, oðókanąąžį (variants of **oðókinąąžį**).

oðókinąąžį (variants: **oðókanąąži, oðókanąąžį,oðókanáaži, oðókinąąži**). N **trousers, pants, underwear.** *oðókanąąžį okíkxą* put on your pants (BE2.144; 04/03/95/PM/pc: *ðókináži* also ok).

•• RB: <ó-tho-kah-náh-zhi, o-thó-ki-náh-zhi>.

•• LFD 123: *oðókinąžį* <o-tho´-gi-no^{n}-zhi^{n}> trousers. LFD 179: *oðókinąžį* <u-thu´-gi-no^{n}-zhi^{n}> pants, pantaloons, trousers. *oðókinąžį aakihpasta* <u-thu´-gi-no^{n}-zhi^{n} a-a-gi-pa-çta> [*aakihpasta* is not acceptable in Mod. Os.] I patch my pants. [Translation should be 'I put my pants on' (PM).] *oðókinąžį akiną braza* <u-thu´-gi-no^{n}-zhi^{n} a-gi-no^{n} btha-ça> I tore my pants. [Verb form for 'I tore it' should be *anąkaabrazé* (PM).]

••• Cf. *oðíkinąąžį.*

oðókinąąžį ákaha. N **overalls.**

•• LFD 179: *oðókinąžį akaha wihta* <u-thu´-gi-no^{n}-zhi^{n} a-ga-ha wi-ṭa> my overalls (03/03/95/FH/pc:ok).

oðóohpa. V [conjug. unknown] *(trans.)* **obey (e.g., the law).** *wahkílaace oðóohpa akxái* it's the rule, he's obeying the law (BE2.76; 02/14/95/FH/pc:ok). *wahkílaace oðóohpa nąpe* he obeys the law (02/15/95/FH/pc).

•• LFD 29: *okíhpa* <u-gi´ pa> obey (to).

oðópše. N **baby board of any type** (MREI/pc/1994; FH); **cradle of any type, cradleboard** (BE2.27; FH 1994/pc).

•• LFD 179: *oðópše* <u-thu´-pshe> cradle board.

••• Cf. *ípše.*

oðóši. ADJ **in the way, in front of and blocking.** *oðóši nįkšé* you're in the way [sitting] (BE2.152).

•• LFD 179: *oðóši ha omąðį* <u-thu´-shi ha u-mo^{n}-thi^{n}> to walk in advance of a group of people. *oðóši ha omąbrį* <u-thu´-shi ha u-mo^{n}-bthi^{n}> I walked in advance. *oðóšiha ąko mąðį pe* <u-thu´-shi-ha o^{n}-gu mo^{n}-thi^{n} i> [expected Mod. Os. form: *oðóši ąkómąðįpe*] we walked in advance.

oðóšimąðį (variants: **oðóšima, oðóšimą**). V [uninfl. or sync., *oðóšimą_ðį*] [*oðóši* + *mąðį*] *(intr.)* **block s.o.'s way or be in the way while moving.** *oðóšimąbrį* I'm just in the way (03/16/95/JS/pc:ok; FH:5/01/96/pc). *oðóšimą ðée apa* he's in the way (lit., 'he's in the way, that one moving'). *ðée apa oðóšimąðį* he's in the way (03/16/95/JS/pc:okc; FH:5/01/96/okc). *oðóšimąšcį* you're in the way [moving].

oðóta, oðótą (apparently variants of **ootá**).

oðótą mązeska. N **interest money (lit., 'use money', 'use of money')** (04/14/95/FH/pc:ok; RBn1-MOJ/p28; FH:4/25/96/tape: *oðótą;* 04/13/95/FH/pc).

••• Cf. *mązeska oðótą, mąžą ootá, ootá mązeska.*

oðówaðe (variants: **oðówai, oðówe**). V [reg., *oðówa_ðe*] [*wa-* VAL + *oðóðe*] *(intr.* [also *trans.?*]*)* **be boss in relation to an event (e.g., a dinner), be in charge of, see to or oversee a certain occasion.** *ónǫbre che oðóawaðe hta mįkšé* I'm going to be taking care of the food (FH:prod). *oðówaðaðe* you are taking care of it. *ónǫbre che oðówaðai hkǫ́bra* I want you to oversee this dinner (FH:prod). *ónǫbre oðówa[ð]i akxa* she's bossing the food; she's in charge of food (01/07/95/FH/pc:prod orig). *Carolyn ónǫbre che oðów[að]e kǫ́ða apai* they want Carolyn to oversee this dinner (FH:prod). *Mary, Darlene ónǫbre che oðóepi wáhkǫ́bra* I want Mary and Darlene to oversee this dinner [*oðóepi* < *oðówaðe api*] (FH:prod). *waaðǫ́ hta apai, oðówaðaðe hta nįkšé?* they're going to sing, are you going to see about things? • **run a business, conduct one's own or s.o. else's affairs, be boss or foreman.** *xuháaska apa táatą ąkóhta oðówa[ðe] apai* white people are running our business, bossing us (01/07/95/FH/pc:prod; BE2.10). • N **boss, foreman.** *oðówai* boss, foreman.

óðoxta. N [*wa-* VAL + *óxta*] **s.t. or s.o. valued, beloved, or treasured (such as a favorite child).** *óðoxta škaaye* you're making it special, you're making it a favorite thing.

oðúluha. ADV **underneath, beneath, below, under** (LF).

•• LFD 349 (unconfirmed): *oðúluha* <u-thú-xthu-ha> underneath.

••• *QU odíxda* under, beneath a solid object (RR).

oðúuc?ake. ADJ, V [sync., *o_ðúuc?ake*] [apparently *ó-* LOC + *ðuuc?áke*] *(intr.)* **(be) lazy.** *waxpéį ąkái, ók?u ąðúuc?ake še nąąhtąhtąą oðúuc?ake wį́* we're too poor to feed that lazy donkey (RBn10-2:MJ/79). *obrúuc?ake* I'm lazy (FH:4/25/96/tape). • V *(trans.)* **be or become tired or weary of.** *níwahce obrúuc?ake* I'm tired of this cold (RBn23-14). *oščúuc?ake* are you getting tired of this? (FH:5/01/96/tape:prod). *obrúuc?ake* I'm getting tired of this (03/22/95/FH/pc:ok; BE2.141). *áwabruuc?áke mįkšé* I've had enough of them; I've gotten tired

oðúuc?ake (*continued*) of them (MSB). *ąwášcuuc?ake nįkšé?* are you tired of me? • N **laziness.** *wáli oðúuc?ake šíe* you have really gotten lazy (lit., 'indeed you arrived at laziness') (02/15/95/FH/pc:ok; BE2.77).

óðuuc?ake. V [sync., *ó_ðuuc?ake*] [*wa-* VAL + *oðúuc?ake*] *(intr.)* **be lazy** (RB; 02/15/95/FH/pc:okc). *hąpái wálį óbruuc?ake mįkšé* I was very lazy today (02/15/95/FH/pc:okc). *tówa apa óðuuc?akape* that person is lazy (02/15/95/FH/pc:ok; FH:4/25/96/tape). *kóota níhka akxa óðuuc?akape* that man is lazy (02/15/95/FH/pc:ok). *kóota wak?ó akxa óðuuc?akape* that woman is lazy (02/15/95/FH/pc:ok).

oðúuxpaðe (variant: **oðúuxpa**). V [sync., *o_ðúuxpaðe*] *(trans.)* **take out or unload s.t. by removing, by extracting, or by lowering from a carrier or storage** (02/27/95/JS/pc:ok; BE2.147; RB). *htáa che oðúuxpaðe* take the meat out (of the car) (FH:5/02/96/prod). *nąγehci obrúuxpaðe hta mįkšé* I'm going to take it out of the refrigerator (FH/09/23/01/pc). *ąkóðuuxpaðe ąkatxái* we're going to take it out (FH/09/23/01/pc).

ohcíle. N [*ó-* LOC + *hcíle*] **home, place to live, abode, household that one lives in (lit., 'wherein one has a household')** (LS). *ohcíle wíhta* my home (RB; 02/09/95/FH/pc:okc). *ohcíle ðáalį wį íiðe ðí aape* she found a good place to live (RBn19-03). • **furnishings, furniture** (HH/pc). [LS contrasts *hcíle* 'household' with *ohcíle* 'house or household as a place that you live in'.]

ohépe (variant: **óhepe**). N **small amount, amount not quite filling a container or vessel, less than the full amount (especially of liquids); portion that fills a container approximately half full.** *níi tóa ąk?ú, ohépe* give me some water, about half a glass, not quite full (FH:prod). *ohépe ąk?ú* give me [it] about half full (01/04/95/FH/pc:ok).

•• LFD 170: *ohépe* <u-he´-be> dose of medicine [expected gloss not limited to medicine].

••• Cf. *hépe.*

óhesaži (variant: **óhesažį**). ADJ, ADV **fast, rough(ly), bad(ly), untamed, forceful(ly), pushy, abrupt(ly), very strong(ly), fierce(ly), hard, with force, quickly, abruptly.** *htaacé óhesažį* the wind is really strong (01/23/95/FH/pc:prod orig; FH:4/18/96/t; BE2.45). *wisǫka akxa wáli íe óhesažįpe* brother is really a strong talker (FH). *wálį hpíižie óhesažį alįį ðáha níi hpáasike* it's awful that I sat down real quick and splattered water (lit., 'it is really bad that when I sat down quickly I splattered water') (04/19/95/FH/pc). *štǫ́pažie ðalįį óhesažį áha níi špáasike* you didn't look when you sat down hard, and you sat in water and splattered it, made it shoot out (04/19/95/FH/pc). *wisǫ́ka akxa wáli óhesažį wáli íe akxai* brother is really talking strong. *wálį hpíižie óhesažį alįį ðáha níi hpáasike* it's awful that I sat down real quick and splattered water (04/19/95/FH/pc). • ADJ **worse, more intense, stronger.** *taaké óhesaži ahí akxa* the war is worse (lit., 'it is becoming worse fighting') (03/24/95/PM/pc; BE2.161). *taaké óhesaži hi chí aapé* [they say that] the war is getting worse, it's getting to where they're really fighting (01/24/95/FH/pc:ok).

•• LFD 170: *óhesaži* <u´-he-ça-zhi> to act in a violent manner, fiery. *hkáwa ohesaži* <ḳa´-wa u-he-ça-zhi> a fiery horse.

ohí. V [reg., *o_hí*] *(trans.)* **beat, conquer, best s.o. in a game (not used for a race).** *ąkóhipe* we beat him. *ąkówahie* we beat them at a game. *owíhie* I beat you. *owáhie* I beat him. *ąwáhipe* he beat me. *áwahíe* I beat them. *oðíhipaži* he didn't beat you. • *(trans.)* **win.** *ówe tóa owáhi* I won some groceries. *mą́zeska ąwáhipe* he won money from me.

•• LFD 170: *ohi* <u-hi> [no accent indicated by LF] to defeat, to overcome, to prevail (03/16/95/MREI/pc:ok). *owáhi* <u-wa´-hi> I win. *oðáhi* <u-tha´-hi> you win. *ą́kohi pe* <o^n´-gu-hi i> we win.

••• Cf. *óhi.*

óhi. V [reg., *ó_hi*] [*wa-* VAL + *ohí*] *(intr.)* **win at a game or contest, defeat others, best everyone in a game, be the winner** (03/16/95/MREI/pc:ok). *oáhi/wáhi/owáhi* I win (03/16/95/MREI/pc:okc). *íkiha owáhi* I win repeatedly (03/16/95/MREI/pc:okc). *wálį óðahi ðąįšé aape* you sure have been winning, they say (BE2.158). *ówaðahi* you broke us. *hóni óhipe* he almost won (03/16/95/MREI/pc:ok). *ąkówahie* we won. *ąkóhipe* we won. *óhištą* winner. *pée óhi?* who won? *óhištą* a winner, someone who always wins. • *(trans.)* **win s.t.** *ówe tóa owáhi* I won some groceries (RBn22-09; 03/16/95/MREI/pc:ok).

ohíiða. N [*ó-* LOC + *hiiðá*] **bathtub, place to bathe, place to swim** (BE2.7; 01/06/95/FH/pc:ok).

ohíiðahci. N [*ohíiða* + *hcí*] **bath house** (01/19/95/FH/pc:ok (BE2.7).

óhipažinai. N [*óhi* + *api* SUFFIX + *aží* NEG + *ną* 'always' + *ðe* DECLARATIVE MARKER] **loser, s.o. who customarily does not win (lit., 'does not win habitually').**

óhištą. N [*óhi* + *štą*] **habitual winner, s.o. who wins constantly or repeatedly.**

óhkace (variant: **óhkaci**). V [conjug. unknown] [*ó-* LOC + *-hkace*] *(intr., trans.)* **cook, grill, barbecue, cook outside (refers only to cooking meat on a rack, as for barbecue)** (RBn1; BE2.86; 01/11/95/FH/pc:ok; 02/24/95/FH/pc:okc; 04/13/95/LS:ok).

••• Cf. *táahkace.*

ohkáðįke (variants: **ohkąįke, ohkáįke**). V [uninfl.?] [*óhką* 'space' + *ðįké* NEG] *(trans.)* **crowd s.o.** *wáli ohkąðįke ąhé ąži ąwáachi ąhé* I'm really crowding everybody but I'm dancing (RBn2-MOJ/p17). *wi ohkáįke* I'm crowding people (RBn2-MOJ/p17; 01/14/95/FH/pc:ok).

ohkáska (variant of **ohkąska**).

óhką (variant: **óhka**). N **space, room (in the sense of an unoccupied area).** *óhka lą́ąðe* a large space (FH/t113). *óhka wahókʔa* a small space (03/13/95/FH/pc:ok). *óhką ecíhta?* is there room over there? (asking for room for someone to sit) (RBn3-51).

•• LFD 173: *ohką lą́ąðe* <u-ḳo^{n} gtho^{n}´-the> a large space, spacious. LFD 172: *ohką́* <u-ko^{n}´> a vacancy, a space. Room for one more person in a house or at a gathering.

••• Cf. *wíohkaðį.*

óhką (variant: **ohką́**). V [reg., *ó_hką*] *(trans.)* **help, help s.o. with a task, assist, aid** (2-10-83). *ówaðahkąį* you help them (2/1/D). *o[w]áhką* I helped her. *wažážeíe ąwą́ðahką hkǫ́bra* I want you to help me with the Osage language (RBn1-58). *óhką mąðí!* go help them! (RBn10-18). *ąwą́hką!* help me! (02/09/95/FH/pc:okc; BE2.66). *ąkóhkąži áha ékiǫží hta apai* if we don't help her she won't do it (MREI 1-14-82). *owíhką hce* I'll just help you, let me help you (2-1-125). *wihé oáhką eeškítą ąwą́hką nąpé* when I help second daughter she helps me (2-1-G). *owáhkąpi!* help us! (MREI 11-1-83-1).

••• Cf. *okíhką.*

ohkąci (variant: **ohkące**). ADJ, ADV, V [uninfl.] *(intr.)* **(be) alone, isolated, by oneself, individual, distinct, single, sole, apart from anyone else, solitary,** *ohką́ci ąhé* I am by myself (01/06/95/FH/pc:ok).

•• LFD 172: *ohką́ci* <u-ḳo^{n}´-dsi> single, distinct, alone separate, sole. *ohką́ci ne ha* <u-ḳo^{n}´-dsi ne ha> [expected Mod. Os. form: *ohką́ci šcée; ne* is not an Osage word; sentence-final *ha* is not used in Mod. Os.] you went alone. LFD 173: *ohką́ci ðe kaɣe* <u-ḳo^{n}´-dsi the ga-xe> to isolate, to make to be apart, to segregate, to make alone. LFD 121: *óhkąci* <o´-ḳo^{n}-dsi> individual, one single person. *ohką́ciðǫðǫ ǫ* <u-ḳo^{n}´-dsi-tho^{n}-tho^{n}> [*ðǫðǫ* unconfirmed] severally, each one apart from the rest. *ohką́cinąžį* <U-ḳo^{n}´-dsi-no^{n}-zhi^{n}> Stands-alone (personal name), refers to the solitary buffalo that stands apart from the herd. *ohką́ciwašką* <O-ḳo^{n}´-dsi-wa-shko^{n}> Struggles-by-himself (personal name): No one to help him fight.

••• Cf. *mįįohką́ce.*

ohkąci káaɣe. VP [sync. *k*>*p*, *ohką́ci _káaɣe*] *(trans.)* **isolate (lit., 'cause to be alone').**

ohkącilą. N [*ohką́ci* + *oolą́*] **ace in a deck of cards** (LF only, unconfirmed).

•• LFD 172: *ohką́cilą* <u-ḳo^{n}´-dsi-gtho^{n}> one-that-is-placed-in-the-center-of-space. *ohką, ci, lą* <u-ḳo^{n}, dsi, gtho^{n}> space, there (in the center), placed: the ace in a deck of cards (unconfirmed; 04/19/95/FH/pc:not quite right, uk; 04/25/95/PM/pc:uk, first part means 'help').

ohkąįke (variant of **ohkáðįke**).

ohkąska (variants: **óhkąska, ohkáska, ohkǫ́ska**). N, ADV **(in the) center, middle, (at the) halfway point** (RBn1-10; 02/24/95/FH/pc:okc; BE2.87; 04/19/95/FH/pc: non-nasal: *ohkáska*).

•• RB: <ó-kah^{n}-skah>.

•• LFD 172: *ohką́ska* <u-ḳo^{n}´-çka> the center. *Ce ohkąska* <Dse u-ḳo^{n}-çka> center of a lake [*ce* is not recognized in Mod. Osage as 'lake']. *ní ohkąska* <ni´ u-ḳo^{n}-çka> center of waters (the earth). "This was a name given to a subgens of the water division (Wa-zha-zhe gens) of the Osage tribal organization." *hta wį cʔe aðe, ðue ohkąska ao* <ṭa wi^{n} ṭs'e a-the, thiu-e u-ḳo^{n}-çka a-u> [expected Mod. Os. form: *htáa wį cʔéaðe, ðúwe ohkáska* 'I killed a deer, (through) the center of the diaphragm'; sentence-final *ao* <a-u> is not used in Mod. Os.] I killed a deer, I shot it through the middle of the body. *íwiðe hkǫbra, ðohtą pši, ðeka ohkąska xci awihkihpa* <I´-wi-the ḳo^{n}-btha, tho-ṭo^{n} pshi the ga u-ḳo^{n}-çka xtsi a-wi-ḳi-pa> [expected Mod. Os. form: *íiwiðe hkǫ́bra, ðóhtą pši, ðéeka ohkáskaxci áwihkihpa* I want to see you, I went in a straight line to find you, but meet you here (lit., 'I wanted to see you,

ohkąska (*continued*)
straight I went there, exactly in the center here I encountered you')]. *mi ohkąska* <Mi u-ḳo^{n}-çka> [expected Mod. Os. form: *mį́į ohką́ska*] mid-heaven or mid-sun. LFD 121: *okxą́ska* <o-ko^{n}´-çka> [incorrect <o-ko^{n}´-çka> for the correct <u-ḳo^{n}-çka>, Mod. Os. *ohką́ska*] the middle part of the house.

ohkí (variant of **ohkíe**).

óhkiache (variants: **ohkíiche, óhkiachi, ohkíechi**). N **quilt (lit., 'sewn together', 'sewn to each other')** (BE2.110; RBn1-MOJ/p54; 04/20/95/LS/pc; 04/19/95/FH/pc:ok; FH/09/21/01/pc; RBn 3/3/77).
•• RB: <ó-kyah-tsi>.
•• LFD 57: *haská ohkihpache* <ha-çka´u-ḳi-p̣a-tse> a patch quilt.

ohkíce. N **goal, curved stick used to play *kašíni* (shinny)** (03/23/95/FH/pc). [This stick is for hitting the ball made out of buckskin in the game of shinny, which was declining in popularity in the early twentieth century, circa 1916 when FH was born.]
•• LFD 171: *ohkíce* <u-ḳi´-dse> a goal, the goals in the game of shinny.

ohkícheðe (variant of **ohkíicheðe**).

ohkíe (variant: **ohkí** [rare, archaic?]). V [reg., *o_hkíe*] [originally a reciprocal form 'speak with each other, converse' (*ó-* LOC + *hkik-* RECIP + *íe*), now used regularly as a transitive form] *(trans.)* **call on the telephone.** *mą́zeohkíe oą́hkie* they called me by phone (RBn10-20). • **converse with, interview, talk with or to.** *owíhki hkǫ́bra įké* I don't want to talk to you (PM/7/7/94; 03/16/95/JS/pc:ok). *owíhkie achíe* I came to talk to you (RBn12-01). *wažáže záani owíhkie akxą́he* I'm talking to all you Osages. *wažáže záani owíhkie mįkšé* I'm talking to all you Osages. *owíhki[e] hkǫ́bra* I want to talk to you (RBn10-5:JW; 03/05/95/JS/pc:ok *owíhki*). *ǫwą́ðahkie šǫ ðaįšé íiðixope* when you [pl.] were talking to me you lied (FH/05/13/94). *oðíhkie kǫ́ða* he wants to talk to you (03/05/95/JS/pc:okc). *oðíhkie hta akxái* he is going to talk to you. *ąwą́hkia* talk to me (FH). *ąwą́ðahkíe šcílą e* you wanted to talk to me (MSB). *owíhkie bríląe* I wanted to talk to you (MSB; BE2.133; 03/05/95/JS/pc:okc).
•• LFD 171: *ohkíe* <u-ḳi´-e> to interview, to speak or to talk to one another, to hold an interview. *owáhkie* <u-wa´-ḳi-e> I had an interview. *ąkóhkia pe* <o^{n}-gu´-ḳi-a i> we had an interview.
••• Cf. *ohkíhkie, okíhkie.*

ohkíe. N **get-together, meeting of a group of people to converse.** [Takes 'standing' positional article *che*.] *hǫ́ǫpaðe wažáže žį́ toa ohkíe che žóąhkile ąkái, wažážeíe íkʔuce ąkáli* today a bunch of Osage young people, we're gathered together, we've come back to study Osage (RBn10-13; FH/11/19/01/pc:okc).

ohkíechi (variant of **óhkiache**).

ohkíetxątxą (variant: **ohkíekxąkxą**), ADV [*ó-* LOC + *hkik-* RECIP + *etxą́* (reduplicated)] **every time, consecutively, one after another, time after time** (04/13/95/FH/pc:okc).
•• LFD 171: *ohkiá txątxą* <u-ḳi-a´ to^{n}-to^{n}> consecutive, one following the other, a series.

ohkíežą. V [conjug. unknown] [presumably *hkik-* REFL + *óžą*] *(intr.)* **care for oneself.** *ohkíežą akxai* they're taking care of themselves (FH; 04/25/95; PM/pc:ok).

ohkíhce (variant: **ohkíhci**). N **tribe other than Osage (including western tribes), "off-tribe"** (FH/09/22/01/pc; FH/09/25/01/prod). *tówa ðe táatą ohkíhce?* what tribe is he? *kóota įkšé ohkíhce hǫ́ǫxce ðįkšé?* that one sitting over there, what kind of tribe is he? (03/23/95/FH/pc). • **enemy, stranger.**
•• RB: <o-kí-tseh, o-kí-tsi>.

óhkihkaše (variant: **óhkihkašą?**). V [reg., *ó_hkihkaše*] [*hkik-* REFL + *okáše*] *(intr.)* **take care of oneself.** *oáhkihkašą hpímą, htáažį akxa waðílą hkihkáayape* I know how to take care of myself, the little deer thought (lit., 'taking care of myself I am skilled at, the little deer made up his own mind') (RBn15-002).

ohkíhkie. V [reg., *o_hkíhkie*] [*hkik-* RECIP + *ohkíe*] **talk with one another, converse with each other (usually more than two people).** *ąkóhkihkie htái* let's talk to each other (03/05/95/JS/pc:okc).
•• LFD 172: *ohkíhkie* <u-ḳi´-ḳi-e> a dialogue. *ohkíhkie* <u-ḳi´-ḳi-e> to speak to one another, to hold a conversation.

ohkíhpa che. NP [presumably *ó-* LOC + *áhkihpa* + *che*] **council (lit., 'wherein they meet each other').** [Includes 'standing' positional article *che*.] *níhka žúuce hcéka nǫ ohkíhpa che apa hąðé waachí hta apai* Indian Youth Council are having a dance tonight (RBn23-14).

óhkihpaache (variant: **hóhkihpaache**) N [*hkik-* RECIP + *ópaache*] **man's blanket (lit., 'sew [to] each other')** (01/07/95/FH/pc). [Refers to the seam in the center of the man's red and blue blanket.]

••• *QU okkippathe* sewed together (RR).
••• Cf. *óhkiache.*

ohkíicheðe (variant: **ohkícheðe**). v [reg., *ohkíiche_ðe*] [*ó-* LOC + *hkícheðe*] *(trans.)* **put down, set down, place.** *aðį́ku, kaðó ohkíche[ð]e* bring it here and put it down (RBn10-21/JW; FW/77). *káa ohkíche[ð]e* put it here (RBn10-21/JW; FW/77). *šeðó ohkíchi[ð]e* put it over there (RBn10-21/JW; FW/77).

ohkík'ǫhe. v [reg.?, *o_hkík'ǫhe?*] [*hkik-* REFL + *ok'ǫ́he*] *(intr.?)* **interrupt (lit., 'insert oneself into').** *óhkik'ǫ́he* he's interrupting.

ohkík'u. v [reg.?, *o_hkík'u*] [*hkik-* RECIP + *ók'u*] *(intr.)* **give away to each other, have a giveaway.** [Giving away is a custom at the annual Osage dances, especially on Sunday, when blankets, shawls, groceries, cash, and other items are given to others in appreciation.] *ohkík'u hta apai hǫ́ǫpa ðé* they're going to give away today (FH/09/21/01/pc).

óhkila, óhkilą (variants of **ohkúlą**).

ohkílaake. v [reg., *o_hkílaake*] [*hkik-* REFL + *óðaake*] *(intr.)* **tell about oneself, speak of oneself** (RBn 3/3/77; FH/09/11/01/pc okc). *ohkílaaka ði!* tell about yourself! (RBn10-6:JW).
•• LFD 171: *ohkílake* <u-ķi´-gtha-ge> to speak of oneself. *owahkilake* <u-wa-ķi-gtha-ge> I spoke of myself. *owáhkilake* <u-wa´-ķi-gtha-ge> [*sic;* expected Mod. Os. form: *oðáhkilaake*] you spoke of yourself. *ąkohkílaka pe* <o^{n}-gu-ķi´-gtha-ga i> we spoke of ourselves.

óhkioolą́ (variants: **óhkulą, óhkilą, ohkílą**). v [conjug. unknown, presumably reg.+reg., *ó_hkioo_lą́*] [*ó-* LOC + *hkik-* REFL + *oolą́*] *(trans.)* **put on oneself or dress in (e.g., a shirt or a dress).** *haaská ohkílą* put the dress on (RBn12-05). *haaská wasúhu wį́ ohkúlą* put on a clean shirt (RBn12-08). • *(intr.)* **dress oneself, put on clothes.**
•• RB: <hó-kyu-lah> (04/07/95/LS/pc:okt; BE2.33).
••• Cf. *ohkúlą.*

ohkíǫðe (variant: **ohkúįðe**). v [reg.+sync., *o_hkíǫ_ðe*] [*ó-* LOC + *hkik-* REFL + *ǫ́ǫðe*] [secondary accent on *ǫ́ðe*] *(trans.)* **throw oneself into, jump into, get tangled in, fall into.** *hkáwa apa mą́ze ohkíǫðe apái* the horses are tangled up in the wire (RBnot-nd-1/p18; FH:ok). • *(intr.?)* **be in trouble for doing s.t. wrong** (04/03/95/PM/pc:ok). *ohkíǫðe nįkšé* you're in trouble (BE2.144). *ohkúįðe mįkšé* I'm in trouble (BE2.144). *oðáhkiǫšce nįkšé* you sure got into trouble. • v, ADJ *(intr.)* **(be) divorced, separated.** *ohkíǫðe mįkše* she divorced me, quit me, let me go (04/03/95/PM/pc). *ohkíǫðe nįkšé* she quit you (04/03/95/PM/pc). • v *(intr.)* **throw each other away, throw each other away, quit or abandon each other** (PM). *Jóhna éeðǫǫpa ąhkíǫðe hta ąðįhé* I'm divorcing John (lit., 'John and I are going to throw each other away').
•• LFD 172: *ohkíǫðe* <u-ķi´-o^{n}-the> to throw themselves into, to become insnared (04/03/95/PM/pc:ok).
••• Cf. *éwahkiǫ́ðe, hkíǫðe.*

ohkísce. N **half (of anything), half dollar** (01/04/95/FH/pc; BE2.63; RB).
•• RB: <o-kí-steh>.
•• LFD 172: *ohkísce* <u-ķi´-stse> half; 50 cents.

ohkížį. v [reg., *o_hkížį*] [presumably *ó-* LOC + *hkížį*] *(intr., trans.)* **be angry, be mad.** *oáhkižį, awáhkižį* I'm angry. *oðáhkižį* you're angry. *ąkóhkižį* we're angry. *awáhkižį mįkšé* I'm mad at him (MSB 03-83).
••• Cf. *ihkížį.*

ohkǫ́ska (variant of **ohkąska**).

ohkúche (variant of **óhkiache**).

ohkúįðe (variant of **ohkíǫðe**).

ohkúlą (variants: **ohkílą, óhkilą óhkila, ohkúla,**). N [*hkik-* REFL + *oolą́*] **clothes (lit., 'that which one puts oneself into')** (FH: 01/08/01). [*óhkilą* is same as *wéhkilį* (EH)] *óhkilą táapuze akxai* the clothes are drying. *ohkúlą weeáhkie mąží* I can't find my clothes [for myself]. *ohkúlą wasú* I washed my clothes (FH/01/03/01/pc). *wažá ohkílą* Osage clothes.
••• *QU ókkíkdaxda* shirt (RR).
••• Cf. *óhkioolą́.*

óhkulą (variant of **óhkioolą́**).

ohláaži (variant of **oolą́ąži**).

ohlé (variant of **olé**).

óhoo. v [conjug. unknown] [probably *ó-* LOC + *hóo*] *(intr.)* **bark, woof (as a dog does).** *hą́ące šǫ́ke wíhta akxa wáli óhoope* my dog sure barked last night (01/06/95/FH/pc:ok; BE2.6). *šǫke apa óhoo apái ðe* the dogs are barking (01/04/95/FH/pc:okc).
•• LFD 171: *óhoho* <u´-hu-hu> the bark or yelp of a dog. (03/01/95/FH/pc:uk).
••• *OM* same as Osage (LFD 171).

ohpáza. v [stat., *o_hpáza* (but 1st dual/pl. has reg. prefix *ąk-*, not stat. *wa-*)] *(intr.)* **be startled (as by a dream or nightmare).** *ąwą́hpaza* I was startled. *oðíhpaza* you were startled. *ohpáza* she was startled. *ąkóhpaza* we were startled. *hǫ́bre*

ohpáza (*continued*)
ohpáza akxai a dream startled him (he had a nightmare). *hǫ́bre ąkóhpaza ąkátxai* we have nightmares. *hǫ́bre oðíhpazái?* did you have a nightmare? (lit., 'dreaming, did it startle you?'). • N **nightmare, bad dream.** *ohpáza che* a nightmare. *hǫ́bre ohpázą che ąkatxą́e* we had a nightmare (lit., 'dreaming, we had a nightmare').

ohpé (variants: **óhpe, ohpéwį**). V [reg., *o_hpé*] *(trans.)* **enter or go in/into, enter formally (as into a peyote meeting)** (04/13/95/FH/pc:ok). *haakxą́ta hci oðáhpe?* when are you going in the house? (04/28/95/LS/pc:okc). *mį́ihiðe tą oðáhpe* you went in at sundown (RBn12-12; CQc). *okahą́ąpa cí ecíha óhpepi áape* the house has been broken into (lit., 'it was through the window that the house had been entered, they said') (05/01/95/FH/pc). *tówa apa háachi hci ohpéwį kǫ́ða apai* those ones [dogs] keep wanting to come inside the house. *mį́ihiðe tą ąkóhpe* we're going in at sundown (RBn12-12).
•• LFD 175: *ohpé* <u-pe´> to enter. *owáhpe* <u-wa´-pe> I enter. *oðáhpe* <u-tha´-pe> you enter. *ąkóhpa pe* <o^{n}-gu´-pa i> we enter.

óhtaiðįke. ADV **safely** (RB, unconfirmed). *óhtaiðįke alí hkǫ́bra* I want to return safely.
•• LFD 175: *ohtáðį* <u-ṭa´-thi^{n}> to spread fame; refers to the courage of warriors.

ohtáza. V, ADJ [uninfl.] *(intr.)* **(be) good looking, handsome, beautiful, very pretty.** *še žą́ąžį akxa ohtáza akxái* the little tree is pretty (1/1/83/30/MSB). *ohtáza nąąžį́* Stands There Beautiful (personal name) [Joyce Stabler's name] (BE2.59).
•• LFD 175: *ohtáza* <u-ṭa´-ça> handsome. *ohtáza walį* <u-ṭa´-ça wa-gthi^{n}> it is very pretty, showy; stateliness; pretty; comely; pleasing to the sight.

ohtázaži. ADJ [*ohtáza* + *aží*] **ugly, homely, not pretty or handsome** (02/27/95/JS/pc:ok).
•• LFD 175: *ohtázaži* <u-ṭa´-ça-zhi> homely; homeliness; ugly.

ohtą́ną (variant: **ohtą́na**). N, PPN **between, in between, the space between things** (FH).
••• *KS ottáną* space between two things (RR).
••• Cf. *ožą́ke ohtą́na.*

óhuheka. N **sickness.** *óhuheka óhesaži wį ąhkíǫ́ðe* we've come upon a bad sickness (02/01/95/FH/pc:prod orig; 03/09/95/MREI/pc:ok).

óie (variant: **óʔie**). V [conjug. unknown] [*ó-* + *íe*] *(intr.)* **discuss, talk about s.t. positively or negatively; worry about or question s.t. verbally, as in a business meeting** (4/17/96/sideB,FH). [The locative prefix *ó-* has recently been added to *íe,* so that speakers may still sense a boundary between *ó-* and *íe;* hence the occasionally (but rarely) heard variant *óʔie.*] *óʔie ąkái* we're discussing it (FH:prod). *óʔie štą* he causes a lot of talk about everything; he brings up any little thing (FH:prod). *óie apai* they're worrying/questioning. • N **argument, problem.** [Takes 'standing' positional article *che.*] *óʔie che kašǫ́e hce* [let's] leave the problem alone (04/26/95/FH/pc).
••• Cf. *áhkie, íkie, ohkíe, ohkíhkie.*

oísi (variant of **wísi**).

ókaayeįke (variant: **ókaayéįke**), ADJ, V [*ó-* LOC + *káaye* + *ðįké* NEG] **(be) idle, useless, with nothing to it, meaningless (lit., 'wherein nothing is done')** (RBn HW8). *okaayéįke!* it's idle [gossip], there's nothing to it! *íe ókaayeįki akxai* his talk is useless, there's nothing to it (03/01/95/FH/pc:ok; 02/27/95/JS/pc:ok; BE2.148). *ókaayeįke žáže aðį́pe* "Useless" was his name (RBn10-2:MOJ/79).
•• LFD 120: *ókaye ðįke* <o´-ga-xe thi^{n}-ge> value-nothing, valueless. LFD 168: *ókaye ðįke* <u´-ga-xe thi^{n}-ge> nonsense, absurd; meaningless; immaterial; a useless person.
••• Cf. *hą́ąpa ókaayéįke.*

okábra. V [uninfl.?] *(trans.)* **disperse a group, scatter (e.g., corn for drying), spread around.** (03/01/95/FH/pc); *(intr.)* **go away, depart, scatter, disband, leave (e.g., a crowd leaving after a dance or other public gathering).** *ąkábra htai* let's scatter [unexpected form, omits *o-*] (RBn HW). *okábra káaya akxai* they are all leaving now (RBn10-7:JW). *okábra káayape* they have already gone (lit., 'they have caused them to scatter') (RBn10-7:JW).
•• LFD 120: *okáe bra* <o-ga´-e btha> to disperse. LFD 167: *okáebra* <u-ga´-e-btha> to scatter; to disband; to scatter in every direction. *okáebra hpaye* <u-ga´-e-btha pa-xe> I made them scatter. *okáebra škaye* <u-ga´-e-btha shka-xe> you made them scatter. *okáebra ąkaya pe* <u-ga´-e-btha o^{n}- ga-xa i> we made them scatter. LFD 28: *brąðálį okábrą* <btho^{n}tha´-gthi^{n} u-ga-btho^{n}> redolence (03/02/95/FH/pc:ok).

okácʔį. V [reg., *o_kácʔį*] *(trans.)* **peer in or into; peep into** (03/01/95/FH/pc).
•• LFD 168: *okácʔį* <u-ga´-ṭs'i^{n}> to peep; stealthily look into the crack of a door or window.

htížepeche oðakáhcį <ṭi´-zhe-be-te u-tha-ga´-ṭsi^n> [expected Mod. Os. form: *hcižépe che oðákacʔį*] you peeped in the door.
••• Cf. *niióhkiacʔį.*

okáhąpa (variants: **okáhąąpa, okáhǫpa**). N [*ó-* LOC + *kaa-* INSTR + *hą́ąpa*] **window; pane of glass, window glass (lit., 'place where by sudden action daylight').** *okáhǫpa áðihtą* close the window (04/28/95/LS/pc:okc: short final *a/ą*). *okáhąpa záani ðuuáza* open [all] the window[s] (04/28/95/LS/pc:okc; RBn1-52; BE2.159). *šį́htožį apa okáhąpa kaalékape* the boys broke the window (04/28/95/LS/pc:okc). *okáhąpa kaaléke che ðe* someone broke a window, that's the way it is (01/07/95/FH/pc:ok; LS:ok). *okáhąpa wahósce* a small window (04/28/95/LS/pc:okc).
•• LFD 168: *okáhąpa* <u-ga´-ho^n-ba> a window glass, pane of glass. *šįhto žįka apa oká hąpa kale ka pi* <shi^n-ṭu zhi^n-ga a-ba u-ga´ ho^n-ba ga-xthe ga bi a> [expected Mod. Os. form: *šį́tožį apa okáhąpe kaalékape*] the boy broke the pane of glass. *okáhąpa wahósca* <u-ga´-ho^n-ba wa-ho-stsa> a small pane of glass for a window.

okáhąpa akáspe. N **window shade** (RBn HW11). *okáhąpa akáspe ðuumą́ši* raise the window shade.

okáhǫpa (variant of **okáhąpa**).

ókahpo. ADJ, ADV **sick from eating too much** (BE2.121; 03/09/95/MREI/pc:ok) [*ókahpo, ókohpa,* and *okúhpu* have similar meanings and may have partially influenced each other in form. *ókahpo* and *ókohpa* possibly contain *wa-* VAL (*wa-* + *o-* > *ó-*).]

okákʔǫ. V [conjug. unknown, presumably reg. *ka-* del., *o_(ká)kʔǫ*] *(intr.)* **make a hole.** *okákʔǫapía* [expected Mod. Os. form: *okákʔǫpe*] they broke a hole in it (RBn10-19).

okále. V *(trans.)* **face a certain direction.** *kóota okála!* face the other way! (RBn19-02).
•• LFD 265: *ehtá okale* <e-ṭa´ u-ga-xthe> facing. *hkímǫhǫ okale* <ḳi´-mo^n-ho^n u-ga-xthe> [expected Mod. Os. form: *hkímąhą okále*] facing (the wind).

okášą (variant: **okáša**). V [reg., *o_kášą*] *(trans.)* **take care of or handle s.t. specific for s.o., take charge of, undertake, supervise or have the responsibility for s.t. specific in response to a formal request (e.g., taking care of the food for an event)** (RBn22-15;04/13/95/LS/pc:ok). *owíkašą hta mįkšé* I'll take care of you (MSB,t9a). *owákašą mįkšé* I'm taking care of it for somebody. *šǫ́ke wíhta akxa hkáwa, hceeská éðǫǫpa owákaša nąpé* my dog takes care of horses and cows (RBn12-03). *hcéska okáša apai* he's taking care of the cattle [for someone else] (FH/09/24/01/pc/prod). *htáa okáša* take care of the meat (includes cutting it up for different dishes, cooking the ribs outside, activities mostly performed by men, with women slicing the meat for meat gravy) (FH/09/23/01/pc). *žįkókaša* taking care of kids (RBn10-6:JW). *xuðókaša* takes care of the eagle (personal name) [*xúða+ okášąa*] (RBn22-04). *šǫ́ke wíhta akxa hkáwa, hceeská éðǫǫpa owákaša nąpé* my dog takes care of horses and cows (RBn12-03). • *(intr.)* **go on an errand, set out on or undertake a new task under one's charge** (03/01/95/FH/pc:ok). *oðákašą šcee?* are you going on an errand? (03/01/95/FH/pc). *ąwą́kašą ąká[ð[ape* [*ąwą́kašą* not the expected form] we're going on an errand (03/01/95/FH/pc). *ąkókašą ąká[ð]ape* we're going on an errand (03/01/95/FH/pc).
•• JOD (slip file): *okášą* <u-ḳa´-ca^n> to travel.
•• LFD 168 (unconfirmed): *okášą* <u-ga´-sho^n> going forth on an errand. *okášą bre ha* <u-ga´-sho^n bthe ha> [sentence-final *ha* is not used in Mod. Os.] I am going on an errand (unconfirmed; 03/01/95/FH/pc:no). *okášą šte a?* <u-ga´-sho^n shde a?> are you going on an errand? *okášą ąkaða pe* <u-ga´-sho^n o^n-ga-tha i> we are going on an errand (03/01/95/FH/pc:no).
••• Cf. *okáše.*

ókašą. V [reg., *ó_kašą*] [*wa-* VAL + *okášą*] *(intr.)* **take charge of things in general for another.** *ókašape ną ðe ánąąžį mąbrį ški tą* even when I get there (go and stand up there), he always takes charge of things (RB; trans by CQ). *žįkážį áwakašą́ hta mįkšé* I'll take care of the kids (lit., 'as for the children, I'll take care of things') (MSBt9a;RB:MSB/02/17/83;CQc).

okáše (variant: **okáši**). V [reg., *o_káše*] *(trans.)* **take care of, see to (especially a person).** *okáši apai* he's taking care of him/her (RB:MSB/02/17/83). *owíkaše hta mįkšé* I'll take care of you (RB:MSB/02/17/83).
••• Cf. *óhkihkaše, okášą.*

ókaše. V [uninfl.] *(intr.)* **be suffering a period of illness, be troubled, distracted, or impeded by problems or sickness** (MREI). *ókaše akxa* he's sick (RBn1-40). *ókaše akxái* she or he is sick or is not feeling very well (03/09/95/MREI/pc:ok). *oðíhtą ókaše apai* his car is holding him back (lit., 'with regard to his car, things are troubling

ókaše (*continued*)
him'). *Preston akxa šáake ókaší akxa* Preston's hands are causing him trouble (lit., 'Preston is suffering with his hands') (05/06/94; MREI:ma).
• N **spell of illness or trouble of any kind** (MREI). [The period of illness is *ókaše*, while the illness itself is *húheka* (02/13/95/FH/pc).]
•• LFD 120: *ókaše* <o´-ga-she> obstacles in the path of life, such as disease and accidents which interfere with the enjoyment of life and health (03/01/95/FH/pc:ok). LFD 168: *ókaše* <u´-ga-she> ailment, not well.

ókašéįke (variant: **ókašéįki**). ADJ, ADV [*ókaše* 'be ill, troubled' + *ðįké* NEG] **untroubled, nothing wrong, well, in good health, free from worry or illness, safely, okay, all right** (BE2.59; 02/01/95/FH/pc:okc),
•• LFD 120: *ókaše ðįké* <o´-ga-she thi^{n}-ge> hearty; no interference in the enjoyment of good health; hale (03/01/95/FH/pc:ok:well). LFD 168: *ókaše ðįke* <u´-ga-she thi^{n}-ge> well; healthy; no interruption to the enjoyment of good health. *ókaše ąðįke mįkše o* <u´-ga-she o^{n}-thi^{n}-ge mi^{n}-kshe o> [sentence-final *o* is not used in Mod. Os.] I am well. *ó kaše ðiðįke nikše a(?)* <u´ ga-she thi-thi^{n}-ge ni-kshe a(?)> are you well(?) [No conjugated forms attested in Mod. Os.]

okáši (variant of **okáše**).

okáške. V [reg., *ka*-ret., *o_káške*] [*ó-* LOC + *kašké*] *(trans.)* **tie (e.g., shoelaces), tie up (e.g., a dog or a horse).** *hǫǫpé okáške* tying shoes (FH:prod). *hǫǫpé oðákaške* tie my shoe (lit., 'you tie the shoe') (03/22/95/FH/pc).
•• LFD 168: *okáške* <u-ga´-shke> to tie or tether a horse or any other animal.
••• Cf. *oðáške, wapíokaške.*

ókawai. ADJ **sickly** (RBn22-09).
••• Cf. *ókaše.*

okáwįye. ADV **around.**
••• Cf. *ákiye, hkilíihkǫįye, hǫǫpé okáwįye, opáwįye.*

okáxpa. N **Quapaw Indians** (BE2.110; 03/08/95/PM/pc:ok).
•• LFD 168: *okáxpa kaxa* <U-ga´-xpa ga-xa> Quapaw Creek; Quapaw, Okla.

okáxpa. V [reg., *o_káxpa*] *(trans.)* **throw off (suddenly severing or moving s.t. or s.o. from s.t.).** *paaxó citxa oákaxpai* I threw him off the hill (RBn19-02). *paaxó kšitxa okáxpape* he threw him off the hill (RBn19-02). *hkáwa ówakaxpa áape* he said the horse threw him off (RBn19-01). *hkáwa apa okaxpápe* he got thrown off the horse (lit., 'the horse threw him') (RBn19-01). *paaxó įkšítxa ąkókaxpai* we threw him off the hill (RBn19-02).

okáxta (variant: **okáxtą**). V [reg. *kaa*-del.?, *o_(ká)xta*] *(trans.)* **pour or dump out (e.g., garbage)** (RBn; HW12).
•• LFD 309: *ní káxtą* <ni´-ga´xto^{n}> pour [water]. *ni áxtą* <ni´ a-xto^{n}> I pour water. *wakáxtą* <wa-ga´-xto^{n}> pour.

okíce (variant: **okíci**). V [reg. *ki*-ret., *o_kíce*] [*kik-* SUU + *océ* (but with unexpected *c* rather than *hc*)] *(trans.)* **look for or search for s.t. or s.o. lost or misplaced (often s.t. or s.o. belonging to oneself)** (FH). *ówakice* look for them. *ðíe okíca* look for it yourself (FH:4/25/96/tape:prod; 02/22/95/FH/pc:okc). *Mary apa iižįke óxpaðe apa ná háaški okíci apái* Mary's son is lost and she's looking everywhere for him (03/23/95/FH/pc). *ákahaamį okíca* look for your shawl (BE2.117).
•• JOD (slip file): *okíce* <u-ḳí-ṭṣe> to hunt, seek, or search for his own.
••• *QU okíhte* to look for one's own (RR); *OM ogine* look for one's own (RR).

okíce. V [conjug. unknown] [*ki-* DAT + *océ*] **look for or search for s.t. or s.o. for another.** [Possibly reg. *ki*-del. conjugation, but there are no examples available.]

okíhką. V [reg. *ki*-ret., *o_kíhką*] [*kik-* SUU + *óhką*] *(trans., intr.)* **help one's own (relative).** [Uninflected form is homophonous with dative form of this verb.] *wažážeíe ąwáðakihką hkǫ́bra* I want you to help me talk Osage (02/09/95/FH/pc:okc; FH:4/25/96/tape; RBn10-5:JW). *okíhkąpái* you all help him [a relative] out [and continue to do so] (02/09/95/FH/pc:okc). *táatą owáðakihką hkǫ́bra* I want you to help me with something (RBn22-02).

okíhką. V [reg., *o_kíhką*] [[*ki-* DAT + *ohką*] *(trans.)* **help another (who is not a relative).** [Uninflected form is homophonous with SUUS form of this verb.] *okíhkąpái* you all help him [not a relative] out [and continue to do so] (02/09/95/FH/pc:okc).

okíhkie. V [reg., *o_kíhkie*] [*kik-* SUU + *ohkíe*] *(trans., intr.)* **speak to one's own relative, family, or friends.**
•• LFD 169: *okíhkie* <u-gi´-ḳi-e> to speak [definition should include 'to a relative']. *owákihkie* <u-wa´-gi-ḳi-e> I spoke to a relative. *oðákihkie* <u-tha´-gi-ḳi-e> you spoke to a relative. *ąkókihkia pe* <o^{n}-gu´-gi-ḳi-a i>

we spoke to relatives; to speak to a friend or some relation.

okíkxą (variant of **okítxą**).

okínąązį. v [reg. (*ki*-ret.?), *o_kínąązį*] [*ki-* DAT + *onáązį*] *(trans.)* **follow (lit., 'stand next to another').** • ADJ **successive, following.**

•• LFD 169 (unconfirmed): *okínąžį* <u-gi´-no^n-zhi^n> to succeed (05/02/95/LS/pc:uk). *owákinąžį* <u-wa´-gi-no^n-zhi^n> I succeed. *oðákinąžį* <u-tha´-gi-no^n-zhi^n> you succeed. *ąkókínąžį pe* <o^n-gu´-gi´-no^n-zhi^n i> we succeed; to stand in the place of; to follow in order.

okípše. v [reg. *ki-ret., o_kípše*] [*kik-* SUU + *opšé*] *(trans.)* **follow one's own, be true to one's own, obey one's own.** *íe owákipše* I have followed their [my parents'] word. *íe ąkókipše hta ąkáðe* we will keep our word.

••• Cf. *íe okípše.*

okítxą (variant: **okíkxą**). v [reg. (*ki*-ret.?), *o_kítxą*] [*kik-* SUU + *otxą́*] *(trans.)* **put on one's own pants or shoes.** *oðíkinąąži okíkxą* put on your pants (RBn10-12:JW).

ókohpa. v [conjug. unknown] *(intr., trans.)* **vomit, regurgitate, or throw up due to overeating or being too full** (PM/pc; 04/26/95/FH/pc:ok). [Possibly based on a borrowed word and partially influenced in form by the semantically similar word *okúhpu.*]

••• Cf. *ókahpo.*

okšéhtą. v [reg., *o_kšéhtą*] *(trans.)* **gain, earn, come into possession of, obtain.** • N **salary, earnings, gain, winnings.**

•• LFD 272: *okšéhtą* <u-kshe´-ṭo^n> gain. LFD 173: *okšétą* <u-kshe´-ṭo^n> wages, pay, salary, compensation, earnings, income. *okšéhtą* <u-kshe´-ṭo^n> to obtain, come into possession of, win, gain, earn.

okúhpu (variants: **oküxhpü, ókuhpi, okúhpe**). v, ADJ [stat., *o_kúhpu*] *(trans.)* **(be) full of, have a fullness of, be filled with (as the stomach is full; said of a person); be full, be flooded (e.g., a creek filled to capacity).** *įįštá níi ąwą́kuhpe* my eyes are full of tears (FH/09/21/01/pc). *įįštá níi oðíkuhpe* your eyes are full of tears (FH/09/21/01/pc). *kaxé akxa okúhpu akxai* the creek is full (flooded) (RB; 04/26/95/LS/pc:ok; FH/09/21/01/pc:ok). • N **full amount; houseful** (LS; RBN1-29). *okúhpu kaaγé* fill it up (lit., 'make it the full amount') (04/26/95/LS/pc:okc). *okúhpu ąwą́žu* fill it up for me (lit., 'pour the full amount for me') (04/26/95/LS/pc:okc; BE2.51).

•• RB: <o-kyú-pu>.

•• LFD 170: *okíhpi* <u-gi´-p̣i> full, will contain no more, replete. LFD 77: *įštá ni ąwąkihpi* <i^n-shta´ ni o^n-wo^n-gi-p̣i> my eyes are full of water.

••• *KS ogíppi* full, filled (RR); *OM* same as Osage (LFD 170).

••• Cf. *ókahpo, ókohpa.*

ókxaži (variant of **ókxąži**).

okxą́ (variant: **otkxą́**). PRON, ADJ [*ó-* LOC + *txą*] **next, following, the following one** (01/11/95/FH/pc).

••• *KS owákhą* next of kin (RR), *owákkihą́he* succession of, one after another, descendants (RR).

okxą́ (variant of **otxą́**).

ókxąkxą (variant of **ótxątxą**).

ókxąži (variants: **ókxaži, ótkxąži**). v, ADJ [*otxą́* + *ažį́*] [uninfl.] *(intr.)* **(be) slow, slow about catching up, always late, never on time** (04/19/95/FH/pc:ok:tk). *hpáze wanǫ́bre ónǫbre ðúwį ókxąži ąhé* I was slow buying groceries for supper (03/10/95/MREI/pc:okc; BE2.123). *hpáze wanǫ́bre ówe brúwį ótkxąži ąhé* I was slow buying groceries for supper (04/19/95/FH/pc:ok).

ókˀą (variant: **okˀą́**). v [uninfl.] *(intr.)* **put on a program, hold an event, have a "doings"** (FH:prod). *ókˀą hta apa* they're going to have a program. *ókˀą hta ąkai tą háachi niižú ną ąpai* when we're going to have something, it always rains. *ókˀą ąkǫ́ða tą háachi niižú nąpe* whenever we want to have something, it always rains (FH). • *(trans.)* **act like.** *įįštáxį ókˀą akxai* he's acting like a white man (03/16/95/JS/pc:ok). • N **act, deed, ways, custom, personality, personal characteristics** (03/16/95/JS/pc:ok). *ókˀą tąhe* he has good ways (FH:prod). *ókˀą ðáalį* good ways, cheerful, easy to get along with (03/16/95/JS/pc:ok). *ókˀą hpííži* bad ways, bad tempered, hard to get along with (03/16/95/JS/pc:okc). *cˀéka ókˀą ée įká* don't try any funny stuff, don't act the fool. *Ed apa ókˀą ðáalįpe* Ed has good ways (03/16/95/JS/pc:okc; BE2.152). *wažáže okˀą́ oxpáðape* Osage ways are all gone (lit., 'Osage ways got lost') (05/01/95/LS/pc).

•• LFD 121: *ókˀą* <o´-ḳ'o^n> habit, a tendency to follow certain inclinations continuously. *ókˀą ðálį pia* <o´ḳ'o^n tha´-gthi^n bia> [*pia* unconfirmed (FH: *pe*, not *pia*)] he has good manners. LFD 172: *ókˀą* <u´-ḳ'o^n> custom, rite, ceremony. *ókˀą tąhe* <u´-ḳ'o^n do^n-he> kindly disposition.

ókˀą axópe. N , VP *(trans.)* **respect (lit., 'honor by acts')** (01/06/95/FH/pc:ok). [Position of accent recorded as different from *áxope* 'honor'.]

ókˀą axópe (*continued*)

•• LFD 172: *ókˀą axope* <u´-ḳ'o^{n} a-xo-be> proper respect for things sacred.

ókˀą ðaalį. ADJP **likable; having good ways, manners, and thoughts; cheerful.** *ókˀą ðáalį hkí[ð]a* have good ways (FH:prod). • NP **good manners, good thoughts.**

•• LFD 172: *ókˀąðalį* <u´-ḳ'o^{n}-tha-gthi^{n}> meek, lovable, a likable disposition.

ókˀą ekǫ́ži. ADJP, ADVP, N **wrongful, wrongly, inappropriate, inappropriate action** (FH:6/25/01/pc:ok; LR:pc/ok).

•• LFD 173: *okˀą ekǫži* <u-ḳ'o^{n} e-go^{n}-zhi> wrongful, wrongly. Any act that is contrary or does not conform to custom.

ókˀą éži. VP [conjug. unknown] **be wrongheaded, act unsuitably.** *ókˀǫ éži ðíepe* he's confused (FH/09/24/01/pc/prod). • N **wrongful acts or bad deeds (such as bad talk or theft).**

ókˀą hpíiži. ADJP **having bad manners or ways, ill-mannered (lit., 'bad ways'), unruly** (FH; BE2.27); **cross, high-tempered, cranky, having a bad disposition, sullen, morose.**

•• LFD 173: *ókˀąhpiži* <u´-ḳ'o^{n}-p̣i-zhi> cruel, wicked, unruly, person with a bad disposition, sullen, morose.

ókˀą wanąðaži. N **perplexity.** [Unconfirmed; possibly an Omaha expression, not Osage.]

•• LFD 121: *ókˀą wanąða ži* <o´-ḳ'o^{n} wa-no^{n}-tha zhi> perplexity, bewilderment (01/06/95/FH/pc:uk; FH:6/25/01/pc, no, LR; no).

ókˀąštą. N [*ókˀą* + *štą*] **busybody (refers to s.o. who is into everything).**

okˀó (variant: **okˀóce**). N [*ó-* LOC + *kˀó*] **hole.** *sį́ice okˀó ce oolą́ą* put your tail in the hole (RBn16-02). *céɣenii okˀóce akxa* the drum has a hole in it (RBn10-21/JW&FW/77). *céɣenii okˀóce ahí akxa* the drum has a hole in it (04/25/95/PM/pc:ok).

okˀǫ́he. V [reg.?, *o_kˀǫ́he*?] [*ó-* LOC + *kˀǫ́he*] *(trans.)* **insert, put into, sheathe, place into, put.** [Implies 'lifting up and putting in', as a baby into a crib or onto a baby board or blankets into a box (FH).] *hpáažį okˀǫ́ha* put the baby on the board (RBn2-MOJ/p30; 04/17/95/LS/pc:ok).

•• LFD 173: *okˀǫhe* <u-ḳ'o^{n}´-he> to sheathe, to place in a scabbard. LFD 179: *oðókˀǫhe* <u-thu´-ḳ'o^{n}-he> to put a horizontal object into a receptacle for another person [not 'for another person']. LFD 66: *hą́nąhpaze okˀǫhe* <ho^{n}´-no^{n}-p̣a-çe u-ḳ'o^{n}-he> to imprison, imprisonment, to place in confinement (02/13/95/FH/pc:okc).

okˀú. V [reg., *o_kˀú*] [apparently *ó-* LOC + *kˀú*] *(trans.)* **lend.** *mą́zeska tóe ąwákˀu* lend me some money (02/15/95/FH/pc:okc; BE2.78). *hcíoka wį ðáalį ówakˀupe* they lent us a nice room (RBn23-14). *waléze toa ąwą́ðakˀu na* these are the books that you loaned me (MSB/ 2/10/83). *áwakˀu* I loaned it to them; I fed them (MSB 2-25-83). • **give, provide, furnish, supply.**

•• LFD 171: *okˀí* <u-ḳ'i´> to lend. *owákˀi* <u-wa´-ḳ'i> I lend. *oðákˀi* <u-tha´-ḳ'i> you lend. *ąkókˀi pe* <o^{n}-gu´-ḳ'i i> we lend. *mąhį spe wihta hpisi owakˀi* <mo^{n}-hi^{n} çpe wi-ṭa p̣i-çi u-wa-ḳ'i> I loaned my ax to Pi-çi. [Vowel *i* rather than *u* in this stem (*okˀí*, etc., seen in LF's examples) is unacceptable to Mod. Os. speakers.]

ókˀu. V [reg. *ó_kˀu*] [*wa-* VAL + *okˀú*] *(trans.)* **give, provide, furnish, give stuff to s.o.** *ókˀupe* it was given (lit., 'they gave it to some folks'; with a nonspecific actor on an active verb in Mod. Os., the gloss is often English passive). *ówakˀupe* it was given to us (lit., 'they gave some things to us'). • **feed.** *hkáwa owákˀu* I fed the horse (01/24/95/FH/pc:okc; BE2.46; 01/24/95/FH/pc:prod). *šǫ́ke ókˀu mąðį́* go feed the dog (RB). *waxpéį ąkái, ókˀu ąðúucˀake še nąąhtąhtąą oðúucˀake wį́* we're too poor to feed that lazy donkey (RBn10-2:MJ/79). *áwakˀu* I fed them (2-25-83). • N **giving, giveaway, event of giving or giving away.**

oláha (variant of **oðáha**).

ólaži (variant of **óðąži**).

ólą (variants: **óolą, olǫ́ǫ, ódla** [rare]). ADJ, V [reg., *ó_lą*] [*ó-* LOC + *lą́*] **pout, sulk; sulky.** *owálą mįkšé* I'm pouting (MSB 03/83; 04/18/95/FH/pc:OK?). *óðalą nįkšé* you're pouting (MSB).

olé (variant: **ohlé**). V [reg., *o_lé*] *(trans.)* **chase, chase away, run off.** *cˀáiži, wakˀóžį apa olé apai* the old man and old woman chased him (RBn10-2:MOJ/79). *owále* I ran him off, chased him away (BE2.18; CQc 'them' changed to 'him').

•• RB: <o-hléh> (01/09/95/FH/pc:ok).

•• LFD 182: *olé* <u-xthe´> to overtake. *oðále* <u-tha´-xthe> you overtake.

olį́į. V [reg., *o_lį́į*] [*ó-* LOC + *lį́į*] *(trans.)* **sit in, occupy (a seat), be seated on, sit down on, take a seat on.** *hówąįki oálįį škǫ́šta?* where do you want me to sit? (RBn10-4:MOJ/79). *hową́įki oðálįį škǫ́šta?* where do you want to sit? (02/16/95/FH/pc:prod orig). *háši olį́į* sit in the back, sit in a certain place, as at a peyote meeting (03/10/95/PM/pc:ok; BE2.119;

03/08/95/MREI/pc:ok). • **ride, ride in.** *oðíhtą žúuce žį́ ðiitą́ owálįį hkǫ́brai* I want to ride in your little red wagon (RBn10-3:MOJ/79). *oðíhtą olį́į* ride in a car (RBn19-01). *oðíhtą olį́į hta apái* they're going in a car (01/09/95/FH/pc:ok). *pacíolįį ąkái hta ąkái* [*pacé olį́į ąkáðe hta ąkáðe*] we are going boating (01/07/95/FH/pc:ok; BE2.9). • **live in or at, dwell in, inhabit, live within metaphorically (e.g., a person's heart).** *túlsa htą́wą owálįį* I live in Tulsa (02/16/95/FH/pc:okc). *howáįki oðálįį?* where do you live? (02/16/95/FH/pc:okc). *níi žópše pšíe ðáha, táatą wį́ mąžą́ olį́į iiðáðe* when I would go to wade in the river, I saw something that was in the woods (lit., 'when I went to wade in the water, I saw a thing that lived in the countryside') (t24b-p17/num4CQ119; 04/27/95/FH/pc:okc, added *iiðáðe*). *ðą́ące oálįį* he lives within my heart (04/04/99/FH/pc). *howáįki olį́į?* where does he live? (02/16/95/FH/pc:okc).

•• LFD 170: *ólį* <u´-thi^{n}> to occupy a seat.

••• Cf. *álįį*.

olǫ́ǫ (variant of **ólą**).

ómahka (variant of **ómąhka**).

omáįhka (variant of **omą́įhka**).

omą́ðį (variants: **omą́į, omę́į**). v [reg.+sync. *o_mą́_ðį*] [*ó-* LOC + *mąðį́*] *(intr.)* **live.** *oámabrį* I live. *oðámąšcį* you live. *kaahúužą mą́žą ðéka omą́įpe* he lived on this earth a long time (RBn10-13:JW). *kaahúužą mą́žą ðéka omą́į apai* he lived on this earth a long time ago (RBn10-13:FH). *wéewina mǫ́žǫ ðé škaškáða oámąbrį* I want to thank you for this good life [that I live] (RBn10-10:JW). • *(trans.)* **walk in, be in, among, or throughout an area or a group of people.** *ožą́ke omą́ðį apai* they're walking in the road (RBn 5/3/79; corrected; FH:5/01/96/tape:prod). • *(intr.)* **be active within (as a substance within a body).** *šée mįkšé, wanǫ́bre akxa omę́į mįkšé* I'm just sitting there, that peyote is working in me (RBn10-6:JW; CQc). *omą́ði apa* (PM: it's [that whiskey is] in him, he's got a little in him [equivalent to 'he's drunk', describing a state equally as drunk as *lǫðį*]).

••• Cf. *omą́įžį, taaké omą́ðį.*

ómąðį. v [reg.+sync., *ó_mą_ðį*] [*wa-* VAL + *omą́ðį*] *(intr.)* **walk among folks, live among others.**

omą́hą. N, ADJ **Omaha (tribe or tribal member)** (BE2.9; 03/08/95/PM/pc).

•• JOD (slip file): *omą́hą* <U-ma^{n}´-ha^{n}> an Omaha, the Omaha.

•• LFD 300, 173: *omą́hą* <U-mo^{n}´-ho^{n}> Omaha, Nebr., the Osage name for Omaha (03/02/95/FH/pc:ok).

••• *KS ǫmǫ́hǫ* Omaha tribe, those who went upstream (RR).

ómąhka (variant: **ómahka**). ADJ **easy, cheap, inexpensive** (RB; 12/30/94/FH/pc). *ómahka apa ahṹ apái* cheap things are coming (FH). *haxį ómąhka káaγi akxai* he made the blankets cheap in value (RBn22-17; BE2.38). *ómąhka xcį́* it's easy (RBn10-18). *táatą ómahką ecíepe éetana ostówe aðíi apai* a whole line of people are running because there's something cheap [*aðíi* from *aðée*] (FHt128).

•• LFD 174: *ómąhka* <u´-mo^{n}-ķa> easy, not difficult.

omą́į (variant of **omą́ðį**).

omą́įhka (variant: **omáįhka**). N **year.** *omą́įhka hcéka* new year (HH/14-A/308; 03/24/95/PM/pc:prod; BE2.162; FH/09/24/01/pc:hk).

•• LFD 173: *omą́įhka* <u-mo^{n}´-i^{n}-ķa> a year (03/24/95/PM/pc:ok). *omą́įhka wį* <u-mo^{n}´-i^{n}-ķa wi^{n}> one year. *omą́įhka satxą* <u-mo^{n}´-i^{n}-ķa ça-to^{n}> [expected Mod. Os. form: *omą́įhka sáhtą*; <ça-to^{n}> is an error for <ça-ţo^{n}>, Mod. Os. *sáhtą*] five years.

omą́įhka háaną (variant: **omáįhka háaną**). INTERR/INDEF NP **how old?** *omáįhka háaną nįkšé?* how old are you? (RBn2-MOJ/p40; 03/02/95/FH/pc:ok). *omą́įhka háaną ðaašé?* how old are you? (02/09/95/FH/pc:ok).

omą́įhka hcéka (variant: **omáįhka hcéka**). N **January** (HH/14-a/249ff); **new year.**

omą́įhka lébrą híeną. N **decade** (LF).

•• LFD 173: *omą́ihka lebrą hieną* <u-mo^{n}´-i-ķa gthe-btho^{n} hie-no^{n}> a period of ten years.

omą́įhka wį hieną. ADVP **annually (lit., 'one year arrives').**

•• LFD 174 (unconfirmed): *omą́įhka wį hieną* <u-mo^{n}´-i^{n}-ķa wi^{n} hi e-no^{n}> yearly.

omą́įžį. V, ADJ [uninfl.] [*omą́ðį* + *-žį* 'little'] *(intr.)* **(be) very active within (as a substance is active within a person's body, such as when alcohol causes drunkenness)** (01/20/95/PM/pc). [Said to be synonymous with *lǫ́ðį*.]

•• RB: <o-máh-i^{n}-zhi^{n}>.

omę́į (variant of **omą́ðį**).

omíže (variant: **omį́že**). N **blanket, quilt, bedclothes, bedding; rug, carpet** (01/07/95/FH/pc:ok; RBn2-MOJ/p3; RBn2-02). [Takes 'sitting' positional article *į́kšé*.] *omíže*

omíže (*continued*) *aðúsu* cover her with a blanket (01/07/95/FH/pc:ma; 04/07/95/PM/pc:uk; 04/07/95/LS/pc:uk,ma; BE2.9). *omíže ąkšixa* fix my bedclothes (RBn12-08). *žįkáži apa taaðúhpiižipe, omíže ðuhpíižipi įkše* children are destructive, they have ruined the rug (lit., 'children are destructive, the rug is sitting there ruined') (01/20/95/FH/pc:ok; BE2.30; 04/07/95/LS/pc:ok; BE2.9). • **mattress, pallet** (01/07/95/FH/pc:ok).

•• LFD 173: *omíže* <U-mi´-zhe> Bedding (personal name), refers to the buffalo hide used for bedding <u-mi´-zhe> mattress, bedding, pallet, carpet.

onáaži (variant of **oną́ąžį**).

ónalį (variants: **ónaxlį** [rare, archaic], **óną le, ónahlį**). V [conjug. unknown] **hurry up!** (FH). [Historically *óną xðį*; Proto-Siouan **xð > hl > l* in Osage.] *ónalįpi, mį́įðohta ahíe akxái* hurry up you all, it's time (02/13/95/FH/t141/pc:prod orig). *ónalįpi, pá húðe ðąąchí akxái* hurry up you all, it's about to snow (02/13/95/FH/pc:prod orig; FH:4/25/96/tape; BE2.70).

•• LFD 122: *ónąlį ðe wakaye* <o´-no^{n}-xthi^{n} the wa-ga-xe> to dispatch, to send them [messengers] in a hurry. *ónąlį ðe wahpaye* <o´-no^{n}-xthi^{n} the wa-p̣a-xe> I dispatched [them] (02/13/95/FH/pc:ma). *ónąlį ðe waškaye* <o´-no^{n}-xthi^{n} the wa-shka-xe> you dispatch [them] (02/13/95/FH/pc:ma). *ónąlį ðe ąwakaya pe* <o´-no^{n}-xthi^{n} the o^{n}-wa-ga-xa i> we dispatch [them] (02/13/95/FH/pc:ma). LFD 174: *ónąlį* <u´-no^{n}-xthi^{n}> to make haste, to hurry. *ónąlį kaye* <u´-no^{n}-xthi^{n} ga-xe> to expedite, to hasten. *ónąlį xci* <u´-no^{n}-xthi^{n} xtsi> hastily, speedily.

ónaxlį (variant of **ónalį**).

oną́ąžį (variant: **onáaži**). V [reg. *o_ną́ąžį*] [*ó-* LOC + *nąąžį́*] *(trans.)* **wear or put on (footwear or clothing)** (RB). *hǫǫpé onáaži* put your shoes on (PM:prod). *ðée onáaži* here, put it/them on; get into these (PM). • *(intr.)* **stand in there, get in or stay in there, as in a room or place** (03/22/95/PM/pc). *ðée onáažį!* stay there! (as in your room) (PM). • *(trans.)* **attend.** *taapóskahci oną́ąžį* attending school.

óną kˀǫ. V [reg., *ó_ną kˀǫ*] [*wa-* VAL + *ó-* + *ną kˀǫ́*] *(intr.)* **hear a rumor, have foreknowledge of an event.** *óðanąkˀǫ́?* did you hear that? (04/20/95/LS/pc:ok). *óðanąkˀǫ?* did somebody else tell you about this? (referring to an event that is happening, such as a knock on the door) (04/20/95/LS/pc:prod; 01/04/95/FH/pc:ok). *owáðanąkˀǫ́?* have you heard [about them]? (01/04/95/FH/pc:prod). • N **rumor, s.t. heard about** (01/04/95/FH/pc:ok; 05/01/95/LS/pc:ok).

•• LFD 174: *oną́kˀǫ* <u-no^{n}´-ḳ'o^{n}> a rumor. *oðake wį aną́kˀǫ* <u-tha-ge wi^{n} a-no^{n}´-ḳ'o^{n}> I heard a rumor. *oðake wį ðaną́kˀǫ* <u-tha-ge wi^{n} tha-no^{n}´-ḳ'o^{n}> you heard a rumor. *oðake wį ąną́kˀǫ pe* <u-tha-ge wi^{n} o^{n}-no^{n}´-ḳ'o^{n} i> we heard a rumor, a report, hearsay.

oní ðįké (variant: **onį́ke**). VP **be quiet, not make noise, no sound!** (04/18/95/FH/pc). *onį́ įká, awáata hta akxą́he* be quiet, I'm going to pray. *onį́ įka!* don't make noises! (RBn11-02/JW&FW&HHsk/c.1976).

ónie. V [conjug. unknown] *(intr.)* **breathe, draw breath** (PM:prod). • N **sound** (RBn22-01, unconfirmed).

•• LFD 174: *óni ožą́ke* <u´-ni-u-zho^{n}-ge> road for the breath, the windpipe, air passage for breathing (lit., 'breathing path') (PM: *ónie* 'breathe', 04/14/95/PM/pc:ok).

ónihkaši. N [apparently *ó-* LOC + *níhkašie* (or *níhkašika* 'live'?)] **place or condition of being saved (in the Christian religious sense), fulfillment as a person, culmination of living.** *ónihkaši ší tą, wašč íhtą tą* when you are a saved person, when your work [on earth] is done (lit., 'when you've arrived there at fulfillment, when you've done work') (RBn12-10/MJ).

oníhkašie (variant: **oníhkaši**). N [apparently *ó-* LOC + *níhkašie* (or *níhkašika* 'live'?)] **life.** *oníhkašie ðáalį waðakšíye iche* you made this good life for us (RBn10-12:JW). *įhtáci wahkǫ́ta, oníhkaši haakǫ ðáalį wakšíapi* our father God, how good you have made our lives (RBn).

ónihkašika. V [conjug. unknown] [apparently *ó-* LOC + *níhkašika* 'live'] *(intr.)* **have or lead a life, live life.** *ónihkašika ðáalį* lead a good life.

ónihkie. V [reg.?, *ónihki_[ð]e?*] *(intr.)* **get well or be healed, be free at last from illness (phrase often used in a funeral service)** (01/04/95/FH/pc:ok; RBn2-MOJ/p14). *oníhkie akxai* he's free at last (said of the deceased who suffered from illness) (RBn23-20).

oníži (variant of **onį́žį**).

onį́ke (variant of **oní ðįké**).

onį́žį (variants: **onį́ži, oníži**). V [reg., *o_nį́žį*] *(intr., trans.)* **be afraid or feel fearful (owing to an indefinite or nonspecific stimulus, such as darkness, being alone, catching a cold, flying, pain in general)** (FH). [Contrast *nǫ́ǫhpe*, said to be used for fear of a specific storm that is occurring; e.g., *šǫ́ke nǫ́ǫahpe* 'I'm afraid of that dog' vs. *šǫ́ke owánįži* 'I'm afraid of dogs'.] *owánįžį* I'm afraid (12/30/94/FH/pc:prod). *owánįži ąži žįkážį apa kíðalį nǫpe* I'm feeling fearful, but the children enjoy it. *íhaa che owánįži* I'm afraid of his mouth [his gossiping about me] (FH/11/18/01/pc:prod). *síʔ aníe owánįži* I'm afraid of my feet hurting (FH/11/18/01/pc:prod). *kį́į owánįži* I'm afraid of flying (FH/11/18/01/pc:prod). *šǫ́ke owánįži mįkšé* I'm afraid of dogs (FH/11/18/01/pc). *oðánįžį nįkšé?* are you afraid? (12/30/94/FH:pc). *ąkónįžį* we're not afraid (RB).

•• LFD 174: *oníží* <u-ni´-zhi^{n}> the fear of darkness, a coward, craven, timid. [This verb in fact does not imply 'darkness' specifically.] *owánižį* <u-wa´-ni-zhi^{n}> I fear darkness. *oðánižį* <u-tha´-ni-zhi^{n}> you fear darkness. *ąkónižį pe* <o^{n}-gu´-ni-zhi^{n} i> we fear darkness. *hta apa onižį ną pe* <ṭa a-ba u-ni-zhi^{n} no^{n} bi a> the deer is timid. *onížį paži* <u-ni´-zhi^{n} ba-zhi> not afraid of darkness. *owánižį mąži* <u-wa´-ni-zhi^{n} mo^{n}-zhi> I am not afraid of darkness. *oðáni ží aži* <u-tha´-ni zhi´ a-zhi> you are not afraid of darkness. *ąkónižį paži pe* <u^{n}-gu´-ni-zhi^{n} ba-zhi i> we are not afraid of darkness.

ónǫ. N [apparently *ó-* LOC + *nǫ́ǫ*] **old age.** *ónǫ kši pšíe ðe* I'm old, I've arrived at old age (FH/6/16/96). *ónǫ ahí akxai* he or she has reached old age (RBn10-6:JW). *ónǫ kši ąkáhi aðį́kše* we [two] are old (FH:prod).

ónǫ ahí. VP **get old (lit., 'arrive at old age').** *koe ónǫ žišǫ ší tą ší tą koe hpíiži žišǫ ší tą koe péeški ðikǫ́ða htai wáščuye ðáalį* before you get old and before you get fat and ugly and nobody wants you, you should get married (RB).

•• LFD 114: *nǫhí* <no^{n}-hi´> senility (unconfirmed; 03/02/95/FH/pc:uk). *nǫhí* <no^{n}-hi´> reaches mature age.

••• Cf. *nǫ́ǫ ahí.*

ónǫbre. N **food, groceries, rations.** *ónǫbre ážupi* serve the food (01/30/95/FH/pc:ok). *ónǫbre húu ážupi ché* there is lots of food set out (01/30/95/FH/pc:produced corrected). *ónǫbre húu oohǫ́pi ché* they cooked many foods, a lot of food (BE2.50; 01/30/95/FH/pc:ok). *hpáze wanǫ́bre ónǫbre ðúwį ókxąži ąhé* I was slow buying groceries for supper (03/10/95/MREI/pc:okc; BE2.123). • **meal, dinner.** *Carolyn ónǫbre che oðówe kǫ́ða apai* they want Carolyn to oversee this dinner (FH:prod).

•• LFD 174: *ónǫbre* <u´-no^{n}-bthe> a grocery.

••• Cf. *wanǫ́bre.*

ónǫbréoožú (variant of **wánǫbréoožú**).

oochí (variant of **ochí**).

óochiže (variant: **oochíže**). V, ADJ [reg., *óo_chiže*, but sometimes stative in 2nd sg.] *(intr.)* **(be) loud or noisy** (03/05/95/JS/pc:ok; RBn22-06; FH/11/17/01/pc; 04/14/95/PM/pc). *ooáchiže* I am noisy. *ooðáchiže, ooðíchiže* you are noisy. *káa įkše óochiže* this is too noisy (speaking of a television) (03/15/95/PM/pc:ok; BE2.133; 02/27/95/FH/pc:ok; BE2.9). *htáhtáze óochižape* grasshoppers are noisy (RBn3-55; 02/27/95/FH/pc:ok). • **(be) talkative in excess, talk too much.** *káa įkše óochiže* this one talks too much (03/15/95/PM/pc). *ðée akxa óochiže* this one talks too much (03/05/95/JS/pc). • N **noise, disturbance, rumpus, turbulence** (FH/11/17/01/pc). *óochiže škáaye* you're noisy (lit., 'you are making noise') (FH). *wáli óochiže škáaye, ąkóhkihkie ąðúucʔake* you're making too much noise, we can't even converse (02/27/95/FH/pc; BE2.94).

•• LFD 180: *óchiže* <u´-tsi-zhe> a row, an uproar, a rumpus; a fracas, riot, disorder, a fray. *óchiže kaye* <u´-tsi-zhe ga-xe> a riot, uproar, tumult [expected gloss: '*cause* an uproar, a tumult,' etc.] (02/27/95/FH/pc:ok). *óchi ži kaye štą* <u´-tsi zhi ga-xe shto^{n}> [expected Mod. Os. form: *óochiže káaye štą* 'always making noise'] riotous, noisy, turbulent. LFD 166: *óčiže* <u´-chi-zhe> [expected Mod. Os. form: *óchiže*, not *óčiže*] disturbance. *owáčiže* <u-wa´-chi-zhe> [expected Mod. Os. form: *óachiže*] I caused a disturbance. *óðičiže* <u´-thi-chi-zhe> [expected Mod. Os. form: *óðichiže*] you caused a disturbance.

óoðąąži (variant of **óðąži**).

óohkihą (variants: **óohkiha, óohkihǫǫ**), V [reg., *óo_hkihą*] [*hkik-* REFL + *óohǫ*] *(intr.)* **cook for oneself** (01/11/95/FH/pc:prod, PM; LS). *hpáata wį oowáhkiha* I cooked myself an egg (RBn22-17). *hpáata wį óohkihą* cook yourself an egg (RBn22-17). • **take care of a meal when asked to do so, put on a feast** (01/11/95/FH/pc:prod; RBn1-41). *óohkiha hta apai* they're going to have a feast (BE2.24; RBn22-17) • **boss, oversee an event (e.g., a naming)** (FH/06/28/01/pc).

•• LFD 172: *ohkíhą* <u-ḳi´ - ho^{n}> to cook something for oneself (LS:ok). *owáhkihą* <u-wa´-ḳi-ho^{n}> I cooked for myself (01/11/95/FH/pc:ok). *oðáhkihą* <u-tha´-ḳi-ho^{n}> you cooked for yourself. *ąkóhkihą pe* <o^{n}-gu´-ḳi-

óohkihą (*continued*)
ho^{n} i> we cooked for ourselves (01/14/95/FH/pc:ok).

oohláaži (variant of **oolą́ąži**).

oohǫ́. V [reg., *oo_hǫ́*] *(trans.)* **cook, prepare (e.g., food).** *ooáhą, ooáha, oowáhą, oowáha* I prepare it. *ooðáhą, ooðáha* you prepare it. *oohǫ́* he prepares it. *ąkóohǫ* we prepare it. *oohǫ́ bríištą* I'm finished cooking (01/12/95/FH/pc:ok). *htáaliko owáhą* I cooked some meat gravy (01/12/95/FH/pc:ok). *súhka háaną ooðáhą ðatxą́šé?* how many chickens are you cooking? (01/12/95/FH/pc:okc). *tóopa oowáhą atxą́he* I am cooking four (01/12/95/FH/pc:ok). *súhkahtą htaaníi oohǫ́ ðáalį káayapi ché* they cooked the turkey soup well (lit., 'cooking the turkey soup they did it well') (01/12/95/FH/pc:okc). *óngbre huukǫ́į oohǫ́pi che* they cooked many foods, a lot of food (01/12/95/FH/pc:ok, prod). *óngbre oohǫ́ ðáalį káaya iché* the food was cooked well (lit., 'cooking the food, they did it well'). *oohǫ́ hpíǫpe* she is a good cook (lit., 'she knows how to cook') (01/14/95/FH/pc:ok; BE2.23). *oowáhai* I cooked it. *ooðáhai* you cooked it (MSB 2-24-83). *ąkóohǫ [ąð] įkšé* we [two] cooked it. *ąkóohǫpe* we [pl.] cooked it. *htóožu ąkóohǫ hta ąkái* we [pl.] are going to cook some meat.
••• Cf. *óohǫ*.

oohǫ́ (variant: **óohǫ** [MSB]). N **cook, person who cooks** (FH/07/09/01/pc). *oohǫ́ akxa tooská ðįké akxa áa akxái* the cook says there are no potatoes (01/12/95/FH/pc:prod).

óohǫ. V [reg., *óo_hǫ*] [*wa-* VAL + *oohǫ́*] *(intr.)* **cook things, cook stuff.** *óohǫ ąwą́ąxta* I love to cook (FH). *wáli táahkaci akxái, óohǫ hkǫ́bra įké* it's hot, I don't want to cook (01/12/95/FH/pc:okc; BE2.24). • N **cooking pot.** *óohǫ ootáapi apai* they're borrowing the pot (04/13/95/FH/pc:ok).
•• LFD 170: *óhǫ* <u´-ho^{n}> to cook. *owáhą* <u-wa´-ho^{n}> I am cooking. *oðáhą* <u-tha´-ho^{n}> you are cooking. *ą́kohǫ pe* <o^{n}´-gu-ho^{n} i> we are cooking, the act of cooking, to cook by boiling or stewing.

óohǫ hcí (variant of **oohǫ́hci**).

óohǫ owáwakʔu. N [*óohǫ* + *wa-* VAL + *wa-* VAL + *ókʔu*] **waiter, waitress (lit., 'one who feeds cooked things [over and over?] to folks').**

óohǫ saakí. N **dried corn (lit., 'hard cooking': dehydrated corn made by boiling ears of corn lightly then drying the kernels in the sun for approximately three days).**

oohǫ́hci (variant: **óohǫ hcí**). N [*oohǫ́* (or *óohǫ*) + *hcí*] **kitchen, cookhouse.** *oohǫ́hci ðuuwásu* clean the kitchen (02/14/95/FH/pc; BE2.74).
•• RB: <ó-ho^{n}-tsi>.
•• LFD 170: *óhǫ hci* <u´-ho^{n} ṭsi> kitchen.

ooláaži (variant of **oolą́ąži**).

oolą́. V [reg., *oo_lą́*] *(trans.)* **put into, place inside of, pour round items into (e.g., fruit into pies), add items to cooking, pour liquid into.** *mą́zeska ooðálą?* have you put your money in? *mį́įhtoeli oolą́ akxa* he's chewing gum (lit., 'he has put gum in') (RBn14-03; HRE/12/29/01/pc:ok). *paazénii wéli pąąšcéka oolą́* put cream on your strawberries. *hpáatažį oðópše oolą́* put the baby in (the baby board). *níi tóe oolą́* add water to it (e.g., the soup) (FH; LS). *kašpéǫpa oolą́* put your 25 cents in. *htáaoolą* sandwich (lit., 'meat-put-inside'). *hkąącóolą lébra oðíhtą ci oolą́ akxa* there are ten pies sitting in the car (lit., 'they have placed ten pies in the car').
•• JOD (slip file): *olą́* <u-k-¢a^{n}´> to put a cv. ob [i.e., curved object], paper, book, piece of cloth, etc., in a receptacle.
••• Cf. *hkąącóolą*.

oolą́ (variant of **oolą́ke**).

óolą (variant of **ólą**).

oolą́ąži (variants: **ooláaži, ohláaži, oohláaži**). V [reg., *oo_lą́ąži*] [*oolą́* + *aží* NEG] *(trans.)* **do (s.t.) not quite right, do imperfectly, make a poor performance of or fail at.** *oowáhlą mažį́* I don't quite do it perfectly; I can't make it, I can't succeed [at it] (03/05/95/JS/pc:ok). *céyenii ochį́ ooláaži káayape* he didn't hit drum quite right (not up to par) (01/20/95/PM/pc:ok). • V, ADJ *(intr.)* **fall short, fail, miss the mark; (be) not up to par, inferior, poor, subpar, inadequate.** *hóo ðáalį aščį ažį́ ąži oohláaži ašččįe* they think you have a good voice, but it isn't right (lit., 'you have a good voice, you think, but you have it not up to par'). *mį́į táahkace oolą́ąži įkši aape éhta pąąščéka cúuce oolą́ąži apa aapé* the sun had not been warm enough to make the strawberries ripe (lit., 'sun warming fell short, they said, therefore strawberries ripening failed, they said'] (RBn18-02). *ąkóolaaži eekǫ́ ąkái* we fall short, being as we are (BE2.43).
•• LFD 182: *oláži* <u-xtha´-zhi> secondary, of less importance, inferior; fail. *owálamąži* <u-wa´-xtha-mo^{n}-zhi> I failed to beat in the race. *oðála aži* <u-tha´-xtha a-zhi> you failed to beat in the race.

oolą́ke. V [reg., *oo_lą́ke*] [probably contains *oolą́*] *(trans.)* **wear on the head, put on the head, don as a hat.** *óoląke oolą́ka* put on your hat (03/22/95/PM/pc:okc; RBn10-12:JW). • ADJ **with the head covered.**

óoląke. N [*wa-* VAL + *oolą́ke*] **hat, head cover, item worn on the head** (RBn1-20). *óoląke sápe še ðíhta?* is that your black hat? (01/04/95/FH/pc:ok; BE2.64).

•• RB: <ó-lu^{n}-keh>.

•• LFD 120: *óląke* <o´-gtho^{n}-ge> a hat, a cap. LFD 170: *óląke* <u´-gtho^{n}-ge> hat. "This article of wearing apparel was not known to the Osage until introduced by the traders."

óošechia, óošechie (variants of **hóšechie**).

óošechiðe (variant of **óšechiðe**).

ootá (variant: **ootą́** [perhaps also **oðóta, oðótą**]). [reg., *oo_tá*] *(trans.)* **ask for (as a loan), request to borrow; borrow, use s.o.'s, ask for s.t. to use it.** *ooðáta* you ask for a loan. *ąkóota* we ask for a loan. *mą́zeska oowáta hkǫbrái* I want to borrow money (01/07/95/FH/pc;ok). *oðíhtą ðíhta oowáta hkǫ́bra* I want to borrow your car (01/07/95/FH/pc:prod *ootá*; BE2.10). *ée ootápe* he borrowed it (01/07/95/FH/pc;ok). *óohǫ ootáapi apai* they're borrowing the pot (04/13/95/FH/pc:ok). *ootá!* borrow it! (01/07/95/FH/pc;ok; 1/20/83-p2/020; RBn2-MOJ).

•• LFD 96: *mą́zeska ota waleze* <mo^{n}´-çe-çka u-da wa-gthe-çe> paper or writing for borrowing money, a note. LFD 178: *oðóta (?)* <u-thu´-da> interest money. [LF's original analysis is <u-da> 'borrow', <thu> 'by which'.]

••• *KS wadá* beg, ask for, request (RR); *QU wahtá* pray (RR).

••• Cf. *mą́zeska ootá waléze, mą́žą óota, oðótą mą́zeska, waatá.*

ootá mą́zeska (variant: **ootą́ mą́zeska**). N **rent.** *mąžą́ ootá mą́zeska* lease money (for land) (lit., 'land usage money') (RBn1-28). *mą́žą ootą mą́zeska* lease money (02/25/95/FH/pc:okc).

óota (variant: **óotą**). V [reg., *óo_ta*] [*wa-* VAL + *ootá*] *(intr.)* **ask for stuff to be loaned, borrow things.**

ootą́ (variant of **ootá**).

óowe (variant of **ówe**).

oožú. V [reg., *oo_žú*] *(trans.)* **pour or serve liquids or small solids such as beans, pour for (s.o.).** *oowížu hce* let me pour for you. *mąhkása toe ooą́žu* pour me some coffee (RBnot 5/3/79/7; 04/17/95/LS/pc:ok). *mą́hkasa ą́ąwąžu* pour me some coffee (03/10/95/MREI/pc). *ąąwážu* pour for me (04/17/95/LS/pc:ok; BE2.106). • **put in.** *wéli tóe oðíhtą ooðážu?* did you put some gas in the car? (RBn12-06). *hkiistómąį háaną oožú nąpé* how many councilmen do they usually put in? (RBn3-01; 04/18/95/FH/pc:okc). *hkíðatoopa oožú nąpé* they put in eight (RB; 4/18/95/FH/pc:ok). *hpéece oožú* put them in the fire (RBn10-16). • **plant or sow (e.g., seed in the ground), "put in" plants.** *oowážu bríištą* I finished planting them. *hápaóožu etkxą́ akxái* it's time to plant corn (lit., 'corn-planting it is time') (03/09/95/FH/pc:ok; BE2.104). • N **receptacle, container, bottle, cup, bowl, jar, shaker, holder (for pourable dry or liquid substances).** [*oožú* follows the noun naming the filler substance.] *žąąníeoožú* sugar bowl (FH: 04/18/95).

••• Cf. *htáanieoožú, mąhkásaioožú, mą́zeskaoožú, níioožú.*

óožu. V [reg., *óo_žu*] [*wa-* VAL + *oožú*] *(intr.)* **put stuff in, plant stuff.** *háaną óožu apái?* how many people have put in? (e.g., if attendees at an event are to bring a certain number of cans of tomatoes, one asks 'how many [people] have put in?') (03/09/95/FH/pc; FH/t116b). • N **pocket, bottle, container, vessel.** *óožu htóho* a blue bottle (FH: 04/18/95).

•• LFD 182: *óži htóho* <u´-zhi ṭo-ho> a blue bottle. *óži* <u´-zhi> to plant. *oží pši aða*<u-zhi´ pshi a-tha> [expected Mod. Os. form: *óožu pší*] I have been to plant [*aða* unconfirmed in all examples] (03/09/95/FH/pc:uk). *óðaži še aða* <u´-tha-zhi she a-tha> [expected Mod. Os. form: *óoðažu ší*] you have been to plant (03/09/95/FH/pc:uk). *oží ąkahi pi aða* <u-zhi´ o^{n}-ga-hi bi a-tha> [second syllable accent in verb is probably an error; expected Mod. Os. form: *óožu ąkáhipe*] we have been to plant.

óožuhaa. N [*óožu* + *háa*] **bag, sack, pouch made of hide or leather (lit., 'skin into which to put stuff').**

ópaache. N [*wa-* VAL + *ó-* LOC + *paaché*] **sewing (lit., 'wherein stuff is sewn').** • ADJ **sewn, sewn together** (RBn1-MOJ/p4304/19/95/FH/pc:okc).

••• Cf. *óhkihpaache.*

opáaɣa. V [sync. fortisizing stop stem?, *o_páaɣa?*] *(intr.)* **open (e.g., flowers opening out).** *hlaaská opáaɣa akxai* the flowers are opening out. *opáaɣa káaɣa!* open it!

••• Cf. *paaɣáce.*

opáahą (variant: **opą́ąhą**). V [sync. fortisizing stop stem, *o_páahą*] *(trans.)* **raise up, hold up**

opáahą (*continued*) (LS/02/95/LS/pc:prod); **put on, don (as clothing)** (04/18/95/FH/pc:ok; 04/18/95/FH/pc:ok). *ákahamį ohpą́ąhą ąhé* I'm putting this coat on (FH:prod). *wéhkili wį ohpáahą mįkšé* I'm putting on my clothes (ERE). *ákahamį ošpą́ąhą ðaįšé?* are you putting this coat on? (FH:prod; BE2.109). *wéhkili wį opą́ąhą* he's putting on his clothes (ERE). *ákahami opą́ąhą* put this coat on. *haaská ðé opáahą* put this shirt/clothing on (04/18/95/FH/pc:ok). *ąkópą́ąhą* we put it on.

••• Cf. *ðuhpáahą, hpaahą́, paahą́, wéhkilį okíhpaahą, wéhkilį opáahą.*

ópaašike. ADJ **overbearing (describes s.o. who is always butting in, interrupting)** (RBn22-01, unconfirmed).

•• LFD 175: *opášie* <U-pa´-shi-e> Counsellor (personal name).

••• *QU pášike* ruin by cutting in or poking a hole in (RR).

opáhce. N **herd** (LF, unconfirmed).

•• LFD 165 (unconfirmed): *opáhce* <u-ba´-ṭse> a herd. "Now applied to a herd of cattle." *įtáci akxa hceeská opáhce hu waðį́ pe* <i^n-da-dsi a-ka tse-çka u-ba´-ṭse hiu wa-thi^n bi a> my father has a large herd of cattle.

opáhce (variant: **opáhcilą**). V *(trans.)* **hang up (e.g., clothing)** (RB; 04/11/95/LS/pc:okc). *ákahamį ðíhta opáhce* hang your coat up (04/11/95/LS/pc:ok; BE2.64). *opáhcila* hang it up (RBn10-21/JW&FW/77). *óoląke opáhcila* hang that hat up (RBn10-21/JW&FW/77, unconfirmed).

•• RB: <o-páh-tsi-nah>.

•• LFD 166: *opáhcilą* <u-ba´-ṭsi-gtho^n> to hang something on a peg or the limb of a tree. *opá hcialą* <u-ba´ ṭsi-a-gtho^n> I hung something on a peg. *opáhciðalą* <u-ba´-ṭsi-tha-gtho^n> you hang something on a peg. *opáhcikilą* <u-ba´-ṭsi-gi-gtho^n> he hung something on a peg. *ópahcižu* <u´-ba-ṭsi-zhu> to hang bunches of ears of corn to dry; to hang clothes to dry (unconfirmed; LS/04/11/95/pc:ma, may mean hanging more than one thing).

opákˀo (variant: **opákˀoe**). V [presumably sync. fortisizing stop stem, *o_pákˀo*] [*ó-* LOC + *paakˀó*] *(trans.)* **punch a hole in, cut a hole in by pushing.** *ną́ye opákˀoe* cut a hole in the ice (RBn16-02).

•• LFD 165: *opáhkuce* <u-ba´-ḳu-dse> [should be <u-ba´-k'u-dse>, Mod. Os. *opákˀoce*] to punch holes in a pair of moccasins or clothing [expected gloss would not include moccasins or clothing].

••• *KS obákˀoǰe (obákˀodabe)* make or enlarge a hole (RR).

opásące. V [conjug. unknown]. *(trans.)* **have it in for; consider (s.o.) an opponent.** *opásące* they've got it in for him, they're "laying for him" (01/09/95/FH/pc:prod).

••• *KS ábasąǰe* to push against something, to have sex with (RR), *áabüsąǰe* to press down on, wrestle (RR).

••• Cf. *áhkiasąci, ásąci, kasǫ́ci.*

opáwįye. V [uninfl.?] *(intr.)* **wander, roam, rove, travel around; go for a ride, drive around for pleasure, go on an excursion.** *opáwįye ąąðįhé* I'm riding around (FH:prod). *oðíhtą opáwįye aðáape* they went riding in the car (RBn10-20). *mą́ąye ðáalį akxa, opáwįye ąkái hce* the weather is good, let's go for a drive [two people]. *opáwįye ąkái htái* let's go for a ride [three or more people]. • N **excursion, ride.** *opáwįye brée ðe* I'm going riding, I'm going for a ride (FH:prod; 01/20/95/PM/pc:ok; BE2.35).

•• JOD (Wolf and Fawn p1 ln2): *ha wižįe ohpáwįye áðįhe* <Ha´, wi´çi ^{n}e´! Upa´wi^n xe a´¢i^{n}he´> [expected form <Uḳa´wi^n xe>] Ho, elder brother, I've been wandering around.

•• LFD 263: *opáwįye* <u-ba´-wi^n-xe> an excursion. LFD 166 (unconfirmed): *opáwįye* <u-ba´-wi^n-xe> to travel, to roam about, to wander, to travel for pleasure to rove, to saunter, to stroll; to swirl in a kettle when cooking. *ohpáwįye* <u-ḳa´-wi^n-xe> I travel for pleasure. *ošpáwįye* <u-shpa´-wi^n-xe> you travel for pleasure. *ąpópawįya pe* <o^n-bu´-ba-wi^n-xa i> [presumably a typographical error for *ąkópawįya pe* <o^n-ku´-ba-wi^n-xa i>] we travel for pleasure. *opáwįye ąðalį* <u-ba´-wi^n-xe o^n-tha-gthi^n> I like to stroll.

opázo (variant: **ópazo**). N [apparently *ó-* LOC + *pázo* 'finger'] **index finger** (RBn10-9:JW; 01/24/95/FH/pc:prod).

••• Cf. *šáake opázo, wéapazo.*

opą́ąhą (variant of **opáahą**).

opéni. V [sync. fortisizing stop stem, *o_péni*] *(trans.)* **detect, find out about or partially uncover an undisclosed idea or plan (such as a surprise party), discover in part but not fully, get wind of, get word of, get a feeling about s.t. without full knowledge of it.** *ohpéni ąįhé* I found out, I have a feeling (LS). *ošpéni* you [sg.] found out, you [sg.] have a feeling (LS). *opéni paašé* you [pl.] found out, you [pl.] have a feeling (LS). *pée John opéni ðe?* who found out about John? who did John find out about? (RBnot-nd-

1/ps; LS/7/27/95, all short vowels). *pée opénipe?* who did they find out about? *opéni kaaɣé į̨ká* don't let them get wind of it (RBnot-nd-1/p2; 01/24/95/FH/pc:ok; 03/09/95/FH/pc).

•• LFD 166: *opéhni* <u-be´-hni> to detect (01/24/95/FH/pc: *opéni*, no preaspiration of *p* or *n*). *ohpéhni* <u-pe´-hni> I detect. *ošpéhni* <u-shpe´-hni> you detect. *ąkópehtą pe* <o^{n}-gu´-be-ṭo^{n} i> [*-htą-* is unexpected in this form; expected Mod. Os. form: *ąkópenipe*] we detect, to discover.

opétxą (variants: **opétkxą, opétxa**). v [sync. fortisizing stop stem?, *o_pétxą?*] *(trans.)* **tie in a bundle or wrap up s.t. specific.** *haxį́ke opétkxą* wrap up those [scattered] blankets (03/22/95/FH/pc). *haxį́ hcéka che haaská wasúhu opétkxą* wrap up those new [stacked] blankets in a clean cloth (03/22/95/FH/pc). *háxį́ toa opétxą* tie up some blankets (RBn2/p18; 03/22/95/FH/pc:ok).

ópetxą (variants: **ópetkxą, ópetxa**). v [sync. fortisizing stop stem?, *ó_petxą?*] [*wa-* VAL + *opétxą*] *(intr.)* **wrap or tie up stuff as a bundle.** *ópetxą* put it inside and wrap it up (as inside a blanket or in a cloth) (BE2.161; 03/24/95/PM/pc:okc; LS). *ópetxa* tie that up (e.g., tie up some blankets) (BE2.140; RBn1-25).

•• LFD 166 (unconfirmed): *opéhtą* <u-be´-ṭo^{n}> [expected LF form would be <u´-be-to^{n}>, expected Mod. Os. form *ópetxą*] to wrap. *ohpéhtą* <u-pe´-ṭo^{n}> I wrap up the goods. *ošpéhtą* <u-shpe´-ṭo^{n}> you wrap up the goods. *ąkópehtą pe* <o^{n}-gu´-be-ṭo^{n} i> we wrap up the goods or envelop (unconfirmed; 03/24/95/PM/pc:no). [In all these LF examples, *-htą* should be *-txą*.]

opíɣą (variants: **opíɣa, opíxą**) v [conjug. unknown (sync. fortisizing stop stem?, *o_píɣą?*)] [*ó-* LOC + *píɣą*] *(trans.)* **blow into or on (e.g., a fire in a fireplace), blow inside, play a horn or other wind instrument** (RBn1-42; FH:ok:[x]). *hpéece škáaɣe ščuucˀake tą, opíɣą* if you can't start the fire, blow on it (FH/11/19/01/pc). *hpéece ščúucˀake tą ópiɣą íkˀuca* if you can't start the fire, try blowing on it (FH/11/19/01/pc:prod; HRE/12/29/01/pc *opíxą*). • N **whistle, horn, flute, wind instrument** (02/09/95/FH/pc:ok; BE2.67).

•• LFD 166: *opíɣą* <u-bi´-xo^{n}> any wind instrument, as a flute or horn.

ópoce (variant: **opóce**). N **trash, things scattered around (as in a messy house), scattering, collection of scattered things** (FH: t119a). *ópoce ášihta aðį́ðaa* take the trash outside (03/23/95/FH/pc:okc; t119a;BE2.144, RBn2-MOJ/p20). *opóce ðaašé* you're falling apart (lit., 'you are a collection of scattered things') (3-10-83C; 03/23/95/FH/pc:okc; RBn10-12:JW).

•• LFD 166: *opóce* <u-bu´-dse> profusion, abundance.

opšáži. v [reg., *o_pšáži*] [*opšé* + *aží* NEG] *(trans.)* **disobey.**

opšé. v [reg. *o_pšé*] *(trans.)* **obey, follow, heed.** *háakǫ́ škǫ́šta tą oðípše hta akxai* however you want it to be, they're going to listen to you.

••• Cf. *íe opšé, okípše.*

opxá. ADV **down the middle.**

opxá (see **kíopxa**).

opxáži (see **kíopxaži**).

opxą́ (variant: **opxá**). v [reg., *o_pxą́*] *(trans.)* **follow (as a path), go through or down (as a road)** (RBn22-04, unconfirmed). *ožą́ke owápxa ąhé* I'm going through that road (RBn22-05 [archaic?]).

•• LFD 192: *wáhkilace owahpa* <wa´-ḳi-gtha-dse u-wa-p̣a> [LF's <p̣> (Mod. Os. *hp*) is probably an error for <p> (Mod. Os. *px*)] I obey the law (02/14/95/FH/pc:uk). *wáhkilace oðahpa* <wa´-ḳi-gtha-dse u-tha-p̣a> [LF's <p̣> (Mod. Os. *hp*) is probably an error for <p> (Mod. Os. *px*)] you obey the law (unconfirmed). *wáhkilace ohpa* <wa´-ḳi-gtha-dse u-p̣a> [LF's <p̣> (Mod. Os. *hp*) is probably an error for <p> (Mod. Os. *px*)] he obeys the law (unconfirmed).

••• Cf. *opxą́pxą́.*

ópxą (variant: **ópxa**). N **elk** (04/25/95/PM/pc:ok; 12/30/94/FH/pc:uk; BE2.41; RBn1-24).

•• LFD 123: *ópxą waðǫ* <o´-po^{n} wa-tho^{n}> Elk Songs.

ópxą hį́į ekǫ́. ADJP, N **light brown, dun colored (lit., 'like the color of elk')** (04/25/95/PM/pc:ok).

•• LFD 122: *ópxą hį ekǫ* <o´-po^{n} hi^{n} e-go^{n}> dun colored, the color of the elk.

ópxąhaa. N [*ópxą* + *háa*] **elk skin** (4/25/95/PM/pc:ok).

•• LFD 122: *ópxą ha* <o´-po^{n} ha> elk skin.

opxą́pxą́ (variant: **opxą́pxą́i**). N [reduplicated form of *opxą́* 'follow'] **chief-to-chief (refers to succession of hereditary chiefs within a family); one of anything following the other** (04/13/95/FH/pc:okc).

opˀą́ða (variant: **opˀą́ðe**).v [uninfl.] *(intr.)* **steam, emit vapors, produce a rising fog (such as fog from water in a pond, lake, or swamp)** (BE2.49; 04/07/95/PM/pc:okc; MSB/pc). *níi akxa opˀą́ðe nąpé* water steams (2-2-670). • N

opˀą́ða (*continued*)
fog rising from standing water when the sun shines on it, steam or vapor arising.
•• LFD 129: *opˀóðą* <u-p'o´-thoⁿ> [expected Mod. Os. form: *opˀą́ða*] steam rising from a kettle over a fire (01/26/95/FH/pc:uk; 03/14/95/FH/pc:uk). LFD 175 (unconfirmed): *pˀóðą* <p'o´-thoⁿ> steam arising from boiling water. *pˀóðǫ́ che ǫ́ðǫ nite akše* <p'o´-tho´ⁿ tse o´ⁿ-thoⁿ ni-de a-ke> the steam burnt my arm [this sentence is not confirmed and is unintelligible].

osái (variant: **ozái** [RB only]). v [reg., *o_sái*] [presumably *ó-* LOC + *sápe*] *(intr.)* **burn, be on fire;** *(trans.)* **set fire to, burn.** [Probably used specifically of lighting cigarettes at a peyote meeting (FH/11/19/01/pc).] *nąníǫpa osái* burn the cigarettes (RBn10-16). *oðásai* you burned cigarettes (in a peyote meeting) (RB).
•• LFD 166: *osá pi o* <u-ça´ bi o> [sentence-final *o* is not used in Mod. Os.] to set fire. *owáse* <u-wa´-çe> I set fire to it. *oðáse* <u-tha´-çe> you set fire to it. *ąkósa pe* <oⁿ-gu´-ça i> we set fire to it.
••• *KS osé* to be burned, to be set afire (RR).
••• Cf. *ðą́ące ósai.*

oscé (variant of **oščé**).

ósi. v [reg., *ó_si*] *(intr., trans.)* **alight (from), get off (e.g., a horse), get out of (e.g., a car).** *ósipi* get out [pl. addressee] (FH/11/18/01/pc). *oðási* you got out (FH/11/19/01/pc:prod).
••• Cf. *wísi.*

óski. N **arch of the foot.**

ostá. v [reg., *o_stá*] *(intr.)* **slide, slip.**
••• Cf. *štáha.*

ostówe. ADJ [apparently *ó-* LOC + *stówe*] **running as a group, hurrying toward s.t., being rushed or rushing in a row** (FHt128). *táatą ómahką ecíepe éetana ostówe aðíi apai* a whole line of people are running because there's something cheap (lit., 'something cheap is there, thus rushing in a line/group they are going there') (FHt128).
•• LFD 167: *ostówe nąží* <u-çtu´-e noⁿ-zhiⁿ> to stand abreast, to stand in a row

oščé (variants: **oscé, oščé**). v [reg., *o_šcé*] *(intr.)* **remain, be left or left over** (02/15/95/FH/pc:okc). *wanǫ́bre níi tóa oščé?* is there any peyote tea left? (02/15/95/FH/pc:ok; BE2.78). *ðekǫ́ǫci áha waxpáðe níhkašika, háaną įksé ški ówašta apa tąha* at the present time we are a pitiful people, and there are even very few of us left [*ówašta apa* is probably a misrecording for *ówaštape* 'we are left'] • *(trans.)* **leave (as leftovers), spare.** • N **remainder, rest, leftover amount.** *oščé ke* remainders or leftovers that are scattered around.
•• LFD 175: *oscéke* <u-stse´-ge> the rest that are scattered about (02/15/95/FH/pc:ok).
••• Cf. *oðáašce.*

oščé che (variants: **oscé che, oščé che**). ADJP **leftover, remaining** (02/15/95/FH/pc:okc). *ówe oščé che ąnáhkilai htai* let's all of us divide these leftover groceries (03/06/95/FH/pc). N **remainder (sg. standing inanimate or pl. sitting inanimate), leftovers.** *htáatą oscé che* whatever is left (PM).
•• LFD 175: *oscé che* <u-stse´ tse> the rest that has been gathered and stands in a pile; the remainder, part left over (02/15/95/FH/pc:ok). LFD 35: *táatą oscé che* <da´-doⁿ u-stse´-tse> what is left over, remainder, residue (04/14/95/PM/pc:ok).

oščé ke. N **remainders, leftovers, or rest (scattered around).**

oscúuce. N **slowpoke, slow person, pokey one.**

oščé (variant of **oščé**).

óše. v [uninfl.] *(intr.)* **exist plentifully** (03/23/95/FH/pc). [Nearly synonymous with *ochí*, but *óše* cannot be used with *žįkážį* 'child' or *haxį́* 'blanket', for example (LS).] *táatą óše* something plentiful (FH). *ónǫbre óše* a lot of food (lit., 'food-wise there is plenty'). *táatą óše* a lot of things (LS/04/17/95/pc). • N **lots, abundance, plenty, profusion of s.t.**
•• LFD 175: *óše* <u´-she> plenty, plentiful.

óšechiðe (variants: **óšechie, óošechiðe**). v [conjug. unknown] *(intr.)* **be much, be many.** *ónǫbre óošechíepe* there's a lot of food.

óšechiðe wakáaye. N **quail.** [Possibly *óšechiðe* here is a variant of *hóšechie* 'jump as when startled'; in that case the expression would literally mean 'make them jump up in a startled fashion', referring to the sudden movement or sound that quail make when flushed (LF, unconfirmed).]
•• LFD 313: *ošechiðe wakaaye* <u'-shi-ṭsi-the wa-ga-xe> quail (unconfirmed).

óškika (variant: **óškike**). ADJ, v [uninfl.] *(intr.)* **(be) mischievous (said of a person who tends to laugh and make fun of people).** *Eddie akxa óškika akxai* Eddie is being mischievous (01/04/95/FH/pc:ok); **(be) unreliable, ornery, worthless, no good** (03/03/95/FH/pc:ok; RBn2-MOJ/p5; 02/27/95/FH/pc:ok; BE2.94). *níhka* *štáke apa wáli óškike apai, taašéðai hta mįkšé* that nice [or 'gentle'] man is really being ornery [or 'a drag'], I'm going to shake him up [or 'hit him on the head'] (FH/98/pc; FH/10//13/96/pc). *óškika!* you're ornery! (a response to someone who has just said something crazy and funny).

•• LFD 175: *óškika pi a* <u´-shki-ga bi a> [expected Mod. Os.: *óškikape*] he is perverse. LFD 256: *óškika* <o´-shki-ga> dissipated, dissolute. LFD 123: *še níhkašika apa óškika pi a* <she ni´-ḳa-shi-ga a-ba o´-shki-ga bi a> [expected Mod. Os. form: *še níhka apa óškikape* 'that man is ornery'] he is very dissipated, dissolute.

ošpéžį. N [*ó-* LOC + *-špé* + *-žį* 'little'] **fragment, small piece, chip, bit, bits and baubles, one's small things** (RB; FH). *ošpéžį nąlǫ́ǫha apái ðée apa ahú apai óceštąpe* they're hiding their things because the people coming are snoops. • **change left over after a purchase, coins, small change, pennies** (RBn2-MOJ/p19; 03/07/95/PM/pc:ok; BE2.102; FH).

•• LFD 175: *ošpé* <u-shpe´> a fragment (03/07/95/PM/pc:ok).

••• Cf. *kašpé, paašpú.*

oštá. N [presumably *ó-* LOC + *štáha*] **yard, lawn, cleared area, bare ground.** *oštá kaasé* mow the lawn (RBn10-16).

otáa. V, ADJ [conjug. unknown] [presumably *ó-* LOC + *táa* 'freeze'] *(intr.)* **(be) frozen.** *htóožu akxa otáa akxai* the meat pie is frozen.

ótaa. V [conjug. unknown] [*wa-* VAL + *otáa*] *(trans.)* **freeze in/to another substance, make s.t. freeze.** *sį́ice akxa ną́ye ótaape* his tail was frozen in the ice (RBn16-02). *htóožu ótaa ðiké* don't freeze the meat pie.

otáhpa. N **entrails, part of the stomach resembling little books or pages, used for soup** (04/07/95/LS/pc:ok; 3/3/83/p2). [Also called "bible," it lies in layers and has a fringe on it; may have grass inside that the animal has eaten earlier.]

•• LFD 167: *otáhpa* <u-da´-p̣a> the third stomach of an ox. LFD 120: *otáhpa* <o-da´-p̣a> the third stomach of an ox, used by the Indians for food and considered a delicacy.

otkxą́ (variant of **okxą́**).

ótkxąži (variant of **ókxąži**).

otxą́ (variants: **okxą́, otxá**). V [reg., *o_txą́*] *(trans.)* **put on (e.g., pants, shoes).** *Į́įka, hǫǫpé ðé otxá* sit down, put these shoes on (RBn1-MOJ/p38).

•• RB: <o-txáh>.

•• LFD 313: *hǫǫpé otxą* <ho^{n}-be´ u-to^{n}> to put on shoes. LFD 65: *hǫǫpéotxą* <ho^{n}-be´-u-to^{n}> to put on moccasins. *hǫǫpé oðatxą* <ho^{n}-be´ u-tha-ṭo^{n}> [LF's *t* <ṭ> here and in the next two examples is evidently an error for *tx* <t>] you put on moccasins. *hǫǫpé owatxą* <ho^{n}-be´ u-wa-ṭo^{n}> I put on moccasins. *hǫǫpéąkotxą pe* <ho^{n}-be´-o^{n}-gu-ṭo^{n} i> we put on moccasins.

ótxątxą (variant: **ókxąkxą** [FH]). ADJ, N [reduplicated form] **time after time, generation, generational, generation after generation, referring to a long line of chiefs, ongoing** (02/14/95/FH/pc: prod). *kahíke ókxąkxą* hereditary chief (FH).

•• LFD 178 (unconfirmed): *oðoátxą* <u-thu-a´-to^{n}> to follow; to be next; sequence. [Related, not identical, to *ótxątxą*.] *oðóawatxą* <u-thu´-a-wa-to^{n}> I follow next. *oðóaðatxą* <u-thu´-a-tha-to^{n}> you follow next. *ąðą́kotxą pe* <o^{n}-tho^{n}´-gu-to^{n} i> we follow next. *oðoáwatxą anąžį* <u-thu-a´-wa-to^{n} a-no^{n}-zhi^{n}> I follow next to him.

••• Cf. *opxą́pxą́.*

ówaachi. N [*ó-* LOC + *waachí*] **dance place or location.** *huukǫ́ða dalípe na, ðe ówaachi ilǫ́ǫška* many of you have come back to this place of the *ilǫ́ǫška* dances (HREsr: 1965 *ilǫ́ǫška*-line 2).

ówaðaace. N [*ó-* LOC + *wa-* VAL + *ðaacé*] **law.**

•• LFD 181: *ówaðace* <u´-wa-tha-dse> the law.

owáhkiha. N [presumably *ó-* LOC + *áhkiha*] **grandchild(?), grandchildren.** *ówahkiha háaną aščį?* how many grandchildren do you have?

••• Cf. *žįká owáhkihą.*

owánǫbrehcí. N [*ó-* LOC + *wanǫ́brehci*] **cafe, restaurant** (BE2.16; 01/09/95/FH/pc:ok). [Preferred to *wanǫ́brehci* (FH).]

ówatoį (variant: **ówatǫe**). N [*ó-* LOC + *wa-* VAL + *tǫ́pe*] **show, picture show, movie, film, theater presentation, exhibition (lit., 'wherein to see things')** (04/19/95/FH/pc:okc; 02/27/95/FH/pc:ok; 04/11/95/LS/pc:ok). *ówatoį ąkái hce* let's go to the show [sg. addressee] (RBn2-MOJ/p5; 03/09/95/MREI/pc:ok). *wíe hą́ące ówatǫe pšíe* I went to the movies last night (02/27/95/FH/pc:ok; BE2.90).

•• LFD 180: *ówatǫpe* <u´-wa-do^{n}-be> a theater, a circus. *ówatǫpe ðe ązo* <u´-wa-do^{n}-be the o^{n}-çu> [expected Mod. Os. form: *ówatǫe ðée ą́ązo*] I like to go to the theater.

ówatǫįhci N [*ówatoį* + *hcí*] **theater, exhibition hall (lit., 'show house')** (MOJt150a).

ówe (variant: **óowe**). N **groceries** (02/03/95/FH/pc:ok). *hpázc wanǫ́bre ówe brúwį*

ówe (*continued*)
ókxąži ąhé I was slow buying groceries for supper (04/19/95/FH/pc:okc). *ówe hcíhta áðįkü* bring the groceries inside (BE2.61). *ówe tóa owáhi* I won some groceries. • **garden, cultivated area, field planted for harvest** (FH). *óowe ðáalį aščį* you have a good garden (01/31/95/FH/pc:ok, prod). • **greens, vegetables, produce** (01/31/95/FH/pc:ok).

ówe hci (variant: **owéhci**). N **grocery store** (BE2.61; 01/11/95/FH/pc:ok). *óweche brée* I'm going to the grocery store (FH).

óweena (variants: **óweeną, ówiina**) V, ADJ [uninfl.] [*ó-* LOC + *wéeną*] *(intr.?)* **(be) glad.** *ðachí che óweena ąškáaɣe* I'm glad you are here (HH/14-a/401ff&pc). [Used in formal speech.] • **(be) thankful, appreciative, grateful** (02/03/95/FH/pc:ok). *óweena ąkxą́he* I'm thankful (03/16/95/FH/pc:ok). *ðachí che óweena ąškáaɣe* thank you for coming (lit., 'you have made me grateful, as you have come here, as is evident') (HH/14-a; pc). *óweena iðá[ð]e hkǫ́bra* I want to say something in appreciation (03/16/95/FH/pc:ok). *ónǫbre ðé waðákikʔupi che ówiina ąkátxą* we are grateful for this food you have given us (part of a prayer).

•• LFD 181: *ówehną* <u´-we-hno^{n}> thankfulness, gratitude.

owéhci (variant of **ówe hci**).

owíhta (variant of **oðíhtą**).

ówiina (variant of **óweena**).

owísi (variant of **wísi**).

ówǫ (variant: **ǫ́wǫ**). V, ADJ [uninfl.] [presumably *ó-* LOC + *wa-* VAL + *éǫ*] *(intr.)* **(be) busy** (BE2.37). *hǫpái wálį ówǫ ąhé* today I was very busy (01/09/95/FH/pc:ok). *wáli ówǫ ąhé* I'm really busy (01/09/95/FH/pc:ok; 04/25/95/PM/pc:ok). *eetą, ówǫ hta mįkšé* well, I'm going to be busy (01/09/95/FH/pc:okc). *kasįe ówǫ hta ðaįšé?* are you going to be busy tomorrow? (01/09/95/FH/pc:prod). *kasįe ówǫ hta nįkšé?* are you going to be busy tomorrow? (BE2.14). *ówǫ ąkxąhé, lįįpi* I'm busy, sit down (FH:prod; RBn2-MOJ). • N **chore, task, errand, duty, things one has to do** (01/20/95/PM/pc:ok). *huuwáli ǫ́wǫ ǫ́ąchi* I've got a lot to do (lit., 'a large number of chores are plentiful to me') (RBn12-07; FH/11/19/01/pc: okc). *wáli ówǫ oðíchi* you're really busy (04/25/95/PM/pc:prod). *ówǫ oðíchi ðaašé íhpahǫ* I know you have had a lot to do (RBn10-4:MOJ/79).

•• LFD 181: *owǫ* <u-wo^{n}> to be busy. *óǫ ǫwąhci* <u´-o^{n} o^{n}-wo^{n} ṭsi> I am busy. *óǫ oðihci* <u´-o^{n} u-thi-ṭsi> you are busy.

ówǫ káaɣe. VP [sync. *k>p, ówǫ _káaɣe*] *(trans.)* **make trouble for s.o., trouble another, be a burden to s.o.** *wáli ówǫ wihpáaɣe* I'm a lot of trouble to you.

ówǫ kšíɣe. VP [reg. *ówǫ _kšíɣe*] *(trans.)* **make trouble for s.o., trouble another, be a burden to s.o.** *ðihkówa akxa wálį ówǫ ąkšíɣe akxai* your friend is making me a lot of trouble (lit., 'your friend really makes tasks for me') (RBn23-17).

óxe. N **grave, ditch, burial place.** *óxe pakʔó apái* they're digging the ditch; they're digging the grave (RB; 02/03/95/FH/pc:ok; 04/25/95/PM/pc:ok). *hlaaská óxe ážu* put flowers on the grave (02/03/95/FH/pc:ok; 04/25/95/PM/pc:ok; BE2.6).

••• *OP óxe* grave.

óxe mą́žą. N **cemetery, graveyard, burial ground.**

óxe sápe. N **coffin** (LF, unconfirmed).

•• LFD 124: *óxe sape* <o´-xe ça-be> a coffin.

óxiða. N [*ó-* LOC + *xíða*] **death** (RBn10-7:JW). *įhtáci wahkǫ́ta akxa óxiða káaɣi akxái* God created this death (said at a peyote meeting).

óxįį. V, ADJ [uninfl. (neither ***oðíxį* nor ***oðáxį* 'you are jealous' is acceptable)] *(trans., intr.)* **(be) jealous, envious (e.g., of another's position)** (RBn10-7:JW). *ée óxįį akxai* they're envious (04/26/95/LS/pc:ok). *óxįe nįkšé* you're envious (04/26/95/LS/pc:ok; BE2.42). • **pout, sulk about another's good fortune** (04/26/95/LS/pc:okc). • N **envy, jealousy** (04/26/95/LS/pc:okc).

•• RB: <ó-xi^{n}, ó^{n}-xi^{n}>.

oxpáðe (variants: **oxpái, oxpáðį**). V [stat., *o_xpáðe*] *(intr.)* **fall from a height.** *oxpáðe įká* don't fall in (RBn23-17). *žą́ą kítxą ąwą́xpaðe* I fell out of a tree. *oxpáðape* he fell from a height, they fell from a height. • **get lost, become lost, be lost.** *o[w]ąxpa[ð]e, ową́xpaðe* I get lost. *oðíxpaðe* you get lost. *owáxpaðape* we get lost. *hǫpá oą́xpai aðįhé* I got lost today (RBn). *oxpáðape* they got lost; it was lost (FHt128). *oxpáðe apai, oxpáðape* they've gotten lost, they're lost. *šǫ́ke wíhta akxa oxpáðe akxa* my dog is lost (04/27/95/FH/pc). *šǫ́ke wíhta akxa oxpáðape* my dog was lost (04/27/95/FH/pc). *wažáže okʔą́ oxpáðape* Osage ways are all gone (lit., 'Osage ways got lost') (05/01/95/LS/pc). • *(trans.)* **lose (s.t. specific or s.o. specific)** (RBn1-23). [Accent tends to fall on the initial *o-* in the 1st pl. form in the transitive use of this verb, as in *ówaxpaðape* 'we lost it', causing this to resemble the valence-reduced form *óxpaðe*.] *ąwą́xpaðe* I lose it. *oðíxpaðe* you lose it. *owáxpaðe* we lose it. *mą́zeskaoožú ąwáxpai* I lost my purse (02/22/95/FH/pc:ok; BE2.82). *waðílą ąwáxpai* I lost my mind (RBn23-20). *haxį́ ąwą́xpaðį* I lost my blanket (02/22/95/FH/pc:okc). *sǫ́ke wíhta ąwą́xpaðe* I lost my dog (04/27/95/FH/pc). *haxį́ oðíxpaðe* you lost your blanket (02/22/95/FH/pc:ok). *wéleze Frances akxa oxpáði akxai* Frances [has] lost her pencil (02/27/95/FH/pc). *haxį oxpáðape* they lost their blanket, she lost her blanket (02/22/95/FH/pc:ok). *hǫǫpé ówaxpa[ðe] ąkáðe* we lost our shoes (RBnotes, MSB). *óoląke oðíxpai ðąįše* you lost your hat (RBnotes, MSB). *ąwą́ðaxpai* you lost me. *ówaðaxpai* you lost us.

•• LFD 181: *oxpáðe* <u-xpa´-the> to grope, to feel around with the hands in the dark; to fall, to become lost. [The gloss 'grope, feel' is unconfirmed.] *ąwą́xpaðe* <o^{n}-wo^{n}´-xpa-the> I felt around in the dark. [A more accurate translation is probably 'I fell'.] LFD 73–74: *ąwą́xpaðe ha íhkišoce kše* <o^{n}-wo^{n}´-xpa-the ha, i´-ḳi-sho-dse ke> [sentence-final *ha* is not used in Mod. Os.] I was lost in the fog. *oðíxpaðe ha íhkišoce kše* <u-thi´-xpa-the ha, i´-ḳi-sho-dse ke> [sentence-final *ha* is not used in Mod. Os.] you were lost in the fog. *páce apa oxpáða pe ha íkišoce kše* <ba-dse a-ba u-xpa´-tha pe ha, i´-ḳi-sho-dse ke> [phrase-final or sentence-final *ha* is not used in Mod. Os.] the boat was lost in the fog.

••• Cf. *óxpaðe*.

oxpáðe káaɣe. VP [sync. *k>p*, *oxpáðe _káaɣe*] *(trans.)* **mislead, cause to get lost.**

•• LFD 181: *oxpáðekaɣe* <u-xpa´-the-ga-xe> to mislead, to lead one into error. *oxpáðe hpaɣe* <u-xpa´-the pa-xe> I misled him. *oxpáðe škaɣe* <u-xpa´-the shka-xe> you misled him. *oxpáðe ąkaɣa pe* <u-xpa´-the o^{n}-ga-xa i> we misled him.

óxpaðe (variant: **óxpaði**). V [stat., *ó_xpaðe*] [*wa-* VAL + *oxpáðe*] *(intr.)* **lose things, lose stuff.** [Note the contrast to transitive *oxpáðe* 'lose it, lose s.t. specific'.] *Frances akxa óxpaði akxai* Frances lost some stuff (FH; RBn).

oxpáðeðe. V [reg., *oxpáðe_ðe*] [*oxpáðe* + *ðe* CAU] *(trans.)* **cause to be lost.** *oxpáðewaðai* you lost them (lit., 'you caused them to be lost').

oxpáði, oxpáðį, oxpái (variants of **oxpáðe** 'lose').

óxta. V, ADJ [uninfl.] *(intr.)* **(be) precious, dear or beloved, valuable, marvelous, important, special, right, respectable.** *žį́ka oxta* honored or favored child (CQ ok; BE2.107). *žúika akxa óxta akxai* my body is precious (RBn10-9:JW). *óxta káaɣe akxai* they're making him important.

óxta káaɣe VP [sync. *k>p*, *óxta _káaɣe*] *(trans.)* **hold sacred, consider precious, regard as holy.** *hą́ąpa ðe óxta káaɣe apai* people hold this day sacred (02/22/95/FH/pc:okc).

•• LFD 181: *óxta* <u´-xta> marvelous, pleasing, mysterious, lovable, to hold precious, to prize highly, to hold a thing as precious or valuable. [LF's definitions 'to hold precious, to prize highly, to hold a thing as precious or valuable' strictly speaking apply to the phrase *óxta káaɣe* rather than to *óxta* alone.] *óxta hpaɣe ekǫ saki obrįke* <u´-xta p̣a-xe e-go^{n} ça-gi u-bthi^{n}-ge> I hold it precious. [A more accurate translation would be 'I made it precious, therefore I hold tightly to it'.] *óxta ąkaɣa pe ekǫ saki ąkoðįka pe* <u´-xta o^{n}-ga-xa pe e-go^{n} ça-gi o^{n}-gu-thi^{n}-ga i> we hold it precious. [A more accurate translation would be 'we made it precious, therefore we hold tightly to it'.]

••• Cf. *kíoxta, óðoxta*.

óxtaðe. V [reg., *óxta_ðe*] [*óxta* + *ðe* CAU] **make precious, special, or important.**

•• LFD 182: *óxtaðe* <u´-xta-the> to be fond of a person. *oxtaaðe* <u-xta-a-the> I am fond of that person. *oxtaðaðe* <u-xta-tha-the> you are fond of that person.

óxtahkiðe. V [reg., *óxta_hkiðe*] [*hkik-* REFL/RECIP + *óxtaðe*] *(intr.)* **make oneself important, make oneself right and respectable.** *óxtaðahkie* you made yourself right and respectable. *óxtahkie* he's making himself important. • **cherish each other.** *óxtahkiapi* cherish each other.

óxtakiðe. V [reg., *óxta_kiðe*] [*ki-* SUU + *óxtaðe*] *(trans.)* **make dear, make special, give special status to a relative or s.o. close.** *žįkówahkihą óxtawakíe akxai* he's making his grandchildren special.

ozái (variant of **osái**).

ozó. N **lowland, low wooded level** (JOD).

•• JOD (Wolf and Fawn p15 ln1): *hcaléže ozó ki áhkihpape ska* <Tca-ḳ¢eçe uʂú ḳi ákipáp̣e ska> he met Fawn on the lowland.

óžą. V [reg., *ó_žą*] [*ó-* LOC + *žą́ą*] *(intr., trans.?)* **lie abed, lie down.** *oážą* I lie abed. *oðážą* you lie abed. *ožą* he lies abed. *ąkóžą* we lie abed. *húhekahci ožą́ akxai* he's [lying abed] in the hospital (RBn12-06). *škáži žą́ą!* lie still! (RBn23-15). • *(trans.)* **lie down in** (02/15/95/FH/pc:ok). *ážą ąkóžą hta [aðįįkšé* we

óžą (*continued*)
[two] are going to lie down in the bed (02/15/95/FH/pc:okc). • N **bed, place one lies in** (FH). *óžą oðážą žąkšé* you're lying in bed (FH/pc).

óžąke (variant: **ožą́ke**). N **road, highway, thoroughfare, route, path, pathway, orbit.** [Takes 'lying down' positional article *kše*.] *ožą́ke kše bráaða* the road is wide. *ožą́ke olį́į* sit in the road, sit at the altar in a peyote meeting, thus be a roadman.
•• LFD 182: *óžąke* <u-zho^{n}-ge> a trail, a path, a route to be taken, a thoroughfare, a road.

ožą́ke ohtą́ną. N **street (lit., 'road between')** (03/03/95/FH/pc:ok).

ožą́ke olį́į. V [reg., *ožą́ke o_lį́į*] *(intr.)* **be a roadman (lit., 'sit in the road [altar in the peyote religion]').** *ožą́ke oðálįį hta nįkšé?* are you going to be roadman? (FH/11/18/01/pc:prod). *pée ožą́ke olį́į hta ðe?* who's going to be roadman? (FH/11/18/01/pc:prod). • N **roadman in the peyote religion, minister of a religious entity, preacher, pastor, priest.**

óžeðe (variants: **ožéðe, ožéða**). V, ADJ [uninfl. or stat. *ó_žeðe*] *(intr.)* **feel tired, (be) fatigued, weary, tired** (03/22/95/FH/pc:ok). *ąwą́žeðe* I'm tired (BE2.141; 03/22/95/FH/pc:ok). *ožéðe mįkšé* I'm tired (03/22/95/FH/pc:prod).
•• LFD 182: *ožéða* <u-zhe´-tha> to be tired, to be weary (03/22/95/FH/pc:ok). *ąwažeða* <o^{n}-wa-zhe-tha> I am tired. *oðížeða* <u-thi´-zhe-tha> you are tired. *owážeða pe* <u-wa´-zhe-tha i> we are tired.

ožéhci (variants: **óžehci, océžehci**). N [*ó-* LOC + *žé* + *hcí*] **bathroom, toilet room, john, w.c., outhouse** (01/19/95/FH/pc:ok; 04/26/95/FH/pc).
•• LFD 182: *ožéhci* <u-zhe´-ṭsi> fireplace [unconfirmed as fireplace, perhaps this gloss is for Omaha?].
••• *OM* <u-zhe´-ti> (LFD 182).

ožížie (variant: **ožíže**). V [reg., *o_žížie*] *(trans.)* **bait or coax s.o. to say or do s.t., egg on, encourage, incite.** *áwažižíe* I egged him on. *éekǫaži ówaðažižíe* you egged them on anyway (RB:MSB/02/17/83). *ékimą hkǫ́bra įké ąži ąwą́ðažižíe* I didn't want to do it, but you egged me on (RB:MSB/02/17/83). *ožížì apai* they egged him on. • **convince.** *ąwą́ðažižie* you convinced me (2/3/83/236; FH:ma).

óžį hpíiži. VP *(intr.)* **become angry, get mad.** *óžį hpíiži ðįké, ókˀą ðáalį hkí[ð]a* don't get angry, have good ways (lit., 'don't become angry, make yourself be of good ways') (01/04/95/FH/pc).
•• LFD 182: *oží akxa/ožú akxa/ožó akxa* <u-zhu´- a-ka> the person himself, personally, self.

óžo áhkižį. VP [reg., *óžo áhkižį*] [*hkik-* REFL + *óžo áži*] *(intr.)* **be proud of oneself, be conceited** (RBn HW). *líe ðáha óžo áhkiži ðí áape* when she came back she was proud of herself (RBn19-03). *súhkahtą́ą mį́įka hcí nalǫ́ǫhkile ðáalį káaye che óžo áhkiži ðí áape* turkey hen was proud [of herself] because she could hide [for herself] her nest so well (RBn19-05).
•• LFD 182: *ožo áhkižį* <u-zhu a´-ḳi'zhi^{n}> conceit, vainglorious, egotism, pride.

óžo ákižį (variant: **óžo ákiži**). VP [reg. *ki*-ret. + sync. nasal vowel stem, *óžo á_kiža_į* (object pronominal or portmanteau subject-object prefix *wi-* in the first slot, subject pronominal in second slot; underlying stem is *ákižaį* (*ákižai*), seen when there is a subject pronominal in the second slot (*akížami* 'I am proud of', *akížaži* 'you are proud of', etc.), but becomes *ákižį* (*ákiži*) when no subject pronominal precedes the *į*)] [*kik-* SUU + *óžo áži*] *(trans.)* **be proud of one's own (as of one's relative).** *žįkážį wíhta óžo áwakižami* I'm proud of my children (RBn HW). *óžo áwikižami* I'm proud of you (RBn HW; RBn22-0). *žįkážį óžo áwakiži akxai* he's proud of his children (RBn10-15; gloss by CQ). *ožo áwikižamí ąhé* I'm proud of you (RBn10-15; RBn HW-MREI).

óžo áži (variants: **ožóažį, óžo ážai, óžo ážaį**). VP, ADJP [reg.+sync. nasal vowel stem, *óžo á_ža_i* (object pronominal or portmanteau subject-object prefix *wi-* in the first slot, subject pronominal in second slot; underlying stem *ážaį/ážai* becomes *ážį/áži* when no subject prefix precedes the *į*)] *(trans.)* **(be) proud, proud of.** *óžo áðiži apai* they're proud of you (RBn HW). *táatą owáðakihką óžǫ [ážį?] mįkšé* I'm proud of what you did to help them (RBn10-21; CQ EN gloss). • **admire.** *hci wį ožóažį akxai* they're admiring a house (FH/09/11/01/pc).
•• LFD 187: *ihkóða wihta ožo aážį mikše o* <i-ḳo´-tha wi-ṭa u-zhu a-a´ zhi^{n} mi-kshe o> [sentence-final *o* is not used in Mod. Os.] he is my friend, I hold him in esteem.
••• Cf. *ažį́*.

óžokˀa. N **bet, wager** (04/07/95/PM/pc:okc, PM, FH ok'd *óžokˀa*, not *óžokˀą*).
•• LFD 183 (unconfirmed): *óžokˀą* <u´-zhu-ḳ'o^{n}> a wager (04/07/95/PM/pc:okc: not *ą*).

[Mod. Os. speakers have *óžokˀa*, not forms with final nasal vowel (***óžokˀą, ** óžokˀǫ*).] *óžokˀą hpaɣe* <u´-zhu-k̦'o^{n} p̦a-xe> I made a wager. *óžokˀą škaɣe* <u´-zhu-k̦'o^{n} shka-xe> you made a wager. *óžokˀą ąkaɣa pe* <u´-zhu-k̦'o^{n} o^{n}-ga-xa i> we made a wager.

óžokˀa káaɣe. VP [sync. *k*>*p*, *óžokˀa _káaɣe*] *(intr.)* **make a bet.**

óˀie (variant of **óie**).

ǫ, ǫ́

ǫ́. V [sync. nasal vowel stem, *_ǫ́* (1st dual/pl. *ąǫ́* 'we do' > *ǫǫ́* or *ǫ́ǫ*)] *(trans.)* **do, engage in (an activity [rare usage]).** *ąhíiða ški ǫ́ǫ hta ąkái* we are also going to swim (RBn3-32). *ónǫbre ąkáðį tą ášihta ąwánǫbre škí ǫ́ǫ htai* we have food, so we will have a picnic (lit., 'since we have food, let's also do a meal outside') (BE2.102; 03/07/95/FH/pc:okc).

••• Cf. *ékiǫ, éǫ, háaǫ.*

ǫ́ðąži (variant of **óðąži**).

ǫǫ́ (variant: **ǫ́ǫ**). V [1st pl. form of *ǫ́* 'do']. **we do (rare usage).**

ǫ́ǫ (variant: **ǫǫ́**). V [sync., nasal vowel stem, *(á)_ǫ́ǫ* (1st sg. and 2nd person subject forms, regularly *mǫ́ǫ* and *žǫ́ǫ*, respectively, may have an additional initial accented *á*, the status of which is unclear: *ámǫǫ, ážǫǫ ážǫ́ę*)] *(trans.)* **suffer from, have as an illness, be sick from.** [Perhaps more literally 'be enveloped by (sickness)', '(sickness) lies upon s.o.'; cf. the meaning 'wear' below.] *Mary mą́ąke púze ǫǫ́ nąðe áape* Mary has tuberculosis (FH/09/24/01/pc/prod). *húheka ški ǫǫ́ ðée apai* sickness lies over them [envelops them] too (FH: prayer). *waðílą waxpáį ǫǫ́ ðée apai* worry is upon them (FH/09/24/01/pc). *húheka ǫǫ́ ðée apai* there are those whom sickness lies over (FH/09/24/01/pc). *hóxpe ǫǫ́ akxai* he's got a cold (5/12/83/4). *Christine akxa hóxpe ǫǫ́ įkše?* does Christine have a cold? (01/19/95/FH/pc:ok). *Smokey akxa hóxpe ǫǫ́ akxai* Smokey has a cold (RBn19-01). *wácini ǫǫ́ akxai* he or she had VD (BE2.31). *hóxpe hpíiži ǫǫ́ akxái* she has whooping cough (FH:08/22/96). *hóxpe hpíiži [m]ǫ́ǫ mįkšé* I have a bad cold (RB). *hóxpe mǫ́ę mįkšé* I have a cold (FH/11/19/01/pc:ok). *hóxpe žǫ́ę?* do you have a cold? • **wear, use.** *mǫ́ę* I wear it. *žǫ́e* you wear it. *íhįhtą mǫ́ǫ mįkšé* I'm wearing earrings (5/12/83/4). *haaská ščúuce ámǫį* I'm wearing warm clothes (FH). *haaská ščúuce ážǫ ðąįšé* you're wearing warm clothing. *haaská ǫǫ́ ąkxai* she's wearing a dress (01/19/95/FH/prod). *įįhį htą ǫ́ǫ akxai* he or she is wearing earrings. *íhįhtą ąkǫ́ǫ ąkatxai* we're wearing earrings (5/12/83/4). *íhįhtą ąkǫ́ǫ ąkáðe* we're wearing earrings (5/12/83/4). *wanǫ́pˀę ǫǫ́* put on the necklace, wear the necklace. *ákahami ǫ́ǫ kšíe* put a shawl on her (03/08/95/FH/pc). *ípehį sí kše ǫ́ǫ kšíe* put a pillow under his foot (lit., 'have him have his foot be enveloped by a pillow') (03/08/95/FH/pc).

•• LFD 8: *ákahami ohpa hą* <a´-ga-ha-mi u-pa ho^{n}> I wear a coat. *ákahami ošpa hą* <a´-ga-ha-mi u-shpa ho^{n}> you wear a coat. *ákaha mi akihpi ðįke xci mǫ ha* <a´-ga-ha mi a-gi-p̦i thi^{n}-ge xtsi mo^{n} ha> [expected Mod. Os. form: *ákahamį akihpi (?) ðįké/ðįkšé xci mǫ́ǫ* 'I am wearing a coat really not (*ahkipi*)'; sentence-final *ha* is not used in Mod. Os.] my coat is threadbare. LFD 37: *tósku mǫ ha* <do´-çkiu mo^{n} ha> [expected Mod. Os. form: *tóoske mǫ́ǫ*; sentence-final *ha* is not used in Mod. Os.] I have the hiccups. *tósku žǫ ha* <do´-çkiu zho^{n} ha> [expected Mod. Os. form: *tóoske žǫ́ǫ*; sentence-final *ha* is not used in Mod. Os.] you have the hiccups.

••• *QU ˀǫ* use, have (as a disease) (RR).

ǫ́ǫða (variant: **óoðaðe**). V [reg.+sync., *_ǫ́ǫ_ða* (possibly *ǫ́ǫða* and *ǫ́ǫðe* have the same base form, [_]*ǫ́ǫ_ða*[_]*ðe*)] *(trans.)* **throw away, throw, leave or quit s.o., discard s.o. or s.t., toss out** (FH,pc, 8/8/94). *aǫ́ǫbra ~ ǫ́ǫbra ~ aǫ́ǫbre ~ ǫ́ǫbre* I throw it away. *ðaǫ́ǫšta ~ ðaǫ́ǫšce ~ ǫ́ǫšta ~ ǫ́ǫšce* you throw it away. *John apa Mary ǫ́ǫðape* John quit Mary (03/22/95/FH/pc).

•• LFD 122: *ǫ́ða* <o^{n}´-tha> to throw away, to dispense. *aǫ́bra* <a-o^{n}´-btha> I throw away (03/22/95/FH/pc:okc). *ðaǫ́šta* <tha-o^{n}´-shta> you throw away (03/22/95/FH/pc: *ðaǫ́ǫšče*). *ąǫ́ða pe* <o^{n}-o^{n}´-tha i> we throw away. (03/22/95/FH/pc:ok).

••• Cf. *hkíǫðe.*

ǫ́ǫðe. v [(reg.+) sync., (_)ǫ́ǫ_ðe (possibly *ǫ́ǫða* and *ǫ́ǫðe* have the same base form, [_]ǫ́ǫ_ða[_]ðe)] *(trans.)* **throw away, discard, leave behind, remove, as from office** (FH). *áǫǫbra* I threw something away (FH/t116b). *káache ǫ́ǫbre hta mįkšé* I'm going to throw away that stuff [stack of trash] (FH/t116b). *níhka akxa hkilíisąpi iáha ǫǫwíbre tą wakˀą́ hta mįkšé áape* the man turned around and said, "I'll sure be glad when I get rid of you" (RBnot 79/p4). *ðaǫ́ǫšče?* did you throw it away? (FH/t116b). *kį́įkįįežį hlaaskážį éðǫǫpa ǫ́ǫðe aðáape* he went leaving the flowers and butterflies behind (RBn15-03). • **quit s.o., divorce or separate from.** *wǫ́ǫbre* I left them, I quit them [from *wa-ǫ́ǫbre*]. *John apa Mary ǫ́ǫðe hta apai* John is going to quit Mary (03/22/95/FH/pc). *Mary apa ǫ́ǫðe ðiištą́ apai* Mary has already quit him (FH/t116b). *John apa Mary ǫ́ǫðape* John quit Mary (03/22/95/FH/pc).

•• LFD 45: *kahíke ǫða pe o* <ga-hi´-ge o^{n}-tha bi o> [sentence-final *o* is not used in Mod. Os.] the chief was removed from his office.

ǫ́pe. n **hip, hips, tail, buttocks** (04/11/95/LS/pc:ok). *ǫ́pe htą́ke* big hips (02/09/95/FH/pc:ok; BE2.67; BE2.74).

•• LFD 121: *ǫ́pe* <o^{n}´-be> the buttocks.

••• Cf. *letą́ ǫ́pe žúuce.*

ǫ́pežahta (variant: **úpežahta**). n **scissortail (lit., 'tail divided')** (BE2.117; 03/08/95/MREI/pc:uk; 04/13/95/FH/pc:uk; 04/20/95/LS/pc:ok).

•• RB: <u -peh zháh-tah>.

•• LFD 121: *ǫ́pežahta* <o^{n}´-be-zha-ṭa> forked tail.

••• Cf. *žáhta.*

ǫ́wǫ (variant of **ówǫ**).

---

p

pa. posit **positional article for pl. nonsubject.** *ecí pa žóąðale šíe ðe* you brought me to them (lit., 'you went with me to those ones there'). *súhkahtą́ą mį́įka éži pa wáðihota įkše ípahǫ įkši áape* turkey hen knew she had done everything she could to fool the others [them] (RBn19-05). *níhkaši pa wáatǫpa* take care of those men [standing or sitting], look after those people.

••• Cf. *tówa pa.*

pa (variant of **pai**).

pá. n **snow.** *pá húðe akxa pá škópe akxá* the snow is deep (lit., 'the snow coming down is a deep snow') (03/13/95/PM; BE2.124). *nuužú pá žóle húði akxai* rain and snow are coming down together (FH:4/24/96/pc; BE2.123). *pá xoce* gray snow, dingy snow.

•• LFD 17: *pa* <ba> snow.

pá húðe. vp [uninfl.] *(intr.)* **snow.** *pá húðe akxa* it is snowing (03/13/95/FH/pc:ok). *pá húðe ðiištą́ akxa* it stopped snowing (03/13/95/FH/pc:ok). *pahúðape* it snowed (03/13/95/FH/pc:ok). n **snow, snowfall, snow coming down, falling snow.** *pá húðe akxa pá škópe akxá* the snow [coming down] is [a] deep [snow] (03/13/95/PM; BE2.124).

•• RB: <pah-hyú-theh> (lit., 'snow coming down') (03/13/95/FH/pc:ok).

•• LFD 21: *pahúðe* <ba-hiu´-the> snowstorm.

pa- (variant of **paa-**).

pá- instr **by use of a sharp edge, by cutting.** [Precedes pronominal prefixes; thus, *páa-* 'I . . . by cutting', *páða-* 'you . . . by cutting', *pá-* 'he/she . . . by cutting', *ąpá-* 'we . . . by cutting'.] *haatxą́ta páðaleke hta nį́kšé súhka?* when are you going to hatch, chicken? (lit., 'when will you shatter it by using a sharp edge, chicken?') (FH).

•• LFD 17: *pa* <ba> a prefix to denote the act of cutting with a knife, a verb prefix denoting an act is done with a stick, spear, or any other sharp thing.

••• *WI mąą-* by cutting (KM); *OM ma-* by cutting (RL); *LAK wa-* by cutting (RL).

••• Cf. *páse.*

paa- (variant: **pa-**). instr **by pushing away or by hand, by pushing or pressing on s.t. (either compacting or spreading it), by pushing up and away with the hands** (FH/04/24/96tape). [Follows pronominal prefixes and takes sync. fortisizing stop stem inflection; thus, *hpaa-* 'I . . . by pushing', *špaa-* 'you . . . by pushing', *paa-* 'he/she . . . by pushing', *ąpaa-* 'we . . . by pushing'. But unexpectedly (probably as a result of language disuse) some Mod. Os. verbs with *paa-* sporadically use reg. inflection: *apaa-* 'I . . . by pushing', *ðapaa-* 'you . . . by pushing', *ąpaa-*

'we . . . by pushing'.] *haatxą́ta špáaleke hta nį́kšé súhka?* when are you going to hatch, chicken? (lit., 'when will you shatter it by pushing outward, chicken?') (FH).

••• *OM ba-* by pushing (RL); *LAK pa-* by pushing (RL); *WI wa-* by pressure or pushing (KM).

••• Cf. *paaɣówe, paahí, paasé, paaxcé.*

paaché. V [sync. fortisizing stop stem, *_paaché*] [perhaps *paa-* INSTR + *che* POSIT] *(trans.)* **sew.** *hpáache* I sewed it. *špáache* you sewed it. *ąpáache* we sewed it.

•• LFD 24: *paché* <ba-tse´> to sew. *hpáche* <p̣a´-tse> I sew. *špáche* <shpa´-tse> you sew. *ąpácha pe* <o^{n}-ba´-tsa i> we sew.

••• Cf. *wapáache.*

paacˀį (variant: **paacˀí** [FH]). V [sync. fortisizing stop stem, *_paacˀį*] [presumably contains *paa-* INSTR] *(intr.)* **stoop over (as to touch one's toes), bend down.** *hpaacˀįe* I stooped over. *špaacˀį* you stooped over. *ée paacˀį akxai* he is stooping over (MSB). • ADJ, V *(intr.)* **(be) crooked** (04/25/95/PM/pc).

•• RB: <pah-ts'í^{n}> (BE2.128; 03/14/95/MREI/pc:prod).

•• JOD (slip file): *žé ðištą tą, pacˀį-aú, ápi aú* <Çe´ ¢ücta^{n}´ - ṭa^{n}, p̣áts'i^{n} -au´, áp̣i au´> [expected Mod. Os. form: *žé ðiištą́ tą, pacˀį-a áape* 'when he finished defecating, bend down, he said'] When he (a child) finished stooling, he said, Turn bottom up!

•• LFD 24: *pacˀį* <ba-ts'i^{n}´> head down and feet up, headlong, head foremost (meanings unconfirmed; MREI).

••• Cf. *paakˀó.*

paacˀó. V [sync. fortisizing stop stem, *_paacˀó*] [presumably contains *paa-* INSTR] *(intr.)* **stoop over.**

paaɣáce. V [sync. fortisizing stop stem?, *_paaɣáce?*] *(intr.)* **open out, spread, spread open, blossom, bloom.** *hlaaská akxa paaɣáci akxai* the flowers opened out.

•• JOD (slip file): *paxáce* <p̣a-qa´-ṭse> crest of hair, parting of man's hair (JK). [Note discrepancy between JOD's *x* and Mod. Os. *ɣ*.]

••• Cf. *opáaɣa.*

paaɣí. V [sync. fortisizing stop stem?, *_paaɣí?*] [presumably contains *paa-*INSTR] *(trans.)* **push to awaken or make active, activate by pushing on** (RBn23-17). *šíi apa oðíhtą paaɣí apai* they're pushing the car (to start it) (RBn23-17).

•• JOD (slip file): *paxí* <p̣a-qi´> to arouse once from sleep by pushing with a stick, etc., held firmly against him (?). [Note discrepancy between JOD's *x* and Mod. Os. *ɣ*.]

••• Cf. *ðixí.*

paaɣó. N **hill, mountain (rare; variant of *paaxó*?)** (LS, JOD); **corner, angle** (JOD).

•• JOD (slip file): *paɣó* <p̣a-xu´> modern word, a hill or bluff, a high hill or mountain. "The ancient word was *p̣ahě*." *paɣó* <p̣a-xu´> an angle or corner. *paɣó tópa* <p̣a-xu´ ṭúp̣a> four-cornered.

paaɣówe (variants: **paaɣó, paaɣóe, páaɣo** [MSB]). V [sync. fortisizing stop stem, *_paaɣówe*) [presumably contains *paa-* INSTR] *(trans.)* **push along, push s.o. or s.t. steadily (making the person or object move along)** (MSB 01/02; FH:4/24/96/tape:ok). *wihpáaɣowe* I'm pushing you (FH). *ą́špaaɣo ðaįšé* you're pushing me (FH/06/16/01/pc). *paaxó paaɣówe apai* he's pushing the mountain (FH:4/24/96/tape). *paaxó paaɣó apai* he's pushing the mountain. *ðée ðe paaɣówe* this one here, push him (FH:4/24/96/tape). *ą́paaɣo įká!* don't push me! (FH/07/02/01/pc).

•• JOD (slip file): *paxówe* <p̣a-qu´-wě> to make an obj., as a book on a table, slide or slip along by pushing it. [Note discrepancy between JOD's *x* and Mod. Os. and KS *ɣ*.]

••• *KS mą baɣówe* the game of 'swing the arrow' (RR).

••• Cf. *ðiiɣó.*

paahą́ (variant: **paahá**). V [sync., fortisizing stop stem, *_paahą́*] [presumably contains *paa-* INSTR] *(trans.)* **raise, hold up** (RBn10-10:JW). *hpáaha* I raise it. *špáaha* you raise it. *ąpáaha* we raise it. *šáake paahápi* raise your hand (instructions uttered by the person saying the prayer to those present, before beginning to say the prayer at a birthday dinner or after a peyote meeting, etc., followed at the end of the prayer by *íistahkie pi* 'bless yourselves with it', instructing supplicants to pass the previously raised hand over their minds and their hearts). *kaakǫ́naa, šáake paahą́pi, íštahkíapai* that's all, raise your hand, use it on yourself (FH). *nǫǫpé paahą́* raise your hand (as when voting by a show of hands) (RBn22-03). *waahkíhta paahá* pray for yourselves, raise it up (RBn10-15). *waahkíhta paahá* pray for each other, raise it up (RBn10-15).

•• LFD 49: *kípaha* <gi´-ba-ha> to show anything to another. *hkawa wihta ehpaha tǫpe ahkiðe ha* <ḳa-wa wi-ṭa e-p̣a-ha do^{n}-be a-ḳi-the ha> [expected Mod. Os. form: *hekáwa wíhta ée*

paahą́ (*continued*)
hpáahą tǫ́pe akšíðe; sentence-final *ha* is not used in Mod. Os. and *kípaahą* not attested] I showed him my horse (lit., 'my horse for him I raised up, I allowed him to see it'). *mąžą́ ðitxaðą ðešpaha* <mo^n-zho^n´ thi-ta tho^n the-shpa-ha> you showed him your land.
••• Cf. *opáahą, táatą paahą́, watáahą.*

paahí (variant: **paahį́**). v [sync. fortisizing stop stem, *_paahí*] [perhaps contains *paa-* INSTR] *(trans.)* **pick or gather (e.g., fruit, flowers), collect together or pick up (many small, scattered things)** (RBnot-nd-1/p21; FH/7/24/95/pc:okc). *hpáahi* I gather it. *špáahi* you gather it. *ąpáahi* she gathers it. *háazu špáahi?* did you pick grapes? *hápa ąpáahi ąkái* we are picking corn. *watástoe paahį́ toe ąkái hce* let's go pick pecans (RBn12-05). • **sort (e.g., beans, clothing to be laundered).** *hǫbrį́ke che hpaahíke* [*ke* 'scattered'] I sorted the beans (FH:ok). *hǫbrį́ke hpáasihi mįkšé* [*hpáasihi* rather than *hpáahi* is unexpected] I'm sorting the beans (FH/11/17/01/pc). *hǫbrį́ke paahí akxai* he's sorting the beans (FH/11/17/01/pc). *hǫbrį́ke che paahí apai* they're sorting the beans (FH/11/17/01/pc). *haaská wasúhuži ke paahípai, ščúuwasu htai* be sorting the dirty clothes [pl. addressee], let's you [pl.] wash them (FH/11/17/01/pc).
•• LFD 21: *pahí* <ba-hí> to pick, as selecting one from many; to sort, to sort the good from the bad; picked, selected, the best. LFD 65: *hǫbrį́ke che hpahi* <ho^n-bthi^n´-ge tse pa-hi> I sorted the beans.
••• Cf. *wapáahi.*

paahí. N **diamonds (suit in a deck of cards)** (03/10/95/FH/pc:ok; (RBn10-21/JW).

páahi [JOD] (variant of **hpaahį́**). [This form perhaps is simply a misrecording by JOD.]

paahį́ (variant of **paahí** 'pick or gather').

paahléke (variant of **paaléke**).

paakíce. v [sync. fortisizing stop stem, *_paakíce*] [probably *paa-* INSTR + an otherwise unattested stem *kice* 'squeak' (LF)] *(intr.)* **play music on an instrument.** • N **musical instrument, piano** [Osage has no special words for other instruments (except drum) (LS)] (02/13/95/FH/pc:ok; RBn1-MOJ/p42; 04/17/95/LS/pc:ok; BE2.91; 02/27/95/FH/pc:ok; FH/09/22/01/pc; BE2.91). • **music.** *paakíce káaye* make music.
•• JOD (slip file): *pakíce* <p̣a-ḳi´-ṭse> to play a fiddle.
•• LFD 20: *pakíce* <ba-gi´-dse> a fiddle. *pakice kše spákice ha* <ba-gi-dse ke spa´-gi-dse ha> [expected Mod. Os form: *paakíce špáakice;* sentence-final *ha* is not used in Mod. Os.] you play the fiddle.

páakʔa (variant: **páaxa**). N **cottonwood** (HRE).
•• RB: <báh-xah, bah´-kʔah> (BE2.25; RBn23-08;HRE/12/29/01/pc: both ok).
•• JOD (slip file): *pákʔa* <p̣a´-k'a> a cottonwood tree, cottonwood.

paakʔó (variant: **paakʔǫ́**). v [sync., fortisizing stop stem, *_paakʔó*] *(trans.)* **dig (e.g., a grave)** (RBnot-nd-1/p22); *(intr.)* **stoop over (a little)** (1/27/83/p1). [The triplet *paacʔį, paacʔó,* and *paakʔó* apparently show consonant and vowel symbolism.]
•• LFD 22: *pákʔo* <ba-ḳ'u´> to dig a ditch. *hpákʔo* <p̣a´-ḳ'u> I dig a ditch. *špákʔo* <shpa´-ḳu> you dig a ditch. *ąpákʔo pe* <o^n-ba´-ḳ'u i> we dig a ditch.

paaléke (variant: **paahléke** [historically *paaxléke*]). v [sync. fortisizing stop stem, *_paaléke*] [*paa-* INSTR + *léke*] *(intr.)* **hatch, shatter by pushing outward.** [Refers to birds pushing outward on the shell of an egg until it breaks; contrasts with *pá_leke* 'hatch, shatter by using a sharp edge' (with instrumental *pá-* 'by using a sharp edge'), which refers to birds' beaks cutting the eggshell (FH).] *hpáaleke* I hatch. *špáaleke* you hatch. *ąpáaleke* we hatch. *haatxą́ta špáaleke hta nįkšé, súhka?* when are you going to hatch, chicken?

páaleze (variant: **páleze**). v [sync. fortisizing stop stem, *_páaleze*] [*paa-* INSTR + *léze*] *(trans.)* **write s.t. or make one's mark upon s.t., vote, vote for or against s.t. or s.o.** (BE2.161; 04/27/95/FH/pc:ok).
••• *KS baléze* to make striped, to write lines (RR).

páalǫðį (variants: **paalǫ́ðį, paalǫ́ðe**). v [sync. fortisizing stop stem? *_páalǫðį*] [*paa-* INSTR + *lǫ́ðį*] *(trans.)* **impel s.o. to drunkenness, push s.o. to be drunk or upset, make s.o. nervous, talk s.o. silly** (FH). *ðée pa páalǫði apai* these here are all upset, all shook up (lit., 'these ones they've pushed them making them nervous') (FH).

paamą́ši (variants: **paamáši, pamáši**). v [sync. fortisizing stop stem, *_paamą́ši*] [*paa-* INSTR + *mą́ši*] *(trans.)* **lift, hold up (e.g., a picture in front of a group of people in an auditorium), raise (e.g., a flag or a window)**

(02/15/95/FH/pc:okc). *hpáažį paamáši akxái* he's holding up the baby (e.g., for people to see it). *įcé waléze hpaamáši hta mįkše* I'll hold the picture up (02/15/95/FH/pc:prod). *haaská paamáši* raise your shirt up (02/15/95/FH/pc:prod).

•• LFD 22: *pamą́ši* <ba-mo^{n}´-shi> to raise an object by pushing it upward with the hands or with a pole. *hpámąši* <p̣a´-mo^{n}-shi> I raised the object with my hands. *špámąši* <shpa´-mo^{n}-shi> you raised it with your hands. *ąpámąši pe* <o^{n}-ba´-mo^{n}-shi i> we raised it with our hands.

paasása. v [sync. fortisizing stop stem, *_paasása*] [reduplicated form of *paasé*] *(trans.)* **dice by cutting over and over (lit., 'cut repeatedly by pushing down on')** (FH). *paasása!* dice it! (RB) .

paasé. v [sync. fortisizing stop stem, *_paasé*] [*paa-* INSTR + *-se*] *(trans.)* **cut up (e.g., meat or potatoes), cut into pieces (e.g., a cake) (lit., 'cut by pushing down on').** *htáa hpáase mįkšé* I cut up meat. *haakǫ́ta wacúe skúe špáase ðikǫ́ða apai?* why did they want you to cut the cake? *htáa špáase nįkšé* you cut up meat. *htáa páase akxai* he cuts up meat. *htáa ąpáase ąkatxą́i* we cut up meat. • **cut off by using a pushing motion.** *žą́ą hpáase* I'm cutting off a limb. *špáase hta ðaįšé?* are you going to cut it off? (FH/11/17/01/pc). *špáasape?* did you all cut it off? (FH/11/17/01/pc). *ąpáasape* we cut it off (FH/11/17/01/pc).

••• Cf. *páse.*

paasíke (variants: **páasike, paasį́ke**). v [sync. fortisizing stop stem, *_paasíke*] *(trans.)* **splatter, spray, splash, squirt, splinter, cause to fly out in pieces.** *wálįį hpíižie óhesažį alį́į ðáha níi hpáasike* it's awful that I sat down real quick and splattered water (04/19/95/FH/pc). *hpáasike* I splattered it (04/19/95/FH/pc). *štǫ́pažie ðalį́į óhesažį áha níi špáasike* you didn't look when you sat down hard, and you sat in water and splattered it, made it shoot out (04/19/95/FH/pc). • *(intr.)* **splatter, spray, splash, squirt, splinter, fly out in pieces.** *žą́ą akxa paasíke akxái* the wood chips are flying out (lit., 'the wood is flying out in pieces') (04/19/95/FH/pc). *žą́ą kaasípi tą žą́ąžį paasíke akxai* when he cuts wood, the little splinters fly out (or 'when he cuts wood, he splinters it'?) (04/19/95/FH/pc).

paaspą́. v [sync. fortisizing stop stem, *_paaspą́*] *(trans.)* **touch with the fingers, nudge, punch.** *hpáaspą* I touch it. *špáaspą* you touch it. *alį́į šǫ mįkšé ąpáaspąpe* I was sitting there and he punched me (03/23/95/FH/pc:okc; 1/20/83/693).

•• LFD 19–20: *paspą́* <ba-çpo^{n}´> to nudge with the hand, the elbow, or with a stick to attract the attention of another. *hpáspą* <p̣a´-çpo^{n}> I nudged with my hand. *špáspą* <shpa´-çpo^{n}> you nudged with your hand. *ąpáspą pe* <o^{n}-ba´-çpo^{n} i> we nudged with our hands.

paastǫ́ka. v [sync. fortisizing stop stem, *_paastǫ́ka*] *(trans.)* **soften by pushing on.**

•• JOD (slip file): *pastǫ́ka* <pa-ctŭñ´-ka> to thrust a stick, etc., into a hole at a soft object, as at an animal covered with hair, or to see if the soft ob. is there. JOD (Devouring Mountain p2 lines 10–11): *wahǫ́ižįka bráani na ną́ące ą́pastǫka ku káaɣape áakxa ska* <Wahu^{n}´içiñ´ka p¢a´hni^{n} -na´ năn´-tse a^{n}´ pa-ctŭñ´-ka ku kaxapi, á akqá ska> [JOD's *ku káaɣape* <ku kaxapi> is likely *kikáaɣape* in Mod. Os.] the orphan that I devoured made my heart turn soft, he said.

paašcéka (variant of **pąąšcéka**).

paašé. CONT **continuative aspect postverbal marker (indicating ongoing action or state in present, past, or future time) for 2nd pl. sitting/moving/lying down subject.** ['Moving' here means 'changing location'; motions or gestures that do not change the entity's location in space do not count.] *žįkóhkiha ðíizo paašé?* are you all enjoying your grandchildren? *íe ąðánąąk?ǫ škǫ́šta įké paašé ąži iðáe ątxąhé* you all don't want to hear me talk, but I'm talking (RBn10-16). *žįkážį ókašeįki paašé?* are your children okay? [note 2nd pl. use with *žįkážį*] [*paašé* in this example pluralizes the understood 2nd person possessor of *žįkážį*] (RBn10-7:JW). *kasį́ táatą hta paašé?* what are you [pl.] doing tomorrow? (03/23/95/FH/pc:okc; BE2.142). *howáįki paašé?* where are you all? (04/28/95/LS/pc:ok:prod). • **you are characterized by [the preceding expression, which may be a noun phrase].** *hį́į hpíiži paašé* you [pl.] have bad teeth. *waðílą hpíiži paašé* you [pl.] have a bad temper.

••• Cf. *ðaįšé.*

paašpú (variant: **paašpé**). N **cut corn, fresh corn cut off the cob** (01/12/95/FH/pc:ok, not preasp). [To prepare *paašpú*, cut the corn off the cob, place it in boiling water, and cook it until it takes on the consistency of gravy.]

páašpue. v [sync. fortisizing stop stem, *_páašpue*] [presumably contains *paa-* INSTR] *(trans.)* **peel** (RBn10-16). *záani hpaašpue* I peeled them all (RBn10-16)

••• Cf. *ðušpú.*

páaxa (variant of **páakʔa**).

paaxcé. V [sync. fortisizing stop stem, _*paaxcé*] [perhaps contains *paa-* INSTR] *(trans.)* **tie down (e.g., a drum), place or push two or more things together and tie them; bind, handcuff, manacle.** *céɣenii paaxcé apai* they're tying a drum (RBn10-7:JW). • **gather and tie in a bundle or bundles** (01/31/95/FH/pc:ok). *hpáaxce* I tied it into bundles (FH). *špáaxce* you tied it into bundles (FH). *ąpáaxcape* we tied it into bundles (FH). *haxį haaskámį ški špáaxce hta nįkšé?* these blankets and shawls, are you going to gather them up and tie them in a bundle? *paaxcí apai* they are gathering [something] up and tying [it/them] in a bundle (01/31/95/FH/pc:ok). *paaxtáži apai, paaxcáži apai* they're not gathering it/them up and tying it/them into a bundle (01/31/95/FH/pc:okc). *paaxtá!* gather it/them up and tie it/them into a bundle! (01/31/95/FH/pc:ok). *haxį che paaxcé* tie those blankets up (FH).

•• LFD 25: *paxcé* <ba-xtse´> to tie up into bundles as a sheaf. *hpáxce* <p̣a´-xtse> I tied it into bundles. *špáxce* <shpa´-xtse> you tied it up. *ąpáxca pe* <o^{n}-ba´-xtsa i> we tied it up. *paxcé* <ba-xtse´> to manacle, handcuff, shackle. *hpáxce* <p̣a´-xtse> I handcuffed [him]. *špáxce* <shpa´-xtse> you handcuffed [him]. *ąpáxca pe* <o^{n}-ba´-xtsa i> we handcuffed [him]. LFD 345: *páxce* <ba´- xtse> [same forms listed as for *paxcé* <ba-xtse´>] to tie a bundle.

••• Cf. *ípaaxce.*

paaxó N **hill, mountain.** [Perhaps lit. 'rise, rise up from the earth' (02/09/95/FH/pc:okc). Also a name, probably shortened from *paaxóska* (Carl Kemohah was often called by this shortened form, used actively in the early 1900s by the other children growing up with him, among whom only Osage was spoken [FH]).] *paaxóžį* low hill, little hill (FH:4/25/96/tape; BE2.66). *paaxó įkšítxa ąkókaxpai* we threw him off the hill (RBn19-02). *paaxó ki ąkáipe* we're going to the mountains (to express 'we're going to Colorado') (02/27/95/FH/pc:ok). *paaxó ki aðáape* they went to the mountains (02/27/95/FH/pc:ok; BE2.90, RBn22-15). *paaxó šcee* a high hill or tall mountain.

•• LFD 26: *paxó* <ba-xu´> a hill, a ridge. *paxó htą́ka* <ba-xu´ ṭo^{n}-ga> a mountain.

••• *OP baɣú* flat topped hill (mesa, butte), hilltop; *KS baxó* mountain (RR).

••• Cf. *paaɣó.*

paaxóska N **White Mountain (personal name).** [Carl Kemohah's name (Joe's brother), possibly an earth clan name.]

paaxǫ́. V [sync. fortisizing stop stem, _*paaxǫ́*] [*paa-* INSTR + *xǫ́*] *(trans.)* **break a long object by pushing, break off by pushing (e.g., a limb)** (01/07/95/FH/pc; 04/19/95/FH/pc:uk).

•• LFD 25: *paxǫ́* <ba-xo^{n}´> to break a stick, tent pole, or an awl by pushing. *hpáxǫ* <p̣a´-xo^{n}> I broke the tent pole by pushing [expected Mod. Os. gloss: 'I broke it by pushing']. *špáxǫ* <shpa´-xo^{n}> you broke the tent pole by pushing. *ąpáxǫ* <o^{n}-ba´-xo^{n}> we broke the tent pole by pushing. *žą́xa kše hpaxǫ* <zho^{n}´-xa ke p̣a-xo^{n}> I broke the stick [expected Mod. Os. gloss: 'I broke the stick that was lying there'].

paazé. N **breast, udder.** *paazé wáli lą́ąðe akxai* she has [lit., 'is characterized by'] really big breasts (BE2.12; 01/19/95/FH/pc:ok).

•• LFD 18: *pazé* <ba-çe´> a woman's breast. [LF's alternate term *mązé* <mo^{n}-çe´> 'woman's breast' (LFD 96) is not Osage; it is probably Omaha.]

paazénii. N [*paazé* + *níi*] **milk (lit., 'breast liquid')** (BE2.87; 02/24/95/FH/pc:okc).

•• RB: <báh-zeh-ni>.

•• LFD 18: *pazéni* <ba-çe´-ni> milk. *pazéni skiðe* <ba-çe´-ni çki-the> sweet milk. *pazéni niwekʔuce(?) wį* <ba-çe´-ni ni-we-ḳ'u-dse wi^{n}> a quart of milk (unconfirmed; 03/01/95/FH/pc:uk 'quart').

paazénii ðiiscúe. VP [sync., *paazénii _ðiiscúe*] *(trans.)* **milk** (LF).

•• LFD 19: *pazéni ðiscue* <ba-çe´-ni thi-stsu-e> to milk. *paséni, briscue* <ba-çe´-ni, bthi-stsu-e> I milk. *paséni ąðiscua pe* <ba-çe´-ni o^{n}-thi, stsu-a i> we milk.

••• *QU distíhte* pull open, milk, pull out (RR).

paazénii saakí. N **cheese** (03/07/95/PM/pc:ok).

•• LFD 18: *pazéni saki* <ba-çe´-ni ça-gi> cheese. *pazéni saki ązo* <ba-çe´-ni ça-gi o^{n}-çu> I like cheese. *pazéni saki ðizo* <ba-çe´-ni ça-gi thi-çu.> you like cheese.

paazénii skúðe. N **sweet milk.**

paazénii wéli. N **butter (lit., 'milk grease')** (BE2.14; 01/09/95/FH/pc:ok); **cream.**

•• LFD 19: *pazéniweli* <ba-çe´-ni-we-gthi> cream. *pazéniweli waskiðe itápe ąso* <ba-çe´-ni-we-gthi wa-çki-the i-da´-be o^{n}-çu> [expected Mod. Os. form: *waskúðe paazénii wéli áažu ą́ązo*] I like cream on fruit.

paazénii wéli saakí. N **cheese (lit., 'hardened cream')** (01/09/95/FH/pc:prod).

pábrakʔa. V [reg., *pá_brakʔa*] [*pá-* INSTR + *brákʔa*] *(trans.)* **flatten by cutting, make flat by using a sharp edge, plane (as wood with a woodplane).**

•• LFD 18: *pábrakʔa* <ba´-btha-k'a> to flatten a piece of wood, or make smooth as with a plane. *páðabrahka* <ba´-tha-btha-ka> you flattened the wood by cutting.

pacé (variant: **páce**). V [reg?., *pa_cé?*] [presumably contains *pá-* INSTR] **butcher.** *hceeská wį́ páce hta apái* they're going to kill a beef (FH: 07/24/95, 4/17/96, FH/4/22/96/tape).

••• Cf. *hpáce.*

páce (variant: **pacé**). N **boat.**

pacíolįį. N [*páce* + *olį́į*] **boating.**

paðe (variant of **pai**).

paðé (variant: **páðe**). N **winter** (03/16/95/MREI/pc:ok; BE2.159). [Takes 'standing' positional article *che.*] *hǫ́ǫpa wį́ páðe ehtáha* one day toward winter, one winter day (RBn16-02).

•• RB: <páh-théh>.

•• LFD 24: *páðe* <ba´-the> winter. *páðe ce žą oðaą htahce ani kše ahį* <ba´-the dse zhoⁿ u-tha-oⁿ ta-tse a-ni ke a-hiⁿ> [expected Mod. Os. form: *páðe che žą́ą ašcį́ hta nįkšé?*] have you wood for the winter? *páðe che žą abrį ha* <ba´-the tse zhoⁿ a-bthiⁿha> [expected Mod. Os. form: *páðe che žą́ą abrį́;* sentence-final *ha* is not used in Mod. Os.] I have my wood for the winter.

paðíhta. ADJ **last.** *mį́įǫpa paðíhta* last month (HH/t38-a-p1; 04/14/95/FH/pc:ok).

páðo (variant: **páðǫ**). N **locust, insect** (RBn3-55; 02/16/95/FH/pc:okc; BE2.80).

•• LFD 24: *páðo* <ba´-tho> harvest fly, locust. *páðo apa žąape ke ðasni a po* <ba´-tho a-ba zhoⁿ-a-be ge tha-çni a bo> [expected Mod. Os. form: *páðo apa žą́ąpe ke ðaachá pe;* the form *ðasni* was never an Osage form (it is probably Omaha), and *a po* is not recognized by Osage speakers] the locust eats the leaves of trees.

pae (variant of **pai**).

paɣíce (variant: **paɣį́ce**). V [stat., *_paɣíce*] *(intr.)* **sweat, perspire** (RBn10-21/JW). *wálį ą́paɣici mįkšé* I'm sure sweating (RBn10-21/JW).

•• LFD 24: *paɣíce* <ba-xi´-dse> to perspire. *ą́paɣice* <oⁿ´-ba-xi-dse> I perspire. *ðípaɣice* <thi´-ba-xi-dse> you perspire. *wápaɣica pe* <wa´-ba-xi-dsa i> we perspire.

••• *KS baɣį́je (baɣį́jape)* sweat, perspire (stative JOD) (RR).

páhįįži (?) (variant: **páįži** [JOD]). V [reg., *pá_hįįži*] [*pá-* INSTR + *hį́į* 'slivers, small strips' + *aží* NEG] *(trans.)* **fail to cut due to dullness of the knife.**

•• JOD (slip file): *páįži, páįpáži* <pa´-iⁿ-çi>, <pa´-iⁿ-pa´-çi> to fail in cutting with a knife, because of its dullness. *páaį máži* <páaiⁿ-máçi> I fail to cut. *páðaįži* <pá¢a-iⁿ-çi> you fail to cut.

••• Cf. *hpaahį́ži.*

pahúkaaski. N [*pá húðe* + *kaaskí*] **snowball (lit., 'compressed snowfall')** (01/10/95/FH/pc:prod).

pai (variants: **paiðe, paðe, pae, pa**). SUFFIX **continuative imperative plural postverbal marker (follows the verb and signals that the speaker desires that the addressee [always pl.] continue the action of the verb into the future; can be approximately translated 'be doing [the action of the verb], continue to do [the action of the verb], go along doing [the action of the verb]' [FH]).** [Replaces *api.*] *ðée ékiǫ pai ąðákisuðe škǫ́štapi tą* do this in remembrance of me (lit., 'be doing this whenever you want to remember me') (FH/09/11/01/pc). *wahkǫ́ta akxa eená hta akxa na, hpahą́le mę́į, ahkílaðį pai* soon it will be only God, put him first, [be] carry[ing] yourself that way (04/04/99/FH/pc). *į́nǫhpa pai, wécʔa ochía* be careful (lit., 'be going along carefully'), there are lots of snakes. *haaská wasúhuži ke paahí pai, ščúuwasu htai* be sorting the dirty clothes, let's you [pl. addressee] wash them (FH/11/17/01/pc). *táatą hǫ́ǫži ecíkie tą ékiǫ ðįkápai* if there's anything bad around, don't do [be doing] that. *hpéece íištahkipa* [*íištahkiðepa*] use [be using] the fire to bless yourselves (PM:04/07/95/pc). *okíhkąpái!* you all help [be helping] him out! (RB; 02/09/95/FH/pc:okc). *ąhkihtǫ́pa pai* you all watch [be watching] each other, take [be taking] care of each other.

•• LFD 24 (unconfirmed): *pa ðį ho* <ba thiⁿ ho> [expected Mod. Os. form: *pái*] an emphatic expression used at the end of a sentence. *onąlį pa ðį ho* <u-noⁿ-xthiⁿ ba thiⁿho> hurry up. *xįðaða pa ðį ho* <xiⁿ-tha-tha ba thiⁿ ho> [sentence-final *ho* in the above examples is not used in Mod. Os.] be quick.

páįži (variant of **páhįįži?**).

páleke. V [reg., *pá_leke*] *(intr.)* **hatch;** *(trans., intr.)* **shatter by cutting or using a sharp edge.** [Contrast with *paaléke.*] *haatxą́ta páðaleke hta nį́kšé súhka?* when are you going to hatch, chicken?

páleze (variant of **páaleze**).

pamáši (variant of **paamáši**).

panáa. v [conjug. unknown; may be reg., _panáa] (*intr., trans.*) **adjourn, be adjourned, stop, pause, recess, disband, end, break up (as a meeting), "let out" (e.g., school for summer recess), be dismissed (as at the end of a school day).** *ą́pánaa hce* let's [two people] adjourn (12/30/94/FH/pc:ok). *ą́pánaa htai* let's [more than two people] adjourn (12/30/94/FH/pc:prod orig). *kaatxá ą́pánaa htai* let's stop a while [more than two people]. *taapóska apa panáipe* school is out (12/30/94/FH/pc:corr). *wažáži íe íkʔuce hą́ðé hǫ́ǫpa tóe ą́pánaa htai* let's adjourn our Osage language class this evening for a few days (lit., 'trying to talk Osage, we're going to let out for a while' [FH]) (12/30/94/FH/pc:ok; BE2.1). *taapóska panáa* school is dismissed [said at the close of the school day], school is out [for the summer] (03/08/95/MREI/pc:okc; BE2.116).

•• LFD 22: *paną́ða* <ba-noⁿ-tha> to disband, to adjourn a meeting. *paną́ðe* <ba-noⁿ-the> recess.

pánihkášie. N [pá + nihkašie] **snowman.** *pánihkašie wį káaɣape* he made a snowman (RBn23-14).

papó. v [conjug. unknown] (*intr.*) **sink, lower, go down (e.g., the sun when setting)** (HRE/01/17/02/pc). [Possibly *hpapó*?]

••• Cf. *mį́įhpapo*.

pásąci. N **north** (LF only, unconfirmed).

•• LFD 19: *pásąci* <ba´-çoⁿ-dsi> north (unconfirmed; 03/01/95/FH/pc:uk; 04/17/95/LS/pc:uk).

pascé (variant: **pašcé**). v [reg., pa_scé] [pá- + scéce] (*trans.*) **cut up, slice into strips or slices using a sharp edge (e.g., bananas, sausage, watermelon).** *wacúe skúe paðášce hta ðąįšé?* are you going to cut up the cake? *hcéska wį pascé hta apai* they're going to cut up a beef.

páse. v [reg., pá_se] [pá- + -se] (*trans.*) **cut with a sharp edge.** *wacúe skúe paðáse kǫ́ða apai* they're wanting you to cut the cake. *páase* I cut it with a sharp edge. *paðáse* you cut it with a sharp edge. *ą́pásape* we cut it with a sharp edge.

• LFD 18: *páse* <ba´-çe> to cut hair, cord, or rope with a knife. *wéðį kše páase o* <we´-thiⁿ ke ba´-a-çe o> [sentence-final *o* is not used in Mod. Os.] I cut the rope. *wéðį kše páðase o* <we´-thiⁿ ke ba´-tha-çe o> [sentence-final *o* is not used in Mod. Os.] you cut the rope. *wéðį kše ą́pasa pe* <we´-thiⁿ ke oⁿ-ba-ça i> we cut the rope. LFD 24

(unconfirmed): *páðase* <ba´-tha-çe> [expected Mod. Os. form *páse*] to cut as when butchering [gloss should probably be 'you butcher'].

páskuha (variant: **paskúha**). ADV, PPN **alongside, beside, adjacent, parallel (to).** *ší kǫ́kǫe apai, žįkáží apa páskuha nąąkí apai* he went round and round, children ran beside him (RBn10-2:MOJ/79). *óžąke paskúha* beside the road.

•• LFD 19: *paskú* <ba-çkiu´> near, side by side, contiguous, adjacent.

••• KS *baskúha* nearby, close, parallel (RR).

pašcé (variant of **pascé**).

pašǫ́ (variant of **pašǫ́we**).

pašǫ́šǫwe v [presumably reg., pa_šǫ́šǫwe] [reduplicated form of *pašǫ́we*] (02/09/95/FH/pc:okc) (*trans.*) **bind.**

•• LFD 358: *pašǫ́šǫ* <ba-shoⁿ´-shoⁿ> zigzag.

pašǫ́we (variants: **pašǫ́, pašǫ́wį**). v [reg., pa_šǫ́we] (*trans.*) **bind (as a blanket), using a zigzag pattern on the edges.** *haxį́ kóoci ščúuwasu tą wíe paašǫ́wį, hcéka éekǫ hta akxai* if you will clean that old [striped] blanket, I'll bind it and it will be like new (FH/11/19/01/pc:prod). *brúuwasu tą ðíe pašǫ́wa* if I clean it, you bind it (FH/11/19/01/pc:prod). *haxį́ įkšé páðašǫ hta ðąįšé?* are you going to bind the blanket? (FH/11/19/01/pc:prod).

pátą. CONJ **when, and.** [Often appears in speeches as a default connector of phrases, pronounced *pǝtǝ*.]

•• JOD (slip file): *pátą* <p̣a´-t̬aⁿ> when, and; it often connects verbs in the pl., but sometimes it refers to the 3rd sg.

páxoce. N [pá + xóce] **Ioway or Iowa Indians (a tribe living in Nebraska, Kansas, and Oklahoma and in earlier days in Iowa) (lit., 'gray snow').** [In the Ioway language, *Baxoje* 'gray snow'; refers to the soot-tainted snow from cooking and lodge fires covering Chakirutha lodges (wigwams, long houses) when the Oto-Missouri reunited with the Baxoje after decades of separation (Jimmy Goodtracks).]

•• RB: <páh-xó-tseh> (02/13/95/FH/pc:ok; BE2.71).

•• JOD (slip file): *páxoce* <p̣a´-qu-t̬se> Ioway.

•• LFD 25: *páxoce* <Ba´-xo-dse> the name of the Iowa tribe of Indians living in the State of Nebraska.

pázą htá hu. N **east wind, "fall winds"** (PM) **(probably lit. 'comes [(a)hú] from the pines [cf. *páze hú*]')** (RB, unconfirmed).

•• RB: <páh-zah-táh-hu or péh-zeh-táh-hu> (BE2.38, unconfirmed; 12/30/94/FH/pc:uk; 04/26/95/LS/pc:uk).

•• LFD 19: *páząhi* <ba´-ço^{n}hi> spruce or pine trees. *pázą* <ba´-ço^n> from the cedars, the north, a ritual term (04/25/95/PM/pc:ma, unconfirmed).

••• *KS bázątta* east wind, power of the east (wind) [may have long vowel: *báa*] (RR).

páze hú. N **pine wood, pine tree** (RBn HW13).

•• JOD (slip file): *pázą hü* <p̣a´-ṣa^n> a pinetree.

pazó. N **inedible red berry that grows in the woods** (FH).

•• LFD 20: *pazó* <ba-çu´> pokeweed (*Veratrum viride*).

••• *KS bazó* pokeberry (RR).

pazó eko̜. ADJ, N **maroon, dark red color (lit., 'resembling berries').**

•• RB: <báh-zó-eh-kó^n> (02/24/95/FH/pc:okc; FH:5/02/96/okc; BE2.84).

••• *KS bazó ego* purple, the color of pokeberries (RR).

pázo. N **finger; score or point(s) in a game** (BE2.117; 03/08/95/MREI/pc:ok: *pazó*).

••• Cf. *opázo, pázo, wéapazo.*

pážahta (variant: **pažáhta**). V [reg., *pá_žahta*] *(trans.)* **brand (lit., 'slit by using a sharp edge'), slit, divide, notch, or make forked.**

•• LFD 26: *pážahta* <ba´-zha-ṭa> to mark an animal, as a horse, cow, or pig, by slitting the ears. *páažahta* <ba´-a-zha-ṭa> I slit the horse's ear to mark it. *páðažahta* <ba´-tha-zha-ṭa> you slit the horse's ear to mark it. *páążahta pe* <ba´-o^n-zha-ṭa i> we slit the horse's ear to mark it.

pažážaki (variants: **paažáža?, paažą́žą?**). N [reg., *pá-* 'by using a sharp edge' + *žáhta* 'forked'] [reduplication of truncated *žáhta*] **zigzag** (FH; 04/20/95/LS/pc:okc), **zigzag pattern on each side of a woman's yarn belt** (04/20/95/LS/pc:prod; BE2.163).

•• RB: <bah-zháh-zhah>.

•• LFD 271: *pažáke* <ba-zha´-ge> forked. LFD 358: *pašó̜šo̜* <ba-sho^n´-sho^n> zigzag cutting.

••• Cf. *pašó̜šo̜we, pašó̜we, pážahta.*

paží (frequent combination of postverbal plural or 3rd person noncontinuative marker *api* plus negative *aží*; see **api** and **aží**).

pą́. V [sync. fortisizing stop stem, *_pą́*] *(intr.)* **holler, yell, scream, shout.** *níhkašie tówa apa pą́ ąpái áapa* those people coming there are just hollering, they're saying (01/04/95/FH/pc:okc; FH/11/19/01/pc:prod). *pą́ ąpai áapa* they're hollering they say (FH/11/19/01/pc:prod).

•• LFD 28: *pą́* <bo^n> to call, to shout. *ąpą́ pe* <o^n-bo^n´ i> we call or shout. *pą hósaki* <bo^n hu´-ça-gi> to call or shout loudly.

••• *KS bą* call out, proclaim publicly (RR).

••• Cf. *kípą.*

pąąšcéka (variants: **po̜o̜ščéka, paašcéka**). N **strawberry.** *pąąšcéka wacúesku hpáaye* I made a strawberry cake.

•• RB: <bah-shtséh-kah> (BE2.129; 03/14/95/MREI/pc:okc).

•• LFD 23: *pascéka* <ba-stse´-ga> strawberry. *pascéka apa no̜bre ðalį* <ba-stse´-ga a-ba no^n-bthe tha-gthi^n> strawberries are good to eat. *pascéka ąðalį ną aða* <ba-stse´-ga o^n-tha-gthi^n no^n a-tha> [expected Mod. Os. form: *pąąšcéka ą́ðaalį*] I like strawberries. *pascékahu* <ba-stse´-ga-hiu> strawberry vine, the berry is called <ba-stse´-ga>.

pe (very frequent combination of postverbal plural or 3rd person noncontinuative marker *api* plus declarative *ðe*; see **api**).

pe POSIT **positional article for a pl. entity in nonrandom arrangement.** *wéewina záani pe* I'm grateful to you all [sitting or standing in rows, not in random pattern] (RBn22-13). *žą́ą pe* trees (planted in a regular formation such as in rows or in a line; contrast *žą́ą ke* 'trees [as in a forest, occurring naturally with no pattern]').

pé ðaha. N [derivation unknown] **diamonds (suit in a deck of cards)** (03/10/95/FH/pc:ok; RBn10-21/JW).

•• LFD 84, 253: *hkéhpa* <ḳe´-p̣a> diamond in a deck of cards [perhaps *hkée* 'turtle' + *hpá* 'head'].

pée. N **springtime, spring.** • V [conjug. unknown] *(intr.)* **be spring.** *pée tą* in the spring, in springtime, when it is spring. *pée tą nuužú štą* in the spring, it rains a lot (03/14/95/FH/okc; BE2.126).

•• LFD 26: *pe* <Be> spring of the year. *pe akxa ni pi a* <be a-ka hni bi a> [expected Mod. Os. form: *pe akxa nípe*] it is a cold spring. *pe tą oi ną pi a laska cuhu apa* <be do^n u-i no^n bi a xtha-çka tsu-hu a-ba> [probable Mod. Os form: *pée tą hlaaskácúuhu apa ówe nąpe*] violets grow in the spring (lit., 'when it's spring, violets grow').

pée. INTERR/INDEF PRON **who, whom, to who(m).** *Johna haxį́ pée kʔú e?* who did John give the blankets to? (MSB 03/93). *Johna pée haxį́ wakʔú e?* who [pl.] did John give the blanket(s) to? (03/16/95/MREI/pc:ok) *šée txa pée ðe?* who is that standing over there? (03/16/95/MREI/pc:ok). *hkáwa ðé txa pée íhta?* whose horse is that over

pée (*continued*) there? (lit., 'that horse standing there, to whom does he belong?'). *káa íe txa pée txa?* who is that who is talking? *ká níhka íe txa pée txa?* who is that person who is talking? *pée oðáake hta įkše?* whose bid is it? *šáake oolǫ́kˀǫ pée íiðaðe?* who did you see at the handgame? *pée ðąįšé?* who are you [sg. moving]? *pée nįkšé?* who are you [sg. sitting]? *pée ðaašé?* who is it? (asking the person who knocked at the door, lit., 'who are you?') (MSB 02583). • **whose turn?** *pée hta įksé?* whose turn? (lit., 'who will it be?') (04/04/95/FH/pc:ok; BE2.146). • **anybody, anyone, nobody, no one.** *pée kípąpažíe* he didn't invite anybody (FH:ok, reconf; 5/12/83/rbnot D). *pée kípąží akxai* he's not inviting anybody (FH:prod). *pée aðée įké hta ðé?* isn't anybody going? (MRB02583). *pée aðée įké hta apai* nobody is going (MRB02583). *pée ðaažį́ hta apai* nobody is going (MRB02583). *hcí wį́ pšíe, pée ðįké* I went to the house, no one was there (lit., 'nobody was at the house that I went to') (BE2.157).

•• LFD 26: *pe* <be> whoever, any one of them, a ritual term. *pe a(?)* <be a(?)> who is it? *pé ewaðakše a* <be´ e-wa-tha-ke a> [expected Mod. Os. form: *pée waðáakše?* sentence-final *a* is not used in Mod. Os.] who do you mean?

pée háaną. INTERR/INDEF PRONP **who all (lit., 'who how many').** *Johna akxa pée háaną wéeðe ðe?* who all did John see?

pée íhta. INTERR/INDEF VP **whose (lit., 'who owns [it]?' or 'to whom does it belong?').** *hkáwa ðé tx̨ą pée íhta?* whose horse is that [standing] over there? (lit., 'that horse standing there, to whom does it belong?') (RBn1-46).

péeški. INTERR/INDEF PRON [presumably *pée* + *ški*] **everybody.** *péeški ípahǫpe* everybody knows him. • **nobody.** *koe ónǫǫ žišǫ ší tą šį́ tą koe hpíiži žišǫ ší tą koe péeški ðikǫ́ða htai wáščuɣe ðaalį* before you get old and before you get fat and ugly and nobody wants you, you should get married. • **anybody.** *péeški kípąpažíe* he didn't invite anybody.

pi (form of the postverbal plural or 3rd person noncontinuative marker *api*; see entry **api**.)

pi (variant of **api**).

pi- INSTR **by blowing (as on a fire to get it started, dust from a table top, dandelion fluff into the wind, anything from the palm of the hand).**

pi ché (see **api** SUFFIX, **che** EVIDENTIAL).

píɣą (variants: **píɣa, piɣą́, piɣǫ́**). V [conjug. unknown (sync. fortisizing stop stem?, *_píɣą?*)] (FH) *(trans.)* **blow (as one's nose), blow on s.t. (e.g., blow into a fire, blow dust off a surface, blow a dandelion away in the wind, blow on a burnt finger to relieve pain)** (FH: *ą*). *hpá piɣą́! hpa piɣǫ́!* blow your nose!

•• LFD 27: *píɣǫ* <bi´-xo^n> to make a fire burn by blowing. *hpíɣǫ* <p̣i´-xo^n> I made the fire burn by blowing. *špíɣǫ* <shpi´-xo^n> you made the fire burn by blowing. *ąpíɣǫ pe* <o^n-bi´-xo^n i> we made the fire burn by blowing [gloss should be 'blow' and should not mention fire burning].

••• *KS biɣą́* blow on a fire to make it burn (JOD) (RR).

••• Cf. *opíɣą.*

pixǫ́. V [sync. fortisizing stop stem?, *_pixǫ́?*] [presumably *pi-* INSTR + *xǫ́*] **break down (presumably by blowing upon)** (LFD 237, unconfirmed). [Based on LF, expected forms are *hpíxą* 'I break down', *špíxǫ* 'you break down', *ąpíxǫpe* 'we break down'.]

pó. N **blackhaws** (JOD only).

•• JOD (Raccoons and Crawfish p21 ln7): *po* <p̣u>.

pó-. INSTR **by means of sudden intrusive action (e.g., 'by shooting', 'by punching').**

••• Cf. *pólǫðį.*

póbraska. V [reg.?, *pó_braska?*] [presumably *pó-* INSTR + *bráaska*] *(trans.)* **flatten by shooting** (LF, unconfirmed).

pólǫðį. V [reg.?, *pó_lǫðį?*] [*pó-* INSTR + *lǫ́ðį*] *(trans.)* **startle, shock (as with suddenly emerging news);** ADJ, V *(intr.)* **(be) startled, shocked.**

pósu. N **rice** (RB; FH).

•• LFD 27: *pósu* <bo´-çu> rice.

••• *KS sį* wild rice (JOD) (RR).

pǫǫščéka (variant of **pąąšcéka**).

pšé. V [reg., *_pšé*] *(trans.)* **pound.** *apšéðe* I pounded it. *ðapšéðe* you pounded it. *ąpšáape* we pounded it. *ée pšápe* they pounded it. *pšá!* pound it! *apšá mąžíe* I didn't pound it (1/20/83). *htaa ðápše hta ðąįšé?* are you going to pound meat? *htáa waðápše hta ðąįšé?* are you going to pound meat? (6-30-94).

•• LFD 129: *pše* <pshe> to pound corn into fine meal. *apšé* <a-pshe´> I pound. *ðašpé* <tha-shpe´> [*šp* <shp> is presumably an error for *pš* <psh>] you pound. *ąpšá pe* <o^n-psha´ i> we pound. *hápa ðišpi che apše he* <ha´-ba thi-shpi tse a-pshe he> [expected Mod. Os. form: *hápa ðušpú che ápše* 'I pounded the shelled corn'] (w. sp. [presumably "woman speaking"]) I pounded the corn.

••• Cf. *kípše, ną́ɣe kípše.*

pu-. INSTR **by pressing down on with movement back and forth (?); by smoothing.** [Verbs with this prefix usually seem to be uninflected.]

••• Cf. *púkxa, puštáha, púze.*

púɣa. V [conjug. unknown, uninfl.?] *(trans.)* **dust off, clean off** (RB, unconfirmed).

••• Cf. *píɣą.*

púkaške (variant: **pṹkaške**). N **drop feathers (feathers such as those hanging on a staff in a Native American Church meeting, above and to the left of the first group of feathers at the top).** [In the *ilǫ́ǫška* dance too, the men's dress has drop feathers; these hang to left side in Hominy, and in Grayhorse to right side (HRE/12/29/01/pc).]

púkxa (variant: **pútkxa**). V [sync./reg., *_púkxa*] *(trans.)* **rub or wipe to efface, obliterate, erase, clean off or dust off by wiping, dry by wiping** (01/09/95/FH/pc; BE2.19). *áwanǫbre ðapúkxa?* did you wipe [clean/dust] the table? (05/01/95/LS). *áwanǫbre púutkxa* wipe off the table (FH:4 /24/96/prod).

•• LFD 27: *pikxá* <bi-ka´> to efface, to erase; to obliterate, to wipe out. *hpíkxa* <p̣i´-ka> I erase. *špíkxa* <shpi´-ka> you erase. *ąpíkxa* <o^{n}-bi´-ka> we erase.

••• *OM* same as Osage (LFD 27).

••• Cf. *hį́ice ípukxa, wépukxa.*

puštáha (variants: **puštá, púštaha**). V [uninfl., or sync. fortisizing stop stem, *_puštáha.*] [*pu-* INSTR + *štáha*] *(trans.)* **iron, smooth by pressing** (02/13/95/FH/pc:ok). *pṹštaha* iron this (BE2.71). *hpuštáha maži* I don't iron (FH).

•• RB: <pú-shtah-hah>.

••• Cf. *wapúštaha.*

pútkxa (variant of **púkxa**).

púuspe (variant: **puuspé**). V [uninfl.] *(intr.)* **hide, conceal oneself;** *(trans.)* **hide or conceal s.t.** *púuspape* they hid it. *puuspé brée* I'm going to go hide (RBn10-3:MOJ/79). *púuspi akxai* he's hiding (RBn12-06). *puuspé mąðį́* go hide (RBn22-06).

púze. V [conjug. unknown] *(intr.)* **dry, wither** (01/20/95/PM/pc:prod; BE2.37; 01/20/95/PM/pc:ok withered). *hápa akxa ášihta púze akxa* corn dries outside (FH:prod).

•• LFD 26: *púze* <biu´-çe> dry, withered. *laska the púze ha* <xtha-çka te biu´-çe ha> [expected Mod. Os. form: *hlaaská ðe púze;* sentence-final *ha* is not used in Mod. Os.] the rose is withered. [In the following examples, all LF *pi* should be *pu*; all these examples are more accurately translated as 'I/you/we caused it to dry by heat', without specific mention of 'sun', 'fire', 'clothing'.] *píze* <bi´-çe> dry. LFD 27: *tápizekaɣe* <da´-bi-çe-ga-xe> to dry wet clothing. *tápize hpaɣe* <da´-bi-çe p̣a-xe> I dried my clothes in the sun. *tápize škaɣe* <da´-bi-çe shka-xe> you dried your clothes in the sun. *tápize ąkaɣa pe* <da´-bi-çe o^{n}-ga-xa i> we dried our clothes by the fire. LFD 6 (unconfirmed): *ápize* <a´-bi-çe> to become dry.

púzeðe. V [reg., *púze_ðe*] [*púze* + *ðe* CAU] *(trans.)* **dry, cause to be dry.** *hápa ášihta púzeða!* dry that corn outside!

••• Cf. *ðuuláwa.*

pxáðaži (variant: **pxáži**). ADJ, V [uninfl.] [presumably contains *aží* NEG] *(intr.)* **(be) off in the head, (be) confused, not understand.** *pxáðaži mįkšé* I don't understand (RBn HW9). *pxáðaži akxai* he doesn't understand (RBn HW9). • N **demented or confused person.**

••• Cf. *kíopxaži.*

S

sa (variant of **sápe**).

saakí. ADJ, ADV **tight, tightly** (03/22/95/FH:ok; RBn2-MOJ/p14). *wahkąta íe saakí oðį́ka* hold tight to God's word (03/22/95/FH/pc). • ADJ **firm, solid, hard (in texture), strong, muscular.** *htaacé saakí* strong wind. *níhkašie saakípe* he's a strong person (FH/06/27/01/pc). • **difficult, hard to do things with.** *níhkašie saakípe* he's a person hard to do anything with (FH/06/27/01/pc).

•• LFD 29: *sakí* <ça-gi´> firm, solid, strong, hard.

saakí šǫǫšǫ́we. ADJP **permanent** (03/23/95/FH/pc:ok).

•• LFD 29: *sakíšǫšǫe* <ça-gi´sho^{n}-sho^{n}-e> permanency, permanent.

saakížįka. ADJ [*saakí + žįká*] **slim (lit., 'hard small')** (LF).

•• LFD 29 (unconfirmed): *sakížįka* <ça-gi´-zhi^{n}-ga> slim, slender, thin.

sáežį (variant: **sáižį**). N [*sápe + -žį* 'little'] **little black person.**

••• Cf. *níhka sápe.*

sáhku. N **watermelon.** *sáhku šúpe zí* yellow-meated watermelon (03/16/95/JS/pc:ok; BE2.152).

•• LFD 29: *sáhku* <ça´-ķiu> watermelon. *sákhu ðache ą̨zo šna aða* <ça´-kiu tha-tse o^{n}-çu shna a-tha> [expected Mod. Os. form: *sáhku ðaaché ą́zo štą* (*šna* was never an Osage form; probably Omaha)] I like watermelon.

sáhtą (variant: **sáhta**). ADJ, N **five.** *htóožu sáhtą abrį* I have five meat pies (BE2.48; 01/26/95/FH/pc:ok, *a/ą*).

sáhtą aži. N [*sáhtą + ážu*] **five-spot (the 'five' card in a deck of cards; perhaps lit. 'five scattered on' [LF])** (LF only).

•• LFD 29: *sáhtą aži* <ça´-ţo^{n} a-zhi> five-spot in deck of cards.

sakí ho. N **Sac and Fox (tribe or tribal member)** (03/08/95/PM/pc:prod).

sakíwa (variant: **sakíwo**). N **Sac and Fox (tribe or tribal member) (lit., 'making it tight' [PM:ok:])** (RBnote; 03/08/95/PM/pc:prod).

•• LFD 29: *sakéwa* <ça-ge´-wa> Sac and Fox. "This term is used when speaking of these tribes by the Osage."

sakížį. N [*saakí + -žį* 'indeed'] **Sac and Fox (tribe or tribal member).**

••• Cf. *sakíwa.*

sápe (variant: **sa**). ADJ, N **black** (01/07/95/FH/pc:prod; BE2.9). [Takes 'standing' positional article *che.*]

•• LFD 28: *sápe* <ça´-be> black. *sápe che hkobra* <ça´-be tse ķo^{n}-btha> I prefer black. *sape che škǫšta* <ça-be tse shko^{n}-shta> you prefer black.

••• *OM* same as Osage (LFD 28).

••• Cf. *šápe.*

sase. N [reduplicated form of *-se*] **shavings.**

••• Cf. *mą́ąsase.*

sáta. ADJ **stiff, rigid, stiffened.** *áa akxá sáta akxái* his arm is stiff (03/14/95/FH/pc:okc). *žeká sáta mįkšé* my legs are stiff (03/14/95/FH/pc; BE2.128).

•• RB: <sáh-táh>.

•• LFD 29: *sáta* <ça´-da> stiff, rigid, stiff-jointed.

są́ą. N **forest.** [LF only, unrecognized by Modern Osage speakers.]

••• Cf. *zą́ące, ząącéolįį.*

scéce (variants: **scé, scée** [JS]). ADJ **tall** (03/16/95/FH/pc:ok; 03/05/95/JS/pc: *scée* only); **long** (03/16/95/FH/pc:ok; 03/05/95/JS/pc: *scée* only). *kahíke scée* Tall Chief, a name (03/16/95/FH/pc; BE2.133). *kahíka scée* Tall Chief (03/05/95/JS/pc:ok). *scéce nį́* you're tall. *paaxó šcee* a high hill or tall mountain. *huuscée* very long in length, very tall (BE2.81; RBn2-MOJ/p3; 02/16/95/FH/pc:okc). *scéce káaye* lengthen, make longer, make taller.

•• RB: <stéh-tseh>.

•• JOD (slip file): *scéce* <sté´-ţşe> long.

•• LFD 134: *scecé* <stse-dse´> tall, a tall man; long. LFD 209: *walélescece* <wa-xthe´-xthe-stse-dse> a tall standard made by the Osage, also by the Kaw and the Omaha.

scúuce (variant: **šcúuce**). ADJ **slow.**

••• Cf. *wascúuce.*

-se. V ROOT **cut.** *mąąhį́se* cut grass (FH/11/17/01/pc:prod). *paasé* cut with any instrument by pushing down on, as cutting grass or cutting s.t. into pieces (e.g., cake, meat, potatoes). *ípaase* cut with. *ðuusé* cut with scissors or knife (e.g., hair). *kaasé* [with reg. *kaa*-del. inflection: 1st sg. *áase,* 2nd sg. *ðáase,* 3rd sg. *kaasé*] chop or cut into long thin sticks, mow lawn, cut down (e.g., a tree with an axe or knife, not by sawing); [with reg. *kaa*-ret. inflection: 1st sg. *ákaase,* 2nd sg. *ðákaase*] cut with a sudden or striking action (e.g., chopping meat, cutting down trees with an axe [not by sawing], cutting grass). *páse* cut by using a sharp edge (as in cutting a cake; contrast *pacé* 'butcher [chop by using a sharp edge]' and *pascé, pašcé* 'cut up, slice into strips').

síekǫ. N [*síi + ékǫ*) **meat pie (lit., 'foot-like', referring to the shape of the traditional meat pie).** [Especially used in the Grayhorse district.] *síekǫ wikšíye* I made a meat pie for you (RB; MREI 11-1-83-8; 02/24/95/FH/pc:ok).

••• Cf. *htóožu.*

síi. N **foot, feet.** *síi yoį́* stinking feet (BE2.50).

•• RB: <sí ɣwí^{n}>.

•• LFD 30: *si* <çi> foot. *si hce* <çi ţse> the foot or the feet. LFD 31 (unconfirmed, unintelligible): *si hce ahkio ha* <çi ţse a-ķi-u ha> [sentence-final *ha* is not used in Mod. Os.] I have a wound on my foot (01/30/95/FH/pc:uk). *sihce ǫðǫpa* <çi-ţse o^{n}-tho^{n}-ba> my feet are swollen (01/30/95/FH/pc:uk). *sihce opaha te eðiðąpe ha* <çi-ţse u-ba-ha de e-thi-tho^{n}-be ha> [sentence-final *ha* is not used in Mod. Os.] your foot protrudes (01/30/95/FH/pc:uk). *si hce opaha hta e ąðąpe ha* <çi ṭse u-ba-ha ṭa e o^n-tho^n-be ha> [sentence-final *ha* is not used in Mod. Os.] my foot protrudes (FH: uk).

siihpó. N **toe.** *siihpóhtą* big toe (RB; 03/23/95/FH/pc). *siihpóžį* any toe or toes other than the big toe (03/23/95/FH/pc; BE2.142).

•• LFD 31: *sihpá* <çi-pa´> toes (unconfirmed: 03/23/95/FH/pc:no).

••• *OM* same as Osage (LFD 31).

síioski (variant: **síioske**). N **arch of the foot** (RBn10-9:JW; RBn22-19).

•• LFD 31: *sióskita* <çi-u´-çki-da> the hollow in the sole of the human foot.

siisí (variant of **sísi**).

síke. N **third daughter** (LF only, unconfirmed).

•• LFD 30: *sike* <çi´-ge> the third daughter, special kinship term.

••• Cf. *asįka.*

sinǫ́bre (variant: **sinǫ́įbrį́** [RB-MSB]). N **kidney (human or animal).** *sinǫ́bre štáache nǫpe?* do you eat kidney? (01/30/95/FH/pc:prod; BE2.73).

•• LFD 30: *sinǫbre ekǫ* <çi-no^n´-bthe e-go^n> resembling a kidney in shape.

sisą́ðe (variant of **sísiąðe**).

sísi (variant: **siisí**). ADJ, V [uninfl.] **(be) strong.** *wíe sisi brį́e ąðįhé* I'm strong (FH; RBn10-6:JW). *íe šǫ ðaašé, sísi mą[ðį] ðaašé* while you're [still] talking, you'll get strong (RBn10-6:JW). *wahéhe mįkšé ąžį sísi nįkšé* I am weak, but thou art strong (line in a Christian hymn) (MOJ). • **(be) energetic, well, doing well, healthy** (LS). *sisípe* he's well, energetic (FH/09/22/01/pc; BE2.129; LS:ok).

•• LFD 30: *sísi* <çi´-çi> stalwart, brave, active. *sísi pe* <çi´-çi bi a> he is stalwart.

sísiąðe (variant: **sisą́ðe**). V [conjug. unknown] [presumed reg., *sísią_ðe*] *(intr.)* **seesaw, make a back and forth movement (as when riding a teeter-totter), wobble or teeter (e.g., a glass when jarred or bumped).** *sisą́ðe akxai* it's teetering (FH:prod).

sitǫ́į. ADV, N **yesterday.** *sitǫ́į Smokey iiðáðe* I saw Smokey yesterday (RBn10-21/JW&FW/77). *Bill akxa sitǫ́į achípe* Bill arrived here yesterday.

•• LFD 30: *sitóci* <çi-do´-dsi> yesterday.

••• *QU sióhti* yesterday (RR); *KS sídoji* yesterday (RR).

sitǫ́į kootáha ce. ADVP, N **(on the) day before yesterday.**

•• RB: <si^n-twí gó-tah-háh-tseh> (04/11/95/FH/pc:okc; BE2.30).

••• *QU sióhti kkohtí htehtá* yesterday, the day before (RR).

sízo (variant: **cízo?**). N **thigh.**

•• RB: <tí-zo> (BE2.138, unconfirmed; 03/20/95/FH/pc:uk; FH/09/23/01/pc:uk).

•• LFD 343 (unconfirmed): *sizó* <çi-çu´> thigh.

••• *KS hížo ~ hį́įžo*femur (JOD), thigh (RR).

sį́įce. N **tail, animal's tail, part of Osage dance costume; tail dancer at Osage War Dances; last part of a dance song** (BE2.131; 02/27/95/JS/pc:ok).

•• LFD 30: *sį́ce che* <çi^n´-dse tse> the refrain, the repetition of the last part of a song to which only two or three select men dance. "This word also means the tail; it is the last of the dance that those, aside from the select men, must pay in order to dance in the tail."

sį́ka. N **squirrel.**

•• LFD 30: *sį́ka* <çi^n´-ga> squirrel. "The squirrel figures in the myths of the Osage and the Omaha." *sį́ka sape* <çi^n´-ga ça-be> black squirrel. "The black squirrel is not known to the Omaha."

••• Cf. *sįkóce, sį́štaa.*

sį́ka hpaléze. N **square dance (lit., 'stripe-nosed squirrel', a square dance call equivalent to "Swing your partners")** (RBn19-06). [Modeled on the English expression.]

sįkóce. N [*sį́ka + océ*] **squirrel hunting.** *sįkóce ąkáðe hce* let's go squirrel hunting (BE2.126; 03/14/95/FH/pc:ok).

sį́štaa. N [*sį́ka + štáha*] **possum (lit., 'smooth squirrel').**

•• RB: <sí^n-shtáh> (BE2.106; 03/10/95/FH/pc:okc).

ska. MODAL **it must be that, it seems that, I suppose that, I guess that, perhaps, I deduce that.** [Impersonal suppositional particle; sometimes implies that the event took place previously, and can then be loosely translated 'before, previously, earlier, already' (04/19/95/FH/pc:ok). Often pronounced *skə*.] *tówa akxa éžixci akxái, lǫ́ði akxa ska* he [that one] looks funny, so he must be drunk (04/26/95/FH/pc). *ðachíe ska* you must have been here before (01/06/95/FH/pc:ok). *hkiistó apá ska* I guess [as I see all the cars around the building] that they are counciling (RBn24). *éekǫ ska* I guess so (RBn23-15). *hące wáli nuužúpe ska, žįkáži apa hǫ́pái niižópši apái* last night it must have rained a lot, the children today are wading (01/24/95/FH/pc:ok). *hą́ąci ðetkxą́ci wacúe bráache mįkšé ska* last night at this time I must have been eating this bread (FH/09/06/95/pc). *tówa akxa éžixci akxái, lǫ́ði akxa ska* he looks

ska (*continued*)
funny [different] so he must be drunk (04/26/95/FH/pc). *kʔǫ́su kʔǫ́ aðáape ska* I guess they went to play dice. *táatą hpíiži wį áðanąąžį ska táabrą ðąįšé* you must have stepped on something bad, because you're smelling bad (FH:prod). *ðachíe ska* you must have come here before (lit., 'you arrived here, it seems') (01/06/95/FH/pc:ok).

ská. ADJ, N **white.** *hci htąą ska ški* a big white house, the big white house. • **bright, clear** (as variant of *skáha*).

•• LFD 31: *skáska* <çka´-çka> [reduplicated form] white spots, flecked with white spots.

••• Cf. *hcéeská, xuháaska.*

skáha (variants: **skáhe** [rare], **ská**). V, ADJ [uninfl.] *(intr.)* **(be) bright, clear** (RBn10-5:MOJ/79; FH/11/19/01/pc:ok). *mihkákʔe skáha, štáha* the stars are bright and shiny (FH/11/19/01/pc:prod). *níi skáha* clear water (01/09/95/FH/pc:ma). *níi ská* clear water (04/13/95/LS/pc). *mą́ąɣe akxa skáha akxa* the weather cleared off (01/09/95/FH/pc:okc; 04/13/95/LS/pc:ok, *skáha* or *skáhe*). • ADV **clearly.** *íe ska* speak clearly (FH). *íiði skáha* [expected form: *íiðe skáha*] see clearly (HRE/12/29/01/pc:ok; BE2.20).

••• Cf. *íe waská, ną́ąɣeska.*

skákaaɣe. V [sync. *k>p, ská_kaaɣe*] [*ská* 'white' + *káaɣe*] *(trans.)* **whiten (lit., 'make white')** (FH/10/09/01/pc). *haaská skákaaɣa* make the buckskin dress white (FH/10/09/01/pc). *hpáxį skákaaɣe* she made her hair white (FH/10/09/01/prod).

•• LFD 31: *skákaɣe* <çka´-ga-xe> whiten.

ską́ą (variant of **šką́**).

skíke (variant: **škíke**). ADJ **heavy, tired, weighted down, heavily laden** (02/09/95/FH/pc:ok: not *šk;* RBn18-06). [One speaker in the early 1980s reported a distinction between *skíke* 'tired' and *škíke* 'heavy'. Possibly such a difference in meaning between the two forms once existed and has been partially lost.] *įį kootáha skíke* that rock over there is heavy (BE2.66; FH/07/31/01). *ðéka hų̃pi waxpáðįpi aha ną́ące skíke paašé aha, ðakʔéwikie hta mįkšé, škaaškáða* come unto me you who are poor and heavy laden and I will give you rest, I will give you peace. *škáace mąðį́pi, wáskike waškáaɣapi* you all go on and play, you make us tired.

••• Cf. *ðiiskíke, kaaskíke.*

skúðe (variants: **skúe, skú**). ADJ **sweet** (BE2.130). *wacúe skúe* cake (lit., 'sweet bread').

•• RB: <skyú-theh> (03/14/95/MREI/pc:ok).

•• LFD 31: *skíðe* <çki´-the> sweet. *mąhką́ sape che skiðe walį* <mo^{n}-ķo^{n}´ ça-be tse çki-the wa-gthi^{n}> the coffee is too sweet.

••• *OM* same as Osage (LFD 31).

••• Cf. *ðą́ące skúðe, níiskue, waskúe.*

stá. ADJ **smooth, clear, bald.**

••• Cf. *nąąstá, ostá.*

staahį́ke (variant of **wastą́įke**).

stáðe. V [reg., *stá_ðe*] [*stá* + *ðe* CAU] *(trans.)* **apply a substance (such as ointment, grease, or cream), smear on, anoint, apply as salve or medicine to a wound (lit., 'cause to be smooth'); paint (e.g., a house or a small object of any kind)** (03/03/95/FH/pc:ok). *stáaðe* I paint it. *stáðaðe* you paint it. *ąstáðe* we paint it. *hcí stáða* paint the house! (03/03/95/FH/pc:ok; BE2.101). *hci staaðe hta mįkše* I'm going to paint the house (03/03/95/FH/pc). • *(intr.)* **paint (engage in painting as a hobby or profession).** • N **cream, paint, grease, ointment (for applying to a surface to make it smooth).** *šáake ni štáðe* analgesic cream for the hands (lit., 'cream for hands hurting') (FH).

•• LFD 31: *snáðe*<çna´-the> [expected form: *stáðe; sná-* is incorrect in all examples here and elsewhere, and is probably Omaha (*sn* has never been a permitted sequence of consonants in Osage; it elicits laughter from Osage speakers)] to heal the wound of a child by using an ointment made from buffalo grease; to grease a wagon or oil machinery. *snáaðe* <çna´-a-the> [expected form: *stáaðe*] I grease machinery ['machinery' is not strictly implied by the example]. *snáðaðe* <çna´-tha-the> you grease [expected form: *stáðaðe*] *snáąða pe* <çna´-o^{n}-tha i> [expected form: *stáąðape* or *ąstáðape*] we grease.

stáko. ADJ **neat, uniform, level, smooth, even, straight, nice-looking.**

•• RB: <stáh-kó>.

•• LFD 32: *stakó* <çta-go´> even, level, uniform, smooth.

••• Cf. *ðuustáko, nąąstá.*

stówe. V **run, flow or emerge from (as a liquid).** *hpalístowe, hpalį́stowe* runny nose (FH/11/17/01/pc:prod; FHt128). *hcí níi stówe* water is running from the house (FH/11/17/01/pc:prod).

••• Cf. *ostówe.*

súhka. N **chicken** (BE2.18; MREI:ok). *wisǫ́ka súhka wį oohǫ́ kšíɣape* they cooked a chicken for Sonny.

súhka húhka. N **needle.**
•• RB: <sóo-kah hí-kah> (02/27/95/FH/pc:okc; BE2.92)
•• LFD 31: *súhkahuhką htaγe* <çiu´-ķa-hiu-ķo^n ţa-xe> pin.
súhka léze. N **guinea hen (lit., 'striped chicken')** (RBn19-02).
súhka mį́įka (variant: **súhka mį́įe**). N **hen.**
súhka oðį́įke. N **hawk (lit., 'catches chickens').**
•• RB: <sóo-kah-o-thí^n-kah> (RBn1-58, unconfirmed; 01/04/95/FH/pc:uk).
súhka saaki. N **banty (bantam chicken).**
súhka tóoka (variant: **súhka tóe**). N **rooster.** *hǫ́ǫpa wį súhka tóoka ók?ą ékǫži káaγe nąpe* sometimes the rooster did things he shouldn't do (RBn18-01).
súhkahtąą. N [*súhka* + *htą́ą*] **turkey (lit., 'big chicken')** (BE2.145; MREI).
súhkahtąą hą́ąpa. N **Thanksgiving Day (lit., 'turkey day').**
•• LFD 31: *súhka ðache hąpa* <çiu´-ķa tha-tse ho^n-ba> [expected Mod. Os. form: *súhka ðaaché hą́ąpa*] Thanksgiving day.
súhkahtąą mą́šǫ oðį́įke. VP [sync., *súhkahtą mą́šǫ _oðį́įke*] *(intr., trans.)* **vote, vote for (lit., 'grasp the turkey feather').** *súhkahtąą mą́šǫ obrį́įke* I've already voted (lit., 'I grasped the turkey feather').
••• Cf. *mą́šą oðį́įke.*

súhkahtąą mį́įǫpa. N **November (lit., 'turkey month')** (HH/14-a/231ff; HH:pc).
súhkahtąą mį́įka. N **turkey hen.** *ąžį howáįki súhkahtą́ą mį́įka hcí káaγe che ípahǫži akxa áape* but they could not guess where turkey hen made her nest (RBn19-05).
súhkahtąą mǫ́šǫ (variant: **súhkahtąą mą́šǫ**). N **turkey feather, any quill** (PM/7/7/94).
••• Cf. *súhkahtąą mą́šǫ oðį́įke.*
-súhu. V ROOT **clean.**
••• Cf. *taasúhu, wasúhu.*
súu. N **seed, pit, kernel.** *hpéγe súu* rattle seeds, gourd seeds.
•• LFD 128: *hpéγe su* <pe´-xe çu> rattle seeds.
••• *QU si* seed, pit, grain or kernel (RR).
••• Cf. *wasúutą.*
súutą (variant: **súuta**). ADJ [*súu* + *tą*] **ripe, ready to pick or harvest** (FH). *hápa akxa súutą akxai* the corn is ripe, ready to pick (01/31/95/FH/pc:prod).
•• LFD 30: *síta* <çi´-da> ripe corn ['corn' is not strictly implied by this form]. *hapa apa sita pi o* <ha-ba a-ba çi-da bi o> [sentence-final *o* is not used in Mod. Os.] the corn is ripe. LFD 186: *wasíta* <wa-çi´-da> the ripening of the corn, the harvest.
••• *KS wasúda* hard or firm, as corn (RR), *wasúdabe* the month when the corn is hard, midsummer, July (RR).

Š

šaáke. N **Cherokee (tribe or tribal member)** (BE218, unconfirmed).
••• Cf. *šálaki.*
šáake. N **hand, claw; handprint, footprint, tracks; hands of the body that are touched by the attendees when passing by it at a funeral** (01/04/95/FH/pc:ok; RBn1-MOJ/p27). *šáake oðį́įke* to shake hands (01/04/95/FH/pc:ok). *šáake oðį́įka!* hold tight! (FH/06/27/01/pc). *súhka šáake* turkey track. *šáake weáchį̨e* I hit him with my hand (01/04/95/FH/pc:ok; BE2.63). • **finger.** *šáake žį* the little finger (RBn1-MOJ/p26b). *šáake ąwą́pazo ðįká* don't point the finger at me (said to the children by FH's mother) (01/24/95/FH/pc:prod; BE2.47; 01/24/95/FH/pc:prod). *šáake ohką́ska owakxą́* [presumed Mod. Os. form based on KS form] ring finger (lit., 'next to the middle finger').
•• LFD 130: *šáke* <sha´-ge> hands, paws, claws, talons (02/13/95/FH/pc:ma). LFD 31: *suhkášake ekǫ* <çiu-ķa´-sha-ge e-go^n> resembling a turkey track, Flat Rock, Okla. LFD 130 (unconfirmed): *šáke ozápe* <sha´-ge u-ça-be> fingers (01/24/95/FH/pc:uk). *šake oscéce che* <sha-ge u-stse´-dse tse> the long or middle finger (01/24/95/FH/pc:uk). *šáke ožį́ka* <sha´-ge u-zhi^n-ga> the small finger, the little finger (01/24/95/FH/pc:uk). *šake nie* <sha-ge ni-e> a run-around ('finger ache') (01/24/95/FH/pc:uk). LFD 112 (unconfirmed): *nąpe ožį́ka* <no^n-be u-zhi^n´-ga> the little finger (01/24/95/FH/pc:uk).

šáake (*continued*)

••• *KS šáge ohkąska owakhą* the next to the middle finger (RR).

••• Cf. *nǫǫpé.*

šáake ípukxa (variant: **šáake íipukxa**). • VP [conjug. unknown] *(intr.)* **wipe one's hands** (01/04/95/FH/pc). *šáake íipukxa* wipe your hands! (BE2.63; FH: without *ði*). N **hand towel, napkin** (01/04/95/FH/pc).

•• RB: <sháh-keh í-pú-xah>.

••• Cf. *htanąkʔa ípukxa.*

šáake oðįįke. VP [sync., *šáake o_ðįįke*] *(trans.)* **shake hands with, touch the hands of s.o.** *šáake oðįįke* shake hands with a person, touch the hands of the deceased when passing by the coffin at a funeral (RBn1-MOJ/p27). *šáake owíbrįįke hkǫ́bra* I want to shake your hand (RBn11-02/JW&FW&HHsk/c.1976; 01/04/95/FH/pc:ok; BE2.63). • **sign, write one's signature or name on (lit., 'grasp in the hand', as in writing one's name on a document)** (HRE/12/29/01/pc, unconfirmed); **endorse (as a check)** (HRE: unconfirmed; 04/27/95/FH/pc:ma). *šáake oscįįke* you endorsed it.

••• Cf. *mą́šą oðįįke.*

šáake opázo. N **index finger (lit., 'hand pointer').**

••• Cf. *wéapazo.*

šáakeðíiskike. V [sync. *šáake_ðíiskike*] [*šáake + ðiiskíke*] *(intr.)* **make a fist.** • N **fist.**

šáakeoolą́kʔǫ. N [*šáake + oolą́ + kʔǫ́*] **hand game.**

šáhpe. ADJ, N **six.** *hką́ące oolą́ šáhpe paasé hta apai* they're going to cut the pie six times (FH:4/24/96/tape:prod).

•• RB: <sháh-xpeh, sháh-peh> (03/10/95/PM/pc:ok; BE2.122).

•• LFD 130: *šáhpe* <sha´-pe> six. *šáhpe ą* <sha´-pe o^{n}> six times. *šáhpe aži* <sha´-pe a-zhi> six spot in a deck of cards.

••• *OM* same as Osage (LFD 130).

šálaki (variant: **šáléke**). N **Cherokee (tribe or tribal member)** (BE2.18;03/08/95/PM/pc: *šálaki;* 01/09/95/FH/pc:uk).

•• RB: <shah-láh-keh, shah-áh-keh>.

••• Cf. *šaáke.*

šápe. ADJ **dark (in color), shaded, darkened.**

••• Cf. *mįįǫpa šápe, sápe.*

šáwanįį. N **Shawnee (tribe or tribal member)** (BE2.120; 03/09/95/MREI/pc:okc).

•• RB: <sháh-wah-nah>.

•• LFD 226 (unconfirmed): *žąní* <Zho^{n}-ni´> Shawnee, the name of an Indian tribe.

šcéðe (variant: **ščéðe** [Hominy]). V [reg., *šcé_ðe*] *(trans.)* **doctor a person, administer medical care to s.o.** (01/20/95/ERE/pc:ok:*šč*). *šcéaðe* I doctor him. *šcéðaðe* you doctor him. *šcéðe* she doctors him. *šcéąðe* we doctor him. *ščéąðe* doctor me (01/20/95/ERE/pc:ok; BE2.33) *šcéąða!* doctor me! *tówa kše šcéða!* doctor that one lying there, doctor him! *ąkóe šcéąðapé* we doctored them.

•• RB: <shchéh-theh>.

••• Cf. *wašcéðe.*

šcį V (variants: **šcįe, ščíe** [Hominy]). V [rare variant 2nd person sg. of *ðį́* 'be a certain way, exist as' (more usual form is *nį́*)] *(intr.)* **you are (a certain way).** *wascúuce ščįe* you're slow (04/26/95/FH/pc).

šcúuce (variant: **ščúuce** [Hominy]). V, ADJ [uninfl.] *(intr.)* **(be) warm (e.g., clothing, a house; not used of people).** *haaská ščúuce mį ąhé* I'm wearing warm clothes (FH/10/12/95/pc). *hci ąkóhta akxa šcúuce akxai* our house is warm. *ákahamį ðíhtapi akxa šcúuce?* are your [pl.] coats warm?

••• *QU štíhte* warm, comfortable (RR).

••• Cf. *mįįtáašcuuce.*

šcúuce (variant of **scúuce**).

ščéðe (variant of **šcéðe**).

ščíe (variant of **šcį́**).

ščúuce (variant of **šcúuce**).

še. ADJ **that (near you).** *še žą́žį akxa ohtáza akxai* that little tree is pretty. *še hką́ące akxa tožáðe akxai* that apple is rotten. *wéhice nąkʔǫ́ še ðíhta?* is that your radio? (RBn1-44). *óoląke sápe še įkšé ðíhta?* is that black hat over there yours? (RBn1-45). *óoląke sápe še ðíhta?* is that your black hat? (01/04/95/FH/pc:ok; BE2.64).

•• LFD 130: *še* <she> that one, there (03/20/95/FH/pc:ok). *še éwakše* <she e-wa-kshe> that in your hand is what I mean.

šée (variant: **šíi** [especially when followed by a subject marker *akxa* or *apa*]). ADV **here near you.** *šée mįkšé, táatą íhpahǫ mąží* I'm just sitting here [near you], I don't know anything (RBn10-6:JW). *šée mįkšé, wanǫ́bre akxa oméį mįkšé* I'm just sitting here, that peyote is working in me (RBn10-6:JW). • **there near you, there (closer to the hearer than to the speaker).** *šée nįkšé óhkie* you're just sitting there, speak to me (RBn10-6:JW). *šée mąðį́* stay where you are (lit., 'go there by you') (PM/109-a). • PRON **him/her/it (closer to the hearer than to the speaker); that, that one near you.** *šée ðe iiðási* I dislike him [he is moving]. *wažážeíe šée ąkšíǫza* teach me that in Osage (03/16/95/FH/pc:ok). *šée bróka sáhta wikʔúe* I'll give you five dollars for it [for that] (RBn10-10:JW).

••• Cf. *šíi akxa, šíi apa.*

šée apa (variant of **šíi apa**).

šée che. PRONP **that one standing (inanimate), those things (sitting or round items).** *šée che* a group of [sitting or round] items sitting there (03/20/95/FH/pc).

šée ðe. PRONP **that one moving (animate or inanimate).** *šée ðe iiðási* I dislike him [he is moving].

šée htaha. ADVP **toward you, along a path toward where you (the hearer) are or toward s.t. or s.o. closer to you (the hearer) than to the speaker** (FH: t119a) *šée htaha aðáape* they went over that way, toward you over that way (BE2.143; 04/26/95/FH/pc:ok)

šée įkšé (variant: **šée ðįkšé**). PRONP **that one sitting (animate or inanimate), that one over there, closer to the hearer than to the speaker.** *šée įkšé, šée ðįkšé* that over there sitting [animate or inanimate] (e.g., referring to sitting sack of flour) (03/20/95/FH/pc:ok, person or thing). *ą́ðikue, šée ðįkše* bring me that thing there.

šée kxą (variant of **šée txą**).

šée mąðį́. VP **stay there!** [Used in imperative sense.] *šée mąðį́* stay where you are (PM/109-a).

šée nąąžį́. VP **wait, stay there (lit., 'there near you stand').**

šée txą (variants: **šée tkxą, šée kxą**). PRONP **that one standing (animate).** *šée txą* that over there [standing, animate: person or animal] (03/20/95/FH/pc). *šée tkxą pée ðe?* who is that [standing] over there? (03/20/95/FH/pc:ok; BE2.136).

šeeðó (variant of **šeeðǫ́**).

šeeðóha, šeeðóhą (variants of **šeeðǫ́ha**).

šeeðǫ́. ADV (variants: **šeeðó, šó**). ADV **there where you are, right there where you are** (FHprod). [Sometimes used in formal speechmaking or lengthy monologue as 'and also' or 'and then' (RB).] *šeeðó brée* I'm coming over there [where you are] (03/20/95/FH/pc:okc; BE2.137). *šeeðó ha bree* I'm going there where you are. *šeeðó akší hta apai* they're going to come back there (PM/7/8/94; 01/06/95/FH/pc:ok). *šeeðó méį* stay where you are (RBn 3/3/77). • PRON **that person there.** *šeeðó nąąžį́ txą hú hce éa* tell the person standing there to come here. *šeeðó aðáape* he went that way.

•• RB: <shéh-tho^{n}> (03/20/95/FH/pc:okc).

•• LFD 131: *šéðo* <she´-thu> yonder, there where you are.

šeeðǫ́ha (variants: **šeeðóhą, šeeðóha**). ADV **that way, along a path toward the hearer, to a place right next to the hearer** (RBn1-23). *šeeðóha aðáape* he went that way [toward where hearer is located].

••• Cf. *šée htaha.*

šéšeka. V [uninfl.?] [reduplicated form] *(intr.)* **stagger.** *šéšeka ąðįhée* I'm staggering around (BE2.126; 03/14/95/FH/pc).

ši. ADV **again, more.** *ší ékia* say that again (BE2.1;12/30/94/FH/pc:ok: but *ékie* preferable). *ši záani ðalípi hkǫ́bra* I want you all to come back again (RBn10-21). *ši ąkálįįpe* we're back again (RBn10-16). *Carolyn akxa šíną wažáže͏íe iðǫ́ye akxa* Carolyn keeps asking about Osage words (01/13/95/FH/pc). *ší tóa ąkʔú* give me some more [e.g., food] (lit., 'again some give me'). *ší mą́ą šó ðée hpáaye* I'm going to let the arrow go again (expression used at peyote meetings) (BE2.4; 01/06/95/FH/pc:okc). *ókaayéįke akxa ší waachípe* "Useless" [a donkey] danced again.

•• LFD 131: *ši* <shi> again; and *šíną* <shi´-no^{n}> again and again (01/13/95/FH/pc:ok).

ší. V [2nd person sg. of *ahí* 'arrive there'] *(intr.)* **you arrive there.** *įį olįį ší hkǫ́bra* I want you to come sweat (lit., 'I want you to go there and sit among the rocks').

ší ǫpe. N **hip joint** (02/14/95/FH/pc:okc).

••• *QU šįhtéhi káxakdé* pelvis, hips (RR).

šiðǫ́ce. N **kneecap** (unconfirmed; 02/14/95/FH/pc:uk).

•• LFD 132 (unconfirmed): *šiðǫ́ce mǫškǫ* <shi-tho^{n}´-dse mo^{n}-shko^{n}> the kneecap.

••• *KS šiyą́je* knee (RR).

••• Cf. *šį́ce.*

šíi (variant of **šée**).

šíi akxa. PRONP [*šée* + *akxa* SUBJECT MARKER] **that one (thing or person not in motion) near you, those ones (not in motion) near you.** *šíi akxa waðíhici akxái* that person is teasing (03/16/95/FH/pc:ok; RBn2-MOJ/p11).

šíi apa (variant: **šée apa**). PRONP [*šée* + *apa* SUBJECT MARKER] **that one (thing or person in motion or deceased) near you; those ones (in motion or deceased) there (near you)** (RBn10-21/JW&FW/77; RBn22-03). *šíi apa cʔápe* that man died (RBn22-17). *šíi apa oðíhtą paaxí apai* they're pushing the car (RBn23-17). *šíi akxa*

šíi apa (*continued*)
waðíhici akxái that person is teasing (03/16/95/FH/pc:ok; RBn2-MOJ/p11).

šíkxą (variant: **šikxą́**). N **my brother's wife, my husband's sister, my husband's brother's wife (used only when speaker is female; more precise than English 'my sister-in-law')** (RBn14-10; 03/10/95/PM/pc:ok; FH/09/22/01/pc:ok). • **her brother's wife, her husband's sister, her husband's brother's wife (more precise than English 'her sister-in-law').** [In this usage, synonymous with *išíkxą*.]

•• RB: *šikxą́* <shi-kxáh^{n}>.

šíkxą ðíhta (variant: **šíkxą ði**). NP **your brother's wife, your husband's sister, your husband's brother's wife (used only when addressee is female; more precise than English 'your sister-in-law').**

••• Cf. *ðišíkxą.*

šíle. V [conjug. unknown] [presumably *ši* + *ki-* INCEPTIVE/VERTITIVE + *ðe* CAU] *(trans.)* **set off, remove from (e.g., remove a kettle from a cooking fire)** (BE2.119; 03/09/95/MREI/pc:ok).

••• Cf. *ále.*

šíną (variant: **šína**). ADV [*ši* + *ną* 'always'] **over and over, again and again (used to express 'keep on, continue to do a thing').** *Carolyn akxa šíną wažážeíe iðǫ́ye akxa* Carolyn keeps asking about Osage words (01/13/95/FH/pc).

•• LFD 131: *šíną* <shi´-no^{n}> again and again (01/13/95/FH/pc:ok).

šíǫce (variant of **šį́įce**).

šį (variant of **wašį́**).

šį́. V, N **(be) fat.**

••• Cf. *wašį́.*

šį́htąką (variant: **šį́htąą**). ADJ [*šį́* + *htą́ka*] **fat, portly.** [The longer variant *šį́htąką* may possibly imply a somewhat greater degree of fatness than does the shortened variant *šį́htąą* (01/23/95/FH/pc:ok).] *wáli šįhtąą ąhé* I'm really fat (01/23/95/FH/pc).

•• RB: <shí^{n}-táh^{n}> (01/23/95/FH/pc:okc).

•• LFD 131: *šį́htąka* <shi^{n}´-ṭo^{n}-ga> portly, fat.

šį́įce (variant: **šíǫce**). N **knee** (FH:4/25/96/tape: *šį́įce* preferred; FH:4/20/96/pc).

•• RB: <shí-ah^{n}-teh>.

•• LFD 132: *šiðǫ́ce* <shi-tho^{n}´-dse> knee, that part of the leg around the kneepan (02/14/95/FH/pc:uk, unconfirmed).

••• Cf. *šiðǫ́ce.*

šį́mįžį. N **girl, baby girl; girlfriend.** *šį́mįžį ihtá apa* that's his girlfriend (RBn19-01; 01/31/95/FH/pc:okc; BE2.54).

•• LFD 131: *šímižįka* <shi´-mi-zhi^{n}-ga> a baby girl, a damsel, a maiden, a lassie.

šį́mįžį ąkóhta. NP **our daughter.**

šį́tožį (variant: **šį́tožįka** [archaic]). N **boy, baby boy, male child** (01/07/95/FH/pc:ok). *Yvonne šį́tožį kíhuheka* Yvonne's boy has a sickness (BE2.10; RBn14-02; FH/11/19/01/pc:uk).

•• JOD (slip file): *šį́htožį́ka* <ci^{n}´-tu-çi^{n}´-a> a boy under five feet high, one under fifteen years of age. [JOD's *ht* (<t> in his transcription) contrasts with Mod. Os. *t* and Kansa *d* (from *t*) in this word.]

•• LFD 131: *šį́hto žįka* <shi^{n}´-ṭo zhi^{n}-ga> a baby boy. LFD 132: *šį́hto žįka* <shi^{n}´-ṭu zhi^{n}-ga> a boy. *šį́hto žįka žáže brace o* <shi^{n}´-ṭu zhi^{n}-ga zha´-zhe btha-dse o> [sentence-final *o* is not used in Mod. Os.] I called the boy by name. *šį́hto žįka žáže štace o* <shi^{n}´-ṭu zhin-ga zha´-zhe shda-dse o> [sentence-final *o* is not used in Mod. Os.] you called the boy by name. [LF *ht* contrasts with Mod. Os. *t* and KS *d* in this word.]

••• *KS šídohįŋ a* boy, young man (RR).

šká. V, ADJ **(be) quiet.** *hpáažį akxa šká akxa* the baby is quiet (FH).

••• Cf. *škaškáða.*

škáce. V [reg., *_škáce*] *(intr.)* **play** (RBn23-17c). *žįkážį apa škáce apa* the children are playing (03/09/95/FH/pc:ok: short *a*). *htaapéškace* play ball (HRE/12/29/01/pc:prod). *žįka akxa škáce akxa* the child is playing. *škáce mąðípi* you all go play (03/09/95/FH/pc:ok; BE2.105). *škáce žówalapi hta paašé?* are you all going to play with us? (03/09/95/FH/pc). *škáce žólaži apai* they won't play with them (2-10-83-p4).

•• LFD 132: *škace* <shka-dse> to play. *aškáce* <a-shka´-dse> I play (03/09/95/FH/pc:ok). *ðaškáce* <tha-shka´-dse> you play. *ąškaca pe* <o^{n}-shka-dsa i> we play, to sport. *škáce kizo* <shka´-dse gi-çu> full of life (sport, play, happy: sportive) (lit., 'likes to play'). *škáce hi waðį* <shka´-dse hi wa-thi^{n}> society, club; sport, play, arrive at, house or place for (03/09/95/FH/pc:uk; unconfirmed sentence).

••• Cf. *kíškace.*

škaškáða (variants: **škaškáðą, škaškáðe**). ADJ [probably contains a reduplicated form of *šká*] **all right, nothing wrong; happy, content.** *škaškáða mįkšé, škaškáða nįkšé* I'm all right, you're all right, I'm OK, you're OK (as book title) (01/04/95/FH/pc:ok: *-ða*). *škaškáða ąkái* we're happy (RBn12-03p5). *hcíle ąkóhta škaškáða ąkái* we are happy in our home (RBn12-03p5).

• ADJ, ADV **peaceful(ly), calm(ly), at rest, still (as a lake), in harmony, harmonious(ly), not worried, satisfied.** *škaškáðe* he's calm (BE2.102; FH:prod). *wéewina mǫ́žǫ ðé škaškáða oámąbrį* I want to thank you for this good life (lit., 'I am grateful, I walk on this earth peacefully') (RBn10-10:JW). *škaškáða mąbrį́ hkǫ́bra* I want to go on in peace, harmony (RBn22-17).

•• LFD 132: *škaškáðą* <shka-shka´-tho^{n}> happy, joyous, facetious, humorous. [Final vowel should be nonnasal *a* rather than nasal *ą* or *ǫ* (FH).]

šką́ (variants: **šką́ą, ską́ą**). V [reg., *_šką́*] *(intr.)* **move, change (as the weather)** (FH:ok) *ąšką́ htai* let's move, let's start (RBn12-11). *háakǫta šǫ́ke apa šką́kąða?* why is this dog moving around so much? • **go on, continue.** *kóoci ašką́ą ąąhé* I've been going on for a long time (MOJ). • **start.** *oðíhtą šką́ káaya* start the car (lit., 'make the car start') (RBn2-MOJ/p35; 03/14/95/FH/pc:ok). *oðíhtą šką́ ché?* is the car started? (FH:prod). *ąšką́ htai* let's get started (03/14/95/FH/pc:ok; BE2.127; RBn2-MOJ/p19b).

•• LFD 132: *šką* <shko^{n}> to be active. *ašką* <a-shko^{n}> I am active. *ðašką́* <tha-shko^{n}´> you are active. *ąšką pe* <o^{n}-shko^{n} i> we are active, to move, to stir. *šką wahtóke* <shko^{n} wa-ṭo´-ge> quick in action.

••• Cf. *šką̨šką́, waašką́.*

šką́ ðįké (variant: **šką́ įké**). ADJP, VP [reg., *_šką́ ðįké*] **(be) quiet, still (lit., 'not move').** *šką́ įká!* be still! (04/18/95/FH/pc:ok; BE2.110).

•• LFD 132: *šką́ ðįke* <shko^{n}´ thi^{n}-ge> motionless.

šką́ąži (variant: **šką́ži**). ADJ, ADV [reg., *_šką́ąži*] [*šką́ + aží* NEG] **still (lit., 'not move') quiet, quietly (as not in movement), unable to move or start (as a motor vehicle).** *oðíhtą akxa šką́ži akxa* the car won't start. *šką́ži lį́į* sit still (RBn23-15). *šką́ži žą́ą* lie still (RBn23-15).

•• LFD 132: *šką́áži* <shko^{n}-a´ zhi> not active, inactive. *žąape ke šką̨štiwą aži* <zho^{n}-a-be ge shko^{n}-shti-wo^{n} a-zhi> the leaves are motionless [unconfirmed sentence; <shti-wo^{n}> is unintelligible].

šką́ą (variant of **šką́**).

šką̨šką́. V [reg., *_šką̨šką́*] [reduplicated form of *šką́*] *(intr.)* **keep moving, move again and again.** *šką̨šką́ðe* keep moving.

šką́ži (variant of **šką́ąži**).

ški. ADV **also, too (often used as a way of implying 'and').** [Often not glossed in English: *hcí htąą ska ški* 'a big white house' (lit., 'big house also white').] *hpáata waší ški toa brúwį hce* let me buy some eggs and bacon, too (RBn1-43). *ðée lípi che ški wéewinai* I'm thankful, too, for these who have come here (FH/10/13/96). *ąhíiða ški hta ąkái* we are also going to swim (BE2.130; 05/02/95/LS/pc:okc). *mąhkása tóa ąwą́žu, wacúe ški tóa ąkʔú* pour me some coffee and give me some cake (RBn1-45; MREI/ok). *hpáata waší ški* bacon and eggs (lit., 'egg, bacon also') (01/04/95/FH/pc:ok; BE2.3). • **even.** *waðíhtaži ški apai* they don't even work (RBn10-2:MOJ/79). *híi ški ðiiskíke akxai* he's even grinding his teeth (FH). *táatąží ški oðáake* she's a blabbermouth (lit., 'she even tells small things'). • **even though, in addition, as well.** *hǫbrįke owáha hta mįkšé, waší ški oðóhkihą* I'm going to cook beans, I add salt meat (lit., 'I'm going to cook beans, I also cook salt meat with it') (01/12/95/FH/pc:prod).

•• LFD 132: *ški* <shki> also.

••• *KS ški* and/also (RR).

••• Cf. *ąkóški, ðiškítą, eeškítą, -škítą, wiškítą.*

škíke (variant of **skíke**).

-škítą. ADV **also, too.** [Suffixed to pronouns.] *wiškítą, wiškí* me too, I too (01/04/95/FH/pc:ok). *ðiškítą, ðiškí* you too. *ąkóški* we also. *eeškítą, éeški* he or she or it/they too (02/09/95/FH/pc:okc; BE2.67). *nǫ́ǫ apa eeškítą íixa apa* the grownups laughed too (lit., 'the grownups they too laughed') (RBn10-2:MOJ/79).

••• Cf. *ški.*

škópe. ADJ **deep.** *pa škópe akxa* the snow is deep (RBn1-11; HH/pc). *pá húðe akxa pa škópe akxa* the snow is deep (03/13/95/PM).

•• LFD 105: *níaxexe škope* <Ni´-a-xe-xe shku-be> Deep Ford. "At this place there was bad crossing. The location was near what is now the cemetery of Pawhuska, Okla. This was the sixth camp of the first trail."

šó (variant of **šeeðǫ́**).

šó chéðe. VP [*šó + che* POSIT + *ðe* CAU] **leave it alone (lit., 'stand it there by you').**

••• Cf. *šǫ́cheðé.*

šo ðíe. VP **leave alone, leave be (command form).** *šo ðíe!* let her alone! leave her be!

šóce. ADV, N **smoke, smoky, dingy, gray** (FH, 03/13/95/PM/pc:ok; BE2.124). [Smoke was the personal name of one of Frances Holding's maternal uncles whose English last name was Petsemoie.]

šóce (*continued*)

•• LFD 132: *šóce* <Sho´-dse> Smoke (personal name). *šóce* <sho´-dse> smoke. *šócenąą* <sho´-dse-no^{n}> turned to smoke, usually smokes. *hpéce hǫ́ži šoce* <p̣e´-dse ho^{n}-zhi sho-dse> a smoky fire [expected Mod. Os. gloss: 'a fire that is bad (*hǫ́ǫži*) because it is smoky'].

••• Cf. *xóce.*

šoðée (variant: **šǫðée**). VP [sync., *šó + (a)ðée*] **go toward you, go to the place where you are or near you** (03/23/95/FH/pc:ok). *ðakínakʔǫ táatą šoðée hpáaye* I'm sending something [this message] along to you so that you may hear about your own people (FH:ok).

•• LFD 134: *šoðé* <sho-the´> come toward you.

šoðée káaye. VP [sync. *k>p*, *šoðée _káaye*] **send, make go where you are.** *John apa íiðiðe kǫ́ðapí apa nąą, šoðée hpaayé hta mįkšé* John wants to see you [pl.], so I'm going to send him to see you (FH:5/01/96/tape119a).

šómihkasi, šómįhkase (variants of **šǫ́mįhkase**).

šooká (variant: **šóoka**). ADJ **thick** (RB; 03/20/95/FH/pc:okc). *haxį́ šooká į́į ðįké* don't wear that thick blanket (FH/09/24/01/prod).

•• RB: <šóká>.

•• LFD 132: *šoká* <sho-ga´> thick, as applied to goods, skin, or any material. LFD 125: *hpáhį ðihta akhi šoká* <p̣a´-hi^{n} thi-ṭa a-ki sho-ga´> [expected Mod. Os. form: *hpáhįį ðíhta kše šooká*] your hair is thick. LFD 190: *walúška hašoka* <wa-gthu´-shka ha-sho-ga> [LF's <ha-sho-ga> is presumably Mod. Os. *háa šooká*] a shard, a bug with a shell or tough skin.

••• *QU ákkišóka* crowded, thick, dense, plentiful (RR); *KS šóoga* thick, dense as a forest (RR).

šǫ́ (variants: **šǫ́e, šǫ́we, šǫðé**). CONJ **while, as, when.** *íe šǫ́ akxá* while they're talking, while they were talking; while he/she is/was talking talking (04/28/95/LS/pc:pl; 04/28/95/LS/pc:ok). *ohkie šǫ́ akxai* while he was talking [conversing]. *owíhką šǫ́we achípe* while I was helping you, he got there. *kṹ šǫ́ apa* while they were coming back (RBn22-07). *owíhką šǫ́we achípe* I was helping you when he came in (lit., 'while I was helping you, he arrived'). *awą́hkie šǫ́ akxa kaðǫ yaaké ahípe* while he was talking to me, he got to crying; he was talking to me then suddenly he started to cry (FH/8/30/94/prod). *lįe šǫ́ įkšé* while he was sitting (04/28/95/LS/pc:prod). *mąðį́ šǫ́ apa, xíðape* while he was walking, he fell down. *alį́į šǫ mįkšé ąpáaspąpe* I was sitting there and he punched me (03/23/95/FH/pc:okc; 1/20/83/693). *ną́ye ðaaxǫ́ke šǫ akxai híi ðiixǫ́kape* while he was chewing ice, he broke his tooth. • ADV **still.** *šǫ átxąhe* I'm still doing it (04/26/95/FH/pc). *wawépaho aní šǫ́ ąhé* I'm a witness and I'm still living. *híi ðáalį šǫ́ ðaašé* your teeth are still good (RBn3-49). *ąną́ži šǫ́ ąkxą́he* I'm still standing here (04/26/95/FH/pc). *wakʔó ðáalį šǫ ðaįše wáščuye ðáalį* you ought to get married while you're still a pretty woman (RBn17-p02). *ątíðe šǫ́ ąnįkšé* we [two] are/were still gossiping (MSB). • **continually.** *kaakǫ́ šǫ́ ðáįše, ðalǫ́šči nónə* keep on [like this] until you get drunk (lit., 'you are this way continually, you will just be drunk') (01/14/95/FH/pc:ok; RBn2-MOJ/p28).

•• LFD 134: *šǫ́ ðįkše į ta* <sho^{n}´ thi^{n}-kshe i^{n} da> even as he sat, while yet he sat. From a ritual. LFD 133: *šǫ átxąhe* <sho^{n}-a´-to^{n}-he> I am still here, standing (04/26/95/FH/pc:ok FH: means 'I'm doing it' or 'I'm still doing it'). *šǫ́ahtąhe aðo* <sho^{n}´-a-ṭo^{n}-he a-tho> [expected Mod. Os. form: *šǫ́ atxąhe; aðo* is not used in Modern Osage] I am still standing. *šǫ́ðahtąše* <sho^{n}´-tha-ṭo^{n}-she> [expected Mod. Os. form: *šǫ́ ðatxą́še*] you are still standing. [All LF examples should contain <t>, which may reflect the correct *tx* in Mod. Os., and not <ṭ>, which equates to *ht* and is erroneous.]

šǫ́ (variant of **šǫ́ke**).

šǫ́ htą (variant of **šǫ́ke htąą** 'wolf').

šǫ́ce. N **penis.** [Not as socially acceptable for 'penis' as *žé*] *oðíkinąąži oðíina šǫ́ce wahtį́į* [Mod. Os. form of *wahtį́į* is *wahcį́į*] zip up your fly (fasten your pants), your penis is showing (RBn2-MOJ/p21; 03/03/95/FH/pc:ok).

•• LFD 133: *šǫcé* <sho^{n}-dse´> the scrotum. *šǫcé ðįke* <sho^{n}-dse´ thi^{n}-ge> gelding.

šǫ́cheðé (variants: **šǫchéðe, šǫ́chíe**). V [reg., *šǫ́che_ðé*] [*šǫ́* 'still' + *che* POSIT + *ðe* CAU] *(trans.)* **leave alone without bothering, touching, or otherwise disturbing it/them [inanimate standing sg. item or sitting pl. items] (lit., 'cause to be still standing')** (BE2.78; 01/04/95/FH/pc:okc; 05/08/01,01/06/95, 02/15/95/FH/pc:prod). *waléze che šǫ́chia* leave the letters alone [as they are] (02/15/95/FH/pc:okc). *šǫ́chéða!* leave that alone! (e.g., to children [RB]) (RBn2-MOJ/p12; BE2.2-3). *šǫ́chie* leave that alone, don't bother that, don't touch that (FH/11/18/01/pc:prod).

•• LFD 134 (unconfirmed): *šǫhce* <sho^{n}´-ṭse> as it is, in fact (02/15/95/FH/pc:uk with this gloss).

šǫcóso. N **scrotum, testicles** (RBn HW13). [Possibly *šǫ́ce* + *ó-* LOC + *súu* (lit., 'place for seeds for the penis').]
•• LFD 325: *osú* <u -çi´> seeds. *sáhku akxa osú ochípe* <ça-çkiu a-ka u-çi´ u-tsi bi a> the watermelon has many seeds.

šǫðé (variant of **šǫ́**).

šǫðéðe (variant: **šǫǫðéðe**). ADV **forever, for always, for good.** *šǫðéðe brée hta mįkšé* I'm going and not coming back (MOJ/RBn2/p21). *šǫðéðe aðáape* she's left for good and not coming back (as when a wife leaves a husband) (PM).

šǫðée (variant of **šoðée**).

šǫ́e (variant of **šǫ́**).

šǫhtą́ą sa. N **black dog (lit., 'black wolf').**

šǫ́įkšeðe (variants: **šǫ́įkšée, šǫ́įkšíe**) V [reg., *šǫ́įkše_ ðe*] [*šǫ́* + *įkšé* POSIT + *ðe* CAU] *(trans.)* **leave it (round or sitting item) alone, leave him/her (sitting) alone, let him/her be, let it alone (includes allowing it/him/her to move freely), not have anything to do with s.o. or s.t.** (MSBt9b;02/15/95/FH/pc:ok). *šǫ́įkše[ð]e!* leave her alone! (RBn HW).

šǫ́ke (variant: **šǫ́**). N **dog.** *kšą́ka šǫ́ke íhta apa zípe* second son's dog is yellow. *šǫ́ke kšé nǫ́ǫðahpe?* are you afraid of that dog [lying down]? (12/30/94/FH/pc:prod orig). *šǫ́ htąą* a big dog. *šǫ́žį* a small dog.
•• LFD 133: *šǫ́ke* <sho^{n}´-ge> dog. *šǫ́ke ðįkše aðanąžį* <sho^{n}´-ge thi^{n}-ke a-tha-no^{n}-zhi^{n}> you stepped on the dog, wolf (01/20/95/ERE/pc:ok).

šǫ́ke. N **wolf.** *šǫ́ke xóce* gray wolf (RBn HW13; RBn22-04). *šǫ́ke sápe* black wolf (RBn HW13; RBn22-04).
•• LFD 133: *šǫ́ke ska* <sho^{n}´-ge çka> white wolf. *šǫ́ke sape* <sho^{n}´-ge ça-be> black wolf.

šǫ́ke htąą (variant: **šǫ́ htą**). N **wolf.**

šǫ́ke sa. N **Black Dog (personal name)** (RBn1-29).

šǫ́kehci. N **doghouse, kennel.**

šǫ́kšeðe. V *(trans.)* **leave it/him/her (lying down) alone** (MSBt9b). *šǫ́kše[ð]a!* leave her alone!

šǫmįe (variant of **šǫmį́įka**).

šǫmį́hka (variants: **šǫmį́hke, šǫ́mįhka**). N **Catholic** (01/09/95/FH/pc:ok, *hke* or *hka*; 04/13/95/LS/pc:ok, definitely *hka* only). [After an early Catholic missionary named Father Shoemaker (RB).]
••• Cf. *šǫ́mįhkase.*

šǫmį́hka kahíke (variant: **šǫ́mį́hke kahíke**). N **pope (lit., 'Catholic chief').** *šǫmį́hka kahíke mą́ze wanǫ́pʔį wį kʔúpi áape* they gave the pope a medal, they say (lit., 'chief of the Catholics, a metal necklace they gave him, it is said') (02/01/95/FH/pc:ok).

šǫmį́hka wakʔó. N **nun (lit., 'Catholic woman').**

šǫ́mįhkase (variants: **šómįhkase, šómihkasi**). N **coyote** (BE2.27; 01/14/95/FH/pc:ok, hk; FH:4/22/96/tape:okc). • **Fox or Wolf (personal name).** [Possibly Henry Haskell's name.] *šǫmihkase žúuce* red wolf.
•• JOD (Wolf and Fawn p15 ln1): *šǫ́mihkase wį aðaape ska* <Cŭ^{n}´mikáse wi^{n} a¢ápe ska> a wolf went out.
•• LFD 133: *šómihkasihtąka* <sho´-mi-ḳa-çi-ṭo^{n}-ga> big coyote; gray wolf. *šómihkasi sape* <sho´-mi-ḳa-çi ça-be> a black wolf.
••• *KS šǫ́mihkase hį htóho (htą́ga)* wolf, grey (RR).

šǫmį́hke (variant of **šǫmį́hka**).

šǫmį́įka (variants: **šǫmį́į, šǫmį́e**). N [*šǫ́ke* + *mį́įka*] **female dog, bitch.**

šǫǫðéðe (variant of **šǫðéðe**).

šǫǫšǫ́we (variants: **šǫ́šǫwe, šǫ́šǫ**). ADV **always, forever; during that time (refers to s.t. going on and on through time, uninterruptedly)** (01/04/95/FH/pc:ok). *wažážeíe šǫǫšǫ́we mąðį́ ðée hkǫ́bra* I want the Osage language to go on and on (BE2.3; 01/04/95/FH/pc:prod orig).
•• LFD 29: *sakíšǫšǫe* <ça-gi´sho^{n}-sho^{n}-e> permanency; permanent. *saki; šąšąe* <ça-gi; sho^{n}-sho^{n}-e> solid, strong; always.

šǫ́we (variant of **šǫ́**).

šǫ́žį. N [shortened from *šǫ́ke žįká* 'small dog'] **puppy** (FH:ok).

-špé. N ROOT **fragment, bit.** • V ROOT **fragment.**
••• Cf. *kašpé, ošpéžį, paašpú.*

špéka. (variant of **xpéka**).

špǫ́ǫ. V, ADJ [uninfl.] *(intr.)* **(be) softened by soaking in water; soften, become soft, sodden.**
•• LFD 134: *špǫ* <shpo^{n}> sodden; softened by soaking in water.
••• *KS špą́ye ~ špą́ąye* to soak something in water (RR); *QU špǫ́* wet (RR).

štá(a) (variant of **štáha**).

štáha (variants: **štáa, štá**) [uninfl.] ADJ, V **(be) shiny and smooth (as a lake surface), slick, bald, hairless, cleared.** *ožą́ke apa štáha apai* the roads are slick (RBn23-14). *mihkákʔe skáha, štáha* the stars are bright and shiny (FH).
•• LFD 134: *štáha* <shta´-ha> slick; smooth (04/06/95/LS/pc:ok).
••• Cf. *ðuuštá, ðuuštáha, haaštáha, hpeeštá, kaaštá, mąąštáha, oštá, puštáha, wéelišta.*

štáke. V, ADJ [uninfl.] *(intr.)* **(be) gentle, mild, or calm (a person or a person's ways); soothing, comforting.** *níhka štáke* a gentle man (FH). • **(be) mild, calm (e.g., weather).** *mą́ąɣe štáke* mild weather (02/24/95/FH/pc:ok; BE2.87; RBn2-MOJ/p19). • **(be) tepid, lukewarm.** *níi akxa štáke akxái* the water is tepid (04/26/95/FH/pc).

•• LFD 110: *ni che štáke ha* <ni te shta´-ge ha> [sentence-final *ha* is not used in Mod. Os.] the water is tepid. LFD 134: *štáke* <shta´-ge> tepid, slightly warmed; stagnant.

••• Cf. *waštáke.*

štą. ADV **all the time, incessantly, always, a lot; constantly, continuously; keep on doing s.t.** [Contrast *ną* (usually followed by *pe*) 'customarily'.] *Preston apa oðíhtą xǫ́ǫ štą* Preston is always having car trouble (01/04/95/FH/pc:prod). *žįkážį ąką́zą štą* we boss the kids around all the time (FH:prod). *pée tą nuužú štą* in the spring, it rains a lot (03/14/95/FH/okc; BE2.126). *žįkážį ąkáazą štą* we boss the kids around all the time (FH:prod). *íxope štą́ akxai* he lies so much (3-1-698). *niižú štą akxái* it keeps on raining, it likes to rain, it's always raining (ok CQ; RBn2-MOJ/p22). *wak^ʔó waðíhtą štą wį* a working woman (a woman who works all the time or constantly).

•• LFD 134: *štą* <shto^{n}> in the habit of. *ekǫ štą pe* <e-go^{n} shto^{n} bi a> he is in the habit of doing it; habitually; constantly.

štǫ́ka. ADJ **soft.** [***štą́ka* would be incorrect (FH); a (rare) clear difference in *ǫ* vs. *ą*.] *wacúe štǫ́ka* cornbread (made from fresh corn) (RB;2/2/07/MSB/849; 03/13/95/FH/pc:ok: final *a* short; BE2.124).

•• RB: <shtó^{n}-káh>.

•• LFD 187: *wacúe štǫka* <wa-dsiu´-e shto^{n}-ga> corn meal.

••• Cf. *mą́įhka íðištǫka.*

šúpe. N **intestines; appendix; colon; entrails, insides; stomach area, stomach** (FH:ok; LS:ok). *šúpe ihúheka kší áape* he [lying down] has intestinal trouble, they said (12/30/94/FH/pc; FH/09/23/01/pc; BE2.1). *šúpe aníe* my stomach hurts (02/13/95/FH/pc:ok; BE2.70).

•• LFD 132: *šúpe* <shiu´-be> intestines.

t

tá. V [reg.(?), *_tá*] *(trans.)* **ask for, request.** *mą́zeska tá akxái, bróka sáhta k^ʔú* he is asking for money, give him five dollars (02/25/95/FH/pc:okc; BE2.89). *kašpéǫpa tá akxai* he's asking for a quarter (RBn3-55).

••• Cf. *ootá, waatá.*

taa- (variants: **tae-, ta-**). N ROOT **behavior (in regard to behavior or conduct).** *žįkážį apa taaðúhpiižipe, omíži ðuhpíižipi įkšé* children are destructive [in their behavior], they have ruined the rug (RBn24). *taeðáalįži* mischievous (04/17/95/LS/pc:ok).

•• LFD 35: *táe ðalį aži* <da´-e tha-gthi^{n} a-zhi> unaccommodating; an unruly person; a disobedient child; willful; obstinate; forward; iniquitous; intractability.

••• Cf. *ootá, waatá.*

táa. V [uninfl.] *(intr.)* **freeze, be frozen.** *wáli táape* he was frozen fast (RBn16-02). *wáli táa akxa sį́įce* his tail was really frozen (FH/11/27/01/pc:prod). *sii ðíhta táa hta apa* you'll freeze your feet. *htóožu akxa otáa akxai* the meat pie is frozen.

•• LFD 117: *ną́ɣe ata* <no^{n}´-xe a-da> [possible Mod. Os.: *ną́ɣe átaa* or *ną́ɣe táa*] iciness; icy.

••• Cf. *átaa, otáa, táalį.*

táa-. INSTR **by extreme of temperature, by heat or cold.** *taazíhi* brown (as when fried food browns) [*táa-* + *zíhi*].

•• LFD 187 (unconfirmed): *watóštaha káaɣe* <wa-do´-shta-ha ga-xe> to iron clothes [presumably *wa-* + *táa-* 'by heat' + *štáha*, but unrecognized, unconfirmed].

••• Cf. *táahkace, táalį.*

táabrą. V [uninfl.] [*táa-* INSTR + *brą́*] *(intr.)* **smell from heating or body heat; emanate an odor while being heated (as in cooking/burning, refers to either a good or bad odor).** *óohǫ akxa táabrą akxai* the cooking is smelling (FH). *óohǫ akxa táalį akxa ska, táabrą akxai* the cooking must be burning, because it's smelling (FH). *táatą hpíiži wį áðanąąží ska táabrą ðąįšé* you must have stepped on something bad, because you're smelling bad (FH:prod).

táaðįke káaɣe. VP [sync. *k>p, táaðįke _káaɣe*] [*táa-* INSTR + *ðįké* + *káaɣe*] *(trans.)* **burn, burn up, burn down, incinerate, reduce to ashes.**

•• LFD 36: *táðįke káɣe* <da´-thi^{n}-ge ga-xe> to make to burn; incinerate; to reduce to ashes. *táðįke hpaɣe* <da´-thi^{n}-ge p̣a-xe> I reduced it to ashes. *táðįke škaɣe* <da´-thi^{n}-ge shka-xe> you reduced it to ashes. *táðįke ąkaɣa pe* <da´-thi^{n}-ge o^{n}-ga-xa i> we reduced it to ashes.

taaðúhpiiži. ADJ [*taa-* 'behavior' + *ðuhpíiži*] **destructive (lit., 'make behavior bad'), engaging in harmful behavior.** *žįkáži apa taaðúhpiižipe, omíže ðuhpíižipi įkše* children are destructive, they have ruined the rug (lit., 'the children have bad behavior, the rug is sitting there ruined') (01/20/95/FH/pc:ok; BE2.30).

•• RB: <táh-thú-pi-zhi>.

táahkace (variant: **táahkaci**). V, ADJ [uninfl.] [*táa-* INSTR + *-hkace*] *(intr.)* **(be) hot to the touch, (be) warm (an object or a substance; or a person only in special circumstances, such as with fever; does not apply to weather).** *tą́ąhkatažį mįkšé* I'm not hot (e.g., in the sweat house) (02/09/95/FH/pc:ok; BE2.68). *táahkata mąží mįkšé* I'm not hot. *táahkace* it's hot [an object]. *htóožu táahkace wį ąkʔú* give me a hot meat pie. *níi táahkace* hot water (02/09/95/FH/pc:ok). *wáli táahkaci akxái, óohǫ hkǫ́bra įké* it's hot [in here], I don't want to cook (01/12/95/FH/pc:okc; BE2.24). *táahkataží akxá* it's not hot to the touch. *táahkace káaɣa!* heat it up! *níhka táahkace* a warm man (02/09/95/FH/pc:okc).

•• LFD 36: *táhkace* <da´-ḳa-dse> hot. LFD 7 (unconfirmed as conjugated verb): *átahkace* <a´-da-ḳa-dse> to be hot from the heat of a fire or from the sun's rays. *ą́tahkace* <o^{n}´-da-ḳa-dse> I am hot from the fire. *táðihkace* <da´-thi-ḳa-dse> you are hot from the fire. *táwahkaca pe* <da´-wa-ḳa-dsa i> we are hot from the fire.

táahkace káaɣe. VP [sync. *k>p, táahkace _káaɣe*] *(trans.)* **heat (lit., 'make it hot; cause it to heat up').**

••• Cf. *taašcúe.*

táahkiðe. V [uninfl.] [*táa* 'freeze' + *hkik-* REFL + *ðe* CAU] *(trans.)* **freeze one's own.** *síi táahkiðe* I froze my feet.

táahpa. ADJ **round, circular.** *niitáahpa* pond (lit., 'round water') (BE2.105; 03/10/95/FH/pc:ok). [Forms diminutives *čáahpa, čáahpažį.*]

•• LFD 36: *tahpa* <da´-p̣a> disk; round, globular, orbicular; rotund. LFD 44: *katatahpa* <ga-da-da´-p̣a> to cut a log into short pieces

••• Cf. *ðutáahpa, wahóohtą táahpa.*

taahpóska (variant of **taapóska**).

taaké. V [reg., *_taaké*] *(intr.)* **fight; go to war.** *atáake* I fought. *ðatáake* you fought. *šǫžį apa taakí apái* the puppies are fighting (01/24/95/FH/pc:prod orig). *taaké apá aape* I heard they're fighting (01/24/95/FH/pc:okc). *ðǫha taaké hta apá aape* they are about to fight or go to war (01/24/95/FH/pc:ok). *ątáakaaži hce* let's don't fight [sg. addressee] (MSB/4/83/p7). • ADJ **fighting.** *taaké níhkašika* a fighting man, a boxer or wrestler (01/24/95/FH/pc:ok). • N **fight, fighting; war.** [Takes 'standing' positional article *che.*] *súhka taaké* a chicken fight (01/24/95/FH/pc:prod). *súhka taaké* cock fight. *taaké óhesaži hi chí aapé* the war is getting worse, it's getting to where they're really fighting (lit., 'they're getting to having fierce fighting, they said') (01/24/95/FH/pc:ok).

•• LFD 35: *také* <da-ge´> to fight; engagement; dissension; battle; pugilism. *atáke* <a-da´-ge> I fight. *ðatáke* <tha-da´-ge> you fight. *ątáka pe* <o^{n}-da´-ga i> we fight. *také che ewǫ akxa eepia* <da-ge´ tse e-wo^{n} a-ka e-e-bia> he is the cause of the fight [lit., 'that fight (*taaké che*), he is doing it (*éwǫ akxa*), they said (*éepe*)'] (01/24/95/FH/pc:uk). *táke nihkašika hpiǫ ðe tǫpe ązo ną aða* <da´-ge ni-ḳa-shi-ga p̣i-o^{n} the do^{n}-be o^{n}-çu no^{n} a-tha> [expected Mod. Os. form: *taaké níhkašika hpíǫ ðe tǫ́pe ą́zǫ ną*] I like to see a good pugilist [lit., 'a fighting man who is skilled, I always like to watch'].

taaké ie. N **verbal fight, fighting or arguing, quarrel (lit., 'fight talk')** (RB; 01/24/95/FH/pc:okc).

•• LFD 35: *také ie* <da-ge´i-e> an angry dispute; quarrel; altercation.

taaké omą́ðį (variant: **taaké omą́į**). VP **be in the armed forces, be a member of the military service; go to war** (BE2.4; 01/06/95/FH/pc:ok). N **armed forces; any branch of the military service.**

taaké oną́ążį (variant: **taaké onáaži**). VP, N **(be in the) armed forces or services** (04/19/95/FH/pc:ok).

•• RB: <tah-kí-o-náh-zhi>.

taakéštą. ADJ **quarrelsome (lit., 'fights continually').** *wakʔó taakéštąpe* she's a quarrelsome woman.

táaliko (variant of **táalįko**).

táalį. V, ADJ [stat.] *(intr.)* **burn; burned.** *ðéeze ątáalį* I burned my tongue (01/09/95/FH/pc:okc; BE2.13). *óohǫ akxa táalį akxa ska, táabrą akxai* the cooking must be burning, because it's smelling (FH). *htáa táalį škaaɣée* you burned the meat (lit., 'you caused meat burning') (01/09/95/FH/pc:prod). *htáa akxa táalį akxai* the meat's burned (01/09/95/FH/pc:prod; BE2.13).

táalįko (variant: **táaliko**). N [probably *táa-* INSTR + *lįkó*] **meat gravy, popular Osage dish made of boiled meat** (BE2.86; FH). [Meat is cut up, washed, rinsed, and stored in a pot overnight. The next day the meat is rinsed off then covered with the rinse water and juices that have exuded and accumulated in the pot. Salt and pepper are added, and the meat is boiled until almost dry, whereupon bacon grease and flour are added and the entire mixture is browned. Water is then added to achieve gravy consistency (FH).]

•• RB: <tah-lí^{n}-ko> (02/24/95/FH/pc:okc).

•• LFD 56: *táli pe* <da´-xthi be> to boil meat till tender. *talípe hpaɣe* <da-xthi´-be p̣a-xe> I boiled it till tender. LFD 220: *li* <xthi> fester, suppurate. [No exact match for *táalįko* has been found in LFD.]

taapóska (variants: **tapóska, taahpóska**). N **school** (03/08/95/MREI/pc:ok: short final *a*). [Borrowed from Pawnee *taapuska* 'school' (Douglas Parks). The Pawnee word may have entered Osage at different times in different forms, with or without preaspiration of the stops *(h)t* and *(h)p* and with a long or short vowel *aa* or *a*; it is losing or has lost the preaspiration in *(h)t* and *(h)p*.] *taapóskahci* school building (03/08/95/MREI/pc). *taapóska mąðį́* go to school [sg. addressee]. *taapóska máðį́pi* go to school [pl. addressee]. *taapóska panáa* school is dismissed [said at the close of the school day], school is out [for the summer] (03/08/95/MREI/pc:okc; BE2.116). *žįkážį apa kasį́xcižį páahą nąpé, taahpóska wábrįbree nai* the children get up early, I take them to school (02/27/95/JS/pc:okc; BE2.131). *taapóska ščée hta ðąįšé tą áhkihtǫ́pa ði* when you're going off to school, take care of yourself.

•• RB: <tah-pó-skah>.

•• JOD (slip file): *htáposka* <ta´-pu-ska> a teacher.

•• LFD 138: *htáposka* <ṭa´-pu-çka> a school-teacher. *htáhposka wihta oxta akiðe* <ṭa´-p̣u-çka wi-ṭa u-xta a-gi-the> I like my school-teacher. *htápxoska hci* <ṭa´-pu-çka tsi> [here LF's <-pu-> is a mistake for <-p̣u-> (Mod. Os. *-hpo-*)] Mission House; School.

taapóska mį́įǫpa. N **September (lit., 'school month')** (HH/14-a/249ff&pc).

taapóskahci. N [*taapóska* + *hcí*] **schoolhouse** (03/08/95/MREI/pc).

táapuɣe. V [uninfl.] *(intr.)* **boil over** (BE2.10; 01/07/95/FH/pc:ok).

••• Cf. *ápuɣe.*

táapuze. V [uninfl.] [*táa-* INSTR + *púze*] *(intr., trans.)* **dry from heat; boil dry (lit., 'by heat dry')** (01/07/95/FH/pc:ok; RBn1-MOJ/p50). [Contrast this word with *htáa púze* 'dried food; dried meat'.] *haxį táapuze mįkšé* [the blanket is drying; *mįkšé* here indicates ownership or interest in the process] I'm drying the blanket (FH). *óhkilą táapuze akxai* the clothes are drying (FH). *watáažoe táapuze mįkšé* I'm drying corn for hominy. • ADJ **boiled dry.**

•• LFD 6: *ápize* <a´-bi-çe> to become dry.

táasaaki. N [*táa-* INSTR + *saakí*] **burned meat, charred meat (the burned black part of meat such as barbecue; lit., 'hard due to heat').**

táaską. V [uninfl.] [presumably contains *táa-* INSTR] *(intr.?)* **melt** (FH:ok). *ną́ɣe akxa táaskąpe* the ice has melted (02/13/95/FH/pc:okc).

••• *KS dáaską* melt (RR); *QU táską* melt (RR).

táaske. ADJ **mellow** (02/27/95/FH/pc, unconfirmed).

taasúhu. V [*táa-* INSTR + *-súhu*] *(trans.)* **be clean or cleanse by heat or cold.**

•• LFD 34: *tásihi* <da´-çi-hi> to cleanse with heat; to purify. *tásihi akšiðe* <da´-çi-hi a-ki-the> [LF's *-kši-* <-ki-> is probably an error for *-hki-* <-ḳi->] I cleansed or purified myself with heat (01/30/95/FH/pc:uk). *tásihi ðakšiðe* <da´-çi-hi tha-ki-the> [LF's *-kši-* <-ki-> is probably an error for *-hki-* <-ḳi->] you cleansed or purified yourself with heat (01/30/95/FH/pc:uk). *tásihi ąkšiða pe* <da´-çi-hi o^{n}-ki-tha i> [LF's *-kši-* <-ki-> is probably an error for *-hki-* <-ḳi->] we cleansed or purified ourselves with heat.

••• Cf. *wasúhu.*

taašcúe (variants: **táašcue, taaščúe** [Hominy]) (BE2.151; 03/16/95/JS/pc:ok). ADJ, V [uninfl.] *(intr.)* presumably reduced from *táa-* INSTR + *šcúuce*] **(be) warm.** *ohkúla taaščúe* warm clothing (lit., 'clothing that warms') (03/16/95/JS/pc). *táašcue akxai* it's warm (speaking of an object such as a food item).

••• Cf. *mįįtáašcuuce.*

táašcue káaɣe. VP [sync. *k>p, táašcue _káaɣe*] *(trans.)* **warm (lit., 'make warm').** *táašcue káaɣa!* warm it up!

táašcuehkíðe. V [reg., *táašcue_hkíðe*] [*taašcúe* + *hkik-* REFL + *ðe* CAU] *(intr.)* **warm oneself, as at a stove or fire (lit., 'cause oneself to be warm')** (MSBt9).

taaščúe (variant of **taašcúe**).

taašéðe. V [reg., *taašé_ðe*] *(trans.)* **thump hard or knock s.o. in the head; shove, shove s.o.'s head quickly in anger.** [Does not apply to thumping watermelon; is not synonymous with *ochį́*.] *taašéwi[ð]e hta mįkšé* I'm going to thump you on the head (FH:5/01/96/tape:prod). *taašéwie hta ąkatxą́* I'll knock you in the head (RBn22-12; CQc). *Bob akxa Mongrain taašéðape* Bob hit Mongrain over the head (RBn22-12). *taašéðe tą, waðílą htǫ́ǫ hta apai* when you hit him on the head, that will make his mind get right (FH/1013/96). *taašéðie hta akxai* they'll hit you over the head (RBn23-20). *oðákie tą káazą, taašéða* when you talk to him, bawl him out, hit him on the head. *taašéðe įką* don't shove (FH:5/01/96/tape:prod).

táata záani (variant of **táatą záanį**).

táatą (variant: **táata**). INTERR/INDEF PRON **what (interrogative).** *htą́wa įkší táatą šíe* what did you all go to town for? (04/27/95/FH/pc:ok). *táatą háakǫ?* what happened? (RBn10-15). *táatokˀą́ apa?* [*táatą okˀą́ apa*] what are they doing? (RBn10-15). *táatą štáachape?* what did you all eat? (04/27/95/LS/pc:ok). *táatą štáahtąpe?* what did you all drink? (04/28/95/LS/pc:ok). *mįįðóhta wanǫ́bre táatą ąðáache hta ąkatxą́?* what are we having [going to eat] for noon meal? (04/28/95/LS/pc:ok). *táatą štáaci nǫpe?* what do you call that? (04/28/95/LS/pc:ok). *táatą štáache nǫpe?* what do you eat? (04/28/95/LS/pc:ok; BE2.154).

• **thing(s); anything, something; what, whatever (indefinite or relative).** *táatą škáaɣe* what you did (lit., 'the thing you did'). *táata ðíhǫǫ íšpahǫ?* do you know what you like? (RBn22-20). *táata ą́hǫǫ íhpahǫ, įcé ðuuhpíiži ą́hǫǫ* I know what I like, I like to make faces (RBn22-20). *táatąžį ðahkíliiski hta nįkšé?* those little things, small items that you've got, are you going to gather them up? *táatą ékipše sitǫ́į, wanáhkai ékimą* what I said yesterday I did it by mistake (lit., 'I said things yesterday, I made a mistake') (RBn10-2). *táatą hpíiži ecíke ta* if there are bad things around. *níi žópše pšíe ðáha, táatą wį mąžą́ olį́į iiðáðe* when I would go to wade in the river, I saw something that was in the woods (lit., 'whenever I went to wade in the water, I saw a thing that lived in the countryside') (T24b-p17/#24CQ119; 04/27/95/FH/pc:okc, added *iiðáðe*). *táatą ízizike ecíke tą, ékiǫ ðįkápi* if there is anything unclean, don't do it (FH: Hǫpétoohka). *táatą ékizǫ ðaįšé che wéeąna mįkšé* whatever you're doing, I'm grateful.

• INTERR ADJ **what kind, what sort, what type, what class of (interrogative).** *káache táatą waaðǫ́?* what kind of song is that? (RB). *táatą ohkíhce kóota įkšé?* what tribe is he [the one sitting over there]? *waskų́e táatą ðíhǫǫ?* what kind of candy do you like? (RBn10-18; CQc).

• INTERR V [uninfl.?] **do what (interrogative).** *kasį́ táatą hta paašé* what are you all going to do tomorrow? [note that no verb appears for 'do'] (04/27/95/FH/pc:okc).

táatą ékǫ ðįké. INDEF VP **nothing like it.** *mą́žą ðekáha táatą ékǫ ðįkí akxai* there's nothing like it here on earth (RBn10-2).

táatą éžiški (variant: **táatąžiški**) INDEF PRONP **anything; any other thing, anything else (lit., 'thing other also'); everything else, all other things.** *wį́ áoxta tą táatą éžiški ékimą ną* [expected Mod. Os. form of 'like': *ą́oxta*] when I like somebody, I'll do anything for them (RBn17-p03; HRE/01/17/02/pc:okc). *táatąžiški káaɣe íisi pe kóe wanǫ́bre, hóo saakí, waachí kíhǫǫpe* he didn't like to do anything but eat, holler, and dance (lit., 'everything else he hated doing, but eating, hollering, dancing he liked') (RBn10-2:MOJ/79; RBn16-01).

táatą howachéeški. INDEF PRONP **whatever; everything, anything at all.** *táatą howachéeški waðákšiɣe hkǫ́bra* whatever it is, I want you to fix it for them. *táatą howachéeški waðákšiɣe hkǫ́bra* anything at all, I want you to fix it for them; everything, I want you to fix it for them.

táatą hǫǫžį. INDEF PRONP **evil, bad things.** *táatą ðeke hǫ́ǫžįke ékiǫ įká* don't do these bad things (RBn10-18).

táatą íbrilą che. INTERR/INDEF VP **guess what? (lit., 'I'm thinking something').** [Contains 'standing' positional article *che*.] *táatą íbrilą che* guess what?

táatą íðilą. INDEF VP [sync., *táatą í_ðilą*] *(intr.)* **think about or consider s.t., have s.t. on one's mind.** [For 'think of us', use *kisúðe* 'remember' (FH).] *táatą íbrilą* I've got something on my mind (03/20/95/FH/pc:ok: short *ą* in verb). *táatą*

táatą íðilą (*continued*)
íbrilą I'm thinking about something (FH; RBn10-21/JW&FW/77). *táatą íščilą ðáįše?* what's on your mind? (03/20/95/FH/pc:prod). *táatą ðáalį na íðilą* think good thoughts (FH/98/pc). *táatą íbrilą che?* do you know what I'm thinking about? guess what? do you know what [I have on my mind]? (as when introducing an unexpected comment) (FH).

táatą ochí. INDEF PRONP **many things, lots of things; disorderly abundance; mixture of items that are out of order, trashy mixture; mess** (PM/pc:prod; 04/17/95/LS/pc:ok).
•• LFD 35: *tatą ochí* <da-do^{n}´ u-ṭsi> superabundance.

táatą paahą́ (variant: **táatą paahá**). VP [sync. fortisizing stop stem, *táatą _paahą́*] *(intr.)* **show things (lit., 'show something'); make a proposition, proposal, or offer.** *brúwį hkǫ́bra éekǫ táatą ée hpáahą* as I wanted to buy I made him a proposition.
•• LFD 34: *tatą paha* <da´-do^{n} ba-ha> an exhibition; an offer; a proposal; a proposition. *bri wį hkǫbra eką táatą éhpaha* <bthi wi^{n} ḳo^{n}-btha e-go^{n} da-do^{n} e´-pa-ha> I made him a proposition.

táatą záanį (variant: **táata záani**). INDEF PRONP **everything, all of it.** *táatą záani šcíištąpé?* have you [pl.] got everything all prepared? (04/13/95/LS/pc:pl) *taátą záani íšpahǫ* you know everything [in a religious sense, talking to God] (04/26/95/LS/pc:ok). *táatą záani ée ecí che?* is everything there? is everything ready? (04/26/95/LS/pc).

táatąžiški (variant of **táatą éžiški**).

táatąžį́ N [*táata* + *-žį* 'little'] **small things.** *táatąžį́ ški oðáake* she tells everything, she's a blabbermouth (lit., 'small things even she tells').

táatąžį́ ški oðáake. N **tell-all, person who tells everything** (RBn14-05), **blabbermouth.**

taazíhi. ADJ, V [uninfl.] [*táa-* INSTR + *zíhi*] *(intr.)* **brown, become brown by application of heat; (be) browned, fried.** *súhka taazíhi akxa?* is the chicken browning? (FH/07/09/01/pc). *htáa taazíhi* fried meat, steak (RBn3-53). *tooská taazíhi tóe oohǫ́* cook some fried potatoes (RBn12-05;CQ;okc). *mį́įðohta ci súhka taazíhi ąðáachape* we ate fried chicken at noon.

taazíhiðe (variant: **taazihíðe**). V [presumed reg., *taazíhi_ðe*] [*taazíhi* + *ðe* CAU] *(trans.)* **fry, brown, cause to brown (as food)** (01/30/95/FH/pc:ok). *Mary akxa súhka taazíhi[ðe] akxa* Mary's browning the chicken (FH/07/09/01/pc).
•• RB: <táh-zi-hí-théh>.
•• LFD 34: *tázihi* <da´-çi-hi> to burn a stick until it becomes yellow.

táaži. V [uninfl.] [*táa-* + *aží* NEG] *(intr.)* **go out, not burn, become extinguished.** *táažipe* it [the fire] went out (01/09/95/FH/pc:ok; 01/26/95/FH/pc:okc). *hpéece akxa táazi akxai* the fire is going out (RB).
•• LFD 36–37: *táži* <da´-zhi> to extinguish a fire [translation should be: '(fire) become extinguished']. LFD 127: *hpéce taži* <pe̱´-dse da-zhi> fire burned out.

tae- (variant of **taa-**).

taeðáalįži (variants: **taiðáalįži, teðáalįži**). V [*taa-* 'behavior' + *ðáalį* + *aží* NEG] *(intr.)* **be mischievous, rowdy, or unruly, show unpredictable behavior, misbehave, "run wild" (lit., 'behavior not good')** (RBn10-21/JW). *wáli taeðáalįži ðąįšé ąc?éðie hta ąkatxai* you're really behaving badly, we're going to kill you (FH/08/15/95; BE2.115). *wak?óhpa apa taiðáalįži apai* my girl is running wild (03/01/95/FH/pc:ok).
•• LFD 35: *táðalį* <da´-tha-gthi^{n}> decency; propriety in conduct, speech. *táe ðalį* <da´-e tha-gthi^{n}> dutiful, obedient. *táe ðalį aži* <da´-e tha-gthi^{n} a-zhi> unaccommodating; an unruly person; a disobedient child; willful; obstinate; forward; iniquitous; intractability. *táe ðalį niaži* <da´-e tha-gthi^{n} ni-a-zhi>you are unaccommodating (03/01/95/FH/pc:ok). LFD 131: *šį́htoži táeðalįži* <shi^{n}-ṭo zhi^{n}-ga da´-e tha-gthi^{n} a-zhi> a willful boy.

tapóska (variant of **taapóska**).

tą (variant: **tǫ** [LH]). SUBORDINATOR **if; provided that.** *mą́zeska abrį́e akxąhé tą, wíbruwį hce ska* if I had money, I'd buy it for you [I guess, but unsure] (FH:4/25/96/tape:prod). *mą́ąye ðáalį tą, hóolą ąkái hta ąkái* if the weather is good, we are going fishing (RBn3-MOJ?/p18). *niižú tą, hcíta küe* if it rains, come inside (04/28/95/LS/pc). *ąkóhkihkąpi tą* if we help each other (108-b/FH/527). *ðíe waðákaaži tą, owé hci ci brée hkǫ́bra* if you drive, I want to go to the grocery store (04/28/95/LS/pc:ok). • **when.** *péehtąą tą niížú nąpé* when it becomes spring, it usually rains (04/28/95/LS/pc:okc). *ðéekaa bríištą tą, htą́wą įkši brée hta mįkšé* when I get through here, I'm going to town (04/28/95/LS/pc:okc; BE2.155). *htą́wa kši śí tą* when you get to town (04/28/95/LS/pc:okc, tape; 03/20/95/FH/pc:prod; BE2.136). *chípi tą íinǫǫhpapai íðaapi tą* when they come, be careful when you [pl.] speak (FH/11/19/01/pc:prod). *chí tą íinǫǫhpapai íðaapi tą* when he comes, be careful when you [pl.] speak (FH/11/19/01/pc:prod). *žą́ą kaasípi tą žą́ąžį paasíke akxai* [(a)pi on 3rd sg. verb *kaasé* is unexpected in this context] when he cuts wood, the little splinters fly out (04/19/95/FH/pc). *wíe bríištą tą waatáihci ci pší hta mįkšé* when I get through, I'm going to go by the church. *ók?ą hta ąkai tą háachi niižú ną apai* when we're going to have something, it always rains. *ók?ą ąkǫ́ða tą háachi niižú nąpe* whenever we want to have something it always rains (FH). • **since; because.** *káakǫ kǫ́ða tą* since he wants it this way (04/11/95/FH/pc:prod).

•• RB: <tah^{n}, tuh^{n}>.

•• LFD 38: *tą* <do^{n}> because; when; did.

tą́ąska. INDEF PRON **what-do-you-call-it, thingamajig, whachamacallit; who's-it, what's-his-name, what's-her-name; item, thing, something** (BE2.154; RBn2-MOJ/p14; 04/28/95/LS/pc:okc ; FH:ok). [May be used in place of a person's or an item's name that one cannot remember or that seems unimportant to state explicitly.]

tąhé (variant: **tąhí**). ADJ, V [uninfl.] **(be) well.** *tąhé mįkšé* I [sitting] am well. *tąhé ąhé* I [moving] am well; I have been well. *tąhé nįkše?* are you well? *tąhé ðatxą́še?* are you [standing] well? *tąhé ðaašé?* are you [moving] well? (LS: or sitting). *tąhé žą́kše?* are you [lying down] well? *tąhé paašé?* are you all well? *ðáalį tą́he nįkšé che* it's good you are keeping well (05/01/95/LS/pc:okc). *wak?ó tąhé įkšé?* is your wife [who is not present] well? *wižǫ́ke akxa tąhé akxa* my daughter has been well (05/01/95/LS/pc). *žįkážį tąhé apai?* are your children well? (BE2.153) *tąhį́ ąkái* we are well. • **(be) wonderful.** *nihkáši tąhápe* he or she is wonderful (1-27-83-p1).

•• LFD 38: *tąhé* <do^{n}-he´> decent, clean, of good character.

••• Cf. *kitą́he.*

teðáalįži (variant of **taeðáalįži**).

tíðe. N **gossip.** [The form of this word is archaic: *ti-* is a rare sequence in Mod. Os.] *tíðe ðįké?* is there [not] any gossip? (05/01/95/LS/pc:ok; FH:4/22/96/tape: prod; BE2.59). *wak?ó tíðe štą* she's a gossipy woman (FH:4/22/96/tape:prod). *ątíðe žǫ́ ąnįkšé* we [two] are/were still gossiping (MSB). *ątíla ąðįkšé hta akxai mą́žą įké etxą́* we will still be gossiping when the world ends.

tó (variant: **tǫ́**). ADV **barely, hardly, only to a limited degree or barely representative amount.** *íixa che tǫ́ ekǫ káaya* don't laugh so much (lit., 'that laughing, like barely make it') (ERE/2/95/pc). *tǫníðe* barely allow to live. *žį́įhe che tó ekǫ káaya!* don't sleep so much! (02/23/95/FH/pc). *taiðáalįži tó ekǫ káaya* don't be so rowdy, mischievous (02/23/95/FH/pc). *lǫ́ðį che tó ekǫ káaya* don't get drunk so much (02/23/95/FH/pc).

tó įkšé (variant of **tówa įkše**).

tóa (variants: **tóe, tó**). ADJ, PRON **any.** *htóožu tóa wéščuwį?* did you sell any meat pies? (RB). *wanǫ́brenii tóa ošcé?* is there any peyote tea left? (02/15/95/FH/pc:ok; BE2.78). • **some.** *mą́hkasa tóe ąwą́žu* pour me some coffee (BE2.125; 03/13/95/FH/pc:ok). *tóa štáache ðáalį* you ought to eat some (RBn1-55). *tóa wéhice ðachípe* some of you came a long ways (RBn11-02/JW&FW&HHsk/c.1976). *ší tóa ąk?ú* give me some more [e.g., food] (lit., 'again some give me'). *wapúška tóe nǫ́p?į akxai* they've got beads around their neck (RBn12-08). *mą́zeska tóa owáhi* I won some money. • **(marker of head within a relative clause).** [Compare *wį* ADJ/PRON.] *hǫ́ǫpa ðé wéeną akxai ðe níhkaši tóa áðixǫpape, hpáðį wéhkili íwehkili į kšíyape* she's grateful today because they honored her, they dressed her in Kiowa clothes (lit., 'today she's grateful to the people that honored her by having her dress with Kiowa clothes') (RBn23-17; CQc). *waléze tóa ąwą́ðak?u na, ðé é í apai* the books that you loaned me are these (2-10-84-p4).

•• LFD 40: *tópa* <du´-ba> some. *tópa* <du´-ba> some. LFD 37: *tópa* <do´-ba> some; a part of. *tópa abrį a ðo* <do´-ba a-bthi^{n} a tho> I have some.

tóa (variant of **tówa**).

tóekǫ́ži. ADJ [*tó + ékǫ + aží*] **greedy, overbearing, excessive, not limited in excessiveness (lit., 'not as if limited')** (RBn18-04; RBn22-0). [Describes someone that takes over, runs over people (RB) (03/03/95/FH/pc:ok; BE2.100).]

toníðe. V [reg., *toní_ðe*] [*tó + níðe* 'allow to live'] *(trans.)* **scold harshly, bawl out, or "get after" s.o.; spare s.o.'s life, barely leave s.o. alive.** *Carolyn, Johna toníðae?* Carolyn, did you scold John? *toníwaðape* they bawled us out, they bawled them out (MOJ; FH:ok). *Smokey akxa toníwaipe* Smokey bawled them out (RB; CQc). *toníðe apai* he's just barely alive (lit., 'they've just barely allowed him to live') (RBnot-nd-1/p9). *iihǫ́ akxa toníwa[ð]ape* their mother bawled them out. *toníðape* they bawled him out

toníðe (*continued*) (MOJ;FH:ok). *toníąðape* they got after me (04/19/95/FH/pc). *toníąðape* they bawled me out, they almost killed me, they barely left me alive (RB; MOJ).

••• Cf. *waníðe.*

tóo-. N ROOT **tuber.**

••• Cf. *tóolehtąą, tóole žúe, tóoleži, tooscée, tóoska, tóoskue, tóožuuce.*

tóoce. N **throat, gullet.** *tóoce ąníe* I have a sore throat (03/22/95/FH/pc:prod). *tóoce ðiníe* you have a sore throat (03/22/95/FH/pc:prod; BE2.140). *tóoce oscį́ike* you took him by the throat (03/22/95/FH/pc:ok).

•• LFD 37: *tóce* <do´-dse> throat; gullet.

tóoce ðiláace (?) (variant: **tóoce ðihláace?**). N **beads** (RBn, unconfirmed). [Presumably either *tóoce* 'throat' + *ðu-/ði-* INSTR 'by hand' + *xláce* 'touch' (root not attested in Os., but cf. KS *xláǰe* 'beads for touching or rubbing worn around the throat') or alternatively *tóoce* + *ðu-/ði-* INSTR + *láace* 'name one's own' (lit., '[something] around the throat for naming, calling, or saying one's own'); both derivations refer to rosary beads.]

•• RB: <to-síe thi-lá-tse> beads.

••• *KS xláǰe ~ xláaǰe* touch; massage, rub (RR).

tóoce níe. VP [stat., *tóoce _níe*] **sore throat.**

tóoce oðį́ike. VP [sync., *tóoce o_ðį́ike*] *(trans.)* **choke with the hands (lit., 'grasp the throat'), strangle** (01/09/95/FH/pc:ok; RBn2-MOJ/p14).

tóoceha (variant: **toocéha** [FH]). V [uninfl.?] *(intr.)* **eat too much, overeat** (FH/11/27/01/pc:prod: 1st syll stress). *wálį tóocehape, waachí ną apái* he eats too much and he doesn't do anything but dance (RBn10-2:MOJ/79). *Dave akxa toocéha akxa* Dave sure likes to eat (RBn 5/3/79). • N **glutton, one who overeats** (01/31/95/FH/pc:ok; BE2.55; RBn2-MOJ/p12).

••• *KS wažį́ga dóoǰeha* pelican (RR).

••• Cf. *tóoce.*

toohká. ADJ **wet, moist, damp** (FH:10/13/96/pc). *hǫpé toohká* Wet Moccasins (a personal name that may refer to dew on moccasins) [Hǫpétoohka was the name of an elderly Osage lady near Hominy in the early 1900s who probably did not have an English name; also Ruth Shackelford's name.]

tooká (variant: **tóoka**). N **male.** *hceetóoka* buffalo bull.

•• LFD 38: *toká* <do-ga´> the male; a ritual expression.

tooká ðįké. VP [stat., *tooká _ðįké*] *(intr.)* **be without males (said of a family with all girls)** (01/14/95/FH/pc). *tooká ðįké* no males (01/14/95/FH/pc). *ðe hcíle akxa tooká ðįké* that family has all girls (01/14/95/FH/pc).

••• Cf. *mįįká ðįké.*

tooké (variants: **tookétą, tookéta**). N **summer, when it is summer, summertime** (MREI; 05/02/95/LS/pc:ok). *tookétą hípe* it's summer (lit., 'summer arrived there') (BE2.129). *tooké tą* when it's summer.

•• RB: <tó-kéh, to-kéh-tah>.

•• LFD 38: toké <Do-ge´> summer.

tookéce. N [*tooké* + *ce* 'last'] **last summer** (FH/pc).

•• JOD (slip file): *tokéci* <ṭu-ḳe ṭṣi> last summer.

••• *KS dogéǰi* last summer (RR).

tookéta, tookétą (variants of **tooké**).

tóole žúe. N **beet** (LF, unconfirmed; FH:4/22/96/tape/ma).

•• LFD 38: *tóle žue* <do´ -gthe-zhu-e> beet, radish.

••• KS *dóole yű́ǰe* radish (RR).

tóolehtąą. N [presumably *tóo-* + *le* (otherwise unattested) + *htą́ą*] **turnip.**

•• LFD 38: *tóle htǫa* <do´gthe -ṭo^{n}-a> pomme blanche.

tóoleži. N **carrot** (BE2.17; 01/09/95/FH/pc:prod).

•• LFD 38: *tóle* <Do´-gthe> *Psoralea esculenta* Pursh, commonly called "pomme blanche" by the whites [densely hairy perennial of central North America having edible tuberous roots; synonymous with breadroot, Indian breadroot, pomme blanche, pomme de prairie; LF has no entry for 'carrot'].

••• *KS*: *dóole zíhi* carrot (RR).

tóopa. ADJ, N **four.** *hcéska tóopa abrį́e* I have four cattle (01/30/95/FH/pc:okc; BE2.50).

•• LFD 37: *tópa* <do´-ba> four.

tooscée (variant: **toošcée**). N [*too-* + *scéce*] **sweet potato, yam (lit., 'long potato')** (03/14/95/MREI/pc:ok; RBn1-MOJ/p14; FH:5/01/96/tape:prod). *tooscée ðe howáįke šcúwį?* where did you buy these sweet potatoes? (RBn1-33).

•• LFD 39: *tóscece* <do´-stse-dse> the sweet potato. *to; scece* <do; stse-dse> potato; long.

tóoska (variant: **tooská**). N [*too-* + *ská* 'white'] **white potato, Irish potato** (01/09/95/FH/pc:prod). *tóoska akʔé hta aðįhé* I'm going to dig potatoes (BE2.31; FH:ok).

•• RB: <to-skáh> white potato (BE2.106).

•• LFD 37: *tóska* <do´-çka> white potatoes, Irish potatoes. *tóska che paažape* <do´-çka tse ba-a-zha-be> I pared the potatoes. *tóska che paðaža pe* <do´-çka tse ba-tha-zha be> you pared the potatoes. *tóska owažu mikše o* <do´-çka u-wa-zhu mi kshe o> [sentence-final *o* is not used in Mod. Os.] I am planting white potatoes.

tóoske. N **hiccup.** *tóoske akxa* it's a hiccup (RBn10-21/JW&FW/77).

•• LFD 37: *tósku* <do´-çkiu> hiccup. *tósku mǫ ha* <do´-çkiu mo^n ha> I have the hiccups. *tósku žǫ ha* <do´-çkiu zho^n ha> you have the hiccups.

••• Cf. *íkaske, tóoce.*

tóoskue. N [*too-* + *skúðe*] **sweet potato.**

tóoskue káxa. N **sweet potato branch (Sweet Potato Creek).**

•• LFD 37: *toskue kaxa* <Do-çkiu-e ga-xa> Sweet potato branch; sometimes called Ni-u-zhu (Neosho); Spring River. *tósku káxa kše áška ci alį̨* <Do´-çkiu ga-xa ke a-shka dsi a-gthi^n> I live near Spring River [Sweet Potato Creek] (unconfirmed; FH:5/01/96/tape:uk).

toošcée (variant of **tooscé**).

tóožuuce. N [*too-* + *žúuce*] **sweet potato (lit., 'red potato')** (RBn14-08).

totá aðíi (variant of **totą́ha aðée**).

totáha (variant of **totą́ha**).

totą́ (variant: **totá**). N **war; warpath; scouting, scouting alone; looking for enemies.** *totá ha bree* I'm going off to war (FH). *totą́ ðée* be on the warpath, go to war. *hkée wį tǫtą́ ðée ná* one turtle went on the warpath (a line from a song). *totá brée* I'm going scouting (RB). *totá ší?* have you been scouting? (lit., 'did you go there scouting?') (RB).

•• LFD 37: *totą́* <do-do^n´> to go to war [translation should be simply 'war'; 'go' is not explicitly mentioned].

totą́ aðée (variant of **totą́ha aðée**).

totą́ha (variants: **totą́hąka, totą́hą, totáha**). N **committeeman, member of war dance committee; one with rank or authority, ranking member.** • ADJ **ranking; with rank and authority** (RB).

•• LFD 11b: *áhkita totą́hąka* <a´-ḳi-da do-do^n-ho^n-ga> an army officer of rank. LFD 222: *totą́hąka* <Do-do^n´-ho^n-ga> chief commander of the army.

totą́ha aðée (variants: **totą́ aðée, totá aðíi**). V [sync., *totą́ha (a_)ðée*] **go to war, go on the warpath.** *hkežį́ totą́ha ðée* the little turtle went to war (line from a children's song). *hkée wį totá aðíi aape* a turtle went on the warpath (RB).

•• LFD 37: *totą́bre* <do-do^n´bthe> I go to war. *totą́ ąkaða pe* <do-do^n´ o^n-ga-tha i> we go to war.

totą́ha wahtą́ka (variant: **totáha hą́hka**). N **head committeeman** (01/04/95/FH/pc:prod).

•• RB: <dó-dah-hú^n-gah> or <do-dáh-hah^n-wah-tú^n-kah> (BE2.65).

totą́hą, totą́hąka (variants of **totą́ha**).

tówa (variant: **tóa**). PRON, ADJ **that, those (of one or more persons or things that are more remote than s.o./s.t. else or whose exact description is unknown or of little importance to the speech event)** (MSB3/1/690). *tówa txą áwak?u mįkše* I'm giving stuff to that bunch of people. *tówa apa óðuuc?akape* that person is lazy (RBn3-39). *tówa níhka hpa éži apai* that man has an odd-looking nose (RBn13-01). *tówa níhka įkšé táatą žáže aðíe?* what is that man's name? *tówa kše šcéða!* doctor that one lying there; doctor him!

tówa akxa. PRONP [*tówa* + *akxa* SUBJECT MARKER] **that one; that person; those ones, those persons** (MREI/6/7/94/#94; 3/1/690). [The combination *tówa akxa* is somewhat unacceptable ("sounds blunt"), while *tówa įkše* is preferred. Presumably this unacceptability arises because the subject marker *akxa* implies a subject that is present and not moving, while *tówa* implies that its referent is not proximate.] *tówa akxa waachípi áape* they said those ones danced.

tówa apa. PRONP [*tówa* + *apa* SUBJECT MARKER] **group of people or single person of unknown or unimportant identity, moving and marked as the subject of a sentence.** *tówa apa aðáapažíe* he didn't go, they didn't go (2-10-83-p2).

tówa che. PRONP [*tówa* + *che* POSIT] **this one (thing) standing here, that one (thing) standing there; those ones, that stuff (a collocation of sitting or round inanimate objects [such as a bunch of grapes] whose exact identity is unimportant or unknown).** *tówa che* those things sitting there (03/20/95/FH/pc).

tówa įkše (variant: **tó įkšé**). PRONP [*tówa* + *įkšé* POSIT] **that one of uncertain or unimportant identity (animate or inanimate); that person sitting; that object or thing sitting there** (03/20/95/FH/pc:ok). [*įkšé* is the default positional article, which may be used even if an item or person is not known to be sitting (especially if not present or in an unknown position). It is more polite to use *įkšé* with *tówa* than to use *akxa*.] *tó įkše iiðási* I don't like that person (RBn19-06). • **that group of objects of**

tówa įkše (*continued*) **uncertain or unimportant identity (not animate if pl.)** (03/20/95/FH/pc:ok).

•• LFD 40: *tóta ðįkšé* <du´-da thi^n-kshe> [*tóta* is unconfirmed; should be *tówa;* possibly an error] the one sitting on this side.

tówa ke. PRONP [*tówa* + *ke* POSIT] **those scattered (e.g., people or leaves)** (03/20/95/FH/pc). *tówa ke* those ones scattered around (BE2.139).

tówa pa. PRONP [*tówa* + *pa* POSIT] **group of people of unknown or unimportant identity.** *tówa pa áwawakˀu mįkšé* I'm giving stuff to that bunch of people.

tówa txą. PRONP [*tówa* + *txą* POSIT] **that one or those ones standing (animate, of unknown or unimportant identity).** *tówa txą áwakˀu mįkše* I'm giving stuff to that bunch of people.

•• LFD 40: *tóta txą* <du´-da to^n> [*tóta* is unconfirmed; should be *tówa*] the one standing on this side.

tožáðe. ADJ **rotten, decomposed, putrefied.** *še hką́ące akxa tožáðe akxai* that apple is rotten.

•• LFD 39: *tožáðe* <do-zha´-the> rotten.

tóže. ADJ **flat, flattened or mashed (said of a soft object); squashed, deflated (e.g., an object that formerly contained s.t.).** *hcéðe akxa tóže akxai* the tire is flat (softened, air has gone out of it) (FH/11/27/01/pc:ok; BE2.49).

••• Cf. *iištáðe ðiitóže.*

tǫ́ (variant of **tó**).

tą (variant of **tą**).

tǫ́, tǫ́e, tǫ́ę, tǫ́į (variants of **tǫ́pe**).

tǫ́ǫpše (variant: **tǫ́pše**). N [*tǫ́ǫ* 'stubby' (?) (root not attested elsewhere in Mod. Os.) + *pšé*] **frankfurter; Indian frankfurters, Indian sausages (made from strips of round steak encased in entrails and broiled until brown; these sausages were cut two to three inches long)** (01/30/95/FH/pc:okc; RBn2-MOJ/p28); **any sausage or baloney** (03/08/95/MREI/pc:ok; BE2.116; 03/08/95/FH/pc:ok).

•• LFD 156: *htǫpše* <ṭo^n-pshe> [expected form (in this and the next example) is <do^n´-pshe>, with plain <d>, not <ṭ>] sausage, made from the tenderest part of fresh meat and the intestines of the buffalo, well seasoned with pepper and salt; before it is inserted in the casing, water is put in and both ends are tied. *htǫ́pše šoce brą* <ṭo^n´-pshe sho-de btho^n> smoked sausage. LFD 39: *tǫ́hka* <do^n´-ḳa> short or stubby, as a bear's tail. [This is a possible source of *tǫ́ǫ* 'stubby'.]

••• Cf. *htáapše.*

tǫ́pe (variants: **tǫ́, tǫ́ę, tǫ́e, tǫ́į**). V [sync. fortisizing stop stem, *_tǫ́pe*] *(trans.)* **see, observe, watch** (RBn10-15). [Truncated variants *tǫ́, tǫ́ę, tǫ́e, tǫ́į* occur frequently in combination with other words, as in *enątǫ́įpe* 'Look Only at Her' (personal name) and *watǫ́ehci* 'store'.] *htǫ́pe* I watch it. *štǫ́pe* you watch it. *tǫ́pe* he watches it. *ątǫ́pe* we watch it. *watǫ́pe brée ðe* I'm going to see it (02/22/95/FH/pc:prod orig). *waachí watǫ́e ąkái hce* let's go watch them dance [sg. addressee] (RBn10-12:JW). *žįkážį nakxą́še wéewina akxą́he, ilǫ́įhpa waachí štǫ́pape* I want to thank you children for watching my son dance. *kį́įkįežį ówaðaha apa, kóe watǫ́pe che* he followed the butterflies so that he could watch them (RBn15-02; FH:ok). • *(intr., trans.)* **look, look at, on, or upon** (02/22/95/FH/pc:okc). *htóį akxąhé* I'm looking (02/22/95/FH/pc:ok; BE2.81). *htǫ́pe tą įcé ąhpáze ną* when I look at it, it makes me dizzy (RBn10-7:JW). *wátǫpapi akxái* someone is looking at us; something is looking at us; someone is staring at us (02/22/95/FH/pc:okc). *tówa įkše tǫ́pa* look at him/her/that. *kóota ðe níhka tǫ́pa* look at that man farther over there. *tǫ́pa mą́ąɣe ðáalį akxa* look, the weather is good (RBn1-33).

•• LFD 38: *tǫ́pe* <do^n´-be> to see. *wahtǫ́pe* <wa-ṭo^n´-be> I saw them. *waštǫ́pe* <wa-shto^n´-be> you saw them.

••• Cf. *átǫpe, hkíhtǫpe, kítǫpe, ówatoį, ówatǫįhci, watǫ́e scee.*

tǫ́pe aðée. V [sync., *tǫ́pe (a)_ðée*] *(intr.)* **go looking.** *kaðǫ́ tǫ́pe aðáape* he started off to see what he could see (lit., 'and he immediately went looking') (RBn15-03).

tǫ́pewaðe (variant: **tǫ́pewai**). V [uninfl. or reg., *tǫ́pewa_ðe*] [*tǫ́pe* + *wa-* VAL + *ðe* CAU] *(intr.)* **be worth looking at (lit., 'causes people to look at it').** *tǫ́pewai akxa* it's worth looking at (1/20/83/p5). • **make s.o. look or appear a certain way, look like or appear.** *lǫ́ðį tǫpéwai* he looks like he's drunk (02/22/95/FH/pc:ma). *hcéka ðahpáahą tǫpéwai* you look like you just got up (02/22/95/FH/pc:ok; BE2.82). *ɣǫ́ǫce tǫ́pewai* it makes you look sloppy. *áalįį wahéhe tǫpéwai* the chair looks weak (BE2.152; 03/16/95/JS/pc:ok).

tǫ́pše (variant of **tǫ́ǫpše**).

túlsa htą́wą. N **Tulsa (a city in northeastern Oklahoma that includes a small part of Osage County).** *túlsa htą́wą owálįį* I live in Tulsa (02/16/95/FH/pc:okc).

••• Cf. *htaasílee htáwą.*

txą (variants: **txa, kxą**). CONT **continuative aspect postverbal marker (indicating ongoing action or state in present, past, or future time) for 2nd person sg. animate standing subject; also may indicate initiation of an activity by subject regardless of position.** *ka níhka íe txa pée txa?* who is that person who is talking? *mą́zeska háaną kǫ́ða txa?* how much money does he want? (RB, unconfirmed). *ðihkówa lǫ́ði txa?* is your friend [standing] drunk? (RBn3-54). *ðihkówa lǫ́ði txa žamíe* I think your friend [standing] is drunk (RBn3-54).

txą (variants: **txa, kxą**). POSIT **positional article for a sg. animate standing entity (usually not the subject of a verb describing action).** *šée ðǫ nąążį txa hú hce éa* tell the person standing there to come here. *hkáwa šé txa pée íhta?* whose horse is that over there? (lit., 'the horse, that one standing there, who does it belong to?'). *šǫ́ke txą kǫ́ða akxai* he wanted that dog. *káa íe txa pée txa?* who is that who is talking? (RB).

•• LFD 155: *htą* <ţo^{n}> [presumably an error for *txą* <to^{n}>; compare next example] the; the one standing; he who is standing. *níhkašika txą* <ni´-ķa-shi-ga to^{n}> the man who is standing.

txą́ha (variant: **kxą́ha**). PPN [*txą* + *ha*] **until, from.** *hǫ́ǫpa ðé kxą́ha* to this day (RBn16-02). *ðetkxą́ha/ðetxą́ha* from here on; from now on.

---

u, ú

úpežahta (variant of **ǫ́pežahta**).

úže. N **vagina.**

•• JOD (slip file): *hceeúže* the vagina of a buffalo cow. *úže* <ü´-çe> vagina; the vagina of a woman.

•• LFD 81: *úže* <iu´-zhe> urethra.

••• *KS üžé* (JOD) vagina (RR).

úžewąąmǫį. N **lizard** (MOJt150; BE2.80). [Folk etymology: 'stealing the female organ'.]

---

w

wa- (variant of **wa- . . . api**).

wa- VAL **things, stuff; people, folks (indefinite; eliminates the need for a direct or indirect object).** [*wa-* VAL + initial *o-* of verbs regularly becomes *ó-*.] *waaðáahtą* drink stuff [*wa-* VAL + *ðaahtą́* 'drink'] (connotes drinking alcoholic beverages). *wahcéka* new things, new stuff [*wa-* VAL + *hcéka* 'new'] (FH/09/24/01/prod, pl.). *waléze* book [*wa-* VAL + *léze* 'striped'] (04/19/95/FH/pc). *šíi apa walǫ́ǫ štą* that person coming sure likes to call people names [*walǫ́ǫ* < *wa-* VAL + *lǫ́ǫ* 'revile s.o.'] (01/09/95/FH/pc:okc; BE2.16). *nąnióǫpažį wakǫ́ða apai* a whole bunch of them wanted cigarettes (from anybody: from folks) [*wakǫ́ða* < *wa-* VAL + *kǫ́ða* 'want'] (3-2-140). *wapą́* holler for folks, invite folks [*wa-* VAL + *pą́* 'holler'].

wa- PRNM **3rd person pl. patient pronominal ('they', subject of stative verb [can be omitted]; 'them', object of active verbs).** *wahkǫ́ða* he wants it for them. *éc wápą káaya* make her invite them. *waátǫpa!* watch over them [sg. or pl. addressees]! (FH/08/01/01/pc; not 'us'). *mą́zeska huuhtą́ą waðák$^{?}$upe* you gave them a lot of money (02/25/95/FH/pc:okc).

• **(agrees with pl. object noun).** *žą́ąhkoke hcéka ðǫǫpá wáabrį mįkšé* I have two new trunks (03/22/95/FH/pc:ok). *hkóða akxa hkáwa ðǫǫpá kǫzéhkihkǫ waaðį́pe* my friend has two horses just alike. *žikóhkiha wahkǫ́bra* I want it for my grandchildren (RBn22-19). *íe wasúhu wáli waðának$^{?}$ǫ hkǫ́bra* I want you to hear very clean words [*wa-* 'them' in *waðának$^{?}$ǫ* refers to 'words']. *žįkážį wíhta wáðohta níhkašika waðákiškaaye hkǫ́bra* I want you to make my children proper people [*wa-* 'them' in *waðákiškaaye* refers to 'my children'] (RBn19-06). *wažį́kake wáðaawa* count the birds. *šǫ́ke wíhta akxa hkáwa, hceeská éðǫǫpa owákaša nąpé* my dog takes care of horses and cows (RBn12-03). *wažážeíe hpíǫ wahkǫ́bra* I want

wa- *(continued)*
them to learn Osage (more literally, 'I want of them that they learn Osage') (RBn10-7:JW). *žįkážį ɣǫ́ǫce hcí ci achípi wahkǫ́bra įké* I don't want sloppy children to come to my home (FH). *Mary, Darlene óńǫ́bre che oðóapi wahkǫ́bra* I want Mary and Darlene to oversee this dinner (FH:prod). *waachí hí žiišǫ́ ðée ðe hpahą́le hą́nahpaze oolą́ąpi wáhkǫ́bra* before the dances start, first I want [them] to put him in jail (more literally, '. . . I want of them that they put him in jail') (FH/09/22/01/pc).
•• LFD 189: *waleze* <wa-gthe´-çe> things striped: a book.

wa- . . . api (variant: **wa-**). PRNM **1st person pl. patient pronominal ('we', subject of stative verbs; 'us', object of active verbs).** *oðówaapi akxai* he's bossing us around [*oðówaapi* < *wa- . . . api* 'us' + *oðóðe*] (FH:prod). *waátǫpapi* watch over us [*wa- . . . api* 'us' + *átǫpe*] (FH/08/01/01/pc). *haakxą́ta waðákištǫ́papi ðachí hta ðąkxą́še?* when are you all going to come see us? (04/28/95/LS/pc:okc). *škáce žówalapi hta paašé?* are you all going to play with us? (03/09/95/FH/pc). *hǫ́ǫpa huuwáli žówaðale hkǫ́bra* I want you to be with us a long time [*žówaðale* < *wa-* 'us' + *ða-* 'you' + *žóle* 'accompany'] (RBn12-10/MOJ). *žówaðale šcée ðáalį* you ought to go with us.

wáache (variant: **waaché**). N **skirt with ribbon work or other decorations.** *waaché wíhta čáahpa* my skirt is short (03/10/95/PM/pc; FH:4/24/96/pc). *wáache ohíži* my skirt does not go around.
•• RB: <wah-tséh>.
•• LFD 205: *waché* <wa-tse´> skirt; dress. LFD 206: *wachéwihta ðą cahpa* <wa-tse´-wi-ṭa thoⁿ dsa-p̣a> my skirt is short. LFD 187: *wáciohiži* <Wa´-dsi-u-hi-zhi> [expected Mod. Os. form: *wáacheoðíšiži*] Skirt-that-does-not-go-around (female personal name).
••• Cf. *mį́waapaache, óhkihpaache, wáakipaache.*

waachí. V [reg., *waa_chí*] **dance.** *áwaachi ~ awáachi* I dance. *waðáachi* you dance. *ąwáachipe* we [pl.] dance. *žįkážį nąkxáše wéewina akxą́he, ilǫ́įhpa waachí štǫ́pape* I want to thank you children for watching my son dance. *waachí hpíǫpe* she is a good [skilled] dancer (lit., 'she knows how to dance'). *káaši wáli ąwáachipe, ąðíištą htai* we've danced a long time, let's stop (BE2.29). *ąwáachi ðíe* dance for me (FH/11/17/01/pc:ok: *awáa*). • N **dance.** *waachí watǫ́į ąkái hce* let's go see the dance [sg. addressee]. *waachí wį wažáže apa húuža ðée aðį́ apa* this dance Osages had a long time (lit., 'Osages had a dance, a long time they've had this one') (PM/7/7/94). *hpáze waachí watǫ́į ąkái hta akái* we are going for the night dance [to observe the dance]. *waachí ąkái hce* let's go to the dance [implies that we will dance]. *waachí ðǫ́hą éetkxą ahí akxai* it's almost time for the dance (FH/t116b).
•• LFD 206: *wahcí* <wa-ṭsi´> dance.
••• Cf. *áwaachi.*

waaðǫ́. V [(reg.)+sync., *waa(_)_ðǫ́*] *(intr.)* **sing.** *waabrǫ́ ~ awáabrǫ* I sing. *waaštǫ́ ~ waaðáštǫi* you sing. *ąwáaðǫpe* we sing. *waabrǫ́ hkǫ́bra* I want to sing (03/09/95/MREI/pc:ok). *wižį́, waaðǫ́ ðáalį škáaɣe hą́ąci* older brother, you sang good last night (03/09/95/MREI/pc:ok). *waaðáštǫ tą ą́hǫǫ* when you sing, I like it (RBn; MREI/01/11/93). *waaštǫ́ che íðibra?* did you get enough [of you] singing? *Mogri akxa wálį waaðǫ́ ðáalį káaɣe akxai* Mogri is really singing pretty (FH:prod). *wažį́ka apa waaðǫ́ apái* the birds are singing (FH). *waaðǫ́ hta apai, oðówaðaðe hta nįkšé?* they're going to sing, are you going to see about it/things? (FH). *ąwáaðǫ htai* let's [three or more] sing (03/09/95/MREI/pc:ok). *waaðǫ́pi awáachi ąkxąhé* you all sing, I'm dancing. • N **song.** [Takes 'standing' positional article *che.*] *įlǫ́ǫška wapą́ waaðǫ́* "calling them" songs (HRE; BE2.121; 03/09/95/MREI/pc:uk; FH:4/24/96/tape:uk). *hcée waaðǫ́* buffalo songs. *káache táatą waaðǫ́?* what kind of song is that? *htáa waaðǫ́* deer songs (RB).
•• LFD 119: *nąžį́ waðǫ* <noⁿ-zhiⁿ´ wa-thoⁿ> the rising song (04/07/95/PM/pc:ok, *nąąžį́ waaðǫ*). "This song refers to the rising of the <Xo-ḳa> after the symbolic moccasins have been placed on his feet." LFD 123: *ópxą waðǫ* <o´-poⁿ wa-thoⁿ> Elk Songs (04/07/95/PM/pc:ok; *ópxą waaðǫ*).
••• Cf. *hkihkǫ́ze waaðǫ́, mįįðóhta waaðǫ́, mįįwáaðǫžį, wapą́ waaðǫ́.*

waaðǫ́ hpíǫ. VP [sync.+sync. nasal vowel stem, *waaðǫ́ _hpí_ǫ*] *(intr.)* **be a singer, be skilled at singing (lit., 'know how to sing').** *waaðǫ́ hpíǫpe* he's a skilled singer (RBn3-42).

waahkíhta. V [reg., *waa_hkíhta*] [*hkik-* REFL/RECIP + *waatá*] *(intr.)* **pray for oneself; pray for each other.** *waahkíhta paahá* pray for yourselves, raise it up (RBn10-15). *waahkíhta paahá* pray for each other, raise it up (RBn10-15).

wáakipaache. N **skirt with ribbon work or other decorations** (03/10/95/PM/pc; FH:4/24/96/pc).

••• Cf. *wáache.*

wáakipetxą. N [probably *wa-* VAL + *ki-* INCEPTIVE(?) + *ápetxa*] **wraparound skirt; blanket wrapped around like a skirt (lit., 'to wrap s.t. around')** (FH:4/24/96/pc; BE2.122; 03/10/95/PM/pc:ok). [Not 'wrap s.t. on top of itself'; the word was definitely heard with *ki-* rather than with reflexive *hkik-*.]

waaláke. V [conjug. unknown] [*wa-* VAL + *áalake*] *(intr.)* **menstruate** (02/24/95/FH/pc:ok; 03/01/95/FH/pc:ok). *wakʔó wíhta waaláke akxai* my wife is menstruating (02/24/95/FH/pc:ok). *waaláki akxái* she's menstruating (02/24/95/FH/pc:ok; BE2.87).

wáalake(?) (or **wálake?**). N **bad or unfavorable impression made upon another by offensive conduct** (LF, unconfirmed). • **taboo** (LF, unconfirmed, 03/01/95/FH/pc:uk as 'taboo').

•• LFD 189: *wálake* <wa´-gtha-ge> an unfavorable impression made by a person upon another or upon a number of persons by his offensive conduct; to come or go for a person that is a relative [unconfirmed: FH: incorrect gloss; uk], a thing sacred which must not be used for profane purposes, and to which is attached a penalty, particularly things consecrated for ceremonial purposes (03/01/95/FH/pc:uk).

••• Cf. *áalake.*

wáali, wáalį (variants of **wálį**).

waanǫ́ǫ. N **elder.** *waanǫ́ǫ wį ecí įkše tą ðáalį* it's good that there is an elder in here (lit., 'if there is an elder here it's good') (01/14/95/FH/pc:prod).

•• LFD 196: *wanǫ* <wa-no^{n}´> the senior; the elder of two persons. "The name of a gens occupying the office of the 'oldest.' Term used in rituals."

waápazo átǫpe. N [*wa-* VAL + *ápazo* + *átǫpe*] **scorekeeper.**

•• RB: <wáh-páh-zo-áh-to^{n}-peh> (RB: e.g., one who keeps sticks in an Indian hand game) (03/23/95/FH/pc:ok; BE2.117).

wáapą. V [*wa-* VAL + *kípą*] [reg. *ki*-del. + sync. fortisizing stop stem, *wáa_(ki)_pą*] *(intr.)* **invite folks to appear before others.** *wáapąži akxai* he's not inviting anybody (he's not issuing invitations to folks) (FH:prod).

wáapįce. N **restraint (such as a bridle?)** (RBn10-5:JW, unconfirmed). [Derivation unknown; possibly a truncated version of LF's *wápisǫce* <wa´-bi-ço^{n}-dse> (see below) and possibly related to *ásąci* 'put to the test'.]

•• LFD 184: *wápįsǫce* <wa´-bi-ço^{n}-dse> to press or hold to the ground, as an animal to prevent its escape. *áhpisǫ́ce* <a´-pi-ço^{n}-dse> I prevented the animal from escaping. *ášpisǫ́ce* <a´-shpi-ço^{n}-dse> you prevented the animal from escaping. *wápice* <wa´-bi-dse> see *huapice* <hu-a-bi-dse>. LFD 67: *huapice* <hu-a-bi-dse> a fish snare, made of willow saplings tied together so as to make one long piece [see LFD 67 for further description of the snare]. LFD 81 (unconfirmed): *iwapį́ akinąžį* <i-wa-bi^{n}´ a-gi-no^{n}-zhi^{n}> stepping in the blood that issues from the mouth of the animal (mythical).

wáaspaži (variant: **waaspáži**). N [*wáaspe* + *aží*] **gadabout, one who seldom stays home, s.o. who won't stay home.** *wáaspaži nį́e* you're a gadabout (2-25-83).

•• LFD 186 (unconfirmed): *wáspaži* <wa´-çpa-zhi> an unprincipled person; mischievous; ill-mannered; boisterous. [LF's translations are not confirmed by Mod. Os. speakers.]

wáaspe (variant: **waaspé**). V [reg. or uninfl., *wáa_spe* (2nd person is seldom inflected)] *(intr.)* **stay, stay quiet.** *awáaspe* I stay. *waaðáspe* you stay. *hcí ci waaspé hta mįkšé* I'm going to wait in the house (RBn22-06). *waaspé hta nįkšé ąži ščée hta nįkšé?* are you going to stay or are you going to go? (BE2.127). *John akxa waaspé hta akxái* John is going to stay. *wáaspi akxái* he is staying (03/14/95/FH/pc:ok). *wáaspe hta apai* they are going to stay. *wáaspi akxái* they are staying (03/14/95/FH/pc:ok). *wáaspa!* stay here! (RBn3-MOJ/p8; 03/14/95/FH/pc:ok). *mąðį́ ðįká ði, wáaspa ði* don't go anywhere, stay here (03/14/95/FH/pc). *ðíi įká, wáaspa ði* don't go anywhere, stay there. *ðée įká ði, wáaspa* don't go anywhere, stay here (03/14/95/FH/pc). *wáaspe hta nįkšé?* are you going to stay? (2-25-83). N **stay-at-home, one who seldom goes out.** *wáaspe nį́e* you're a stay-homer.

•• RB: <wáh-speh> (03/14/95/FH/pc:ok).

•• LFD 186: *wáspe* <wa´-çpe> tranquil; quiet; well behaved; good habits. *zani wáspe pe* <ça-ni wa´-çpe i> [expected Mod. Os. form: *záani wáaspape*] all is tranquil.

wáasta (variant: **waásta**). ADJ [*wa-* VAL + *ásta*] **sticky.**

waašką́. V [reg., *waa_šką́*] *(intr.)* **try hard; do one's best; make an effort; struggle** (RBn16-02; RBn10-18: FH). [Used especially when congratulating young people; for example, telling them to try hard upon graduating from high

waašką́ (*continued*)
school (FH).] *ąwáašką hkǫ́bra* I want to do my best (03/14/95/FH/pc). *awáašką hta mįkšé* I'll try my best, I'm going to try hard (04/04/95/FH/pc:okc; RBn10-9:JW). *waaðáška hta nįkšé* you will do your best (04/04/95/FH/pc:okc; BE2.145). *waaðášką škǫ́ǫšta?* do you want to do your best? (03/14/95/FH/pc). *ðiitą́ waaškápe* he pulled harder (lit., 'pulling, he did his best'). *céɣenii ochį́ waašką́pi aha ðáalį ché aha, ahú ókašeįke céɣenii ðée įkše* whenever they're doing their best hitting the drum, when it's good, it's an untroubled, peaceful drum (RB; CQ gloss). *waašką́* try your best (FH/09/22/01/pc). *waašką́ ðį!* try hard! *waašką́ pai* do your best [pl. addressee, continuative imperative] (01/07/95/FH/pc:prod). *ąwáašką hta ąkáðe* we'll do our best. • N **strength, might, force, power** (04/04/95/FH/pc:ok).

•• LFD 199: *wašką́* <wa-shko^{n}´> to make an effort; to struggle hard. *awášką* <a-wa´-shko^{n}> I made an effort. *waðášką* <wa-tha´-shko^{n}> you made an effort. *ąwą́šką pe* <o^{n}-wo^{n}´-shko^{n} i> we made an effort. LFD 121: *ohką́ciwašką* <O-ķo^{n}´-dsi-wa-shko^{n}> Struggles-by-himself (personal name); No one to help him fight. LFD 199: *wašką́ htąka* <wa-shko^{n}´ ţo^{n}-ga> great strength. *wašką́* <wa-shko^{n}´> strength; might; force; power.

waašką́ðįké. V [stat., *waašką́_ðįké*] [*waašką́* + *ðįké*] *(intr.)* **be frail; lack strength** (LF).

•• LFD 199: *wašką́ðįke* <wa-shko^{n}´-thi^{n}-ge> disability; weak, having little or no strength; frail.

waašką́htąka. V [stat., *waa_šką́htąka*] [*waašką́* + *htą́ka*] *(intr.)* **strong, having great strength** (LF).

•• LFD 199: *wašką́ htąka* <wa-shko^{n}´ ţo^{n}-ga> great strength. *waðišką htąka* <wa-thi-shko^{n} ţo^{n}-ga> you have great strength.

waatá. V [reg., *waa_tá*] *(intr., trans.)* **pray; pray for s.o. or s.t.** *awáata* I'm going to pray (04/18/95/FH/pc:ok). *éekǫ awáata nai* I pray that way all the time. (RBn12-10/MOJ). *waawítai hta mįkšé* I'm going to pray for you (04/18/95/FH/pc:prod). *awáatai hta mįkšé* I'm going to pray (04/18/95/FH/pc:okc; BE2.107). *ąwą́ąta ąkái* we [sitting] are praying (04/18/95/FH/pc:ok). *ąwáata htái* let us pray (04/18/95/FH/pc:okc). *wawáatapi* pray for all of us (04/18/95/FH/pc:okc). *wawáata* pray for them (04/18/95/FH/pc:ok). *Johna akxa žįkážį waatá apa íistahkiepi* John is praying for the children and the children are asking God for a blessing (lit., 'John is praying for the children and they are blessing themselves with it'). • **ask a favor, request s.t.; solicit, petition, or beg for s.t. from s.o.** *waawítai hta mįkšé* I'm going to ask you for a favor (04/18/95/FH/pc:prod). *awíwaata achíe ðe* I came to ask for a favor [from you] (01/23/95/FH/pc:prod orig; BE2.45). • N **grace (as said at mealtime), prayer of any kind.**

•• LFD 186: *watá* <wa-da´> speaking; to solicit; to petition.

••• *KS da* ask, beg, demand (RR) (type [reg., conj).

••• Cf. *kaašéną, waatášta.*

waatáihci. N [*waatá* + *í-* LOC + *hcí*] **church.** *wíe bríištą tą, waatáihci ci pší hta mįkšé* when I get through, I'm going to go by the church (FH10/7/94).

waatášta (variant: **waatáštą**). N [*waatá* + *štą*] **beggar** (04/18/95/FH/pc:prod).

wáawažį (variant of **waðáawažį**).

waazó. V [uninfl.] *(intr.)* **be fun.** *ášihta wanǫ́bre waazóe* it's fun to eat outdoors (RB; 01/30/95/FH/pc:okc).

••• Cf. *kízo.*

wabrą́lį. N **perfume.** *wabrą́lį brą́ akxai* he/she smells like perfume (RBn10-20).

wachú (variant: **wachúe**). V [presumably reg., *wa_chú*] [*wa-* VAL + *chúe* (but sometimes used as transitive)] *(intr., trans.)* **copulate, have intercourse, have sex.**

wácinie (variants: **wáchini, wáchinie**). N **venereal disease, sexually transmitted disease (STD)** (01/20/95/FH/pc:ok). [Probably from 'Virginia' (which may have been used to mean 'white man'). Perhaps venereal disease was later associated with *wachú* 'copulate' and thus may have substituted *ch* for *c*, giving the variants *wáchini* and *wáchinie* (Robert Rankin, personal communication). Additionally, *wácinie* may contain or be influenced by *níe* 'hurt'.] *wácini ǫǫ́ akxai* he had venereal disease (BE2.31).

•• RB: <wah-tsí-ni>, <wah-tsí-ní-eh>.

•• LFD 187: *wácini* <wa´-dsi-ni> a disease, a malady.

wacípxaį (variants: **wacípxa, wacípxą, wacípxai**). N **crier, town crier, announcer** (01/14/95/FH/pc;prod; BE2.27; HH/pc); **crier at ilǫ́ǫška dances** (RB).

•• LFD 187: *wacéhpaį* <wa-dse´-p̧a-i^{n}> [*px* <p> rather than *hp* <p̧> would have been expected, given the Mod. Os. form] meaning lost; used as an official title among the Osage for a crier.

wacúaxą (variant of **wacúexą**).
wacúe. N [probably *wa-* VAL + *cúuce*] **bread; any kind of bread whether corn or wheat, in any shape or size; piece of bread of any kind** (RB). [Takes 'standing' positional article *che.*] *wacúe che ípasą [ð]į* turn that bread over. *wacúe štǫ́ke* 'soft bread', refers to fresh cornbread (01/07/95/FH/pc:ok; BE2.11). *wį̨céke, wacúe wį škǫ́šta?* uncle, do you want a [piece of] bread? (RBn1-17). • **any kind of flour or grain (such as wheat, oats).**
•• LFD 187: *wacúe* <wa-dsiu´-e> flour.
wacúe bréhka. N **pancake(s)** (03/20/95/FH/pc:ok).
•• LFD 187: *wacúe brekxa* <wa-dsiu´-e bthe-ka> [*hk* <ķ> rather than *kx* <k> would have been expected, given the Mod. Os. form] thin bread.
wacúe ðiiskí (variant of **wacúe kaaskí**).
wacúe ðubráaska. N [*wacúe* + *ðu-/ði-* INSTR + *bráaska*] **dumplings made of wheat flour or corn flour (lit., 'bread made flat')** (01/07/95/FH/pc). *súhka htaaníi wacúe ðubráaska žóle hpáaɣe* I'm going to make chicken and dumplings (BE2.9; FH:prod). *súhka htaanį škáaɣe tą wacúe ðubráaska oozú* if you're going to make chicken soup, put dumplings in it [in chicken soup, these would be cornmeal dumplings made from squaw corn and dropped into the soup and would float to the top when done] (FH:prod).
wacúe ðutáahpa. N **biscuit (lit., 'bread made round')** (01/07/95/FH/pc:ok; FH:4/22/96/tape:prod).
•• LFD 187: *wacúe tahpa* <wa-dsiu´-e-da-p̣a> biscuit, round bread.
••• Cf. *wacúe táahpa.*
wacúe ikaažį. N [*wacúe* + *í-* LOC + *kaaží*] **grain sieve (lit., 'drive grain with it').**
•• LFD 187: *wacúe ikažį* <wa-dsiu´-e i-ga-zhi^n> sieve used for screening grain.
wacúe kaascú. N **frybread (for which the dough is cut, sliced, or slit through)** (01/07/95/FH/pc:okc).
wacúe kaaskí (variant: **wacúe ðiiskí**). N **cornmeal dumplings (cornmeal dough compressed into balls and dropped into chicken or turkey soup to cook)** (FH:prod).
wacúe kˀąsaaki. N **noodles (lit., 'fast bread').**
wacúe skúðe (variant: **wacúesku**). N **cake (such as a birthday cake) (lit., 'sweet bread')** (RB; 01/09/95/FH/pc:prod). *wacúesku tóa ąk'ú* give me some cake (BE2.16). *pąąšcéka wacúesku hpáaɣc* I made a strawberry cake.
•• LFD 187: *wacúe skuðe* <wa-dsiu´-e çkiu-the> sweet-corn-cake. [Sweet bread, not corn (RB).]
wacúe sóso. N **dumplings; bread cut into little pieces** (RBn22-13, unconfirmed). [Possibly mistranscription for *wacúe sása*, where *sása* is reduplicated form of root *-se* 'cut'.]
wacúe štǫka, wacúe štǫke (variants of **wacúeštǫ**).
wacúe táahpa. N **dumplings (lit., 'round bread')** (04/07/95/LS/pc:okt; t14a-p5).
wacúe wéli. N **frybread** (FH).
wacúe xúɣa. N **crackers (lit., 'bread that makes a noise or is crumbly')** (BE2.27; 01/14/95/FH/pc:ok).
•• LFD 187: *wacúe xuxu ɣe* <wa-dsu´-e xu-xu xe> crackers. *wacoe; xuxuɣe* <wa-dsu-e; xu-xu-xe> bread; that cracks or crumbles.
••• Cf. *kaaxúɣe.*
wacúe žéela. N **cornbread or grated fresh corn baked in an oven (lit., 'fried bread')** (01/13/95/FH/pc:ok; FH/09/24/01/pc); **turnover bread (cornbread fried in a little grease in a skillet)** (01/13/95/FH/pc:ok; FH/09/24/01/pc); **deep-fried frybread (rarer usage)** (01/13/95/FH/pc:ok; FH/09/24/01/pc).
wacúesku (variant of **wacúe skúðe**).
wacúeštǫ (variants: **wacúe štǫka, wacúe štǫke**). N **cornbread (lit., 'soft bread')** (FH/09/24/01/ok; RBn14-13; 01/13/95/FH/pc). *wacúe štǫ́ke* soft cornbread (lit., 'soft bread'; *wacúe štǫ́ke* is fresh cornbread, never refers to wheat bread) (01/07/95/FH/pc:ok; BE2).
•• LFD 187: *wacúe štǫka* <wa-dsiu´-e shto^n-ga> corn meal [translation is unexpected and may be erroneous].
wacúexą (variants: **wacúexǫ, wacúaxą, wacúxa**). N **cornshuck, corn husk.** *wacúaxą hkǫ́bra* I want the cornshuck (BE2.25) [Saying this signals 'I want to make a smoke' so as to make a prayer at a peyote meeting (04/25/95/PM/pc:ok).]
•• JOD (slip file): *wacúcexa* <wa-ţsü´-ţse-qa> corn husks.
•• LFD 187: *wacúexǫ* <wa-dsiu´-e-xo^n> corn husks.
wacúexo (variant: **wacúexoe**). N **flour** (BE2.49; 01/26/95/FH/pc:ok).
•• RB: <wah-tsú-eh-xó> (01/26/95/FH/pc:ok; BE2.49).
•• LFD 187: *wacúe* <wa-dsiu´-e> flour.
wacúexǫ (variant of **wacúexą**).
wacúexǫ oðiši. N **dumplings, tamales (lit., 'wrapped in husks').**
•• LFD 187 (unconfirmed): *wacúexǫ oðišį* <wa-dsu´-e-xo^n u-thi-shi^n> corn dumplings,

wacúexǫ oðiši (*continued*)
rolled up in corn husks and boiled. Green corn is generally used. Very similar to tamales.

wacúhta. N **animal** (JS). *wacúhta záani eeškítą ípahǫpe* all the animals knew him, too (JS: Osage Stories: Coyote and Bear).

•• LFD 188: *wacúhta* <wa-dsu´-ṭa> living creatures; animals; a term used in rituals.

wacúxa (variant of **wacúexą**).

wac?é (variant of **wac?éka**).

wac?éðe. V [reg., *wac?é_ðe*] [*wa-* VAL + *c?éðe* (but sometimes used as transitive)] *(intr., trans.)* **kill others; kill folks.** *wac?éąðe ðįké* we don't kill at all (FH:ok). *awác?eðai* I killed [unexpected form] (FH: prod). *wac?éaðe* I killed. *wac?éðaðe* you killed. *wac?éąðape* we killed. *wac?éaðe* I killed him. *wac?éðaðe* you killed, you killed him (FH).

•• LFD 206: *wac?éðe* <wa-ṭs'e´-the> the act of killing in battle or in a quarrel at home. *wac?eáðe* <wa-ṭs'e-a´-the> [position of accent is unexpected] I killed him. *wac?eðaðe* <wa-ṭs'e-tha-the> you killed him.

wac?éka (variant: **wac?é**). ADJ **gentle, docile, tame, not wild, not difficult, easy to do** (01/31/95/FH/pc). *wac?éka akxai* he's gentle (FH/09/24/01/okc; BE2.53). *šǫ́žį apa wac?éka* the little puppy is gentle (FH/09/24/01/prod). *hkáwa akxa wac?éka akxai* the horse is gentle (FH/09/24/01/pc:prod). *wažážeíe wac?éka škáaye* you make Osage language easy (01/31/95/FH/pc:prod orig). • **tender** (LF) ['Tender' only as describing materials, not as a personality trait (RB).]

•• LFD 206, 205: *wac?éka* <wa-ṭs'e´-ga> tender; as meat, grains of corn; not difficult; easy, docile, gentle; easily managed (01/31/95/FH/pc:ok).

••• Cf. *hápa wac?éka.*

waðáahtą. V [sync., *wa_ðáahtą*] [*wa-* VAL + *ðaahtą́* (but sometimes used as transitive)] *(intr., trans.)* **drink alcohol.** *níhka akxa wáli lǫ́ði akxai, hpéecenii huuwáli waðáahtąpe* that man is really drunk, he's drunk a lot of liquor (RBn12-06). *wižį́ke akxa waðáahtą kíðalįpe* Sonny really likes to drink.

•• LFD 142: *wabráhtą* <wa-btha´-ṭo^n^> I drank. *waštáhtą* <wa-shda´-ṭo^n^> you drank.

wáðaaska. ADV, V [sync., *wá_ðaaska*] [*wa-* + *ðaa-* 'by mouth' + *ská* 'white, clear'] **(speak) clearly; (make) plain, distinct, or clear, clarify, elucidate (lit., 'by mouth make it clear to folks').** *íe wáðaaskape* he makes the words plain. *íe wábraaska* I explained it, I made it plain (FH/11/19/01/pc:ok).

••• Cf. *wáðuuska.*

waðáašoe. V [sync., *wa_ðáašoe*] [*wa-* VAL + *ðaašóe*] *(intr.)* **smoke.** *wabráašoe* I'm smoking.

waðáawa. V [sync. *wa _ðáawa*] [*wa-* VAL + *ðaawá*] *(intr.)* **count, say numbers.** *waðáawa ðatxą́še* you count. *wabráawa ątxą́he* I'm counting. *waðáawa akxai* he's counting. *waštáawa nįkšé* you're counting. • N **counting, number(s).**

•• LFD 201: *waðáwa* <wa-tha´-wa> counting. *wabráwa* <wa-btha´-wa> I am counting. *waštáwa* <wa-shda´-wa> you are counting.

waðáawa htą́ke (variant: **waðáawa htą́ka**). ADJP, N **million (lit., 'big count')** (02/24/95/FH/pc:ok; BE2.87).

•• RB: <wah-tháh-wah tú^n^-keh>.

•• LFD 201: *waðáwahtąka* <wa-tha´-wa-ṭo^n^-ga> a million, counting big.

waðáawa lébrą. N **dime, ten cents (lit., 'ten count')** (01/20/95/FH/pc:ok; BE2.31).

•• LFD 201: *waðáwalebrą* <wa-tha´-wa-gthe-btho^n^> a dime. *waðáwa; lebrą* <wa-tha´-wa; gthe-btho^n^> cents; ten: ten cents.

waðáawa sáhtą. N **nickel, five cents (lit., 'five count')** (02/27/95/FH/pc:ok; BE2.93).

waðáawa žúuce (variant: **waðáawa žúu**). N **penny (lit., 'red count')** (03/07/95/PM/pc).

waðáawažį (variant: **wáawažį**). N [*waðáawa* + *-žį* 'little'] **penny, cent, change, coins (lit., 'little count')** (03/07/95/PM/pc:ok). *wáawažį ðiðúuze hta apai* they are going to take pennies away from you (03/15/95/PM/pc:ok; 03/16/95/JS/pc:ok). *wáawažį ąšcúuze hta níkšé?* are you going to take pennies away from me? are you going to take the change away from me? (03/15/95/PM/pc:okc; 03/16/95/JS/pc:ok; BE2).

waðáaxtake. V [sync., *wa_ðáaxtake*] [*wa-* VAL + *ðaaxtáke*] *(intr.)* **bite folks, bite people.** *waðáaxtake!* he bites people! (BE2.9).

waðáazo. V, N [sync.?, *wa_ðáazo*] [*wa-* VAL + *ðaazó*] *(intr.)* **lulu, ululate (i.e., produce the high-pitched, shrill sound that the women singers around the drum sometimes make at an event such as a dance to show that they are pleased by gifts they have just received or by the dancing or some other stimulus; a sound similar to yodeling)** (FH/08/22/96).

••• Cf. *kízo.*

waðák?eðe. V, ADJ [stat., *waðák?e_ðe*] [*wa-* VAL + *ðak?éðe*] **(be a) kind or generous person.** *waðák?eðíðe nįkšé aape, ðe etą, ðak?éwaðapi* they said you were kind, so pity us.

waðánii. N **Tonkawa (tribe or tribal member)** (BE2.143; 03/23/95/FH/pc:ok).

•• LFD 200: *waðáhni* <Wa-tha´-hni> Tonkawa Tribe.

wáðastástá. ADJ [*wa-* VAL + + reduplicated form of *ásta* (*ð* is epenthetic)] **sticky (lit., 'keeps sticking to stuff')** (MSB 2-25-83).

waðe. CAUSATIVE STEM [reg., *wa_ðe*] [*wa-* VAL + *ðe* CAU] **make one, make people, make folks.**

••• Cf. *kǫ́ðawaðe, tǫ́pewaðe.*

waðíhohota (variant: **waðíhoohta**). N [reduplicated form of *wáðihota*] **clown** (BE2.21; 01/19/95/FH/pc:ok).

•• LFD 202: *waðíhohota* <wa-thi´-ho-ho-da> a droll. *wisąka ata waðihohota kiðalį pe* <wi-ço^{n}-ga a-da wa-thi-ho-ho-da gi-tha-gthi^{n} bi a> my brother is fond of joking; one fond of practical jokes.

wáðihota. V [*wa-* '3rd person pl. patient' + *ðíhota*] **fool them.**

waðíhta. V [uninfl./stat., *wa_ðíhta*] *(intr.)* **be one's turn.** *waðíðihta ðinįe* it's your turn to take over, you're it (said to next one whose turn it is to hit drum in a meeting) (RBn23-16). [Expected 1st sg. form: *ą́wąðihaą* 'it's my turn'; expected 1st pl. form: *wáwaðihtapi* 'it's our turn'; expected 3rd pl. form: *wáwaðihta* 'it's their turn'.] *waðíhta ðíe* it's your turn (said to fire chief at peyote meeting when it is his turn to carry drum) (RB; 03/24/95/PM/pc:ok). *waðíhta ðíe* it's your turn (to hit drum) (RBn3-22).

waðíhtą. V [sync., *wa_ðíhtą*] *(intr.)* **do work, farm.** *ónihkaši ší tą, waščíhtą tą* when you are a saved person, when your work [on earth] is done (lit., 'when you arrive at fulfilment as a person, when you do work') (RBn12-10/MOJ). *hową́įki waścihtą ðą́įše?* where are you working? where are you farming? (03/24/95/PM/pc:ok). *kasíe wašcíhtą hta paašé?* are you all going to work tomorrow? *waðíhtą aðáape* he/she went to work (03/24/95/PM/pc:ok; BE2.160). *waðíhta ąkái* we work (RBn12-03p3). • N **work, employment, job; place of employment, workplace, office** (03/24/95/PM/pc:okc). *hǫpá waðíhtą pšíe* I went to work today (03/24/95/PM/pc:ok). *waðíhtą aðáape* he or she went to work (03/24/95/PM/pc:ok; BE2.160).

•• LFD 202: *waðíhtą* <wa-thi´-ṭo^{n}> to farm, to work in the field; a household servant, a domestic [unconfirmed gloss]; any kind of work or labor. *wabríhtą* <wa-bthi´-ṭo^{n}> I work. *ąwą́ðihtą pe* <o^{n}-wo^{n}´-thi-ṭo^{n} i> we work. *waðíhtą olį kšiðe* <wa-thi´-ṭo^{n} u-gthi^{n} kshi-the> to install a man into an office.

••• Cf. *waðíhtąštą.*

waðíhtą olį́į. VP [reg., *waðíhtą o_lį́į*] *(intr.)* **occupy an office, serve in a post.**

•• LFD 202: *waðíhtą olį kšiðe* <wa-thi´-ṭo^{n} u-gthi^{n} kshi-the> to install a man [could probably be a woman as well] into an office.

waðíhtą wakáaži. N **foreman; driver, chauffeur** (03/24/95/PM/pc).

•• LFD 201: *waðíhtą wakaži* <wa-thi´-ṭo^{n} wa-ga-zhi> a foreman.

waðíhtąštą. N [*waðíhtą +štą*] **workaholic, one who works all the time** (03/24/95/PM/pc:ok).

•• LFD 202: *waðíhtąštą* <wa-thi´-ṭo^{n}-shto^{n}> industrious; hard-working. *wabríhtąštą* <wa-bthi´-ṭo^{n}-shto^{n}> I am industrious. *ąwą́ðihtąštą pe* <o^{n}-wo^{n}´-thi-ṭo^{n}-shto^{n} i> we are industrious. *wakʔo akxa waðihtó inąhi pe* <wa-ķ'u a-ka wa-thi-ṭo´ i-no^{n}-hi bi a> the woman is industrious [better translation: 'the woman is willing to work'].

waðíiðiiski. V [uninfl.?] [reduplicated form of *waðíiski*] *(intr.)* **gather together with folks** *ðǫ́ha waachí hta apa, háatkxąta waðíiðiiski hta nįkšé?* it's almost time for the dances, when are you [sg.] going to get together [with them]? (FH:4/24/96/tape).

waðíihice. V [sync., *wa_ðíihice*] [*wa-* VAL + *ðiihíce*] *(intr.)* **tease people.** *šíi akxa waðíihici akxái* that person is teasing (03/16/95/FH/pc:ok; RBn2-MOJ/p11). *waðíihice kízope* he likes to tease (03/16/95/FH/pc:okc; MREI/t116a). *waðíihice štąpe* he is always teasing. *wabríihice ąhe* I was playing with him, teasing him (01-27-83).

•• LFD 201: *waðíhice* <wa-thi´-hi-dse> meddler; a mischief-maker. *waðíhice akxa* <wa-thi´-hi-dse a-ka> persecutor.

waðíiski (variant: **wawáðiiski**). V [inflected only for object in available data] [*wa-* VAL + *ðiiskí*] *(intr.)* **gather together;** *(trans.)* **gather with s.o.** *hą́ąpa ðé wawáðiiski nįkše, wéewinai* I'm glad you [sg.] have gathered [with them] here today (FH:4/24/96/tape; BE2.53; 04/06/95/LS/pc:ok). N **gathering of people (e.g., at a dance)** (FH:4/24/96/tape).

•• LFD 201: *waðíski* <wa-thi´-çki> to assemble, to gather together men for council.

••• Cf. *waðíiðiiski.*

waðíiški. V [sync., *wa_ðíiški*] [*wa-* VAL + *ðiiškí*] *(intr.)* **do laundry, wash clothes, wash s.t.** • N **laundry (clothes needing washing).** *waščíiški* you wash clothes (02/14/95/FH/pc:ok).

waðíiški (*continued*)

•• LFD 202: *waðíški* <wa-thi´-shki> to wash clothes. *wabríški* <wa-bthi´-shki> I wash clothes (02/14/95/FH/pc:ok).

waðíiškihci (variant: **waíiškihci**). N [*waðíiški* + *hcí*] **laundry (the place), laundry house.** *waðíiškihci ci šcée tą žówile brée hkǫ́bra* when you go to the laundry, I want to go with you.

•• RB: <wah-í-shki-tsi> (04/11/95/LS/pc:ok; BE2.76).

•• LFD 202: *waðíški hci* <wa-thi´-shki ţsi> a washhouse, laundry.

waðílą. V [sync., *wa_ðílą*] *(intr.)* **think things; think about, think on, ponder, muse about (especially about things in the past or events that have already occurred).** *wabrílą mįkšé* I'm thinking about it (03/20/95/FH/pc:okc; RBn10-05:JW). *ąwáðilą* we're thinking. • N **mind, brain, thought, soul, thinking** (RBn10-5:JW; RBn2-MOJ/p8ff). *waðílą wákalą ą́ðiiciza* take these dirty thoughts away (RBn10-3:MOJ/79).

•• RB: <wah-thí-d-?-lah>.

•• LFD 201: *waðílą* <wa-thi´-gtho^{n}> to meditate; reverie, day dreaming. intellect, sense; sound judgement. *wabrílą* <wa-bthi´-gtho^{n}> I meditate. *ąwąðilą pe* <o^{n}-wo^{n}-thi-gtho^{n} i> we meditate. *áwabrilą* <a´-wa-bthi-gtho^{n}> I considered it (03/20/95/FH/pc:ok). *waðíląðįke* <Wa-thi´-gtho^{n}-thi^{n}-ge> No-mind (personal name) (unconfirmed as a name: 03/01/95/FH/pc:ok, but unknown as a name).

••• Cf. *áwaðilą*.

waðílą áška. ADJP, VP [conjug. unknown] *(intr.)* **(be) irritable, easily angered, cranky, irascible.** *waðílą áškape* he gets mad easily (RBn23-14).

•• LFD 113: *nǫ́ce áška* <no^{n}´-dse a-shka> heart quickly moved; quick to anger; a quarrelsome disposition.

waðílą ðáalį mąðį́. VP [(reg.+) sync., *waðílą ðáalį (_)mą_ðį́*] *(intr.)* **be satisfied (lit., 'walk with a good mind').**

waðílą eekǫ́ įké (variant: **waðíląekǫįké**). ADJP, VP [uninfl.] *(intr.)* **(be) wayward, unruly, not in one's right mind.** • N **crazy person, person of unsound mind, demented person.** *waðíląekǫįkí apai, ðekǫ́ǫci áhkihtǫpa ðį* there are crazies around, now watch out for yourself.

waðílą hkihkáaye. VP [reg.+sync. *k>p*, *waðílą _hkih_káaye*] **make up one's mind on one's own, decide for oneself.** [For example, a young woman deciding to get married without permission of her parents, who should marry her off (FH). (In the 1980s, it was still thought by some elders to be improper for a young woman to make up her own mind about whom to marry and when.)] [Expected (but unattested) inflectional forms: *waðílą áhkihpaaye* 'I decide for myself'. *waðílą ðáhkiškaaye* 'you decide for yourself'. *waðílą ąhkíhkaaye* 'we decide for ourselves'.] *waðílą hkihkáaye akxai* they made their own mind up (03/20/95/FH/pc:ok, prod). *waðílą hkihkáayipe, koe šómįhkasi hǫ́ǫe éekǫ ší íiðe htai* [expected Mod. Os. form: *waðílą hkihkáayape koe šómįhkasi hǫ́ǫe éekǫži íiðe hta ðe*] she made up her mind, the coyote would never see anybody like her again (RBn17-p03). *oáhkihkašą hpímą, htáažį akxa waðílą hkihkáayape* I know how to take care of myself, the little deer thought [decided, made up his mind] (RBn15-002).

waðílą hpíiži. N **bad temper.** *waðílą hpíiži ąhe* I've got a bad temper (lit., 'I am characterized by a bad temper') (03/16/95/FH/pc:ok; MREI/t95).

waðílą káaye. VP [sync. *k>p*, *waðílą _káaye*] *(intr.)* **decide, make up one's mind.** *waðílą káaya!* make up your mind! (04/07/95/LS/pc:okc; RBn2-MOJ/p21).

waðílą kikáaye. VP [sync. *k>p*, *waðílą _ki_káaye*] [*waðílą* + *ki-* INCEPTIVE + *káaye*] *(intr.)* **change one's mind (lit., 'make up one's mind anew').** *waðílą ši kikáaye tą ée kǫ́ðažipe* he didn't want her to change her mind again (RBn17-p04).

waðílą ochí (variant: **wailą ochí**). ADJ **wise.** *súhkahtą́ą mįka wailą ochí hcí wį káaye, aną́ðapaži che ažį ðíaape* that wise turkey hen has made a nest where she thinks we can't find it (RBn19-05).

waðílą waxpáðį. N **worry (lit., 'mind suffering').** *waðílą waxpáį ǫǫ́ ðée apai* worry is upon them (FH/09/24/01/pc).

waðíląekǫįké (variant of **waðílą eekǫ́ įké**).

waðíląhtąą (variant: **waðíląhtǫǫ**). ADJ, V [uninfl.] **(be) smart, intelligent; (be) a smart person; have a good mind** (BE2.124); **learn, adjust the mind.** *taašéðe tą, waðíląhtǫǫ hta apai* shake him up, he is going to learn (FH:98/pc). *taašéðe tą, waðíląhtǫǫ hta apai* when you hit him on the head, that will make his mind get right (FH/10/13/96). • N **good mind, intelligence, large brain** (RBn10-5:JW; RBn2-MOJ/p8ff).

waðį́. N **drumkeeper.** [Shortened version of **céyenii aðį́**.]

waðįpe. V [1st person pl. of *ðį́* 'be' + *api* 'pl.' + *ðe* DECL] **we are.**

wáðohtą (variants: **wáðohta, waðóhta**). ADJ **straight; reliable, respectable, proper, honest** (04/19/95/FH/pc). [Refers to a person's way of living rather than to conduct of the moment and hence is often used in admonishments (as in making one's ways straight, reforming, straightening out, going straight in one's behavior); contrasts with *óðohtą*, which refers to immediate behavior or conduct of the moment and thus may be used, for example, to scold childen for their current actions.] *wáðohtą mą́į* keep yourself straight (BE2.129). *wáðohtą ahkílaðį* keep yourself straight (FH:4/24/96/prod). *wáðohta ahkílai* I behave myself/carry myself straight (RBn; MREI/01/11/93?). *žįkážį wíhta wáðohta níhkašika waðákiškaaɣe hkǫ́bra* I want you to make my children proper people (RBn19-06). *níhkašie wáðohtapi ną* he's proper/reliable/good/respectable (RBn22-17). *wáðohtą mįkšé* I'll behave myself (MOJ-11-19-83). *wasái waðóhta ípahǫpe* they knew the bear was honest/respectable (RBn16-02). • ADV **clearly, straight, properly, truthfully.** *íe wáðohtą* speak clearly, straight or truthfully (FH).

waðótaðe. V [presumably reg., *waðóta_ðe*] [*wa-* VAL + *ðótaðe*] **make peace** (LF only).

•• LFD 202: <wa-tho´-da-the>.

wáðuɣaži (variant: **waðúɣaži**). N [*wáðuɣe* + *aží*] **female who has not married; virgin.**

•• LFD 352: *wáðiɣaži* <wa´-thi-xa-zhi> virgin.

wáðuɣe. V, ADJ [sync., *wá_ðuɣe*] [*wa-* VAL + *áðuɣe*] *(intr.)* **(be or get) married (said of a female).** *wáščuɣe ðaašé?* are you married? *wáščuɣe?* did you marry? (FH:4/25/96/tape). *koe ónǫǫ žišǫ ší tą šį́ tą koe hpííži žišǫ ší tą koe péeški ðikǫ́ða htai wáščuɣe ðáalį* before you get old and before you get fat and ugly and nobody wants you, you should get married (RB). *ehta wábruɣe mąží hta akxai* maybe I better not get married (RBn17-p02). • N **wedding (used by bride's friends or family).** *wáðuɣe brée ðe* I'm going to a wedding [spoken by family or friend of the bride] (02/27/95/JS/pc; CQc).

•• RB: <wah-thú-xeh, wáh-thu-xeh>.

•• JOD (slip file): *waðúɣe* <wa-¢ü´-xĕ> to take a husband, to marry.

•• LFD 204: *wáðuɣe* <wa´-thu-xe> to marry; to take a husband. LFD 122: *ąžį́ka xci tą wabriɣe* <o^{n}-zhi^{n}´-ga xtsi do^{n} wa-bthi-xe> I married when I was a young woman.

••• Cf. *wéðuɣe*.

waðúupxai. V [presumably sync., *wa_ðúupxai*] [presumably *wa-* VAL +*ðuupxáðe*] *(intr. or trans.?)* **investigate** (RBn22-17, unconfirmed).

wáðuuska. V [(reg.)+sync., (_)*wá_ðuuska*] [presumably *wa-* VAL + *ðu-/ði-* INSTR + *skáha*] *(intr.)* **make things plain (such as words or lines on a paper, borders on land); clarify or elucidate things** (FH).

waðúuštaha. V [(reg.)+sync., *(_)wa_ðúuštaha*] [*wa-* VAL + *ðuuštáha*] *(intr.)* **iron s.t., iron.** *hǫ́ǫpa ðé awábrúuštaha hta mįkšé* I'm going to iron all day [secondary accent on *-brúu-*]. *hą́ąpa záani wabrúuštaha* I ironed all day.

waðúwį. V [sync., *wa_ðúwį*] [*wa-* VAL + *ðuwį́*] *(intr.)* **buy things.**

waðúwį aðée. VP [sync., *waðúwį (a)_ðée*] *(intr.)* **shop, go shopping (lit., 'buy stuff').** *waðúwį brée* I'm going shopping.

wahą́. N **yarn** (BE2.162 & FH:ok; 03/24/95/PM/pc:ok).

•• LFD 191: *wahą́* <wa-ho^{n}´> the cross threads in weaving, the woof, a single thread or strand of worsted yarn.

wahą́ káaɣe. N **yarn work (as product or activity) (lit., 'yarn making')** (03/24/95/PM/pc:okc; FH/09/24/01/pc/ok; BE2.162).

•• RB: <wáh-háh^{n}-gáh-xeh>.

wáhce tooka. N **star, morning star or male star.**

•• LFD 205: *wáhce toka* <wa´-ṭse do-ga> the male star, the morning star (unconfirmed).

wahcéehtą. N **first son, in *hcížo* clan** (FH/11/17/01/pc). [The name that everyone would use for the male if no boy name was given to him when young; sometimes this adult name is used constantly by all, even if a boy name has been given (FH).]

wahcéka. N [*wa-* VAL + *hcéka*] **treasure; valuable or special things, things a person has put away as special, keepsakes** (HHtape9, sideb/p2); **new things.** *wahcéka owákihce* I'm looking for new things (FH/09/24/01/prod).

wahcéxi. V, ADJ [uninfl.] [*wa-* VAL + *hcéxi*] **(be) difficult, hard, challenging, not easy to do** (FH). *wažážeíe wahcéxi* Osage language is difficult (01/20/95/FH/pc:ok). *óðohta ahkílai wahcéxi* it's difficult to live a straight life, it's hard to keep yourself straight (RBn23-17; BE2.31; 01/20/95/FH/pc:ok).

•• LFD 206: *wahcéxi* <wa-ṭse´-xi> difficult to destroy, to be tenacious of life (term used in some of the rituals of the tribal rites); stingy,

wahcéxi (*continued*)
ungenerous, not liberal, penurious. *wahcéxi walį pe* <wa-ṭse´-xi wa-gthi^{n} bi a> he is very stingy.
••• *KS waččéxi* hard, difficult to endure (RR).

wahcį́į (variants: **wahcį́e; wahtį́į** or **wahtį́e** [archaic]). V [conjug. unknown] [*wa-* VAL + *hcį́į*] *(intr.)* **appear, show, be showing or visible, appear suddenly.** *žé wahtį́e apái* his penis is showing. *oðíkinąąži oðíina šǫ́ce wahtį́į* fasten your pants, your penis is showing (RBn2-MOJ/p21; 03/03/95/FH/pc:ok).

wahéhe. ADJ **weak (e.g., a human, an animal, an object, or a material).** *áalįį wahéhe tǫpéwai* the chair looks weak (BE2.152; 03/16/95/JS/pc:ok). *wahéhe mįkšé ąžį sísi nįkšé* I am weak, but thou art strong (line in a Christian hymn) (MOJ; 03/16/95/JS/pc:ok).
•• LFD 191: *wahéhe* <wa-he´-he> weak, feeble, soft. *wahéhe kaɣe* <wa-he´-he ga-xe> [expected Mod. Os. form: *wahéhe káaɣe* 'to make someone weak'] to weaken. *wahéhe hpaɣe* <wa-he´-he p̣a-xe> I was made weak [rather, 'I made him/her/it weak']. *wahéha škaɣe* <wa-he´-ha shka-xe>you were made weak [rather, 'you made him/her/it weak'] . *wahéhe ąkaɣa pe* <wa-he´-he o^{n}-ga-xa i> we were made weak [rather, 'we made him/her/it weak'].

wahélele (variant of **waléle**).

wáhice. V [presumed reg., *wá_hice*] *(trans.)* **hurry s.o. along, make s.o. hurry.** [Expected (but unattested) inflectional forms: *áwahice* 'I hurry folks', *waðáhice* 'you hurry folks', *ąwáhice* 'we hurry folks'.]
••• Cf. *íhice.*

wahitǫ́ci (variant of **wihtǫ́ce**).

wáhkie (variant: **áwahkie**). N [presumably *wa-* VAL + *áhkie*] **lawyer, attorney (lit., 'taking up for a person').**
•• RB: <wah-kai-ah> or <wáh-ki-eh> (02/15/95/FH/pc:prod; BE2.76) [FH prefers the version *wáhkie.*]
••• Cf. *áwahkie.*

wahkílaace (variant: **wahkílaa**). N [*wa-* VAL + *hkik-* RECIP/REFL + *ðaacé* 'name, say'] **law, regulations, rules (lit., 'things spoken about to each other' by a group of people)** (02/14/95/FH/pc:okc; RBn1-MOJ/p43). *wahkílaace áðihtą* he violates the law (02/15/95/FH/pc:okc). *wáhkilaace akxai* it's the rule (BE2.76). *wahkílaace oðóohpa akxái* he's obeying the law (02/15/95/FH/pc). *wahkílaace oðóohpa nąpe* she obeys the law (02/15/95/FH/pc). *wahkílaace káaɣe apai* they're making it into law.
•• LFD 192: *wáhkilace* <wa´-ḳi-gtha-dse> statute, law: things, possessive sign, spoken: words spoken by a group of persons for their own use or benefit, law; any rule of action agreed upon by the male members of a tribe, ordinance (02/14/95/FH/pc:okc, but accent on second syllable: *wahkílaace*). *wáhkilace owahpa* <wa´-ḳi-gtha-dse u-wa-p̣a> [*hp* <p̣> is presumably an error for *px* <p>] I obey the law (02/14/95/FH/pc:uk). *wáhkilace oðahpa* <wa´-ḳi-gtha-dse u-tha-p̣a> [*hp* <p̣> is presumably an error for *px* <p>] you obey the law. *wáhkilace ohpa* <wa´-ḳi-gtha-dse u-p̣a> [*hp* <p̣> is presumably an error for *px* <p>] he obeys the law.

wahkílaace áðihta (variant: **wahkílaace áðihtą**). VP [sync., *wahkílaace á_ðihta*] **violate the law, break a rule.** *wahkílaace áðihtą* he violates the law 0 (02/15/95/FH/pc:okc).
•• LFD 192: *wáhkilace aðihta* <wa´-ḳi-gtha-dse a-thi-ṭa> to violate [the law].

wahkílaace káaɣe. VP [sync. *k*>*p*, *wahkílaace _káaɣe*] **legislate, make laws (as in Congress).**
• N **lawmakers, legislators, congressman, congresswoman, representative** (02/15/95/FH/pc:ok).
•• LFD 193: *wáhkilace kaɣe* <wa´-ḳi-gtha-dse ga-xe> to make laws, legislate, legislation, law makers.

wahkílae wakášupe. N [presumably *wahkílai* (or perhaps *wahkílaace*?) + *wa-* VAL + *kašúpe*] **cash payment.**
•• LFD 193: *wahkílae wakašipe* <wa-ḳi´-gtha-e wa-ga-shi-be> a money payment to members of the tribe by the Government (03/06/95/FH/pc:ok).

wahkílai (variants: **wahkílae, wáhkila**). N **payment (the quarterly payment some Osages receive)** (RB). [It is not certain whether this word can be used of other kinds of payment.] *Mongrain akxa wahkílai kízo akxá ska* Mongrain is enjoying his payment [I suppose] (RBn10-9:JW; CQc; 03/06/95/FH/pc:okc).
• **rations from the government** (03/06/95/FH/pc:ok).
•• RB: <wah-kí-lai^{n}>.
•• LFD 193: *wahkílae* <wa-ḳi´-gtha-e> issue of Government rations.

wahkǫ́ (variant of **wahkǫ́ta**).

wahkǫ́i. ADV **hurried, in a hurry, rushed.** *wahkǫ́į brée hta mįkšé* I'm in a hurry (RBn14-05, unconfirmed).

•• LFD 217 (unconfirmed): *wąkǫ́* <wo^{n}-go^{n}′> soon. *wąkǫ́ ða ðį ho* <wo^{n}-go^{n}′ tha thi^{n} ho> [sentence-final *ho* is not used in Mod. Os.] go in haste, in haste.

••• *KS wakkǫ́ya* rush to rescue somebody (RR).

wahkǫ́ta (variant: **wahkǫ́**). N **God.** *įhtáci wahkǫ́ta* our heavenly father (lit., 'father God') (02/01/95/FH/pc:ok; BE2.59).

•• LFD 193: *wahkǫta* <Wa-ḳo^{n}′-da> God. "[T]he name applied by the Osage to the mysterious, invisible, creative power which brings into existence all living things of whatever kind." LFD 54: *letą́wahkǫ* <Gthe-do^{n}′-wa-ḳo^{n}> Mystery-hawk (personal name).

wahkǫ́ta íe oðáake. N **preacher (lit., 'tells God's word')** (BE2.107, RBn2-MOJ/p11; 04/17/95/LS/pc:ok).

wahkǫ́ta ižį́ke. N **Jesus Christ (lit., 'God's son')** (02/13/95/FH/pc:ok). *wahkǫ́ta ižį́ke iihǫ́* mother of Christ (02/13/95/FH/pc:ok; BE2.72). *wahkǫ́ta ižį́ke íe* Jesus' teachings.

wahkǫ́ta ižį́ke hą́ąpa iðáalį. INTERJ [*í-* LOC + *ðáalį*] **Merry Christmas! (lit., 'good with God's son's day')** (DN-WHM, unconfirmed).

wahkǫ́ta ižį́ke iihǫ́. N **mother of Jesus, Mary (lit., 'God's son's mother')**. *wahkǫ́ta ižį́ke iihǫ́ hpaxį́į įkše xǫ́ǫce íkǫce káaɣi apai* they're making the cedar like Mary's hair (FH).

wahkǫ́ta ižį́ke íikitaðe (variant: **wahkǫ́ta ižį́ke íikita[e]**). N [*wahkǫ́ta* + *ižį́ke* + *ki-* INCEPTIVE + *iitáðe*] **Christmas (lit., 'God's son is born again'; implies the day recurs)** (FH; RB).

wahkǫ́ta mą́žą. N **heaven (lit., 'God's land')**.

wahkǫ́tahci. N [*wahkǫ́ta* + *hcí*] **church, house of God.**

wahkǫ́taki. V, N [stat., *wa_hkǫ́taki*] *(intr.)* **(be a) doctor, physician, healer, minister of a religious group, preacher** (04/07/95/LS/pc:prod). *waðíhkǫtakie* you are a doctor (RB, LS:ok). *wahkǫ́taki nį́ áapie* [Mod. Os. form: *áape* instead of *áapie*] they said you were a doctor (BE2.33) *wahkǫ́taki kši pšíe ðe* I went to the doctor [*kši* is optional in this sentence; reference to the office of the doctor is implied] (04/26/95/FH/pc:okc). *wahkǫ́taki pšíe* I went to the doctor (03/08/95/MREI/pc; BE2.118).

•• LFD 194: *wahkǫ́taki* <wa-ḳo^{n}′-da-gi> a person who has knowledge of medicine; a physician; a doctor; one who pretends to communicate with the dead; a necromancer; occult; magic; holy; sacred; anything held sacred. *wahkǫ́taki kipą́ ðe awa hkiðe ha* <wa-ḳo^{n}′-da-gi-bo^{n} the a-wa ḳi-the ha> [expected Mod. Os. form for 'I send for' is *áwakšíðe* rather than *awa hkiðe*; sentence-final *ha* is not used in Mod. Os.] I sent for a physician. LFD 142: *ðawáhkǫtaki* <tha-wa′-ḳo^{n}-da-gi> to represent a sacred object as having supernatural powers [*ðaa-* INSTR 'by mouth' + *wahkǫ́taki*, i.e., 'call/designate it as supernatural'].

wahkúcˀa. ADJ **lame** (RB).

•• LFD 193: *wahkílicˀake* <wa-ḳi′-gthi-ṭs'a-ge> cripple.

wahléhle, wahléle (variants of **waléle**).

wahóhota. N [reduplicated form of *wahóta*] **funny, amusing, or comical person, one who is always making people laugh, joker, clown.** • ADJ **funny, amusing, comical** (BE2.21, 01/19/95/FH/pc:ok).

•• LFD 202: *waðíhohota* <wa-thi′-ho-ho-da> a droll. *wisǫka ata waðihohota kiðalį pi a* <wi-ço^{n}-ga a-da wa-thi-ho-ho-da gi-tha-gthi^{n} bi a> [expected Mod. Os. form: *wisǫ́ka apa waðihohota kiðaalį pe*] my brother is fond of joking.

••• Cf. *waðíhohota.*

wahókˀa. V, ADJ [stat., *wa_hókˀa*] *(intr.)* **(be) small, little; (be) young** (03/10/95/MREI/pc:ok). *ąwą́hokˀa* I'm small. *waðíhokˀa* you're small. *óhka wahókˀa* a small space (03/13/95/FH/pc:ok). *ąwą́hokˀa tą* when I was little (RBn21-01HL, FH:okc). • N **small amount; reduced quantity.** *wahókˀa óožu* [pour] just a little (lit., 'little bit pour') (03/10/95/MREI/pc:ok, RB).

•• LFD 191: *wahókˀa* <wa-ho′-k'a> a young person ['person' unconfirmed]. *waðíhokˀa* <wa-thi′-ho-ḳ'a> you are young, a juvenile.

wahókˀažį. V, ADJ [stat., *wa_hókˀažį*] [*wahókˀa* + *-žį* 'little'] *(intr.)* **(be) very small or very young** (RB: MREI:ok).

wahóohtą (variant: **wahóohta**). N [*wa-* VAL + *hóohtą* (or perhaps *wa-* VAL + *hóohtą* + *ðe* CAU [LF])] **gun, handgun, rifle, shotgun, pistol, revolver (perhaps lit. 'cause things to cry out' [LF]).** *wahóohta aščį htape?* are you all going to have guns? (03/10/95/PM/pc:ok). *wahóohtą lókialą [lóhkialą?]* shotgun with a big trigger (RBn HW10, unconfirmed).

•• LFD 192: *wahóhtąðe* <wa-ho′-ṭo^{n}-the> a gun.

wahóohtą ápahazi. N [*ápaha* (not otherwise attested)+ *zí*] **rifle (lit., 'gun with yellow [on top back(?)]', referring to the brass sight on top of a rifle).**

•• LFD 192: *wahóhtąðe apahazi* <wa-ho′-ṭo^{n}-the a-ba-ha-çi> a rifle with a brass sight.

wahóohtą ápahazi (*continued*) (unconfirmed; 03/02/95/FH/pc:uk; 03/10/95/PM/pc:uk).

wahóohtą hpa (variant of **wahóohtą táahpa**).

wahóohtą opáaxǫ. N [*ó-* LOC + *paaxǫ́*] **breech-loading shotgun (lit., 'gun that breaks by pushing on').**

•• LFD 192: *wahóhtąðe opaxǫ* <wa-ho´-ṭo^n-the u-ba-xo^n> a breech loading gun. (03/02/95/FH/pc:ma; 03/10/95/PM/pc:uk).

wahóohtą táahpa (variant: **wahóohtą hpa**). N **pistol (lit., 'round gun')** (02/03/95/FH/pc:ok; RBn3-MOJ/p5; 04/11/95/LS/pc:uk; BE2.103). [Refers to the round chamber in pistols as opposed to the rectangular chamber in rifles and shotguns (except breech-loading ones) in early days. Pistols were the first guns to have round chambers.]

•• RB: <wah-hó-tah-páh> (04/11/95/LS/pc:okc).

•• LFD 192: *wahóhtąðe tahpa* <wa-ho´-ṭo^n-the da-p̣a> a pistol. *wahóhtąðe hpa* <wa-ho´-ṭo^n-the p̣a> a pistol.

wahóohtąžį (variant: **wahóohtąhpažį́**) (RB; 04/11/95/LS/pc:ok). N [*wahóohtą* + *-žį* 'little'] **revolver (lit., 'small gun').** [Early revolvers were much smaller than pistols of the time.]

•• LFD 192: *wahóhtąðe hpa žįka* <wa-ho´-ṭo^n-the p̣a zhi^n-ga> a revolver.

wahóšce (variants: **wahóšče, wahósce, wahóšča**). ADJ, V [uninfl. or stat., *wa_hóšce*] **(be) small, little** (RBn10-5:MOJ/79; 7/8/94/PM/num98b; 02/16/95/FH/pc:prod); **(be) narrow, slim.** *wahóšce bríe* I'm small. *wahóšce ąkai* we're small (FH:08/05/99). *šǫ́ke akxa wálį wahóšče akxa* that dog is really little (FH:08/05/99/DNpc; BE2.123). *okáhąpa wahósce* a small window (04/28/95/LS/pc). *šǫ́ke wahóšce* a little dog (BE2.80). *wahóščažį* tiny, quite little.

•• RB: <wah-hó-shchiah, wah-hó-stseh, wah-hó-shtah> [note all three grades: *sc, šcm, šč*].

•• LFD 192: *wahósta* <wa-hu´-sta> small, tiny. LFD 168: *okáhąpa wahosca* <u-ga´-ho^n-ba wa-ho-stsa> a small pane of glass for a window.

wahóšča, wahóšče (variants of **wahóšce**).

wahóščažį. V, ADJ [uninfl. or stat., *wa_hóščažį*] [*wahóšče* + *-žį* 'little'] *(intr.)* **very little, quite small, tiny** (7/8/94/PM/num98b).

•• LFD 192: *wahósca žįka* <wa-hu´-stsa zhi^n-ga> very small, minute. *wahósca žįka* <wa-ho´-stsa zhi^n-ga> small, tiny, minute.

wahóta. ADJ, V [uninfl.] *(intr.)* **(be) funny, amusing, comical** (FH). *táatą wahóta wį* something funny (lit., 'a funny thing') (3-3-83-p2).

•• LFD 192: *wahóta* <wa-hu´-da> amusing.

••• Cf. *ðíhota, wahóhota, žáže wahóta.*

wahótaðe. V [reg., *wahóta_ðe*] *(trans.)* **make fun of s.o.** (LS).

wahówahá. N **Potawatomi (tribe or tribal member)** (ERE, unconfirmed; 03/08/95/PM/pc:uk; 04/18/95/FH/pc:uk).

••• *KS wáhi óyaha* Potawatomie (JOD) (RR), *badó wadǫ́be* Potawatomie (RR). **tribe**

wahǫ́į (variant: **wahǫ́ǫ**). V [reg., *wa_hǫ́į*] *(intr.)* **address folks with respect** (MREI; HRE/01/17/02/pc). *áwahǫį* I address folks with respect. *waðáhǫį* you address folks with respect. *wahǫ́ǫ hpážįka* I don't know how to address folks (RBn1-41). *wahǫ́ǫ na ðáalį áapa nǫ́ǫ apa* they said we should show this respect, the elders (RBn1-41). • *(trans.)* **address as friends and relatives.** *záani wawíhǫįpi* I address you all as friends and relatives (FH/10/30/9/pc/ok). *wihtą́ke, wižį́, wisǫ́ka, wawíhǫįpi* sisters, elder brothers, younger brothers, I wish to address you with respect [man speaking] (MREI). *wižǫ́a, wihtáežį, wihcį́to, wisǫa, wawíhǫįpi* elder sisters, younger sisters, elder brothers, younger brothers, I wish to address you with respect [woman speaking] (MREI).

wahǫ́įke. V, N [stat., *wa_hǫ́įke*] [*wahǫ́į* +*ðįké*] **(be an) orphan.**

•• JOD (Wasápežįka letter, ln2, 3): *waðíhǫįke* <wa-¢íhŭ^n-iñ´ḳi au> you are an orphan. JOD (Devouring Mountain p1 ln4): *wahǫ́įžįka* <wa-hŭ^n´-içiñḳa> little orphan [*wahǫ́įke* + *žįká*] (BE2.99; 03/03/95/FH/pc:ok).

•• LFD 191: *wahǫ́įke* <wa-ho^n´-i^n-ge> no mother, an orphan. "The word was used among the Indians when speaking of a child with neither father nor mother, an orphan."

wahǫ́ǫ (variant of **wahǫ́į**).

wahpáce (variant: **wáhpace**) V [reg., *wa_hpáce*] [*wa-* VAL + *hpáce*] *(intr.)* **perform surgery on folks; butcher, cut up meat** (BE2.14; 02/08/95/FH/pc:okc; FH:4/22/96/tape). [The original meaning of this word may be 'perform surgery'; the normal Mod. Os. form for 'butcher' is *wapáse.*]

•• RB: <wah-páh-tseh>.

•• LFD 239 (unconfirmed): *wahpáce* <wa-p̣a´dse> butcher.

wahpíǫ. V [conjug. unknown] [*wa-* VAL + *hpíǫ*] *(intr.)* **learn, learn how to do s.t., be skilled at doing things** (04/14/95/PM/pc:ok).

•• RB: <wah-pyú^n>.

wahpóka (variant: **wáhpoke**). N **owl** (03/03/95/FH/pc:okc; RBn1-MOJ/p58). [The call of any kind of owl at night is considered bad luck (FH).]

•• LFD 198: *wahpóka* <wa-p̣o´-ga> the gray owl, an Osage symbol of night, also a life symbol. "It is a bird that succeeds in bringing its young safely to maturity." *wahpóka htąka* <wa-p̣o´-ga ṭo^{n}-ga> the great gray owl. *wahpóka waðǫ* <wa-p̣o´-ga wa-tho^{n}> Songs of the Gray Owl.

••• *KS wappǫ́ga* owl (not the screech owl), hoot owl.

wahríše. N **Generous (non-Osage surname).** [Hazel Harper's family's name. *wahríše* is not an Osage word; it may be an Omaha cognate of Osage *walíži* 'generous, not stingy'.] • ADJ **generous.** *ąkóhta wahríše wahkǫ́ta ižį́ke* [expected Mod. Os. form: *ąkóhta wahkǫ́ta ižį́ke walíži*] ours through the bounty of Christ (DN-WHM, unconfirmed; FH: no).

wahtą́ą. N **king (in a deck of cards)** (RBn12-10/MOJ).

wahtį́e, wahtį́į (archaic variants of **wahcį́į**).

wahtóke. V, ADJ [stat., *wa_htóke*] **(be) industrious, have the qualities of a good worker, alert, not lazy, quick to do things, quick-acting** (FH:ok). *wahtóke apa* he's a good worker (BE2.71;02/13/95/FH/pc:ok).

•• LFD 206: *wahtóke* <wa-ṭu´-ge> to be active, alert. *ąwą́htoke* <o^{n}-wo^{n}´-ṭu-ge> I am active. *waðíhtoke* <wa-thi´-ṭu-ge> you are active. LFD 204: *wahtóke* <wa-ṭo´-ge> alert, quick, active. *ąwą́htoke* <o^{n}-wo^{n}´-ṭo-ge> I am alert. *waðíhtoke* <wa-thi´-ṭo-ge> you are alert. *wahtóke* <Wa-ṭo´-ge> Active (personal name).

wahtǫ́ka (variant: **wahtą́ka**). ADJ, N [possibly *wa-* VAL + *htą́ka*] **authoritative; authority, s.o. with authority.** *áhkita wahtǫ́ka* a soldier with authority (FH).

••• Cf. *totą́ha wahtą́ka.*

wahtǫ́pe. N **onlookers.** *xóhka ški, wahtǫ́pe ški, haaną́, hpáze ðe* you singers and drummers, you onlookers, too, however many there are this evening (HREsr: 1965 *ilǫ́ǫška*, lines 1–2).

••• Cf. *watǫ́pe.*

wahú. N **bone** (01/06/95/FH/pc:ok). *wahú wanǫ́pʔį* a bone necklace (BE2.10).

•• LFD 191: *wahí* <wa-hi´> bones. *wahú* <wa-hiu´> a bone. *wahúsąį* <Wa-hiu´-ço^{n}-i^{n}> White-bones-woman (female personal name), refers to the story of bones left to whiten on the ground [*są* is not recognized as 'white' in Mod. Os.].

wahúąkʔį (variant of **wahúįkʔį**).

wahúhka. N [*wa-* VAL 'stuff' + *húhka*] **fork** (01/30/95/FH/pc:ok; BE2.50).

•• LFD 191: *wahúhka žahta* <wa-hiu´-ḳa zha-ṭa> a fork, an awl, forked (01/30/95/FH/pc:uk with *žáhta*).

wahúį (variants: **wahų́ų, wahų́e**). V [reg., *wa_húį*] [probably *wa-* VAL + *híǫ*; for variation between *iǫ* and *uį*, see *kšíǫze*] *(intr.)* **move to another location, migrate** (02/27/95/FH/pc). *áwahųe* I'm moving (02/27/95/FH/pc). *wahų́ę hta akxai* he's going to move. *hcí hcéka ąwáhųe hta mįkšé* I'm going to move into the new house (FH/06/20/95). *hcí hcéka ðiištą́pi áape wahų́e hta akxai* they said that the new house is finished, so she's going to move in (FH/06/20/95). *ważį́ka ški wahúį nǫpe* even birds migrate.

•• LFD 191: *wahíǫ* <wa-hi´-o^{n}> to pack up, as when preparing to break camp to move from place to place, to migrate, to remove, to depart, to break camp (02/27/95/FH/pc: pronunciation unconfirmed). *awáhiǫ* <a-wa´-hi-o^{n}> I broke camp. *waðáhiǫ* <wa-tha´-hi-o^{n}> you broke camp. *ąwą́hiǫ pe* <o^{n}-wo^{n}´-hi-o^{n} i> we broke camp.

••• *OM* same as Osage (LFD 191).

wahúįkʔį (variant: **wahúąkʔį**). V [conjug. unknown] [*wahúį* + *kʔį́*] *(trans.)* **load for moving.**

•• LFD 191: *wahíąkʔį* <wa-hi´-o^{n}-ḳ'i^{n}> to load, a load.

wahúni. N [*wahú* + *níe*] **arthritis, rheumatism, lumbago (lit., 'bone hurt')** (01/06/95/FH/pc: ok; BE2.4).

•• LFD 191: *wahínie* <wa-hi´-ni-e> aching bones, lumbago, rheumatism.

wahúžįka. N [*wahú* + *žįká*] **button (lit., 'little bone')** (04/07/95/LS/pc:ok).

•• LFD 191: *wahúžįka* <wa-hiu´ zhi^{n}-ga> button.

wahų́e, wahų́ų (variants of **wahúį**).

waíįškihci (variant of **waðíįškihci**).

waíląą ochí (variant of **waðíląą ochí**).

wą́įɣaaké (variant: **wéuɣaake**). N [*wa-* VAL + *į́* + *ɣaaké*] **Carrying and Wailing (personal name)** (04/25/95/PM/pc:ok: *wą́į ɣaake* ok). [Wéuɣáake was the father of John Oberly, who was Frances Holding's father.]

•• LFD 192: *wą́į ɣake* <Wa´-i^{n} Xa-ge> Carrying and Wailing, Carrying (a pipe) and Wailing. "The wailing is an appeal to the <No^{n}-ho^{n}-zhi^{n}-ga> to recite the <Wi-gi-e> (ritual) in its entirety."

wakaacˀáiži. ADJ **disrespectful, rude, insolent, failing to show respect to people or property, forward** (BE2.32; 04/07/95/LS/pc:okc).
•• RB: <wah-káh-ts'áh-zhi>.
•• LFD 188: *wakácˀaeži* <wa-ga´-ṭs'a-e-zhi> impudence, rude, forward, insolence, officious.

wakáaɣe. N, V [sync. k>p, *wa_káaɣe*] [*wa-* VAL + *káaɣe*] **(be) boss** (03/24/95/PM/pc, unconfirmed).

wakáahcįe (variant: **wakáahcįi**). N [*wa-* '3rd person pl. patient' ('to them') + *káa-* INSTR + *hcįį*] **Appear Suddenly to Them (personal name referring to the moment the deer look up, disturbed by the appearance of s.t.).** [George Shannon's name.] *wakáahcįe* it appears to them suddenly.
••• Cf. *wahcįį*.

wákaapše N [*wa-* VAL + *káapše*] **wire brush** (FH).

wakáaxa. V [reg. *ka*-del. *wa_(ká)axa*] [*wa-* VAL + *káaxa*] **beat folks at a race.**

wakáaži (variant: **wakáažį**). V [reg., *wa_káaži*] [*wa-* VAL + *kaažį́*] *(intr.)* **drive.** *wakáaži hpímǫ* I know how to drive. *ðíe waðákaaži tą owé hci ci brée hkǫ́bra* if you will drive, I want to go to the grocery store (01/20/95/PM/prod). • N **driver, chauffeur.** *wakáaži wihta hcúɣežį* that's my driver, he's a little dried up guy (PM). • **garage** (RBn12-07; 01/20/95/ERE/pc:ok).
•• RB: <wáh-gah-zhi>.

wakái (variant: **wákai**). V [presumably *wa-* VAL + *kaa-* INSTR + *ce* (root not attested independently; cf. *pacé*)] **cut meat (cutting or slicing meat as for barbecue) (lit., 'slice stuff with sudden motion' [?])** (02/24/95/FH/pc:ok; *wákai;* 01/14/95/FH/pc:ok; RBn1-MOJ/p50).
•• RB: <wah-kái>.

wákalą. ADJ **dirty** (RBn10-3:MOJ/79; 01/20/95/FH/pc:uk; MSB 2-25-83). [Possibly borrowed from Spanish *guácala* or *guácatela* 'yuck! ugh! dirty!'] *waðílą wákalą ą́ðiicíza* take these dirty thoughts away (RBn10-3:MOJ/79). *híihka wákalą akxái* your ankles are dirty (RBn10-3:MOJ/79).

wákaštǫ. N [*wa-* VAL + *štǫ́ka*] **cushion or pillow to sit on (as for a sofa, chair, or other seat)** (BE2.28); **saddle blanket; blanket folded to cushion a seat** (RB; 04/25/95/PM/pc:ok; 01/14/95/FH/pc:uk). [Takes 'sitting' positional article *įkšé*.] *wákaštǫ įkšé hkáwa áalą* put that saddle blanket on that horse.

wákazo. N, V [reg.?, *wá_kazo?*] [*wa-* VAL + *ákazo*] **judge, examine an issue (lit., 'examine things')** (BE2.72; 02/13/95/FH/pc:ok).

wakíkˀu. V [reg., *wa_kíkˀu*] [*wa-* VAL + *wakˀú* (valence-reduced form, but may be used transitively)] *(trans.)* **give away to folks who are family.** *waðákikˀue* you gave it away to family. *ąwákikˀupe* we gave it away to our own.

wakíšupe. V [reg.? *wa_kíšupe*] [*wa-* VAL + *kíšupe*] *(trans.)* **repay for, reimburse (for)** (03/06/95/FH/pc). [Expected (but unattested) inflectional forms: *áwakišupe* 'I reimburse her for it', *waðákišupe* 'you reimburse her for it', *ąwákišupape* 'we reimburse her for it'.]
•• LFD 189: *wakíšipe* <wa-gi´-shi-be> to remunerate, to repay.
••• Cf. *kašúpe*.

wakǫ́ða. V [sync. fortisizing stop stem+sync., *wa_kǫ́_ða*] [*wa-* VAL or *wa-* '3rd person pl. patient' + *kǫ́ða*] **want s.t. for s.o. else.** *žikóhkiha wahkǫ́bra* I want it for my grandchildren (RBn22-19).

wakǫ́ze (variant: **wákǫze** [JS]). • V [sync. k>p, *wa_kǫ́ze*] [*wa-* VAL + *kǫ́ze* 'teach'] *(trans.)* **teach** (03/05/95/JS/pc; 03/16/95/FH/pc:ok). *wažážeíe wakǫ́ze mįkšé* I'm teaching Osage language (RBn10-12:JW). • N **teacher, minister** (FH, RB). *wažážeíe wakǫ́ze mįkšé* I'm a teacher of Osage language. *wakǫ́zažį* little teacher [expected Mod. Os. form: *wakǫ́zežį*].
•• RB: <wah-kó^{n}-zeh> (BE2.133;03/05/95/JS/pc: *wákǫze*).
•• LFD 189: *wakǫ́ze* <wa-go^{n}´-çe> an instructor, a preceptor, a teacher, a preacher; to teach, to instruct, to preach. *wahpǫ́ze* <wa-p̣o^{n}´-çe> I teach. *waškǫ́ze* <wa-shko^{n}´-çe> you teach. *ąwą́kǫza pe* <o^{n}-wo^{n}´-go^{n}-ça i> we teach. *wakǫ́ze wakˀo* <wa-go^{n}´-çe wa-ḳ'o> a woman instructor, a preceptress (CQ: ok).

wakšé. V [reg., *wa_kšé*] *(trans.)* **mean, intend, have in mind.** *ðíe wawíkše* I mean you (RBn22-01). *šée ée awákše* that [item near you] is what I meant, that is what I was talking about (03/20/95/FH/pc:ok).
•• LFD 130: *še ewakše* <she e-wa-kshe> [expected Mod. Os. form: *šée ée awákše* that in your hand [rather, 'that near you'] is what I mean. LFD 26: *pé eawakše a* <be´ e-a-wa-ke a> [expected Mod. Os. form: *pée ée awákše?*; sentence-final *a* is not used in questions in Mod. Os.] who do I mean? *pé ewaðakše a* <be´ e-wa-tha-ke a> [expected Mod. Os. form: *pée ée waðákše?*; sentence-final *a* is not used in questions in Mod. Os.] who do you mean? *pé ewakše a* <be´ e-wa-ke a> [expected Mod. Os. form: *pée ée*

wakšé akxa?; sentence-final *a* is not used in questions in Mod. Os.] who does he mean?
••• *KS wakhé* mean something, refer to, intend (RR).

wakšíǫze. V [reg.+(sync. nasal vowel stem), *wa_kší(_)ǫze*] [*wa-* VAL + *kšíǫze*] *(trans.)* **teach things to s.o.**
•• LFD 192: *wakčíǫze* <wa-kchi´-o^{n}-çe> [expected Mod. Os. form *wakšíǫze*] instruction, to give instruction to a pupil, to teach.

wakxázu (variant of **watxázu**).

wakxą́ (variant of **watxą́**).

wakˀą́. V, ADJ [uninfl. (but reg., *wa_kˀą́*, in LF examples)] *(intr.)* **(be) glad, happy, joyous; exult.** *wakˀą́ mįkšé* I'm glad (01/31/95/FH/pc:ok). *wakˀą́ apai* they're glad (01/31/95/FH/pc:ok; BE2.55). *wakˀą́ ðąįšé* you're glad (9/17/94/FH/p.c.).
•• LFD 193: *wakˀą* <wa-ķ'o^{n}> to exult. *awákˀą* <a-wa´-ķ'o^{n}>I exulted. *waðákˀą* <wa-tha´-ķ'o^{n}> you exulted. *ąwákˀą pe* <o^{n}-wa´-ķ'o^{n} i> we exulted.

wakˀó. N **woman.** *wakˀó taaké štą́* a woman who likes to fight (03/24/95/PM/pc:ok; BE2.160). *wakˀó wíhta* my woman, my wife. • **wife; my wife.** *wakˀó wíhta!* wife! [man calling his wife]; my wife. *wakˀó ðíhta* your wife. • **queen (in a deck of cards)** (RBn23-17c).
•• RB: <wah-k'ó, wáh-k'o>.
•• LFD 193: *wakˀó* <wa-ķ'o´> woman, or women. *wakˀó kahike* <Wa-ķ'o´-ga-hi-ge> Woman-chief (female personal name) (03/24/95/PM/pc:ok).
••• Cf. *ðiwákˀo, iwákˀo.*

wakˀó ðílą. VP [sync., *wakˀó _ðílą*] **flirt with a woman** (RB; 01/26/95/FH/pc:okc).

wakˀó ðįké. N **widower (lit., 'woman none').**
•• LFD 195: *wakˀó ðįke* <wa-ķ'o´ thi^{n}-ge> has no woman, a widower.

wakˀó éekǫ (variant: **wakˀó ékǫ**). VP [uninflected] *(intr.)* **be womanly (lit., 'like a woman')** (03/24/95/PM/pc:ok; 04/06/95/LS/pc:ok).
•• LFD 193: *wakˀó ekǫ* <wa-ķ'o´ e-go^{n}> womanly.

wakˀó mąąðǫ́štą. N [*wakˀo* + *mąąðǫ́* + *štą*] **wife stealer (lit., 'steals wife/wives constantly').**

wakˀó nǫǫhǫ́. N **prostitute, woman of bad reputation** (RBn11-02/JW&FW; RB/HHsk/c.1976).
•• JOD (slip file): *wakˀó nǫ́hǫ́* <wa-k'u´ nú^{n}-hú^{n}> a woman who has been married, but who is now alone, a widow.

wakˀó wéðuɣe (variant: **wakˀó weúɣe**). N **married woman** (04/18/95/FH/pc:both okc: *wakˀó weúɣe* is preferred; 04/17/95/LS/pc:ma).
•• LFD 195: *wakˀo waðiɣe* <wa-ķ'o wa-thi-xe> a married woman.

wakˀó wíhta. NP **my wife (claimed** [perhaps wrongly] **to be used to refer to her but not to address her)** (03/16/95/MREI/pc:ok; RB).

wakˀóhpa. N **eldest daughter.** [Kinship terms ending in *-hpa* may be baby names; at any rate they seem to be infrequently used except with 1st or 2nd person possessor (e.g., for 'my eldest daughter' and 'your eldest daughter').]

wakˀóhtą. N **(my/your/his/her, etc.) eldest daughter, first daughter** (01/09/95/FH/pc:prod). [Used by Grayhorse and Hominy Osages.] *wakˀóhtą hcí ðe ée aðį́ apa, hcílepa ðée káaɣe* my daughter has this house, she's making a home in it (PM/7/7/94; 02/03/95/FH/pc:ok). *wakˀóhtą apa ðéka hcíle apái* that's where eldest daughter lives.

wakˀóžį. N **my mother-in-law; mother-in-law.** [According to some speakers, used only for the mother of the wife of a male (RB; 02/25/95/FH/pc:okc); according to others, it can also be used for the mother of the husband of a female (04/17/95/LS/pc).] *wakˀóžį wíhta apa htóolą káaɣe kǫ́ða įkí apá* my mother-in-law doesn't want to make meat pies (T24b-p15/24; CQ105; BE2.90: 'man speaking'). *wakˀóžį ðíhta* your mother-in-law. • **crone, elderly woman, little old woman, little woman (used both to refer to her and to address her)** (03/02/95/FH/pc:ok; BE2.98).
•• LFD 195: *wakˀó žįka* <wa-ķ'o´ zhi^{n}-ga> mother-in-law, a crone, an aged woman (02/25/95/FH/pc:ok). *wakˀó žįka hi* <wa-k'o´ zhi^{n}´-ga hi> a woman who has reached old age.
••• Cf. *ðíwakˀóžį, íwakˀóžį.*

wakˀú. V [reg., *wa_kˀú*] [*wa-* VAL + *kˀú* (but sometimes used as transitive)] *(trans.)* **give away to folks.** *ðíe waðákˀue* you gave it away. *ąwákˀu ą[ð]įkšé* we [two] gave it away, we gave it to them. • **loan, provide for, feed folks.** *íkiha táatą áwawakˀeu ąhé* I loan them [people] stuff all the time (5-12-83). *áwawakˀúe* I fed them, provided for them (5-12-83). *waléze tóa ąwą́ðakˀu na, ðée é í apai* the books that you loaned me are these (2-10-84-p4).

wálake(?) (see **wáalake**).

waléle (variants: **wahléle, wahléhle, wahélele**) (FH: all variants ok; PM: *waléle* only). N **flag,**

waléle (*continued*)
American flag, staff with feathers (BE2.126; 04/07/95/PM/pc:ok; RB; 01/26/95/FH/pc:prod).
•• RB: <wah-hléh-hleh>.
•• LFD 209: *waléle* <wa-xthe´-xthe> a war standard. *waléle wahkątaki* <Wa-xthe´-xthe Wa-ḳo^{n}-da-gi> Mysterious War standards. *waléle cˀįša* <wa-xthe´-xthe ts'-i^{n} sha> the standard made with a crook by the Osage and Omaha. *waléle scece* <wa-xthe´-xthe-stse-dse> a tall standard made by the Osage, also by the Kaw and the Omaha. LFD 189: *wale* <wa-gthe> a symbolic plume made of a downy feather of an eagle.
••• Cf. *haawálele.*

waléze. N [*wa-* VAL + *léze*] **paper, stationery, posterboard, or any other paper or document containing text (lit., 'something striped').** [Contrasts with *htanąkˀa* 'stationery, paper for making signs, blank paper'; *waléze* already has text on it.] *óðaake waléze* newspaper (03/06/95/FH/pc:okc; BE2.101). *mązeska ootá waléze* note, loan document (document of borrowed money). • **book** (04/19/95/FH/pc:pl)
•• LFD 189: *waléze* <wa-gthe´-çe> book, mail, a script, writing.
••• Cf. *óðaake waléze.*

waléze hpíǫ. VP [sync. fortisizing stop stem, *waléze _hpíǫ*] *(intr.)* **be educated, literate, learned (lit., 'know books').**
•• LFD 189–90: *waléze hpiǫ* <wa-gthe´-çe p̣i-o^{n}> educated, literate, learned. *waléze hpimǫ* <wa-gthe´-çe p̣i-mo^{n}> I am educated. *waléze špižǫ* <wa-gthe´-çe shpi-zho^{n}> you are educated. *waléze ąhpiǫ pe* <wa-gthe´-çe o^{n}-p̣i-o^{n} i> we are educated.

waléze káaye. N **secretary, record-keeper for tribal council** (RB).

waléze sápe (variant: **wáleze sápe**). N **Bible (lit., 'black book')** (BE2.8; 01/07/95/FH/pc:ok).

wáleze. N **letter.** *wáleze ðée kši[ð]e* mail this letter [for him/her] (lit., 'make the letter go for another person' [the sender or the recipient]) (02/15/95/FH/pc:okc). *wáleze ðée káaya* send a letter (02/15/95/FH/pc:okc). *wáleze ðalúuze?* did you get your letter? (02/15/95/FH/pc:ok; BE2.78).
•• RB: <wáh-leh-zeh> letter (02/15/95/FH/pc:ok).

wáleze wį kšíye. VP **write a letter to s.o. (lit., 'make a letter to another').** *wáleze wį ąkšíya* write me a letter (RBn10-20; CQ:okc).

walézeáace (variant: **walézeáaci**). N [presumably *waléze* + *ðaacé*] **school, learning, class, reading, schooling, education (lit., 'read books')** (01/09/95/FH/pc; 03/08/95/MREI/pc:ok). *hąąðé walézeáace ščée hta ðaašé?* are you going to class tonight? (RBn12-08). *žįkážį apa záani walézeáace apái* my children are all in school (RB). *walézeáace pée wakǫ́ze ðįkšé?* who is teaching the class? (RB). *walézeaaci mąðį́* go to school (RBn2-MOJ/p5; MREI).
•• LFD 190: *waléze ðace* <wa-gthe´-çe tha-dse> to read. *waléze brace* <wa-gthe´-çe btha-dse> I read. *waléze scace* <wa-gthe´-çe stsa-dse> [expected Mod. Os. form: *waléze štáace* 'you read'; <stsa-dse> is presumably an error for <shda-dse>] you read, to read to someone.

walí. ADJ, V [conjug. unknown] *(intr.?)* **(be) selfish, stingy.** [Only found in LFD; Mod. Os. has *kíwalį.*]
•• LFD 209: *walí* <wa-xthi´> stingy, uncharitable, unwilling to give, selfish, undue value placed upon certain property. *walí walį hi a* <wa-xthi´ wa-gthi^{n} hi a> [expected Mod. Os. form: *wáli kíwalipe*] he is very stingy. LFD 325: *walí walį pe* <wa-xthi´ wa-gthi^{n} bi a> [from *kíwali*, expected 3rd person form: *kíwali wálipe*] he is very selfish.
••• Cf. *wáawali.*

wáli (variant of **wálį**).

walíži. V, ADJ [stat., *_(kí)walįži*] [*kíwalį* + *aží* NEG] **(be) generous, not stingy.**
•• LFD 209: *walíži* <wa-xthi´-zhi> Generous (personal name), refers to the man who always shared his spoils, taking in his war exploits, with the people; generous, liberal, munificent.
••• Cf. *wahríše.*

wálį (variants: **wáalį, wáli, wáali**). ADV **very, indeed, really, extremely, so very, a great deal, a lot, so very much (used also in expressions with 'too much').** *wáli hó lą́ąðe!* what a big fish! (lit., 'it's really a big fish!'). *hą́ące wáli nuužúpe ska, žįkáži apa hǫ́pái niižópši apái* last night it must have rained a lot, the children today are wading (01/24/95/FH/pc:ok). *wálį tóocehape, waachí ną apái* he eats too much and he doesn't do anything but dance (lit., 'he is really a glutton, he only dances') (RBn10-2:MOJ/79).
•• JOD (slip file): *wálį* <wa´-ḳ¢i^{n}> very, greatly, very much.
•• LFD 190: *wálį* <wa´-gthi^{n}> very much; greatly; a great many; beyond description. LFD 100: *mąhką sape che skiðe walį* <mo^{n}-ḳo^{n}´ ça-be tse çki-the wa-gthi^{n}> the coffee is too sweet.

••• *QU walí, walį́* very, really, so (RR).

••• Cf. *kíwalį.*

walǫ́ǫ. v [conjug. unknown, presumed reg., _*walǫ́ǫ*] [*wa-* VAL + *lǫ́ǫ*] *(intr.)* **call folks names.** *šíi apa walǫ́ǫ štą* that person coming sure likes to call people names (cuss them out) (01/09/95/FH/pc:okc; BE2.16). *tówa ðe hų́ ðée walǫ́ǫ šta* that person coming there likes to call people names.

•• LFD 190: *walǫ́* <wa-gtho^n´> to revile; to heap reproach or scandal upon another (01/09/95/FH/pc:ok). *walǫ́lǫ* <wa-gtho^n´-gtho^n> to curse. *ąwąlǫlǫ pe* <o^n-wo^n-gtho^n-gtho^n i> we curse (unconfirmed gloss).

walúška. N **bug, insect, worm, vermin, joker (in a deck of cards)** (RBn12-10/MOJ01/19/95/FH/pc:ok; BE2.13). [A purported word *wákluška* 'witch' that appears in some teaching materials probably actually represents an older pronunciation of *walúška* 'bug, vermin' (perhaps *waglúška*?). The consonant cluster *kl* is otherwise unattested in Osage.]

•• LFD 190: *walúška* <wa-gthu´-shka> bug, any kind of bug, a worm, an insect. *walúška hašoka* <wa-gthu´-shka ha-sho-ga> a shard, a bug with a shell or tough skin. *walúška sape* <wa-gthu´-shka ça-be> black bug, a cricket. LFD 191: *walúška žįka* <wa-gthu´-shka zhi^n-ga> little bugs. *walúška ochí* <wa-gthu´-shka u-ṭsi> wormy, full of worms.

walúška háa šooká. N **beetle or other bug with thick outer layer or exoskeleton.**

•• LFD 190: *walúška hašoka* <wa-gthu´-shka ha-sho-ga> a shard, a bug with a shell or tough skin.

walúška įįštá htąka. N **praying mantis (lit., 'bug with big eyes').**

•• LFD 191: *walúška įšta htąka* <wa-gthu´-shka i^n-shta ṭo^n-ga> praying mantis.

wamą́ą (variant of **wamą́ąðǫštą**).

wamą́ąðǫ (variant: **wamǫ́ǫ**). v [sync., *wamą́ą_ðǫ*] [*wa-* VAL + *mąąðǫ́*] *(intr.)* **steal, steal s.t., steal things** (03/14/95/FH/pc:ok). *wamą́ąbrǫðe* I stole. *waðímǫǫ akxai* he stole from you. *ąwámąąaðǫ* we [two] stole things. *ąwámąąðǫpe* we [three or more] stole things (BE2.127). • N **thievery, theft, stealing, robbery.** [Takes 'standing' positional article *che.*]

•• RB: <wáh-máh>.

•• LFD 196: *wamą́ðǫ* <wa-mo^n´-tho^n> to steal, to take that which belongs to another, to pilfer. *wamą́brǫ* <wa-mo^n´-btho^n> I steal. *wamą́štǫ* <wa-mo^n´-shto^n> you steal. *wamą́ðǫ asila* <wa-mo^n´-tho^n a-si-gtha> I accuse you of stealing [*asila* 'accuse' is unattested]. *wamą́ðǫ che hpiaži* <wa-mo^n´-tho^n tse p̣i-a-zhi> [expected Mod. Os. form: *wamą́ąðǫ che hpíiži*] it is bad to steal.

••• Cf. *wamą́ąðǫštą.*

wamą́ąðǫštą (variants: **wamą́ą, wamǫ́ǫįštą**). N [*wamą́ąðǫ* + *štą*] **thief, robber** (03/14/95/FH/pc:ok). *amą́ąðǫštą ðe obrį́ike* I caught the thief (BE2.138; ok; BE2.127; 03/20/95/FH/pc:ok).

•• LFD 196: *wamą́ðǫštą* <wa-mo^n´-tho^n-shto^n> one who is in the habit of stealing, a thief. *wamą́ðǫštą ðe obrį́ke* <wa-mo^n´-tho^n-shto^n the u-bthi^n-ge> I caught the thief, one who is in the habit of stealing.

wamą́ðį. v [sync., *wamą́_ðį*] [*wa-* VAL + *mąðį́*] *(intr.)* **travel, go on a mission or on a journey, be engaged in going places (such as going over to s.o.'s house to ask for s.t.)** (03/23/95/FH/pc:ok). *wamą́ðį brée* I'm going on a trip, I'm going to go do something (03/23/95/FH/pc; FH:5/01/96/tape; 05/02/95/LS/pc:ok). • N **errand, mission.**

•• LFD 195: *wamǫ́ðį* <wa-mo^n´-thi^n> to travel, to go forward from one place to another on a mission as a delegate, to go on a journey. *wamą́ðį ą́zo* <wa-mo^n´-thi^n o^n-çu a-tha> I like to travel.

wamǫ́ǫ (variant of **wamą́ąðǫ**).

wamǫ́ǫįštą (variant of **wamą́ąðǫštą**).

wanáaye (variant of **waną́ąye**).

wanáhkai. N [presumably *wa-* VAL + *ną́hka* + *ðe* CAU] **mistake (not a particularly serious mistake).** *wanáhkai škáaye* you made a mistake (02/25/95/FH/pc). *táatą ékipše sitǫ́į, wanáhkai ékimą* what I said yesterday I did it by mistake (RBn10-2; 02/25/95/FH/pc:ok).

•• LFD 197 (unconfirmed gloss): *waną́hkaðe* <wa-no^n´-ḳa-the> to injure. *ną́hka aðe* <no^n´-ḳa a-the> I injured him. *ną́hka ðaðe* <no^n´-ḳa tha-the> you injured him, to maim.

wanáše (variant: **wanášį**). v [conjug. unknown] *(trans.)* **take care of.** *waxópe wanáše* take care of the bundle (RBn 10-16). • N **whipman, whip, soldier.** *waną́šežį* Little Soldier (personal name).

•• RB: <wah-náh-sheh> (03/16/95/MREI/pc:ok; BE2.156).

•• LFD 197: *waną́šežįka* <Wa-no^n´-she-zhi^n-ga> Little-soldier (personal name).

waną́ąɣe (variants: **wanáaɣe, wánąąɣe**) N **spirit, holy spirit** (LS, FH). *waną́ąɣe ðáalį* the good spirit, the holy spirit. • **ghost, soul** (01/31/95/FH/pc:ok; RBn2-MOJ/p8; 03/14/95/FH/pc:okc; BE2.126). *waną́ąɣe ðáalį* the holy ghost.

•• RB: <wáh-nah-xeh, wáh-nah-xeh tháh-li^{n}>.

•• LFD 197: *waną́ɣe* <wa-no^{n}´-xe> the spirit (used in rituals), the soul of man, a ghost. *waną́ɣe waðǫ* <wa-no^{n}´-xe wa-tho^{n}> Spirit songs. LFD 272: *waną́ɣe įlǫ́ɣe* <wa-no^{n}´-xe i^{n}-gtho^{n}´-xe> ghost.

••• Cf. *ną́ąɣe.*

waną́ąɣe mą́žą (variant: **wanáaɣe mą́žą**). N **spirit land.** [Takes 'lying down' positional article *kše.*] *wanáaɣe mą́žą kši brée hta mįkšé* I'm going to spirit land.

waníðe. V [reg., *waní_ðe*] [likely a borrowing from Ponca] *(intr.)* **give things away, hold a giveaway.** [Giving away is a custom at the annual Osage war dances on the last day, when blankets, shawls, groceries, cash, and other items are given to others in appreciation.] *waníðe hta apái* they are going to give away [stuff] (01/31/95/FH/pc:ok). *waníðe hta akxai* he's going to give away [stuff]. *waníða[ð]e tą, táatą ðáalį níwaeðéða* when you give away, give good things (MSB 2-24-83). • N **giveaway (ceremony at *ilǫ́ǫška* dances and other special occasions).**

waníe (variant: **wanįe**). V [conjug. unknown] [presumably *wa-* VAL + *níe*] *(intr.)* **be in labor, be birthing (refers to the accompanying pain)** (01/06/95/FH/pc). *waníekxą* boyhood name of A. C. Oberly, brother of Frances Holding: a boy's name in the Eagle clan [the ending *ekxą* is a variant of *éetxą* 'it is time' (FH)]. • N **labor during childbirth** (01/06/95/FH/pc).

wanǫ́braži. V [reg., *wa_nǫ́braži*] [*wanǫ́bre +aží*] *(intr.)* **fast, not eat, not be eating, have no appetite** (01/06/95/FH/pc). *wanǫ́braži akxa* he/she is not eating, he/she has no appetite (RBn1-55).

wanǫ́bre. V [reg., *wa_nǫ́bre*] *(intr.)* **dine, eat** (01/06/95/FH/pc). *áwanǫbre* I eat. *waðánǫbre* you eat. *wanǫ́brape* he eats, they eat. *ąwanǫ́brape* we eat. *ðáalį áwanǫbre che bráašta* it is good that I have eaten, I'm finished (RBn1-3). *áwanǫbre ~ awánǫ́bre* I ate (RBn22-03). *waðánǫbre?* did you eat? *waðánǫbre hkǫ́bra* I want you to eat. *waðánǫbrape?* have you [pl.] eaten? (RBn10-5:MOJ/79). *hkáwa akxa wanǫ́bre akxa* the horse is eating [while standing still]. *wanǫ́braži akxa* he/she is not eating (has no appetite). *wanǫ́brape* they've already eaten. *wanǫ́brape?* did they eat? *wanǫ́bre hú ði* come over and eat [sg. addressee]. *záani wanǫ́bre húðapi* come over and eat [pl. addressee]. *ą́wanǫbre htai* let's all eat. *wanǫ́bre kú* come and eat [sg. addressee]. *wanǫ́bre kúpi* come and eat [pl. addressee]. • N **dinner, supper (meal served at noon or in the evening)** (01/04/95/FH:pc). *hǫpái wanǫ́bre ąkái htai* let's go to the dinner today. *hǫpái wanǫ́bre ąkáða pe* we're going to the dinner today (01/31/95/FH/pc:ok). *hpáze wanǫ́bre ónǫbre ðúwį ókxąži ąhé* I was slow buying groceries for supper (03/10/95/MREI/pc:okc; BE2.123). • N **peyote.** *wanǫ́bre pšé* pounded peyote (01/06/95/FH/pc:ok). *wanǫ́bre štǫ́ka* pounded peyote (01/06/95/FH/pc:ok). *wanǫ́bre htóho* green peyote (01/06/95/FH/pc).

•• LFD 196: *wanǫ́bre* <wa-no^{n}´-bthe> a meal, breakfast, dinner, or supper; nourishment, food, to eat, to dine. *awánǫbre brišta* <a-wo´-no^{n}-bthe bthi-shto^{n}> [expected Mod. Os. form: *awánǫbre bríištą* 'I finished eating'] I have had my dinner. *wanǫ́bre čopa abrį mįkše o* <wa-no^{n}´-bthe dsu-ba a-bthi mi^{n}-kshe o> [sentence-final *o* is not used in Mod. Os.] I have a scant supply of food (01/20/95/FH/pc:ok). LFD 112: *nǫ́bre* <no^{n}´-bthe> [not recognized by Mod. Os. speakers] to eat. [Mod. Os. has *wanǫ́bre* for the meaning 'to eat'. Note that what LF gives as inflectional forms of *nǫ́bre* (immediately following) are in fact forms of *wanǫ́bre,* as seen from the fact that they contain *wa-*.] *awanǫ́bre* <a-wa-no^{n}´-bthe> I eat, I am eating. *waðánǫbre* <wa-tha´-no^{n}-bthe> you eat, you are eating. *ąwą́nǫbra pe* <o^{n}-wo^{n}´-no^{n}-btha i> we eat, we are eating.

••• Cf. *hpáze wanǫ́bre, mįįðóhta wanǫ́bre, ónǫbre.*

wanǫ́brehci N **cafe, restaurant (lit., 'eating house')** (BE2.16; 01/09/95/FH/pc:ok). [Less preferred than *owánǫbrehcí.*]

•• LFD 196: *wanǫbre hci* <wa-no^{n}-bthe-ṭsi> hotel. [Not confirmed as 'hotel'.]

••• Cf. *owánǫbrehcí.*

wanǫ́brenii. N [*wanǫ́bre + níi*] **peyote tea.** *wanǫ́brenii tóa oščé?* is there any peyote tea left? (02/15/95/FH/pc:ok; BE2.78).

wánǫbréoožú (variant: **ónǫbréoožú**). N [*wanǫ́bre + oožú* (note adjusted accent in compound)] **stomach, abdomen** (FH:ok); **pantry** (04/14/95/FH/pc:ok); **food bag** (FH).

•• LFD 196: *wanǫ́bre oži* <wa-no^{n}´-bthe u-zhi> the abdomen, a place for keeping food or provisions, food bag, pantry.

wanǫ́pʔį (variants: **wanǫ́pʔe, wanǫpxį** [FH]). N [*wa-* VAL + *nǫpʔį́*] **necklace, gorget, choker, medallion, medal (part of Osage dance clothing) (lit., 's.t. worn around the neck')** (RB). *šǫmį́hka kahíke mą́ze wanǫ́pʔį wį kʔúpi áape* they gave the pope a medal, they say (02/01/95/FH/pc:ok). *wanǫ́pʔę ǫǫ́* put on the necklace, wear the necklace.

•• RB: <wáh-nó-p'i^{n}> (01/19/95/FH/pc:ok; BE2.19; 02/27/95/FH/pc:ok).

•• LFD 197: *wanǫ́pʔį* <wa-no^{n}´-p̣'i^{n}> necklace. "These were made of shells, nuts of trees, elk teeth [02/27/95/FH/pc:ok]. Pendants were made of the mussel shells also. This is also the name applied to the symbolic neck ornament: gorget." LFD 116: *wakʔo ðe wánǫpʔį htą akšiðe ha* <wa-ḳ'u the wa´-no^{n}-p̣'i^{n} ṭo^{n} a-kshi-the ha> [expected Mod. Os. form: *wakʔó waánǫpʔį htą́ akšíðe*; sentence-final *ha* is not used in Mod. Os.] I caused the woman to wear a [large] necklace.

wáopxa. V [stat., *wá_opxa*] [*wa-* VAL + *kíopxa*] *(intr.)* **find out or understand things.** *waðíopxa* you understand things.

••• Cf. *ðuupxáðe, waðúupxai.*

waǫ́. V [sync. nasal vowel stem, *wa_ǫ́*] [*wa-* VAL + *ǫ́*] **do stuff, do things.** *wamǫ́* I do things. *wažǫ́* you do things.

wápa níhka. N **Delaware (tribe or tribal member).** [Claimed to mean 'water nation' (RB).]

•• RB: <wáh-páh-ni-kiu, wáh-bah-ní-kah> (01/20/95/FH/pc:ok; BE2.30; 03/08/95/PM/pc:ok; ERE).

•• LFD 183: *wápanihki* <Wa´-ba-ni-ḳi> the Osage name for the Delaware Tribe.

wápaace (variant of **wáapaache**).

wapáache. V [sync. *k>p*, *wa_páache* [*wa-* VAL + *paaché*] *(intr.)* **sew, sew things together** (RBn1-MOJ/p50; 03/08/95/FH/pc:okc: *wáa*; BE2.119; 03/09/95/MREI/pc:ok). [Contrast *wáapaache* 'ribbon work'.]

•• LFD 183: *wapáche* <wa-ba´-tse> to sew. *wahpache* <wa-p̣a-tse> I sew. *wašpáche* <wa-shpa´-tse> you sew. *ąwą́pacha pe* <o^{n}-wo^{n}´-ba-tsa i> we sew. *wapáche wakʔo* <wa-ba´-tse-wa-ḳ'o> a sewing woman, a seamstress, one who sews. *wapáche wakʔo wį iðaðe hkǫbra* <wa-ba´-tse wa-ḳ'o wi^{n} i-tha-the ḳo^{n}-btha> I want to find a seamstress.

••• Cf. *mą́ze wépaache.*

wápaache (FH) (variants: **wáapache, wápaace** [PM]). N **ribbon work, sewing** (FH, PM).

•• LFD 183: *wápahce* (or *wápache*) [LF ambiguous] <wa´-ba-ṭse> ribbons.

wapáahi. V [reg.+sync. fortisizing stop stem *_wa_páahi*] [*wa-* VAL + *paahí* (but sometimes used as transitive)] *(trans.)* **pick, choose, or select people [or things?].** [Expected (but unattested) inflectional forms: *waðášpaahi* 'you choose', *wapáahi* 'he chooses', *ąwápaahi* 'we choose'.] *níhka ðǫǫpá awáhpaahi hta mįkše* I am going to choose two men (03/07/95/FH/pc:okc).

•• LFD 87: *níhka ðǫpa awahpáhi hta mįkše* <ni´-ḳa tho^{n}-ba wa-p̣a´-hi ṭa mi^{n}-ke> I choose [rather, 'I will choose'] two men (03/07/95/FH/pc:okc). *wahko ðǫpa ði wapahi o* <wa-ḳu tho^{n}-ba thi wa-ba-hi o> [expected Mod. Os. form: *wakʔó ðǫǫpá wápaahi* 'choose two women' (imperative form); sentence-final *o* is not used in Mod. Os.] you choose two women (03/07/95/FH/pc:okc).

wapáaleze. N [*wa-* VAL + *paa-* + *léze*] **pencil, pen (lit., 'makes marks on stuff by pushing down on').** *wapáaleze wį ąkʔú* give me a pencil or a pen (RBn 10-20).

wápaase (variant: **wápase**). V [sync., *wá_paase*] [*wa-* +*paasé*] *(trans.)* **cut, splice (lit., 'cut something by pushing').** • N **cutting, cut** (04/25/95/PM/pc:ok; FH).

wápaya. N **man's or woman's ornamental pin or brooch** (FH/06/16/01/pc; 03/08/95/FH/pc:ok; BE2.103).

••• *KS wabáyą* safety pin (RR).

wapáleze. N [*wa-* VAL + *páaleze*] **pencil, pen.**

wápaleze. N [*ó-* LOC + *á-* LOC + *páaleze*] **writing (such as a letter)** (FH/09/24/01/pc/ok: synonym of *wáleze*). ["A scratching of some lines" (FH).] *wápaleze škáaye?* did you write something? (FH/09/24/01/pc/prod).

wápaleze káaye. VP [sync. *k>p*, *wápaleze _káaye*] **be a writer (lit., 'make writings')** (FH/09/24/01/pc/prod).

wapáse. N [*wa-* VAL 'stuff' + *páse*] **butcher, one who cuts things up (lit., 'cuts things using a sharp edge').**

wápase (variant of **wápaase**).

wapázike. N **wasp (archaic)** (RB; 03/16/95/JS/pc:ok). [JS prefers *mąąpíaza* to *wapázįke*, which she says is archaic.]

•• LFD 353: *wapázike* <wa-ba´-çi-ge> wasp.

wapą́. V [reg.+sync., *wa_ _pą́*] [*wa-* VAL + *pą́*] *(intr.)* **call, holler for folks, invite people.** *wapą́*

wapą́ (*continued*)
mąðį́ go invite people (04/11/95/LS/pc:ok). *waðášpa nįkšé?* are you inviting? *wáahpą* I invited.

wapą́ waaðǫ́. N **calling songs (sung at the start of the annual war dances, in a fixed order).**

wapéį (variant of **wapį́**).

wapíokaške (variants: **wapúške** [HRE], **wapíokaški**). N [probably *wa-* VAL + *púkaške*] **drop feathers.** [In the *ilǫ́ǫška* dance, the men's dress has drop feathers, or brow feathers, which hang down from the roach to the left side for Hominy dancers and to the right side for Grayhorse dancers (HRE/12/29/01/pc).] *wapíokaške* drop feathers (RBn14-03 unconfirmed; HRE/12/29/01/pc: wapúške only).
••• Cf. *okáške.*

wapį́ (variant: **wapéį**). V [stat., *wa_pį́*] **bleed.** *hpá wapéį akxái* his nose is bleeding (RBn2-MOJ/p35; 01/07/95/FH/pc:ok). • N **blood** (BE2.9; 03/02/95/FH/pc:ok; 01/07/95/FH/pc:prod).
•• LFD 184: *ąwą́pį* <o^n-wo^n´-bi^n> I am bleeding. *waðípį* <wa-thi´-bi^n> you are bleeding. *wapį́* <wa-bi^n´> blood, bleeding (03/02/95/FH/pc:ok). *wapį itxaži* <Wa-bi^n i-ta-zhi> [expected Mod. Os. form: *wapį́ ðiihtą́aži*]. Those-who-do-not-touch-blood, the name of a subgens of the <Ṭsi´-zhu Wa-shta-ge>, the Peacemaker gens.

wapóške ówe. N **wheat, wheat field, wheat crop, harvest** (LS04/28/95/pc:prod).
•• LFD 196: *wamóske owe* <wa-mu´-çke u-we> [expected Mod. Os. form *wapóške ówe; wamóske* is likely an Omaha term] wheat field.

wapúška. N **beads** (BE2.7; 01/06/95/FH/pc:ma).

wapúške (variant of **wapíokaške**).

wapúštaha. V [reg+sync. fortisizing stop stem, *_wa_púštaha*] *(intr.)* **iron, smooth, or press s.t. (e.g., cloth with an iron).** *hǫ́ǫpa ðé awahpúštaha hta mįkše* I'm going to iron all day. *ąwą́puštaha ąkái* we've been ironing.

wasápe (variants: **wasá, wasái**). N **bear (especially black bear).**
•• LFD 185: *wasape* <wa-ça-be> black bear (01/07/95/FH/pc:ok; BE2.7; RB note: black bear). *wasápe ochi* <Wa-ça´-be u-tsi> where bears are plentiful, Bear Creek. *wasape ska* <Wa-ça-be çka> the white bear, a subgens of the <Wa-ça´-be ṭo^n> gens. *wasápe waðǫ* <Wa-ça´-be wa-tho^n> Black Bear Songs.

wasápe íikitali. N [*wasápe* + *ki-* INCEPTIVE + *iitáðe*] **January (lit., 'again time when bears are born').**

wasápe iitáipi. N [*wasápe* + *iitáðe*] **December (lit., 'bears give birth').**

wasápežį. N [*wasápe* + *-žį* 'little'] **bear cub (any species of bear)** (04/13/95/LS/pc); **Little Black Bear (personal name)** (FH/pc). [Name of Henry Petsemoie, who was Frances Holding's maternal uncle, and also of Jess Townsend.]
•• LFD 185: *wasápe hpata* <wa-ça´-be-p̣a-da> cub, bear cub.

wascúuce. ADJ, ADV **slow, pokey, slowly; late, overdue (describing a person** [RB]**).** *wascúuce brįe* I'm slow (04/25/95/FH/pc). *wascúuce ščį́e* you're slow [*ščį́* is an unusual alternate form for *nį́*, 2nd person sg. of *ðį́* 'be'] (04/26/95/FH/pc). *šímižį apa įcé káaɣe éena wáli wascúutape* the girls put on their makeup, which makes them very slow (RBn3-19). *wascúuce ąkáe* we're slow (BE2.123). *íe wascúuce* speak slowly, drawl (FH). *wascúuce nįe* you're late! (FH:08/22/96;04/25/95/PM/pc:ok; 03/10/95/MREI/pc:uk).
•• LFD 331: *wastúce* <wa-çtu´-dse> slow movements. LFD 71: *íe wastuce* <i´-e wa-çtu-dse> to drawl.
••• *QU óstihte* (stative) slow, late, be, to delay (RR).

waséhtą. N **sycamore tree.**

waséhtą xóe. N [*waséhtą* + *xóce*] **Verdigris River (lit., 'gray sycamore')** (RBn22-03; CQc).
•• LFD 351: *waséhtą xoe* <Wa-çe´-ṭo^n xo-e> Verdigris River, Oklahoma.

waséhtąhü. N **sycamore** (RBn22-03, unconfirmed; CQc).

wáseska. N **suitcase, purse, handbag** (BE2.129; 03/14/95/MREI/pc:ok).

wasísi. ADJ **strong, energetic, elastic.** • N **elastic.**

waskúe. N [*wa-* VAL + *skúðe*] **fruit, dessert, any sweet food or sweet sauce** (BE2.51).
•• RB: <wáh-skyu> (01/30/95/FH/pc:prod).
•• LFD 186: *waskíðe* <wa-çki´-the> sauce, fruit, sweet food.

waskúe ðibrúbruɣe (variant: **waskú ðibrúbruɣe**). N **gelatin, Jell-O (lit., 'sweet, shimmering/shaking')** (02/12/95/FH/pc:okc).

waskúe sápe. N **blackberry (lit., 'sweet black fruit')** (FH:4/22/96/tape:ok).

waskúe šką́šką. N [*waskúe* + reduplicated form of *šką́*] **Jell-O, gelatin (lit., 'sweet thing moving')** (FH/11/19/01/pc:ok; BE2.72).

waskúežį. N [*waskúe* + *-žį* 'little'] **cookie (lit., 'small sweet thing')** (FH:4/22/96/tape:ok).

wastą́įke (variant: **staahį́ke**). N **persimmon** (RBn HW13;HRE/12/29/01).

wásueži. ADJ [*wa-* VAL + *kisúðe* + *aží*] **forgetful (lit., 'not remember things').**

wasúhu. ADJ, ADV [*wa-* VAL (?) + *-súhu* 'clean' (root not attested as independent word)] **clean(ly), clear(ly)** (01/09/95/FH/pc:prod). *íe wasúhu* clean talk. *níi wasúhu* clear water. (01/09/95/FH/pc:ok; BE2.19). *íe wasúhu* speak clearly (01/09/95/FH/pc:ok).

•• LFD 186: *wasíhi* <wa-çi´-hi> clean in character, without reproach, free from blame, tidy, neat. *ą́wąsihi* <o^{n}´-wo^{n}-çi-hi> I am neat. *óðisihi* <u´-thi-çi-hi> you are neat. *wasíhi kaγe* <wa-çi´-hi ga-xe> to cleanse, to purify. *wasíhi ahki hpaγe* <wa-çi´-hi a-ḳi p̣a-xe> I cleanse. *wasíhihkiðe* <wa-çi´-hi-ḳi-the> to cleanse oneself.

••• Cf. *taasúhu.*

wasúhuži. ADJ [*wasúhu* + *aží*] **dirty, soiled, unclean.** *žįkážį apa omíže wasúhuži káaγapi ché* the children have dirtied the rug (BE2.31: FH okc). *įįštáxį šímižį wasúhuži wahókʔa* a dirty little white girl (FH/04/14/94, t76b). *haaská wasúhuži ke paahípai, ščúuwasu htai* be sorting the dirty clothes, let's you wash them (FH/11/17/01/pc; 01/20/95/FH/pc:ok).

•• LFD 186: *wasíhi aži* <wa-çi´-hi a-zhi> impure, unclean, dirty, poverty stricken.

wasúutą. N [*wa-* VAL + *súutą*] **vegetable, greens, garden produce (lit., 'ripe stuff')** (02/03/95/FH/pc:ok; RBn2-MOJ/p28). *wasúutą ąkʔú* give me the garden stuff (01/31/95/FH/pc:ok; 05/01/95/LS/pc).

•• RB: <wah-sú-tah>.

wašápe. N [*wa-* + *šápe*] **coal, charcoal.**

wašápe aðį (variant: **wašápe waðį**). N **mourning dance (lit., 'carrying the charcoal', an expression historically used at Osage funerals)** (BE2.90, unconfirmed; PM:uk).

•• LFD 198: *wašápe aðį* <wa-sha´-be a-thi^{n}> carrying the charcoal. "This was a very important part in the formation of a war party. Each warrior was to carry a piece of charcoal in a buckskin pouch with which to blacken his face before attacking the enemy." [Such older terms as *wašápe aðį, wašápe aðį wažówale*, and *wašápe wažówale* are now unknown to most Osages; they were part of the old religion now replaced by the Native American Church and other Christian religions (FH). Early sources such as LF apply these terms to usages followed by war parties and in related ceremonies. In the mid-twentieth century, speakers who knew the terms applied them to usages connected with funerals, as reported by Bristow.]

wašápe aðį wažówale. N [*wašápe* + *aðį* + *wa-* (?) + *wa-* 'them' + *žóle*] **title of two officers chosen to accompany warriors of the two great tribal divisions (lit., 'he who, having charcoal, accompanies them').**

•• LFD 198–99: *wašápe aðį wažowale* <wa-sha´-be a-thi^{n} wa-zho-wa-gthe> the title of the two officers chosen at the ceremonial organization of a war party to accompany the warriors of the two great tribal divisions throughout the great ceremony. "The warriors were called Wa-sha´-be a-thi^{n} because they were to carry with them the dark symbolic charcoal by which each warrior who carries a small pouch of it declares his determination to show no mercy to the foe."

wašápe waðį (variant of **wašápe aðį**).

wašápe wažówale. N **charcoal accompanying them** (RB). *wašápe wažówale* 'charcoal accompanying-them', the name of a dance that messengers, announcers, conducted (BE2.90).

•• LFD 99: "The two men who accompany the two bodies of warriors bear the title [*wažówale* <wa-zho´-wa-gthe>], Accompanying the Warriors."

wašcéðe (variant: **waščéðe**). V [reg., *wašcé_ðe*] [*wa-* VAL + *šcéðe*] *(intr.)* **doctor folks, treat others.** *wašcéðe hkǫ́bra* I want to doctor people.

waší. V [reg., *wa_ší*] *(trans.)* **hire, employ, ask a favor of s.o., prevail upon s.o. to do s.t.; ask s.o. to help out.** *áwaši* I hire him. *awáši* I hire him. *waðáši* you hire him. *wawíši hkǫ́bra* I want [to hire] you to do something for me (RBn10-16; 02/09/95/FH/pc:ok). *ąwą́ši apái* they're hiring me (02/09/95/FH/pc). *ąwą́šipe éci brée* he's/they've asked me to work, so I'm going (03/24/95/PM/pc:ok). *ąwą́šipe oláha brée* he hired me, so I'm going (03/24/95/PM/pc). *Eddie a[w]áši hkǫ́bra mįkšé* I want to ask Eddie to help me (03/24/95/PM/pc:ok; BE2.161). *wawíši* I asked you to help out. *wižį́e awáši hkǫ́bra* I want to get my older brother to help me (01/06/95/FH/pc:okc). *ðée įkše awáši hkǫ́bra* I want that person to help me (01/06/95/FH/pc:prod; BE2.5). *wapáache ą́wašipe* someone asked me to sew (RBn3-41). *wisǫ́ka akxa ąwáši akxa* younger brother is asking me to help (01/06/95/FH/pc:prod). *žą́ą kaasé ąwą́šipe* they asked me or hired me to cut wood (FH:prod, ok). *oohǫ́ ąwą́šipe* they've asked

waší (*continued*)
me to cook [it] (01/06/95/FH/pc:ok). *mąąhí̜ kaasé ąwą́šipe* they've asked me to cut the grass (01/06/95/FH/pc:ok). • N **hired person, worker, employee, hired hand.**
•• LFD 199: *waší* <wa-shi´> to employ one to run on an errand or to do some work; a hireling, a person serving for hire with pay or the equivalent. *waši* <wa-shi> to employ; to ask for services. *awáši* <a-wa´-shi> I employed him. *waðáši* <wa-tha´ shi> you employed him. *wawíši athi* <wa-wi´-shi a-ti> [expected Mod. Os. form: *wawíši achí*] I come to ask for your services. *wawíši hkǫbra* <wa-wi´-shi ḳo^{n}-btha> I wish to secure your services. *wawíši mąži̜* <wa-wi´-shi mo^{n}-zhi^{n}> I do not ask for your services.
••• *OM* same as Osage (LFD 199).
••• Cf. *wawáši.*

wašíži̜. N [*waší* + *-ži̜* 'little'] **hired help, hired worker**.

waší̜ (variant: **ší̜**). • V [uninfl.?] *(intr.)* **be fat, be overweight.** *koe ónǫǫ žišǫ ší tą ší̜ tą koe hpíiži žišǫ ší tą koe péeški ðikǫ́ða htai wáščuye ðáali̜* before you get old and before you get fat and ugly and nobody wants you, you should get married (lit., 'so before you arrive at old-age, before when you are fat and therefore ugly and when nobody would want you, you ought to take a husband'). N **bacon, fat meat, salt pork (of the type cooked with beans)** (01/06/95/FH/pc: prod). *wiži̜ke, waší̜ toe šcúwi̜?* son, did you buy some bacon? (BE2.6; RBn1-18). *waší̜ hpáata žóle* bacon and eggs (RBn12-05).
•• RB: <wah-shí^{n}, shi^{n}> (01/23/95/FH/pc:ok; BE2.45).
•• LFD 199: *waší̜* <wa-shi^{n}´> fat meat, meat with very little lean.

waší̜haa. N [*waší̜* + *háa*] **Baconrind (personal name)** (01/06/95/FH/pc:prod; BE2.6). [Baconrind was a historic Osage leader.]

wašóše. V, ADJ [stat., *wa_šóše*] **(be) brave** (FH). *wašóše achí nąąží̜* name of a solo dance by one who has been in a war (lit., 'one who is brave arrives here and stands') (RB2:90).
•• LFD 237: *wašóše* <wa-sho´-she> brave (to be), courageous, dauntless, brave, gallant. LFD 199: *ąwąšoše* <o^{n}-wo^{n}-sho-she> I am courageous. *waðišóše* <wa-thi-sho´-she> you are courageous. *wawašóša pe* <wa-wa-sho´-sha i> we are courageous.

wašóše achí nąąží̜. N **name of a solo dance by one who has been in a war (lit., approximately: 'a brave one comes and stands before us')** (RB2:90).

waštáke. ADJ [presumably contains *štáke*] **gentle.** *hcížo waštáke* Gentle Eagle, a name. *ók?ą waštáke akxa* he's got gentle ways (RBn17-p03).

watáabrą. N [*wa-* VAL + *táabrą*] **smell of s.t. cooking** (04/06/95/LS/pc:ok). *watáabrą ðáali̜* the cooking smells good (lit., 'the cooking smell is good').
•• LFD 186: *watábrą ðali̜* <wa-da´-btho^{n} tha-gthi^{n}> a savory smell of things cooking.

watáahą. N [*wa-* VAL + *táa+* *-hą*] **light bread, leavened wheat bread (as opposed to cornbread) (lit., 'something that rises with heat')** (01/07/95/FH/pc:ok).

watáažoe. N [*wa-* VAL + *táa+* *žoe* (not otherwise attested)] **hominy (any kind, cracked or not)** (04/11/95/LS/pc:ok; t14a-p4; 02/09/95/FH/pc:ok). *watáažoe oohǫ́ apai* they're cooking hominy (BE2.67; FH/09/22/01/pc). *watáažoe táapuze mi̜kšé* I'm drying corn for hominy.
•• LFD 187: *watážoe* <wa-da´-zhu-e> hominy.

watástosta (variants: **watástoe** [RB], **watáščoče** [PM]). N **pecan nut** (BE2.102). *watástosta žą́ą* pecan wood. *watástoe paahí̜ toe ąkái hce* let's go pick pecans (RBn12-05).
•• RB: <wah-táh-sto-stah, wah-táh-stoi> (03/07/95/PM/pc:okc) .
••• *QU watástohta* pecan (nut) (RR).

watástostahú. N [*watástosta* + *hú*] **pecan tree** (03/07/95/PM/pc:ok).
•• LFD 200: *wahtástosta hu* <wa-ṭa´-ço-çta hiu> the pecan (*Hicoria pecan*).
••• *QU watástohtá hi* pecan tree (RR).

watáščoče (variant of **watástosta**).

watkxázu, watkxą́zu (variants of **watxázu**).

watkxą́, wátkxą (variants of **watxą́**).

watǫ́e, watǫ́ę, watǫ́i̜ (variants of **watǫ́pe**).

watǫ́e scee (variant: **watǫ́i̜ scee**). V [uninfl.] [*watǫ́pe* + *scéce*] *(intr.)* **stare (at people, not at inanimate things)** (03/14/95/FH/pc:ok). *watǫ́i̜ scee ékiǫ ði̜ká!* don't stare! (lit., 'staring, don't do that!') (RBn1-25). *watóe scee akxa* they are staring at people. *watǫ́e scee ąði̜kšé* we [two] are staring [at folks].

watǫ́ehci. N [*watǫ́pe* + *hcí*] **store, shop, place where things are exhibited (lit., 'house in which to look at things').** *Johna táatą íiðe ðe watǫ́ehci ce?* what did John see in the store?

watǫ́i̜ scee (variant of **watǫ́e scee**).

watǫ́ǫžu. N [presumably *watǫ́e* + *oožú*] **store, trading house.**

watǫ́pe (variants: **watǫ́į, watǫ́ę, watǫ́e**). v [conjug. unknown] [wa- VAL + *tǫ́pe*] *(intr.)* **see or watch people or events, look on at an event (e.g., a dance** [RB]**)** (03/02/95/FH/pc:okc). *waachí watǫ́į ąkái ðe* we are going to see the dance (03/02/95/FH/pc; BE2.97). *waachíe watǫ́į šcée ną hta akxai* you're always going to go to [to watch] dances (MSB-9-3-82). *waachí watǫ́e* watch the dances. N **spectators, onlookers, audience, public** (03/14/95/FH/pc:ok; BE2.125).
 •• LFD 187: *watǫ́pe* <wa-do^{n}´-be> the act of seeing, applied to a runner in search of buffalo.
 ••• Cf. *wahtǫ́pe.*

watxázu (variants: **wakxázu, watkxázu, watkxą́zu**). N **dried corn, preparation of dried corn soup** (LS; FH/09/11/01/pc:ok; RBn1-14). [Some families dried corn on the ear, tying it up with twine to hang it a cob at a time. The children would be in charge of keeping the flies off during the day, and the ears would be taken inside at night if it had been drying outside on tables. If hanging on a screened-in porch, it would be left about three days to dry.]

watxą́ (variants: **watkxą́, wakxą́, wátxą, wátkxą**). N **pumpkin.** *hką́ącezi akxa watkxą́ kǫzékǫ akxai* the orange is just like the pumpkin (FH:4/24/96/tape:prod). • **squash (the vegetable).**
 •• RB: <wah-txáh^{n}, wah-kxáh> (BE2.108; PM/7/7/94; FH: *wakxą́*; 03/14/95/FH/pc:okc).
 •• LFD 204: *watxą́* <wa-to^{n}´> pumpkin, squash, or any of the vegetables of that family. LFD 205: *watxą́ hkące olą* <wa-to^{n}´ ko^{n}-dse u-gtho^{n}> pumpkin pie.

watxą́ púze (variant: **watkxą́ púze**). N **dried squash.**

wawáðiiski (variant of **waðíiski**).

wáwalį. v [stat. *ki*-del, *wá_walį*] [*wa-* VAL + *kíwalį*] *(intr.)* **be a stingy person, be stingy (lit., 'stingy with stuff').** *wą́ąwalį, wáawalį* [from *wa-ą́-walį*] I'm stingy. *waðíwalį* you're stingy. *wakíwalį ~ wáwalį* he's stingy. *wá[w]awalį* we're stingy. *wáawali mįkšé* I'm really stingy (04/26/95/FH/pc:okc). *John akxa wáli wawálipe, John akxa wáli walípe* John is really a stingy person (04/26/95/FH/pc:okc; BE2.128). *hką́ącezi záani ðuuzí akxái wáli wawálį akxai* she took all the oranges, she's really stingy (04/26/95/FH/pc).

wawáši. v [presumed reg., *wa_waši*] [*wa-* VAL + *waší*] *(intr.)* **hire or employ folks to work.** *áwawaší hkǫ́bra* I want to ask someone to work (03/24/95/PM/pc:ok).

wawéeðe. v [reg., *wawée_ðe*] [*wa-* VAL + *wa-* VAL + *íiðe*] *(intr.)* **see things (as in a dream or hallucination), see multiple things or persons one after another.** *hą́ące wawéeaðe* last night I saw something in a dream (RBn12-10). *wawéeða[ð]e nįkšé?* are you seeing things? (FH/6/16/95; FH/1/17/96:prod). • **see, have normal eyesight.** *wawéeðe hǫ́ǫži brį́* I see poorly (RB). *wawéeðe mąžíe įįštóolą ðįké* I can't see without my glasses (RB). *wawéeðe hǫ́ǫži nį́* you see poorly (RB). *wawéeðe hǫ́ǫžipe* she sees poorly (RB). *wawéeðe hǫ́ǫži ąðé* we [two] see poorly (RB). • N **vision, sight, seeing.**

wawéešce. N [*wa-* VAL + *wa-* VAL + *iišcéwai*] **shame** (04/06/95/LS/pc:ok).
 •• LFD 207: *wawéšce* <wa-we´-shtse> ignominy, shame.

wawékˀo. v, N [reg., *wawé_kˀo*] [*wa-* VAL + *wa-* VAL + *íkˀo*] *(intr.)* **belch, burp.** *wawéakˀoe* I belched. *wawéðakˀoe* you belched. *wawéąkˀope* we belched.

wawépahǫ. v [sync. *k>p, wawé_pahǫ*] [*wa-* VAL + *wa-* VAL + *ípahǫ*] *(intr.)* **be a witness, give testimony** (BE2.159; 03/16/95/MREI/pc:uk). • N **witness.** *wawépaho aní šǫ́ ąhé* I'm a witness and I'm still living (RB note: as in a courtroom; 04/06/95/LS/pc:ok).
 •• LFD 206: *wawépahǫ* <wa-we´-ba-ho^{n}> a deponent, a witness; to give testimony. *wawéhpahǫ* <wa-we´-p̣a-ho^{n}> I was a witness. *wawéšpahǫ* <wa-we´-shpa-ho^{n}> you were a witness. *wawépahǫ ǫlake che hǫži hpaye* <wa-we´-ba-ho^{n} o^{n}-gtha-ge tse ho^{n}-zhi p̣a-xe> I gave poor testimony [expected Mod. Os. phrasing: *wawépahǫ hǫ́ǫži hpáaye* 'I did badly as a witness'].

wawíhǫįpi. v [*wi-* '1st person sg. subject–2nd person pl. object' + *wahǫ́į* 'address folks with respect, address as friends and relatives' + *api* 'plural'] **I address you as friends and relatives.** [A very common expression in opening Osage speeches.]

wawį́kšaži. N [*wawį́kše + aží*] **s.o. who doesn't keep his/her word, disloyal person.** • ADJ **unfaithful, untruthful.** *níhkaši wawį́kšapažíe* she's an untruthful person (RB:MSB).

wawį́kše. ADJ [*wa-* VAL + *wį́kše*] **truthful.** *níhka wawį́kšape* he's a truthful person (MSB/2-24-83; FH:prod).

waxáka. N [*wa-* VAL + *xáka*] **stickers, thorns, briars, cocklebburs.** *waxáka olį́į* dwell in the thorns [an infinitive or imperative form].

waxáka (*continued*)
• **thorny, burry, prickly** (FH:5/01/96/tape,ok). *waxákahtóho* a certain plant or plants called green briar (04/06/95/LS/pc:ok).

•• JOD (slip file): *waxáka žį́a* <wa-qa´-k̥a çi^{n} ´-a> small thorns which grow on plants resembling grass.

•• LFD 207: *waxáka* <wa-xa´-ga> any plant that has prickly spines, like the sand bur, cactus, cocklebur, prick-ash. *waxákahtoho* <wa-xa´-ga-ṭu-hu> a green briar.

waxákaolį́į. N [*waxáka* + *olį́į*] **Pawhuska district, Pawhuska Osages (lit., 'dwelling in the thorns' or 'living in the cockleberry land')** (FH/06/16/01/pc). *waxákaolį́į* Pawhuska Osages (03/06/95/FH/pc:ok; BE2.101).

•• LFD 207: *waxákaolį* <Wa-xa´-ga-u-gthi^{n}> Dwellers-in-the-Thorny Thicket. "This was the name by which a group became known who fled from the overflowing banks and were caught in a thicket of thorny trees and bushes. They live in Pawhuska, Okla."

waxópe (variants: **wáxope** [RB], **waxópi** [HRE]) N [*wa-* VAL + *xópe*] **medicine bundle, sacred object, things consecrated or honored** (02/24/95/FH/pc:ok). *waxópe wanáše* take care of the bundle (RBn 10-16).

•• RB: <wáh-xo-peh> (BE2.87).

•• LFD 208: *waxópe* <wa-xo´-be> a talisman, or something worn about the person to ward off evil; anything consecrated for ceremonial use. "A portable symbol, like the hawk, that represents or symbolizes the courage of a warrior." *waxópe* <wa-xo´-be> a whistle used as a sacred symbol after victory (unconfirmed, 02/24/95/FH/pc:uk as 'whistle'). *waxópe kaɣe* <wa-xo´-be ga-xe> to make sacred, to consecrate some object to religious use. *waxópe škaɣe* <wa-xo´-be shka-xe> you consecrated it. *waxópe ąkaɣa pe* <wa-xo´-be o^{n}-ga-xa i> we consecrated it.

waxpáðį (variants: **waxpáį, waxpéį**). ADJ **poor, poverty stricken.** *níhkašika apa waxpáðįpe* the people are poverty stricken (FH/pc). *waxpéį ąkái, ókʔu ąðúucʔake še nąąhtąhtąą oðúucʔake wį́* we're too poor to feed that lazy donkey (lit., 'we are poor, we couldn't feed that donkey who was lazy') (RBn10-2:MOJ/79). • **pitiful, humble, long-suffering (as the victim of pain, poverty, or ill fortune).** *ąwáxpaðį* I'm pitiful. *waxpáðį ną ahkílaipi* carry yourself humbly [to two or more people] (RB). *waxpáðį ąnąbra xcį* I'm pitiful with suffering (lit., 'I've had my fill of being pitiful') (RBn1-56; FH/09/23/01/pc:ok). *waxpéį įðąbrą* I've had enough of being pitiful (12/30/94/FH/pc:ok).

•• LFD 108: *níhkašika apa waxpaðį pi aða* <ni´-k̥a-shi-ga a-ba wa-xpa-thi^{n} bi a-tha> [expected Mod. Os. form: *níhkašika apa waxpaðįpe*] the people are poverty stricken.

wáxta. N **worm, caterpillar.**

wazóeðe. V [reg., *wazóe_ðe*] [*wa-* '1st pl. patient' + *kízo* + *ðe* CAU] *(trans.)* **make s.o. enjoy.** *wazóewa[ð]ape* we [two or more] had a good time (lit., 'they made us enjoy ourselves') (FH/08/01/01/pc).

wazóekšiðe (variant: **wazóokšiðe**). V [reg., *wazóe_kšiðe*] [*wa-* '3rd pl. patient' + *kízo* + *kšíðe*] *(trans.)* **make s.o. enjoy (s.t.), show s.o. a good time, make s.o. have a good time.** *wazóowakšíe* make them have a good time, show them a good time (FH/08/01/01/pc).

wažá (variant: **wažáže**). V [reg., *wa_žá*] [presumably contains *wa-* VAL but is used as transitive] *(trans.)* **doubt.** *áwaža* I doubt it, I don't believe it (04/25/95/PM/pc:okc; 01/20/95/ERE/pc:ok; 04/13/95/FH/pc:ok; ERE prod: *awáža*). *wáðaža?* are you doubting it? (04/13/95/FH/pc). *ąwážaže* he doubts me (04/25/95/PM/pct). *awážažai eekǫ́ žažį́ ahí* I doubt it and he doesn't believe it (RB). *wáža apai* he doubts it (RB; CQc).

•• LFD 209: *wažá* <wa-zha´> to disbelieve, to discredit, to doubt the statement, to express doubt. *awáža* <a-wa´-zha> I discredit it. *waðáža* <wa-tha´-zha> you discredit it. *ąwą́žape* <o^{n}-wo^{n}´-zha i> we discredit it. *wawíža* <wa-wi´-zha> I expressed doubt as to your statement. LFD 17 (unconfirmed): *éža* <e´-zha> I doubt his statement. *ðeža* <the-zha> you doubt his statement. *kíža* <gi´-zha> they doubt his statement (01/20/95/ERE/pc:uk, unconfirmed). [LF's forms *éža* 'I doubt' and *ðeža* 'you doubt' are unusual and probably incorrect.]

••• *KS gíža* (JOD) doubt someone's word (RR), *wagíža* (JOD), *wagíža* ~ *waagíža* doubt one's own (child, etc.) (RR).

wažáe wéhkilį (variant of **wažáže wéhkilį**).

wažáihci (variant: **wažáehci**). N [*wažáže* + *hcí*] **tipi (lit., 'Osage house')** (MREI; 03/16/95/FH/pc:ok; RBn2-MOJ/p2); **long house covered with brush or canvas (like the houses Osages used to live in)** (04/28/95/LS/pc:ok; BE2.158; MREI); **tent, arbor** (RB; FH).

wažáwa. N **dance.** [A rare word; may be Ponca (RB).]

wažáxį. N **Josephine Walker's name, Myrtle Oberly Jones's name** (RB).

wažáže (variant: **wažáži**). ADJ, N **Osage (tribe, tribal member, or language).** *wažáže níhkaši* an Osage person. *háakǫ wažáže?* how much Osage are you? (this question is considered impolite). *wažái wéhkilį* dress in Osage clothes (03/03/95/FH/pc:ok; BE2.99). *wažáže nįpe* you Osages (lit., 'those of you who are Osage'). *wažáže huuwáli íhpahǫ* I know a lot of Osages (RBn10-2).

•• RB: <wah-zháh-zhi> (03/03/95/FH/pc:ok).

•• LFD 209–10: : *wažáže* <Wa-zha´-zhe> name of the Osage Tribe, corrupted by the French to Osage. The name of the subdivision which refers to the water portion of the earth. It is also a personal name belonging to the <Wa-ṭse-ṭsi> [Mod. Os.: *wahcéhci*] or <P̣oⁿ-ḳa Wa-shta-ge> [Mod. Os.: *hpǫ́hka waštáke*] gens. "In the mythical story of this gens the people came from the stars to the earth. In their wanderings they came suddenly upon a man who stood in the midst of the waters that rushed noisily over the rocks. The man leading the way turned around and said to his followers: 'Here stands Wa-zha´-zhe, a person who has made the waters of the earth his body.' . . . The meaning of the name is obscure. Even some of the older Osage fail to give satisfactory interpretation of the name."

wažáže (variant of **wažá**).

wažáže wéhkilį (variants: **wažáe wéhkilį, wažáže óhkilį**). N **Osage clothes** (RB, FH, ERE).

wažážeíe. N [*wažáže* + *íe*] **Osage language** (03/03/95/FH/pc:ok).

wažážemįįhcexį. N [*wažáže* + *mįįhcéxi*] **name for a first daughter (possible interpretations are 'precious Osage female', 'difficult Osage woman', 'stout Osage daughter', 'sacred Osage sun').** [Name of Armeda Lookout (RB), Robin Bristow (RB), and Priscilla Iba.]

wažáži (variant of **wažáže**).

wažį́. N [*wa-* VAL + *ažį́*] **will, mind, idea.**

•• LFD 211 (unconfirmed): *wažį wihta hpaye* <wa-zhiⁿ´ wi-ṭa p̣a-xe> I did it of my own free will, it was my own idea.

wažį hpíiži. ADJ **enraged, mad (angry).**

••• Cf. *óžį hpíiži.*

wažį hpíiži káaye. VP [sync. *k*>*p*, *wažį hpíiži _káaye*] *(trans.)* **make a person angry, enrage s.o.**

•• LFD 211: *wažį hpiži kaye* <wa-zhiⁿ´ p̣i-zhi ga-xe> to enrage a person. (LF here provides several inflected forms that are not from *wažį hpíiži káaye*, but rather are from a verb *ðuuwážįhpíižį* or *ðiiwážįhpíižį* 'make angry' [not attested in Mod. Os.]: e.g., *bríwažį hpiži* <bthi´-wa-zhiⁿ p̣i-zhi> I angered him.)

wažį ihta. ADVP, ADJP **determinedly, determined** (RB); **of his/her own free will.**

•• LFD 211: *wažį ihta* <wa-zhiⁿ´ i-ṭa> of one's own free will and accord.

wažįhtąą. N [*wažį́ka* + *htą́ka*] **hawk (lit., 'large bird')** (RBn14-13).

wažį́ka. N **bird.** *wažį́kake wáðaawa* count the [scattered] birds (BE2.8; 01/07/95/FH/pc:ok). *wažį́ka hį́į* bird feathers. *wažį́ka šáake* bird claws, talons. *wažį́ka ški wahúį nąpe* even birds migrate. *wažį́ka hpažúuce* red-headed woodpecker. *wažį́ka sápe* the blackbird.

•• LFD 210: *wažį́ka* <wa-zhiⁿ´-ga> any bird or fowl. [But note *míya* 'duck, goose, any large bird or fowl'.]

wažį́kaíe. N [*wažį́ka* + *íe*] **parrot, macaw (any bird that can be taught to "speak").** *wažį́ka íe mǫ́šǫ* parrot feathers (01/24/95/FH/pc:ma; BE2.45).

wažį́žue. N [*wažį́ka* + *žúuce*] **cardinal (the bird; lit., 'red bird').**

wažóla (variant: **wažóole** [PM]). N **Oto (tribe or tribal member).**

•• RB: <wah-zhó-d-?-lah> (BE2.99; RBn23-11; 03/03/95/FH/pc:ok).

•• LFD 211: *wažóla* <Wa-zho´-xtha> a name given to the Oto Tribe.

wážu (variant of **oážu**).

wažúpe. N **marrow** (FH:4/22/96/tape:prod; 10/13/96).

••• *QU wahí žiwe* marrow (RR); *KS wažű́be* (JOD), *-žű´we* marrow, a long bone in the shin (RR).

wąkóižį, wąkǫ́įžį (variants of **wąkǫ́ǫžį**).

wąkǫ́ǫ. ADV **quickly.** *wąkǫ́ǫ alí hta mįkšé* I'll be back quickly (01/06/95/FH/pc:prod).

•• LFD 313: *wąkǫ* <woⁿ-goⁿ> I'll come right back quickly.

wąkǫ́ǫžį (variants: **wąkǫ́įžį, wąkóižį**). ADV [*wąkǫ́ǫ* + *-žį* 'little'] **right away, immediately.** *wąkóižį alí hta mįkšé* I'll come right back (RBn3-21).

wé-. PREFIX [The prefixes *wa-* VAL (or in some cases '1st pl. object' or '3rd pl. object') + *í-* LOC regularly combine to form *we-*. This formation is

wé- (*continued*)
regularly seen in the ordinal numerals and in several names of tools.]
••• Cf. *wéðaabrį, wéðį, wéðǫǫpa, wéðušupe, wesáhtą, wešáhpe, wétoopa.*

wéapazo (variants: **weápazo, wepázo**). N [*wa-* VAL + *í-* LOC + *ápazo*] **index finger, pointing finger (lit., 'with which to point at things').**
••• Cf. *šáake opázo.*

wécʔa. N **snake, serpent, viper.** *íinǫǫhpapai, wécʔa ochíe* be careful, there are lots of snakes (BE2.124; 03/13/95/FH/pc:okc).
•• LFD 215: *wécʔa* <we´-ṭs'a> reptile, snake. *wécʔa hcihciži* <we´-ṭs'a ṭsi-ṭsi-zhi> snake brittle, name given to the glass snake by the Osage. *wécʔa niciwaǫ* <we´-ṭs'a ni-dsi-wa-o^{n}> water snake. *wécʔa hpahta žįka* <we´-ṭs'a p̣a-ṭa zhi^{n}-ga> [expected Mod. Os. form: *wécʔa hpáatažį*] a young snake [that has] just hatched. *wécʔa sape* <we´-ṭs'a ça-be> black snake.

wéðaabrį (variant: **weðáabrį**). ADJ [*wé-* PREFIX + *ðáabrį*] **third, number three.**
•• RB: <weh-tháh-bri^{n}> (03/20/95/FH/pc:ok; BE2.139).
•• LFD 214: *wéðabrį* <we´-tha-bthi^{n}> the third.

wéðaawa. V [*wé_ðaawa*] [*wa-* VAL + *í-* LOC + *ðaawá*] *(trans.)* **count or measure s.t. with.** *žą́ą wéðaawa* measuring stick (lit., 'measure stuff using wood') (05/02/95/LS/pc:prod).

wéðahpe. V [reg.-*iða, wéð_ahpe*] [*wa-* VAL + *iðáhpe* (but sometimes used as transitive)] *(intr., trans.)* **wait for folks.** *wawé[ð]ahpi akxai* he's waiting for them (FH). *wéąðahpe ąkakxái* we were waiting for people (FH).

wéðišipe (variant of **wéðušupe**).

wéðį. N [presumably *wé-* PREFIX + *oðįįke*] **rope, cord (lit., 'with which to hold stuff').**

wéðǫǫpa (variant: **weðǫ́ǫpa**). ADJ [*wé-* PREFIX + *ðǫǫpá*] **second, number two.** *hpéece íhta weðǫ́ǫpa* second fireman in peyote meeting (05/02/95/LS/pc:ok; BE2.117). *hǫ́ǫpa wéðǫǫpa* Tuesday (lit., 'second day') (RB).
•• LFD 215: *wéðǫpa* <we´-tho^{n}-ba> the second: from a ritual.

wéðuɣe (variant: **wéuɣe**). V [sync., *wé_ðuɣe*] *(intr.)* **get married, follow a man as his wife, take a husband, marry (said of a woman)** (02/24/95/FH/pc:ok). *wéðuɣe? wéšcuɣe?* did you marry? did you get married? [asking a woman] (02/24/95/FH/pc). *wéščuɣe hta ðąiší aape* they said you were going to get married. *hatkxą́ci wéščuɣe?* when did you get married? • N **wedding.** *Carolyn apa wéðuɣe aðeé hta apá apai* Carolyn is going to a wedding [they say] (02/27/95/JS/pc).
•• RB: <wéh-u-xeh> (02/24/95/FH/pc:okc).
••• Cf. *áðuɣe, íðuɣe, wáðuɣe.*

wéðuɣekíðe (variant: **wéuɣekiðe**). V [reg., *wéðuɣe_kíðe*] [*wéðuɣe* + *kíðe*] *(trans.)* **make one's own relative take a husband, marry off a female relative (e.g., marry off one's daughter).** *wéðuɣekíðe* they made her [the young woman who was their own] marry (FH/prod). *šímižį wéuɣekí[ð]e akxai, wáðohta hta ną* they married their girl off so she would be proper, respectable (RBn22-17).

wéðušupe (variants: **wéðišipe, wéušupe**). N [*wé-* PREFIX + *ðuušúpe*] **key (lit., 'with which to open').** [Takes 'lying down' positional article *kše.*] *wéðušupe ašč́į ðaašé?* have you got the key? (BE2.73). *wéðišipe kše ąwą́xpaðe mįkše* I lost my door key (02/14/95/FH/pc:okc).
•• RB: <weh-ú-shu-peh> (02/14/95/FH/pc:okc).
•• LFD 215: *wéðišipe* <we´-thi-shi-be> a key. *wéðišipe kše ąwą́xpaðe mįkše o* <we´-thi-shi-be ke o^{n}-wo^{n}-xpa-the mi^{n}-kshe o> [sentence-final *o* is not used in Mod. Os.] I lost my door key.

wéðuwį. V [sync., *wé_ðuwį*] [*wa-* VAL + *íðuwį*, but used as transitive] *(trans.)* **sell s.t. by bartering for other stuff.** *wébruwį mįkšé* I'm selling it. *wébruwį* I sold it. *haxį́ wébruwį* I sold the blanket *htóožu tóa wéščuwį?* did you sell any meat pies? (RB). *htóožu wéðuwį akxái* he or she is selling meat pies (BE2.118). *htóožu wéðuwį kǫ́ða apai ąžį oðóóai hce ée apai* they want to sell meat pies but they want you to oversee it [they're saying] (FH:prod). *wéðuwį iká* don't sell it (04/26/95/LS/pc:ok). *ðúwį iká, wéðuwį!* don't buy it, sell it! (04/26/95/LS/pc:ok). • **buy or acquire stuff with s.t.** *haxį́ wébruwį* I bought it [some stuff] with a blanket (or 'I traded the blankets for them'). *wéðuwį ðįké atxą́he* I have nothing to buy [stuff] with (lit., 'I am without anything to exchange stuff for') (RBn1-58).
•• RB: <wéh-thu-wi^{n}> (03/08/95/MREI/pc:ok).
•• LFD 215: *wéðiwį* <we´-thi-wi^{n}> to sell or to purchase. *wébriwį* <we´-bthi-wi^{n}> I sell. *wésciwį* <we´-stsi-wi^{n}> you sell. *wéðiwį ðištą* <we´-thi-wi^{n} thi-shto^{n}> sold. *nihkašika akxa hkawa ðǫpa ąðiwį akxa o* <ni-ḳa-shi-ga a-ka ḳa-wa tho^{n}-ba o^{n}-thi-wi^{n} a-ka o> [expected Mod. Os. form: *níhkašika akxa hkáwa ðǫǫpá ąðúwį akxa* 'the man has bought two horses from me'; sentence-

final *o* is not used in Mod. Os.] I sold two horses to the man. *hci che webriwį brištą ha* <ṭsi tse we-bthi-win bthi-shton ha> [expected Mod. Os. form: *hcí che wébruwį bríištą* 'I finished selling the (standing) house'; sentence-final *ha* is not used in Mod. Os.] I sold the house. LFD 116: *nąníhi weðiwį* <non-ni´-hi we-thi-win> a tobacconist, one who deals in tobacco.

wéehkile. N [*wa-* + *hkik-* RECIP + *íiðe*] **visit, means to see each other.**

wéehlihpíiži (variant: **wéelihpíiži**). ADJ, V [uninfl.] *(intr.)* **(be) extremely drunk (lit., 'bad head'), very badly inebriated, very drunk, "crazy" drunk.** *wéehli hpíiži akxa* he's crazy drunk (WF/12/30/01:prod).

wéeli. N **head (human or animal)** (BE2.65, CQc; FH:ok/pc). *wéeli hóxpe záani ąwážu mįkšé* I have a head cold (lit., 'a head cold is all through me') (01/19/95/FH/pc:uk; BE2.21).

•• RB: <wéh-'l-?-din>

•• LFD 215: *wéðili* <we´-thi-xthi> the head of a man or of an animal.

wéelihpíiži (variant of **wéehlihpíiži**).

wéelihtąą (variant: **wéelįhtąą**). N **cabbage (lit., 'big head')** (01/09/95/FH/pc:ok; BE2.16; 01/09/95/FH/pc:ok, *htąą*).

•• LFD 215: *wéðili htąka* <we´-thi-xthi ṭon-ga> big head: cabbage.

wéelišta. N, ADJ [*wéeli* + *štáha*] **bald head, bald headed** (BE2.6; FH: preferable to *hpeeštá;* 04/07/95/PM/pc:ok).

wéenacehkiðe (variant of **wéenącehkiðe**).

wéeną (variant: **wéena**). V [reg., *wée_ną*] *(intr.)* **be thankful, grateful, or appreciative, be glad.** *wéewinai ąkxą́he* I'm thankful to you (03/16/95/FH/pc:ok). *wéeana ąkxą́he* I'm thankful (03/16/95/FH/pc). *wéena íe iiðáe hkǫ́bra* I want to say something in appreciation (lit., 'I want to say grateful words') (03/16/95/FH/pc; BE2.136). *wéewina* I am grateful to you. *wéeana mįkšé záani ðachípe* I'm glad you all came (BE2.60). *wéenąpi* they're thankful (02/03/95/FH/pc:prod orig). • *(trans.)* **be thankful or grateful for, be appreciative of, be glad about.** *ąną́ðapi che wéeąna mįkše* I'm glad you all saw me (FH/07/27/95/pc:prod; LS/07/28/9?pc:ok). *tąhé paašé wéeąna mįkšé* I'm glad you [pl.] are well (FH:7/27/95:prod). *žįkážį nakxą́še wéewina akxą́he, ilǫ́įhpa waachí štǫ́pape* I want to thank you children for watching my son dance. *hǫ́ǫpa ðé wéena akxai ðe níhkaši tóa áðixǫpape, hpáðį wéhkili íwehkili į kšíɣape* she's grateful today because they honored her, they dressed her in Kiowa clothes (lit., 'today she's grateful to the people that honored her by having her dress with Kiowa clothes') (RBn23-17; CQc). *wéewinai, mąąhí wíhta ðákaase* thank you for cutting my grass (01/14/95/FH/pc:prod; BE2.28).

wéenące. V [reg., *wée_nące*] [presumably *wa-* VAL + *ínące* 'satisfied with food' (*ínące* appears in LFD 76, but is not attested not in Mod. Os.)] *(intr.)* **be full, filled; have one's hunger sated.** [According to some, this is a way for a male speaker to express appreciation to the host at a dinner (RB); according to others, both men and women use this expression (FH) (01/25/95/FH/pc:okc).] *weeą́nące* I'm full (RBN3-21; FH:okc). *weeðánące* are you full? (BE2.51).

•• LFD 214: *wénące* <we´-non-dse> to feed [rather, 'eat'] until filled to satisfaction. *weánące* <we-a´-non-dse> I am satisfied (my hunger [is satisfied]). *weðánące* <we-tha´-non-dse> you are satisfied (your hunger [is satisfied]). *wénąte* <we´-non-de> gratified, satiated. [LFD lists *wénąte* <we´-non-de> as a separate word, but it is probably an error for *wénące* <we´-non-dse>.] LFD 76 (unconfirmed): *ínące* <i´ -non-dse> to be full and satisfied with food.

wéenącehkiðe (variant: **wéenacehkiðe**). V [reg.+reg., *wée_nące_hkiðe*] [*wéenące* + *hkíðe* CAU (reflexive form)] *(intr.)* **cause oneself to be satiated with food, satisfy oneself with food, make oneself full.** *pąąšcéka bráache weeą́nącheahkí[ð]e hta mįkšé* I will eat strawberries until I'm satiated (RBn18-02; CQc).

wéetaðaži. ADJ [*wéetaðe* + *aží*] **barren, childless.**

•• LFD 212: *wétaðaži* <we´-da-tha-zhi> without a child, barren, childless.

wéetaðe (variant: **wéetai**). V [reg., *wée_taðe*] [*wa-* VAL +*íitaðe*] *(intr.)* **give birth, have a baby** (01/31/95/FH/pc:ok). *wéeta[ð]ape* she had a baby (FH:4/18/96/tape; BE2.55). *wéeðatai?* did you give birth? • N **childbirth, birth** (01/31/95/FH/pc:ok).

•• LFD 212: *wétaðe* <we´-da-the> childbirth, the act of giving birth to a child. *wétaaðe* <we´-da-a-the> I gave birth to a child. *wétaðaðe* <we´-da-tha-the> you gave birth to a child. [Note contrast between LF *wéta_ðe* and Mod. Os. *wée_taðe*.]

••• *OM* same as Osage (LFD 212).

wéetaha. N **lap (part of the body)** (RBn22-09, unconfirmed).

wéetai (variant of **wéetaðe**).

wéewiną (variant: **wéewina**). INTERJ [*wi-* '1st person sg. subject–2nd person object' + *wéeną*] **thank you (lit., 'I'm grateful to you')** (BE2.136; 03/16/95/FH/pc:ok). [Not used as frequently as 'thank you' in English.]

wéhice. ADV **far, far away, from afar, a long way** (BE2.44; FH). *wéhice pši* I went far away (03/02/95/FH/pc:ok). *wéhice pšíeðe* I went far away (01/23/95/FH/pc:prod). *alée, wéhice achíe* I'm going, I have a long way to go (lit., 'I'm returning there, from far away I arrived here'). *wéhice ší* you went far away (01/23/95/FH/pc:ok; 03/02/95/FH/pc:ok). *tóe wéhice ðachípe* some of you have come from far off (01/23/95/FH/pc:ok:prod). *wéhice hí áape hcí káaɣe káaši ðí áape* she went a long way and took a long time to build her nest [they said] (RBn19-03). *wéhice ąkáchie* we [two] came from a long ways away (RBn3-47). *ąkále, wéhice ąkáchie* we're going, we [two] came from far away (as if to say: we're going because it's a long ways home) (FH).

•• LFD 213: *wéhice* <we´-hi-dse> far away, distant (01/23/95/FH/pc:ok). *wéhice pši* <we´-hi-dse pshi> I went far away. *wéhice ši* <we´-hi-dse shi> you went far away.

wéhice anąkʔǫ (variant: **wéhice nąkʔǫ́**). N **radio (lit., 'listen from far away')** (BE2.111; RBn1-9, unconfirmed; 04/20/95/LS/pc:no).

wéhkikʔǫ. N [*wé-* PREFIX + *hkik-* REFL + *éǫ* 'do'] **tool, implement, machinery, gadget, piece of equipment (lit., 'things with which to do for oneself')** (HH/pc).

••• Cf. *éwahkikʔǫ*.

wéhkilį. N [possibly *wé-* PREFIX +*hkik-* + *į́*] **clothes, dress, costume, pants, coat, vest, any item of clothing or suit of clothes** (RB note: for man, woman, or child) (04/07/95/LS/pc:ok). *wažái wéhkilį* Osage clothes (01/09/95/FH/pc:ok). *wéhkilį ðuustáko* straighten up your clothes (01/09/95/FH/pc:ok; BE2.20). *hǫ́ǫpa ðé wéeną akxai ðe níhkaši tóa áðixǫpape, hpáðį wéhkili íwehkili į kšíɣape* she's grateful today because they honored her, they dressed her in Kiowa clothes (lit., 'today she's grateful to the people that honored her by having her dress with Kiowa clothes') (RBn23-17; CQc). *wažái wéhkilį į́* dress in Osage clothes.

•• LFD 213: *wéhkiliwį* <we´-ḳi-gthi-wi^{n}> clothing. *wéhkiliwį okíhpahą* <we´-ḳi-gthi-wi^{n} u-gi´-p̣a-ho^{n}> to dress. *wéhkiliwį okíhpahą* <we´-ḳi-gthi-wi^{n} u-gi´-p̣a-ho^{n}> to dress.

wéhkilį okíhpaahą. VP [reg., *wéhkilį o_kíhpaahą*] [*wéhkilį* + *kik-* SUU+ *opáahą*] *(intr.)* **dress in or put on one's own clothes.** *wéhkilį okíhpaahą́pi* put on your clothes (01/20/95/ERE/pc; 04/18/95/FH/pc:okc).

•• RB: <ó-kyu-lah o-kí-pah-háh^{n}-pi>.

•• LFD 213: *wéhkiliwį okíhpahą* <we´-ḳi-gthi-wi^{n} u-gi´-p̣a-ho^{n}> to dress [specifically 'in one's own clothes']. *wéhkiliwį owákihpahą* <we´-ḳi-gthi-wi^{n} u-wa´-gi-p̣a-ho^{n}> I dress [in my own clothes] (01/20/95/ERE/pc:ok). *wéhkiliwį oðákišpahą* <we´-ḳi-gthi-wi^{n} u-tha´-gi-shpa-ho^{n}> you dress [in your own clothes] (01/20/95/ERE/pc:ok). *wéhkiliwį ąkokihpahą pe* <we´-ḳi-gthi-wi^{n} o^{n}-gu-gi-p̣a-ho^{n} i> we dress [in our own clothes].

••• *KS obáhą ~ obáahą* wear (RR).

wéhkilį opáahą. VP [sync. fortisizing stop stem, *wéhkilį o_páahą*] **dress in or put on clothing (not one's own).** *wéhkili wį ohpáahą mįkšé* I dress (lit., 'I put on an outfit'—as when I check out some clothing and put it on) (01/20/95/ERE/pc).

wéhpiiži. V, ADJ [conjug. unknown, presumed reg., *wé_hpiiži*] [*wa-* VAL + *í-* LOC + *hpííži*] **(be) destructive, damaging, harmful** (RBn17-p02). • **cause trouble or disturbance for others.** *wéhpiiži apai* they're causing trouble, they're causing a disturbance (lit., 'folks are troubled [by them]' or 'they are troubled [by them]').

•• JOD (Raccoons and Crawfish p20 ln5): *wéhpįįmaži* <we´pii^{n}-máçi>. [No appropriate gloss given, but the form appears to contain the 1st person sg. negative *maží* 'I do not, I did not'—as if *wéhpiiži* were *wéhpii* (unattested) + *aží* 'not'. In Mod. Os., however, *hpííži* and *wéhpiiži* are clearly not *hpíi* or *wéhpii* + *aží*.]

wéhuu. V [uninfl., presumably also reg., *wé_huu*] [*wa-* VAL + *í-* LOC + *húu* 'many'] *(intr.)* **make a crowd** (RBn22-17). *wéhuu mįkšé* I'm here making a crowd (RBn22-17).

wéhuukǫ́į. V [conjug. unknown] [*wa-* VAL + *í-* LOC + *huukǫ́ða*] *(intr.)* **make a crowd** (FH).

wéhuužį. V [uninfl.] [*wa-* VAL+ *í-* LOC + *húu* 'many' + *-žį* 'little'] *(intr.)* **increase in size a bit by more (number or amount) being added; help to make a bit of a crowd.** *wéhuužį brée ðe* I'm just going to help make a crowd, I'm going to make a little bit more (BE2.27; FH; 01/14/95/FH/pc:okc).

wékaacuxe (FH) (variant: **wékaacuɣe** [LS]). N [*wé-* PREFIX + *kaacúxe*] **broom** (BE2.12; 01/09/95/FH/pc:ok; 04/13/95/LS/pc:ok).

•• LFD 212: *wékacuxe žį̨ka* <we´-ga-dsu-xe zhiⁿ-ga> small broom.

••• *KS ččígaɣe* broom (RR), *gaɣé* sweep (RR).

wékaaɣe. V [sync. *k>p, wé_kaaɣe*] [*wa-* VAL + *íkaaɣe*] *(trans.)* **make from, make using.** • N **tool used to make s.t.**

wékaapše (variant: **wekáapše**). N [*wé-* PREFIX + *káapše*] **brush or comb (for the hair), hairbrush** (01/09/95/FH/pc:ok; 04/20/95/LS/pc:ok; 04/17/96).

wékaaspe (variant: **wékaaspa**). N **hammer** (02/09/95/FH/pc:prod orig). *wékaaspe háažǫ́?* what did you do with the hammer? (02/09/95/FH/pc:prod orig; BE2.63).

•• LFD 212 (unconfirmed): *wékasta* <we´-ga-çta> with which to pound: hammer (FH:uk).

wékaaži (variant: **wékaažį**). N [*wé-* PREFIX + *kaaží*] **horse whip, quirt, stick to drive people or animals, stick that tail dancers carry at war dances** (05/02/95/LS/pc:ok). *wékaaži ąnáchįpe* he hit me with a stick (05/02/95/LS).

•• LFD 212: *wékažį* <we´-ga-zhiⁿ> whip, quirt.

wéleze. N [*wé-* PREFIX + *léze*] **pencil, pen (lit., 'with which to make marks')** (RBn10-20; 03/07/95/PM/pc:ok). [The corresponding form in LFD has final *ðe* (see below), but this is not found in the Mod. Os. data.]

•• LFD 213: *wélezeðe* <we´-gthe-çe-the> a pen, or pencil. *wélezeðe ðihta žúce* <we´-gthe-çe-the thi-ṭa zhu-dse> your pencil is red. *wélezeðe wihta sape* <we´-gthe-çe-the wi-ṭa ça-be> my pencil is black.

wéli. N **oil; lard; grease or similar substance (such as shoe polish)** (HH). *wéeli weli* hot oil treatment for the hair or scalp (lit., 'head oil') (01/07/95/FH/pc:prod). *hkohkósa wéli* pork lard. *wéli hǫǫpé ápuštai* polish your shoes. • **gasoline, kerosene.** *wéli tóe oðíhtą oožú ði* put some gas in the car (RBn12-06). *wéli tóe oðíhtą ooðážu?* did you put some gas in the car? (RBn12-06).

•• LFD 213: *wéli* <we´-gthi> grease, oil, kerosene (03/02/95/FH/pc:ok). LFD 88: *hkohkosa weli* <ḳo-ḳo-ça, we-gthi> hog, grease: lard.

••• Cf. *átahką wéli níini, paazénii wéli, wacúe wéli.*

wéli mąhką́. N **castor oil** (03/02/95/FH/pc:ok).

•• LFD 213: *wéli mąhką* <we´-gthi moⁿ-ḳoⁿ> castor oil (oil, medicine).

wélisaaki. N [*wéli* + *saakí*] **tallow** (03/02/95/FH/pc:ok).

•• LFD 213: *wélisaki* <we´-gthi-ça-gi> tallow.

wéoohǫ́. N [*wé-* PREFIX + *oohǫ́*] **cooking utensils** (JS).

wépaase. N [*wa-* VAL + *ípaase*] **any tool for cutting wood (such as a saw; lit., 'with which to cut things by pushing down on them')** (RB).

••• Cf. *žą́ąpaase.*

wepázo (variant of **wéapazo**).

wépše. N [*wé-* PREFIX + *pšé*] **pestle (lit., 'with which to pound things')** (RBn23-07).

wépukxa. N [*wa-* VAL + *ípukxa*] **soap, detergent (lit., 'with which to rub things')** (RBn1-MOJ/p49b; 03/13/95/FH/pc:ok). *hį̨cé íðuuža wépukxa* dish soap (03/13/95/FH/pc:ok). *wépukxa íhkiluužaa* wash yourself with soap (03/16/95/JS/pc:okc; BE2.124).

•• LFD 212: *wépukxa* <we´-biu-ka> soap. *wépukxa topa ąðiwį a he* <we´-biu-ka du-ba oⁿ-thi-wiⁿ a he> [expected Mod. Os. form: *wépukxa tóa ą́ðuwį*] buy me some soap.

wesáhtą. ADJ [*wé-* PREFIX + *sáhtą*] **fifth.**

wešáhpe. ADJ [*wé-* PREFIX + *šáhpe*] **sixth.**

wéšį. N **oatmeal** (RB, unconfirmed, BE2.97). [Possibly *wé-* PREFIX + *wašį́* (lit., 'with which to eat bacon or fat'?); perhaps a borrowing.]

•• RB: <wéh´-shiⁿ>

wétoopa (variant: **wetóopa**). ADJ [*wé-* PREFIX + *tóopa*] **fourth.**

•• RB: <wéh-tó-pah> (01/30/95/FH/pc:ok; BE2.50).

•• LFD 212: *wétopa* <we´-do-ba> the fourth.

wéuɣaake (variant of **wáįɣaaké**). N **Carrying and Wailing (personal name).**

wéuɣe (variant of **wéðuɣe**).

wéuɣekiðe (variant of **wéðuɣekíðe**).

wéušupe (variant of **wéðušupe**).

weúuze. N [*wé-* PREFIX + *ðuuzé*] **debt, s.t. owed.** *weúuze htą ášupe hta mį́kše* I'm going to pay this big debt (03/06/95/FH/pc:prod). • **instrument for picking s.t. up (tongs, fork, etc.).** [By analogy with Omaha *wéðize* (RL).]

wí (variant of **wíe**).

wi-. PRNM **combined marker of 1st person sg. subject and 2nd person object ('I . . . you').** [Used both with reg. and sync. verbs (whose subject may also be expressed by agent pronominal prefixes) and with doubly stative verbs (whose subject may also be expressed by patient pronominal prefixes). The object 'you' may be pluralized by addition of *api* in postverbal position.] *šée wihkǫ́bra* I want that for you (03/16/95/JS/pc:ok). *wikˀú* I give [it] to you. *wíbruwį atxąhé* I am buying it for you. *wawíhǫ́ipi* I address you all as friends and family. *íiwinǫhpe* I'm afraid of you. *wikíkxopi achíe* I

wi- (*continued*)
have come to invite you all to eat (04/14/95/FH/pc:okc; 04/25/95/PM/pc:ok; t14b-p3/170). *žįkážį nakxą́še wéewina akxą́he, ilǫ́įhpa waachí štǫ́papa* I want to thank you children for watching my son dance. *mąhká owíbrikʔe* I gave you a shot (FH:4/25/96/t141, prod).

wi-. PRNM **1st person sg. inalienable possessive pronominal ('my'; used with many kinship terms, e.g., *wihcíko* 'my grandfather').**

wíaðaaspe (variant of **wíoðaaspe**).

wícihta. N **Wichita (tribe or tribal member)** (RBn HW13; FH/10/09/01/prod).

••• *KS mítsitta, wítsitta* Wichita, people or tribe [*ts* is not a Kansa phoneme; therefore this a borrowing] (RR).

wíe (variant: **wí**). PRON **me, I (emphatic).** *wí, ąðáhice* as for me, I'm ready to go (RBn10-5:JW). *wíe hta mįkšé?* is it I? • **it is my turn.** *wíe hta mįkšé* [it will be I] it's my turn (RB note: Mr. Maten said this to the fireman when it was his turn to hit drum in a peyote meeting) (04/04/95/FH/pc:ok; RB).

•• LFD 216: *wíe* <wi´-e> I, me.

wíexci. PRON [*wíe* + *xci*] **I myself (more emphatic form of *wíe*).**

wíeži. ADJ **bashful** (RBn10-18, unconfirmed).

wihą́ka. N **my wife's sister, my brother's wife (used only when speaker is male** [RB]**; more precise than English 'my sister-in-law').** [Traditionally men liked to tease their sisters-in-law with jokes.]

wihcíko. N **my grandfather.** *wihcíko hpéece* grandfather fire (RB; FH/09/24/01/ok). *wihcíko mį́į* grandfather sun (BE2.59). • **my father-in-law** (02/03/95/FH/pc:ok).

•• LFD 217: *wihcikóe* <wi-ṭsi-go´-e> [02/03/95/FH/pc: wrong pronunciation, should be *wihcíko*] my grandfather. "The term <ṭsi-go> is applied to a father's father, to his father, to a mother's father, to his brother, to a father-in-law, and to a wife's maternal uncle. It is also used as a term of reverence for God and for natural objects, such as the sun, the morning star, the dipper, Orion's belt, the pole star, and living objects whose mysterious habits inspire in the Osage mind a feeling of reverence for the Creator."

••• Cf. *hcíko.*

wihcími. N **my father's (older or younger) sister (my paternal aunt; used when speaker is male or female)** (FH/09/22/01/pc; 01/06/95/FH/pc:prod).

wihcíni (variant: **wihcínį**). N **my daughter-in-law (used when speaker is male or female)** (01/19/95/FH/pc:ok).

wihcióžąke (variant: **wihcóžąke**). N **my brother's daughter (used only when speaker is female; more precise than English 'my niece')** (02/27/95/FH/pc:okc; BE2.93).

wihcížo (variant: **wihcížoe**). N **my sister's daughter (used only when speaker is male; more precise than English 'my niece'); my father's sister's daughter (used when speaker is male or female; more precise than English 'my cousin').** [*wihcížo* as 'cousin, my paternal aunt's daughter' is said by some to be used only by a female speaker.]

•• LFD 81: *ihcížǫ* <i-ṭsi´-zhoⁿ> niece, daughter of a sister or a father's sister.

wihcį́to. N **my older brother (oldest of speaker's brothers, not necessarily older than the speaker; used only when speaker is female; more precise than English 'my older brother')** (01/09/95/FH/pc:ok).

•• LFD 217: *wichį́to* <wi-tsiⁿ´-do> brother, older (than myself), woman speaking.

wihcóška. N **my sister's son, my wife's brother's son (used only when speaker is male; more precise than English 'my nephew')** (02/27/95/FH/pc:ok; BE2.92); **my brother's son (used only when speaker is female; more precise than English 'my nephew'); son of my father's sister (my paternal aunt's son; used when speaker is male or female; more precise than English 'my cousin'); my grandchild (my granddaughter or my grandson; used when speaker is male or female)** (04/17/95/LS/pc; 04/18/95/FH/pc:ok). [Historically, 'grandchild' is an unexpected gloss (perhaps used only by extension to one's grandniece or grandnephew: i.e., one's sibling's grandchild?).]

••• *KS iččóškayą* woman's sister's son (RR).

wihcóšpa (variant: **hcošpá**). N **my grandchild** (05/01/95/LS/pc). *wihcóšpa, ðéka ku* grandchild, come over here (RBn1-18).

•• LFD 217: *wihcóšpaži xci ðǫ* <wi-tsu´-shpa-zhi xtsi thoⁿ> [*xci* is not confirmed as 'dear' and *ðǫ* is not used in Mod. Os.] my dear grandchild (woman speaking).

••• Cf. *wihčóšpa.*

wihcóšpa áhkiha. N **my great-grandchild(ren).**

wihcóžąke (variant of **wihcióžąke**).

wihčóšpa. N **my grandchild.** [Endearing or diminutive in comparison to *wihcóšpa.*]

wihé. N **second daughter** (02/27/95/FH/pc).

•• LFD 215: *wihé* <wi-he´> special kinship term, the name by which the second daughter is called (04/07/95/LS/pc:ok).

wíhta. PRON **mine, my.** *óoląke ðé wíhta* this hat is mine (PM:ok; BE2.88).

•• LFD 217: *wíhta* <wi´-ṭa> mine, denoting possession, my. *mąžą wíhta* <mo^{n}-zho^{n} wi´-ṭa> my land. *hkawa wihta* <ḳa-wa wi-ṭa> my horse. *hci wihta* <ṭsi wi-ṭa> my house or tipi (CQ:ok).

wihtáežį (variant of **wihtéžį**).

wihtąha. N **my father's sister's husband (my paternal uncle by marriage; used when speaker is male or female; more precise than English 'my uncle'); my sister's husband, my wife's brother (used only when speaker is male; more precise than English 'my brother-in-law')** (01/09/95/FH/pc:prod; BE2.12).

••• Cf. *htąhą, ihtąha.*

wihtąke (variant: **wihtąke**). N **my older sister (used when speaker is male or female); my sister (loosely used mutually among unrelated younger and older female speakers to show respect); my wife (lit., 'my sister'; used to refer to speaker's wife when they have no children and possibly to address her)** (RBn12-12; 03/16/95/MREI/pc:ok; BE2.158). [This is the default vocative 'sister' term; the person so addressed need not be older than the speaker. As illustration of this, Mrs. Josephine Walker always called Mrs. Frances Holding, who was younger, *wihtąke* (FH10/13/96). When used to mean 'older sister', the sister in question may be either older than the speaker or the oldest of the group of sisters.]

wihtéžį (variant: **wihtáežį**) N **my younger sister (used when speaker is male or female)** (03/09/95/MREI/pc:ok).

wihtǫce (variant: **wahitǫci**). N **my son-in-law (used when speaker is male or female).**

•• RB: <wi-tó^{n}-tsi> (03/13/95/FH/pc:okc; BE2.125).

wíkie. N **prayer; church (meeting)** (RBn10-18). *óchį ðáalį káaγį aha wíkie* whenever he hits drum well, there's a prayer (RBn10-18; gloss by CQ). *žáže kʔú wíkie* prayer for name-giving (LF; CQc). • V [reg., *wí_kie*] *(intr.?)* **pray** (LF only).

•• LFD 216: *wíkie* <wi´-gi-e> orison, prayer, to pray. *wíakie* <wi´-a-gi-e> I pray. *wíðakie* <wí´-tha-gi-e> you pray. *wiąkiape* <wi-o^{n}´-gi-a i> we pray.

••• Cf. *wíkiehci.*

wíkie hįįska. N **prayer beads, rosary.**

••• Cf. *hįįskawáata.*

wíkiehci. N [*wíkie* + *hcí*] **church.** *šįtožį akxa wíkiehci ci aðée apai* that boy [who is now absent but was just present] is on his way to church.

wíkihcižį. N [*wíkiehci* + *-žį* 'little'] **little church (lit., 'little house of prayer'; used to refer to the Friends' Church [Quaker Meeting] in Hominy by its members).** (DN/FH980930).

wíną (variants: **wįną, wína**). V, PRON [1st person sg. of *eeną́* 'be the only one'] *(intr.)* **(be) only I.** *winą́*, it is only I.

••• Cf. *ąkóną, ðíną.*

winíhka. N **my husband.**

••• Cf. *níhka.*

wíoðaaspe (variant: **wíaðaaspe**). N **cork** (BE2.25; RBn3-07, unconfirmed; 01/12/95/FH/pc:uk; 04/25/95/PM/pc:uk) **(specifically a fishing cork [RB]).**

•• LFD 216 (unconfirmed): *wéoðatą* <we´-u-tha-do^{n}> a stopper of any kind. [A different word from *wíoðaaspe.*]

••• *KS oyáadą* to cork, to put a stopper in (RR).

wíohkaðį. V [uninfl.] [probably contains *óhką* 'space, room'] *(intr.)* **in the way, not fitting in the available space.** *wíohkaðį nįkšé* you're in the way (FH:5/01/96/okc). *wíohkaðį ąðįhée* I'm in the way (FH:5/01/96/prod).

wióohǫ. N [*wa-* VAL + *í-* LOC +*oohǫ́*] **cooking utensils (lit., 'with which to cook things').** *wióohǫžį alábrįbrée hta ąhé* I am going to take my little cooking utensils along (BE2.25; 01/12/95/FH/pc:ok; RBn3-MOJ/18).

wísi (variants: **oísi, owísi, wíse**). V [reg., *o_ísi, o_wísi*] *(trans.)* **get off, alight from (e.g., a vehicle), dismount from (e.g., a horse)** (BE2.72). *hkáwa owéisi hta mįkše [hkáwa owáisi hta mįkšé(?)]* I'm going to get off the horse (01/31/95/FH/pc:ok; BE2.53). • *(intr.)* **jump** (02/13/95/FH/pc: *wíse*).

•• LFD 181: *owísi* <u-wi´-çi> to leap, to jump in play; to alight, to dismount. *oðáwisi* <u-tha´-wi-çi> you dismount. *ąkówisi pe* <o^{n}-gu´-wi-çi i> we dismount. LFD 216: *wísi* <wi´-çi> to jump, alight from a horse, leap.

••• *KS oyúsį* (JOD) jump down, get off, dismount (reg. conjugation) (RR).

••• Cf. *ósi.*

wisíkxą. N **my sister-in-law (used only when speaker is female).**

wísikʔǫ. N **jumping game** (RB).

wísisi. N [reduplicated form of *wísi*] **flea** (01/26/95/FH/pc:ok; BE2.49).

•• LFD 216: *wísisi* <wi´-çi-çi> flea.

wisǫ́ežį (variant: **wisǫ́ažį**). N **my younger brother (used only when speaker is female)** (BE2.12; 01/09/95/FH/pc:prod; 04/13/95/LS/pc:ok). ['Younger' here probably means 'younger than the speaker'.]

wisǫ́ka. N **my younger brother (younger than the speaker; used only when speaker is male)** (04/13/95/LS/pc:ok). [Also used by both men and women for a related or unrelated younger male.]

•• JOD (Raccoons and Crawfish p21 ln7): *wísǫká* <Wi´sañk̥a´> my younger brother. [Historically, it appears that when this word was used vocatively, its accent would shift to the first and third syllables.]

•• LFD 216: *wisǫ́ka* <wi-çoⁿ´-ga> brother (younger than myself). "This is the ordinary use of the kinship term for my younger brother. But the same term is used ceremonially when no blood relationship exists. One member of a tribe may address members of the other gentes of the same division with this term." *wisǫ́ka owa hkihkie mį kše o* <wi-çoⁿ´-ga u-wa gi-ḳi-e mi kshe o> [sentence-final *o* is not used in Mod. Os.] I spoke to my younger brother.

wišík?e. N **my sister's husband, my husband's brother (used only when speaker is female; more precise than English 'my brother-in-law')** (RB; 01/09/95/FH/pc:prod orig).

wiškítą (variants: **wiškíta, wiškí**). PRON [*wíe* + *-škítą, ški*] **me too, I too** (02/24/95/FH/pc:okc). *wiškítą!* me too! (BE2.85). *wiškí* me too, I too (01/04/95/FH/pc:ok).

•• LFD 217: *wíški* <wi´ -shki> I also. *wíškitą* <wi´ shki-doⁿ> I too, for my part.

••• *KS wiškédą* (JOD) I too (RR).

wižį́ðe (variants: **wižį́, wižį́e**). N **my older brother (used only when speaker is male)** (01/09/95/FH/pc:ok). [When used in the extended sense outside the immediate family, this brother must only be older than the speaker and is not necessarily the eldest son of a family.] *wižį́e ą́wahką hkǫ́bra* I want older brother to help me (01/06/95/FH/pc:prod). *wižį́, waaðǫ́ ðáalį škáaye hą́ąci* older brother, you sang good last night (03/09/95/MREI/pc:ok).

•• JOD (Raccoons and Crawfish p21 ln9): <Wi´çiⁿ¢e´>. [Historically it appears that when this word was used vocatively, its accent would shift to the first and third syllables.]

•• LFD 217: *wižį́ðe* <wi-zhiⁿ´-the> my elder brother, my brother older than myself.

wižį́ke. N **my son (any of my sons, including a first son; in this meaning, used regardless of whether speaker is male or female); my brother's son (used only when speaker is male; more precise than English 'my nephew')** (02/27/95/FH/pc:ok); **Sonny (as a nickname, used by either male or female speakers for a son or a friend).** [Used also, perhaps more recently or only in certain dialects or families, by female speakers, as either 'my brother's son' or even 'my sister's son' (RB, CQc). Historically, it appears that when this word was used vocatively, its accent would shift to the first and third syllables (*wížįké*).] *wižį́ke líi tą, húu hce éa* when Sonny gets back here, have him come over here (03/13/95/FH/pc:ok).

wižį́ke iðáce. NP **my husband (lit., 'my son's father') (used to speak about or address one's husband if the first child is a boy).**

wižį́ke iihǫ́. NP **my wife (lit., 'my son's mother') (used to speak about or to one's wife if the first child is a boy)** (RBn12-12; 03/16/95/MREI/pc:ok).

wižǫ́ą. N **my older sister (i.e., older than the speaker; used only when speaker is female)** (BE2.122; HH/pc, 03/09/95/MREI/pc:ok).

wižǫ́ke. N **my daughter (used when speaker is male or female); my brother's daughter (used only when speaker is male; more precise than English 'my niece'); my sister's daughter (used only when speaker is female; more precise than English 'my niece')** (BE2.29).

•• RB: <wi-shóⁿ-keh, wi-zhóⁿ-keh>.

wižǫ́ke iihǫ́. NP **my wife (lit., 'my daughter's mother') (when the oldest child of the husband and wife is a girl, this is what a man calls his wife [RB])** (03/16/95/MREI/pc:okc).

wį. ADJ, PRON **a, an, one, single, anyone.** *wak?ó wį achípe* a woman came (FH/pc:ok). *hǫpái wacúe skúe wį hpáaye* I made a cake today (RBn10-2:MOJ/79). *wį́ ą́ðuwį ðáalį* we ought to buy one (RBn1-44). *wį́ nąhka álįipi tą, ílǫǫška waachí nąpe* when he carried anyone on his back, he would war-dance (RBn10-2:MOJ/79; HRE/12/29/01/pc). *táatą wahóta wį* something funny (lit., 'a funny thing') (3-3-83-p2). • **one of a group.** *níhka wį akxa aðáape* one of these men went. • **(marker of sg. head within a relative clause).** [Compare *tóa.*] *waachí wį wažáže apa húuža ðée aðį́ apa* Osages had this dance a long time (lit., 'this is the dance that for a long time Osages had it') (PM/7/7/94). *hcí wį́ pšíe, pée ðįké* no one was at the house I went to (lit., 'I went to a house, no one was there') (BE2.157). *waxpéį ąkái, ók?u ąðúuc?ake še nąąhtąhtąą oðúuc?ake wį́* we're too poor to feed that lazy donkey (lit., 'we are poor, that donkey who is/was lazy, we can't/couldn't feed him') (RBn10-2:MOJ/79). *nihkáši wį sitǫ́į achípe haxį́ wį ąk?úpe* the man that came yesterday gave me a blanket. *šį́htožį wį iiðáðe hkóopši apai* the boy that I saw was running away (3-2-163). *hǫ́ǫe wį ahú apa ðak?éðie hta ðe* nobody will be coming to take care of you (FH).

•• LFD 216: *wį* <wi^n> one, single. *níhka wį* <ni´-ķa wi^n> one man. *wak?o wį* <wa-ķ'o wi^n> one woman. LFD 219: *xǫ́cewį* <Xo^n´-dse-wi^n> Cedar-woman (female personal name), refers to the cedar tree.

wį. N **female, woman (used only in personal names for females).** [Historically related to *mį́į, mį́įka.*] *letǫ́ wį/letǫ́wį* Hawk Woman (personal name). [Frances Holding's name.]

wį́ (variant of **wį́xce**).

wįcéki (variant: **wįcéke**). N **my mother's brother (my maternal uncle; more precise than English 'my uncle')** (02/27/95/JS/pc:ok). [Accent may change to *wį́ceki* in vocative use.]

-wįɣe (variant: **-įɣe**). V ROOT **turn, spin, whirl, around (as in drive around, turn around, etc.).**

•• LFD 218: *xúða apa káawįɣe nąpe* <xi-tha´ a-ba ga-wi^n-xe no^n bi a> the eagle soars [around] (CQc).

••• *QU bakkówįɣáɣa* push round and round (RR), *kakóįɣaɣa* go around and around (RR), *kkówįɣáɣa* turn round and round (RR); *OP wįɣe* turn, spin, whirl.

••• Cf. *ákiɣe, hkilíihkǫįɣe, -hkóįɣe, hǫǫpé okáwįɣe, okáwįɣe, opáwįɣe.*

wį́hkikše. V [reg., *wį́_hkikše*] [*hkik-* REFL + *wį́kše*] *(intr.)* **be true to oneself.** *wį́hkikša!* be true to yourself!

wįįðé. N **that unique thing, that single item or event.** • ADV **this particular way, solely or uniquely so.** *wįįðé níhkašie mǫ́pšewaa hpíǫ apa* this particular way our people's forefathers knew it (HREsr-1965 *ilǫ́ǫška*-line 2).

wį́kše. V [reg., *wį́_kše*] *(intr.)* **speak the truth, tell the truth.** *wį́akše* I speak the truth (04/03/95/PM/pc:ok). *wį́ðakše* you speak the truth (04/03/95/PM/pc:ok). *wį́ðakše?* are you telling the truth? (04/03/95/PM/pc:okt). *wį́kše akxá* he/she is telling the truth (04/03/95/PM/pc:okt; BE2.145). *wį́kše akxai* he's telling the truth (RBn12-11). • *(trans.)* **be true to.** *wį́ąðakše hta ðąįšé?* will you be true to me? (04/03/95/PM/pc:okt). • ADJ **true.** *wį́kše žóąðále hta ðáaše?* will you be true with me? (04/03/95/PM/pc:ok). • N **truth.** *wį́kše oðáaka!* tell the truth! (04/03/95/PM/pc:ok). *wį́kše owíbraake mįkšé* I'm telling you the truth. • INTERJ **golly! gosh! (female exclamation of surprise)** [As an exclamation, *wį́kše* is not vulgar and is not a statement about truth or question about truth.] *wį́įkšé!* golly! (RBn2-MOJ/p5; 04/06/95/FH/pc:ok).

•• LFD 216: *wį́hke* <wi^n´-ke> [expected Mod. Os. form *wį́kše*] truth, sincere, genuine, sincerity, sure. *wiáhke* <wi^n-a´-ke> [expected Mod. Os. form: *wį́akše*] I speak the truth. *wį hkaži* <wi^n ķa-zhi> [expected Mod. Os. form *wį́kšaži*] he speaks not the truth.

••• Cf. *wawį́kše, wį́hkikše.*

wį́ną (variant of **wíną**).

wį́xce (variants: **wį́xci, wį́**). ADJ, N **one, a, an** (BE2.98). *hǫ́ǫpa wį́xci nąški níhkaši aní hkǫ́bra* (lit., 'one day at a time only, as a person, I want to live') I want to live one day at a time (RBn10-21).

•• RB: <wí^n-xtsi>.

•• LFD 217: *wį́xci* <wi^n´-xtsi> one of a kind, a single piece. *wį́xci hkǫ́bra* <wi^n´-xtsi ķo^n-btha> I want one (03/02/95/FH/pc:ok).

X

xáða ADV **back, backward, in reverse, retrograde** (JS). *xáða mąðį́* step backward.

•• LFD 218: *xáða mąðį* <xa´-tha mo^{n}-thi^{n}> the act of stepping backward. *xáða mąbrį* <xa´-tha mo^{n}-bthi^{n}> I walk backward. *xaðámąscį* <xa-tha´-mo^{n}-stsi^{n}> you walk backward, the act of stepping backward. *xaðalé* <xa-tha-gthe´> retrograde, to appear to move backward. *xáðe* <xa´-the> backward.

••• *OP xáða* back.

xáhtape. ADJ **dry grass, dried grass** (unconfirmed).

•• JOD (slip file): *xáhtape* <qa´-ta-p̣e> dried grass.

xáka. ADJ **rough, prickly.** *ðéeze xáka* thorny tongue (03/23/95/FH/pc:prod).

•• JOD (slip file): *xáka* <qa´-ka> rough, as a tongue.

•• LFD 217: *xáka* <xa´-ga> bristling, rough in appearance.

••• Cf. *ɣáɣaka, waxáka.*

xáxa (variant: **xą́xą**). ADJ [reduplicated form?] **ruffled, ruffly, having leaves or leaflike layers** (FH).

••• Cf. *hceeníxaxa, waxáka.*

xą́xą. ADJ [reduplicated form?] **shiny** (RBn22-04).

•• LFD 219: *xąxą́mąį* <Xo^{n}-xo^{n} ´ -mo^{n}-i^{n}> Shines-as-he-moves (personal name), refers to the reflection of the sun on the outspreading [*sic*] of the eagle.

xci (variant: **xcį**). ADJ, ADV **real, really, exactly, very, fully, indeed, precisely** (MREI). *žą́ąxežį ðuuzái cʔéða xci* take a stick and really kill someone (FH:prod). *wažáže xci bríe* I'm a real Osage. *kasį́excį mį́į ątǫ́pe htái* let's go see the morning sun coming up (as in a peyote meeting) (BE2.129; 01/14/95/FH/pc).

•• JOD (slip file): *xci* <qtsi> adv. very, real, used only in composition. *xúða-xci* <qu¢a-qtsi> real eagle.

xée. V [conjug. unknown] *(intr.)* **roar, patter.** *nižu xée wálį* the rain patters very much.

•• JOD (slip file): *xe* <qe> v. to roar, as running water, to patter, as rain.

xéka. V, ADJ **dead (from drying up; e.g., a vegetable), dried.**

••• Cf. *nąąɣúce xéka.*

xémąke. N **dew, frost** (BE2.30; 01/20/95/FH/pc:prod).

•• LFD 218: *xémąke* <xe´-mo^{n}-ge> frost, hoarfrost.

xépe (variant: **ɣépe?**). ADJ **shallow.** [Possibly related to *hépe* 'small amount'.]

•• LFD 218: *ɣépe* or *xépe* <xe´-be> shallow, not deep (unconfirmed).

••• *OP ɣébe* shallow.

-xi. V ROOT *(intr.)* **wake, awaken.**

••• Cf. *ðixí, nąąxí.*

xíatǫ. N [*xúða* + *tǫ́pe*] **name for an eldest daughter (*hcížo* clan) (lit., 'looking at the eagle')** (HRE/pc/2002).

xíða. V [reg.+sync. *_xí_ða*] *(intr.)* **fall, stumble, fall down, stumble and fall; euphemism for 'die', pass away; topple (as a tree topples).** [It is not clear whether *xíða* is related to *xį́na* 'hurry', even though *xį́na* has variants such as *xį́ða* and *xíða*.] *xíðape* he died (04/26/95/LS/pc:okc). *xíða akxa* he fell down (RBn10-18). *hóni axíbra* I almost fell (FH:4/18/96/okc). *mąðí šǫ́ apa, xíðape* while he was walking, he fell down/he died (04/26/95/LS/pc: identical fall down/die). *axíbra* I fell down (04/26/95/LS/pc:okc). *axíbra tą* if I fell down (04/26/95/LS/pc). *íinǫǫhpa, ðaxíšta hta akxai* be careful, you might fall (04/26/95/LS/pc:ok; BE2.43). *mašcį́ íðakʔuce ąži ðaxíða* you tried to walk but you fell down.

•• LFD 218: *xíða* <xi´-tha> to fall; to topple. *axíbra* <axi´-btha> I fall. *ąxíða pe* <o^{n}-xi´-tha i> we fall. *žą akxa xiða txa txa iche eci ahi akxa ha* <zho^{n} a-ka xi-tha ta ta i-tse e-dsi a-hi a-ka ha> [expected Mod. Os. form: *žą́ą akxa xíða che ecí ahí akxa*; sentence-final *ha* is not used in Mod. Os.] the tree is ready to topple.

••• Cf. *xíxiða.*

xíða. N **eagle.** [Archaic variant of *xúða*.]

xíða (variant of **xį́na**).

xíðaxa (variant: **xíðaha**). N **breechcloth, loincloth, diaper** (FH),

•• JOD (slip file): *xíðaaxáðe* <qi´-¢a-a-qa´-¢ĕ> a breech-cloth.

xína (variant of **xį́na**).

xíxiða. V [reg.+sync., *_xíxi_ða*] [reduplicated form of *xíða* 'fall, stumble'] *(intr.)* **stumble repeatedly, go stumbling along.** *cʔáižį akxa xíxiða akxái* the old man is stumbling (RBnot 5/3/79/3; FH:okc).

xį́ (variant of **ɣį**).
xį́na (variants: **xína, xíða, xį́ða**). ADJ, V [presumed reg., *_xį́na*] *(intr.)* **go fast.** • ADV **hurriedly.** [Adverbial meaning 'hurriedly' is typically associated with the pronunciation *xį́ða*, and vice versa.]
•• RB: <xí-nah> or <xí-thah> (04/25/95/PM/pc: *xíða káaɣe* 'hurry it up' plain *í*, not *į́*).
•• LFD 218: *xį́ðaða* <xi^n´-tha-tha> to hurry, make haste, to hie. *xį́ðaða bre* <xi^n´-tha-tha bthe> [expected Mod. Os. form: *xį́ða brée*] I hurry [rather, 'I go making haste']. *xį́ðaða sce* <xi^n´-tha-tha stse> [expected Mod. Os. form: *xį́ða ščée*] you hurry [rather, 'you go making haste']. *xį́ðaða ąkaða pe* <xi^n´-tha-tha o^n-ga-tha i> [expected Mod. Os. form: *xį́ða ąkaðape*] we hurry [rather, 'we go making haste'].
xį́na káaɣe (variant: **xį́ða káaɣe**). VP [sync. *k>p*, *xį́na _káaɣe*] *(trans.)* **make s.t. go faster, hurry s.t. up, step s.t. up (as in 'hit drum faster', 'hit it faster')** (04/25/95/PM/pc:ok: *xínạ*; RBn10-5:MOJ/79; HH/t9b-p1; BE2.45).
xóce (variant: **xóe**). ADJ **gray, dull (color or finish), faded, grayish like ashes, smoky** (BE2.61; 02/03/95/FH/pc:ok; FH/09/21/01/pc). *hkáwa xóce* gray horse, the town of Grayhorse (02/03/95/FH/pc:ok).
•• JOD (slip file): *xóce* <qu´-ţșe> n. and adj. gray.
•• LFD 219: *xóce* <xo´-dse> gray, a gray line. *hkáwa xoce* <ķa´-wa xo-dse> gray horse. LFD 159: *hceehéxoce* <ţse-he´-xo-dse> a young buffalo with gray horns; one whose horns are not yet turned black with age.
••• Cf. *páxoce, šóce.*
xoé (variant of **xowí**).
xóhka. V [reg., *_xóhka*] *(intr.)* **sing dancing songs.** • N **singers and drummers** (FH:4/22/96/tape); **all singers of dancing songs** (RB; 03/09/95/MREI/pc:okc). *xóhka nąkxą́še* all you singers (RB; 03/09/95/MREI/pc:okc).
•• JOD (slip file): *xóhka* <qu´-ka> to sing dancing songs.
••• *QU xókka* sing dancing songs (RR).
xóhtą. ADJ **small, little, fine (e.g., fine raindrops).** *níižuxóhtą* fine rain, mist (FH/pc).
••• *QU nižíxohtá* mist, drizzle (N) (RR).
••• Cf. *hpéže xóhtą.*
xoį́ (variant of **ɣoį́**).
xóoka. N **badger.**
•• JOD (slip file): *xóka* <qu´-ķa> a badger.
••• *KS xǫ́ǫga ~ xóoga* badger (RR); *QU xóka* ground hog, 'badger' in several other languages (RR).
xópe. ADJ **sacred, consecrated, holy.** *mąhká xópe* sacred medicine, peyote, as used in a peyote meeting (RB).
•• LFD 221: *xópe* <xu´be> holy, supernatural power; sanctity.
••• Cf. *áxope, ðixópe, waxópe.*
xowí (variant: **xoé**). V [conjug. unknown] *(intr.)* **growl, roar, sigh, rumble, resound.** *hcéze xowí akxai* my stomach is growling (RBn10-21/JW&FW/77, unconfirmed).
•• LFD 219: *xoé* <xo-e´> to roar, as the wind or the waterfall, to sigh, to sough, as the wind.
xǫ́. ADJ, V [reg., *_xǫ́*] *(intr.)* **break, (be) broken.** *oðíhtą akxa xǫ́pe* the car broke, the car is broken. *ną́ące xǫ* broken heart. *žékaxǫ́ akxai* his leg is broken (FH). *žékaxǫ́ mįkšé* my leg is broken (FH). *mǫ́ǫ xǫ́* broken arrow (RBn10-6:JW). *xǫ́pe* it broke (MSB 2-24-83). *ðą́ące xǫ́* a broken heart. *mą́ą xǫ́* a broken arrow (MSB 2-24-83). • **(be) broke, without money or penniless (a loan translation).** *axǫ́ ątxą́he* I'm broke [I'm standing] (04/13/95/LS/pc:ok: *aɣǫ́*). *áxǫ mįkše* I'm broke [I'm sitting] (04/13/95/LS/pc:ok: *ɣ*; BE2.12). *ðáxǫ nįkšé?* are you broke?
•• LFD 219 *xǫ* <xo^n> to break; just a simple break. [LF erroneously lists *bríxǫ* <bthi´-xo^n> 'I break (s.t.)' and *ąðíxǫpe* <o^n-thi´-xo^n i> 'we break (s.t.)' as if they were forms of this verb; actually they are forms of *ðiixǫ́* 'break (s.t.) by hand'.]
xǫ́ǫce. N **cedar** (01/09/95/FH/pc:prod; PM:ok). *wahkǫ́ta ižį́ke iihǫ́ hpaxį́į įkše xǫ́ǫce íkǫce káaɣi apai* they're making the cedar like Mary's hair (FH).
•• RB: <xo-tséh>.
•• JOD (slip file): *xǫ́ce hu* <qŭ^n´- ţșĕ hú> a cedar tree.
•• LFD 219: *xǫ́ce* <xo^n´-dse> the red cedar. "Used as a symbol among the Osage, found in ritual." *xǫ́ce hi* <xo^n´dse hi> the cedar tree. *xǫ́ce hi* <Xo^n´-dse hi> Cedar Hills. *xǫ́ce omąį* <Xo^n´-dse u-mo^n-i^n> Dwell-among-the-cedars (personal name). "Refers to the thunder and lightning which are supposed to live among the cedars. There is also another meaning to this word, which is Walks-among-the-cedars, a personal name; refers to the habit of the bears." *xǫ́cewį* <Xo^n´-dse-wi^n> Cedar-woman (female personal name), refers to the cedar tree.

xǫ́ǫce (*continued*)

••• *KS xǫ́je* the red cedar (RR); *QU xǫhté* cedar wood (RR).

••• Cf. *xǫǫcóðibra.*

xǫ́ǫce mą́į. N **Walks among the Cedars (personal name that refers to thunder and lightning).** [The Bear Dwells among the Cedars, name of Henry Pratt, Jr. (02/22/95/FH/pc).]

xǫǫcéhu. N [*xǫ́ǫce* + *hú* 'trunk'] **cedar tree.**

xǫǫcéhu káaɣe hǫ́ǫpa. N **Christmas (lit. 'cedar tree preparation day')** (RBn10-18, unconfirmed).

xǫǫcénii. N [*xǫ́ǫce* + *níi*] **cedar tea** (01/09/95/FH/pc:prod; BE2.18). [Used in a sweathouse before a peyote meeting to induce vomiting for cleansing, a custom said to be learned by watching bears (RB).]

xǫǫcóðibra. V [conjug. unknown] [*xǫ́ǫce* + *oðíbrą*] **smoke cedar (cause cedar to smoke), smell cedar, smoke a house with cedar or use in a peyote meeting to smoke a person** (BE2.18).

xpéka (variant: **špéka** [PM]). V, ADJ [stat., *_xpéka*] **(be) dull** (MSB/pc), **not shiny** (MSB/pc; RBn10-5:MOJ/79; BE2.37; PM:uk); **languid or "blah" feeling one gets in winter.**

•• LFD 219: *xpéka* <xpe´-ga> languid. *ąxpéka* <o^{n}-xpe´-ga> I am languid. *ðixpéka* <thi-xpe´-ga> you are languid, drooping.

xpi. N **flatulence, fart.** • V [conjug. unknown] *(intr.)* **expel gas from the body.**

xtoe. V, ADJ [stat.?, *_xtoe*?] *(intr.)* **(be) snotty, filled with mucus.** *ðíxtoe!* you're snotty! (RB, unconfirmed).

•• LFD 221: *xtǫ* <xto^{n}> to spill, to slop over.

••• Cf. *hpahlíxtoe.*

xúða. N **eagle.** *xúða akxa ɣaakí akxái* the eagle is crying (01/14/95/FH/pc).

•• JOD (slip file): *xúða léže* <qü-¢á k¢e-çe> the spotted eagle, same as *hą́ka ǫ́pe léže* 'spotted tail eagle'. *xúða hpasą* <qü-¢á paça^{n}> the eagle with a whitish head, the bald eagle, a sub-gens of the *hcížo waštáke. xúða wáðalǫ žįké* <qü-¢á wa´-¢a-ķ¢ü^{n} ¢iñ-ķe´> an eagle that differs from the *hą́ka ǫpe léže;* its tail is about six inches long with black feathers, the rest of the feathers are white, the toes are yellow, no feathers on lower legs (CQ paraphrase of JOD gloss).

•• LFD 221: *xuðá* <xu-tha´> eagle, the adult golden eagle. *xuðá ekǫ žįka* <xu-tha; e-go^{n}; zhi^{n}-ga> resembles a young eagle. LFD 218: *xiða* <xi-tha> [pronunciation unacceptable to Mod. Os. speakers, should be *xúða* or *xuðá*] eagle. *xiðá apa kawįxe ną pi a* <xi-tha´ a-ba ga-wi^{n}-xe no^{n} bi a> [expected Mod. Os. form *xúða apa káawįɣe ną pe*] the eagle soars. *xiðá ðįkše ahį che ðixǫpi a* <xi-tha´ thi^{n}-ke a-hi^{n} te thi-xo^{n} bi a> [expected Mod. Os. form: *xúða įkše áahu che ðiixǫ́pe*] the eagle's wings are broken.

••• Cf. *xíða* 'eagle'.

xuðáchewį. N [*xúða* + *che* (?) + *wį*] **Eagle Woman (personal name).** [Yvonne Lookout's name.]

xúðalą́ke. N [*xúða* + *oolą́ke*] eagle headdress.

•• JOD (slip file): <qü-¢a´ ķ¢añ-ķĕ> a headdress made of entire eagles.

xúðawį. N [*xúða* + *wį*] **Eagle Woman (personal name).** [Anita Lookout's name.]

xuðážuuce. N [*xúða* + *žúuce*] **Red Eagle (name for first boy in *hcížo* clan, used until he becomes a teenager)** (FH).

•• JOD (slip file): *xuðá žuuce* <xü-¢á çü´ţşe> a red eagle, the name of the *hcížo waštáke* gens.

xuðókašą. N [*xúða* + *okášą*] **Take Care of the Eagle (personal name)** (RBn22-04).

•• JOD (slip file): *xuðókašą* <qü-¢u´-ķa-ca^{n}´> name of gens or sub-gens, referent of *aahu-okʔoce* <ahü-ukʔoce>, a personal name.

xúe tǫ́į. N [*xúða* + *tǫ́pe*] **Looking at the Eagle (personal name)** (RB). [Jeanna Redeagle's name.]

xúɣa (variant of **xúhaa**?). ADJ **skin.**

xúhaa (variants: **xuháa, xúha, xúɣa?**). N **skin, hide, bark.** *xuháa ska* white skin, white person.

•• RB: <xu-háh> (03/10/95/PM/pc:okc; BE2.122).

•• JOD (slip file): *xúha* <qu´-ha> skin of a person or animal.

•• LFD 218 (unconfirmed): *xįha* <xi^{n}-ha> skin of a human being or bark of a tree. *xį́ha šape* <xi^{n}´-ha sha-be> dark skin, swarthy. LFD 221: *xúha* <xu´-ha> the skin of a person or an animal.

••• Cf. *háa.*

xuháaska. N [*xúhaa* + *ská* 'white'] **white person, Caucasian.** *xuháaska brį́e* I'm a white person (FH:08/22/96:x, not ɣ). *xuháaska apa táatą ąkóhta oðówa[ðe] apai* white people are running our business, bossing us (01/07/95/FH/pc:prod; BE2.10).

•• JOD (slip file): *xúha* <qu´ha> the skin of a person or animal.

•• LFD 218: (unconfirmed): *xįhá ska* <xi^{n}-ha´ çka> white skin, the white race.

xúuða. ADJ **wrinkled** (01/14/95/FH/pc:ok; 03/24/95/PM/pc:ok;04/06/95/LS/pc). *haaská xúuða* your clothes are wrinkled (FH:prod).
• **ragged** (PM only; PM/03/10/95/pc).

Z

záani (variant: **záanii**). ADJ **whole, all.** *kį́į ékimą hta akxai, kóe mǫ́žǫ záani iiðáðe hta akxai* if I could fly, then I could see the whole world (RBn15-02). *žįkážį záani wéeðai?* did you see all the children? (MSB; FH). *hką́ące záani ą́ðuwi hcé* let's [two people] buy all the apples (01/04/95/FH/pc:ok). *súhka záani abráani* I ate all the chicken (PM). *niiǫ́tą záani* all the universe (01/04/95/FH/pc:ok, according to HH, who used to employ this expression). *įlǫ́ǫška záaní* all the dance (the event participants; form of address when making a speech at the *ilǫ́ǫška*) (01/04/95/FH/pc:ok). *mą́žą záani* all the world (01/04/95/FH/pc:prod). • PRON **all, every one, everyone, everybody.** *záani wanǫ́bre hipi* you all come over and eat (01/04/95/FH/pc: ok). *záani wanǫ́bre hípai* you all be there to eat. *záani aðįalaape* they took all of it (01/04/95/FH/pc:ok; BE2.2). *hkáwa záani aðį́ apai* all of them own the horse. *Johna záani wéeðape?* did John see all of us? (3-2-26). *Johna apa záani wéeðapí apai* John saw every one of us (3-2-274).

•• LFD 29: *zani* <ça-ni´> total, all.

zą́ą. N **country, prairie** (FH); **timbers** [not 'timbers' or 'woods' in Mod. Osage, possibly archaic?]. *ząącé* a valley with trees, a grove of trees (RBn19, unconfirmed).

zą́ące. N **prairie, country (i.e., rural area), countryside.** *hcížį wį ząącíolįį akxai* little house on the prairie (RBn22-08).

ząącéolįį (variants: **zą́ąceolį́į, ząącólįį**). N **Hominy district (lit., 'dwelling in the country' or 'dwelling on the prairie'; no reference to 'timber')** (02/09/95/FH/pc:okc; FH/6/16/01)**; dwelling in the timbers** (RB; BE2.67; unconfirmed). [Note that sources disagree as to whether this term refers to 'timber'.] *hcížį wį ząącíolįį akxai* little house on the prairie (lit., 'the little house that dwells on the prairie') (FH; RBn22-08).

•• RB: <sáh^{n}-so-li^{n}, sah^{n}-tsí-o-li^{n}, sah^{n}-tséh-o-lí^{n}a>

•• JOD (slip file): *zącé* <ṣan-ṭṣĕ´> a highland containing many trees. *zącolį* <ṣanṭṣuḳ¢i^{n}> (cited as a source by JOD, see <ca^{n}-q¢u-k'u-pe>). *zącólį* <Sanṭṣuk¢i^{n}> dialect or subdialect [given as a dialect of Osage] (e.g., under <káwa> 'a horse').

•• LFD 32: *ząceólį* <ço^{n}-dseu´-gthi^{n}> Dwellers-in-the-upland-forest ['upland forest' unconfirmed by modern speakers]. "This was a name given to a group of Osage Indians who fled from their village at the time of an overflow of the river, and halted at the forest, there pitching their camp. This group now dwells in what is known as Hominy, Okla." *ząceólį* <Co^{n}-dse-u´-gthi^{n}> Dwellers-in-upland-forests (personal name).

zą́zi. N **sour odor, acrid smell (such as armpit odor or onion smell)** (RB, unconfirmed).

zí. ADJ, N **yellow** (FH). *kšǫ́ka šǫ́ke íhta apa zípe* second son's dog is yellow (2-1-Fl; BE2.162; PM03/24/95/pc: *zi* only; RBn10-5:MOJ/79: *zíhi* only).

•• RB: <zí-hi>.

•• LFD 30: *zi* <çi> yellow. *zíhi* <çi´-hi> pallor, an unhealthy color (03/24/95/PM/pc:ma). *zízie* <çi´-çi-e> spotted with yellow, a ritual term (unconfirmed; 03/24/95/PM/pc:uk). LFD 89: *hką́ce hįscee che zi akxa cuuce akxa* <ḳo^{n}´-dse hi^{n} stse-e tse çi a-ka dsu-dse a-ko> the peach is mellow [expected Mod. Os. gloss: 'these peaches are yellow, they're ripe'] (03/07/95/PM/pc:ok for 'ripe').

••• *OM* same as Osage (LFD 30).

••• Cf. *zíhi.*

zí žuuce ékǫ. ADJP **orange (lit., 'yellow that is redlike')** (BE2.99; 04/17/95/LS/pc:ok/ma).

zíhi. ADJ, N **brown** (05/01/95/LS/pc:brown only, also *zi*, no distinction); **yellow** (FH, same as *zi*). [For the meaning 'yellow', some speakers use both *zí* and *zíhi*, while other speakers prefer one form or the other.]

••• Cf. *žíhi.*

zízi. ADJ, N [reduplicated form of *zí*] **brown** (03/24/95/PM/pc/prod, unconfirmed; 05/01/95/LS/pc:uk).

ž

žaamí (variant of **ážamį**).
žaaníe, žaaníi (variants of **žąąníi**).
žáhke. N **jack (in a deck of cards)** (LF; 04/14/95/FH/pc:uk). [Borrowed from English.]
•• LFD 285: *žáhke* <zha´-ke> jack (playing card).
žáhta. ADJ **divided, forked, notched, branded, split, cut, sliced** (04/20/95/LS/pc:prod). *ǫ́pe žáhta* bird's tail divided, scissortail flycatcher (BE2.117; 04/20/95/LS/pc:ok).
•• LFD 222: *žáhta* <zha´-ta> cloven, parted, as the foot of a deer, buffalo, or cow.
••• Cf. *íhaa žáhta, ǫ́pežahta, pažážaki.*
žamí, žamį́, žámį (variant of **ážamį**).
žápe. N **beaver** (RB).
•• JOD (slip file): *žápe* <ça´-pe> a beaver.
•• LFD 221: *žápe* <zha´-be> the beaver (04/07/95/PM/pc:no). "This animal figures prominently in Osage tribal rites." *žápe toka* <zha´-be do-ga> the male beaver.
žápuška. N **ant** (BE2.3; 01/04/95/FH/pc:prod).
•• LFD 222: *žápuska* <zha´-biu-çka> an ant. "In the war rites the ant represents the weapons of the warriors." *žápuska sape* <zha´-biu-çka ça-be> black ant. *žápuska zi* <zha´-biu-çka çi> yellow ant. *žápuska žúuce* <zha´-biu-çka zhu-dse> red ant.
žáže (variant: **žáži**). N **name; signature** (HRE; 02/27/95/FH/pc:ok). [Males have a childhood name and an adult name, while girls keep their name all life long (HRE); all these are denoted by *žažé*.] *táata žáže ašcį́e?* what is your name? (lit., 'what name do you have?') (02/27/95/FH/pc:ok). *táatą žáže aðį́e?* what is his name? (02/27/95/FH/pc:ok). *į́įštáxį žáže táatą ašcį́e?* what is your English name? (02/27/95/FH/pc:ok). *tówa níhka įkšé táatą žáže aðíe?* what is that man's name? *Bob žáži abrį́e* my name is Bob (02/27/95/FH/pc:ok; BE2.92). *Mary žáže aðį́pe* her name is Mary (RBn12-08). *šį́tožį wíhta žáže ðakˀú hkǫ́bra* I want you to give my boy a name (RBn10-21/JW&FW/77). *žį́kážį žáže* child's name (RBn10-21/JW&FW/77). *nǫ́ǫ žáže* adult name (RBn10-21/JW&FW/77; 02/27/95/FH/pc:ok). *žáže kˀú* give an Indian name (02/27/95/FH/pc:ok)
•• RB: <zháh-zhi>.
•• LFD 222: *žáže akˀǫhe* <zha´-zhe a-k'o^n-he> to sign name, a signature (02/27/95/FH/pc:okc). *žáže kšihtǫ wikie* <Zha´-zhe Ki-to^n Wi-gi-e> [expected Mod. Os. form: *žáže kˀú wíkie*] prayer for name taking (02/27/95/FH/pc:uk). *žaže kˀu* <zha-zhe k'i> to dub.
žáže kikáaye. VP [reg. *ki*-del.?, *žáže _(ki)káaye?*] [*žáže + ki-* DAT + *káaye*] *(intr.)* **sign (as a document), subscribe, undersign, affix one's signature (lit., 'produce one's name for others')** (05/02/95/LS/pc:prod, non-preasp; HRE/12/29/01/ok).
žáže wahóta. N **nickname; name used to make fun of s.o. (lit., 'funny name')** (02/27/95/FH/pc:ok).
•• LFD 222: *žáže wahota* <zha´-zhe wa-ho-da> nickname.
žáže wéleze. N **signature.** *žáže wéleze káaye* sign it (lit., 'make the name with a pen') (HRE/12/29/01/pc:ok).
žáži (variant of **žáže**).
žáˀaži (variant of **ažážį**).
žą́ą. N **tree, log, wood, lumber** (03/16/95/MREI/pc:ok); **stick, pole; woods, forest** (03/16/95/MREI/pc:ok). *žą́ą kše ą́ąhǫǫ* I like that tree [lying down]. *še žą́ąžį akxa ohtáza akxai* that little tree is pretty. *žą́ą įkše ší tą hkilísąða* when you get to that particular tree that stands there, turn. *žą́ą íichįpe* he was hit with a stick (lit., 'they hit him with a stick') (FH: prod).
žą́ą. V [reg., *_žą́ą*] *(intr.)* **sleep, go to sleep, lie down to sleep, go to bed; sleep over, stay all night** (RBn10-5:MOJ/79). *žą́ą kši áape* that person's lying down, they said (02/15/95/FH/pc:prod orig). *žą́ą kše* they're lying down (BE2.76). *žą́ą kše* the one sleeping over there (03/24/95/PM/pc). *šką́ži žą́ą* lie still (RBn23-15). *šǫ́ke akxa hci ápetxa žą́ą nąpé* those dogs just lie around the house. *wáli níhka kǫ́ða, íhpiiži akxai, ąžą́ą htai* she really wants a man, she's bad off, let's have her stay all night (lit., '. . . let's all go to sleep'). *ðažą́ą hta paaše?* are you all going to sleep? *ðažą́ą hta nįkšé* are you [sg.] going to sleep here? *ðažą́ą hta paašé?* are you [pl.] going to sleep here? [implying staying over, sleeping all night] are you going to stay all night (lit., 'are you going to go to sleep?')

(RBn10-21/JW&FW/77). N **sleep, night's rest, overnight stay.** *ðáabri žą́ą tą* in three sleeps hereafter (FH:ok).

•• JOD (slip file): *žą* <ça^{n}> to sleep, a sleep, a day.

•• LFD 224: *žą* <zho^{n}> to sleep. *ažą́* <a-zho^{n}´> I sleep. *ðažą́* <tha-zho^{n}´> you sleep. *ąžo pe* <o^{n}-zho' i> [LF's <o^{n}-zho'> is presumably an error for *ąžą́* <o^{n}-zho^{n}´>] we sleep. LFD 225: *žą́ihe* <zho^{n}´-i-he> to sleep.

••• *KS/QU žą* sleep (RR); *WI nąą* sleep, fall asleep, *haną* I sleep, *raną* you sleep (KM).

••• Cf. *ážą, óžą.*

žą́ą áace. N **vine (lit., 'embraces the tree').**

žą́ą ákaastowe. N [*žą́ą + á- + kaa- + stówe*] **sleigh, sled.**

žą́ą háa. N **outer bark of a tree.**

•• LFD 233: *žą́ha* <zho^{n}´-ha> outer bark of a tree.

žą́ą káahtahta. N **woodpecker (lit., 'pecking on wood')** (RBn HW13; FH:uk).

•• LFD 357: *hpakátataye* <pa-ga´-da-da-xe> downy woodpecker.

••• *KS ppagádadaye ppa žűüje* red-headed woodpecker (RR).

••• Cf. *htáhtaze.*

žą́ą káxa. N **tree branch, limb, tree branching out** (FH).

žą́ą kʔa. N **cottonwood** (RBn HW13, unconfirmed FH:uk).

žą́ą kʔą. N **root or roots (of a tree, bush, etc.).**

•• JOD (slip file): žą́ kʔą <ça^{n}´ k'ă^{n}>.

žą́ą olį́į. VP [reg., *žą́ą o_lį́į*] *(intr.)* **live in the woods, dwell in the forest.**

žą́ą pe. N **trees growing in a nonrandom pattern.** [Contrast *žą́ą ke* 'trees growing in random pattern'.]

••• Cf. *žąąpé.*

žą́ą tái įké. VP *(intr.)* **talk in one's sleep** (RBnot3/3/77; 05/02/95/LS/pc:ok; 03/15/95/PM/pc:uk; 03/16/95/JS/pc:uk).

žą́ą waxáka. N **thorny tree.**

žą́ą wéðaawa. N **measuring stick, ruler, yardstick** (05/02/95/LS/pc:prod).

žą́ąhcuke. N [*žą́ą + hcúke*] **wooden spoon.**

žąąhcúkʔa. N [*žą́ą + hcúkʔa*] **punk, tinder, fine kindling (dried decayed wood used for tinder to strike a flint fire** [RB]**).**

•• RB: <zháh^{n}-tsu-kah^{n}> (04/18/95/FH/pc:okc; BE2.108).

•• LFD 227: *žą́hcikʔa* <zho^{n}´-tsi-ķ'a> decayed-wood, punk, touchwood.

žą́ąhkoke (variants: **žą́ąhkoe, žą́ąhkoa**). N **box, coffer, trunk; thousand.**

žą́ąhlaa, žą́ąhlaaská (variants of **žą́ąlaa**).

žą́ąhpaye. N **bat (the flying mammal)** (RB; HRE/12/29/01/pc:okc).

žąąhpáto. N **beaver** (BE2.7; RBn1-24).

•• RB: <zhuh^{n}-páh-to>.

••• Cf. *žápe.*

žą́ąhpeece. N [*žą́ą + hpéece*] **fire-making wood (piece of wood laid on ground and rubbed to make fire).**

•• JOD (slip file): *žą́ hpece* <ça^{n}´ pe -tse>.

žą́ąkaaxǫ́. N [*žą́ą + kaaxǫ́*] **branch or limb that has been broken off a tree; bridge.**

•• LFD 225: *žą́kaxǫ* <zho^{n}´-ga-xo^{n}> a bridge. "This word originated from the fact that streams were frequently crossed by using fallen trees that had been blown down into the streams by the wind."

žą́ąlaa (variants: **žą́ąhlaaská, žą́ąhlaa, žąąláa**). N [*žą́ą + laaská*] **blossom or flower on a tree.**

žąąníe wapeį huukǫ́ða óožu (variant: **žąąníe wapį huukǫ́ða óožu**). N, VP [uninfl.] *(intr.)* **(suffer from) diabetes, (have a) high blood glucose level (lit., 'put a lot of sugar in your blood').** *žąąníe wapį huukǫ́ða óožu ékǫ ðaįšé tą, žąąníežį ðaaché ížoši apai* if you have sugar in your blood/diabetes, they said don't eat candy (FH:4/18/96/tape:prod).

žąąníežį. N [*žąąníi + -žį* 'little'] **candy (lit., 'little sugar')** (BE2:16; 01/09/95/FH/pc:prod).

žąąníi (variants: **žaaníe, žaaníi**). N [*žą́ą + níi*] **sugar (lit., 'tree water', originally referring to maple sap or syrup).** *paašcéka žaaníi ážu* put some sugar on the strawberries (03/14/95/MREI/pc:ok, also ok: *paašcéka žaaníi tóa ážu*). *paašcéka žaaníi ážu bríišta* I already put some sugar on the strawberries (03/14/95/MREI/pc:okc; BE2.129).

•• LFD 226: *žąní* <zho^{n}-ni´> sugar; candy. *žąni tópa ąhkío* <zho^{n}-ni do´-ba o^{n}-ķi´-o> [expected Mod. Os. form: *žąąníi tóa ąkʔú*] give me some sugar. *žąni akxa waðasta* <zho^{n}-ni a-ka wa-tha-çta> [expected Mod. Os. form: *žąąníi akxa waastá*] the candy is sticky.

žąąníi nížǫe. N **syrup** (DN-WHM, unconfirmed; FH:uk). [It is doubtful that this expression is a real Osage form.]

•• LFD 295: *žǫní sápe* <zho^{n}-ni´ ça-be> molasses.

••• Contrast *QU wažǫ́ke skíde kdókdo* syrup, molasses (RR).

žąąníioožu. N [*žąąníi* + *oožú*] **sugar bowl** (MSB, 3-3-83-p4, 03/14/95/MREI/pc:ok).

žą́ąpaase. N [*žą́ą* + *paasé*] **saw (for cutting wood).**

žąąpé. N [possibly *žą́ą* + *ápe*] **leaf.**

•• RB: <zhaⁿ-béh>, <zháhⁿ-ah-péh> (04/14/95/FH/pc:ok; BE2.77).

žą́ąxe (variant: **žą́ąxa**). N **pole, stick** (RBn10:21/JW). *hóįze žą́ąxe* a fishing pole (RBn3-05; FH:prod). *žą́ąxe ąnáchįpe* he hit me with a stick. • **baby board** (FH: prod). *žą́ąxe wį aðįhú hta apai* they're going to bring a board [for the baby] (FH:prod).

•• JOD (slip file): *žą́xa* <çaⁿ´-qa> a stick, a pole.

•• LFD 227: *žą́xa* <zhoⁿ´-xa> a yardstick, a counting stick used in counting songs in a ceremony (unconfirmed; 05.02.95.LS.pc:uk).

žą́ąxe céɣenii. N **drumstick** (BE2.36; 01/20/95/PM/pc:ok).

••• Cf. *céɣenii ochį́*.

žą́ąxežį. N [*žą́ąxe* + *-žį* 'little'] **stick, branches, small limbs or twigs (of a tree or bush).**

••• Cf. *žą́ąžį*.

žąąxúhaa. N [*žą́ą* + *xúhaa*] **inner bark of a tree.**

•• JOD (slip file): *žąxúha* <çaⁿ-qü´-ha>.

žą́ąže. V [uninfl.]? *(intr.)* **smell as spoiled food smells, have a stinking odor or a bad odor (e.g., underarm odor)** (t109/PM/506; 01/13/95/FH/pc:ok). *žą́ąže ðáįše* you smell bad.

žą́ąžį. N [*žą́ą* + *-žį* 'little'] **splinters** (FH); **small branches, small limbs or twigs (of a tree or bush).**

žą́kše. CONT **continuative aspect postverbal marker (indicating ongoing action or state in present, past, or future time) for 2nd sg. lying down subject.** *óžą oðážą žąkšé* you're lying in bed (FH/pc). *tąhé žą́kše?* are you well? (05/01/95/LS/pc:ok).

žą́kxa žįįhé. VP [reg., *žą́kxa _žį́įhe*] *(intr.)* **sleep sitting up.** *žą́kxa žįhé akxa* he's sleeping sitting up (FH/06/16/01/pc). *žą́kxa ažį́įhe hta mįkšé* I'm [going to be] sleeping sitting up (FH/06/16/01/pc).

žą́xta. N **body odor, any soured odor (such as the smell of clothes, shoes, feet, or a refinery).** *hǫǫpé akxai žą́xta akxai* the shoes smell bad (03/02/95/FH/pc). • V, ADJ [conjug. unknown] *(intr.)* **smell unpleasantly sour, have a sour odor; stinky, sour-smelling.**

•• RB: <zhúⁿ-xtah>.

žé. V [reg., *_žé*] *(intr.)* **defecate, have a bowel movement; be excreted, ooze, be emitted.** *ažé hkǫ́bra* I want to shit (BE2.120;CQc: *a* not *ą*, not stative). • *(trans.)* **excrete, emit.** • N **penis, male organ.** *žé wahtįe apái* his penis is showing.

•• JOD (slip file): *že* <çe> to stool. *žé ðištą tą, pac*ˀ*į́-aú, ápi aú* <Çe´ ¢ücta^n´-ţaⁿ, ṗáts'iⁿ-au´, áṗi au´> [expected Mod. Os. form: *žé ðiištá tą, pac*ˀ*į́, áape*] When he (a child) finished stooling, he said, Turn bottom up!

••• *OM* same as Osage (LFD 81).

••• Cf. *céže, óochiže, ožéhci, úže*.

-žé. ADV [contraction of *aží* NEG + *ðe* DECLARATIVE MARKER (extremely rare)] **not, never.** *htáažį akxa kį́įkįežį íiðaapižé* the little deer has never seen butterflies.

žeká. N **leg.** *iiséwai žeká akxa ą́nąk*ˀ*ǫ́ži akxái* the thing hateful [i.e., 'hateful thing'] is that my legs won't listen to me (01/09/95/FH/pc:prod; HRE:ok). *žékaxǫ́ akxai* his legs are broken (FH). *žékaxǫ́ nįkšé* your legs are broken [unexpected stress on first syllable may be due to reassignment of accent due to following accented *xǫ́*] (FH).

•• LFD 222 (unconfirmed): *žeká* <zhe-ga´> the upper part of the leg. *žekáole* <zhe-ga´-u-gthe> the muscles and nerves around the thigh bone, the femoral circumflex.

••• Cf. *žekáxǫ*.

žeká óhkiche. N **knee joint.**

•• LFD 222 (unconfirmed): *žeka óhkiche* <zhe-ga u´-ḳi-tse> knee joint.

žékaxǫ́. N [*žeká* + *xǫ́*] **broken leg(s).**

žekáxǫ letǫ́. N **Crippled Hawk (personal name).**

žekážįka. N [*žeká* + *žįká*] **queen (in a deck of cards) (lit., 'little legs')** (LF only).

•• LFD 222: *žekážįka* <zhe-ga´-zhiⁿ-ga> little legs. "This name was given by the Osage to the queen in a deck of cards. It is said that the picture of the queen on the old-style cards was in full figure with very small legs."

ži (variant of **aží**).

žíhi (variant: **ží**). ADJ, N **brown** (01/09/95/FH/pc:prod; 05/01/95/LS/pc). *haaská žíhi ðíhta íiðahkie?* did you find your brown dress [for yourself]? (BE2.13; RBn1-45; BE2.162).

•• LFD 222: *žíhi* <zhi´-hi> reddish, pink. *žíhi htąka* <zhi´-hi ţoⁿ-ga> yellow-billed cuckoo.

••• Cf. *zí, zíhi*.

žišǫ́ (variant: **žiišǫ́**). PPN **before.** *hą́įnį žišǫ́ ąkále* we'll go home before dark (RBn10-7:JW). *koe ónǫǫ žišǫ ší tą šį́ tą koe hpíiži žišǫ ší tą koe péeški ðikǫ́ða htai wáščuɣe ðáalį* before you get old and before you get fat and ugly and nobody wants you, you should get married (RB).

-žį (variant: **žíka** [archaic]). ADJ **a little, small amount of s.t.** *wihtáežį akxa ékipše kǫ́ða akxa, hǫ́ǫpa ðé wéeðina akxai, mą́zeskažį níðe kǫ́ða akxa* [younger] sister wants me to say something, she's grateful today and wants to give away a little money (RBn23-17). • **small, little.** *hkąącóolążį* a little pie (FH: not *žįka*). *kóe htáa htóhožį wį pe* once there was a little blue deer (RBn15-01). *ážąžį* cot, small bed. *níhkažį* a little man, little men. *níhkažíka* a little person, little men [*níhkažį* is more common (FH)]. *nihkašikažį* little people (7/8/94/PM/num98b). • ADV **really, very, indeed.** *wąkóižį alí hta mįkšé* I'll come right back [*wąkǫ́ǫ* + *-žį*] (RBn3-21). *wahók?ažį* very young. *áskažį*very close [*áška* + *-žį*]. *hcékažį* just now [*hcéka* + *-žį*].

žį́. V [2nd sg. of *į* 'wear'] **you wear.**

žį́įhe (variants: **žį́įha** [PM], **žįhé, žįįhé, žį́įhi**). V [reg., *_žį́įhe*] *(intr.)* **sleep, slumber** (02/15/95/FH/pc:ok). *ažį́įhi, ažį́įhe* I sleep (02/15/95/FH/pc:prod). *ðažį́įhe* you sleep (02/15/95/FH/pc:prod). *ąžį́įhe* we sleep (02/15/95/FH/pc:prod). *žį́įhe brúuc?ake ąįhé* I can't sleep (RBn22-08). *žį́įhe ðáalį hpáaye* I slept well. *ðóha ažį́įhe* I'm about asleep (MREI/04/27/94). *ðóha ðažį́įhe nįkšé* you're about asleep (MREI/04/27/94). *žį́įhe ðáalį škáaye?* did you sleep well? (03/10/95/MREI/pc:okc). *žį́įhe ðáalį škáayapi?* did you [pl.] sleep well? (03/10/95/MREI/pc:ok). *žį́įhe akxái* he/she is asleep (PM:ok; BE2.123). *ðóha ąžį́įhe aðįkše* we [two] are about asleep (MREI/04/27/94). *ąžį́įhe ąðįkšé* we [two] are sleeping (02/15/95/FH/pc). *ąžį́įhe ąkakxái* we [pl.] are sleeping (02/15/95/FH/pc). *žį́įha* go to sleep! (03/10/95/MREI/pc:prod). *žįįhápi* go to sleep [pl. addressee]! (02/15/95/FH/pc:okc; RBn23-09; 03/10/95/PM/pc:ok).

•• LFD 225 (unconfirmed): *žą́ihe* <zho^{n}´-i-he> to sleep. LFD 224: *žį́ha o* <zhi^{n}´-ha o> [sentence-final *o* is not used in Mod. Os.] lie down.

žįká (variant: **žį́ka).** ADJ, V [uninfl.] **(be) little, small** (7/8/94/PM/num98b; 02/16/95/FH/pc:ok). [A somewhat archaic variant of *žį*. Use of *žįká* instead of *žį* sounds old-fashioned in most contexts (FH; 02/16/95/FH/pc; BE2.80).] • N **child(ren), little one(s), kid(s)** (BE2.19; 01/19/95/FH/pc:ok). *níi táahpa įkší žįka nǫ́ǫðe ðáalį, ecíe ska ąąžį ąkátxa* the pond is a good place to raise children, we think it's there (from a fable) (RBn19-04).

•• RB: <zhí^{n}-kah>.

•• LFD 331: *žį́^{n}-ga* <žįka>. LFD 222: *žįká* <zhi^{n}-ga´> small, little children. "When used in the ritual its meaning is young, as reference is made to a sapling." *žįkáe* <zhi^{n}-ga´-e> this term is found in a ritual, meaning little ones. LFD 224: *žįkáoxta* <Zhi^{n}-ga´-o-xta> favored little ones, a title among the Osage. LFD 224 (unconfirmed): *žįkáhtą* <zhi^{n}-ga´-ṭo^{n}> to have children, to generate. *žįká ahtą* <zhi^{n}-ga´ a-ṭo^{n}> I have children. *žįká ðahtą* <zhi^{n}-ga´ tha-ṭo^{n}> you have children. *žįká ąwąhtą pe* <zhi^{n}-ga´ o^{n}-wo^{n}-ṭo^{n} i> we have children. [All these sentences with *-htą* are unconfirmed and are unrecognized by Mod. Os. speakers.]

••• Cf. *žįkážį.*

žįká owáhkihą (variants: **žį́ka owáhkiha**).

•• RB: <zhí^{n}-kah o-wah-kí-hah^{n}>.

•• LFD 224: *žįká owahkihą* <zhi^{n}-ga´ u-wa-ḳi-ho^{n}> grandchild; a descendant; to issue, to bring forth.

••• Cf. *owáhkiha.*

žįkážį (variant: **žįkáži**). N **child(ren), little one(s), kid(s); childhood** (RB; BE2.19; 01/19/95/FH/pc:ok). *žįkážį nakxą́še wéewina akxą́he, ilǫ́įhpa waachí štǫ́pape* I want to thank you children for watching my son dance.

•• LFD 222: *žįká žįka* <zhi^{n}-ga´ zhi^{n}-ga> baby [now archaic]. *žįká žįka wakilą pi o* <zhi^{n}-ga´ zhi^{n}-ga wa-gi-gtho^{n} bi o> [sentence-final *o* is not used in Mod. Os.] he plans for the good of his children. LFD 217: *žįka žįka wihta* <zhi^{n}-ga zhi^{n}-ga wi-ṭa> [expected Mod. Osage: *žįkážį wíhta*] my child.

žįkókašą (variant: **žįkókaša**). V [reg., *žįkó_kašą*] [*žįkážį* + *okášą*] *(intr.)* **babysit, take care of kids** (RBn10-6:JW). • N **babysitting, childcare.**

žóhkile. V [reg., *žó_hkile*] [*hkik-* RECIP + *žóle*] *(intr.)* **be with each other.** *žóąhkile ðálį žamíe* I think we ought to get married [marry each other] (RBn17-p1). *žóhkile apái* they are going with each other (02/01/95/FH/pc:okc).

žóika (variant of **žúoka).**

žókile. V [reg. *ki*-ret., *žó_kile*] [*kik-* SUU + *žóle*] *(trans.)* **be with one's own people.** *žóðakile ðąįšé* you are with him [your own].

žóle. V [reg., *žó_le*] *(trans.)* **marry, accompany, go with, come with, date, be in a courtship with (lit., 'be with').** *žówile hkǫ́brai* I want to marry you (RBn17-p01). *žówile hkǫ́brai įké* I don't want to marry you (RBn17-p01). *žówile* I [am] with you. *žówile brée hce* I'll just go with you

žóle (*continued*) (02/01/95/FH/pc:okc). *žóawale brée hta mįkšé* I'm going to go with them (02/01/95/FH/pc:okc). *lį́į žóąle* sit with me (02/01/95/FH/pc:okc). *žóðale ðachíe?* did you come with her? (02/01/95/FH/pc:okc). *žóðale ðaįšé?* are you with him? are you going with him? (02/01/95/FH/pc:okc). *žówaðale šíe?* did you go with them? (02/01/95/FH/pc:ok). *žówaðale ščee ðáalį* you should go with them/us (02/01/95/FH/pc:ok). *žówaðale škǫ́šta?* do you want to go with us? (02/01/95/FH/pc:ok). *ecí pa žóąðale šíe ðe* you brought me to them (lit., 'you went with me to them'). *Eddie akxa žóąle achíe* I came with Eddie (lit., 'Eddie came with me') (02/01/95/FH/pc:okc). *žóle mąðį́* go with her. *žówalape* he went with them. *žówale mąðį́* go with them. *žówale* with us, with them. *žówalapi* with us (FH). *škáce žólaži apai* they won't play with them (2-10-83-p4). • PPN **with (often glossed 'and' in English).** *súhka htaaníi wacúe ðubráaska žóle hpáaɣe* I'm going to make chicken and dumplings (lit., 'I make chicken soup with dumplings') (BE2.9; FH:prod).

•• LFD 224: *žóle* <zho´-gthe> to accompany, to go with some one. *žóale* <zho´-a-gthe> I am with him, I accompany. *žóðale* <zho´-tha-gthe> you accompany. *žóąla pe* <zho´-o^{n}-gtha i> we accompany. LFD 228: *žóle* <zhu´-gthe> with him or her. *žóale bre* <zhu´-a-gthe bthe> I went with him. *žóðale sce* <zhu´-tha-gthe stse> you went with him.

••• Cf. *žóhkile, žókile.*

žópše. V [reg., *žó_pše*] *(intr.)* **wade** (JS, FH). *níi žópše pšíe ðáha, táatą wį mąžą́ olį́į iiðáðe* when I would go to wade in the river, I saw something that was in the woods (lit., 'when I went to wade in the water, I saw a thing that lived in the countryside') (t24b-p17/num24CQ119; 04/27/95/FH/pc:okc, added *iiðáðe*). *níi žópše hkǫ́bra* I want to wade in the water (04/27/95/FH/pc). *hą́ące wáli nuužúpe ska, žįkáži apa hǫ́pái nii žópši apái* last night it must have rained a lot, the children today are wading (01/24/95/FH/pc:ok).

•• LFD 228: *žópše* <zhu´-pshe> to wade, as in the water. *žóapše* <zhu´-a-pshe> I wade. *žoðápše* <zhu-tha´-pshe> you wade.

žówale. V [reg., *žówa_le*] [*wa-* VAL + *žóle*] *(intr.)* **be with folks.**

•• LFD 228: *žówale* <zhu´-wa-gthe> to be with [rather, 'to be with them']. *žoáwale brée* <zhu-a´-wa-gthe bthe> I am with them [rather, 'I went with them']. *žówaðale scée* <zhu´-wa-tha-gthe stse> you are with them [rather, 'you went with them'].

••• Cf. *žóhkile, žókile.*

žǫ́. V [2nd sg. form of *ǫ́* 'do'] **you do (rare usage).**

žǫ́e, žǫ́ę (variants of **žǫ́ǫ**).

žǫhpáleze (variants: **žǫ́hpaze, žǫ́hpoize**). N [probably contains *hpá* 'head' + *léze* 'striped'] **quail, stripe-headed quail, bobwhite** (FH:4/24/96/tape,ma; 04/20/95/LS/pc). *žǫ́hpázi mǫnoį océ pšíe* I went to look for quail and prairie chicken (BE2.110; RBn3-11; RBn3-MOJ/p1).

•• RB: <zhó^{n}-páh-zeh> quail.

•• LFD 134: *šǫ́hpaleze* <shó^{n}-p̣a-gthe-çe> quail, bobwhite, striped headed. "This word in modern times is spelled sho^{n}´-p̣a-'the-çe."

žǫ́ǫ (variants: **žǫ́e, žǫ́ę**). V [2nd sg. form of *ǫ́ǫ* 'wear'] **you wear.**

žúe (variant of **žúuce**).

žúoka (variant: **žóika**). N **human body** (01/07/95/FH/pc:ok). *žúoka ahkílazo mįkšé* my body is recovering, my body is healing (01/07/95/FH/pc:prod, no nasal; BE2.9). *mą́hka žóika mą́į akxai, kitą́he hta akxa hǫ́ǫpa hu* he's haywire with peyote [medicine is moving in his body], but he'll be all right at daylight (01/06/95/FH/pc:prod; BE2.102; RBn HW). *hpéecenii akxa žúoka ðíðuuhpíiži hta akxai* whiskey is bad for your health (lit., 'whiskey will make your body bad') (JS).

•• LFD 224: *žóika* <zho´-i-ga> their bodies, ceremonial ritual term. LFD 228: *žóika* <zhu´-i-ga> body, flesh. *žóika ląðe* <zhu´-i-ga gtho^{n}-the> large-body, stocky. *žóika nie* <zhu´-ga ni-e> ache, pain in any part of the body. *žóika anie* <zhu´-i-ga a-ni-e> I have a pain. *žóika ðinie* <zhu´-i-ga thi-ni-e> you have a pain. LFD 228 (unconfirmed): *žo* <zhu> flesh, or body.

žúuce (variants: **žúe, žúu**). ADJ, V [uninfl.] *(intr.)* **(be) red** (FHt128). *ákahamį žúuce ðée, pée ðuuštáke hta ðe?* who is going to undress that one with the red coat? (spoken at the ceremony of paying for the drum, where a woman's red wedding coat is being given to the former drumkeeper). *žúuce, ska kaðǫ́ htóho* red, white, and blue. *htaaníi žúe tóe káaɣa* make vegetable soup (RBn12-06, unconfirmed).

••• Cf. *hką́ące žúe.*

žúuce sápe. ADJP, N **purple, burgundy (lit., 'black [i.e., dark] red').**

••• Cf. *htóho sápe.*

English-Osage Index

Introduction

Following is an index to the Osage entries in the dictionary by their English meanings. Most entries consist of an English word or phrase matched with one or more Osage terms, which refer to entries in the Osage-to-English part of the dictionary. This is not a full English-to-Osage dictionary. Entries in this index do not provide full information on the ranges of meaning and use of Osage terms; Osage entries should be consulted for that information, even when additional clarification of meaning or usage appears in the index entry. An Osage word identified in the index as the equivalent of an English word may well have a wider range of meaning or a more specific meaning than the English word does. An Osage word that has multiple English equivalents appears in multiple places in the index. If a particular English word is not found in the index, try looking for words of similar or related meaning.

In some entries the English word or phrase is the technical term for a class of grammatical elements, and the Osage terms are the members of that class; for example, the entry "continuative aspect markers" lists the set of Osage words that follow the verb to mark ongoing action and simultaneously convey something about the stance (lying down, sitting, standing, etc.) of the subject of the sentence; the entry "pronominal prefixes" lists the various prefixes by which Osage usually conveys notions such as "I," "you," "us," and so forth.

In a few cases, cross-references to other entries in the index are provided; these are noted as "*see* xxxx" (or "*see also* xxxx"), where "xxxx" is another index entry. In some cases the reader is referred to an Osage entry that is not the exact equivalent of the English expression but that provides some discussion relevant to that expression; such cases are noted as "*see discussion under* **xxxx**" (where "**xxxx**" is an Osage entry). Occasionally, too, it has seemed useful to note that Osage has no direct equivalent of an English expression. (This does not represent a deficiency of Osage; it would be just as easy to compile a list of Osage expressions for which English has no direct equivalent.)

Certain English phrases are listed in the index by a word other than the first. In such entries, the word by which the phrase is listed is separated from the rest of the phrase by a colon (:), and its place in the phrase is represented by a tilde (~). Thus, the phrase "make friends" is indexed as "friends: make ~" (under F). When looking for the Osage equivalent of an English phrase whose first word is a common word with a general meaning, such as "make," "have," or "be," it is a good idea to look first under a more specific word later in the phrase; for example, look for "make friends" or "be good" first under "friends" or "good."

Abbreviations for grammatical categories ("N" for noun, "V" for verb, "CAU" for causative, etc.) are the same as those used in the Osage-to-English part of the dictionary.

In a few entries in the index (which were noticed after it was no longer possible to ask Carolyn Quintero about them), a form is listed that, as far as we can determine, does not appear in the Osage-English part of the dictionary, but nonetheless looks as if it might conceivably be a genuine Osage form that was inadvertently omitted. Although these forms are not guaranteed to be Osage words, it seemed worthwhile to retain them in the index in case it later turns out that they are. They are signaled by the notation "no Osage entry; possibly not a genuine form" in square brackets.

a, an. **wį, wį́xce**
abalone. **hcúke**
abandon s.o. **kíhkoopše, ohkíǫðe**
abdomen. **hcéze, wánǫbréoožú**
abhor. **íisi**
abnormal in appearance. **éžixci**
abode. **ohcíle**
abound. **ochí**
about (i.e., 'almost', as in 'about asleep'), about to. **ðóha**
above. **mąšíhta**
above: be ~ others. **álįįha**
above: go, be, or place s.t. ~. **ámąši**
above: place ~. **mąšíhta**
above s.t. else. **ámąši**
abroad. **níimąse**
abrupt, abruptly. **óhesaži**
absent: be ~. **ðįké**
absurd. **ókaayeįke** [LFD]
abundance. **óše**
abundance: disorderly ~. **táatą ochí**
abundant: be ~ in quantity. **óše**
accept. **iinąhi**
accompany. **žóle**
accomplish a task for s.o. (especially drumming for s.o. else's singing in a peyote meeting). **áwaši**
ace (in a deck of cards). **ohkącilą**
achieve success for s.o. **ðáalį kšíðe**
acorn. **hposú**
acquainted: be ~ with. **ípahǫ**
acquainted: get or become ~ with each other. **ðótahkiðe**
acrid smell. **zązi**
across. **áðuuhta**
act (N). **ókˀą**
act a certain way. **mąðį́**
act like. **íkǫskahkíðe, ókˀą**
act unsuitably. **ókˀą éži**
act with rectitude. **óðohtąhkiðe**
activate by pushing on. **paaɣí**
active. **wahtóke** [LFD]
add a little more to. **wéhuužį**
add in cooking. **oðóhkihą**
add items to cooking. **oolą́**
address as friends and relatives, address with respect. **wahǫ́į**
adhere to. **ásta**
adjacent. **páskuha**
adjourn. **panáa**
administer medical care to s.o. **ščéðe**
admire. **óžo áži**
adulthood, adults. **nǫ́ǫ**
advance: in ~. **hpahą́le** [LFD]
advanced age. **nǫ́ǫ**
affect a person. **omą́ðį**
affected: have one's body ~ by peyote. **mąhkažóika**
afraid. **ðą́ące óðisąha, ðą́ące ósai**
afraid: be ~ (of). **nǫ́ǫhpe, onį́žį**
afraid: be ~ of. **íinǫǫhpe**
afraid: s.t. to be ~ of. **nǫ́ǫhpewaðe**
African American. **mįhkása, mįįása, níhka sápe**
after. **álįįha**
after the present event. **ákahahta**
afternoon. **mįįðóhta ðiištą́**
afternoon: late ~. **mį́įhpapo**
afterward. **álįįha**
afterward (after the present event). **ákahahta**
afterward (following, next). **áhkiha**
again. **aðóoha, ši** (*see also* inceptive prefix)
again and again. **šíną**
against: be ~. **ížoši**

against: place vertically ~. **álą**
against all odds. **ðąącháži**
ago. **haašíhta**
ago: a long time ~. **kaahúuža**
agree, agree with. **iináhi**
agree with s.t. **íištą**
ahead. **kootáha**
ahead: go ~. **mąðį́**
ahead: go ~ with s.t. **ékįǫ**
aid (v). **óhką**
air. **htaacé**
airplane: ride or fly in an ~. **kį́į̨**
alcohol: drink ~. **waðáahtą**
alcoholic beverage. **hpéecenii**
alert. **wahtóke**
alight (from). **ósi, owísi**
alight from (e.g., a vehicle or a horse). **wísi**
alive: be ~. **ní**
all. **záani**
all: that's ~. **kaašéną, kaašǫ́įke**
all day (long). **hą́ąpa záani**
all night: stay ~. **žą́ą**
all other things. **táatą éžiški**
all over, all paths and directions (e.g., children running off in all directions). **háaški**
all right. **škaškáða**
all the time. **háachi, štą**
all the world, all the universe. **níǫhta záani**
allotment. (*see discussion under* **mą́žą**)
allow. (*see injunctive markers*)
allow s.o. to do s.t. **kšíðe** (*see also* causative markers)
allow to live. **níðe**
almost. **ðóha, hóni**
alone, be alone. **éwažį̌**
alone: leave ~ (a sitting person or thing). **šǫ́įkšeðe**
alone: leave ~! (command). **šo ðíe**
alone: leave it ~. **kaašǫ́e che**
along: leave ~ without bothering, touching, or otherwise disturbing. **šǫ́cheðé**
along, alongside. **páskuha**
along a path. **ha**
along that way. **ée htáha**
already. **ðiištą́** (*see also* evidential marker; *see also discussion under* **ska** [MODAL])
Alred: Jo Ann Shunkamolah ~ (personal name: Looking Only at Her). **eeną́tǫįpe**
also. **éški, ški, -škítą**
always. **'háachi, íkiha, kaašǫ́e, ną** [ITERATIVE], **šǫǫšǫ́we, štą**
always did. **nąpe**

always late. **ókxąži**
amen. **kaašéną**
among: be ~. **oðízą, omą́ðį**
among: be ~ a group of people. **omą́ðį**
among: be ~ others. **oðízą**
among: mixed ~. **íwihe**
amount: large ~. **huuhtą́ka**
amount: small ~. **hépežį̨**
amount: small ~ (approximately half a container). **hépe**
amount: small ~ (not quite filling a container). **ohépe**
amusing. **wahóhota, wahóta**
amusing person. **wahóhota**
ancestors. **mópše**
ancient. **kóoci**
and. **kóe, pátą** (often not overtly expressed in Osage)
and (in addition). **ški**
and (in numbers only). **éci**
and then. **káakǫ tą, kaðǫ́, kóe**
anew. (*see* inceptive prefix)angel. **áahualį̨į**
angle. **paaγó**
angry. **wažį́ hpííži**
angry: be ~. **lǫ́ǫ**
angry: be ~ at s.o. **ohkížį̨**
angry: be ~ at s.o. or at each other. **hkížį̨**
angry: be ~ with. **ihkį́žį̨**
angry: become or get ~. **óžį̨ hpííži**
angry: feel ~ at. **hkížį̨**
angry: make s.o. ~. **ðúulą, wažį́ hpííži káaγe**
animal. **wacúhta**
animal sounds: make ~ (moo, bark or howl, sing [as a bird], quack, etc.). **hóo, hóohtą**
ankle. **hį́ihką**
announcer. **wacípxaį**
annoyed: be ~ by. **áalake**
annually. **omą́įhka wį̨ hieną**
anoint with. **stáðe**
another one. **éži wį̨**
ant. **žápuška**
anus. **įléha**
anxious: be ~ for. **íhice**
anxious: feel ~ about. **óðąąceši** [LFD]
any. **tóa**
any other thing. **táatą éžiški**
anybody. **howaðéeški, pée**
anyhow. **óðąži**
anyone. **pée,' wį̨**
anything. **howachéeški, táatą**
anything, anything else. **táatą éžiški**
anything at all. **táatą howachéeški**

anything one doesn't like. **kihǫ́ǫži**
antique. **kóoci**
anyway. **óðą̨ži**
apart: be ~. **kíðahapa**
apart: pull or tear ~ (e.g., a tree limb from the trunk). **ðupáxa**
apart from anyone else. **ohką́ci**
appear. **hcį́į, íðǫpe, wahcį́į**
appear a certain way: make one ~. **tǫ́pewaðe**
appear so. **tǫ́pewaðe**
appear suddenly. **wahcį́į**
Appear Suddenly to Them (personal name). **wakáahcį̨e**
appendix (the internal organ). **šúpe**
appetite: have no ~. **wanǫ́braži**
apple. **hką́ące**
apply (a substance such as ointment, grease, or cream). **stáðe**
apply makeup. **į̨cé káaɣe**
apportion. **íhkilai**
appreciative. **óweena**
appreciative: be ~ (of). **wéeną**
approach. **mąðį́**
appropriate. **ðą̨ąché, ékǫ**
appropriate: be ~. **íhta**
appropriately. **ékǫ**
approve of. **iinąhi**
apricot. **hką́ące zi žį́**
April. **mį́įǫpa šápe, mį́įǫpa wetóopa**
Arapaho (tribe or tribal member). **aį́paxo**
arbor. **áhcihtą, wažáihci**
arbor house: long ~. **haaskáhci**
arch of the foot. **óski, síioski**
area: cleared off ~. **oštá**
argue on behalf of (e.g., as an attorney). **áhkie**
argument. **óie, taaké ie**
arise (from a bed or chair). **hpaahą́**
arm. **áa**
armband. **áahkǫ, áapiolą**
armed forces. **áhkita, áhkita omą́ðį, taaké omą́ðį, taaké oną́ąžį**
armed forces: be in the ~. **taaké omą́ðį, taaké oną́ąžį**
armed person. **áhkita**
army. **áhkita , áhkita omą́ðį**
around. **okáwį̨ɣe** (*see also discussion under* **ke**)
around: be ~ close. **ákiɣe**
around: go ~. **kǫ́kǫe**
around: go, pass, or walk ~. **ákiɣe, ápše**
around: go ~ s.t. **íðišąha**
around: move or be all ~. **ákiɣe**
around: turn oneself ~. **ámąhta hkilíikoį̨ɣe, hkilíisą**
around: turn s.o./s.t. ~. **ðiihkóį̨ɣe**
around: twist ~ (e.g., a crepe paper streamer). **ðusą́sąwį**
around (as in drive around, turn around, etc.). **-wį̨ɣe**
around (e.g., a house, tree, tipi, drum). **ápetxa**
around the edge (e.g., of a pond). **ákiɣe**
around this way. **ðeekáiha**
Aroused by Something That Suddenly Appears (personal name, referring to a deer suddenly looking up). **wakáahcį̨e**
arrange. **ðuustáko**
array (v) (multiple items) on top of s.t. else. **ážu**
arrest (put s.o. in jail). **hą́ąnahpazé oolą́**
arrive back here. **alí**
arrive back there. **akší**
arrive here. **achí**
arrive here with (motion accomplished). **aðį́achi**
arrive home. **akší**
arrive home here (motion accomplished). **alí**
arrive there (motion accomplished). **ahí**
arrow. **mą́ą**
arrow shaft. **mǫ́ǫse**
arrow shaft tree. **mǫ́ǫsa hu**
artery (blood vessel). **hką́, lušúpe**
arthritis. **wahúni**
artichoke. **hpǫ́ɣe**
as. (*see* because)
as. **šǫ́**
as . . . as. **ékǫ**
as soon as. **áha**
as well. **ški**
ashamed, feel ashamed. **iiščéwai**
ashes. **níixoce**
ashtray. **niixócoožu**
ask a favor. **waatá, waší**
ask a question. **íðǫɣe**
ask concerning one's own people or things. **ilǫ́ɣe**
ask folks to work for one. **áwawaši**
ask for. **tá**
ask for (as a loan), ask for s.t. to use it. **ootá**
ask permission. **íihǫ**
ask s.o. questions. **ðuupxáðe**
ask s.o. to do s.t. **ée, íihǫ**
ask s.o. to help out. **waší**
aspirin or any other kind of medicine. **mąhká**
ass, asshole. **į̨léha**
ass (donkey). **nąąhtą́htąą**
assassinate. **c?éðe**

assemble (as for a council). **kiistó**
assign a name to s.t. or s.o. **ðaacé**
assist. **óhką**
assistant chief. **kahíke ók?ą, kahíke otxą́**
at. **ci, ki**
at (s.t. lying or spread out). **kši**
at a time (e.g., a bit at a time, two at a time). **nąðé**
at least. **našǫ**
at rest. **škaškáða**
at that place or time: be ~. **ecí**
at this time. **ðetxą́ci**
attend. **oną́ąžį**
attend to. **óðąąceši**
attention: act of paying ~. **nąąɣúce**
attorney. **wáhkie**
attractive. **ðáalį**
augment. **htą́ą**
August. **hlaazípe, mį́įǫpa hkíetoopa**
aunt: maternal ~ (specifically, mother's older sister). **iiną́** or **iinąhtą** 'my mother's older sister', **ðiihǫ́htą** 'your mother's older sister', **iihǫ́htą** or **iihǫ́** 'his/her mother's older sister'
aunt: maternal ~ (specifically, mother's younger sister). **iiną́žį** or **iiną́** 'my mother's younger sister', **ðiihǫ́žį** 'your mother's younger sister', **iihǫ́žį** 'his/her mother's younger sister'
aunt: paternal ~ (i.e., sister of father of male, either older or younger). **wihcími** 'my father's sister', **ðihcími** 'your father's sister', **ihcími** 'his/her father's sister'
authoritative, authority. **wahtǫ́ka**
authority: one with ~. **totą́ha, wahtǫ́ka**
automobile. **éwažį nąąke**
automobile tire or wheel. **hcéðe**
autumn, in the autumn. **htąątą́**
avoid s.t. **íðišąha**
awaken *(intr.)*. **iihkíðe, -xi**
awaken *(trans.)* by foot. **nąąxí**
away: a short distance ~. **áška**
away: give ~. **níðe, wak?ú**
away: give ~ by pressing or pushing away (e.g., the *ilǫ́ǫška* drum). **kaaðéešpa**
away: give things ~. **waníðe**
away: give ~ to each other. **ohkík?u**
away: give ~ to one's own people. **kík?u**
away: giving ~. **ók?u**
away: go ~. **mąðį́, okábra**
away: pass or give ~ (e.g., the drum at *ilǫ́ǫška* dances). **kaaðée**
away: take ~. **aðį́aðee, aðį́mąðį, ðicíze**
away: take ~ from s.o. s.t. of his/her own. **kilúuze**
away: take ~ one's own. **lúuze**
away: throw ~. **ǫ́ǫðe**
awful. **hpíiži**
awhile. **katxą́**
axe. **mą́ąhįska(?), mą́ąhįspe**

baby. **hpáažį**
baby: have a ~. **wéetaðe**
baby: place or put a ~ on the baby board or inside. **hpáažį ok?ǫ́he**
baby boy. **šį́tožį**
baby girl. **šį́mįžį**
baby board. **oðópše'**
baby board: place a baby on the ~. **hpáažį ok?ǫ́he**
babyhood. **hpáažį**
babysit, babysitting. **žįkókašą**
back. **xáða**
back: attached to the ~. **oðáha**
back: arrive, come, or get ~. **akší, akú, alée, alí**
back: bring or take ~. **aðį́akši, aðį́aku, aðį́alee, aðį́ali**
back: give ~. **kík?u**
back: go ~. **mąlį́**
back: in the ~ of. **haaší**
back: some days ~. **hǫpái hašíhta**
back (in return, again). **ki-**
back (of the body). **nąhka**
back and forth: pass or go ~. **ihkílašą**
back and forth movement: make a ~ (as when riding a teeter-totter). **sísiąðe**
backward. **xáða**
bacon. **wašį́**
Baconrind (personal name). **wašį́haa**
bad. **hǫ́ǫži, hpíiži, óhesaži**
bad: make s.t. ~. **ðuhpíiži**
bad deeds (such as bad talk or theft). **ók?ą éži**
bad disposition: having a ~. **ók?ą hpíiži**
bad dream. **ohpáza**
bad manners: having ~. **ók?ą hpíiži**
bad medicine. **mąhká hpíiži**
bad reputation: of ~. **nǫhǫǫ**
bad shaft of an arrow. **mą́ąhpiiži**
bad shape: be in ~. **íhpiiži**
bad temper. **waðílą hpíiži**
bad things. **ízizike, táatą hǫ́ǫžį**
bad things about s.o.: say ~. **hkiláažoži**
bad weather. **mą́ąhpiiži**
bad words. **íe hpíiži**
bad words: say ~. **lǫ́ǫ**
badger. **xóoka**

badly. **óhesaži**
bag. **óožuhaa**
bag: tobacco ~. **nąnúhuoožúhaa, nąnįǫ́kužu**
bait s.o. to say or do s.t. **ožížie**
bake in an oven. **mą́zeǫ́ohǫ oohǫ́**
bald. **stá, štáha**
bald: make ~. **ðuuštá, ðuuštáštai**
bald head. **hpeeštá, wéelišta**
bald headed. **wéelišta**
ball (used in a game). **htaapé**
baloney. **tǫ́ǫpše**
banana. **htóžąke**
bank. **mą́zeskahci**
banner. **haawálele**
banty (bantam) chicken. **súhka saaki**
bar. **hpéecenii ðaahtą́ hci, hpéeceniihci** [archaic]
barbecue (refers only to cooking meat on a rack). **óhkace**
barbecue meat: the black part of ~. **táasaaki**
barbecue rack. **oážu, wážu**
bare: make ~. **ðuuštá**
bare ground. **oštá**
barely. **tó**
barely touch. **ðiihcé**
bark (as a dog does). **hóo, hóohtą, óhoo**
bark of a tree. **hį́ce, xúhaa**
bark of a tree: inner ~. **žąąxúha**
bark of a tree: outer ~. **žą́ą háa**
barren. **wéetaðaži**
Bartlesville (Oklahoma). **hkáwažį htą́wą**
base (ADJ). **iiséwaðe**
basement. **mą́įhkaši**
bashful. **wíeži**
basta! **kaašǫ́ka**
bat (flying mammal). **žą́ąhpaye**
bath house. **ohíiðahci**
bathe, take a bath. **hiiðá**
bathe: place to ~. **ohíiða**
bathroom. **ožéhci**
bathtub . **ohíiða**
baubles: bits and ~. **ošpéžį**
bawl out. **kaazą́, toníðe**
be. **ðį́** (note that there are many constructions in which forms of English 'be' occur but where Osage *ðį́* is inappropriate; *see also* continuative aspect markers)
be alive, be in good health. **ní**
be characterized by. **ðį́** (*see also* continuative aspect markers)
be here. **ðeeká**
be here or there. **ecí, ecíke** (scattered)
be in, among, or throughout an area or a group of people. **omą́ðį**
be so. **ékǫ**
be there. **ahí**
be there, be at that place, be at that time. **ecí**
beads. **hį́ska, tóoce ðiláace (?), wapúška**
beads: prayer ~. **wíkie hį́ska**
beadwork (N). **hį́ska káaye**
beadwork: do ~. **hį́ska káaye**
bean vine. **hǫbrį́ hi**
beans. **hǫbrį́ke**
beans: green ~. **hǫbrį́ke, hǫ́brįke htóho žį**
bear (especially black bear). **wasápe**
bear cub. **wasápežį**
beard. **hį́į, į́hį**
beat (conquer). **ohí**
beat (e.g., a drum). **kaaštá**
beat of a drum, beating sound. **hcíce**
beat s.o. in a race. **káaxa**
beat things (such as a drum). **óchį**
beat up. **ochį́**
beautiful. **ðáalį, ohtáza**
beaver. **žąąhpáto, žápe**
because. **tą** ('because' is often not expressed directly but implied by the logical or pragmatic relationship of one clause to another; for examples, *see under* **táalį** 'burn', **tóa** 'some', **wéeną** 'be thankful, grateful', **wéhice** 'far')
become (suddenly?). **ahí**
become a person. **ínihkašie**
become angry or mad. **óžį hpíiži**
become embarrassed. **iizíke**
become extinguished. **táaži**
become soft or sodden. **špǫ́ǫ**
bed. **ážą, óžą**
bed: go to ~. **žą́ą**
bed: have s.o. in ~, put s.o. to ~. **áðižą**
bedclothes, bedding. **omíže**
beef: head of ~. **hcéeska**
beer. **hkáwaceženii, níi ápuye** [archaic]
beet. **tóole žúe**
beetle. **walúška háa šooká**
before (ADV). **haašíhta**
before (PPN). **žišǫ́** (*see also discussion under* **ska** [MODAL])
beggar. **waatášta**
begin. **hínąąžį**
begin to. **ahí**
beginning: from the ~. **hpahą́le**
behave. **óðohtą**
behave oneself. **óðohtąhkiðe**
behavior: good ~. **óðohtą, óðohtąhkiðe**

behavior: in regard to ~. **taa-**
behind. **haaší**
behind: be ~. **oðáha**
behind: leave ~. **ǫ́ǫðe**
behind s.o.'s back: ~. **nąlǫ́ǫha**
belch. **ík?o, wawék?o**
believe. **ažį́, éðe**
believe regarding s.o. **ažį́**
belittle. **ðaažóži**
belittle s.o. **hkiláažoži**
bell **íikaahtamą**
bell: ring like a ~. **kaahtáama**
bell: ring the ~. **ðuuhkáamą**
bells (such as the ones dancers tie around their legs). **mą́zeštahižį**
belly. **hcéze**
belong to (a group). **oðízą**
belong to him. **íhta** (*see also* pronominal prefixes; suus prefix)
belong to s.o. **íhta**
belong to them. **íhta, íhtaapi**
beloved. **óxta**
beloved: s.o. or s.t. ~ (such as a favorite child). **óðoxta**
below. **oðúluha**
belt. **íhpią**
belt: men's dance ~. **íišupe**
belt: woman's yarn ~. **hceehį́į**
belt (worn by men outside a blanket). **íišupe**
belt (worn by men with dance clothes or outside a blanket). **íhpią**
beneath. **oðúluha**
bend: make ~ (e.g., a tree branch using the hands). **ðiizó**
bend down. **paac?į́**
bend one's body part (e.g., leg or arm). **ðuušǫ́**
bend one's own (body part or possession), bend oneself. **líizoke**
bend over. **kaapáac?į**
bent over (as a person, a tree, or a hooked staff). **c?įša**
bent over (referring to a human body). **c?į́xa**
berry (inedible). **pazó**
beside. **páskuha**
beside each other. **hkiðé**
best: be the ~ (above all others in a certain aspect). **ochí**
best: do one's ~. **ík?uce, waašką́**
best everyone in a game. **óhi**
best s.o. in a game. **ohí**
bet (N). **óžok?a**
bet: make a ~. **óžok?a káaɣe**
better: get ~ (in regard to illness). **kiní, kitą́he, kítąhe**
between. **ohtą́ną**
bewitch or "witch" s.o. **kilǫ́že**
beyond. **kootá, kootáha**
beyond a certain point. **kootáha**
beyond another thing. **áhkiha**
Bible. **waléze sápe**
bicycle. **hcéðe álįį, hcelį́ álįį**
bid (N). **oðáake**
big. **htą́ą, htą́ka, lą́ąðe**
big goose or big duck. **míɣa htą́ka**
big mouth. **íhcuke**
bill (paper money). **htaną́k?a, htaną́k?a mą́zeska**
billfold. **mą́zeskaoožú**
bind (V). **paaxcé**
bind (as a blanket). **pašǫ́we**
bird. **wažį́ka**
bird: game ~. **míɣa**
birth. **wéetaðe**
birth: give ~ (to). **iitáðe**
birthday: have a ~. **iitáðape ékitxą**
birthing: be ~. **waníe**
biscuit. **wacúe ðutáahpa**
bit: a ~ (of). **hépe, huužį**
bit: a ~ (slightly). **ékǫ**
bit (fragment). **kašpé, ošpéžį**
bit of a whole coin (twelve and a half cents). **kašpé**
bitch (female dog). **šǫmį́įka**
bite (V). **ðaaxtáke**
bite folks, bite people. **waðáaxtake**
bite into small pieces. **ðaaxǫ́ke**
bite oneself. **hkilaaxǫ́**
bits and baubles. **ošpéžį**
bitter. **hpá**
blabbermouth. **táatąžį́ ški oðáake**
black. **sápe**
black dog. **šǫhtą́ą sa**
Black Dog (personal name). **šǫ́ke sa**
black person (African American). **mįhkása, mįįása, níhka sápe**
black person: little ~. **sáežį**
black walnut. **htákue**
blackberry. **waskúe sápe**
blackhawk. **letǫ́sape**
bladder. **céženiioožú**
blanket. **haxį́, mį́, omį́že**
blanket: man's ~. **óhkihpaache**
blanket: saddle ~. **wákaštǫ**
blanket: woman's ~. **mį́waapaache**

blanket folded to cushion a seat. **wákaštǫ**
blanket wrapped around like a skirt. **wáakipetxą**
blazing star *(Liatris punctata)*. **mąhká saakí**
bleed. **wapį́**
blend. **oðóhkiðe**
bless. **ðakʔéðe, ðuðáalį**
bless: use to ~. **íištope**
bless: use to ~ oneself. **íistahkiðe**
bless or give a blessing with the hand. **ðistópe**
bless with. **íista, íištope**
blind: be ~. **įįštá wawéeðeži**
blind (covering, e.g., for a window). **akáaspe**
blink (v). **ðupʔį́ze**
blink at each other. **iištáðe ahkíliitože**
blink repeatedly. **ðupʔį́pʔįze**
blink the eyes (at). **iištáðe ðiitóže**
block s.o.'s way. **oðóšimąðį**
blood. **wapį́**
blood vessel (vein or artery). **hką́, lušúpe**
bloom (v). **opáaɣa, paaɣáce**
blossom (v). **paaɣáce**
blossom on a tree. **žą́ąlaa**
blow *(trans.)*. **ðaažóce**
blow (as one's nose). **píɣą**
blow inside, into, or on (e.g., a fire in a fireplace). **opíɣą**
blow on. **ðaažóce**
blow on s.t. **píɣą**
blow with force (as in blowing one's nose). **kaaží**
blowing: by ~ (as on a fire to get it started). **pi-**
blue. **htóho**
blustery. **htaacé hpíiži** [LFD]board: baby ~. **oðópše**
boat. **páce**
boating. **pacíolįį**
bobcat. **įžį́akika, lį́xa**
body (human). **žúoka**
body odor. **žą́xta**
boil (N). **ðéskali**
boil (as food boils when cooking). **ápuɣe**
boil dry, boiled dry. **táapuze**
boil over. **táapuɣe**
bois d'arc. **mį́ceštá hu**
bone. **wahú**
book. **waléze**
boot. **hǫǫpésce** [LFD]
born. **iitáðe**
borrow. **ootá**
boss (N, V). **oðówaðe, wakáaɣe**
boss: be a ~. **oðóðe**
boss: be ~ of (e.g., an event). **oðówaðe**
boss an event. **oðóðe, óohkihą**

both of them. **ðǫǫpá, éeðǫǫpa**
both of us. **éeðǫǫpa**
bothered: be ~ by **áalake**
bottle. **oožú, óožu**
bottle: pop ~. **niikáapxokeoožú**
bottom (buttocks). **įléha**
bounce up (as in a car or wagon). **kaamą́šąšie**
bouncy (as in a rough ride). **kaamą́šąšie**bow (N). **mį́ce**
bowel movement: have a ~. **žé**
bowl (N). **hį́įce, htáanieoožú, oožú**
bowstring. **mį́cehką**
box (N). **žą́ąhkoke**
boy. **šį́tožį**
bracelet. **áahkǫle**
braid (N). **hpáxįįsą**
braids. **héðǫǫpa**
brain. **waðílą**
branch: tree ~. **žą́ą káxa**
branch (of a tree or a stream). **káxa, káxa žį**
branch of a tree: broken ~. **žą́ąkaaxǫ́**
branches: small ~. **žą́ąxežį, žą́ąžį**
brand (v). **pážahta**
branded (with a notch or cut, etc.). **žáhta**
brave. **wašóše**
bread: light or leavened ~ (wheat bread, as opposed to cornbread). **watáahą**
bread (or 'piece of bread'; any kind of bread: cornbread, wheat bread, etc.). **wacúe**
break. **kaaléke, xǫ́**
break a long object by pushing **paaxǫ́**
break by biting. **ðaaxǫ́**
break by foot, break with the foot. **nąąxǫ́**
break by hand. **ðiixǫ́**
break by mouth. **ðaaxǫ́**
break by striking (a long object such as a stick). **kaaxǫ́**
break down. **pixǫ́**
break into pieces by mouth. **ðaaxǫ́ke**
break into two parts. **ðiixǫ́**
break off (a long object such as a stick). **kaaxǫ́**
break off a long item by using the hands (e.g., a limb, sofa, car antenna). **ðiixǫ́**
break off by pushing (e.g., a limb). **paaxǫ́**
break off s.o.'s (e.g., body part). **kíðiixǫ**
break one's own (e.g., a body part). **kiixǫ́, líixǫ**
break one's own by mouth. **láaxǫ**
break one's own by shattering. **kíleke**
break s.o.'s (e.g., a body part). **kíðiixǫ**
break s.t. of one's own by mouth. **láaxǫ**
break up (e.g., a meeting). **panáa**

break with the hands (e.g., a dish, an egg, a light bulb, a window). **ðuuléke**
break wind. **ðiipíɣą**
break wind (with a small noise, by letting the air out slowly). **ðižíce**
break wind noisily. **ðibrį́ɣa**
breakfast. **kaasįexci wanǫ́bre**
breakfast food. **kaasįexci ónǫbre**
breast. **paazé**
breath: run out of ~ from. **íkaske**
breath: short of ~. **hehé**
breathe. **ónie**
breathe hard. **heháha**
breathless: become ~ from. **íkaske**
breechcloth. **xíðaxa**
breechloading shotgun. **wahóohtą opáaxǫ**
breeze. **htaacé**
briars. **waxáka**
bridesmaid: have as a ~. **íðuɣe**
bridge (N). **žą́ąkaaxǫ́**
bright. **skáha**
bright colors. **hį́į**
bring. **akú**
bring back here (motion underway). **aðį́aku**
bring back here, bring back home (motion accomplished). **aðį́ali**
bring back s.t. that belongs to oneself. **aláðįku**
bring back there (motion accomplished). **aðį́akši**
bring here (motion accomplished). **aðį́achi**
bring here (motion underway). **aðį́ahu**
bring home (motion accomplished). **aðį́akši**
bring the parts of a whole together with pressure, bring components into contact. **ðiiskíke**
bring there (motion accomplished). **aðį́ahi**
bring up (rear or raise). **nǫ́ǫðe**
Bristow: Robin ~ (personal name). **wažážemį́įhcexį**
broad. **bráaða, lą́ąðe**
broadcloth. **haaštáha**
broke (without money [a loan translation]). **xǫ́**
broken. **xǫ́**
broken: be ~. **kaaléke, kaaxǫ́** (when used with continuative aspect marker *akxa* or *apa*), **xǫ́**
broken heart. **ðą́ące ðuusáaki, ðą́ące xǫ́**
brooch. **wápaɣa**
broom. **wékaacuxe**
broth. **htaaníi**
brother (specifically, older brother of a female). **wihcį́to** 'my older brother' (speaker is female), **ðihcį́to** 'your older brother' (addressee is female), **ihcį́to** 'her older brother'
brother (specifically, older brother of a male). **wižį́ðe** 'my older brother' (speaker is male), **ðižį́ðe** 'your older brother' (addressee is male), **ižį́ðe** 'his older brother'
brother (specifically, younger brother of a female). **wisǫ́ežį** 'my younger brother' (speaker is female), **ðisǫ́ežį** 'your younger brother' (addressee is female), **isǫ́ežį** 'her younger brother'
brother (specifically, younger brother of a male). **wisǫ́ka** 'my younger brother' (speaker is male), **ðisǫ́ka** 'your younger brother' (addressee is male), **isǫ́ka** 'his younger brother'
brother: baby ~ (of a female). **kxáhpą**
brother-in-law (specifically, brother-in-law of a male). **wihtą́ha** or **htą́ha** 'my brother-in-law' (speaker is male), **ðihtą́ha** 'your brother-in-law' (addressee is male), **ihtą́ha** 'his brother-in-law'
brother-in-law (specifically, brother-in-law of a female). **wišík^{ʔ}e** 'my brother-in-law' (speaker is female), **ðišík^{ʔ}e** 'your brother-in-law' (addressee is female), **išík^{ʔ}e** 'her brother-in-law'
brow. **hpée**
brow: smooth ~. **hpeeštá**
brown (ADJ). **zíhi, zízi, žíhi**
brown: light ~ (like the color of elk hide). **ópxą hį́į ekǫ́**
brown (become brown by application of heat). **taazíhi**
brown (i.e., to brown food). **taazíhiðe**
browned. **taazíhi**
brownie (elf). **míalǫška**
brush (V). **kaaɣú**
brush: wire ~. **wákaapše**
brush (for the hair). **wékaapše**
brush arbor. **áhcihtą, wažáihci**
brush s.o.'s hair. **kípše**
brush the mane or coat of an animal. **kípše, wákaapše**
buck. **htáa, htáa htą́ka**
bucket. **céɣe**
buckeye tea. **htáška hí**
buckskin. **htaaháa**
buckskin dress. **haaská**
bud on a tree. **žą́ąlaa**
buddy. **hcošpá**
buffalo. **ðóxe, hcée**
buffalo: small ~. **hceežį́**
buffalo: young or small male ~. **hceetóežįká**
buffalo calf: unborn ~. **hceežį́**
Buffalo Chief (personal name). **ðóxe kahíke**
Buffalo Clan. **ðóxe**
buffalo horn(s). **hcehé**

bug. **walúška**
bug with thick outer layer or exoskeleton. **walúška háa šooká**
build. **káaɣe**
build a fireplace or fire. **océðe**
build for oneself. **hkihkáaɣe**
bulge. **hpá**
bulk, in bulk. **bróka**
bull. **hceeskátóoka**
bun (woman's hairdo). **hpáxį̣ ðuutáahpa**
bunch: a whole ~ of. **huuhtą́ka, huuwáli**
bundle: gather and tie in a ~. **paaxcé**
burden: be a ~ to s.o. **ówǫ káaɣe**
burdened: be ~ (e.g., with excessive woe). **íibrąxcį**
burgundy (color). **žúuce sápe**
burial ground. **óxe mą́žą**
burial place. **óxe**
burial stick (red stick put into a coffin at the head or foot, made of special wood). **hką́ące žąą**
burn (v). **osái, táaðįke káaɣe, táalį**
burn cigarettes (as in a peyote meeting). **osái**
burn down, burn up. **táaðįke káaɣe**
burned. **táalį**
burned meat. **táasaaki**
burning. **íwili**
burp. **íkˀo, wawékˀo**
burro. **nąąhtą́htąą**
burry. **waxáka**
burst. **kaapxóhke**
bushy head. **héxpa**
business: run a ~. **oðówaðe**
busy. **ówǫ**
busybody (refers to s.o. who is into everything). **ókˀąštą**
but. **ąži, kóe, ną** [INTERJ]
butcher (N). **wapáse**
butcher (V). **hpáce, wahpáce**
butt in. (*see discussion under* **ópaašike**)
butter. **paazénii wéli**
butterfly. **kį́įkįįežį**
buttocks. **įléha, ǫ́pe**
button. **wahúžįka**
button up. **oðíiną**
button-snake-root (*Liatris punctata*): dotted ~. **mąhká saakí**
buy. **ðuwį́**
buy for one's own (people, family). **lúwį**
buy for oneself. **hkíluwį**
buy for s.o. **áðuwį, kíðuwį**
buy from s.o. (s.t. that belongs to that person). **kíðuwį**
buy s.t. of one's own (buy back). **lúwį**
buy stuff with s.t. **wéðuwį**
buy things. **waðúwį**
buy with. **íðuwį**
buzzard. **héka**
by: pass ~. **ákiɣe, ípše**
by car. **éwažį ną́ąke, oðíhtą olį́į**
by extreme of temperature. **táa-**
by foot: go ~. **mąðį́**
by hand. **ðu-**by heat or cold. **táa-**
by means of. **í-**
by mouth. **ðaa-**
by oneself. **éwažį, ohką́ci**
by striking. **kaa-**
by way of. **ha**

cabbage. **wéelihtąą**
cable. **mą́ze**
cache. **nąlǫ́ǫhkile**
Caddo (tribe or tribal member). **hįįšá**
cafe. **owánǫbrehcí**
cake (e.g., birthday cake). **wacúe skúðe**
calf: unborn ~. **hceežį́**
call: phone ~ (N). **mą́zeie**
call by name (V). **ðaacé**
call by phone. **mą́zeie híðe, ohkíe**
call by phone: have s.o. ~. **mą́zeohkíhkie hükšíe**
call each other names. **hkílǫ(lǫ)**
call folks names. **walǫ́ǫ**
call for folks (V). **wapą́**
call loudly. **hóosaaki**
call names. **lǫ́ǫlǫǫ**
call on s.o.'s name. **ðaacé**
call one's own, call one's own by name. **láace**
call one's relative(s). **kíhpą**
call s.o. a bad name. **lǫ́ǫ**
call to ask or summon s.o. to attend or appear before others. **kípą**
calling songs. **wapą́ waaðǫ́**
calm (V). **ðuuštáka**
calm, calmly. **škaškáða**
calm (a person's ways or the weather). **štáke**
camp (V). **ahcí, hcí**
can or other container for soda pop. **niikáapxokeoožú**
Canadian person. **įįštáxį**
candy. **žąąníežį**
cane. **íisa**
cannot. **ðąącháži, ðuucˀáke**
cannot understand. **kíopxaži**
cantaloupe. **įįštáxį sáhku**
cape. **ákahamį**

car. **oðíhtą**
car, by car. **éwažį nąąke**
car door. **oðíhtą hcižé**
card: greeting or gift ~. **íe ðáalį žį**
card: lead or play a ~ (in a card game). **ðée káaɣe**
card game. **htanąk?a k?ǫ́**
cardinal (bird). **wažįžue**
cards. **htanąk?a k?ǫ́**
cards: play ~. **htanąk?a k?ǫ́**
cards: playing ~ (N). **htanąk?a, htanąk?a ðiihíce**
care: have a ~ with regard to s.t. or s.o. **íinǫǫhpe**
care: take ~ of. **átǫpe, ðak?éðe, okášą, okáše, wanáše**
care: take ~ of a meal oneself when asked to do so. **óohkihą**
care: take ~ of a task or an event. **oðówaðe**
care: take ~ of oneself. **óhkihkaše**
care for kids (babysit). **žįkókašą**
care for oneself. **ohkíežą**
care for the sick. **húheka okášą**
careful: be ~ with. **íinǫǫhpe**
careful: not ~. **íinǫǫhpaži**
caress. **íiščįka**
caress one's own. **íikiščįka**
carousel. **kǫ́kǫe**
carpet. **omíže**
carrot. **tóoleži**
carry. **aðįaðee, į, k?į, k?įahi**
carry on in a certain way. **ahkílaðį**
carry on the back. **k?į**
carry one's items, carry along one's items. **aláðį**
carry one's own. **aláðį**
carry oneself. **ahkílaðį**
carry piggyback. **ðuškápa**
Carrying-and-Wailing (personal name). **wáįɣaaké**
carrying the charcoal (mourning dance). **wašápe aðį**
cash payment. **wahkílae wakášupe**
cast a spell on s.o. **kilǫ́že**
castor oil. **wéli mąhką**
cat. **ilǫ́eži**
catch. **oðįįke**
catch on s.t. **íhkowa**
categorize. **hpahíke**
caterpillar. **wáxta**
catfish. **htóze**
Catholic (N, ADJ). **šǫmįhka**
cattle: head of ~. **hcéeska**
caught on s.t.: get ~. **íhkowa**
causative markers. **ðe** [CAU], **hkiðe** [CAU], **káaɣe, kíðe** [CAU], **kšíðe** [CAU], **kšíɣe** (*see also* instrumental prefixes)
cause oneself ill or harm. **hkilúhpiiži**
cause oneself to be or do. **hkíðe**
cause s.t. to be a certain way. **káaɣe** (*see also* causative markers; instrumental prefixes)
cause to be for s.o. **íkikaaɣe**
cause to be or get lost. **oxpáðe káaɣe, oxpáðeðe**
cause to fly out in pieces or splinter. **paasíke**
cause to go. **ðéeðe**
cause to smell, as in making cedar smoke for a cleansing or a blessing. **oðíbrą**
cedar. **xǫ́ǫce**
cedar tea. **xǫǫcénii**
cease (*trans.*). **kaaštą́, kaakǫ́ną káaɣe**
cellar. **mąįhkaši**
cemetery. **óxe mąžą**
censure (v). **kaazą́**
cent. **waðáawažį**
center. **ohkąska**
center: at the or in the ~. **mąché,ohkąska**
center: toward the ~. **mąchéhtaha**
cents: five. **waðáawa sáhtą**
cereal. **kaasįexci ónǫbre**
ceremonial dances of the Osages. **ilǫ́ǫška**
certain way: live or be a ~. **ðį, mąðį**
certainty of a future event. **ðée hta ché**
chair. **áalįį, álįį**
chaise longue. **álįįscee**
challenging. **wahcéxi**
change (*trans.*). **ðúeži**
change: make or make a ~. **íhkihkawį káaɣe**
change (as the weather). **šką́**
change (money, coins). **íhkihkawį, ošpéžį, waðáawažį**
change one's mind. **waðílą kikáaɣe**
change one's ways. **hkilíisą**
change (*intr.*). **íhkihkawį káaɣe**
changeable. **éžixci**
characteristics: personal ~. **ók?ą**
charcoal accompanying them (ceremonial title). **wašápe aðį wažówale** [LFD]
charge: be in ~ of. **oðóðe**
charge: in ~. **oðówaðe, óohkihą**
charge: take ~ of. **ókašą**
charred meat. **táasaaki**
chart of land. **mąžą́waleze**
chase (v). **ðuxí, olé**
chase away. **olé**
chastise. **kaazą́**
chauffeur. **waðíhtą wakáaži, wakáaži**
cheap. **ómąhka**
check a horse's forward movement. **oðíitą**
cheerful. **ók?ą ðaalį**

cheese. **paazénii saakí, paazénii wéli saakí**
cherish each other. **óxtahkiðe**
cherish one's own. **kíoxta**
cherished. **óxta**
Cherokee (tribe or tribal member). **šaáke, šálaki**
chest (box). **žą́ąhkoke**
chest (of the body). **mą́ąke**
chew. **ðaaškíke**
chew, chew into pieces. **ðaaxǫ́ke**
chewing gum. **mį́įhtǫeli**
Cheyenne (tribe or tribal members). **htáaceomą́i**
chicken. **súhka**
chicken: banty (bantam) ~. **súhka saaki**
chicken: prairie ~. **mǫ́nǫį**
chief. **kahíke**
chief: be ~ (over a people). **kíhike**
chief-to-chief (succession of hereditary chiefs within a family). **opxą́pxą́**
child, children. **žįká, žįkážį**
childbirth. **wéetaðe**
childcare. **žįkókašą**
childhood. **žįkážį**
childless. **wéetaðaži**
children: take care of ~. **žįkókašą**
children in their teens. **hcéka nǫ́ǫ**
chin. **ðéepa**
chip (N). **ošpéžį**
choke from. **íkaske**
choke with the hands. **tóoce oðį́įke**
choker (necklace). **wanǫ́pʔį**
choose. **ðuuzé, hkíhpaahi**
choose people (or things?). **wapáahi**
chop (V). **ðilǫ́že**
chop by striking with. **íkaase**
chop down, chop up (e.g., with an axe or knife). **kaasé**
chop with a blade (e.g., wood for a fire). **kaasé**
chore. **ówǫ**
chorus (female). **oðáazo**
Christmas. **wahkǫ́ta ižį́ke íikitaðe, xǫǫcéhu káaɣe hǫ́ǫpa**
chubby. **lą́ąðehtą**
church. **waatáihci, wahkǫ́tahci, wíkiehci**
church: little ~. **wíkihcižį**
church bell. **íikaahtamą**
church house: Native American ~. **hcipóɣa**
cigarette. **nąnį́ǫpažį**
cigarette: roll a ~. **nąnį́ǫpa káaɣe**
circle around. **ákiɣe**
circular. **táahpa**
circulate. **ápše**
circus. **ówatoį** [LFD]
clan. **htą́wąla, ínihkašie**
clan subdivision (of Deer clan). **nǫ́pxata**
clap (e.g., the hands). **nąsą́sąwa**
clarify. **wáðaaska**
class. **íkʔuce, walézeáace**
class: what ~ of. **táatą**
classify. **hpahíke**
clatter (V). **htáhtaze**
claw. **šáake**
clay. **mą́įhka**
clean (V). **ðuuwásu**
clean, cleanly. **wasúhu**
clean (e.g., the house). **ðicíze**
clean off. **púɣa**
clean off by wiping. **púkxa**
clean oneself. **hkilúuwasu**
clean talk. **íe wasúhu**
clean up. **ðuuwásu**
cleanse. **ðuuwásu**
cleanse or be clean by heat or cold. **taasúhu**
clear (ADJ). **ská, skáha, stá, wasúhu**
clear: make ~. **wáðaaska**
clear (as the weather). **ðáalį**
clear language. **íeska**
clear sky (as after a storm). **hkéðo**
clear speaking. **íe wasúhu**
clear words. **íe waská, íeska**
clearance (space). **ohtą́ną**
cleared off area. **oštá**
clearly. **skáha, ská, wáðohtą, wasúhu**
clearly: speak ~. **íe ðáawaska, íeska, wáðaaska**
clear-minded. **nąąɣeska**
clicking noise against metal (as made by a typewriter). **mą́ze htáhtaze**
clicking sound. **htáhtaze**
cliffs: dwelling on the ~. **hpasú olį́į**
climb, climb onto (by using the arms). **áace**
climbing (by wrapping around?). **átxą**
clock. **mį́įoðaake**
close (V). **kaasį́ce**
close (e.g., one's eyes). **ápisą**
close (near), closeby. **áška**
close by grasping. **áðiihtą**
close by pulling. **áðiitą**
close by zipping, tying, fastening, or buttoning. **oðíiną**
close on. **ákaasįce**
close one's eyes. **ðupʔį́ze**
close suddenly or by striking. **kaasį́ce**
closing of a prayer. **kaašéną**
cloth. **háa, haaská**
clothe oneself with. **íwehkilį**

clothes. **haaská, ohkúlą, wéhkilį**
clothes: Osage ~. **wažáže wéhkilį**
clothes: put on ~ (one's own). **wéhkilį okíhpaahą**
clothes: put ~ on oneself. **óhkioolą́**
clothes: take ~ off (another person or oneself). **ðuušáwa**
clothes: wash ~. **waðíiški**
clothes: wash ~ for oneself. **hkilíiški**
clothing. **haaská**
clothing: any item of ~. **wéhkilį**
clothing: put on ~ (not one's own). **wéhkilį opáahą**
clothing: relieve s.o. of ~. **ðuuštáke**
cloud, cloudy. **mą́xpu**
clown. **waðíhohota, wahóhota**
clubs (suit in a deck of cards). **cˀáaži**
coat. **ákahamį, mǫkápo, wéhkilį**
coax s.o. to say or do s.t. **ožížie**
cobbler. **hǫ́ǫpekaaɣe**
cock: turkey ~. **áahu mą́ðį**
cockleburs. **waxáka**
coffee. **mąhkása**
coffer. **žą́ąhkoke**
coffin. **óxe sápe**
coin. **mą́zeska**
coins. **mą́zeska zí, ošpéžį, waðáawažį**
cold. **níni**
cold: be or feel ~. **níhce**
cold: have a ~. **hóxpe ǫ́ǫ**
cold (used of weather). **níwahce**
cold with sniffles and fever (N). **hóxpe**
collect together (many small scattered things). **paahí**
colon. **šúpe**
color bright colors. **hį́į**
Comanche (tribe or tribal member). **hpá tóohka, wátoohka** (?) [no Osage entry **wátoohka**; possibly not a genuine form]
comb (N). **hpahúze, wékaapše**
comb one's hair. **káapše**
comb s.o.'s hair. **kípše**
come back. **alí**
come back here (motion underway). **akú**
come back with s.t. that belongs to oneself. **aláðįku**
come by (i.e., pass). **ípše**
come by (i.e., stop in). **ahí**
come here: cause to ~. **húðe**
come here (motion accomplished). **achí**
come here (motion underway). **ahú**
come here with. **akú**
come home (motion underway). **akú**
come into possession of. **okšéhtą**
come there (motion accomplished). **ahí**
come to (after being unconscious), come to one's senses. **hkilázo, iihkíðe**
comfort. **kiɣúhke(?)**
comfortable. **hkikˀą́ze**
comfortable: make oneself ~. **hkikˀą́ze**
comforting. **štáke**
comical. **wahóhota, wahóta**
comical person. **wahóhota**
command s.o. to do s.t. **ákaaži, kaaží**
commit suicide. **cˀéhkiðe**
committeeman. **totą́ha**
compete with one another. **áhkihkie**
complementizer. **che**
complete. **bróka**
completive markers. (*see* noncontinuative markers)
compress **kaaskí**
conceal, conceal oneself. **nąlǫ́ǫha, púuspe**
conceited: be ~. **óžo áhkižį**
concern: feel ~ over, be ~ed about. **óðąąceši**
conduct one's own or s.o. else's affairs. **oðówaðe**
conduct oneself. **ahkílaðį**
conference held by a group of people. **hkiistó**
confused: be ~. **ážąį ðuucˀáke**
confused, confused person. **pxáðaži**
congested. **ocˀį́ze**
congressional representative. **hkiistó omąðį**
congressman, congresswoman. **wahkílaace káaɣe**
conquer. **ohí**
consciousness: regain ~. **iihkíðe**
consecrated. **xópe**
consecutively. **ohkíetxątxą**
consider. **áwaðilą, éðe, ékiðe, íðilą, waðílą**
consider precious. **óxta káaɣe**
consider s.t. **táatą íðilą**
consommé. **htaaníi**
constantly. **štą**
consume. **ðaanį́į**
consumption (tuberculosis). **mą́ąke ní, mą́ąke púze**
contact: bring components into ~ (e.g., parts of a blanket). **ðiiskíke**
container. **oožú, óožu**
contaminate (e.g., water or air). **ízizike káaɣe**
contempt: hold s.o. in ~. **hpíiži ažį́**
contemptible. **iiséwaðe**
contend with one another. **áhkihkie**
content (happy). **škaškáða**
contest (V). **áhkihkie**

continually. **háachi, ną** [ITERATIVE], **nąną, šo̜,**
štą
continuative aspect markers [CONT]. **akxa,**
apa, ąðé, ąðįhé, ąðįkšé, ąhé, ąkáðe, ąkatxą́,
ątxą́, ątxąhé, ðaįšé, ðatxą́še, įkšé, kše, mįkšé,
nąkxáše, nįkšé, paašé, pai (imperative),
txą, žą́kše
continue. **šką́**
continue, continue to. **šíną, šo̜** (*see also* iterative
markers)
continuously. **štą**
contrarily. **óðąži**
contrary: go or be ~ to. **áðihta**
converse, converse with. **ohkíe**
converse with each other. **ohkíhkie**
convince. **ožížie**
cook (N, V). **oohó̜**
cook, cook outside (refers only to cooking meat on
a rack, as for barbecue). **óhkace**
cook for oneself. **óohkihą**
cook things, cook stuff. **óoho̜**
cook together. **oðóhkihą**
cooked. **cúuce**
cookhouse. **oohó̜hci**
cookie. **waskúežį**
cooking: add in ~. **oðóhkihą**
cooking pot. **óoho̜**
cooking utensils. **wéoohó̜, wióoho̜**
cookstove. **mą́zewéooho̜**
cool (as weather), cool to the touch. **níni**
coon (raccoon). **mį́hkaa**
copperhead. **aį́paxo**
copulate. **wachú**
copulate with. **aðį́ažą, chúe**
cord. **wéðį**
cork, fishing cork. **wíoðaaspe**
corn. **hápa**
corn: cracked ~. **hápa waléke**
corn: cut ~ (fresh corn cut off the cob). **paašpú**
corn: dried ~. **óoho̜ saakí, watxázu**
corn: fresh ~. **hápa, hápa wacˀéka**
corn: fresh ~ cut off the cob. **paašpú**
corn: grated fresh ~ baked in oven. **wacúe žéela**
corn: ripe ~ (just at the point of ripeness). **hápa**
wasúta
corn: squaw ~ (white term). **hápa wacˀéka**
corn husk. **wacúexą**
cornbread. **hápa wacúe, wacúe žéela, wacúešto̜**
corner. **paaɣó**
cornmeal dumplings. **wacúe kaaskí**
cornshuck. **wacúexą**
correct, correctly. **éko̜**
correctly: say s.t. ~. **éko̜ ðaacé**
cosmetics. **kikˀó̜**
costume. **wéhkilį**
cot: small ~. **ážąžį**
cottonwood. **páakˀa, žą́ą kˀa**
couch. **álįįscee, ážą, óžą**
cough (N and V). **hóxpe**
cough: have or be suffering from a ~. **hóxpe ó̜o̜**
could. **ðąąché** (*see also* potential marker)
council. **ohkíhpa che**
council house. **hkiistóhci, kiistohcí** (?) [no Osage
entry **kiistóhci**; possibly not a genuine form]
council meeting. **hkiistó**
council member. **hkiistó omąðį**
council session: tribal ~. **hkiistó**
count (V). **ðaawá, waðáawa**
count on. **íkinaaži**
count oneself. **hkiláawa**
count out. **ðaawá**
counting. **waðáawa**
country (land). **mą́žą**
country (nation?). **níhkašika ochí**
country (rural area). **zą́ą, zą́ące**
countryside. **mą́žą, mąžą́htą, zą́ą, zą́ące**
couple, pair, two of them. **nahko̜į́**
courageous. **wašóše**
court (woo). **ðílą**
courthouse. **hkiistóhci**
courtship: be in a ~ with. **žóle**
cousin: male ~ (specifically, father's sister's son).
hcióška 'my/your/his/her father's sister's son',
wihcóška 'my father's sister's son' (perhaps also
ihcóška [LFD] 'his/her father's sister's son')
cousin: female ~ (specifically, father's sister's
daughter). **wihcížo** 'my father's sister's
daughter', **ðihcížo** 'your father's sister's
daughter', **ihcížo** 'his father's sister's daughter'
cover: pull or tug s.t. over in order to ~. **áðuzu**
cover (for a tipi, sweat lodge, pillow, etc.). **oðíši**
cover oneself up. **áhkihkaaspe**
cover over, cover up. **ákaaspe**
cover over by spreading some material upon.
ákaaɣace
cover with earth. **áðikˀo**
covered with: be ~ (as a garment). **į́**
covering (e.g., a windowshade). **akáaspe**
covering wrapped around s.t. **ápetxa**
covert, covertly. **nąló̜o̜ha**
cow. **hcéeska, hceeská mį́įka**
coyote. **šó̜mįhkase**
crack (*intr.*). **kaaléke**
crack from sudden impact. **kaaxúɣe**

crackers. **wacúe xúɣa**
cradle of any type, cradleboard. **oðópše**
crafts: small ~. **hįįcéžį**
cranky. **ókˀą hpííži, waðílą áška**
cranky: feel ~. **hkížį**
crash (V). **kaapxóhke**
crave. **kǫ́ða** [LFD]
crawl on, crawl upon. **ámįce**
crazed with medicine. **mą́hkažóika**
crazy. **cˀéka**
crazy, crazily. **ekǫ́įke**
crazy person. **waðílą eekǫ́ įké**
cream. **paazénii wéli**
cream (for applying to a surface to make it smooth). **stáðe**
creek. **káxa**
creek: small ~. **káxa žį**
Creek Indians. **muskóke**
crescent moon. **mį́įǫpa aðikeže**
crestfallen. **kízoži**
cricket. **htáhtaze**
crier. **íekie, wacípxaį**
Crippled Hawk (personal name). **žekáxǫ letǫ́**
crockery. **hį́įce**
crone. **wakˀóžį**
crooked. **cˀįša, paacˀį́**
crooked (referring to a human body). **cˀį́xa**
crop: wheat ~. **wapóške ówe**
cross (ADJ). **ókˀą hpííži**
cross (N). **cˀáaži**
cross (V). **áðuuhta ðée**
crow (N). **hkáɣe** [LFD]
crowd: help to make a bit of a ~. **wéhuužį**
crowd: make a ~. **wéhuu, wéhuukǫ́į**
crowd s.o. **ohkáðįke**
crucifix. **cˀáaži'**
crumbly: bread that is ~ (i.e., crackers). **wacúe xúɣa**
crutch. **íisa**
cry *(intr.)*. **ɣaaké**
cry for. **áɣaake**
cub (of any species of bear). **wasápežį**
cucumber. **hkohkóma**
culmination of. **ó-**
cunning. **nąlǫ́ǫha**
cup. **hcéheska, hcéhežį, mąhkásaioožú, oožú**
curb motion. **oðíitą**
curl (as a person's hair). **ðuuhkíhkį**
curly. **hkíhkįnį**
currency (paper). **htaną́kˀa mą́zeska**
curry the mane or coat of an animal. **káapše, kípše, wákaapše**
curse (N). **íe hpííži**
curse (V). **lǫ́ǫ**
curse over and over. **lǫ́ǫlǫǫ**
curse s.o. **hkiláažoži, kilǫ́že**
curses. **íe okaaɣéįke**
curve (N). **koša**
curved. **cˀįša**
curved stick used to play *kašíni* (shinny). **ohkíce**
cushion to sit on (as for a sofa, chair, or other seat). **wákaštǫ**
custom. **ókˀą**
customarily. **ną** [ITERATIVE]
cut (ADJ). **žáhta**
cut (N). **wápaase**
cut (V). **kaasé, paasé, -se, wápaase**
cut: one who ~s things up. **wapáse**
cut (e.g., with an axe, lawnmower, or knife). **kaasé**
cut (e.g., with scissors). **ðuusé**
cut a hole in by pushing. **opákˀo**
cut into pieces (e.g., a cake). **paasé**
cut meat (e.g., slice meet for barbecue). **wakái**
cut off. **paasé**
cut s.t. for s.o. **kíse**
cut s.t. with s.t. else by pushing down on the item being cut. **ípaase**
cut the grass. **mąąhį́ paasé**
cut up (e.g., meat, potatoes). **paasé**
cut up into slices (e.g., bananas, sausage, watermelon). **pascé**
cut with. **íkaase**
cut with a sharp edge. **páse**
cutthroat. **hpápaxǫ**
cutting, cut (N). **wápaase**
cutting: by ~. **pá-**
cyclone. **htaacé óhesaži**

daily. **hą́ąpa záani**
damage one's reputation or standing by doing s.t. inappropriate. **ílaną**
damaging. **wéhpiiži**
damp. **toohká**
dance (N, V). **waachí**
dance: *hé ðúška* ~ (name of a Ponca dance). **hé ðúška**
dance: mourning ~. **wašápe aðį́**
dance: night ~. **hpáze waachí**
dance: soldier ~. **áhkitaną́ąžį waachí**
dance: solo ~ by one who has been in a war. **wašóše achí nąąžį́**
dance arbor. **áhcihtą**
dance for. **áwaachi**
dancc placc or location. **ówaachi**

dances: *ilǫ́ǫška* ~ (war dances or ceremonial dances of the Osages). **ilǫ́ǫška**
dancing songs: sing ~, singers of dancing songs. **xóhka**
dare not: I ~. **ą́žǫ ðįké**
dark. **hą́įnį**
dark: become or get ~. **hą́ąnahpazé**
dark (in color). **šápe**
dark night. **hą́ąnahpazé**
darken. **hą́ąnahpazé**
darkened. **šápe**
darkness. **hą́įnį**
darkness of night. **hą́ąnahpazé**
date (be in a courtship with). **žóle**
dative prefix [DAT]. **ki-**
daughter: baby ~. **asíhpa**
daughter: first (eldest) ~. **míina, wakʔóhpa, wakʔóhtą**
daughter: fourth ~ (or subsequent daughter). **asížį**
daughter: second ~. **wihé**
daughter: third ~. **asį́ka**
daughter (without reference to age). **wižǫ́ke** 'my daughter', **ðižǫ́ke** 'your daughter', **ižǫ́ke** 'his/her daughter'
daughter-in-law. **wihcíni** 'my daughter-in-law', **ðihcíni** 'your daughter-in-law', **ihcíni** 'his/her daughter-in-law'; **míaɣe**
daughter name: second ~ (*hcížo* clan). **eeną́tǫįpe**
dawn. **hǫ́ǫpahu, mį́įhuðe**
day. **hą́ąpa**
day: a ~ or two. **hǫ́ǫpa wį́xci ðǫǫpá hta ški**
day: last ~. **hą́ąpa oðóhake**
day: this ~ some time back, this day back in time. **hǫpái hašíhta**
day after tomorrow. **kaasį́ kootáha**
day before yesterday. **hą́ąpa kootáha ce, sitǫ́į kootáha ce**
daybreak. **hǫ́ǫpahu, mį́įhuðe**
daylight, daylight: be ~. **hǫ́ǫpahu, hǫ́ǫpaskaha**
Daylight Approaches, It's Coming Daylight (personal name). **hǫ́ǫpahu**
days to come: in ~ **ihtǫ́į ðéha**
dead: the ~. **cʔé**
dead (e.g., a vegetable). **xéka**
dead person. **cʔé**
deaf. **nąąɣúcexéka**
deal with. **ðuhcépe**
dear. **óxta**
dear: hold each other ~. **ðótahkiðe**
dear: make ~. **óxtakiðe**
death. **cʔé, óxiða**
death: be near ~. **íhpiiži**
debt. **weúuze**
decade. **omą́įhka lébrą híeną**
deceitful: be ~ toward. **ðiihíce**
deceive oneself. **mąɣíhkiðe**
deceive s.o. **ðiihíce, mąɣíðe**
December. **mį́įǫpa álįį ðǫǫpá, mį́įǫpa wahkǫ́ta ižį́ke iitáe ékitxą, wasápe iitáipi**
decide. **waðílą káaɣe**
decide for oneself. **waðílą hkihkáaɣe**
deck of cards. **htaną́kʔa ðiihíce, htaną́kʔa kʔǫ́**
declarative sentence-final marker [DECL]. **ðe**
decomposed **tožáðe**
decrease *(trans.)*. **čóopa ekǫ́ káaɣe**
deduce: I ~ that. **ska**
deed (act). **ókʔą**
deed (document). **htaną́kʔa**
deep. **škópe**
deer. **htáa**
deer: female ~. **htáa mį́įka**
deer: male ~. **htáa htą́ka**
Deer clan. **htáanihkáši**
deer mating moon (October). **htáa hkiðíɣepi**
deerskin. **htaahháa**
defeat others (in a game or contest). **óhi**
defecate. **žé**
define as. **ðaacé**
deflated. **tóže**
defraud s.o. **mąɣíðe**
Delaware (tribe or tribal member). **wápa níhka**
deliberate over. **áwaðilą**
demented. **cʔéka , pxáðaži**
demented person. **pxáðaži, waðílą eekǫ́ įké**
denude. **ðuušáake, ðuušáwį, ðuuštá**
depart. **aðée, okábra**
depend on. **íkinaaži**
desire (v). **kǫ́ða**
despair (v). **hkíxiða**
despicable. **iiséwaðe**
despise. **íisi**
despite: have one's way ~ s.t. **óðąži**
despite the odds. **óðąži**
despondent. **kízoži**
dessert. **waskúe**
destructive. **taaðúhpiiži, wéhpiiži**
detain s.o. who is passing by. **nąąží**
detect s.t. (without getting full knowledge of it). **opéni**
detergent. **wépukxa**
detergent: dish ~. **hį́įce íðuuža wépukxa**
determined. **níhka wažį́htąą, wažį́ ihta**
determinedly. **wažį́ ihta**
determined person. **níhka wažį́htąą**

detest. **íisi**
detestible. **iiséwaðe**
detour around s.t. **íðišą̨ha**
devil. **c?á htą̨ą, ilǫ́ɣe**
devoid: be ~ of. **ðį̨ké**
devour. **ðaaníį̨**
dew. **xémą̨ke**
Dhegiha. **ðeekíha**
diabetes, suffer from diabetes. **žą̨ąníe wapeį̨ huukǫ́ða óožu**
diamonds (suit in a deck of cards). **pé ðaha**
diaper. **híðaxa, xíðaxa**
diaphragm. **ðúwe**
dice (N). **k?ǫ́su**
dice: play ~. **k?ǫ́suk?ǫ́**
dice by cutting over and over. **paasása**
dice game. **k?ǫ́suk?ǫ́**
die (V). **c?é, xíða**
die: make ~. **c?éðe**
different. **éeži**
different kind: of a ~. **éeži**
different one: a ~. **éži wį̨**
different-looking. **éžixci**
difficult. **hcéxi, saakí, wahcéxi**
Difficult Female (name for a first daughter). **mį̨įhcéxi**
dig, dig up. **k?é**
dig (e.g., a grave). **paak?ó**
dime. **waðáawa lébrą**
diminish s.o. by slandering, maligning, or belittling him or her. **hkiláažoži**
dine. **wanǫ́bre**
dine outdoors. **ášihta wanǫ́bre**
dingy. **šóce**
dinner (meal served at noon or in the evening). **mį̨įðóhta wanǫ́bre, ónǫbre, wanǫ́bre**
dinner bell. **íikaahtamą**
dinnerware (e.g., a set of plates, cups, and bowls). **hcéhežį̨**
dipper. **níiðaahtą**
direction: in a ~. **ha**
direction: in that ~. **ée htáha**
direction: in the ~ of. **ée htáha, hta, htáha**
direction: in the other ~. **ámą̨htaha**
direction: that ~. **émą̨hta**
dirt. **mą́įhka**
dirt: cover with ~. **áðik?o**
dirty (sick, evil). **ízizike**
dirty (unclean). **wákalą, wasúhuži**
dirty s.t. **ízizike káaɣe**
disagree, disagree with. **iiną́hiži**
disallow. **ížoši**
disband. **okábra, panáa**
discard (V). **ǫ́ǫðe**
discard s.o. or s.t. **ǫ́ǫða**
discern s.t. **íikiðe**
disconsolate. **kízoži**
discouraged: become ~. **hkíxiða**
discover in part but not fully. **opéni**
discover s.t. **íikiðe**
discuss. **íe, óie**
disease: venereal ~. **wácinie**
disgrace: be in ~. **ílaną**
dish. **hcéhežį̨, hį́įce**
dish: flat and wide ~. **hį́įce braaka**
dish soap, dish detergent. **hį́įce íðuuža wépukxa**
dish towel. **hį́įce ípukxa**
dishes (e.g., a set of plates, cups, and bowls). **hcéhežį̨**
disheveled. **héxpa**
disinfect (e.g., a buffalo hide). **ðuuwásu**
dislike. **íisi**
dislike s.t. **kihǫ́ǫži**
disliked. **iiséwaðe**
disloyal person. **wawį́kšaži**
dismissed (as at the end of a school day): be ~. **panáa**
dismount from (e.g., a horse). **owísi, wísi**
disobey. **opšáži**
dispatch (V). **ðée káaɣe**
disperse *(trans., intr.)*. **okábra**
dispirited. **kízoži**
display (multiple items) on top of s.t. else. **ážu**
disposition: having a bad ~. **ók?ą hpíiži**
disregard. **óðą̨ąceši ðį̨ké**
disrespectful. **wakaac?áiži**
dissect. **hpáce**
distant: be ~ (e.g., an estranged married couple). **kíðahapa**
distant (in space). **wéhice**
distant in space or time. **kootáį̨ke**
distinct. **ohką́ci**
distinct: make ~. **wáðaaska**
distracted: be ~ by problems or sickness. **ókaše**
distraught: be ~ from. **íhpiiži**
disturbance. **óochiže**
disuse (V). **óðą̨ąceši ðį̨ké**
ditch. **óxe**
ditch: small ~ around tipi for drainage. **ną́ceaha**
divan. **álį̨įscee, ážą žį̨ka**
divest oneself of. **níðe**
divide (V). **íhkilai, kíðahapa**
divide in two. **ðǫǫpáha káaɣe**
divided. **žáhta**
divided: be ~. **kíðahapa**

divorce. **hkíǫðe, ohkíǫðe**
divorce, be divorced. **kíðahapa**
divorced: become ~ from. **ohkíǫðe**
dizzy. **į̨cé hpáze**
do. **ékiǫ, éǫ, káaɣe** (not always overtly expressed in Osage; e.g., *háakǫ kóða tą* 'whatever he wants to do', *káakǫ kǫ́ða tą* 'that's the way he's going to do it'; *see also discussion under* **táatą**)
do (engage in an activity). **ǫ́** [rarely used]
do for oneself. **hkihkáaɣe**
do good works, do good. **ðáalį káaɣe**
do harm to. **ðuhpíiži**
do how/however, do in whatever way, do what about (indefinite). **háaǫ**
do no more. **kaakǫ́ną káaɣe**
do nothing. **ókaaɣeįke**
do one's best. **íkˀuce, waašką́**
do oneself ill or harm. **hkilúhpiiži**
do over. **kikáaɣe**
do s.t.: make s.o. ~. **ákaaži**
do s.t. poorly. **oolą́ąži**
do s.t. to oneself. **éwahkikˀǫ, éwahkiǫ́ðe**
do to oneself, do s.t. to excess while paying no heed to others. **éhkiǫ**
do what, do what with, do what about. **háaǫ**
do whatever with, do whatever. **háaǫ**
do work. **waðíhtą**
docile. **wacˀéka**
doctor (N), be a doctor. **wahkǫ́taki**
doctor s.o. **šcéðe**
document (legal or otherwise). **htaną́kˀa**
document containing text. **waléze**
document of borrowed money. **mą́zeska ootá waléze**
doe **htáa, htáa mį́ka**
dog. **šǫ́ke**
dog: black ~. **šǫhtą́ą sa**
dog: female ~. **šǫmį́ka**
dogwood. **mǫ́ǫsa hu**
"doings": have a ~. **ókˀą**
dollar. **bróka**
dolled up. **íišcewai**
don (as clothing). **opáahą**
done (cooked). **cúuce**
donkey. **nąąhtą́htąą**
door. **hcižé**
doorbell: ring or press the ~. **ðuuhkáamą**
doorway. **hcižépe**
dotted button-snake-root, dotted gay feather (*Liatris punctata*). **mąhká saakí**
dotted with small dots. **léže**
doubt (V). **wažá**
doubt oneself. **hkíxiða**
down, downward. **húuce, mą́le**
down: go ~ (as a road). **opxą́**
down: go ~ (e.g., the sun when setting). **papó**
down: put or set ~. **hkícheðe**
down: take ~. **ðuuhúuce, ðuxpáwį**
downcast. **kízoži**
drag. **ðiiɣó, ðiitą́**
draw water (e.g., in a bathtub). **ðixtą́, ðuuzé**
dream (N, V), have a dream. **hǫ́bre**
dream: bad ~. **ohpáza**
dress (N). **haaská, wéhkilį**
dress in. **íwehkilį, óhkioolą́**
dress in (e.g., a shirt or a dress). **óhkioolą́**
dress in clothing (not one's own) **wéhkilį opáahą**
dress in one's own clothes. **wéhkilį okíhpaahą**
dress oneself. **óhkioolą́**
dress up in one's best attire. **íišcewai**
dressed up. **íišcewai**
dried. **xéka**
dried corn. **óohǫ saakí**
dried fruit. **hką́ące púze**
dried meat. **htáa púze**
dried squash. **watxą́ púze**
dried up. **hcúɣe**
drill: conduct a ~. **áhkita okˀą**
drink (V). **ðaahtą́**
drink: soft ~. **niikáapxohke**
drink alcohol. **waðáahtą**
drink soup. **ðaazúpe**
drink up. **ðaanį́į**
drive *(intr.)*. **wakáaži**
drive (a vehicle). **kaaží**
drive (animals). **mąðį́ káaɣe**
drive around for pleasure. **opáwįɣe**
drive for s.o. **kíži**
driver. **waðíhtą wakáaži, wakáaži**
drizzle (N). **íhkišoce, níišoce, niižú xóce, níižu xohtą**
droopy. **cˀóka, xpéka**
drop (e.g., an object or a comment into a conversation). **ðikšį́ce**
drop feathers. **púkaške, wapíokaške, wapúške**
drop s.t. into (e.g., eyedrops into eyes). **oðíkˀe**
drown *(intr.)*. **níipxaðe**
drub. **ochį́**
druggist. **mąhká aðį́**
drum. **céɣenii**
drum: pass the ~. **céɣenii ðée káaɣe**
drum: tie the ~ (involves wrapping the drum up and tying it). **céɣenii káaɣe**
drum boss. **céɣenii ochį́**

drumbeat. **hcíce**
drumkeeper. **céɣenii aðį́**
drumkeeper and committee. **ilǫ́ǫška záani**
drumstick. **céɣenii ochį́, céɣenii ochį́ scée, žą́ąxe céɣenii**
drunk. **lǫ́ðį, omą́įžį**
drunk: extremely or "crazy" ~. **wéehlihpíiži**
drunk: get ~. **álǫðį**
drunkenness: push or impel s.o. to ~. **páalǫðį**
dry *(intr.)*. **ðipúze**
dry *(trans.)*. **púze, púzeðe**
dry by wiping. **púkxa**
dry from heat. **táapuze**
dry grass, dried grass. **xáhtape**
dry with (by wiping). **ípukxa**
duck. **míɣa**
duck: big ~. **míɣa htą́ka**
duck: mallard ~. **hpáhiihto**
due to. **í-**
dull (color or finish). **xóce, xpéka**
dull (not sharp). **hpaahį́ži**
dump out (e.g., garbage). **okáxta**
dumplings. **wacúe sóso, wacúe táahpa, wacúexǫ oðiši**
dumplings: corn meal ~. **wacúe kaaskí**
dumplings: wheat flour or corn flour ~. **wacúe ðubráaska**
dun colored (like the color of elk hide). **ópxą hį́į ekǫ́**
dung. **įlé**
during that time. **šǫǫšǫ́we**
during the night. **hą́ą**
dust (e.g., the house). **ðicíze**
dust off. **púɣa**
dust off by wiping. **púkxa**
dusty (as of a table top). **mąąšóce**
duty. **ówǫ**
dwell (in a place). **olį́į**
dwell in the forest. **žą́ą olį́į**
dwelling on the cliffs. **hpasú olį́į**
Dwells among the Cedars (personal name). **xǫ́ǫce mą́į**
dying from hunger: be ~. **nǫhpéhicˀe**

each. **kiðá, nąðé**
each: belong to ~, one for each one. **ihtá na**
each other. (*see* reciprocal prefix)
eager: be ~ that s.t. take place. **íhice**
eagle. **xúða**
eagle: bald ~. **hą́ka**
eagle: golden ~. **hcížo**
eagle headdress. **xúðalą́ke**
Eagle Woman (personal name). **xuðáchewį, xúðawį**
ear, inner ear. **nąąɣúce**
ear, outer ear. **nąąhtą́**
ear pop. **nąąɣúce oðipxokši**
ear wax. **nąąɣúhaše**
earache. **nąąɣúce níe**
earlier. **haašíhta** (*see also discussion under* **ska** [MODAL])
earlobe. **nąąhtą́**
early in the morning. **kaasį́exci**
early morning. **hą́ąekǫ́žį, kaasį́exci, kaasį́excįžį**
earn. **okšéhtą**
earnings. **okšéhtą**
earring(s). **į́įhtǫ**
earth. **mą́žą**
earth, Earth (name for a second son). **mą́įhka**
earth: cover with ~. **áðikˀo**
earthquake. **mąžą́ šką́**
easily angered. **waðílą áška**
east. **mį́į íðǫpe įkšé**
east wind, "fall winds." **pázą htá hu**
easy. **ómąhka**
easy to do. **wacˀéka**
eat *(intr.)*. **wanǫ́bre**
eat (*trans.*). **ðaaché**
eat: not ~, not be eating. **wanǫ́braži**
eat too much. **tóoceha**
eat up. **ðaanį́į**
eat with. **íðaache**
eavesdrop. **nąlǫ́ǫha waną́kˀǫ**
economical. **ómąhka**
edge. **bráaɣe, hkǫ́ha**
edging (e.g., fabric sewn round the edge of a blanket). **bráaɣe**
educated: be ~. **waléze hpíǫ**
education. **walézeáace**
efface by rubbing or wiping. **púkxa**
effort: make an ~. **íkˀuce, waašką́**
egg. **hpáata**
egg s.o. on. **ožížie**
egg yolk. **hpáatazi**
egg white. **hpáataska**
eggshell. **hpáata xúha**
eight. **hkietóopa**
eighteen, eighteenth. **lébrą álįį hkietóopa**
eighty, eightieth. **lébrą hkietóopa**
either. **ímąðe**
elbow. **iistó**
elder (N). **waanǫ́ǫ**
elderly man. **cˀáižį**
elderly woman. **wakˀóžį**

elders in times past. **haašíhta, kóoci, nǫ́ǫ**
eldest. **htą́ą**
eldest son. **ilǫ́ǫhpa**
elephant. **níita**
eleven, eleventh. **lébrą álįį wį́xce**
elf. **míalǫška**
elk. **ópxą**
else. **éški**
else: anything ~. **táatą éžiški**
elucidate. **wáðaaska**
embarrassed: be or become ~. **iizíke**
embarrassing: be ~. **iizíke**
embrace. **áace, oðį́įke**
embrace as tradition. **oðį́įke**
emerge from (as a liquid). **stówe**
emit, be emitted. **žé**
employ. **waší**
employ folks. **wawáši**
employee. **waší**
employment, place of employment. **waðíhtą**
encircle a place or a person (especially in an annoying way). **ákiɣe**
encounter (v). **áhkihpa** [LFD, JOD], **áhkiǫðe, áhkoopše**
encourage. **híce, ožížie**
end *(intr.)*. **panáa**
end (N). **kaašǫ́**
end *(trans.)*. **kaaštą́, panáa**
end: living on the ~. **hpasú olį́į**
end: make s.o. ~ s.t., make s.t. ~. **ðiištą́ káaɣe**
end: put an ~ to s.t. **kaaštą́**
end: that's the ~ (INTERJ). **kaaštą́**
end: (it's) the ~. **kaašǫ́įke**
end: the ~ of earthly living (exclamation). **kaašǫ́eðe**
end (e.g., of one's earthly existence). **kaašǫ́**
end an activity involving the mouth. **ðaaštą́**
end of an activity. **kaakǫ́ną**
ended. **kaašéną**
endorse (as a check). **mą́šą oðį́įke** [LF], **šáake oðį́įke**
enemies: looking for ~. **totą́**
enemy. **ohkíhce**
energetic. **sísi**
engage in. **káaɣe**
English (language). **įįštáxį íe**
English person. **įįštáxį**
enjoy. **kiðálį , kízo**
enjoy: make s.o. ~. **wazóeðe, wazóekšiðe**
enjoyment: feel ~. **kiðálį, kízo**
enlarge. **htą́ą**
enormous. **lą́ąðe wálį**

enough. **eená, kaakǫ́ną, kaašǫ́**
enough: get or have ~ of. **íibrą**
enough: have more than ~. **íibrąxcį**
enough: it's ~. **kaašǫ́ka**
enough: make ~. **kaašǫ́ káaɣe**
enrage s.o. **wažį́ hpíiži káaɣe**
enraged. **wažį́ hpíiži**
enter, enter formally (e.g., a peyote meeting). **ohpé**
entire. **bróka**
entrails. **otáhpa, šúpe**
envious (e.g., of another's position). **óxįį**
envy. **óxįį**
epistemic marker. (*see* evidential marker)
equal: make ~ to. **íkǫskahkíðe**
equal in appearance to. **íkǫska**
equipment: piece of ~. **wéhkikʔǫ**
erase by rubbing or wiping. **púkxa**
errand. **ówǫ, wamą́ðį**
errand: go on an ~. **okášą**
error: commit an ~ (e.g., dropping something at a dance, causing a commotion). **ílaną**
espionage: conduct ~. **nąlǫ́ǫha átǫpe**
estranged: be ~. **kíðahapa**
even. **ški**
even (level). **stáko**
even only. **ną́ški**
even so. **óðąži**
even though. **ški**
evening. **mį́įhiðe**
evening, in the evening time. **hpáze**
evening: last or yesterday ~. **hpázece**
evening meal. **hpáze wanǫ́bre**
event: have or hold an ~. **ókʔą**
every day. **hą́ąpa ke záani, hą́ąpa ohkíeche, hą́ąpa záani**
every one. **záani**
every time. **háachi, ohkíetxątxą**
everybody, everyone. **howaðéeški, huukǫ́ða, péeški, záani**
everything. **howachéeški, táatą howachéeški, táatą záanį**
everything else. **táatą éžiški**
everywhere. **háaški**
evidential marker. **che**
evil (ADJ). **hǫ́ǫži, hpíiži**
evil, evil things. **ízizike, táatą hǫ́ǫžį**
exactly. **xci**
examine. **ákazo, ákǫze**
examine an issue. **wákazo**
excel, be excellent. **álįįha**
excessive. **ochí, ochíchacha**
exchange (N). **íhkihkawį**

exchange one item for another. **íhkihkawį káaɣe**
excited: be ~. **hóšechie** [LF]
excrement. **įlé**
excrete. **žé**
excursion, go on an excursion. **opáwįɣe**
exhausted (tired). **kaaskíke**
exhibition. **ówatoį**
exhibition hall. **ówatǫįhci**
exist. **ecí, ecíke** (scattered), **níhkašika**
exist: not ~. **ðįké**
exist as. **ðį́**
exist in large quantity. **ochí**
exoskeleton. **háa šooká**
expel gas from the body. **xpi**
experience pain. **níe**
expert: be ~ in. **hpíǫ**
explode (e.g., a balloon). **kaapxóhke**
extinct: be ~. **ðįké**
extinguish. **ðuutáaži**
extinguished: become ~. **táaži**
extremely. **wálį**
eye (N). **įįštá**
eyebrows. **įįštáhįį**
eyeglasses. **mą́ze įįštóolą**
eyelid. **įįštáhaa**
eyes: light ~. (*see discussion under* **įįštáxį**)
exult. **wakˀą́**

fable (Osage children's story in which animals are the main characters). **híko**
fabric. **háa, haaská**
face (N). **įcé**
face a certain direction. **okále**
faces: make ~. **įcé ðuuhpííži**
faded. **xóce, xpéka**fail. **ðikšį́ce**
fail at doing s.t. **oolą́ąži**
failing to show respect to people or property. **wakaacˀáiži**
Fairfax group of Osages. **hpasú olį́į**
fairy. **míalǫška**
fall, fall down. **xíða**
fall (autumn), in the fall. **htąątą́**
fall from a height. **oxpáðe**
fall into. **ohkíǫðe**
fall short. **oolą́ąži**
falling snow. **pá húðe**
false gossip: malicious ~. **íe okaaɣéįke**
falsehood (N). **íxope**
family. **hcíle**
famished: be ~. **nǫhpéhicˀe**
fan (N), fanning. **kíhką**
fan (V). **kahką́**
fan: electric ~. **htaacéxowe**
fan made of feathers. **mą́šą**
fan made of tail feathers. **íhkuáci**
fan off s.o. **kahką́**
fan off, as at a peyote meeting. **kíhką**
far, far away, from afar. **wéhice**
far: how ~. **háatxą**
far back in time: from ~. **kóoci**
farewell (to a dead person). **kaašǫ́eðe**
farm (N). **mą́žą**
farm (V). **waðíhtą**
fart (N). **xpi**
fart (V). **ðiipíɣą, xpi**
fart: make a loud ~, fart loudly. **ðibrį́ɣa**
fart (with a small noise, by letting the air out slowly). **ðižíce**
farther, farther away, to/from farther, farther back in time or space, farther forward. **kootáha**
farther one: the ~, in space or time. **kóota**
farther over there **kootá**
fast (ADJ, ADV). **óhesaži**
fast: go ~. **xį́na**
fast: walk or move ~. **htą́ąðį**
fast (not eat). **wanǫ́braži**
fast in movement. **kˀą́saaki**
fasten. **aðímą, oðíiną**
faster: make s.t. go ~. **xįna káaɣe**
fat. **hį́še, lą́ąðe, šį́, šį́htąką**
fat: be ~. **wašį́**
fat: pork ~. **hkohkósa wéli, wéli**
fat meat. **wašį́**
father. **įhtáci** 'my father', **ðiðáce** 'your father', **iðáce** 'his/her father'
father-in-law. **wihcíko** 'my father-in-law', **ðihcíko** 'your father-in-law', **ihcíko** 'his/her father-in-law'; **cˀáke** 'wife's father; my wife's father'
fatherless. **íðace įké**
fatigued. **óžeðe**
favor: ask a ~. **waší**
fawn (deer). **htáa**
fear (V). **nǫ́ǫhpe**
fear: instill ~ in. **ðusáaki**
fearful: feel ~. **onį́žį**
Fearful One (personal name). **nǫ́ǫhpewaðe** (specifically, variant form **nǫ́ǫhpewali**)
fearful thing. **nǫ́ǫhpewaðe**
fearless. **nǫ́ǫhpaži, wašóše**
feast (N). **kíkxo**
feast: put on or prepare a ~. **kíkxo, óohkihą**
feather: turkey ~. **súhkahtąą mǫ́šǫ**
feathers: drop or brow ~. **púkaške, wapúške**

feathers: fan made of ~. **mą́šą**
feathers of certain kinds of birds (such as eagle, hawk, and macaw). **mą́šą**
February. **hǫ́ǫpa scée, mį́įohką́ce, mį́įǫkʔaįke, mį́įǫpa weðǫ́ǫpa**
feces. **įlé**
feed (V). **ókʔu, wakʔú**
feel ashamed. **iišcéwai**
feel cranky. **hkížį**
feel fearful. **onį́žį**
feel good. **kiðálį**
feel good about. **íhtąą**
feel good or well. **ðáalį**
feel oneself to be a certain way (?). **áhkiži**
feel s.o. or s.t. **ðiihtą́**
feel sorry for. **áacexcį, ðakʔéðe**
feel sorry for one's own or s.o. close. **ðakʔékiðe**
feel sorry for oneself. **ðakʔéhkiðe**
feeling: get a ~ about s.t. (without full knowledge of it). **opéni**
feign. **kǫzé** [JOD, LFD]
female. **mį́į, mį́įka**
female (used in personal names for females). **wį**
female dog. **šǫmį́įka**
females: without ~ (said of a family with all daughters and no sons). **mįįkáðįke**
fence. **ápahta**
fence: wire or metal ~. **mą́ze ápahta**
fetch. **akú**
fetid odor: have a ~. **ɣoį́**
fever: sick from or running a little ~, feverish. **áachi**
few, a few. **čóopa**
few: a ~ (e.g., people). **huužį**
fib (N). **íxope**
fiddle with s.t. **ðiihíce**
field. **ówe**
field: wheat. **wapóške ówe**
fierce, fiercely. **óhesaži**
fifteen, fifteenth. **lébrą álįį sáhtą**
fifth. **wesáhtą**
fifty, fiftieth. **lébrą sáhtą**
fight (N). **taaké**
fight (V), fight against or with. **taaké**
fight (verbal). **taaké ie**
fighting. **taaké**
fill: have one's ~ of. **íibrą**
filled: be ~ (sated). **wéenące**
filled: be ~. **okúhpu**
film (N). **ówatoį**
final. **oðóhake**
final: be ~. **ecí che**
final event in life: the ~ (exclamation). **kaašǫ́eðe**
final part of s.t. **kaakǫ́ną**
final point. **kaašǫ́**
find (V). **íiðe, íikiðe**
find bothersome. **áalake**
find for oneself; find one's own. **iihkíðe**
find out *(trans.)* (e.g., about s.o.'s activities). **ðuupxáðe**
find out about (without getting full knowledge of). **opéni**
find out things. **wáopxa**
fine (N). **ílanąwakíšupe**
fine (e.g., fine rain). **xohtą**
fine (of high quality). **ðáalį**
finely. **ðáalį**
finger. **pázo, šáake**
finger: index ~. **opázo, wéapazo**
finish, be finished **ðiištą́**
finish eating. **ðaaštą́**
finished, the thing is finished. **kaašéną**
fire (e.g., a cooking fire, meeting fire, or cooking-stove fire). **hpéece**
fire: build a ~. **océðe**
fire: build a ~ on. **áceðe**
fire: set ~ to. **osái**
fire a gun. **hkúce**
fire-drill stick. **hį́įcecʔohu**
fire-making wood (a piece of wood used in making fire). **žą́ąhpeece**
fireman (a position in Native American Church meetings). **hpéece íhta**
fireplace: build a. **océðe**
fireplace (in a home or ceremonial). **océhci**
fireplace or fire (of any kind, to cook or to warm oneself). **océðe**
Fire-walker (personal name and family name). **hpéece mąðį́**
firewater (whiskey or any strong alcoholic drink). **hpéecenii**
firewood. **hpéece žą́ą**
firm. **saakí**
first. **hpahą́le**
first: place s.t. or s.o. ~. **hpahą́le mąðį́**
first son in *hcížo* clan. **wahcéehtą**
First Striker (personal name). **hpahą́le ákaaleke**
fish. **hó**
fishhook. **íhkǫe**
fishing. **hóolą**
fishing cork. **wíoðaaspe**
fishing line. **hóize**
fishing pole. **hóize žą́ąxe**
fist. **nǫǫpé, nǫǫpé aski**

fist: make a ~. **ðiiskíke, šáakeðíiskike**
fit (v). **íhta**
fitting in the available space: not ~. **wíohkaðį**
five. **sáhtą**
five cents. **waðáawa sáhtą**
five-spot (in a deck of cards). **sáhtą aži** [LFD]
fix (e.g., repair a torn place in a dress). **kikáaɣe**
fix (prepare). **káaɣe**
fix (prepare or repair) for s.o. **kšíɣe**
fix (remedy). **ðuðáalį**
fix one's own, fix up s.t. of one's own. **lúðaalį**
flag **haawálele**
flag, U.S. flag. **waléle**
flashlight. **ðuuhpéece**
flask for gunpowder. **níixoce weoožu**
flat. **bráaska, brákˀa, brúuska**
flat, flattened (said of a soft object). **tóže**
flatten. **ðibrúuska**
flatten by cutting. **pábrakˀa**
flatten by shooting. **póbraska**
flatten by striking. **kaaštá**
flatten with the feet. **nąąstá**
flatulence. **xpi**
flea. **wísisi**
flee. **hkóopše**
fleet (as a runner). **kˀą́saaki**
flint. **kaalį́įže**
flirt with. **ðílą**
flirt with a woman. **wakˀó ðílą**
flooded (e.g., a creek). **okúhpu**
flooding water. **níita**
floor. **ánąąhkoe**
flour. **wacúexo, wacúe**
flow (v). **stówe**
flower. **laaská**
flower on a tree. **žą́ąlaa**
fluid. **níi**
flute. **opíɣą**
fly (N). **hą́hceka**
fly (as birds do or in an airplane). **kį́į**
fly out in pieces: cause to ~ or splinter. **paasíke**
foam up. **ápuɣe**
focus on. **óðąąceši**
fog. **íhkišoce**
fog rising off standing water. **opˀą́ða**
follow. **íe opšé, opšé**
follow. **oðáha, opxą́**
follow (succeed), following. **okínąąžį**
follow one's own. **okípše**
following (ADV). **áhkiha**
following (PRON, ADJ), the following one. **okxą́**
following: go ~. **oðáhaaðee**
Follows-the-Sun (an Eagle clan name). **mį́įšechie**
food. **ónǫbre**
food: sweet ~. **waskúe**
food bag. **wánǫbréoožú**
food taken home from a feast. **óðaašce**
fool s.o. **ðiihíce, mąɣíðe**
fool s.o. **wáðihota**
foolish acts. **cˀéka ókˀą**
foot. **síi**
foot: by ~. **nąą-**
footprint. **šáake**
for. (*see* dative prefix)
for a day or so. **hǫ́ǫpa wį́xci ðǫǫpá hta ški**
forbid. **ížoši**
force (N). **waašką́**
force over or through s.t. **ákaaži**
force s.o. to do s.t. **kaaží**
forceful, forcefully. **óhesaži**
forebears, forefathers. **mǫ́pše, nǫ́ǫwaapi**
foregoing: the ~. **ée**
forehead. **hpée**
forehead: smooth ~. **hpeeštá**
foreknowledge: have ~ of an event. **ónąkˀǫ**
foreman. **oðówaðe, waðíhtą wakáaži**
forenoon, in the forenoon. **mįįðóhta žišǫ́**
forest. **są́ą (?), žą́ą**
forest: dwell in the ~. **žą́ą olį́į**
forever. **šǫǫšǫ́we**
forget. **áalǫðį, kisúðaži**
forgetful. **wásueži**
fork. **wahúhka**
forked. **žáhta**
forked: make ~. **pážahta**
forked lightning. **ðiléleze**
forty, fortieth. **lébrą tóopa**
foward: go ~. **aðée**
forward (rude). **wakaacˀáiži**
four. **tóopa**
Four Cliffs (personal name). **hpásitoopa**
fourteen, fourteenth. **lébrą álįį tóopa**
fourth. **wétoopa**
Fox (personal name). **šǫ́mįhkase**
fracture (e.g., one's head). **kaaléke**
fragment. **ošpéžį**
fragrance: give off a ~. **brą́**
frail: be ~. **waašką́ðįké**
frankfurter, Indian frankfurter. **tǫ́ǫpše**
free: be: ~ at last from illness. **ónihkie**
free from worry or illness. **ókašéįke**
free will: of his/her own ~. **wažį́ ihta**
freeze. **táa**

freeze: make s.t. ~. **ótaa**
freeze in or to another substance. **ótaa**
freeze one's own. **táahkiðe**
freeze to, freeze sticking to s.t. **átaa**
French (ADJ). **íšpaðǫ**
French language. **íšpaðǫ**
French person. **įįštáxį, íšpaðǫ**
frequently. **íkiha**
fresh. **hcéka**
Friday. **hą́ąpa htaaðáachaži**
fried. **taazíhi**
friend. **hcošpá, hkóða, ihkówa**
friend: make a ~ of. **iiðótahkiðe**
friend: person who is made into a ~. **iiðótahkiðe**
friend: regard as a ~. **ðótaðe**
friends: make ~ with each other, regard each other as ~. **ðótahkiðe**
Friend's Church (Quaker) in Hominy. **wíkihcižį**
frog. **hcéokˀa**
from. **ci txą, ha, hta, í-, íhtą, txą́ha**
from now on. **ðetxą́ce, ðetxą́ha, ihtǫ́į ðéha**
from the beginning. **hpahą́le**
from this time on. **ðetxą́ha**
frost. **xémąke**
frowzy. **héxpa**
frozen: be ~. **táa**
fruit. **hkąące, waskúe**
fruit juice. **hkąącenii**
frustrated: be or become ~ (?). **níǫhta**
fry. **taazíhiðe**
frybread. **wacúe wéli**
frybread: deep-fried ~. **wacúe žéela** [more commonly means 'cornbread']
frybread that is slit through. **wacúe kaascú**
fulfillment as a person. **ónihkaši**
full: be ~. **okúhpu**
full: be ~ (sated) **wéenące**
full: make oneself ~. **wéenącehkiðe**
full amount. **okúhpu**
full moon. **mį́įǫpa táahpa**
full size. **htą́ą**
fully. **xci**
fun: be ~. **waazó**
fun: have ~. **kízo**
fun: make ~ of s.o. **wahóta**
funny. **wahóhota, wahóta**
funny: be ~. **íixaéewaðe**
funny-looking. **éžixci**
funny person. **wahóhota**
funny stuff. **cˀéka ókˀą**
fur. **hį́į**

furnish. **okˀú**
furnish to folks. **ókˀu**
furnishings, furniture. **ohcíle**
further over. **kootáha**
future (N). **hą́ąpa ihtóį ðeha, kóota ðée**
future: in the ~. **hą́ąpa ihtóį ðeha, ihtǫ́į ðéha, ihtǫ́į ðihé, kóota ðée**
future months. **kóota ðée**
future tense marker. (*see* potential marker)
fuzz (as on a peach). **hį́į**
fuzzy. **héxpa, hį́įšce**
fuzzy balls (e.g, on yarn garters), fuzz (as on a sweater). **hį́įšcežį́**

gadabout. **wáaspaži**
gadget. **wéhkikˀǫ**
gain (N and V). **okšéhtą**
gale. **htaacé óhesaži, htaacé saakí**
gallant. **wašóše**
gamble. **kˀǫ́**
game bird. **míɣa**
gap. **ohtą́ną**
garage. **oðíhtąhci, wakáaži**
garage door. **oðíhtąhci hcíže**
garden. **ówe**
garden produce. **ówe, wasúutą**
garlic. **mą́ąžąxe**
garment. **mį́**
garter. **híǫnįį**
gas: pass ~ or air. **ðiipíɣą**
gasoline. **wéli**
gather *(trans.)*. **ðiiskíke**
gather (e.g., fruit). **ðuuzé, paahí**
gather and tie in a bundle. **paaxcé**
gather for council. **kiistó**
gather together, gather with. **waðíiski**
gather up. **ðiiskíke**
gather up for oneself, gather together for oneself. **hkilíiski**
gather up with a sudden movement. **kaaskí**
gather with each other, gather together. **hkilíiski**
gathering of people (e.g., at a dance), people gathering with each other. **hkilíiski, waðíiski**
gaunt. **lažį́į**
gay person. **miixóke**
gayfeather (*Liatris punctata*). **mąhká saakí**
gelatin. **waskúe ðibrúbruɣe, waskúe šką́šką́**
generation: older ~. **mǫ́pše**
generation after generation, generational (referring to a long line of chiefs). **ótxątxą**
generous. **waðákˀeðe, wahríše (?)**

Generous (non-Osage surname). **wahríše**
gentle. **štáke, wacˀéka, waštáke**
Gentle Man (personal name). **níhka watą́įke**
get. **akú, ðuuzé**
get (i.e., 'become'; e.g., get old). **ahí**
get a feeling about s.t. (without full knowledge of it). **opéni**
get back here. **alí**
get better (in regard to illness). **kiní, kitą́he, kítąhe**
get drunk. **álǫðį**
get here. **achí**
get it anyway. **óðąži**
get lost. **oxpáðe**
get moving, get going. **mąðí**
get moving! (command). **mąðį́ ðíe**
get off (e.g., a horse). **ósi, wísi**
get one's own. **lúuze**
get oneself into s.t. by oneself. **éwahkiǫ́ðe**
get oneself ready. **hkíliištą**
get oneself tangled in. **ohkíǫðe**
get out of (e.g., a car). **ósi, wísi**
get ready. **háhahkie**
get rid of. **ǫ́ǫðe**
get stuck to. **káataace**
get the idea: not quite ~. **hahkíe**
get there (as in a room or a place). **onąą́žį**
get undressed. **hkilííša, hkilúušawa, hkilúuštake**
get up (from a bed or chair). **hpaahą́**
get up (preparatory to departing). **nąąžį́**
get well. **kiní,' kítąhe, ónihkie**
get word of. **opéni**
get-together. **ohkíe**
ghost. **ilǫ́ɣe, wanąąɣe**
giddy. **cˀélǫðį**
gift card. **íe ðáalį žį**
girl, girlfriend. **šį́mįžį**
give. **kˀú, okˀú**
give a name for s.t. or s.o. **ðaacé**
give away. **níðe, wakˀú**
give away (e.g., the drum at *ilǫ́ǫška* dances). **kaaðée**
give away by pressing or pushing away (e.g., the *ilǫ́ǫška* drum). **kaaðéešpa**
give away to each other. **ohkíkˀu**
give back. **kíkˀu**
give birth. **iitáðe, wéetaðe**
give birth to. **iitáðe**
give each other. **hkikˀú**
give out in portions (e.g., food). **íhkilai**
give stuff to s.o. **ókˀu**
give testimony. **wawépahǫ**
give things away. **waníðe**
give to one's own, give away to one's own people. **kíkˀu**
give up. **hkíxiða**
giveaway. **nąnįǫ́kužu** [archaic], **ókˀu, waníðe**
giveaway: have or hold a ~. **ohkíkˀu, waníðe**
glad. **kízo, óweena**
glad: be ~. **kiðálį, wéeną**
glad: be ~ of. **wéeną**
glass (N). **íkǫpa**
glass: pane of ~ , window glass. **okáhąpa**
glasses (eyeglasses or any device worn over the eyes). **mą́ze įįštóolą**
glutton. **tóoceha**
go. **mąðį́**
go: let ~. **ðée káaɣe**
go: make or cause to ~. **ðéeðe**
go ahead. **mąðį́**
go ahead with s.t. **ékiǫ**
go around. **ákiɣe, ápše, kǫ́kǫe**
go around s.t. **íðišąha**
go away. **mąðį́, okábra**
go back and forth. **ihkílašą**
go behind s.o.'s back. **nąlǫ́ǫha**
go by (i.e., stop in). **ahí**
go by (go past). **ípše**
go by foot, by walking. **mąðį́**
go by using. **iiðée**
go down (as a road). **opxą́**
go down (e.g., the sun when setting). **papó**
go fast. **xį́na**
go faster: make s.t. ~. **xį́na káaɣe**
go following. **oðáhaaðee**
go for a ride. **opáwįɣe**
go for a walk. **mąðį́ aðée**
go forward. **aðée**
go home, go back. **mąlį́**
go home, go back there (motion underway). **alée**
go hunting (for). **htáabre aðée, océ**
go in, go into. **ohpé**
go looking. **tǫ́pe aðée**
go on. **mąðį́**
go on! (command). **mąðį́ ðíe**
go on (continue). **šką́**
go on a mission or journey. **wamą́ðį**
go on an excursion. **opáwįɣe**
go on horseback. **hkáwaalįį aðée**
go out (become extinguished). **táaži**
go out (in a card game). **ííðį**
go or be up above. **ámąši**

go past. **ípše**
go shopping. **waðúwį aðée**
go table-hopping. **ákiɣe**
go there (motion accomplished). **ahí**
go there: make s.t. ~. **ðée káaɣe**
go there (motion underway). **aðée**
go through (as a road). **opxą́**
go to bed. **žą́ą**
go to war. **taaké, taaké omą́ðį**
go toward you, go to the place where you are or near you. **šoðée**
go walking. **mąðį́ aðée**
go where you are: make ~. **šoðée káaɣe**
go with. **oðáhaaðee**
goal. **ohkíce**
goat. **į́hįhkicéže**
God. **hpahą́le mąðį́ ąðíðaace** [archaic or idiosyncratic?], **wahkǫ́ta**
going: get ~. **mąðį́**
gold (in color), golden, goldlike. **mą́zeska zí ékǫ**
gold (metal). **mą́zeska zí**
golden eagle. **hcížo**
golf. **htaapéskažįkˀǫ́**
golf: play ~. **htaapéskažįkˀǫ́**
golly. **éeše** [slang]
golly! (female exclamation of surprise). **wį́kše**
gone (finished). **kaašéną**
gone: be ~ (absent, nonexistent). **ðįké**
good. **ðáalį**
good: be ~ to. **ðakˀéðe**
good: be ~ to each other. **ðakˀéhkiðe**
good: feel ~. **kiðálį**
good: make oneself ~ (e.g., in respect to one's behavior). **ðáalįhkiðe**
good behavior. **óðohtą, óðohtąhkiðe**
good grades in school: have or make~. **álįįha**
good health: be in ~. **ní**
good health: in ~. **ókašéįke**
good manners, thoughts, or ways: having ~. **ókˀą ðaalį**
good time: have a ~. **kízo**
good time: show s.o. a ~. **wazóekšiðe**
good to one's own or to s.o. close: be ~. **ðakˀékiðe**
Good Voice (personal name). **hooðáalį**
good works or good: do ~. **ðáalį káaɣe**
good-bye. **kaašǫ́įke**
good-bye (to a dead person). **kaašǫ́eðe**
good-looking. **ðáalį, ohtáza**
goodness! **ą́žǫ ðįké**
goof, goof up. **ílaną**
goose. **míɣa, míɣa htą́ka**
gorget. **wanǫ́pˀį**
gosh! (female exclamation of surprise). **wį́kše**
gossip. **tíðe**
gossip: malicious and false ~. **íe okaaɣéįke**
gourd, gourd rattle. **hpéɣe**
government. **mą́ąhį htą́ą**
grab hold of. **kaaskí**
grab s.o. **ðiiskí**
grace (as said at mealtime). **waatá**
grain: any kind of ~ (such as wheat, oats). **wacúe**
grain sieve. **wacúe ikaažį**
grand. **htą́ka, lą́ąðe**
grandchild. **wihcóšpa** (also **wihcóška**) or **hcošpá** 'my grandchild', **ðihcóšpa** (also **ðihcóška**) 'your grandchild', **ihcóšpa** (also **ihcóška**) 'his/her grandchild'; **íihkoahkiha, žįká owáhkihą**
grandfather. **wihcíko** or **hcíko** 'my grandfather', **ðihcíko** 'your grandfather', **ihcíko** 'his/her grandfather'
grandmother. **iihkó** 'my/his/her grandmother', **ðiihkó** 'your grandmother'
grandmother lightning. **iihkó lǫ́ǫ**
grandmother thunder. **iihkó lǫ́ǫ**
grandparents. **ðiihkówa** 'your grandparents' (plural only)
grape. **háazu**
grape juice. **háazunii**
grasp. **ðiihtą́, oðį́įke**
grasp s.o. by the scruff of the neck. **ðiiskí**
grass. **mąąhí**
grass: cut the ~. **mąąhí kaasé**
grass: dry or dried ~. **xáhtape**
grass: sweet-smelling ~. **hpéže brąðáalį**
grasshopper. **htáhtaze, įįštáxį htáhtaze**
grateful. **óweena**
grateful: be ~ (for). **wéeną**
grave. **óxe**
graveyard. **óxe mą́žą**
gravy. **htáa lįkó, lįkó**
gray. **šóce, xóce**
grayish (like ashes). **xóce**
grayhorse. **hkáwa xóe**
Grayhorse camp (near Fairfax, Oklahoma). **hkáwaxoce**
Grayhorse group of Osages. **hpasú olį́į**
grease. **stáðe, wéli**
grease: meat ~. **htáaweli**
greasy. **ðóðo**
great. **htą́ka, lą́ąðe**
great deal: a (a lot). **wálį**

great-grandchild. **wihcóšpa áhkiha** 'my great-grandchild', **ihcóšpa áhkiha** 'his/her great-grandchild'
greed. **íibrąži**
greedy. **íibrąži, tóekǫ́ži**
green (color). **htóho** [LFD], **mąąhį́ htóho**
green (unripe). **cúutaži**
green beans. **hǫbrį́ke, hǫ́brįke htóho žį**
green onion. **mąąžą́xe htóho**
green tea. **hpéže htóho**
greens (vegetables). **ówe, wasúutą**
greeting card. **íe ðáalį žį**
grief, grieve. **kihǫ́ǫži**
grill (refers only to cooking meat on a rack, as for barbecue). **óhkace**
grimace (v). **įcé ðuuhpíiži**
grin (N), with a grin. **íixažį**
grind, grind up. **ðilǫ́že**
grind together (e.g., the teeth). **ðiiskíke**
grinder. **hówe**
grinningly. **íixažį**
groceries. **ónǫbre, ówe**
grocery store. **ówe hci**
ground (earth). **mą́įhka**
ground (earth): bare ~. **oštá**
group including individuals just mentioned. **éeðǫǫpa**
grow in size. **htą́ą**
grow up. **nǫ́ǫ ahí, nǫ́ǫ ðiištą́**
grow up to adulthood. **nǫ́ǫ**
growl. **xowí**
grownups. **nǫ́ǫ**
guess. **ípahǫ**
guess: I ~ that. **ska**
guess what? **táatą íbrilą che**
guinea hen. **súhka léze**
gullet. **tóoce**
gum. **mį́įhtǫeli**
gun. **wahóohtą**
gunpowder: flask for ~. **níixoce weoožu**

habitually. **ną** [ITERATIVE]
haggard. **lažį́į**
hair. **hį́į**
hair: roached ~. **hé káaɣe**
hair (of the head or neck of a human or an animal). **hpaxį́į**
hairbrush. **wékaapše**
haircut. **hpáxį ðuusé**
haircut: roach ~. **hpaxáce**
hairdo: woman's bun ~. **hpáxį ðuutáahpa**
half. **ohkísce**
half a container. **hépe**
half dollar. **ohkísce**
half moon. **mį́įǫpa aðikeže** [LFD]
halfway point, at the halfway point. **ohką́ska**
halt. **kaaštą́**
halt s.o. who is passing by. **nąąžį́**
halt s.t. (e.g., the horse pulling a buggy, the motion of a car). **oðíitą**
halve. **ðǫǫpáha káaɣe**
hammer (N). **wékaaspe**
hammer (V). **kaaštá**
hand: pass by ~. **kˀú huu**
hand (also used in referring to the hands of the body that are touched by the attendees when passing by a body at a funeral). **šáake**
hand game. **šáakeoolą́kˀǫ́**
hand over, hand to. **húðe**
hand towel. **šáake ípukxa**
handbag. **mą́zeskaoožú, wáseska**
handcuff. **paaxcé**
handgun. **wahóohtą**
handkerchief. **haaléžowaake, haaská wanǫ́pˀį**
handle. **ðuhcépe, okášą**
handle meat with the hand. **htaaðíihtą**
handle s.t. with the hand. **ðiihtą́**
handprint. **šáake**
handshake: have a ~. **šáake oðį́įke**
handsome. **ðáalį, ohtáza**
hang around. **ákiɣe**
hang up (e.g., clothing). **opáhce**
hanging on the back of or behind s.t. else: be ~. **oðáha**
happen. **ékǫ, híeną**
happen upon. **áhkiǫðe**
happy. **škaškáða, wakˀą́**
happy: be ~ about s.t. **kiðálį, kízo**
hard (difficult). **wahcéxi**
hard (in texture). **saakí**
hard (with force). **óhesaži**
hard to do things with. **saakí**
hardly. **to**
hare. **mąšcį́ka**
harelip. **íhaa žáhta**
harm (v). **ðuhpíiži**
harm: do or cause oneself ~. **hkilúhpiiži**
harm oneself by making a serious mistake. **hkilúhpiiži**
harm s.o. physically, mentally, or emotionally. **ðiižóži**
harmful. **wéhpiiži**

harmful behavior: engaging in ~. **taaðúhpiiži**
harmony: in ~, harmoniously. **škaškáða**
harness. **hkáwa hkihkáaɣe** (?) [no Osage entry **hkáwa hkihkáaɣe**; possibly not a genuine form]
harvest. **wapóške ówe**
harvest: ready to ~. **súutą**
hat. **óoląke**
hat: don as a ~. **oolą́ke**
hat: Osage wedding ~ (a top hat with plumes optionally worn by the bride). **lǫǫhúu**
hatch. **paaléke, páleke**
hatchet. **mą́ąhįspežį**
hate. **íisi**
hate a person. **hpíiži ažį́**
hateful. **iiséwaðe**
have. **aðį́**
have: not ~. **ðįké**
have as one's own. **ahkílį, aláðį**
have for oneself. **ahkílį**
have nothing. **ðįké**
have one's way despite s.t. **óðąži**
have s.o. do s.t. (*see* causative markers; *see also discussion under* **hce ée**)
have s.o. do s.t. for his/her own benefit. **kšíðe**
hawk. **héka, letǫ́, súhka oðį́įke, ważį́htąą**
hawk: black ~. **letǫ́sape**
hawk: redtailed ~. **letą́ ǫ́pe žúuce**
Hawk Woman (personal name). **letǫ́wį**
hay. **mąąhį́**
haywire from medicine. **mą́hkažóika**
haze. **níišoce**
Hcížo (an important Osage tribal division). **hcížo**
he. (There is no direct equivalent of 3rd person pronouns 'he', 'him', 'she', 'her', 'it' in Osage. Unemphatic 3rd person pronouns are usually not overtly expressed; *ée* and demonstratives such as *še* can be used as emphatic 3rd person pronoun ['he himself', 'she herself', etc.].) (*see also* pronominal prefixes; this; that)
he too. **eeškítą**
head. **hpá, hpée, wéeli**
head: bald ~. **hpeeštá**
head: item worn on the ~. **óoląke**
head: under the ~. **į́pehi**
head: wear or put on the ~. **oolą́ke**
head: with the ~ covered. **oolą́ke**
head committeeman. **totą́ha wahtą́ka**
head cover. **óoląke**
head of cattle. **hcéeska**
headdress. **htaasį́įce**
headdress: eagle ~. **xúðalą́ke**
headright. **hcíwažu**

heal. **kiní, kiní káaɣe**
heal fully. **kítąhe**
healed: be ~. **ónihkie**
healer. **wahkǫ́taki**
health problems: have ~. **íhpiiži, íhuheka**
healthy. **sísi**
hear, hear about. **nąkˀǫ́**
hear a rumor. **ónąkˀǫ**
hear of one's own. **kínąkˀǫ**
heard: s.t. ~. **ónąkˀǫ**
hearing: (act of hearing). **nąąɣúce**
hearing (legal proceeding). **áhkiisto**
hearsay. **ónąkˀǫ**
hearsay: known by ~. **áape**
heart. **ðą́ące**
heart attack. **ðą́ące ðuusáaki**
heart: broken ~. **ðą́ące ðuusáaki, ðą́ące xǫ́**
heart: have a pain in the ~. **ðą́ącenie**
heartache. **ðą́ącenie**
hearts (suit in a deck of cards). **ðą́ące, nį́cekˀa**
heat *(trans.)*. **táahkace káaɣe**
heater: hot water ~. **mą́ze níi táahkace káaɣe**
heating: smell (good or bad) from ~. **táabrą**
heaven. **mą́žą ðáalį, wahkǫ́ta mą́žą**
heavy, heavily laden. **skíke**
heed (V). **ánąkˀǫ, opšé**
heifer. **hcéeska, hceeská mį́įka**
hellcat. **ilǫ́eži iiséwai**
hello. **hawé**
help. **óhką**
help one's own. **okíhką**
help s.o. (who is not a relative). **okíhką**
help s.o. with a task. **óhką**
help: hired ~. **wašížį**
hen. **súhka mį́įka**
hen: guinea ~. **súhka léze**
hen: turkey ~. **súhkahtąą mį́įka**
henceforth. **ðetxą́ha**
her. (There is no direct equivalent of 3rd person pronouns 'he', 'him', 'she', 'her', 'it' in Osage. Unemphatic 3rd person pronouns are usually not overtly expressed; *ée* and demonstratives such as *še* can be used as emphatic 3rd person pronoun ['he himself', 'she herself', etc.].) (*see also* pronominal prefixes; this; that)
her, hers (possessive). **íhta** (*see also* pronominal prefixes; suus prefix)
herd (N). **opáhce**
herd (V). **kaaží, mąðį́ káaɣe**
here near you. **šée**
here, be here. **ðeeká**
here (in this place). **káa**

hernia. **hcéze bráze**
hers. (*see* her, hers [possessive]).
herself. (*see* reflexive prefix)
hiccup. **tóoske**
hickory nut. **hpáhtąą**
hidden item. **nąlǫ́ǫhkile**
hide (v). **nąlǫ́ǫha, púuspe**
hide (animal skin). **háa, xúhaa**
hide (animal skin): remove the ~ from anything. **ámaxa**
hiding place. **nąlǫ́ǫhkile**
high: hold ~. **ðumáða**
high noon. **mįįðóhta**
high quality: of ~. **ðáalį**
high-tempered. **ók[?]ą hpíiži**
highway. **óžąke**
hill. **paaɣó, paaxó**
him. (There is no direct equivalent of 3rd person pronouns 'he', 'him', 'she', 'her', 'it' in Osage. Unemphatic 3rd person pronouns are usually not overtly expressed; *ée* and demonstratives such as *še* can be used as emphatic 3rd person pronoun ['he himself', 'she herself', etc.].) (*see also* pronominal prefixes; this; that)
himself. (*see* reflexive prefix)
hip. **ǫ́pe**
hip joint. **ší ǫ́pe**
hire. **waší**
hire folks to work. **wawáši**
hire people to work for oneself. **áwawaši**
hired hand, hired person. **waší**
hired help. **wašížį**
his, be his, belong to him. **íhta** (*see also* pronominal prefixes; suus prefix)
hit (e.g., a drum). **kaaštá**
hit (e.g., a drum or a person). **ochį́**
hit (e.g., s.o. on the side of the head). **kaabráze**
hit hard, hit with a stunning blow. **káasaaki**
hit s.o. in a way that shakes him/her up badly. **kaaníeži**
hit s.o. in the head. **taašéðe**
hit s.o. on the back, knocking the wind out. **kaapxóhke**
hit things (such as a drum). **óchį**
hit with. **iichį́**
Hochunk (Winnebago) (tribe or tribal member) . **hóhtąka**
hoe. **mą́įhka íðištǫka**
hog. **hkóhkosa**
hoggish. **hkohkósa ékǫ**
hold: have or take ~ of. **oðį́įke**
hold: take ~ of one another. **mą́hki**
hold an opinion of s.t. **ažį́**
hold down (e.g., a lid or a person). **ápisą**
hold each other dear. **ðótahkiðe**
hold high. **ðumáða**
hold military maneuvers. **áhkita ok[?]ą**
hold oneself in a certain way. **ahkílaðį**
hold onto, hold. **oðį́įke**
hold sacred. **ðixópe, óxta káaɣe**
hold up. **ðuumą́ši, opáahą, paahą́**
hold up (to display). **paamą́ši**
hold up s.o. or s.t. **ðiihą́**
holder (container). **oožú**
Holding, Frances Oberly (personal name: Hawk Woman). **letǫ́wį**
hole. **k[?]ó, ok[?]ó**
hole: make a ~. **okák[?]ǫ**
hole: punch or cut a ~ in. **opák[?]o**
Holes in the Wings (personal name). **áahuk[?]oe**
holler **hóohtą, pą́**
holler for folks. **wapą́**
holy. **xópe**
holy: regard as ~. **óxta káaɣe**
home. **hcíle, ohcíle**
home: bring or take ~ (motion accomplished). **aðį́akši**
home: go ~. **mąlį́**
home: make a ~. **hcíle**
home: my ~ (similar to *chez moi* in French). **ecí mįkšé**
home: return or go ~ (motion underway). **alée**
home: take ~ (motion underway). **aðį́alee**
home: take ~ for oneself or as one's own. **ahkílįalée**
homely (not pretty or handsome). **ohtázaži**
hominy. **watáažoe**
Hominy. **hą́ąmąðį**
Hominy district. **ząącéolįį**
homosexual. **miixóke**
honest. **wáðohtą**
honey. **hkilǫ́ɣemąį**
honor (v). **áxope, ðixópe, kíoxta**
honored. **óxta**
hook. **íhkǫe**
hook and line. **hóize, íhkǫe**
hook of any kind. **húhka**
hook s.t. (e.g., clothing or a tree by using a thrown line). **húhka**
hopeless: feel ~. **hkíxiða**
horn (of animal). **hé**
horn (wind instrument). **opíɣą**
horned toad. **kalǫ́eže**
horse. **hkáwa**

horse: wild or untamed ~. **hkáwa wahcéxi**
Horse Feeder (personal name). **hkáwa óˀku** [may be an error for **hkáwa ókˀu**]
Horse Giver (personal name). **hkáwa wakˀú**
horse herder, horse watcher. **hkáwatǫpa**
horse whip. **wékaaži**
horseback. **hkáwaalįį**
horseback: go on ~. **hkáwaalįį aðée**
horserace. **hkáwa hkipáną**
hosiery. **hį́įǫke**
hospital. **húhekahci**
hot (said of objects or substances; not usually used of persons). **táahkace**
hot water heater. **mą́ze níi táahkace káaɣe**
hour. **mį́įoðaake ohtáną**
house. **hcí, hcíle**
house: long ~ covered with brush or canvas. **wažáihci**
house of God. **wahkǫ́tahci**
housefly. **hą́hceka**
houseful. **okúhpu**
household. **hcíle, ohcíle**
housekeeping: set up ~, set up a household. **hcíle**
how. **haakǫ́, hǫ́ǫche**
how about. **hą́ą**
how big. **háaðaską**
how far. **háatxą**
how long. **háatxą**
how many. **háaną**
how much. **haakǫ́, háaną**
how small. **háaðaską**
however. **óðąži**
howl. **hóohtą**
hug. **oðį́įke**
huge. **lą́ąðe wálį**
human. **níhkašie**
human: be ~. **ínihkašie**
human body. **žúoka**
humble. **waxpáðį**
humorous. **wahóhota, wahóta**
hunchback. **cˀóxe**
hundred, hundredth. **lébrą huužį́**
hungry. **nǫhpéhi**
hunt for. **océ**
hunting. **htáabre**
hunting: go ~ (for). **htáabre aðée**
hunting: squirrel ~. **sįkóce**
hunting expedition: go on a ~. **kaalǫ́ðe**
hunting time. **hceetóoka kišipi**
hurriedly. **xį́na**
hurry (v). **híce**
hurry: cause to ~. **híceðe**
hurry: in a ~. **wahkǫ́i**
hurry: make s.o. ~. **wáhice**
hurry along. **htą́ąðį**
hurry s.o. **híceðe**
hurry s.o. along. **íhice, wáhice**
hurry s.t. up. **xį́na káaɣe**
hurry up! **ónalį**
hurrying toward s.t. **ostówe**
hurt. **níe**
hurt one another physically or emotionally. **hkilíižoži**
hurt s.o. physically, mentally, or emotionally. **ðiižóži**
husband. **winíhka** or **níhka wíhta** 'my husband' (also **wižį́ke iðáce** if the couple's first child is a boy, or **cˀáižį** when the husband is elderly), **ðiníhka** or **níhka ðíhta** 'your husband', **iiníhka** or **níhka íhta** 'her husband', **ilǫ́ǫhpa iðáce** 'my/your/her husband'
husband: take as a ~. **áðuɣe**
husk (N): corn ~. **wacúexą**
husk (V) (e.g., corn). **ðuušáake**

I. **wíe** (emphatic) (*see also* pronominal prefixes)
I too. **wiškítą**
Iba: Priscilla ~ (personal name). **wažážemį́įhcexį**
ice. **ną́ɣe**
ice cream. **ną́ɣe kípše, ną́ɣe paazénii**
ice tea. **hpéženii ną́ɣe oolą́**
ice water. **ną́ɣenii**
icebox. **ną́ɣeoožú**
idea. **waðílą, wažį́**
identical to. **kǫzékǫ** idle. **ókaaɣeįke**
if. **tą** (often not overtly expressed in Osage)
ignorant: be ~ (about s.t., of s.t.). **kíopxaži**
ill: be gravely ~. **íhpiiži**
ill: be ~ with. **íhuheka**
ill: do oneself. **hkilúhpiiži**
ill fortune: having ~. **waxpáðį**
ill-advised. **ékǫži**
illegitimate, illegitimate child. **íðace įké**
ill-mannered. **ókˀą hpíiži**
illness. **húheka**
illness: be free at last from ~. **ónihkie**
illness: be suffering a period of ~. **ókaše**
illness: have as an ~. **ǫ́ǫ**
illness: suffer from an ~. **kihúheka**
ill-tempered. **ókˀą hpíiži**
imitate. **íkǫskahkíðe**
immaterial. **ókaaɣeįke** [LFD]
immature. **nǫ́ǫhiži**
immediately. **wąkǫ́ǫžį**

immediately when: and ~. **áha, iáha**
impatient: be ~. **íhice**
impeded: be ~ by problems or sickness. **ókaše**
impel s.o. to drunkenness. **páalǫðį**
imperative markers. **a, ði , pai**
imperfectly: do (s.t.) ~. **oolą́ąži**
implement (tool). **wéhkikˀǫ**
important. **lą́ąðe, óxta**
important: make ~. **óxtaðe**
important: make oneself ~. **óxtahkiðe**
impossible, impossibly. **ðąącháži**
improbable. **ékǫžie ska**
improbably. **ðąącháži**
improve with regard to an illness. **kitą́he**
in. **ci, ki**
in: be ~ an area or a group of people. **omą́ðį**
in: go ~. **ohpé**
in: live ~. **olį́į**
in: put ~. **oožú**
in: put stuff ~. **óožu**
in (s.t. lying or spread out). **kši**
in (s.t. sitting or round). **įkší**
in a direction. **ha**
in addition. **ški**
in an offhand manner. **íðilą ðįké**
in attendance: be ~. **ahí**
in between. **ohtą́ną**
in bulk. **bróka**
in charge: be ~. **oðóðe**
in charge: be ~ of. **oðówaðe**
in front of and blocking. **oðóši**
in harmony. **škaškáða**
in order to, so that. (usually not overtly expressed in Osage, but only implied)
in place of. (*see* dative prefix)
in spite of. **óðąži**
in that time. **ée htáha**
in the direction of. **ée htáha, hta, htáha**
in this manner. **kaakǫ́**
in this place. **káa**
inadequate: be ~. **oolą́ąži**
inappropriate. **éeži, ékǫži**
inappropriate, inappropriate action. **ókˀą ekǫ́ži**
inappropriately. **ekǫ́įke, íhtaháaži**
inceptive prefix. **ki-**
incessantly. **štą,**
incinerated: be ~. **táaðįke káaɣe**
incite. **ožížie**
incorrect: be ~. **ðikšį́ce**
incorrectly. **ekǫ́įke**
increase in size. **htą́ą**
increase s.t. a bit. **wéhuužį**
indeed. **wálį** (*see also* declarative sentence-final marker)
indeed (ADV). **xci, -žį**
index finger. **opázo**
Indian, Indians. **níhka žúuce**
"Indian butter" (i.e., meat grease). **htáaweli**
individual. **níhkašie, ohką́ci**
indoors. **hcíhta**
industrious. **wahtóke**
inebriated. **lǫ́ðį, omą́įžį**
inebriated: very badly ~. **wéehlihpíiži**
inefficient. **hǫ́ǫži**
inevitably. **óðąži**
inexpensive. **ómąhka**
infamous. **iiséwaðe**
infant, infancy. **hpáažį**
inferior. **hǫ́ǫži**
inferior: be ~. **oolą́ąži**
inflict upon oneself. **éhkiǫ**
inform. **óðaake**
inhabit. **olį́į**
inherit. **aláðį**
injunctive markers. **hce, htai**
inner ear. **nąąɣúce**
innocent. **ilánąðįké**
inoculation: administer an ~. **mąhká oðíkˀe**
inquire after one's own people or things. **ilǫ́ɣe**
inquire into. **ákazo**
insane. **cˀéka**
insect. **páðo, walúška**
inside, in (as in 'come in/inside [the house]'). **hcíhta**
inside: place ~ of. **oolą́**
inside out. **háašįðe**
inside out: make ~. **ðuháašįðe**
insides (entrails). **šúpe**
insolent. **wakaacˀáiži**
inspect. **ákazo**
instill fear in. **ðusáaki**
instruct. (*see discussion under* **hce ée**)
instrument: musical ~. **paakíce**
instrument: wind ~. **opíɣą**
instrumental prefixes [INSTR]. **ðaa-, ðu-, kaa-, nąą-, pá-, paa-, pi-, pó-, pu-, táa-**
insufficient. **eeną́ži**
insufficient (said of clothing). **cúuða**
insult by word. **ðaažóži**
intelligent, intelligence. **waðíląhtąą**
intend. **wakšé**
intense: more ~. **óhesaži**
intercourse: have ~. **wachú**
intercourse: have ~ with. **aðįažą¸ chúe**

interest money. **mą́zeska oðótą, oðótą mą́zeska**
intermingle. **oðóhkiðe**
interpret for another. **íe waská íkikaaɣe**
interpreter. **íe waská**
interrogate. **íðǫɣe**
interrupt. **ohkík?ǫhe**
interview, interview a person. **ohkíe**
intestines. **šúpe**
into. **hta, ki**
into: fall or jump ~. **ohkíǫðe**
into: get ~. **ohkíǫðe**
into: get oneself ~ s.t. by oneself. **éwahkiǫ́ðe**
into: go ~. **ohpé**
into: put ~. **ok?ǫ́he, oolą́**
intoxicated. **lǫ́ðį, wéehlihpíiži**
invert. **ðiisą́ða**
invert one's own. **liisą́ða**
investigate. **ðuupxáðe, waðúupxai**
invite folks. **wapą́**
invite folks to appear before others. **wáapą**
invite one's relative(s). **kíhpą**
invite others to feast. **kíkxo**
invite s.o. (not a relatives). **kípą**
inward. **mąchéhtaha**
Iowa or Ioway Indians. **páxoce**
irascible. **ók?ą hpíiži , waðílą áška**
iron (v). **ðuuštáha, puštáha, wapúštaha**
iron (v), iron s.t. **waðúuštaha**
iron (metal). **mą́ze**
Iron Hawk (personal name). **letą́mąze**
Iron Necklace (personal name). **mą́ze wanǫ́p?į**
irrelevant. **ée htáhaži**
irritable. **waðílą áška**
irritated: be ~ by. **áalake**
island. **níǫhta žį́ka**
isn't it so? **hį́**
isolate. **ohką́ci káaɣe**
isolated. **ohką́ci**
isolated from. **ákahahta**
it. (There is no direct equivalent of 3rd person pronouns 'he', 'him', 'she', 'her', 'it' in Osage. Unemphatic 3rd person pronouns are usually not overtly expressed; *ée* and demonstratives such as *še* can be used as emphatic 3rd person pronoun ['he himself', 'she herself', etc.].) (*see also* pronominal prefixes; this; that)
it is time. **éetxą, mįįðóhta**
it is time again. **ékitxą**
itch: scratch an ~. **k?úe**
item. **tą́ąska**
iterative markers. **ną, nąpe**
itself. (*see* reflexive prefix)

jack (in a deck of cards). **žáhke**
jack mule. **nąąhtą́htąą**
jail, jailhouse. **hą́ąnahpazéhci**
jail: put s.o. in ~. **hą́ąnahpazé oolą́**
January. **hą́ąpascee, mį́įohką́ce, mį́įǫpa hpąhą́le, omą́įhka hcéka, wasápe íikitali**
jar. **oožú**
jaw. **ðéepa**
jealous (e.g., of another's position). **óxįį**
jealous (used of a man), man who is jealous. **míwatą**
jealous: be ~ about (used of a woman), woman who is jealous. **ną́wązi**
jealousy. **óxįį**
Jell-O. **waskúe ðibrúbruɣe, waskúe šką́šką́**
jerk hair out. **ðuuštáštai**
Jesus Christ. **wahkǫ́ta ižį́ke**
job. **waðíhtą**
john (toilet). **ožéhci**
joke: make a ~ of s.t. **ixaéewaðe**
joke: play a ~ on. **ðíhota**
joker (clown). **wahóhota**
joker (in a deck of cards). **walúška**
Jones, Myrtle Oberly (personal name). **wažáxį**
journey: go on a ~. **wamą́ðį**
joyous. **wak?ą́**
judge (v). **wákazo**
judgment: use bad ~. **ílaną**
juice: fruit ~. **hką́ącenii**
July. **mį́įǫpa hpeðǫ́ǫpa**
jump *(intr.)*. **owísi, wísi**
jump, as when startled. **hóšechie**
jump over. **áwisi**
jumping game. **wísik?ǫ**
June. **hceetóoka kišipi, hceetóoka mąąną́ɣape, mį́įǫpa wešáhpe**
just. **na, ną́ški**
just now, just a while ago. **hcéka**
just right, just the right amount. **káaną**

Kansas gayfeather *(Liatris punctata)*. **mąhká saakí**
Kaw, Kansa (tribe or tribal member). **hką́ąze**
keep (as a souvenir, memento, or treasure). **kícheðe**
keep on (doing s.t.). **šíną, štą**
keep on (with the action of the verb). **nąną**
keep true to s.o.'s word. **íe opšé**
keepsake(s). **wahcéka**
Kemohah: Carl ~ (personal name: White Mountain). **paaxóska**

kerosene. **wéli**
kettle. **céɣe**
kettle: small ~. **céɣeží̜**
kettle: soup ~. **htaaníe céɣe**
key. **wéðušupe**
kick *(trans.).* **ną̜ąstá**
Kickapoo Indians. **kihkápo**
kidney (human or animal). **sinǫ́bre**
kid(s). **ží̜ká, ží̜káží̜**
kids: take care of ~. **ží̜kókašą**
kill. **cˀéðe**
kill oneself. **cˀéhkiðe**
kill others, kill folks. **wacˀéðe**
kind. **waðákˀeðe**
kind: be ~. **íðakˀéðe**
kind: be ~ to each other. **ðakˀéhkiðe**
kind: be ~ to one's own or to s.o. close. **ðakˀékiðe**
kind of (somewhat). **ékǫ**
kind: what ~. **hǫ́ǫxci̜, táatą**
kindling: fine ~. **žą̜ąhcúkˀa**
kindness: show or use ~. **íðakˀéðe**
king (in a deck of cards). **wahtą́ą**
kinky. **hkíhki̜ni̜,**
Kiowa (tribe or tribal member). **hpá tóohka, hpáði̜**
kiss. **íišci̜ka**
kiss one's own. **íikišci̜ka**
kitchen. **oohǫ́hci**
knead meat with the hand. **htaaðíihtą**
knead s.t. with the hand. **ðiihtą́**
knee. **ší̜i̜ce**
knee joint. **žeká óhkiche**
kneecap. **šiðǫ́ce**
knife. **mą́ąhi̜**
knock s.o. in the head. **taašéðe**
knock s.o. out. **kaalǫ́ði̜, kaaníeži, káasaaki**
knot: tie a ~. **ákaške**
know (e.g., a fact, the answer to a question). **ípahǫ**
know as a person, know s.o. as. **ípahǫ**
know for oneself. **hkihpíǫ**
know how: not ~ (to). **kǫ́ži̜ka**
know how to do s.t. **hpíǫ**

labor: bc in, labor (during childbirth). **waníe**
lack, be lacking. **ði̜ké**
lack strength. **waašką́ði̜ké**
lacking: be ~. **níðe**
ladle. **hcú hápa, níiðaahtą**
lame. **wahkúcˀa**
lamp. **átahką**
land. **mą́žą**
language. **íe**
languid. **xpéka**
lap (part of the body). **wéetaha**
lard. **hkohkósa wéli, wéli**
large. **htą́ą, htą́ka, lą́ąðe**
large: exceedingly ~. **lą́ąðe wáli̜**
large: very ~. **lą́ąðehtą**
large amount. **huuhtą́ka**
large number of. **huuhtą́ka, huuwáli**
large quantities: in ~. **bróka**
last (ADJ). **haaší, haašíhta, oðóhake, paðíhta**
last: the one before ~. **kootáha**
last (the most recent). **ce**
last day. **hą́ąpa oðóhake**
last evening. **hpázece**
last night. **hą́ące**
last summer. **tookéce**
late. **wascúuce**
late: always ~. **ókxąži**
late afternoon. **mí̜i̜hpapo**
laugh, laugh at. **íixa**
laugh: cause folks to ~. **íixaéewaðe**
laughable: be ~. **íixaéewaðe**
laughing stock. **ixaéewaðe**
launder. **ðiiškí**
laundry: do ~. **waðíiški**
laundry: do ~ for oneself. **hkilíiški**
laundry (clothes to wash). **waðíiški**
laundry (place), laundry house. **waðíiškihci**
law. **ówaðaace, wahkílaace**
law enforcement. **áhkita**
lawmaker. **hkiistó omąði̜, wahkílaace káaɣe**
lawn. **oštá**
laws: make ~ (as in Congress). **wahkílaace káaɣe**
lawyer. **wáhkie**
lay (have sex with). **aðí̜ažą, chúe**
lay into. **kˀǫ́he**
laziness. **oðúucˀake**
lazy. **oðúucˀake**
lazy: be ~. **óðuucˀake**
lead (in a card game). **ðée káaɣe**
lead (metal). **mą́ze**
lead a life. **ónihkašika**
leaf. **žąąpé**
lean. **bréhka**
lean (used to describe a person or animal). **laží̜i̜**
lean up against. **áakxą, áðiikxą**
learn. **hpíǫ, waðílą̜htąą, wahpíǫ**
learn for oneself. **hkihpíǫ**
learn how to do s.t. **wahpíǫ**

learned: be ~. **waléze hpíǫ**
learning. **walézeáace**
lease money. **mą́zeska oðótą, oðótą mą́zeska, ootá mą́zeska**
leasing of land. **mą́žą óota**
leastways. **našǫ**
leave (as leftovers). **ošcé**
leave (depart). **aðée**
leave (e.g., a crowd leaving after a dance or other public gathering). **okábra**
leave (s.o.). **kíhkoopše**
leave alone. **šǫ́įkšeðe**
leave alone (a sitting person or thing), leave it alone. **šǫ́įkšeðe**
leave alone! (command). **šo ðíe**
leave alone without bothering, touching, or otherwise disturbing. **šǫ́cheðé**
leave be! (command). **šo ðíe**
leave behind. **áalǫðį, ǫ́ǫðe**
leave it alone. **kaašǫ́e che**
leave it/him/her (lying down) alone! (command). **šǫ́kšeðe**
leave s.o. **ǫ́ǫða**
leave s.o. barely alive. **toníðe**
leaves. **žą́ąpe**
leaves or leaflike layers: having ~. **xáxa**
left, lefthand. **ðáhta**
left over: be ~. **ošcé**
leftover. **ðaacˀáke, ošcé che**
leftover amount. **ošcé**
leftovers (scattered around). **ošcé ke**
leftward. **ðáhta**
leg. **žeká**
leg (e.g., of spider). **hú**
legal proceeding. **áhkiisto**
legend. **óðaake**
leggings. **hį́įǫke**
legislate. **wahkílaace káaɣe**
legislator. **hkiistó omąðį**
lemon. **hką́ące zi cˀáaðe**
lend. **okˀú**
leprechaun. **míalǫška**
lesbian. **miixóke**
less than the full amount. **ohépe**
lessen. **čóopa ekǫ́ káaɣe**
let, let's. (*see* injunctive markers)
let go. **ðée káaɣe**
let it alone, let it be, let it sit. **kaašǫ́e che**
let s.o. be. **šǫ́įkšeðe**
let s.o. do s.t. **kšíðe** (*see also* causative markers)
let slip (as a comment), let slip away. **ðikšį́ce**
letter. **óðaake waléze, wáleze**
lettuce. **hpéžehtoho**
level (ADJ). **stáko**
liar. **íxopeštą́**
Liatris punctata (gayfeather, blazing star). **mąhká saakí**
lice. **hée**
lick (V). **ðaaštápe**
lie (N, V). **íxope**
lie abed. **óžą**
lie down. **ážą, óžą**
lie down against. **áðiikxą**
lie down, as to sleep or rest. **áakxą**
lie down in. **óžą**
lie down to sleep. **žą́ą**
lie to. **mąɣíðe**
lie up against. **áakxą**
life. **oníhkašie**
life: lead or live a ~. **ónihkašika**
life: live this ~. **mą́žą ðé ómąðį**
lift (V). **ðuhcépe, ðumáða, ðuumą́ši, paamą́ši**
lift off. **ðuxpáwį**
lift s.o. or s.t. **ðiihą́**
light (N). **átahką**
light in color. **ɣį**
light weight. **háha** [LFD]
lighten. **ðuuhépe**
lighter (N). **ðuuhpéece**
lightning. **lǫ́ǫ waléze, níǫpapa**
lightning: forked ~. **ðiléleze**
lightning: grandmother ~. **iihkó lǫ́ǫ**
lightning strike(s). **kaalį́**
likable. **ókˀą ðaalį**
like (V). **kiðálį, kíhǫǫ, kízo**
like: act ~. **íkǫskahkíðe, ókˀą**
like (similar to). **kǫzékǫ**
like each other (resembling each other). **kǫzéhkihkǫ**
like that or this. **ékǫ**
like this or that: not be ~. **ékǫži**
likewise. **ékǫ**
limb of a tree. **káxa**
limb of a tree: broken ~. **žą́ąkaaxǫ́**
limbs of a tree or bush: small ~. **žą́ąžį, žą́ąxežį**
line (fishing line). **hóize**
lined (having lines). **léze**
lion. **michó**
lip: broken or split ~. **íhaa žáhta**
liquid. **níi**
liquid medicine. **mąhká oðáahtą eeną́**
liquor. **hpéecenii**
liquor store. **hpéeceniihci**
listen, listen to. **ánąkˀǫ**

literate: be ~. **waléze hpíǫ**
little. **wahók?a, wahóšce, xohtą, -žį, žįká**
little: a ~. **-žį**
little: a ~, a little bit. **čóopa**
little: a ~, a little piece. **hépežį**
little: very ~. **wahóščažį**
Little Black Bear (personal name). **wasápežį**
little black person. **sáežį**
little one(s). **žįká, žįkážį**
little people (small beings in Osage mythology). **míalǫška, níhkašikažį**
little star. **mihkák?ežįka**
live (v). **hcíle, ní, níhkašika, omą́ðį**
live (in or at a place), live within (e.g., a person's heart). **olį́į**
live a certain way. **ðį́, mąðį́**
live a life. **ónihkašika**
live among others. **ómąðį**
live as. **ðį́**
live as a person. **ínihkašie**
live for another or others. **kiní**
live in the woods. **žą́ą olį́į**
live this life. **mą́žą ðé ómąðį**
liver. **hcehpé**
living on the end. **hpasú olį́į**
lizard. **úžewąąmǫį**
load for moving (v). **wahúįk?į**
loan (N). **mą́zeska ootá waléze**
loan (v). **wak?ú**
locative prefixes [LOC]. **á-, í-, ó-**
lock (e.g., a house door, a trunk, a car door). **oðį́įmą**
locomotive. **oðíhtą k?ą́saaki**
locust. **páðo**
lodge: sweat ~. **ítaasuhu, į́įolįįhci**
log (wood). **žą́ą**
loincloth. **híðaxa, xíðaxa**
lonesome. **kízoži**
lonesome: be ~ (for s.o.). **íkišike (stative)**
long (ADJ). **húuscee, scéce**
long ago. **kóoci**
long ago: those (who lived) ~. **haašíhta, kóoci**
long house covered with brush or canvas. **wažáihci**
long legs: having ~. **húuscee**
long time. **hǫ́ǫpa huuwáli, kaahúuža, káaši**
long time: for a ~. **kaahúuža, káaši, kóoci**
long time ago: a ~. **kaahúuža**
long way: a ~ (ADV). **wéhice**
long-suffering. **waxpáðį**
look a certain way: make one ~. **tǫ́pewaðe**
look after oneself, look at oneself. **áhkihtǫpe**
look after or look at (one's own things or people). **ákihtǫpe**
look at, look on, look upon. **tǫ́pe**
look at one's own. **hkíhtǫpe**
look at one's own things. **kihtǫ́pe**
look at oneself. **hkíhtǫpe**
look at s.t. that belongs to s.o. **kítǫpe**
look down on (benevolently). **kitǫ́pe**
look for (s.t. lost or misplaced, s.t. of one's own, or s.t. belonging to s.o. else). **okíce**
look for s.t. or s.o. **océ**
look for things. **óce**
look into. **óðąąceši**
look like (appear so). **tǫ́pewaðe**
look like (be at the point of happening). **ðąąché**
look like (resemble). **íkǫska**
look on at an event. **watǫ́pe**
look over (supervise). **oðóðe**
look with regard to s.o. **kitǫ́pe**
looking: go ~. **tǫ́pe aðée**
Looking at the Eagle, (personal name). **xúe tǫ́į**
looking for enemies. **totą́**
Looking Only at Her, Look Only at Her (personal name). **eeną́tǫįpe**
Lookout: Anita ~ (personal name: Eagle Woman). **xúðawį**
Lookout: Armeda ~ (personal name). **wažážemį́įhcexį**
Lookout: Dora ~ (personal name: Sacred Arrow Shaft). **mą́ąsihcexi**
Lookout: Smokey ~ (personal name: Follows-the-Sun). **mį́įšechie**
Lookout: Yvonne ~ (personal name: Eagle Woman). **xuðáchewį**
lorgnette. **mą́ze įįštóolą**
lose one's own. **lúuxpaðe**
lose some things, lose stuff. **óxpaðe**
lose s.t. **ðuuxpáðe**
lose s.t. or s.o. specific. **oxpáðe**
loser (one who customarily does not win). **óhipažinai**
lost: be, get, or become ~. **oxpáðe**
lost: cause to be or get ~. **oxpáðe káaɣe, oxpáðeðe**
lot: a ~ (a great deal). **wálį**
lot: be a ~ of. **ochí**
lots. **óše**
lots: be ~. **óše**
lots (of), a lot of. **huuhtą́ka, huuwáli**
loud: be ~. **óochiže**
lounge (N). **ážą**
lounging chair. **álįįscee**

louse (N). **hée**
love (v). **ðą́ąceíki, kiðáli̜, kíhǫǫ**
love one's own. **kíoxta**
loved. **óxta**
lower by pulling (e.g., a window shade). **ðuuhúuce**
lowland. **ozó**
lukewarm. **štáke**
lulu. **ðaazó, waðáazo**
lumbago. **wahúni**
lumber. **žą́ą**
lunch. **mi̜i̜ðóhta wanǫ́bre, óðaašce**
lung. **ðǫ́ɣu**
lying down (position). (*see* continuative aspect markers; positional articles)

macaw. **waží̜kaíe**
machine or machinery. **wéhkikˀǫ**
mad (angry). **lą́, waží̜ hpíiži**
mad (angry): be ~. **ohkíži̜**
mad (angry): become or get ~. **óži̜ hpíiži**
mad (angry): feel ~ at s.o. **hkíži̜, ohkíži̜**
magazine. **óðaake waléze**
maiden. **kažą́si**
mail (v). **ðéeðe, ðée káaɣe**
mail to another person. **ðeekšíðe**
make. **káaɣe**
make (s.o. do s.t. or be a certain way). **káaɣe, kaaží** (*see also* causative markers; instrumental prefixes)
make (up) for oneself (e.g., one's bed). **hkihkáaɣe**
make a crowd. **wéhuu, wéhuukǫ́i̜**
make a fist. **ðiiskíke, šáakeðíiskike**
make a hole. **okákˀǫ**
make a home. **hcíle**
make a joke of s.t. **íixaéewaðe**
make a phone call. **mą́zeie híðe**
make a recording with an audio device. **íe ðuuzé**
make a talk or speech. **íe**
make an effort. **waašką́, íkˀuce**
make bald or bare. **ðuuštá, ðuuštáštai**
make believe (v). **kǫzé** [JOD, LFD]
make-believe. **ékǫska ha**
make camp. **ahcí, hcí**
make change, make a change. **íhkihkawi̜ káaɣe**
make curly. **ðuuhkíhki̜**
make dear. **óxtakiðe**
make die. **cˀéðe**
make equal to. **íkǫskahkíðe**
make faces. **i̜cé ðuuhpíiži**
make folks want to, make one want to. **kǫ́ðawaðe**
make for s.o. **íkikaaɣe**
make for s.o. (e.g., food or a bed). **kšíɣe** (*see also* causative markers)
make forked. **pážahta**
make friends with each other. **ðótahkiðe**
make from. **wékaaɣe**
make fun of s.o. **wahóta**
make go. **ðéeðe**
make go where you are. **šoðée káaɣe**
make good. **ðuðáali̜**
make it (in a card game). **káaɣe**
make it anyway. **óðąži**
make it slow. **lúžihkiðe**
make laws (as in Congress). **wahkílaace káaɣe**
make lie down or be in bed, have another in bed. **ðížąą** (?) [no Osage entry **ðížąą**; possibly not a genuine form]
make lighter. **ðuuhépe**
make no more (of). **kaakǫ́ną káaɣe**
make one look or appear a certain way. **tǫ́pewaðe**
make one's best effort. **íkˀuce**
make one's mark upon s.t. **páaleze**
make oneself (to be or do). **hkíðe**
make oneself comfortable. **hkikˀą́ze**
make oneself full. **wéenącehkiðe**
make oneself important. **óxtahkiðe**
make oneself ready, make yourself ready. **háhahkie**
make oneself right and respectable. **óxtahkiðe**
make oneself straight. **óðohtąhkiðe**
make out of. **íkaaɣe**
make over. **kikáaɣe**
make plain or distinct. **wáðaaska**
make round. **ðuutáahpa**
make sick. **húheka káaɣe**
make slower. **lúži káaɣe**
make smaller. **ðuuhépe**
make s.o. do s.t. **ákaaži, kaaží**
make s.o. hurry. **wáhice**
make s.o. nervous. **páalǫði̜**
make s.o. put on an article of clothing. **i̜kšíðe**
make s.o. successful. **ðáali̜ kšíðe**
make special. **óxtaðe, óxtakiðe**
make s.t. bad. **ðuhpíiži**
make s.t. go faster. **xí̜na káaɣe**
make s.t. go to another person. **ðeekšíðe**
make things plain (e.g., words or lines on a paper, borders on land). **wáðuuska**
make trouble ~ for s.o. **ówǫ káaɣe**
make up (apply makeup). **i̜cé káaɣe**
make up one's mind. **waðílą hkihkáaɣe, waðílą káaɣe**
make using. **wékaaɣe**

makeup. **kikˀǫ́**
makeup: apply ~. **į̨cé káaɣe**
male. **tooká**
male child. **šį́tožį**
males: be without ~ (said of a family with all girls). **tooká ðįké**
male singers at a dance. **xóhka**
malicious false gossip. **íe okaaɣéįke**
malign. **ðaažóži**
mallard duck. **hpáhiihto**
malodorous. **ɣoį́**
man. **níhka, níhkašie**
man: elderly ~. **cˀáižį**
manacle. **paaxcé**
manage. **ðuhcépe**
manage (e.g., an event). **oðóðe**
mandible. **ðéepa**
mane. **hpaxį́į**
maneuvers: hold military ~. **áhkita okˀą**
mangy. **hcúxe**
manner: in this ~. **kaakǫ́**
manners: having no ~. **ókˀą hpíiži**
mantle. **ákahamį, mǫkápo**
many. **huuhtą́ka, huuwáli**
many: be ~. **ochí, óšechiðe**
many people. **huukǫ́ða**
many things. **táatą ochí**
map. **mąžą́waleze**
March. **hą́ąpa ohkísce, mį́į okˀą́įke, mį́įǫpa weðáabrį**
marines. **áhkita omą́ðį**
mark: make one's ~ upon s.t. **páaleze**
maroon (color). **pazó ekǫ́**
marriage (term used by friend or family of groom). **mį́įląke**
married: be or get ~ (said of a man). **mį́įląke**
married: be or get ~ (said of a woman). **wáðuɣe, wéðuɣe**
married woman. **wakˀó wéðuɣe**
marrow. **wažúpe**
marry *(trans.)*. **žóle**
marry: make one's own relative ~, marry off a female relative (e.g., one's daughter). **wéðuɣekíðe**
marry (a man). **áðuɣe**
marry (a woman). **lą́ke**
marry a woman. **mį́įląke**
marry each other. **hkilą́ke**
marvelous. **óxta**
Mary (mother of Jesus). **wahkǫ́ta ižį́ke iihǫ́**
mash down. **ápisą**
Mashunkashey: Russell Koshehe ~ (personal name: Buffalo Chief). **ðóxe kahíke**
match (for lighting a fire). **ðuuhpéece**
mate *(trans.)*. **ðúɣe**
material. **haaská**
mattress. **omíže**
mature. **nǫ́ǫ**
may, might. (*see* potential marker)
May. **mį́įǫpa wesáhtą**
maybe. **nąka**
me. **wíe** (emphatic) (*see also* pronominal prefixes)
me too. **wiškítą**
meadowlark. **mǫ́ǫke zí htą́ą**
meal. **ónǫbre**
meal: evening ~. **hpáze wanǫ́bre**
meal: noon or evening ~. **wanǫ́bre**
meal: noon or midday ~. **mįįðóhta wanǫ́bre**
meal: take care of a ~ oneself when asked to do so. **óohkihą**
mean (hateful). **iiséwaðe**
mean (have a certain meaning). **ékǫ**
mean (intend). **wakšé**
meaningless. **ókaaɣeįke**
means: by ~ of, a means to. **í-**
means to see each other again. **wéehkile**
meantime. **ihtǫ́į ðéha**
meanwhile. **katxą́**
measure (v). **ðaawá**
measuring stick. **žą́ą wéðaawa**
meat. **htáa**
meat: burned or charred ~. **táasaaki**
meat: fat ~. **wašį́**
meat candy (pounded meat). **htáa štǫ́ka, htáapše**
meat gravy (popular Osage dish made of boiled meat). **táalįko**
meat pie. **htóolą** (old meaning), **htóožu, síekǫ**
meatball. **htáa štǫ́ka**
medal, medallion. **mą́zeska wanǫ́pˀį, wanǫ́pˀį**
medical care: administer ~ to s.o. **šcéðe**
medicine. **mąhká**
medicine: liquid ~ (medicine that comes in liquid form only). **mąhká oðáahtą eeną́**
medicine: one who has ~. **mąhká aðį́**
medicine bundle. **mąžáhku, waxópe**
meditate on. **áwaðilą**
meet *(trans.)*. **áhkihpa** [JOD, LFD], **áhkiǫðe, áhkoopše**
meet and talk things over. **kiistó**
meet each other, meet s.o. **íihkihkiðe**
meeting. **hkilíiski**

meeting: hold a Native American Church or peyote ~. **hkihkǫ́ze**
meeting: peyote or Native American Church ~. **hkihkǫ́ze, mąhkáðaaché**
meeting held by a group of people. **hkiistó**
meeting of a group of people to converse. **ohkíe**
mellow (ADJ). **cúuce, táaske**
melt. **táaską**
member: be a ~ (e.g., of a club). **oðízą**
memento: keep as a ~. **kícheðe**
men. **níhka, níhkašie**
men: young ~. **nǫ́hǫžį**
menstruate. **waaláke**
"mentally retarded," mentally unstable. **cˀéka**
merciful: be ~ to. **ðakˀéðe**
merely. **ną́ški**
Merry Christmas. **wahkǫ́ta ižį́ke hąąpa iðáalį**
merry-go-round. **kǫ́kǫe**
mess (trashy mixture). **táatą ochí**
message sent by wire. **mązekˀąsaaki**
messed up. **ɣǫ́ǫce**
metal of any kind. **mą́ze**
meteor. **mihkákˀe oxpáðe**
Mexican or other native Spanish-speaking person. **íšpaðǫ**
midday. **mįįðóhta**
midday dinner or meal. **mįįðóhta wanǫ́bre**
middle. **ohką́ska**
middle: be in the ~. **iðǫ́eðįhé**
middle: down the ~. **opxá**
middle: in the ~. **ohką́ska**
midnight. **hąą ohkáska, hąą ohtąka**
might. (*see* potential marker)
might (N). **waašką́**
migrate. **kalǫ́ðe, wahúį**
mild (a person's ways or the weather). **štáke**
military maneuvers: hold ~. **áhkita okˀą**
military service: be in ~. **taaké omąðį**
milk. **paazénii paazénii ðiiscúe**
milk: sweet ~. **paazénii skúðe**
mill. **hówe**
million. **waðáawa htąke**
mind. **waðílą, wažį́**
mind: have a good ~. **waðíląhtąą**
mind: have in ~. **wakšé**
mind: have on one's ~. **íðilą**
mind: have s.t. on one's ~. **táatą íðilą**
mind: I don't have the ~! **ąžǫ ðįké**
mind: in one's right ~. **nąąɣeska**
mind: make up one's ~. **waðílą hkihkáaɣe, waðílą káaɣe**
mine (PRON). **wíhta**
minister of a religious group. **ožąke olį́į, wahkǫ́taki, wakǫ́ze**
mink. **hį́įzįį**
mirror. **niióhkiacˀį**
misbehave. **taeðáalįži**
mischievous. **iiscéwai**
mischievous: be ~. **ðiihíce, taeðáalįži**
mischievous (said of a person who tends to laugh and make fun of people). **óškika**
misconstrue. **íe ðaaéži**
mislead. **oxpáðe káaɣe**
misrepresent oneself. **mąɣíðe**
miss (a target). **kakšį́ce**
miss (be lonesome for, long for). **íkišike**
miss (not get right). **ðikšį́ce**
miss each other. **íhkišike**
miss out on (e.g., a dinner by arriving late). **kakšį́ce**
miss the mark. **ooląąži**
mission, go on a mission. **wamąðį**
Mississippi River. **níi htąka**
mist. **íhkišoce, níišoce, niižú xóce, níižu xohtą**
mistake: make a ~. **hkilúhpiiži**
mistake: make a (disgraceful) ~ that brings attention to oneself. **ílaną**
mistake (N) (not a particularly serious mistake). **wanáhkai**
mistaken: be ~. **mąɣíhkiðe**
misting rain. **íhkišoce**
mistreat. **ðiižóži**
mistreat (an animal or person). **ðiihíce**
mistreat one another. **hkilíižoži**
mistreat s.o. **ðišǫ́ži**
mistrust oneself. **hkíxiða**
mixed blood: person of ~. **įįštáxįžį́**
mixed in, mixed among. **íwihe**
mixture: trashy ~ (of items that are out of order). **táatą ochí**
moccasins. **hǫǫpé**
moist. **mąątóohka, toohká**
moment: at this ~. **ðekǫ́ǫce**
moment: the ~ for s.t. **éetxą**
Monday. **hąąpa hpahąle**
money. **mązeska**
money: paper ~. **htanąkˀa mązeska**
money bag. **mązeskaoožú**
monkey. **héeoce**
month, month's time. **mį́įǫpa**
month before last. **mį́įǫpa kootáha**
moo (V). **hóohtą**
moon (N). **mį́įǫpa**

moon: crescent ~. **mį́įǫpa aðikeže**
moon: full ~. **mį́įǫpa táahpa**
moon: half ~. **mį́įǫpa aðikeže** [LFD]
more. **oðóhake, ši**
morning. **mį́įhuðe**
morning: early ~. **hą́ąekǫ́žį, kaasį́exci, kaasį́excįžį**
morning: late ~. **mįįðóhta žišǫ́**
morning star. **mihkákˀe hą́ąpa tą ðįkše, mihkákˀe hą́ąpaska tą, mihkákˀehtąą**
morose. **ókˀą hpíiži**
mortar (for grinding). **hówe**
mosquito. **brápxąąke, lápxąąke**
most recent: the ~. **ce**
mother. **iiną́** 'my mother', **ðiihǫ́** 'your mother', **iihǫ́** 'his/her mother, the/a mother'
mother of Jesus. **wahkǫ́ta ižį́ke iihǫ́**
mother-in-law. **wakˀǫ́žį (wíhta)** 'my mother-in-law' (for some speakers, specifically 'my wife's mother'), **ðíwakˀóžį** or **wakˀǫ́žį ðíhta** 'your mother-in-law' (for some speakers, specifically 'your wife's mother'), **íwakˀóžį** 'his/her mother-in-law'; **iihkó** 'my husband's mother', **ðiihkó** 'your husband's mother'
Mother's Day. **íihǫhą́ąpa**
mound. **hpá**
mountain. **paaɣó** (variant, rare), **paaxó**
mounted on a horse. **hkáwaalįį**
mourn *(trans.)*. **kíkxą**
mourning dance. **wašápe aðį́**
mouse. **įchóka**
mouth. **íhaa**
mouth: big ~. **íhcuke**
move *(intr.)*. **šką́** (*see also* continuative aspect markers; positional articles; subject markers)
move *(trans.)*. **ðicíze, ðuušką́**
move: unable to ~ (as a motor vehicle). **šką́aži**
move all around. **ákiɣe**
move fast. **htą́ąðį**
move to another location. **wahúį**
movement: make a back and forth ~ (as when riding a teeter-totter). **sísiąðe**
movie. **ówatoį**
movies. **hkéetaxewatǫ́e**
moving: get ~. **mąðį́**
much: be ~. **ósechiðe**
much: this ~. **káaną**
mucus: filled with ~. **xtoe**
mucus from the nose. **hpahlíxtoe, hpalį́**
mud. **mąąstósto, mą́įhka**
muddy. **mąąstósto**
mule. **nąąhtą́htąą**
murder. **cˀéðe**
muscle. **áahkǫ**
muscular. **saakí**
muse about. **waðílą**
mushroom. **mihkákˀe**
music. **paakíce**
music: play ~ on an instrument. **paakíce**
muskrat. **htachí, įchóhtąą**
must: it ~ be that. **ska**
mutter in complaint. **lǫ́ǫ**
my. **wíhta** (*see also* pronominal prefixes; suus prefix)
my goodness! **ą́žǫ ðįké**
my home (similar to *chez moi* in French). **ecí mįkšé**
myself. (*see* reflexive prefix)
mysterious power. **wahkǫ́ta**

naked. **hį́ðohkižį**
name. **žáže**
name: assign, give, or use a ~. **ðaacé**
name: call on s.o.'s ~. **ðaacé**
name: call s.o. a bad ~. **lǫ́ǫ**
name: say the ~ of s.t. or s.o. **ðaacé**
name one's own. **láace**
name used to make fun of s.o. **žáže wahóta**
names: call ~. **lǫ́ǫlǫǫ**
names: call each other ~. **hkílǫ(lǫ)**
names: call folks ~. **walǫ́ǫ**
napkin. **íhaa ípukxa, šáake ípukxa**
napkin: paper ~. **htaną́kˀa ípukxa**
narrate. **oðáake**
narrative. **óðaake**
narrow. **wahóšce**
nation. **níhkašika ochí**
Native American Church (the religion given this name). **hkihkǫ́ze**
Native American Church meeting. **mąhkáðaaché**
Native American Church meeting: hold or put on a ~. **hkihkǫ́ze**
Navajo (tribe or tribal member). **haxį́ležekáaɣe**
navy. **áhkita omą́ðį**
near, nearby. **áška**
near the time of that. **ée htáha**
nearly. **ðóha, hóni**
neat. **stáko**
neaten. **ðuustáko**
neck. **htáhu**
neck: wear around the ~. **nǫpˀį́**
neckerchief. **haaléžowaake, haaská wanǫ́pˀį**
necklace. **wanǫ́pˀį**
necklace of iron or other metal. **mą́ze wanǫ́pˀį**
needle. **súhka húhka**

negative markers [NEG]. **aží, ðįįké, ðįké, maží**

negatively affected by too much of s.t.: be ~. **íibrą**

Neosho (in Oklahoma). **niióšo**

nephew (specifically, son of brother of female). **wihcóška** (also **wižį́ke**) 'my brother's son' (speaker is female), **ðihcóška** (also **ðižį́ke**) 'your brother's son' (addressee is female), **ihcóška** 'her brother's son'

nephew (specifically, son of brother of male or son of sister of female [same as terms for 'son']). **wižį́ke** 'my brother's son' (speaker is male) or 'my sister's son' (speaker is female)', **ðižį́ke** 'your brother's son' (addressee is male), **ižį́ke** 'his brother's son, her sister's son'

nephew (specifically, son of sister of male or son of brother of wife). **wihcóška** 'my sister's son, my wife's brother's son' (speaker is male), **ðihcóška** 'your sister's son, your wife's brother's son' (addressee is male), **ihcóška** 'his sister's son, his wife's brother's son'

nerve: I don't have the ~! **ą́žǫ ðįké**

nervous: make s.o ~. **páalǫðį**

nest. **hcí**

never. **aži ną** (no Osage expression exactly matches the range of use of English 'never')

never on time. **ókxąži**

never will. **aži hta** (for future time only; no Osage expression exactly matches the range of use of English 'never')

nevertheless. **óðąži**

new, newly. **hcéka**

new things. **wahcéka**

new year. **omą́įhka hcéka**

news. **óðaake**

news: shocking or startling ~. **hóšechie**

newspaper. **htaną́kˀa waléze, óðaake waléze**

newsprint. **htaną́kˀa waléze**

next. **áhkiha, ímąche, okxą́**

next: and ~. **kaðǫ́**

next: the one after ~. **kootáha**

next-to-last. **kootáha**

nice. **ðáalį**

nice-looking. **stáko**

nickel (five cents). **waðáawa sáhtą**

nickname (N). **žáže wahóta**

niece (specifically, daughter of brother of female). **wihcióžąke** 'my brother's daughter' (speaker is female), **ðihcióžąke** 'your brother's daughter' (addressee is female), **ihcóžąke** 'her brother's daughter'

niece (specifically, daughter of sister of male). **wihcížo** 'my sister's daughter' (speaker is male), **ðihcížo** 'your sister's daughter' (addressee is male), **ihcížo** 'his sister's daughter'

niece (specifically, daughter of brother of male or daughter of sister of female [same as terms for 'daughter']). **wižǫ́ke** 'my brother's daughter' (speaker is male) or 'my sister's daughter' (speaker is female), **ðižǫ́ke** 'your brother's daughter' (addressee is male) or 'your sister's daughter' (addressee is female), **ižǫ́ke** 'his brother's daughter, her sister's daughter'

night. **hą́ą, hpáze**

night: at ~. **hą́ą**

night: darkness or dark of ~. **hą́ąnahpazé**

night: last ~. **hą́ące**

night: late ~. **hąą káaši**

night: stay all ~. **žą́ą**

night before last. **hą́ące kootáha ce**

Night Walker (personal name). **hą́ąmąðį**

night woman. **hą́ą wakˀó**

nightmare. **ohpáza**

nighttime. **hą́ą**

nine, ninth. **lébrą hce wį́įke**

nineteen, nineteenth. **lébrą álįį hce wį́įke**

ninety, ninetieth. **lébrą lébrą hce wį́įke**

no (INTERJ). **hą́ąhkaži**

no ears (a person who won't listen). **nąąɣúce ðįké**

no good. **óškika**

no more: make ~ (of). **kaakǫ́ną káaɣe**

no more: there is ~ (INTERJ). **kaaštą́**

no value: s.t. of ~. **mą́ąhpiiži**

nobody. **pée, hǫ́ǫe wį, péeški** (*see also* anybody)

nocturnal. **hą́ą**

noise. **óochiže**

noise: not make ~. **oní ðįké**

noise: ticking, tapping, or clicking ~ against metal (as made by a typewriter). **mą́ze htáhtaze**

noisy: be ~. **óochiže**

noncontinuative markers (3rd person). **api, i**

none: be ~. **ðįké**

nonexistent: be ~. **ðįké**

nonsense. **ókaaɣeįke** [LFD]

noodles. **wacúe kˀą́saaki**

noon. **mįįðóhta**

noon meal. **mįįðóhta wanǫ́bre**

normal eyesight: have ~. **wawéeðe**

normally. **ną** [ITERATIVE]**, nąpe**

north. **níwahcekši htáha, pásąci** [LFD]

north wind. **nį ké hta huðe**

nose. **hpá**
nose: runny ~. **hpahlíxtoe, hpalį́**
Nose Cutter (personal name for a second son). **hpápaxǫ**
not. (*see* negative markers)
not anything else, not anything but. **na**
not be present. **ðįké**
not be thus. **ékǫži**
not careful. **íinǫǫhpaži**
not difficult. **wacˀéka**
not easy to do. **wahcéxi**
not enough. **eeną́ži**
not exist. **ðįké**
not fitting in the available space. **wíohkaðį**
not get s.t. right. **ðikšį́ce**
not have anything, lack. **ðįké**
not have anything to do with s.o. or s.t. **šǫ́įkšeðe**
not in one's right mind. **waðílą eekǫ́ įké**
not know how (to). **kǫ́žįka**
not lazy. **wahtóke**
not make noise. **oní ðįké**
not pay attention to. **óðąąceši ðįké**
not quite dark yet. **hpáze**
not quite get the idea. **hahkíe**
not quite right: do (s.t.) ~. **oolą́ąži**
not right. **eekǫ́ ðįké, ékǫži**
not satisfied anywhere. **cˀélǫðį**
not trust oneself. **hkíxiða**
not understand. **kíopxaži, pxáðaži**
not up to par: be ~. **oolą́ąži**
not where or how it is supposed to be. **ekǫ́įke**
not wild. **wacˀéka**
not worried. **škaškáða**
notch. **pážahta**
notched. **žáhta**
note (document of borrowed money). **mą́zeska ootá waléze**
nothing: it's ~. **ókaaɣeįke**
nothing: say ~. **íeži**
nothing like it. **táatą ékǫ ðįké**
nothing more. **kaašǫ́įke**
nothing wrong. **ókašéįke, škaškáða**
notwithstanding. **óðąži**
November. **mį́įǫpa álįį wį́xci, súhkahtą mį́įǫpa**
now (ADV). **ðekǫ́ǫce**
now (INTERJ). **ną** [INTERJ]
now: from ~ on. **ðetxą́ha, ihtǫ́į hta**
nude. **hį́ðohkižį**
nudge. **paaspą́**
number(s). **waðáawa**
nun. **šǫmį́hka wakˀó**
nurse (N, V). **húheka okášą**

oak. **hpisúhu**
oatmeal. **wéšį**
Oberly: Frances ~ Holding (personal name: Hawk Woman). **letǫ́wį**
Oberly: Myrtle ~ Jones (personal name). **wažáxį**
obey. **íe opšé, opšé**
obey (e.g., the law). **oðóohpa**
obey one's own. **okípše**
object: sacred ~. **waxópe**
object to. **iiną́hiži**
obliterate by rubbing or wiping. **púkxa**
observe. **tǫ́pe**
observe people or events. **watǫ́pe**
obtain. **okšéhtą**
occupation. **oðíhtą**
occupy a seat. **olį́į**
ocean. **níi htą́ka, níimąse**
o'clock. **mį́įoðaake**
October. **htáa kiðíɣepi, mį́įǫpa lébrą**
odd. **éeži**
odd-looking. **éžixci**
odor: body or soured ~. **žą́xta**
odor: emanate an ~. **brą́**
odor: have a (good or bad) ~ from heating. **táabrą**
odor: have a stinking ~. **žą́ąže**
odor: sour ~. **zą́zi**
off. **ekǫ́įke**
off: get ~ (e.g., a horse). **ósi, wísi**
off: switch ~. **ðuutáaži**
off: take ~ a garment. **ðiištówe**
off: take ~ a person's clothes. **ðuušáwį**
off: take ~ by pulling. **ðiištówe**
off: throw ~ (suddenly severing or moving s.t. or s.o. from s.t.). **okáxpa**
off: turn ~. **ðiistą́, ðuutáaži**
off (s.t. round or sitting). **įkšítxą**
off in the head. **pxáðaži**
off target. **ekǫ́įke**
off the record. **ákahahta**
off the subject. **ée htáhaži**
offend. **ílaną**
offensive smell: have an ~. **ɣoį́**
offer: make an ~. **táatą paahą́**
offhand: in an ~ manner. **íðilą ðįké**
office. **waðíhtą**
officer. **áhkita, áhkita totą́hąka**
officer or other white person of rank. **mą́ąhį htą́ą**
"off-tribe" (tribe other than Osage). **ohkíhce**
oil. **wéli**
oil well. **átahką wéli níini**
oily. **ðóðo**

ointment. **stáðe**
old. **kóoci**
old: be ~. **nǫ́ǫ**
old: get ~. **ónǫ ahí**
old: how ~ ? **omą́įhka háaną**
old age. **nǫ́ǫ, ónǫ**
old and stacked or piled. **kóoche**
old folks, the old ones. **haašíhta, kóoci, nǫ́ǫ, nǫ́ǫwaapi**
oldest. **htą́ą**
old-fashioned. **kóoci**
old-time. **kóoci**
Omaha (tribe or tribal member). **ámaxa, omą́hą**
on. **á-, ki**
on: put ~. **álą**
on: put ~ (e.g., pants, shoes). **opáahą, otxą́**
on: put ~ one's own pants or shoes. **okítxą**
on: put ~ oneself (e.g., a shirt or a dress). **óhkioolą́**
on: turn ~. **káaɣe**
on (s.t. lying or spread out). **kši**
on and on. **nąną**
on one's own. **éwažį**
on time: never ~. **ókxąži**
on top. **ákaha**
once upon a time. **kóoci**
one. **wį, wį́xce**
one another. (*see* reciprocal prefix)
one of several, one to be chosen among many. **ą́mą**
one of these. **ðéeka wį**
one's own. (*see* suus prefix)
ongoing (recurring one after another). **ótxątxą**
onion. **mą́ąžąxe**
onion: green ~. **mąąžą́xe htóho**
onlookers. **wahtǫ́pe**
only. **na, ną́ški**
only (one): be the ~. **eená**
only I. **wíną**
only this much. **káaną**
only to a limited degree. **to**
ooze. **žé**
open (ADJ). **íðoce**
open *(intr.)* (e.g., a flower). **opáaɣa**
open *(trans.)* (e.g., a door or a box). **ðiišúpe, ðuuáze**
open *(trans.)* (e.g., one's eyes or arms). **ákabra**
open out. **paaɣáce**
operate on (perform surgery on). **hpáce**
operation: place in ~. **ðuušką́**
opinion: hold an ~ of s.t. **ažį́**
or. **ąži, ímąðe** (*see also discussion under* **ímą**)
orange (color). **zí žuuce ékǫ zí žuuce ékǫ**
orange (fruit). **hką́ące zi**
orbit. **óžąke**
order s.o. not to (do s.t.). **ížoši**
ordure. **įlé**
ornery. **óškika**
orphan (N). **wahǫ́įke**
Osage (tribe, tribal member, or language). **wažáže**
Osage language. **wažážeíe**
Osage orange. **mį́ceštá hu**
other. **ą́mą, éeži, ímą, ímąkše**
other: the ~ (one of two). **ą́mą**
other (different). **éeži**
other (one). **ímąche**
other side: (location) of the ~. **áðahtaha**
other side: on or to the ~. **mąchéhta, mąsį́ha**
other side: on the ~. **ákahahta, ámąhta, ámąhtaha**
other side: on the ~ of s.t. **kootá**
other side: turn oneself to the ~. **ámąhta hkilíikoįɣe, hkilíisą**
other thing: any ~. **táatą éžiški**
other things. **táatą éžiški**
other way. **émąhtaži, émąhtažíha**
other way: turn oneself the ~. **ámąhta hkilíikoįɣe, hkilíisą**
otherwise. **éeži, éški**
otherwise: be ~. **ékǫži**
Oto (tribe or tribal member). **wažóla**
otter hide or skin. **htónąke**
ought to. (*see discussion under* **ðáalį**)
our(s). **ąkóhta, ąkóhtapi** (*see also* pronominal prefixes; suus prefix)
ourselves. (*see* reflexive prefix)
out: be ~ (e.g., school for summer recess). **panáa**
out: be ~ of. **níðe**
out: get ~ of (e.g., a vehicle). **ósi, wísi**
out: give ~. **wahkílai**
out: put or set ~ (multiple items). **ážu**
out: take ~ (unload). **oðúuxpaðe**
out: toss ~. **ǫ́ǫða**
out of breath. **íkaske**
out of line. **ekǫ́įke**
outdoors, out-of-doors. **ášihta**
outer ear. **nąąhtą́**
outhouse. **ožéhci**
outset: at the ~. **hpahą́le**
outside. **ášihta**
outside of a certain area. **ákahahta**
outside of the main events or activity, outside of someone's social circle. **ákahahta**
outskirts: on the ~ of . **ákahahta**

outstanding: be ~. **álįįha**
oven. **mą́ze oohǫ́**
over: make over or do ~. **kikáaɣe**
over: put ~. **ákaaspe**
over: turn ~ *(trans.)*. **ðiisą́ða , ípasą**
over: turn ~ one's own. **liisą́ða**
over again. (*see* inceptive prefix)
over and above: be ~. **álįįha**
over and over. **šíną**
over and over: turn ~ *(trans.)*. **ðusą́sąwį**
over here. **ðeeká ci**
over there. **ée htáha, kaaðó, kootáįke**
over there: farther ~. **kootá**
overall. **bróka**
overalls. **oðókiną́ąžį ákaha**
overbearing. **ópaašike, tóekǫ́ži**
overburdened: be ~. **íibrąxcį**
overdue. **wascúuce**
overeat. **tóoceha**
overeater. **tóoceha**
overseas. **níimąse**
oversee. **oðóðe**
oversee an event. **oðówaðe, óohkihą**
overweight. **lą́ąðe**
overweight: be ~. **wašį́**
overwhelming. **hóšechie**
owed: something ~. **weúuze**
owl. **wahpóka**
own (my own, your own, his/her own, our own, their own, one's own). (*see* suus prefix)
own (possess). **aðį́**
owned by, be ~. **íhta**

Pahsetopa (a family name among the Osages). **hpásetoopa**
pail. **céɣe**
pain: experience ~. **níe**
pain: suffering ~. **waxpáðį**
pain in the heart: have a ~. **ðą́ąceníe**
paint (N, V). **stáðe**
paint the deceased, apply face paint. **kik?ǫ́**
pair, couple, two of them. **nahkǫį́**
paisley. **hpasúkoša**
pal. **hcošpá**
pallet. **omíže**
palm (of the hand). **nǫǫpé**
pancake. **wacúe bréhka**
pane of glass. **okáhąpa**
pant (v). **heháha**
pantry. **wánǫbréoožú**
pants. **oðíkinąąžį, oðókinąąžį, wéhkilį**
papaw. **hį́įce hu**
paper. **htanąk?a**
paper: toilet ~. **íkahci**
paper containing text. **waléze**
paper money. **htanąk?a, htanąk?a mą́zeska**
paper napkin. **htanąk?a ípukxa**
paper towel. **htanąk?a ípukxa**
parallel (to). **páskuha**
parasol. (*see discussion under* **oðíni**)
parents: your ~. **ðiihǫ́ ðitáce**
parrot. **wažį́kaíe**
part: be a ~ of. **oðízą**
part (of the whole). **hépe**
part in the hair. **hpióka**
pass *(trans.)*. **húkaaɣe**
pass air (gas). **ðiipíɣą**
pass around. **ákiɣe, ápše**
pass away (e.g., the drum at *ilǫ́ǫška* dances). **kaaðée**
pass away (euphemism for 'die'). **xíða**
pass away (vanish). **ðįké**
pass back and forth. **ihkílašą**
pass by. **ákiɣe, ípše**
pass by hand. **k?ú huu**
pass gas. **ðiipíɣą**
pass s.t. to s.o. (e.g., at the table). **k?ú**
pass the drum. **céɣenii ðée káaɣe**
pass to (by hand or other means). **húðe**
past (in time). **álįįha**
past: go ~. **ípše**
past: in the ~. **haašíhta**
past the next: the one ~. **kootáha**
path, pathway. **óžąke**
path: along a ~. **ha**
path: along a ~ to the hearer. **šeeðǫ́ha**
path: on the ~ to a certain point. **htáha**
pathway: by what ~. **howaįkíha**
patter (v). **xée**
pause. **panáa**
Pawhuska. **hpahį́ska**
Pawhuska district, Pawhuska Osages. **waxákaolį́į**
Pawnee (Indians). **hpaðímaha, hpáðį**
pawpaw. **htóžąke** [archaic meaning]**, htóžąke eekǫ́**
pay (a debt). **kašúpe**
pay attention to. **óðąąceši**
pay back. **kíšupe**
pay for (a purchase). **kašúpe**
pay s.o., pay for s.o. **kíšupe**
paying attention: act of ~. **nąąɣúce**
payment. **wahkílai**
payment: cash ~. **wahkílae wakášupe**
peaceful. **škaškáða**

peach. **hkąące hį́įšce**
pear. **hkąące hpá álą**
peas. **hǫ́brįke htóho žį**
pecan nut. **watástosta**
peel (v). **ðiilóce, ðuušáake, páašpue**
peep into, peer in or into. **okácʔį**
peeved: be ~. **ólą**
pemmican. **htáapše**
pen. **wapáleze, wéleze**
penalty. **ílanąwakíšupe**
pencil. **wapáleze, wéleze**
penis. **šǫ́ce, žé**
pennies (small change). **ošpéžį, waðáawažį**
penny. **waðáawa žúuce, waðáawažį**
people. **níhkašie, níhkašika** (*see also* valence reducer prefix)
people: little ~ (small beings in Osage mythology). **míalǫška**
people: many or a lot of ~. **huukǫ́ða**
people gathering with each other. **hkilíiski, waðíiski**
pepper. **mąhkáhpa**
pepper: black ~. **mąhkáhpa sápe**
pepper: red ~. **mąhkáhpa žúuce**
pepper shaker. **mąhkáhpaóožu**
perch (fish). **hó bráaska**
perform. **káaɣe**
perform surgery on. **hpáce**
perfume. **wabrą́lį**
perhaps. **ska**
permanent (ADJ). **saakí šǫǫšǫ́we**
perplexity. **ókʔą wanąðaži**
persecute (an animal or person). **ðiihíce**
persimmon. **wastą́įke**
person. **níhka, níhkašie**
person: become or live as a ~. **ínihkašie**
person: young ~. **hcéka nóǫ**
person of mixed blood. **įįštáxįžį́**
person of unsound mind. **waðílą eekǫ́ įké**
person who cooks. **oohǫ́**
person who is always making people laugh. **wahóhota**
person who talks too much or too long. **íe scece, íeštą**
person who tells everything. **táatąžį́ ški oðáake**
person who won't stay home or seldom stays home. **wáaspaži**
personal name in the Eagle clan (**mǫ́žǫ**). **mą́žą**
personal name (perhaps that of Charlie Pasetopah). **hcí tóopa**
personality, personal characteristics. **ókʔą**
perspire. **paɣíce**

pestle. **wépše**
petition. **waatá**
Petsemoie (family name). **hpéece mąðį́**
Petsemoie: Herman ~ (personal name: Daylight Approaches). **hǫ́ǫpahu**
peyote. **wanǫ́bre**
peyote: have one's body affected by ~. **mą́hkažóika**
peyote meeting. **hkihkǫ́ze, mąhkáðaaché**
peyote or any other kind of medicine. **mąhká**
peyote song. **hkihkǫ́ze waaðǫ́**
peyote tea. **wanǫ́brenii**
pharmacist. **mąhká aðį́**
phlegm. **hóxpe léle, íli**
phone (N). **mą́zeie**
phone: call by ~. **mą́zeie híðe**
phone: have s.o. call by ~. **mą́zeohkíhkie hükšíe**
phone call. **mą́zeie**
phone call: make a ~. **mą́zeie híðe**
photograph. **įcé waléze**
physician. **wahkǫ́taki**
piano. **paakíce**
pick (choose). **hkíhpaahi**
pick (e.g., flowers or fruit). **paahí**
pick fruit. **ðuuzé**
pick or pluck (e.g., a chicken). **ðuušáake**
pick people (or things?). **wapáahi**
pick up. **ðiihą́, hkíhpaahi**
pick up (many small scattered things). **paahí**
pickle. **hkohkóma**
picnic (v). **ášihta wanǫ́bre**
picture of anything. **įcé waléze**
picture show. **ówatoį**
pie of any sort (fruit, cream, etc.). **hkąącóolą**
piece. **hépe**
piece: small ~. **ošpéžį**
pig. **hkóhkosa**
piggyback: carry ~. **ðuškápa**
pillow. **ípehi**
pillow to sit on (as for a sofa, chair, or other seat). **wákaštǫ**
pillowcase. **ípihį oðíši, oðíši**
pin (ornamental). **wápaɣa**
pinch (v). **ðilǫ́ke**
pinch off (e.g., in making balls out of cornmeal for cornmeal dumplings). **kaaskí**
pine wood, pine tree. **páze hú**
pipe. **nąnį́ǫpa**
pistol. **wahóohtą, wahóohtą táahpa**
pitch (and other card games). **oðáake kʔǫ**
pitcher (container). **níioožú**
pitiful. **lažį́į, waxpáðį**

pity (v). **ðakˀéðe**
pity: show or use ~ with. **íðakˀeðe**
pity each other. **ðakˀéhkiðe**
pity one's own or s.o. close. **ðakˀékiðe**
pity oneself. **ðakˀéhkiðe**
place: at their ~. **ecí pa**
place: be at that ~. **ecí**
place: in ~ of. (*see* dative prefix)
place a baby on the baby board or inside. **hpáažį okˀǫ́he**
place a standing item on a surface. **hkícheðe**
place above. **mąšíhta**
place an item upright on another item. **ále**
place at which. **ó-**
place in operation. **ðuušką́**
place inside of. **oolą́**
place into. **okˀǫ́he**
place multiple items on top of something else. **ážu**
place right next to the hearer: to a ~. **šeeðǫ́ha**
place s.t. or s.o. first. **hpahą́le mąðį́**
place s.t. up or above. **ámąši**
place to bathe. **ohííða**
place to live. **ohcíle**
place together (as when cooking two or more items together). **oðóhkiðe**
place two or more things together and tie them. **paaxcé**
place upon or on. **álą, álįį**
place vertically against. **álą**
plain: make ~. **wáðaaska**
plain: make things ~ (e.g., words, lines upon a paper, borders on land). **wáðuuska**
plant (e.g., seed in the ground). **oožú**
plant stuff. **óožu**
plant to mix with tobacco (a small, sweet-smelling plant with yellow flowers that is mixed with tobacco). **nąnúhu íkiahį**
planting. **ówe**
plants: "put in" ~. **oožú**
plat. **mąžą́waleze**
plate. **hį́įce**
platter. **hį́įce apakˀą́, hį́įce braaka**
play *(intr.)*. **škáce**
play *(trans.)*. **kˀǫ́**
play a card (in a card game). **ðée káaɣe**
play dice. **kˀǫ́sukˀǫ́**
play a horn or other wind instrument. **opíɣą**
play a joke on. **ðíhota**
play cards. **htaną́kˀa kˀǫ́**
play golf. **htaapéskažįkˀǫ́**
play music on an instrument. **paakíce**
play slyly or meanly with. **ðiihíce**
play with s.o. related to oneself or animate being of one's own. **kíškace**
play with s.t. **ðiihíce**
player: tape ~. **mązeie**
playing cards (N). **htanąkˀa, htanąkˀa ðiihíce**
pleased with: be ~. **kiðálį**
plentiful. **ochí**
plentifully: exist ~. **ochí, óše**
plenty. **kaakǫ́ną, óše**
pluck (e.g., a chicken). **ðuušáake**
plum. **hkąące xóce, níižue hkąące**
plural marker. **api** (*see also* continuative aspect markers; positional articles)
plus. **éci**
pneumonia. **ðúwenie**
pocket. **óožu**
pocketbook. **mązeskaoožú**
point at, point to. **ápazo**
point (in a game). **pázo**
point (of an object). **hpasú**
pointing finger. **wéapazo**
pointless, pointlessly. **ée htáhaži**
poison. **mąhká hpíiži**
pokey (slow). **wascúuce**
pokey one (slow person). **oščúuce**
pole. **žą́ą, žą́ąxe, žą́ąxežį**
pole: fishing ~. **hóize žą́ąxe**
police. **áhkita**
polish. (*see discussion under* **ápuštai**)
pollute (e.g., water or air). **ízizike káaɣe**
Ponca (tribe or tribal member). **hpǫ́hka**
pond. **niitáahpa**
ponder. **waðílą**
pony. **hkáwa**
ponytails (one on each side of the head). **héðǫǫpa**
poor (of poor quality). **hǫ́ǫži**
poor (pitiful). **lažį́į**
poor (poverty stricken). **waxpáðį**
poor: be ~, do s.t. poorly. **oolą́ąži**
poor performance: make a ~ of. **oolą́ąži**
poorly. **hǫ́ǫži**
pop (e.g., a balloon). **kaapxóhke**
pop: soda ~. **niikáapxohke**
pop bottle or can. **niikáapxokeoožú**
pope. **šǫmį́hka kahíke**
porch. **ánąąhkoe**
porcupine. **hpáhį**
pork. **hkóhkosa**
pork fat. **hkohkósa wéli, wéli**
porter. **hcížepe ahkita**

portion that fills a container to approximately half full. **ohépe**
portly. **šį́htąką**
portrait. **įcé waléze**
position (occupation). **oðíhtą**
positional articles [POSIT]. **che, ðe, įkšé, ke, kše, pa, pe, txą** (*see also* subject markers)
positioned so that it surrounds a part of the body: have s.t. ~. **į́**
possess. **aðį́**
possession: come into ~ of. **okšéhtą**
possible. **ðąąché**
possum. **sį́šta**
posterboard containing text. **waléze**
pot. **céɣe**
pot: cooking ~. **óohǫ**
potato: white or Irish ~. **tóoska**
Potawatomi (tribe or tribal member). **wahówahá**
potential marker. **hta**
pouch: tobacco. **nąnįǫ́kužu**
pouch made of hide or leather. **óožuhaa**
pound (v). **pšé**
pound, (measure of weight). **íðuspa**
pour. **ðixtą́, okáxta**
pour (liquids or pourable solids such as beans), pour for (s.o.). **oožú**
pour round items into (e.g., fruit into pies). **oolą́**
pour s.t. on or over another surface. **ážu**
pout. **ólą**
pout about another's good fortune. **óxįį**
poverty stricken. **waxpáðį**
power. **waašką́**
practice (N), practice session. **ík?uce**
prairie. **zą́ą, zą́ące**
prairie chicken. **mǫ́nǫį**
prance. **ðihcíceðe**
Pratt: Henry ~ (personal name). **nǫ́ǫhpewaðe** (specifically, variant form **nǫ́ǫhpewali**)
Pratt: Henry ~, Jr. (personal name). **xǫ́ǫce mą́į**
pray. **waatá, wíkie**
pray for. **kíwaata**
pray for oneself, pray for each other. **waahkíhta**
pray for s.o. or s.t. **waatá**
prayer. **íe, waatá, wíkie**
prayer: closing of a ~. **kaašéną**
prayer beads. **wíkie hį́iska**
praying mantis. **walúška įįštá htąka**
preacher. **ožą́ke olį́į, wahkǫ́ta íe oðáake, wahkǫ́taki**
precede. **hpahą́le ðée**
precious. **hcéxi, óxta**
precious: consider ~. **óxta káaɣe**
precious: make ~. **óxtaðe**
precisely. **xci**
prepare. **káaɣe**
prepare (e.g., food). **oohǫ́**
prepare a feast for another or others. **kíkxo**
prepare for s.o. (e.g., food or a bed). **kšíɣe** (*see also* causative markers)
president. **ihcíkoapí**
press s.t. (e.g., cloth with an iron). **wapúštaha**
press together. **ðiiskíke'**
pressing, by ~. **paa-, pu-**
pretend. **kǫzé** [JOD, LFD]
pretty. **ðáalį**
pretty: very. **ohtáza**
prevail upon s.o. to do s.t. **waší**
previously. (*see also discussion under* **ska** [MODAL])
prickly. **waxáka, xáka**
priest. **ožą́ke olį́į, wahkǫ́taki**
prior. **hpahą́le '**
prize s.t. **kíwalį**
probable. **ðąąché**
probe. **ákazo**
problem. **óie**
problem: discussion of a ~. **óie**
proceed. **ékiǫ**
proclaim. **oðáake**
produce: garden ~ (vegetables). **ówe, wasúutą**
profusion. **óše**
program: put on a ~. **ók?ą**
prohibit. **ížoši**
promise-keeper. **íe okípše**
pronominal prefixes [PRNM]. **a-** 'I', **ą-** 'me, I', **ąk-** 'we', **ða-** 'you', **ði-** 'you', **ði-** 'your', **wa-** 'them, they', **wa- . . . -api** 'us, we', **wi-** 'my', **wi-** 'I . . . you' (the **i** at the beginning of many kinship terms might also be considered a 3rd person possessive prefix 'he, hers')
pronounce. **ðaacé**
proper, properly. **wáðohtą**
proposal or proposition: make a ~. **táatą paahą́**
propose. **hce ée**
prostitute. **wak?ó nǫǫhǫ́**
protrude. **ðuhtáža**
protuberance. **hpá**
proud, proud of. **óžo áži**
proud: be ~ of one's own. **óžo ákižį**
proud: be ~ of oneself. **óžo áhkižį**
provide. **ok?ú**
provide for. **wak?ú**
provided that. **tą**
prune. **hką́ące sápe**

níhka watą́įke
puff, puff on. **ðaahtá**
pull. **ðiitą́**
pull (e.g., a tooth) to remove it. **ðiištówe**
pull apart (e.g., a tree limb from the trunk).
  ðupáxa
pull dirt over. **áðikʔo**
pull down. **ðuuhúuce**
pull off. **ðiištówe**
pull out (e.g., all of one's hair). **ðuušáake**
pull over to cover. **áðuzu**
pull to, pull shut. **áðiitą**
pull up. **ðuumą́ši**
puma. **ilǫ́eži**
pumpkin. **watxá**
punch. **paaspá**
punch (e.g., ~ s.o. on the side of the head).
  kaabráze
punch a hole in. **opákʔo**
punch through. **kaascú**
punching: by ~. **pó-**
punk (tinder). **žą́ąhcúkʔa**
puppy. **šóžį**
purchase. **ðuwí**
purple. **htóho sápe, žúuce sápe**
purse. **mázeskaoožú, wáseska**
push along, push s.o. or s.t. steadily. **paaɣówe**
push aside. **kaacį́že**
push down on. **ápisą**
push s.o. onward. **hpánąąke**
push to awaken or make active. **paaɣí**
push to drunkenness. **páalǫðį**
push two or more things together and tie them.
  paaxcé
pushing: by ~. **paa-**
pushy. **óhesaži**
put (e.g., a baby on a baby board). **okʔǫ́he**
put a pourable substance on s.t. else. **ážu**
put an end to s.t. **kaaštą́**
put away to keep. **kícheðe**
put clothes on oneself. **óhkioolą**
put down. **hkícheðe**
put each other to a test. **áhkiasąci**
put in. **oožú**
put into. **okʔǫ́he, oolá**
put on: cause s.o. to or make s.o. ~ an article of
  clothing. **įkšíðe**
put on (e.g., pants, shoes). **álaha, oną́ąžį,**
  opáahą, otxą́
put on (place on). **álą**
put on clothing (not one's own). **wéhkilį opáahą**

put on clothing (one's own). **wéhkilį okíhpaahą**
put on one's own pants or shoes. **okítxą**
put on oneself (e.g., a shirt or a dress). **óhkioolá**
put on the head. **oolą́ke**
put out (multiple items). **ážu**
put over, put upon. **ákaaspe**
put s.o. in jail. **hą́ąnahpazé oolą́**
put s.o. to bed. **áðižą**
put stuff in. **óožu**
put to the test. **ásąci**
putrefied. **tožáðe**

quack (like a duck). **hóohtą**
quail. **óšechiðe wakáaɣe, žǫhpáleze**
Quapaw Indians. **okáxpa**
quarrelsome. **taakéštą**
quarrelsome: feel ~. **hkížį**
quarter (25-cent piece). **kašpéǫpa**
queen (in a deck of cards). **wakʔó, žekážįka**
queen of spades (in a deck of cards). **mą́ąhįsu**
  wakʔó
question about one's own people or things. **ilǫ́ye**
question s.o. **íðǫye**
question s.t. verbally (as in a business meeting). **óie**
quick to do things, quick-acting. **wahtóke**
quickly. **óhesaži, wąkǫ́ǫ**
quiet. **níažį, šká**
quiet: be ~. **oní ðįké**
quiet (not in movement). **šką́ ðįké, šką́aži**
quietly (not in movement). **šką́aži**
quill. **súhkahtąą mǫ́šǫ**
quilt. **óhkiache, omíže**
quirt. **wékaaži**
quit. **kaaštą́, panáa**
quit s.o. **ǫ́ǫða**
quit s.o. (divorce or separate). **ǫ́ǫðe**
quite a while: for ~. **kaahúuža**
quiver. **ðibrúbruɣe**

rabbit. **mąščíka**
raccoon. **míhkaa**
race (N). **hkipáną**
rack (barbecue rack). **oážu, wážu**
radio. **htaacé oðį́įke, mázeie, wéhice anákʔǫ**
radish. **hpǫ́ɣe**
ragged. **cúuða, xúuða**
ragweed. **mąąhíhpa**
rain (N, V). **níižu**
rain: fine ~. **níižu xóhtą**
rain: gray ~. **níišoce, niižú xóce**
rain: light ~. **niižúžu**
rain: misting. **íhkišoce**

rain lightly. **nuužúžu**
rain shower. **níižužį**
rainbow. **htoníle**
raindrops: fine ~. **níižu xóhtą**
raise (e.g., a flag). **paamą́ši**
raise (lift). **ðuhpáahą, ðumáða, ðuumą́ši, paahą́, paamą́ši**
raise (rear). **nǫ́ǫðe**
raise s.o. or s.t. **ðiihą́**
raise up. **ðumáða, opáahą**
raised us: those who ~. **nǫ́ǫwaapi**
rank and authority: one with ~. **totą́ha**
ranking member. **totą́ha**
rape (v). **mąąðǫ́**
rat. **įchóhtąą**
rate: at any ~. **óðąži**
rather (ADV). **ékǫ**
rather (CONJ). **kóe**
ration (give out in portions). **íhkilai**
rations (food). **ǫ́nǫbre**
rations (from the government). **wahkílai**
rattle: gourd ~. **hpéɣe**
raven. **hkáɣe, hkáɣe htą́ka**
raw. **cúutaži**
reach as a location or place. **achí**
read *(trans.)*. **ðaacé**
reading. **walézeáace**
ready (ADJ). **háha, íðiištą**
ready: be ~. **ðiištą́, íhice**
ready: get or make oneself ~. **háhahkie**
ready oneself, get oneself ready. **hkíliištą**
ready to pick or harvest. **súutą**
real. **xci**
really. **wálį, xci, -žį**
rear (raise). **nǫ́ǫðe**
reason: out of ~ (unreasonable). **ée htáhaži**
recent, recently. **hcéka**
recent: the most ~. **ce**
receptacle. **oožú**
recess (v). **panáa**
reciprocal prefix [RECIP]. **hkik-**
recite. **oðáake**
reckless. **íinǫǫhpaži**
recline. **áðiikxą, áðiikxą žąą**
recognize (a person). **ípahǫ**
recognize oneself (as). **íhkihpahǫ**
reconsider. **oðóhake íðilą**
record (make a recording with an audio device). **íe ðuuzé**
recorder: tape ~. **mą́zeie**
record-keeper for tribal council. **waléze káaɣe**
recover (from illness). **kiní, kítąhe**
recover consciousness. **hkilázo, iihkíðe**
rectitude: act with ~. **óðohtąhkiðe**
rectitude: acting with ~. **óðohtą**
rectum. **įléha**
recuperate. **kiní**
recurring one after another. **ótxątxą**
recurringly. **ną** [ITERATIVE], **nąpe**
red. **žúuce**
red: dark ~. **pazó ekǫ́**
Red Eagle (name for first boy in *hcížo* clan). **xuðážuuce**
Redeagle: Jeanna ~ (personal name: Looking at the Eagle). **xúe tǫ́į**
redo. **kikáaɣe**
reduce *(trans.)*. **čóopa ekǫ́ káaɣe**
reduced quantity. **wahókˀa**
reflexive possessive. (*see* suus prefix)
reflexive prefix [REFL]. **hkik-**
reform (v). **kikáaɣe**
refrigerator. **ną́ɣeoožú**
refuse to do something. **ížoši**
refuse to talk. **íeži**
regain consciousness. **iihkíðe**
regard as holy. **óxta káaɣe**
regard each other as friends or relatives. **ðótahkiðe**
regardless. **óðąži**
regulations. **wahkílaace**
regurgitate due to overeating. **ókohpa**
reimburse. **kíšupe**
reimburse (for). **wakíšupe**
reject. **ðuuzáži**
relate (narrate). **oðáake**
related: be ~. **ðótahkiðe**
relatives: regard or take each other as ~. **ðótahkiðe**
relax. **hkilázo**
reliable. **wáðohtą**
relieve s.o. of clothing. **ðuuštáke**
reluctant to do s.t.: be ~. **ížoši**
reluctant to share s.t. of one's own. **kíwalį**
rely on. **íkinaaži**
remain. **ošcé**
remainder. **ošcé**
remainder (singular standing inanimate, or plural sitting inanimate). **ošcé che**
remainders (scattered around). **ošcé ke**
remaining. **ošcé che**
remedy (v). **ðuðáalį**
remember. **kisúðe**
remove. **ðicíze, ðuxpáwį**
remove a garment. **ðiištówe**

remove, as from office. **ǫ́ǫðe**
remove by pulling. **ðiištówe**
remove from (e.g., remove a kettle from a cooking fire). **šíle**
remove some substance from a surface. **kaací**
remove s.t. by extracting or lowering it. **oðúuxpaðe**
remove the hide from anything. **ámaxa**
rent (N). **ootá mą́zeska**
repair (v). **kikáaɣe**
repair for s.o. **kšíɣe**
repay. **kíšupe**
repay for. **wakíšupe**
repeatedly. **háachi, íkiha, ną** [ITERATIVE], **štą**
reportative markers. **áakxa, áapa, áape**
represent (as an attorney at law argues on behalf of a client). **áhkie**
representative: congressional ~. **hkiistó omąðį**
representative (in legislature). **wahkílaace káaɣe**
reprimand (v). **kaazą́**
request (v). **tá**
request marker. **hce**
request s.t. **waatá**
request that s.o. do s.t. **íihǫ**
request to borrow s.t. **ootá**
resemble (visually). **íkǫska**
resembling each other. **kǫzéhkihkǫ**
reside. **hcíle**
resound. **xowí**
respect (v). **ðixópe, kíxope, ókˀą axópe**
respect: address folks with ~. **wahǫ́į**
respectable. **óxta, wáðohtą**
respectable: make oneself ~. **óxtahkiðe**
responsibility: have the ~ for s.t specific in response to a formal request (e.g., taking care of the food for an event). **okášą**
rest (v). **áðiikxą, áðiikxą žąą, hkikˀązehkiðe**
rest: a night's ~. **žą́ą**
rest: at ~. **škaškáða**
rest (remainder): **ošcé, ošcé che**
rest (remainder, scattered around). **ošcé ke**
restaurant. **owánǫbrehcí**
restrain by tying. **ðuušáwį**
restraint (such as a bridle?). **wáapįce**
retarded: "mentally ~." **cˀéka**
rethink. **oðóhake íðilą**
retrograde. **xáða**
return here (motion accomplished). **alí**
return home, return there. **akší**
return home, return there (motion underway). **alée**
return point. **ípaašąha**
revere. **ðixópe**
reverse (v). **ðiisą́ða**
reverse: in ~. **xáða**
revile. **lǫ́ǫ**
revile over and over. **lǫ́ǫlǫǫ**
revolver. **wahóohtą, wahóohtąžį**
rheumatism. **wahúni**
ribbon. **háabrehka**
ribbon work. **wápaache**
ribcage. **ðúwe**
rice. **pósu**
rid: get ~ of. **ǫ́ǫðe**
ride. **olį́į, opáwįɣe**
ride: go for a ~. **opáwįɣe**
ride horseback. **hkáwaalįį**
ride in. **olį́į**
ride in an airplane. **kį́į**
ride on. **álįį**
rifle. **wahóohtą**
right (correct). **ékǫ, óxta**
right, on the right, rightward, to the right. **íštǫka**
right: I guess that's ~. **ékǫ ska**
right: just ~, just the right amount. **káaną**
right: make oneself ~. **óxtahkiðe**
right: not ~. **eekǫ́ ðįké,ékǫži**
right: not get s.t. ~. **ðikšį́ce**
right: say s.t. ~. **ékǫ ðaacé**
right: that is ~. **ékǫ**
right away. **wąkǫ́ǫžį**
right mind: not in one's ~. **waðílą eekǫ́ įké**
rigid. **sáta**
rind. **háa**
ring (*intr.*). **hkaamą́, kaahtáama**
ring (*trans.*), ring the bell. **ðuuhkáamą**
ring (for wearing on the finger). **nǫǫpióolą**
ringing noise: make a ~. **kaahtáama**
rip (v). **kaabráze**
ripe. **cúuce, súutą**
ripped (said of clothing). **cúuða**
rise. **-hą, hpaahą́**
risk (v). **íkˀuce**
river. **níižuuce**
roach bone. **htaasį́įce wahú**
roached hair. **hé káaɣe, hpaxáce**
road. **óžąke**
roadman, be a roadman. **ožą́ke olį́į**
roam. **opáwįɣe**
roar (v). **xée, xowí**
robbery. **wamą́ąðǫ**
robe. **mį́**
rock (N). **į́į**
roll (v), rolling. **htą́ąða**
roll a cigarette. **nąnį́ǫpa káaɣe**

room. **hcíohka**
room (in the sense of an unoccupied area). **óhką**
rooster. **súhka tóoka**
root (of a tree, bush, etc.). **žą́ą kˀą**
rope (N). **wéðį**
rope (V) (e.g., a calf). **oðíiną**
rosary. **hį́įskawáata, wíkie hį́įska**
rotten. **tožáðe**
rough. **ɣáɣaka, óhesaži, xáka**
roughly. **óhesaži**
round. **ðą** [LFD], **táahpa**
round: make ~. **ðuutáahpa**
round about this way. **ðeekáiha**
rounded and squat. **čáahpa**
rove. **opáwįɣe**
rowdy: be ~. **taeðáalįži**
rub off to efface. **púkxa**
rude. **wakaacˀáiži**
ruffled, ruffly. **xáxa**
rug. **omíže**
ruin. **ðuhpíiži**
ruined. **hǫ́ǫži**
ruler (measuring stick). **žą́ą wéðaawa**
rules. **wahkílaace**
rumble (V). **xowí**
rumor. **óną kˀǫ**
rumpus. **óochiže**
run *(intr.)*. **htą́ąðį, ną́ąke**
run (as a liquid). **stówe**
run away, run off. **hkóopše**
run in a competition. **hkipáną**
run into. **áhkoopše**
run off. **olé**
run off (on s.o.). **kíhkoopše**
run out of breath from. **íkaske**
run water (e.g., into a bathtub). **ðixtą́, ðuuzé**
run wild. **taeðáalįži**
running as a group. **ostówe**
running here and there. **cˀélǫðį**
Running Man (personal name). **níhkahkipáną**
runny nose. **hpahlíxtoe, hpalį́**
rupture (hernia). **hcéze bráze**
rushed. **wahkǫ́i**
rushed: being ~, rushing in a row. **ostówe**

Sac and Fox (tribe or tribal member). **sakí ho, sakíwa**
sack (bag). **óožuhaa**
sacred. **hcéxi, xópe**
sacred: hold ~. **ðixópe, óxta káaɣe**
Sacred Arrow Shaft (personal name for a female). **mą́ąsihcexi**
sacred object. **waxópe**
sad. **kíhpiiži, kízoži**
saddle. **ną́hkai**
saddle blanket. **wákaštǫ**
safely. **óhtaiðįke, ókašéįke**
sage. **hpéže xóhtą**
sage (sage bush or sagebrush). **hpéže**
said: it is ~. (*see* reportative markers)
salary. **okšéhtą**
saliva. **íli**
saloon (bar). **hpéeceniihci** (old meaning), **hpéecenii ðaahtą́ hci**
salt. **níiskue**
salt pork. **wašį́**
salt shaker. **níiskueoožú**
same: the ~ as. **kǫzékǫ**
sand. **hpuzá**
sand-in-eyes. **įcóolą**
sandwich. **htóolą**
sash. **íhpią** [LFD]
Satan. **ilǫ́ɣe**
sated or satiated: be ~ with. **íibrą, wéenące**
satiated with food: cause oneself to be ~. **wéenącehkiðe**
satisfied. **škaškáða, waðílą ðáalį mąðį́**
satisfy oneself with food. **wéenącehkiðe**
Saturday. **hą́ąpa ókaaɣéįke**
sauce: sweet ~. **waskúe**
sauerkraut. **mą́ąsase**
sausage. **tǫ́ǫpše**
save (as a memento or treasure). **kícheðe**
saved: place or condition of being ~ (in religion). **ónihkaši**
saw (for cutting wood). **žą́ąpaase**
saw or other tool for cutting wood. **wépaase**
say. **ðaacé, ée, ékie, íe** (*see also* reportative markers)
say bad things about s.o. **hkiláažoži**
say bad words. **lǫ́ǫ**
say nothing. **íeži**
say so. **oðáake**
say s.t. right or correctly. **ékǫ ðaacé**
say the name of s.t. or s.o. **ðaacé**
scales (for weighing). **íðuspa** [LFD]
scarecrow. **níhkaši íkǫske**
scared: be ~. **nǫ́ǫhpe**
scared: be ~ of. **íinǫǫhpe**
scarf. **haaléžowaake**
scary. **nǫ́ǫhpewaðe**
scatter *(trans. and intr.)* (e.g., corn for drying). **okábra**
scheme against s.o. secretly. **nąlǫ́ǫha**

school. **taapóska, walézeáace**
schoolhouse. **taapóskahci**
schooling. **walézeáace**
scissors. **hpahúuse**
scissortail. **ǫ́pežahta**
scold. **kaazą́**
scold harshly. **toníðe**
score (points in a game). **pázo**
scorekeeper. **waápazo átǫpe**
scouting, scouting alone. **totą́**
scrambled (e.g., eggs). **nílǫze**
scrape aside. **kaacį́že**
scratch. **ðikˀíðe**
scratch an itch. **kˀúe**
scream (v). **pą́**
screw (have sex with). **aðį́ažą, chúe**
scrotum. **šǫcóso**
sea. **níi htą́ka, níimąse**
search for (s.t. lost or misplaced, s.t. of one's own, or s.t. belonging to s.o. else). **okíce**
search for s.t. or s.o. **océ**
search for stuff. **óce**
seat (N). **áalįį, álįį**
seat: take or occupy a ~. **olį́į**
seated: be ~. **olį́į**
second. **wéðǫǫpa**
secret: in ~. **ákahahta**
secret society. **nǫ́hǫžį**
secretary. **waléze káaɣe**
secretly scheme against s.o. **nąlǫ́ǫha**
see *(intr.)*. **wawéeðe**
see *(trans.)*. **íiðe, tǫ́pe**
see about. **oðóðe**
see each other again: means to ~. **wéehkile**
see people or events. **watǫ́pe**
see s.o. **kitǫ́pe**
see things (as in a dream or hallucination), see multiple things or persons one after another. **wawéeðe**
see to. **okáše**
seed. **súu**
seems: it ~ that. **ska**
seesaw (v). **sísiąðe**
seize. **oðį́įke**
select. **ðuuzé**
select by pointing to. **ápazo**
select for oneself. **hkíhpaahi**
select from one's own people or items. **kíhpaahi**
select people (or things?). **wapáahi**
self. (*see* reflexive prefix)
selfish. **wáli**
selfish: be ~ with. **kíwalį**
sell for. **íðuwį**
sell s.t. by bartering for other stuff. **wéðuwį**
senator. **hkiistó omąðį**
send, send by mail. **ðéeðe, ðée káaɣe**
send by wire, send there by telegraph. **mą́zekˀąsaaki ðée káaɣe**
send here. **húðe, hukšíðe**
send there. **híðe**
send to another person. **ðeekšíðe**
send to where you are. **šoðée káaɣe**
separate (as a couple). **ohkíǫðe**
separate, separated (e.g., an estranged couple, egg yolks from whites). **kíðahapa**
separated: be ~. **kíðahapa**
separated: become ~ from. **ohkíǫðe**
September. **mį́įǫpa lébrą hce wį́įke, taapóska mį́įǫpa**
serpent. **wécˀa**
serve (liquids or pourable solids such as beans). **oožú**
set: go ~ (as in a card game). **ðuucˀáke**
set aside. **kícheðe**
set down. **hkícheðe**
set fire to. **osái**
set off (e.g., set a kettle off a cooking fire). **šíle**
set on (e.g., set a kettle on a fire). **ále**
set out (go). **aðée**
set out (multiple items). **ážu**
set out on a new task under one's charge. **okášą**
seven. **hpéeðǫǫpa**
seventeen, seventeenth. **lébrą álįį hpéǫǫpa**
seventy, seventieth. **lébrą hpéðǫǫpa**
sever by striking with. **íkaase**
several days: for ~. **kahą́naže**
sew *(intr.)*. **wapáache**
sew *(trans.)*. **paaché**
sew things together. **wapáache**
sewing. **ópaache, wápaache**
sewing machine. **mą́ze wépaache**
sewn, sewn together. **ópaache**
sex: have ~. **wachú**
sex: have ~ with. **aðį́ažą**
sexual partner: take as a ~. **ðúɣe**
shack. **hcí hpíiži**
shackle. **paaxcé**
shade: window. **akáaspe, okáhąpa akáspe**
shaded. **šápe**
shadow. **hkeetáxe**
shake (*intr.*). **ðibrúbruɣe**
shake *(trans.)*. **ðusą́sąwį**
shake (a person, an object, or one's own body part). **ðižáža**

shake hands. **šáake oðį́įke**
shake one's own (body part or possession). **ližážai**
shaker (container). **oožú**
shallow. **xépe**
shame (N). **wawéešce**
Shannon: George ~ (personal name: Aroused by Something That Suddenly Appears). **wakáahcįe**
sharp. **hpaahį́**
sharp edge: by using a ~. **pá-**
sharpen. **ðiimǫ́**
shatter *(intr.)*. **kaaléke, léke**
shatter *(trans.)*. **kaaléke**
shatter by cutting or using a sharp edge. **páleke**
shatter by foot or with the foot. **nąąléke**
shatter by pushing outward. **paaléke**
shatter by striking or sudden movement. **kaaléke**
shatter one's own. **kíleke**
shatter with the hands. **ðuuléke**
Shattered Forehead (nickname). **hpéeleke**
shave the head. **kaacˀó**
shavings. **sase**
shawl. **haaskámį**
Shawnee (tribe or tribal member). **šáwanįį**
she. (There is no direct equivalent in Osage of 3rd person pronouns 'he', 'him', 'she', 'her', 'it'. Unemphatic 3rd person pronouns are usually not overtly expressed; *ée* and demonstratives such as *še* can be used as emphatic 3rd person pronouns ['he himself', 'she herself', etc.].) (*see also* pronominal prefixes; this; that)
she too. **eeškítą**
shears. **hpahúusehtąą**
sheathe. **okˀǫ́he**
sheep. **htaaská**
shinny stick, the curved stick used to play *kašíni* (shinny). **ohkíce**
shiny. **xą́xą**
shiny and smooth (as a lake surface). **štáha**
ship. **páce**
shirt. **haaská**
shit (defecate). **žé**
shiver. **ðibrúbruɣe**
shoat. **hkóhkosa**
shock. **ðusáaki**
shock s.o. **hóšechie**
shock s.o. (as with suddenly emerging news). **pólǫðį**
shocked. **pólǫðį**
shocking, shocking news or report. **hóšechie**
shoemaker. **hǫ́ǫpekaaɣe**
shoes. **hǫǫpé**
shoot (a gun or a bow and arrow), shoot at. **hkúce**
shoot at each other, shoot each other. **hkihkúce**
shooting: by ~. **pó-**
shop (commercial establishment). **watǫ́ehci**
shop, (go shopping). **waðúwį aðée**
short, short and small. **čáahpa**
short distance: a ~ away. **áška**
short of breath, shortwinded. **hehé**
shot: administer a ~. **mąhká oðíkˀe**
shotgun. **wahóohtą**
shotgun: breechloading ~. **wahóohtą opáaxǫ**
should. (*see discussion under* **ðáalį**)
shoulder. **ábro**
shoulder blade. **áahu**
shout. **hóohtą, pą́**
shove, shove s.o.'s head quickly in anger. **taašéðe**
shovel. **hcúke**
show *(intr.)*. **hcį́į, wahcį́į**
show (N). **ówatoį**
show s.o. how to do s.t. **kǫ́ze, kšíǫze**
show things. **táatą paahą́**
shower (of rain). **níižužį́**
showing: be ~. **wahcį́į**
shroud. **haažúuce**
shut: pull ~. **áðiitą**
shut (e.g., one's eyes). **ápisą**
shut by pulling. **áðiitą**
sick: be ~. **íhpiiži, kihúheka**
sick: be ~ from. **ǫ́ǫ**
sick: be ~ with. **íhpiiži, íhuheka**
sick: make ~. **húheka káaɣe**
sick from eating too much. **ókahpo**
sick with fever. **áachi**
sicken *(trans.)*. **húheka káaɣe**
sickly. **ókawai**
sickness. **húheka, óhuheka**
side: (on the) other ~. **ákahahta, ámąhta, ámąhtaha**
side: take s.o.'s ~. **áhkie**
sides: take ~ with respect to s.o. **íkie**
sieve: grain ~. **wacúe ikaažį**
sigh (as wind through trees). **xowí**
sight. **wawéeðe**
sight: have normal ~. **wawéeðe**
sign (e.g., a document). **šáake oðį́įke, žáže kikáaɣe**
sign with a thumbprint (in lieu of a signature). **íkuspe**
signature. **žáže, žáže wéleze**
signature: affix one's ~. **žáže kikáaɣe**

signify. **ékǫ**
silly: talk s.o. ~. **páalǫðį**
silver. **mą́zeska**
similar in appearance to. **íkǫska**
similar to. **ékǫ**
similar to another. **kǫzékǫ**
similar to each other. **kǫzéhkihkǫ**
similarly. **ékǫ**
since (because). **tą** (often not expressed directly, but implied by the logical or pragmatic relationship of one clause to another; for examples, *see under* **táalį** 'burn', **tóa** 'some', **wéeną** 'be thankful, grateful', **wéhice** 'far')
sing. **waaðǫ́**
sing (like a bird). **hóohtą**
sing dancing songs. **xóhka**
singer: be a ~. **waaðǫ́ hpíǫ**
singers and drummers. **xóhka**
singers: female ~. **oðáazo**
singers of dancing songs, singers at a dance. **xóhka**
singing: be skilled at ~. **waaðǫ́ hpíǫ**
single. **ohką́ci, wį**
single (unmarried) person. **kažą́si** [JOD]
single item or event: that ~. **wįįðé**
Sioux (tribe or tribal member). **hpápaxǫ**
sister: baby ~. **asíhpa**
sister (specifically, older sister of female). **wižǫ́ą** or **wihtą́ke** 'my older sister' (speaker is female), **ðižǫ́ą** or **ðihtą́ke** 'your older sister' (addressee is female), **ižǫ́ą** or **ihtą́ke** 'her older sister'
sister (specifically, older sister of male). **wihtą́ke** 'my older sister' (speaker is male), **ðihtą́ke** 'your older sister' (addressee is male), **ihtą́ke** 'his older sister'
sister (specifically, younger sister). **wihtéžį** 'my younger sister', **ðihtéžį** 'your younger sister', **ihtéžį** 'his/her younger sister'
sister-in-law (specifically, sister-in-law of male). **wihą́ka** 'my sister-in-law' (speaker is male), **ðihą́ka** 'your sister-in-law' (addressee is male), **ihą́ka** 'his sister-in-law'
sister-in-law (specifically, sister-in-law of female). **wisíkxą** or **šíkxą** 'my sister-in-law' (speaker is female), **ðišíkxą** or **šíkxą ðíhta** or **ðisíkxą** 'your sister-in-law' (addressee is female), **išíkxą** or **šíkxą** 'her sister-in-law'
sit. **lį́į** (*see also* continuative aspect markers; positional articles)
sit down. **lį́įke, olį́į**
sit in a place. **olį́į**
sit suddenly. **lį́įke**
sit upon. **álįį**
six. **šáhpe**
sixteen, sixteenth. **lébrą álįį šáhpe**
sixty, sixtieth. **lébrą šáhpe**
skilled: be ~ at. **hpíǫ**
skilled: be ~ at doing things. **wahpíǫ**
skillfully. **ðáalį**
skin (V) (as an animal). **ámaxa**
skin (of an animal). **háa**
skin (of an animal): thick ~. **háa šooká**
skin (of a person or animal). **xúhaa**
skinny (e.g., a person or a tree). **lažį́į**
skirt: wraparound ~. **wáakipetxą**
skirt with ribbon work or other decorations. **wáache, wáakipaache**
skirting the edge of s.t. **ákiɣe**
skunk. **mą́ka**
sky. **mą́ąɣe, hkéðo**
slam *(trans.)*, slam closed. **kaasį́ce**
slam on s.t. **ákaasįce**
slander (V). **hkiláažoži, ðaažóži**
slap (N). **įcé bráaska, įcé bráze**
slave. **mą́ąhpiiži**
slay. **cʔéðe**
sled. **žą́ą ákaastowe**
sleep (N). **žą́ą**
sleep (V). **žą́ą, žį́įhe**
sleep: lie down to ~. **žą́ą**
sleep-matter-in-eyes. **įcóolą**
sleep over (stay all night). **žą́ą**
sleep sitting up. **lįlį́įe, žą́kxa žįhé**
sleepy: be ~. **įįštáha cʔóka**
sleepy-in-eyes. **įcóolą**
sleet. **nąɣežį, niižúpa**
sleigh. **žą́ą ákaastowe**
slender. **lažį́į**
slice (V). **kaascú**
slice by using a sharp edge. **pascé**
slice meat (as for a barbecue). **wakái**
sliced (ADJ). **žáhta**
slick. **štáha**
slide *(intr.)*. **mašcúce, ostá**
slightly. **ékǫ**
slim. **bréhka, lažį́į, saakížįka**, **wahóšce**
slip *(intr.)*. **ostá**
slip or slip away: let ~. **ðikšį́ce**
slippery. **mąąštáha**
slit (V). **kaascú, pážahta**
sloppy, slouchy. **ɣǫ́ǫce**
slow (ADJ). **lúži, ókxąži, scúuce, wascúuce**
slow: take or make it ~. **lúžihkiðe**
slow about catching up. **ókxąži**

slow down *(intr.)*. **lúžihkiðe**
slower. **lúži**
slower: make ~, slow down. **lúži káaɣe**
slowly. **lúži, wascúuce**
slowpoke, slow person. **ošcúuce**
slumber (v). **žį́įhe**
sly, on the sly, be sly. **nąlǫ́ǫha**
small. **wahókʔa, wahóšce, xóhtą, -žį, žįká**
small: quite or very ~. **wahóščažį**
small amount. **hépe, hépežį, huužį, ohépe, wahókʔa**
small amount of s.t. **-žį**
small amount or number. **čóopa**
small change (money). **ošpéžį**
small items, pieces, or things. **ošpéžį**
small number of (e.g., people). **huužį**
smaller: make ~. **ðuuhépe**
smart. **waðíląhtąą**
smear on. **stáðe**
smell (N and *intr.*). **brą́**
smell *(trans.)*. **ðíbrą**
smell: acrid or sour ~. **zą́zi**
smell: cause to ~, as in making cedar smoke for a cleansing or a blessing. **oðíbrą**
smell: have an offensive ~. **ɣoį́**
smell bad. **žą́ąže**
smell (good or bad) from heating. **táabrą**
smell of s.t. cooking (N). **watáabrą**
smell unpleasantly sour. **žą́xta**
smile (N). **íixažį**
smoke (N). **šóce**
smoke *(intr.)*. **waðáašoe**
smoke *(trans.)* (e.g., tobacco). **ðaahtą́, ðaašóe**
smoke *(trans.)*, as in making cedar smoke for a cleansing or a blessing. **oðíbrą**
smoke: make a ~ (e.g., roll a cigarette). **nąnį́ǫpa káaɣe**
smoky. **šóce, xóce**
smooth. **stá, stáko**
smooth and shiny (as a lake surface). **štáha**
smooth by pressing (iron). **puštáha**
smooth out. **ðuustáko**
smooth s.t. (e.g., cloth with an iron). **wapúštaha**
smoothed out (e.g., icing on a cake). **bráaða**
smoothing: by ~. **pu-**
smother with smoke or dust. **íkaskike**
snake. **wécʔa**
snap in two. **ðiixǫ́**
sneak off. **hkóopše**
sneaky ~. **nąlǫ́ǫha**
sneeze (v). **héchį**
snicker (v). **íixažį**
snoop (v, N), snoopy. **océštą**
snore (v). **lóce**
snot. **hpalį́**
snotty. **xtoe**
snout. **hpá**
snow (N). **pá, pá húðe**
snow (v). **pá húðe**
snowball. **pahúkaaski**
snowfall. **pá húðe**
snowman. **pánihkášie**
so (therefore, that's why). **éetana, káakǫ tą**
so! (an exclamation used especially in storytelling). **hą́ą**
so very, so very much. **wálį**
soap. **wépukxa**
soap: dish ~. **hį́įce íðuuža wépukxa**
soar, as an eagle. **káawįɣe**
sober. **ną́ąɣeska**
sober up. **ną́ąɣeskahkiðe**
socially distant from. **ákahahta**
society: secret ~. **nǫ́hǫžį**
socks. **hį́įǫke, hį́įǫke xóe, hǫǫpé okáwįɣe**
soda. **niikáapxohke**
soda bottle or can. **niikáapxokeoožú**
sodden. **špǫ́ǫ**
sofa. **álįįscee**
soft. **štǫ́ka**
soft drink. **niikáapxohke**
soften, become soft, softened. **špǫ́ǫ**
soften by pushing on. **paastǫ́ka**
softly: touch ~ as with a feather fan. **ðiihcé**
soil (N). **mą́įhka**
soiled. **wasúhuži**
soldier. **áhkita, áhkita ną́ąžį, wanáše**
soldier dance. **áhkitanąą́žį waachí**
sole (solitary). **ohkąci**
solely. **na, nąški, wįįðé**
solicit. **waatá**
solid. **saakí**
solitary. **ohkąci**
solo dance by one who has been in a war. **wašóše achí nąąžį́**
some. **hépe, tóa**
some day, some days. **hǫ́ǫpa wį**
someone (whose name one doesn't remember). **tą́ąska**
something. **táatą**
something (the name of which one doesn't remember). **tą́ąska**
something scattered. **ðéeke ci**
sometime. **hǫ́ǫpa wį**
sometimes. **ðéeke ci, hǫ́ǫpa wį**

somewhat. **ékǫ**
son: baby ~ (used by a woman of her youngest son if there are at least two older sons). **kxáhpą**
son: first or eldest ~. **ilǫ́ǫhpa, ilǫ́ǫhtą**
son: second ~. **kšǫ́ka**
son: third ~ (or subsequent son). **kxáke, kxážį**
son (without reference to age). **wižį́ke** 'my son', **ðižį́ke** 'your son', **ižį́ke** 'his/her son'
song. **waaðǫ́**
song: peyote ~ (song sung in a peyote meeting). **hkihkǫ́ze waaðǫ́**
songs: calling ~. **wapą́ waaðǫ́**
songs: sun ~. **mįįwáaðǫžį**
son-in-law. **wihtǫ́ce** 'my son-in-law', **ðihtǫ́ce** 'your son-in-law', **ihtǫ́ce** 'his/her son-in-law'
Sonny (nickname) . **wižį́ke**
soothing. **štáke**
sore (N). **ðéskali**
sorry: be ~ (used to apologize). **ékǫ kǫ́ðaaži**
sorry: feel ~ for. **áacexcį, ðakˀéðe**
sorry: feel ~ for one's own or s.o. close. **ðakˀékiðe**
sort (e.g., beans, clothing to be laundered). **hpahíke, paahí**
sort: what ~. **táatą**
soul. **waðílą, wanáąɣe**
sound (N). **ónie**
sound: beating ~. **hcíce**
sound out. **hóohtą**
sounds: make animal ~ (e.g., sing like a bird, moo, bark, howl). **hóohtą**
soup. **htaaníi**
soup: drink ~. **ðaazúpe**
soup: preparation of dried corn ~. **watxázu**
soup kettle. **htaaníe céɣe**
sour (taste). **cˀáaðe**
sour odor: have a ~. **žą́xta**
sour smell. **zą́zi**
sour-smelling. **žą́xta**
south. **mąąšcé kšíhtaha**
south wind. **ákˀahúe**
souvenir: keep as a ~. **kícheðe**
sow (e.g., seed in the ground). **oožú**
space (in the sense of an unoccupied area). **óhką**
space between things. **ohtą́ną**
spade (e.g., as gardening tool). **mą́ąhįspe, mą́ąhįsu**
spades (suit in a deck of cards). **hámąsi, mą́ąhįspe, mą́ąhįsu**
Spaniard, Spanish person. **íšpaðǫ**
Spanish (ADJ). **íšpaðǫ**
Spanish language. **íšpaðǫ**
Spanish-speaking: any native ~ person (especially Mexican). **íšpaðǫ**
spank. **ochį́**
spare (V). **ošcé**
spare s.o.'s life. **toníðe**
sparks that are struck. **kaalį́įže**
speak, speak of. **íe**
speak a language. **íe**
speak clearly. **íe ðáawaska, íeska, wáðaaska**
speak ill of. **ðaažóži**
speak of oneself. **ohkílaake**
speak positively or negatively of s.o. **íkie**
speak to each other using (a certain language or the hands). **íhkihkie**
speak to one's own relative, family, or friends. **okíhkie**
speak the truth. **wį́kše**
speak truthfully. **íe wáðohta**
speaking: clear or clean ~. **íe wasúhu**
special. **óxta**
special: make ~, give ~ status to. **óxtaðe, óxtakiðe**
special things. **wahcéka**
speckled. **léže**
spectacles. **mą́ze įįštóolą**
spectators. **watǫ́pe**
speech, make a speech. **íe**
spell of illness or trouble of any kind. **ókaše**
spider. **hcéxope**
spin, spin around. **-wįɣe**
spirit. **ilǫ́ɣe, nąąɣe, wanáąɣe**
spirit: holy ~. **wanáąɣe**
spirit land. **wanáąɣe mą́žą**
spit, spit on, spit out. **ðaakˀį́**
spittoon. **íluekˀí**
splash, splatter. **paasíke**
splendid. **ðáalį**
splice. **wápaase**
splinter (V). **paasíke**
splinter from sudden impact. **kaaxúɣe**
splinters. **žą́ąxežį, žą́ąžį**
split (ADJ). **žáhta**
split (V), split open. **kaaxúɣe**
split lip. **íhaa žáhta**
spoil s.t. (by making it dirty). **ízizike káaɣe**
spoiled. **hǫ́ǫži**
spoiled food: smell like ~. **žą́ąže**
spoon. **hcéhapa, hcúke**
spoon: wooden ~. **žą́ąhcuke**
spotted. **léže**
spray. **paasíke**
spread *(intr.)*. **paaɣáce**

spread *(trans.)*. **ðíbra, ðuuláwa**
spread on (as shoe polish). **ápuštai**
spread open. **paaɣáce**
spread out (e.g., a cloth). **ðíbra, ðuuláwa**
spread over, spread upon. **áðubra**
spreader for Osage headdress. **htaasį́ įce wahú**
spring (natural water spring). **níini**
Spring River. **tóoskue káxa** [LFD]
springtime, spring. **pée**
sprinkle (light rain). **niižúžu**
sprinkle (rain lightly). **nuužúžu**
sprite. **míalǫška**
square dance (N). **sį́ka hpaléze**
squash (vegetable). **hpǫ́ɣe, watxą́**
squash (vegetable): yellow climbing ~ (now extinct). **hpǫ́ɣe áace žį**
squashed. **tóže**
squat and rounded. **čáahpa**
squaw corn (i.e., fresh corn). **hápa wacˀéka**
squirrel. **sį́ka**
squirrel hunting. **sįkóce**
squirt. **paasíke**
staff used at peyote meetings. **mą́ą**
staff with feathers. **haawálele, waléle**
stagger. **šéšeka**
stain. **ðóðo** [LFD]
stairs. **ánaašile**
stalk (N). **hú**
stammer. **ðéeze opásike**
stand, be standing. **nąąžį́** (*see also* continuative aspect markers; positional articles)
stand on top of (used in comparisons). **ánąąžį**
stand there (as in a room or place). **onį́ąžį**
stand up (preparatory to departing). **nąąžį́**
standard (flaglike object). **haawálele**
star. **mihkákˀe**
star: evening ~. **mihkákˀe hą tą ðįkšé**
star: falling ~. **mihkákˀe oxpáðe**
star: little ~. **mihkákˀežįka**
star: morning ~. **mihkákˀe hą́ąpa tą ðįkše, mihkákˀe hą́ąpaska tą, mihkákˀehtąą**
star: morning or male ~. **wáhce tooka**
star: orbit of a ~. **mihkákˀe óžąke**
stare (at people). **watǫ́e scee**
start. **šką́**
start: unable to ~ (as a motor vehicle). **šką́aži**
start (e.g., a car motor). **ðuušką́**
start off. **aðée**
start to, suddenly start to. **ahí**
startle s.o. **hóšechie**
startle s.o. (as with suddenly emerging news). **pólǫðį**
startled. **pólǫðį**
startled: be ~. **hóšechie**
startled: be ~ (as by a dream or nightmare). **ohpáza**
startling, startling news or report. **hóšechie**
starving: be ~. **nǫhpéhicˀe**
starwort (*Liatris punctata*). **mąhká saakí**
statement: make a ~, state. **oðáake**
stationery with writing. **waléze**
stay. **mąðį́, wáaspe**
stay all night. **žą́ą**
stay-at-home. **wáaspe**
stay quiet. **wáaspe**
stay there (as in a room or place). **oną́ąžį**
stay there! (command). **šée mąðį́**
stay there (wait). **šée nąąžį́**
steak. **htáa taazíhi**
steal *(intr.)*, steal things. **wamą́ąðǫ**
steal *(trans.)*. **mąąðǫ́**
stealing. **wamą́ąðǫ**
steam *(intr.)*. **opˀą́ða**
steam (N). **íopˀąðą**
steam rising off standing water. **opˀą́ða**
steer. **hceeskátooka**
step on, step in. **ánąąžį**
steps (stairs). **ánaašile**
sterile (childless). **wéetaðaži**
stick *(intr.)*. **káataace**
stick (N). **žą́ą, žą́ąxe, žą́ąxežį**
stick: burial ~ (red stick put into coffin at head or foot, made of special wood). **hką́ące žą**
stick: shinny ~ (curved stick used to play *kašíni*). **ohkíce**
stick: small ~. **žą́ąxežį**
stick out. **ðuhtáža**
stick to. **ásta**
stick to drive people or animals, stick that the tail dancers carry. **wékaaži**
stick used to rub the fire-making wood. **hį́icecˀohu**
stickers, stickery. **waxáka**
sticky. **wáasta, wáðastástá**
stiff, stiffened. **sáta**
still (as a lake). **škaškáða**
still (not in movement). **šką́ ðįké, šką́aži**
still (yet). **šǫ́**
stingy: be ~. **kíwalį, wáli, wáwalį**
stingy person: be a ~. **wáwalį**
stink, it stinks! (an exclamation). **ɣoį́**
stinking odor: have a ~. **žą́įže**
stinky. **ɣoį́, žą́xta**

stippled. **léže**
stir (e.g., food when cooking). **oðókahi**
stockings. **hį́įǫke**
stomach. **hcéze, šúpe, wánǫbréoožú**
stomach: part of the ~ resembling little books or pages (used for soup). **otáhpa**
stomp the ground. **nąąstá**
stone (N). **į́į**
stoop over. **paacˀó, paakˀó**
stoop over (as to touch toes). **paacˀį́**
stop (INTERJ). **kaaštą́**
stop *(intr.)*. **ðiištą́, panáa**
stop *(trans.)*. **ðiištą́, kaašǫ́ káaɣe, nąąžį́le, panáa**
stop! wait! (used to get someone to pause or suspend an activity). **katxą́**
stop an activity. **kaaštą́**
stop an activity involving the mouth. **ðaaštą́**
stop in. **ahí**
stop s.o./s.t. **nąąžį́**
stop s.t. (make it end). **ðiištą́ káaɣe**
stop s.t. (make it halt). **oðíitą**
stopped up. **ocˀį́ze**
store (commercial establishment). **watǫ́ehci, watǫ́ǫžu**
storm with strong winds. **htaacé hpíiži, htaacé óhesaži**
story. **híko, óðaake**
stove. **océðe**
stove: heating or wood-burning ~ (for heat, not cooking). **hpéece íiška**
stove: metal ~. **mą́zewéoohǫ**
straight (even). **stáko**
straight (virtuous). **óðohtą, wáðohtą**
straight: make oneself ~. **óðohtąhkiðe**
straight: talk ~. **íe wáðohta, íeska**
straight up. **óðohtą**
straighten, straighten out, straighten up. **ðuustáko**
strange. **éeži**
stranger. **hpáðįhǫka, ohkíhce**
strangle. **tóoce oðį́įke**
strawberry. **pąąšcéka**
stream: small ~. **káxa žį**
street. **ožą́ke ohtą́ną**
strength. **waašką́**
strength: having ~. **waašką́htąka**
strength: lack ~. **waašką́ðįké**
stretch *(trans.)*. **ðiizíðe**
stretch oneself. **hkilíiziðe**
strike (e.g., a drum or a person). **ochį́**
Strike Axe (name of a band). **mą́ąhįspe**
strike with. **iichį́**
striking: flint for ~. **kaalį́įže**
strip s.t. (e.g., husk corn or peel a banana). **ðuušáake**
striped. **léze**
strong. **saakí, sísi, waašką́htąka**
strong: very ~. **óhesaži**
stronger. **óhesaži**
strong-willed. **níhka wažį́htąą**
stroud (cloth). **haažúuce**
struggle (V). **íkˀuce, waašką́**
stuck: get or be ~ to. **ásta**
study. **íkˀuce**
stuff. (*see* valence reducer prefix)
stuffed up. **ocˀį́ze**
stumble. **xíða**
stumble and fall. **hípše**
stumble repeatedly. **xíxiða**
stun. **ðusáaki, kaapxóhke, káasaaki**
stutter. **ðéeze opásike**
subject markers. **akxa, apa** (*see also* positional articles)
subpar: be ~. **oolą́ąži**
subscribe. **žáže kikáaɣe**
succeed (follow); successive. **okínąąžį**
succeed anyway. **óðąži**
success: achieve ~ for s.o. **ðáalį kšíðe**
successful: be ~. **ðáalį káaɣe**
successful: be ~ anyway. **óðąži**
successful: make s.o. ~. **ðáalį kšíðe**
succession (e.g., of chiefs; also one of anything following another). **opxą́pxą́**
suck. **ðaašóe**
sudden application of force or sudden movement: by ~. **kaa-**
suddenly start to. **ahí**
suffer from. **ǫ́ǫ**
suffer from an illness. **kihúheka**
suffer from heartache. **ðą́ącenie**
suffering (ADJ). **waxpáðį**
sufficient. **kaakǫ́ną**
sufficient, it's sufficient. **kaašǫ́ka**
sugar. **žąąníi**
sugar bowl. **žąąníioožu**
suicide: commit ~. **cˀéhkiðe**
suitable. **ðąąché**
suitable: be ~. **íhta**
suitcase. **wáseska**
sulk. **lǫ́ǫ, ólą**
sulk about another's good fortune. **óxįį**
sulky. **ólą**
sullen. **ókˀą hpíiži**
summer, summertime, when it is summer. **tooké**

summer: last ~. **tookéce**
summit. **ákaha**
sun. **mį́į**
sun seen straight overhead (high noon). **mįįðóhta**
sunbeam. **mįįtáašcuuce**
Sunday. **hą́ąpa wahkǫtáki, hą́ąpa wahkǫ́taki**
sundown. **mį́įhiðe**
sundown: toward ~ (as a time of day). **mįįáðee ehtáha**
sunflower. **mį́įhtǫeli**
sunglasses. **mą́ze įįštóolą sápe**
sunrise. **mį́į íðǫpe**
sunset. **mį́įhiðe**
superintendent, as of the Osage Agency. **mą́ąhį htą́ą**
superior: be ~ to in some quality (used in comparisons). **ánąąžį**
supervise. **oðóðe**
supervise s.o. specifically in response to a formal request (e.g., taking care of the food for an event). **okášą**
supervisor. **oðówaðe, wakáaɣe**
supper (evening meal only). **hpáze wanǫ́bre**
supper (noon or evening meal). **wanǫ́bre**
supply. **ok?ú**
supply to folks. **ók?u**
suppose: I ~ that. **ska**
surface. **háa**
surgery. **hpáce**
surprise: interjection expressing ~ (said to be a woman's exclamation). **íto**
surround. **ákiɣe, oðíši** [LFD]
surroundings: in the ~ of. **ákahahta**
surveillance: have under ~. **nąlǫ́ǫha átǫpe**
suus prefix [SUU]. **kik-**
swallow (v). **ðaašcúe**
swallow: a ~ or two (of a liquid). **huužį**
swan. **míɣa ska**
swap (N). **íhkihkawį**
sweat. **į́į olį́į, paɣíce**
sweat lodge, sweat house. **ítaasuhu, į́įolįįhci**
sweep *(trans.)*. **kaacúxe**
sweet (N). **waskúe**
sweet food or sauce. **skúðe, waskúe**
sweet milk. **paazénii skúðe**
sweet potato. **tooscée, tóoskue, tóožuuce**
sweet potato branch (Sweet Potato Creek). **tóoskue káxa**
sweetheart. **ðą́ące skúðe**
sweets. **waskúe**
swim. **hiiðá**
swim: place to ~. **ohíiða**
swim supporting a child in the water. **ðuškápa**
swindle. **mąɣíðe**
switch off. **ðuutáaži**
sycamore. **waséhtąhü**

table. **áwanǫbre**
tablecloth. **áwanǫbre aðibra**
table-hop (v). **ákiɣe**
taboo. **wáalake(?)** [LFD]
tail (animal's tail or part of Osage dance costume), tail dancer. **sį́įce**
tail (hip or buttocks). **ǫ́pe**
tail feathers: fan made of ~. **íhkuáci**
take (select, take out). **ðuuzé**
take (take along, carry). **k?į́ahi**
take a bath. **hiiðá**
take a seat. **olį́į**
take a wife. **mį́įląke**
take as a husband. **áðuɣe**
take each other as relatives. **ðótahkiðe**
take as a sexual partner. **ðúɣe**
take as a wife. **lą́ke**
take away. **aðį́aðee, aðį́mąðį, ðicíze**
take away from s.o. s.t. of his/her own. **kilúuze**
take away one's own. **lúuze**
take back (motion underway). **aðį́alee**
take back there (motion accomplished). **aðį́akši**
take care of. **áhkihtǫpe, ákihtǫpe, ákitǫpe, átǫpe, ðak?éðe, okášą, okáše, wanáše**
take care of a meal oneself when asked to do so. **óohkihą**
take care of a task or an event. **oðówaðe**
take care of kids or children. **žįkókašą**
take care of oneself. **óhkihkaše**
Take Care of the Eagle (personal name). **xuðókašą**
take charge of. **ókašą**
take clothes off (another person or oneself). **ðuušáwa**
take down. **ðuuhúuce, ðuxpáwį**
take each other as relatives. **ðótahkiðe**
take hold of. **oðį́įke**
take hold of one another. **mą́hki**
take home (motion accomplished). **aðį́akši**
take home (motion underway). **aðį́alee**
take home for oneself, take home as one's own. **ahkílįalée**
take it slow. **lúžihkiðe**
take off a garment. **ðiištówe**
take off a person's clothes (e.g., a child's clothing before a bath). **ðuušáwį**
take off by pulling. **ðiištówe**

take one's own. **aláðį, aláðįðee, lúuze**
take out s.t. by removing, extracting, or lowering it. **oðúuxpaðe**
take sides with respect to s.o. **íkie**
take s.o.'s side. **áhkie**
take there (motion accomplished). **aðíahi**
take there (motion underway). **aðíaðee**
take up for s.o. **áhkie**
talk, talk about. **íe**
talk: clean or clear ~. **íe wasúhu**
talk about s.t. positively or negatively. **óie**
talk clearly. **íeska**
talk for another, talk in the presence of others. **ékie**
talk for or against s.o. **áhkie, íkie**
talk in one's sleep. **žą́ą tái įké**
talk s.o. silly. **páalǫðį**
talk straight. **íe wáðohta**
talk to each other using (a certain language or the hands). **íhkihkie**
talk too long. **íe scece**
talk too much. **óochiže**
talk up or talk down, as when expressing one's emotions with respect to some topic. **áhkie**
talk with one another. **ohkíhkie**
talkative in excess. **óochiže**
talker (person who talks too much). **íe scece, íeštą**
tall. **húuscee, scéce**
taller. **húuscee**
tallow. **wélisaaki**
tamales. **wacúexǫ oðiši**
tame (ADJ). **wacˀéka**
tame (V) (e.g., a horse). **ðiwáštake**
tangled. **hkíhkįnį**
tangled: get oneself ~ in. **ohkíǫðe**
tape (make a recording with an audio device). **íe ðuuzé**
tape recorder, tape player. **mą́zeie**
tapping noise against metal (as made by a typewriter). **mą́ze htáhtaze**
tapping sound. **htáhtaze**
tarantula. **hcéxopehuuscee**
task. **ówǫ**
taste (V). **íkˀuce**
tea. **hpéže mą́hka**
tea: buckeye ~. **htáška hí**
tea: cedar ~. **xǫǫcénii**
tea: green ~. **hpéže htóho**
tea: iced ~. **hpéženii nąye oolą́**
tea: peyote ~. **wanǫ́brenii**
teach. **wakǫ́ze**
teach s.t. to s.o. **kǫ́ze, kšíǫze**
teacher. **wakǫ́ze**
teachings. **íe**
tear (N), teardrop. **įįštábri**
tear (V) (rip). **kaabráze**
tear apart (e.g., a tree limb from the trunk). **ðupáxa**
tease: be a ~, tease s.o. **ðiihíce**
tease people. **waðíihice**
teenager. **hcéka nǫ́ǫ**
teeter. **sísiąðe**
teeth. **híi**
telegraph. **mą́zekˀąsaaki**
telegraph: send there by ~. **mą́zekˀąsaaki ðée káaye**
telephone. **mą́zeohkíhkie**
television. **mą́ze íe ówatǫe**
tell (e.g., news, stories). **oðáake**
tell about oneself. **ohkílaake**
tell s.o. not to (do s.t.). **ížoši**
tell s.o. to do s.t. **ée, hce ée**
tell the truth. **wíkše**
tell untruths. **íxope**
tell-all. **táatąží ški oðáake**
telling: a ~ of s.t. **óðaake**
temper: bad ~. **waðílą hpíiži**
tempest. **htaacé hpíiži, htaacé óhesaži**
ten, tenth. **lébrą**
ten cents. **waðáawa lébrą**
tend (take care of). **átǫpe**
tend s.o. **ákitǫpe**
tender. **wacˀéka**
tent. **haaskáhci, wažáihci**
tepid. **štáke**
terminate an activity preparatory to departing. **nąąží**
terrapin. **hkée**
test (V). **íkˀuce**
test: put each other to a ~. **áhkiasąci**
test: put s.o. to the ~. **ásąci, kasǫ́ci**
test by questions. **ákazo**
test s.o. **ásąci, kasǫ́ci**
testicles. **šǫcóso**
testimony: give ~. **wawépahǫ**
text: document or paper containing ~. **waléze**
thank you. **wéewiną**
thank you ('feel good' used as an equivalent of thank you). **kiðálį**
thankful. **óweena**
thankful: be ~ (for). **wéeną**
Thanksgiving Day. **súhkahtąą hą́ąpa**
that (complementizer connecting subordinate clause to the following main clause). **che**
that, this, those, these. **ðée**

that, those (near you). **šée**
that, those (person[s] or thing[s] that are relatively remote or whose exact description is unknown or of little importance). **tówa**
that direction. **émąhta**
that one, that person (emphatic pronoun). **ée**
that only. **eená**
that way. **kaakǫ́**
that way: along ~. **ée htáha**
that yonder. **kóota**
that's all. **kaakǫną́**
that's why. **eená**
the. (no exact Osage equivalent; *see* positional articles; subject markers; that; this)
theater. **ówatǫįhci**
theater presentation. **ówatoį**
theft. **wamą́ąðǫ**
their, theirs. **íhta, íhtaapi** (*see also* pronominal prefixes; suus prefix)
their place: at ~. **ecí pa**
them. (There is no direct equivalent in Osage of 3rd person pronouns 'he', 'him', 'she', 'her', 'it', 'they', 'them'. Unemphatic 3rd person pronouns are usually not overtly expressed; *ée* and demonstratives such as *še* can be used as emphatic 3rd person pronouns ['he himself', 'she herself', etc.].) (*see also* pronominal prefixes; these; this; that; those)
themselves. (*see* reflexive prefix)
then, and then immediately or right away. **kaðǫ́**
then: and ~. **kaðǫ́, káakǫ tą**
there. **ðeeká**
there: be ~. **ecí**
there: get, stand, or stay ~ (as in a room or a place). **oną́ąžį**
there: go, come, or arrive ~ (motion accomplished). **ahí**
there: go ~ (motion underway). **aðée**
there: over ~. **ée htáha, kaaðó, kootáįke**
there (near you). **šé, šeeðǫ́**
therefore. **ðekáhtą, eená, éetana, ékǫ, étą, káakǫ tą**
these. **ðee, ðeeká**
these, this (animate or inanimate, emphatic or expressing certainty or immediacy). **káa**
these scattered. **ðéeke**
they. (There is no direct equivalent in Osage of 3rd person pronouns 'he', 'him', 'she', 'her', 'it', 'they', 'them'. Unemphatic 3rd person pronouns are usually not overtly expressed; *ée* and demonstratives such as *še* can be used as emphatic 3rd person pronouns ['he himself', 'she herself', etc.].) (*see also* pronominal prefixes; these; this; that; those)
they too. **eeškítą**
thick. **šooká**
thick skin. **háa šooká**
thief. **wamą́ąðǫštą**
thievery. **wamą́ąðǫ**
thigh. **sízo**
thin. **bréhka, lažį́į**
thing. **tą́ąska** (*see also* valence reducer prefix)
thingamajig. **tą́ąska**
thing(s). **táatą**
things: many or lots of ~. **táatą ochí**
things: small ~. **táatąžį**
things one has to do. **ówǫ**
things scattered around (as in a messy house). **ópoce**
think. **waðílą**
think about. **éðe, ékiðe, íðilą, óðąąceši, waðílą**
think about again. **oðóhake íðilą**
think about s.t. **táatą íðilą**
think ill of s.o. **hpíiži ažį́**
think on. **waðílą**
think oneself to be a certain way (?). **áhkiži**
think regarding s.o. **ažį́**
think so. **ékiðe**
thinking. **waðílą**
third. **wéðaabrį**
thirsty: be ~ for. **ípuze**
thirteen, thirteenth. **lébrą álįį ðáabrį**
thirty, thirtieth. **lébrą ðáabrį**
this. **ðée, ée, káa**
this time. **ðétxą**
thorns, thorny. **waxáka**
thorny tree. **žą́ą waxáka**
thoroughfare. **óžąke**
those, that. **ðée**
those, that (near you). **šée**
those, that (person[s] or thing[s] that are relatively remote or whose exact description is unknown or of little importance). **tówa**
those from around here. **ðeekíha**
thought. **waðílą**
thoughtlessly. **íðilą ðįké**
thousand. **žą́ąhkoke**
thrash. **ochį́**
thread. **háaweáze**
three. **ðáabrį**
threshold. **hcižépe**
throat. **tóoce**
throat: sore ~. **tóoce níe**

through (direction). **ha**
through: be ~ (be finished). **ðiištą́**
through: go ~ (as a road). **opxą́**
through the action of. **í-**
throughout: be ~ an area or a group of people. **omą́ðį**
throughout: be ~ a person's body. **omą́ðį**
throw. **kį́įðe, ǫ́ǫða**
throw away. **ǫ́ǫða, ǫ́ǫðe**
throw each other away. **hkíǫðe, ohkíǫðe**
throw off (suddenly severing or moving s.t. or s.o. from s.t.). **okáxpa**
throw oneself into. **ohkíǫðe**
throw s.o. away. **ohkíǫðe**
throw up due to overeating. **ókohpa**
thumbprint: make a ~ on a document in lieu of a signature. **íkuspe**
thump hard. **taašéðe**
thumping sound (e.g., footsteps). **hcíce**
thunder (N). **lǫǫhǫ́, lǫǫhóohtą**
thunder (V). **lǫǫhóohtą**
Thunder clan, person of the Thunder clan. **lǫ́ǫ iníhkašika**
thunder people. **lǫ́ǫ níhkašika**
thunder: grandmother ~. **iihkó lǫ́ǫ**
thunder: lots or large amount of ~. **lǫǫ húu**
Thursday. **hą́ąpa wétoopa**
thus. **éetana, ékǫ**
thus with certainty. **kaakǫ́**
tick (e.g., a clock or an insect making noise). **htáhtaze**
ticking noise against metal (as made by a typewriter). **mą́ze htáhtaze**
ticking sound. **htáhtaze**
tickle. **ðikˀíðe**
tidy, tidy up. **ðuustáko**
tie (e.g., shoelaces). **oðáške, okáške**
tie down (e.g., a drum). **paaxcé**
tie in a bundle s.t. specific, tie stuff up as a bundle. **opétxą**
tie the drum; (involves wrapping the drum up and tying it). **céɣenii káaɣe**
tie to s.t. **ákaške**
tie up. **ákaške, ápetxa, ðuušáwį, kašké, oðíiną, okáške**
tight, tightly. **saakí**
tight (inebriated). **lǫ́ðį, omą́įžį**
timbers. **zą́ą**
time: a long ~ (which has passed). **káaši**
time: at this ~. **ðetxą́ci**
time: be at that ~. **ecí**
time: from this ~ on. **ðetxą́ha**
time: in or near that ~. **ée htáha**
time: it is ~. **éetxą, mįįðóhta**
time: it's ~ again. **ékitxą**
time: this ~. **ðétxą**
time after time. **ohkíetxątxą, ótxątxą**
time of day (as told by the clock). **mį́įoðaake**
tinder. **žąąhcúkˀa**
tiny. **wahóščažį**
tip (of an object). **hpasú, ihtáɣe**
tipi. **wažáihci**
tire (of a vehicle). **hcéðe**
tired. **kaaskíke, skíke**
tired: be ~ of. **íibrą**
tired: become or be ~ of. **oðúucˀake**
tired: feel ~. **óžeðe**
to. **ci, įkší, ki, kši** ('to' is often implied rather than overtly expressed in Osage, especially with motion verbs; *see also* dative prefix)
toad. **níižu oxáke**
toad: horned ~. **kalǫ́eže**
tobacco. **nąnúhu**
tobacco bag. **nąnįǫ́kužu, nąnúhuoožúhaa**
tobacco boss (who sits to the left of the roadman in a peyote meeting). **nąnįǫ́pa olį́į**
tobacco pouch. **nąnįǫ́kužu**
today. **hą́ąpa, hǫ́ǫpa ðé**
toe. **siihpó**
together: place ~ (as when cooking two or more items together). **oðóhkiðe**
toilet, toilet room. **ožéhci**
toilet paper. **íkahci**
told: as it is or was ~ (e.g., as in a story or in the Bible). (*see* reportative markers)
tomato. **hką́ące žúe**
tomorrow. **kaasį́**
tongue. **ðéeze**
tongue-tied: be ~, tongue splayed or split. **ðéeze opásike**
tonight. **hąąðé**
Tonkawa (tribe or tribal member). **waðánii**
too (also). **ški, -škítą**
too (excessively). **wálį**
too: he/she, it, or they ~. **eeškítą**
too much or too long: person who talks ~. **íe scece, íeštą**
tool. **wéhkikˀǫ**
tool for cutting wood. **wépaase**
tool used to make s.t. **wékaaɣe**
tooth. **híi**
toothless. **híi įke**
top, on top. **ákaha**

top: on ~ of s.t. else. **ámąši**
topple (as a tree topples). **xíða**
torn. **bráze**
torn (said of clothing). **cúuða**
tornado. **htaacé hpíiži, htaacé óhesaži**
tortoise. **hkée**
toss. **ǫ́ǫða, ǫ́ǫðe**
totter. **sísiąðe**
touch softly as with a feather fan, barely touch. **ðiihcé**
touch the hands of s.o. **šáake oðį́įke**
touch with the fingers. **paaspą́**
touch with the hand. **ðiihtą́**
toward. **hta, htáha**
toward: not ~ that way. **émąhtažíha**
toward the center. **mąchéhtaha**
toward you: go ~. **šoðée**
toward you (along a path toward where you [the hearer] are or toward s.t. or s.o. nearer to you than to the speaker). **šée htaha**
towel: hand ~. **šáake ípukxa**
towel: dish ~. **hį́įce ípukxa**
towel: paper ~. **htaną́kˀa ípukxa**
town. **htą́wą**
Town Builder (personal name). **htą́wakáaɣe**
town crier. **íekie, wacípxaį**
toy with. **ðiihíce**
tracks. **šáake**
trade (N). **íhkihkawį**
trade (V). **íhkihkawį káaɣe**
trade for. **íðuwį**
trading house. **watǫ́ǫžu**
traditiong. **óðaake**
tradition: embrace as ~. **oðį́įke**
trailer. **oðíhtą hcí oðáha**
train. **oðíhtą kˀą́saaki**
trample. **nąąstá**
tranquil. **škaškáða**
transport (V). **kˀį́ahi**
trap (N). **mą́ze oðóbrįįke**
trash (N). **ópoce**
travel. **kaalǫ́ðe, wamą́ðį**
travel around. **opáwįɣe**
travel on (e.g., certain funds). **iiðée**
traverse (e.g., a street). **áðuuhta ðée**
Treadway: George ~ (nickname: Shattered Forehead). **hpéeleke**
treasure. **wahcéka**
treasure: keep as a ~. **kícheðe**
treasure one's own. **kíoxta**
treasure s.t. **kíwalį**
treasured: s.o. or s.t. ~ (such as a favorite child). **óðoxta**
treat others (medically). **wašcéðe**
tree. **žą́ą**
tree: thorny ~. **žą́ą waxáka**
tree branch, tree branching out. **žą́ą káxa**
Tree-killer. **kaalį́** [LFD]
trees growing in a nonrandom pattern. **žą́ą pe**
tremble. **ðibrúbruɣe**
trench (N). **ną́ceaha**
trench (V). **ną́ce káaɣe**
trial. **áhkiisto**
tribal council session. **hkiistó**
tribe: western ~ or tribal member (refers to any tribe from the western United States). **hpáðį**
tribe other than Osage (including western tribes). **ohkíhce**
trick (V). **mąɣíðe**
trick them. **wáðihota**
trigger. **mį́cehką**
tripe. **hceeníxaxa**
trouble: be in ~ for doing s.t. wrong. **ohkíǫðe**
trouble: have health ~ with. **íhuheka**
trouble: make ~ for s.o. **ówǫ káaɣe**
trouble s.o. **ðišǫ́ži, ówǫ káaɣe**
troubled: be ~ by problems or sickness. **ókaše**
troubled: be very ~ by (e.g., an illness, an ailing body part). **íhpiiži**
trousers. **oðíkinąąžį**
true. **wį́kše**
true! **ékǫ**
true: be ~ to. **wį́kše**
true: be ~ to one's own. **okípše**
true: be ~ to oneself. **wį́hkikše**
trunk (box). **žą́ąhkoke**
trunk (e.g., of a tree). **hú**
trust oneself: not ~. **hkíxiða**
truth. **wį́kše**
truth: speak or tell the ~. **wį́kše**
truthful. **wawį́kše**
truthfully. **wáðohtą**
truthfully: speak ~. **íe wáðohta**
try (V), try on. **íkˀuce**
try hard, try one's best. **íkˀuce, waašką́**
tuberculosis. **mą́ąke ní, mą́ąke púze**
tuberculosis. **hóxpe hpíiži** (?), **hóxpe zúpe** (?)
Tuesday. **hą́ąpa wéðǫǫpa**
tug (V). **ðiitą́**
tug s.t. over in order to cover s.t. or s.o. **áðuzu**
Tulsa (Oklahoma). **htaasílee htáwą, túlsa htą́wą**
turbulence. **óochiže**
turkey. **súhkahtąą**
turkey buzzard. **héka**
turkey cock. **áahu mą́ðį**
turkey feather. **súhkahtąą mǫ́šǫ**

turkey hen. **súhkahtąą mį́ka**
turn (root). **-hkóįɣe, -wįɣe**
turn *(trans.)*. **ðiisą́ða**
turn: be one's ~. **waðíhta**
turn: it is my ~. **wíe**
turn: whose ~. **pée**
turn: your ~. **ðíe**
turn around (root). **-hkóįɣe, -wįɣe**
turn in the road. **ípaašąha**
turn off. **ðiistą́, ðuutáaži**
turn on. **káaɣe**
turn one's own. **liisą́ða**
turn oneself around. **ámąhta hkilíikoįɣe, hkilíisą**
turn over *(trans.)*. **ðiisą́ða , ípasą**
turn over and over *(trans.)*. **ðusą́sąwį**
turn over one's own. **liisą́ða**
turn s.o. or s.t. around. **ðiihkóįɣe**
turn up. **ðumáða**
turn wrong side out. **ðuháašįðe**
turnaround place. **ípaašąha**
turnip. **tóolehtąą**
turnover bread. **wacúe žéela**
turtle. **hkée**
twelve, twelfth. **lébrą álįį ðǫǫpá**
twenty, twentieth. **lébrą ðǫǫpá**
twenty-one, twenty-first. **lébrą ðǫǫpá álįį wį́xci**
25-cent piece. **kašpéǫpa**
twice. **ðǫǫpá**
twigs of a tree or bush: small ~. **žą́ąžį, žą́ąxežį**
twin (N). **ðǫǫpátą**
twist, twist around (e.g., a crepe paper streamer). **ðusą́sąwį**
two. **ðǫǫpá**
two of them, couple, pair. **nahkǫį́**
type: what ~. **táatą**
typewriter. **mą́ze htáhtaze**

udder. **paazé**
ugly. **ohtázaži**
ululate. **ðaazó, waðáazo**
umbrella. **oðínii**
unable. **ðąącháži**
unable: be ~ to do. **ðuuc?áke**
unable: be ~ to understand. **hahkíe, kíopxaži**
unable: items one was ~ to eat. **ðaac?áke**
unable to move or start (as a motor vehicle). **šką́aži**
unafraid. **nǫ́ǫhpaži**
unafraid of. **íinǫǫhpaži**
uncle (specifically, brother of father). **įhtáci** or **įhtáciżį** 'my father's brother', **ðiðáce** or **ðiðácežį** 'your father's brother', **iðáce** or **iðácežį** 'his/her father's brother'
uncle (specifically, brother of mother). **wįcéki** 'my mother's brother', **ðįcéki** 'your mother's brother', **įcéki** 'his/her mother's brother'
uncle (specifically, husband of sister of father). **wihtą́ha** 'my father's sister's husband', **ðihtą́ha** 'your father's sister's husband', **ihtą́ha** 'his/her father's sister's husband'
unclean (dirty). **wasúhuži**
unclean (sick, evil). **ízizike**
unconcerned with: be ~. **óðąąceši ðįké**
uncooked, undercooked. **cúutaži**
uncover partially. **opéni**
under, underneath. **mąché, mąchéhta, oðúluha**
under the head. **įpehi**
undergarment (for men or women). **mą́che oðúxa**
undersign. **žáže kikáaɣe**
understand. **íiðe, ípahǫ, kíopxa, nąk?ǫ́**
understand: be unable to ~. **hahkíe, kíopxaži**
understand: not ~. **kíopxaži, pxáðaži**
understand things. **wáopxa**
understanding: act of ~. **nąąɣúce**
undertake, undertake a new task under one's charge. **okášą**
underwear. **mą́che oðúxa, oðíkinąąžį**
undivided. **bróka**
undress. **ðiištówe**
undress (another person or oneself). **ðuušáwa**
undress oneself, get undressed. **hkilíiša, hkilúušawa, hkilúuštake**
undress s.o. **ðuušáwį, ðuuštáke**
uneaten item. **ðaac?áke**
unfaithful. **wawį́kšaži**
unfavorable impression made upon another by offensive conduct. **wáalake**
unfitting. **ékǫži**
unhappy. **kízoži**
unhappy: be ~. **kihǫ́ǫži**
uniform (even). **stáko**
uninterruptedly. **šǫǫšǫ́we**
unique. **éžixci**
unique thing: that ~, uniquely so. **wįįðé**
universe. **mą́žą záani**
universe, all the universe. **níǫhta záani**
unkempt. **ɣǫ́ǫce, héxpa**
unlikely. **ée htáhaži**
unload (remove). **ðuxpáwį, oðúuxpaðe**
unmarried female. **wáðuɣaži**
unmarried person. **kažą́si** [JOD]
unobserved: be ~ (as a custom). **óðąąceši ðįké**

unpredictable behavior: show ~. **taeðáalį̨ži**
unreasonable, unreasonably. **ée htáhaži**
unreliable. **óškika**
unripe. **cúutaži**
unruly. **ók'ą hpíiži, waðílą eekǫ́ įké**
unruly: be ~. **taeðáalįži**
unseemly. **ékǫži**
unskilled: be ~ (at). **kǫ́žįka**
unsound. **eekǫ́ ðįké**
unstable: mentally ~. **c'éka**
unsuitable. **éeži, ékǫži, íhtaháaži**
unsuitably. **ée htáhaži, ekǫ́įke, íhtaháaži**
unsuitably: act ~. **ók'ą éži**
unsure: be ~ (of s.t.). **hahkíe**
untamed. **óhesaži**
untamed horse. **hkáwa wahcéxi**
untie (e.g. horse). **ðuuškáke**
until. **txą́ha** (*see also* complementizer)
untroubled. **ókašéįke**
untruth. **íxope**
untruthful. **wawíkšaži**
untruths: tell ~. **íxope**
unusual. **éeži**
unwell: be ~. **íhpiiži**
unwilling: be ~ to. **iiną́hiži**
up. **ámąši**
up: get ~ (from a bed or chair). **hpaahą́**
up: hold or pull ~. **ðuumą́ši**
up: hold or raise ~. **opáahą, paahą́**
up: raise or turn ~. **ðumáða**
up: take ~ for s.o. **áhkie**
up: wake or get ~. **hpaahą́**
up above, in the upper part. **ámąši**
upon. **á-**
upon: place ~ (e.g., a suitcase on a table). **álįį**
upon: put ~. **ákaaspe**
upon (used in numbers). **álįį**
upright: be ~. **mą́ši**
upright: place an item ~ on another item. **ále**
upset: make s.o. or push s.o. to be ~. **páalǫðį**
upstairs. **ámąši**
upward: be ~. **mą́ši**
urinal. **océže**
urinate. **céže, hkilúuhepe**
urine. **céženii**
us. **ąkóta** (emphatic) (*see also* pronominal prefixes)
use a name for s.t. or s.o. **ðaacé**
use s.o.'s. **ootá**
use to bless oneself. **íistahkiðe**
used to (do, be). **ną** [ITERATIVE], **nąpe**
using: go by ~. **iiðée**
using (by means of). **í-**
useless. **ókaaɣeįke**
usually. **ną** [ITERATIVE], **nąpe**
utensils: cooking ~. **wéoohǫ́, wióohǫ**
U-turn. **ípaašąha**

vacant space. **óhką**
vagina. **úže**
vague: be ~ about. **kíopxaži**
valence reducer prefix [VAL]. **wa-**
valuable. **óxta**
valuable things. **wahcéka**
value: s.t. of no ~. **mą́ąhpiiži**
value s.t. **kíwalį**
valued: s.o. or s.t. ~ (such as a favorite child). **óðoxta**
valueless. **ókaaɣeįke**
vanish. **ðįké**
vapor rising off standing water. **op'ą́ða**
vegetables. **ówe, wasúutą**
vein (blood vessel). **hką́, lušúpe**
venerate. **óxta káaɣe**
venereal disease. **wácinie**
Verdigris River. **waséhtą xóe**
vermin. **walúška**
very. **wálį, xci, -žįvessel. óožu**
vest (N). **ákahahpa, wéhkilį**
vile. **iiséwaðe**
vine. **žą́ą áace**
vine: bean ~. **hǫbrį́ hi**
vinegar. **níi c'áaðe**
viper. **wéc'a**
virgin (N). **wáðuɣaži**
Virgin Mary. **ižį́ke iihǫ́, wahkǫ́ta ižįke iihǫ́**
virtuous. **óðohtą**
vision (sight). **wawéeðe**
visit (N). **wéehkile**
visit a relative or one's own (family). **íkihtǫpe**
visit to ask or summon s.o. to attend or appear before others. **kípą**
visiting, on a visit. **íihkiðemąðį**
voice. **hóo**
vomit. **lépe**
vomit due to overeating. **ókohpa**
vote, vote for. **mą́šą oðį́įke**
vote, vote for or against s.o. or s.t. **páaleze**

wad together with a sudden movement. **kaaskí**
wad up. **ðibrúuska, ðiiskíke**
wad up, wad together (e.g., clothing at the back of the neck). **ðiiskí**

wade. **žópše**
wager (N). **óžok?a**
wagon. **oðíhtą**
wail. **ɣaaké**
waist. **ðúwe**
wait. **šée nąąží**
wait, wait for. **iðáhpe**
wait for folks. **wéðahpe**
wait for one's own family or close persons. **iðákihpe**
waiter, waitress. **óohǫ owáwak?u**
wake *(trans.)*. **ðixí**
wake by foot. **nąąxí**
wake up, wake *(intr.)*. **hpaahą́, iihkíðe, -xi**
walk. **mąðį́**
walk: go for a ~. **mąðį́ aðée**
walk among folks. **ómąðį**
walk around. **ákiɣe, ápše**
walk fast. **htą́ąðį**
walk in. **omą́ðį**
walk on or upon. **ámąðį**
Walker: Josephine ~ (personal name). **wažáxį**
walking: go ~. **mąðį́ aðée**
walking stick. **íisa**
Walks among the Cedars (personal name). **xǫ́ǫce mą́į**
wallet. **mą́zeskaoožú**
walnut, black walnut. **htákue**
wander. **opáwįɣe**
want. **íðilą, kǫ́ða** (*see also discussion under* **hce ée**)
want: make folks/one ~ to. **kǫ́ðawaðe**
want as one's own, want for oneself. **hkihkǫ́ða**
want s.t. that is another's. **kíkǫða**
war (N). **taaké, totą́**
war: go to ~. **taaké, taaké omą́ðį**
war dances of the Osages. **ilǫ́ǫška**
warm (ADJ and *intr.*). **šcúuce, táahkace, taašcúe**
warm *(trans.)*. **táašcue káaɣe**
warm oneself, as at a stove or fire. **táašcuehkíðe**
warpath. **totą́**
wary: be ~ of. **íinǫǫhpe**
wash '(e.g., clothes, hair). **ðiiškí**
wash (e.g., dishes, parts of the body, food items, a car). **ðuužá**
wash clothes, wash stuff. **waðíiški**
wash clothes for oneself. **hkilíiški**
wash one's own (body parts or possessions). **lúuža**
wash one's own (e.g., clothing or hair). **líiški**
wash oneself with. **íhkiluuža**
wasp. **mąąpíaza, wapázike** [archaic]
watch (v). **tǫ́pe**
watch (some entity or some process). **átǫpe**
watch one's own things. **kihtǫ́pe**
watch out for. **íinǫǫhpe**
watch over (one's own things or people). **ákihtǫpe**
watch over (some entity or some process). **átǫpe**
watch over each other. **áhkihtǫpe**
watch over oneself, watch oneself. **áhkihtǫpe**
watch over s.o. **ákitǫpe**
watch over things for oneself, watch over one's own things. **áhkihtǫpe**
watch people or events. **watǫ́pe**
water. **níi**
water: flooding ~. **níita**
water moccasin. **níi wéc?a**
watermelon. **sáhku**
water-strider bug. **ámąðį, niiámąðį**
way: be in the ~. **iðǫ́eðįhé**
way: be in the ~ while moving. **oðóšimąðį**
way: by ~ of. **ha**
way: in the ~. **oðóši, wíohkaðį**
way: on the ~ to a certain point. **htáha**
way: other ~. **ámąhta**
way: that ~. **émąhta, šeeðǫ́ha**
way: the other ~. **ámąhtaha, ímąhtaha**
way: this ~. **ðeekáha**
way: this particular ~. **wįįðé**
way over there, way back in time or distance. **kootáįke**
ways. **ók?ą**
wayward. **eekǫ́ ðįké, íinǫǫhpaži, nǫhǫ, waðílą eekǫ́ įké**
w.c. (toilet). **ožéhci**
we. **ąkóta** (emphatic) (*see also* pronominal prefixes)
weak. **wahéhe**
wear. **áǫ, į́, oną́ąžį, ǫ́ǫ**
wear: have s.o. ~. **įkšíðe**
wear around the neck. **nǫp?į́**
wear on the head. **oolą́ke**
wear one's own. **álaha**
Wearing Bright Colors (personal name). **hį́įhkiąpi**
weary. **óžeðe**
weary: become or be ~ of s.t. **oðúuc?ake**
weather. **mą́ąɣe**
weather: warm, hot, or sunny ~. **mąąšcé**
wedding. **wéðuɣe**
wedding (term used by a friend or family of the bride). **wáðuɣe**
wedding (term used by a friend or family of the groom). **mį́įląke**

wedding hat: Osage ~ (a top hat with plumes optionally worn by the bride). **lǫǫhúu**
Wednesday. **hą́ąpa wéðaabrį**
weed. **hpéže**
week. **hą́ąpa wahkǫtáki**
weep. **ɣaaké**
weighted down. **skíke**
well (ADJ). **ókašéįke, sísi, tąhé**
well (ADV). **ðáalį**
well (INTERJ). **ehtą́, ną**
well (INTERJ) (often precedes a statement or command). **há**
well (of water). **níini**
well: be ~. **ní**
well: doing ~. **sísi**
well: get ~. **kiní, kítąhe, ónihkie**
west. **mįįáðee ehtáha**
west wind. **mǫ́ǫhahtáhu**
western tribe or tribal member (refers to any tribe from the western United States). **hpáðį**
wet. **toohká**
whachamacallit. **tą́ąska**
what. **haakǫ́**
what (interrogative), whatever. **táatą**
what: do ~ for. **háažǫ**
what for? (as a one-word question). **táatą**
what if. (*see* potential marker)
what if, what would you think if. **ną́htą**
what kind. **hǫ́ǫxcį, táatą**
what pathway: by ~. **howaįkíha**
what sort, type, or class of. **táatą**
what time. **mį́įoðaake háaną**
what time in the future: at ~. **haatxą́ta**
what time in the past: at ~. **haatxą́ci**
what-do-you-call-it. **tą́ąska**
whatever. **haakǫ́, táatą, táatą howachéeški**
whatever (thing). **howachéeški**
what's his/her name. **tą́ąska**
wheat, wheat field, wheat crop. **wapóške ówe**
wheel. **hcelį́**
wheel: automobile ~. **hcéðe**
wheelchair. **álįįhceðe**
when (ADV). **éetxą**
when (CONJ). **ðáha, pátą, šǫ́, tą**
when in the future. **haatxą́ta**
when in the past. **haatxą́ci**
whenever. **áha**
where, wherein, where at, where to, be where. **howáįki**
where: through ~. **howaįkíha**
wherever. **háaški**
wherever, be wherever. **howáįki**
whereupon. **áha, káakǫ tą**
which. **íma̧**
which, which one. **hówa**
which one: exactly ~. **hówaxcį**
which way (manner). **haakǫ́**
which way (path). **howaįkíha**
whichever one (inanimate). **howachéeški**
while. **šǫ́**
while, for a while, after a while, a little while. **katxą́**
whip, horse whip. **wékaaži**
whip strongly. **ochį́**
whipman, whip. **wanáše**
whirl. **-wįɣe**
Whirlwind (name of a character in an Osage fable). **htaacéžį**
whiskers. **hį́į, į́hį aok**
whistle. **opíɣą**
white. **ská**
white hair (of the head). **hpahį́įska**
white man's language. **įįštáxį íe**
White Mountain (personal name). **paaxóska**
white person (Caucasian). **įįštáxį, mą́ąhį htą́ą** [archaic or rare], **xuháaska**
whiten. **skákaaɣe**
whizzing sound. **htáhtaze**
who, whom. **pée**
who all. **pée háaną**
whoever. **howaðéeški**
whole. **bróka, záani**
wholesale. **bróka**
whoop (N) (applies only to the noise women make). **oðáaze**
whoop (V). **ðaazó, hóosaaki**
whooping cough. **hóxpe hpíiži, hóxpe zúpe**
whose. **pée íhta**
who's-it. **tą́ąska**
why. **háakǫta**
why: that is ~. **éetana**
Wichita (tribe or tribal member). **wícihta**
wicked. **hpíiži, hǫ́ǫži**
wide. **lą́ąðe**
wide and smooth, as a prairie. **bráaða**
widower. **wakˀó ðįké**
wife. **wakˀó (wíhta)** 'my wife' (**wižį́ke iihǫ́**, or son's name + **iihǫ́**, can be used if the couple's oldest child is a boy; **wižǫ́ke iihǫ́** can be used if their oldest child is a girl; **wihtą́ke** 'my sister' can be used when there are no children), **ðiwákˀo** or **wakˀó ðíhta** 'your wife', **iwákˀo** 'his wife'; **ilǫ́ǫhpa iihǫ́** 'my/your/his wife'; **wakˀó** 'wife'
wife: take a ~. **mį́įlą̧ke**

wife: take as a ~. **lą́ke**
wife stealer. **wakʔó mąąðǫ́štą**
wild: not ~. **wacʔéka**
wild horse. **hkáwa wahcéxi**
wildcat. **ilǫ́ǫka**
will (mind). **wažį́**
willing: be ~ (to). **iiną́hi**
willow. **mǫ́ǫsi céɣe**
win *(intr.)*. **íiðį, óhi**
win *(trans.)*. **ohí**
win over s.o. in a race. **káaxa**
wind. **htaacé**
wind: break ~. **ðiipíɣą**
wind: get ~ of. **opéni**
wind: strong or violent ~. **htaacé saakí**
wind instrument. **opíɣą**
window, window glass. **okáhąpa**
window shade. **akáaspe, okáhąpa akáspe**
windstorm. **htaacé hpííži, htaacé óhesaži, htaacé saakí**
windy: be ~. **htaacé saakí**
wing. **áahu**
wink (at). **iištáðe ðiitóže**
wink at each other. **iištáðe ahkíliitože**
Winnebago (Hochunk) (tribe or tribal member). **hóhtąka**
Winnebago (Hochunk) language. **hóhtąka íe**
winner: be the ~. **óhi**
winner: habitual ~ (one who wins constantly or repeatedly). **óhištą**
winnings. **okšéhtą**
winter. **paðé**
wipe (any surface). **kaací**
wipe clean (after using the toilet). **kaací**
wipe off. **púkxa**
wipe one's hands. **šáake ípukxa**
wipe oneself (in the bathroom, after using the toilet). **hkíaci**
wipe to clean or remove dust. **púkxa**
wipe with. **ípukxa**
wire. **mą́ze**
wire: send by ~. **mą́zekʔąsaaki ðée káaɣe**
wire: telegraph. **mą́zekʔąsaaki**
wire brush. **wákaapše**
wise. **waðílą ochí**
wish *(trans.)*. **íðilą**
with. **í-, žóle**
with: be, come, or go ~. **žóle**
with: be ~ each other. **žóhkile**
with: be ~ one's own people. **žókile**
with: go ~. **oðáhaaðee**
wither. **púze**
within: live ~ (e.g., a person's heart). **olį́į**
without: be ~. **ðįké, níðe**
witness: be a ~. **wawépahǫ**
wobble. **sísiąðe**
wolf. **šǫ́ke,**
Wolf (personal name). **šǫ́mįhkase**
woman. **wakʔó**
woman: elderly ~. **wakʔóžį**
woman: married ~. **wakʔó wéðuɣe**
woman (used in personal names). **wį**
woman of bad reputation. **wakʔó nǫǫhǫ́**
woman of the night (possibly a clan name?). **hą́ą tą wakʔó**
womanly. **wakʔó éekǫ**
wonder: I ~ (in speculative questions). **ną** [INTERJ]
wonderful. **tąhé**
woo. **ðílą**
wood. **žą́ą**
wood: fire-making ~. **žą́ąhpeece**
wooden spoon. **žą́ąhcuke**
woodpecker. **žą́ą káahtahta**
woods. **žą́ą**
woods: live in the ~. **žą́ą olį́į**
word, words. **íe**
word: get ~ of. **opéni**
word: one's ~. **íe**
words: clear ~. **íe waská, íeska**
work (N). **oðíhtą, waðíhtą**
work: do ~. **waðíhtą**
work for. **áwaši**
work meat with the hand. **htaaðíihtą**
work s.t. with the hand. **ðiihtą́**
workaholic (one who works all the time). **waðíhtąštą**
worker: have the qualities of a good ~. **wahtóke**
worker: hired ~. **waší, wašížį**
workplace. **waðíhtą**
workshop (for practicing or learning). **íkʔuce**
world. **mą́žą**
world, all the world. **níǫhta záani**
world, whole world. **mą́žą záani**
world: upper ~. **mą́ąɣe**
worm. **htamá, walúška, wáxta**
worn, worn out (said of clothing). **cúuða**
worn out (tired). **kaaskíke**
worried: not ~. **škaškáða**
worry (N). **waðílą waxpáðį**
worry about. **óðąąceši**
worry about s.t. verbally (as in a business meeting). **óie**
worse. **óhesaži**

worst: be the ~. **ochí**
worth: be ~ looking at. **tǫ́pewaðe**
worthless. **óškika**
worthless thing. **mą́ąhpiiži**
would. **ðąąché** (*see also* potential marker)
would be. (*see* potential marker)
wrap (V). **oðíši**
wrap one's arms around. **áace**
wrap stuff as a bundle. **ópetxą**
wrap up. **ápetxa**
wrap up s.t. specific. **opétxą**
wrapping, wrapper. **ápetxa**
wrestle one another. **mą́hkisǫce**
wrinkle (N). **cˀį́ða**
wrinkled. **xúuða**
write a letter to s.o. **wáleze wį kšíɣe**
write s.t. **páaleze**
writer: be a ~. **wápaleze káaɣe**
writing (such as a letter). **wápaleze**
wrong: what is ~ with. **haakǫ́**
wrong. **ée htáhaži, ékǫži, íhtaháaži**
wrongful, wrongly. **ókˀą ekǫ́ži**
wrongful acts (such as bad talk or theft). **ókˀą éži**
wrongheaded: be ~. **ókˀą éži**
wrong side out: turn ~. **ðuháašįðe**

yam (sweet potato). **tooscée, tóoskue, tóožuuce**
yard: by the ~ (fabric). **bróka**
yard (lawn). **oštá**
yardstick. **žą́ą wéðaawa**
yarn. **wahą́**
yarn belt: woman's ~. **hceehį́į**
yarnwork (as product or activity). **wahą́ káaɣe**
year. **omą́įhka**
yearly. **omą́įhka wį hieną**
yell. **hóohtą, pą́**
yellow. **zí, zíhi**
yes (female speaking). **ą́ą, ąhą́į**
yes (male speaking). **howé**
yes (response when listening to a story). **hąąé**
yesterday. **sitǫ́į**
yolk of an egg. **hpáatazi**
yonder. **kootáha, kootáįke**
yonkapin. **hcéwa**
you. **ðíe** (emphatic) (*see also* pronominal prefixes)
you know? (INTERJ). **hį́**
you only. **ðíną**
young. **wahókˀa**
young men. **nǫ́hǫžį**
young person or people. **hcéka nǫ́ǫ**
your(s). **ðíhta, ðíhtaapi** (*see also* pronominal prefixes; suus prefix)
yourself, yourselves. (*see* reflexive prefix)
youth (young person or people). **hcéka nǫ́ǫ**

zigzag. **pažážaki**
zip. **oðíiną**

Printed in the USA
CPSIA information can be obtained
at www.ICGtesting.com
LVHW070842100124
768548LV00012B/516

9 780806 138442

GENERAL CHAMBERLIN:

America's Equestrian Genius
The US Cavalry's Greatest Horseman
and The Evolution of American Horsemanship

XENOPHON PRESS

GENERAL CHAMBERLIN:

America's Equestrian Genius
The US Cavalry's Greatest Horseman
and
The Evolution of American Horsemanship

A BIOGRAPHY OF HARRY DWIGHT CHAMBERLIN,
BRIGADIER GENERAL OF CAVALRY, UNITED STATES ARMY

XENOPHON PRESS

Photos of the Inter-Allied Games of 1919 and the practice sessions related to those games are private photos that reside in the author's private collection.

All quotations from *A Life of Duty, The Autobiography of George Willcox McIver 1858-1947 Edited by Jonathan Dembo* are printed with the permission of the publisher The History Press, Charleston, South Carolina 29403

All re-prints of articles from *The Cavalry Journal* are with permission from The US Cavalry and Armor Association. The reprints of other Chamberlin articles and monographs reside in the public domain in that they were originally printed at US Government expense via *The Rasp* or as US Army training materials.

The extended quotation printed under the heading "A Remembrance" is an excerpt from a memorial to General Chamberlin and is printed with the permission of the West Point Association of Graduates.

Extended quotations from the works of Jean-Claude Racinet are used with the permission of the publisher Xenophon Press.

The photos of the various Olympic competitions in which Chamberlin participated are used with the permission of the US Olympic Committee. Other photos supplied by the United States Equestrian Team Foundation are re-printed here with the Foundation's permission. Other photos reside in the public domain or are photos of the US Army Signal Corps.

Published by Xenophon Press LLC
7518 Bayside Road, Franktown Virginia 23413
XenophonPress@gmail.com

ISBN: 9781948717236

Cover photo: Major Chamberlin on Tanbark jumping a 5'3" gate fronted by a 3' wide hedge as they train for the Olympics of 1932.

***Figure 1** In the mid-1930s, then Lt. Colonel Harry D. Chamberlin rides in a Pariani Borsarelli model 320 saddle. Here, Chamberlin "rides in the stirrups." His seat remains continuously out of the saddle. His hip joints remain flexed. Photo courtesy of Ms. Lydia Moore.*

Each day from August 1939 through early March 1942, first Colonel and then Brigadier General Harry Dwight Chamberlin rides his horse from his quarters on the main post at Ft. Riley to his headquarters at the main post and later either to Camp Funston or to Camp Forsyth, both also at Ft. Riley. On his way home, at about the same time each late afternoon, he passes the home of a sergeant, the sergeant's wife, and their young son.

More than sixty years later, the son recalls that Chamberlin's face displays the heavy burdens and responsibilities that he shoulders. The son also recalls that every Friday afternoon, his mother waits for Chamberlin to pass by. Without fail, she bakes an apple, peach, or strawberry pie for the general. She presents it to him to take home to his family. She really does not know Chamberlin. She only knows *of* him. He is an officer admired in the enlisted ranks as well as in the officer corps. He is known as an excellent and fair officer and the great horseman who brought Olympic and other international honors to the cavalry. With her pies, she shows her admiration and respect and that of her husband as well. The son recalls that for his father and mother and for all of their friends who serve in the cavalry at Ft. Riley, Brigadier General Chamberlin remains a source of great pride; in fact, everyone in the cavalry knows of him, respects him, and admires him.

Dedication

To my father, Warren E. Matha
Staff Sargent, 2nd Squadron, 5th US Cavalry, First Brigade, 1st Cavalry Division
And

To the other cavalrymen of the 2nd Squadron, 5th US Cavalry who landed on an island named Los Negros in the Admiralty Island chain of the Bismarck Archipelago. There, on the morning of February 29, 1944, the 2nd Squadron's 800 troopers land, with General Douglas MacArthur personally commanding. Brig. General William C. Chase leads the assault. The 800 troopers, together with another 200 support troops, fight to hold the island beach-head for four days and three nights without sleep. Re-supplied by air, with their backs to the sea, with no chance to evacuate, the 800 fight to hold the beachhead against 4,500 Japanese fanatics.

On the third day, the 1st Squadron of the 5th Cavalry joins them. Still without sleep, the troopers of the 2nd Squadron continue to fight infiltrators by day and to fight off charge after charge each night. On the third night, the cavalry's machine gun barrels melt. Out of ammunition, riflemen use their rifles as clubs; others fight with knives and bayonets. The Japanese penetrate the American lines at a dozen places. Still the 5th Cavalry holds. One 2nd Squadron trooper, Sgt. Troy McGill, will receive, posthumously, the Medal of Honor for his heroism that night. Relief finally arrives late afternoon of the fourth day. Only then, do the troopers of the 2nd Squadron sleep. The 5th Cavalry's achievement makes the liberation of the Philippines possible. Of all the actions in the Pacific War, General MacArthur says the 5th Cavalry's achievement on Los Negros Island fills him with the most pride. He personally chose them for the mission.

On October 20, 1944, a reinforced 2nd Squadron assaults the island of Leyte. There they fight for 71 straight days in the mud and mountains against an enemy who refuses to surrender. They suffer 50 percent casualties. Without rest, refitting, or reinforcement, the remaining 400, as part of the 1st Cavalry Division, land on the island of Luzon. The next day, MacArthur looks to them again: he selects the 400 of the 2nd Squadron, 5th Cavalry to lead "a flying column" of 800 troopers and a tank battalion to dash 100 miles behind enemy lines to Manila to rescue almost 4,000 men, women, and children prisoners of the Japanese just hours before their guards are to burn them alive. The troopers of the 2nd Squadron 5th, along with 400 troopers of the 2nd Squadron 8th Cavalry, kill the guards, secure the prison, and protect the prisoners for four days as 16,000 Japanese begin to destroy Manila around them. On the fourth day, the main US forces arrive. Thereafter, the 2nd Squadron fights in the Battle of Manila, block by block, building by building, floor by floor, room by room to crush the Japanese resistance and to secure the city.

For action on Los Negros, the 2nd Squadron, 5th US Cavalry, receives a Presidential Unit Citation with Arrowhead, the highest honor the President of the United States may bestow and an honor, for each trooper, second only to the Medal of Honor. In 1939, Army Chief of Staff Malin Craig says that the 1st Cavalry Division is the Army's best trained. At that time, the core of the 2nd Squadron's professional soldiers trains under the officer responsible for Division-wide training; that officer's name: Col. Harry Dwight Chamberlin.

Foreword

One of the biggest regrets of my life, and I mean this from my heart, is that I did not meet Harry Chamberlin, ride with Chamberlin, be a pupil of Chamberlin. Unfortunately, I was born a good twenty years too late.

Oh, how I would have loved to have been a resident at the Cavalry School at Fort Riley, Kansas during the 1920s and 1930s. How I would have loved to be indoctrinated by Chamberlin with the principles of the French School (Saumur) and the Italian School (Pinerolo and Tor di Quinto); perhaps with a bit of Hanover (German) and Weedon (English) thrown in.

Luckily, we have a man today, Warren C. Matha, who is so convinced and dedicated to Harry Chamberlin that he has made it his life's work, his passion, his obsession to bring this equestrian genius back to us. If it were not for Mr. Matha, Chamberlin would recede into history as only a dim memory, the only tether being his brilliant literature. With Mr. Matha's biography, we have a tangible reference that makes Chamberlin relevant now in the twenty-first century. We are now able to really know Chamberlin.

Harry Chamberlin has to go down in history as America's greatest horseman. There really is no contest. Not only was he a great rider (medalist Olympic Games) be it on a show jumper, event horse, dressage horse, hunter, polo pony, race horse, but he was the consummate horseman. This man understood the points of the horse, conformation, soundness, ailments, horse management, veterinary science, horseshoeing better than most.

Obviously, through his results and literature, he became a great horse trainer. And because of this man's intellect, horse background, and education he became a great instructor. So when you take all of these abilities combined, and then add his ability to transfer his knowledge through the written word (his books are the best!), Chamberlin must go to the top of the list.

Even if America and the world doesn't know it (and most don't), our country's incredible and consistent success in international competition,

World Championships, Pan American and Olympic Games, in all disciplines, traces back to Fort Riley and to Harry Chamberlin.

In my opinion, this one man is the founding father of equestrian sport in the United States. And the United States has had a tremendous influence on the sport over the last sixty years, especially in riding methodology in show jumping.

And I thank Warren Matha for his tremendous effort in giving us Chamberlin. I have been on the fringe of his work for some time and know that it has been a labor of love. My hat goes off to him. And may Brigadier General Harry Dwight Chamberlin never be forgotten.

George H. Morris
Wellington, Florida
2019

Foreword

I stand only one degree of separation from Brig. Gen. Harry D. Chamberlin. My father and most of his friends—my 'Dutch Uncles'—were students of his. I therefore grew up immersed in his techniques and teachings without knowing it. During that period, my father and others often spoke of "Col. Chamberlin." All the members of the US Army horse show team knew very well that Chamberlin had reached high rank during World War II, but that was their nickname for him, always said with respect and approval. I never heard a comment from any of his students that implied that his behavior was less than admirable, or his judgment regarding any matters of the horse was somehow lacking. To a man, they spoke of his riding as being on a higher plane than they could ever achieve.

For instance, when I asked one of my Dutch Uncles, Gen. Frank Henry, about the practice of "timing" (a technique by which the rider selects a take-off spot for his horse before a jump), Gen. Henry said, "Oh, you mean 'hand riding.' Col. Chamberlin would never let us hand ride." Gen. Henry paused a moment, chuckled, and said, "But Col. Chamberlin was doing something different." By this he meant it was widely known that Chamberlin, in addition to all his other gifts, was possessed of an uncanny ability to predict his stride long before his horse did, and to arrange things so that the horse got to the jump in the correct place without knowing that his rider had predetermined that takeoff spot.

By the time I became aware of such things, these students of Col. Chamberlin were coming to the end of their army careers, or were already retired. They were Olympic veterans with medals on their walls to prove it, and world-famous horsemen in their own right. In addition, they were members of the "Greatest Generation," survivors of a global conflict that took so many of their West Point classmates. They had other medals as well—Purple Hearts, Silver Stars, and Distinguished Service Crosses—but these were never mentioned or displayed. I learned of such awards for extraordinary bravery in combat from these men's obituaries.

What they loved to speak about, and practice, and possibly most importantly to teach, was their system—Col. Chamberlin's system. What a system it was, and remains to this day, as Warren Matha makes clear in this extraordinary book. He explains in detail how one man traveled the world to study and learn about riding and training horses, and then returned home to synthesize what he had learned into a new approach toward those subjects.

It takes a certain amount of genius, not just to see what others have seen, but to say things others have never said. Chamberlin started writing about what he had learned in the 1920s, and continued writing until the outbreak of WWII. Much of his fame is based on those writings and his literary work reminds us of the power of the simple declarative sentence. Before publication, Chamberlin sent his manuscript to a non-riding friend, with instructions to mark any passage in which the actions of the rider were not understood. Writing in clear, understandable prose, Chamberlin laid out his system, a system still in use nearly a century later. Until that time such a unique combination of techniques had never been seen ; indeed it was a combination that horse world experts of the era said would not work. Not only could Chamberlin, a genius in the saddle, make it work, but his students and their students could make it work. He was the leading light of the military horse world for three decades, and his influence continues to the present day.

Seminal figures in the civilian horse world, who succeeded the military horse show teams, applied his techniques; we can trace a clear path from Chamberlin to Gordon Wright, on through world-famous riders such as George Morris, Bill Steinkraus, Frank Chapot, Mike Plumb, Michael Page, Kevin Freemen, right up to today. I have been riding and teaching for half a century, and can safely say not a day goes by without my quoting from one of Chamberlin's works, or applying his methods. We are the beneficiaries of Col. Chamberlin's genius, and horses around the world live far more comfortable and productive lives because of his work. With his writings and teachings, Chamberlin satisfied one of the most sacred duties of a horseman: He produced a system of riding and training that truly preserves "the tranquility of the horse."

James Wofford
Fox Covert
Upperville, Virginia
2019

Introduction

By
Lieutenant-Colonel Louis A. DiMarco
US Army (Retired) PhD.
Author of
War Horse: A History of the Military Horse and Rider (2008)
Concrete Hell: Urban Warfare from Stalingrad to Iraq (2017)

Beyond his horsemanship, in an era that produced the greatest crop of outstanding soldiers in America's history, Harry Chamberlin was a soldier's soldier. His peers, men whose names will forever be associated with the great American military that won World War II, Marshall, MacArthur, Eisenhower, Bradley, Patton and Truscott among many others, respected him, admired him, and valued him as a colleague and friend. This personal and professional respect was not because of their admiration for him as a horseman but rather because of his abilities as an Army officer and leader.

Several factors make up the ideal soldier. One of them is leadership. Leadership is the art of motivating others to work hard and accomplish sometimes unpleasant tasks under often adverse conditions, and have them do it willingly. A good leader builds on the talents of his subordinates and helps them exceed what they believe they are capable of. Chamberlin's leadership is evident in all that he did—and more, it echoes in the respect and regard that his subordinates had for him. He was a natural coach and mentor who treated everyone with whom he came into contact with respect. His influence on training methods and the ability to pass his knowledge on to others distinguishes him from being merely a talented rider. In the Army, no higher praise can be made of an army officer's leadership than the respect and admiration of the sergeants who served with them, and thus at the end of his career the loyalty of Staff Sergeant Noble is representative of the type of loyalty only the best leaders inspire.

Another characteristic of the soldier is service and sacrifice. A military life is full of sacrifices and compromises of self for the good of the organization, fellow soldiers and country. Chamberlin's life and career represents the price one pays in service to the country: years away from the United States in dangerous and less than ideal surroundings including combat zones in France in World War I and the Pacific in World War II. As a horse cavalryman, life in the field was months of hard riding and hard living in rugged conditions without shelter and in many cases adequate food and water. Long separations from family were the norm. Throughout his career, Chamberlin sought out dangerous assignments and active service. He wanted to be in the midst of the action.

A final attribute of the ideal professional soldier is technical and tactical competence. Harry Chamberlin is renown today for his insights, theories and contributions to the art and science of equestrian sport. What often is under-appreciated is that to Chamberlin and the Army of his time, the goal of equestrian excellence was not about sport, sport was merely a way of demonstrating the true objective—military technical and tactical excellence. To cavalrymen like Chamberlin horsemanship did not win cups and trophies, it won battles and wars. Training the horse and rider was not about athletic achievement, it was about the ability to maneuver on the battlefield, the ability to march long distances, the ability to carry weight over difficult terrain, and finally about the ability to mass hundreds of horses and riders in precise formations, under disciplined control in order to harness the speed, shock, and power of the horse to deliver the critical cavalry charge at just the right time and place to achieve victory. This was the ultimate goal of Chamberlin's study and practice and why his horsemanship was so professionally admired by his peers, subordinates and superiors. Harry Chamberlin's superior horsemanship translated directly into the abilities of the US Army, and the US Cavalry in particular, to fight and win the nation's wars.

Harry Chamberlin left a legacy of equestrian excellence and knowledge that continues to influence equestrians all over the world. His stamp in the US military is more modest but equally important. He represents the model military professional: a caring leader who set the example in all things for his subordinates; a soldier who put duty first and made the sacrifices and bore the burdens of a life of service to his country; and finally, the expert professional whose tactical and technical knowledge, whose expert horsemanship and training methods, had the primary purpose of contributing to the ability of the US military to support and defend the interests of the citizens of his country. In this regard, Harry Chamberlin was an outstanding professional, perhaps the greatest American equestrian, and finally, a great American.

I am profoundly grateful that Warren Matha has devoted so much time and effort to presenting the truly inspiring story of a particularly great leader, soldier, and horseman.

Louis A. DiMarco,
Lieutenant Colonel, US Army
(Retired), PhD
2019

Acknowledgements

I must thank so many people I fear that I may leave someone out. If I do, then please forgive me. I thank General Chamberlin's daughter Ms. Lydia Moore and his granddaughter Ms. Tracey Reese Brown for their help, photos, and General Chamberlin's letters. Thanks also to Ms. Marianne Murphy of London, England for sending me the letters of her uncle, Sgt. Reginald Noble; to Mr. Jack Wetzel and the late Mr. Bruce Duchossois for their friendship and encouragement regarding this biography; to Mr. James Wofford for his insights, recommendations, and encouragement. I would have never finished this book were it not for Mr. Wofford's encouragement and for reading an early draft of this biography. So too, I thank the late Mr. William Steinkraus for his insights and guidance; Mr. George H. Morris, for his interest, encouragement, and for his kind words in the Foreword to this book as well as for writing *The American Jumping Style* which inspired me to delve deeper into work of the US Cavalry officers who influenced that style. I also thank Lt. Col. Louis DiMarco, (retired) PhD historian at the US Army's Command and General Staff School at Fort Leavenworth, Kansas for his insights, encouragement, and for reading the book and for writing the Introduction to this biography.

Thanks go to Thomas Poulin for the many hours that he shared with me discussing François Baucher, Étienne Beudant, as well as the art of dressage; to Mrs. Paul A. (Dodie) Seymour, Jr. for the photos and recollections she shared; to Sharon Poulin for all of my hours on a longing line; to the late Jean Claude Racinet for his time in explaining to me his views on the French seat, the theories of François Baucher, and the glories of French equitation in general; to Robert d'Artois, the Director of the French National Riding School at Saumur, for his insights regarding the *Cadre Noir* and the Cavalry School at Saumur when I visited in 2009; to the librarians at the Texas A&M University and the University of Florida for guiding me through ancient records, journal articles, and newspapers; to Ms. Pam Bell of the United

States Cavalry Association; to Lt. Col. Mark S. Gavula (retired.), Executive Director of the US Cavalry and Armor Association; to the members of the Society of the Military Horse; to the staffs of: the US Army's *Artillery Journal*, the magazine *Armor*; the United States Olympic Committee, the United States Equestrian Team Foundation, the Association of West Point Graduates, the United States Military Academy at West Point, the George C. Marshall Foundation; the Elgin Illinois Historical Society; the German National Riding School at Warendorf, Germany. Thanks go to Robert Matha for trudging through drafts of this book and making so many corrections and suggestions, I hazard to guess at how many.

Thanks also to Richard Williams of Xenophon Press for publishing all of this. And last but not least: thanks to my late father, Warren E. Matha, Staff Sgt. 2nd Squadron, 5th US Cavalry, who shared with me his experiences as an 18-year-old recruit in a squad of "A" Troop, 1st Squadron, First Training Regiment at Fort Riley's Cavalry Replacement Training Center in 1942; his recollections of the last days of the horse-mounted US Cavalry; his recollections of Drill Sgt. William Offill, Gen. Innis Palmer Swift, and Col. Hiram Tuttle; his memories of the cavalry Sergeants at Fort Bliss who recounted their days pursuing Pancho Villa into Mexico; and above all, for his recommendation, when I was about fourteen years old, that I study the teachings of Army *Field Manual 25-5, Animal Transport: Horsemanship and Horsemastership 1942 Edition,* the US Cavalry's bible. In no way am I qualified to be called a "horseman." So, I am sure that mistakes arise here and there. When you find them, please forgive me. All mistakes that you find arise from me and from me only.

Warren C. Matha

Author's Note

By
Warren C. Matha

As you read this book, you will share time with a remarkable man—the greatest equestrian in American history; and most certainly, a man of genius, a distinguished officer in the United States Army; a doting father, and a loving husband. A look at his life instructs and inspires from any vantage point. Among even the most informed equestrians, however, Harry Chamberlin remains a figure of vague legend about whom very little is known. In the John Ford film, *Who Shot Liberty Valance?* an actor says: "When the legend become fact, print the legend." In Chamberlin's case, the facts prove far more inspiring and exciting than whatever legend attaches to his name.

My main purposes here are to survey his life as it relates to his contributions to horsemanship and to equestrian sport; and then, to put his contributions in historical context. The information you will find concerning horsemanship will offer value to any serious equestrian. The descriptions of the "Chamberlin Seat," of the approaches for caring for horses, and of the techniques for training them remain worthy of strong consideration. Context remains, however, important in that consideration.

Harry Dwight Chamberlin did not toy casually with horses as a dilettante. He did not casually discover his approaches to horsemanship, nor did he simply adopt the teachings of others or follow long standing norms. During the better part of his life, he studies, learns, tests, integrates, applies, questions anew, and then transcends the equestrian concepts of masters and schools throughout Europe as well as America. All of this effort, he pursues for one overriding purpose: to maximize the mobility of horse and trooper for the twentieth-century United States Cavalry.

Even before Chamberlin's time as a cavalryman and until the early years of World War II, the horse mounted US Cavalry performed service integral to American defense. The Cavalry protected the southern border of the country on a continuous basis until 1943. In 1916, the Cavalry pursued the Mexican revolutionary and border raider Pancho Villa for more than 1,000 miles round trip over some of the most difficult terrain on the planet. For the first half of the twentieth century, the Cavalry prepared for battle in theaters ranging from the Philippine Islands to Italy, from the plains of central Europe to the mountains of the Sierra Madre. Horses and troopers regularly crossed rivers and streams; climbed and overcame hills and cliffs; navigated forests, swamps, marshes, grasslands, mountains, and deserts. At all times, regardless of terrain and weather, the Cavalry kept its horses fit and its cavalrymen ready to give battle. The US Cavalry was the greatest long distance riding force of the mid-nineteenth and the early twentieth centuries.

The preparation, training, and style of riding developed over time by Chamberlin and the US Cavalry influences every aspect of present-day casual riding and competitive horsemanship in the sports of Eventing, Show Jumping, Endurance riding and more. Tom Dorrance, of Western horsemanship and teaching, attributes many of his own concepts to Harry Chamberlin's influence. While Harry Chamberlin and the US Cavalry did not develop their approaches to horsemanship primarily to win Olympic medals, they enabled the Cavalry's officers to do so and, after the horse-mounted cavalry's passing, they enabled others to do so.

With this context in mind, you will find included in this biography snap shots of the history surrounding the evolution of equestrian thinking during Chamberlin's life. This thinking greatly influences horsemanship to this day. You will find Chamberlin's professional writings about horsemanship. You will find many of Chamberlin's own letters to home during the early days of World War II. Those letters deal with the stress of his responsibilities in the earliest days of his country's most terrible war, and most of all, with the stress of perhaps never seeing his wife and two little girls again.

You will find snapshot appraisals of Chamberlin's personality, abilities, and accomplishments presented by his peers, subordinates, and superior officers as well as by horsemen who knew him or who followed him long after his passing. As you learn of his equestrian life, keep in mind that first and foremost, Harry Chamberlin was a father and husband as well as a soldier. And as you read you may begin to wonder more and more about the man in each of those roles.

In addition, in this biography and in its companion volume, *The Chamberlin Reader*, you will see many photos, of Chamberlin, of the US Cavalry, of the Olympics of 1932, but also of the Inter-Allied Games of 1919 which were a turning point in not only Chamberlin's equestrian career, but in the horsemanship of the US Cavalry. To my knowledge, these photos from 1919 have not been published previously. You also will find in *The Chamberlin Reader,* a rare booklet published in 1923 by the French Cavalry School at Saumur at the very time Chamberlin studied there. A fellow officer brought the booklet to the United States shortly after World War I. We include all of these items in the hope that, as snapshots of history, they will survive and be enjoyed by equestrians everywhere.

You also will find in *The Chamberlin Reader* the US Cavalry's protocol for long distance riding distributed in 1942, the Cavalry's checklists to evaluate horses for purchase and for hoof care, as well as the foundation text for horse training used by the Cavalry's Mounted Service School and distributed in 1912. Each of these offers practical knowledge valuable to this day.

To help you navigate the biography, the table of contents that follows provides a map of highlights: of equestrian theory and technique, of the historical background, and of the key turning points in Brigadier General Harry D. Chamberlin's life. I respect the man immensely and treasure my time with him. The study of his life took me to parts of the United States, France, Germany, and the Philippine Islands. It remains a privilege to share what I learned about him with you.

Warren C. Matha
New Port Richey,
Florida
2019

Contents

PHOTOS AND ILLUSTRATIONS

A Remembrance

"He was a most gallant officer and the spirit of West Point was strongly entrenched in his being."

Everyone who knew Harry Chamberlin was immediately impressed by his enormous personality and charm. He was one of the most widely known and most talked of officers in the Army. In addition to his great ability and brillance as an officer, which his record amply proves, he had the rare quality of making and holding friends, to which his wonderful sense of humor and dry wit added in no small degree.

His joy of life was so infectious that he lent a zest to every activity in which he took part. He had an innate kindliness and wanted everyone to enjoy himself whether at work or play. He was intensely loyal to the Army and to his friends and subordinates.

His sense of fair play was paramount; he was never spiteful, was absolutely open-minded and at the same time set the highest of standards; so high, in fact, that occasionally some of his subordinates could not "make the grade;" corrective measures were promptly and habitually taken. His many years of service at Fort Riley contributed in no small way to the character and atmosphere of that post.

He was a most gallant officer and the spirit of West Point was strongly entrenched in his being. He never complained about any "job" he had to do, no matter how dour it might seem. Instead he put his whole heart into it and made it interesting and glamorous. His friends were legion—of all classes, types and nationalities. He had great ability in this respect for sizing up people for what they were and not merely for their station in life. He could, and did, associate with kings, and never lost the common touch. All will agree that there was never a dull moment when Harry was present. He worked hard when he worked and played with zest when he played. He will always be remembered for his outstanding accomplishments and by many anecdotes and bon mots connected with his life…

The above resume…was compiled and written by one who has been associated with him for nearly 25 years. He has been my brother officer, commanding officer, commanding General, and above all, my devoted friend. My association with him, in each of the aforementioned capacities, has been an inspiration and has enriched my life. His loss, to me, can never be replaced.

—B. P [1]
1944

1 Excerpt reproduced with the permission of The Association of West Point Graduates. The author of the document is known only as B.P. See Association of West Point Graduates https://www.westpointaog.org/memorial-article?id=f3efb07e-1306-45c3-86dd-780dd099a6a0

Chapter 1

The Evening Before Major Chamberlin's Ride

"The finest horseman in the army...He was tall, handsome, a magnetic personality—the very beau ideal of a cavalryman." [2]
—General Lucian K. Truscott, Jr

"He was one of the ablest and most popular men in the Regular establishment..."
—General George C. Marshall [3]

Late in the evening of Saturday, the 13th of August 1932, the United States Cavalry's greatest horseman, Major Harry Dwight Chamberlin relaxes quietly and prepares his mind to meet the challenge of tomorrow's *Prix des Nations* stadium jumping competition. Tomorrow, he faces the most difficult jumping course in Olympic history.

All of Chamberlin's years as a horseman, all of his education, all of his training and experience prepare him for tomorrow's challenge. Tomorrow brings an event of particular significance: He rides in the last event, in the last Olympics of his equestrian career—for Chamberlin privately knows that tomorrow, as the sun sets over the Great Stadium, his Olympic riding career ends forever.

His military superiors require that he retire from international competition. He is 45 years old. His superiors consider him one of the more competent, respected, and well-liked younger officers in the Army. And

2 See General Lucian K. Truscott, Jr. *The Twilight of the US Cavalry. Life in the Old Army 1917-1942*, University Press of Kansas, 1989.

3 See Association of West Point Graduates https://www.westpointaog.org/memorial-article?id=f3efb07e-1306-45c3-86dd-780dd099a6a0

so, they order him to report to The Army War College in Washington, DC immediately after the Olympic Games conclude. Only the Army's elite study there. With this appointment, Major Chamberlin's role as rider-captain and trainer of the Army Equestrian Team draws to a close and the door to the Army's highest commands opens. His new appointment remains a coveted honor for any officer so chosen. But tomorrow's challenge looms large on his mind, most certainly.

From the day more than 35 years ago that his father Dwight buys him a horse, Chamberlin's athletic prowess remains well recognized. He is a natural athlete. Twenty-six years ago, he enters West Point where he boxes, swims, and plays football. He runs ninety-five yards on a punt return to set up a winning touchdown against Navy in 1908. This record remains the stuff of legend among the Army's West Point educated officer corps. Most of all, however, he excels at riding horses. On this August evening of 1932, his accomplishments as a horseman remain the stuff of legend in the US Cavalry and among others who ride and compete in the world of horses.

Only one other officer in the United States Army and very few others in the world equal Chamberlin's equestrian education and training; no other American and only a few riders internationally equal his range of experience and the height of his accomplishment. Chamberlin rides in childhood. He studies, in depth, all things equine at West Point. He then graduates first in his class from the basic and the advanced horsemanship courses at Fort Riley's Mounted Service School. Later, shortly after the Great War in which he serves near Verdun and in the Meuse-Argonne Offensive, he returns to his passion: horses.

As the US Army's official observer, he analyzes the riding and training methods of the French at Saumur, the Germans at Hannover, the Belgians at Ypres, and the British at Weedon. He studies. He evaluates. He synthesizes the riding, teaching, and training methods of each school. French lightness and German precision appeal to him.

Later still, as a "distinguished" graduate of Saumur, he understands and applies French dressage expertly. As a "distinguished" graduate of Tor di Quinto, he masters Italian forward riding. In every field of horsemanship, he proves himself a star student of rare athletic ability. On graduation day eight years ago at the Italian Cavalry's advanced school at Tor di Qunito, the school's Commandant takes Chamberlin's hand, presents a diploma, and says: "The pupil has surpassed his master." [4]

---

4 See Louis A. DiMarco, Major USA, *Brigadier General Harry D. Chamberlin, The Cavalry's Greatest Horseman 1887-1944*, unpublished manuscript.

Not only does he excel at equestrian academics and apply such concepts with a mastery that few others attain, Chamberlin develops his own theories of horsemanship. His "Chamberlin seat" modifies the Italian forward method to render the rider more secure and more precise with the aids. He applies French dressage to train jumpers and cavalry mounts, something the Italian theorists and many others refuse to do. Ultimately, Chamberlin synthesizes and then transcends the equestrian theories of France, Germany, Italy, and the United States to create a mode of riding and training that elevates the US Cavalry's horsemanship to its highest plain and, in the future, will influence Olympic riders throughout the world well into the twenty-first century. When one considers his career, one considers a genius not only in the development of theory but in its application as well.

So what might Chamberlin be thinking this night before his last Olympic ride? Certainly, he might reflect on the great victory won earlier today: The Chamberlin led and Chamberlin trained Three-Day Event team wins the Team Gold Medal for The Three-Day Event, the first Olympic Gold Medal ever won by an American equestrian team. The Americans dominate the event as they ride in the Chamberlin style on horses trained in the Chamberlin fashion. For the first time in Olympic history, a team other than one from Sweden or Holland wins the Team Gold Medal in Eventing. The American victory breaks the European lock on the sport.

Perhaps Chamberlin, on this night, thinks back on his many other experiences over the years. Only a few horsemen in the world come close to the wide range of his experience: In 1912, he rides with the 7th Cavalry in the Philippines where heat prostration causes cavalrymen to fall from their saddles. In 1916, he rides with the 5th Cavalry over 1,000 miles round-trip through Mexico under war-time conditions, over the most difficult terrain on earth, where temperatures soar to 120 degrees by day and canteens freeze solid at night. In 1919, at the Inter-Allied "Pershing" Games, he impresses all as a *Prix des Nations* and a Three-Day Event rider. In 1920, in the Olympics at Antwerp, he participates in all three equestrian disciplines: Dressage, the Three-Day Event, and the *Prix des Nations.*

In 1925 and 1926, he captains and trains the 8th Cavalry polo team. Chamberlin and his team win the national polo championship in both years (an Army first) and he achieves a three-goal (professional) handicap. In 1928, in the Olympics at Amsterdam, he competes in the *Prix des Nations,* where he comes under the eye of the President of the American Olympic Committee, Major General Douglas MacArthur (whose support proves crucial for the Olympics of 1932). Throughout the 1920s and into 1931, on his horses Nigra, Tanbark, Huron Girl, and Gary Owen, he defeats the finest horseman of Germany, Ireland, Poland, Holland, France and Britain in successive international show jumping competitions in America and in Europe. Chamberlin's jumping style proves so spectacular that Vladimir Littauer at the time tells his students: "...don't bother to try to go over obstacles the way Major Chamberlin does, because you will never be able to do it anyway..." [5]

Perhaps this evening before his last Olympic ride, Chamberlin reflects on just a few of his past victories: In 1928, at Madison Square Garden, out of eighteen riders who compete from the United States, Poland, Holland, Germany, Belgium, and Canada, only Chamberlin jumps a clean round. In 1929, to win the Challenge Cup against horsemen from Italy, Ireland, Poland, and Germany, he rides Gary Owen and wins the hunter class by achieving a flawless, clean round in record time. In 1930, at the Boston Horse Show, in a long drawn out battle between Chamberlin on Huron Girl and the German Army's Lt. Ernst Hasse on the gelding Elan, each rides a clean round. The judges raise and widen the jumps. After two jump-offs, each with higher and wider jumps, both riders and horses achieve clean rounds; in the third jump off, over still higher and wider jumps, Chamberlin and Huron Girl make it clear with no faults. Hass and Elan falter and topple a bar to the ground. Chamberlin wins the Millwood Hunt Challenge Trophy. In 1931, against some of the finest military horseman in the world, he wins the International Military Trophy at Madison Square Garden in what the New York Times describes as "*one of the most exciting performances in the history of the National Horse Show to date, Major Chamberlin on Tan Bark wins the International Military Stakes.*" [6]

Perhaps this evening Chamberlin thinks of the many officers who mentor him, support him, and contribute to this success. Chamberlin's superior officers—especially General Guy V. Henry, Jr., the Chief of Cavalry and General Douglas MacArthur, the Army Chief of Staff and Olympics enthusiast—in unprecedented fashion, put all of the resources of the United States Army behind Chamberlin and his team. MacArthur authorizes General Henry to support the team to the fullest extent possible. MacArthur delivers the entire resources of the Army: Officers all over the country search for talented horses. The Army Corps of Engineers constructs special facilities around the country that include jumping courses that Chamberlin designs.

---

5 See Vladimir S. Littauer, *Common Sense Horsemanship*, Second Edition, D. Van Nostrand Company, 1963.

6 See *New York Times* https://spiderbites.nytimes.com/1931/articles_1931_10_00000.html.

General Henry sponsors events across the country to qualify riders with the most potential for success. Never before and never again will the Army devote so much time, effort, personnel, construction resources, and money to such an endeavor. A year before the start of the Games, Chamberlin and his team work six days a week with only occasional breaks to prepare for the Olympics of 1932.

Chamberlin's traits as a leader prove perfect for the task. He recognizes a fact far too often neglected in the "brown-shoe US Army." He understands the difference between "command" and "leadership." In the Army of that day, many officers "teach" with insults, intimidation, fear, accusation and abuse. Chamberlin in his role as teacher offers praise. He forgives and encourages. He expects the highest standards of his charges. If a subordinate fails to meet his high expectations, Chamberlin goes out of his way to find a position for that man better suited to the man's abilities. From the time he first leads and trains cavalrymen as a Second Lieutenant until now as Captain of the Army's Equestrian Team, he builds the strongest organizations and inspires the greatest loyalty, friendship, and enthusiasm.

Perhaps Chamberlin thinks about those who will witness his team's performance a few hours from now. Tomorrow, so many luminaries will watch and cheer the American team on: Charles Curtis, the Vice-President of the United States; Jim Thorpe, against whom Chamberlin played football; General Guy Henry, his old West Point horsemanship instructor, mentor, and now Chief of Cavalry; everyone who is anyone in the horse world plus the elite of Hollywood; the millionaires of New York, Boston, Chicago, and Washington; and many others from the major cities of Europe as well.

Perhaps he thinks of the 100,000 or more other spectators who will fill the stands tomorrow and of his many friends and his superiors at posts all over the United States who will listen by radio once the radio blackout lifts including MacArthur, Patton, Swift, and Truscott.

Perhaps he thinks of his horse Tanbark, his splendid brown Thoroughbred gelding, at 15-3 hands, supremely athletic, intelligent, courageous, well experienced, and a jumper of immense scope and power. Of all the horses that Chamberlin rides over the years—Nigra, Gary Owen, Huron Girl, High Hat, and Tanbark, Tanbark proves best able to negotiate the difficult jumps that tomorrow presents.

So far, we have speculated about Chamberlin's thoughts. We know three things for certain: One, his prized jumper Tanbark rests lame in his stall. Two, Chamberlin knows that he must ride over a jumping course that he has not seen before—on a substitute horse on which he has not competed before. Some say that he has never jumped the horse before. And three, he knows that tomorrow presents his last chance to win the crowning glory of his equestrian career: The Gold Medal in the *Prix des Nations* stadium jumping competition, the last and the most dramatic event of the Olympic Games.

And so, on this Saturday evening, Major Chamberlin makes ready for his last Olympic ride.

Chapter 2

Major Chamberlin's Ride

"He was one of those rare individuals who excelled in everything that he did..."
—General George C. Marshall [7]

"...to come right down to it, don't bother to try to go over obstacles the way Major Harry Chamberlin does, because you will never be able to do it anyway..."
—Vladimir Littauer [8]

It is Sunday, August 14, 1932. On this morning of the last day of the Olympic Games of 1932, the captain, trainer, and star rider of the US Army's Olympic Equestrian team, Major Harry Dwight Chamberlin stands in the open window of his room at the Olympic Village outside of Los Angeles. He fills his lungs with fresh air as he completes his daily regimen of calisthenics. The air feels cool, fresh and clean; the weather remains perfect—a southern California day of mild temperature and low humidity with clear skies—ideal for the stadium jumping competition, known as the *Prix des Nations*, traditionally the last and most dramatic event of the Olympic Games.

As his morning routine of calisthenics progresses, his physical condition remains stellar: even under stress, his heart rate maintains at a steady fifty-five beats per minute; at 5'11" tall, he maintains his weight at 160 pounds,

---

7 See Association of West Point Graduates https://www.westpointaog.org/memorial-article?id=f3efb07e-1306-45c3-86dd-780dd099a6a0.

8 See Vladimir S. Littauer, *Common Sense Horsemanship*, Second Edition, D. Van Nostrand Company, 1963.

the insurance company ideal. At age 45, this tall, handsome, "beau ideal" of the US Cavalry remains at the height of his powers as a horseman.

He finishes his morning regimen of exercise and begins to dress. He dons his riding breeches, tailored in the pattern favored by British and American cavalry officers by Albert More and Company of Junction City, Kansas near Fort Riley. He pulls on his riding boots, shined to a mirror finish, custom made for him by R. Thomas and Son, LTD, St. James Street, London, the boot makers to the King of England.

As Chamberlin finishes dressing, he begins his last-minute mental preparation for his last appearance in Olympic competition. Tanbark was to carry Chamberlin in the *Prix des Nations* this day. But his prized jumper Tanbark came up lame and remains in his stall. So, Chamberlin focuses his concentration on Show Girl, the substitute horse. To scratch would be unthinkable. Show Girl, the team's only back-up, remains his only option. Some sources write that before this day, Chamberlin has not even taken a jump on Show Girl. At least (as far as we know), he has never ridden Show Girl in competition. How will the mare perform under the unique pressures of the Los Angeles Colosseum not to mention the most difficult jumping course in Olympic history? How will Chamberlin anticipate Show Girl's unique quirks? Regardless, Chamberlin knows that he has no choice. Show Girl it will be. And, as events unfold, Chamberlin, riding this gray mare, remains the only hope of the United States to win a Gold medal in the *Prix des Nations.*

Figure 2 *The Trumpets sound. The riders take to the field.*
Photo courtesy of the US Olympic Committee.

In the Great Stadium: Ten Olympic trumpets sound "Attention." The 105,000-spectator crowd falls silent. The procession of horses and riders begins. From each nation, the riders on their mounts trot onto the track of the Great Stadium. In rows of two's, three's, and four's they proceed: 53 riders in all. By nation, they enter in alphabetical order. First, the riders of France: Hector, Le Sage, Marion, Jousseaume; then the riders of Holland: Labouchere, de Mortanges, Schummelketel, Van Lennop; then, seven from Japan; ten from Mexico; eight from Sweden; and finally, nine riders from the United States of America by order of rank: Scott, Chamberlin, Bradford, Kitts, Argo, Tuttle, Moore, Wofford and Thomson.

As the United States Army Olympic Equestrian Team enters onto the track, perhaps ninety thousand or more spectators rise to their feet and yell out a deafening cheer and offer a standing ovation. Timers, starters, checkers, scorers, judges at jumps and in the official's box all prepare themselves for the *Prix des Nations*, the *Grande finale* of the Xth Olympiad.

THE *PRIX DES NATIONS*

"Horse, thou art truly a creature without equal,
for thou fly without wings and conquer without sword."
—Job 39:19-22

"This dramatic closing of one of the greatest of all Olympics took place...
in the hardest of all equestrian tests, harder than the Grand National."
—Grantland Rice, *L.A. Times* [9]

"...the two 1.60m fences, the wall and the five-meter
wide water jump were far too much."
—The International Olympic Committee [10]

The *Prix des Nations* competition of the Xth Olympiad, the greatest jumping event the people of the United States ever witness to date, begins. Lt. Colonel John A. Barry, US Cavalry, designs the most difficult *Prix des Nations* jumping course thus far experienced in Olympic history. In fact, it proves to be the most difficult in all of Olympic history.

9 See Grantland Rice, *Los Angeles Times* August 14, 1932.
10 See *The Official Report of the Games of the Xth Olympiad Los Angeles* 1932.

It extends 1060 meters (1150 yards) long. It consists of eighteen stiff obstacles. It demands twenty jumps. It presents jump heights between four-feet-three inches and five-feet three inches high and spreads as wide as sixteen-feet, five-inches. As one commentator writes: "A whirl-around of impressive fences, ditches and water." [11] The jumps remain much higher—at times, eight inches higher than any jumps riders face in 1928 or at any other previous Olympic competition.

The rules impose a time limit that requires horse and rider to travel at a gallop of 400 meters (437 yards) per minute to avoid a time penalty. They must clear an old-fashioned snake fence, a Tennessee stake, and then a rock fence; an oxer; a post and rail fence; an Aiken Brush; a water jump sixteen-feet five-inches wide; an obstacle consisting of a ditch with a bar and bank five-feet, three inches high followed by another bar; various kinds of gates and wide ditches; a chicken coop five-feet, three inches high "seeming to be as high as the Olympic peristyle, with its white sides appearing to protrude abruptly out of the green carpet of the stadium's floor," as the Grimes account states. [12] To clear a water-jump 16-feet and 5-inches wide requires the horse to leap 25 feet clear in order to land free of the water. The course presents obstacles more difficult than the Grand National Steeplechase.

Figure 3 *The International Olympic Committee writes that the two 1.6-meter fences, the 1.6-meter wall, and the five-meter wide water jump were far too much for Olympic competition. On a substitute horse, Chamberlin shows his mettle. Photo courtesy of the US Olympic Committee.*

11 See Major W.M. Grimes, Cavalry, "Equestrian Sports—Games of the Xth Olympiad," *The Field Artillery Journal*, Vol. XXII, September-October 1932, No. 5. p 477.

12 Ibid.

The competition begins. Riding first, the Mexican Army's Captain Bocanegra enters the course. Bocanegra approaches the first obstacle: clear. The second, third and fourth obstacle: clear. The fifth obstacle, a ditch and bank. The horse refuses. Bocanegra tries again. The horse refuses. He tries one more time. The horse refuses! Horse and rider eliminated.

Next, the United States Army's Lt. Wofford starts his ride on Babe Wartham. Wofford and Babe Wartham approach the first obstacle: clean. The second obstacle: clean. Obstacles three, four, five, six and seven: clean! On the eighth barrier, a ditch and bar, Babe Wartham leaps forward but falls back into the ditch. Lt. Wofford falls into the ditch with her. After what seems like eternity, the horse rises to her feet. Wofford climbs out of the ditch and remounts. The crowd goes wild with their cheers. Wofford and horse confront the ditch and bar again. They barely clear the top bar but clear it they do! Wofford and Babe Wartham continue. The horse refuses on fence number ten. On the second try, success! Babe refuses again on number eleven! Three refusals. Wofford and Babe Wartham: eliminated. The Jury allows them, however, to complete the course which they do. Over 100,000 voices cheer their approval.

Figure 4 *Lt. Wofford of the United States on Babe Wartham shows perfect jumping form as taught by Major Chamberlin. Photo courtesy of the US Olympic committee.*

The Japanese Army's Kido gallops into the course. Within twenty seconds, horse and rider crash and roll along the ground. The fall seriously hurts both horse and rider. Eliminated.

The Japanese Army's Major Imamura takes his turn. Imamura's horse refuses at fence eight. The horse refuses two more times at fence ten. Three refusals! Eliminated.

All eyes turn to the Army of Sweden's Lt. von Rosen. He and his horse hit three close calls over rock and fence, water obstacles, and a high gate but make it through with 16 faults. Most significantly, von Rosen's horse puts two feet into the water at jump number thirteen, the 16-foot 5-inch water jump. Nonetheless, horse and rider make it through. They are the fifth horse and rider to try but the first to succeed. The crowd roars. After a bit, the stadium announcer asks for silence to give the horses and riders a chance to focus on the challenge of the course.

Next, Major Mejia of Mexico gallops into the course. The first fence: clean. The second fence: the horse refuses. Mejia tries again. The horse refuses! A third try and the horse refuses! Eliminated.

Figure 5 *Captain Bradford (USA) rides Joe Aleshire as they topple first hurdle of the obstacle that Lt. Wofford and Babe Wartham clear. US Olympic Committee photo.*

Now comes Captain Bradford of the USA on Joe Aleshire. They bash through top rail after top rail. At the water jump number thirteen, Joe

Aleshire puts two feet into the water but they make it through the course with twenty-four faults: only the second pair make it through! The 105,000 roars its approval. The stadium announcer, again, asks for silence. The crowd slowly calms down.

Lt. Francke of Sweden starts his ride. He and his horse jump the first nine obstacles well. But then, his horse refuses three times at barrier number ten, the Aiken Brush! Eliminated.

Next, Captain Hallberg of Sweden bashes through the course. Like the others, his horse puts two feet into the water at jump thirteen. Hallberg and horse approach the chicken coop. The horse lunges over the ditch and then smashes against the near wall of the coop tossing Hallberg off to the side in what looks like a disastrous fall with the horse's neck stretched out over the edge of the coop. Horse and rider recover. Hallberg remounts and on the second try they barely negotiate the coop, but they do get to the next obstacle. Horse and rider complete the course with 50½ faults but at least, horse and rider get through.

Figure 6 *Captain Hallberg of Sweden and horse Kornett take a tumble at the chicken coop. Hallberg remounts Kornett and they try again! Photo courtesy of the US Olympic Committee.*

Captain Ortiz of Mexico tries next. The first obstacle: clean. Obstacles two, three, four, five, six, and seven: clean! At number eight: the horse refuses! Ortiz tries again. The horse refuses! Ortiz tries once more. The horse refuses! Eliminated.

The standings so far: In first place, Rosen of Sweden with 16 faults; in second place, Bradford of the USA with 24 faults; in third place, Hallberg of Sweden with 50½ faults. The Olympic officials will award no Team Medals since no three-member team will manage to get through the course.

Now comes Major Harry Dwight Chamberlin on Show Girl, the graceful, back-up gray mare. The stadium announcer intones: "Major Chamberlin for the United States on Tanbark." [13] The cheering, pro-American crowd of 105,000 people, one of the largest audiences ever to witness, in person, an equestrian competition, rises to greet them. Far from the Great Stadium after the radio blackout lifts, Army Chief of Staff, General Douglas MacArthur and Chamberlin's friends George Patton, and Lucien Truscott will listen by radio at Fort Meyer; Innis Swift, another friend, will listen from Fort Bliss along with an estimated 25 million plus other radio listeners.

Surely, Chamberlin will win the Gold Medal the horse show enthusiasts say to themselves. After all, many times before, Chamberlin and Tanbark turn in clean rounds to win medal after medal. But Tanbark rests lame in his stall. Chamberlin rides Show Girl, a horse that before this day, he has not ridden in competition. And now they face a course that has brought down some of the most accomplished horses and horsemen in the world.

The noise on the field remains deafening. The announcer asks for silence and slowly the crowd complies. All eyes of the 105,000 focus on Chamberlin and Show Girl: Hollywood luminaries Douglas Fairbanks, Jr. and Mary Pickford, John Barrymore, Marlene Dietrich and Charlie Chaplin; columnist Will Rogers; the Harrimans, Vanderbilts, and Morgans of New York; the McCormicks, the Armours, and the Swifts of Chicago, and many other Madison Square Garden horse-show regulars watch from the stands of the Great Stadium. Many of them personally know, respect, and like Chamberlin. The Madison Square Garden elite recognizes, however, that Chamberlin rides not the dark brown gelding Tanbark but a gray mare not seen before with Chamberlin in the Garden.

As those in the Great Stadium watch, Major Chamberlin begins his ride. Horse and rider confront the first fence, a tall rail with brush: they take it clean! The second fence, a wide-spread oxer: clean! They approach the third fence, a tall gate. Clean. The fourth fence: clean! So far, flawless! The crowd roars its approval as well as its relief with each clean jump. Still more

13 See short newsreel film clip at https://www.efootage.com/stock-footage/55623/Prix_De_Nations_Event_-_1932_Summer_Olympics/.

spectators rise to their feet; others hunch over with intense concentration. They alternate between breathless silence and roaring applause and screams. Obstacle five: the ditch, bar and bank followed by another bar: a knock down. Four faults! Obstacle six: the bar over a water jump: one foot in the water! Four faults. Obstacle seven: the 5-foot-3-inch tall chicken coop. Show Girl, cat like, leaps over the ditch and scrambles onto the top of the chicken coop with Chamberlin in an extreme position. She takes one stride, then another, and then leaps off of the coop and over the bar: Clean!!! Obstacle eight: clean. Obstacles nine, ten, eleven and twelve—all clean!

More spectators rise to their feet. The stadium noise rises to a deafening level; then silence. Obstacle thirteen: the wide, gaping 16-foot, 5-inch water-jump that Show Girl must leap 25 feet to clear. One foot, just barely in the water—four faults! Again, a loud sigh from the crowd. Obstacle fourteen: clean! Obstacle fifteen: clean! Obstacles sixteen, seventeen and eighteen: all clean! Chamberlin and Show Girl break to a full gallop. They race to the finish. Tenths of a second speed by. They finish within the time allowed! Their total: twelve faults! The United States, Chamberlin, and Show Girl lead!

Surely, Chamberlin has won. Perhaps 90,000 people rise to their feet and scream after Chamberlin and Show Girl surmount the last obstacle and gallop to the finish. 100,000 voices of the pro-American audience roar almost in unison. Hands applaud and feet stomp. Men embrace each other and women as well. Some jump up and down. Hands and arms raise to the air. Many faces show tears. The sound of the audience drowns out all comprehension. They have witnessed a great performance on this, the most difficult *Prix des Nations* course ever, by Major H. D. Chamberlin, United States Cavalry, the greatest American horseman on a horse, that before this day, he has never ridden in competition.

Chamberlin surely has won! And with time to spare! On the floor of the stadium, riders, judges, attendants cannot hear above the roar of the crowd. Horses become wide eyed. They fidget as they gaze at the roaring crowd surrounding them on all four sides. The stadium announcer asks for silence. He waits. Still the crowd roars. He asks again. And then, he asks a third time. Finally, the crowd falls silent.

One rider and one rider alone remains: Lt. Nishi of The Empire of Japan. He starts his ride on Uranus, a 14-year-old French Half-Thoroughbred. Over the first jump: clean. Over the second, clean; over the third, fourth, and fifth: clean. On the sixth obstacle, the bar over water jump: a foot in the water, four faults! On the seventh: clean. On the eighth, clean. On the tenth, the Aiken Brush, a refusal! Three faults! And then, a second try over the Aiken Brush: clear! Obstacles eleven and twelve: clean. Obstacle thirteen, the massive water jump: clean! Jump fourteen: clean. Obstacles fifteen, sixteen, seventeen and eighteen: clean! Nishi and Uranus gallop to the finish line. They complete the ride with a time penalty of one fault. Total faults: eight. Nishi and Uranus for The Empire of Japan win the Gold Medal!

The Japanese victory stuns the American crowd. Silence for perhaps five seconds. Then, they cheer the winner but many spectators break down in tears. Major Chamberlin's Staff Sergeant, a veteran of the Great War, walks under the stadium stands, breaks down, and cries for his friend.

America's Chamberlin wins the Individual Silver; Sweden's Von Rosen, wins the Individual Bronze. Japan's Lt. Nishi and Uranus win the Individual Gold. The Committee awards no team medals because no team completes the course. Nishi on Uranus takes the victory lap around the Great Stadium track. Nishi, with arm raised high, carries in his right hand the staff that displays the red circle on white flag of the Empire of Japan.

And now the concluding ceremony begins: The Dutch flag rises and the national anthem of Holland fills the air for the Dutchman de Mortanges as he receives his Individual Eventing Gold medal and Thomson of the USA receives his Individual Eventing Silver medal. Next, the American Three-Day team: Chamberlin, Argo and Thomson receive their Team Gold medals. The Olympic band strikes up the Star-Spangled Banner and the American flag rises. Almost the entire audience again rises from their seats. Many in the audience begin to sing the national anthem. Tears flow down the faces of many as they sing.

And now, for the *grand finale,* the *Prix des Nations* victory of Japan: the officials award the Gold medal to Lt. Nishi, the Silver to Chamberlin and the Bronze to von Rosen. The Olympic band plays the national anthem of The Empire of Japan and the red circle on white flag of The Empire rises.

Shortly thereafter, the sun begins to set over the Pacific. The ceremony concludes with 1,200 choral voices singing the melody "Aloha" and the report of cannons firing in the distance.

Chamberlin slowly rides Show Girl out of the stadium. When he arrives at the stabling area, he dismounts. He says nothing. He gently pats Show Girl on her neck. And then, in silence—he turns away.

Would Chamberlin have won the Gold medal had he and Tanbark jumped that course? Chamberlin and Tanbark racked up a record of successive triumphs in Europe and in America. Time after time when the US team needed a "clean round," Chamberlin and Tanbark came through.

Figure 7 *The Prix des Nations awards. Left to right: von Rosen, Chamberlin, Nishi.*

Regardless, Major Chamberlin's accomplishment this day, bitter sweet though it is, places him in a select group of competitors who win medals in two different Olympic events at the same Olympiad. His success over such a difficult course on a substitute horse presents further testament to Chamberlin's skill. Many years later, the official Olympic Committee commentary discusses the *Prix des Nations* as follows:

> "The Jumping competition of 1932 was a disaster. The first known Olympic course designer, John A. Barry (who rode for the USA in the 1920 and 1924 Olympics) supported by Sloan Doak (also a multi Olympic rider) built a course that was much more difficult than 1928. It had 18 obstacles and 20 jumping efforts over a length of 1,060m.... the two 1.60m fences, the wall and the five-meter wide water jump were far too much. No team finished the competition and the team medals remained unclaimed." [14]

A few evenings later, the US Army Equestrian Team sponsors a dinner for the Equestrians of the 1932 Olympics. Earlier, the members of the American team purchase a chrome plated, Colt M-1911 semi-automatic pistol. At the dinner, Major Chamberlin formally presents the pistol to Baron Lt. Nishi as a gift of friendship. In a few days, Lt. Nishi returns to Japan. Major Chamberlin goes to Fort Riley to pack, and then goes on to Washington, DC

14 See *The Official Report of the Games of the Xth Olympiad Los Angeles 1932.* See also *Olympic Summer Games, Fonds List, Historical Archives,* Olympic Studies Center, International Olympic Committee, April 2011.

MAJOR CHAMBERLIN'S RIDE

A SEQUENCE

Figure 8 *Chamberlin immediately prepares for the upcoming jump.*
Photo courtesy *of the US Olympic Committee.*

Figure 9 *Chamberlin sits deep in the saddle in anticipation of the upcoming jump. As Eventing coach Jim Wofford points out: Chamberlin enjoys "...an uncanny ability to predict his stride long before his horse did... "*
Photo courtesy *of the US Olympic Committee.*

Figure 10 *Show Girl's upward thrust to meet the jump brings Chamberlin* ***out of*** *the saddle. Photo courtesy of the US Olympic Committee.*

Figure 11 *A clean jump and Chamberlin stays out of the saddle.* ***US Olympic*** *Committee.*

Figure 12 *Off to the next obstacle. Chamberlin sits deep since the next jump* ***is seconds*** *away. Photo courtesy of the US Olympic Committee.*

Figure 13 *Chamberlin remains deep in the saddle to prepare for the jump and to* ***enable Show*** *Girl to feel his position. Photo courtesy of the US Olympic Committee.*

Figure 14 *Chamberlin stays deep in the saddle to feel his horse's every move. The jump is a fraction of a second ahead. Photo courtesy of the US Olympic Committee.*

Figure 15 *This jump is five feet and three inches high. Note Chamberlin's body position: upper body parallel with Show Girl's neck, hands in contact with her mouth. He never drops contact. His calves remain tight. His weight stays in his heels. His lower leg position remains perfect. Photo courtesy of the US Olympic Committee.*

Figure 16 *They clear the jump and Chamberlin remains out of the saddle until Show Girl's hind end is ready to push forward. His hands never lose contact with the mare's mouth. His weight remains in his heels. His calves softly remain in contact with her flanks. He nudges her forward with a tickle of his spur. Photo courtesy of the US Olympic Committee.*

Figure 17 *A full gallop to beat the time limits. US Olympic Committee*

Figure 18 *Back in the saddle to keep contact with the horse.*
US Olympic Committee photo.

Figure 19 *As fractions of a second speed by, Chamberlin takes a two-point to maintain speed. As he draws close to the jump he will move back into the saddle. Photo courtesy of the US Olympic Committee.*

Figure 20 *Chamberlin stays in a two-point position to keep moving fast. US Olympic Committee photo.*

Figure 21 *Still out of the saddle to maintain top speed. Only fractions of **a** second speed by. Photo courtesy of the US Olympic Committee.*

Figure 22 *Chamberlin is out of the saddle to keep up top speed. US Olympic Committee photo.*

Figure 23 *A wide turn and breakneck speed to avoid a time penalty. Photo courtesy of the US Olympic Committee.*

Figure 24 *Chamberlin is deep in the saddle as he and Show Girl size up the obstacle to come. As James Wofford points out, Chamberlin would "… arrange things so that the horse got to the jump in the correct place without knowing that his rider had predetermined that takeoff spot." US Olympic Committee photo.*

Figure 25 *Chamberlin makes a wide turn and heads directly into the jump and firmly planted in the saddle. Photo courtesy of the US Olympic Committee.*

Figure 26 *Chamberlin stays deep into the saddle so the Show Girl knows exactly where he is. His hands maintain soft contact throughout. Photo courtesy of the US Olympic Committee.*

Figure 27 *Chamberlin and Show Girl clear this jump and make ready for the next jump to come. Photo courtesy of the US Olympic Committee.*

Figure 28 *On to the next jump. Photo courtesy of the US Olympic Committee.*

Figure 29 *Up and over the chicken coop. On the back of this photo, Major Chamberlin writes: "Over a deep ditch onto a bank at Olympic Games— "Show Girl." Notice horse's 'cat-like' action going into this strange obstacle seen for the first time." Photo courtesy of the US Olympic Committee and Ms. Lydia Moore.*

Figure 30 *Over the jumps and now the dash to the finish. Chamberlin and Show Girl make it with time to spare. Photo courtesy of the US Olympic Committee.*

AFTER CHAMBERLIN'S LAST OLYMPIC RIDE

After the Olympics of 1932, Chamberlin attends the Army War College and succeeds there.

In 1935, after he graduates from the Army War College, now Lt. Col. Chamberlin authors his first book *Riding and Schooling Horses.* Chamberlin's friend, Ambassador John Cudahy writes in his introduction to the book that few people enjoy the education, experience and genius of a Chamberlin. More than 70 years of perspective confirms Cudahy's opinion.

In 1937, Chamberlin writes another book: *Training Hunters Jumpers and Hacks,* [Xenophon Press, 2019]. One great teacher, Vladimir Littauer, hails Chamberlin's book to be "... in its field, the greatest book of the century, not only in the United States but in the world." [15]

His two books, together with his other writings, establish a standard of riding and training in many ways unique in equestrian literature. But Chamberlin's talents and accomplishments go well beyond equestrian pursuits. It remains true that in the pre-World War II Army, an officer's accomplishments in sports (or lack thereof) typically would forward or retard that officer's future prospects as a soldier. Chamberlin's equestrian accomplishments deliver visibility and generate admiration and respect. His intellectual accomplishments, however, remain distinguished in the Army's advanced schools. They open the doors of the army's elite ranks to him. He will become one of the most well-liked and respected military officers of his generation.

"He...excelled in everything he did," writes Army Chief of Staff George C. Marshall.[16] Chamberlin vindicates Marshall's opinion: as a "distinguished" graduate of the US Army Command and General Staff School; as a graduate of the Army War College; as "G-3" and then Chief of Staff for the 1st Cavalry Division where he trains the division to peak performance; as a commander of the 2nd US Cavalry Regiment for which he assembles a staff that shines in European combat during World War II; as the Commandant of the Cavalry Replacement Training Center at Fort Riley where he refines the curriculum to produce what one authority calls "absolutely first rate riders." [17]

Finally, as a Task Force commander in World War II, he performs his first mission in the Pacific Theater in stellar fashion and demonstrates strategic

15 See Vladimir S. Littauer, The *Development of Modern Riding*, Howell Book House, 1991.

16 See Association of West Point Graduates https://www.westpointaog.org/memorial-article?id=f3efb07e-1306-45c3-86dd-780dd099a6a0.

17 See George H. Morris, *Four Show Jumping Masters—Part 4: Gordon Wright* https://www.horsemagazine.com/thm/2010/07/four-showjumping-masters-part-4-gordon-wright/.

acumen of great value to the Allied cause. He remains the only Allied officer in World War II to hold a "unified" command of all Army, Army Air Corps as well as Navy, Marine Corps and Sea-Bee personnel in a combined operations Task Force. It will be more than 40 years before the armed forces of the United States implement such an approach as standard operating procedure.

Early in World War II, now Brigadier General Chamberlin's performance puts his career on the fast track with other cavalrymen like Patton, Swift, and Truscott. He looks forward to completing his assignment, making full General, and even begins thinking long term of his future retirement from the Army after the war. From the Pacific, he writes to his wife Helen: "If fortune continues to smile, I will make it all the way to the top." [18]

Sadly, fortune fails to smile. On the South Pacific Island of New Caledonia, his doctors diagnose an enemy that to this day, no one really knows how to cure. The illness derails his career and ultimately strikes him down. In June of 1942, he returns home and undergoes two years of operations and other treatments in the United States. His once powerful, athletic build withers. Regardless, he remains on active duty until the very end. After two years of constant illness, he passes away on September 29, 1944 leaving behind those he treasures most of all: two young girls, Lydia, age ten and Frederica, age eight and his widow, Helen Bradman Chamberlin, age thirty-one. The officers with whom he served take his passing as if he were a brother as well as a devoted and respected friend.

Military fame will not be his. The respect of his follow officers and especially of Army Chief of Staff George C. Marshall, however, remains firm: In 1941, when Third Army Lt. General Walter Krueger asks Marshall for an officer to turn around a unit in need of rehabilitation, Marshall replies to Krueger that he cannot find someone of the caliber of a Chamberlin.[19] Nothing changes Marshall's opinion in 1944. Marshall writes of Chamberlin: "He was one of the ablest and most popular men in the Regular establishment, and his loss to the Army is a great one…" [20]

Today, the horse cavalry, World War II, and the forgotten islands of the Pacific recede into the past. Still, Chamberlin's contributions to horsemanship continue. Chamberlin's genius links a modified concept of Italian forward riding with French dressage and the American cavalry's vast

---

18 Chamberlin personal letter to Helen Chamberlin in the papers of Harry Chamberlin.

19 See: Marshall Memorandum #2-570 to Lt. General Walter Krueger, October 11, 1941, George C. Marshall Papers, Pentagon Office Collection, Selected Materials, George C. Marshall Research Library, Lexington, Virginia.

20 See Association of West Point Graduates https://www.westpointaog.org/memorial-article?id=f3efb07e-1306-45c3-86dd-780dd099a6a0.

experience in riding long distances. His enduring legacy provides not only the foundation for what George Morris calls the "American jumping style" but also for so much more. The totality of Chamberlin's writing provides a complete protocol to train both horse and rider for Eventing, Show Jumping, Endurance Riding, Hunting, and just plain hacking for fun.

To this day, many Olympic equestrians from all over the world and others with competent instructors apply his riding and training concepts even though most do not know his name. In the twenty-first century, many of the most knowledgeable riders and trainers admire, respect, and follow Chamberlin's lead: William Steinkraus writes in 2008, "So often, I think I have come up with an idea of my own, only to find it in one of Chamberlin's books." [21] James Wofford contends that Chamberlin remains second only to Caprilli in international influence and that "Chamberlin is to horsemanship as Mozart is to music." [22] Charles Chenevix-Trench writes that Chamberlin "...had an influence on American riding second to none..." [23] George Morris ranks Chamberlin, all things considered, as "the 20th Century's greatest combined horseman, theorist, teacher, and writer." [24]

In our current era of professional riders whose only pursuit remains riding almost to the exclusion of all else, we must remember: the equestrian sports of Dressage, Eventing, and Stadium Jumping as well as horse shows and exhibitions are neither the main focus of Chamberlin's professional life nor the main focus of his professional consideration. Relatively speaking, such pursuits take up only a small portion of his life. As Chamberlin points out, rarely does a cavalryman in the field jump over anything other than a mud hole or a ditch. Rather, he may confront and negotiate steep slides, ford rivers, travel faster than infantry over rough terrain to flank an enemy. A cavalryman moves faster than infantry where tanks, trucks and other motorized transport cannot move at all.

On what manner of issues does he focus most of the time? Cavalry officers of his generation debate whether cavalry should deploy in large concentrations masse as typical of European concepts or whether, in most circumstances, the horse should serve as a means of transport not as a weapons platform; that when engaged, troopers should dismount quickly and fight as infantry; that cavalry should devote itself to reconnaissance on the flanks of an army. They focus on technical questions of performance.

---

21 William Steinkraus email to author June 3, 2008.

22 James Wofford response to questions submitted by author May 2008.

23 Charles Chenevix-Trench, *A History of Horsemanship*, Doubleday & Company, 1970.

24 George H. Morris response to questions submitted by author May 2008.

Exactly 57 years after Chamberlin's passing, American soldiers enter combat mounted on horses. On October 23, 2001, men of the 5th Special Forces Group ride with Afghan cavalrymen of the Northern Alliance to attack Taliban forces in the Darya Suf River Valley of northern Afghanistan. Later, those same Special Forces troops, mounted on horses, scout out targets for B-52 bombers and move faster than infantry under conditions of terrain where armor and other motorized transport cannot deploy, exactly as Chamberlin and his friends Truscott and Patton argue.

At this writing, more than 70 years after Chamberlin's passing, some of the US Army's Special Forces receive a rudimentary introduction about riding horses and deploying pack horses and mules over terrain too rough for motorized transport and through mountain passes too narrow for helicopters. So, in the long run, Chamberlin might leave a legacy valuable not only to equestrian sport but, in limited circumstances, also to the Army he loved so well. This would be especially true if today's military consults the manuals that Chamberlin helps produce in the early 1940s and applies the tactical doctrines of "mounted infantry" that his friend Major General Innis P. Swift develops and implements back then as well.

Chamberlin's career as a cavalry officer, as well as an Olympic competitor, inspires many questions. As the years pass and Chamberlin learns more and more about the horsemanship and the other training most important to his professional life—the life of a cavalry officer—what does Chamberlin learn about horses and horsemanship at West Point? At Fort Riley? At Saumur? At Tor di Quinto? At three Olympiads? During the grueling 1,000-mile round-trip march into Mexico and back? During the long patrols as he rides over the parched desert of the American southwest, along the Rio Grande, and in the humidity of the Philippines? How does this learning and experience mold his views and what might we learn from them as well?

Of course, learning of Chamberlin's schooling and experience will offer only a few insights into the man. In the words of Chamberlin's friend John Cudahy, himself an Ambassador to Poland, Ireland, Belgium and Luxembourg:

> "Impressive as this great range of training and experience is, it cannot account for a Chamberlin, for a truly great horseman is a genius, endowed with the fine sensibilities of an artist, combined with keen perception, cool judgment, courage, discretion, unfailing patience and infinite tact." [25]

25 John Cudahy Introduction to Lt. Col. Harry D. Chamberlin, *Riding and Schooling Horses*, Derrydale Press, 1934.

How does this son of an insurance agent living in the light-manufacturing town of Elgin, Illinois surrounded by a vast Midwestern corn field, become the US Cavalry's greatest horseman; an equestrian theorist and teacher second in international influence only to Federico Caprilli; an Olympic Gold and Silver Medalist; and one of the most respected and well-liked military officers of his generation?

Let us inquire.

Chapter 3

Beginnings

"It's a piece of New England that got lost, but it knows what time it is."
—A writer refers to Elgin, Illinois [26]

"Why would anyone choose a vocation in which the pay was low, the outlook for advancement uncertain, and the business is neglected by its owners?"
—An unknown old soldier regarding joining the Army [27]

Little written record survives regarding the early life of Harry Dwight Chamberlin. As far as his immediate family knows, he does not keep a diary. And it seems, that during Harry Chamberlin's youth, his family finds little need to communicate by letter. In the 1950s, a fire destroys his Olympic medals, his saddles, and most of his papers and other personal effects. In the 1970s, a fire at the US government records center in St. Louis destroys his military records.

A picture of Chamberlin's early life emerges, however, through his family background; through the origins and activities of his father, Dwight Chamberlin and of his mother, Corrine Orth Chamberlin; through the history and the values of Elgin, Illinois where he grows up; and through the typical pursuits of boys living in a Northern Illinois town in the last years of the nineteenth-century. Three facts seem clear: Harry's winning personality he learns from his father; his ambition to become an officer in the Army stems

26 See E.C. Alft, Elgin, Days Gone By and Elgin: *An American History*. Internet website, 2001. www.elginhistory.com.
27 See Victor Vogel, *Soldiers of the Old Army*, College Station, Texas A & M University 1990.

from his father and from the traditions of Elgin, Illinois; and his concept of public service stems from both his father and his mother.

Yet, unlike his closest army friends, Chamberlin does not come from a military family; nor does he come from an equestrian family. He does not hail from a frontier cavalry post in Texas or from the rolling hills of Northern Virginia. He comes from an Illinois manufacturing town, a town known for watch-making and dairy products, centered in the middle of dairy-cow country and surrounded by almost a million acres of corn and hay fields.

Chamberlin's army friends, in later years, come from entirely different backgrounds. Cavalryman George S. Patton, Jr., steeped in the equestrian tradition of Virginia, rides the hills of California with Confederate Major John Mosby, "The Grey Ghost" of Civil War fame. Patton thrives on Mosby's stories and cavalry exploits. Several of Patton's ancestors die as Confederate war heroes.

Another Chamberlin friend, Major General Innis Palmer Swift, a cavalryman to his core, is born in a covered wagon while his father, Eben Swift, a Captain of E Troop, 5th US Cavalry, moves the family from one frontier post to another. Swift's father eventually rises to the rank of Major General. Swift also descends from maternal grandfather, Major General Innis N. Palmer and paternal grandfather Brigadier General Ebenezer Swift.

Chamberlin enjoys no such ancestors or riding companions. Yet, Chamberlin becomes "the beau ideal of a cavalryman" to borrow Lt. General and cavalryman Lucian Truscott, Jr's words. He becomes an Olympic rider of the highest order, an internationally respected theorist second only to Caprilli. He remains the finest teacher of the equestrian arts ever to grace the United States Cavalry and overall, probably the finest horseman ever produced in the United States.

Let us begin at the beginning.

Harry Chamberlin's grandparents are born in the first decade of the nineteenth century on the East Coast of the United States. They hail principally from Vermont, Massachusetts, and New York. Sometime in the 1830s, Albert and Nancy Chamberlin move west to Illinois just after the Black Hawk War of 1832, where American officials mobilize an army to drive Black Hawk and his band west over the Mississippi River. In the early 1850s, Chamberlin's maternal grandparents, John and Mary Orth emigrate from New York to Boone County, Illinois near the town of Belvidere. As this migration takes place, Chamberlin's parents are born.

In Rockford, Illinois on June 2, 1849, Harry's great grandparents, Alfred and Nancy, celebrate the arrival of a fourth child : Dwight Allen Chamberlin.

Little remains known of Dwight's early life. He attends school in Rockford. When he reaches age 10, he and his family move to a town called Cherry Valley just southeast of Rockford. Alfred abandons the foundry business in Rockford for something better in Cherry Valley: milling. And in Cherry Valley, Alfred Chamberlin engages in the milling business until his retirement many years later.

The Chamberlin family seems to do well in Cherry Valley. They live a life typical of those living on the Illinois frontier that fast becomes "civilization." For the Chamberlins and for most other families in northern Illinois, life settles into the normal routines until events in South Carolina stun the nation.

On April 12, 1861, eleven-year-old Dwight and his family hear the news that forces of the State of South Carolina fire on Fort Sumter. The Civil War begins. In July of 1862, the Union army establishes a training camp near Rockford called Camp Fuller. Several thousand Union troops, all from Illinois counties surrounding Rockford, train there. Frequently, local residents from Rockford and Cherry Valley including Dwight Chamberlin, now twelve years old, visit the camp to watch marching drills and dress parades.

In particular, they watch the 74th Illinois Infantry Regiment march out of Camp Fuller in 1862 to face the full fury of the Civil War. In all, the 74th fights 16 bloody engagements. The regiment marches to war in with 950 troops; the regiment marches back to Illinois in 1865 with 170 survivors. The regiment's heavy losses inspire reverence in almost every citizen of the Rockford area including Dwight Chamberlin. Dwight will pass this reverence on to his son Harry. To this day, the 74th Regiment's battle flag hangs in Rockford's Memorial Hall.

In 1865, when Dwight reaches age 16, General Ulysses S. Grant visits Rockford on his way home to Galena, Illinois. Thousands turn out to see the general as he rides through the streets. Most certainly, the Chamberlin family join the crowd. The Civil War and Ulysses S. Grant make a deep impression on Dwight. For his entire adult life, Dwight Chamberlin respects Grant as the hero who saves the Union. Dwight remains proud of the fact that he casts his first vote, at age 21, for US Grant as President and mentions this fact frequently. The United States Army, US Grant, and later the Republican Party form three pillars of Dwight's thinking and values.

In 1871, at age 22, Dwight Chamberlin begins work in the insurance business. For the next 14 years, he lives first in Cherry Valley and then in Rockford. Probate records disclose that sometime in the mid-1870s, Dwight marries and then divorces. During this time, he travels throughout the region on behalf of the Rockford Insurance Company. He sells farm insurance and becomes well known around the northwestern portion of the state as a successful insurance agent.

In 1885, at age 36, Dwight Chamberlin moves from Rockford to Elgin, Illinois, a town on the Fox River 50 miles southeast of Rockford and almost 40 miles west of Chicago. For the rest of his life, he establishes himself as one of Elgin's most prominent citizens. The history, traditions and values of Elgin, Illinois offer insights into the motivations, values and choices of Dwight and his son, Harry.

Elgin, Illinois in the 1880s presents a neat, clean, orderly and quiet atmosphere in its factory and residential areas thus inspiring comparisons with New England. A watch factory shapes the pattern of Elgin life. Massachusetts watch makers arrive in Elgin to work at the Elgin National Watch Company. They further affirm and strengthen Elgin's New England associations. The firm's managers, New Englanders all, enjoy respect from local citizens and enjoy their place in the top tier of Elgin society.

A writer who visits Elgin's watch factory observes: "the introduction of watch making into this Illinois country was a refining influence upon the population. There is a neatness, orderliness, cleanliness, and extreme quietness not often seen in a factory..."[28] This combination of factors makes Elgin different from most manufacturing towns: it maintains a middle class feel not usually related to manufacturing. Its industries make watches and process dairy products. Such industries remain "clean." Much later another Chicago newspaper writes of Elgin: "It's a piece of New England that got lost, but it knows what time it is." [29]

The surrounding countryside also reinforces this impression: "While strolling over the hills and through the groves, one can hardly realize that he is in the heart of the West; hills and dales, and groves and sparkling streams, elegant residences, charming views, and thriving manufactories are all suggestive of New England," reports one Chicago paper in 1867.

In Elgin Township which surrounds the city of Elgin, dairy cows and the refined breeding of dairy cows dominate the agrarian culture. Cows and more cows grow to support the growing dairy industry that supplies Chicago with milk, butter and cheese. By 1885, when Dwight Chamberlin moves to Elgin, at least twelve thousand dairy cows outnumber the human population. When it comes to animal husbandry, cows rather than horses dominate the attention of Elgin area farmers.

---

28 See E.C. Alft, *Elgin, Days Gone By* and *Elgin: An American History.* Internet website, 2001. www.elginhistory.com.

29 Ibid.

By 1898, farmers around Elgin milk, each day, over 55,000 cows and pour half a million quarts of milk into 14,000 cans just to satisfy one company's requirements. Over 50 cheese, butter and milk producing companies operate in Elgin at that time. Definitely not fox-hunting country!

Elgin's watch and dairy product industries draw more women than men to Elgin. This remains unique for a manufacturing town in Illinois. One young woman, Corrine Leone Orth whose friends call her "Cora" comes to Elgin from Belvidere, Illinois. In the mid to late nineteenth century, Belvidere offers a life typical of a sleepy farming community. The Orth family works their farm just as hundreds of other families in the region. Life on the farm demands a life of hard work. Medical care remains primitive to non-existent. Many die young. Cora's father, John Orth, dies on October 10, 1877 at age 59; Cora's sister, Ida, dies on November 1, 1878 at age 24. In August of 1880, Cora leaves the farm of her birth to build a new life in Elgin, Illinois. She is 21.

Miss Corrine Orth finds a job at the Elgin National Watch Company. She starts out as a waitress at the factory's boarding house to pay for her meals. After about six months, she earns one dollar and fifty cents to two dollars a day on piecework. Since women outnumber men in Elgin, the town remains a good place for a single man to find a wife. Most likely, the divorced Dwight Chamberlin leaves his lucrative insurance business in 1885 to work in the watch factory for about 12 dollars a week for this reason.

Shortly after starting at the factory, Dwight meets Cora. A romance ensues and evolves into marriage one year later. The couple marries at the Palmer House Hotel in Chicago on July 2, 1886. Cora will turn 27 the following month, and Dwight has just turned 37.

The couple returns to Elgin after their wedding and makes the town their home. Shortly after his marriage, Dwight leaves the watch company and returns to the insurance business. In insurance, he will prosper for the rest of his life. During his previous 14 years of insurance work, he develops many clients. Dwight Chamberlin re-establishes those relationships and hits the bricks running. His patronage grows rapidly. Soon, he becomes a prominent businessman.

On May 19, 1887, Dwight and Cora welcome the birth of a son whom they name Harry Dwight Chamberlin. Almost four years later, on February 20, 1891, Cora gives birth to a daughter whom they name Marie. Sometime after Marie's birth, Cora also gives birth to a third child named Alice. Alice does not survive.

As the years pass, Dwight prospers in the insurance business. From his offices in the Elgin National Bank building, Chamberlin works hard. His contemporaries recognize him as a "hustler" in the best sense of that word. For over forty years, he serves as one of Elgin's most accomplished and respected insurance and real estate agents. Politics also engages Dwight's time. He serves as a respected local public office holder in Elgin for 16 years and as an effective Republican Party organizer all of his life. For example, well into the twentieth-century, Republicans comment on Dwight Chamberlin's hard work during the campaign of 1896.

The election of that year for President proves to be one of the most hotly contested on record. The Republican, William McKinley of Ohio, the last Union Civil War veteran to run for president, stands against Democrat William Jennings Bryan of Nebraska, one of American history's greatest orators.

Dwight Chamberlin campaigns hard for McKinley. William Jennings Bryan campaigns personally in the city of Elgin. Turnout reaches an astounding 90 percent of eligible voters. The Elgin vote creates a Republican landslide. Less than 24 percent vote for Bryan. Through his efforts, Dwight gathers political influence that will benefit his son Harry in later years.

Also important to Harry's development is Dwight's reverence for US Grant, the general who saved the Union and for the soldiers that served under him in the Civil War. The record of Elgin's Civil War regiments reinforces Dwight Chamberlin's politics formed outside Camp Fuller and in Cherry Valley. And the record of Elgin's Civil War regiments inspires Harry who, like every other boy in Elgin, hears of the battles and heroes from the veterans who fought the war.

In 1861, many of the first volunteers to heed Lincoln's call for troops to suppress the South come from Elgin. They form Company A of the 7th Illinois Regiment. It is the first regiment formed in the state. Others from Elgin join the Illinois Cavalry. Ulysses S. Grant of Galena, Illinois leads all of these troops south.

Recruits from Elgin follow Grant into battle at Fort Donnellson and again at Shiloh Church. At Shiloh, one Elgin regiment, the 58th Illinois, suffers more than 75 percent casualties before the Confederates take the regiment prisoner. A year later, at Vicksburg, the siege creates heavy Elgin casualties. For example, in the 127th Regiment, all but three men become casualties from disease and privation.

In particular, the Elgin's 36th Illinois Regiment fights some of the bloodiest battles of the war: Shiloh, Perryville, Stones River and Chickamauga. One engagement during the war becomes a legend, however, to surpass all legends in Elgin: the assault of November 25, 1863. For months, around Chattanooga, Tennessee, the Union and Confederate forces grapple with each other. The Confederates stop cold the Union offensive of the West at the Battle of Chickamauga. When the Union troops retreat into Chattanooga, the Confederates lay siege to the city in an effort to starve the Union forces into surrender.

In hopes of breaking the Confederate siege, Grant orders Union troops to seize a series of rifle pits at the base of Missionary Ridge. This, they do. As they take the rifle pits, however, the Confederates from above fire down upon them a withering barrage of rifle and cannon. Suddenly, the Union troops break ranks and charge up the hill against the theretofore impregnable Confederate line at the top of Missionary Ridge!

Generals Grant and Sherman look on amazed and frustrated because the troops exceed their orders. Elgin's 36th and Rockford's 74th Illinois Regiments charge the Ridge along with the 24th Wisconsin. They all follow 19-year-old Arthur MacArthur as he yells "On Wisconsin." Up the steep and rugged slope, they charge to overwhelm the Confederate defenders who serve under General Braxton Bragg. The 74th Illinois plants their battle flag on Missionary Ridge as one of the first regiments to do so; Elgin's 36th Regiment follows suit. The charge destroys the Confederate line and opens the way to Atlanta. The stunning success at Missionary Ridge transforms the war in the West and inspires Elgin for a generation and Harry Chamberlin throughout his life.

Later, the Elgin Regiments fight their way south under Sherman to Atlanta; from Atlanta they march to the sea. From Savannah, they march north to Charleston and then to Columbia; then to Danville, Virginia. From there, they march to Washington, not to fight, but to celebrate the war's end. Together with over 140,000 other Union troops, they march in "The Grand Review of the Armies," the procession through the streets of Washington by the Army of the Potomac and the Army of the West to celebrate their victory and the Union preserved. And then, they march home.

Elgin's regiments suffer heavily in the war. The veterans who survive and return home meet regularly well into the twentieth-century to remember their dead as well as their deeds and to celebrate their Union victory. They establish traditions that will mold Harry Chamberlin's life. They sit in corner grocery stores and speak of the war. Many return to Elgin from the war missing an arm or a leg and for the next 50 or more years, people recognize them for that reason. Young Harry Chamberlin grows up surrounded by these veterans and vicariously shares their remembrances.

Every July 4th and every other public function well into the 1930s, Union Army veterans lead parades, public meetings and memorial remembrances.

They begin a Memorial Day observance in 1868 that, to this day, continues in the exact pattern they establish. To ensure that the observance will continue long after the last of their kind passes into history, they form the Elgin Patriotic Memorial Association. The Association presides over the observance throughout Harry Chamberlin's life and operates to this day.

Every Memorial Day, 500 large American flags line the city cemetery's main drive. For that day, the main drive becomes the "Avenue of Flags." At 11 a.m. sharp, people from Elgin assemble at the cemetery. Someone reads Lincoln's Gettysburg Address; another reads the exact words of General John A. Logan's proclamation of May 5, 1868 establishing Memorial Day.

The day's most solemn moment occurs just as the Civil War veterans prescribe: a military honor guard places a wreath at the base of the Grand Army of the Republic Memorial. The guard performs this ceremony in the same fashion as those who lay wreaths at the Tomb of the Unknowns at Arlington National Cemetery. Every year, the Chamberlin family attends this ceremony. And from the first time his mother carries him in her arms to this ceremony on Memorial Day of 1887 to Memorial Day of 1906, Harry Chamberlin, together with his family, goes to the City Cemetery. Each year, Harry hears General Logan's proclamation and, in the presence of living veterans of the Civil War, he and his family decorate the graves of the fallen.

Stories of the exploits of Elgin's Civil War regiments inspire Harry's imagination along with the imagination of every school boy in Elgin. On July 4, 1896, Dwight takes eight-year-old Harry to hear the words of Major General Oliver O. Howard, Commander of a Union Army of the Potomac Corps at Gettysburg. General Howard speaks to a huge crowd in Elgin filled with Civil War veterans, their families, and almost all the other citizens of the town.

Though Elgin maintains a strong foothold in the past, Elgin enters a new age in 1885, when Dwight arrives in town. Elgin's electric company installs city-wide service with the capacity to feed the "remarkable" number of five thousand bulbs.

By the time their son Harry reaches age ten, Elgin's first electric street cars begin carrying passengers; the St. Mary's Academy and the Elgin High School line up for the first football game; and a few years later, the high school plays its first night football game under lights at Elgin's King Park where Harry will play as star half-back on the high school football team.

Yet during Harry's childhood, most families use gas lamps for light, and maintain chicken pens and large vegetable gardens in their backyards. Behind the Chamberlin home during this period, in addition to the familiar chicken pen and vegetable garden, stands a large horse barn. It still stands as of this writing. In that barn, Harry keeps the horse he will ride until he leaves Elgin for West Point.

In Elgin, people typically depend on horses to pull carriages. The pursuits of an equestrian such as horsemanship, obstacle jumping, fox hunting and the like, however, prove foreign in Elgin's dairy farm country. Harry rides his horse but possibly not in a fashion approved by the military. Several cavalrymen live in Elgin who rode with Grierson on his daring 600-mile raid through the Confederacy in 1863. Perhaps Harry receives pointers as well as inspiration from them.

Most articles regarding Chamberlin report that Harry mounted his first horse at West Point. This is mistaken as Chamberlin, himself, states in a November 10, 1930 interview with *New York Times* reporter, Walter Fleisher. Chamberlin says that he "rode a pony almost as soon as I could walk."

An April 3, 1968 column in *The Elgin Free Press* newspaper discusses the "Elgin Pony Club" active at the turn of the century. One of the "club" members, a Helen Higginbotham recalls Harry, the Pony Club and her Shetland pony. The article mentions Harry's membership as one of four children in the Douglas neighborhood who owned and rode their own horse or a pony as a member of the club. [30] Miles of dirt roads, and prior to 1904, no autos made distance riding in between corn fields something easy and fun to do.

No record thus far located discusses Harry's proficiency as a rider during grammar school and high school. It seems clear that he does gain experience, however elementary, with horses and ponies while living at 711 Douglas, the house with the large barn in the rear. The Chamberlins live at that address from the time Harry is age five until he reaches age 16.

In the 1890s, while Harry Chamberlin studies in grammar school, drivers of skittish carriage horses protest against the bicycle riders who ride in Elgin's streets. Much later during Harry's junior year at Elgin High School, another reason to protest appears. For the first time, a "machine" known as the "Red Devil" zooms through Elgin's streets. The driver dashes around town at unsafe speeds as fast as thirty miles per hour! The new technology, however, does not seem to inspire Harry.

Nor does this new technology change the past-times of Elgin boys. They swim and fish. They play baseball in vacant lots. They go to the circus when it comes to town once a year. At Elgin's Trout Park, they ride a roller coaster. Since Elgin resides "on the political map" in Illinois, they leave school to see and hear Theodore Roosevelt, William Jennings Bryan and other political figures who speak in town.

30 See article on Elgin Pony Club, *The Elgin Free Press*, April 3, 1968.

In 1900, when Harry reaches age 13, another presidential campaign rages and another candidate, Theodore Roosevelt, visits Elgin. At that time, Filipino guerrillas resist the US occupation of their Philippine Islands. Opinion in town divides between the views of Republican vice-presidential candidate, Roosevelt and those of Chicago lawyer, Clarence Darrow. At Elgin, the two men debate American policy in the Philippines. The Chamberlin family attends.

Waving his Rough Rider hat, Roosevelt loudly proclaims to the audience "where the American flag has been hoisted in honor, let it not be hauled down in dishonor." Darrow responds "...the Filipinos haven't done anything..." to justify American bullets fired by Elgin boys. [31] Dwight Chamberlin works hard for the Republicans McKinley and Roosevelt. Again, Elgin carries overwhelmingly for the Republican ticket top to bottom. Again, Dwight gathers political "markers" soon to be important to Harry's future.

In 1904, Harry reaches age 17. Roosevelt runs again, this time as president. He wins 82 percent of the Elgin vote. Again, Dwight Chamberlin labors hard and long to elect the Republican Roosevelt and his party's down-ticket candidates. And again, Dwight Chamberlin accumulates influence to prove invaluable to Harry shortly thereafter. As the local paper relates:

"He has always taken an active interest in political affairs and for the success of his party has labored hard in season and out in the dissemination of party principles. In the campaign of 1896, he gave much time to the work and of his means he has usually given with a generous hand...," writes the *Elgin Herald* in 1923. [32]

Dwight Chamberlin does not serve, however, the Elgin community alone. Cora Chamberlin, like her husband Dwight, participates in the political, charitable, and social life of Elgin. Like her husband, Cora also is "a joiner and a doer." She devotes much time and energy to the Congregational Church. She serves on the Board of Directors of Elgin's Sherman Hospital. She participates in the Elgin Women's Club which founds the Sherman Hospital. She becomes a leader of "The Court of Honor," a fraternal organization with over 400 Elgin members in 1905.

Such community service and the insurance business create continued and expanded prosperity for the Chamberlin family. The address of each new home they occupy speaks to their growing prosperity. Dwight Chamberlin lives alone at 163 South Grove between 1885 and 1886 and then with Cora until 1887. As one moves north, Grove Street changes into Douglas

31 See E.C. Alft, *Elgin, Days Gone By* and E.C. Alft, *Elgin: An American History*. Internet website, 2001. www.elginhistory.com.

32 See Dwight Chamberlin Obituary, *Elgin Herald*, 1923.

Street. And as one moves north along Douglas Street, the higher the address number, the more prestigious the address.

In 1887, the year Harry comes into the world, Dwight and Cora move to 296 Douglas. From 1889-91, they live at 317 Douglas. This area comprises mostly of modest, Queen Anne style, single family residences. From 1892 to 1904, (for Harry, from kindergarten until his junior year in high school), the family lives at 711 Douglas in a large home with the large barn in back. Finally, in 1904, the Chamberlins build a home at 714 Douglas Ave in the ornate style of the times.

Newspaper reports from the time refer to the area as the "Elgin's Gold Coast" and the "exclusive upper Douglas area district." The mansions of the Bordens of Borden Milk, the Lords of Elgin National Watch Company, and the other wealthy and respected families in Elgin society sit a block or so north of the Chamberlin homes. The Chamberlin houses on Douglas appear tastefully modest and middle class, when compared to the elaborate mansions in the area.

"Old" Elgin High School: In 1901, Harry attends Elgin High School as a freshman. At that time, the entire school holds 450 seats to accommodate all four years of school. Unfortunately, no records exist of Harry's grades in high school. For Harry to aspire to West Point, however, suggests that he achieves exemplary grades. The school yearbook does attest to his leadership skills and to his athletic abilities. His classmates elect him president of the senior class. The football team, the Maroons, elect him captain of the team. For the Maroons, he plays varsity half-back.

In Harry's high school days, football prowess depends on pure strength. Without the "forward pass," which enters later, football teams use the "hurdle" to move the ball forward. To execute the "hurdle," the half-back (in this case Harry) carries the ball. He jumps onto the back of the quarterback and then hurdles himself over the offensive and defensive lines in hopes of moving the football forward.

In high school, Harry's combination of athletic prowess, intellectual ability, and leadership skill well qualify him for any college and any career that he might desire. His father's business success assures him of financial support at whatever college he might choose. As Harry considers colleges, he knows that upon graduation, he can join his father's insurance business and live a lucrative life. Instead, Harry chooses West Point and embraces the financially strapped, essentially ignored US Army.

To borrow a question that an old soldier of that era poses: "Why would anyone choose a vocation in which the pay was low, the outlook for advancement uncertain, and the business is neglected by its owners?" [33] In the case of Harry Dwight Chamberlin: The culture of Elgin; the Civil War reminisces of its veterans; the "Avenue of Flags;" the ceremony each Memorial Day; the speech of General Howard regarding Gettysburg; his mother's community service; the example of his staunchly Republican father proud to cast his first vote in a presidential election for Ulysses S. Grant—all combine to motivate him to aspire to West Point and to serve as a soldier in "the Army which he loved so intensely" to borrow General George C. Marshall's words about Harry. [34]

Aspiring and becoming, however, remain two different things. Dwight certainly develops the right political resume and contacts. Even if the Congressman agrees to appoint Harry, however, he might not be able to do so before Harry reaches the maximum age of 22. In those days, the local Congressman's power to appoint lapses until his previous appointee either graduates, drops out, or is expelled from the Academy. And of course, though admission requires an appointment, an appointment does not assure admission. The Academy requires all appointees to pass rigorous physical and intellectual examinations.

The last appointment to the Corps from the 11th Congressional District occurs in 1901. At that time, the local Congressman appoints Julius Charles Peterson. Another opportunity for the Congressman from the Illinois 11th District to appoint a Cadet remains closed until after Peterson either leaves the Academy or graduates. So, Harry might have to wait. George Patton faces exactly the same hurdle when his father begins lobbying for Patton's appointment to West Point in 1903.

Often, the Academy requires cadets to repeat a year for poor academic performance. This would defer by another year or longer, the Congressman's power to appoint a new cadet. At the turn of the century, this problem occurs frequently.

Most likely Dwight, like George Patton's father, lobbies for Harry's appointment long before the potential year of appointment. Thankfully, Julius Peterson graduates from the Academy in June of 1905. Immediately, Congressman Harold Snapp of the 11th Congressional District of Illinois appoints Harry. Most Congressmen usually hold competitive examinations to assist them in making such an appointment. Congressman Snapp holds no such examination, probably a testament to Dwight's political stature.

---

33 See Victor Vogel, *Soldiers of the Old Army,* College Station, Texas A & M University 1990.

34 See https://www.westpointaog.org/memorial-article?id=f3efb07e-1306-45c3-86dd-780dd099a6a0

Formal notice will come from the War Department the first week of January 1906. Dwight Chamberlin's long years of service to the Republican Party opens the door. Now, only the physical and mental examinations stand in Harry's way. One might imagine how the Chamberlin family celebrates upon hearing the news of Congressman Snapp's decision but soon, sadness overwhelms any thoughts of celebration.

Harry graduates from the Elgin High School on June 17, 1905. The day after Harry's mother, Cora Chamberlin, attends Harry's graduation ceremony, she suddenly falls ill, seriously ill for the first time in her life. Her doctors ascribe her first illness to "inflammatory rheumatism." Her sudden illness comes out of nowhere. Unable to get out of bed, she grows worse for the next two months. During the last week of August, she enters the Sherman Hospital. On Tuesday, August 30, 1905, she feels just as ill but wants to go home. The doctors approve. Back home she goes. She lingers bed ridden. Her condition grows worse. On Friday, Sept. 1st, her doctors abandon all hope for her recovery. [35]

She dies at 10 a.m., Monday, September 4, 1905, in her home at 714 Douglas. Her death stuns the family as well as the people of Elgin. Longevity seems the norm in the Chamberlin family: Cora's mother, Mary Orth, passes away in her late 70's; Dwight's father, Alfred, passes away at age 93; Dwight's mother, Nancy, passes away at age 88. The month before her death, Corrine Orth Chamberlin turned 46.

How Harry Chamberlin mourns the loss of his mother, no discovered record discloses. Perhaps, as a means of grieving, he throws himself into preparing for the West Point examinations. One fact remains certain: he studies from the day after his graduation and almost every day thereafter for eleven months. Harry well knows that a Congressional appointment to the Academy provides only the first step in the admissions process. He faces arduous mental and physical examinations in May 1906. Harry uses the time to prepare.

On January 27, 1906, The Military Secretary of the War Department at Washington, DC sends to Harry Chamberlin a letter which states in part:

> Sir:
> I have the honor to inform you that you have been selected for appointment as a cadet for the United States Military Academy at West Point, NY. Should you desire the appointment, you are authorized by the Secretary of War to present yourself before a board of officers at Fort Sheridan,

35 See *Elgin Herald*, Sept 1905.

Illinois, on the first day of May 1906, before 9 o'clock in the morning for mental and physical examination...Upon it having been found that you possess the requisite qualifications, you will be admitted to the Academy, without further examination... on the 15th day of June 1906...You are requested immediately to inform this office of your acceptance or declination of the contemplated appointment...

Very respectfully,
The Military Secretary. [36]

Academic Requirements;

The following paragraph describes the academic examinations Harry must pass:

"Each candidate before admission to the academy, must show by examination as prescribed in paragraph 19 that he is well versed in algebra, to include quadratic equations and progressions, plane geometry, English grammar, composition and literature, descriptive and physical geography, and general and United States history, as explained in the circulars of notification."

—*The Official Register of the Officers and Cadets of the United States Military Academy,* West Point, New York, June 1905

The whole exercise plays out at Fort Sheridan in May 1906. It seems rote and exhausting. The methods remain consistent with the practices of the times. The examiners perfect their own methods to assess the level of competence in each area. The candidate must write answers to parts of the examination and also must answer other parts orally. The examiners test Harry in the fields the official announcement describes and a host of other subjects to determine whether Harry shows promise as a future West Point cadet.

Physical and Other Requirements:

The Academy bars any candidate under seventeen, or over twenty-two years of age. The Academy sets 5'-5" as the minimum height requirement for candidates eighteen years old and up. The regulations also ban any candidate "who is deformed, or afflicted with any disease or infirmity which would render him unfit for the military service, or who has, at the time of presenting himself, any disorder of an infectious or immoral character. Candidates must be unmarried."

The candidate needs to demonstrate "normal" hearing in both ears.

36 Letter in Chamberlin's papers.

His vision cannot fall below 20/40 in either eye, and not below 20/20 unless the defect were a simple refractive error entirely corrected by proper glasses. The Academy rejects any candidate who displays color blindness for red, green, or violet. [37]

The Results:

At 5'-11" and 160 pounds; in perfect health and physical condition; with sufficient competence in all intellectual fields examined, Harry Dwight Chamberlin passes all examinations, physical and mental. In June of 1906, Chamberlin departs from his home above the Fox River to take up residence on the plain above the Hudson.

Harry Chamberlin begins the next phase of his life: life as a soldier in the United States Army.

---

37 See *The Official Register of the Officers and Cadets of the United States Military Academy* West Point, New York, June 1905.

Chapter 4

West Point: School for Officers 1906

"If Sherman's definition of war be right, then West Point is war."
—Cadet George S. Patton, Jr. [38]

When Harry Chamberlin departs from his home on the Fox River and arrives at West Point on the Hudson in 1906, the academy maintains a rigid protocol that stifles creativity, frowns on independent thought, and depends on rote memory and recitation. Once there, Chamberlin lives in cloistered isolation. This isolation, in the opinion of the Academy Board, enables West Point to mold a young man into the officer that the Board thinks the Army needs. Clearly, the academy remains stuck in the early nineteenth-century. The West Point of 1906 differs little from the West Point of 1856 or of 1836. Regarding the teaching methods and the tenor of the place, one of Douglas MacArthur's classmates in the Class of 1903 writes: "West Point made human turnips out of perfectly good young men." [39]

But not Harry Chamberlin. He endures the rigid atmosphere, sublimates his inquiring mind, and focuses on working through the four years of cumbersome regulations, rote classroom recitation, and unending drudgery. Once he graduates, his natural intellect reasserts itself and for the rest of his life, he delves into subjects deeply, questions everything, and focuses his intellect to achieve precise goals. The spirit and *esprit de corps* of West Point, however, resonates within him for the rest of this life.

38 See Carlo D'Este, Patton: *A Genius For War*, Harper Perennial, 1995.

39 See Geoffrey Perret, *Old Soldiers Never Die, The Life of Douglas MacArthur*, Random House, 1996.

During his four years at the Academy, what does he endure? What does he learn? What does he achieve? Who does he meet? What influence, long term, does the Academy, its history and its methods have on him?

The Academy's history exerts a strong influence on Chamberlin. For centuries European settlers recognize the Hudson river's strategic importance as a gateway from the South into the interior of New England and as a gateway from the North to New York City. By the time of the American Revolution, the plateau overlooking the Hudson 55 miles north of New York City becomes the most strategic point in North America: West Point.

In 1778, General Washington commissions Continental Army engineers to fortify the plateau and to draw a large chain across the Hudson to interdict British ships sailing south toward the city. The engineers design and built forts, ramparts and other fortifications high on the plateau to command the Hudson's west bank and the river below. To this day, West Point remains the oldest continuously occupied and active military post in the United States.

In 1802, President Thomas Jefferson signs into law the Act of Congress that establishes the United States Military Academy at West Point, New York. Initially, the school's sponsors seek to free the country from its dependence on foreign engineers and artillerists. In addition, Washington, Hamilton, Adams and others recognize the need for a school devoted to the study of war and fortifications as well as to the study of bridge, harbor, and road building. Under Superintendent Sylvanus Thayer, the school focuses on civil engineering as its core curriculum to achieve these purposes.

For the first 50 years of the school's existence, West Point graduates design almost all of the bridges, roads, harbors and fortifications for the country. For example, Robert E. Lee designs a series of levies to discipline and direct the flow of the Mississippi River and thereby preserve the City of St. Louis's role as a river port. When the Mississippi changes course and threatens to leave St. Louis "high and dry," Lee's engineering feat redirects the river's flow and preserves St. Louis as a river town. His design remains effective to this day.

The Mexican War of the 1840s, as well as the Indian Wars prior to the Civil War, establishes West Point's graduates as the nation's military leaders. During the Civil War, West Point graduates lead armies on both sides. In fact, in almost every major battle of the war, a West Point graduate leads at least one and usually, both sides. When Chamberlin arrives at West Point in 1906, Lee, Jackson, Longstreet, Grant, Stuart, Sheridan and Sherman—West Point graduates all—achieve legendary status. Their exploits inspire Chamberlin's generation of West Point cadets and graduates alike.

When Chamberlin arrives at the Academy, the American Civil War stands as the world's bloodiest and most recent major war and it forms the major portion of military education at West Point for Chamberlin's class. And so, West Point classes study, therefore, all aspects of that war as well as the successes and failures of its military leaders. Their stories inspire Chamberlin just as do the stories of the Union veterans back home in Elgin.

Upon his son's acceptance to the Academy, Chamberlin's father Dwight must deposit the sum of $100 with the Academy's Treasurer. Like all other cadets, Chamberlin must use this money, as far as it goes, to defray the expense of his cadet outfit. The Academy allows cadets to bring with them only enough money to pay for their travel to the Academy. The Academy prohibits parents from sending money with the exception of the initial $100 deposit.

Before he arrives, Harry must purchase items the Academy requires that each bring with them; eight white shirts; two gray shirts; eight summer undershirts; five night-shirts; six winter undershirts; twelve white linen collars; twelve pairs of white linen cuffs; eight pairs of summer drawers; six pairs of winter drawers; eight pairs of socks; twelve pocket handkerchiefs; twelve towels; one clothes brush; one hair-brush; one toothbrush; one comb; one trunk, no more, no less. It prohibits any other personal items that parents might supply.

After he arrives, Chamberlin must purchase at the Academy: one black tie; two clothes bags, made of ticking; two pairs of uniform shoes; six pairs of uniform white gloves; two sets of white belts; one mattress; one pillow; four pillow-cases; six sheets; two blankets; one quilted bed cover; one chair; one tumbler; one account book; one wash basin. Cadets buy and wear only the uniform the Academy prescribes in a pattern that it designates.

For the next four years, the same regimen governs Chamberlin's life as that of Lee, Grant, McClellan, Stuart and Sheridan: life by the book; life by the Regulations of the Army; life by the Regulations of the United Stated Military Academy; life by the Regulations of the Corps of Cadets. Every aspect of their lives submits to Regulations and more regulations stacked high. His life remains cloistered with few opportunities outside of the Academy. Reveille sounds at 5:30 a.m. with roll call at 6:00 a.m. Each day consists of military drills, rituals and seven hours of classroom time. Taps sounds at 10:00 p.m. and lights go out.

The regulations require that a cadet stay on the West Point campus almost his entire four years. When he passes into the last semester of his second year at the Academy, he may ride a horse outside the Academy up to a distance of six miles. According to the rules, he must not stop. He must not dismount. He must not talk to anyone. At the end of his second year, he might earn a ten-week leave if his grades meet accepted standards and if his number of demerits stay below a set threshold.

After that single ten-week leave, he must remain at West Point until he graduates with only short leaves of from four to six days at Christmas, but only if his conduct during the preceding six months meets a satisfactory standard. When he reaches his senior year, he might enjoy a leave of no more than seventy-five hours at the beginning of the summer encampment and a leave of no more than 27 hours at Thanksgiving, but only if he meets, once again, a satisfactory standard.

During the balance of his four years at the Academy, when he does not pursue academic duties, Chamberlin like all other cadets, engages in "military duties and exercises and receives practical instruction in military and other subjects," says a military manual of the day. Luckily, the Academy's history, the friendships that he develops there, and his intense desire to serve as a soldier outweigh the academy's unending drudgery and rigid requirements.

When Harry Chamberlin enters West Point, the Corps of Cadets remains relatively small: 522 cadets consisting of four classes: "Plebe," "Yearling," "Third Class," and "Fourth Class." Recent graduates as well as members of Chamberlin's class will achieve high rank 25 years later. At the same time, Chamberlin follows, by three years, First Captain and first in his class of 1903, Douglas MacArthur. Chamberlin misses, by three days, First Captain Jonathan Wainwright, who graduates in the Class of 1906. MacArthur will further Chamberlin's career and offer opportunity for his equestrian talent. Wainwright will become a good friend.

When Chamberlin enters West Point, he meets several members of the Corps of Cadets who torment him and all other new comers in "Plebe Camp" but later become life-long friends who achieve military fame in World War II: George S. Patton, Jr, admitted '04, commands the 3rd Army and leads armored thrusts in Africa and Europe; Robert Eichelberger, admitted '05, commands the 8th US Army in the Pacific under General MacArthur; William Simpson, '05 commands the 9th Army which, as the first Allied army to cross the Elbe River, awaits orders to march on Berlin in April 1945; Simon Bolivar Buckner, Jr, admitted '04 and the son of the Confederate general who surrenders Fort Donelson to US Grant in the Civil War, leads the 10th Army's assault on Okinawa and there, Japanese shrapnel kills him, the highest-ranking American officer to die in command of troops during World War II. [40]

In addition to Chamberlin, 21 others of the Class of 1910 achieve the rank of Brigadier General or above during World War II. Chamberlin marches in good company. Of course, in 1906, World Wars I and II remain in the distant and unknown future. Aircraft flies for the first time only three years earlier. Machine guns frequently jam and a reliable version remains six years in the future. Mechanization, which ultimately will replace the horse in warfare, remains virtually unknown.

In June of 1906, Chamberlin and the other "Plebes" (the name the Academy gives to first year cadets) report to a tent city on the plain that overlooks the Hudson River. There, tailors measure him for his uniforms and he joins a squad of four men based on his height. Two Third-Classmen focus on each squad and haze each squad member without mercy. "Welcome to Beast Barracks" or "Plebe Camp" as they call it.

Hazing, as a West Point tradition and integral part of the program, emerges shortly after the Civil War. Technically, the practice violates Academy regulations. The rules fail to describe accurately, however, the prohibited practices. Tactical Officers typically turn a blind eye to the practice. In addition, every cadet that the Academy expelled for hazing eventually returns either by presidential appointment or by act of Congress.

Beast Barracks consists of constant physical and mental harassment, military drill, saluting and constant exercise. Second Corporal George S. Patton, Jr (admitted in '04 but held back for deficiency in mathematics) greets the newcomers including Harry Chamberlin. In time, Patton's words and conduct prove so harsh that he irritates not only the "Plebes" but the Tactical Officers as well. His actions so upset the officers, that finally, in August, they demote him!

For the first month of June, Chamberlin and the other Plebes learn military and ceremonial drill. They exercise to the point of exhaustion. Third-Classmen manage the misery and hand out demerits for the most minor infractions of military discipline and demeanor. Plebes walk punishment tours that sometimes last twenty-four hours. During such "tours," they carry a rifle and full pack—and back and forth, they march.

In addition to military drill, marching, and calisthenics, cadets also engage in swimming drills. On July, 9, Chamberlin's swimming instructor

---

40 See Cullum, Brevet-Major General, George W. *Biographical Register of the Officers and Graduates of the US Military Academy at West Point, New York Since its Establishment in 1802 Supplement, Volume IX 1940-1950* Edited by Col. Charles N. Branham, USA Retired.

had "the honor to report that Cadet Chamberlin, 4th Class, qualified in swimming today." Chamberlin keeps this report in his personal papers for the rest of his life.

In mid-July, Upper Classmen integrate with the Plebes in a summer encampment. Hazing intensifies: Upper Classmen harass the Plebes at meals, on the parade ground, and in their tents. They demand spur and saber shining, leather polishing, and gun cleaning; they dream up other exhausting physical exercises. They put Tabasco sauce in Plebes' food, order them to sweep the streets, carry water, and conduct mock funerals for dead rats. One hour of daily dancing classes where a tent-mate acts as a partner provide the only respite from the otherwise endless toil.

On the last day of August, the Corps leaves summer camp and departs for the Academy proper. Hazing abates but marching continues. Cadets march everywhere. They march to breakfast. They march to the bath house. They march from class to class. They march to and from lunch, to and from afternoon drill, to and from athletics, to and from dinner; and then, they march to the barracks for the night.

The next morning, they march anew. This goes on every day, seven days a week. The regimentation and routine, the discipline and punishment finally cause some cadets to snap mentally. More than one attempts suicide. Others attempt homicide against upper classmen. Cadet George Patton writes home: "If Sherman's definition of war be right, then West Point is war." [41] Sherman famously said: "War is Hell." Many Plebes quit in disgust and despair. Chamberlin presses on.

The cadets describe the food as putrid; the housing as slum-like. Cadet George Patton writes home saying that the meat is so tough "the more you chewed it, the bigger it got!" The housing conditions come right out of a Charles Dickens novel. Cadets live in Spartan barracks. They shiver in winter cold and sweat in summer heat. The Academy assigns two cadets to a room. Each cadet sleeps on his own iron bed "softened" with a hair mattress and made "comfortable" with one pillow, a sheet, two blankets and a bed cover. Each cadet enjoys his own chair and his own table with a wash basin. The Academy allows no other furniture. Due to the room's small size, its occupants cannot not stand together in the room at the same time.

No running water services the rooms so Chamberlin and the other cadets haul water in a bucket up several flights of stairs. Since the buildings enjoy no central heat, when water spills on the iron stair risers, it freezes and makes the dash down the stairs for morning roll call a dangerous endeavor.

---

41 See Carlo D'Este, *Patton: A Genius For War*, Harper Perennial, 1995.

The building enjoys no electricity. Gas lamps light the rooms. The squalor equals what the poor in a big-city slum endure during the late nineteenth-century. So much for the accommodations.

Chamberlin and his fellow "plebes" attend academic classes for the first time on September 1, 1906. Regulations govern the manner in which instructors carry on classes. Each day, instructors teach from assigned textbooks and grade cadets on "recitations" from those assigned texts. These "recitation regulations" dull the mind, strangle creativity, discourage independent thinking, and reduce cadets to nothing more than automatons. To follow the regulations, the cadet must stand at the blackboard in a certain way, hold the pointer at a certain angle, and recite answers in a certain manner to instructor questions regarding the previous night's reading assignment. The answers, for the most part, constitute rote recitation of memorized facts without the meaningful exploration of ideas and constructive dialogue between cadet and instructor.

During Chamberlin's first semester of the first year, each morning the he and the other cadets recite on mathematics. They devote three 80-minute classes per week to Algebra and three 80-minute classes per week to Geometry. Each afternoon, they devote five 60-minute classes per week to English. Each week, cadets devote one 60-minute class to artillery and infantry tactics. The balance of their day they devote to bayonet practice; to target practice with rifle, revolver, mountain and field gun; and finally, to athletics. [42] At night, the cadets read and prepare to recite the next day.

During Chamberlin's second semester of the first year, he and the other cadets devote five one-hour classes per week to French; one hour per week to tactics; three 80-minute classes per week to Algebra; three 80-minute classes per week to Trigonometry. Later in the term, they devote six 80-minute sessions to Conic Sections. The balance of the day, they devote to target practice; and then cavalry, artillery and infantry drill. At night, again, the cadets read and prepare to recite the next day.

At the end of his first year, Chamberlin fairs well enough. In a starting class of 116, he ranks 33rd in math; 26th in English; 21st in French; 67th in Drill; 54th in Conduct. He amasses 88 demerits. By way of comparison, during Patton's first year, Patton fails mathematics; stands 69th in English; 109th in French; 2nd in Drill; 19th in Conduct; and he amasses 45 demerits. [43] One must keep in mind, however, that Patton suffers from dyslexia. Often, he

---

42 *Official Register of the Officers and Cadets of the United States Military Academy*, West Point, New York, June 1907.

43 Ibid.

cannot read the bulletin board for daily orders not to mention the classroom blackboard for daily lessons.

At this point, of great importance to Chamberlin's future career, three officers serve on the West Point staff: Lt. Col. Robert Howze, Commandant of Cadets, will become the first commander of the 1st Cavalry Division. Captain Charles F. Summerall, Instructor of Artillery Tactics, will become the Army Chief of Staff. Captain Francis C. Marshall, Senior Instructor of Cavalry Tactics and Commander of West Point's Cavalry Detachment, will teach Chamberlin to ride "the army way." Most importantly, Captain Marshall proves to be a great horseman, a prolific writer, an excellent instructor of horsemanship, and a model of leadership. In addition, Marshall breaks the West Point mold and pushes his students to go beyond the mere rote recitation of memorized facts.

SUMMER ENCAMPMENT: JUNE 30, 1907

For the summer encampment of 1907, Chamberlin achieves the rank of Corporal of the Corps, 17th out of 29 so appointed. Patton, who is one year ahead of Chamberlin, achieves the rank of Sergeant-Major of the Corps. [44]

Whether now Corporal Harry Chamberlin delights in tormenting the newly appointed Fourth Classmen during their initiation to "Beast Barracks" remains unknown. One might infer, however, that Harry devotes himself to his perceived responsibilities with a certain level of enthusiasm. And of course, once "Beast Barracks" ends, the Academy expects the hazing and harsh treatment of "Plebes" to end as well. An incident that occurs six months after the cadets depart from "Beast Barracks" might offer insight into how Chamberlin conducts himself.

His mode and tone of address toward a fourth classman comes to the attention of the Commandant of Cadets, Lt. Col. Robert Howze. On February 23, 1908, Lt. Col. Howze orders Cadet Chamberlin "to submit an explanation, in writing," with regard to a charged offense of "using harsh language towards a fourth classman while leaving the mess hall after dinner." [45]

Just as the Tactical Officers demote 2nd Corporal George S. Patton, Jr. for harsh conduct regarding "Plebes," so too do they demote 17th Corporal

44 *Official Register of the Officers and Cadets of the United States Military Academy*, West Point, New York, June 1908.

45 Col. Howze order found in Chamberlin's personal papers.

Harry D. Chamberlin. Pursuant to Special Order No. 42 at West Point on February 27, 1908:

1. For 'Making unauthorized and harsh correction of a fourth classman while leaving the mess hall after dinner," 23rd instant, the appointment of Cadet Harry D. Chamberlin, third class, as a corporal in the Battalion of Cadets is revoked, and he will be confined to barracks, area of barracks, and gymnasium until Mary 13, 1908, and during that period will serve punishment tours every Wednesday and every Saturday at the usually prescribed hours.

By ORDER OF COLONEL SCOTT:

J. S. HERRON,
Captain, 2d Cavalry
Adjutant.

A copy of this order remains one of the few items to survive in Harry Chamberlin's personal papers.

Regardless of Chamberlin's demotion, the summer encampment of 1907 offers an event of particular importance for Chamberlin: his class studies horsemanship. For the first time, the class mounts horses. The formal equestrian education of Harry D. Chamberlin begins.

Chapter 5

Horsemanship at West Point
The Summer Encampment of 1907 and Thereafter

"First Class cadets ride like Indians..."
—*The New York Times* 1887 [46]

"For teaching a firm, close seat, and giving the recruit confidence in himself, nothing is as good as the trot without stirrups."
—General Carter 1906 [47]

"Unfortunately, our officers and troopers were taught to ride with the buttocks pushed under them so that they were seated on the ends of their spines..."
—Harry Chamberlin 1937 [48]

"...the French position...there is a tendency toward riding with the weight somewhat to the rear."
—Col. Albert Phillips 1935 [49]

Harry Chamberlin begins his formal training in military horsemanship at West Point's summer encampment in the year 1907. At this time, most

---

46 *The New York Times*, May 22, 1887.

47 General William H. Carter, United States Army, *Horses Saddles and Bridles*, The Lord Baltimore Press, The Friedenwald Company, 1906.

48 Lt. Col. Harry D. Chamberlin, *Training Hunters, Jumpers, and Hacks* Derrydale Press, 1937.

49 Col. Albert Phillips, "The Phillips Cross Country Saddle," *The Cavalry Journal March–April* 1935.

of what West Point and the cavalry schools of Europe teach about training riders and training horses relies, in large measure, on the theories of the French Cavalry School at Saumur. In fact, American officers of the nineteenth and early twentieth centuries view the French Army as the world's preeminent military organization.

Most of the French theory regarding training horses and riders, especially the "military seat" as defined by the French, the Americans view as valuable for cavalry. The French theory of the rider's aids and the various rein effects remains solid, in the American view, and West Point teaches these concepts with slight modification. West Point departs, however, from other French practices: For example, the Academy does not adopt extreme "collection," i.e. the controlled, precise, elevated movements of the horse as advocated by François Baucher. The Academy prefers the free-flowing, natural way of going typical of the Thoroughbred in the hunt field as opposed to the horse performing, in a high state of collection, artistic movements in the dressage ring.

Keep in mind that in 1907, the forward riding theories of Federico Caprilli remain "revolutionary," unknown in the United States, and (outside of Italy) deemed unsuitable for cavalry by most of Europe's military. When compared to the Italian concepts, the French theories of the "military seat," of jumping obstacles, and of traversing down steep grades, together with some of the French theories of dressage for horses prove flawed for cavalry purposes. But recognition of these flaws remains more than 15 to 20 years in the future in spite of the disastrous results experienced in the early days of World War I by the French and Russian cavalries trained in these theories.

Keeping these introductory facts in mind, let us explore what Chamberlin learns, how he learns, and from whom he learns in the year 1907. Space requires that we choose only a short list of topics drawn from the exhaustive and in-depth study of horsemanship that West Point requires its cadets to master over a period of three years. We will explore the basic objectives of the West Point program, the personnel in charge, the two textbooks the cadet must master; the theory of the "military seat" circa 1907 (also known as the "Saumur Seat"); and finally, the teaching process that the instructors employ.

In the companion to this biography, we explore in depth some of the principles that instructors teach that may be of value to contemporary readers who ride: their concept of ideal equine conformation; and finally, their recommendations regarding horse shoeing faults to avoid.

The summer encampment of Chamberlin's second or "yearling" year at the Academy takes place prior to the start of classes. Once summer camp ends, Chamberlin and the other cadets continue their study of horsemanship from November 1st through March 15th of the following year. Thereafter, they study horsemanship each year until they graduate two years later. In their final year, cadets learn to play polo and ride in "flat" English saddles as opposed to the regulation McClellan saddles in which the other classes ride.

BASIC OBJECTIVES OF THE PROGRAM: TO CREATE HORSEMEN NOT JUST RIDERS

To the instructors, the term "horsemanship" means far more than equitation; in fact, most of the written curriculum deals with the wide-ranging subject of "Hippology" a term derived from Greek which means "the study of the horse." At the Academy, cadets study the horse from a number of different angles. To do this, they study two text books written for the Academy program. The first is: *Elements of Hippology* by Francis C. Marshall. Marshall writes: "The effort has been made to write a comprehensive book that will cover, in outline only, all general subjects that a horseman should know." [50] In the second text, *Horses, Saddles, and Bridles* by General William H. Carter, Carter writes to provide the "...elementary facts and principles essential to the well-being and efficiency of the mounted branches of the army..." including "...some information usually found in books on horsemanship..." [51]

All of the "book" learning takes place through the study of those texts at night and "recitation" in the classroom the next day. The curriculum offers knowledge beyond what the army shares with the cavalry ranks of that era. Academy instructors view this as a serious weakness and the status of horsemanship in the ranks helps to understand the objectives of the Academy's curriculum and the responsibilities for which the instructors hope to prepare Chamberlin and the other cadets.

For the troopers in the ranks and non-West Point officers, the *"Cavalry Drill Regulations, 1891"* addresses horsemanship in the context of mounted drill and maneuver for squads, squadrons and regiments. The manual ignores equitation in the French sense and, to the extent the manual touches on that subject, it does so in paragraphs of squadron drill. In the *Regulations,* equitation as a discipline separate and apart from drill does not exist.

The Academy textbooks discuss basic, elementary equitation only in passing since most of the skills-oriented learning takes place outside the

50 F.C. Marshall, *Elements of Hippology*, US Military Press at West Point, 1906.

51 General William H. Carter, United States Army, *Horses Saddles and Bridles*, The Lord Baltimore Press, The Friedenwald Company, 1906.

classroom in the round pen, in the riding hall, and in the countryside under the critical eye of instructors. After a discussion of the "military seat" and the use of the aids, the written course materials offer an exhaustive treatment of all other things equine, everything from what makes a solid cavalry horse capable of traveling long distances to every equine disease then known, to strengths and weakness in conformation, to the equine musculature and skeletal framework, to proper and improper shoeing; to stable management, forage selection and feeding and far more.

When the well-experienced cavalrymen of the Civil War and of the Indian Wars pass from the scene, their knowledge and experience pass with them. For the most part, the officer corps and the ranks remain inconsistent in their understanding and in their approach to horsemanship. In fact, whatever level of elevated understanding exists in the ranks regarding horsemanship exists for the same reasons that American marksmanship in the First World War so impresses the Germans. As one German officer remarks after the war, the average nineteenth-century American farmhouse contains more rifles than a German infantry platoon and so American youth know how to shoot. So too with horses: many troopers mount horses from time they learn to walk and care for horses on the family farm until the day the leave home to join the army. They transfer their horse-keeping and horse-riding knowledge to their military careers.

As noted above, West Point instructors take a different approach. They expect their students to master the basic French skills of the military seat and the application of the aids together with an exhaustive understanding of all aspects of Hippology. The goal: to enable the West Point trained officer to train troopers in garrison, to lead troopers in the field, and to supervise all aspects of horse care for thousands of horses.

PERSONNEL IN CHARGE OF THE PROGRAM AND THEIR INFLUENCE ON CHAMBERLIN

The Academy views experience in the field equally important to the mastery of theory, and the backgrounds of the Academy's horsemanship instructors reflect this. During Chamberlin's time at the Academy, four officers mold the curriculum and the methods of instruction: initially, General William H. Carter, Captain Llewellyn W. Oliver, Captain Francis Cutler Marshall; and later, Captain Guy V. Henry Jr. The military records of each demonstrates that West Point values a combination of theory with extensive, practical field experience.

General Carter begins his career as a mounted messenger in the Civil War and offers extensive experience in mounted action against the Apaches and other tribes in the American Southwest. Through his book *Horses, Bridles, and Saddles,* Carter exerts direct influence on the content of the West Point program and the theory of horsemanship taught.

Captain Oliver rides with the 12th Cavalry and attends the French Advanced Cavalry School at Saumur. From Oliver, Chamberlin learns his first exposure to the "military seat."

Captain Marshall, in particular, influences both Patton and Chamberlin as future cavalrymen since he teaches both men much of their initial understanding of horsemanship and cavalry tactics during their time as cadets. Captain Marshall serves on the American frontier with mounted scouts, goes to Asia where he leads the 6th Cavalry and 500 British Bengal Lancers in a cavalry charge against the Boxers, and then moves to the Philippines where he fights the Filipinos in successive mounted actions. Marshall conducts himself, in the words of Patton biographer, Carlo D'Estes, as "a man of dignity, patience, and quiet but very effective leadership." [52] He proves himself not only a capable leader but also a superb horseman steeped in experience as well as in the theories of that era. Carlo D'Estes writes that Captain F.C. Marshall remains one of the few men in Patton's life that George Patton truly reveres. Most likely, Harry Chamberlin holds a similar opinion. In fact, what Carlo D'Estes writes of Marshall as "a man of dignity, patience, and quiet but very effective leadership" applies to Chamberlin as well. Captains Marshall and Oliver exert direct, day to day influence on Chamberlin in the first year of his West Point horsemanship experience.

Captain Guy V. Henry, Jr. In August, 1908, Chamberlin meets his future mentor, teacher, and perhaps the most important contact of his early military career: Captain Guy V. Henry, Jr. Captain Henry's experience, accomplishments, and education merit a detailed discussion since, from 1908 until at least 1934, he influences Chamberlin's career as no other officer in the Army.

By the time he meets Chamberlin, Henry combines advanced equestrian education, higher staff responsibility in the Cavalry, and practical field experience. Born in Fort Robinson, Nebraska, Captain Guy V. Henry, Jr comes into the world on

January 28, 1875. His father, Guy V. Henry, Sr. graduates from West Point, wins the Medal of Honor for action at Cold Harbor in 1864, and ultimately achieves the rank of general in the army. Guy Henry, Jr. graduates from West Point in 1898. He fights in the Spanish American War and wins the Silver

52 Carlo D'Estes *Patton: Genius For War,* Harper Perennial 1995.

Star in the Philippines. Later, he studies equitation under Edward Anderson whom General Carter in his book *Horses, Saddles and Bridles* acknowledges as one of the great horsemen and authors of the age.

In 1902, Henry becomes adjutant at Fort Riley where he begins lecturing on equitation. He also becomes a member of the Cavalry Board. Through his efforts and his critique of horsemanship in the US Cavalry, Henry persuades the army to transfer Captain Walter C. Short, an accomplished horseman, to Fort Riley where he establishes the rudiments of school for farriers. By 1904, Henry and Short help Brig. General Godfrey establish the Mounted Service School at Fort Riley.

In 1905, Henry helps persuade the cavalry to abandon the severe Shoemaker Bit in favor of the bit and bridoon. He also persuades the artillery to adopt the straight bar snaffle as its standard bit. In April 1906, Henry's career takes a pleasant turn. He writes:

> "Major General J. Franklin Bell was the Army's first Chief of Staff, and about April 1906, he sent for me one day and told me that he desired to send me to the French Cavalry School at Saumur, France, for a year's instruction...." [53]

Several US Cavalry officers attend Saumur prior to Henry including Captain Llewellyn Oliver, Chamberlin's first horsemanship and cavalry tactics instructors at West Point. While he attends the French Cavalry School at Saumur, Captain Henry studies and adopts many of the theories of François Baucher. After a year of instruction, he returns to the United States and to the Mounted Service School in 1907. He then serves as Senior Instructor under Brig. General Godfrey, the school's Commandant.

As Senior Instructor, Henry continues his innovations: In horse training, Henry introduces "breaking" horses on the longe line as opposed to "breaking" them in the western manner by bucking to exhaustion. In equitation, he favors the Baucheriste methods to apply the lower leg as opposed to the German methods and adopts Baucher's maxim: *"hands without legs; legs without hands."*

In August of 1908, Captain Henry succeeds Captain Francis C. Marshall as Senior Assistant Instructor of Cavalry Tactics when Marshall's tour of duty ends at West Point. Henry takes special notice of Chamberlin due to the latter's riding proficiency and interest in the subject of horsemanship.

---

53 Guy V. Henry, Jr. *A Brief Narrative of the Life of Guy V. Henry, Jr.* Military History Research Collection, Carlisle Barracks Pennsylvania. 1974

During Chamberlin's last year at the Academy, Henry spends considerable time watching Chamberlin's progress as a horseman. Henry also conducts Chamberlin's last course in Hippology at the Academy.

***Figure 31** Captain Guy V. Henry, Jr. placed fourth in Prix des Nations jumping at the Olympics of 1912. US Army photo.*

***Figure 32** Major General Guy V. Henry, Jr, Chief of Cavalry 1930-1934, supports Chamberlin and the Army Olympic effort whole heartedly. US Army photo.*

Throughout his life, Henry remains an expert horseman. He participates in the 1912 Olympics in Sweden as a member of the Army Equestrian Team. He competes in all three equestrian disciplines. In Eventing, He wins the Bronze Team Medal and places 11th individually. He ranks fourth in show jumping. Henry remains at West Point to become Commandant of Cadets from 1916-1918, graduates from the Army War College in 1921, the Army School of the Line in 1922, and General Staff School in 1923. Most importantly for Chamberlin, Henry becomes Chief of Cavalry during the years 1930-1934.

As Chief of Cavalry, General Henry makes sure that then Major Harry Chamberlin enjoys every advantage that the United States Army might offer as Chamberlin and the other members of the Army Equestrian Team ready themselves for the 1932 Olympic Games at Los Angeles. From 1931 through 1935, Henry serves as President of the *Fédération Equestre Internationale* (the FEI). He remains the only American in history to achieve this status.

TEACHING IN THE CLASSROOM:

Much of what Chamberlin studies about horsemanship occurs in the classroom. He learns about the "center of motion," the "center of gravity," the "base of support" and the "proper distribution of load in order to retain the normal position of the Center of Gravity." He learns that a horse and rider must remain "in equilibrium" so that the horse may obey the rider's commands without "unnecessary effort."

Chamberlin and the others study all areas valuable to the true horseman. To demonstrate the level of detail the course requires: they learn the range of equine body temperatures from normal to potentially fatal and all variants and potential exposures in between. They memorize the range of acceptable pulse rates for various breeds of horses at various rates of exercise. They study every disease known then as well as recommendations for treatment. They study the strengths and potential defects in equine conformation. They study horseshoeing and bad practices associated with same. In short, the exploration of "non-riding" aspects of horsemanship prove exhaustive. A more detailed discussion of conformation as well as points to consider regarding hoof care and the pre-purchase examination as taught at West Point appears in *The Chamberlin Reader.*

The theory of the Military Seat circa 1907, also known as the "Saumur Seat," forms the cornerstone of West Point horsemanship during this era.

In his book *Horses, Saddles and Bridles,* General Carter describes the "military seat" in detail. Essentially, it mirrors the seat that the French cavalry teaches recruits and its officers. Once in the saddle, the rider places his shoulders back, a trifle behind the vertical. He tucks his spine under his torso. He places his legs a bit forward with stirrup straps a trifle ahead of the vertical. He keeps his feet parallel to the horse. The rider's seat bones and the buttocks slightly behind the seat bones form his base of support.

General Carter quotes a noted horseman and famous equestrian writer of that era, Edward Anderson, who states that the "military seat" of the American army circa 1907 is "the seat of François Baucher." The cadets learn the following rationale and theory of the "military seat" as taught at Saumur. Carter writes:

"It has been shown that the center of gravity lies somewhat nearer the shoulders than the center of motion. It is a very natural question, therefore, as to whether the load should be adjusted so as to leave the center of gravity where nature placed it, or to move it further back..." [54]

"To use a saber on horseback it is necessary to have the horse balanced more with a view to quick turns on the hind rather than the forehand. One reason exists for throwing the balance of the horse somewhat to the rear, which alone makes it expedient to do so. This is the necessity for preventing the fore feet and legs from becoming prematurely ruined. It is not a matter of theory merely, but a well-known result of actual experience, that horses carrying weights upon their backs become broken down in front, as a rule, long before they suffer any deterioration of the hind legs. The date of breaking down is much hastened by saddling far forward over the withers, and by an improper use of the stirrups, which will be explained later." [55]

While this is the seat Chamberlin learns at West Point, and was the standard of the time, Chamberlin will write more than 25 years later: "Unfortunately, our officers and troopers were taught to ride with the buttocks pushed under them so that they were seated on the ends of their spines..."

In future years, Chamberlin and a number of select other officers will change these practices.

---

54 General William H. Carter, United States Army, *Horses Saddles and Bridles,* The Lord Baltimore Press, The Friedenwald Company, 1906.

55 Ibid.

Figure 33 *The military seat circa 1906 as taught at West Point Horses. Photos of the seat typically show the rider's shoulders a trifle behind the vertical à la Saumur as opposed to almost upright as shown here. From* Horses, Bridles, and Saddles. *Carter. Public domain.*

Figure 34 *Another view of the military seat circa 1906 as shown in Horses, Saddles, and Bridles, the West Point textbook. Notice the shoulders well back to put the upper body a trifle behind the vertical as taught at Saumur. As Col Albert Phillips writes, the French maintain "a tendency toward riding with the weight somewhat to the rear."*

***Figure 35** The military seat of 1906 as applied in polo as shown in* Horses, Saddles, and Bridles. *Notice the rider's "tendency toward riding with the weight somewhat to the rear." Public domain.*

TEACHING OUTSIDE THE CLASSROOM IN THE ROUND PEN, IN THE RIDING HALL, AND IN THE FIELD

Participants in the summer camp, the "yearlings" as everyone now calls Chamberlin's class, number 82 cadets. They assemble into small groups of eight to ten. Both Marshall and Oliver supervise a cavalry sergeant or a corporal assigned to West Point's Cavalry Detachment. Each takes one group and begins to teach "the army way of riding" the "army way." Each day, both Oliver and Marshall quickly assess each cadet's progress.

"The army way." No previous experience necessary; in fact, no previous experience preferred. The army views previous riding experience as a potential liability since only a few civilians ride "the army way." No experience proves a definite plus since someone with little or no experience will harbor few or no bad habits that the army must break. Such a cadet offers the West Point instructors a "clean slate."

The following describes a composite of various discussions, articles and recollections which, hopefully, will give the reader a feel for the process.

Antidotal descriptions from the 1900s include comments that bring some levity and personality to the otherwise harsh teaching practices at West

Point. For example, the instructors tend to pick the stubborn and unruly horses for those who had the least experience; and the instructors often pick the tallest fellow in the class to mount the shortest horse. In one situation, the fellow's legs almost touch the ground while mounted. Everyone around him snickers and tries not to laugh. Finally, the sergeant, the rider, and the whole class break down and share a hearty laugh. So, at least, the horsemanship classes offer lighter moments in the regulation bound West Point.

On their first day of horsemanship, the yearlings assemble and hear: "Gentleman, for this morning—THIS—is your horse." The sergeant points to a wooden "horse" consisting of four wooden legs affixed to a barrel with an outstretched 2" x 8" board attached to the front end as a "neck." The wooden legs raise the "back" of the wooden horse to a height of about 15 hands. Across the top of the barrel sits a folded saddle blanket affixed to the barrel with a surcingle.

The sergeant explains how to mount and dismount a bare back horse and then orders a corporal to demonstrate the proper military way to perform each command: "Stand to horse," he commands. A corporal stands to horse. "Mount!" The corporal mounts. "Prepare to dismount. (long pause) Dismount!" The corporal dismounts. Each cadet, in turn and upon command "stands to horse" and then, upon command, attempts to mount. Once up, the sergeant assesses the cadet's seat (initially without saddle or stirrups). The sergeant corrects the cadet's position until the cadet's "military seat" reflects the form the army mandates and that General Carter described earlier.

"Prepare to dismount! (pause) Dismount!" The cadet attempts to dismount in proper fashion. Once the cadet mounts and dismounts in the regulations mandated manner, a corporal demonstrates several "monkey drills" that each cadet attempts, in turn, on the wooden horse. Each cadet practices on the wooden horse in his off hours to perfect his mounting and dismounting skills as well as each of the "monkey drills." Many years later, most of these "monkey drills" the cavalry calls "suppling exercises."

After a few days, each cadet understands the exercises and performs them well on the stationary, wooden horse. Then, the group moves to a round pen and to live horses. Their instruction continues in this new venue.

"Gentleman... this...IS a horse," the sergeant says as he points to a horse. The sergeant describes the various points of confirmation. "This is the head. The hay goes in there. This is the dock. The manure comes out here. This is the tail. The horse swats the fly with his tail. This hump right here, we call this hump the withers. This hump here, we call the croup. In between the withers and the croup, we have the back. In good time, you will learn how to stay up on the back without falling off and breaking your neck."

The sergeant discusses various points of confirmation; then corporals bring ten or so horses up to the round pen. They outfit each horse with a halter, a lead rope, and a folded saddle blanket held in place by a surcingle. Half the class vaults onto horses in the military fashion as practiced on the wooden horse. The other half remains on the ground. Each takes a lead rope and leads a horse and rider around the perimeter of the round pen at a slow walk.

The sergeant assesses each cadet's position and recommends changes as he sees fit so the cadet's position conforms to the "military seat." The sergeant reminds each rider to try to feel how the horse's back moves in relation to the rider's seat bones. "Close your eyes and try to feel which hind hoof hits the ground and when," the sergeant says. "Try to feel, don't look. Try to call it out." After several times around in a large circle, the mounted cadet reverses roles. He dismounts, his comrade mounts and the exercises start anew. Whether a cadet plays polo with a 3-goal handicap, rides steeplechases as a hobby, or rides on a merry-go-round as his sole mounted experience, he starts out exactly the same way.

The next day, the cadets seem comfortable being led and leading. The sergeant brings his group of cadets to a picket line of horses. Folded on a nearby fence, a saddle blanket and surcingle await each horse. The sergeant demonstrates how to fold a saddle blanket properly with "all four corners of the blanket to the near and rear." Once the cadet understands how to fold the blanket, the sergeant teaches him, first, to pass the blanket over the horse's back from withers to loin two times so as to smooth the hairs on the horse's back. Next, the sergeant shows how to attach the surcingle. The army proscribes a set procedure for each activity.

Once the cadets properly equip their assigned horses for that day, the sergeant orders each cadet to mount his assigned horse. In the first year of training, cadets never ride the same horse twice. Once the cadets master mounting in proper fashion as the army prescribes, they mount and then attempt to assume the "military seat" of that era, on a live as opposed to a wooden horse.

Once the cadets master prescribed form at the walk, they start work at the trot, either independently or on the lunge line. Since, at this time, cavalry horsemen do not post at the trot, Chamberlin learns to sit the trot expertly. Usually, the work with blanket and surcingle continues with the canter and then into the gallop.

Once a cadet seems confirmed in his position at a halt, the instructor either orders him to "Take reins" or, if it seems that the cadet might rely on the reins to preserve his position, then the instructor orders an assistant to take hold of a lunge line and lead the cadet forward without the reins in his hand but with his forearms horizontal and his wrists turned in slightly as if he were holding reins.

The instructors teach the cadets how to hold the snaffle reins as well as the reins for a bit and bridoon. When discussing the application of the reins, Carter suggests "pulling" the reins and using "wrist action" to guide the horse. In 1907, the concept of "squeezing" the fingers to communicate with the horse's mouth, it seems, remains unknown.

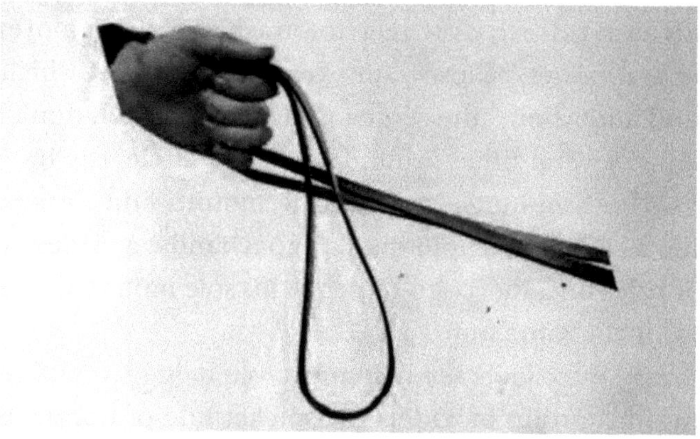

Figure 36 *Photo from the West Point text* Horses, Saddles, and Bridles *by General Carter. Carter advises that this is the "best method to handle a set of curb reins because you can get so much more wrist action to bear and the reins run through more of a grasp."*

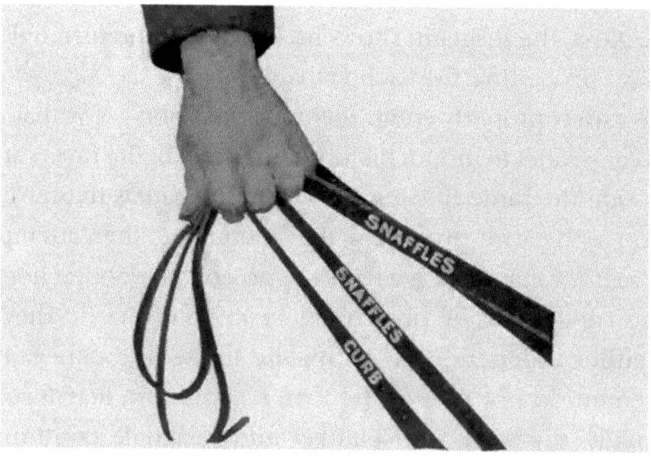

Figure 37 *From* Horses, Saddles, and Bridles. *Carter writes: "Shows the reins as they should be held with the back of the hand up when no special signal is intended for the horse's mouth."*

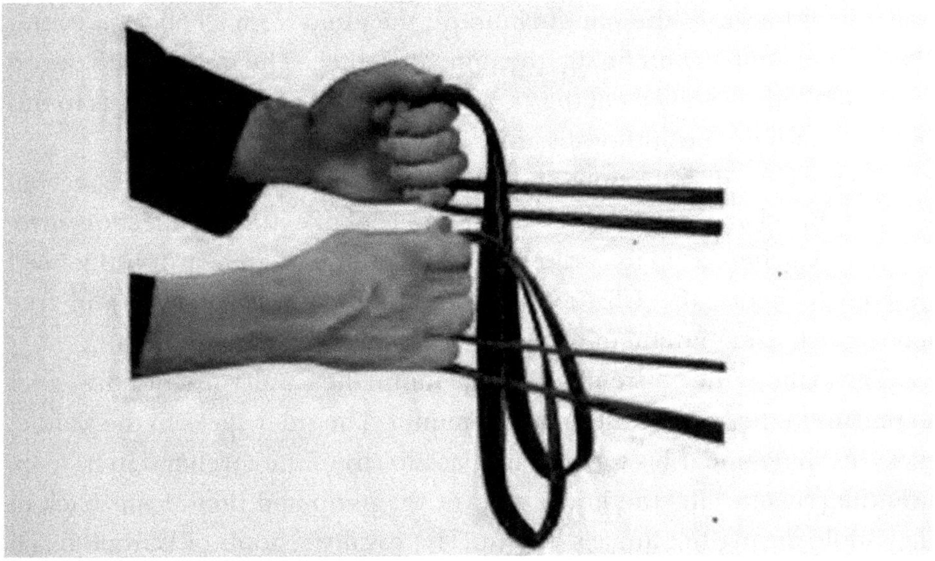

Figure 38 *From* Horses, Saddles, and Bridles. *Carter writes: "Shows four reins used in two hands, curb below little finger and snaffle above, or snaffles can be used in one hand and curb in one hand as desired."*

As the cadet moves forward at the walk, he performs each "monkey drill" that he learns and practices on the wooden horse. The first drill requires the cadet to lean back and lay his head on the horse's loin without dislodging the position of his legs and then to resume the upright position. Once a cadet performs the drill adequately at the walk, he executes the drill at the trot and then at the canter. In all, the cadet executes 17 separate drills many of which make "circus" like demands.

In time, the cadet rides with his horse equipped with a 1904 model McClellan Saddle and a snaffle bridle. In his saddle, the cadet sits the slow trot without stirrups for extended periods. As General Carter writes: "For teaching a firm, close seat, and giving the recruit confidence in himself, nothing is as good as the trot without stirrups."

As he progresses, the cadet works at transitions up and down through the gaits: walk-trot; trot-extended trot; trot-halt; halt-trot; trot-canter; canter-trot; walk-canter; canter-halt; halt-canter; canter-gallop and so on. He performs various riding hall movements: spirals, circles, abouts, and obliques. In time, he learns turns on the forehand; turns on the haunches; leg yields (which the instructors called "passage"); the rein back; and finally, the canter and gallop depart.

In time, the cadet starts jumping. In keeping with the teachings of Saumur, the cavalry categorizes jumps into three types: the jump from the walk which they call "the standing jump"; the jump from a collected canter ("the flying jump"); and finally, the jump of a ditch. The only time the word "collected" appears in any of the cavalry's literature of that era occurs in this one place: where the author discusses the "flying jump."

On the issue of collection: Even though the cavalry teaches the "seat" of François Baucher, the cavalry rejects the concept of extreme collection advocated by Baucher. From its earliest days, and even though heavily influenced by French theory, the US Cavalry favors the "natural balance" and free moving style and movement of the horse at liberty in its natural state.

Throughout the entire phase of the jump, the cavalry teaches the cadet to remain in the "firm, close" seat of Saumur. The rider sticks to the saddle, tucks his spine under his torso, leans back to "free" the forehand in its leap, uses the reins to "lift" the horse up over the jump and then, leans back in the saddle during the horse's decent. The cavalry schools of Europe teach this same jumping style, with the exception of the Italian cavalry school once Caprilli's theories take hold (which we will review in detail later).

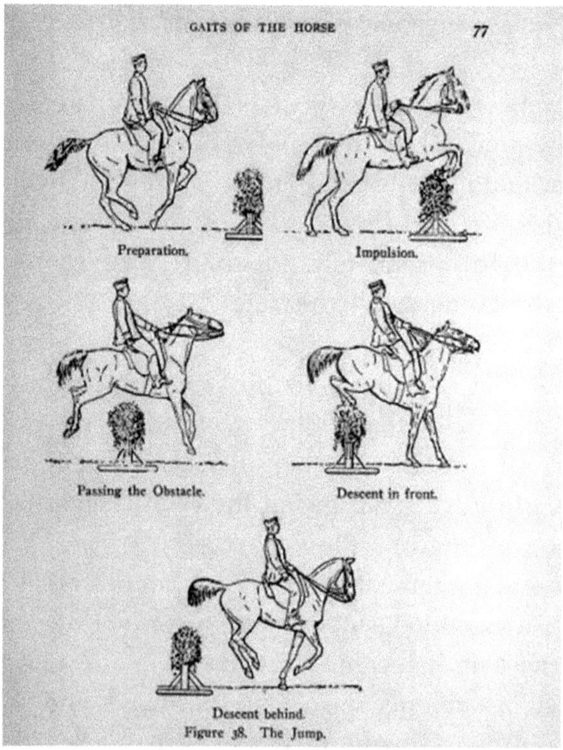

Figure 39 *From Horses, Saddles, and Bridles. Carter adopts the jumping concepts of Saumur for West Point. The French resist Caprilli's theories well into the 1930s after the US Cavalry adopts a more Caprillist method as modified by then Major Harry D. Chamberlin. Public domain.*

Figure 40 *Chamberlin friend, polo teammate, and the future commander of the 1st Cavalry Division, Captain Innis Palmer Swift shows the "firm, close seat" at the top of the jump as taught at West Point and at Fort Riley during the early twentieth-century. US Army photo.*

Figure 41 *Lt. Adna R. Chaffee displays the jumping form during the descent phase of the jump taught at West Point during the early twentieth-century. Chaffee translated into English the Manual of Equitation of the French Army for 1912. US Army photo.*

INSTRUCTION IN YEARS THREE AND FOUR

The instruction for third-year cadets mainly expands on and reinforces those concepts and skills the cadet acquires in his "yearling" a.k.a. second year. In addition, the third-year mounted curriculum focuses on complex drill involving the movement and coordination of large bodies of cavalrymen as well as how to train troopers in the ranks. Topics include: the school of the trooper in the riding hall; the school of the troop, the formation of the troop, the division into platoons, the formation of columns on the right or on left into line, platoon columns, and the charge with saber. These are just a few of the technical points the curriculum covers for the cadet in his third school year.

Figure 42 *The riding hall at West Point, completed in 1909 is large enough to host polo matches in doors. US Army photo.*

In the fourth and final year at West Point, cadets experience a much more varied and more detailed instruction regimen in the saddle to refine skills. Military and reconnaissance rides into the countryside surrounding West Point make up a good part of these details. Once competent on a horse, even "yearlings" ride for please up to six miles into the surrounding countryside on Wednesdays and Saturdays, at their option. On these excursions, the cadet must not stop, must not dismount, and must not speak to anyone. Also, in the final year, Chamberlin and the other cadets learn the game of polo and play often. Such riding serves to round out and complete the course.

In addition, in their last year, Chamberlin and the other cadets delve more deeply into Hippology. The course expands on the earlier general discussion of breeds: their confirmation, characteristics and the work best suited to each. The course and the text *Elements of Hippology* devotes additional and much more detailed attention to each of the following topics: how to determine a horse's age by examining the teeth; the causes and effects of inflammation and how to treat same; the characteristics of the equine head and neck together with the strengths and weaknesses of each; the action, influence, and proper use of bits; the front leg, its structure and role; the proper position of the saddle; the equine trunk, its components, strengths and weaknesses; the hind leg, its structure and role; the horse's foot, its structure and how it functions; the diseases of the foot and how to avoid, cure or mitigate same; the principles of horseshoeing for horses with ordinary feet and what shoeing practices to forbid; characteristics and function of the heart, lungs, and air passages; how the digestive system operates; the principles of effective stable management; the endurance of horses together with their vices and the punishments for each; how to care for sick horses; how to recognize preventable diseases; how to spot irregularities of gait and the effects of each; and finally, how to judge horses and examine them for soundness.

Most importantly, the Academy expects those cadets who report to the cavalry branch upon graduating to view their Academy instruction as an "introduction" to horsemanship. Ultimately, each cavalry bound cadet will attend the Mounted Service School at Fort Riley for at least one more year of instruction and possibly two years.

For the rest of his life, riding horses remains Chamberlin's passion. At West Point, he pursues, however, an additional passion: Football.

Chapter 6

West Point, 1907–1910
Academics, Football, and Graduation

"Man of the hour Chamberlain (*sic*) paved the way to a glorious victor"
—*The New York Herald* [56]

"May West Point have more like him."
—*Howitzer*, West Point graduation notes on Chamberlin [57]

After the examinations of June 1907, Chamberlin ranks thirty-fourth out of a class of 108. During the first term of Chamberlin's second year at West Point (commencing September 1907), he studies various branches of mathematics: conic sections, analytical geometry, descriptive geometry. He also studies English, history, surveying, French, and drawing.

During the second term (ending June of 1908), he studies calculus, mechanics, French, chemistry, topography and Spanish. As previously mentioned, by February of 1908, Chamberlin achieves the rank of Corporal, only to be demoted because he uses harsh language to a plebe. In June of 1908, Chamberlin stands forty-third in a class that now numbers eighty-five.

There is more to Chamberlin's West Point experience, however, than academics and horses.

56 *New York Herald*, November 29, 1908.
57 *Howitzer 1910, Yearbook of the United States Military Academy at West Point, 1910.*

FOOTBALL 1908-1909

By the time Harry Chamberlin attends West Point, the academy fields athletic teams in a variety of sports. Steeped in tradition, the academy names each of its teams "The Black Knights of the Hudson." Chamberlin's natural athleticism shows in a variety of sports. He qualifies as an "expert rifleman." He rides better than any other cadet at the Point. In inter-collegiate sports, Chamberlin excels in track and boxing; but most of all, he achieves legendary status in football. Of all of its teams, West Point adores its football team. It ranks first in the hearts of both cadets and alumni.

Patton tries out for the football team several times. Each time he fails to make the squad but does play third-string as a "scrub" practice player. That means, he serves as a tackle-dummy for the squad in which Harry Chamberlin earns his West Point "A." Douglas MacArthur, at 130 pounds, does not even try out for the football team choosing to play baseball instead. Yet, for the rest of MacArthur's life, he avidly follows West Point football and MacArthur's enthusiasm for the sport will benefit Harry Chamberlin. MacArthur surely notes Chamberlin's stunning performance against Navy in 1908, for example (recounted below). The impact of such displays of athletic ability cannot be over stated. An intense football rivalry exists between the Army and the Navy which is played out on the gridiron. As early as 1893, a dispute regarding the game almost leads to a duel between a Rear Admiral and a Brigadier General.

During the twentieth-century's first decade, football players pursue their game brutally. (In fact, not until 1939 will the rules require football helmets for all players!) The rules enable brutality and foul play. In 1905 to no avail, President Theodore Roosevelt demands "that football change its rules or be abolished...Change the game or forsake it!" The "flying wedge" and other massing plays often prove fatal and, ultimately, the sponsoring schools ban such practices.

Nonetheless, at the end of the 1905 season, the Chicago Tribune reports eighteen deaths and fifty-nine injuries across the nation. Columbia University and two other colleges ban football in 1905. In 1909, football causes twenty-six deaths and seventy serious injuries. During that same year—Chamberlin's senior year—West Point cadet Eugene Byrne dies as a result of injuries sustained in the Army-Harvard game. Byrne's death and the death of Navy's Early Wilson that same 1909 season ends collegiate football early that year. The authorities cancel the Army-Navy game scheduled for 1909.

Not only does Chamberlin face brutal competition. He faces competition of the highest quality at a time of great creativity in football. For instance, Chamberlin plays against the legendary hero, Jim Thorpe of Carlisle College. In Chamberlin's plebe year, 1906, John Heisman, coach of Georgia Tech, creates the forward pass.

In the spring of 1907, Chamberlin participates in "class football," meaning intra-murals. In September of 1907, he makes the football team's second squad as a half-back substitute. In September of 1908, in his third year at West Point, Chamberlin makes the first squad as a full-back weighing in at 163 pounds.

Chamberlin's performance on the gridiron creates an academy legend that makes him stand out in the Corps of Cadets. And this legend endures beyond his own lifetime amongst West Point educated officers. Playing at Philadelphia's Franklin Field in the 1908 Army-Navy game, Chamberlin plays in front of an important audience. According to the *New York Times* article of November 28, 1908, "From a social standpoint the game eclipses all others, as it attracts a most representative gathering of society leaders, army and navy officers, diplomats, and others prominent in all walks in life."

On that day, Harry Chamberlin performs magnificently. As the *Howitzer* recounts the day:

> "Northcroft won the toss and chose to defend the west goal. A hush of expectancy settled as Dean poised the ball on the little mound at the center of the field. The whistle blew, a dull thud and a curving yellow streak rose in the air, and the fight was on. Scarce three minutes had passed when the play was made that brought joy and exultation to every Army man. Greble, standing on his twenty-five-yard line got off a punt that went to the Navy Forty-five-yard line. The ball got away from Lang, and Chamberlin, coming down the field like a whirlwind, leaped high into the air and clutched it. Without slackening speed, he was off for the Navy goal line, with Lange close behind. Ten, twenty, thirty yards he made before Lange brought him to earth on the four-yard line. No power on earth could have kept the Army team from gaining the coveted distance and in two smashes, Dean was pushed over Captain Northcroft for the winning touchdown." [58]

The *New York Sun,* on November 30,1908, writes:

---

58 *Howitzer 1908 Yearbook of the United States Military Academy at West Point, 1908*

"When it came right down to football, the Navy eleven was outclassed... the backfield worked like a piece of well-oiled machinery and during the second half did so much effective battering that the Annapolis Eleven was literally cut to pieces, so that before the game ended, the Navy had six substitutes in the lineup...."

The hometown *Elgin Daily Courier* writes of Chamberlin:

As Army's starting fullback, he is "...responsible for the victory over the Navy in the annual football game." (*Elgin Daily Courier*, November 30, 1908) In the closing minutes of the game, Chamberlin returns a Navy punt 92 yards to the Navy five-yard line and set up the wining Army touch down.

In a memorial to Chamberlin published by the Association of West Point Graduates, a memorialist known only as "B.P" writes:

"Chamberlin ran 95 yards for a touchdown, winning the game for the Army in the last few minutes of play—an almost unprecedented feat." [59]

According to another account, he runs 110 yards from his own end zone to score the winning touchdown against Navy. Whether he runs 92 or 110 yards, one fact stands out: as the *Elgin Daily Courier* quoted from the *New York Herald*: "Man of the hour Chamberlain (*sic*) paved the way to a glorious victory." 30,000 fans watch the game. The final score: Army 6; Navy 4. [60]

Later, Chamberlin plays in the 1909 season which opens with better than average prospects as the *Howitzer* again recounts:

"Of the veterans of a winning team Bryne, Pullen, Chamberlin, Wier, Dean, Hyatt, Devore and Walsmley were left as a nucleus." [61]

Injuries put Chamberlin out of several of the games in the 1909 season including the games against Yale and Harvard. Death on the field causes West Point and Annapolis to cancel the Army-Navy game of that season.

---

59 See https://www.westpointaog.org/memorial-article?id=f3efb07e-1306-45c3-86dd-780dd099a6a0.

60 See *New York Times* article of November 28, 1908; *The New York Herald*, November 29, 1908. *Elgin Daily Courier*, November 30, 1908; *The New York Sun*, November 28, 1908; *Howitzer 1908 Yearbook of the United States Military Academy at West Point, 1908*. Association of West Point Graduates 1944 See https://www.westpointaog.org/memorial-article?id=f3efb07e-1306-45c3-86dd-780dd099a6a0

61 *Howitzer 1909 Yearbook of the United States Military Academy at West Point*, 1909.

His injuries do not affect, however, his marksmanship with a rifle. He scores fourth in the Expert Rifleman's competition that year. Chamberlin also participates in discus and shot-put competitions: in 1909, he comes in sixth in hurling the sixteen-pound shot put; in 1910, he comes in second. In the discus, Chamberlin places second in 1910.

In September 1910, after Harry graduates, 110 cadets come out for the football squad. The only positions open: that of two graduates, Daniel Pullen at tackle and Harry Chamberlin at full back. A *New York Times* article of September 1910 covers the massive turn out for the West Point team and refers to the full-back position as the "Chamberlin position." Regardless of its popularity, the sport remains so dangerous that finally, in 1910, reformers create the National College Athletic Association (The NCAA) to impose reforms and rule changes to make the game safer. Changes in both rules and player equipment brought about by the reform movement lead to the immensely popular modern game.

ACADEMICS

During the first term of Chamberlin's third year (commencing September 1908), he studies gunnery, chemistry, geology and philosophy. During the term ending June 1909, he studies field sketching, building construction, geometry, tactics, hygiene, and Spanish. In June 1909, Chamberlin's class rank stands at 24th out of a class of 81. He also achieves the rank of Sergeant and of Acting Color Sergeant. [62]

During the term commencing in September 1909, Chamberlin studies Engineering, law and Spanish. During his final semester at West Point which ends in June 1910, he studies engineering, law, Spanish, Hippology, and tactical map problems. He graduates 29th out of a class of 82. Among the subjects tested, his highest and his lowest class rankings: in history, 6th; in Conduct 68th. At 68th in Conduct, Harry proves to be an individualist of sorts. [63] At the same time, his personality attracts friends throughout the entire Corps. In the opinion of his peers: "May West Point have more like him." [64]

62 *Official Register of the Officers and Cadets of the United States Military Academy*, West Point, New York, June 1909.

63 *Official Register of the Officers and Cadets of the United States Military Academy*, West Point, New York, June 1910.

64 *Howitzer* 1910 yearbook, West Point page 56.

CONDUCT, LETTERS AND DISTINCTION

Chamberlin's *Howitzer* yearbook entry discloses the letter "A" for football; A.B. for "Area Bird" and B.A. for "Busted Aristocrat." In West Point parlance of that day, "Area Bird" means the recipient walks punishment guard duty for a grave breech of discipline; "Busted Aristocrat" means the designee suffers a reduction in rank. Chamberlin shares the "A.B." on his record with men like John J. Pershing. He shares his "B.A." with the likes of George S. Patton, Jr. Each will achieve acclaim and the coveted General's rank in future years. Even though once demoted, Chamberlin rises to the rank of Acting Color Sergeant for the Corps of Cadets. Chamberlin also serves as Hop manager for several Academy social functions and is called upon to deliver an opening toast at the Athletics New Year's Banquet. Usually, New York debutantes and the daughters of higher-ranking Army officers attend such functions.

GRADUATION

June 15, 1910: Graduation Day. In the bright blue sky, the sun shines brightly at West Point. At 10:30 a.m. that morning, the Military Academy Marching Band marches across the plain and takes its position directly in front of the speaker's podium. The Academy Superintendent, Col. Hugh Scott delivers an opening address:

"This is a particular fitness in my being selected to address you this morning for I am the oldest graduate of the Academy, save one, on the active list of the army…and I have seen more years of active service than any other officer in the army, save one. I will also add incidentally, that I have taken all the horsemanship tests up to date, which is not an unimportant matter." [65]

(An interesting aside regarding Col. Scott: he graduates from the Academy in 1876. As his first assignment, he marks the graves of the fallen at the Little Big Horn. Later in 1876, he interviews many of the Sioux warriors who massacred Custer's command. He serves the first 20 years of his military career as an officer in the 7th US Cavalry.)

After Scott concludes his speech, the Secretary of War, Jacob Dickinson, addresses the audience. He concludes his address by saying:

65 *New York Times* June 17, 1910.

"No man is so great or so good in a republic that he can be permitted to govern outside of the law and the constitution. No public good, however attractive, is worth gaining at the price of setting aside a fundamental principle of government. This is substituting a government of men for a government of law, and this is the beginning of the end of the republic." [66]

Under a large canopy erected near the Battle Monument on Trophy point, Secretary of War, Dickerson delivers to each of the 82 cadets a diploma that makes him a Second Lieutenant in the United States Army. On each side of the canopy sit hundreds of distinguished visitors including Harry's father Dwight Chamberlin and Harry's sister Marie and "several hundred pretty girls who had come to witness the transformation of the first classmen into army officers." [67]

The Secretary of War, Jacob Dickinson hands out the diplomas according to class rank. He calls out the name: "Cadet Fredrick S. Strong, Jr. first in the Class of 1910." Strong and the next nine cadets in class rank will go to the Corps of Engineers. Interesting aspects of the Class of 1910 include: Cadet Beverly C. Drum ranks 7th in the class; his brother, Walter K. Drum ranks 53rd in the same class. Cadet Barr ranks 47th and marries his sweetheart from Missouri in the new West Point chapel immediately after the ceremony that day. Cadet Oscar Griswold graduates 77th and Cadet Emil Reinhardt graduates 79th. In World War II, Major General Griswold commands a Corps under MacArthur during the liberation of the Philippines and Major General Reinhardt reaches the Elbe River in Germany as the first American General officer to do so and the first to meet the Russians there in 1945. The army assigns both men to the infantry upon their graduation from West Point.

Chamberlin's 29th class rank enables him, however, to choose the branch of the army that he desires except for the Engineers. The natural athleticism that enables him to triumph in football also makes him a natural horseman. By the time he graduates, he rides horses better than any other cadet in the Corps. So, he chooses the Cavalry, the army's most glamorous, and in 1910, its elite branch. He joins the men with the mirror polished, high boots and spirited horses, men like the old veteran cavalrymen from Elgin, Illinois who helped save the Union and whose recollections Chamberlin heard as a boy. To join troopers like them, Harry Chamberlin will go.

---

66 Ibid.

67 Ibid.

Immediately after the graduation ceremony, father Dwight and sister Marie present Harry with a pocket watch as a graduation present that he will carry for the rest of his life. As he leaves West Point, his classmates write of him in the *Howitzer*:

"But, faith, he had a way with him
that never came amiss—
No man that wouldn't follow him, no
girl he couldn't kiss..."
"May West Point have more like him." [68]

And so, Harry Chamberlin, Second Lieutenant of Cavalry, leaves West Point and the Corps of Cadets on the plain above the Hudson and travels to Fort Riley on the Republican River and to the 7th United States Cavalry.

Figure 43 *West Point graduation photo of now Second Lieutenant of Cavalry, Harry Dwight Chamberlin: "No man that wouldn't follow him...May West Point have more like him." Photo courtesy of the United States Military Academy at West Point.*

68 *Howitzer 1910, Yearbook of the United States Military Academy at West Point,* Page 56.

Chapter 7

Fort Riley and the 7th Cavalry 1910–1911

"Officers will not shoot buffalo on the parade ground from the windows of their quarters."
—By Order of the Commanding Officer [69]

Fort Riley, Kansas sits near the exact geographical center of the United States on a plain overlooking the Kansas River Valley. Named after Major General Bennett C. Riley who led the first military escort along the Santa Fe Trail in 1829, Fort Riley enjoys a long association with the Cavalry. The Army names Fort Riley's airport after Brig. General Francis C. Marshall, Chamberlin's first instructor of horsemanship and cavalry tactics who, as Assistant Chief of Cavalry, died in an airplane crash in 1922. As Patton biographer, Carlo D'Estes writes: "If the Old Army was the western frontier, then Fort Riley was its heart and soul." [70]

During the late spring and early summer, bright green grass covers the rolling hills and the deep gorges that surround Fort Riley in every direction. In the late fall, the grass turns a parched brown. In winter, the weather turns bitter cold and fierce winds blow snow-blizzards over the open plain. In summer, the sun and the heat stifles. In fact, cavalrymen riding out of Fort Riley in a column of twos in the summer heat often quip: "After a visit to Kansas in the summer, the devil went to hell to cool off."

69 Carlo D'Estes, *Patton: Genius For War*, Harper Perennial, 1995.
70 Ibid.

The army establishes Fort Riley in 1853 as a cavalry post to support western expansion to Oregon, California, and New Mexico. The post remains integral to western security for the balance of the nineteenth Century. In 1876, Custer and his 7th Cavalry set out from Fort Riley to the Little Big Horn. In 1884, General Philip Sheridan recommends that Fort Riley become the headquarters of the US Cavalry. By 1904, Fort Riley houses the Mounted Service School as well as the 7th Cavalry Regiment.

"HONOR AND COURAGE"
MOTTO OF THE 7TH CAVALRY

The 7th Cavalry influences Harry Chamberlin's life well into the twentieth-century. The 7th provides Chamberlin with his first command. The 7th offers a unique and somewhat burdensome history for a young officer. Historians favor the 7th, the press embellishes the 7th, Hollywood romanticizes the 7th. Massacres, blunders, and high casualties perhaps offer interesting stories of sacrifice while successful military feats often remain ignored.

When the Sioux massacre Custer and his troopers on the Little Big Horn, the 7th Cavalry loses its battle standards and its regimental dignity exactly thirty-four years prior to the time that Chamberlin's arrives.

But the 7th Cavalry provides more to Harry Chamberlin than his first command and a weighty and somewhat checkered history. Many of the Army's then highest-ranking officers serve with the 7th Cavalry at some point in their careers. Two Indian fighters of great repute will influence Harry's future well into his own career: The Inspector General of the Army, Ernest Albert Garlington and the Army's first Chief of Staff, James Franklin Bell. Both serve with the outfit in their younger days. In fact, Inspector General Garlington writes a book entitled *Historical Sketches of the Seventh Cavalry Regiment.*

Though Chamberlin does not know it in the summer of 1910, when Chamberlin arrives at Fort Riley, both Garlington and Bell will exercise great influence over Chamberlin's early career and beyond, especially, given the close-knit society that makes up the US Army during the first half of the twentieth-century. Chamberlin's future wife, born at Fort Riley and known as the "finest equestrienne in the cavalry," is born at Fort Riley while her father serves in the 7th Cavalry. So, the regiment's history offers an insight into the Army in which Chamberlin serves and into the family into which he marries.

After the end of The Civil War in 1865, the West and the Mexican border explode as critical trouble spots. The Sioux skirmish daily with white settlers in Minnesota and the Dakotas; the Utes make war in Idaho; the Navajo attack in New Mexico; the Apaches raid in Texas. In response, Congress authorizes the US Cavalry to form four additional cavalry regiments to restore order. Pursuant to this authorization, in 1866, the Army forms the 7th Cavalry Regiment.

In August 1866, the regiment concentrates at Fort Riley. The army assigns Lt. Col. George Armstrong Custer to command regiment's Troop D but later, he becomes the Acting Regimental Adjutant. George Armstrong Custer's brother, First Lieutenant T.W. Custer serves as the Acting Regimental Quartermaster.

In March 1867, the 7th embarks on its first mission on the barren and bleak plains to engage the Cheyenne and the Sioux. During the campaign, Lt. Col. Custer kills Indians with such relish that many of his troops refuse to continue and others desert in droves. Custer orders bounty hunters to shoot these men on sight and to bring them back dead, never alive.

Outraged at Custer's treatment of both Indians and his own men, higher authority relieves Custer of his command. A court of inquiry investigates and then court-marshals Custer. The court suspends his rank, pay and command for one year. After reading the court testimony, the reviewing officer decides to impose a more lenient sentence due to Custer's past record in the Civil War. After serving his punishment, Custer returns to the 7th. Not an auspicious start for the regiment.

From 1865 through 1891, the entire US Cavalry wages thirteen campaigns and fights at least 1,067 engagements with the western tribes. The Cavalry's experiences in the Black Hills of the Dakota Territory, where the 7th US Cavalry and both Garlington and Bell fight, represent the general trend.

General Sheridan, on behalf of President Grant, confidentially writes to General Terry (who commands the territory) that while the administration would not revoke the orders commanding the Cavalry to evict any settlers or miners who penetrate into the Black Hills, "the troops should make no efforts to keep them out…therefore quietly cause the troops of your Department to assume such attitude as will meet the views of the President in this respect." [71]

As prospectors, settlers, and the Indian Bureau commit outrage after outrage and violate treaty after treaty, bands of young braves from the Sioux, the Cheyanne, and other tribes slip away from various reservations to join Sitting Bull, the great and charismatic Lakota-Sioux war-chief. As Sitting Bull and his followers become more and more defiant regarding violations of

71 Herr and Wallace, *The Story of the US Cavalry*, Little Brown 1953.

relevant treaties, the Indian Bureau orders that all Sioux must be on their reservations by January 31, 1876, or the United States will consider them hostiles subject to military action.

Usually, the cavalrymen sympathize with the Indian's plight. After all, the Cavalry typically suffers the brunt of the Indian's displeasure. But orders remain orders and "confidential suggestions" remain orders too. The 7th Cavalry, under Custer, departs from Fort Riley for the Dakota Territory to force Sitting Bull and his followers back onto the reservation.

Ultimately, Custer divides the 7th Cavalry into three commands at the Little Big Horn. Custer leads one such command himself. On that fateful Sunday afternoon in June 1876, a group of officers assemble on the edge of a bluff overlooking the Little Big Horn Valley. Watching the scene unfold below, a veteran of the cavalry, Captain Moylan says to the group: "Gentlemen, in my opinion General Custer has made the biggest mistake of his life..." [72] At that moment, a large group of Lakota-Sioux, Northern Cheyenne, and Arapaho horsemen suddenly gallops down the valley and wipes out Custer's command. George A. Custer, his brother, T.W. Custer, and all of the troopers under Custer's then direct command die at the Little Big Horn. The combined Native tribes achieve their greatest victory and the US Army suffers its worst defeat in the long war on the Great Plains.

Journalists, novelists, historians, and motion picture writers propagate more legends, half-truths and exaggerations; in fact, they produce more fiction about the 7th Cavalry and this battle than any other single event in US military history. Yet, the writers seldom mention that though the 7th Cavalry continued fighting in small skirmishes with the Apaches as late as 1896, the Cavalry high command refuses to restore to the 7th Cavalry its regimental battle flags lost at the Little Big Horn (its "standards" in cavalry parlance) until 1919. Only then does the 7th live down some of the official and unofficial internal Army shame of the Little Big Horn.

Chamberlin joins the regiment, 34 years after the massacre. Top-Sergeants and other troopers still serve with him who witness its aftermath. In late June 1910, Second Lieutenant Harry D. Chamberlin presents his calling card to Colonel George K. Hunter, the recently appointed commander of the 7th Cavalry Regiment at Fort Riley. Long standing custom in the Cavalry requires every new officer to dress smartly in his best uniform and to present his calling card to the post commander and to every other officer at the post.

---

72 Shirley A. Leckie, *Elizabeth Bacon Custer and The Making of a Myth*, University of Oklahoma Press, 1998.

As Chamberlin crosses the parade ground to visit Hunter's quarters, undoubtedly, he reads the sign which states: "Officers will not shoot buffalo on the parade ground from the windows of their quarters. By Order of the Commanding Officer"

THE MAKING OF A SECOND LIEUTENANT OF CAVALRY

As the Commanding Officer's warning regarding the shooting of buffalo suggests, in many ways, Fort Riley still resides in the "Wild West." When Harry arrives his schooling, like all junior officers new to the fort, starts with a long ride on horseback with a fellow officer to familiarize him with the grounds of Fort Riley and to introduce him to a cavalryman's rigorous life. After a few easy rides, the work in earnest begins.

Regardless of whether a new Second Lieutenant holds equestrian honors from West Point or has never before ridden on the back of a horse, the training regimen remains the same: hour after hour, the Second Lieutenants and enlisted men alike work on their position with suppling exercises and by sitting the slow trot without stirrups. As Chamberlin reads in *Horses, Saddles and Brides,* at page 155: "For teaching a firm, close seat, and giving the recruit confidence in himself, nothing is as good as the trot without stirrups."

And trot without stirrups they do hour after hour. Second Lieutenants participate in all drills and formations with their assigned troops. In each troop, along with the Second Lieutenant, serves a "Top-Sergeant." This Top-Sergeant offers an average of 24 years of cavalry experience and almost as many years of experience leading men. He also earns a dollar a month more than does the Second Lieutenant.

Harry's Top-Sergeant teaches Harry Chamberlin the job of an officer. From him, Chamberlin gradually learns the techniques of command. He learns how to put a platoon through its equitation paces by commands of voice, hand signal, and whistle.

In addition to the Top-Sergeant's tutelage, each Second Lieutenant studies, if serious about his profession, a number of texts:

Cavalry Drill Regulations, 1891
Field Service Regulations
Rules of Lands Warfare
Manual of Interior Guard Duty
Engineer Field Manual
Army Regulations

War Department General Orders and Bulletins
Manual of Physical Training
Manual for Stable Sergeants
Army Cooks Manual

The Cavalry also recommends that a Second Lieutenant purchase and read a copy of *Breaking and Riding* by James Fillis. Harry Chamberlin acquires a copy, and reads it cover to cover, and refers to it often. He will later study Fillis in depth at the Mounted Service School in the future.

The Top-Sergeant tutors Chamberlin in leadership and also helps with morning reports, sick reports, duty rosters, council books, troop administration, and correspondence. Chamberlin learns to inventory property, inspect feed, sketch roads, signal by flag. He also inspects horseshoeing since all West Point graduates use F.C. Marshall's checklist regarding horseshoeing and hoof care.

He also learns the basics of pack transport: the various rolls of the "bell mare," the riding mules, and the pack mules. He learns the terminology and the technique of how to pack a 250-pound load on the back of a pack mule. These tasks combine with the work on horseback and demand almost all of Chamberlin's time, from dawn until dusk.

At 5:30 a.m. each morning the bugle sounds of Reveille penetrate every corner of the camp. In 1910, no bells, no public address systems, no telephones, no radios communicate among the troopers. The bugles and only the bugles sound the orders of the day. The bugle sounds from Reveille in the morning, to Retreat in the early evening to Taps at 11 p.m. each night. Chamberlin, like all troop officers, will stand for roll call with his unit at Reveille, again at Retreat; and finally, at Taps. The bugle blows throughout the day for Mess call, Police call, Sick call, Water call, Feed call, Drill call, Recall, Stable call, Officer's call, Sergeants call, and Boots and Saddles.

Throughout the cavalry, for the Second Lieutenant, morning equitation drill with his troopers lasts three hours and often longer. During this time, he leads his command in exercises: drills at the walk, trot, and gallop without stirrups; and then, suppling exercises at the slow trot without stirrups. Add to all of this the exercises in dismounted fighting and various complex cavalry movements—all as specified in the *Cavalry Drill Regulations, 1891.*[73]

At this time, all discussion of equitation in the Regulations remains in the context of drill and maneuver. For the line unit, and those in the ranks, equitation as a separate discipline remains unknown until 1929.

---

73 All references to drill movements and exercises see *Drill Regulations, Cavalry 1891*, United States War Department adopted October 3, 1891.

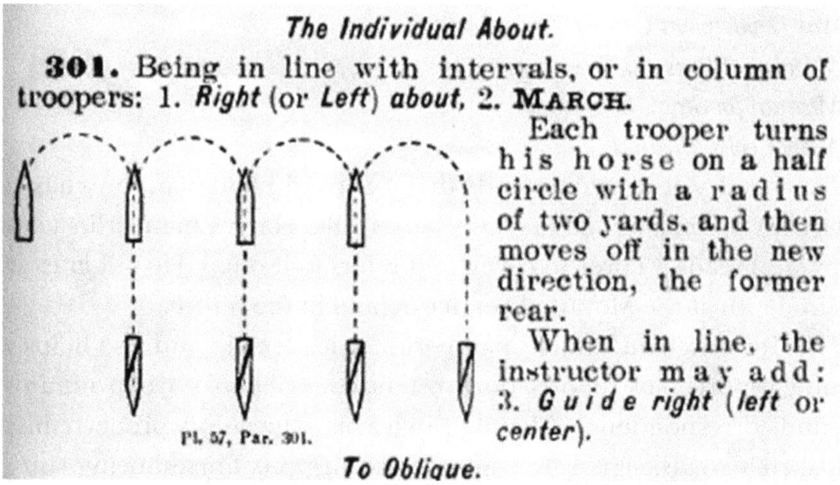
The Individual About.

301. Being in line with intervals, or in column of troopers: 1. ***Right*** (or ***Left***) ***about,*** 2. **MARCH.**

Each trooper turns his horse on a half circle with a radius of two yards, and then moves off in the new direction, the former rear.

When in line, the instructor may add: 3. ***Guide right*** (***left*** or ***center***).

Pl. 57, Par. 301.

To Oblique.

Figure 44 *From Drill Regulations, Cavalry 1891.*
Drill after drill, day after day. Public Domain

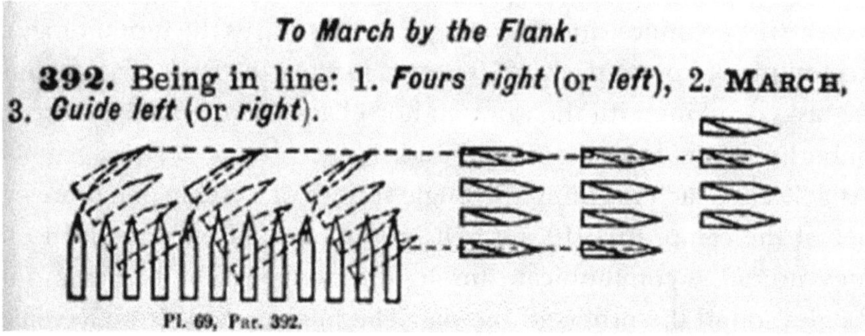
To March by the Flank.

392. Being in line: 1. ***Fours right*** (or ***left***), 2. **MARCH,** 3. ***Guide left*** (or ***right***).

Pl. 69, Par. 392.

Figure 45 *From Drill Regulations, Cavalry 1891 Public Domain.*

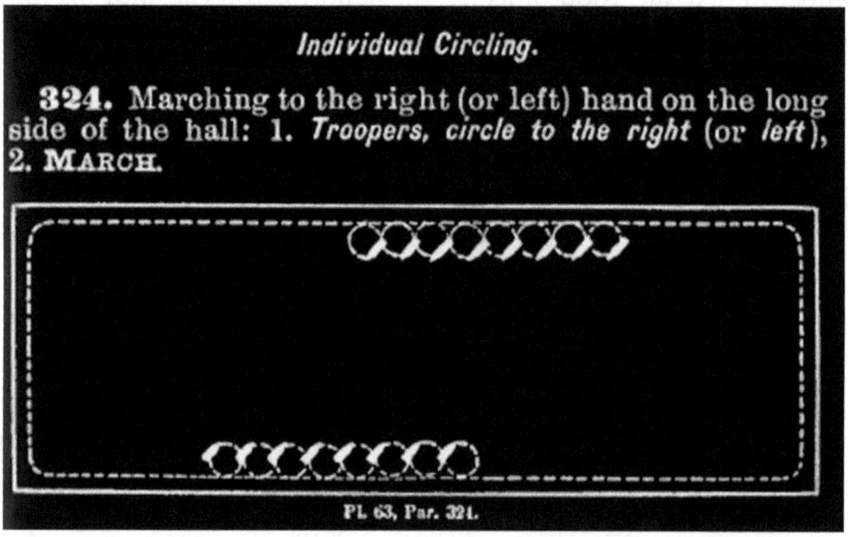
Individual Circling.

324. Marching to the right (or left) hand on the long side of the hall: 1. ***Troopers, circle to the right*** (or ***left***), 2. **MARCH.**

Pl. 63, Par. 321.

Figure 46 *From Drill Regulations, Cavalry 1891 Public Domain.*

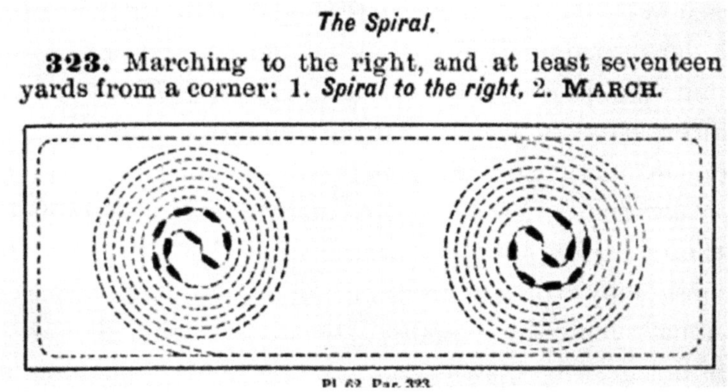

The Spiral.

323. Marching to the right, and at least seventeen yards from a corner: 1. ***Spiral to the right,*** 2. **MARCH.**

Figure 47 *From Drill Regulations, Cavalry, 1891 Public Domain.*

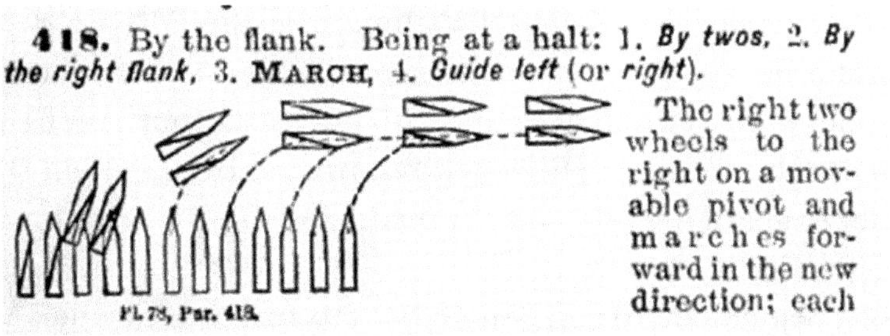

418. By the flank. Being at a halt: 1. ***By twos,*** 2. ***By the right flank,*** 3. **MARCH,** 4. ***Guide left*** (or ***right***).

The right two wheels to the right on a movable pivot and marches forward in the new direction; each

Figure 48 *From Drill Regulations, Cavalry1891 Public Domain.*

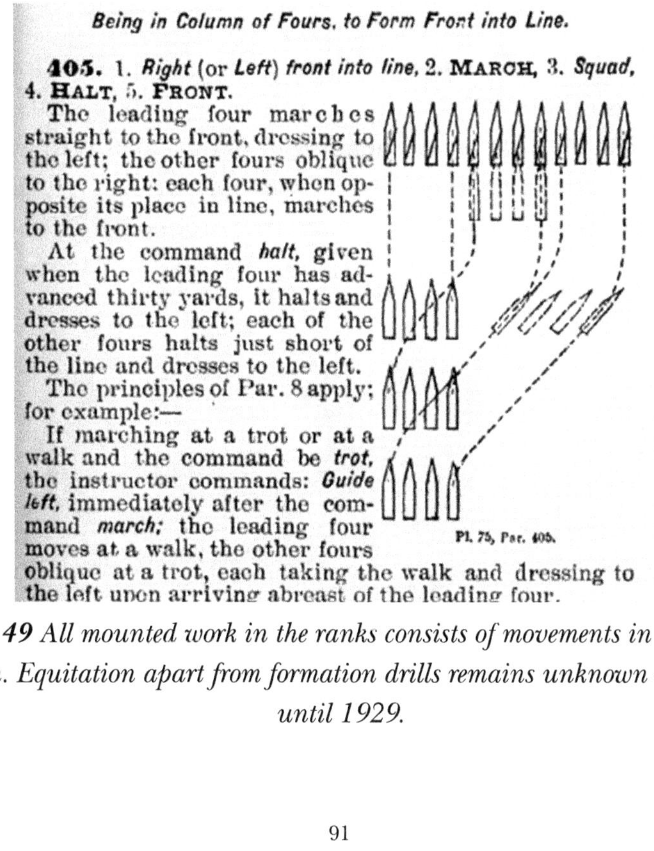

Being in Column of Fours, to Form Front into Line.

405. 1. ***Right*** (or ***Left***) ***front into line,*** 2. **MARCH,** 3. ***Squad,*** 4. **HALT,** 5. **FRONT.**

The leading four marches straight to the front, dressing to the left; the other fours oblique to the right: each four, when opposite its place in line, marches to the front.

At the command ***halt,*** given when the leading four has advanced thirty yards, it halts and dresses to the left; each of the other fours halts just short of the line and dresses to the left.

The principles of Par. 8 apply; for example:—

If marching at a trot or at a walk and the command be ***trot,*** the instructor commands: ***Guide left,*** immediately after the command ***march;*** the leading four moves at a walk, the other fours oblique at a trot, each taking the walk and dressing to the left upon arriving abreast of the leading four.

Figure 49 *All mounted work in the ranks consists of movements in groups in formation. Equitation apart from formation drills remains unknown in the ranks until 1929.*

Once each week, the units perform for higher authority. The units work through the formations, drills, parade maneuvers, and various mounted ceremonies they practice all week. At 11:45 a.m., Officer's Call sounds.

All officers gather in a circle near the center of the drill field. The regimental adjutant announces the regimental commander's appearance on the field. Typically, the 7th Cavalry's regimental commander, Colonel Hunter, comments on what he observes during his ride around the drill field that day. He consistently expresses his displeasure regarding poor performance and occasionally expresses his approval regarding a job well done.

Target practice—both rifle and pistol—follows equitation drill. All troops take their regular turn on the rifle range and then later on the pistol range. The unit follows this routine day after day, week after week.

At one point during Chamberlin's time with the 7th Cavalry, the War Department orders that the regiment exercise under battlefield conditions. And so, under wartime conditions and with full packs, four Troops of the 3rd Squadron march 143 miles in five days. Two troops, Troops C and D, remain at Fort Riley to guard the post and to prepare for an equestrian tournament at Des Moines, Iowa.

Between September 16 and September 29, Troops E through M march 232 miles. On October 9, they start their march back to Fort Riley, travel another 224 miles by the time they arrive on the 18th of October. Their total march, principally at the walk and trot: 454 miles.

For the remainder of the year 1910, the regiment prepares for its change of station which resides 9,881 miles away. The beginning of the year 1911 marks the closing days of the regiment's tour of duty at Fort Riley. Soon, the Regiment will experience an entirely new people, an entirely new climate, an entirely new culture. The War Department orders the 7th Cavalry to the Philippines.

Chapter 8

To the Philippine Islands and Miss Sally 1911-1914

"Sally is considered one of the best equestriennes in the army..."
—*The Washington Post* 1912 [74]

On January 30, 1911, the first wave of the 7th Cavalry departs Fort Riley for San Francisco. At noon, February 4, the regiment boards the *USS Sheridan.* On March 4, the regiment lands at Manila and prepares to march to Fort William McKinley, a cavalry post located just south of Manila. (Today, Fort McKinley serves as the final resting place for over 17,000 American soldiers killed during the liberation of the Philippines in World War II. Many of the 7th Cavalry rest there along with others from the 1st Cavalry Division.)

The Philippines present a new people, a new climate, and a new culture to the Americans of the 7th Cavalry when they arrive in the islands. The Filipinos resent the American presence and show their resentment with periodic outbreaks of fighting especially on the southern islands of the archipelago—Mindanao and smaller islands further southeast. The Philippine archipelago consists of approximately 7,000 islands. Chamberlin and the 7th Cavalry will serve principally on the largest and the northern most island: Luzon. For the most part, on Luzon, the people "go along to get along." But privately, the Filipinos remain fiercely independent, view the American presence in their country as a betrayal of the ideals expressed by the founders of the American Republic, and cannot wait until the "Yankees" go home. In fact, the Japanese invaders of the 1940s achieve something in

74 *The Washington Post,* February 17, 1912.

four weeks that the Americans fail to achieve in forty years: The Japanese make the Filipinos love the Americans.

The climate in the islands proves initially hard on most troopers of the 7th Cavalry. The humidity around Manila remains high throughout the day and night; the temperatures range from the high 90's by day and, on a cool night the temperature might drop to 75 or 80 degrees. In the mountains near Fort Stotsenberg, about 60 miles north of Manila the night time temperatures remain relatively more comfortable. Mold and mildew infest all leather unless stored in a closet with an electric light bulb burning throughout the day and night. Troopers typically take two showers and make two changes of uniform per day; some might take three showers and three changes of uniform per day when possible. Filipina maids remain more than happy to wash and iron clothes every day so everyone has a fresh uniform whenever desired. Young Filipino men, for less than 25 cents per day, offer their services to clean saddles, boots, bridles, and even groom horses for the lowliest private or the highest General.

The culture of the islands remains a combination of devout Spanish Catholicism among the poorer classes and Western-European sophistication combined with Catholicism among the ruling elites. Both strata populate Manila and the central plain of Luzon. In the more remote regions of Luzon and in the mountains north of Manila, some people live in stone-age conditions. They continue to take the severed heads of their enemies as prizes of war. When aroused, Filipinos prove to be ferocious warriors. For now, most tolerate the Americans because fighting proves ineffective.

Chamberlin and his unit's activity in the Philippine Islands focuses primarily on practice marching, routine training, and topography studies. For most of their initial time in the islands, the troopers prepare for and engage in rifle and pistol practice. The balance of time, they spend in equitation drills and suppling exercises sitting the slow trot without stirrups. In the field, they practice swimming horses over the many rivers that bisect the central Luzon plain. They perform extended order drills and maneuvers, and of course, they march long distances on horseback.

The long-distance rides often prove unusual. For example, on one ride through the Zambales Mountains north of Fort Stotsenberg, troopers ride along a path through the rain forest. Suddenly, a giant python slithering above drops its head from a tree immediately to the front of a Second Lieutenant staring him right in the eyes. The officer draws his revolver and shoots the snake dead-on in the mouth! For certain, the Lieutenant takes a stiff drink upon his return to the post. In addition, newly arrived troopers often drop from their saddles due to the high humidity and heat. The cavalry sends back to the United States many troopers who cannot tolerate the climate. At the same time, the cavalrymen take such good care of their horses and the Cavalry's march protocol proves so effective, that (as far as we can discover) no horses drop from heat prostration.

The marching protocol of the US Cavalry in the Philippines remains similar to that practiced in the deserts of the American Southwest. Due to the humidity, however, the rest periods extend a little longer and the marching pace remains a little slower. This preserves both horses and troopers. When marching with full equipment each horse carries approximately 250 pounds of combined rider and equipment weight. The officers and troopers give constant attention to the proper adjustment of the saddle and equipment packs.

When traveling in the mountains, the cavalrymen dismount and lead their horses to move up and down steep grades. For the first mile to two miles out of camp at the beginning of a march, they walk at a speed of something less than four miles per hour. At the end of the first mile, they dismount for about ten minutes and check to be sure all equipment rides properly on the horse's back. They readjust anything that seems out of whack. Every hour, they dismount and walk five to ten minutes to allow the horses to rest, to allow blood and air to recirculate under the saddle, and to enable troopers to stretch their own legs. At every opportunity, the troopers water their horses. At noon, the command takes an hour to two hours of rest and uses the time to feed horses and troopers.

During the month of December 1911, their practice rides total 717 miles. During January 1912, their practice rides total 120 miles. During February, they ride over 250 miles. During the month of May, they ride 562 miles. For all such rides, troopers proceed, for the most part, at the walk and trot. They also practice mounted rifle and pistol drills. The new Colt .45 caliber M-1911 pistol becomes standard equipment and remains standard for the army until 1985. Riding, target practice, more riding, more target practice takes up each day. War games, maneuvers, and more maneuvers hone skills. The 7th Cavalry, like the other cavalry regiments stationed in the islands, maintain this routine day in and day out. During these maneuvers and training sessions, Harry meets Col. George Willcox McIver, the army's machine gun and musketry expert who conducts several courses for troopers of the 7th Cavalry. McIver will play an important role in Chamberlin's future career as a soldier. Harry's winning personality makes its mark with McIver.

All of this work proves highly valuable. Thirty years later, under the considerably different circumstances of World War II, the regiment will pass through the same villages so familiar during the mounted marches and maneuvers of 1913-1915 and thereafter. The Army uses similar maneuvers against the Japanese invasion of the Philippines in early 1942. The 26th Cavalry Regiment (Philippine Scouts) will cover the withdrawal of General MacArthur's forces into the Bataan Peninsula in 1942. Many historians consider the 26th Cavalry's rear-guard action to be as fine as any performed by any cavalry unit in military history. Their predecessors worked out much of their tactics in 1913.

Team sports provide the only breaks from field exercises and maneuvers, equitation and marching, pistol and rifle practice. Polo continues to be the officer's favorite sport. Their teams compete against all comers. The officers from Fort McKinley compete with the officers at Fort Stotsenberg. Polo dominates the athletics of the Cavalry in the Philippines. The officers of the 7th Cavalry dominate polo in the islands with Chamberlin as one of the very best players in the regiment. Riding for pleasure also occupies much of the trooper's free time as well. On Sunday mornings, before the heat sets in, officers and enlisted men alike ride into the countryside or along the seashore.

One "non-riding" event, in particular, merits special mention. Second Lieutenant Thomas Christian and Privates Eckton, Huthmacher, Sanderson and Silet ascend to the top of Mount Pinatubo. For more than 400 years, this mountain peak defies all others who attempt to climb: Spanish explorers, insular government, and military parties. Private Eckton gains the highest point, slightly higher than the nearby second highest peak that his comrades reach.

HARRY MEETS SALLY

In between the equitation and distance riding, the rifle and pistol practice, the polo and hacking, Second Lieutenant Harry Chamberlin meets or renews the acquaintance of Miss Sally Garlington, the sister of Creswell Garlington, one of Chamberlin's classmates in the West Point class of 1910. Sally stands tall both physically and in the eyes of the upper echelons of the US Cavalry.

Some newspaper articles state that Sally visited West Point often. Most likely, since Sally spends time at West Point during her teens and also due to her brother's enrollment there, she and Harry probably meet. At West Point, Harry takes charge of some of the hops and dances that the Academy sponsors for cadets and the daughters of the Army's social elite. Whether any romantic inclinations emerge at that time, remains unknown. Other articles say that she first meets Harry in the Philippines. Nonetheless, as "one of the best equestriennes" in the army, she shares a great deal in common with Second Lieutenant Harry Chamberlin.

And Sally is not just "anybody." She is the daughter of the Army's Inspector General, Brig. General Earnest Garlington. In 1911-1912, Sally makes a round-the-world tour. She spends the winter in the Philippine Islands with her aunt and uncle, Major General and Mrs. Franklin Bell. Bell now commands The Philippine Department and thus all U.S troops in the Philippines from 1911 to 1914. The 7th Cavalry Regiment, therefore, resides within his command.

Major General Bell, an "old time" cavalryman, serves in the 7th Cavalry back in 1878. He loves riding horses and so does his niece Sally. Sally rides horses everywhere, especially as a member of Washington, DC's highest social circles. "Sally is considered one of the best equestriennes in the army circle here," writes the *Washington Post.* Highly intelligent, tall, slender, blond, athletic and beautiful, Sally surely captures more than one young officer's eye.

Figure 50 *Sally Garlington: tall, blond, willowy, daughter of the Army's Inspector General, Niece of the first Army Chief of Staff, and the finest horsewoman in the US Cavalry.* Washington Post *photo 1912. Public domain.*

Sally and Harry share so much in common that a romance blooms. They ride horses together all through Fort McKinley just south of Manila. Sally watches Harry play polo at Fort McKinley and also 60 miles north of Manila at Fort Stotsenberg. Harry takes Sally to the Army and Navy Club of Manila, a "dignified white structure, nearly hidden by beautiful palms and acacia trees, and guarded by a well carved wrought iron fence..." near Luneta Park along the shores of Manila Bay. The club is the best of its type in the world with excellent food and a superb staff. The club remains the center of Manila's burgeoning social life. (Today, the building houses the magnificent Rizal Park Hotel.) [75] Together, they walk on the promenade along Manila Bay. From that promenade, they watch the most beautiful sun sets over the bay that one might imagine with the island fortress of Corregidor in the distance. They also walk through the splendid Rizal Park as the Manila Hotel nears completion—all in Manila's central district planned by the great urban planner Daniel Burnham.

On Saturday, February 17, 1912, the *Washington Post* announces Sally's engagement to Second Lieutenant Harry D. Chamberlin of the 7th United States Cavalry. Sally is "one of the best-known army girls. She spent part of each year at West Point. Like the daughters of most army officers, Miss Garlington is an accomplished horsewoman," writes the *Elgin Daily News,* 22 July 1912. [76]

Harry and Sally return to the United States for their wedding. When they arrive in Washington, Washington society welcomes the couple with dinners in Sally's honor at places like the Chevy Chase club. According to the *Washington Post* article of June 25, 1912: On Wednesday, June 24, 1912, in the presence of Sally's family, Harry's family, the President of the United States, the Army Chief of Staff, and the Secretary of War, Sally Garlington, age 22, marries Harry Chamberlin, age 25. [77] Years later, in 1918, the *Washington Post* still refers to her as a former Washington "debutante and belle."

At 6 o'clock that day, the ceremony takes place in St John's Protestant Episcopal Church on Lafayette Square in Washington, D.C across from the White House. As customary at military weddings, the groom and all the Ushers wear full dress, white military uniforms. Attending as Ushers: Harry's West Point classmates Lieutenants Donald Connelly, Daniel Pullen, Beverly

75 https://www.realliving.com.ph/lifestyle/arts-culture/the-former-army-navy-club-is-now-the-rizal-park-hotel-a247-20170825-lfrm2

76 *Elgin Daily News,* July 22, 1912.

77 For all references to Garlington-Chamberlin wedding see Washington Post June 25, 1912; *Elgin Daily News,* 22 July 1912.

Dunn, and Harry's classmate and Sally's brother, Creswell Garlington. Lt. Dwight Shurtleff serves as best man.

Figure 51 *Father of the bride, Inspector General of the Army Earnest Garlington escorts his daughter Sally down the center aisle of St. John's Episcopal Church on Lafayette Square across from the White House. The President of the United States William Howard Taft, The Secretary of War, high ranking officers of the Army and public officials attend the wedding of Sally Garlington and Second Lieutenant Harry Chamberlin. US Army photo.*

Sally's father, Brigadier General Garlington, dressed in his full-dress uniform, escorts his tall, blond, blue eyed daughter, dressed in a white satin gown trimmed with cavalry-yellow roses, down the aisle of St. John's Church. The President of the United States, William Howard Taft, General Leonard Wood, the Secretary of War, and other dignitaries attend not only the ceremony but also the reception General and Mrs. Garlington hold thereafter at their Washington, DC residence.

The newly wed Mr. and Mrs. Chamberlin take a few days' trip to New York City and to Philadelphia. Later, they return to Elgin, Illinois and tour the Wisconsin lake region, according to the *Elgin Daily News*, 22 July 1912. Harry and Sally remain married for 21 years.

Harry Chamberlin marries "well" in army circles. Not only does Sally's father serve as the army's Inspector General and her uncle, General J. Franklin Bell, serve as the army's first Chief of Staff, Sally's mother and her aunt (Bell's wife) are the nieces of Major General John Buford of Civil War fame. Union cavalry General Buford (West Point '48) holds the field on the first day at Gettysburg against Confederate Harry Heath (West Point '47) until the Union infantry of General Reynolds arrives to reinforce the Union position.

Sally's maternal great, great grandfather serves in the Revolutionary War as a cavalryman under Light Horse Harry Lee, the father of Robert E. Lee. Sally's grandfather, Creswell Garlington, serves as a General in the Army of the Confederacy. Two of her great-uncles die in the Civil War fighting for the South. (Of course, Sally and her family refer to the Civil War as The War Between the States.) Sally's uncle Franklin Bell's influence extends all the way to World

War II in the person of then Chief of Staff, General George C. Marshall. Bell furthers Marshall's career when the latter serves as a Captain on Bell's staff. Marshall never forgets the help. The Garlington, Bell, Buford, Marshall linkages serve as only one example of the close-knit society of the US Army that endures well into the mid-twentieth century. One important thing to remember: *they* remember—always.

Since an officer's tour of duty in the Philippines lasts three years, Chamberlin and his wife return to the Philippines in September of 1912. The differences between Harry Chamberlin and his friend, George S. Patton come into relief regarding the Philippines. Patton successfully exercises all of his family's influence to avoid service in the Philippines and thus never serves there. Harry easily might wrangle a transfer given his wife's family connections. Harry does not.

Harry and Sally remain stationed in the islands until February of 1914. In February of that year, the Chamberlins return to the United States where Second Lieutenant Chamberlin joins a regiment stationed at Fort Bliss, Texas near the Rio Grande: the 5th US Cavalry.

Chapter 9

The 5th US Cavalry
And
The Mounted Service School
1914–1917
"Loyalty...Courage"
From the motto of the 5th US Cavalry

Harry and Sally Chamberlin travel to Fort Bliss, Texas to join one of the oldest and the most illustrious regiments in the army, the 5th United States Cavalry. The regiment's first commander: Albert Sidney Johnston in 1855; its second: Robert E. Lee in 1857. Lee resigned his commend of the 5th Cavalry to return to Virginia after refusing the command of all Union armies.

The regiment serves with distinction during the Civil War when it saves the Union at the Battle of Gains Mill and fights from Bull Run to Appomattox. It serves with distinction in the Indian Wars as well. The regiment takes the surrender of Chief Joseph of the Nez Perce, a military genius who repeatedly outmaneuvered and battled against army pursuers, travelling across present day Oregon, Washington, Idaho, Wyoming and Montana, and surrendering just 40 miles from the Canadian border. Throughout the latter part of the 19th Century, the regiment pursues and fights the Comanches, the Apaches, the Nez Perce, the Cheyenne, the Utes.

Perhaps most significant: The regiment never loses its battle "standards"—the Cavalry's term for battle flags. This fact enables officers and enlisted men alike to look down on Chamberlin's previous regiment, whose battle standards, lost at the Little Big Horn, would display only six campaign streamers once the War Department awards the regiment new standards in 1919 to ameliorate the 7th Cavalry's disgrace.

At the time Chamberlin joins the regiment, the 5th Cavalry's battle standard, however, carries 27 campaign streamers: 13 from the Civil War and 17 from the Indian Wars. In the eyes of the troopers of the 5th Cavalry, Chamberlin now belongs to the best cavalry regiment in the army and their battle standards show the campaign streamers to prove it. The intra-service rivalry and the feelings of resentment that troopers of the 5th Cavalry hold for what they consider the unearned and maudlin fawning by the press and public over the 7th Cavalry remains intense.

From Fort Bliss, the 5th patrols the Mexican Border along the Rio Grande. Its mission: to protect the southern border of the United States from smugglers, gun runners, and other unsavory characters including Mexican bandits. Day to day activities involve long patrols. When not patrolling the border, the troopers train themselves and their horses each morning. The quality of this training depends on the horsemanship of the officer in command.

Second Lieutenant Harry Chamberlin, one of the most athletic of West Point officers and a natural horseman with training to boot, works his troopers with exercises at the sitting trot and the canter without stirrups hour after hour, day after day. The troops then practice equitation at the walk, trot, and canter executing abouts, circles, serpentines, obliques, turns on the forehand and on the haunches, two-tracking; changing leads. Ten minutes out of each hour, the troops dismount, loosen cinches and rest the horses.

And again, all equitation takes place in the context of maneuver and drill. Troopers first practice movement of a platoon in close order; then, from the platoon level to the squadron; then, from the squadron to the regiment. The afternoons might consist of rifle and pistol practice on the firing range, physical exercise, and then marching on foot.

On border patrol days, the troop leaves Fort Bliss for the border. These patrols involved long, grueling, sometimes multiple day tours. The horses and troopers encounter rough terrain characterized by steep slides, rocky soil, and uphill climbs to overlooks as well as the Rio Grande River itself. They endure air full of dust, grit and grime; a blazing hot sun by day with temperatures over 100 degrees and a shivering cold by night where canteens often freeze.

Even as they patrol, horses and troopers train as they march alternating between the trot and the walk. Over rough ground, the troopers dismount and lead their horses to easier going. Ten minutes out of every hour, the troops loosen the cinches of their McClellan saddles and lead their mounts at a slow pace; or if near water, then the horses drink and the troopers rest. At noon, for at least an hour, sometimes longer, the troop halts, dismounts, loosens tack, feeds and rests.

Before halting at the end of the day, the entire command dismounts, loosens cinches and leads the horses at a slow walk for about one mile to cool out the horses before making camp. Once in camp, the trooper removes all tack; shakes out his saddle blanket; massages his horse's back and legs; grooms the horse on a picket line; waters and feeds his horse (and also a pack horse if so assigned), and then rests for the night. Officers and NCO's inspect the backs of horses to watch out for sores. The next morning, each trooper refolds his saddle blanket with "four corners to the rear and the near" being careful to put a fresh side down on his horse's back. Then, the trooper saddles up and the routine begins anew from start to finish.

Chamberlin leads his men, trains them, and patrols the border day in and day out. The routines remain the same. The pattern remains the same throughout the life of a cavalry officer until the end of the horse cavalry. As an officer's rank progresses upward (always slowly), privileges accrue but riding continues non-stop, and so does learning.

On July 1, 1915, the cavalry sends Second Lieutenant Harry Chamberlin to the Mounted Service School at Fort Riley, Kansas. There, he studies equitation as a separate discipline on the French model of Saumur and concentrates all of his efforts to master horsemanship. For all cavalry officers, this opportunity remains a key to a successful future. Highly prized, the enrollment potentially means a bright future for Harry Chamberlin.

THE MOUNTED SERVICE SCHOOL
FORT RILEY, KANSAS
1915

"This is the most strictly army place
I have ever been in and also the most strictly business...
more work than I have ever done in the army,"
—George S. Patton, Jr.
Letter to his father, 1913 [78]

78 See Carlo D'Estes, *Patton: Genius For War*, Harper Perennial, 1995.

A cavalry training school, in one form or another, exists in the US Army since the Spanish American War of 1898. Initially, the training school focuses on topics *other* than equitation and horsemanship. For a number of years, Col. Edward S. Godfrey lobbies the army to create a school devoted to equitation.

Finally, in 1904 the school focuses on equitation and horsemanship as a formal, free standing discipline. By 1907, now Brig. General Godfrey becomes the school's Commandant. Godfrey engages Captain Guy V. Henry Jr. as chief instructor, Henry recently returns from a year studying French equitation at Saumur, the school for advanced horsemanship of the French Cavalry. Henry successfully lobbies the army to transfer Captain Walter C. Short, also a Saumur graduate, to the school to expand the horsemanship and equitation curriculum as well.

Through the efforts of Godfrey, Henry, and Short, the Mounted Service School concentrates exclusively on equitation and horsemanship as opposed to treating the discipline as an adjunct to drill and maneuver. They also agree that the army should study the methods of all of the cavalry schools of Europe to create a curriculum aimed at making US Cavalry officers, in equitation, the equal of their counterparts in Europe.

To chart this curriculum and mode of instruction, an American Army Board of Officers visits the various cavalry schools around the world including Weedon in Britain, Saumur in France, Hanover in Germany, Vienna in Austria, Pinerolo in Italy as well as the Russian cavalry school at St. Petersburg. In time, the officers will also visit the cavalry schools of Sweden, Portugal, and Spain. When each officer returns home, the Board studies and then compares and contrasts the equitation and horsemanship training techniques and literature of each school.

In October 1907, the Board decides to adopt the "French System of Equitation" as applied by the instructors of the French Cavalry School at Saumur. Of course, from the end of the Napoleonic Wars of the early nineteenth-century forward, the "French System" influences not only the US Cavalry but the cavalries of the world, particularly the Germans who adopt the concepts of the Comte D'Aure, the chief instructor at Saumur until the 1850s.

The US Cavalry's methods, however, do not totally mimic the French. Minor variations exist. For example, in 1834, the United States War Department publishes its first manual entitled *A Complete System of Tactics for Cavalry.* The manual shows a solid French imprint but differs from the French by reinforcing the concept of natural balance and a free way of going for the horse as opposed to collecting the horse and modifying its balance as in "classical" equitation or French *Haut École.*

In 1841, the War Department replaces its 1834 manual with *A System of Tactics, adapted to the Organization of Dragoon Regiments.* To produce this manual, the army directly translates, word for word, a copy of the French *Drill Regulation of 1829.* (The French continued to apply, with only minor revisions in 1888, the principles of their *Drill Regulations of 1829* into the first decade of the twentieth-century.) [79] This long-standing affinity for French concepts combines with the Saumur education of the key instructors, Henry and Short. They make French equitation the core of the school's curriculum.

Captain Henry, the Mounted Service School's senior instructor, also studies under Edward Anderson, an American proponent of François Baucher's methods. (General Carter in his West Point text book *Horses, Saddles and Bridles* quotes Anderson when the latter describes the "military seat" as the "seat of Baucher.") In addition, during Henry's recent year's study of equitation at Saumur itself, many elements of Baucher's theory appeal to him as well.

The instructors at Saumur teach much of Baucher's theory in an unofficial, low keyed manner. While the elite riders of the French cavalry adopt most of Baucher's theory in their riding, the school "officially" rejects the concepts that its instructors privately practice. A later chapter on Saumur and Chamberlin's experiences there will elaborate on this point.

To implement this "French System of Equitation," the Board of Officers initially choose as a text for instruction the French Cavalry manual entitled, *Notes on Equitation and Horse Training in Answer to the Examination Questions at the School of Application for Cavalry at Saumur, France ("Saumur Notes ").* The Board chooses *Saumur Notes* as an interim measure since it will give them time to develop a text of their own. Using *Saumur Notes,* they push forward. The Board omits the original French version's "Notes on High School," "Training of Sauteurs," "Work between the Posts" and "Class Exhibitions," as not applicable to American cavalry service.

(One will learn a great deal about horsemanship, about training a green—or not so green—horse, and about Harry Chamberlin's background by reading *"Saumur Notes."* The reader will find in *The Chamberlin Reader* an edition abridged and edited for the civilian rider. The *"Notes"* discuss concepts of horse training that remain as valuable today as they were in Chamberlin's time. Everyone interested in horses will profit from this reading.)

---

79 For a discussion of the evolution of the US Cavalry's Drill regulations see James A. Ottevaere, *American Military Horsemanship, The Military Riding Seat of the United States Cavalry,* Author House 2005.

A short time after incorporating "Saumur Notes" into the curriculum, the Cavalry Board adds the text of the French influenced, Russian cavalry school: *Principles de Dressage et d'Equitation* by James Fillis, written in French in 1890. In 1902, M.H. Hayes translates the book into English under the title *Breaking and Riding*. Fillis studies equitation under François Caron, a François Baucher disciple, as did many of the instructors at Saumur. He follows the precepts of Baucher with subtle differences, especially regarding direct and lateral flexions as well as the concept of forward movement that we will discuss in a later chapter. Fillis serves as the chief instructor for the Russian Cavalry School at St. Petersburg from 1898 to 1910. Chamberlin highly values the book *Breaking and Riding* and studies it intensely before attending the Mounted Service School and, now at the school, expands his knowledge even further.

THE MOUNTED SERVICE SCHOOL REJECTS CAPRILLI AND THE ITALIAN SCHOOL FOR "ALL-AROUND MILITARY WORK"

By 1912, US Cavalry officers, along with their French counterparts, evaluate the "Italian seat" that Caprilli espouses and the Italian Cavalry adopts. To evaluate the Italian method in 1911, American officers travel to Rome with Colonel Blacque-Belair, head riding instructor at Saumur. Belair rejects the Italian methods. [80] Col. Blacque-Belair and the French influence carry the day with the Americans. Lt-Col T. Bentley Mott, Second Field Artillery, writes in *The Rasp,1912*, at pages 270-2:

"It would be unintelligent to dismiss the Italian seat because it offends ideas of 'cross-country horsemanship' long accepted in both England and France and believed in and practiced by our Mounted Service School. ...The Italian seat is probably a superior seat for races and exhibition jumping... But is it a good seat to teach officers? I believe not, and this opinion is supported by the best authorities in France.

> At Tor di Quinto this year were Colonel Blacque-Belair, the head riding instructor of Saumur...and other eminent masters. We talked of this point in all its aspects, and while admiring what was accomplished by the Italians and confessing that results alone count, these officers believed that their seat was not the proper one to teach military men.

80 Lt-Col T. Bentley Mott, Second Field Artillery, *The Rasp*, Mounted Service School, 1912.

The reasons may be briefly alluded to. An officer… should use the seat most suitable for all-around military work…Speed is important, but not all-important. The Italian seat does not appear to be as safe for either man or horse as the French. In going across country, even at top speed, an officer must see—must observe the ground…the military features of the terrain, the landmarks. If a man habitually gallops with his body inclined far forward, his head is inevitably down, and he sees about him only with an effort…

When we come to the every-day work of the mounted soldier there is still less reason for adopting the cramped far-forward position preferred by the Italians. In mounted combat a man in that position is far less free to use his weapons and less secure on his horse than when, by long habit, he sits well down in the saddle, his body inclined only slightly forward and the stirrups long enough to enable the calves of the legs to grip the horse...The best authorities in military horsemanship in France… do not permit…a system believed faulty for military work. These matters have been considered at Saumur and the instructors there are careful to indicate the narrow limits within which they believe the Italian seat finds a useful application.

As our ideas in military horsemanship now closely follow the French, it seems well to have enlarged upon this point. I can only add as a personal conviction that nothing which was to be seen at Rome last May or in London last June, where French officers made so brilliant an impression, is calculated to make us feel anything but satisfaction in having chosen the French as our models." [81]

81 Lt-Col T. Bentley Mott, Second Field Artillery, *The Rasp*, Mounted Service School, 1912.

Figure 52 *Patton displays the seat taught at the Mounted Service School. This photo originates in the year 1922. It will be several more years before the entire cavalry abandons the Saumur seat. Photo courtesy of International Museum of the Horse.*

In 1913, the Board of Officers adds to the Mounted Service School's curriculum the Manual of Equitation of the French Army 1912. This manual, to quote the words of the manual's forward: "contains…no innovations, but merely sums up the advice of de Pluvinel, de la Guérinière, the Comte d'Aure, Boucher, Generals L'Hotte, Faverot de Kerbrech, de Beauchesne and Jules de Benoist…as well as the traditional principles of the Cavalry School."

This manual is of specific interest especially regarding the use of the reins which the French classify into five different rein effects. The School of Versailles originated the diagrams shown and the explanations given for each of the five rein effects. Count d'Aure, (a student and then instructor at the School of Versailles and then Chief Instructor at Saumur) transmits them to Saumur and Gen. J. de Benoist makes them generally known.

Later, the authors of the US Cavalry's bible, *Horsemanship and Horsemastership* and Chamberlin in his two books adopt the concepts and the diagrams verbatim. The *Chamberlin Reader* displays the diagrams that Chamberlin uses in the final written work of his career: *Horsemanship and Horsemastership*, the 1942 edition.

For the right hand, the manual describes the 5 rein effects:

The right opening rein;

The right direct rein of opposition;

The right bearing rein;

The right bearing rein of opposition (in front of the withers);

The right bearing rein of opposition (in rear of the withers);

Of course, the rein effects follow for the left hand as well.

Of additional interest, the manual offers training pointers for Chamberlin and other who serve as instructors. It states a "commands" protocol to direct the students' use of the aids:

"By the right *opening* rein, by the right flank."

"By the right *bearing* rein, volt to the left;"

"By the *left direct rein of opposition*, half turn to the left."

"Half turn in reverse, leave the track by the *bearing rein.*"

"*Right rein of opposition*, on two-tracks on the diagonal."

"Turn to the right, by the right *opening rein.*"

"By the right *opening rein*, half turn."

"By the *left bearing rein of opposition*, on two-tracks on the diagonal"

The manual also suggests how the hands should be used to guide the horse:

> "The hand should know how to resist authoritatively when necessary, but should give way as soon as the resistance disappears and should return to the softness which is always the union between lightness and firmness. It is in this sense that a good hand has been defined as 'a force in the fingers equal to the resistance of the horse, but never greater.' (de Lancosme-Breves)" FEM p. 38. [82]

Having decided on the school's main textbooks, the faculty and the Board decides that the Mounted Service School will offer three courses along the Saumur pattern: a year-long Basic Course; a second, year-long Advanced Course; and a third-year course that focuses on *Haute École* riding. Circumstances on the international scene preclude the school from implementing

82 *Manuel of Equitation of the French Army*, 1912 translated by Lt. A. Chaffee, Jr., US Cavalry, Mounted Service School, Ft. Riley. 1913.

the third-year course and it never comes into fruition. In fact, with the advent of World War I, the school suspends operations for five years.

In the "Basic Course," approximately 60 officers study the French concepts of equitation together with American doctrine regarding how to use the pistol and saber mounted; how to care for horses; how to judge a farrier's work; how to march long distances and yet maintain equine fitness; and finally, how to care for horse equipment. The basic course intends to create first-rate horsemen by the standards of that era. Participants devote more than 1400 hours to the study of such topics. They spend 7½ hours each day in the saddle or in the classroom. They study well into the night to prepare for the next day's work.

Figure 53 *At the Mounted Service School, just as at West Point and at most cavalry posts around the United States, the wooden "horse" makes its appearance. US Army photo. Public domain.*

The school assigns to each student a green remount to train. The faculty believes that training a horse gives the student a solid foundation to understand the aids and their application. In pursuit of this principal, each night, the student studies French equitation and Hippology in books. When not riding the hills, slides, canyons, wooded and open plains, natural and artificial jumping courses of Fort Riley's then 22,000 acres, the student studies French equitation on "schooled" horses in the school's two immense riding halls. At mid-day, the student studies in the classroom. Each afternoon, he applies these French principles to training the remount entrusted to his care. Learning how to train contributes to learning how better to ride.

The student trains the same remount during his time at the school. He rotates schooled horses and jumpers twice a week, however, so that in a year's time, he rides almost 100 horses over the course of the year's study.

The officer-students at the school put in long hours in the saddle and in the classroom. The work proves demanding physically and intellectually. For hours on end, they slow trot without stirrups, longe remounts, jump obstacles, ford rivers, traverse slides, and ride into the countryside both by day and by night. They ride and attend class from 8 a.m. to 3:30 p.m. (with the exception of night rides which might endure the whole night). After hours, they read assignments late into the night to prepare for the next day's work "...which is more work than I have ever done in the army," writes George Patton to his father.

By 1915, the Mounted Service School establishes a fine reputation. All cavalrymen hold its graduates in the highest regard. Graduating from the Mounted Service School's Basic Course affects the balance of an officer's military career. One's academic standing at the school affects future promotion. Admission into the Advanced Equitation Course signifies an officer's potential for higher command in the cavalry.

Figure 54 *The West riding hall of the Mounted Service School at Fort Riley. Both the East and the West riding halls continued to serve when the Cavalry School was established at Fort Riley as the Cavalry's new school to train officers and NCO's. US Army photo.*

Figure 55 *The East riding hall of the Mounted Service School at Fort Riley. US Army photo. Each of the riding halls were large enough in which to play polo.*

Only the top ten graduates of the Basic Course qualify to take the Advanced Course. George S. Patton, Jr. qualifies and so does Harry D. Chamberlin. Upon graduating first in his class from the school's Basic Course, Chamberlin immediately receives his appointment to the school's Advanced Equitation course class of 1916. In addition, on January 7, 1916, the army promotes Chamberlin to First Lieutenant.

The Advanced Equitation Course, focuses more deeply into the theories that James Fillis expresses in his book *Breaking and Riding.* In addition, students devote deeper study to the "Baucheriste" *Manual of Equitation of the French Army 1912.* French equitation and horse training continue to form the pillars of the advanced equitation curriculum. The Advanced Course, however, pushes riders to their limits over still higher jumps, over wider gullies and through deeper ravines, down steeper slides and up higher hills. They complete night rides over rough terrain and complete long marches over varied terrain. As George Patton writes again in a second letter to his father: "I never worked so hard in my life." [83]

Events along the Rio Grande River interrupt Chamberlin's studies, however, during the Advanced Course. The nation's newspaper headlines focus on a Mexican revolutionary named Jose Doroteo Arango Arámbula—better known as Pancho Villa.

---

83 D'Este, Carlo, *Patton: A Genius For War,* Harper Perennial, 1995.

Chapter 10

Into Mexico 1916

"The Last Campaign of the Old Cavalry"
—Col. Frank Tompkins [84]

The 1916 expedition into Mexico teaches Harry Chamberlin and other younger cavalry officers like George Patton and Innis Swift a great deal about horsemanship. Most of this knowledge, they will not find in European books nor manuals of that day. With the exception of the British punitive expedition into Afghanistan in the 1870s, no recent European cavalry encounters terrain and climate as forbidding as what Chamberlin, Swift, Patton, and the US Cavalry encounter in Mexico.

At the same time, Gen. Eben Swift (Innis Swift's father) and Col. George Dodd, two commanders under Pershing, fought Apaches all along (and at times, across) the border in the 1880s and 90's. The Mexican experience will teach the entire cavalry's officer corps much of what those two men know about horses and endurance.

In 1916, horses and men demonstrate to the cavalrymen of Chamberlin's generation what horses and men will endure and achieve in difficult terrain and in an adverse climate. Even in our own day, machines fail to operate effectively in such areas. Of the other places on earth, perhaps Afghanistan provides the best geographic analogy to Mexico of that era. [85]

---

84 Major Frank Tompkins, Chasing Villla: *The Last Campaign of the Old Cavalry*. Military Service Publishing Company 1934.

85 For a detailed discussion of the Pershing Punitive Expedition see Herbert Mason, Jr. *The Great Pursuit*, Random House, 1970.

Why did this expedition begin? What did it achieve? How did it end? What did Chamberlin and his fellow officers learn from the experience?

In April of 1915, Mexican irregulars stop a train inside the United States. They order 18 Americans to exit the train and to strip naked. The Mexicans then shoot and kill each person execution style with a bullet to the back of the head. Violence of this sort occurs often along the Mexican-United States border. Mexican regular and irregular troops routinely violate the borders of the United States to steal cattle, weapons, and other material—as well as to rob and to kill Americans living north of the border. These assaults foreshadow things to come.

When the violently anti-American General Pancho Villa first crosses the Rio Grande into the United States in April of 1913, he commands eight men. Six months later, he commands 10,000 cavalry irregulars. Villa poses as Robin Hood to many in Northern Mexico. He serves as arch-villain to almost everyone else. Villa neither smokes nor drinks. (This makes him a hero in the eyes of US Secretary of State, William Jennings Bryan who also neither smokes nor drinks.) Critics say that Villa fights, rapes, pillages, loots, and steals so consistently that he has little time for the minor vices.

On March 9, 1916, Villa marches once again into the United States. Just before 4 a.m. on that morning he attacks Columbus, New Mexico with about 500 men. Villa's elite, 300-man bodyguard leads the attack. They are known as the Dorados because of the gold insignia on their olive uniforms and Stetson hats they wear.

When Villa attacks Columbus, US Cavalry kitchen crews initially fight back with pots of boiling hot water, axes, baseball bats and a few shotguns. They kill their share of raiders. After organizing themselves, dismounted troopers blast the Villistas with withering machine gun and rifle fire. The Americans inflict a heavy toll. In the end, the Columbus raid proves costly for Villa. The US troopers gather sixty-seven dead Villistas and burn the bodies the next day. American losses total seven troopers killed and five wounded along with eight civilians killed and two wounded. Though the Columbus raid offers him little of military significance, it enhances Villa's prestige.

As Villa retreats from Columbus, Major Frank Tompkins gathers 32 mounted troopers and pursues Villa about 15 miles into Mexico. The cavalrymen shoot stragglers and the Villista rear guard killing an additional 75 to 100 of the enemy. The very next day, President Woodrow Wilson announces that a "Punitive Expedition" will enter Mexico to capture Villa and destroy his forces. Yet privately, Wilson orders his military commanders to achieve something different: he orders the expedition "to pursue and disperse" Villa's band, not to capture them.

The night of March 15, 1916, the cavalry columns assemble and concentrate at the border under the Command of Brigadier General John Pershing. Horses and men do not sleep that night. Nonetheless, at 12:30 a.m., March 16, 1916, elements of the 5th, 7th, 8th, 10th, 12th and 13th Cavalry Regiments cross the Mexican border. By 8:00 p.m., the evening of March 17th—in just under 32 hours after crossing the border and traversing some of the roughest terrain on earth—the cavalry penetrates 125 miles into Mexico.

On March 25, 1916, 1st Lieutenant Harry Chamberlin receives orders to leave the Advanced Equitation Course at Fort Riley and report back to his regiment, the 5th Cavalry. A few days later, Chamberlin and the balance of the entire regiment cross the border. Ultimately, the regiment rides over 500 miles south to the outskirts of Satevo and then, near San Antonio, Mexico. They fight Villa's irregulars, as well as the Mexican Army, in a sequence of hit and run engagements further south through mountainous terrain and clouds of dust.

The Mexican experience proves invaluable for Chamberlin as well as for Swift, Patton and a number of other cavalry officers who achieve fame in future years. The experience leading men serves them well in two world wars. The experience riding horses teaches them about the strengths and the limitations of mounted troops operating in hostile country and over difficult terrain; the experience operating in foreign territory provides insights into living off the land and about the effect of restrictions imposed by higher authority on action, movement, and firepower.

President Wilson restricts the cavalry expedition in ways that limit its effectiveness. Initially, Wilson refuses to allow the cavalrymen to bring their rifles into Mexico. He limits their fire power to .45-caliber, 1911 semi-automatic pistols; (ultimately, Pershing protests and this order changes). Wilson refuses to allow them to enter any Mexican town (where Villa hides). He refuses to allow them to use the telegraph lines. He refuses to allow them to use the railroads to move supplies and to save horseflesh. Pershing and his officers object and argue: How much easier it would be to put the cavalry on trains, speed them 200 miles south and then let the cavalry ride north to cut off Villa's line of retreat. Wilson refuses these recommendations.

Obeying Wilson's restrictions, the cavalry lives off of the land and travels more than 30 miles each day. Each horse, each day, carries an average of 250 pounds. By day, they travel through sweltering heat as high as 120 degrees and stifling dust that hampers the breathing of men and horses. By night, they shiver in freezing cold. The hot days and freezing nights torture both horses and men. Temperatures usually drop *90 degrees* between noon and midnight.

Each morning, troopers find the water in their canteens frozen solid, their facial hair and their horses' mussels covered with frost, and their weapons slow to function due to the cold. Throughout the day, the wind blows sand or snow or both. It cuts like knives at horses and men. Mexico's drought adds to the misery, with no rain for nine months. The cavalry moves through the terrain—broken, rutted, uneven; up hills, down into gullies; over sharp rocks. Much of the campaign takes place in higher altitudes—about 7,500 feet. The movement of horses and men produces massive clouds of white alkaline dust that clog the nostrils of trooper, horse, and mule. Troopers tie wet rags across their horses' muzzles to keep the nostrils moist.

Since Pancho Villa knows that Pershing's orders prohibit the Cavalry from entering towns and villages, Villa hides in those towns and villages high in the rough, mountainous countryside. Even with these limitations and hurdles, the Cavalry presses on and engages bands of Villistas. At 7 a.m. on March 29, after a 17-hour march through freezing weather over a steep mountain range, 400 cavalrymen of the 7th US Cavalry engage Villa and 500 of his men. The 7th kills 60 and wounds Villa himself. The cavalrymen pursue Villa until his army evaporates into the mountain villages that Wilson forbids the US cavalrymen to enter.

As German Field Marshall Erich von Falkenhayn pursues his strategy to bleed white the armies of France at Verdun, General Pershing penetrates 516 miles into Mexico. The hostile local population hides Villa. The "friendly country and government of Mexico" (Wilson's words) attacks the US Cavalry with hit and run tactics that the Mexican army and irregular forces carry out.

Even though the American government continues to forbid them to enter towns and to use the railroads to supply the expedition, the US Cavalry puts Villa and his band "on the ropes." Then, in January of 1917, American relations with Germany reach a critical stage. As Pershing degrades Villa in Mexico, German Field Marshall Erich von Falkenhayn bleeds white the armies of France at Verdun. The infamous Zimmerman Telegram proposes a military alliance between Germany and Mexico offering Texas, Arizona, and New Mexico as payment for entering World War I, should the United States enter the war against Germany. As a consequence, Wilson orders the cavalry out of Mexico. Pancho Villa escapes as the United States prepares for a larger war.

On February 5, 1917, the last US Cavalry unit crosses back into the United States. (As late as 1942, the author's father serves in the 5th Cavalry with veterans of the Mexican campaign who remain bitter about the restrictions; the hardships caused thereby; and the fact that, but for the restrictions, they would have captured or killed Pancho Villa.)

Nonetheless, the expedition breaks the back of Villa's forces. The experience also demonstrates the US Cavalry's ability to operate in difficult terrain, to live off of the land, and to travel long distances under harsh conditions. The experience teaches Chamberlin and other cavalry officers a number of lessons that challenge and modify their conception of horsemanship and of the utility of horses in general. According to Major Frank Tompkins:

> "...we passed mostly through a mountainous country devoid of trails... Wherever the country was sufficiently level we moved at a slow trot of about seven miles per hour regardless of time, trotting wherever the country would permit. This was easier on the horse than the constant walk, and covered the ground with no strain on the animals' heart, lungs, or feet, and it enabled us to constantly cut down the lead of Villa and his band. In the very hilly regions and rough parts of the trail each officer and man dismounted and led his horse. We halted every two hours... These two-hour halts averaged about ten minutes each...
>
> "This service demonstrates that the compactly built horse endures a campaign much better than the tall, leggy type. Our horses never even got half feed and it was a constant effort to keep the big ones on the job. The little fellows also did better in the mountains and the rough places. The cavalry horse should be an animal low on his legs, of full form, one that when in low flesh does not show it—a horse whose bone, muscular development, energy and reserve power are denoted by a certain balance not often seen in horses over 15 hands 2 inches. The height of the cavalry horse should range between 14-2 and 15-2." [86]

Colonel Tompkins' horse "Kingfisher," a pureblooded Arabian, stands 14 hands 3 inches tall; carries "a load well over 200 pounds"; and marches round trip about 667 miles during the expedition.

Unfortunately, many of the higher command levels of the US Cavalry do not recognize these insights. Many Field Grade and staff officers still base their riding theory on the doctrines published by the French. The higher echelons regret that their troopers fail to ride as the French ride at Saumur. In the world's military circles, this remains typical. Military officers from

---

86 Major Frank Tompkins, *Chasing Villa: The Last Campaign of the Old Cavalry*. Military Service Publishing Company 1934.

around the globe view the French army as the planet's greatest and refuse to question, learn, and evolve.

Given the new knowledge, the most troubling aspect of training proves to be the French "Military Seat." But, at this time, no substitute theory of the "seat" exists. To ride "in the French manner," a trooper takes a deep "static seat"; he sits bolt upright or leans a trifle back behind the vertical; he tucks his spine under his torso and then sits on his spine. To ride down a steep slide or hill, French theory directs the trooper to lean back over the horse's loins (thus over-burdening the horses' hindquarters and straining the rider's jockey muscles). To jump an obstacle like a mud hole or a ditch or a fence, French theory commands that the rider remain upright, tight in the saddle; and that with his reins, he will "lift" his horse over the obstacle. Thankfully, for both horse and rider, in the field during the Mexican campaign, jumping proves a rare occurrence.

At least, in theory, the army wants its troopers to ride that way. Many troopers do not. The fact remains that French theory does not filter down consistently into the ranks. Perhaps it is just as well that it does not. Just two years earlier in 1914, the French cavalry and the French-influenced, Russian cavalry perform poorly during the early days of World War I. Horses break down, collapse from exhaustion, suffer from sore backs in as little as two weeks of action. It seems that the near century of relative peace in Europe from 1815 to 1914, enables the French cavalry to become more interested in form than in effective results.

Military historian John Keegan describes how "the main French reconnaissance force, Sordet's Cavalry Corps, had criss-crossed the Ardennes between 6 and 15 August without detecting the enemy's presence. The troopers had ridden raw their horses' backs—French cavalry had the bad habit of not dismounting on the march—but had seen neither hide nor hair of the enemy." (See the *First World War*, John Keegan.) [87]

Vladimir Littauer describes how, throughout the late nineteenth and early twentieth-centuries, horses trained and ridden in the classical French tradition, when exposed to a rigorous field campaign, lost flesh, broke down early on the march, and "...began to collapse and the great majority was found to be completely incapable of field service." (See *The Development of Modern Riding*, Littauer.) [88]

87 John Keegan, *The First World War*, Alfred A. Knopf, 1998.

88 Vladimir A. Littauer, *The Development of Modern Riding: The Story of Modern Riding From Renaissance Times to The Present.* Howell, 1991.

In the 1916 Mexican expedition, the US Cavalry's experience proves far different. The US expedition rides over terrain more difficult and endures a climate more unforgiving than anything the French encounter in the Ardennes. And yet, the Americans suffer no massive breakdowns as the French suffer. For example, the 11th Cavalry Regiment, Col. Robert Howze commanding, covers almost 700 miles during the expedition. The regiment's complement of horses consists of just over 760 animals. During the entire expedition, the regiment loses only 30 horses—and those due to exhaustion.

Three factors perhaps contribute to this different performance:

First, all US Cavalrymen in the ranks are "regular army." Most of them grow up as children with horses. Many learn to ride shortly after they learn to walk. They care for the family horses on the farm prior to joining the cavalry. Some join the cavalry at age 14 and 15 lying about their age; many drink hard and live hard; they prove to be tough soldiers who love soldering and riding—above all, they lavish care on their horses. They serve as career troopers who typically spend their entire careers in the same cavalry regiment.

As author Herbert Mason writes: "For the job at hand, they were the best soldiers Pershing could ask for, better than the Prussian Guards or anybody else." [89]

In the French cavalry, except for the officers and the NCOs, most cavalrymen serve as two-year conscripts with limited riding experience and even less knowledge of horsemanship.

Second, most US troopers are not as well indoctrinated as their French counterparts in the French "Military Seat" with the legs slightly forward, the torso a trifle behind the vertical and with the spine tucked under and the fleshy part of the buttocks as the primary point of balance. Many troopers ride in the manner most natural for them as opposed to following theories the regulations prescribe. Keep in mind that the fathers and grandfathers of many of these troopers rode with JEB Stuart, John Mosby, and Bedford Forrest. Their fathers and grandfathers learned to ride under war-time conditions in the Civil War and later, in the Plains wars. Much of this knowledge may have passed down to the sons and grandsons.

---

89 Herbert Mason, Jr. *The Great Pursuit,* Random House, 1970. The author's father was able to speak with several of the men who rode into Mexico in 1916 with General Pershing. Some, at the time of the expedition, were only 15 and 16 years old. They resented the restrictions that President Wilson placed upon the cavalry in Mexico. They insisted that but for those restrictions, they would have destroyed Villa's army

Third, US troopers, as a matter of standard procedure, dismount and walk their horses, at least, every two hours. (In later years, after considerable analysis, the cavalry adopts a dismounted walk and halt 10 minutes out of every hour.) The US Cavalry's long experience in long distance riding proves decisive. The French fail to dismount periodically, however, and thus ride their horses' backs raw.

Even though the troopers of the US Cavalry might not consistently display the "theoretical refinements" of Saumur's "Military Seat," they function far better than the French perhaps for that very reason. At the same time, no theoretical framework exists to offer alternatives. In future years, Chamberlin, Bradford, Henry, Doak, Phillips and other officers of insight and distinction will pick and choose concepts from France, Italy, Germany, Sweden, Poland, Austria and England and will combine them with American experience wrought during the Indian Wars and on the harsh and unforgiving terrain of Mexico to create a most effective mode of riding and theory of horsemanship for cavalry purposes of riding long distance and surmounting the obstacles most often encountered on the long march.

To summarize what Chamberlin and his fellow officers learn from the Mexican experience and of particular value to modern riders:

1) Smaller horses, closely coupled and compact, between 14.3 and 15.2 hands prove the best animals for riding with the maximum height limit being 16.1 hands tall. Those horses over 16.1 hands break down faster, suffer from poor balance, and are prone to leg injuries. This opinion extends to hunters and hacks as well as to horses needed to endure the rigors of a cavalry campaign. As we will discuss in a later chapter, Chamberlin writes that effective show-jumpers might display different characteristics.

2) A rider should dismount and lead the horse over rough terrain and steep hills except under exceptional circumstances that preclude this practice;

3) Smaller horses carry more weight more effectively than larger horses: a horse 14.3 hands will carry as much as 250 pounds provided the rider remains in balance; the smaller horse remains proportionally stronger than the larger horse.

4) The conformation recommended by General William Carter in *Horses, Saddles and Bridles* proves best. (Carter's discussion of conformation appears in *The Chamberlin Reader.*)

5) In subsequent years, the cavalry decides that the rider must dismount, loosen the girth and practice a combination of halt and leading for 10 minutes out of every hour. This practice enables blood to circulate under the saddle and thereby to rejuvenate the muscles and flesh of the equine back (as well as the posterior of the rider). The rider should "dismount and walk the last mile" of any long ride to cool out the horse and to rejuvenate the equine back prior to making camp. Failure to follow this practice, impedes blood flow, leads to muscular degeneration that impedes the performance, and shortens the life of the horse;

6) A marching regimen consisting of short periods of trot at approximately eight miles per hour alternated with short periods of walk at four miles per hour combined with ten minutes of halt and leading on the hour with a longer rest a mid-day enables the rider to achieve a rate of march as high as six miles per hour at 30 miles per day, day in and day out. Using this protocol for a one-day effort, horses and riders achieve 100 to 125 miles or slightly more in 24 hours. In the most extreme exertions, a cavalry courier riding alone and pushing his horse to the extreme might achieve 170 miles in 24 hours.

Figure 56 *Lt. Harry Chamberlin's regiment of the 5th US Cavalry, on patrol south of El Valle, Mexico, 1916. In later years, Cavalry endurance studies reveal that a properly conditioned horse will carry up to 20 percent of its body weight without undue strain. US Army photo.*

Figure 57 *The 5th US Cavalry in Mexico. Horses at 15 hands 2 prove proportionally stronger than larger horses. 15 hands 2 becomes the Cavalry's optimal size for purchase. US Army photograph.*

Figure 58 *The 5th US Cavalry in Mexico. The campaign reveals that horses 16 hands and larger break down under the rigors of campaigning more often than horses in the 15.2 range. In the future, for an exceptional horse, the Cavalry will go as high as 16.2 hands but seldom larger. US Army photograph*

Figure 59 *The 5th Cavalry in Mexico, 1916. As much as possible, the horses live off of the land. US Army photograph.*

Figure 60 *The 5th Cavalry in Mexico, 1916. The Americans preserve their horses better in Mexico than do the French near the Ardennes in 1914. The French ride their horses for hours on end without dismounting. In a matter of days, the French horses' backs turn raw. Author's collection. Public domain.*

After the 5th Cavalry's Mexican punitive interlude, Chamberlin earns his Mexican Campaign Medal and returns to Fort Riley to complete the Advanced Equitation course at the Mounted Service School.

Chapter 11

Back to the Advanced Equitation Course 1917

"...we must continually practice the great principle of *taking* and *giving*; The former to stop resistance, the latter to reward obedience..."
—James Fillis [90]

In February of 1917, Chamberlin returns to Fort Riley to complete the Advanced Equitation Course.

Just as in the Basic Course, Chamberlin's day starts with an hour or more in the gymnasium with fencing, calisthenics, vaulting and other exercises to "limber up" his body. The balance of his day focuses on horses. The school believes that proficiency comes from riding and more riding; jumping and more jumping; with saddle and without; with stirrups and without. Jumping still proceeds in the "old" fashion of the French with the close, static seat.

The faculty designs The Advanced Course to approach more complex issues of equitation and aims to train instructors who, upon graduation, will train other officers and enlisted men in equitation and horsemanship. The rudiments continue for "weary hours" as one graduate remarked: longing remounts; rotating horses twice a week; slow trotting without stirrups; jumping without stirrups; long, cross country rides through the canyons; down the steep slides; over the rocky terrain and through every other type of terrain, that in one way or another, in summer and in winter, a cavalryman

90 James Fillis, *Breaking and Riding with Military Commentaries. Aka Principles of Dressage and Equitation*, Xenophon Press, 2017.

might encounter on campaign. Students ride in French saddles and shun the McClellan. They study *Saumur Notes* in detail. [91]

Figure 61 *Interior of one of the riding halls at Fort Riley's Mounted Service School. US Army photo.*

The Mounted Service School expects graduates to shoe a horse, to perform all equitation movements up to and including the flying change of leads, to train a green horse from initial gentling to a clean execution of the flying change of leads; to understand in detail, elements of Hippology with special emphasis on diseases, hospital work, dissections and operations; to understand all elements of care for horses and equipment in garrison and in the field.

Students study, in detail, the training concepts of James Fillis as discussed in his book *Breaking and Riding with Military Commentaries.* The book discusses all aspects of training the horse, and thus the rider. Students study direct flexions of the equine jaw and how to achieve those flexions from the ground (which Chamberlin later decides only an expert should attempt). They study the rotation of the croup and of the shoulders. They study the rein back. They study the "ramener" (meaning the direct flexion of the lower jaw and of the neck as the first step to achieve equilibrium). They study collection (the second step in achieving equilibrium). They study the "rassembler" (whereby the horse comes up on the hand when the impulsion

91 *Saumur Notes, Notes on Equitation and Horse Training, In Answer to the Examination Questions at the School of Application for Cavalry at Saumur, France,* Translated from the French by Captain George H. Cameron, Assistant Commandant, The Mounted Service School, Ft. Riley, Kansas 1909.

communicated by the legs brings the hocks strongly under the animal's body and sends him freely onto the bit but only when the horse is "in hand" to a maximum extent). Finally, they study the concept of equestrian tact. The rider achieves this "tact" once he applies his "aids" with absolute precision at each stride; once he correctly combines and times his "aids," and asks the hind quarters to exert only the force necessary to maintain equilibrium with maximum propulsion).

Students practice and refine changes of direction at the walk, trot and canter. They execute the "doubler," the volte, the demi-volte, the diagonal change of hand, the reverse change of hand, and the counter change of hand. They work on side steps and two-tracks (including shoulder-in). They refine changes of lead at the canter and at the gallop. They learn to execute the well-collected canter (where the horse covers little ground and carries his head and neck high). They perfect the hand gallop (where the rider gives the horse liberty to extend). And finally, they develop the full-speed gallop (where the horse extends the head and neck fully).

The students delve deeply into all areas of horsemanship. For example, Chamberlin attaches particular importance to James Fillis' discussion of the concept of "*give* and *take*" with the rider's hands. The sections of Fillis' work that Chamberlin finds most valuable on this topic, we include in *The Chamberlin Reader.*

In addition to the detailed discussion of the rider's hands, principles of note taught in the program through *Breaking and Riding* include:

1. Horses that work on soft ground in garrison should remain without shoes;
2. A horse always will escape *from* strength *with* strength. The rider must prevent the horse from knowing his own strength;
3. For every longe lesson, the horse should wear flannel bandages on his forelegs, from the fetlock to the knee, so as to support the flexor tendons and to guard the horse from getting splints which are often caused by a green horse hitting himself;
4. At first, the trainer should teach at the walk all changes of direction and then, all other movements;
5. To move forward, the leg should precede the hand; to turn, the hand should precede the leg;
6. The resistance of the horse never should interrupt or terminate a lesson;

7. Of all the gaits, the rider will find the canter the most difficult and complicated. Few riding masters succeed in making a horse do the movements they require at the canter;
8. Since with the forehand, a horse begins the movement he desires, we say that "the hand ought to feel the ideas of the horse."
9. One cannot practice good horsemanship without progressive and delicately effected transitions;
10. Gripping too tightly with the knees pushes the thighs upwards, and causes the rider, more or less, to rise out of the saddle. By gripping with the hollow of the leg just behind the knee, we have, on the contrary, perfect adherence from the buttock to the heel.

Chamberlin respects Fillis and his book. He recommends its contents to anyone interested in furthering an equestrian education. At the same time, Chamberlin reflects on and evaluates everything he reads. Some points he adopts. Others, he rejects or modifies to meet his own objectives. For example, he rejects as absurd the Fillis argument that a woman's confirmation precludes her riding a horse astride. He reserves to the expert, as opposed to the general rider, the exercise of lateral and direct flexions of the horse's jaw when executed from the ground. He differs sharply with Fillis on the issue of collection. At the same time, he recognizes that Fillis offers the rider and trainer a great deal of practical and solid information.

In addition to studying *Saumur Notes*, and *Breaking and Riding*, advanced students at the Mounted Service School study the *Manual of Equitation for the French Army, 1912* (the "*Manual of Equitation*"). Of particular interest remain the five rein effects (discussed earlier) and depicted along with their coordinated leg effects. (The concepts and the diagrams originated with the School of Versailles and were introduced to Saumur by D'Aure and General Benoist. The diagrams appear in *The Chamberlin Reader.*) Chamberlin adopts into his own writings and practice these concepts as well as the diagrams shown in the *Manual of Equitation.*

***Figure 62** Officers continue to lean back over horse's loins while traversing a slide. From the Cavalry Journal, April, 1915. Vol. XXV, No 106. Chamberlin will change this method to a forward inclination of the upper body over the withers.*

The year 1917 proves to be an important year in Chamberlin's life for a number of reasons. On April 6, 1917, the United States formally declares war on Germany and Austria. On May 15, 1917, the army promotes Chamberlin to the rank of Captain.

On June 15, 1917, Chamberlin graduates first in his class from the Advanced Course at the Mounted Service School. He then returns to Fort Bliss and the 5th Cavalry. Chamberlin's graduation from the Advanced Equitation Course and his promotion to Captain culminate into a fortuitous advancement: the army appoints Chamberlin an instructor of Cavalry Tactics. He becomes and a member of the Tactical Department of the US Military Academy at West Point.

In July of 1917, Captain and Mrs. Chamberlin depart Fort Bliss on the Rio Grande and to return to the plain above the Hudson.

Chapter 12

An Instructor of Tactics
West Point
July 1917–June 1918

"...commanders of genius were to demonstrate how, boldly handled, cavalry could yet be employed to good purpose."
—Lt. Col. James P. Lawford,
the Royal Military Academy, Sandhurst [92]

Chamberlin arrives at West Point in July 1917. Of great importance to his career, his appointment to the West Point faculty enables Chamberlin to renew his "life-long association with one of the most distinguished and influential cavalry officers and horsemen of the twentieth century, then Lieutenant Colonel Guy V. Henry, Jr. who, as Commandant of Cadets, serves as Chamberlin's direct superior at West Point." [93]

Recall that Lt. Col. Guy V Henry, Jr. studies equitation in the United States under Edward Anderson, a Baucher disciple; he then studies equitation for a year at Saumur. Thereafter in 1907, he serves as chief instructor at Fort Riley's Mounted Service School. Next, in August of 1908, he becomes Senior Instructor of Cavalry Tactics and Commander of the Cavalry Detachment at West Point. For the next two years at West Point, he teaches Harry Chamberlin cavalry tactics and horsemanship. After Chamberlin graduates

92 John Ellis, Cavalry: *The History of Mounted Warfare* G.P. Putnam's Sons, 1978.
93 Major Louis A. DiMarco, *Brig. General Harry D. Chamberlin, The Cavalry's Greatest Horseman 1887–1944*, unpublished manuscript.

from West Point in 1910, Henry continues his teaching at the military academy with time off to compete in the Olympics.

In 1912, Henry represents the United States at the Olympic Games Equestrian competition in Sweden. He wins a Team Bronze Medal for Eventing and comes in 4th in *Prix des Nations* jumping. From 1916 to 1918, he serves as West Point's Director of Equitation and Commandant of Cadets. Now that Chamberlin also serves at West Point, Guy V. Henry, Jr. makes Chamberlin his protégé and guides his career as a soldier, horseman, trainer, and teacher. As later chapters will reveal, after both men leave West Point, Henry continues to sponsor Chamberlin's career into the 1930s.

At West Point, Chamberlin teaches cavalry tactics that evolve over approximately 80 years of continuous action. Prior to and after his West Point teaching, Chamberlin devotes almost all of his efforts to improve horsemanship and to develop better techniques of riding with one main purpose in mind: to increase the mobility of the American horse cavalry to meet the tactical requirements of twentieth-century warfare and the tactical doctrines of the US Cavalry. As a side line, he works on jumping mostly for sport and for improving a rider's balance. He recognizes that seldom will a cavalryman on campaign in the field confront an obstacle to jump. More likely, they will face steep slides and hills, wide ditches and ravines, narrow and rocky paths. This is because, in accordance with Cavalry doctrine, regiments of horse cavalry operate on the flanks of an army, to seize bridge heads far in an enemy's rear, to ford rivers, to traverse rugged terrain inhospitable to machines, and to hold ground until infantry arrives.

This emphasis on mobility departs from European norms concerning the use of cavalry. It becomes controversial among cavalry strategists, and given Chamberlin's contribution to the debate and final outcome, it is worth considering in detail.

While the American cavalry adopts many, but not all, French equitation concepts (just as do the German and other European militaries), the American cavalry develops its own "home grown" tactical doctrines by the time Chamberlin enters the debate as part of the West Point faculty in 1917. Historically, the American cavalry grew out of the "dragoons" or "mounted infantry."

With this heritage, the American cavalry typically viewed the horse as a means of transport from one place to another and not as a weapons platform. The long-distance rides around enemy flanks and deep penetration raids of the Civil War inspire American cavalrymen to seek ever greater mobility. As a result of this evolution, much of the equestrian theory that Chamberlin develops is to further this quest for greater mobility.

For the next 25 years leading up to the Second World War, however, arguments would rage regarding the prime mission of troopers on horseback. Would they be members of a combat arm or members of a reconnaissance unit? Would they operate like traditional European cavalry or would they operate like mounted infantry? Unlike European tactics, American tactics depend on mobility. In reality, though sometimes not in theory, those tactics depend on dismounted, ground combat troops. In most circumstances, in the final analysis, American cavalrymen will ride horses to the point of encounter, dismount, and fight as well as the finest infantry in the world.

True, they still practice firing pistols at targets while galloping on horses; some still revel in the idea of the massed attack. Until 1934, they still pay homage to the saber but even Custer left his saber home when he set out for the Little Big Horn. Cherished ideas give way to practical experience. Ultimately, in the 1940s, the last commander of the horse-mounted 1st Cavalry Division and Chamberlin friend, Major General Innis Palmer Swift, opts for the mounted infantry model much to the distaste of cavalry traditionalists, including his superior, the then Chief of Cavalry. But actually, this decision by Swift remains in keeping with the actual (as opposed to the perceived) activities of the cavalry during much its history. Except in rare circumstances, in the US Cavalry, the horse offered a means of mobility, not a method of attack.

European cavalry doctrine evolved, however, from a different historical experience and often, from a miss-perception of that experience. By 1914, Europe enjoyed almost 100 years of relative peace broken by minor outbreaks in the Crimea as well as in Europe. The Austrians and the Prussians fought in 1866 and the French and Prussians fought in 1870. These wars remained short encounters but proved costly nonetheless.

In particular, the French cavalrymen suffered great losses due to faulty tactical doctrine that they refused to recognize or admit. For example, at the Battle of Sedan in 1870, with unbelievable gallantry, through four successive attacks, the French cavalry galloped down on the advancing Prussian infantry, only to carpet the ground with dead and dying horses and cavalrymen. The casualties in both horses and men reached appalling levels and to no purpose.

The reason: European tactics remain fixed on faulty recollections of Napoleonic triumphs, one-off exceptions, and fantasy based on myth as opposed to experience. The art work popular in nineteenth and early twentieth-century England, for example, displays this mentality. *"Scotland Forever,"* Lady Butler's famous 1881 painting, "reconstructs" the charge of the Scots

Greys at Waterloo. The painting dramatizes the charge to the point of fiction. The horses move too fast over a plowed field and on a collision course.

The experience at Waterloo proves far different. Artillery firing "grape shot" or "canister" equating to huge shot guns, fires thousands of ball bearings into lines of charging horsemen. This causes the lead horses to fall which, in turn, causes the horses immediately behind to crash into those ahead. Of course, that assumes that the riders can spur their horses into such a melee. Often, horses refuse no matter what their riders demand. And, as one sergeant at Waterloo shouts to his assembled "square" of musket men: "They're wearing armor; shoot the horses." [94]

Nevertheless, Europe maintains its fictions and fantasies, and clings to those exceptions to the more typical results they experience. The realities of nineteenth-century warfare diminish the powers of cavalry. As applied in Europe, cavalry wanes even though European generals refuse to give up their head-long charges. The idealistic rendition of the attack of the Scots Greys at Waterloo sticks in the modern mind as cavalry's "standard operating procedure." Even as late as World War I, a painting of the same unit charging at St. Quentin in 1914 shows another artist's attempt to perpetuate or to resuscitate the myth of the cavalry charge.

Hopelessly out of date, European cavalry perhaps never recognizes reality or at least, holds on to a few exceptional successes which they establish as the rule rather than the exception. After all, more than 500 years prior to the invention of the machine gun, English archers with bow and arrow slaughter the French mounted knights in their frontal assault at Crecy in 1346; the Scots at Bannockburn put pikes into the ground to impale the charging English horses in 1314; the French dig a maze of holes every few feet simulating a modern-day minefield to break the legs of a charging mounted enemy throughout the eighteenth-century and before.

During the Napoleonic Wars, the French cavalry applies maneuvers other than the "charge" of course. Napoleon's cavalry abandons the training of the Manege and "artistic dressage" often to great tactical success (when not charging artillery or lines of musketry). Under Napoleon, they achieve exceptional mobility all the way from Paris to Moscow. After the Napoleonic Wars, the Cavalry of France returns, however, to the ways of the Manege.

Even though the British never adopt the "manage style" of riding, their tactics remain European. The British cavalry regulations of 1907 state: "It must be accepted as a principle that the rifle, effective as it is, cannot replace the effect produced by the speed of the horse, the magnetism of the charge

94 V. Vuksic and Z. Grbasic, *Cavalry: History of a Fighting Elite 650 BC–AD 1914*, Cassell, 1993.

and the terror of cold steel." [95] And so, they perpetuate the fantasy. Even *after* World War I, British General Sir Douglas Haig's answer to the machine gun: The cavalry charge en masse. It remains true that in certain situations, a cavalry charge with troopers riding boot to boot at a full gallop will panic infantry and cause them to break. This result remains the spectacular exception.

From Europe, on the issue of horsemanship, but not regarding tactics or the artistic ways of the French, the American Cavalry borrows much. From America, the cavalries of Europe learn nothing. According to Helmut von Moltke, Chief of the Imperial German General Staff in 1870, the American cavalry "was a disorganized, amateur collection of rabble." [96] In Europe, to call a military organization "rabble," one spews the highest insult.

On this point, Lt. Col. James P. Lawford, Senior Lecturer at the Royal Military Academy, Sandhurst writes: "While the generals in Europe groped for a solution, it was to be in the American Civil War that commanders of genius were to demonstrate how, boldly handled, cavalry could yet be employed to good purpose." [97]

J.E.B. Stuart comes into his own, not through the frontal assault but through swift, long-distance raids—often as long as 1000 miles—around the enemy's flanks and behind the enemy's lines. Generally, he avoids mounted assaults on the actual battlefield; so too with Bedford Forrest and John Hunt Morgan as well as with Grierson, Sheridan, Stoneman and McPherson. To understand the potency of their tactics, one only need recall Grierson's 1863 raid 600 miles through the Confederacy where troopers under his command suffer only three fatalities but reap havoc in the western Confederacy. Of course, exceptions occur like the battle at Yellow Tavern where cavalrymen meet head on and J.E.B. Stuart meets his death.

Lt. Col. Lawford's focus on the Civil War, however, may remain too limited. One should look back further in the American experience. The US Cavalry learns how to operate from the greatest light cavalry in the world: The Crow, the Cheyenne, the Wichita, the Pawnee, the Lakota Sioux, and the Nez Perce. The American cavalry faces brilliant, horse-mounted tacticians like Geronimo, Sitting Bull, and Chief Joseph who use the horse for mobility and mobility only. That mobility enables them to strike at will and to vanish into the countryside. They fight dismounted, not only to preserve

95 Edward Spiers, "The British Cavalry, 1902–1914," *Journal of the Society for Army Historical Research, Vol. 57, No. 230, Summer 1979.*

96 Lt. Col. John Moncure, *The Cowpens Staff Ride and Battlefield Tour,* Combat Studies Institute, US Army Command and General Staff College, Ft. Leavenworth, Kansas, 1996.

97 Ellis, John, Cavalry: *The History of Mounted Warfare* G.P. Putnam's Sons, 1978.

their horses (and thus their ability to remount and flee), but also to lay down more accurate fire. The horse, after all, offers a wobbly weapons platform.

In addition, for the Western tribes, the frontal charge remains almost unknown. They rely on mobility to outdistance their enemies not the charge to meet them head on. For example, the Apache leader Josanie covers over 1000 miles in less than four weeks. The brilliant tactician of the Nez Perce, Chief Joseph, his tribe riding toward sanctuary in Canada, succumbs only to freezing cold and to overwhelming force. He surrenders to the 5th US Cavalry merely 40 miles south of the Canadian border. The US Cavalry never defeats him in pitched combat.

These tribes and their chiefs ride horses to convey them to the battlefield. Once there, they dismount and search for cover from which to fight. Recent research into Custer's "Last Stand" reveals this tactic clearly. Many historians now believe that Custer's defeat not only results from his vainglorious misjudgments. They also attribute the defeat to the accepted tactical doctrine. Custer and his troopers dismount at the Little Big Horn to use their long-range rifles to shoot the attacking enemy at a distance. They do not have repeating rifles. The Indians dismount, encircle Custer on foot, and close in for the kill with Winchester repeating rifles.

Overwhelmed, Custer and his troopers do not have adequate fire power to fight off the assault nor do they have time to remount and retreat. As mentioned earlier, had they remained on their horses, perhaps they might have galloped to safety; but then again, Custer drives his mounts and men hard. By the time they arrive at the Little Big Horn, most likely, the endurance of horse and man is sapped. Nonetheless, for the American cavalry, (thankfully) dismounted combat remains the rule; mounted combat and the charge remains the exception.

So, therefore, American tactics evolve from ongoing, practical experience as opposed to European theory—from fighting the marauding bands of Indians before the Civil War to McClellan's observations during the Crimean War; to the flanking rides and raids of Forrest, Morgan, Buford, Stoneman, Grierson, Sheridan and Stuart during the Civil War to the Indian campaigns of the 1860s through the 1890s; from the "pacification" of the Philippines to Pershing's expedition into Mexico. The American Cavalry traverses wide open prairies, parched deserts, woodlands, mountains and rain forests. They ford rivers. They endure tropical heat and winter cold, sand storms and torrential rains. The campaigns typically demand movement, long marches, hit and run battles against a highly mobile enemy usually living off the land. Chamberlin hones his experience in several of these domains. These experiences mold the US Cavalry into the best endurance riding force of the nineteenth and the twentieth-centuries.

True, the American cavalry practices the charge with .45-caliber pistols drawn. But the charge remains the exception as opposed to the rule. One such exception: Lt. Edwin Ramsay of the 26th US Cavalry (Philippine Scouts) orders his troopers to charge a Japanese infantry position in the village of Morong on the Bataan Peninsula in 1942. The charge breaks the Japanese line as the infantrymen flee in panic. As Lt. Col. Eliseo Mallari, USA (Ret.) writes of the charge:

> "...our casualties in the battle were one killed, PFC Mallaris, and three wounded who were Ramos, PFC Ricardo Lopez, and PSC Pedro Euperio, along with Capt. Wheeler with a bullet through his leg and Lt. Ramsey with a small mortar fragment above his knee which did not require hospitalization...Summarizing the outstanding victory we had over the enemy in the battle of Moron, with an overwhelmingly advantageous casualty ratio in our favor, it can mainly be attributed to the shock resulting from the aggressiveness of Lt. Ramsey's Platoon charging unexpectedly into the of their advance guard and to the good training, discipline, leadership and loyalty of our troops." [98]

Another spectacular exception: The charge of the 4th Australian Light Horse at Beersheba on October 31, 1917. It is worthy to note that the 4th Australian Light Horse and Gen. Innis Swift's 1st Cavalry Division of 1942 generally apply the same tactical doctrines and for each, the successful charges mentioned in this chapter stand as exceptions to typical procedure.

Until 1934, Americans practice mounted saber drill and George Patton even designs a special saber. Long before 1934, however, the cavalry informally puts the saber on the shelf where, in reality, it rests since even before the Indian Wars. (As mentioned earlier, even Custer leaves sabers behind at Fort Riley as worthless weight when he marches to the Little Big Horn.)

It remains difficult to dispel the widely held Hollywood myth that the American cavalry typically "charged" at the full gallop, boot to boot with sabers drawn. Nothing could be further from the truth. True, the American cavalry galloped to the rescue in perhaps more than 1000 separate engagements—just not "Hollywood Style." Even US Army documents drafted in

---

98 Affidavit of Lt. Col. Eliseo Mallari, USA (Ret.) who, at the time of Lt. Ramsey's charge was a Second Lieutenant, the leader of the 2nd Platoon of Troop E, 26th Cavalry Regiment, Philippine Scouts. USAFE. Copy of Affidavit in author's possession.

the year 2004 and articles written about the horse-mounted, air supported, Special Forces contingent operating in Afghanistan drift into this mode when writers lament that modern firearms remain too heavy for riders to use on horseback. In the opinion of one former horse-mounted cavalryman from the early 1940s, trying to shoot accurately while mounted, regardless of whether the horse moves or remains stationary, remains a tall order. Much better, he said, to dismount, find cover, and shoot from the ground.

Even the Polish cavalry of 1939 never charged tanks not withstanding German propaganda to the contrary. To charge tanks: "That would be stupid," says Edwin Ramsey in the year 2001. (This is the same Ramsey who leads the successful cavalry charge against Japanese infantry in the 1942 Philippines campaign. Reporters interview Ramsey regarding the horse mounted US Special Forces in Afghanistan who locate targets for massive B-52 bombing raids in 2001.)

Twentieth-century American cavalry experience combined with the threats posed by mechanization ultimately defines the method of riding the cavalry needs to develop and to adopt. By the early1920's, American officers begin to question their old theories of horsemanship. Chamberlin and other officers attempt to fashion a new theory of riding to accommodate changes in technology, tactics, and combat that develop over so many years during so many campaigns against so many opponents. For them, horsemanship should reflect the tactical and strategic practice in war, not in parades, in spectator demonstrations, or in tactical fantasy. Of course, throughout the 1930s and 40's arguments rage as to what the "cavalry" should be: fully mechanized, horse mounted, or a combination of the two.

Greater mobility and more fire power after World War I become more important than ever. What counted most? The horse advocates argue the mission should be to travel long distances, to maximize endurance and speed, to live off of the land, to traverse rough terrain in bad weather, to ford rivers to establish bridgeheads, to reconnoiter on the flanks. By the 1930s, upon hearing the order to dismount, the cavalrymen responsible for heavy weapons, for example, must dismount, unpack a mortar or machine gun on a companion pack horse, assemble the weapon, and commence firing within 20 seconds or less from the moment the order to dismount is given.

In the 1930s, many American cavalrymen resist and resent Army Chief of Staff, General Douglas MacArthur's mandate toward mechanization. As a later chapter will describe, other officers like Guy V. Henry, Jr., accept MacArthur's mandate and integrate horses with machines with the hope to improve the combat effectiveness of both. But while Harry Chamberlin teaches cavalry tactics at West Point, issues of mechanization remain in the future. The immediate present offers challenges of its own: Congress declares war against Germany, Austria, and Turkey in April 1917.

By May of 1918, Captain Chamberlin worries that the action will pass him by; that as a West Point instructor of cavalry tactics, he will miss the war even though the army expands dramatically and it needs officers overseas. Promotion often depends on an officer's actual experience in actual war not on what he does in peace and certainly not what he does as an instructor of cadets. Without that vital experience, his career might stagnate. The key question of the hour: How to get an overseas assignment? How to get into the war? At the same time, Chamberlin's commitment to West Point remains in full force. He promised not to attempt to transfer until the end of his tour of duty at the Academy. Will the authorities at the Academy ever allow him to leave prior to his tour's end?

Chapter 13

World War I
Service "Over There"
1918–1919

"Major Chamberlin was an excellent officer
and he made a valuable addition to the brigade.
I can never forget his service with me."
—General George W. McIver [99]

When the United States enters the "Great War" raging in Europe, every officer in the army hopes to secure a place in the American Expeditionary Force soon to cross the Atlantic to fight in France. Chamberlin, however, recently joins the faculty at West Point. He cannot request a transfer. Of course, if a general officer going overseas were to request his services, then the army most probably would honor that general's request.

Keep in mind that Chamberlin married into two of the most prominent, extended families in the United State Army: The Garlingtons and the Bells. Sally Chamberlin's aunt marries General J. Franklin Bell, the first Army Chief of Staff. Sally's father serves as the army's Inspector General until retiring in 1917.

Fortune smiles on Harry since the commanding officer of Camp Upton, on Long Island in New York proves to be none other than General J. Franklin Bell, Sally's Uncle Franklin. It just so happens that in New York City, Harry meets Lt. Whitelegg. Lt. Whitelegg serves as an aide to General George

99 See Jonathan Dembo, Editor, *A Life of Duty, The Autobiography of George Willcox McIver 1858-1947* The History Press, Charleston, South Carolina 2006.

Wilcox McIver then at Camp Upton as commander of the 161st Brigade of the 81st Infantry Division ("The Wildcat Division"). Most of the division's infantrymen hail from the Carolinas and Tennessee. General McIver hails from North Carolina. Keep in mind that Sally's family remains prominent in South Carolina, which cannot hurt.

Lt. Whiteleg mentions to Harry that General McIver needs a brigade adjutant and hopes to find one before sailing for France. Harry mentions that he would be happy to become that adjutant. As General McIver writes:

"I was again without an adjutant until July 1918, when I found another one at Camp Upton, Long Island, just before sailing for France. He was Harry Chamberlin, then holding the rank as major, but without any assignment which would take him to France. I had known him several years before in the Philippines when he was a lieutenant in the 7th Cavalry. Having learned that he would be very glad to accept the detail as brigade adjutant, I at once requested his assignment. To make my request effective, I had to go and interview Gen. J. Franklin Bell, who was then the commanding general at Camp Upton. It was a matter in which General Bell was personally interested because Mrs. Chamberlin was his own wife's niece. The interview I had with General Bell was a pleasant one and prompt action was obtained. He at once sent a telegram to the War Department at Washington and the detail was made in a day or two. Chamberlin always seemed very grateful to me for having provided him with the opportunity for going to France with a combat division. He turned out to be a very competent assistant and along with this he had a very pleasing personality. Later on, in recognition of his services, I recommended him for promotion to the next higher grand and the promotion was made...." [100]

Later, McIver writes:

"The availability of Major Chamberlin was made known to me by my aide, Lieutenant Whitelegg, who met him by accident in New York after we had arrived at Camp Upton. Major Chamberlin was on duty at the time as instructor at West Point and was under some sort of a pledge not to make any effort to get a detail which would take him away from the duty he was performing. At the same time, a large number of officers were eager to go overseas, but were unable to get the proper assignments.

100 Ibid.

When I took the initiative and asked for his detail as brigade adjutant, the pledge apparently became inoperative and the detail was promptly made by the War Department at Washington. It was a great help to get General Bell's approval. Major Chamberlin was an excellent officer and he made a valuable addition to the brigade. I can never forget his service with me. He is still on the active list of the Army, holding the rank of lieutenant colonel. For many years he has been looked upon as one of the finest horsemen in the whole Army." [101]

So begins Chamberlin's journey to France and to the Great War. In the early morning of July 30, 1918, with less than four months of war remaining, Chamberlin and McIver arrive at the Hoboken dock and board the *Scandinavian*, a ship of British registry and manned by a British crew. The voyage across the Atlantic proves uneventful. On the morning of August 11, they land at Liverpool in the British Isles. After five days at a camp in Winchester, they move to Southampton on August 16. Shortly thereafter, they board the ship for Cherbourg, France. Chamberlin and the rest of the brigade staff sleep on the ship's steel floor because troops take up every birth and every square foot of the ship other than the deck. The following morning, after an uncomfortable night, they reach the French Port of Cherbourg.

From Cherbourg, the 81st Division travels to near the town of Tonnerre, about 100 miles south of Paris. And then, on the 19th of August, they settle into their main encampment at Flogny. On the 21st of August, General McIver writes to his wife:

"I am very well satisfied with Major Chamberlin. He a very good military man and speaks the language quite fluently, an accomplishment that has been very helpful at times...." [102]

The 81st Division spends just over three weeks in the Flogny area. It fills its days with several divisional maneuvers in the form of terrain exercises, communications work, and target practice. McIver and Chamberlin make their quarters in a chateau and enjoy dinner with the owners, members of the French nobility "which flourished under the old royalist regime in France," writes McIver. On or about September 14th, 1918, the Division moves to a front-line sector of St. Die in the Vosges Mountains in eastern France near the Alsace-Lorraine frontier. The Germans sit entrenched across "no man's

---

101 Ibid.
102 Ibid.

land." The trenches run through rough, rugged, and partly wooded terrain. The American and German forces fire artillery shells back and forth, a common practice on the Western Front. While in the St. Die sector, the Americans get first-hand knowledge about trench warfare from the officers of the 20th French Division.

On October 12th, the Germans launch a massive artillery barrage that lasts several hours. Under cover of the barrage, German infantry attacks the American trench line. When the artillery fire ceases, the Americans spring up to meet the enemy, some of whom just arrive at the edge of the front-line trench. Armed with repeating shot guns (known as "trench sweepers"), the Americans kill most of the German attackers. The loss to the Americans: nine men wounded; none killed. The losses to the division mainly arise from artillery fire, machine-gun fire, hand grenades, shrapnel, and sniping. During the 30 days they occupy the St. Die sector, the Americans lose about 45 officers and men. Even though Chamberlin serves as a staff officer, he comes under artillery fire with each engagement of the Brigade.

On or about November 7th, the division moves from the St. Die sector to five kilometers east of Verdun. On the evening of November 8, orders arrive to form for an attack the following morning at eight o'clock. The final attack of the Muse-Argonne offensive begins. At about 3:30 am, McIver transmits orders of the attack to the assembled officers of the division. The American attack will focus on the German lines east of Verdun in the direction of Metz. The Germans have held these lines since early in the war. Through their long occupancy, the Germans develop an exceptionally strong defensive system of great depth that they reinforce with concrete pill boxes, dugouts, and other strong centers of resistance. The Germans convert the ruins of several destroyed villages into fortresses. Further complicating the attack, the ground's low-lying marshland maximizes the defense, which the Germans reinforce with heavy concentrations of barbed wire.

Despite the strength of the German defenses, General Pershing's headquarters command assumes the Germans are beginning their retreat. This proves a mistake of the first magnitude. The 161st Brigade advances some five and a half kilometers over the marshy ground covered with heavy barbed wire against strong machine-gun positions. The Brigade captures three villages and suffers heavy losses from shell fire but keeps its organization in tact throughout the advance. Total casualties: 535.

At about 9 a.m. on November 9th, McIver, Chamberlin, and other staff officers take up a forward position in the ruins of the village of *Châtillon-sous-les-Côtes*, a village very close to the front line from which that day's attack will launch. The attack keeps McIver and Chamberlin busy well into the night and for the next two days of heavy fighting right up until the moment of the armistice at 11 a.m., November 11, 1918.

Late on the night of November 10th, McIver receives information that all combat will cease at 11 a.m. the next morning. A few seconds prior to 11 a.m. on the 11th of November, the Germans fire an artillery shell directly at the command point that houses McIver, Chamberlin, and the other staff officers of the 161st Brigade. At the moment, they all stand in the street in front of the command post. The shell explodes almost directly over McIver and Chamberlin spewing shrapnel in all directions. A large number of men stand in the shell's bursting radius. Had the shell exploded a bit lower to the ground, it would have killed several men including Chamberlin. Luckily, not a man receives a scratch.

After that explosion, silence. The armistice begins. The 161st Brigade remains along the lines it reaches in its final advance. They remain in place until November 16. Thereafter, they withdraw and assemble in a rear area in the Sommedieue Sector and then, on December 9, they reach the end of their march at Laignes in the Province of Côte-d'Or. Laignes sits southeast of Paris almost on a direct line between Paris and Dijon. They remain at Laignes for several months. McIver and Chamberlin secure lodgings in a beautiful house of a prosperous family. The lady of the house, a Madam Quenot, proves to be a patriotic woman who converts the house at the war's beginning into a hospital for wounded soldiers and maintains it herself for the duration of the war.

On about the 10th of December, McIver asks permission for himself, Major Chamberlin, and Lt. Whitelegg to visit Paris for one week. Headquarters grants permission and McIver and staff decide to embark for Paris the day after Christmas and stay there through New Year's Day. The group hears that Paris is crowded with visitors and accommodations remain hard to secure. Chamberlin writes to a Madam Leclerc, a French lady he and General McIver met at Flogny, their first station in France. Madame Leclerc secures accommodations for the group at the Hotel Moderne in Paris.

On about December 20, Chamberlin receives orders relieving him from duty as the 161st Brigade's adjutant and assigning him to duty at the corps headquarters at Bar-sur-Aube where he will take charge of the 1st Army School for the Care of Animals. General McIver writes:

> "I regretted this change very much since he had been a very competent assistant and a pleasant companion. His attitude towards me was always

very respectful and his personality made him well liked by the officers of the brigade. The new assignment did not please him at all. The duties were somewhat restricted in their scope and they might very well have been performed by a veterinarian. From a professional standpoint, the detail might have been considered as inferior in importance to that of brigade adjutant...On receiving word of his relief from duty with brigade, Major Chamberlin asked for and obtained permission to delay reporting to his new station until after January 1st. He was anxious to go on the trip to Paris as we had planned..." [103]

On Christmas Day, Chamberlin and McIver share a great dinner with a family in the town of Laignes. On the 26th, they depart for Paris. They visit historic sites, attend the Folie Bergere, dine with French friends, and enjoy themselves thoroughly. During this time, for his service in the Great War, Chamberlin receives a Campaign Medal with two battle stars as well as the Belgian Military Cross.

On January 3, Chamberlin reports to his new duty at Bar-sur-Aube. McIver and Chamberlin will periodically visit each other while they both remain in France. In his new role, Chamberlin will not only command the facility, but also will act as an instructor at the School for the Care of Animals. On January 3, 1919, he begins his new role. The role remains short lived, however, because on February 15, Corps Headquarters appoints him Inspector of Animal Transportation, 1st Army. This new roll offers duty highly valuable to Chamberlin's future as a horseman, theorist, and teacher.

In his new role, on March 4, 1919, he undertakes an inspection trip to England, France, Belgium, and Germany. On this trip, he visits cavalry regiments and remount depots of each country and he studies the methods and curriculum of each country's Cavalry School. This tour proves enlightening and highly beneficial: he decides that Weedon in England offers little that the US Cavalry does not already know; that Saumur in France impresses him and he decides that someday, he will try to study there; that the school in Belgium offers little beyond what one would find in France; that Hanover in Germany offers precision, but far too much collection and heavy aids—each unsuited to the hot-blooded horses that the US Cavalry favors. On April 7th, the army promotes him to Lt. Colonel of Cavalry. He ends his tour on April 10, 1919.

A few days later, an intriguing announcement comes from General Pershing's headquarters. The US Army soon will field teams in a number

---

103 Ibid.

of sports, including horsemanship, to compete with the teams of all other Allied Armies in Paris in a novel event called "The Inter-Allied Games."

Hoping to secure a position on the US Military Horsemanship Team that will compete in the Games, Chamberlin trains at Coblenz, Germany from April 22 to May 29, 1919. For Chamberlin, it means hours of slow trotting without stirrups to get back into shape, jumping over in-and-outs, ditches, and hedges. For hours on end, horse after horse, Chamberlin works to retrieve balance and achieve equilibrium—all the things he learned at the Mounted Service School back in 1915 and 1916. He and General McIver ride for recreation during the 161st Brigade's training period and before going into the line during the Meuse-Argonne offensive. Yet, he has not ridden seriously in a long while. Of course, all cavalrymen turned infantry officers will suffer from the same limitations.

The competition for a place on the team proves fierce. Almost every American cavalry officer in Europe—and there are many—aspires to make that team. Distance riding competitions and jump offs will weed out all but seven men. Chamberlin desperately hopes to be one of the seven.

Rumor has it that since the "Games" remain General Pershing's brain child, everyone who is anyone will be at those Games—watching. If—if he finds a suitable horse, if he makes the team, if he achieves some level of merit at this new and unknown event—Chamberlin believes something good might come of it. Above all, the very top ranks of the Army will notice—If.

Chapter 14

The Inter-Allied Games of 1919

"Lt. Col. H. D. Chamberlain *(sic)* on the 7-year-old American mare, Nigra, took the obstacles in brilliant fashion..."
—The Inter-Allied Games Committee [104]

In December 1918, General John Pershing invites the victors of the Great War (as everyone then calls the war) to participate in a series of "Inter-Allied Games" to celebrate the Allied victory. Pershing suggests the event will break down cultural barriers and language differences. The Games also will substitute for the 1916 Olympics which the war canceled. The Games will begin at a time and place the American Army will designate. The only qualification for a soldier to participate: an affirmative answer to the question "Were you a soldier in the Great War?"

The commanders of each of the 18 Allied militaries that fought in Europe and remain with troops there, together with their governments and people, respond positively to a "great athletic competition." The idea develops great public momentum. In fact, the Paris newspapers devote more copy space to the Games at Paris than to the Peace Conference at Versailles. The games begin June 22 and extend to July 6, 1919.

To prepare for the competition, each Allied army pursues its own methods. For just over four months, the Americans work through a rigorous selection process to choose their teams: In the preliminary "qualifying"

104 *Report of the Games Committee* compiled under the direction of Major George Wythe, Infantry, United States Army, 1919. https://ia800201.us.archive.org/18/items/cu31924014114353/cu31924014114353.pdf for all quotations in this chapter.

matches, 75,000 American soldiers compete in the football tryouts; 400,000 American riflemen compete in the rifle tryouts.

Ultimately, from just over two million AEF troops, 5,000 officers and enlisted men make it through the four months of qualifying matches to make the final tryouts. Further competition whittles the 5,000 down to 600 and then down to 80. Another 50 well recognized athletes, who had already shipped home, return to Europe from the USA to participate. Of the 400,000 American riflemen who compete for a position on the team, the series of competitions whittles this number down to 12 who represent the United States.

For the events, the Allied governments construct "Pershing Stadium" just outside of Paris. One-hundred officers and 3,300 American enlisted men, in three 8-hour shifts, work each day and night around the clock for four months to construct the stadium while 300 French troops work on the interior track and the infield. The flags of France, the United States, Great Britain, Italy, and Belgium wave on poles immediately in front of the *"Tribune D'Honneur,"* while the flags of the other 13 Allied nations rim the stadium's interior track. The stadium provides a seating capacity for 25,000.

On 22 June 1919, 90,000 spectators attend the opening day. Thousands more show up on each of the 15 days of competition. Each day, the crowds in throngs spill out onto the interior field and surge against every entrance. All in all, over one-half million spectators watch as 1500 athletes, representing the forces of 18 Allied nations, compete in 24 sports over 15 days. The Allies award to each of the 1500 competitors a bronze badge with blue ribbon to symbolize their participation.

Figure 63 *General Pershing, Marshall Foch, and General Weygand and staffs watch the equestrian competition of the Inter-Allied Games. Photo from the report of the Inter-Allied Games Committee. Public Domain.*

The Games Committee awards an "Inter-Allied Medal" to each competition's first, second, and third place winners individually and then also to each winning team. The French Minister of War awards to each first-place winner a gold medal and to each second-place winner, a silver medal. The Belgian King Albert, who enjoys military equitation, presents a silver cup surmounted by the figure of Winged Victory to the team that performs best in horsemanship.

The Games committee members wait to adopt the final program for riding until they know the exact number of nations that will compete. Ultimately, the finest horseman from seven of the victorious Allied nations compete: The United States, Belgium, Italy, France, Portugal, Romania, and Hedjaz. The other Allied nations cannot gather together the necessary horses to compete in a responsible manner.

In addition, the Games Committee members wait to decide on a program until they form an accurate judgment on the limitations the Stadium imposes for certain events. Ultimately, the committee members decide on a program that consists of four days of riding. The events themselves will number three: The Military Competition, The Pairs Jumping Competition, and The Individual Jumping Competition.

The Military Competition will last two days. On the first day of the Military Competition riders will compete on a long-distance and cross-country course 34 miles long. On the second day, they will compete in military jumping.

The Pairs Jumping Competition will last one day. Teams of two riders and horses will simultaneously jump obstacles in the stadium.

The Individual Jumping Competition will last one day. Riders will jump obstacles in the stadium subject to a strict time limit.

Initially, the Games Committee members want to include a steeple chase in the Military Competition. To arrange a suitable course in the short time available, however, proves impractical. Most equestrian competitors regret that practicality forces the Games Committee to omit the steeple chase.

Only officers of the Allied armies compete in the equestrian events. The Committee members set the minimum weight for riders in the Military Competition at 165 pounds. They leave rider selection, bitting, and saddling to the discretion of each army. Some armies pick the best known among their available riders. Other armies, including the American Expeditionary Force, chose team members, however, by elimination contests.

The Italian army enters seven riders and twenty horses. The French army enters ten competitors and nineteen horses. The Belgian army enters nine officers and nine horses. The Hedjaz army enters three riders and three horses. The Portuguese army enters one rider and one horse. The Romanian army enters three riders and five horses. The American Expeditionary Force enters seven officers and nine horses.

Through a series of competitive rides and jump offs, on June 1, 1919, Chamberlin makes the team. He wins his first opportunity to ride for the United States in international competition. The rules permit competitors to ride either private or government-owned horses. While the French, Italian and Belgian riders bring to the Games private horses as well as the best government-owned stock, the Americans make do with whatever mounts they locate in the American remount depots. After a prolonged search, Chamberlin finds a black mare of uncertain lineage to ride in the competitions: "Nigra." Nigra is a black mare from an American remount station foaled in 1913 of unknown breeding. Presumably, she descends from at least part Irish Thoroughbred lineage. She measures at 16 hands 2 inches and weighs 1,200 pounds. The AEF purchases her in France.

Figure 64 *Chamberlin chooses "Nigra" as his competition horse. She measures 16-2 and weighs 1200 pounds. The American Expeditionary Force purchased her in France. Chamberlin will ride Nigra in the games of 1919 and also in Olympic competition in 1920 and 1928. US Army photo.*

To practice and to prepare for the event, each Allied equestrian team quarters itself at Fort de Champigny, one of the outer rings of forts constructed to protect Paris. The competitors themselves build the obstacles over which the jumpers train. The obstacles, together with their arrangement and distances, remain identical to those both horse and rider will face in the Pershing Stadium. Each competitor trains on this obstacle course from the time he arrives at Champigny until the day he competes at Pershing Stadium. The Italian team reaches the practice course, however, only two days before the competitions began. The other teams practice for several weeks before the competition.

The following photos show some of the practice jumping prior to the event. The riding events begin on June 30, 1919.

Figure 65 *This French officer displays the Saumur "close seat" jumping style taught to French and American cavalrymen prior to World War I. Photo from the author's private collection.*

Figure 66 *Another French officer who displays the accepted jumping style of Saumur: the "close seat." Photo from the author's private collection.*

Figure 67 *Notice the rider's buttocks almost behind the cantle of the saddle in this jump. Photo from the author's private collection.*

Figure 68 *This Italian cavalryman displays the Caprillist "forward seat." The Italians practice only two days to negotiate successfully every jump. The French and Americans who use the "close seat" of Saumur practice for weeks and fail to equal the Italian level of success. The Americans take note. Author's collection.*

Figure 69 *Another Italian officer clears the jump with the jumping style of Caprilli. The French refuse to adopt the style. Author's collection.*

THE MILITARY COMPETITION.

The Military Competition lasts two days. On the first day, the riders confront a 34-mile zig-zag course that combines a long-distance course with a series of cross-country jumps. On the second day, the riders confront a Stadium Jumping course.

The First Day: The 34-Mile Course

The rules require each horse and rider to complete the course in four hours or less. The judges time each rider individually. Three riders from France, three from Hedjaz, four from Italy, one from Portugal, two from Romania, four from Belgium and four from the United States wait their turn. At the drop of a yellow flag, the stop watch starts and horse and rider dash on their way.

The 34-mile course begins at Chennevières on the Marne River, about seven-and one-half miles outside of Paris. Riders find the ground hard. Yet, the Committee selects the best location obtainable near Paris. Chamberlin and Nigra hold start position Number One as they wait for the drop of the yellow flag. They must cover thirty-four miles in four hours or less. The flag drops; the stopwatch starts; they dash off.

They ride the zig-zag course through Ormesson to Noiseau past the Bois de Notre Dame; then they cross a bridge over the River Seine at Choisy le Roi and ride on to the Chateau du Piple. There, Chamberlin stops, dismounts, and waters Nigra. Next, they circle through the village of Chatenay to Pattie d'Oie in the Bois de Meudon. At Pattie d'Oie, again, they stop for water.

Next, in the Bois de Meudon, the three-mile cross-country ride begins. Two yellow flags mark the start of the course. The rules require each horse and rider to complete this ride in fifteen minutes from the drop of the timekeeper's flag. A second timekeeper clocks their progress.

The flag drops; the stopwatch starts. Chamberlin and Nigra dash off. They confront twelve jumps marked with red flags. The jumps consist chiefly of fences, ditches, and imitation stone walls, none exceeding three feet in height or eight feet in width. Nigra and Chamberlin negotiate each jump without a single fault in ten minutes and thirteen seconds, well under the fifteen-minute time limit.

Figure 70 *Chamberlin on Nigra as he negotiates a jump in the three-mile cross country ride in the Bois de Meudon. Notice he uses the "close seat" of the French. Chamberlin comes in second in the Military Competition. A splendid showing for his first time in international competition. Photo from the Report of the Inter-Allied Games Committee. Public domain.*

After this cross-country phase, their long-distance ride continues. Chamberlin and Nigra reach the finish line at Croix de Berny with a time of three hours, forty-seven minutes and twenty-seven seconds.

Along the ride at two places, railroad tracks cross the trail. At each crossing, a passing train might delay a rider's forward progress. If so, a judge at each crossing logs any time delay. Later, the judges subtract the time delay (if any) from a rider's all-in time to calculate the rider's record time. Chamberlin rides Nigra straight through the entire course. He stops twice only to water Nigra; otherwise, Chamberlin and Nigra continue without delays.

A railroad train and another problem hold up the leading French rider for a total of five minutes and forty-five seconds. The judges subtract this delay from the leading French rider's time.

The weather remains good and all horses and men finish in excellent condition without undue physical strain and within the required time. Two riders of the Hedjaz team cannot take the jumps in the cross-country because their mounts are not trained to jump. This eliminates them from the competition but they finish the ride and stun the spectators as their Arabian horses pass seven riders who start long before them.

The French supply the day's stars: Major Joseph de Soras and his mount, Le Minotier, a nine-year-old gelding Thoroughbred, place first and dominate the field. Major de Soras and mount complete the course more than three minutes ahead of any other entry. The judges subtract from the time, the five minute and forty-five second time delay that Major de Soras experiences along the railroad track. Did this time delay offer de Soras and his mount time to replenish their reserves or did it break their momentum for the rest of the ride? Regardless, de Soras covers the thirty-four miles in three hours, forty-two minutes, and five seconds.

The Romanians come second in terms of time: Major Felip Jacob, on a twelve-year-old Irish bay mare, finishes at three hours, forty-five minutes, and twenty-seven seconds but Jacob knocks down one obstacle which will affect his placement overall. The Belgians make the third best time: Lt. de Brabandere, on Pilouche finishes at three hours, forty-six minutes, and thirty-three seconds (with a one-minute hold at the start of the Cross-Country course deducted); The Americans come in fourth in time: Lt. Col. Chamberlin on Nigra, finishes at three-hours, forty-seven minutes, and twenty-seven seconds.

Since Romania's Major Jacob knocks down one obstacle, however, he places below Chamberlin who turns in a clean ride. So, at this point, Chamberlin ranks in third place in the standings overall. Each of the contestants named above, except Major Jacob of Romania, wins the maximum number of points for the ride: 130.

After a day's rest, the same horses and riders enter the Stadium Jumping Phase of the Military Competition which takes place in Pershing Stadium.

The Second Day: The Military Competition's Stadium Jumping Phase

During the four days of competition, the weather remains exceptionally clear and sunny except during this Stadium Jumping phase. A heavy downpour temporarily delays the start of the riding. Although the rains cover the ground with water and make the footing soft and slippery, the event proceeds after the temporary delay without apparent difficulty.

To begin that day, the sound of 100 bugles and even more drums fill the air as regiments of the French Army carry into the stadium battle flags tattered in wars since the time of Napoleon. The stadium seats fill to capacity. Thousands more stand in the infield and at the stadium gates. Generals Pershing, Foch, Weygand, Howze and others take their seats. The Stadium Jumping phase of the Military Competition will soon begin.

The rules allow each rider three minutes and forty-five seconds to complete the jumping course that consists of twenty-three jumps: Stone walls, fences, hedges, hedges with top rails, two railroad gates, a brick wall, two dykes, an earthen wall with a top bar, and various triple and double bar obstacles. Each rider will enter the stadium alone in accordance with a prescribed protocol. Again, Chamberlin holds starting position Number One.

Outside Pershing Stadium, Chamberlin mounts Nigra. Alone, horse and rider walk through the Stadium's West Entrance. They cross a bridge over the running track and proceed to a point in the center of the "*Tribune D'Honneur.*" A lone bugler sounds "Attention." The thousands of spectators fall silent. The American, French and other Allied Generals focus their attention on Chamberlin and Nigra. One of Chamberlin's first riding instructors at West Point, Brig. General Francis C. Marshall looks on; so too do five future Army Chiefs of Staff: John Pershing, Charles Summerall, Peyton March, Malin Craig, and George C. Marshall.

Clouds fill the sky but no rain falls just yet. Chamberlin and Nigra stand quietly. Chamberlin watches the yellow flag. The flag drops; the stop watch starts. Chamberlin and Nigra dash toward the first obstacle, a hedge. They clear it. On the second fence: a fault. Over a stone wall: clean. Over the two railroad gates: clean. Over the triple bar: clean. Over the fence on a dyke: clean. Over a hedge with a top bar: clean. Over the next fence: clean. Over the next hedge: two faults. Over the next fence: clean. Over a brick wall: clean. Over an earthen wall with a top bar: two faults. Over a stone wall, a dyke, and then another stone wall: all clean. Over a bar: clean. On the next obstacle, a knock down: four faults. Over another bar, two more fences and another dyke: all clean. They race to the finish. Their time: three minutes and two-tenths of a second. Well under the time limit. Total faults: nine.

Most importantly: the future Commandant of Fort Riley's new Cavalry School and future Chief of Staff, Malin Craig takes note of Chamberlin. So too does one Col. George C. Marshall, the future Army Chief of Staff during World War II.

Next up, the Italian, Ubertalli: thirty-four faults in just over three minutes and fifty-five seconds.

Next up, the Belgian, de Brabandere: eleven faults in four minutes and forty-one seconds.

Next up, the Frenchman, Larregain: eliminated, rider thrown.

Next up: Major de Soras of France. On a hedge: one fault. On a bar: four faults. On a triple bar: two faults. Time: three minutes, 30.4 seconds. Total faults: seven.

The other riders in succession by number of faults: Thirteen, ten, twenty-five, forty-nine, twenty-six, eleven, nineteen, sixteen twenty-two and thirteen.

Major de Soras of France wins First Place. With nine faults each, Morel of Belgium and Chamberlin of the United States tie for Second Place. Taulbee of the USA comes in fourth with ten faults.

To break the tie between Chamberlin and Morel, the competitors and the Games Committee agree that the riders' performance in the Individual Jumping Competition of July 9, 1919 will break the tie.

The Inter-Allied Committee writes:

> "Although rain fell intermittently all through the contest the jumping was marked by brilliant riding. Major de Soras, France, whose thoroughbred, Le Minotier, had registered the best time over the previous day's ride, lived up to his reputation as one of the finest horsemen on the Continent by lifting his horse over the obstacles and coming within seven points of the perfect 240 in spite of the adverse field conditions..."
>
> "The American team captured a tie for second place and won fourth Place...Lt. Col. H. D. Chamberlain *(sic)* on the 7-year-old American mare, Nigra, took the obstacles in brilliant fashion and captured a tie for second place... Colonel Chamberlain held her well in hand and gave a splendid exhibition of horsemanship...The Belgian, Major Morel rode Miss Daisy into the tie with Chamberlain. The Irish mare refused the brick wall and ditch. The latter jump occasioned the downfall of nearly every rider and mount..." [105]

105 Ibid.

After the three sections of the Military Competition, the riders place as follows:

de Soras, France with 29.708 points;
Chamberlin, U. S.A with 29.625 points
Morel, Belgium with 29.625 points;
Taulbee, U. S.A with 9.583 points.

On July 5, in the Individual Stadium Jumping Competition, neither Morel nor Chamberlin finish among the high point scorers. Chamberlin leads Morel, however, and wins second place in the Military.

The winning teams, therefore, in the Military Competition are:

France
The United States
Italy

At age 32, Harry Chamberlin wins his first four medals in international competition: The Games Committee presents him with the Bronze Competitor's Badge, the Individual Inter-Allied Medal and the Team Inter-Allied Medal. The French Minister of War presents him with the Silver Medal for the Military Competition. Chamberlin's accomplishment in the Military enhances his standing among the other American officers: Taulbee ranks fourth; Merchant ranks ninth; and West ranks fourteenth.

THE JUMPING IN PAIRS COMPETITION

This Jumping in Pairs Competition dazzles both the spectators and the competitors alike. It proves to be the most entertaining and impressive exhibition of all the equestrian competitions. Most importantly, the Italian team and their revolutionary jumping style impresses the Americans. The Italians dominate the Jumping in Pairs event. Two of their pairs win first and second place. The ditch jump, which gives the Italian team so much trouble in the Military Competition, no longer seems a mental or physical hazard. Both Italian teams jump it in excellent form.

Captain Alessandro Alvisi, on his Irish bred gelding Voli and Major Giacomo Antonelli, on his Italian bred Otello, finish first with 236 points. Major Ruggero Ubertalli on Ernani and Major Ettore Caffaretti on Nabucco win second place with a score of 234 points. The French team of Captain Antoine Costa on Gayeuse and Lt. Paul Larregain on Tapageur capture third place with a score of 231 points. The American team of Lt. Col. C. L. Stevenson on Raven and Major D. L. Henderson on Moses secure fourth place with a total score of 229.5 points. Both AEF horses are American bred.

The previously unpublished (to our knowledge) photos that follow show the actual Pairs Jumping in Pairs competition and the Individual Jumping Competition of the Inter-Allied Games.

Figure 71 *Majors Ubertalli and Caffaratti of Italy astound the Americans with their pairs jumping triumph. Photo from the author's collection.*

Figure 72 *Captain Alvisi and Major Antonelli of Italy take first place in the pairs jumping competition. Photo from the author's private collection.*

THE INDIVIDUAL STADIUM JUMPING COMPETITION

The last day of the Games provides spectacular performances in the Individual Jumping Competition. The Games Committee expands the fifteenth and last obstacle on the course, a water jump, to four meters in width. It proves to be a Waterloo for many of the contestants. Ten horses and riders fall at this obstacle. Each of those riders fail to complete the course and the judges eliminate them. Ten more horses land in the water but do not suffer a fall.

The Italian team achieves a national triumph. The Italian Major Ruggero Ubertalli—who studied jumping directly with Caprilli—achieves a personal triumph. His brilliant horsemanship wins both first and third places for his team. On his first round, Ubertalli rides the ten-year-old Irish bay gelding, Treviso. They come within one point of a perfect 240. They suffer only one fault. Then, on the second ride, Ubertalli and his horse Ernani score a 237. Finally, on Ubertalli's third ride, achieved on Sprone, horse and rider score a 235. Only two other riders out of fifty-five riders beat Ubertalli's worst score of 235.

Second place goes to Major Felip Jacob of Romania on Beby, a twelve-year-old Irish bay mare. The Italian, Caffaretti finishes fourth. His fourth place, combined with Ubertalli's first and third, enables the Italian team to win three of the four top places in Individual Jumping.

In the two Jumping venues: In the Pairs Competition and the Individuals Competition, the Italian riders show brilliantly. By taking first and second in the Pairs and first, third, and fourth in the Individuals, the Italians overshadow the French and the individual victors who prevail in the Military Competition. Chamberlin is not among the high score riders in the Individual Stadium Jumping Competition, but he does better than Morel of Belgium and thus he achieves the second place ranking in the Military. Regarding the Italian style and their victories: Chamberlin and the other American officers take note.

From June 1 to July 11, 1919, Chamberlin excels as a member of the US Military Horsemanship Team at the Games. In Chamberlin's first international competition, two factors prevail over all others.

The first factor: Five future Army Chiefs of Staff watch Chamberlin's performance. General Malin Craig takes special note of Chamberlin and soon he will command the new Cavalry School at Fort Riley. Future Chief of Staff George C. Marshall takes special note of Chamberlin and this will take on decisive importance for Chamberlin's future assignments just before and during World War II.

Top left—Lieut. Colonel Chamberlain of America. *Top right*—Lieut. de Rivoyre of France. *Center*—General Blague-Belair of France, senior judge in horse-riding competition. *Bottom left*—Lieut. Colonel Chamberlain of America. *Bottom right*—Major Ubertalli and Major Caffaratti of Italy.

Figure 73 *From the Report of the Inter-Allied Games Committee.*

Figure 74 *The American Team at the Inter-Allied Games of 1919. Chamberlin stands fifth from the left. Chamberlin placed second overall in the "Military" competition. From the Report of the Inter-Allied Games Committee.*

The second factor: The Italian forward seat and the Italian performance in the Games impresses Chamberlin and all other American cavalrymen at the Games. Within three years, the Italian influence of the Games will make a mark on an evolving American jumping style which will culminate with Chamberlin's theories of the late 1920s to mid-1930s. Even before attending the Italian Cavalry's Advanced School at Tor di Quinto, however, Chamberlin will begin to modify his thinking regarding jumping obstacles. He will not immediately abandon the "close seat" of the French and the French style will still dominate his performance at the Olympic Games of 1920, but the seeds of change have been planted.

On July 13, 1919, Chamberlin departs France. On the sea voyage home, he faces an uncertain future. Will he return to West Point as an instructor of Cavalry Tactics? Might the "old guard" at West Point resent the fact that he left the Academy before completing his commitment? Or might the Army find something new for him to do? Only time will tell. Hopefully, he will find out before his short furlough at home with Sally comes to a close. He arrives back in the United States on July 21, 1919.

Chapter 15

Back to Fort Riley, To Weapons, Horsemanship, and The Olympics 1919–1922

"There is not in the world today an officer of distinction, recognized as an authority on military matters in a broad way, who does not declare with emphasis that cavalry is as important today as it ever was."
—General of the Armies, John J. Pershing, 1920 [106]

As the only Allied general who experiences trench warfare and a campaign of cavalry movement within the same year, General Pershing speaks with authority. As Army Chief of Staff in 1921, Pershing strongly supports the cavalry's effort to create a first-class Cavalry School at Fort Riley. In time, it will become one of the finest, if not the finest, school of its kind in the world. Harry Chamberlin will serve there "at the creation."

Chamberlin's horsemanship in Paris impresses everyone, especially Malin Craig, the recently appointed Commandant of the newly opened Cavalry School at Fort Riley. Craig asks that Chamberlin join the faculty at the Cavalry School. Chamberlin gets his new orders while at home with Sally.

On August 19, 1919, Harry Chamberlin, Lt. Colonel of Cavalry, National Army of the United States, returns to Fort Riley, but not to the new Cavalry School's Horsemanship Department. For his first assignment at the Cavalry School, he teaches in the Department of Cavalry Weapons. In addition, on September 25, 1919, Chamberlin reverts back to his permanent grade of Captain of Cavalry, United States Army. His monthly pay: $220 plus a

106 General John K. Herr and Lew Wallace, *The Story of The US Cavalry*, Little Brown, 1953.

monthly allowance for food. This equates to approximately $39,000 per year in 2019 dollars. Few officers, if any, stay in the United States Army for the pay.

One might imagine Chamberlin's sadness when the army reduces his grade from Lt. Colonel to back to his pre-war rank of Captain. Only Chamberlin's love for the Army and his dedication to service soothes the frustration when Congress tightens its purse strings and reduces his rank to save money. After all, Congress reasons "the War to End all Wars" ends, and with it ends the need for a strong military. The army begins its decent into a budgetary wilderness just as the United States Cavalry begins its climb to heights of professionalism unmatched in its history, before or since.

Figure 75 *Chamberlin shortly after his return from the Great War. Photo courtesy of Ms. Lydia Moore.*

The new Cavalry School takes the place of The Mounted Service School that suspended operations due to the Declaration of War on Germany in April of 1917. The school's facilities: the riding halls, the stables and library, howe-ver, remain at Fort Riley. The Horsemanship Department of the new Cavalry School starts, therefore, where the old Mounted Service School leaves off.

When it forms the Cavalry School, the Cavalry expands the curriculum beyond horsemanship. The new curriculum includes tactics, weaponry, and a host of other topics important to a cavalry officer in the field. The faculty periodically modifies the curriculum but the essentials remain relatively constant.

Beyond the Horsemanship Department, the other departments of the new school remain "blank slates" with no course materials ready for classes to begin on January 3, 1920. To correct this situation for the Department of Cavalry Weapons and the Department of Tactics, from August of 1919 until January 1, 1920, Chamberlin and the other instructors work night and day to prepare course materials.

Instructors in Chamberlin's Department of Cavalry Weapons teach officer students and selected enlisted men everything anyone would want to know or need to know about machine guns, rifles, marksmanship, musketry, the Browning Automatic Rifle (BAR), and other weapons of war that the Cavalry deploys. Students rip down all of the machine guns, rifles, and the M-1918 BAR into their component parts, reassemble each, and learn how to maintain them as well as how to fire them. The course follows the same protocols that the Infantry applies to teach its soldiers at Fort Benning, Georgia.

The Cavalry School goes one step further, however, because the Cavalry integrates all of these weapons with horses and mules. Horses carry troopers. Horses carry machine guns and mortars. Mules carry pack artillery, specifically "the French 75's" and ammunition for each weapon the Cavalry uses. Horses and mules also carry additional supplies beyond weapons and ammunition to sustain a combat unit in the field.

The Cavalry specially trains certain horses to work as "machine gun and mortar horses." They carry their loads on a specially made pack saddle that Col. Albert Phillips designs. A mounted trooper guides the machine gun horse with a lead-rope in his right hand and guides his riding horse with reins in his left hand. Together, the mounted trooper and the machine gun-mortar horse trot, canter, and gallop. Together, they jump over obstacles and ditches, traverse down steep slides, ford rivers, climb steep hills, and do everything that a horse and rider performs alone.

If the combination of mounted rider and his machine gun horse comes to a tree, the trooper drops the lead rope; the pack-horse gallops to the right of the tree, the trooper on his mount gallops to the left; once beyond the tree, the pack horse, without fail, returns to the trooper's side and, grabbing the lead rope again in hand, the mounted trooper and his pack horse continues forward.

Heavy-weapons troopers responsible for machine guns and mortars together with their riding and their pack horses train hour after hour, day after day. Under the time pressure of stop watches, they hone their skills so that when riding at a full gallop and upon the order to dismount: they halt from a gallop, dismount, unpack their weapon, assemble it, move the horses out of the line of fire, and commence firing—all in 20 seconds or less. Also under the time pressure of a stop watch and on signal, they dismantle the weapon, repack it on the horse, remount, and gallop off. Chamberlin concentrates on weapons training for six months.

Finally, on June 20, 1920, Captain Chamberlin transfers to the Cavalry School's Department of Horsemanship. He now teaches horsemanship for the Troop Officer's Class. As an instructor, Chamberlin continues his life-long, intense study of the more theoretical aspects of the art and science of riding and training horses.

At the time, the Cavalry School continues to use as texts *Breaking and Riding* by James Fillis, the English translation of *Saumur Notes,* and an English translation of *The Manual of Equitation of the French Army 1912* published at Saumur, the French Cavalry School.

Figure 76 *The Cavalry School Polo Team: Majors Doak, Erwin, Swift, West, Chamberlin. Typically, polo matches take up Sunday afternoons and practice session occur during the week. Chamberlin also acts as the "Head of the Department of Jazz" at the school. He plans most Saturday night parties and dances. US Army photo.*

The Cavalry School now offers three full year classes: The Troop Officer's Class, the Advanced Class, and the Advanced Equitation Class.

The Troop Officer's Class consists of equitation, mounted pistol and saber work, animal management, horseshoeing, marching, cavalry drill; and finally, the care of horse equipment. In addition to this curriculum, officers enrolled in the Troop Officer's Class also study courses presented by the Department of Tactics (which presents the Cavalry Drill Regulations and other such materials), by the Department of Cavalry Weapons, and by the Department of General Instruction. The Troop Officer's class consists mostly of captains and a few lieutenants totaling fifty in all.

The Advanced Class consists of twenty-five field grade officers, usually colonels and generals. Advanced and higher equitation dominates the curriculum in the Advanced Course. This horsemanship curriculum consists of mastering more advanced equitation, negotiating extreme conditions of terrain, practicing endurance marching, caring for horses in the field, and shoeing horses. Each student must work with four horses including a green horse, a made jumper, a green jumper, and an equitation horse.

The Advanced Equitation Class consists of twelve students selected from the fifty officers graduating from the Troop Officer's Class the previous year. Obviously, students face intense competition for a place in the Advanced Equitation Class. Selection depends on performance throughout the entire course of study. The Advanced Equitation Class focuses on the most advanced concepts of horsemanship over the most demanding terrain that Fort Riley presents. At this stage of his career, Chamberlin's role focuses, however, on the more basic Troop Officer's Course.

The Cavalry School's facilities and terrain offer superior training opportunities. Two large indoor riding halls, multiple Hitchcock pens, jumping chutes, miles and miles of bridle paths, slides as high as 75 feet, rivers to ford, gorges to negotiate, woods to traverse, miles of open country where one could gallop for miles and miles. Such magnificent facilities present the horseman with every type of terrain and problem that he might ever encounter.

For a cavalry officer, graduation from the Cavalry School provides an important milestone. Graduation and an officer's class standing upon graduation determine the officer's position in the cavalry and his opportunities for advancement throughout the rest of his career. Officers remain anxious to attend the school and work hard once there.

The workload remains intense, even more intense than when George Patton writes home in 1915 that he never worked harder in the Army than he does at the Mounted Service School. Lucien Truscott, in his book *Twilight of the Cavalry*, reveals the school's curriculum when he attends in the mid-1920s. At that time, out of 1,402 hours of instruction, officers receive 573 hours of instruction in horse related topics:

455 hours of horsemanship;
40 hours of horseshoeing;
8 hours of transportation.

In addition, students ride and study texts during their out of class hours. Students spend at least one half of every work day, usually in the morning hours, devoted to horsemanship. The balance of the day they devote to academic subjects in the classroom or in private study sessions. After an 8-hour a day, 5-day work week, students also ride on Saturdays and Sundays to hone their skills, exercise remounts, hunt on horseback, play or practice polo. and ride for pure pleasure. The instructors play polo against military and civilian teams throughout the southwest. Majors Sloan Doak, William Erwin, Innis Palmer Swift, William W. West, and Harry Chamberlin make up the Cavalry School Team of 1921-22. Each becomes a friend for life.

The school holds drag hunts three times each week and usually the field in attendance grows large. On Sundays, student officers attend to make the field even larger. During the fall, spring and summer, students in the Advanced Equitation Class play polo. (According to Truscott, only the Advanced Equitation Class students have the time to play.) Throughout the winter, the school holds horse-shows to give all students showing experience.

Of course, all is not work and no play. In the 1921 issue of *The Rasp,* the editors refer to Harry Chamberlin as the Chief Instructor of the Department of Jazz. Harry plans all parties for every Saturday evening at the school. In the Cavalry, (and it seems more so than in the other branches of the military), the alcohol flows freely in spite of the Volstead Act.

Officers and enlisted men alike are known as heavy drinkers. After the Saturday night dances that Harry coordinates, stone drunk officers often go to one of Riley's immense riding halls, mount up on jumpers and take high jumps. The jumps go higher and higher, wider and wider until the horses crash through the barriers or the riders fall off in a drunken stupor. Comments by Harry's contemporaries, however, suggest that Harry holds his liquor well and rarely drinks to excess. This trait proves an exception in the Cavalry. The School's curriculum imposes intense pressures on its students. They seek respite somehow. Alcohol seems to be the remedy of choice.

During June graduation week, tests of horsemanship skill, prowess, and ability take place. Instructors observe, record, and rank the performance of each graduating student. During this week, many legends develop that will follow a cavalryman for the rest of his years in the Cavalry. Future promotion and prime command opportunities often depend on one's rank in these tests.

A point-to-point race tests the remount that each student officer trains. The races extend 5 to 8 miles over a measured course. In a test of gaiting, each student on his horse must complete a specified stretch in a specified time in a specified gait. The instructors flag the courses for walk, trot, and gallop. Though the students must ride without watches, they must complete each course within the specified time.

Next, an outdoor and then an indoor jumping regimen tests the newly trained remount and his rider over a series of well selected jumps. After the jumping tests, students perform in schooling competition that consists of basic dressage tests. In addition, each graduating student also competes in "The Standard Stakes" which the student newspaper called the *Standard* sponsors. A cup and prize money are presented to the winner. The competition unfolds as follows:

1. Horses unknown to each rider stand tied to a picket line 300 yards away with saddles and bridles on the ground.
2. Each student dashes the 300 yards to his assigned horse, saddles and bridles the animal, mounts, then rides down a course of jumps.
3. At the end of the course of jumps, the student grabs a saber while still mounted and on the run; he then slashes at three dummies and continues to a pistol range.
4. At the pistol range, the rider dismounts, takes up a pistol and, from twenty-five yards away, fires at a bottle marked with his number. He continues to fire until he breaks the bottle.
5. Once he breaks the bottle, the student remounts and gallops to the Republican River. He fords the river, dismounts, and on foot leads his horse for one mile to a second river ford. He remounts, fords the second river, and rides to the foot of Sherman Heights (a steep precipice). He dismounts and leads his horse up the steep climb.
6. At the top of the climb, he remounts, gallops to a rifle range and dismounts. He takes up a rifle and from a range of 100 yards, fires at a bottle marked with his number until he breaks the bottle.
7. Once he breaks that bottle, he remounts and rides to the finish line.

Referees assign penalties for failure to break bottles, to miss jumps, or to miss saber dummies. The winner suffers the least number of penalties combined with achieving the fastest time to complete the course.

Next, the students complete the "Night Ride." This grueling test truly constitutes a "rite of passage." The rider negotiates a sixty-mile course in the dead of night. Each student takes a map that shows the route and each starts the course at three-minute intervals. The student must check in at four different monitoring stations along the route at an appointed time though the student carries no watch. Again, the student must estimate his rate of march to reach each station within the required time frame. Referees assign penalties if a rider exceeds the allotted time between stations. The faculty expects the rider to complete the course within five to six hours.

On the afternoon after the ride, the referees inspect the horse's condition and assign penalties if the horse proves not serviceable and in poor condition. The rider with the best time and the least penalties wins.

The caliber of horsemanship practiced and the level of instruction offered equals that offered at any other cavalry school in the world. At one time or another, the most respected horseman in the cavalry serve as instructors: Walter C. Short, Hiram Tuttle, Leonard Kitts, William W. West, Sloan Doak, John Barry, Innis Palmer Swift, Benjamin Lear, Harry Chamberlin.

THE OLYMPICS OF 1920 AT ANTWERP [107]

In March of 1920, someone in the United States Army realizes that the Olympic Games in Antwerp begin in August of 1920! Thankfully, the equestrian competitions begin on September 6, 1920. This gives the Americans six months to select a team and then, to prepare. The Americans choose Majors Chamberlin, West, Doak and Barry for the Three-Day Event team. They choose Chamberlin, Barry, and Doak to represent the United States in the Dressage competition. They choose Chamberlin again for *the Prix des Nations* jumping competition along with Doak, Erwin, and Greenwald.

Of course, horses remain a major question for the American team. The finest horses of Sweden, Norway, France, Italy, Belgium and the other nations of Europe (except Germany and Austria) will compete. The Swedish government and people make *every* horse in Sweden available to their team. The Swedes purchase and field horses costing, in 1920, as much as $30,000.

107 Information regarding the Olympic Games of 1920 derived from *Olympic Games 1920 Official Report* https://digital.la84.org/digital/collection/p17103coll8/id/9586/.

The only horses available to the Americans: remounts the Cavalry purchases for $165 each.

Chamberlin chooses to ride Nigra, his fabulous remount of unknown breeding from the Inter-Allied Games of 1919. Major Barry rides Raven, whom team captain Major Berkeley Merchant describes as a "big headed, slim-gutted scrub" of a remount with breeding unknown. Major West rides Black Boy who pulled a wagon during the last days of the Meuse-Argonne Offensive. Major Doak rides Deceive, an 18-year-old Thoroughbred who saw service in the Olympics of 1912. With these horses, the American team will compete against the best horses and riders of competing countries.

The US Cavalry's riding and jumping style slowly transitions to a rider who inclines more forward than in the past. This move to a more forward inclination slowly gains favor after the American officers witness the Italian performance at the Inter-Allied Games of 1919. At the Olympics of 1920, American riders maintain, however, their "close and static seat" with only intermittent forward inclination over jumps.

On July 7, 1920, the army promotes Chamberlin to the rank of Major.

Figure 77 *Newly promoted to Major, Chamberlin takes a jump on Nigra at the Olympics of 1920. He displays the "close seat" but a much more forward upper body when compared to his style at the Inter-Allied Games of 1919. Photo courtesy of the US Olympic Committee.*

In memory of the victims of The Great War, the International Olympic Committee awards the Olympic Games to Antwerp, Belgium. Two-thousand-six-hundred athletes compete, but the Committee refuses to invite Germany, Austria or any of the other "Central Powers" of the Great War. Baron de Coubertin creates an Olympic flag for the 1920 Games. It displays five interlocking rings. Each ring represents one of the five continents on Earth. Displayed for the first time, the flag flies over the Olympic Stadium at Antwerp.

The Americans arrive in Antwerp on July 6, 1920. To prepare for the Games, they train themselves and their horses along the Rhine River in Germany. To gain experience, they compete outside the cities of Cologne, Bonn, Coblenz, and Wiesbaden. On September 1, 1920, they return to Antwerp.

Eight nations compete in the Equestrian games: Sweden, The Unites States, Italy, Belgium, France, Finland, The Netherlands. In all, the competition includes 72 riders, 87 entries: 45 in jumping, 17 in Dressage, 25 in Eventing or in the term of the day: "The Military."

SEPTEMBER 6, 1920. THE OLYMPIC GAMES, ANTWERP, BELGIUM. [108] THE MILITARY "THREE-DAY EVENT"

The First Day: The first day of the Military Three-Day involves thirty-one miles of riding in three-and-one-half hours. This includes three miles of cross-country riding over natural obstacles at rate of fifteen miles per hour. Chamberlin and all other riders experience heavy going due to rains most of the day. They confront twenty-two obstacles. Major Barry falls at the first jump. He breaks two bones in his right hand. He remounts and continues on.

They traverse down an almost vertical, eighty-five-degree angled slide softened and muddied by rain. They slog their way up muddy slopes of seventy degrees. At another point, they jump down an approximate forty-five-degree slope into a gully and then slog their way up a slope of approximately seventy degrees. They jump in-and-outs as well as two and three-rail fences of various heights with slippery footing everywhere.

They face a particularly difficult water obstacle: a brook with steep and muddy banks. To surmount the brook, they jump from mid-way down the steep and muddy bank, over the two-meter brook to reach a muddy and

108 Also see Robert D. Thompson, *US Army Olympic Equestrian Competitions 1912-1948*, Schiffer Military History, 2008.

slippery, forty-five-degree angle landing on the other side. There, Chamberlin and Nigra make it over the brook, but Chamberlin falls off Nigra on the landing. Unhurt, he remounts and rides forward.

Chamberlin's teammate, Major West achieves a perfect score. Major Doak loses time, however, on the cross-country phase. US Individual scores at end of the First Phase:

West with 900
Chamberlin with 870
Barry with 870
Doak with 810

Relative standings at end of the First Phase:

Sweden
The United States
Italy
Belgium
France
The Netherlands
Norway
Finland

The Second Day: On this day of the Military, each rider must cover twelve and one-half miles in one hour over roads and bridle paths. Heavy rains render the bridle paths soggy. The rain and paths impose extremely heavy going. The Americans pace their rides to complete a twelve and one-half mile distance in the hour or less. Yet, the distance proves to be at least two miles and one-quarter longer than the twelve and one-half miles stated! This puts the American time table way behind what they need to finish the course on time. They fall so far behind between the fourth and fifty control points, that all of them gallop as fast as possible for the last fifteen minutes as they try to finish within the hour. None finish on time. The judges impose a heavy penalty for overtime.

At the end of this ride, the judging committee examines each horse to decide whether it remains fit to go on. Each of the remaining American horses: Nigra, Raven, and Black Boy, the judges classify as "fit." Major Doak's eighteen-year-old Thoroughbred, "Deceive" pulls a ligament in the right-hind pastern. The judges eliminate him—a considerable blow to USA

The riders now move to a regular steeple-chase track. They gallop two-and-one-half miles over jumps, some formidable. The rules allow a twenty miles per hour minimum rate. At twenty-two miles per hour a rider gains a certain percentage advantage and at twenty-four miles per hour, he gains another percentage advantage. The three remaining American horses make a clean score over this part of the test but not one of the three averages the twenty-two miles per hour rate, not to mention the twenty-four miles per hour rate.

The American riders achieve the following Individual scores end of the Second Phase, with a score of 1,500 being the maximum possible:

West with 1,470
Chamberlin with 1,440
Barry with 1,350
Doak with 855

Team standings at end of the Second Phase:

Sweden
USA
Italy
Belgium
France
The Netherlands
Norway
Finland

The entire Second Phase imposes a grueling test on the thoroughbred horses and riders alike. The steeple-chase of the Second Phase exhausts the non-thoroughbreds or the otherwise underbred horses. Yet, the U.S. Cavalry's $165 remounts keep close behind Sweden's $30,000 horses and ahead of the best horses of Italy, Belgium, and France. After this grueling Second Phase, will they muster the energy, however, they need to compete in the Third Phase? Will Major Barry, with his broken hand, remain competitive?

The Third Day: the riders compete in stadium jumping.

Not until the day before this jumping competition do the judges allow the riders to walk the course for one "look." The Americans face a course entirely new to them: one far different from what they expect and for which they train. In fact, few of the jumps resemble anything like what the Americans see before. On one obstacle, horse and rider confront a two-rail fence, followed by a ditch, immediately followed by narrow strip of ground that provides a narrow landing space, immediately followed by another two-rail fence, followed by another ditch.

Another obstacle directs the rider down a narrow, sloped corridor with earthen sides covered with trees on both sides, almost like the entrance to a subway station. Down the continuous slope goes horse and rider to a depth of about three feet below grade; at the corridor's end, they confront a post and rail jump with a top rail about two feet above grade for a total jump of about four feet.

Another obstacle requires horse and rider, at a gallop, to jump a three to three-and-one-half-foot oxer; then on the decent, the rider must gallop a few yards into a sand box, twenty feet square. From a full gallop, horse and rider must then halt in the box, turn around, gallop back in the reverse direction, and jump again over the oxer. Major Barry, with one hand broken, cannot halt quickly enough and make the reverse turn. So, the American team lost time points there.

All three American horses tire and show a lack of recuperative power unlike the better-bred Swedish, Italian, and French horses. Nevertheless, the Americans do well but slip from second place to fourth place in the Team standings.

At end of the Military Three-Day competition, the Americans achieve the following individual standings:

Chamberlin	6th
West	7th
Barry	16th
Doak	eliminated

The Team Standings

Sweden
Italy
Belgium
USA
France
The Netherlands
Norway
Finland

The Dressage Event

The Dressage test in 1920 includes the collected walk, trot and canter; the extended trot; the counter canter; and four-tempi, three-tempi, two-tempi, and single-tempi flying-lead changes. Horse and rider perform a five-loop serpentine at the canter with: flying changes of lead and counter canter loops; and then, counter canter changes of hand with flying changes of lead. The rider performs the halt through the walk. The rules require that the rider perform the test from memory, in ten minutes or less, on a 50 meter by 20-meter arena.

Chamberlin rides Harebell, 16.1 mare, 1125 pounds. Harebell performs as the best schooled mare at Riley. Out of a maximum score of thirty, Chamberlin's score 19.321. He places fourteenth. The two other Americans place fifteenth and sixteenth. The Swedes win First, Second, and Third. The quality of Sweden's horses and the brilliance of their performance stands second to none. It seems, however, that political bias intrudes on the scoring as well.

In the opinion of the Americans, one French entry and one Belgian entry seemed "good," but the rest perform way below the USA The Americans label the judges' placement of USA team as "ridiculous." So "...absurd that we didn't't even protest it. We could have put Nero and Santa Claus in that class and made a better showing than some of the Belgians did," writes Major Berkeley Merchant in the 1921 edition of *The Rasp.*

THE *PRIX DES NATIONS* TEAM JUMPING EVENT

In this event, each nation enters a team of four riders and the scores of the three highest riders count. The nature of the jumps changes from what the Americans saw in the Three-Day. The jumps stand higher. They average four feet seven inches. Other jumps rise higher still with doubles about six-and one-half feet wide. (They consist of two gates or two fences, configured as in-and-outs, six-or seven-feet apart).

Chamberlin rides Nigra. Doak rides Rabbit Red. Chamberlin and Nigra commit a number of faults as do the other American horses. The American team finishes fifth with forty-two collective faults. Sweden places First with fourteen collective faults.

THE *PRIX DES NATIONS* INDIVIDUAL JUMPING EVENT

Since the Individual Jumping and the Team Jumping take place on the same day, the rules bar from the Individual Jumping competition any horse and rider that competes in the Team competition. Chamberlin, therefore, cannot enter. The Italian team takes first and second place with only two faults for first place; three faults for second place.

Figure 78 *Major Karl Greenwald on Miss Armory displays the close seat but with a more forward upper body. The Italian influence of the Inter-Allied Games of 1919 shows its mark. Photo courtesy of the US Olympic Committee.*

Chamberlin's record at the 1920 Antwerp Games:

Chamberlin finishes sixth individually in the Three-Day; fourth in the Three-Day Team; fourteenth in Dressage; and fifth in Team Jumping. Not a bad showing for his first Olympic Games, for competing in all three disciplines, and for riding $165 remounts. For most of his career, Chamberlin will ride $165 remounts or in some instances horses that race tracks in the United States donate to the US Cavalry.

The Americans must wait for truly great horses until the late 1920s and early 1930s, after Thoroughbred breeder August Belmont places all of his finest stallions at the service of the United States Cavalry. Other multi-millionaire breeds follow suit. In the future, therefore, the United States Army's remount program begins to yield the progeny of the nation's greatest Thoroughbreds. For example, Sir Barton, the first Triple Crown winner in the history of racing, becomes an Army stallion.

At the Antwerp Games, the other United States teams in other sports fare much better than the American equestrians: the USA wins forty-one Gold Medals, the best of any nation in 1920.

After the Olympics of 1920, Chamberlin returns to Fort Riley and continues to teach in The Cavalry School's Horsemanship Department.

By 1922, Chamberlin sees and experiences a great deal in his Army career: He rides with the 7th Cavalry at Fort Riley and in the Philippine Islands; he pursues Villa into Mexico with the 5th Cavalry; he places first in both the Basic and the Advanced course at the Mounted Service School; he teaches as an instructor of cavalry tactics at West Point; he performs staff work in World War I; he impresses all at the Inter-Allied Games; he teaches horsemanship at Fort Riley; he competes in all three equestrian disciplines in the Olympics at Antwerp. All such experience combines to give him perspectives shared by few.

In 1922, Chamberlin writes an article on jumping obstacles for *The Rasp*, The Cavalry School 's yearbook. He discusses the impact of the Italian jumping triumphs at the Inter-Allied Games in 1919 on American thinking. He also discusses the Italian performance at the Olympics in 1920. Both events reaffirm his thinking regarding a more forward seat. The experiences accelerate the transition to a more forward seat for the upper reaches of the cavalry.

The Rasp Article Reveals Chamberlin's Thinking as of 1922. [109]

A complete reprint of Chamberlin's 1922 *Rasp* article appears in *The Chamberlin Reader.* The article offers a complete discussion of Chamberlin's thinking as of that year. A short summary follows below:

Chamberlin slowly begins to depart from the Saumur system of jumping. The rider should incline his body slightly forward without stirrups and without reins in hand. The rider should never lean back behind the vertical. He should secure his position with a strong grip of the legs *below* the knee and never with the knee.

Chamberlin rejects the older French concept of keeping the foot parallel to the horse's sides since the knee can flex only in one direction and if the foot remains parallel to the horse, then the lower leg cannot wrap around the horse's sides. The rider should turn his toes out slightly, writes Chamberlin, with his legs hanging naturally without stirrups "to wrap the lower leg around the horse." Equestrians will profit much from reading the whole article. It presents Chamberlin's thinking at an early stage of his transition to what ultimately, in a few years, will become "the Chamberlin seat."

---

109 All quotes and summary of Chamberlin article on jumping taken from: "Observations on Riding and Training Jumpers" by Major Harry D. Chamberlin *The Rasp 1922*, The Cavalry School, Ft. Riley, Kansas.

Though departing somewhat from the French theory of the jump, Chamberlin recognizes the value of French dressage training for horsemanship. He also recognizes that since the time of George McClellan, up and coming American cavalry officers study horsemanship and horsemastership at the French Cavalry's school for advanced horsemanship at Saumur in the Loire Valley of France.

In June 1922, the Chief of Cavalry grants the request of Major William W. West, Jr. and Major Harry Dwight Chamberlin to attend *L'École d'application de Cavalerie de Saumur* and later, the Italian Cavalry School for Advanced Cross-Country Riding at Tor di Quinto. Majors West and Chamberlin will be the only two officers from the US Cavalry to study at both schools.

In June 1922, Chamberlin's tour of duty at The Cavalry School ends. For the next year, he will devote himself to the study of French horsemanship and horsemastership at Saumur. He will follow in the footsteps of George McClellan, Walter Short, Llewellyn Oliver, Guy V. Henry, Jr.; Benjamin Lear, Adna Chaffee, Jr., and others to study the works of François Robichon de La Guérinière, the Count d'Aure, François Baucher, General L'Hotte, and the other masters of the French classical tradition both in the classroom and on horseback. He and Sally depart for Saumur, France in August of 1922.

Chapter 16

Saumur Part I
1922–1923

"Calme, en avant, et droit"
"Calm, Forward, and Straight"
—The Motto of Saumur

Two hundred miles southwest of Paris, the town of Saumur, France sits on the Loire River, an hour and a half's drive south of Le Mans in the green and bountiful Loire Valley. Some of the finest vineyards of France surround the town. Today, just as in 1922 and in the year 922, the *Chateau de Saumur* holds a commanding view of the river. Since 1906, the chateau houses a group of museums: The Museum of the Horse being one.

Imagine that you walk from the *Chateau de Saumur* south to the *Rue Jean Jaures*; you continue east to the *Rue St. Nicolas.* You proceed down a narrow, cobblestone paved street. On both sides of the street, you observe buildings hundreds of years old with shops on the ground floor and apartments above. After walking about four blocks along the *Rue St. Nicolas,* you come to the *Rue du Colonel Michon*; there, *Rue St. Nicolas* sharply turns to the left; but you look straight ahead. Nothing bars your view. To your left sits *Rue Manège des Écuyers*

Straight ahead you face the sand covered dressage arenas of the French Cavalry's school for advanced riding at Saumur: *L'École d'Application de Cavalerie de Saumur.* No pastures, no tall fences, no gates, no guards, no barricades separate you or the town from the school's grounds. Look to your left. You see the *Manège des Écuyers,* the old riding hall of the *Cadre Noire.* Look to your right. You see a line of stables that connects in the distance to other stables that extend around the dressage area on three sides. The stables form the boundaries of a huge plaza.

This first line of stables serves as a museum today: *Le Musée de la Cavalerie.* You walk into the stable turned museum. You see displays in glass cases. You study closely the paintings, the saddles, the swords, the uniforms, and the other memorabilia. They reveal the history and the evolution of the French cavalry. In so doing, they survey the history of Europe's wars from the time of Louis XIV to the early days of World War II.

Now, walk outside and look to your right. You see, in the distance, the other stables that border the dressage plaza. They now serve as a garage for tanks of the French Army. You walk toward the dressage area fences. Between the stables and the dressage areas proper, you come to a tree lined promenade: a continuous archway formed by centuries old trees that shield a bridle path from the sun. You look to your right and you survey the tree covered lane that extends into the distance. This tree shaded path circumnavigates the school's immense central, dressage plaza. An officer of the modern French Army rides his horse down the promenade.

Now, you turn to your left and walk forward into the middle of the dressage area. Make another left for ninety degrees. Look straight ahead. You now gaze upon a breath-taking site: the school's main building; a grand, four story, "U" shaped, Palladian-inspired structure, classical in design, over 240 years old with a huge equestrian tableau out front. Walk straight ahead. Today, you cross a parking lot that in Chamberlin's time accommodated more dressage arenas. You cross *L'Avenue du Marechal Foch.* You walk past the immense equine monument and enter into the main building's center courtyard.

Figure 79 *The main building at L'École de Cavalerie as it appeared during Chamberlin's tour of study at Saumur. In 2009, the dressage area directly in front of the building consists of a paved parking lot. A postcard in the author's collection printed in 1919.*

As you walk through these grounds and along the tree lined promenade; as you look at the exhibits in the stable turned museum; as you stand in the *Manège des Écuyers;* as you gaze at the central building that defines the magnificence of this place, as you ascend the staircase of that central building, let your mind focus on the past, to the year 1922 when Major Harry Chamberlin studies here.

Even prior to the American Civil War and well into the 20th Century, the United States Army sends promising cavalry officers here to study. Guy V. Henry, Jr. studies equitation here in 1906. George Patton, Jr. studies swordsmanship and takes cavalry classes here in the summer of 1913. American cavalry Majors Chamberlin, West, and Rayner study equitation here from August 1922 until June 1923. They learn much. They also impress their instructors with their prowess. Majors West and Chamberlin prove themselves to be expert polo players and equally adept students of equitation. At the same time, most certainly, they stand in awe of the place. Unlike Fort Riley, circa 1910, no buffalos wander into the parade ground here.

By 1922, *L'École d'Application de la Cavalerie de Saumur* offers more than 200 years of equestrian tradition and learning. It enjoys an equal number of years in which to evolve a well-defined equestrian theory. The school's facilities span the centuries. The French army finished the main building in 1771. The *Manages des Écuyers* dates from the time of Napoleon III. The stables date from the early to mid-19th Century.

In 1922, you see that the school's library contains over 18,000 volumes, mostly devoted to horsemanship with some volumes dating back to the year 1240. Next to the school's library, you find the *Salon d'Honneur.* There, you see the names of the school's former Commandants chiseled into the room's marble walls. Portraits of the Marshalls of France and of the Generals of the French cavalry hang on these walls as well. Beneath the portraits and along the walls, glass table-cases hold relics of the French cavalry: the saddles, helmets and spurs of some of Napoleon's cavalry commanders; the spurs of Count d'Aure, one of the school's celebrated Commandants; the saber of General Michel who, to cover a French retreat in 1870, leads a suicidal charge of his cavalry brigade against Prussian cannons at Reichshoffen. You see officers moving about: the officers who teach military science wear blue; the officers who teach equitation wear black. *Le Général* Thureau commands the school ; *Le Commandant* Watel serves as Chief Instructor of Equitation.

To teach equitation, the faculty divides its horses into three categories: trained horses for the riding hall or as the French say *la manège*; trained horses for jumping and cross-country riding (*carrière*); and finally, green or partially trained horses that students will train (*dressage*). The total number of horses at the school approximates 1400. Of these, 800 enjoy the finest Thoroughbred blood lines in Europe.

What does Major Chamberlin experience upon commencing his studies at this famed institution? What theoretical perspectives and established principles does he learn from *Le Commandant* Watel, *Le Général* Thureau and the other instructors and officers at the school? What controversies of equestrian theory does he explore? What concepts does he retain? What concepts does he modify? What does he discard?

In the evening classes, Chamberlin studies mounted military tactics, Hippology and its allied subjects such as sanitation and equine hygiene, the care of horses, horse breeding and horse-shoeing, all very much like at Fort Riley's Mounted Service School in 1915 and 1916. In the mornings from 7 a.m. to 10 a.m., to refine his horsemanship, he rides a trained Thoroughbred in the riding hall. Each afternoon from 12:30 to 2:15, he rides and trains a green (*dressage*) horse. In late afternoon, from 2:30 to 5:00, he rides a Thoroughbred cross-country (*carrière*).

During early evenings and on Saturdays, he attends classes. Each weekday evening, he studies into the night. Six days a week, he practices riding or training horses. Every few days, he rides a different horse. He observes. He reflects. He refines his skills.

Recall that Chamberlin, a serious rider for eleven years, places second and well ahead of most of the riders in the Inter-Allied Games of 1919. He rides well in the Olympics of 1920. Nonetheless, during his first three months of riding at Saumur, he rides in the riding hall without stirrups on a trained Thoroughbred. He rides cross-country without stirrups on a different trained Thoroughbred. During this initial three-month period, he rides with stirrups only on the green horse that he trains.

Starting in his fourth month and thereafter, he rides *with* stirrups on trained horses and on the green horse in the riding hall and cross-country. In addition, he rides and jumps *without* stirrups on a trained jumper three days a week. He rides and trains *with* stirrups on a green jumper on the other three days of the week.

Following the French theory, he maintains the "close seat" jumping style first enunciated by the Count d'Aure, currently practiced by both the French and the American cavalries, and first taught to Chamberlin at West Point. In fact, just prior to World War I, Lt. Col. Blacque Blair, chief instructor at Saumur, rejects the forward "Italian" style of Caprilli. The "close seat" of

France, he reasons, offers more security for true military work. The leaders of the US Cavalry agree, for now.

Once or twice a week, depending on his schedule, Chamberlin witnesses the French *Cadre Noire* demonstrate the finest in French equitation. In *Le Manège des Écuyers,* an eerie silence pervades the hall, the same silence one hears today at the Spanish Riding School in Vienna and at the new French National Riding School just outside the town of Saumur. Three galleries overlook *la manège*: two accommodate the public, one accommodates the military. Upon entering, all visitors remove their hats and remain silent so as not to distract the horses or the riders.

Each of the *Cadre Noire* rides a Thoroughbred of the highest quality. The officer in command breaks the silence with clear, concise commands. With each command, each horse and rider moves in uniform cadence and performs intricate maneuvers at the walk, trot, and canter. The riders apply their aids with barely discernible movement: an almost invisible touch of the spur; a slight pressure of the thigh or calf; a delicate flexing of the fingers; an imperceptible shift of the weight, often just a shift of the seat bones, either laterally to one side or to the other, and either forward or back. All takes place in a dim, soft light. All remain silent except for the commands of the commandant, the sound of leather against leather, and the displacement of air and sand by horses and riders.

The evolution of horsemanship: Night readings and classroom work begin with a summary of how European horsemanship evolves from the earliest times of Xenophon to the Middle ages where equitation equates to brute force; then to the Italian school of the sixteenth-century where brutal training and vicious bits dominate; next, to the French school of the sixteenth-century where a straight, stiff seat in a high saddle and the "immoderate" use of the sharp spur and the whip rule the day; then into the seventeenth-century where the same "immoderate" and brutal equitation combines with work outdoors but when on campaign in 1691, the horses "stumble and seem to have scarcely enough strength to stand up." Then into the eighteenth-century with the advent of Fredrick the Great and his cavalry tactics of maneuver, the founding of the French School of riding at Versailles; and finally, with the writings of *de la Guérinière* who recommends that the saddle's pommel and cantle be cut down, that the rider adopt a more natural, firm and deep seat with an upright position for the rider, and that the rider apply the aids with a subtle finesse. The foundations of modern French equitation develop.

By 1770, the French army applies Prussian cavalry tactics but hones French equitation doctrine. The French cavalry establishes regimental riding schools at all cavalry stations. The three most famous: Versailles, Saint Germain, and Saumur. Each focus on equitation to enable squadrons to maneuver in the field. Nineteen years later, the French Revolution's extremists close the schools, calling them a "relic of the aristocracy." Yet, a short time later, the cavalry of Napoleon becomes an effective combat arm without the formal equitation training of a cavalry school.

At the close of the eighteenth-century and the dawn of the nineteenth, the cavalry of Napoleon simplifies campaign riding to its bare essentials. The Dressage teachers of the Monarchy flee France to escape the ravages of the Revolution. At the same time, the new-born French Republic requires legions of cavalry to defend its borders. Attacked by the Royal Concert of Europe seeking to destroy the Republic, France tackles the military emergency with a cavalry barely trained to ride forward for the charge and the long march.

The elaborate, scholarly schooling and riding of the seventeenth and eighteenth centuries vanishes as the emergency demands more and more cavalrymen and the horses to carry them. The manège trained cavalry of the Monarchy (even if available) cannot support victory after victory under Napoleon. Gunpowder, musket and cannon make short shrift of manège trained horses. Such horses, if ever useful in war, better suit the 17th century positional warfare where the well maneuvered position decides the day with few or no casualties. The Napoleonic shock attack requires something far different. Using a simplified approach, raw recruits learn as they ride. Napoleon's cavalry rides from battle to battle between Paris and Moscow and back again. The return trip, however, decimates the cavalry of France.

Finally, after the fall of Napoleon and the restoration of the French king, and after several closings and re-openings, in 1824 the Monarchy finally and formally re-establishes Saumur as the cavalry school of the French army. The now almost defunct sister institutions at Versailles and Saint Germain offer only an illustrious past of courtly, academic equitation designed principally for the spectator. Saumur's primary mission now differs though it tries to preserve the past.

In the words of General Albert Decarpentry:

> "What remains of the academic tradition was passed on by the subalterns of the Royal Stables and by the former grooms of Versailles, and that was how Saumur was able to benefit from it. It is, therefore, only by a somewhat tenuous thread of indirect transmission that the School of Saumur was linked in its beginnings to the School of Versailles...The School,

however, had an essential mission which had to take precedence over all considerations of tradition: this was to establish, to fix and to elaborate a Military Equitation, because Saumur is a Cavalry School rather than an Academy of Equestrian Art..." [110]

La manière française: General Pierre Durand (former Cadre Noire Chief Rider and father of the Gold Medal winner in the 1988 Olympics for *Prix de Nations* jumping) publishes, in 2008, *L'Équitation Francaise, Mon Choix de Coeur et de Raison.* (*French Equitation, My Choice and My Reason*). He writes that *la manière française* (the French manner) owes its equestrian past primarily to three names: de la Guérinière, Baucher, and L'Hotte. Chamberlin owes much of his theory of training horses and his theory of "lightness" in the application of the aids primarily to the same three gentlemen.

The works of these three, together with the insights of Count d'Aure and a host of other French theorists, their agreements, disagreements, and settled principles, Chamberlin studies in the classroom by night and applies on horseback by day.

To understand the roots of Chamberlin's own theory, one must understand, at least, some of the basic principles of de la Guérinière, d'Aure, Baucher, and finally, L'Hotte who harmonizes the theories of the other three.

DE LA GUÉRINIÈRE
A THEORETICAL FRAMEWORK

In 1733, François Robichon de la Guérinière finishes his book *L'École de Cavalerie* [Xenophon Press 1994, 2015]. He creates a theoretical framework for French equitation. To supple and develop balance in the horse, he develops the "shoulder-in," the "haunches in" and the "counter canter." He also develops the flying change of leads. He advocates a soft, yielding hand (the *decente de main*) and a secure seat. He tries to combine the "*le manège*" with exterior equitation.

He states that while riding the outdoor horse, a rider should *not* ask for "collection" or for a vertical placement of the head; but rather, the rider should enable the horse to gallop as he would without being mounted. Chamberlin absorbs much of this theory into his own concepts. He takes special note of *de la Guérinière's* admonition regarding collection; of his

110 See General Albert Decarpentry, *Academic Equitation,* Crowood Press, 2012; also General Decarpentry, Baucher *and His School,* Xenophon Press, 2011.

recommendation regarding the natural placement of the horse's head; and of his advocacy for the rider's soft and yielding hand. These concepts will become a cornerstone of Chamberlin's own theory.

THE RISE OF CONTROVERSY

Toward the middle of the nineteenth-century, French equitation splits into two schools of thought: that of François Baucher and that of the Count d'Aure. Baucher sponsors several new concepts in equitation. Ultimately and after years of revising his theories, he argues that for the rider and the horse to *achieve* equilibrium, the horse must relax; to relax the horse, the rider must relax the equine jaw. He argues that for the rider and horse to *maintain* equilibrium, the rider must apply the leg without the hand, and the hand without the leg; and most important, the rider must bring lightness to both. He argues that the rider must position the horse before the rider directs the horse to move and that the rider must release the aids completely once the horse moves as the rider directs. These concepts exert strong influence on Chamberlin and the other officers responsible for the US Cavalry's concepts of horsemanship.

The Count d'Aure rejects most of Baucher's theories. He advocates a more vigorous approach. He argues that rider must push the horse forward with vigorous legs into firm hands and thereby coil the equine body as one coils a spring. At the same time, the Count d'Aure insists that riding instructors and students venture out of the riding hall and into the outdoors.

In the early to mid-nineteenth-century, these two rival horsemanship theories vie for supremacy at Saumur. The clash of theory causes several duels. The Count d'Aure and Baucher write pages of arguments and counter arguments in books and newspaper columns. Their followers produce even more.

François Baucher emphasizes the delicate dressage of the manège. Count d'Aure emphasizes daring cross-country riding. By 1906, General L'Hotte merges the theories of de la Guérinière,

Baucher, and d'Aure into a harmonious theory of French equitation. General L'Hotte studies under both d'Aure and Baucher, serves as the chief instructor at Saumur during the 1870s, and retires to write his book *Questions équestres*. L'Hotte's book becomes the equestrian bible of France. [111] Major Chamberlin evaluates, for his own purposes, the theories of all three.

---

111 See General Albert Decarpentry, *Academic Equitation*, Crowood Press, 2012; also General Decarpentry, Baucher *and His School*, Xenophon Press, 2011.

***Figure 80** A French instructor demonstrates the jumping form taught to Chamberlin at Saumur. Photo of a postcard printed in 1919 in the author's collection. This photo brings to mind the technique of some Eventers in the twenty-first century.*

***Figure 81** Another view of the Saumur jumping method taught while Chamberlin studies at Saumur. A postcard printed in 1919. Part of the author's collection.*

Figure 82 *This photo displays some of the stables and ancillary buildings of Saumur. Notice also, the rider's seat while going over the jump. Photo of a postcard in the author's collection. Saumur continues this jumping style until the early 1930s.*

Chapter 17

Saumur Part II
François Baucher: The Poetry of Equitation

Gifted as a trainer of French *Haute École,* Baucher develops methods that train his horses in a remarkably short time, by any standard. Only in rare cases does Baucher take more than a year to prepare horses for *Haute École* performances in the circus manège. (Note: Col. Hiram Tuttle of the US Cavalry trains his horse Olympic to Olympic standards in one year as well.) Usually, Baucher works his "magic" with horses after only a few months. Baucher's results prove spectacular. His reputation grows. In time, the instructors at Saumur take notice but ultimately, for political reasons, the high command banishes Baucher and his theories from the school. Still, many instructors study his concepts privately.

Figure 83 *François Baucher on Partisan cantering backwards. Illustration from F. Baucher, Souveniers Équestres, Paris, Manage Baucher et Pellier, 1840 Public Domain.*

His theories evolve over time. He observes. He reflects. He modifies his theories with each passing edition of his book, 14 editions in all. Ultimately, his refinements culminate in *"La deuxième manière"*—the second method of Baucher. These last theories prove to be the most valuable. Baucher teaches in the riding hall, however, much better than he writes in his study. A literate and lucid discussion of the *"deuxième manière"* must wait for a literate and lucid writer.

Figure 84 *General Thureau, Commandant of Saumur, is mounted on Raquetier, an English Thoroughbred. Chamberlin admires Thureau and uses this photo in his own book Riding and Schooling Horses. Public Domain. From the author's collection.*

In 1891, the Baucher disciple, General Faverot de Kerbrech, a great writer and horseman, publishes a literate and lucid discussion of Baucher's deuxième manière. General de Kerbrech titles his book Dressage methodique du Cheval de Selle d'apres leas derniers enseiqnements de F. Baucher, Recueillis par un de ses élèves. [Methodical Dressage of the Riding Horse after the Last Teachings of Baucher, Collected by One of His Students, Xenophon Press 2010]. The key words to remember in de Kerbrech's title are: The Last Teachings of Baucher. These "last teachings" contribute key elements to the equitation that the Americans Carter, Henry, and others import into the US Cavalry's horsemanship and constitute the components of "French lightness" that Chamberlin imports into his own theory.

THE LAST TEACHINGS OF BAUCHER

"Hands without legs, legs without hands." [112] This concept remains Baucher's cornerstone principle. He applies the principle throughout *all* training and riding even to the level of *haute école.* Baucher and his disciples, General de Kerbrech and Captain Beudant, state that except in certain rare circumstances, the hands should act only when the legs remain silent and the legs should act only when the hands remain silent.

Rather than opposing the hand to the leg and the leg to the hand, Baucher advises the rider to alternate actions of the hand and leg, even to achieve high states of collection. This principle of "hands without legs; legs without hands" remains true even with the most highly trained horse. The timing of hand and leg action may move closer together, but the leg and the hand must always act separately. This concept, Chamberlin adopts in full. He and the other members of the Cavalry Board graft the concept into the US Cavalry manual *Horsemanship and Horsemastership.*

"The Fixed Hand:" Another key point of Baucher's last teachings that Chamberlin and the other American cavalrymen adopt involves the use of the "fixed" hand. Captain Étienne Beudant explains:

> "Here lies the secret which alone allows one to master a horse's mouth, whether outside or in High School riding; that is to say, to obtain the relative lightness which suffices to check a bolting horse, or the almost complete lightness which, in High School work, places a horse at the disposal of this rider (the hand acts without taking from the impulsion). But one has to know how to fix the hand."
>
> "Fixing the hand is not giving the horse a support with the bit in order to help his gallop, because this would mean pulling, opposing to the horse's mouth a force equal to that he himself is using. One succeeds, on the contrary, by fixing the hand absolutely without any pulling and by squeezing the reins with one's fingers in a convulsive way if necessary, so as to prevent the hand from being attracted by any force: the horse's mouth, or the rider's wrist...With the fixed hand, it is the horse who

112 For this and all other quotations of Baucher (each of which is stated in bold face type and derived from de Kerbrech), see *Methodical Dressage of the Riding Horse, From The last teachings of Francois Baucher as recalled by one of his students: General Francois Faverot de Kerbrech.* Translation by Michael L. M. Fletcher, Edited by Richard and Frances Williams, Xenophon Press LLC 2010.

yields to himself, who rewards himself, who takes pleasure in chewing his bit, therefore giving suppleness and mellowness to his mouth…" [113]

Contemporary French author, Jean Claude Racinet elaborates on the concept:

"If the hand or the legs act alone, they will have to reach their *optimal threshold of efficacy*. The rider will become efficient *and subtle*; the horse will become attentive *and calm*… But the horse will become not only calm but also *highly sensitive to the legs*, since hand and legs will no longer *erase each other's conditioning*…And so a new style of riding will become possible: riding in the release of hand *and legs*, that is, in the "release of aids," the horse being left in "liberty on parole" and the aids wielded *only for transitions*: the legs (alone) for the "up" transitions, and the hand (alone) for the "down" transitions. When there is no need for a modification of the speed, movement, gait, or direction of the horse, the aids *remain silent*." (Italics provided by Racinet.) [114]

Chamberlin and his fellow officers graft most of these concepts into the cavalry's manual *FM 25-5, Animal Transport, Horsemanship and Horsemastership*.

Work on the parts, not the whole*; *position before movement: First, Baucher relaxes the horse's jaw and then separates various exercises into discrete parts. For example, he isolates the horse's jaw, then the pole, then the forehand and then the hindquarters. Where de la Guérinière and his disciples work on "the whole horse" simultaneously through various movements, Baucher concentrates on each individual part of the horse. Baucher trains his horses at first from the ground and later mounted, without moving much at all except the specific part of the horse on which he concentrates at the time.

When Baucher breaks down each aspect of a movement into a single part, he reasons that the horse understands and assimilates more easily what Baucher expects. As he works on each component part of a movement, Baucher first manipulates the horse to position itself to set up the movement. Until the horse assumes this position, movement itself, remains an enemy. In the words of Jean Claude Racinet, Baucher introduces movement "as an eye-dropper releases droplet of water…" Slowly and deliberately, one must proceed.

---

113 See Captain Etienne Beudant, *Horse Training Out-Door and High School*. Translated by Lt. Col. John A. Barry, US Cavalry, Charles Scribner's Sons, 1931.

114 See Jean-Claude Racinet, *Racinet Explains Baucher, Xenophon Press, 1997; See also Jean-Claude Racinet, Another Horsemanship: A Manual of Riding in the French Classical Tradition.* Xenophon Press, 1994.

"Relax the jaw through flexion:" From the very beginning of his research, Baucher focuses the *core* of his method on lightness of the horse's mouth and jaw. He believes that the mouth and the jaw provide the seat of all resistance, resistance of the horse's weight and of his strength, to the rider's will. He reasons that if one relaxes the jaw then, in turn, one relaxes the whole the horse. Relax the horse and one will remove resistances to the rider's will.

The *Baucheriste* trainer performs relaxation exercises, called direct and lateral flexions, first from the ground and then later, mounted. If well skilled, then the trainer uses a bit and bridoon for these exercises. The trainer manipulates first the curb and later the snaffle. If less well skilled, then the trainer manipulates only the snaffle bit. The American officers decide that to perform these exercises from the ground proves too difficult for all except for the true expert. They mandate, therefore, that the trainer perform direct and lateral flexions only when mounted.

While mounted, the trainer commences "direct flexion." The trainer gently moves the snaffle bit back and forth to massage the horse's lower jaw. The trainer continues this maneuver—always gently—until the jaw "gives" and relaxes. As the jaw relaxes, the trainer will feel tension vanish and will feel the horse "chew the bit." The trainer immediately must cease all action to reward this relaxation. Once horse and trainer achieve "direct flexion" easily, the trainer moves to "lateral flexion."

The trainer works toward "lateral flexion" when mounted as follows: by squeezing the fingers convulsively, the trainer "flexes" (turns) the horse's head slightly from the poll (not the neck); first to the right, and then to the left. Again, Chamberlin (and Carter before him) limits "direct and lateral flexions" from the ground only to experts. Both Carter and Chamberlin advocate the lateral and direct flexions, however, but only when a rider applies them when mounted.

"Range the haunches:" Once horse and trainer easily achieve both direct and lateral flexion, the trainer works to "range the haunches." Working from the ground, the trainer holds both reins in his left hand. He equips his right hand with a lunging whip and gently touches the horse's flanks where the boot would apply the leg aids to move the haunches to the left. Next, the trainer moves to the other side of the horse, equips the left hand with the lunging whip and touches the flanks to moves the haunches to the right.

Once the horse understands the exercises with the trainer applying the technique from the ground, the trainer mounts and repeats the sequence mounted. The process requires patience, a gentle touch, and a perceptive sense of feel.

"The Gather: [*Rassembler*]" Baucher "gathers" the muscular energy of the horse between the rider's hands and legs by alternating the action of the leg with the hand, but never at the same moment. Thus the "gather" readies the horse to move in the intended direction and to obey whatever command the rider asks. Chamberlin and the other officers responsible for writing the US Cavalry's manual *Horsemanship and Horsemastership* teach the concept of the "gather." In *Horsemanship and Horsemastership*, the Americans use the term "gather" for the French term "*Rassembler.*"

By 1873, Baucher completes his life's work. His highest-ranking military student, General L'Hotte stands next to Baucher's bed as the equestrian master dies. Near death, Baucher takes L'Hotte's hand. He positions it to apply the "fixed hand" and squeezes strongly. "Always do this," Baucher says. Then, he says "Never this," as he pulls L'Hotte's hand toward him. Always, according to Baucher, the rider should "fix the hand" and then, squeeze the fingers. This concept, Chamberlin adopts in his own theory and he and his fellow officers adopt the concept in *Horsemanship and Horsemastership.*

The American cavalry officers continue their interest in Baucher beyond Chamberlin's time at Saumur. In 1929, another self-taught disciple of Baucher, Étienne Beudant writes a book entitled *Horse Training: Out-Door and High School* [Xenophon Press, 2014]. In 1931, The Cavalry School at Fort Riley publishes the work in English. Many consider Beudant's book to be one of the greatest training manuals ever written. The book, with its *"Baucheriste"* outlook, significantly influences Chamberlin and American cavalry training of both horse and of rider.

François Baucher and his theories, at first, remain officially rejected but privately practiced by the *Ecuyer* of Saumur. In time, they become only an unacknowledged part of the theories that Saumur will teach. The concepts of the Count d'Aure present a hostile and often contradictory set of theories officially accepted and openly acknowledged at Saumur. These concepts exert great influence on German equitation but a lesser influence on Chamberlin. The Count d'Aure's outdoor spirit appeals to Chamberlin; some of the Count d'Aure's techniques do not. It takes the synthesis fashioned by General L'Hotte to bridge the differences and to create a unified theory of French equitation that Saumur presents to Harry Chamberlin and that Chamberlin modifies and then applies to his own theory.

Chapter 18

Saumur Part III

"To observe and to reflect, these are the rider's surest means of success."
—E. Beudant [115]

Count d'Aure: Forward! and General L'Hotte: The Synthesis

In 1847, the Count d'Aure, Baucher's chief equestrian rival, takes charge as Saumur's Chief of Instructors. As stated earlier, d'Aure teaches that a rider must push the horse forward with vigorous legs into the firm hand and thereby coil the equine body as one coils a spring. Under d'Aure, riding instructors and students venture out of the riding hall and into the outdoors. They continue the academic and artistic training fostered by the School of Versailles but with a difference: d'Aure institutes radical changes with boar hunting, jumping, and rough riding over rough terrain.

General Decarpentry states with approval:

"The school…had an essential mission which had to take precedence over all considerations of tradition: this was to establish, to fix and to elaborate a Military Equitation, because Saumur is a Cavalry School rather than an Academy of Equestrian Art…. Count d'Aure devoted himself

115 See E. Beudant, *Horse Training Out-Door and High School.* Translated by Lt. Col. John A. Barry, US Cavalry, Charles Scribner's Sons, 1931.

to this task and in this he was remarkably successful... The riding masters under his command, besides giving the riding instruction prescribed by their chief, were allowed to continue with the dressage of their own horses far beyond the requirements of military equitation...Each one of them was free to use the methods of his earlier teachers be it Baucher or those of Vienna... and they all upheld a classical correction and elegance of which the Riding Master in Chief was a shining example. Thus, although it remained confined to the 'Cadre' of the Manege, artistic equitation lived on at the Cavalry School." [116]

Count d'Aure elegantly rides *haute école.* But also, he rides audaciously outdoors. He avidly hunts, races, jumps, and negotiates all types of terrain—all skills that cavalry demands in war. He rides with legendary hands. While fixed, they remain light. His fingers—always gentle and with a constant rapport—communicate with the horse's mouth as if through reins of thread. The tension on his reins corresponds with the intensity of the gait.

Impulsion with extensions of head and neck: With d'Aure up, the horse's head and neck extend and retract with ease. For d'Aure, impulsion remains paramount. One of the major differences between Baucher and d'Aure arises when d'Aure argues that the legs must force the horse into a strong hand, in essence, the hand opposes the leg into order to coil the horse like a spring.

A more natural approach: Count d'Aure expresses his reasoning for a "more natural" approach to horsemanship in his book *Traité d'équitation,* published in 1847:

"The art ...should be simplified: it should no longer consist of producing elevated gaits and forced movements, which serve only to display the skill and patience of the rider. Today, on the contrary, it should be applied to regularizing gaits and to controlling the horse, while permitting him to retain all his natural energy, and to helping him to develop almost by himself those which are proper to him." [117]

Outdoor riding: As Vladimir Littauer points out, d'Aure sounds very much like Caprilli, only 50 years earlier. Prior to d'Aure, outdoor riding

---

116 See General Albert Decarpentry, *Academic Equitation,* Crowood Press, 2012; also General Albert Decarpentry, Baucher and His School, Xenophon Press, 2011.

117 See Count d'Aure, *Traite d'Équitation,* as quoted in *Notes on Equitation and Horse Training, translated from the French* by Major George H. Cameron, Fourteenth US Cavalry, Assistant Commandant, The Mounted Service School, Ft. Riley, Kansas 1910.

at Saumur consists mainly of a simple hack in the woods. With d'Aure, the school varies the forms of exterior riding as well as the terrain and the pace. He also introduces wild boar and fox hunting, obstacle jumping, steeple chasing, racing, and cross-country riding into the Saumur curriculum. He divides riders into groups of four and makes them ride abreast. If a rider's horse moves faster, then the rider must moderate his pace; if the rider falls behind, then he must quicken his pace. The Count also requires riders to leave the line either by extending or shortening the gait.

Count d'Aure requires riders to sit deep in the saddle and to sit with ease so that the rider's suppleness unites with the horse. He advocates the "close seat" so riders remain secure in the saddle. The Americans hold fast to this method into the 1920s; the French hold fast to the "close seat" until Col. Danloux pries them loose in the 1930s.

Just as Chamberlin and other American officers will do 80 years later, the Count looks beyond the borders of his own country for concepts useful in cavalry training. In this vein, D'Aure writes:

> "England and Germany differ in their principles: the former are occupied with racing and hunting, and consider speed as the most important quality. In training young horses, they employ means that serve to push them forward; also, generally English horses are more on the shoulders than on the haunches...The Germans, on the other hand, work particularly in the manège and are occupied with military riding. They want to have horses that are slowed-down and handy. To obtain this result, they make their horses carry more weight on the hindquarters than on the forehand...We, in our riding should look for a middle way, and do something to come closer to the English principles, without taking over what is bad in them; as we also should modify the German system, which is the one to which we are the closest. These results should be that much easier to obtain in that they are closer to nature." [118]

Many of the "natural" methods foreshadowed by d'Aure would find expression in the United States 80 years later through Chamberlin's writings. For example, d'Aure writes regarding the canter depart:

> "Work on straight lines, devised to some extent for the trot, becomes difficult as soon as it is a question of practicing it at a gallop...the order

118 Count d'Aure as quoted by Vladimir A. Littauer, *The Development of Modern Riding: The Story of Modern Riding From Renaissance Times to The Present.* Howell, 1991.

in which the legs move at the gallop *naturally entails a gallop departure from an oblique position...* [119]

Chamberlin writes in *Training Hunter, Jumpers, and Hacks* that:

"...no attempt to compel a canter with the quarters directly in rear of the shoulders should be made. This is neither natural nor beneficial, although it is considered important in high-school work."

Six years after taking command at Saumur, d'Aure writes a second book entitled *Cours d'Equitation.* In this work, the Count expands upon his theories. "Impulsion is like vapor," he writes. "The rider holds in his hand the outlet valve of a boiler and allows the vapor to escape but at a constant rate." [120]

By the 1910, with both d'Aure and Baucher long gone, the instructors at Saumur achieve a synthesis that melds the theories of both horsemen. This synthesis arises from the posthumously published work of General Alexis-François L'Hotte.

GENERAL ALEXIS-FRANÇOIS L'HOTTE THE SYNTHESIS OF D'AURE AND BAUCHER

With the Comte d'Aure's retirement from Saumur, Alexis-François L'Hotte becomes *Ecuyer* in Chief. During his early career, L'Hotte studies under both Baucher and d'Aure. In private, L'Hotte applies Baucher's principles with his personal horses. As chief instructor (*"Ecuyer")* at Saumur, L'Hotte strictly enforces the French army's ban on Baucher.

Yet, L'Hotte never conforms completely to the past. He never enslaves himself to the procedures and techniques of the present. In the 1870s, *Captain* L'Hotte introduces "*le trot Anglais*" (the posting trot) to his unit despite official skepticism. As *Ecuyer* at Saumur, *General* L'Hotte teaches the entire French cavalry to post at the trot. The American cavalry follows suit some years later in the 20th Century.

---

119 Ibid.
120 Ibid.

Figure 85 *General L'Hotte, Instructor-in-chief and author of Questions Équestres, the "Bible of Saumur" rides his horse Laruns. Photo from a postcard in the author's collection. Public domain.*

Figure 86 *Commandant Watel, Instructor-in-chief of Equitation during Chamberlin's stay at Saumur rides Venus, an Anglo-Arab. Photo from the author's collection.*

General L'Hotte retires from the army in 1880 as a much-admired officer of the French Army. During his retirement, he writes a book entitled *Questions Équestres.* He dies in 1904. Saumur publishes his book in 1906.

As the faithful successor to d'Aure at Saumur and the diligent student of Baucher in private, the now retired General L'Hotte synthesizes the theories of each. General Albert Decarpentry writes that in *Questions Équestres,* General L'Hotte gives "a corpus of doctrine to that modern French School that owes almost everything to him."

L'Hotte's *Questions Équestres* becomes the "Bible of Saumur." [121] By the time Chamberlin arrives in 1922, the theories of Baucher and d'Aure as synthesized by L'Hotte permeate Saumur's curriculum and become the cornerstone of the "French School" of riding.

This "French School," as communicated by *Questions Équestres,* provides a central component to the American army's equitation and to Harry Chamberlin's thinking. Even L'Hotte's guidance as to the manner of the effective teacher make their way into Chamberlin's thinking and practice. L'Hotte's work enables horses and riders to perform savant equitation in the *manège* and the French view of military equitation outdoors. (Even after World War I, however, Saumur has not yet addressed the weaknesses in French cavalry performance that show up in 1914.) Nonetheless, this junction of the two riding purposes fixes itself in Chamberlin's mind.

The following principles of *Questions Équestres* make their way into American military equitation and, most importantly, into Chamberlin's mode of thinking. For L'Hotte, three words express the primary goals of horse training: ***calm, forward, straight.*** The rider must seek to achieve each goal *in the order stated.* Only the *calm* horse can respond correctly to the rider's requests:

Calm: Once the rider's horse is calm and "has put his forces at the disposal of the rider, it becomes a matter of channeling them."

Forward: "A free and positive movement forward is the first test," writes L'Hotte. The horseman achieves this goal "...only when the horse executes every movement and, in all situations, and shows the desire to go *forward.*"

The forward impulse resides in "the haunches... which must ...vibrate at the slightest touch of the heels...The activity or diligence of the haunches affects the totality of the horse and provokes animation. It is there that everything hangs together...the horse...in all circumstances, will seem to be

121 Short quotations in this chapter from L'Hotte *Questions Equestre* as translated by Hilda Nelson in *Alexis-Francois L'Hotte: The Quest for Lightness in Equitation,* J.A. Allen, 1998. And Jean-Claude Racinet, *Another Horsemanship: A Manual of Riding in the French Classical Tradition.* Xenophon Press, 1994.

saying: 'I want to go forward'...What is important in the long run, is that preoccupation with impulsion is of greater importance than the demands which follow."

Straight: When one thinks of straight, L'Hotte does not insist on a "rigorously exact position." ...He writes: "With this goal in mind, it is a question of walking in a straight line; but it is not too important if the neck or the haunches do not follow exactly the straight line, as long as the horse, as a whole, does not deviate." [122] For L'Hotte, this standard applies to military equitation.

After the trainer achieves with the horse these three primary goals, the trainer then considers other issues.

No Impulsion, no horse: L'Hotte reinforces the impact of forward impulsion and straightness on movement when he says: "This kind of perfection in execution—and one cannot state this too often—depends upon the regularity of the energy of impulsion...If impulsion begins to weaken, there is also a weakening in whatever support is needed for the procedures that require a straight horse and the positions that command the different movements...All can be summarized in only two words: no impulsion, no horse."

The Ramener: "The Ramener, as it is understood in higher equitation," L'Hotte writes, "is not concerned with the direction of the head alone. It concerns itself as much in the submission of the jaw, which is the first articulation (or spring) to receive the effect of the hand. If this spring responds with softness to the actions which solicit its play, it will bring about the flexibility of the neck and will provoke the tying to it of all the other parts, because of the relationship existing among all the muscles. If to the contrary, the jaw resists and refuses to be mobile, then there will be no more lightness, for by nature the resistances mutually sustain themselves, and one resistance will set up numerous others. Thus, in higher equitation, the "Ramener" represents a general state of submission of all parts of the horse rather than a fixed direction of the head." (Chamberlin and his fellow American officers will adopt these concepts in *Horsemanship and Horsemastership*, under the term "to gather" the horse.)

Co-coordinate the muscular forces of the horse: To control a horse, the rider must co-ordinate the horse's muscular action and weight. In fact, for L'Hotte equitation remains the art of co-coordinating these elements. He adds further that one will master these elements the moment one combines

---

122 See Nelson, Hilda, *Alexis-Francois L'Hotte: The Quest for Lightness in Equitation*, J.A. Allen, 1998

"...impulsion with the elastic flexibility of all joints and muscles." L'Hotte contends that depending on the rider's purpose, the two elements—impulsion and flexibility—will differ in the proportion required. L'Hotte breaks down the various purposes as follows.

For race horses, impulsion dominates. The race horse needs flexibility only sufficient to enable the horse to make a large turn, and to halt by slowing down gradually.

For cross county horses, impulsion dominates as well. The cross-country horses need more flexibility than the race horse, however, since the cross-country horse must negotiate varied terrain and often move on a shorter arch.

For military horses, the proportions between flexibility and impulsion remain similar to the cross-country horse but with impulsion "raised to a higher degree due to more diverse and pressing requirements."

Therefore, depending on the goals and purposes of the rider, the relative importance of impulsion and flexibility will vary; naturally, these variations impact the training of the horse.

A fundamental point in L'Hotte makes fundamental point to govern all training as follows.

The Trainer must, in the beginning, school all horses along similar lines regardless of discipline: L'Hotte insists that no matter what their discipline, all horses must share a common training as the foundation for all equitation. The horse of "savant equitation" as well as the outdoor horse should share the same essential rudiments in their training. *Chamberlin adopts this principle in total.*

A great deal of theory absorbs Chamberlin's time at Saumur. Keep in mind, Saumur remains a school, however, primarily for the "application" of theory, not so much the study of theory itself. Chamberlin devotes his nights to the classroom and to the study of theory. He devotes his days, six days each week for a minimum of five hours each day to riding; at all times, under the critical eyes of Saumur instructors. And then, he plays polo on Sundays. For several years after Chamberlin departs Saumur, French cavalry officers there speak with admiration of how well he succeeds at the school and how he dominates the polo field.

Figure 87 *The rear of the main building at Saumur during an honors presentation. Photo of a postcard in the author's collection. Public domain.*

While studying at Saumur in February of 1923, sadness descends on Chamberlin's life: On February 10 of that year, Harry's father Dwight, age 73, passes away from complications of pneumonia. As the *Elgin Daily Courier* of February 12, 1923 writes:

> Major Chamberlin will be unable to attend his father's funeral. The army officer is now stationed in a French cavalry school at Faumir, France (*sic*) [123]

In June of 1923, Chamberlin and West complete their tours of study at Saumur. Chamberlin wins honors at Saumur as a "distinguished graduate." He and Major West request and receive permission from the Chief of Cavalry to attend Tor di Quinto, the Italian Cavalry's School for Advanced Cross-Country Riding. Chamberlin and West remain the only American cavalry officers to study at both Saumur and Tor di Quinto. As guests of the Italian Cavalry, they will study the methods of Captain Federico Caprilli.

123 The *Elgin Daily Courier* article mistakenly refers to the location of Chamberlin's residency at the French Cavalry School at Saumur as "a French cavalry school at Faumir, France" as opposed to the correct location: Saumur.

Chapter 19

Tor di Quinto
1923-1924

"The pupil has surpassed his master."
—Lieutenant-Colonel Starita, Commandant of Tor di Quinto [124]

Today, Tor di Quinto, Italy's Cavalry School for Advanced Cross-Country Riding, located five miles north of the center of Rome, occupies an area about the size of a large race track. An airport, super highways, housing and commercial developments encroach upon its site.

In 1923, however, the school ranks as one of the largest and the greatest in the world. Many different nations send cavalry officers to study, to evaluate, and to learn "the Italian System" based on the school's fundamental premises: the "*impulso in avanti*" (the "forward impulse") and the "horse's natural way of going." [125] In time, officers from Britain, the United States, Russia, Sweden, Switzerland, Poland, Argentina, Rumania, Bulgaria, and Japan study at the famous Italian cavalry schools of Pinerolo and Tor di Quinto. Significantly, France and Belgium, however, send none; Germany sends only one. Until the mid-1930s, officers from France and Germany, reject the school's concepts. By 1933, the United States will send seven officers to Pinerolo and eight officers to Tor di Quinto.

---

124 See Louis A. DiMarco, Major USA, *Brigadier General Harry D. Chamberlin, The Cavalry's Greatest Horseman 1887-1944*, unpublished manuscript.

125 See Captain Piero Santini, *The Forward Impulse*, Huntington Press, 1936; *Riding Reflections*, Huntington Press, 1933.

THE ITALIAN SYSTEM OF FEDERICO CAPRILLI

The Italian cavalry officer Federico Caprilli spends ten years analyzing the free movements of the horse and develops his "revolutionary" concepts. He rejects the French and German concepts that have the rider lean back at a jump and attempt to lift the horse over with the reins. He rejects the five rein effects of Saumur and insists that the rider control the horse with fingers on the snaffle reins. He advocates riding with a short stirrup, with the knee snug to the saddle, and with the ankle forced well down. The rider's knee and ankle position, together with the upper body's forward position from the hips with either a flat or a concave position of the small of the rider's back govern the overall approach.

The rider must not apply the "close seat" of the French but rather remain light in the saddle at the walk, trot, and canter; and off the saddle at the fast gallop. The rider remains perched over the horse's withers with the buttocks barely on the saddle in all circumstances: up-hill, down-hill, over jumps of all type including drop jumps, and even when backing the horse. Caprilli argues that if the rider places his weight to conform to the horse's natural equilibrium, the need to "rebalance" the horse in accordance with French theory vanishes into thin air. Caprilli also rejects Count d'Aure's requirement that the rider must bring the horse's forehand and hind-quarters together "like the two ends of a curved whip" by placing the effect of the legs against the effect of the reins.

Beyond Caprilli's pamphlet, *Principi di Equitazione di Compagna* only a brief outline that Caprilli dictates exists. To learn Caprilli's theory and the "Italian System," therefore, one must depend on the *Principi* and on the writings of Caprilli's disciple, Captain Piero Santini. Santini serves as an officer in the Italian army's cavalry reserve. In the 1930s, he establishes himself as Caprilli's principle expositor in two books: *Riding Reflections* first published in 1933 and *The Forward Impulse* [Xenophon Press 2016] published in 1936. For a complete understanding of the Italian method, the reader should consult both of these books.

According to Santini, Caprilli's theory extends beyond "the forward seat." Caprilli's Italian System encompasses, not only the rider's position and how he applies the aids but also encompasses the horse's training and manner of going. According to Santini, the Italian System rejects the theories of François Baucher as well as the earlier classical principles of de la Guérinière. As an example of the concepts that Caprilli rejects, one of his disciples quotes (with distain) from the French cavalry regulations:

"Should the horse not respond to the action of the closed fingers, the legs must act in such a manner as to force him on to the bit so strongly that it causes him pain and makes him seek to escape it." Caprilli rejects such thinking.

The Italian "natural way of going" and "natural balance" take the place of the French "enforced equilibrium." [126] At Tor di Quinto, the "forward impulse" governs mental attitude, rider position, communication through the aids, horse training, and all other aspects of equestrian theory and practice. No longer should riders lean back while negotiating down a steep grade. No longer should they lean back and "lift" their horses over jumps with a jerk of the reins. Forever more, the rider keeps the upper body forward with the knees, legs and feet stationary. And so, Caprilli's horses jump higher, gallop faster, and endure longer than those trained under French or German theory.

In 1893, the horse Svoltsoi holds the international jumping record at 1.10 meters. Applying his theories, Caprilli jumps his horse Molopo and clears 2.08 meters—a new international record.

In 1894, the Italian Cavalry appoints Caprilli Instructor of Horsemanship at Tor di Quinto and later at Pinerolo.

In 1901, Caprilli writes his brief pamphlet: *Principi di Equitazione di Compagna.* He argues that effective horsemanship depends not on force but on gentle persuasion; in modern terms, teamwork between horse and rider. Caprilli puts the natural movements and inclinations of the horse into the service of his rider. As stated earlier, he rejects the concepts of force and the imposition of pain advocated by the French and the Germans.

So "revolutionary" and so contrary to classical precepts do his ideas strike his superiors that the cavalry establishment moves against him. They remove him from his instructor's position and they ban him from all cavalry training. Fortunately, his training concepts come to the attention of the Italian Chief of Cavalry, General Luigi Berta. Berta gives Caprilli a chance to vindicate his training concepts for horses and troopers. The experiment proves a spectacular success. Not only do horses and riders make fast progress, but horses became so willing that riders complete the training course without reins!

In 1904, the Italian cavalry officially adopts Caprilli's philosophy and methods.

---

126 See Captain Piero Santini, *The Forward Impulse*, Huntington Press, 1936; *Riding Reflections*, Huntington Press, 1933.

Figure 88 *An instructor at Tor di Qunito demonstrates the revolutionary new jumping theory of Federico Caprilli. Photo in the public domain.*

In 1906, Caprilli represents Italy in the Olympic Games. From all over Europe, few cavalrymen recognize his superior methods. Most significant, the French and Germans reject his new way.

In 1907, Caprilli and his horse slip on ice. Caprilli falls to the ground seriously injured. He dies as a result. Never an enthusiastic writer, he leaves only brief written notes regarding his theory of "natural horsemanship." And even then, most of what he puts to paper deals with the rider's mental attitude toward the horse.

In 1908, at the Olympics, the Italian cavalry team stuns international observers and competitors alike with their revolutionary methods and epoch-making show ring victories. Since in 1908, the United States does not compete in equestrian events, the Americans miss the Italian victories and learn nothing of the Italian method.

In 1911, an American observer visits Tor di Quinto with Lt. Col. Blacque Blair, chief instructor at Saumur. Blair rejects the Italian method. The American observer follows Blair's lead.

In 1912, Italy opts not to compete in the Olympics' equestrian competitions, so the Americans, especially Guy V. Henry, Jr., miss a potentially stellar performance.

In 1916, The Great War cancels the Olympics.

In 1919, Italy competes in the Inter-Allied Games. American officers take note of the Italian system and victories. They bring home to Fort Riley some of these new ideas. The American cavalry's seat and the American jumping style begins a slow, gradual process of change.

In 1922, for *The Rasp,* Chamberlin writes that the Italian performance at the Inter-Allied Games of 1919 inspires American officers to re-think their position on "position." A few years later, he writes: "... 'going with the horse has been adopted to some extent, although there is still much difference between the two methods, due principally to fundamental differences in the seats themselves.'"

CHAMBERLIN AT TOR DI QUNITO

In 1923, Chamberlin and West complete their studies at Saumur. In the month of September, as the first Americans ever to study at Tor di Quinto, they mount their horses. Chamberlin and West learn "the Italian system."

On the first day of the course, the school's Commandant, Lt. Colonel Starita addresses the class. Chamberlin listens closely. Tor di Quinto "is a school of morale," says Starita. It molds a "state of mind." What purpose does Tor di Quinto serve? Tor di Quinto develops the most essential characteristics of the cavalryman: boldness and daring across country at fast paces. "You will encounter little elementary instruction at Tor di Quinto. You will devote your time to jumping obstacles. You will ride at gaits and at speeds as if at war," says Starita.

Tor di Quinto serves as a school of application not of theory. Chamberlin rides horses an average of five hours each day. As Colonel Starita warns on the first day, the curriculum focuses on fast paces cross-country. Chamberlin devotes all work to mastering the seat, to jumping obstacles, and to riding at the speeds and the gaits necessary in time of war. The difficulty of the jumps, the courage required to negotiate the slides and other obstacles vindicates Commandant Starita's by-words of "boldness and daring." One might think of Count d'Aure's "break neck" exploits at Saumur. Multiply that by a factor of 50!

Chamberlin, among 30 other students in his class, negotiates almost vertical slides; steep inclines, drop jumps and water obstacles; brick walls, bank jumps, and rail fences. He gallops through mud and uneven terrain in all manner of weather, under all conceivable conditions, over the most dangerous obstacles at the highest, full gallop speeds of an Irish-Thoroughbred or a one-half Thoroughbred. The class of 30 divides into two platoons of 15 riders each. Each platoon reports to a Captain-instructor.

Figure 89 *Students at Tor di Qunito gallop at breakneck speed down slides and over obstacles in all conditions of weather and footing with the upper body always forward from the hips. Photo in the public domain.*

The range of Chamberlin's athletic ability displays its full extent at Tor di Quinto. Chamberlin excels at riding in "the Italian system." He makes a stunning and complete shift in seat and method in a short span of time. To practice the "close seat" of France at Saumur for almost a year, and then, a few months later, to master in stellar fashion, the entirely different "forward seat" of Italy at Tor di Quinto demonstrates intellect and athletic ability of the highest order. How many riders abandon the practices of a life time in such short order?

Chamberlin's performance attracts the attention of Tor di Quinto's Commandant, Lieutenant-Colonel Starita. Starita serves as a fearless cavalryman during World War I. In the war, he suffers one heel shot away during a cavalry engagement. He appears everywhere, constantly on his horse at Tor di Quinto. In Chamberlin's words, Col. Starita is "superb and fearless…over any obstacles or country." Chamberlin's performance and abilities attract Starita's attention. Starita closely watches Chamberlin's progress. Chamberlin astounds him.

Figure 90 *Chamberlin astounds the Commandant of Tor di Quinto with his fearless riding down steep slides and over dangerous obstacles. Photo in the public domain.*

At the graduation ceremony, as Chamberlin arrives at the podium to receive his diploma, the Commandant Starita salutes and then takes Chamberlin's hand. As he presents the diploma, Starita says: "The pupil has surpassed his master." No higher complement may a teacher bestow; no higher complement may the cavalryman of one nation bestow upon the cavalryman of another.

In January of 1924, Chamberlin and Sally leave Tor di Quinto and travel to Great Britain. Throughout February and March, he acts as an official observer (once again) at the British cavalry school at Weedon. As usual, Chamberlin assimilates and evaluates everything that he observes. His "sabbatical" ends at the end of March 1924. He and Sally then depart from England and sail for the United States.

In early April 1924, Chamberlin arrives home. After a leave that lasts until the beginning of May, he and Sally travel to Fort Riley where Chamberlin delivers his report regarding his Tor di Quinto experience and his evaluation of the Italian system.

CHAMBERLIN'S REPORT ON THE ITALIAN SYSTEM

And what conclusions does Chamberlin report to the command at Fort Riley? He provides a synopsis of his report, describes his experiences at Tor di Quinto, and also evaluates the Italian system in a *Cavalry Journal* article entitled "*The Italian Cavalry School at Tor di Quinto*" written shortly after his report to Fort Riley. [127]

Chamberlin points out that the Italian horses rank in quality no better—and actually far below the average cavalry horse at Weedon, the British Cavalry School and even further below that of Saumur, the French Cavalry School. Nonetheless, he writes:

> "The horses...are not as handy as ours; nevertheless, they go beautifully across country, extending themselves naturally and making the greatest use of neck and head in clearing obstacles. The most remarkable characteristics of the horses at Tor di Quinto are the calmness and willingness with which they jump. These horses are all ridden in snaffle bits, as are all Italian horses in jumping competitions, with but rare exception.
>
> "Briefly stated, the Italian rides with a very short stirrup, keeps the heels and knees driven down as far as possible, and at the fast gallop does not sit down in the saddle, only the knees, thighs, and stirrups serving as the seat. Contrary to appearances, this seat is very secure and the legs can be employed very vigorously...With such short stirrups, the rider not accustomed to the seat becomes tired in the knees and loin at first. After one or two weeks, one finds it a very easy way of riding at fast gaits.
>
> "The country is quite varied and difficult to negotiate in many places. One finds few obstacles that come down, but as the horses are always trained over fixed obstacles, they jump very cleanly...this horse is usually not very large, about 15-0 to 15-3, but very agile, courageous, and remarkably good at obstacles of a reasonable height."

The Italian superiority in jumping stems from three reasons, writes Chamberlin:

> "First.... They have developed the most advantageous seat for the horse in getting his own and the rider's mass over an obstacle..." They achieve "maximum efficiency from the machine.

127 See Major Harry D. Chamberlin, "The Italian Cavalry School at Tor di Quinto" *The Cavalry Journal,* 1924.

"Second...the Italians specialize in cross-country work...and spend but little time at anything else, such as schooling and polo, they ride over many more obstacles per day than do the French, English, or American officers...

"Third...The training of their horses is eminently correct. The horse is taught to jump when mounted as he does at liberty...."

And Chamberlin concludes:

"The Italian system of equitation is not, in my opinion, suitable for our cavalry...our type of mounted action requires a very 'handy' horse.... the Italian system does not produce. However, I believe an adaptation of our military seat along Italian lines, when riding across country and when jumping, is practicable and advisable, for it saves both horse and man and gives better general results.

"These ideas were carried to Fort Riley, and 'going with the horse' has been adopted to some extent, although there is still much difference between the two methods, due principally to fundamental differences in the seats themselves.

"The rider does not 'tuck under' the seat, as in the French, English and American schools but keeps the loin straight or even a bit concave. There is no exception to the rule that the body must be inclined forward *at all times,* whether backing a horse or racing him."

During his short stint at Fort Riley and over the next several years, Chamberlin reflects on his experiences at Saumur and at Tor di Quinto. He accepts certain principles and rejects others. At this stage, he settles on the following ideas.

THE ITALIAN SYSTEM'S BEDROCK PRINCIPLES THAT CHAMBERLIN ACCEPTS:

1. The horse's natural sense of balance, without undue effort, will accommodate the additional weight of the rider so long as the rider adopts the correct forward position toward the withers;

2. Collection, imposed over long periods, unduly taxes the horse, inhibits mobility, and destroys "the forward impulse;"
3. With the "Italian seat," the rider's position frees the animal's hindquarters to maximize impulsion and positions the rider's weight where nature would have intended the horse to carry it: over the withers;
4. In natural carriage, the horse holds its head at a 45-degree angle and extends the head and neck with forward movement, something the rider's hands should accommodate;
5. The vertical head position that classical dressage imposes impedes forward mobility and, for an "outdoor" horse, the rider should avoid that position;
6. The rider must reject, in total, the French concept of jumping obstacles;
7. The rider should "ride the angles." The tibia and the foot always form acute angles. The thigh and the tibia approximate a right angle to each other. When jumping, the rider's angles widen to a greater or lesser degree to bring the body forward. At the same time, the right angle that the pelvis forms, in the beginning, with the thigh bone reduces to an acute angle;
8. The rider should not 'tuck under' the seat, as in the French, English and American schools but rather should keep the loin straight or even a bit concave. There is no exception to the rule that the body must be inclined forward *at all times,* whether backing a horse or racing him.

THE ITALIAN ARGUMENTS THAT CHAMBERLIN REJECTS:

1. The Italian argument that dressage exercises work against nature and constrict movement.
2. The Italian argument that artificial gymnastics of the French and Germanic schools provide a horse with less benefit than what natural outdoor work provides—so long as the work entails all manner of obstacles and terrain. "By exercise, not exercises," the Italians achieve their goals.
3. The Italian requirement that (a) the stirrup iron treads must be "full home" and thereby touch the forward portion of the rider's boot

heel, (b) that the rider's ankle must incline toward the horse, and (c) that the sole of the rider's boot must be visible to spectators.

ITALIAN CONCEPTS THAT CHAMBERLIN ADOPTS WITH MODIFICATION:

1. Italian theory places the rider well forward in the saddle with his loin either flat or bent inwards and his fork close to the pommel. The rider reduces, as much as possible, contact between the buttocks and the saddle. This puts the bulk of the rider's weight where the horse feels it the least: the forehand. The rider's weight no longer encumbers the horse's loins and hindquarters. As a result, the horse gains maximum propulsion. Above all, the rider must *not* use the saddle as the "family armchair" of James Fillis or adopt the "close seat" of Saumur. The more the rider "sits," the heavier the rider will be.
2. Italian theory maintains that even while negotiating down steep inclines or slides, the position from hip to heel, from knee to toe remains fixed. The rider keeps the upper body forward with the knees, legs and feet stationary. This position applies whether up or down inclines and slides, -gradual or steep; over every sort of jump: high, broad or drop; uphill or down; cross country or in a show ring; over a steeplechase or during a hack in the countryside. In negotiating a steep downward incline or slide, the rider keeps the horse "between the legs and on the aids" to assure a straight decent. The rider's forward position frees the hindquarters which act as a break on the rate of decent, puts weight on the forehand to push the hooves into the ground; and thus, avoids slipping and tumbling down.
3. Italian theory maintains that the rider's toe should remain perpendicular to the knee as if a straight line were dropped from the knee to the ground. The Italians maintain that the rider's foot should extend outward from the horse in natural fashion but should *not* remain parallel with the horse as French equitation requires.

Figure 91 *The method of Tor di Quinto radically differs from the method taught at Fort Riley. Fort Riley will change its method soon. Photo in the public domain.*

FROM FORT RILEY TO FORT BLISS

In June of 1924, Harry and Sally leave Fort Riley and travel to Fort Bliss near El Paso, Texas. Harry reports for duty and takes command of the 1st Squadron, 8th United States Cavalry, a regiment of the recently formed 1st Cavalry Division. While riding along the Mexican Border with the 8th Cavalry, Chamberlin reflects long hours on his European experiences at Saumur and Tor di Quinto. In the rough and unforgiving terrain along the border, he begins to develop his own major contributions to educated riding.

Chapter 20

1924–1926
The 8th Cavalry

"...the beau ideal of a cavalryman"
—Lucian Truscott on Chamberlin [128]

"Major Chamberlin...had the faculty...beyond any player I have ever seen of relaxing both himself and his mount whenever speed was not necessary. He could stand at times with his pony as quiet as though tied to a picket line and then dash at top speed to the point where he was needed."
—Harry Cottingham on Chamberlin playing polo [129]

In typical army fashion, rather than assign Chamberlin to the Horsemanship Detachment at Fort Riley where he might share his new knowledge with his fellow instructors and his students, the army sends him to command the 1st Squadron of the 8th Cavalry at Fort Bliss. The 8th constitutes a part of the recently formed 1st Cavalry Division whose shoulder patch is the bright yellow Norman shield with the head of a black thoroughbred horse in the upper right quadrant and a black bar diagonally dividing the patch. The army's decision to place Chamberlin with the 8th Cavalry proves fortuitous, however, for Chamberlin's growth as a theoretician as well as a practical horseman. It gives him time to think.

From June 1924 through August 1926, Chamberlin, for days on end, leads his troopers through the rough terrain along the border with Mexico.

---

128 See General Lucian K. Truscott, Jr. *The Twilight of the US Cavalry: Life in the Old Army, 1917-1942.* University Press of Kansas, 1989.

129 See Harry Cottingham, *"Polo Here and There," New York Times,* November 1925.

Long, dusty rides through gorges, up steep inclines and through the desert dominate Chamberlin's equestrian diet day in and day out. Often, his border patrols extend 25 miles a day, six days a week. In the field, Chamberlin must remember to empty his boots every morning to rid them of scorpions and other predators.

When not on patrol, the squadron engages in the normal morning training exercises of equitation, rifle practice, and marching. Of course, as a Squadron Commander, Chamberlin enjoys a great deal of latitude regarding how he will spend his time. He enjoys polo, jumping, and hacking for leisure.

At the same time, the long, grueling patrols enable Chamberlin to reflect on the various theories from France, Italy, Germany and England that he studies or observes immediately after The Great War and more recently while on his overseas "sabbatical" at Saumur and Tor di Quinto. While riding with the 8th Cavalry, Chamberlin assimilates what he learns in Europe. He begins to modify and transform what he learns to suit the US Cavalry's experience, mission, and methods of warfare.

On those long, dusty marches, numerous questions probably pass through his mind: What horsemanship best suits a cavalry that often marches long distances over rough, unforgiving and often mountainous terrain and whose mission demands an agile and responsive horse capable of quick turns and instant halts as well as a fast gallop? What methods serve a cavalry that, but for drills, seldom charges over grassy plains directly on a battlefield but must still be able to do so, if necessary? What methods suit a cavalry that usually fights on foot, regardless of what some of the more romantic souls of the cavalry might hope? What mode of riding enables a trooper and horse to jump obstacles; march 30 miles a day, day in and day out; and if necessary, march 100 miles in 24 hours with the trooper still able to fight and the horse still able to carry on? What mode of riding might enable a courier to cover 170 miles in 24 hours at the extreme?

Mobility—always, mobility—remains the object of his thinking. Jumping obstacles occurs only occasionally on campaign or patrol. Of course, he loves obstacle jumping as a sport. Its challenges and intricacies engage his mind and his competitive spirit. The military application of horsemanship in which jumping anything other than mud hole or a ditch proves rare dominates his thinking.

Of course, all is not work. When not out on patrol, Chamberlin supervises the normal troop functions during the morning training periods but devotes his afternoons to polo. Chamberlin excels at the game ever since graduating from West Point. He plays at Fort Riley in Kansas as well as at Fort McKinley and Fort Stotsenberg in the Philippines. Later, as an instructor at the Cavalry School, Chamberlin plays polo with his friend Innis Palmer Swift and together, the two hone their skills. He also plays polo at Saumur where he impresses the French and dominates the field. Back in the United States, he becomes a rated player of considerable repute: In 1925, The American Polo Association rates Chamberlin with a three-goal handicap. (More than two-thirds of all players rate below two. A handicap of two or higher indicates a professional player.)

Figure 92 *Chamberlin demonstrates unusual abilities as a polo player and ranks a three-goal (professional grade) handicap. Chamberlin is second from the left. Truscott is third from the left. Photo courtesy of The US Cavalry and Armor Association.*

During his term of service as Commander of the 1st Squadron of the 8th Cavalry, Chamberlin also captains the 8th Cavalry's polo team. In early 1925, Chamberlin befriends Lucian Truscott after Truscott's team defeats Chamberlin's team at Marfa in a hard-fought game. After the game, Chamberlin and Truscott "talk horse" well into the night. Chamberlin's magnetic personality, range of knowledge, and outstanding horsemanship impresses Truscott. Truscott's aggressive polo playing style and superb horsemanship impresses Chamberlin. Truscott's credo in polo: "no S.O.B., no winner." The two men become friends for life.

Men of the Cavalry play polo seriously; in fact, deadly so. Originally, Fort Bliss sports five polo fields with each regiment maintaining its own practice area and therefore, its own regimental designation. The designations change over time because when a cavalryman dies playing polo, the post command names the field after the deceased player. Therefore, Bosserman Field honors the deceased player Lieutenant Raymond Bosserman who dies on the field of honor playing polo; so too with Noel Field named for deceased Lieutenant Paul Noel; and Armstrong Field, named for deceased Lieutenant Eugene Armstrong. Most die in intramural competition among the four regiments that make up the 1st Cavalry Division: the 5th, 12th, 7th, and 8th. The 8th Cavalry tends to win most of the time.

Ultimately, Chamberlin's 8th Cavalry team wins the 1st Cavalry Division Polo Championship. The victory enables his team to compete in Philadelphia at the United States Polo Association's National Competition. Chamberlin invites Truscott to join the Fort Bliss Polo team to play in those polo championship games. Chamberlin intends to win and he wants Lucian Truscott to play on his team. To enable Truscott to play, Chamberlin arranges (pulls strings) to assign Truscott to command temporarily to Troop E, 1st Squadron, of the 8th Cavalry.

During the play-off rounds, the 8th Cavalry team bests Fort Oglethorpe by a score of 17 to 3. On September 20th, the final playoff for the National Inter-Circuit Championship takes place at the Philadelphia Country Club. The Cavalry plays against the Rockaway Club four. The 8th Cavalry team of Fort Bliss, says Associated Press, "outplayed its more experienced rivals at every stage of the game." [130] They display wonderful teamwork and excellent horsemanship. They also prove themselves lethal with the mallet. With a neat backhand stroke, Truscott scores after 32 seconds of play. Playing under a three-goal handicap, Chamberlin leads the field with four of his team's goals. Captain Truscott, "one of the longest hitters in the Army" [131] meets all expectations. Like Chamberlin, he rides aggressively without fear. The combined force of Chamberlin and Truscott enables the Fort Bliss team to defeat the famed Rockaway Club by a score of 12 to 8. The 8th Cavalry team takes a trophy back to El Paso and Fort Bliss.

Seven days later, at the Championship games of the United States, on September 27, the Fort Bliss team of Chamberlin, Truscott, Wood and Hutsteiner prove unstoppable. Associated Press writes: "Displaying the same brilliant form that gave them the Inter-Circuit Championship a week

---

130 *Associated Press,* September 20, 1925.
131 *Ibid.*

ago, the Fort Bliss polo players captured the 12 Goal Championship of the United States by defeating the Midwick Club of Pasadena, California 14 to 5." [132] The Cavalry's "desperate" riding causes them many penalties but the penalties prove no handicap. Captain Wood, playing in the No.1 position proves to be a "tower of strength" with seven goals. Chamberlin, Truscott and Hutsteiner score two goals each. The team takes home The United States Polo Association's Julius Fleishmann Trophy.

A commentator observes Chamberlin on the polo field: "Major Chamberlin...had the faculty...beyond any player I have ever seen of relaxing both himself and his mount whenever speed was not necessary. He could stand at times with his pony as quiet as though tied to a picket line and then dash at top speed to the point where he was needed." [133]

In November of 1925, in an article entitled "Polo Here and There," Harry Cottingham comments on the year's play. He writes of the outstanding developments that year: the spread of polo in the ranks of the United States Army, the skills they show, and the proliferation of first-class tournaments. The "Fort Bliss Four" of team captain, Major Chamberlin, Captain Wood, Captain Truscott and Captain Hutsteiner—a new team, new to polo circles—competes amongst 190 teams, 40 of which are military. The Fort Bliss Four "defeats Rockaway Hunt Club captained by the internationally renowned player, J. Cheever Cowdin." (Cowdin was the son of John E. Cowdin who achieved a remarkable 10-goal handicap in 1894.)

After the September 1925 championship match, Truscott heads to Fort Riley to attend the Troop Officer's Course at The Cavalry School. The Chamberlin-Truscott friendship endures for the rest of Harry Chamberlin's life. And after Chamberlin's passing in 1944, Truscott never forgets his friend. To Truscott, Chamberlin represents the ideal cavalryman and military officer. Truscott's evaluation of Chamberlin reveals something about Chamberlin, the man: Chamberlin remains at peace with himself. Competitive, yes. An achiever, for certain. An intellectual, absolutely. A gifted athlete, definitely. A horseman of the first order striving for excellence, of course.

But in Chamberlin, one perceives more: There is no "lying in him." While others might attempt to portray externally to the world something different than the reality of the man, with Chamberlin, what you see is what he is. George Patton, Jr., for example, feels compelled to conceal his sensitive nature, tries to be someone other than himself, and impersonates what he thinks a "warrior" must be. Chamberlin feels no compulsion to do so.

---

132 *Associated Press* September 27, 1925.

133 Ibid.

On the polo field, the conduct of each man reveals this dichotomy of personality: Patton rides like a mad man dashing all over the field to be noticed. Chamberlin chooses a corner of the field to conserve his horse, watches, waits, and then pounces on an opponent with devastating result. This is how Chamberlin conducts himself in every quarter, from the polo ground to the battlefield, from the barracks with sergeants and other enlisted men to the army headquarters with superior and subordinate officers alike.

In 1926, again with Chamberlin as captain, the 8th Cavalry polo team wins the National Twenty-Goal Championship. In winning the Joseph Jessop Challenge Trophy Series, "The Cavalry" beats Midwick by a score of 12 to 5.

"Major Chamberlin, playing the No.2 position, showed a marked ability to follow the ball and drove the oval between the posts for five of his team's tallies," a newspaper writes. [134] The team wins by defeating the teams of three other cavalry regiments, two field artillery regiments, the Second Division team, the Eighth Corps Area team; and civilian teams from San Antonio, Austin, and Detroit. That year, Chamberlin and his team also win the National Twelve-Goal Polo Championship at the Westchester-Biltmore Club at Rye, New York.

In June of 1926, Chamberlin receives word that he will attend The Command and General Staff School at Fort Leavenworth, Kansas. This most prestigious opportunity confirms that the army recognizes his superior talents and his capacity for high levels of command in United States Army. Success "at Leavenworth" will elevate Chamberlin into an elite group of the Army's most celebrated officers. In August of 1926, the Chamberlins leave Fort Bliss for Fort Leavenworth.

134 *New York Times*, May 22, 1926.

Chapter 21

The Command and General Staff School Fort Leavenworth, Kansas, 1926–1927

"I have been studying to beat hell...
I doubt that I will stand relatively as high as I did at Riley...
I think some of the others will crack—I sure hope so."
—George S. Patton, Jr. letter to home 1924 [135]

"At the completion of your schooling here, the foundation has been laid,
and the framework of your future life is erected."
—General Edward King, Commandant,
Command and General Staff School, 1926 [136]

General William Tecumseh Sherman establishes The School of Application for Infantry and Cavalry at Fort Leavenworth in the year 1881. In 1907, the army changes the school's name to The School of the Line. In Chamberlin's time, the army changes the name to The Command and General Staff School.

Regardless of the school's name, in 1926, it stands as the most important military school in any American officer's career. Those who rise to the army's highest positions of responsibility attend this school. Graduates include celebrated officers such as George Patton and George Marshall. To become

135 See Carlo D'Estes, *Patton: Genius For War,* Harper Perennial, 1995.
136 See Elvid Hunt, *History of Fort Leavenworth 1827–1937,* Second Edition, Command and General Staff School Press, 1937.

"a Leavenworth man," as George Marshall calls its graduates, means that the army recognizes an officer's talent.

Without this mark of success, no officer may aspire to future high command in the army. Chamberlin achieves this essential mark *before* a host of others who become famous in World War II: Wainwright, Buckner, Bradley, Devers, Hodge, Arnold—all follow Chamberlin by several years. Patton precedes Chamberlin by two years; Eisenhower precedes him by one year. Obviously, the army recognizes Chamberlin as a potential future commander of the *highest* caliber.

The school imposes immense pressures on its students. The pressures—or at least, a student's response to the pressures—make and break careers as well as marriages. Those fortunate enough to attend take the school's rigors seriously. Each student knows that success here assures a future career of high command and responsibility; failure, assures oblivion. The results: Pressure and stress are constants. Depression and insomnia are common. Nervous collapse is frequent. Divorce is not unusual; suicide, occasional.

Here in the 1920s, the army trains an officer to prepare for the highest staff responsibilities. Here, the army evaluates an officer to determine whether he possess the mental and emotional qualities that make for a General Officer. Students study military history, leadership and decision making. They work through problems of command, logistics and maneuver. They attend conferences, lectures, and map and field exercises.

Rather than present students with case problems for which no "right" answer exists, the faculty presents problems with secretly pre-determined "right" answers—at least, "right" in the faculty's mind. In all, by graduation, an officer will attend over 1,000 hours of theory and more than 350 hours of practice implementing the theories discussed.

The long, pressure filled and highly structured days absorb almost all of their time. The faculty does its best to create the stress and strain of war to test the officer's mettle. They demand that he think and decide while exhausted. Students study into the night to prepare for the next day; a day in which they might face the most challenging problems of any officer's peace-time career.

During what little time the students have to themselves on weekends during the day, Chamberlin rides horses—always horses and more horses. For others, alcohol in abusive amounts eases the pressure. And on some weekends, an occasional cocktail party and formal dinner enable students and faculty to get to know each other. In the Cavalry especially, alcohol flows often too freely; but not with Chamberlin. He is not a teetotaler but, unlike many others in the Cavalry, he does not drink to excess. At the same time, he often remains the life of the part with his warm personality and winning ways.

At the end of the program, how does Chamberlin's record compare with others who attend the school? Patton attends the school in 1924, Eisenhower in 1925, Chamberlin in 1926. Eisenhower ranks first in his class, but enjoys Patton's class and examination notes while he studies. Patton graduates in the top 25 percent of the class and thus graduates as an "Honor Graduate." In June of 1927, Chamberlin ranks just below the 25th percentile and graduates as a "Distinguished Graduate." He secures his future. The Army's high-level responsibilities open up to him.

After the intense pressures and the intellectual challenges of the Command and General Staff School, any sane man would welcome some fun for a change. Chamberlin's next assignment, thankfully, frees him from the pressures of simulated war-time command as well as from the relative drudgery of peace time administrative work. It offers him an enjoyable pursuit that nonetheless calls upon all of his previous training as a leader, all of his intellectual resources as a teacher and a trainer, all of his athletic abilities as a rider, and all of the competitive spirit that he can muster.

In September of 1927, he departs the classrooms and pressure cooker of Fort Leavenworth to enter the open spaces, jumping arenas, and riding halls of Fort Riley. Chamberlin becomes the Captain of the newly established United States Army Horse Show Team.

Chapter 22

The United States Army Horse Show Team
September 1927–August 1932

"If I become a horseman, I shall be a man on wings."
—Xenophon, 400 B.C.

"Nothing, aside from the dearest human relationships, can give the pleasure found in working and playing with a horse."
—Harry Dwight Chamberlin [137]

"In one of the most exciting performances in the history of the National Horse Show to date, Major Chamberlin on Tan Bark wins the International Military Stakes."
—*The New York Times* [138]

American military equestrians did not win a single medal in the 1924 Olympic Games, a failure that disappoints then Chief of Cavalry, Major General Herbert Crosby. Crosby meets with Army Chief of Staff, General Charles Summerall and asks Summerall to authorize him to establish an Army Horse Show Team in hopes that American Olympic performance will improve. Summerall agrees.

Crosby decides that of all the American riders since the end of World War I, Major Chamberlin remains the ideal choice to lead the team. Crosby notes that Chamberlin turns in the best international showing when he

137 See Harry D. Chamberlin, *Riding and Schooling Horses*, Derrydale Press, 1934.
138 *The New York Times* November 10, 1931.

places second in the Military Competition of the Inter-Allied Games of 1919. Plus, Chamberlin offers experience in all three Olympic equestrian venues from the Olympics of 1920. Chamberlin graduates from Saumur and Tor di Quinto as a "distinguished graduate" from both schools to boot. Also, Chamberlin graduates from the Command and General Staff School at about the same time as Crosby secures Summerall's approval for the Army Horse Show Team. These factors combine to make Chamberlin Crosby's natural choice. Chamberlin, however, offers more to the challenge than just his schooling and his experience: He brings a penetrating intellect and an equestrian athleticism that few, if any, other officers in any army offer. His keen and analytical mind rarely accepts any theory unquestioned or unchanged. He observes. He reflects. He experiments.

When one views the Chamberlin of 1927 in the perspective of 92 years later, one sees the same genius that resides in Baucher, L'Hotte and Caprilli. Recall Baucher, who constantly evaluates, re-evaluates, and challenges established concepts, as he revises his own methods; ultimately, Baucher influences the *Écuyers* of Saumur. Recall L'Hotte, who synthesizes, balances, and then integrates the theories of Baucher with those of d'Aure; ultimately, L'Hotte transforms French equitation to achieve "lightness." Recall Caprilli, who observes, evaluates, and tries new approaches. Ultimately, Caprilli influences the entire equestrian world. So too with Chamberlin: He draws from Baucher and d'Aure; he combines parts of L'Hotte with Caprilli. He takes some here, rejects some there, and develops his own contributions. Ultimately, he influences the equestrian world well into the twenty-first century.

Evidence of genius: creative people of genius often refer to their labors as "play" as they tinker with ideas, build on what has preceded, and engage in a process of elimination to achieve what others only dimly perceive, if at all. Writes Chamberlin:

> "Nothing, aside from the dearest human relationships, can give the pleasure found in working and playing with a horse." [139]

In his new position as leader of the Army Horse Show Team, Chamberlin plays as he develops and incorporates new concepts into the US Cavalry's equestrian thinking. Drawing from his Saumur experience, in the words of his student John Tupper Cole, he develops "a progressive, related series of equine calisthenics which balance the horse, make him supple and 'instantly

139 Harry D. Chamberlin, *Riding and Schooling Horses*, Derrydale Press, 1934.

obedient.'" [140] He works so "the horse finally almost falls into obedience if the rider can put him in a position which makes the new demand logical and comfortable." (Baucher: first the position, then the movement.) He constantly puts "emphasis on keeping the horse calm." (L'Hotte: "calm, forward, straight.") He provides a protocol of equine gymnastics that logically progresses from the previously learned skill to the next new skill to achieve "mastery of balance, obedience and power." (L'Hotte.)

Through these concepts, he strives to perfect a mode of riding effective for the rider and humane for the horse so as to develop the natural gifts of both. Ultimately, Chamberlin develops a mode of riding that combines, in the words of his student General John Tupper Cole: "a delightful blend of French lightness, Italian balance and German accuracy."

Crosby gives Chamberlin six riders for special duty with the team and authority to sequester any horse at the Cavalry School. Each team member will serve a maximum of four years. After such term, each participant must spend two years in a line command of troops to become eligible to rejoin the team. In 1927, Chamberlin's six initial riders join the team: Major Sloan Doak; Captains F.H. Waters, Frank L. Carr, William B. Bradford, Norman McMahon, and Richard Gordon.

Over the next few years, team members will come and go. To name a few: Thomson, Wofford, Cole, and Rodgers rotate in and out over time. The American officers train principally at Fort Riley, Kansas; though later, at times, they train also at Fort Robinson, Nebraska; the Presidio near San Francisco; and the Remount Station at Front Royal, Virginia.

Chamberlin surveys the facilities at Fort Riley and The Cavalry School. The terrain and the existing facilities offer superior training opportunities: two large indoor riding halls, multiple Hitchcock pens, jumping chutes, miles and miles of bridle paths, slides as high as 75 feet, rivers to ford, gorges to negotiate, woods to traverse, miles of open country where one gallops for miles. All challenge the horseman with every type of terrain.

When Chamberlin takes command of the Army Horse Show team, he adds to the challenges when he persuades the School to build a "hippodrome" which consists of a large jumping arena that presents every jump a rider might encounter at Aachen, Dublin, Lucerne, Warsaw, Cologne, Madison Square Garden or any other show in the world. Under Chamberlin, the US Army Horse Show Team will train each year to participate in

140 For all quotes in this section see General John Tupper Cole, Introduction to *Chamberlin Training Hunters, Jumpers, and Hacks*, Arco, Second Edition, 1973.

international shows in Canada, England, Ireland, France, Italy, Belgium, Holland, Germany, Poland, and Sweden and throughout South America.

Next, Chamberlin teaches his team to apply what he calls a "modified Italian seat." The team, and later the whole army, calls it the "Chamberlin seat" which we will describe in a later chapter. He teaches the team to ride with short stirrups and to place themselves well forward but *not* with the stirrups as short or the rider as far forward as the Italians practice at Tor di Quinto. By 1930, Chamberlin finalizes his thoughts regarding "the seat." The reader will find Chamberlin's expanded explanation in this biography's companion volume, *The Chamberlin Reader.* A bare-bones summary follows:

1. The heels forced well down to contract the calf muscles;
2. The feet turned out about 45 degrees; no effort to "splay' the outside of the foot upward;
3. The calf clings gently to the horse's side; the position of the foot enables the rider, in an emergency, to maintain the seat with the calf muscles;
4. The knees remain as low as the stirrups permit
5. The thighs remain flat against the saddle;
6. The fleshy parts of the buttocks remain well to the rear;
7. The backbone remains in a normal, erect position with the small of the back slightly hollowed out;
8. The seat bones rest lightly on the saddle;
9. The upper body inclines forward from the hip joints
10. The length of the stirrup strap depends on the type of riding;
11. The head and chest should remain raised;
12. Due to the relaxed knee and forward inclined upper body, the rider's weight rests lightly on the seat bones, the thigh, the knee, and the heel of the boot.

THE "MILITARY SEAT" ADOPTED

Chamberlin's work regarding the development of the "seat" at this time goes beyond his work with the team. As part of his responsibilities, for two years, he also participates in a Cavalry Board decision to finalize the concept of "the military seat" which will form the basis for military riding in the United States. In time, this "seat" will be known as "the Chamberlin Military Seat."

The board of officers consists of:

Brig. Gen Walter C. Short
Lt. Col. John A. Barry
Lt. Col. B.T. Merchant
Lt. Col. W.W. West
Col Guy V. Henry
Col. Benjamin Lear
Major H.D. Chamberlin (added to consider the "military seat.")
Captain W.B. Bradford (added to consider the "military seat")

In later years, cavalry officers will refine the board's recommendations in the Cavalry's manual *Horsemanship and Horsemastership* with periodic revisions between 1929 and 1953. Chamberlin's influence remains evident throughout the early editions of the manual and he makes his final contributions in the 1942 edition for which he supervises the manual's revision and updating.

Among many concepts the Cavalry Board defines, the foundation principle remains the position of the "seat." The Board abandons the "close seat" and the bolt upright and often behind the vertical upper body of French practice. As Chamberlin writes:

> "Unfortunately, our officers and troopers were taught to ride with the buttocks pushed under them so that they were seated on the ends of their spines..."

Also, given the habit of many cavalrymen (officers and enlisted men alike) to "slouch" in the saddle or to apply "western" modes of riding with the lower legs placed well forward of the saddle and the buttocks pressed against the saddle's cantle, the Board pays special attention to defining "the buttocks," and to prescribing their placement for military riding.

The Board Report defines the buttocks as "...that portion of the rider's anatomy upon which he rests when sitting naturally erect. *It extends no farther to the rear that the points of the pelvic bone* and merges forward into the thighs. The "leg" is that portion of the limb between the knee and the ankle." [141]

They go on to describe the rider's position mounted at the halt:

> "The rider sits squarely in the middle of the saddle, his weight distributed on this buttocks, thighs, and stirrups.
>
> "The positions of the buttocks and the upper body are interdependent. For the buttocks to bear their proper portion of weight, the upper body must be erect; its center of gravity is slightly in *front* of the points of the buttocks facilitating the correct placing of the thighs, and the proper distribution of weight. Inclining the upper body to the rear or convexing the loins to the rear places the center of gravity of the upper body in rear of its base of support and causes the rider to sit on the fleshy parts of his buttocks, or upon the end of his spine. This faulty position raises the thighs and knees, weakens the seat, concentrates the weight toward the cantle, is unmilitary in appearance, injurious to the horse's back, and places the rider *behind* his horse." [142]

Further down in the order, the board report states:

> "...The buttocks are the cornerstone of the rider's base of support, and are placed first. When properly placed, the rider has the sensation that their points are almost in contact with the saddle; their fleshy portion is in rear of their points, and is never part of the seat. *"Tuck your buttocks under you"* is misleading and causes some riders, in an attempt to obey, to sit not on the points of the buttocks, but on their fleshy portion; such a position is the cause of many faults of the seat. To sit on this fleshy portion tends to produce insecurity by causing the rider to "roll" on the saddle, to bow his back to the rear at the loins, to raise his knees, to derange his thighs, and to *"get behind his horse,"* all unsightly and insecure." [143]

At the same time that Chamberlin participates in the Cavalry Board's determinations regarding the "military seat," which reflects more Italian

---

141 Report of the Cavalry Board on the Adoption of the Military Seat, *The Cavalry Journal, 1929.*

142 Ibid.

143 Ibid.

influence than the French influence of the past, he does not abandon French concepts all together. He focuses his team on certain select dressage concepts taught at Saumur. He teaches them to approach dressage, not as an "art form," but rather as a means to train the horse to respond to the slightest hint of the aids and to train the rider to apply the aids in an almost imperceptible and precise manner.

He subscribes to General L'Hotte's view that all horses, no matter what their discipline, should learn a common foundation of skills. Unlike the Italians, he wants his horses to respond to the subtlest of aids and thus be agile and "handy." Unlike the French, he wants his riders to float over jumps as if they were part of the horse and not try to "lift" them over jumps.

Chamberlin produces almost immediate results with his six student-team. Through Chamberlin's riding and teaching, the Army Horse Show Team demonstrates what American horseman and horses will accomplish with new training and riding methods. As a result, the riding of the United States Cavalry reaches its zenith.

In time, Chamberlin's concepts extend beyond the Army Horse Show Team. His ideas, ultimately, contribute to the riding mode that the cavalry adopts for its officers and ranks as a whole. Not until 1929, however, with the initial promulgation of the "military seat" by the Cavalry Board, will the cavalry begin revamping its riding method in a long process that culminates in successive editions of the Cavalry School's manual: *Horsemanship and Horsemastership.*

During this time, Chamberlin continues to refine his concepts. He will achieve his full mastery of training methods and apply them at the Cavalry Replacement Training Center (the "CRTC") which the Cavalry establishes at Fort Riley in 1940. Chamberlin will command the CRTC in 1941 to train cavalrymen during World War II.

Only yellowed newspaper clippings, some now more than 90 years old, and a few journal articles filed away on microfilm chronicle the events of these times. Only a few salvaged, sterling silver trophies remain that attest to the achievements of so long ago.

The newspapers: *The New York Times, the Los Angeles Times, the Chicago Tribune, The Washington Post,* and a few other papers write of these events as they unfold in cities of North America and of Europe; among them: Boston, New York City, Los Angeles and Toronto; Amsterdam, Warsaw and Posen; Cologne, Hamburg and Berlin; Dublin, Aachen and Lucerne.

The list describes the venues where the United States Army Horse Show Team competes against the greatest riders of Germany, Italy, France, Belgium, Holland, Poland, Hungary, Sweden, Ireland and Canada to name a few.

Engraved upon the silver cups that survive or that one might see in old photos found tucked away, one sees the names Tanbark, Suzanne, Nigra, High Hat, Benny Grimes, Show Girl, Dick Waring, Joe Aleshire, and Babe Wartham. Many of these horses now rest under stone markers in a special cemetery at the old remount station at Front Royal, Virginia.

The headlines describe the highlights of Chamberlin's time with the US Army Horse Show Team—the pride of the Cavalry. They depict the team's progress and eventual triumph. [Except where otherwise specified, the bold faced headlines are re-writes and related copy are summaries of longer articles found in *The New York Times* depicting the events described from 1927 through 1932.]

1927

NOVEMBER 10, 1927. US ARMY TEAM SHUTS OUT FRANCE, CANADA AND OTHERS. POLAND TAKES THE WESTCHESTER CUP. THE AMERICAN TEAM SHOWS WELL!

While the Polish Team wins the *International Military Trophy*, the Americans take second, third and fourth place. They shut out two French teams, two Canadian teams, another Polish team and several civilian teams. The American team does better in this show than did the Polish team that last year won the *International Military Trophy*.

Chamberlin, riding Benny Grimes, wins the *Challenge Cup*. The event spans two days and requires a twenty-mile ride through Central Park in New York City that includes jumping over twenty obstacles twice—once up and once back. On the second day, the second part of the event takes place in the Madison Square Garden show ring. Chamberlin on Benny Grimes clears the four jumps. Then Benny Grimes stands quietly as Chamberlin dismounts and remounts. Horse and rider then perform a turn on the forehand. Then they walk, then trot, and then canter with several flying changes of lead in a straight line.

For the next event, *Spur Cup*, with 34 mounts competing, the Polish win after two jump offs and the US Army's Captain Bradford takes second.

1928

During part of 1927 and much of 1928, the US Army Horse Show Team takes time out for the Olympics of 1928. Four of the six horse-show team members go to Amsterdam. At Fort Riley, intense training of horses and riders proceeds in earnest. The team gives the three-day horses a two-hour cross-country workout three days a week. The workout consists mostly of walk and trot up and down gentle slopes. On the remaining three days of the week, riders walk or lead the horses up and down steep inclines. In addition, the three-day horses devote two hours each day to schooling, jumping on the longe or to jumping under saddle depending on individual requirements. The team also includes a period of schooling in the Dressage ring six days each week.

June 2, 1928. The US Olympic Team Picks Its Athletes. Brigadier General Walter C. Short, manager of the Olympic Equestrian Team, selects the members of the team. He chooses Chamberlin, Doak, George, Bradford, and Carr from the cavalry and Argo from the artillery. Doak will serve as team captain. Short reports his selections to Major General Douglas MacArthur who heads the 1928 Olympic effort for The United States.

The riders train at Rye, New York. On July 10, they board a ship for Europe at Hoboken, New Jersey. The army installs two giant treadmills on which the horses exercise each day of the journey. Horses and riders arrive in Amsterdam on July 20. Major General MacArthur addresses the Olympic Team: "We did not travel 3,000 miles to lose gracefully. We come here to win and win decisively." [144]

August 8, 1928. The Military Competition (Three-Day Event) of The Olympic Games at Amsterdam begins.

Twenty-one nations send a combined 114 riders to the Games. Fourteen teams compete in the "Military" or "Three-Day Event" as we now call it. Just before the Three-Day, General Short replaces Chamberlin with Charles George. The original schedule calls for Chamberlin to ride Benny Grimes in the Three-Day Event.

The endurance test is 22½ miles—4 1/5 miles on roads and paths at nine miles per hour; 2½ miles of steeplechase over obstacles at 20 miles per hour; nine and 2/5 miles on roads at nine miles per hour; five miles across country over obstacles at 17 miles per hour; one and 1/4 miles on road to finish at 11½ miles per hour. The obstacle jumping, which is the third part

144 See Arthur Herman, *MacArthur: American Warrior*, Random House, 2016.

of the main event, occurs in the stadium where horses and riders must jump 14 obstacles of every variety at a rate of 12 miles per hour.

For some reason, George misses a jump on the cross-country course. This mishap costs the American team the Silver Medal. Why Short substitutes George for Chamberlin remains unknown.

THE *PRIX DES NATIONS*.

Sixteen nations enter the jumping competition. Chamberlin rides Nigra, his horse of the Inter-Allied Games of almost ten years before. Chamberlin confronts 16 obstacles between four feet and four feet nine inches—and a spread of 14 feet wide—none of which the rules allow him to see before the day of the competition. He must clear the course at a pace of 43 yards per minute, about 14 miles per hour. Chamberlin clears all but one obstacle—a front knockdown—four faults. Nonetheless, the other two American team members rack up a combined 18 faults. This puts the team into 9th place.

Spain wins the gold medal; Poland, the silver; and Sweden, the bronze. The individual gold goes to Captain Ventura of Czechoslovakia with zero faults through two rides of a jump off; the silver goes to Captain de Belinda of France with two faults on his second ride; the bronze goes to Major Kuhn of Switzerland with two faults on the second ride and a longer time than the Frenchman de Belinda. Chamberlin scores 18th individually with four faults and a time of one minute and thirty-four seconds (1:34).

Regardless of Chamberlin's individual ranking, the most important benefit of his Olympic participation beyond additional international experience in 1928 is that Major General Douglas MacArthur, the President of the Olympic Committee takes note of Chamberlin's performance. MacArthur remembers Chamberlin's 95-yard ball return in the football game against Navy in 1908 and hears of his performance at the Inter-Allied Games of 1919. Chamberlin's participation in the 1928 Olympics further bolsters his reputation with MacArthur and this will pay great dividends in 1930 and after.

MacArthur's "earnest efforts and zeal" in cajoling and leading the American Olympic team gains the admiration of most Olympic athletes. As MacArthur biographer Arthur Herman writes "the United States won twenty-four gold medals, more than the next two countries, Finland and Germany, put together. The US team had set no less than seventeen Olympic records and seven world records."[145] Yet, no equestrian medals come home to the United States. MacArthur will do all that he can to see that 1932 proves far different.

Figure 93 *Chamberlin on Nigra at the Olympics of 1928 Prix des Nations competition. He has completely abandoned the "close seat" jumping style. Courtesy U. S.E.T.*

OTHER INVITATIONS FOR THE ARMY RIDING TEAM

The Secretary of War receives a note from the Minister of Poland inviting the US Army Horse Show Team to compete in the International Jumping Competition at the horse show in Warsaw, Poland, September 12 to 28, 1928. The Secretary of War declines the invitation because the Equestrian team must return to the United States on the chartered boat, the *President Roosevelt,* which sails from Amsterdam on August 15, 1928.

Beyond the Olympic invitation, the Army Team receives four other initiations to send riding teams to continental horse shows during the summer of 1928. In addition to the Polish invitation, the other invitations come from the Olympia Horse Show in London, England; the Military International Horse Show at Nice, France; and the International Horse Show to be held at

145 See Arthur Herman, *MacArthur: American Warrior,* Random House, 2016.

Lucerne, Switzerland, July 7 to 15. In the future, the United States makes an effort to compete in these events.

Once back to the United States after the Olympics, the horse show team gathers momentum.

October 1, 1928. The New York State Fair, Syracuse, NY. The US Army Horse Show Team wins two firsts, two seconds, and two thirds.

November 4, 1928. At the National Horse Show at Madison Square Garden, The United States Army Horse Show Team wins the largest number of prizes. Only one rider turns in a clean round: Major H.D. Chamberlin!

The event draws a spectacular group of army officers from Poland, Germany, Holland, Belgium, Canada and The United States. 18 riders, three from each nation compete. Germany wins *The International Military Trophy* by½ of one point. Germany wins with nine faults; The United States and Poland tie for second place with 9½ faults each. Only one of the 18 riders takes his horse over every fence, start to finish with no faults and turns in a clean round: Major Harry D. Chamberlin of the United States Cavalry riding the gelding, Dick Waring.

November 11, 1928. Army's Major Chamberlin and Jumper Score in Cup Event.

Major Chamberlin sails over the jumps in flawless performance on Buckaroo and captures *Brooks-Bright Cup*!

1929

April 19, 1929. US Army Team Accepts Invitation for Fourth Show Abroad.

April 24, 1929. On the pick of their mounts, and headed by Major H.D. Chamberlin, the members of the team circled the ring and then drew up before the reviewing stand to accept show honors.

April 26, 1929. Chamberlin on Huron Girl Takes Blue for Jumping. Army Horse Also Second. Dick Waring Puts up Hard Fight for Laurels.

April 27, 1929. Miss America Wins...Army Mare Jumper shows Brilliantly at Brooklyn Show—Team Mates 2nd and 3rd...Dick Warning Runner Up in "Touch and Go."

May 3. 1929. Chamberlin and the other members of the Unites States Army Horse Show Team board the steamship Dresden bound for Europe.

Chamberlin, now of the 9th US Cavalry, captains a team that consists of Captain William Bradford, 9th Cavalry; Lt. Edwin Argo, 1st Field Artillery; Lt. Earl F. Thomson, 9th Cavalry. They take nine horses: Dick Waring, a black gelding, 16-1 hands; Tanbark, a brown gelding, 15-3 hands; Proctor, a brown gelding 16 hands; Jack Snipe, brown gelding, 16 hands; Buckaroo, brown gelding15-3 hands; Huron Girl, a chestnut mare, 16-1 hands; Miss America, a brown mare 16-2 hands, Garçon, a brown gelding 16 hands; St. Paul, a brown gelding 16.1 hands.

They will compete in five international events and a number of local, European competitions; the most important of which are: The international jumping competition at Warsaw, Poland, June 1-12; then the *International Concours Hippique* at Cologne, Germany, June 16-24; and finally, the Dublin Horse Show at Dublin Ireland, August 6-9.

For the trans-Atlantic voyage, each horse enjoys a large, well-padded box stall. To keep the horses fit, the army installs a treadmill on which the horses exercise every day. (The Team uses the same treadmill that the Olympic team of 1928 uses during its trans-Atlantic voyage to Amsterdam.)

A few words about the American team's mounts: The army bought each one for a price of $165 each. Jack Snipe served as a French coach horse which pounded the streets of Paris. Proctor, a fine old English Thoroughbred carried General Pershing down the Champs-Elysées during the Allied Victory Parade in Paris. Buckaroo began his career as a trooper's horse on the Mexican Border.

June 25, 1929. The Army team scores high in five international classes in Europe. Chamberlin Wins at Dublin! Bradford wins at Cologne!

They compete in the equestrian tournament at Hamburg as well as the tournaments in Warsaw, Posen and Cologne. In the Cologne Grand Prix, Bradford wins first prize with Buckaroo; Chamberlin wins two, second place prizes and Lt. Thomson wins a second-place prize. Later that month, Chamberlin wins first place the International Individual Jumping Championship at the Dublin Horse Show in Dublin, Ireland.

August 31, 1929. Horse Show Opens at Newark Tonight. Title Jump Stake to Miss America. Dick Waring and Buckaroo, Second and Third at Syracuse. Hunter Title to Proctor. Chamberlin: Two Perfect Performances; Two Jump-Offs Held.

The Army again dominates the jumping events. Chamberlin turns in two perfect performances at Syracuse, New York and at Newark, New Jersey.

October 16, 1929. Proctor Wins Cathedral Cup. Army Gelding. One of Pershing's String During the War Named Champion Hunter. Major H.D. Chamberlin dominates!

Proctor shows faultlessly as he walks around the ring and captivates both the judges and the audience. The United States Army Team adds two more blues to its long list of wins. Major Chamberlin rides Gary Owen and dominates the hunter class by giving a flawless, no fault performance in record time over the course. Fort Riley sweeps all in their path.

November 12, 1929. Dick Waring wins for US Places Second.

November 13, 1929. 20,000 Cheer Competitors as US Army Team's Buckaroo Wins Challenge Cup. Polish team takes International Military Trophy beating out Italian, Irish, American and Canadian teams.

1930

April 15, 1930. US Army Horse Show Team to Compete in Brooklyn Show.

Major Harry D. Chamberlin announces that he has entered his horses in the thirty-eighth annual Brooklyn Horse Show. Major Chamberlin, Captain W. B. Bradford and Lt. J.W. Wofford will ride for the Army.

June 3, 1930. Army Entry Takes Horse Show Honors. Captain W. D. Bradford Wins the Annual West Point Horse Show.

The *"Touch and Go Sweepstakes"* of the annual West Point Horse Show require two jump offs to determine the winner. Four riders tie for first with clean rounds; after the first jump off, two more riders tie for first. The win finally goes to Captain W. D. Bradford on the army's bay gelding Joe Aleshire. Major Chamberlin, riding Tan Bark, takes third place. In the lady's division, Sally Chamberlin, Harry's wife, gives a fine exhibition of jumping skill on her husband's bay gelding Sun Magic; but Mrs. Chamberlin loses, in the eyes of the judges, on conformation and thus takes a third place.

June 8, 1930. Major Harry D. Chamberlin on Dick Waring wins the annual Jumping Championship at the Tuxedo Park Horse Show.

June 21, 1930. Army Jumping Horses Thrill the Crowds...Show Jumping Skill at Governor's Island Annual Tournament.

Team members Major Harry D. Chamberlin, Captain W.B. Bradford and Lt. John W. Wofford mount some of the most celebrated horses in the US Cavalry and ride and jump as the crowd cheers.

October 28, 1930. —Boston: US Major Chamberlin Welcomes Swedish Team Here for The Horse Show...To Compete in Military Jumping Event.

October 29, 1930. US Army Scores Again at The Boston Horse Show. Chamberlin Wins in Dramatic Jump-off!

Lt. Rogers Rides Proctor to Victory in the Class for Officer's Chargers. The Germans take Second Place. Lt. Gordon Rogers, a new US Army team member, carries the day over Elan, the chestnut gelding of the German Army ridden by Capt. Freiherr V. Waldenfels. Captain John Tupper Cole takes third place on Avocat. Fourth Place goes to The Irish Free State rider T. P. Finlay on Carobh Ruadh.

The most spectacular jumping of the evening occurs in the Triple Bar Jump for the *Millwood Hunt Challenge Trophy*. The long drawn out battle between US Army Team's Major Harry D. Chamberlin on Huron Girl and the German Army's Lt. Ernst Hasse on the chestnut gelding Elan. With each clean round between the two, the judges raise and widen the jumps. After two jumps offs, both riders and horses achieve clean rounds. On the third jump off, Chamberlin and Huron Girl turn in a clear round. Hass and Elan of Germany falter on the third jump off as Elan kicks off a bar. Chamberlin wins the *Millwood Hunt Challenge Trophy* at the Boston Horse Show.

October 30, 1930. The US Army Team Triumphs at the Boston Horse Show. Lt. Rogers Rides Proctor to Victory in Class for Officers' Chargers. Military Stakes Goes to US Army Team. Chamberlin Wins Without a Single Fault!

With Chamberlin riding Both Dick Waring and Tanbark, he wins a first and a second place in International Military riding. He clears both rides over a difficult international course without a single fault. Of the 27 riders jumping, this night enjoys only four clean rides. To decide which horse takes first place, Chamberlin flips a coin to preserve his horses. The German Army provides an excellent display of horsemanship but the Canadian horse Sergeant Murphy ridden by Capt. Hammond edges them out of second place. The Irish Free State gelding Oisin ridden by Capt. O'Dwyer takes third with the US Army's Huron Girl with Lt. E.F. Thomson up takes fourth. Capt. O'Dwyer on Finighin of the Irish Free State finishes fifth.

In the Scurry Sweepstakes competition, Lt. John W. Wofford riding the bay gelding Babe Wartham takes a first place. On Miss American, Wofford takes a third. In a separate competition, Capt. John Cole wins the "Jumper Stakes."

November 7, 1930. US Army Team One of Yesterday's Winners in National Show.

November 10, 1930. Players of the Game; Major Chamberlin—Leader of the US Horse Team.

November 11, 1930. Three US Army mounts tie in the International Military Stakes competition at the National Horse Show in Madison Square Garden. Giving what commentators call "the most brilliant exhibition of horsemanship they have ever displayed in an international competition..." the American riders sweep all before them in the Remount Cup, the Ciechanowski Challenge Cup, and the Bowman Challenge Cup!

Major Chamberlin on the brown gelding, Tanbark wins First Prize and the Remount Cup in a toss for position. To break the tie, the three officers decide not to jump off. Rather, they decide the winner by a toss of the coin since they want to preserve their horses for the *International Military Trophy* competition the following night. Second place goes to the bay mare Suzanne, ridden by Captain William Bradford. Chamberlin also takes third place on the bay gelding Dick Waring. Bradford riding, Joe Aleshire, wins fourth place. The German Army's Lt. Harmann Freiheer von Nagel on the gray gelding, Dedo wins sixth. The Canadian Major Grant, on Pericles, takes seventh.

The Americans win with three perfect scores. Frantic spectators in the crowded Madison Square Garden cheer the American officers at every clean jump over the difficult international course. All three American horses jump clean with faultless performances. The dangerous German Army Team jumps six of their best horses and commits only six faults. Two Swedish competitors jump well but fail to offset the American performance. The two Canadian riders commit only four faults. The Irish Free State National Team fails to catch the Americans. The Americans achieve victory but at a cost: Bradford injures himself while riding his last mount over the jumps. Springing back from his injury, Captain Bradford wins the *Ciechanowski Challenge Cup* the next evening.

In the final competition of the event, *The Bowman Challenge Cup,* Major Chamberlin on the bay gelding Tan Bark takes first place. Lt. Wofford rides the chestnut gelding Hindustan and takes second.

November 12, 1930. The International Military Trophy competition at Madison Square Garden, the US Army Team comes in second.

The German Army Team wins the *International Military Trophy* for 1930 with only 5½ faults. The US Army comes in second with 10 faults. Hungary takes third place with 16 faults and the Irish Free State takes fourth with 17½ faults. Both Sweden and Canada remain out of the money with 21 faults each.

In a separate competition, Major Chamberlin gambles with fate and wins... He enters an unknown gelding Geraldyn into the competition at the last minute. The US Army team rider Lt. J.W. Wofford mounts Geraldyn and "electrifies the audience by his magnificent performance" on Geraldyn with only ½ fault... "a virtually flawless performance."

November 27, 1930. Toronto, Canada: US Riders Win the International Military Trophy; Germans take second.

US Riders Win in Canada Show. Take First Place in International Team Jumping with a Perfect Performance. Germans in second place with 1½ Faults; Irish take third with five faults, and Canada takes fourth with 10.

1931

November 6, 1931. Horse Show Honors to US Army Team! The US Army team the victor with Major Chamberlin Commander!

November 9th, 1931. Chamberlin on Tan Bark, US Jumper Wins Military Stakes!

Major Harry D. Chamberlin rides to his second victory before a cheering crowd of 10,000. Tan Bark and Chamberlin offer a perfect performance and win in an exciting jump off against riders from France and the Irish Free State.

November 10, 1931. US Army Team's Tan Bark Captures the Military Stakes at Madison Square Garden.

Tanbark Triumphs; the US Army Team Star, Ridden by Major Chamberlin, Scores in National Horse Show Test. French Jumper Is Second. ***In one of the most exciting performances in the history of the National Horse Show to date, Major Chamberlin on Tan Bark wins the International Military Stakes. (The New York Times)***

Twenty-eight horses go over the jumps. Four horses tie with perfect scores: The US Army's Tan Bark, Chamberlin up; Ugly, Raguese up; The Irish Free State Army's Turoe, Capt. Ahern up; The French Army's Cherubin, Capt. Nobili up. The decision comes after a jump off with three countries battling. The officers of the United States, The Irish Free State and France jump off to determine the winner. Chamberlin on Tan Bark goes first: One-half fault. Nobili on Cherubin goes next: three faults. Raguese on Ugly goes: 4½ faults. Ahern on Turoe finishes with 5½ faults. The US Army takes first and third.

For the *Bowman Challenge Cup* at Madison Square Garden, the US Army Team mare Suzanne with W. Bradford up captures the prize.

November 11, 1931. US Army Wins International Military Team Trophy at Garden Horse Show; Military Stake Also Won by U. S.

The Army Team Captures International Trophy at Garden Show before Crowd of 10,000. The Army exhibition remains faultless as the Americans turn in a perfect performance. Second place goes to France. Canadians finish third. British riders place forth. Irish Free State places fifth. Show Girl Has Walk Over. With three faultless exhibitions of jumping, the United States Army wins the International Military Trophy for the first time since the event was inaugurated at Madison Square Garden in 1925.

December 27, 1931. US Army Team Reaches the Pinnacle of Perfection! Capture Victory in the International Military Trophy Event. Army Wins with a Perfect Score!

The United States Army's horse show team triumphs in the contest for the International Military Trophy at the National Horse Show at Madison Square Garden. It marks the fulfillment of hopes and ambitions of several years.

1932

For most of the year, Chamberlin and his team prepare for the Olympic Games at Los Angeles. With the end of the Olympic Games in August of that year, Chamberlin's time with the US Army Horse Show Team ends. His legacy, however, continues into the future.

November 15, 1932. US Army Officers Triumph at Garden.

Again, the US Army Team Wins the International Military Trophy with only four faults total. Lt. Raguse and Major Cole clinch victory with two perfect scores and clean performances over the jumps. For the second year in a row, the United States Army team captures the International Military Trophy. More than 12,000 spectators cheer the winners in Madison Square Garden as Major John Tupper Cole, last of the American Riders, completes a perfect round. Total faults for the team: four.

The United States Army Horse Show Team continues to rack up victories in competitions in the United States and in Europe. Of course, by September 1939, war engulfs Europe. The world puts international competition on hold.

Figure 94 *The National Horse Show in New York City's Madison Square Garden, 1931. Tanbark and Suzanne win the Officer's Jumper's Cup for Pairs. Courtesy Ms. Tracey Reese Brown.*

Figure 95 *The National Horse Show Association of America International Military Trophy for the year 1931 won by Chamberlin. Courtesy of Ms. Tracey Reese Brown*

Figure 96 *Trophy Inscription. Courtesy Ms. Tracey Reese Brown.*

Chapter 23

The Xth Olympiad, Los Angeles, 1932

"The wind of heaven is that which blows between a horse's ears."
—Arabian proverb

"To win and to win decisively"
—MacArthur [146]

Our exploration of Chamberlin's life, and his impact on equestrianism, began with his thrilling ride in the final event of the Xth Olympiad at Los Angeles, California. He won the Silver Medal on Show Girl, a last-minute substitute for his prized jumper Tanbark. That accomplishment captured Chamberlin's greatness as a horseman like no other.

Looking behind the scenes of that event will show the preparations for the Olympics that Major General Guy V. Henry, Jr. Chief of Cavalry and General Douglas MacArthur, Army Chief of Staff authorize Chamberlin to pursue. The chapter will focus on the Three-Day Event itself and the United States Team Gold victory.

In the Fall of 1928, Major General Douglas MacArthur, as President of the American Olympic Committee, submits his report on the Olympics of 1928. As part of his report, he recommends that the U.S. Cavalry immediately begin to prepare and train for the Olympics of 1932. By early spring of 1929, Chief of Cavalry Crosby authorizes the training of individual horses and riders at various army stations where facilities exist. This gives the Army just more than three years to prepare for the games.

146 See Arthur Herman, *MacArthur: American Warrior*, Random House, 2016.

In March of 1930, Brigadier General Guy V. Henry, Jr., becomes Major General Henry, Chief of Cavalry. On November 21, 1930, General Douglas MacArthur becomes Army Chief of Staff MacArthur. He views Henry as "one of the best officers in the service." [147] Henry enjoys MacArthur's ear. The two men agree on all things cavalry, from the need to mechanize and to enhance its firepower to the Army's fielding a great equestrian team to the Olympics. Henry remains a far-sighted officer and a devoted horse cavalryman who also recognizes the need for change and modernization. For example, he introduces the 4 x 4 truck and the .50 caliber machine gun into the Cavalry's (and the whole Army's) repertoire.

MacArthur, as the former head of the American Olympic Committee, remains an Olympic enthusiast and requires no persuasion to back the army's Olympic effort to the maximum. As Arthur Herman has written; "If Douglas MacArthur of the 1920s was the father of the modern West Point, one could also argue he was the father of modern American Olympic sports." [148] Recall that in 1928, he then greets American Olympic Team that arrives in Amsterdam with the words: "We did not come 3,000 miles just to lose gracefully; we are here to win and win decisively."

By 1930, nothing changes MacArthur's opinion or cools his enthusiasm. Adding to his competitive frame of mind is the fact that the Olympics of 1932 will play out on American soil in Los Angeles. And so, from the first day Henry assumes the role of Chief of Cavalry and when MacArthur becomes Army Chief of Staff, together they focus their eyes on the Olympics of 1932. MacArthur states the goal anew to Henry: "To win and to win decisively."

From March 21, 1930 forward, Henry delivers whatever help he can to Lt. Col. Scott, the Manager of the Olympic Equestrian Team and to Major Chamberlin, the team's chief trainer. Their mission: to hone the future Olympic Equestrian team's skills and record of accomplishment. The Olympics are still two years off. Henry directs Scott and Chamberlin to begin preparations at once.

With General MacArthur's full concurrence, the new Chief of Cavalry, Henry, redoubles previous efforts surrounding the Army Horse Show Team and mobilizes other units in the Cavalry and the Field Artillery to train for the Olympics of 1932. Never before has the United States Army expended such effort for such purpose: Henry authorizes full time Army Equestrian Teams for the Cavalry and for the Field Artillery. He designates training locations

147 Guy V. Henry, Jr. *A Brief Narrative of the Life of Guy V. Henry, Jr.* Military History Research Collection, Carlisle Barracks Pennsylvania. 1974

148 See Arthur Herman, *MacArthur: American Warrior*, Random House, 2016.

at Fort Riley, Fort Sill, Fort Meyer, Fort Bliss, Fort Clark. He appoints specific Cavalry regiments to develop horses for each of the Olympic disciplines. He orders the army to construct Olympic style hippodromes at various sites around the country to forward the Olympic training of horses and riders. The pace of this activity proves aggressive:

June 1, 1931 : Preliminary Olympic Equestrian tryouts take place at Fort Bliss, Texas. Lts. Frierson and Curtis of the Cavalry make the grade for the Three-Event.

October 1, 1931: Preliminary Olympic Equestrian tryouts take place at Fort Riley, Kansas. Lts. Raguse, Wofford, and Haines, each of the Cavalry, make the grade for the *Prix des Nations.* For the Three-Day Event, Captain Koester and Lt. Hains make the grade. For Dressage, Captain Kitts and Lt. Stewart, both of the Field Artillery, make the grade.

October 15, 1931: Semi-Final Olympic Equestrian tryouts take place at Fort Riley. For the *Prix des Nations,* Captain Bradford and Lts. Raguse and Wofford make the grade. For the Three-Day Event, Captain Argo of the Field Artillery, Captain Cole of the Cavalry, and Major Thayer of the Cavalry make the grade. For Dressage, Captain Tuttle of the Quartermaster Corps, Captain Kitts of the Field Artillery, and Captain Moore of the Cavalry Reserve make the grade.

October 25, 1931: Final Olympic Equestrian tryouts take place at Fort Riley. The results: Tuttle, Kitts, and Moore make the first string Dressage team; Chamberlin, Bradford, and Wofford make the first string *Prix des Nations* team; Chamberlin, Argo, and Thomson make the first string Three-Day Event team.

Intermediate training of horses and riders finalizes at Fort Riley in 1931. Fourteen riders (including alternates) make the team:

Major Harry D. Chamberlin, Cavalry
Captain W. B. Bradford, Cavalry
Captain I. L. Kitts, Field Artillery.
Captain E. Y. Argo, Field Artillery
Captain H. E. Tuttle, Quarter Master Corps
Captain J.T. Cole, Cavalry
Captain Alvin C. Moore, Cavalry Reserve
Lt. J. W. Wofford, Cavalry
Lt. E. F. Thomson, Cavalry
Lt. C.W. Raguse, Cavalry
Lt. A.A. Frierson, Cavalry

Lt. L.J. Stewart, Cavalry
Lt. R. Curtis, Cavalry
Lt. P. Hains III, Cavalry

Figure 97 *Major Harry Chamberlin on Pleasant Smiles the former race horse that Chamberlin trains off of the track. For a "how to" primer, readers interested in off-the-track Thoroughbreds should consult Chamberlin's monograph reprinted in The Chamberlin Reader: Breaking, Training, and Reclaiming Cavalry Horses. Photo courtesy of the US Cavalry Association.*

The team now transfers to Fort Rosecrans in California to finish training and to acclimate riders and horses to the California climate and altitudes. They work full time at honing their riding skills and training their horses.

At the same time, due to the Great Depression, serious questions arise as to whether some countries possess the financial capacity to send teams or enough tickets at $1 to $3 will sell to support the Games. Hollywood greats Douglas Fairbanks, Jr. and Mary Pickford, Louis B. Mayer and Samuel Goldwyn, Will Rogers, John Barrymore, Marlene Dietrich, Charlie Chaplin, among others, raise funds and rally the community. The Games sponsors come up with the novel idea of an "Olympic Village" in which to house the athletes at a cost of two dollars per day. This saves each sponsoring nation an immense amount of money. In response, many governments reverse policy and agree to send teams.

Yet, President Herbert Hoover opposes holding the Olympics. He states, "The Olympics are the wrong thing at this time." [149] Traditionally, the host nation's head of state opens the Games. Hoover refuses to attend. His opposition, however, fails to discourage MacArthur and Henry. The Army continues its preparations even without President Hoover's full support and probably without his full knowledge.

One week before the Olympics begin, Lt. Col. L.G. Scott, manager of the Olympic Equestrian Team, submits to Major General Henry the official Olympic entries for the *Dressage* Competition, the Three-Day *Militaire* a.k.a. *Concours Complet d'Équitation* competition and for the *Prix des Nations* Jumping competition.

Initially, Lt. Col. Scott lists Chamberlin as a primary rider for the *Dressage* competition as well as for the other two Olympic disciplines. Ultimately, Scott lists him, however, as an "alternate" for the *Dressage* team.

For the *Dressage* event:

Rider	*First Horse*	*Alternate*
Captain H.K. Tuttle	Olympic	SI Murray
Captain L.L. Kitts	American Lady	SI Murray
Captain A.C. Moore	Waterless Pat	Troubles
Alternate		
Major H.D. Chamberlin		

For the Three-Day a.k.a. *Concours Complet d'Équitation a.k.a. Militaire*:

Rider	*First Horse*	*Alternate*
Major H.D. Chamberlin	Pleasant Smiles	Frilles
Captain E.Y. Argo	Honolulu Tomboy	Directrix
Lt. E.F. Thomson	Jenny Camp	Frilles
Alternates		
Captain J.T. Cole		
Lt. L.J. Stewart		

For the *Prix des Nations*:

Rider	*First Horse*	*Alternate*
Major H.D. Chamberlin	Tan Bark	Show Girl
Captain W.B Bradford	Joe Aleshire	Show Girl
Lt. J.W. Wofford	Babe Wartham	Show Girl

149 See *Official Report of the International Olympic Committee Xth Olympiad.*

Alternates

Lt. C.W. Raguse

Lt. A.A. Frierson

Major General Henry submits the list to the Olympic Committee. Now, no changes may take place.

1932

THE XTH OLYMPIAD AT LOS ANGELES

"My treasures do not clink together or glitter.
They gleam in the sun and neigh in the night."
—Arabian proverb

Opening Day: July 30, 1932. In the Great Stadium: 105,000 people fill every seat. The Vice-president of the United States, Charles Curtis, opens the Games. All 105,000 people stand as a 1,200-member chorus sings and 250 members of the Olympic band play the Star-Spangled Banner. The Olympic flag raises; the Olympic torch lights. The procession of nations begins. Starting with the team from Greece, the athletes of each nation march into the Great Stadium.

The 105,000 stadium seats and the seats of the other Games' locations remain filled almost every day. Somehow, during the depths of the Great Depression, people scrape together the $1 to $3 per day to attend. Attendance breaks all previous Olympic records. (In the end, the 1932 Olympics achieves a rare feat: it becomes the first Olympic Games to turn a profit—a feat not equaled until the 1984 Olympics—again at Los Angeles.)

Wednesday, August 10th, 1932. At the Riviera Country Club: The Games' Equestrian events begin on the Club's polo field. Approximately 25,000 spectators attend each day. First up: The Individual Dressage competition.

The 1932 games require much more difficult movements than those required in previous games. The new movements of *piaffer* and *passage,* for example, create a much higher standard of competition.

Commandant Lesage of France, riding *Taine,* presents a beautiful performance. He wins the Individual Gold Medal. Commandant Marion, also of France wins the Individual Silver Medal. Captain Tuttle of the USA, riding *Olympic,* wins the Individual Bronze Medal after the judges eliminate the Swedish rider Bertil Sandstrom for "clucking" to inspire his horse to greater effort.

Captain Tuttle's Individual Bronze Medal win remains an historic accomplishment in American equitation given that *dressage* remains virtually unknown in the USA at this time. Making that win even more significant is the fact that, like Étienne Beudant, Tuttle is self-taught. Tuttle teaches himself and his horse *Olympic* all the required movements in *one year* with *no formal dressage trainer to guide him.* Chamberlin offers benefit of his own Saumur dressage experience, but Tuttle's accomplishment against the Europeans remains a singular one. Tuttle outscores three Swedish and one French rider each of whom enjoys a multitude of trainers and centuries of experience behind him.

Thursday, August 11th, 1932. At Riviera Country Club: The Three-Day Event a.k.a. *Concours Complet d'Équitation* Training Test takes place.

The teams staff up as follows:

Holland

Lieutenant Charles F. P. de Mortanges, on *Marcroix.*
Lieutenant Jonkheer A. Van Lennop, on *Henk.*
Lieutenant Karel J. Schummelketel, on *Duiveltie.*

Sweden

Captain Ernst Hallberg, on *Marokan.*
Lieutenant Clarence von Rosen, Jr., on *Sunnyside Maid.*
Lieutenant Arne Francke, on *Fridolin.*

Japan

Lieutenant-Colonel Shunzo Kido, on *Kyu Gun.*
Captain Taro Hara, on *Sonshin.*
Captain Morishige Yamamoto, on *Kinge.*

Mexico

Captain Armando Barriguete, on *Monza.*
Captain Jose P. Allende, on *El Torero.*

United States

Major Harry D. Chamberlin, on *Pleasant Smiles* (Thoroughbred, G, 16.1, 1100, 8 yrs.)
Captain Edwin Y. Argo, on *Honolulu Tom Boy* (Thoroughbred, M, 15.2½ ,1050, 6 yrs.)

Lieutenant Earl T. Thomson, on *Jenny Camp* (½ Thoroughbred, M, 16, 1000, 6 yrs.)

With a FEI rules change, the *dressage* or "Training Test" for the Three-Day event becomes more crucial. The *FEI* increases the test's relative importance by an additional 100 points. The committee subtracts those 100 points from the Endurance Test. This transfer of weight makes the rider's *dressage* performance count for 20% of a rider's final Three-Day score. The *FEI* makes *dressage* much more important than in previous years. Because of this rules change, the concepts that Chamberlin learns through the *Saumur Notes* and his time at Saumur together with his study of the works of François Baucher and General L'Hotte as well as the concepts of James Fillis serve him well.

A seriously poor performance in this test denies a rider any hope of a medal for the Three-Day. Failure to achieve at least a score of 150 disqualifies a rider from continuing in the remaining two tests. Fourteen riders compete from Holland, Sweden, Mexico, The United States and Japan. The number of riders may seem slight, but the competition from Holland and Sweden proves strong. Those two countries dominate the Three-Day in the Olympics of 1912, 1920, 1924 and 1928. They remain the favorites in 1932. In all of previous Olympic history, only Holland and Sweden have won the Individual and the Team Gold Medals in the Three-Day Event.

Lt. Thomson rides first on *Jenny Camp*. His riding remains "easy and graceful." [150] His transitions prove a bit flawed. He places 6th.

The second American to ride: Captain Argo on *Honolulu Tomboy*. Argo's performance: "almost perfect." [151] He places second.

Now, Chamberlin rides the Training Test for the American team. Chamberlin's horse *Pleasant Smiles* races on the tack at Havana, Cuba until age six—only two years before this competition. A "hot as they come" Thoroughbred, *Pleasant Smiles* races four years on the track and remains sound. *Dressage* on such a horse requires a rider of exceptional skill as well as a trainer of keen insight and great patience. Chamberlin both rides and trains this horse. The performance of the horse reflects the skills of the rider and trainer. Writes one commentator: "There is no question as to Chamberlin's deserving first place." [152]

---

150 See comments of Captain Good in Robert D. Thompson, *U. S. Army Olympic Equestrian Competitions 1912-1948*, Schiffer Military History, 2008.

151 Ibid.

152 Ibid.

The results of the Three-Day Event *Dressage* a.k.a. "Training Test:"

Major H.D. Chamberlin	(USA)	1st
Captain E. Argo	(USA)	2nd
Lt. de Mortanges	(Holland)	3rd
Lt. von Rosen	(Sweden)	4th
Lt. Francke	(Sweden)	5th
Lt. Thomson	(USA)	6th
Captain Hallberg	(Sweden)	7th
Lt. van Lennop	(Holland)	8th
Lt. Schummelketel	(Holland)	9th
Captain Yamamoto	(Japan)	10th
Captain Nara	(Japan)	11th
Lt. Kido	(Japan)	12th
Captain Allende	(Mexico)	13th
Captain Barriguete	(Mexico)	14th

So, the United States, through Major Chamberlin, wins the first phase of the Three-Day event. His French *dressage* experience shows. Now, on to the Endurance Test.

Friday, August 12th, 1932. The Three-Day Endurance Test begins starting at the Riviera Country Club and progressing through the foot hills of the Pacific Palisades.

The course stretches 22½ miles. The terrain is hilly, the ground hard. Cracks and ridges mar the ground and predominate along the entire course. Horse and rider must complete the entire course in less than 2 hours, 5 minutes and 6 seconds. The course designer intends to test the courage, skill, and endurance of mount and rider. He succeeds. The course breaks down into five phases:

Phase 1. Four-and-one-half miles of roads and paths on a winding trail that leads into a canyon in the Pacific Palisades foot hills. The hills and gullies prove difficult. The rider must travel at least at a speed of nine miles per hour.

Phase 2. Two-and-one-half miles of steeplechase presenting 15 obstacles including brush, ditches, water jumps. The course designer fashions each obstacle according to the National Steeplechase and Hunt Association specifications. The horse and rider must negotiate this course at a speed of no less than 22½ miles per hour.

Phase 3. Nine-and-one-half miles of road and track. City streets make up some of the roads that lead into the high mesa area of Los Angeles. Horse and rider must travel at no less than a speed of nine miles per hour.

Phase 4. Five miles of trail presenting 34 obstacles: brush, post and rail fences, ditches, in-and-out across a road, stone fences, concrete culverts, logs, a water trough, bales of hay, a chicken coop, bank jumps, and the like. The fences remain solid and imposing. The horse and rider must travel at least 17 miles per hour to avoid a time penalty.

Phase 5. One-and one-half miles at the gallop over a flat road. Horse and rider must complete the gallop in six minutes or less.

The day before the Endurance Test, Lt. Thomson of the USA walks the course *two* times to examine its challenges. His two walks pay off.

In First Place: Thomson and his mount, *Jenny Camp,* travel the entire course—approximately forty jumps—without a single penalty. *Jenny Camp* and Thomson travel at such a speed that the judges award them a six-point bonus for their steeplechase performance.

In Second Place: Lt. de Mortanges and *Marcroix,* his great Eventing horse, represent Holland. The judges assess a 70-point penalty against the pair in the first phase of the test but award a 6-point bonus for the cross-country phase and another 6-point bonus for the steeplechase phase.

In Third Place: Lt. von Rosen of Sweden. The judges charge a 50-point penalty against them in the steeplechase and a 12½-point time penalty for the cross-country phase.

In Fourth Place: Capt. Hallberg of Sweden.

In Fifth place: Major H.D. Chamberlin. Chamberlin and *Pleasant Smiles* achieve a perfect, no fault performance on the steeplechase phase. On the cross-country course, however, *Pleasant Smiles* plows through jump number 32. Both *Pleasant Smiles* and Chamberlin fall. This fall unseats Chamberlin and Pleasant Smiles roles over. Chamberlin suffers a badly wrenched shoulder. *Pleasant Smiles* cuts a foreleg and possibly pulls a tendon. The horse rises off of his back and onto his feet. Chamberlin rises from the ground. He remounts. They continue on and complete the test within the required time.

In Sixth Place: Lt. Schummelketel of Holland.

In Seventh Place: Capt. Yamamoto of Japan.

In Eighth Place: Captain Argo of the USA and his horse *Honolulu Tomboy offer* a spectacular performance. Prior to the games, Argo slips and falls. He dislocates his shoulder. Doctors tape him up and strap his shoulder tightly into his side to keep it in place. Argo clears the steeplechase obstacle until he comes to the water jump. Here, his shoulder pops out. Somehow, he and

Honolulu Tomboy surmount the obstacle and push on. In excruciating pain, Argo continues. He radically changes his seat to cope with the pain of his shoulder. In this compromised position, he rides approximately 20 miles suffering in pain. He negotiates approximately 40 jumps with his shoulder dislocated. He and his horse complete the course without time penalty. They place eighth.

Eliminated: Capt. Kido of Japan. He gallops 20 miles and negotiates 40 fences through multiple phases...only to be eliminated of jump number 34...the chicken coop...the last jump of the Endurance phase!

Eliminated: Capt. Nara of Japan. The horse refuses three times on steeplechase jump number 12.

Eliminated: Capt. Allende of Mexico. He fails to keep the course between obstacle number 12 and 13.

Eliminated: Lt. Francke of Sweden. The judges eliminate him three jumps from the finish of the cross-country phase!

Only two teams finish the Endurance Test with three riders still in the competition: The United States and Holland.

The Endurance Test results for the Individual medal:

Lt. Thomson	(USA)	1st
Lt. de Mortanges	(Holland)	2nd
Count von Rosen	(Sweden)	3rd

The Endurance Test Results for the Team medal:

The United States	1st with 3236 points
Holland	2nd with 3144.5 points

Team Standing after Training Test and Endurance Test:

The Unites States	1st with 4259.33 points
Holland	2nd with 4001.33 points

Individual Standing after the Training Test and the Endurance Test:

Lt. Thomson on Jenny Camp	1st with 1571 points
Lt. de Mortanges on Marcroix	2nd with 1553 points
Lt. von Rosen on Sunnyside Maid	3rd with 1552.1 points

Thus far, a United States Team member wins first place in the Training Test and first in the Endurance Test. Thirteen riders start the endurance phase. The judges eliminate two in the steeplechase course and two in the cross-country phase. Three riders get through the steeplechase and cross-country courses free from faults at fences (Schummelketel, of Holland; Thomson, of the U. S., and Yamamoto, of Japan). The judges award Lieutenant Mortanges, of Holland, a bonus on both the steeplechase and cross-country phases, six each, for a total of twelve—the only rider they so award.

The finish of the endurance phase presents a scene of intense activity, as each horse and rider draw up after the long, twenty-two-mile ride. Only two teams finish with three riders up—Holland and the United States. Both teams finish with all three horses in good shape.

By far, *Jenny Camp*—the US Army Remount Service bred descendant of the first Triple Crown Winner and Army Stallion Gordon Russell—remains the most alert, the most unconcerned, the least fatigued, the boldest, and the most courageous horse. Alert, keen and wide awake, she remains a picture of perfect health and condition as she nibbles on hay a few minutes after she completes the course.

And another champion: the courageous, big hearted, extremely fit thoroughbred *Pleasant Smiles* carries on and finishes after the horrendous fall he and his rider, Major Chamberlin, take toward the end of the cross-country phase. With a cut foreleg, the horse continues on the next day.

Saturday, August 13th, 1932. In the Great Stadium: The Three-Day *Militaire* Jumping Test and then, the presentation of the winners of the Individual *Dressage* Test of August 10th.

The Jumping Test: The riders and horses now face the final test of the Three-Day. They perform this test in the Great Stadium in front of a huge crowd of spectators. They face twelve jumps. The fences rise between three feet seven inches and three feet nine inches. Each horse and rider must travel the course at a gallop of 14 miles per hour to avoid a time penalty.

Captain Argo, with dislocated shoulder, rides *Honolulu Tomboy* to a stunning performance. Horse and rider commit not one fault but incur a time penalty of 0.75! Lt. Tompson leads the great de Mortanges and the horse *Marcroix* of Holland by 17.2 points going into the Jumping Test. Jenny Camp suffers one knock down and puts a foot into the water at obstacles 4 and 8. De Mortanges and *Marcroix,* however, get through the course with one knock down and only one foot in the water. This difference in performance costs Lt. Tompson the Individual Gold medal and Tompson ties for seventh place along with Major Chamberlin.

So, in the Three-Day Event Jumping Test, Captain E. Argo (USA) places first. With Argo's performance, a United States Olympic Equestrian

Team member places first in each of the three *Concours Complet d'Équitation* Tests. The United States wins the Gold Team medal for the entire event. Lt. Thomson wins the Silver Individual medal. Major Chamberlin comes in fourth overall. Holland's de Mortanges on Marcroix wins the Individual Gold medal. Holland wins the Team Silver. The Olympic Committee awards no Bronze Team medals since Mexico, Sweden and Japan failed to place.

Only three points separate Thomson and *Jenny Camp's* Silver from de Mortanges and *Marcroix*'s Gold. With their 1932 Individual Gold, de Mortanges and *Marcroix* equal their performance of 1928. Winning Individual Gold back to back over two Olympics puts them in a unique category. To this day, their feat remains unequaled. During his career, de Mortanges wins four Gold and one Silver—all in the Three-Day.

Saturday, August 13, 1932. *The Presentation of Medals for the Individual Dressage Competition:* The Olympic Committee presents medals to the Dressage Test winners: Individual Gold to Lesage of France riding *Taine*; Individual Silver to Marion of France riding *Limon*; Individual Bronze to Tuttle of the United States riding *Olympic*. Team Gold goes to France; Team Silver to Sweden; Team Bronze to The United States. The military band plays the national anthem of France and the flag of France rises. The Olympic Committee will award the Three-Day medals on the afternoon of August 14 after the *Prix des Nations*.

Sunday, August 14th, 1932. After the *Prix des Nations* competition that we describe in Chapter 1 concludes, The Olympic Committee awards the Three-Day Medals. As the Committee awards the Team Gold Medals the national anthem of the United States plays and almost the entire audience of 105,000 spectators rise to their feet.

SCENES FROM THE THREE-DAY EVENT

Figure 98 *Major Chamberlin loses his hat in a tumble on an earlier jump. Photo courtesy of Ms. Lydia Moore.*

Figure 99 *A long trudge up the hill in the cross country phase of the Three Day Event. Photo courtesy of the US Olympic Committee.*

Figure 100 *The cross-country phase of the Three-Day Event proves treacherous. Photo courtesy of the US Olympic Committee.*

Figure 101 *Hallberg of Sweden takes a spill on the cross-country course. Photo courtesy of the US Olympic Committee.*

Figure 102 *The USA's Captain Argo, with his shoulder dislocated, clears the jump that foiled Hallberg of Sweden. Photo courtesy of the US Olympic Committee.*

Figure 103 *The USA's Lt. Thomson, on Jenny Camp, wins the Individual Silver Medal overall and achieves the best score on the cross-country phase. Photo courtesy of the US Olympic Committee.*

Figure 104 *Major Chamberlin and Pleasant Smiles clear a jump in the Stadium Jumping phase of the Three-Day Event. Captain Argo achieves the best Stadium Jumping score to clinch the Team Gold Medal for the United States. Photo courtesy of the US Olympic Committee*

Figure 105 *Captain Argo, Major Chamberlin, Lt. Thomson receive the Team Gold Medal for the Three-Day Event. The first time in Olympic history that a team other than one from Holland or Sweden wins this event. Chamberlin scores best in dressage, Thomson scores best cross-country, and Argo scores best in the stadium jumping phase to secure the win. Photo courtesy of the US Olympic Committee.*

Figure 106 *Sweden's Lt. von Rosen on Empire takes Bronze, the USA's Major Chamberlin on Show Girl takes Silver, the Empire of Japan's Lt. Nishi on Uranus takes Gold in the Prix des Nations of 1932. Photo courtesy of the US Olympic Committee.*

A few days after the Olympic Games conclude, the US Army Equestrian Team hosts a dinner in honor of Baron Lt. Nishi. The American officers pool their funds to purchase a chrome plated M-1911 semi-automatic pistol that, on their behalf, Major Chamberlin presents to Nishi. Nishi returns to Japan and during the World War II battle on Iwo Gima, he commits ritual suicide rather than surrender. Many years later, this pistol will take on a prominent place in the Clint Eastwood film *Letters from Iwo Gima.*

The *Prix des Nations* course and the Three-Day Event in the 1932 Olympics prove so difficult that no team medals can be awarded for the Prix des Nations and no bronze Team medal can be awarded in the Three-Day Event. This result leads Major General Henry, in his capacity as President of the FEI, to recommend to the International Olympic Committee the following:

> "The fact that no team completed the course in this latter event, and only two teams out of five starting completed the course in *Concours Complet d'Equitation,* indicates that the International Equestrian Federation rule permitting each nation four entrants—the scores of the highest three to count for team competition—should be followed, rather than Section X, of the International Olympic Committee." [153]

153 "Report of Major General Guy V. Henry, Jr. President of the FEI 1932." *Official Report of the International Olympic Committee Xth Olympiad.*

For all future Olympics, The International Olympic Committee changes the rules. Henry's recommendations apply to this day.

Major Chamberlin returns to Fort Riley, but only for a short while to pack for Washington, DC and the Army War College. His time with the Army Horse Show Team ends. With a Team Gold medal for the Three-Day "*Concours Complet d'Équitation*" and with the Individual Silver medal for the *Prix des Nations,* Major Harry D. Chamberlin ends his international riding career.

Even after leaving the Army Horse Show Team, Chamberlin continues his work with horses. In time, he develops equestrian training and riding concepts that endure to this day as his most lasting contribution to horsemanship. As a soldier, he undertakes other horse related assignments far more important to his country than any Olympic effort.

The United States Army plans bigger things for Major Chamberlin. At the Army's elite "post graduate school" for its top officers, Chamberlin will work through matters of high policy. The school resides at Fort McNair, Washington, DC In late August of 1932, Major and Mrs. Chamberlin depart Fort Riley, Kansas for Fort McNair and for a major change in their lives.

Chapter 24

Personal Change and Professional Challenge August 1932–April 1936

To the Army War College August 1932–July 1, 1933

"While Leavenworth had been the stepping-stone to higher staff duty, the elite War College existed to prepare its students for future high command and staff."

—Carlo D'Estes, *Patton, A Genius for War*[154]

In 1932, The Army War College defines its mission: to train elite officers to conduct the Army's field operations at the highest echelons; to prepare officers for War Department General Staff duties; to train officers for joint operations by the Army and the Navy; to instruct officers in the strategy, tactics and logistics of large operations in past wars with special reference to the world war.

By 1932, Chief of Staff, General Douglas MacArthur transforms the school from a leisurely conclave of soon to retire Colonels to an intellectually rigorous curriculum that prepares officers, as best as a classroom might, for high command in the Army. The pressure breaks many, drives some to suicide, damages marriages, and weeds out those mentally unsuited for the highest commands in the army.

Chamberlin follows Patton to the College by one year and precedes Omar Bradley by one year. The students write papers and discuss their

---

154 See Carlo D'Estes, *Patton: Genius For War,* Harper Perennial, 1995.

findings. These papers span a host of topics of interest and importance to the professional soldier:

> "Procurement of Personnel by voluntary enlistment and under "Selective Service;" "G-2 Activities in Theater of Operations;" "Concentration of Enemy Man Power Upon the North American Continent;" "Joint and Army Strategic War Plans;" "Joint Operations-Russo-Japanese War, 1904-5;" "Operations on Interior Lines;" "Basic Tactical Considerations Affecting Our Cavalry Division Organization;" "War Plans–Red Coalition, Branch and Corps Area Plans." Issues of mechanization for the cavalry, enhanced firepower, and logistical support also provide topics for study. Technical issues revolving around the use of motor vehicles for tactical reconnaissance and the use of large trucks to transport horses to areas of terrain unsuitable for motorized transport remain hotly debated. Will the horse surrender to motorized transport? Should it? How might a motorized logistics train support horse cavalry unit? [155]

From the standpoint of *individual mobility* nothing else will equal a man on a horse (a point made many years later by General Hamilton H. Howze, the founding father of the airmobile concept that took cavalrymen to the air in helicopters in the 1960s). From the standpoint *of unit mobility*, however, motorized transport offers great advantages. Officers at the Army War College, and throughout the military considered some challenging questions during this time period in the Army's development.

Might some combination of horse and motor offer the optimal solution to enhance both unit and individual mobility? What about off-road reconnaissance under cover of darkness—does a horse the most effective solution or perhaps a scout car? Or is a combination of both the answer? How might more effective radios be best integrated into cavalry units to improve communications? How much firepower should be sacrificed to achieve mobility? How much mobility must be sacrificed to enhance firepower? What balance between the two proves optimal? Will pack horses carrying machine guns and mortars insure that superior mobility and firepower shall be retained? Should horse cavalry and mechanized cavalry exist in the same organization? Should the two be joined or be separated? What is the impact of the availability of water and fuel on the mobility and the range of horse units? Of mechanized units?

155 See https://www.armywarcollege.edu/overview.cfm.

As these questions are answered, a key point to remember: Chamberlin serves as a professional soldier. Olympic competition, horse shows, polo, fox hunts, the romance of the cavalry and its equestrian rituals—the traditions of the old army—all remain secondary to a professional officer's main purpose: to manage and to fight wars.

In so doing, the professional must understand logistics and supply, battle readiness and weaponry. In the 1930s, horses and riding make up a large but not an exclusive part of a cavalry officer's knowledge base. His primary responsibility in peace remains to train troopers to fight in war. Horses remain a mode of transport to move those troopers into position to engage an enemy. These somewhat sterile topics of procurement, logistics, war planning and management make up the daily issues that a senior officer must consider and confront.

Just as at Leavenworth's Command and General Staff School, the War College imposes intense pressures on each student. Such is the work of an Army staff officer, especially, an officer that the 1930s Army grooms for higher command responsibilities. On July 1, 1933, Chamberlin graduates from the Army War College but the long hours and stress take a toll on his personal life.

DIVORCE

July 28, 1933

A little over three weeks after he graduates from the Army War College, Chamberlin and Sally divorce. Sally Chamberlin seems to be a vivacious, articulate woman and obviously an expert horsewoman. She routinely goes out of her way to help a friend in need. For example, in September of 1925, the cavalry selects Lucien Truscott to attend the Troop Officer's Course at the Cavalry School. Family accommodations remain almost impossible to find at Fort Riley. The Chamberlins reside at Fort Riley at the time.

Mrs. Truscott mentions their housing predicament to Sally. Without even being asked, Sally locates an apartment and has the place ready—furniture and all—for the Truscott's to move in. According to General Truscott, Sally Garlington Chamberlin was "...known as Sally to almost everyone in the cavalry, was truly a lovely woman in every way that a woman can be. She was tall, graceful, blond, lovely looking, athletic, a wonderful horsewoman, and she was loved and respected by all who knew her."

Figure 107 *Chamberlin in the late 1920s early 1930s.*
Photo courtesy of Ms. Lydia Moore.

On July 28, 1933, however, the Nevada State Journal announces the disposition of a court case filed at Reno, Nevada: *Sally G. Chamberlin v. Harry D. Chamberlin.* Sally and Harry Chamberlin's divorce case. Grounds in Nevada remain the most liberal in the USA: incompatibility satisfies the statute. The state requires that only one litigant reside in Nevada for six weeks. Since Sally's name appears first on the case "style" as lawyers call it, Sally files the action. The divorce proceeds by agreement "uncontested."

In a world where Secretary of War Stimson refuses to invite divorced individuals into his home, one does not divorce lightly. Any dishonorable conduct related to a divorce would destroy an officer's career, especially given the family relationships that Sally Garlington Chamberlin might call upon. Keep in mind the interrelationships in the close-knit society that makes up the upper echelons of the US Army in the first 50 years of the twentieth-century.

Before World War I, a certain Captain George C. Marshall serves as an aide to General Franklin Bell, Sally's uncle. Marshall owes Bell a debt of gratitude for sponsoring and forwarding Marshall's career. By the same measure, in World War II, Marshall forwards Harry Chamberlin's career. General Marshall respects Harry Chamberlin. Even before the war, Marshall laments to Lt. General Krueger that he does not have more officers like Chamberlin. It seems that military society accepts the Chamberlin divorce. And definitely, no evidence exists of dishonor in Harry Chamberlin's actions.

Harry and Sally remain married for 21 years. They have no children. The reasons for the divorce? One may speculate but never know for certain. The fact that after 21 years, the marriage produces no children leads one to speculate that this causes the break up. Infertility might be a factor. In addition, the pressures of the Army War College damage many marriages and destroy some.

After the divorce in 1933, Sally keeps the Chamberlin name. Until she passes away in 1949, officers in the highest reaches of the Army still refer to Sally as "Mrs. Chamberlin." After the divorce, Sally Garlington Chamberlin becomes a stenographer and secretary. First, she works in the Department of Agriculture; then she tries for a position with the Army Remount Service but the position is filled.

In June 1940, at the behest of Major Harry Leonard, she writes General George Marshall a letter requesting employment. At first, Marshall can offer no position since the Secretary of War freezes all hiring. She perseveres. Ultimately, just before Pearl Harbor, she becomes General Marshall's personal secretary. Her hand written and typed letters to, and on behalf of, General and Mrs. Marshall communicate a compelling enthusiasm and exuberance.

In time, it seems as if she were a member of the Marshall family. She works for Army Chief of Staff, General Marshall as his secretary throughout World War II. When Marshall becomes Secretary of State, Sally follows him to the State Department in the same capacity. After an illness of several months, Sally dies on December 4, 1949 of Addison's disease in Washington, DC. General Marshal arranges a grave for her at Arlington National Cemetery next to her father, General Ernest Garlington and her mother Ann Buford Garlington. The tombstone shows her full name as Sally Garlington Chamberlin.

REMARRIAGE

August 13, 1933

Helen Bradman turns 21 on April 25, 1933. Harry Chamberlin turns 46 in May of the same year. Family recollections suggest that the two meet at a horse show outside Washington, DC A *Chicago Tribune* article states that Helen shares Harry's enthusiasm for horses. On August 13, 1933, Harry and Helen marry. On September 9, 1933, *The Washington Post,* announces that: "Cards have been received announcing the marriage of Miss Helen Bradman to Maj. Harry D. Chamberlin, USA" Helen is the daughter of Marine Corps Brigadier General and Mrs. Frederick Bradman. Brigadier General Bradman commands the Marine base at Quantico.

Figure 108 *Helen Bradman Chamberlin. Photo courtesy of Ms. Tracey Reese Brown.*

Fort Sheridan, Illinois
September 1933–April 1936
"Das Paradies der Erde liegt auf den Rucken der Pferda."
("Paradise on earth is on the backs of horses.")

Immediately after their marriage, Harry and the new Mrs. Chamberlin depart for duty at Fort Sheridan, a cavalry post on Lake Michigan north of Chicago, Illinois. At Fort Sheridan, Major Chamberlin commands the 1st Squadron of the 14th Cavalry. Chamberlin's time at Fort Sheridan combines his favorite pleasures of horsemanship and polo with writing books and, most important of all, with starting a family. In October of 1933, Helen becomes pregnant.

Beginning in the fall of 1933 and into early 1934, Chamberlin writes his first book *Riding and Schooling Horses.* He publishes the book in 1934. The book aims for the general reader and clearly states Chamberlin's basic theories of riding in an easy to follow style. A synopsis of *Riding and Schooling Horses* and of Chamberlin's other writings during this period follows in the next chapter.

Immediately upon assuming command of the 14th Cavalry's First Squadron, Chamberlin participates in horse shows and enjoys the company of horse people in and around Chicago. A month after assuming his command at Fort Sheridan, for example, Chamberlin judges a horse show for the Onwentsia Hunt Club in Milburn. Amazingly, President Roosevelt's decision to cut military pay by 15% does not seem to infringe on Chamberlin's equestrian activities and his loyalty to the Army.

But horses definitely take second place behind Helen and then slip a bit further behind on July 10, 1934 when Helen gives birth to a girl at Fort Sheridan, Illinois. They name their child Lydia. A few months later, the Army also bestows new status upon Chamberlin: On November 1, 1934, the Army promotes him to the rank of Lt. Colonel of Cavalry.

During Chamberlin's time at Fort Sheridan, he joins a polo team. As Captain of the "Fort Sheridan Four," Chamberlin and the Fort Sheridan team plays polo against the Metropolitan League of Chicago and the Chicago Riding Club. The Fort Sheridan team also plays against the Chicago Black Horse Troop. They play against the Oak Brook team at the Oak Brook Polo Club in the western suburbs of Chicago. They play polo at Olympia Fields in the far south suburbs of Chicago as well.

During this timeframe, Chamberlin rides with Chicago's elite: The McCormick's of the *Chicago Daily Tribune,* Paul Butler of Butler Aviation, Henry Crown of the future corporation called General Dynamics. Shortly after arriving at Fort Sheridan in 1933, Chamberlin meets multi-millionaire John Cudahy, an accomplished horseman and electronics manufacturer who lives near Milwaukee, Wisconsin. Chamberlin spends eight months commuting to Wisconsin to coordinate the efforts of the Civilian Conservation Corps, a

Depression-era civilian program to help the unemployed by building public works in national parks and other places. Cudahy and Chamberlin become best friends. In fact, Cudahy writes the introduction to Chamberlin's first book.

In addition to the Cudahy friendship, Chamberlin becomes friends with the elite of Chicago's horse-oriented society: The McCormick's of *The Chicago Tribune*, the Butlers of Butler Aviation and the Oak Brook Polo Club, the Crown family of what will become General Dynamics Corporation, the Walgreen family of the drug store chain of the same name, and the Wrigley family that owns the chewing gum company and the famous Wrigley building on Chicago's Magnificent Mile. Chamberlin social graces combined with his equestrian expertise attracts many admirers.

For instance, Mrs. McCormick commissions an oil painting that she proudly displays in her drawing room: Chamberlin taking her prized jumper over an obstacle. These Midwest names add to an already long list of luminaries that Chamberlin's winning personality and personal charm attract: on the East Coast, the Harrimans, Morgans, and Cromwells; on the West Coast, Douglas Fairbanks, Jr. and Mary Pickford, and a host of other Hollywood personalities as well as journalists and commentators such as Will Rogers. Among all, the initial common interest remains horses; the bond that endures springs from Chamberlin's wit, humor, and social grace not to mention his riding skills.

On December 4, 1934, Chamberlin competes on his horse High Hat in a show at Chicago's International Amphitheater before an audience of 25,000 spectators. He wins the Military Charger competition. Two days later, Chamberlin competes at the show again and wins going over jumps 4'-6" high on a horse named Johnny Walker. Throughout this period, The *Chicago Daily Tribune* features him often in articles regarding horse shows in the Chicago area. The September 25, 1935 edition of the *Chicago Daily Tribune,* for example, calls him "the world's best rider" in a full-page spread showing him taking a jump at a Fort Sheridan horse show.

During this period, Chamberlin also leads an endurance march of his 1st Squadron of the 14th Cavalry. They ride their horses from Fort Sheridan on the shore of Lake Michigan to Rock Island, Illinois on the shore of the Mississippi River. Some writers suggest that the horse cavalry's role in the Bonus March of 1932, where the government used the Army to break up a protest of World War I veterans concerning a bonus not due until 1945, turns the people of the United States against the cavalry, equating them to Russian Cossacks. If the public response along the route of Chamberlin's march from

Fort Sheridan to Rock Island, Illinois represents the public's perceptions and mood regarding the Cavalry, then nothing could be further from the truth.

As word spreads by telephone and by word of mouth that: "the cavalry is coming," people line the sides of US Rt. 30 to cheer them on. Through small towns like Rochelle and Sycamore, Illinois, the 1st Squadron, 14th Cavalry rides one way 182 miles to Rock Island and then back another 182 miles to Fort Sheridan. Even people from Dixon, Illinois, the home town of Ronald Reagan, travel several miles just to stand on the side of the road to cheer the 14th Cavalry as they ride past. As is typical, Lt. Col. Chamberlin reflects on the effects of asphalt and concrete roads on horseshoes and on the legs of his outfit's mounts. In the following chapter, we will focus on Chamberlin's writings and other activities during his tour of duty at Fort Sheridan.

Chapter 25

Articles for *The Cavalry Journal*, *Riding and Schooling Horses*, Contributions to a New Saddle Design and Other Writings 1933-1936

"...the perfect handbook to horsemanship amply illustrated and scrupulously simple in language."
—*The Washington Post* review of *Riding and Schooling Horses* [156]

"If you read only one book on riding, then it should be *Riding and Schooling Horses*."
—Captain Paul Kendall,
Instructor of Horsemanship,
The Cavalry School, Fort Riley [157]

Once Chamberlin graduates from the Army War College and rebuilds his personal life, he takes time to reflect and to write. During the years 1933 through 1936, Chamberlin contributes to the Army's new horsemanship manual. He writes a number of articles on the "seat." He helps design a new saddle for cavalry officers. He writes a book on forward riding entitled *Riding and Schooling Horses*. During this period, he also begins a second book to be published in 1937.

156 See *Washington Post* review 1935.
157 See Captain Paul Kendall, "Horseman's Primer", *Horse and Horseman Magazine*, November 1938.

In 1933 and for several years thereafter, as a member of the Cavalry Board, he contributes to Fort Riley's revisions of the manual *Horsemanship and Horsemastership.* The manual reflects a great deal of Chamberlin's thinking regarding "the Military Seat" as well as training horses. Not only does *"H and H"* become the US Cavalry's "bible," it achieves worldwide respect as a treatise on riding and training horses.

In 1934, Chamberlin writes an article for the *Cavalry Journal* entitled: *"The Modern Seat...A Discussion of the Differences between the Seats of Various Countries."* He describes the differences between the seats of various countries and then describes the seat that he teaches to the US Army Horse Show Team of 1932, in essence "The Chamberlin Seat."

Chamberlin first distinguishes the seat that he teaches from the riding concepts that other nations apply such as Germany, Sweden, Italy, and France. He compares and contrasts the French school with the Italian school. He describes the early concepts taught at Fort Riley. He then describes the Swedish and German methods. He then goes on to describe the seat that he developed through his own research and study.

In brief summary:

The heels forced well down;

The feet turned out naturally, about 45 degrees from the horse's side;

The calf clings lightly to the horse's side;

The knees remain as low as the stirrups permit and remain in position by slight pressure;

The thighs remain flat against the saddle;

The fleshy part of the buttocks should not be pushed under the rider by convexing the loin to the rear but should be kept well to the rear

The backbone is held in a normal erect position with the loin slightly hollowed out;

The pelvis bones rest lightly on the saddle;

The upper part of the body is inclined forward *from the hip joints*;

The length of the stirrup strap depends on the type of riding;

The chest and head should be kept raised;

"Normally the rider, due to his relaxed knee and forward inclination of the body, has his weight resting on the pelvis bone, the thigh, the knee, and the heel...

The reader will find Chamberlin's complete article in this biography's companion volume, *The Chamberlin Reader.*

CHAMBERLIN AND SADDLE DESIGN

In 1934 and 1935, Chamberlin argues that the American Cavalry's officer's saddles remain too short to ride properly. The Army needs a saddle that supports the Army's newly emerging "Military Seat," which is based largely on Chamberlin's concepts. In response, and to solve other problems well recognized by the cavalry, Col. Albert Phillips develops a preliminary design for a new "Officer's Field Saddle" to take the place of the M-1917 model, a French design. Chamberlin tests and contributes ideas to the new saddle. A copy of Chamberlin's suggestions to Col. Phillips, the reader will find in *The Chamberlin Reader.*

Col. Phillips writes his observations about riding and the "forward seat" in an article about his new saddle (*The Cavalry Journal,* Mar-Apr 1935):

"It has only been for the past few years that we have really begun to appreciate the many advantages of the "forward seat." The Italians were the first to adopt the forward-seat position for the rider, it differing from the French position in that in the latter there is a tendency toward riding with the weight somewhat to the rear and to keeping the horse closely collected and flexed..."

"The 'forward seat' is both technically and scientifically correct for all types of military riding, from ordinary marching to cross-country work, and it is the most secure position for the rider and the easiest for the horse. For High School work, however, and for polo, other "seats" perhaps may be found more desirable..." [158]

---

158 See Col. Albert Phillips, "The Phillips Cross Country Saddle." *The Cavalry Journal, Mar–Apr 1935.*

The M-1917 saddle that most cavalry officers use until 1936 supports the "close and static seat" of Saumur. In addition, many officers require an additional saddle for training and for jumping due to the M-1917's design. The saddle's long side bars extend well behind the horse's 15th and 16th dorsal vertebrae to support a cantle roll and other equipment that an officer carries in the field. This feature creates at least two problems.

First: when a rider jumps in the M-1917 saddle, the extended rear side bars dig into the horse's loin. Second: the weight of the cantle roll and saddle bags that the M-1917's side bars support bears down on the horse's back beyond the 16th dorsal vertebra. This ultimately causes the horse severe back problems, especially on long marches or endurance rides.

Col. Phillips designs his saddle to solve these problems as well as to provide the larger seat that Chamberlin requests. He follows along French lines with one exception: he removes the extended rear panels and replaces them with an ingenious "shelf" that screws into the cantle. This detachable cantle "shelf" carries the items that an officer needs but keeps those items off of the horse's back. When the horse and rider jump an obstacle, no extended panels dig into the horse's loin. When in garrison, the officer unscrews the "cantle shelf" since he carries nothing while training. When "on campaign" in the field, the officer attaches the shelf to support his equipment.

Phillips asks Chamberlin to test successive iterations of the saddle. To accommodate Chamberlin's use of a stirrup leather longer than what the Italians use for ordinary riding in the field, Phillips places the saddle skirts relatively straight following the French practice. To accommodate the new Military Seat, Chamberlin, Bradford and other accomplished riders recommend that Phillips put the front edge of the stirrup loops three inches behind the front edge of the saddle. This he does.

Chamberlin also recommends that Phillips change the configuration of the saddle's seat. In his original design, Phillips follows the French configuration: He puts the deepest point of the seat in the center. Chamberlin argues that to place the deepest point of seat directly in the seat's center supports the French *"haute école"* seat as opposed to the American cavalry's new "Military Seat."

Chamberlin recommends that Phillips position the seat's deepest point one inch *forward* of the center. Chamberlin reasons that this placement, ever so slight, puts the rider closer to the horse's withers and accommodates a riding style more forward than what the French pursue. Phillips changes his design to accommodate Chamberlin's recommendations.

Phillips also concludes that the seat of all saddles, no matter what the rider's size, must measure 18½ inches in length and enjoy 19½ inches of bearing surface. He argues that a smaller size fails to distribute the rider's weight across the horse's back and thus causes back problems for the horse. He also argues that a saddle's seat must not be larger than 18½ inches and it's bearing surface must not extend longer than 20 inches. If longer, the saddle extends beyond the 15th vertebrae and then encroaches upon the horse's loins.

Phillips also advises how the rider should place the saddle properly on the horse's back. He states that many riders place their saddles too far forward and thus place them high upon the withers. This encroaches on the shoulder musculature, impedes free movement of the scapula, raises the pommel higher than the cantle, and improperly throws the rider's weight toward the cantle. In addition, to place the saddle too far forward causes "bridging" and places pressure at the withers and toward the loins, thus injuring the horse's back.

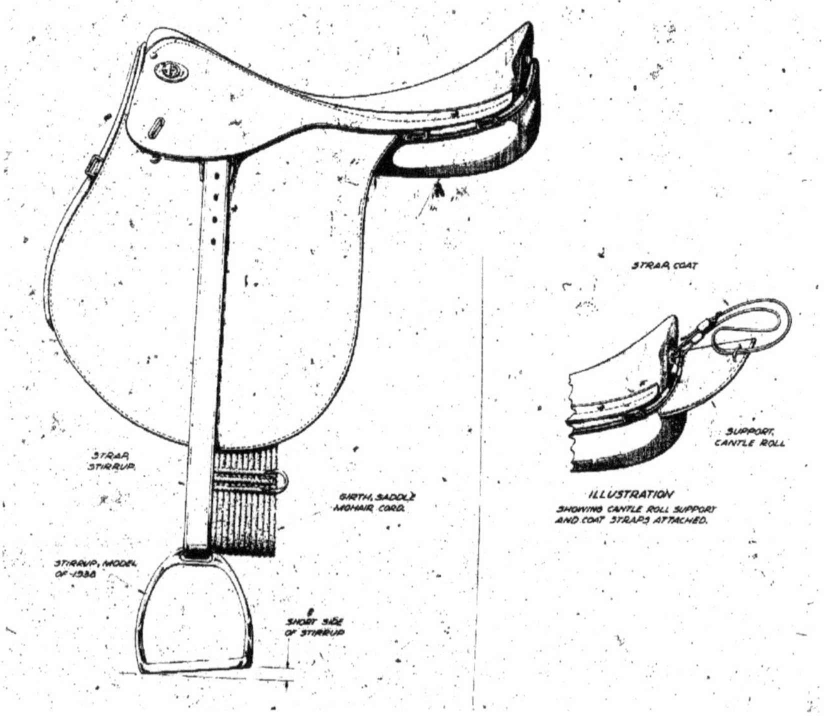

***Figure 109** The Phillips Saddle. Notice the position of the saddle skirt. This supports the "Chamberlin seat" for normal, military riding in the field. The skirt does not extend as far forward as most Italian saddles of that era. Chamberlin would object, however, to the slanted stirrup iron which reflects French influence. Though it forces the knee into the saddle, it also draws the calf away from the sides of the horse.*

Courtesy of the US Army Quartermaster Museum, Fort Lee, Va.

The proper place for the saddle's front bars, he states, remains in the "pocket" just in rear of the withers and clear of the shoulder's scapula to allow unimpeded movement. This also enables the saddle to achieve a *level* surface with pommel and cantle approximately the same height. *Achieving this "level" surface remains most important.* The rider should place the saddle, therefore, "well forward" but not "too far forward."

In 1936, the Cavalry Board approves the Phillips saddle to replace the M-1917 as the recommended Officer's Field Saddle. The Phillips becomes the "M-1936."

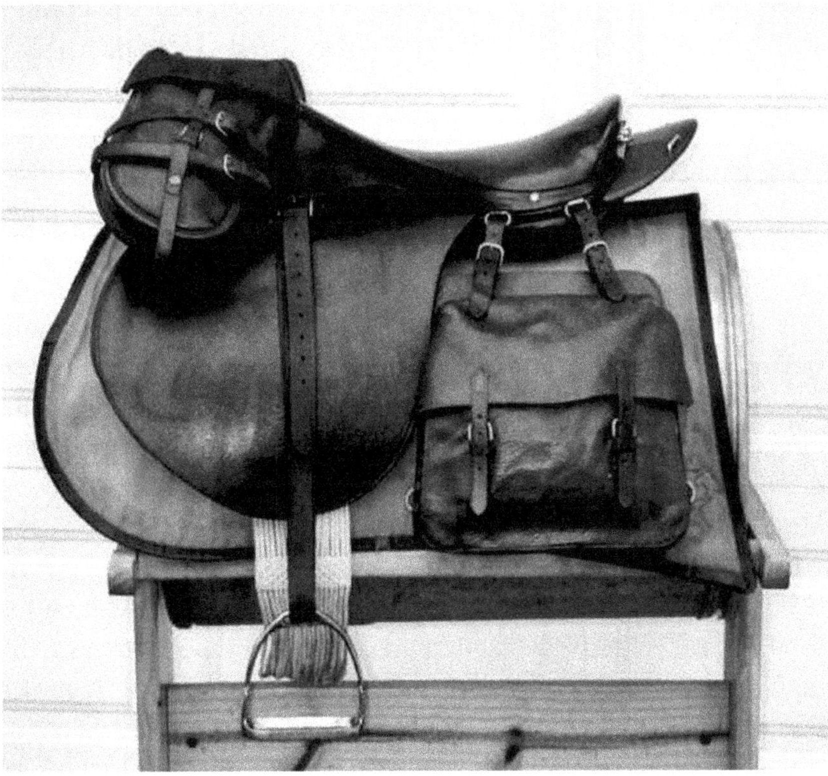

Figure 110 *The Phillips Saddle with cantle shelf, pommel pockets, and saddle bags attached. The attachment of the lower strap of the pommel pocket to the cross strap is in error. The lower strap attaches to the saddle's forward billet strap. The pommel pocket's cross straps are to secure a rain coat across the pockets and the saddle pommel. The cantle shelf is detachable. When attached, it supports the officer's bed roll. The mohair girth was standard. Author's photo.*

RIDING AND SCHOOLING HORSES

In 1935, Chamberlin releases to the public his book *Riding and Schooling Horses* [Xenophon Press 2020]. The *Washington Post* review calls it "...the perfect handbook to horsemanship amply illustrated and scrupulously simple in language."

By the time Chamberlin writes this book, as a horseman, he offers experience equaled by few and surpassed by none:

He leads "C" Troop, 7th Cavalry on forced marches though the tropical heat of the Philippines. He leads "B" Troop, 5th Cavalry several hundred miles into Mexico under wartime conditions, over desert and mountainous terrain, and in a climate that tests the outer limits of horse and rider endurance;

He competes in *Dressage*, Three-Day Event and *Prix des Nations* competitions in three Olympiads and he wins medals in two of those disciplines. He trains riders, both beginners and Olympic competitors. He trains his own horses: green colts, off-the-track Thoroughbreds, endurance horses, and Olympic champions. He wins accolades in horse shows all over the United States and in Europe at venues such as Aachen, Cologne, Dublin, Warsaw, and Paris. He excels at the horsemanship he studies in three of the world's great cavalry schools. He reviews the methods of three other cavalry schools and compares methodology with great horseman from all over the world.

He synthesizes what he learns at each school, develops his own way of "sitting a horse," and then helps revise the curriculum and methods at one of those schools. Chamberlin reconfigures the Italian method, helps develop the American "military seat," integrates French dressage with concepts of Caprilli's "natural" horsemanship, and develops a superior way of riding for military purpose. As we shall see, his work constitutes as an original and enduring contribution to the history, theory, and practice of horsemanship that ranks with the contributions of the European theorists. He does all of this as he works at his full-time job as an officer in the United States Army training troopers, performing staff work, and completing the Army's advanced education programs.

Through the entire body of his writings, Chamberlin offers insights valuable to students of almost every equestrian discipline be it dressage, endurance and trail riding, Gran Prix jumping and Three-Day Eventing, from the back-yard horse owner to the Olympic Gold Medalist. Even the Western horseman and author Tom Dorrance attributes many of his own concepts to Chamberlin.

Just as General L'Hotte, merges D'Aure and his predecessors at the School of Versailles with much of Baucher and thus refines French equitation, Chamberlin merges L'Hotte with Caprilli and then modifies both. In so doing, he achieves his own original contribution to educated riding and horse training.

This spirit of "synthesis" motivates Chamberlin and other American Cavalry officers in their pursuit of maximum mobility for a cavalry challenged by mechanization and the harsh requirements of war in the twentieth-century. Such thoughts may seem out of place and archaic to contemporary people whose love of horses stems from horses as hobby or as professional sport.

To the American cavalrymen of the first 40 years of the twentieth-century, however, these concepts rise to a matter of survival not only for their branch of the military service, but also for the troopers who rely on these doctrines in actual combat. True, some compete in Olympic sport, most ride six days a week professionally and also out of love for hunt and horse; but all focus their doctrine to serve a far more serious purpose: war.

At the same time, Chamberlin's first book directs its message to the civilian rider. In *Riding and Schooling Horses,* Chamberlin writes:

> "The correct principles of equitation and horse training are in themselves simple and well defined, and easily within the comprehension of any intelligent mind."

He strives to communicate the "indispensable" principles in a concise and clear manner so that even the most elementary beginner will understand his concepts. In his first chapter, he describes his concept of the "Seat;" in chapter two, he describes how to maintain that seat while horse and rider move forward; in chapter three, he discusses equine psychology; in chapter four, he discusses "the aids"—the hands, the legs, the rider's weight; in chapter five, he describes various bits and their uses; in chapter six, he summarizes the traits of a well-trained mount; in his final chapter, he discusses what he calls *"an unusual incident in riding:"* jumping obstacles.

Chamberlin's writings remain a trove of wisdom wrought from years of experience and of theory learned from years of study. As Captain Paul Kendal, one of the best instructors in the Horsemanship Detachment at Fort Riley, advises: "if you read only one book on riding, then it should be *Riding and Schooling Horses.*"

In *Riding and Schooling Horses,* Chamberlin states his essential principles of horsemanship. Just a few of the insights one finds in its pages:

The seat: The upper body always must incline at least a trifle to the front; ever so slightly with long stirrups; progressively more forward the shorter the stirrups. Except for variations in the length of the stirrups and the forward inclination of the upper body, the seat remains the same throughout all aspects of riding.

The secure seat: No matter how experienced the rider, **ride** without stirrups as often as possible.

The posting trot: let *the thrust of the horse* push you forward and slightly upward out of the saddle and then let yourself come back down lightly and sparingly. Note again: the thrust of the horse pushes the rider out of the saddle. The rider's leg muscles do *not* lift the rider up and forward. This concept proves extremely important in long distance riding to conserve the rider's strength.

The horse's personality: the horse remembers everything. "His memory… is infallible." *"Reward should instantly follow obedience; and punishment, disobedience"*

The hands: Chamberlin discusses the "hands" at length and refers to the writings of James Fillis on this issue. The reader will find in *The Chamberlin Reader* the James Fillis discussion of "the hands." Chamberlin repeatedly warns against "over flexion" especially direct flexion. Chamberlin adopts the concept of the "fixed hand" in that the rider should fix the position of the hand with reins stretched, arms and elbows set; then the fingers tighten intermittently if necessary. Once the horse "gives" the fingers immediately give, the hands and arms relax and also give. He discusses the concept of "vibrations" on the rein. When closing the fingers does not suffice, he recommends the French concept: The wrist bends inward and upward so that the palm of the hand turns toward the rider's chest to apply additional tension.

The legs: Chamberlin writes that the legs should ask for impulsion but only when necessary to maintain or to change the gait. Chamberlin writes the "calves of rider's legs *squeeze when necessary* to make horse walk fast and freely." (*Italics added*) This recommendation to "squeeze when necessary" comports with the French concept of squeezing the legs only when the rider requires a change in gait or when the horse slows the gait without the rider's asking for same. Like the Frenchman Jean-Claude Racinet, he reasons that to apply the leg constantly merely communicates "my leg means nothing; my leg means nothing; my leg means nothing."

Chamberlin discusses, at length, the French theories regarding the coordination of hands with leg for changes in direction and reproduces the diagrams depicting this coordination originated at the School of Versailles and introduced at Saumur by General Benoist.

The Issue of Collection: Chamberlin writes that the French school of training produces a "more clever and pleasant horse to ride *if it is done* *properly.*" He writes: "In general, these horses are over-bitted and poorly ridden. As a result, the necks are too much arched and over flexed...It is undoubtedly true that except when executed by expert riders, too much collection and schooling are apt to ruin a horse entirely, than are too little."

Regarding collection, itself, Chamberlin warns: "For the most part, a high state of collection is totally unnecessary, and except with the most finished riders, is the proverbial 'razor in the hands of a monkey.' The almost invariable result of demanding high collection is over-flexion. The horse finally develops a permanently over-arched neck; his gaits become high and short; he loses the faculty of extending his neck and going calmly... *The moral indicated is that direct flexion should be very carefully and sparingly employed.*" He repeatedly cautions against "over flexion." Recall that the French master de la Guérinière advises against collection for the outdoor horse in his writings as well.

While Chamberlin opposes heavy handed collection, he suggests a more "natural" collection that the horse would develop on its own or through exercises such as riding down hills to bring the horse's rear legs underneath the horse. In this respect, he seems more Italian than French

Jumping: Chamberlin breaks jumping down into four phases: the approach, the take-off, the period of suspension, the landing. One should read these sections repeatedly.

Figure 111 *Chamberlin student, Lt. Wofford up. Chamberlin writes: "Beautiful balance. Rider's hands correctly following horse's mouth." US Army photo.*

The "Saumur" seat, of which Chamberlin writes and which the American Cavalry (but not the Chamberlin trained Army Equestrian Team) applies in one fashion or another until at least 1929, differs from Chamberlin's concepts in many ways. One of the more significant differences focuses on the rider's balance and base of support. The difference arises principally due to the difference in purposes to be served: The French think in terms of Dressage. Chamberlin thinks in terms of long-distance riding, jumping, and campaigning over harsh terrain.

Both Saumur and Chamberlin agree that for the rider the center of gravity rests slightly in front of the rider's pelvis. Chamberlin and Saumur differ, however, as to what constitutes the "base of support" and how one best achieves "balance" over the rider's base of support in light of the position of the center of gravity.

For the French, the rider's base of support remains, at all times, the seat bones. Hence, they develop a "close and static seat" that General Carter recommends and West Point teaches Chamberlin in 1907. The French reason that, mounted on a horse, the rider cannot keep his legs completely vertical. They must point more or less forward. Since the legs point forward, the rider's upper body must *balance this forward inclination.* To achieve balance, therefore, the French argue that the rider's torso must reside slightly *back behind the vertical.*

At the same time, the rider places his knees as low and as far back as possible to achieve maximum extension of the thighs but the rider must never achieve his knee and thigh position at the expense of the correct position of his upper body. The rider's seat bones, as the base of support, act almost as a fulcrum. The seat bones provide the base of support. On the seat bones, the backward inclination of the rider's upper body balances the forward inclination of the rider's legs.

The French reason that if the rider constantly keeps his torso more or less back behind the vertical, then the rider not only achieves proper balance but also achieves the "position of power." In addition to offsetting the forward inclination of the legs, the torso acts as a "buttress" against the power of the horse. The French argue that with the torso slightly behind the vertical, the rider easily displaces his weight by displacing the pelvis in various directions. Therefore, to put the rider's weight to the right, the rider tips the pelvis to the right. To put the weight to the left, the rider tips the pelvis to the left. To put weight forward, the rider tips the pelvis forward by arching the back; to put weight to the rear, the rider tips the pelvis under backwards by rounding the back.

The French insist that regardless of how the rider shifts his pelvis, the rider's shoulders must remain horizontal at all times. The rotations of the pelvis: forward, back, to the right and to the left must not change the general but slight rearward incline of the rider's torso. For the French, the base of support remains always the seat bones but used as a fulcrum between the rearward inclination of the upper body and the forward inclination of the legs.

To keep its own balance within its vertical base of support, the horse will move to the right when the pelvis weights the right; to the left, forward and back in the same fashion. Always, the horse moves to keep its base of support under the rider's weight as it changes from time to time.

For Chamberlin, the base of support expands or contracts depending on the gait and the rate of forward motion. At the walk or when standing still, the base of support consists of the forward portion of the seat bones, down the inner side of the thigh, to and including the inside of the knee bone that contacts the saddle skirt. The base of support, Chamberlin says, differs when horse and rider travel at the posting trot and the fast gallop. In this situation, the rear part of the seat rises slightly out of the saddle a portion of the time and thus the weight concentrates on the lower thigh, the knee through the calf into the relaxed ankle and ultimately, into the heel of the boot (not the ball of the foot on the stirrup). When his buttocks rise out of the saddle, the rider's base of support narrows to the distance between the inside of the knee and the heel of the boot.

To keep balanced over the base of support, the center of gravity of all portions of the body above and not in contact with the saddle must rest somewhere between the front edge of the seat bones and the area just behind the ball of the foot and into the heel. When posting, fast galloping, or jumping, this base of support narrows to the area between the boot heel up the calf and to the knee in contact with the saddle.

Chamberlin reasons that at the walk, the torso must incline forward slightly ahead of the seat bones and of the boot heel which forms the *center* of the base of support. At the posting trot and the fast gallop, when the rider's buttocks leave the saddle, the torso must incline forward from the hips further than at the walk since the base of support becomes shorter. To avoid the backward inertia that the horse's forward motion causes, the rider must constantly remain a trifle in advance of the center of his base of support.

So, therefore: for the French, the base of support consists of the seat bones. For Chamberlin, the base of support fluctuates. At the walk and sitting trot, it consists a trifle in advance of the seat bones down the thigh to the knee. At the trot, canter, and gallop, and when the buttocks rise slightly out of the saddle, then down the thigh, the calf, and into the boot heel.

In 1935, Chamberlin begins work on his second book *Training Hunters, Jumpers and Hacks* [Xenophon Press 2019] that he publishes in 1937. His wife Helen, an accomplished artist, draws all of the diagrams for the book.

In 1936, toward the end of his tour of duty at Fort Sheridan, he prepares an article on the rudiments of riding for the *Chicago Daily Tribune* which the *Tribune* titles *The World's Best Rider Demonstrates Correct Technique"* and runs in two segments, the first dated May 31, 1936 and the second dated June 7, 1936.

Later in his career, he writes articles that discuss *Haute École* riding as well as various topics about riding and horse training of interest to riders who ride outside the show ring such as endurance riders, trail riders and the like. Much of this writing, we have included in the companion volume to this biography, *The Chamberlin Reader.*

While at Fort Sheridan, Lt. Colonel and Mrs. Chamberlin entertain visitors, attend horse shows and polo matches. For example, with Mrs. George C. Marshall, the Chamberlins attend a Yale Polo contest held in Chicago on Jan 31, 1936.

On April 17, 1936, Lt. Col. Chamberlin's tour of duty at Fort Sheridan ends. The Army transfers him to Fort Bliss, Texas outside El Paso, Texas to serve as the "G-3" General Staff Corps officer for the 1st Cavalry Division, the home to some of the oldest and the most illustrious cavalry regiments in the United States Army and back to a familiar home for Harry Chamberlin.

Chapter 26

To Fort Bliss and The First Cavalry Division, 1936–1939

"The Army's proudest division before Pearl Harbor was its Cavalry Division."
—Ralph Peters. Lt. Col. US Army (*Retired*) [159]

"The Best Trained Division in the Army..."
—Outgoing Chief of Staff Gen. Malin Craig to
in-coming Chief, Gen. George Marshall, 1939 [160]

And
Training Hunters, Jumpers, and Hacks

"...it is, in its field, the greatest book of the century.
I know of nothing comparable produced abroad."
—Vladimir Littauer [161]

On April 17, 1936, Chamberlin joins the First Cavalry Division's Headquarters Staff as "G-3." In this role, Chamberlin serves as the Division's Operations Officer. As such, he must prepare the division for combat. With this focus in mind, he takes responsibility for all Division operations. Staff duties, exercise planning and training, the assessment of operational

159 See Ralph Peters, *Fighting For The Future*, Stackpole Books, 1999.
160 George C. Marshall Papers, Pentagon Office Collection, Selected Materials, George C. Marshall Research Library, Lexington, Virginia
161 See Vladimir A. Littauer, *The Development of Modern Riding: The Story of Modern Riding From Renaissance Times to The Present.* Howell, 1991.

requirements, and combat development and tactical doctrines take up his day. He takes charge of the Division's "war fighting capacity" and its "readiness to fight." Four subordinate officers report to him.

Three months after joining the Division, Harry and Helen Chamberlin welcome a second child into the world. On June 1, 1936, at El Paso, Texas, Helen gives birth to Helen Elena Bradman Chamberlin. The Chamberlins later change their daughter's name to Frederica.

Personal letters and photos clearly demonstrate that Harry Chamberlin absolutely adores his wife and his two little children. The demands of his new role as "G-3" together with writing his second book *Training Hunters, Jumpers and Hacks,* absorb much of his time. Nonetheless, he makes time for his family.

In addition, Helen, an accomplished artist, prepares all of the diagrams that Harry needs to illustrate the training movements in his upcoming book. Helen's pregnancy and Frederica's birth delays publication, however, since Helen cannot complete all of the drawing in time for the intended book release that summer. She finishes the drawings later that fall. The book ultimately reaches the public in 1937.

Figure 112 *Chamberlin with daughter Frederica up. Trooper holding the horse is unknown. Photo courtesy of Ms. Tracey Reese Brown.*

During this time frame, Chamberlin renews many old acquaintances. Personal relationships among US Cavalry officers develop over many years in the close-knit Cavalry. During Chamberlin's time with the First Cavalry, he serves under Brig. General Hamilton Hawkins, Major General Benjamin Lear and Major General Kenyon Joyce. Years ago, Hawkins commands the horsemanship detachment at the Cavalry School while Chamberlin teaches horsemanship there. Lear serves with Chamberlin as a member of the Cavalry Board. Joyce and Lear, along with Chamberlin, carry on a series of experiments regarding how best to integrate the horse with mechanized units on a battlefield.

During this period, Chamberlin writes an article defending horse mounted units as being essential for mobility in terrain unsuitable for machines. He argues that harsh terrain will confine scout cars to roads; that horse-mounted troops with pack horses will move faster to outflank an enemy in these areas than will infantry. More than 60 years later, experience in Afghanistan will vindicate his arguments at least in limited circumstances and adverse terrain. The reader will find this article in *The Chamberlin Reader*.

Figure 113 *His horse at a walk, Chamberlin rides with stirrups shortened for jumping. He rides in a Pariani Borsarelli series 320 saddle probably in 1937. His hands follow the movements of the horse's head. His body inclines forward. His elbows remain relaxed and fall naturally in front of his body. Photo courtesy of Ms. Lydia Moore.*

Chamberlin's main concern focuses on training. One of the most famous and most decorated divisions in the United States Army, the First Cavalry Division consists entirely of "Army regulars." Recall that its oldest regiment, the 5th Cavalry, harkens back to 1855. The National Defense Act of 1920 creates the division as the Army's first complete cavalry division. Like the rest of the Army in 1936, the division's troopers serve as professionals. Conscription does not exist. So, the troopers take training seriously. As a result, Army Chief of Staff, General Malin Craig considers the division to be the "crack" outfit in the Army. Not only do the troopers of the division agree, they do everything they can to prove it. As twenty-first-century commentator Lt. Col. Ralph Peters (*ret*) mentions, the troopers of the division, at this time, remain the army's proudest. The division's personnel proudly wear the largest divisional shoulder patch in the army: a distinctive, bright-yellow, Norman shield with a diagonal black stripe and a silhouette of a horse's head in the upper right-hand corner.

The patch originates with the wife of 7th Cavalry Regiment commander Col. Ben H. Dorcey. The story goes that as Mrs. Dorcey cut up an old blue and yellow cavalry cape of her husband's. Meanwhile, a trooper rides past her window riding a blue-black thoroughbred. The patch quickly takes shape in her mind. The material from Col. Dorcey's cape becomes the material for the first patch. Originally, in blue and yellow, the Dorcey's change the patch to black and yellow: yellow to stand for cavalry; black to stand for iron.

The Division consists of horse mounted cavalry: two brigades of two regiments each together with a headquarters troop and various support elements. The First Brigade consists of the 5th US Cavalry and the 12th US Cavalry. The Second Brigade consists of the 7th US Cavalry and the 8th US Cavalry. In the past, Chamberlin serves with three of the Division's four regiments. In 1934, and extending until 1943, the Division patrols the Mexican Border along the Rio Grande. The horse mounted troopers remain the only force capable of patrolling the harsh terrain along the Mexican Border and of halting the smugglers operating along that border. If all four regiments assemble in a column of two's, (horsemen only, no wagons, trucks, or other support) the column stretches six miles long.

During the 1930s, each cavalry regiment contains 690 troopers. The headquarters staff numbers 78. Each regiment holds four rifle troops containing 119 men each and 108 men serve in a special machine gun troop: Troop "H" for "heavy weapons." Since 1929, as new tensions erupt along the border with fighting in Northern Mexico, the division takes up positions from El Paso, Texas to Douglas, Arizona.

In 1934, then Chief of Staff, General Douglas MacArthur writes: "the horse has no higher degree of mobility today than he had a thousand years ago. The time has therefore arrived when the Cavalry arm must either replace or assist the horse as a means of transportation or else pass into the limbo of discarded military formations." [162] Of course, the same might be said about the infantryman.

Following MacArthur's mandate, and under the guidance of Chief of Cavalry, Major General Guy V. Henry, Jr., the First Cavalry Division begins to mechanize but also preserves its horses. The cavalrymen use 4 x 4 trucks to transport their horses long distances to keep horses and troopers fresh so that once they take the field where machines cannot go, they will surmount any obstacle. In addition, the army adds the .50 caliber machine gun to the division's firepower. Both innovations remain the handiwork of Chief of Cavalry, Major General Guy V. Henry, Jr. (And the 4x4 truck and the .50 caliber machine gun remains with the army to this day.) In 1934, the cavalry officially discontinues the saber as an item of issue. Of course, the cavalry put the saber "on the shelf" since before Custer's time.

Also, by 1934, the international scene darkens. By that time, Hirohito's armies have fought three years in their conquest of Manchuria. In 1934, Hitler expands the German Army. In 1936, Hitler violates the Versailles Treaty and occupies the Rhineland. In 1937, Hirohito expands his conquests in China with savage crimes in Nanking that kill 300,000 or more civilians. Ultimately, the Japanese will kill some 15 million Chinese. The United States Army expands its preparations for war but still suffers from budgets far too low to keep pace with international events. During this period, the United States Army remains the size of the army of Peru.

During this time, most officers assume a role for the horse because horses go places where no machine travels. In fact, the Army intends to keep two full strength, horse-mechanized cavalry divisions operational. Technical issues that revolve around how to organize a cavalry division, either as a "triangular division" or a "square division" take up much of Chamberlin's time. A "triangular division" contains three regiments; the "square division" contains four regiments. Issues such as what specialized troops might the division include: signal troops, ordinance troops, medical units; engineer, reconnaissance and observation squadrons together with a chemical

162 See *The First Team, History of the 1st Cavalry Division,* The 1st Cavalry Division Association, Taylor Publishing Company, 1984; *The 1st Cavalry Division in World War II,* compiled by Major C.B. Wight, Turner Publishing Company, 2000.

warfare unit, also take up Chamberlin's time. He analyzes each and makes his recommendations.

Chamberlin and his commander Major General Kenyan Joyce reject the "triangular model" and thus, the division continues as two brigades with two regiments each. They add to the division other support troop organizations as separate elements but decide not to include a chemical weapons unit or an observation unit.

They do reorganize, however, each cavalry regiment. As G-3, Chamberlin supervises the reorganization. Each regiment now will have a headquarters and headquarters troop; a machine gun and special weapons troop; and three squadrons of three rifle troops each. Divisional war time strength, the army sets at 10,680. This structure carries the division through its campaigns in the Pacific during World War II. Ultimately, Chamberlin becomes Chief of Staff for the Division under General Kenyon Joyce.

TRAINING HUNTERS, JUMPERS AND HACKS

1937

After the birth of her second child, Helen completes the diagrams for Harry's second book: *Training Hunters, Jumpers and Hacks.* The publisher releases the book to the public in 1937. This book, just as Chamberlin's *Riding and Schooling Horses,* stands the test of time. As Vladimir Littauer writes: "...I believe that it is, in its field, the greatest book of the century, not only in the United States but in the world." [163]

In this new book, Chamberlin acknowledges that he learned much from his time at Saumur. He writes: "Credit for the system of training enunciated herein is due to the French Cavalry School at Saumur. Evolved by many generations of skilled and highly intelligent horseman, there is no system more scientifically founded or practically efficacious. Guérinière, Baucher, L'Hotte, d'Aure, Saint Phalle, Beauchesne, Champsavin are the names of but a few among the distinguished Frenchmen whose composite teachings and writings have aided in formulating the principles, doctrines and methods used at Saumur. This system of training, borrowed from the French School,

163 See Vladimir A. Littauer, *The Development of Modern Riding: The Story of Modern Riding From Renaissance Times to The Present.* Howell, 1991.

has long dominated the instruction at the United States Cavalry School at Fort Riley, Kansas...Nothing in equitation is new." [164]

He writes further: "Unfortunately, some equestrians erroneously consider the exercises as the ends to be attained, rather than as a means of making the horse obedient and clever at his normal work...If the French precepts are correctly understood and applied, they will develop calmness, boldness, suppleness, brilliance and all other requisites of a well-trained horse."

Chamberlin divides the subject into its component parts:

I Generalities Concerning Selection, Confirmation and Gaits;
II Details of Conformation;
III Head Carriage and Objectives of Training;
IV Breaking;
V Training;
VI Training the Horse to Jump;
VII Conclusion.

To the topic of conformation, Chamberlin devotes 93 pages. To the topic of head carriage, Chamberlin devotes 33 pages and stresses the importance of allowing the horse to find his own natural head carriage. He breaks down the issue of head carriage into three separate phases, through each of which the trainer must guide the horse slowly. Under no circumstances should a trainer force a horse into a "frame" or seek to position the head so that the horse's face forms a 90-degree angle with the ground since horses forced into this position often lose the ability to fully extend and gallop with long and low strides.

Chamberlin points out the dangers of collection for the outdoor horse, as does the French theorist de la Guérinière. Chamberlin writes:

> "As a matter of fact, many experienced riders, in their efforts to proceed too far in collection and high-schooling, succeed in inculcating nothing more than irritability, nervousness and inability to jump or gallop fast across country."
>
> *"Dangers of Over-Flexion...To the great detriment of the horse, poll flexion easily may be overdone, causing an exaggerated rounding of the neck. This brings the horse's face to a position back of a vertical plane so that his nose is near the neck or breasts.* Poor or inexperienced horseman frequently obtain this faulty over-flexion..."

164 Lt. Col. Harry D. Chamberlin, *Training Hunters, Jumpers, and Hacks* Derrydale Press, 1937.

Regarding the final phase of work on head carriage, he writes:

> "In this third and last phase, the head and neck generally will continue to rise to a greater elevation, still without conscious effort on the trainer's part. When, as a result of training, there normally rests at all times a suspicion of flexion at the poll and the face makes an angle of approximately fifty-five degrees with the horizontal when the horse, lightly on the bit, is moving at slow gaits, the head is termed 'well placed.'"

The objectives of all training must be "calmness...boldness and frank forward movement...relaxation and suppleness...balance and agility...long low strides"

The concept of "breaking," Chamberlin defines "...as the time necessary to gentile the colt, teach him to work on the longe, bear the saddle and rider, gain strength and generally good condition, and accept his bit calmly with an extended head and neck at the walk, trot and gallop. Having accomplished these purposes in the breaking period, the succeeding period is called "training."

"Training" for Chamberlin includes select exercises to improve balance, "natural collection" (as opposed to the full collection practiced by the French). The horse learns each of the five rein effects of French equitation. The horse also learns the half-halt, the extended gallop, backing, the half-turn in reverse, turns and half-turns on the forehand, turns and half-turns on the haunches, the shoulder-in, the false gallop (counter canter in modern parlance), flexions of the jaw while mounted, vibrations of the reins to relax the jaw, division of supports (while using a full bride of bit and bridoon), lateral flexion of the neck, flexion of the poll, placing the head (Ramener), the gallop depart (canter depart in modern parlance), the change of leads; and finally, the horse learns to jump. At this time, the rider corrects refusals, run-outs, and other vices while teaching the horse to jump.

Chamberlin argues that to absorb the book's principles remains a worthy goal even for those who ride but do not consider themselves trainers. The protocols that *Training Hunters, Jumpers, and Hacks* explains apply to the US Army Horse Show Team, to the hunt rider, to the rider on a leisurely hack in the woods, to the endurance rider traveling 100 miles in twenty-four hours, and to a cavalry courier, in extreme circumstances, traveling 170 miles in twenty-four hours.

In addition, the methods apply equally well to train horses for the cavalry. Whole sections of Chamberlin's book appear in Part Two of Fort

Riley's manual *Horsemanship and Horsemastership, 1942 Edition*. Chamberlin provides an updated, step by step, and refined explanation of the horse training methods of Saumur without stressing the collection practiced at that school since he focuses on the outdoor campaigner not the Dressage horse of academic equitation. He explains the approach in a clear, concise, and lucid discussion of the entire training process that one will be hard pressed to find elsewhere. The entire protocol takes approximately two years to turn out a well-trained cavalry campaigner, hunter, jumper, or hack.

THE CONFORMATION OF THREE-DAY HORSES

Chamberlin's work on his book clearly takes third place behind his family and his duty as an officer. In 1937, he does take time, however, to write the article *The Confirmation of Three-Day Horses* as part of a series of articles by cavalrymen on the topic of conformation for the Three-Day Horse. We reprint the full article in this biography's companion volume, *The Chamberlin Reader*. Of particular interest is Chamberlin's suggestion that the short-backed horses favored by the Cavalry for field campaigns do not meet the needs of the Event rider; that a longer backed horse will do better in the Three-Day Event but will not perform as well as the cavalry's favored horse in long distance campaigning. Also, Chamberlin favors smaller horses as opposed to larger. He writes:

"The only test of a horse regardless of his beauty and presumable quality is actually riding him through the phases involved in the particular competition. This alone will determine his fitness. If he has true quality, he may be 15-2 or 16-2. It comes in all sizes and, I believe, most often in smaller horses. In general, however, the medium-sized thoroughbred horse from 15-2 to 16-1 is best for three-day purposes."

As time goes on and the international situation darkens further, the professional demands on Chamberlin mount. He prepares exercises to bring the division up to peak performance. In 1937, the division conducts training maneuvers and participates with the infantry in their "Provisional Infantry Tests" near Fort Sam Houston, Texas. Harry also sends a note to 8th Cavalry Regiment commander, Col. Innis Palmer Swift, his old friend and polo teammate from the Cavalry School, to congratulate him on the success of his unit's 150-mile endurance ride. In May of 1938, the division conducts maneuvers in the mountains near Balmorhea, Texas. In these maneuvers, horse mounted units and mechanized units practiced coordinated movement through rough terrain.

In these maneuvers as well as those the Army holds later in Louisiana and Texas in 1940, Chamberlin argues that the horse mounted units vindicate the view that "In some special cases of difficult terrain, the horse, properly supplemented by motorized transportation, may still furnish the best mobility…." And so, many in the War Department view the horse as an asset for difficult terrain and special tactical missions.

Figure 114 *All is not work at Fort Bliss. Here Chamberlin plays with Lydia, age two, and his horse High Hat. Courtesy of Ms. Lydia Moore.*

Figure 115 *The Chamberlin children: Frederica (left), Lydia (right) Easter 1938. Photo courtesy of Ms. Lydia Moore.*

In 1938, the British and French surrender the strategic areas of Czechoslovakia to Germany. Also in 1938, Hitler annexes Austria into the Third Reich. The United States Army accelerates its preparations for war. In addition to working on how to coordinate machines with horses, Chamberlin integrates an ordinance unit, a signal unit and a medical unit into the First Cavalry Division.

In November of 1938, when Major General Kenyon Joyce takes command of the division, Chamberlin becomes the Division's Chief of Staff. In December of 1938, *The Washington Post* writes that General and Mrs. Bradman and their daughter Mary Jo will travel to Fort Bliss to spend Christmas with son-in-law Lt. Col. Chamberlin and his wife and family. Thereafter, General Bradman intends to retire from the Marine Corps and reside with Mrs. Bradman in San Diego, California. In May 1939, the Army promotes Chamberlin to the rank of Colonel of Cavalry. All goes well in the Chamberlin family.

The state of the world, however, goes not so well. In March 1939, Hitler's Germany absorbs the rest of Czechoslovakia. That same month, Joyce and Chamberlin put the 1st Cavalry Division through its paces with training maneuvers at Fort Bliss. At this time, the division packs the greatest fire power, man for man, of any unit in the army and reaches its objectives three times faster than an infantryman on foot in rough terrain were motorized vehicles cannot go.

At the conclusion of the training maneuvers, the entire 1st Cavalry Division passes before Joyce and Chamberlin in review. The horse mounted units of the Division's 5th, 8th, 7th and 12th Cavalry Regiments—more than 5,000 mounted cavalrymen—ride in a column of two's. (without wagons, trucks or pack trains). The line stretches six-and-one-half miles long.

In May 1939, Chamberlin prepares for the fifth set of training maneuvers in ten years. Prior to the beginning of these maneuvers, Chamberlin learns that he will command the 2nd Cavalry Regiment stationed at Fort Riley. In August of 1939, Chamberlin, Helen, Lydia and Frederica move back to Fort Riley. That same August, Hitler and Stalin sign their non-aggression pact. They secretly divide Poland between them. They set the stage for World War II.

In late August of 1939, Chamberlin leaves Fort Bliss and returns to Fort Riley to command the 2nd Cavalry Regiment. That same month, Army Chief of Staff, Malin Craig tells the incoming Chief, George C. Marshall that the 1st Cavalry Division is the best trained Division in the Army. Marshall assumes the role of Army Chief of Staff on September 1, 1939. The German Army invades Poland that same day.

Chapter 27

Back to Riley
The 2nd US Cavalry Regiment, 1939–1941

"Moreover, *officers of the horse cavalry should maintain abiding faith in our arm!* Until something yet unheard-of appears on the field of battle, the horse cavalry—*properly trained*—has definite and vital functions and missions which no other arm can execute with similar speed or thoroughness...Scout cars by themselves are hopelessly road-bound... While the importance of mechanized and armored forces is evident to all, many officers were struck by the vast amount of terrain found in the Louisiana maneuver area...over which it was utterly impractical to employ tanks."

—Chamberlin, *Cavalry Training* 1940 [165]

In late August 1939, Chamberlin takes command of the 2nd Cavalry Regiment. On September 1st, 1939, General George C. Marshall becomes Army Chief of Staff. That same day, the German Army attacks Poland. Three days later with the British and French Declaration of War against Germany. The Second World War begins.

The 2nd Cavalry Regiment, stationed at Fort Riley, assists the Cavalry School in training officers. Twenty years earlier, Chamberlin's West Point horsemanship instructor, Llewellyn W. Oliver commanded this same 2nd Cavalry Regiment. Now, Chamberlin commands the regiment.

---

165 See Colonel Harry D. Chamberlin, "Cavalry Training," *The Cavalry Journal,* September–October 1940.

Chamberlin fills his time while commanding the 2nd Cavalry Regiment with building an excellent staff (that will serve well in Europe in the coming war), writing articles, training troopers, and training horses. Regarding the training of troopers, traditionally, the army relegates trooper training to the individual field units. This creates problems because as troopers come into the unit, each offers a different level of experience, thus complicating training.

In an October 1940 article entitled *Cavalry Training,* Chamberlin calls for the army to establish a central training center where each trooper will learn the basics of horsemanship and soldiering. His criticism of then existing practice and his recommendations for the future comes to the attention of General George C. Marshall the Army Chief of Staff. By November of 1940, General Marshall directs the Army to start constructing a Cavalry Replacement Training Center at Fort Riley to implement Chamberlin's recommendations in *Cavalry Training.* For the first time, the army abandons the practice of training new recruits in the line regiments.

In his *Cavalry Training* article, Chamberlin also argues that the "scout cars" the army plans to use for close-in reconnaissance for infantry divisions will prove worthless in gathering information due to their road bound limitations. The Army's later experience with mechanized "cavalry" reconnaissance units in Tunisia, Sicily, and Italy vindicate his arguments. A reprint of this article appears in this biography's companion volume, *The Chamberlin Reader.*

Chamberlin publishes another article entitled *Crossing Rivers* in January of 1941. He deals with every conceivable problem and approach to training horses and riders to ford rivers. Much of this article stems from his experiences in the Philippines back in the first decade of the twentieth-century when crossing the Pampanga River in Central Luzon proves a difficult exercise for all involved. This writing and all of his other articles display a depth of knowledge unsurpassed and, as of this writing, often lost to contemporary horsemen. A copy of Chamberlin's article appears in *The Chamberlin Reader.*

From the fall of 1939 and the early spring of 1941, Chamberlin continues to build an excellent staff of officers who will perform superbly in the European Theater during World War II. He continues to prepare articles on cavalry issues as well as regarding how to train troopers and horses. He also takes time to write an article entitled *The Modern Jumping Seat* for *Country Life Magazine.* This article restates his concepts of the jumping seat already expressed through his books but also through his articles in *The Cavalry Journal.*

In April 1941, General Marshall recommends and Congress approves Chamberlin's promotion to the rank of Brigadier General. A month earlier, the army opens the Cavalry Replacement Training Center (the "CRTC") which offers the basic training that Chamberlin's October 1940 article, *Cavalry Training*, advocates.

Upon his elevation to Brigadier General, Chamberlin leaves the 2nd US Cavalry Regiment to command the CRTC.

***Figure 116** On April 11, 1941, Chamberlin becomes a Brigadier General of Cavalry. US Army photo.*

Chapter 28

The Cavalry Replacement Training Center, Fort Riley April, 1941–October, 1941

"They taught me how to ride all over again."
—William Steinkraus [166]

"In my opinion the people that came out of that school: Billy Steinkraus, Cappy Smith, Gordon Wright were fabulous, fabulous horsemen."
—George H. Morris [167]

In December 1940, adjacent to the Cavalry School at Fort Riley, the army creates Camp Forsyth on an expanse of sand dunes along a bend in the Republican River locally known as Republican Flats. Here the cavalry creates The Cavalry Replacement Training Center (the CRTC) to implement the training concepts that Chamberlin recommends in his article *Cavalry Training*. Now, all recruits will receive basic cavalry training in one place. No longer will active cavalry units in the field train raw recruits.

At Republican Flats, in a matter of weeks, the Army creates a city to house thousands of men who will learn the fundamentals of horsemanship and receive basic military training. Barracks, mess halls, chapels, theaters, garages, stables, classrooms, and basic battle training facilities dot the "Flats" virtually overnight. Once at full capacity, with a training staff of 207 officers and 1,175

166 William Steinkraus email to author June 3, 2008.
167 See George H. Morris *Four Show Jumping Masters—Part 4: Gordon Wright* https://www.horsemagazine.com/thm/2010/07/four-showjumping-masters-part-4-gordon-wright/

enlisted men, the school will train more than 6,500 recruits at a time. They will live in 210 barracks buildings. They will eat in 50 mess halls. They will train in round pen after round pen and training field after training field.

The Cavalry Replacement Training Center and the concepts Chamberlin implements there exert immense influence on equestrianism in the United States and much of the world to this day. Given the CRTC's enduring influence, we will deal with its operation in detail and recount the actual experience of 14 recruits in a squad of a platoon of "A" Troop, First Squadron, 1st Training Regiment training under Sergeant William H. Offill early in the year 1942.

It may seem strange to the twenty-first century reader that the United States Army would devote so many resources to horse-mounted cavalry. Throughout 1941, war in Europe and mainland Asia rages as the United States gears up for war as yet undeclared. Massive numbers of men enter the armed forces through enlistment and conscription. General Marshall decides to maintain two horse-mounted cavalry divisions, the 1st Cavalry and the 2nd Cavalry as well as a small number of National Guard mounted units. In fact, the only time that General Marshall waives the age limit for officers is in 1942 when he does so to enable Jack Holt to join the Army to buy more horses for the Cavalry.

Each division, at full strength, will number approximately 11,000 troopers. The Army reasons that horse-mounted troops would prove invaluable in areas of hazardous terrain where mechanized units cannot operate effectively. And since the majority of actual enemy engagements occur fighting dismounted, the Army's command reasons that on such ground, supported by its own artillery, the 1st Cavalry Division, for example, would defeat any enemy tanks that penetrate the harsh terrain.

The Division's horses and mules carry a complete mobile arsenal of seven hundred .30 caliber machine guns, two hundred sixty-five .50 caliber machine guns, five hundred sub-machine guns, sixty-seven 37mm anti-tank guns, twenty-eight 81mm mortars, twenty-four 75mm howitzers; four-thousand semi-automatic rifles, and ten-thousand four-hundred .45 caliber pistols. That level of firepower combined with the fact that horse mounted troops travel twice as fast as infantry makes the Cavalry exceptional in flanking and envelopment maneuvers in harsh terrain.

Once the United States enters the war, however, a major impediment stands in the cavalry's way. When the United States enters World War II and the Battle of the Atlantic rages between the US Navy and the German U-Boats, so many merchant ships fall prey to German torpedoes that not enough shipping remains available to transport the 1st Cavalry Division or any other horse mounted units with their horses and equipment to North Africa, Sicily, or

Italy in Europe. Nonetheless, General Truscott creates ad hoc mounted units among his infantry in Sicily and Italy. In the Pacific, early in 1942, the 112th Cavalry Regiment deploys with all of its equipment, but not with its horses, to the island of New Caledonia where the Army decides that the terrain is ideal for horse-mounted cavalry. The Army plans to use horses the Australians supply. But the horses the Australians send are green or poorly trained, thus rendering them useless. So, the unit operates on foot with mules to transport equipment. The regiment ultimately transfers to the Burma Theater of war.

As a result of the German U-Boat campaign and its success in early 1942-1943 against Allied shipping, the Army dismounts the US Cavalry. In February 1943, the 1st Cavalry Division receives the order to turn in its horses; then in July, the division heads for the Pacific to serve under General MacArthur as light infantry. The 2nd Cavalry Division turns in its horses in early 1944. In preparation for the invasion of Japan in 1945, however, when shipping no longer imposes limitations, the Army considers remounting the horse cavalry for use in the mountainous regions of Japan. All of that remains, however, far into the future.

In late March of 1941, the first recruits arrive at the CRTC to commence 120 days of intensive training. In April 1941, before the first recruits start their horsemanship training, newly promoted Brigadier General Chamberlin takes command of the CRTC. This command offers Chamberlin the opportunity to develop and to implement training techniques that aim to train horseman for the line cavalry regiments on a massive scale. The CRTC will not seek to create Olympic horseman. The objective now will be to offer basic training in military horsemanship to newly enlisted recruits. Chamberlin reviews the curriculum and the training schedules. He revises both.

Between April and October 1941, as Commandant of the CRTC, Chamberlin also writes his last thoughts regarding the rider's seat, application of the aids, and jumping style in the new 1942 edition of *FM 25-5 Animal Transport, Horsemanship and Horsemastership, Part One, Education of the Rider.* He also grafts his concepts of horse training into the manual's *Part Two, Education of the Horse.* One honestly may call the 1942 edition of *FM 25-5* "The Chamberlin Edition." It presents significant revisions of the 1935 edition of the manual and contains considerable material not published previously in *FM 25-5.* Chamberlin himself appears in photos to demonstrate various riding concepts. Chamberlin takes the concepts found in his prior books, refines his thinking further, and grafts all into the manual's military style.

While at Fort Riley, he also writes: "thank you" notes to various officers who submit comments for the new manual and the revised cavalry drill regulations. Several officers ask Chamberlin to autograph their personal copies of *Training Hunters, Jumper, and Hacks* and *Riding and Schooling Horses.* For the rest of their lives, those officers keep the "thank you" notes and the autographed books as treasured remembrances from a remarkable man from an era long past.

As horsemanship training progresses at the CRTC, every morning Chamberlin rides on horseback from his quarters on the main post at Fort Riley to Camp Forsyth where the CRTC conducts its classes. Chamberlin rides through the camp observing from his horse all that transpires. The officers, NCO's, and other enlisted troopers on the faculty of the CRTC respect and like Chamberlin. At least once a week, a Sergeant's wife meets the General on his rounds to give him an apple, peach, or strawberry pie to take home to his wife and two daughters. She does not know Chamberlin but she knows *of* him and of his fame in the cavalry.

When the Center achieves full operation, more than 6,500 recruits train simultaneously, each in a different stage of training. Approximately 3,900 of each increment will train in horsemanship. Never before and never again, in one place, will so many in the United States train on horses. In 1942, approximately half of the 6,500 recruits will go to horse-mounted cavalry units and the other half will go to mechanized cavalry units.

And what of the recruits that Chamberlin's officers and enlisted men train? Once the Japanese attack Pearl Harbor, Army enlistments skyrocket. By early 1942, the CRTC becomes a magnet for "the who is who" of the horse world and of Hollywood. Champion rodeo riders like Turkel Greenough, internationally known polo players like Peter Bostwick, multi-millionaires like Paul Mellon arrive having enlisted as privates in the Cavalry. Later in 1942, Oleg Cassini, accomplished civilian horseman, polo player, and Hollywood fashion designer married to actress Gene Tierney arrives also as a private. He creates "the look" for Hollywood's most glamorous actresses. After the war, he will design movie gowns for Grace Kelly, Marilyn Monroe, Audrey Hepburn and every other famous actress of the post war period. He also designs the wardrobe of First Lady Jacqueline Kennedy. One wonders what he thinks of the "cut" of the cotton, government issue riding breeches and the three-buckle riding boots he and every other recruit wears. To be close to her husband, his wife Gene buys a home near the fort. For the rest of his life, he remembers the CRTC as a place reminiscent of the Imperial Great Britain "Raj" in India.

As Cassini writes in his autobiography:

I felt quite at home in Fort Riley society—a term that I do not use lightly, since the very best horsemen and polo players from all over the country had congregated at the cavalry school (and it had some of the best horses Darryl Zanuck, Jock Whitney, and others had donated their strings of polo ponies to the cause for the duration). Our neighbors were the Bostwicks, the Van Stades, and others of the horsey set. Paul Mellon was there, and Cappy Smith, who was one of the finest equestrians in the country. Nor was Gene the only celebrity wife in camp. Gloria Vanderbilt was there, married then to my friend and fellow man-about-town Pat De Cicco. [168]

Highly significant for the future of the equestrian sports of Eventing, Hunting, and Show Jumping, the former cow puncher and rodeo rider Gordon Wright, age 39, who served a stint in the Cavalry in the 1920s, re-enlists as a private and arrives at the CRTC for training in 1942; so too does the 1938 National Horse Show title-holder Morton Smith. In 1943, the winner of the Maclay Trophy of 1941, William Steinkraus, age 18, arrives at the CRTC thinking that horse mounted cavalry will play a role in the Second World War.

Many other recruits, however, offer little or no previous experience with horses. For example, one 18-year-old, whose only experience with a horse has been on a merry-go-round, joins because in Chicago, Illinois the lines at the Navy and the Army Air Corps recruiters stretch over a block long while no one stands at the Cavalry Recruiting Sergeant's desk. Another recruit, Boxing's World Heavy-Weight Champion Joe Lewis reports to Fort Riley's Camp Funston for training at the CRTC as well. As a CRTC publication states: "Farm boys from Iowa, cowboys from Wyoming, machinists from Michigan, garment workers from Brooklyn, artists, writers, school teachers, lawyers, businessmen, factory, and mill workers" make up the 2,000 or more recruits who report to the CRTC every five weeks.

Regardless of one's past experience, every recruit who receives training in horsemanship—from Gordon Wright, William Steinkraus, and Paul Mellon to the 18-year-old from Chicago and the boxer Joe Louis—everyone learns the "Army way of riding" from the ground up in accordance with the "Chamberlin way of teaching." This new way of riding and the new way of teaching challenges and humbles many an expert horseman. Even the most accomplished civilian horsemen of that era—not to mention the champion rodeo riders—do not ride what the CRTC calls the "Chamberlin Military Seat" nor do they apply the aides in the manor or with the discipline demanded by the Army way of riding and the Chamberlin way of teaching.

168 See Oleg Cassini, *In My Own Fashion, An Autobiography*, Simon and Schuster, 1987 p.146.

Trophy-winning Madison Square Garden horse show riders, veterans of the Virginia hunt field, and east coast polo players of that era must unlearn and discard their established equestrian preferences. They must adopt the close order drill, the cross-country methods, and the long-distance riding concepts that the cavalry develops for military purposes. The officers and enlisted staff of the CRTC banish the methods of "the experienced," initiate the novices, and indoctrinate all in the Army way of riding.

And what horsemanship training protocols do Chamberlin and his subordinates create for this group, diverse in experience and outlook? To learn the basics of the curriculum that Chamberlin and his subordinates devise for new recruits, we will summarize the experience of actual recruits enrolled in one squad in a platoon of "A" Troop of the First Squadron of the 1st Training Regiment early in 1942. The platoon consists of fifty-five recruits who share the same barracks. The squad consists of 14 recruits. We base what you read here on the recollections of a recruit in this squad. Among the recruits are:

Pat DiCicco, age 33, an accomplished civilian horseman, polo player, and prominent Hollywood "man about town" known as "The Glamor Boy of Hollywood," co-producer of films with Howard Hughes, and married to the multi-millionaire socialite Gloria Vanderbilt. DiCicco is well connected having introduced actor George Raft to Ben "Bugsy" Segal. He allegedly serves as Lucky Luciano's "man in Hollywood." His cousin and good friend will own the franchise and produce all of the James Bond films of the 1960s and after. His wife Gloria buys a home in Manhattan, Kansas to be near him and visits every Sunday driving a Lincoln Continental convertible bright yellow in color with a black "rag" top. At the CRTC, DiCicco stands as an equal to any and every recruit no more, no less.

Henry Morgenthau, III, age 25, the son of Secretary of the Treasury, Henry Morgenthau, Jr. and the Hyde Park, New York next-door neighbor of President Franklin D. Roosevelt. He grows up with horses from an early age and begins his training anew at the CRTC. His father, the Secretary of the Treasury, visits once a month and arrives at the barracks in his chauffeur driven, black Packard limousine.

Thurkel (Turk) Greenough, age 37, six-time National Champion rodeo rider, married to the famous fan dancer Sally Rand, remains one of the few rodeo riders ever to stay on the notorious horses Midnight and Five Minutes to Midnight. He performs as a stunt double for John Wayne, Gene Autry, and Roy Rodgers. He eventually is inducted into the National Cowboy Hall of Fame and Western Heritage Center. His glamorous wife Sally visits periodically. He begins his training with the 18-year-old recruit whose first ride on a horse was on a merry-go-round.

Add to these notables, a Hollywood stunt man who routinely performs horseback stunts in films such as *The Charge of the Light Brigade* with Errol Flynn, two polo players of great family wealth, one young man of great wealth who rides with the Middleburg Hunt in Virginia, three cowboys who work horses and cattle and who have ridden all of their lives (one of whom trains horses for Howard Hughes); three others with no riding experience; and the 18-year-old from Chicago, Illinois whose only previous mounted experience occurs on a merry-go-round when he was about six.

Every one of the recruits volunteered for the Cavalry. This class contains no draftees. During the first four weeks after they arrive at Fort Riley's CRTC, the recruits learn the basics: how to wear the uniform; how to care for equipment; how to march, how to perform the manual of arms. They learn basic Garand M-1 and M-1903 rifle and caliber .45 pistol marksmanship. They learn to operate and maintain the 60-and the 80-mm mortar, the caliber .30 machine gun, and the caliber .50 machine gun. They learn basic military protocol. They study personal hygiene, sanitation and first aid. At this point, a major portion of their training also focuses on physical conditioning.

Figure 117 *Sergeant William H. Offill responsible for the training of recruits in the First Platoon, "A" Troop, First Squadron, 1st Training Regiment, CRTC 1942. US Army photo.*

On the first day of their fifth week at the CRTC, the recruits begin horsemanship training under their instructor Sergeant William H. Offill and specialists from the CRTC's Horsemanship Department. (The Sergeant's last name is pronounced "awful" as in "it was an awful day of heat and drudgery under our Drill Sergeant.") Sgt. Offill and the specialists of the Horsemanship Department are expert military horsemen. Sgt. Offill offers years of experience in training new recruits. Under Offill and the instructors from the Horsemanship Department, these recruits will now focus five or more hours each day, six days each week on horsemanship with the balance of their time devoted to pistol and rifle marksmanship as well as to physical conditioning.

Regardless of whether the recruit ranks as a five-goal polo player, a champion rodeo rider, a Hollywood stunt man, or has never mounted a horse, he takes the same training. Actually, no prior experience with horses proves a benefit because the novice offers no bad or ingrained habits to break. The more "accomplished" horsemen often experience the most difficulty adjusting to the discipline and the techniques of military horsemanship.

On the first morning of their first day of horsemanship training, all recruits fall into line. Every recruit has spent hours polishing his boots, pressing his shirt and breeches, brushing his field service hat. Sergeant Offill walks down the line and inspects the deportment of each recruit. He insists on a spit polished shine to the boots, perfectly pressed shirts and breeches. Offill insists on meticulous deportment. With the inspection finished, Sergeant Offill asks each recruit one question:

"Have you ever been on a horse before?" [169]

The Sergeant begins with Private Morgenthau, the son of the Secretary of the Treasury and asks the question.

"Yes, Sergeant," says Private Morgenthau.

"And what type of riding did you do?"

"I fox hunt. I play polo. I started riding when I was six."

"I see," says Sergeant Offill.

Private Pat DiCicco, the "The Glamor Boy of Hollywood" stands next in line.

"Have you ever been on a horse before and if so, what have riding have you done?"

"Yes, Sergeant, I play polo."

169 All quotations attributed to Sgt. William H. Offill and the other members of the Frist Platoon, "A" Troop, First Squadron, 1st Training Regiment, CRTC 1942 are based on the recollections of recruit Warren E. Matha.

And on down the line Sergeant Offill goes.

He comes to one of the cowboys who says that he started riding horses at age 5 and worked as a cowhand for Mr. Howard Hughes.

The next recruit in line explains that before joining the Cavalry, he rides almost every day and owns all of the horses, stage coaches, and wagons used in Hollywood's Western movies.

Offill comes to the 18-year-old Private from Chicago who says the only horse he has ever been on was on a merry-go-round.

Offill smiles and says, "Don't worry about that, you'll learn soon enough."

Offill comes to Private Greenough who says "I've ridden some. Rodeos mostly. I've also done stunts in the movies as a stunt double."

"Really, I am *truly* impressed," says Drill Sgt. Offill perhaps with a hint of sarcasm.

And on down the line, so it goes: the cowboys, the Middleburg Hunt rider, the Hollywood stunt man, the other polo players. Each recruit explains something of his past experience. Clearly, a love of horses motivates almost all of these recruits to join the Cavalry. When he reaches the end of the line, Offill returns to the center, takes a deep breath, and speaks to all assembled in words something like this:

"Ok, gather around me here. Those of you who have experience with horses, place close attention. Playing polo, fox hunting, driving cattle, riding in the movies—those kinds of riding serve very different purposes from what we do here. Army riding is different, *very* different.

"And the *reason* you ride determines the *way* you should ride. Not one of you has military riding experience. So listen up. Listen very carefully. Everything you've done in the past, everything you think you know: *forget it all.* It's irrelevant. It will hold you back. Very little of it applies here.

"This man's Army took 80 years, traveled all over the world, and spent thousands of taxpayer dollars to figure out the best way to ride a horse for military purposes" Sgt. Offill continues: "And from now on, that's the way you need to ride. The bible of the Cavalry, *your* new bible, is *Field Manual 25-5 Animal Transport: Horsemanship and Horsemastership.* That's *the book, your bible: 25-5* will guide you every step of the way. Read it. Read it again. Study it. Memorize it. It tells you all you need to know.

"Here at Riley, you're gonna learn the Army way a riding. And when you ride the Army way, your position is everything. Position. Position. Position. You'll learn what we call the 'Chamberlin Military Seat.' That seat, General Chamberlin refined over many years. He was an Olympic champion and for a while he served as the Commandant of the CRTC. And you're gonna learn that seat through the Army way a teaching. You're also gonna learn more than that seat and riding in general. You're gonna learn to groom your horse the Army way. You're gonna learn to tack up your horse the Army way. You're gonna learn to water your horse the Army way. You're gonna feed your horse the Army way. You're gonna learn to maneuver your horse the Army way. You're gonna do everything the Army way. And the Army way is the *only* way as long as you're in this man's army. And to learn all this, you'll work with a different horse every day. By the time you're through here, you'll ride at least 60 or more different horses, sometimes two different horses in a single day."

"If you've thrown a leg over a horse before: I say *again*—forget everything you *think* you know. I can tell ya, 'you're gonna have lots a habits to break. Face it right now. Almost everything you think you know won't apply here. At first, you might have a hard time. In fact, I *guarantee that some of you* are gonna have a hard time. Accept it. Work through it. You're here now in this man's Army. And in this man's Army, the Army way is the *only* way.'

"Now, if you've *never* been on a horse before, don't worry about it. That's a *positive.* You've got no bad habits to break. And remember this about horses: the horse is a child. Treat him like one. He has a memory that never fails. He remembers everything. Remember that the horse learns through reward and punishment. And by punishment, I don't mean cruelty or harshness. Punishment always must remain gentile and subtle. Usually, just a squeeze of the leg, a nudge of the spur, and twitch of the finger. And ya don't want your fingers to contradict your legs and your legs to contradict your fingers. That's something to remember."

"And another thing: The Army paid 165 dollars for every horse in this man's army. I can get another one a *you* for the cost of a penny postcard. So who do you think the army values more? The horse or you? So take care of your horse better than you take care of yourself."

"Now, if for some reason you don't learn the Army way, then I've got a special job for you. You'll shovel horse manure. You'll shovel all day. Day in and day out *for the duration of this war.* You'll shovel every pile a manure crapped by every single one of the four-thousand-two-hundred horses we have here at Riley. And then, you'll shovel for the 12,000 horses down at Fort Bliss. And those manure piles down there at Bliss, trust me: Those manure piles are a good three stories high. And they stretch more than a mile long. Each. And there's a dozen of 'em down there. That's a whole lot a shovel'n. And it never stops. Don't forget that."

"This afternoon, you're gonna see a demonstration of horsemanship. You'll see what an expert military rider achieves with a well-trained horse.

Col. Hiram Tuttle has graciously agreed to demonstrate for you the highest level of equitation. Col. Tuttle won a Bronze Medal in the Olympics of 1932. He knows what he is doing. Keep in mind, we don't expect you to ride as well as Col. Tuttle. And you won't learn all that he demonstrates this morning. But Col. Tuttle will show you what a military expert can achieve with a well-trained horse. And he'll demonstrate the movements you need to learn. I'll tell ya what those movements are as he shows them. All right, we're gonna march over to the main drill field and watch."

The troopers watch Col. Hiram Tuttle demonstrate a wide variety of movements. He performs *single tempi* flying changes of lead down the center of the drill field. But most importantly, Col. Tuttle demonstrates each of the maneuvers each recruit will need to learn.

Col. Tuttle's performance—especially the successive flying changes of lead down the center of the drill field—impresses the 18-year-old from Chicago. For the next 68 years of his life, he will remember that day and describe Tuttle's performance to his children and grandchildren.

Figure 118 *The self-taught Col. Hiram Tuttle demonstrates a variety of movements on one of his dressage horses for the recruits at the CRTC. He impresses them with singe tempi lead changes down the center of the drill field. At a rodeo organized by Turk Greenough in June of 1942, Tuttle not only performs the single tempi lead changes but he also canters backwards to his original point of departure. He impresses even the championship rodeo riders. US Army photo.*

After the demonstration, Sgt. Offill gives his recruits their reading assignments for the night and dismisses the recruits. The recruits read and memorize as much as they can of the first three chapters of *FM 25-5:* Chapter I, General Considerations; Chapter II, Knowledge and Utilization of the Mental and Moral Faculties of the Horse; Chapter III, Articles of Equipment and Their Adjustment.

The next morning, a group of corporals stands waiting at a corral with a sufficient number of horses to accommodate half the group. Sgt. Offill discusses the horse's memory, level of intelligence and the other concepts of the first two Chapters of *FM 25-5.* He then proceeds to explain the various parts of the McClellan saddle, the bridle, and the bits. He calls upon each recruit to point out the various components of each based on their previous night's reading and his explanation this morning.

Then, Sgt. Offill looks to Private DiCicco, changes his demeanor, and shouts: "Hey you, DiCicco, step over here. And come to think of it, what should we call you from now on? Moe? Larry? How about Curly? Nah—from now on you answer to the name Bur-head. Got that?"

Private DiCicco breathes deeply, smiles broadly, and answers: "Yes Sergeant."

"Ok Bur-head, jump up on this horse."

DiCicco vaults up onto the bareback horse.

"All right, you over there, Morgenthau, come 'ere. You take this lead rope and lead Bur-head up there around the outer edge of this corral. And the rest of you, count off one's and two's. And when I order you to do so: The number one's jump up on a horse; the number two's lead. And Bur-head, you shout out every time your left and right seat bone rises as the horse walks along. And the rest of you children watch and pay close attention until I say otherwise. Notice that our glamor boy up there counts off each move of the horse's hind-end. He feels the horse's hind leg movements through his seat bones and the calves of his legs. You will do likewise. It'll teach you to feel the horse and help ay' develop a sense of timing so that later you can coordinate your aids with the movement of the horse."

On command, half the recruits vault onto the bareback horses and the other half lead both horse and rider at a walk in a circle along the outer edge of the round pen. Turk Greenough, the rodeo champion, mounts up. The 18-year-old recruit from Chicago leads the six-time rodeo champion around the outer edge of the round pen. Quietly, Greenough seethes and rolls his eyes. At least, the novices learn the feel of the horse's movements, especially the hind legs, as they all shout out "left, right, left, right, left."

Sgt. Offill shouts “Halt!” “OK. Now switch roles.”

The mounted recruits dismount. The other recruits mount. The protocol repeats. After the exercise extends for several minutes, Offill shouts “Halt!”

The recruits lead their horses to the fence rail. A corporal shows them how to secure the lead rope to the fence rail in Army fashion using a special knot. Sgt. Offill assigns the class to read Chapter Four in *Field Manual 25-5* about the military way to mount the horse, to assume the military seat, and to dismount. The recruits spend the balance of the day on physical conditioning.

The polo players, the champion rodeo rider, the Hollywood stunt man, and the cowboys quietly seethe. Back at the barracks, they curse, shake their heads, and complain. Yet, they know that Sgt. William Offill might send them to the manure pile at any time to shovel forever if need be. So they persevere. And they read and study the sections regarding the military way to mount, to assume the military seat, and then to dismount as described in *FM-25-5* until “lights out.”

The next morning, Sgt. Offill arrives at the barracks just before dawn. He wakes everyone by pounding on the lid of a trash can. He orders all to wash up and dress. Then, he directs all recruits to gather at a raised wooden barrel on legs about five feet off the floor with a 2 x 6 “neck” simulating the neck of a horse. Each of the 250 barracks buildings at the CRTC contains a duplicate wooden “horse.”

“This fine morning: *This* is your horse,” says Offill.

A corporal comes with a saddle blanket and a McClellan Saddle in hand. The corporal blankets and saddles the barrel. He responds to Offill’s commands: “Stand to horse—Prepare to mount—mount.” The corporal, on command, stands to horse, prepares to mount, and then mounts—all in strict military fashion. He assumes the “Chamberlin Military Seat” as the seat is called at the CRTC. As the corporal performs each move, Offill describes the details of mounting and points out the rider’s body position from the heel of his boot up to the top of his head.

Offill then yells out: “Dismount.” The corporal dismounts, again, in strict military fashion as described in *FM 25-5* and he “stands to horse.” Offill describes the correct manner to dismount. On Offill’s command, each recruit now attempts to mount and assume the military seat. Offill critiques the effort of each. He adjusts the position of each “rider” on the wooden “horse.” He explains that each recruit must learn the military seat as second nature. “You must master each step completely before you move to the next step,” says Offill. “And that is what we will try to do here.”

He then orders the mounted recruit to dismount. Each recruit repeats the procedure: mount, assume the seat, dismount. Each recruit does this several times until he gets it "right." Of course, *FM 25-5* defines "right." No other way will do. Sgt. Offill tells the group to practice on the "wooden horse" as much as possible when in the barracks. He dismisses the recruits for breakfast. Later, he orders the group to a corral where Sgt. Offill delivers a lecture on the day's material. Then, the recruits break down into groups of ten. A corporal attends to each group as Sgt. Offill supervises.

To begin, a corporal stands waiting with a horse. First, the corporal demonstrates the proper Army way to groom the horse. On the fence rail sits a saddle blanket, a McClellan Saddle, and a bridle. The corporal again demonstrates the proper Army way to fold a saddle blanket to six thicknesses: "with all four corners to the rear and near." The corporal shows the proper Army way to apply the blanket to the horse's back upon hearing the command "Blanket." He shows the proper Army way to saddle the horse—again, upon hearing the command "Saddle." The same with putting on the bridle. He then orders: "Stand to horse."

On Sergeant Offill's command, the corporal prepares to mount and then mounts the horse in military fashion and takes the military seat. Offill again describes the characteristics of a good "mount." He then describes the proper "Chamberlin Military Seat." Now on command, the Corporal demonstrates *at the walk* each riding hall movement that the recruits must master as Offill calls out commands: "Circle." "Figure Eight." "Serpentine." "Turn on the forehand." "Turn on the hindquarters." "Oblique to the left." "Two-track to the right." And so on. "Don't worry about these movements now, we'll get to them soon enough. But now you have an idea as to where we are going."

Now a group of corporals brings up enough horses for each recruit to groom, blanket, saddle, and bridle. Supervised by a corporal, each recruit grooms and tacks up his horse (in proper military fashion of course). On command, each recruit "stands to horse." Sgt. Offill inspects each horse to be sure blankets, saddles and bridles are perfectly placed. He inspects closely the saddles and brides. Every fold in the leather must be spotlessly clean, every buckle polished. Sgt. Offill then puts on a white glove and passes his gloved hand over the croup of each horse. If any dust appears, he orders the recruit to untack the horse and once again groom the horse from the tip of the lips to the dock and then to the tip of the tail. Almost half the class must repeat the grooming and, once again, clean the tack even to the point of disassembling the bridles to remove every hint of grime. Everything must be in perfect order down to the most minute detail. The recruits tack up their horses again.

Each recruit then attempts to mount, assume the Chamberlin Military Seat (called the military seat for short), and then dismount, all on command and under the watchful eye of Sgt. Offill and his corporals. After this, he orders the recruits to lead their horses (in correct military fashion) to the stables and to untack, groom, water and feed them. He reminds the recruits to practice on the wooden horse in the barracks. He then calls it a day. The recruits spend the rest of their day in physical conditioning.

The recruits return to the barracks and grumble. When they will actually ride? Those "more experienced with horses" grumble the most. Suddenly after dinner, Sgt. Offill appears in the barracks and calls all to attention at the "wooden horse." A corporal walks to the saddled "wooden horse," mounts in military fashion and assumes the military seat. Each recruit follows suit in the prescribed mounting pattern or at least close to what they saw. Each takes the military seat or tries to do so, hears Offill's corrections, and then dismounts, all on command.

For the rest of their waking hours that night, the group practices mounting the barrel, taking the seat, and then dismounting as supervised by a corporal. For the next several nights in addition to the practice of mounting the "horse," they read and re-read the descriptions of the prescribed mounting and dismounting procedures together with the military seat found in *FM 25-5*. Sgt. Offill demands perfection. He also assigns the recruits to read Chapters Five and Six of FM 25-5 that deals with "taking reins," the five "rein effects," and the application of the "aids."

The next morning, with the group at a large round pen, Sgt. Offill reviews the previous day's lessons. Several other corporals bring up enough horses for each recruit to groom, saddle, and bridle his own horse. Sgt. Offill and the corporals supervise to be sure the recruit performs all of this in the prescribed Army manner. Then, on command, each recruit attempts to mount in the military fashion and to take the military seat.

Sgt. Offill assesses the effort of each recruit and corrects any flaws he sees. On command, he orders all to dismount. He then orders: "Mount." He orders "Dismount." He orders again "Mount." And then, he orders "Dismount." They continue until each recruit mounts and dismounts perfectly. He then commands all to mount and assume the military seat. He checks the seat of each recruit and makes corrections as required. He orders all to dismount and to tie their horses to the fence rail.

Sgt. Offill demonstrates the proper manner to "take reins." He stresses that the fingers should communicate a soft feel with the horse's mouth; that the position of the wrists and their rotation in or out provide either a soft feel or a firm feel to the horse: thumbs up and toward each other offers a soft feel; thumps up and away from each other offers a firm feel. Offill says that if the horse fails to respond to the soft approach, the rider rotates the wrists to bring the fingers up and the thumbs out to provide a firmer feel to gain obedience.

A corporal mounts a horse and demonstrates the application of each of the five "rein effects" in combination with the "leg aids." Offill orders all recruits to "stand to horse, prepare to mount, mount." He commands that each recruit use the opening rein to enter the round pen and ride along the pen's edge in a large circle at the walk. He commands "Halt." The mounted corporal now demonstrates another rein effect. Each recruit then applies the same rein to achieve (hopefully) the same result. The corporal demonstrates another one of the five rein effects to achieve a movement, then another, and another until the recruits see and apply each of the of the five rein effects with a corresponding movement.

After working on applying the rein effects, Offill orders the corporal to perform the suppling exercises one by one and the recruits follow suit. Finally, all dismount, return the horses to the stable. They untack, groom, water and feed each horse. Offill instructs the recruits to continue their practice in the barracks on the wooden "horse," to re-read again Chapters Five and Six in *FM 25-5* regarding the suppling exercises, how to take reins, the five rein effects; and then read Chapter Seven of *FM 25-5* which deals with the control and management of the horse. After this, Sgt. Offill dismisses the group to go to pistol practice for the rest of the day.

The recruits return to their barracks. The cowboys and polo players grumble and complain amongst themselves. That evening after dinner, each recruit reads and re-reads the assigned sections in *FM 25-5*. Each works through the five rein effects and the position of each.

The next morning at the stable, the recruits groom and tack up their horses as corporals watch to be sure all follow the precise military methods. They then "stand to horse" and hold the reins in the required manner. Upon command, they "prepare to mount." On command, they mount and assume the military seat. By now, most recruits mount and dismount well enough at least when the horse stands still.

Sgt. Offill comments on the procedures of each recruit. He then walks back and forth down the line and corrects the position of each trooper to refine the "military seat" of each. Sgt. Offill then orders each trooper to "take reins." The Sergeant or a corporal watches each recruit do so. Each recruit "takes reins" several times upon hearing the command "take reins."

Sgt. Offill then describes the various aids and how to apply them in coordination with each other. Then, at the walk, the mounted troopers drop the reins and perform the various suppling exercises that they learned earlier while being led in the large round pen.

Then Offill orders all to push the gait up to the trot, drop the stirrups and sit the trot. The recruits do so for about 15 minutes. Offill orders them to return to the walk. They walk for a few times around the round pen. Then, Offill commands a trot. Some riders kick their horses. Offill, yells: "NO, just squeeze first. Be subtle. Appear to do nothing!" The recruits trot then walk, walk then trot and continue with upward and downward transitions. Then, they return to the stables, untack the horses, groom and water and feed them. Sgt. Offill assigns for reading Chapter Eight of FM 25-5 regarding riding hall movements. The rest of the day, the recruits take marksmanship exercises and also physical conditioning exercises.

Back at the barracks, the cowboys quietly seethe at what they insist to be ridiculous. Whether they like it or not, the methods and the regimentation prepare them to coordinate well with larger groups of horsemen and to surmount the obstacles of military riding. Back at the barracks after the day's work, the polo players shake their heads and the cowboys curse. But learn the Army's way, they must.

Over the next several days, the cowboys experience the most difficult time perfecting their "military seat." The process of unlearning past habits proves a difficult one. The regimentation connected with "taking reins" and all the other rules and protocols frustrate them as well. Nonetheless, they again read and re-read the manual sections regarding the five rein effects and the other "aids" and also the section that deals with various riding hall movements.

Over the next several days, they learn *at the walk* to apply and coordinate the aids, principally the hands, legs, and weight, as specified by *FM 25-5*. Sgt. Offill says: "You must learn to put your leg in exactly in the same place every time" They begin, also at the walk, the various riding hall movements. Those "most experienced" with horses find much of this frustrating because the Cavalry has specific methods to achieve various movements and does not allow deviance or variation. Offill calls out commands such as:

"By the right bearing rein, volt to the left. March!"

"By the left direct rein of opposition, half turn to the left. March!"

"Turn to the right, by the right opening rein. March!"

"By the left rein of indirect opposition, on two-tracks on the diagonal. March!"

"Half turn in reverse, leave the track by the bearing rein. March!"

"By the right opening rein, half turn. March!"

The cowboys feel that the neck rein is good enough to achieve all they want. They view the five rein effects as nonsense. So, the experienced recruits must continue to unlearn as well as learn. The experienced have lifelong habits to undo. Those with no prior experience but with athletic talent learn quickly and without resistance. They learn to apply the five rein effects as described in the manual: the opening rein, the direct rein of opposition, the bearing rein, the indirect rein of opposition in front of the withers, the indirect rein of opposition behind the withers. "Place your hand in the proper position and then squeeze the fingers intermittently. Do Not Pull on those reins!" yells Sgt. Offill. "Hey, trooper, get those arms in close to your sides! Make like Captain Hook with your arm from the elbow through the reins to that horse's mouth form a straight line with your arm hugging your side! No more flapping around with those elbows!"

They learn to coordinate hands with legs by practicing everything at the walk, "the mother of all gaits" as the Sgt. Offill calls it. "Coordinate your hand with your leg as we told you! Legs first, then hands. Keep your hands light! Move the fingers! Don't pull on those reins. The horse moves from the rear, so legs first. Leg to hand, leg to hand! When the horse does what you want, then stop squeezing those legs, stop everything. Don't do anything more until you want a change or the horse changes on his own. The idea is to do nothing more once the horse obeys. Once the horse obeys, then go back to your original position and do nothing more until you want a change or the horse changes on his own!"

"Your legs: start with a gentile squeeze, work up to a little stronger pressure. If that doesn't work, then tickle him with your heel. But don't start with a strong kick! Where do you go from there if it doesn't get what you want? Plus, don't ride with your feet parallel to the horse. Keep your feet at about a 45-degree angle. That way you can use your legs more effectively. And if the horse bolts, you can stay on the horse with your calves. Don't depend on your knees and don't squeeze with your thighs. You'll pop out of the saddle and down you'll go. Keep your heels down, put the weight of your lower body into those heels. If your leg is wrong, then your seat is wrong."

Sometimes humor shows itself during this timeframe: On a lark, Sgt. Offill chooses a horse just over 14 hands high and puts the tallest recruit (at 6'5") in the group on that horse. The man's feet hang so low as to stretch down perhaps one foot from the ground. He "rides" this horse all day long.

Everyone, including the rider get a laugh out of this. Still, the cowboy's and polo player's sense of frustration grows—but the prospect of shoveling horse manure day in and day out disciplines the frustration. They persevere. Every recruit realizes that the Cavalry "owns' them. It is the Army way as the only way and they have no other choice.

On the more serious side, by now at the start of each riding session, the recruits sit the trot without stirrups for extended periods up to 30 minutes, sometimes more. The cowboys keep slipping into the western mode of riding and often break into a canter. Of course, Sgt. Offill yells at them to transition back to the trot. In time, each recruit learns to sit the trot.

Next, each learns to post at the trot. The cowboys suffer the hardest time as they try to learn the rhythm of posting. "Remember, rotate on your thighs," Sgt. Offill yells out. The polo players and hunt riders understand the rhythm of the post and the rise at the trot, but some fail to post *exactly* as prescribed by *FM 25-5*. Sgt. Offill calls them out. "You'll never make 100 miles in a day by lifting yourself so high off the saddle. Don't do that. Let the thrust of the horse's hind legs push you slightly out of the saddle and forward." He calls out when he wants each recruit to change diagonals periodically to develop the horse's hindquarters evenly. Offill orders all to reduce the gait to the walk. He then calls out each riding hall movement he wants the recruits to execute and calls out the rein effect that he wants them to use. He often varies the rein effect or combination of rein effects to execute the same movement.

The next day after sitting the trot without stirrups for about 30 minutes, its back to the walk, the "mother of all gaits" as Sgt. Offill constantly reminds them for what seems like the 50th time. More than one recruit says under his breath: "I can't wait to meet the mother's daughter." The recruits work to apply the aids to achieve the basic riding hall movements. Over time, and always at the walk, the recruits learn the turn on the forehand, turn on the haunches; the rein back; and two-tracking at the walk. They ride circles, serpentines, and obliques, the shoulder-in, the haunches-in and a host of other movements, initially, all at the walk and always applying the aids the Sgt. Offill calls out.

Once they understand the aids and perform to Offill's satisfaction the movement at the walk, they move into the trot. Then they attempt the canter depart and perform all movements at the canter. In time, each trooper learns to ask for the canter depart three different ways: by outside lateral aids, by inside diagonal aids, and by inside lateral aids. They apply each method on command. With each riding hall movement, Sgt. Offill specifies the rein effect the rider will apply. He yells out:

"By outside lateral aids, ask for the canter depart."

"Now, back down to the trot."

"Now by inside diagonal aids, ask for the canter depart."

"On the forehand, half turn in reverse. March!"

"On two-tracks. Haunches-In. March!"

"Right Oblique. March !"

"On two-tracks. Right Oblique. March !"

And so on. Sgt. Offill stresses the fact the rider's hands and legs must coordinate to achieve the results intended as shown in the diagrams of *FM 25-5*. Sgt. Offill or a corporal watch each recruit to be sure the rider's hands and legs coordinate properly.

Sgt. Offill recommends more advanced methods for more advanced horses. For the canter depart, he recommends inside lateral aids on the more highly trained horses even though *FM 25-5* relegates this method to "higher equitation" and is not found in the manual. For example, for the canter depart to take the left lead, the rider applies with his left hand the indirect rein of opposition in front of the withers, he weights his right buttock, and then he slides his left leg forward to just behind the horse's left elbow, and lightly taps the horse with his toe. The horse breaks into the canter on the left lead. To ask for a flying change of leads, Sgt. Offill recommends this specific method on the better trained horse. At the same time, he requires that each recruit learn each of the three methods to ask for the canter depart so that no matter what horse the recruit mounts, he will have a method that the horse understands.

By now, during each training session, the recruits work through serpentines, obliques, circles, figures-of-eight, and other movements—always first at the walk, then at the trot. In time, some (but not all) recruits possess the reflexes and the necessary "feel" to ask for flying changes of lead at each change in direction while at the canter. The polo players and hunt riders understand the movements but often find it difficult to execute them using the method Offill commands. The cowboys continue to quietly complain that neck reining is good enough and all this other five rein effects nonsense is just that: nonsense. Nonetheless, they learn in time.

At each gait, they practice upward and downward transitions. They extend and then shorten the gait." At the walk: calm, forward and straight," yells Offill. "Remember, the horse moves from his rear end not his front end." In time, recruits go from the halt to gallop and then from a gallop to halt with a rapid dismount followed a rapid remount and an instant gallop. They halt, drop the reins, and immediately ask for the canter and then pick up the reins, drop down to the trot and then to the walk. They do all of this again and again until each trooper achieves the level of competence that Sgt. Offill demands. Now for the night's reading: Sgt. Offill assigns Chapters Nine and Ten in *FM 25-5*: the chapters that deal with jumping and cross-country riding.

As training progresses, a corporal demonstrates to the class how to jump an obstacle. He does this several times as Sgt. Offill explains the phases of the jump and what the corporal does in each phase. After the demonstration, the recruits groom and tack their assigned horses for this day. They mount on command and move to a jumping chute. Each recruit knots and drops the reins and ties his belt around the neck of the horse about mid-way between the withers and the horse's head. A recruit enters the jumping chute. He gently places his hands on the belt. He knows *not* to balance himself on the belt, but rather stays lightly in the saddle, sinks much of his weight into his boot heels, grips principally with his calves, keeps his center of gravity low, balances his upper body without leaning on the horse's neck, and places his hands at the appropriate position at the sides of the horse's neck.

With hands on the belt and reins knotted on the pommel, the recruit won't jerk the horse's mouth as horse and rider enters the jumping chute and negotiates a series of jumps. Sgt. Offill cautions the recruits to stay in the saddle until the upward thrust of the horse's forelegs causes the rider to leave the saddle. They must take care *not* to anticipate the jump which could lead to disaster. He cautions each rider that once over the jump, the rider must stay out of the saddle until the descent phase of the jump completes. Once he and his horse completes the jump, he must return to the saddle.

Over the course of several days, again and again, the recruit on horseback goes through the chute which presents a series of approximately ten "ins and outs" of moderate height. Some of the horse show riders want to stay out of the saddle throughout their trip through the chute. Sgt. Offill yells: "No. Get your rear back into that saddle once you complete the jump's descent. Every time you confront a jump, be sure your rear is in that saddle. Sit deep in that saddle. Let the action of the horse move you up and out the saddle. Don't anticipate it." Each well-experienced horse takes each jump in stride. This exercise continues part of each day until the recruits perform well.

With repetitions through the chute, in time, the trooper refines his balance by also performing many of the suppling exercises while going through the chute. He refines his body position. He improves his seat. He learns the mechanics of the jump. He learns not to balance on the reins because, as yet, he has not jumped with reins in hand. He learns not to lean on the horse's neck. He learns to place his hands on the sides of the horse's neck while negotiating a jump, all without ever holding the reins. Offill stresses that once the rider holds the reins during the jump that the elbows must stay relaxed to enable the hands to follow the movements of the horse's mouth without losing a soft contact between rider's fingers and horse's mouth. "Never rest your hands on the horse's mouth, but don't lose the gentle contact with his mouth either," says Offill.

Once the recruit masters his balance and position by going through the chute dozens of times and satisfies Sgt. Offill that he has confirmed his position, the recruit attempts his first jumps with hands positioned properly on the sides of the horse's neck without the neck strap but still without holding the reins. Later, when totally confirmed in his seat and in the method of the jump, the recruit ultimately negotiates the series of jumps with reins in hand. Offill yells out, "relax your elbows so that your hands follow the horse's mouth. Flexible and following elbows! Don't forget that." The best recruits maintain a soft connection with the horse's mouth throughout the series jumps. "Keep the gentle contact with the horse's mouth throughout the whole jump," says Offill.

Once the recruits start holding the reins, some to try to manage the horse's progress over the jumps. "No. No. NO!!!, yells Sgt. Offill. "Let the horse do it himself. Don't try to tell him what to do. He will size the obstacle up all by himself. If you think he will refuse the jump, then be firm with your legs. But otherwise, let the horse do his job! Somebody watching should think you are doing *nothing*!" In time, each recruit meets Sgt. Offill's expectations. Sgt. Offill assigns the recruits to re-read Chapter Ten in *FM 25-5*, the chapter regarding cross-country riding.

As the recruits further develop their "Chamberlin Military Seat," they better coordinate their legs and weight with the five rein effects. As their physical condition improves, and their "riding muscles" strengthen, they practice six to seven hours each day, six days each week by riding through open country at Fort Riley's 53,000 acres of prime riding land. At this point, recruits learn to negotiate down steep slides and to leap from ledges four feet high. For both such obstacles, they must keep the seat slightly out of the saddle with weight in the boot heel and the upper body positioned well forward from the hips and parallel to the horses' neck with the rider's weight well over the horse's withers.

For steep slides, the recruit learns to lean from the hips forward over the horse's neck, to put most of his weight into his boot heels with the seat slightly out of the saddle, and to bridge the reins across the horse's withers as horse and rider go down the slide. In the beginning, most recruits struggle with this concept. Their intuition suggests that they should lean back not forward while negotiating such obstacles. Again, the cowboys and some of those who play polo or ride in horse shows experience the most frustration and trouble when they think of leaning forward while going down a steep grade or as they leap off of a ledge and then descend downhill. Leaning forward from the hips, rising slightly out of the saddle with most of one's weight in one's boot heels seems so counter-intuitive. Sgt. Offill also demands that the rider descend down the slide straight, never on an angle.

As the Hollywood stunt man who rode in the film *The Charge of the Light Brigade,* moans: "I never heard of such a thing like leaning forward. What is to keep the horse from tumbling forward let alone the rider." The cowboys and some of the polo players agree. Nonetheless, when each recruit on his horse walks over a cliff and descends a steep 70-foot slide in correct, military fashion, both horse and rider perform well. Says one former trooper 65 years later: "Looking down that slide for the first time put a knot in the pit of my stomach. The thought of leaning slightly up out of the saddle with all the weight in your depressed heels and leaning forward as you go over that cliff and down that slide seems to be the opposite of what you should do. You can't imagine the sense of relief I felt when I made it to the bottom without falling off." As the days progress, the recruits learn to ride up steep hills and down even steeper (but shorter) slides: "Be slightly up out of the saddle with your weight in your depressed heals and lean forward from the hips when you go down a steep hill or slide and when you leap off a ledge. When you go down a slide, this position puts the weight on the forehand, pushes the front hooves into the dirt, and frees up the hindquarters to control the descent," says Sgt. Offill. "When going up a steep hill, the rider's forward position frees up the horse's hindquarters to push the horse and rider up the hill."

Figure 119 *A slide tests the mettle of trooper and horse and is not for the faint of heart. The CRTC teaches troopers to lean forward with weight into the depressed heels while descending a slide. The trooper must guide the horse straight down the slide. To attempt to descend at an angle might cause the horse to lose balance and to tumble down to disaster. US Army photo.*

Figure 120 *In 1942, this trooper shows the proper way to descend a slide. He keeps his seat well forward, pushes his buttocks well to the rear with most of his weight in his depressed heels and braces against the stirrups. He bridges the reins over the withers. This position drives the forelegs deeper into the soil, frees up the hindquarters so the horse's legs come well under, and helps to control the pace of the descent. US Army photo.*

Now, the recruits cross gullies and mud holes; in time, the will ford streams and swim rivers. For narrow rivers, they will swim mounted. For wider rivers, they will learn to either hold the horse's tail or to swim alongside the horse as they guide the horse across to the opposite shore remembering to unbuckle the snaffle reins so that the horse does not become entangled. They jump over ever wider mud holes, ditches, and ravines. They ride down the steep side of ravines and then immediately ride up the other side. Sometimes they face a low obstacle that they must jump on the way out of the ravine.

When Sgt. Offill looks the other way, the cowboys sometimes lean back on the downward ride but experience great difficulty going up the other side. They cannot adjust position—from leaning back to bending forward—fast enough. And then, when they try to jump the obstacle that obstructs their way, their upper body position is all wrong. Sometimes a recruit will fall off his horse even when no obstacle obstructs the path.

For some reason, it seems the Sergeant always sees them when they fall off. Sgt. Offill makes these recruits repeat the obstacle a few times until they get it right. Once the recruit accepts the fact that he must remain forward at all times, the forward position enables him, and more importantly, the horse to take the obstacle in stride.

At this stage, when no-longer being closely checked by a corporal or by Sgt. Offill, a recruit might forget something basic. One example involves the correct way to put a McClellan Saddle on the horse. One recruit, a scion of a famous wealthy East Coast family with previous experience with horses, rides the whole day with his McClellan Saddle on backwards. A Major rides up and asks, "You have a new style saddle there trooper?" The entire class smiles at that.

In the field, troopers learn to jump all manner of obstacles three feet high. Yet, Offill tells them that they will seldom meet a fence they must jump in the real world. "Much better to knock the fence down if you can and ride through. It saves the horse," Offill says. The recruits also jump ditches, mud holes, and bogs up to ten feet wide. These obstacles, says Offill, they will see and jump often. They learn to negotiate combinations of multiple jumps, steep inclines followed by even steeper slides. They learn to ride up and down steep wooded slopes; through brambles, marshes and swamps, and over sand and rocks.

They learn to dismount and lead their horses to conserve energy over exceptionally rugged terrain. Every hour, they dismount and lead their horses for ten minutes. This allows vital blood supplies to filter into the compressed areas of their horses' backs (and thus keep the horse's back muscles from degenerating). The practice also enables the riders to stretch their legs. In time, they will adopt the Cavalry's special distance marching protocol (a copy of which the reader will find in *The Chamberlin Reader).* They also learn to ride at night without a flicker of light except the glow of the stars. Sargent Offill stresses that they must pay close attention to their horses well-being in the summer heat. He says: "Just remember, the Devil went to Hell to cool off after suffering a hot summer in Kansas."

After riding seven and sometimes eight or more hours in a day, they dismount and walk their horses for the last mile before reaching the stable area. This usually cools out the horse. Once home with the horse cooled out, the recruit waters and grooms the horse thoroughly. He then feeds the horse (more water first, then hay, then grain). He massages the horse's legs and cleans the hoofs—all according to established Army protocols. He also learns how to inspect the hoof for problems and to remove and replace a shoe in the field when necessary.

On a set day of the week, all recruits spend hours grooming their horses. They and their horses form a line for inspection. An officer wearing a white glove passes the gloved hand over all areas of the horse to test for clean grooming. Woe unto any recruit whose horse fails inspection. After inspection, the meticulously groomed horse, as if out of spite, roles in the dust or mud! Of course, the horse then requires another session of grooming before returning to the stable.

Then one morning Sgt. Offill arrives at the barracks and yells: "Rise and shine children. You're going swimming today!" Offill orders the recruits to dress as usual with three-buckle cavalry boots and riding breeches. As they file out of the barracks, a corporal stands at the door and gives each recruit a life jacket to wear. More than one recruit wonders "What now?" Offill orders the whole group to the stables, where they saddle up and mount their assigned horses. Offill leads them to the Republican River and orders all to dismount and to gather near.

"Ok listen up," Offill says. "Today, you get swimming lessons. What you are going to do is ride your horse into the river. Once the horse begins to swim, you slide off the horse onto the up-current side of the river, which right now is to your right as you cross the river.

"And don't worry, we've got several boats downstream to keep you from drowning if you and your horse fail to make it across. And if you don't know how to swim, then this is a good time to learn. But, even if you don't learn, the life jacket will keep you afloat. And if you do swim well, wear the life jacket regardless. It will keep you afloat if your horse knocks you unconscious and we'll fish you out of the river.

"Now the horse you've been assigned this morning is a fair to good swimmer. So don't worry about the horse. At the same time, there are several things you must know:

> First, unbuckle your reins. That way, your horse won't catch his legs or become entangled in the reins.
>
> Next, tighten the girth on your saddle super tight. That way, it won't slide off. Also, cross your stirrups over the saddle.
>
> And now listen *very carefully*: Do not hold the reins or use them in any way. In fact, take the reins off of the bit and buckle them to the D-ring of your halter.
>
> Also, don't under any circumstances try to turn the horse suddenly. Don't try to pull your horse's head back to you if he swims out and away from you. Turn your horse loose if that happens.
>
> As you swim the river, you can hang on the mane, the saddle, the stirrup, or your horse's tail.
>
> But never, I repeat, never hold on to the reins. And be careful. Relax. Don't get all tense and pull the horse over backwards. That could kill you if you end up under the horse in that deep water. From time to time, I've seen recruits get kicked in the head and others go under but nobody has drowned on me—yet.
>
> If it looks like you'll have trouble, then let the horse go his own way. You take care of yourself and swim to shore.
>
> And one other thing: keep your campaign hats on. If your horse starts flailing around and his hoof hits your head, maybe the hat will save you from a bruise or worse. Plus, I want you to look like cavalrymen when you reach the other shore.
>
> And no we won't have milk a cookies waiting for you when you reach the other side—that is, if you do. Any questions?"

No questions. Just more than a few deep breaths and a few dropped jaws. Clearly not one of the recruits—including the horse show riders, cowboys, and polo players—have ever gone swimming with a horse across a deep river. Puddles and knee-deep water, yes; but never fully clothed with a saddled horse through a deep river with a relatively strong current.

In they go mounted on their horses. As they enter the water, Sgt. Offill yells, "Remember to slide off—remember to slide off to the up-current side once your horse begins to paddle in the deep water."

Each recruit slides off, some better than others. And across they swim. Some hold onto the mane. Some hold the saddle pommel. A few hold the horse's tail. Everyone makes it. They perform this exercise four times over the course of a few days. In the end, many recruits master the techniques well enough to remain mounted all the way across the river (if mounted on a horse who is a strong swimmer; if not, they slide off as originally instructed).

The next concept to learn: The recruits practice maneuvers in squad formation and perform close order drill on horseback. They learn to watch Sgt. Offill for hand signals that communicate what the they must do. They maneuver on the drill field. First, they practice at the walk and then the trot. Later, they maneuver in the field as if on campaign. Upon seeing Offill's hand signal, they move in a well-orchestrated maneuver from a column of twos to form a straight line. Upon another hand signal, they go from the trot to the canter; and then from the canter to the full gallop into a "hell for leather" charge at the maximum speed that their Thoroughbred and half-Thoroughbred horses can achieve. At the gallop, the recruits rise slightly from the saddle well forward with most of their weight through the thighs and down into their heels. "It was great fun to ride in a charge like that, after all, I was only 18," said one participant more than 65 years later.

Once the recruit achieves a satisfactory level of competence, he learns, while mounted, to lead a pack-horse carrying a machine gun or mortar. The mounted recruit guides his riding horse by holding the reins in his left hand. With his right hand, he holds the lead rope to guide the pack-horse who follows behind. He learns to ride at the walk, trot, canter, and full gallop with the second horse at his side. He also learns to jump obstacles on his riding horse while leading the pack-horse over the jump as well. One thing amazes many: as a rider approaches a tree with the lead rope guiding the pack-horse in his right hand, the tree might separate the two. The recruit learns that he can drop the lead rope, pass by the tree on the left as the pack horse passes the tree on the right. Once beyond the tree, the pack-horse brings his head close to the rider's right hand so that the rider may gab the lead rope. The mounted rider grabs the lead rope and thus enables horse, rider, and pack-horse to continue as a team. The pack-horses are so well trained that this "team work" occurs every time without fail.

Figure 121. *Troopers learn not only to jump mounted; they learn to take a pack horse with them over the jump. US Army photo.*

Figure 122 *The troopers gallop at full speed. When they see the hand signal to dismount, they halt, dismount, unpack the machine gun or mortar from the pack horse, set up the weapon, and are ready to fire—all within 20 seconds. One trooper will take four horses in hand and withdraw to a place out of the line of fire. US Army photo.*

Ultimately, the whole class performs a 21-mile, cross-country ride late at night. No Corporals and no Sergeants accompany the class. The recruits are on their own. On this night ride, they jump 17 obstacles; negotiate down three steep slides; ride up and down numerous hills; jump gullies, mud holes, and bogs. They swim four rivers. They travel through pathless, rough and rocky terrain strewn with heavy underbrush with only a map to guide them and a flashlight with which to read the map.

When the recruits successfully complete this exercise, and upon Sergeant Offill's recommendation, the Director of the Horsemanship Department of the CRTC awards each recruit his spurs and the yellow "acorn" hat-band for their stiff brimmed campaign hats. Recruits no longer, they are troopers in the Cavalry now. And the Cavalry expects them to continue learning and sharpening their equestrian skills once they reach their assigned regiments.

Toward the end of "A" Troop's training in the summer of 1942, the CRTC grants the recruits some time off—more than the typical week end pass or Sunday rest. They work together to put on a rodeo for the people living in the towns surrounding Fort Riley, principally Manhattan and Junction City, Kansas. Turk Greenough manages the whole enterprise and the cowboys, rodeo riders, polo players, and others from Troop "A" as well as from the other regiments, squadrons and troops at the CRTC put on a grand show for the local townspeople. Private Greenough even calls civilian rodeo riders from all over the country and asks them to participate—and they do! Even Col. Tuttle participates. He amazes the crowd when he performs single-tempi flying changes of lead down the center of the field and then canters backwards on one of his Olympic Dressage horses. (Something he will do again six months later at the Casablanca Conference in a demonstration for President Roosevelt and Prime Minister Churchill.) The officers of the CRTC and of the Cavalry School also join in and put on a show jumping demonstration as well.

By mid-1942, over 21,000 men learn Army horsemanship at the CRTC. Already experienced riders before enlisting in the Army like Paul Mellon, Gordon Wright, Morton "Cappy" Smith, and William Steinkraus start out like all the rest and learn "the Army way" of riding there. For the balance of their careers as horseman, their riding reflects the Chamberlin influence of the CRTC. Of those four, the CRTC's Horsemanship Department selects Paul Mellon and Gordon Wright to remain at the CRTC as instructors. From Sgt. Offill's Troop "A" described above, the Horsemanship Department retains as instructors one private who demonstrates exceptional skill in the

Army's way of riding: and the 18-year-old private from Chicago, Illinois who experienced his first horse on a merry-go-round.

In a few months, the 18-year-old requests and receives a transfer to the 1st Cavalry Division which he joins in late November of 1942. He sees horrendous combat in the Southwest Pacific as an NCO in the Division's 5th Cavalry Regiment. Paul Mellon rises to the rank of Lieutenant, becomes an instructor and in 1943 transfers out of the CRTC to a line unit. Before the war ends, Mellon achieves the rank of Major. The 1943 CRTC graduate William Steinkraus serves with the 124th US Cavalry in Burma. Privates Oleg Cassini and Gordon Wright rise to the rank of Lieutenant and teach at the CRTC until the Army discharges them in January 1946.

Throughout the 1950s and 60's, Gordon Wright teaches the concepts of Fort Riley's CRTC as a famous and influential instructor of horsemanship. ("...the premier teacher in the country," says George H. Morris.[170]) He abridges and edits a "civilian" version of the 1942 edition of *FM-25-5 Horsemanship and Horsemastership, Part One, The Education of the Rider*—the "Chamberlin edition." In his introduction to his abridgment, he writes that the original manual not only offers a workman-like, step by step method to learn horsemanship but also serves as an inspiration for all who aspire to educated riding.

CRTC graduate William Steinkraus applies much of what he learns a "at Riley" and achieves that which eluded Major Harry Chamberlin: In 1968, he wins the Gold Individual Medal in the Olympic *Prix des Nations*, the first American to do so.

Thirty years after World War II, one polo player who spent two years at the CRTC as a member of the staff called his time there "two wasted years." Upon hearing this man's assessment, the 18-year old recruit who made instructor and later requested and received the transfer to the 1st Cavalry Division said: "If he thought he was wasting his time, then why the hell didn't the guy transfer out? No one would block a transfer from Riley to a combat division. We had several replacements in late 1944 and '45 from the CRTC. On second thought, maybe we were lucky the guy stayed in the USA I wouldn't want to share a fox-hole with him." 171 The former cavalryman added additional comments that remain unprintable.

In 1987, Oleg Cassini looks back fondly at his days "at Riley" and concludes that once he became an instructor, the post was like what Imperial British

170 See George H. Morris *Four Show Jumping Masters—Part 4: Gordon Wright* https://www.horsemagazine.com/thm/2010/07/four-showjumping-masters-part-4-gordon-wright/

171 Interview with Warren E. Matha.

India must have been at the height of the British Empire. Cassini writes: "Graduating training school and becoming an officer of the U.S. Army Cavalry was very important to me, perhaps even a turning point in my life..." [172] In the year 2008, the Olympic champion and winner of over 100 international competitions, William Steinkraus recalls his time "at Riley" fondly saying that at the CRTC: "They taught me how to ride all over again. Before the war and after, I studied General Chamberlin's books. The time at the CRTC also influenced my riding in a major way. And of course, we didn't get the even more intensive program offered at the Cavalry School before the war." [173]

By the time these troopers "earn their spurs" at the CRTC, however, Chamberlin has departed. With the basic format complete and the school up and running, Chamberlin leaves the CRTC in October of 1941 to command the 1st Brigade of the Second Cavalry Division (horse mounted). The Academic Division of the Cavalry School at Fort Riley releases the "Chamberlin" edition of *FM-25-5, Animal Transport, Horsemanship and Horsemastership* three months later in January 1942. For the United States, World War II enters its first full month. For Brigadier General Harry Dwight Chamberlin: the command responsibilities for which he prepares his entire adult life now begin in earnest.

Figure 123 *Training Unit of Fort Riley's Cavalry Replacement Training Center. Training at the CRTC continued throughout World War II. Photo courtesy of Sam Cox and The Society of the Military Horse.*

172 Oleg Cassini, In My Own Fashion: An Autobiography, Simon and Schuster, 1987 p.148.
173 William Steinkraus, conversation with author June 2008.

Chapter 29

Chamberlin Prepares War
To the 1st Brigade, Second Cavalry Division
Breaking, Training and Reclaiming Cavalry Horses.
And then, to the Pacific

In October 1941, Chamberlin leaves the CRTC and takes command of the 1st Brigade of the horse mounted Second Cavalry Division. On 12 November 1941, he publishes a 22-page tract titled: *Breaking, Training and Reclaiming Cavalry Horses.* In this publication, Chamberlin recommends "Four Simple Exercises" to achieve the goals of the publication's title. Chamberlin uses much the same protocol to transition the horse Pleasant Smiles from the race track to the Olympic Eventing field. The reader will find the entire publication in the companion volume to this biography, *The Chamberlin Reader.* A quick summary of the "Four Simple Exercises" follow:

> I—Riding the horse on a circle using the opening rein with absolutely no rearward tension. (Chamberlin devotes six pages to elaborate on this exercise and its benefits.)

> II—Halting and changing gaits literally hundreds of times during an hour's training. (Chamberlin devotes three pages to elaborate on this exercise and its benefits.)

III—Schooling the horse, first on serpentines described on large curves, and later as his training progresses on zig-zags which are arrived at by progressively reducing the radii of the serpentine curves until sharp changes of directions of an approximately 180 degrees are executed on the hindquarters as a pivot. The rider employs only "bearing" or "neck" rein to effectuate these movements. (Chamberlin devotes two-and one-half pages to this exercise and its benefits.)

IV—Shoulder-In. Chamberlin writes: "This exercise is not difficult and is *the most valuable of all gymnastics given a horse.*" (Chamberlin devotes five pages to this exercise and its benefits.)

Two months later, the United States enters World War II.

TO THE PACIFIC

On December 7, the United States enters World War II. In a few short months, the Japanese sweep through the Pacific and threaten Australia. The Australians press both the United States and Great Britain to defend their island. They threaten to withdraw all Australian troops from North Africa regardless of consequences if the Allies fail to protect Australia. General Marshall recommends that President Roosevelt order General Douglas MacArthur to leave Corregidor in the Philippines, to travel to Australia, to defend the island, and to give the Australians the assurance they require. MacArthur arrives in Australia shortly thereafter.

The Japanese and the Americans engage in a race for control of the south and southwest Pacific areas. Thus far, the Japanese prevail almost everywhere. They seize Wake, Guam, Singapore, all of the Philippines except the Bataan Peninsula and the island of Corregidor held by a doomed garrison. Next, they seize the Admiralties and the remaining Bismarck Archipelago. They create a massive naval and army base on the island of Rabaul. They land on the island of New Guinea. They enter the Solomons. As the Japanese press into the Solomon Islands, one of their ultimate objectives resides further south: to seize the New Hebrides Islands and thereby sever or, at least, lengthen further, the lines of supply and communication between Australia and the United States.

Once permitted to establish control over the New Hebrides, the Japanese will threaten far more than the line of communications between Australia and the United States. They will disrupt not only the Pacific theater, but global planning as well. Already hard pressed to allocate scarce shipping capacity to serve Australia, the Allies will face even more pressure if the existing sea route to Australia must move still further south. The resulting drain on shipping resources will undermine shipping plans for the European theater as well as for the Pacific. Even worse, if the Japanese cut the supply line to Australia, then New Zealand and Australia might fall to the Japanese.

To defend against these threats, Brig. General Dwight Eisenhower, chief planner for Pacific Operations, recommends to Chief of Staff General Marshall in his words: "a joint project with rather far-reaching implications." [174] The far-reaching implications to which Eisenhower refers include keeping open Australia's current Pacific lifeline to the United States, but also keeping Australia's troops fighting in North Africa. It also will keep the limited shipping resources balanced between Europe and the Pacific.

For "the joint project," Eisenhower recommends a novel approach: for the first and only time in World War II, a General officer will command a Task Force with "unified" authority over all air, sea and ground forces related to the military operation. General Marshall decides that General officer will be Brigadier General Chamberlin.

With this command structure, all Army, Army Air Corps, Navy, Marine Corps, Marine Air Corps, and Seabee lines of command pass directly and exclusively to the Task Force Commander and not through their traditional chains of command. Admiral King, Chief of Naval Operations agrees. The task force structure for this mission remains unique in World War II and will not become standard procedure for US military forces until more than 40 years later.

The Task Force's mission: to secure the New Hebrides Islands; to hack out of the jungle, as quickly as possible, a 6,000 foot long airstrip that will provide the only land based air support for future Marine and Army combat operations in the Solomon Islands; *to complete that airstrip before the Japanese complete their own airstrip on the island of Guadalcanal*; to defend the New Hebrides against an expected Japanese attack; and finally, at all costs, to hold the islands and to preserve the existing supply line between Australia and the United States. The New Hebrides remain the Allies' last line of defense to preserve this vital link.

---

174 See statement of General Eisenhower in "Hyper-War Strategic Planning for Coalition Warfare", *American Military History*, Maurice Matloff, Gen. Ed. (Center of Military History: 1973) http://www.ibiblio.org/hyperwar/.

In the race against the Japanese, if the Americans complete their airstrip in the New Hebrides before the Japanese complete their airstrip in the Solomons, the American forces will seize the advantage. If the Japanese advance to the New Hebrides, then it will be Brigadier General Chamberlin's job to repel them.

General Marshall summons Chamberlin to Washington, DC on short notice in March 1942. The order specifies that Chamberlin must leave for Washington "immediately" and gives Chamberlin a general indication of what General Marshall has in mind. Chamberlin leaves for Washington in an "unceremonious and hasty" manner to borrow Chamberlin's own words. He immediately leaves for Washington as his daughter Frederica age five, Lydia age seven, and his wife Helen remain behind.

***Figure 124** Lydia, Helen Chamberlin, and Frederica at about the time Brig. General Chamberlin departs for the Pacific. Photo courtesy of Ms. Lydia Moore.*

From this point on in this and the next chapter, we will reprint edited Chamberlin letters in this biography's normal type font and our commentary will appear in bold faced print.

The following letters Chamberlin sends to his wife, Helen. They give insights into the operation as well as into Chamberlin's state of mind and concerns, especially the concerns of a soldier with small children who serves in a combat theater. We have edited the letters somewhat to focus on pertinent points.

22 March 1942, Sunday: From Washington, DC
Kiss the babies—tell them I love them and watch them constantly. I fear my departure was a bit unceremonious and hasty. I wired Johnny and Jean when I sent yours as I felt I had been ungracious.

24 March 1942, Tuesday: From Washington, DC:
I haven't slept much since I left. It is a great adventure after all and occurs at an opportune time in my career—if fate smiles on me.... I expect to get home by the end of the week and leave very promptly for the west coast. I hope you can get packed so I can go with you in the car ...I leave on April 12th but don't mention the date to anyone. It's ghastly to think of leaving you all—God help me bear it! Continue to write c/o Lt. Col. Walter Todd—Room 2534 Munitions Bldg. Kiss my babies. I love you desperately.

Tuesday, 5:00 pm: Offices of Lt. Col. W. E. Todd W.P.D. War Dept.

"Read your letter today. Was happy indeed to hear from you, also your telegrams at the train helped a lot.

"I can't tell just how long I shall be here but will be back in a couple of weeks or earlier—I believe earlier. I suggest you start packing up at once and you probably will have to stay near your family. I have had Johnny ordered here. Brock arrived and wants to be with me. Shall try to take them both. Say nothing to anyone about where I am going. I shall tell you when I return. Jean better prepare to leave, too.

"I may be able to go west with you as I shall assemble my staff out there some place. Tell people I am staying in Washington permanently—which is, as you know, not so. Make no exceptions. Say nothing to a soul. What I told you that night at Jean's is approximately correct concerning the nature of my job. Take care of yourself and my babies. Be assured I shall come to you at the earliest possible moment and keep you with me as long as possible... I am pretty tired—it's been so long since I saw you. Kiss my blessed babies for me and you are my blessed wife. Stay very brave because I love you so. Haven't time for more now. Haven't been out of the office since I landed here..."

Chamberlin flies directly from Washington to San Francisco. Helen, the two children, as well as their friend Jean (the wife of another officer on

Chamberlin's staff) relocate from Fort Riley to the San Francisco area. Helen, Jean, and the two children share a house together.

12 April 1942: With staff assembled, Chamberlin boards his ship at San Francisco and departs for the Pacific. Operation "ROSES" begins.

Chapter 30

Task Force Command, April–June 1942

"...a joint project with rather far-reaching implications."
—Brig. General Dwight Eisenhower [175]

At sea, Chamberlin writes to Helen almost every day. The American and Filipino garrison on the Bataan Peninsula in the Philippines falls on April 9, 1942. Troops on the island fortress of Corregidor keep fighting but are doomed. The Japanese penetrate the Solomons. The New Hebrides are next. Chamberlin knows that the islands he must fortify and defend are, for all practical purposes, a last line of defense against the Japanese to preserve the effective link to Australia. This chapter will allow Chamberlin himself, through his letters to his wife, to communicate directly to the reader. We feel that this shows the inner man and the challenges, concerns, and fears that a soldier in the early days of World War II with a wife and two small children faces when deployed into what potentially might be harm's way.

17 April 1942. ...last night was sticky! I read and study most of the time. To think of anything save my work is too demoralizing. Again, at lunch today, a wave of loneliness overwhelmed me. I couldn't take another bite. Yet, I know I should thank God and I do that we are thus far safe. But to look forward to the months, and probably years, without you just crushes my soul and makes me physically ill... Being bareheaded I see I became very well burned—although the sky is partially overcast.

---

175 Ibid

20 April 1942. Beloved—Just wrote the angels a little note each—enclosed herewith. Make them write me if you can get them to enjoy it. Two weeks gone—it is a century! I think we shall get there about May 5th and hope there will be mail on the boat that comes a week or so later...

Slept on deck last night—It has been frightfully muggy and hot—a little cooler now as it has been sprinkling. At night the lights are poor and the cabins too hot to stay in. On deck it is beautiful—but each star stabs at my heart. ... Don't forget me and care for yourself. I love the job but losing you for so long is awful. Pray that we can get there and get set before being attacked.

One ship dropped behind last night. I do hope she catches up-much important property aboard. Haven't felt well Friday or yesterday—headache—nothing serious, I think. ...I wonder if you and Jean have a house now. When you get one send me pictures of it and you immediately so I'll know where you are.

It's all so gloomy—the whole world situation. God help our country. Everything brings you to my heart.

20 April 1942, 4:30 pm. Darling, just a week ago about this time we left the harbor. How many weeks will pass before we see the N. Y. again? Today we learned of a report that an enemy sub has been seen near the Christmas Islands—directly on our route—about 800 miles away! That is of concern—very cheering! Pray heaven we can avoid it. Each day will be more of a risk now. Tomorrow I believe we shall cross the equator!

Fortunately, I have many things to think about and to plan for—if and when we reach our destination. There will be so much to do—in setting up supplies later—The terrific job of installing the big guns with the necessary preliminary reconnaissance. Sanitation will be a frightful job. We all commence taking quinine before leaving the boat. We must—we and all—take 5 grains daily all the time we are there—another pleasant prospect. All enteric diseases prevail too—which means immersing all vegetables (if we ever get any) and fruits in a permanganate solution. No ice; no laundry—no nothing! It is hard to picture, but the necessities of life—to make us livable—will keep us occupied—even if the Japanese don't.

I pictured you all at 4:00 pm and tried to bring you close, but oh you are so far away. I've been thinking I must devote all my moments to thinking and planning for all these men under me. It's my only salvation.

22 April 1942. Little beloved wife. —At last we have excitement. Last night about 9:00 general alarm sounded as three of our lookouts at gun stations simultaneously thought they saw an airplane. It was a bright starry night—so I finally decided (and hoped!) that they only saw a meteor or star fall. We quieted down and their apprehension disappeared after an hour. This morning a signal from the Middleton stated an unknown plane was approaching from the southwest. Later it did not materialize—Thank heaven!

I didn't know whether it was picked up by radar, The Honolulu's listening devices, or by a lookout. The fear of course that such a plane might be a spotter for the hostile [Japanese]. It is becoming very hot and sticky as we near the equator—today it is overcast which I believe is fortunate for us since visibility is cut down…I have great responsibility and there is such an element of chance in it all that at present we are entirely God's hands. If safely unloaded and with time to perfect our defense, I feel we can put up a great fight. I pray for the time …

We are getting in more critical areas daily now—pray hard that we elude the [Japanese] air and sub forces.

23 April 1942, 9:00 am. Yesterday, dearest, I was about to write you when a general alert sounded. I discovered our five troop vessels (two have vanished going to some place unknown to us) were turning tail as fast as possible and as the horizon loomed, thru glasses, there were vessels. The cruiser sent up planes and advanced while we retreated. It was certainly exciting and frightening, too—as we seemed helpless. After what seemed an interminable time, the units proved to be American destroyers and you can imagine our relief!

I didn't have the chance to write after that. This morning the destroyers are still with us—thank heaven. Evidently, they were sent to intercept and protect us. I told you of the submarines (hostile) previously reported near the Christmas Islands. We haven't met any other ships yet and we seem to be on a totally different course—running northward in part. It's still a bit apprehension that we feel! (I hope you'll extract the historical data from these letters as I suggested. Later I'd like to recall these incidents if we're blessed with the opportunity!) Keep the dates. It's cooler when we head northward.

…It made my heart tighten painfully to find I still have one of the children's little worn out blue socks! Well, dearest one, news just came an enemy carrier plane has been sighted in the area. We are now in a truly perilous position, I fear. God help us.

23 April 1942–5:00 pm. We continued to steam north until 2:30 with an additional alarm that an unknown plane had been sighted...directly overhead in broad daylight and looking exactly like a plane. At 2:30 we joined our other ships—the Tyler, Ben Franklin, Paul Jones and another with a very modern cruiser St. Louis. We now have 8 ships, passenger and freight, 4 destroyers and 2 cruisers. I pray they stay with us! About 4:00 pm, after heading south again, we saw two planes astern but they were finally identified as two reconnoitering from the St. Louis. No further word of the enemy carrier has been received.

As a result of our retreat yesterday and turning back north for 2 hours today we haven't gained much ground (or sea) in the last 24 hours. We are still about 120 miles north of the equator and will pass it early tomorrow morning. It is exceedingly hot again. Enough history—it is a little hard on the nerves though! I hope Jeannie is out by now all well. I'll write her a note before we land—God permitting! Right now, it is 8:10 pm with you and I suppose those darlings are using all their excuses and kisses to delay going to bed! Ah, if I could see you all!

28 April 1942-7:00 am. Beloved—Had a pleasant night's sleep on deck the night before. The rain chased Johnny and me in. Bill slept thru' it. Just a sheet is all we needed...Land is in sight, faintly, to our starboard—you can guess what it is—we'll leave submarines and ships here tonight.... The sea is calm and it's warm, but not uncomfortable—how I'd love to have you in this big cabin.

Tell Dodi [176] a little Javanese boy goes about the ship playing a little tune (of deadly sameness) on a type of marimba to announce all meals. She'd love it. Help them in their singing and make them keep up their little dances, both for exercise and to develop coordination. Will you find time for all their things that mean so much? Just tell people you can't break your routine for anything... Neal, Johnny and I usually have a highball before dinner—though I have been skipping occasionally. Have been exercising systematically and am becoming harder and a bit trimmer.

29 April 1942. It's foggy and raining—we have British friends with us now in the escort. Tomorrow's the silly time when we pass the date line—skip Thursday and now its Friday, may 1st...I'm terribly perturbed—Col. Bolten (the doctor) is extremely sick. (Don't tell anyone). I pray he'll pull through—influenza, I think. If God is willing, we'll arrive on Monday—3 more days.

---

176 Chamberlin refers to his daughter Frederica as Dodi.

I'll try to get word to you by cable and radio. Please take steps to see the children are in no danger in crossing streets going to school. Please do.

I worry about the children and autos. Check their safety in every way across streets, no matter how extreme.

We turned back and picked up the ship that was left behind. I'm much behind. The destroyer had gone back to escort her and now we're altogether. One of our escort, British, took part in a famous Naval battle early in the war. Remind me sometime and I'll tell you about her.

How I wish I knew how you all are. We are 5 hours earlier than you now. Two more days'—how I pray we can make it and unload before attacks by air....

Today two yellow flares appeared from the sea! I suppose it was a signal from a friendly sub as nothing further occurred and no one except the escort knew the code signals...Kiss my babies and care for their minds and bodies. They need much psychological education to perfect their little souls and minds and fill them with appreciation of proper standards.

2 May 1942, Saturday 10:00 am. I was awakened by the ship's doctor at 4:00 a.m. who told me Col. Bolten died. In the haste of sending us away they cannot find sufficient embalming materials. They may have to bury him at sea—but I hope not. We are passing south of the islands next and east to our destination. You can see on the maps where they are. We are unable to see them as visibility is low. It is 3:10 in San F. I wonder where you all are. Be awfully careful driving the car. Be on the lookout for some friend who can get some extra second hand tires, too. Be so cautious and keep out of heavy traffic.

3 May 1942. Beloved, we should reach our destination sometime tonight. Oh, I hope we can get unloaded, but it will take days, I worry about air attack. The men of course will be hurried off tomorrow—if all goes well—but all the food, equipment, etc. in the ship's hold will take a long time, with no docking facilities...

We have started taking quinine daily as malaria is the biggest natural enemy we have. Pray for us darling—I want our expedition to acquit itself successfully and well. I feel a personal responsibility for everyone in it and hope I shall be wise foreseeing enough to give them every chance. There goes the marimba for lunch—it makes my heart yearn for Dodi. I have Dodi's boat on my desk (the flags at each end turn towards each other! I worship you all with deepest devotion).

On May 6, 1942, the Island fortress of Corregidor falls to the Japanese.

6 May 1942. All personnel except unloading details got action yesterday, and unloading is proceeding Monday. We go in—for which I was duly grateful—although unloading will take maybe a month. The place is beautiful—fruits, palms, etc. English are largely evacuated—except a few men—some French left. Rain just ceased and for two days the weather has been glorious beyond description.

Quite a lot of hostile activity not far away and I only hope we can get organized before something breaks. It is very simulating and exciting. I haven't had a minute until now to write. Must get on the move now. There is so much to do. A Gen. Rose was here and has done a great deal and is most helpful. Col. Fosset has the Marines—tell your father. I dare not look into the future too far. We can only pray for the success of our arms.

I'm going to try to get a commercial radio to you or your dad Friday... My task is a big one and the responsibility enormous. Am seeking a house in the little town. I shall be more comfortable. The unloading is a great worry. Our escort remains to help us—thank heaven! God has been very kind to us thus far. I pray he will keep us in mind...

12 May 1942. Have a chance to send this letter by plane to a place nearby from whence it may get to you earlier. I am tired so can't write much. There is so much to worry about and to accomplish. It is well, though, or I should die of loneliness.

How are my darlings? I want to see them so much. Mail is still not off the boat. I do pray your letters are in it. Another one left there yesterday which should have many precious messages from you. I do hope I can hear from you by cable or radio someday....It is so long and so bitterly lonely...

13 May 1942. I learn that the boat which we came on, and which left yesterday...will go back via the East Coast—so I fear all the letters will get to you much later than I had hoped. One of our last 'boats' came in yesterday, but the mail's not off yet. I should get some letters. I do hope so.

Each day, except possibly 2 or 3, I have written you—so you can ultimately connect up my life's history. It rains a great deal, but now the climate is lovely. I have a heavy and light blanket over me. From my office the view is one of ravishing beauty. Would that we were here on a cruise. We've gotten an ice box and electric lights in the house. Also, a native cook, one car, and Hellmas, Kelly, and Kiamco as body guards!

I was frightfully blue last night—The air field was unsatisfactory—so the 'boys' couldn't come in! We needed them terribly of course. Don't know how long it will be—make notes and I'll tell you all about it someday. However, I thought this morning, I must be cheerful for God-he's been very good to us so far—after all, we're here and alive and each day gets us closer to preparedness for attack. It still will take a long time though!!

You have no idea of the enormity of this task. We have active 800 natives working also—5th Columnists to watch—reconnaissance for many miles by plane and boat. We are right where the next mass action will occur. I wish we were far stronger.

Helen darling—you are never out of my mind—my heart beats your name! When I think of our nice home at Riley—my heart fairly breaks! Will we ever be together like that again? I pray constantly each day that we shall be. Kiss my babies.

Sunday a.m. Beautiful Wife—Two Engineer Officers from Washington came in yesterday about fields, etc., and were guests overnight so I wrote no letter—but loved you...More and more to do. It's hard to sleep at night—between aching for you and thinking of all there is to accomplish. Sleep is elusive.

Am striving to clean up the whole place of mosquitos, improper sanitation, etc. Luckily the weather now is perfectly gorgeous—rains not heavy—so as I say the scenery is beautiful beyond description... I'll write more later today...Crush the babies to your heart for me and tell them I love them so much— 'more than (as Dodi used to say) than all the world." God bless and keep you my exquisite wife—Harry.

When Chamberlin writes of the "lovely" surroundings and scenery "beautiful beyond description," he is not alone in his appraisal of the island's beauty. James Michener, a year later, will spend much of his World War II service on the same island. In fact, the island inspires the imaginary place depicted in his book *Tales of the South Pacific* and the Rogers and Hammerstein musical *South Pacific.*

15 May 1942, Friday. Darling, did not have time to write yesterday as urgent radios etc. came in and we are working under great pressure...This area is getting very 'hot,' I believe.

You didn't tell me a word about what you did all day the 14th after I left. I want to know the details of your life and the babies—every item is precious to me... Some of the Australians here have had amazing experiences and escapes from spots not far from here. Wish I could tell you about them... The view from my window is exquisite beyond description, palms; the blue, blue bay and sea-pines, flowers, etc. I hope someday we can take a trip to see it together.

16 May 1942, Saturday. I am busy every second—so much occurs and there is so much to do. Am sending Bill out to a ship and this should get to you possibly before any of my many other letters. I've told you so often all that's in my heart that you will tire of hearing it. Malaria is hitting quite a few already and there's a shortage of quinine—a stupid blunder on the part of both Army and Navy Surgeons General.

Oh, to see you all for a moment—my three lovely, beautiful girls. I worry myself sick lest something happen to any one of you.

Planes whining—cars rushing about. Navy, natives, French, English—soldiers, marines, etc. just like many movies you've seen of this area.... Must send this now as Bill is going to take them out to the boat.

19 May 1942. Just sent a note by Gen. Rose to you. He has been with a detachment before we arrived and is now going back to Caledonia. In the note—to repeat—I said to wire me to Noumea—by my regular name 'c/o General Wm. Rose, Noumea, New Caledonia.' It can go by cable, I guess, or radio. I don't know which. Just say 'all well—as ever.' I'll know you are all well and that you love me as much as you did when I left. Do you?

An admiral was here today and liked my plans, etc. Also, General Richardson is on his way here as the C of S's representative. All this should be kept to your sweet self although it has no military significance...It's a long time, darling, since I saw you or heard from you. Your last message and only one received so far has the note you wrote the day after I left.

The days go by quickly because I am terribly busy constantly. There is so much to be done and always more things coming up. My heart breaks if I stay quiet for a moment—consequently, I try to keep going constantly. At night it is too awful. Well, I'll not tell you that stuff anymore—it doesn't help you any more than it does me. The amount to be done is tremendous and progress seems so slow—although I know it is coming along.

How I wonder how the babies are—I also worry terribly about their getting hurt—or being in the street!

Well, I'm going to look around—it's an involved command—so many things to check on. The future looks awfully black as to when I'll ever see my loved ones. However, we must get this job done. I can't write any more now—there doesn't seem to be much to say except I love you and am aching for you all. Give Jeannie my love. As ever—Harry.

The "plans" to which Harry refers in the above letter involve his recommendation to secure the New Hebrides Island of Espiritu Santo which will move US land-based airpower 400 miles closer to Guadalcanal in the Solomons.

21 May 1942. Darling, we were so busy all day I didn't have a chance to write you yesterday. There's no end in sight to complete all the plans. We're under the Navy now—I believe. Heaven knows what the next moves will be. We were lucky that the last big fight set the [Japanese] back on their tails for a while. Otherwise we'd have been in for it while in the throes of 'unpacking.'

A boat should leave in about 10 days. It should have many letters from you all. It's hell not to know where you are—if you are well. Please don't neglect to tell me everything about yourself and the children. Don't always be in a hurry to finish writing to me to go someplace. The little details are very important to me, darling.

I do hope Jeannie got entirely well. I often worry that she had a relapse. Johnny got one note from her when I got yours. All my love—I need you more each minute—its' hellish! Harry.

The "last big fight" that "set the [Japanese] back on their tails for a while" to which Chamberlin refers is the Battle of the Coral Sea which takes place on 7 May 1942 as the very first carrier-on-carrier conflict in history. Overall, the Japanese loose so many planes and pilots in the battle that their invasion force headed for Port Moresby on the southeastern tip of New Guinea must turn back.

22 May 1942, Friday. Beloved one—time rolls by in a peculiar manner. The days are quick in passing and full of duties, decisions and worries—yet the whole elapsed period seems frightfully long and dreary. Each evening, before during and after—is an eternity. My heart sinks with the sun, and despite the radiant beauty of flowers, trees, birds, skies and seas about me, I am plunged into an cxcruciating depression...There are many interesting things in the making, but I can't tell you them now.

You may radio or cable me when you want to do so. I'll ask Benny Hoge or Ray Williamson who are in N.C. to send them on. General Rose is back here to take part in a plan I have. However, if you send it to me to Noumea, New Caledonia in his care I'll get it. Just to send a word once a month as

'Love' it will mean so much. That will tell me you are all well... I pray over and over and over each day—each time I awaken, that God will keep you all and thank him for giving you all to worthless me.

The plan to which Chamberlin refers is his plan to secure the island of Espiritu Santo, the northern most island of the New Hebrides. Chamberlin reasons that the airfield on Efate will protect the supply line from Australia to the United States but remains a bit far from the current line of Japanese advance. Strategically, as stated earlier, Chamberlin's plan moves American air power 400 miles closer to the Solomon Islands to support American forces who may commence fighting on Guadalcanal. Generals Eisenhower and Marshall see the wisdom in Chamberlin's recommendation. They authorize Chamberlin to implement his plan to hold Efate to protect the supply line and to fortify and develop an airstrip on Espiritu Santo to support any future action in the Solomon Islands.

On 28 May 1942, troops under Brig. General William I. Rose occupy Espiritu Santo to keep the Japanese out. General Rose immediately begins to survey a site for an airstrip, starts constructing a road to that site, and awaits resources to begin construction of the airstrip.

1 June 1942. My precious Dodi's birthday! Kiss her for me. Yesterday at a tea for the Red Cross (natives, French, soldiers of all races present) I bought a couple of stuffed dogs from them which I shall send soon—nothing much ... Tell Dodi I'm sorry I'm not there... The days now—when it doesn't rain—are like exquisite spring days. ... The nights are exquisite—a full moon—palms—mountains, sea—soft balmy air—how I wish you could be here. Rain in this season—winter—is of shower kind normally.

I feel quite recovered today from my little illness. Haven't time for more at present—it's always the same anyhow... a depressed sense of time escaping—escaping with my happiness, my loved ones, my home and now hope of ever having those hours again! It breaks my heart and yes, I must never give way to what's torturing me—the business at hand must be finished. Thank heaven that's so—for it keeps me busy, as I've said—and keeps the loneliness from completely smothering me.

Care for yourself in all the ways I've begged you to my Helen and for our beautiful gifts from God. You will I know. They and our love deserve your daily, concentrated effort to keep yourself and them as lovely as God made you all! Affection to your family, including Fred and muffin and to Jeannie and others I know. As ever, Harry.

4 June 1942. Beloved—didn't write yesterday—forgive me please. Was busy as usual and too tired at night. Generally, go to bed about 8:45 and read until I fall asleep. It's the only way I can forget my loneliness and the evenings are insupportable.

Today a hot wind is blowing and nature as usual presenting a gloriously beautiful time. The sea from my office window is magnificent—but as I said, the more beautiful the things my eyes see the more poignant the longing in my heart becomes. No hope for mail until the 9th and in all probability we'll get none then—something will have gone wrong! I knew yesterday from two people who came from Australia that there were 600 pounds of mail for us there!

There are a multitude of little civil difficulties which arise with the government here—which really annoy. However, that's a good thing too, I believe. It keeps me occupied. Anyhow—I shouldn't complain, we are safely here and each day permits steps in preparation.

Oh! I am dying to hear about you and the babies. I do pray you've found time to write a great deal—all details. I know your letters never have been long enough darling! So, fear they won't be now! Do write me anything—or are you by now *en train de m'authier*? I'm getting quite a lot of practice in French here—and reading it mostly... There is an amazing amount of activity here but lots to be done still—lots and lots.

Does my Dodi suck her thumb anymore and do she and Didi [177] keep their nails clean and long? Tell them to do so for their Daddy! How I long to see them! Do you remember how they'd both hug us when I'd come home to hold you in an embrace? The precious darlings! Don't forget to try to send a radio or cable to me....

Keep well and think of the many things I want you to do! Are you entirely and perfectly well? How much do you weigh? How much do the babies weigh? and Jeannie too! Incidentally I've quit drinking entirely for a time—not one at night. I feel I have too much responsibility and should keep in the best shape I can—which I am sure is not helped by alcohol. More soon... Harry.

5 June 1942, Friday. Helen mine—how I wish you were here. The day is simply gorgeous—temperature varies between 60 to 80 degrees during each 24 hours. We have started many things toward mosquito control. Luckily, we asked for a sanitation expert and got the former Sanitation Officer of Los Angeles County ordered with us. Another man is a naval doctor who was on

177 Chamberlin refers to his daughter Lydia as Didi.

mosquito control in Panama... Hope the entire malaria curse will be about wiped out before we leave—in case we soon do. Got away a lot of plans, etc., today also to W. Dept....Am going out to the air field now-lots of business in that direction.

Last night I was at an all-time low—more than on the boat—but feel a little healthier and consequently a little higher in morale today. All I can do is hope and pray that the glorious day will come when we—all of us well and unharmed—shall form our little groups and join hands again at our own table! One just cannot and dare not think of the happiness—nor of the long, long sorrowful time which will intervene. If it only comes true—I can bear it...Hug my darlings! I mailed them two silly homemade dogs—lucky to get them at the Red Cross benefit. Yours, Harry

Under Chamberlin's direction, the 1st Naval Construction Battalion (Seabees) continues construction of the airstrip on Efate. According to plan, it must be ready on June 23, 1942 for the first B-17 Bomber test landings. Soon, in record time of only 20 days' work, the Seabees carve out of the swamp and jungle a 6,000-foot-long airstrip ready to receive B-17 bombers and fighter aircraft. The project is completed ahead of schedule. But a lethal enemy lies hidden and waiting that will change Chamberlin's life forever.

Chapter 31

A New Enemy, 6 June 1942–29 September 1944

"...serving his country and the Army which he loved so intensely."
—General George C. Marshall [178]

"It is awful to have one's hopes and all of one's future snatched away!"
—Harry Chamberlin [179]

On 6 June 1942, the day ends with news that turns Chamberlin's life upside down. "N.C." refers to the island of New Caledonia.

6 June 1942, Saturday. Darling mine—Just finally got a thorough exam and must leave at one for Honolulu—or maybe Letterman. Have a bad spot high in the rectum—it may be an ulcer but must get immediate attention. Have asked for a flying boat to go to N. C. tomorrow and will get a plane to Honolulu and after they look at me—I don't know what the news will be. If it's a long treatment will ask to come to San F. and be near you all. Will add to this and carry it along and mail it later. I can't write any more—I'm too disturbed—All my love to you. I love you—God bless you. Harry.

7 June 1942, Sunday. Darling—Didn't sleep last night—the exam made me hurt all night and my thoughts are none to gay. There's a 50-50 chance this won't amount to anything and 2 weeks of treatment will fix it up—if it's the

178 See Memorial Association of West Point Graduates See https://www.westpointaog.org/memorial-article?id=f3efb07e-1306-45c3-86dd-780dd099a6a0.

179 Chamberlin letter to his wife Helen Bradman Chamberlin.

bad type, I'll have to have an operation, but the surgeon assures me I have a 9 out of 10 chance to come out all right. I don't know. I hope so. It is not so cheerful and if I'm of no use afterwards—I'll not bore you...

Tomorrow I fly to Noumea and get the earliest flying ship to Honolulu and will get another exam there to determine whether it's a malignant ulcer or non-malignant. If the former, I shall come home for the operation and see you all. Oh, what a heaven to see you and hear you! To see the living likeness of you too! God keep you well. Of course, if the thing is not serious, I'll come back here.

You may well imagine my distress. It's a blow. I know I should have gone sooner but the doctors say it probably has been coming on for at least a year. Nevertheless, I should have gotten care sooner—but I thought it was nothing. The mail comes Tuesday and I must leave tomorrow. I'll try to have mine flown to Noumea. I am so heartsick—almost two months and no word from you except the note written the day I left! You have mail by now, I'm certain...

Oh Helen—I love you three beyond expression! They scared me so at first that I nearly died last night—I was afraid I might never see you!

Discussions with an oncologist and a gastroenterologist in the year 2016 reveal the following: When the doctors tell Chamberlin that his problem "has been coming on for at least a year," they are mistaken. The medical science of 1942 really does not know how long cancer cells of the type Chamberlin fears must multiply to become even detectable. Current medical thinking suggests that such cells multiply for up to 20 years before the medical technology of the year *2016* can detect their presence. By the time the patient notices symptoms, or by the time medical science of the year 1942 would detect the problem, the affliction may advance beyond the colon and beyond medicine's ability to cure.

9 June 1942, Monday. Noumea. Darling. Flew over here yesterday. Staying with General Patch. Don't know when I'll get a ride to Honolulu. My heart is like lead—it's so humiliating to be sent to a hospital and give up a command. However, if I can be fixed up—I guess I'll have nothing to complain about. I pray it won't be malignant—but fear it is. I am frightfully despondent.

General Richardson just arrived here—he goes on to Australia and is making a tour as General Marshall's representative. Kenny Hoge and Ray Williams... are here as I told you...All I can do now is pray I'm not in terrible shape. I'll not send this until I know—after I get to Honolulu. What a wash-out I am. I make me hate myself and I'm trying so hard to be game about is all. I need your help terribly. Harry.

13 June 1942. Beloved—still here at Noumea. Haven't written for a couple of days my depression is so great that I am fighting constantly to keep from going mad! I feel perfectly well—although I realize that why I have gotten tired so easily and needed more sleep for the last year is due to this condition. I dare not look to the future! I may well be retired, I suppose, if the serious operation is necessary. Then too, I may soon be OK again. They say I will be, but I don't know. I know you may not want me around and yet I need you so now. The uncertainty and mental anguish are frightful. I went up the island 80 miles day before yesterday and saw Alec George who put on a demonstration with his art just for me—and review, etc. I do anything to try to forget.

Upon returning I found Johnson had sent my mail south. Where General Patch was to visit by air—but didn't go. Now it is doubtful whether I shall be able to have it flown here before I go! It will finish me! It is awful to have one's hopes and all of one's future snatched away! I feel certain that my case is a serious one...I'll not mail all this unless I feel I can't see you again for a long time. They may not let me leave Honolulu—but I shall insist on coming home if it can be done in any way! ...

How can I bear to be retired—to be nothing! Would you mind living quietly someplace with just the babies and me? I fear you'd be bored to death and want to leave. Surely God will let things turn out so I can have you all again for a while.

My mind and heart are boiling with things I want to know and want to tell you. My darling wife—I need you so and you are so far away and I am so desolate—so blue—so hopeless. God keep you. I wonder if my babies ever think of me. I'm so humiliated to have to quit my job—not to get to the top for you and them. I did so hope I'd make full general for you and now this physical calamity has knocked me flat. My thoughts are awful—I don't know how I can go on . . .

16 June 1942, at Noumea. Discovered they have here the 52nd Evacuation Hospital which is a unit from Pennsylvania—complete doctors, nurses and all. So before going to Honolulu I came here where I have had a complete going over by those who are obviously very high-class physicians. My physical condition is excellent—heart, throat, lungs, etc. They even took x-rays of me—after a preliminary enema followed by a second filling of a barium solution. They also looked at me with a fluoroscope.

These exams displayed no malignant or other observable bad condition. There now remains another proctoscope and exam tomorrow for as yet the source of the blood is undetermined. Of course, I have more hope now that I can be quickly fixed up! Oh darling—I feel I have walked through the valley of the shadow of death!

I have prayed and prayed that God would let me escape a malignant condition which, as you know, will mean a serious operation from which I shall probably never fully recover—although they say I probably would! My misery and mental anguish have been overpowering. They are keeping me abed until tomorrow and administering belladonna internally in order to secure relation of my big intestine, etc., which are exceedingly spastic—which means nervous and tense. If all this turns out too badly—I may never send this letter.

It if is not too bad, I'll wrap it up on a paper with an exterior announcement telling you that I am not critically affected—thus you need not suffer through the pages recently written—but may realize what I have undergone knowing that I'll be all right soon. Of course, it may be that I have a terrible condition—but there is far more hope...

As I've never had any mail from you, I have had to send all communications c/o your father. If I don't have to go to Honolulu, I'll miss you again. I know there is mail at Rose's for me—if it isn't sent to Honolulu before I get it sent here...Over two months and no word at all from my loved ones... As I told you previously, I have had no physical pain—don't worry about that.

Chamberlin returns to the United States and immediately enters the hospital for treatment in late June of 1942. Tests confirm: he suffers from colon and rectal cancer.

23 September 1942. Staff Sgt. Reginald Noble (one of Chamberlin's very loyal aides) writes his mother:

"... General C. was brought back to this country for an abdominal operation. In the middle of June when he learned that I was off duty for three weeks, he got his wife to ask me to go out to California for a visit. I was there in San Francisco for two weeks, with expenses paid and was able to see him at the hospital every day; and his two little girls were delighted to have me stay there."

Chamberlin remains in treatment enduring a number of operations from late June 1942 until March of 1943. Nonetheless, General Marshall keeps Chamberlin on the active duty list. Emaciated upon his leaving the hospital, Chamberlin first heads the Western Defense Command. Later, he takes command of the Southwestern Security District at La Jolla, California. He holds this command from March 1943 through September 30, 1943.

During this timeframe, his good friend John Cudahy dies in a horseback riding accident in Wisconsin. Chamberlin, sits on his living room sofa and stares into the distance for hours as he mourns his friend's death. On October 1, 1943, Chamberlin takes command of Fort Ord in Monterey, California.

Figure 125 *Frederica Chamberlin, Col. Hiram Tuttle, Lydia Chamberlin. Courtesy Mrs. Paul Seymour, Jr.*

In March 1944, Chamberlin enters the hospital and endures two more operations in hopes of eradicating the cancer. He returns to duty toward late April.

During the first week of May 1944, General Marshal arrives at Fort Ord on a secret inspection trip. He stays with the Chamberlin family as a house guest. While staying at the Chamberlin home in the Presidio of Monterey, Marshall plays with the Chamberlin children. (Marshall remembers Lydia's birthday, June 1st and sends her a pair of roller skates from Washington, DC) The Army releases no news of the Marshall visit until he returns to Washington, DC

On 12 May 1944, the Fort Ord local newspaper covers the Marshall's visit and shows a photo of General Marshal and Brig. General Chamberlin. Chamberlin appears emaciated, just skin and bones.

On 29 June 1944, Thursday: Chamberlin's aide, Staff Sgt. Reginald Noble writes his mother in Britain. He refers to Chamberlin as "the G."

"The G gave me a cat at La Jolla...so I have plenty of company. I am sorry to tell you that he has been very ill again; nearly as bad as he could be. It had been getting worse for months, and he went in hospital two months ago; and has had two more operations. You know he has the same thing that father had, and I can only hope that he will come back here. He can't keep any food down at all; he has been fed with tubes all this time. I go to see him now and again; and the last time he gave me his gold watch and chain. It is a beautiful Swiss one, and very thin. He has recovered from the operations; but he goes up and down. One day better and then not so well again. I wish he could only get well enough to take a rest here at home.

"I have been keeping house and landscaping the garden. He said I was to have anything and any help I needed. So, I have two or three workmen with me. I have changed the whole thing here.... Everyone has told me as soon as he sees it, he'll get better at once...."

From his hospital bed, to show his appreciation for Staff Sgt. Noble's efforts to help Helen and the children as well as for his support of Chamberlin himself, Chamberlin gives Sgt. Noble the pocket watch that Noble mentions in his letter to keep as a remembrance. This pocket watch, engraved with his monogram, Chamberlin has carried since graduating from West Point in 1910.

4 August 1944. Staff Sgt. Reginald Noble writes to his mother:

"The G has been moved to a hospital here where they have the most up to date equipment. I'm afraid there is not much hope."

Nobles' support, loyalty, and care for the Chamberlins goes beyond the call of duty. Staff Sgt. Noble visits Chamberlin in the hospital every day of August. He runs errand after errand for Mrs. Chamberlin to ease her burdens.

29 September 1944: at Letterman Hospital in San Francisco, Chamberlin's 27-month ordeal ends. He passes away. The time for remembrance begins. The local newspaper headlines read "Brilliant Career Ends."

The symbols of the military funeral extend far back into history: The rider-less horse with boots reversed in the stirrups symbolizes the fallen leader who will ride his horse no more. The flag covered casket stems from the time of the Emperor Napoleon when flags often covered the bodies of those killed in battle. The triangular fold of the flag represents the three-cornered hat of the Continental Army of George Washington. The firing of three volleys over the grave hails from two different traditions. In Roman times, members of the Roman legions would hail three loud chants over the grave of a fallen hero to ward off evil. At other times and for other armies, the three volleys served as a signal that the dead had been retrieved from the field of battle and that the fighting could begin anew. The bugle melody of Taps originates in the American Civil War to mark the end of the day.

3 October 1944, Tuesday: Beginning at 1p.m., a large number of officers and enlisted men take part in a final tribute to Harry Dwight Chamberlin, Brigadier General, United States Army. A short ceremony takes place at the Chamberlin home in the Presidio of Monterey. Then, the military escort moves Chamberlin's casket to Fort Ord where immediately all flags drop to half-mast. At the Fort Ord Chapel, the post Chaplain conducts "short but impressive funeral rites" as a military guard of honor stands at parade rest outside. Throughout the ceremony, at one-minute intervals, cannons fire in the distance. Their report echoes in the chapel.

After the Chapel ceremony finishes, the procession moves to the Military Cemetery at the Presidio of Monterey. An enlisted man follows. He leads the rider-less horse with spurred cavalry boots reversed in the stirrups. Among the pall bearers who carry the American flag draped casket are Staff Sgt. Crispulo Kaimco and Staff Sgt. Reginald Noble. Sgt. Kamico served as Chamberlin's bodyguard on Efate in the New Hebrides Islands and Sgt. Noble served as Chamberlin's aide for many years. At the grave site, the Army renders final honors. Members of the Honor Guard lift the flag from the coffin and fold it with precision into a triangle. The officer of the guard presents the folded flag to Helen Bradman Chamberlin. The Honor

Guard fires three rifle volleys over the grave. A bugler of the 11th US Cavalry sounds Taps.

Sometime later, Army Chief of Staff, General George C. Marshall writes of Harry Chamberlin:

> "He was one of the ablest and most popular men in the Regular establishment, and his loss to the Army is a great one. He was one of those rare individuals who excelled in everything that he did, and if his overseas service had not been terminated so prematurely by his health, I am confident he would have accomplished great things in combat. He died while serving his country and the Army which he loved so intensely." [180]

***Figure 126** Chamberlin's final resting place: The Presidio of Monterey. Photo courtesy of Ms. Carley Velasquez.*

---

180 See Memorial Association of West Point Graduates https://www.westpointaog.org/memorial-article?id=f3efb07e-1306-45c3-86dd-780dd099a6a0

Chapter 32

Afterword

"Genius is finding the invisible link between things."
—Vladimir Nabokov [181]

"People in Europe now are riding in a softer school with lighter ways, they are riding Chamberlin. See Marco Kutscher, that's Chamberlin. Rodrigo Pessoa, that's Chamberlin...my personal "horseman of the century."
—George H. Morris on Chamberlin [182]

"...a soldier's soldier...He represents the model military professional... a particularly great leader, soldier, and horseman."
—Louis A. DiMarco, Lieutenant Colonel, US Army, (*Ret.*) PhD. on Chamberlin [183]

After Chamberlin's passing, Mrs. Chamberlin and her daughters Lydia and Frederica continue to live in California. Helen Bradman Chamberlin's parents, General and Mrs. Bradman stay close and supportive. Helen applies her artistic talents and becomes a portrait painter in Hollywood. She paints family oil portraits for actors like Alan Ladd and other Hollywood luminaries. In addition, she and her daughters create a number of products like umbrellas sold by I. Magnin and Company.

181 Vladimir Nabokov https://www.goodreads.com/quotes/495657
182 George H. Morris, *Four Show Jumping Masters—Part 4: Gordon Wright* https://www.horse-magazine.com/thm/2010/07/four-showjumping-masters-part-4-gordon-wright/
183 Lt. Col. Louis DiMarco, Introduction to this biography.

Daughter Lydia remembers her mother "as a most beautiful woman." According to Ms. Lydia, Mrs. Chamberlin truly never recovers from her husband's death. As of this writing, Mrs. Chamberlin and her daughter Frederica have passed away. Daughter Lydia now lives with her husband in Texas and stays close to her family. Harry Chamberlin has many grandchildren and great grandchildren of whom he would be proud.

Col. Earl "Tommy" Thomson, the Chamberlin student who wins the Olympic Individual Silver Medal for Eventing in 1932, wins the Olympic Individual Silver Medal in Eventing in 1936, and a Team Silver Medal in Dressage in 1948. To date, the 1948 Team Silver remains the highest team medal won by any US team in Dressage competition. He rises to the rank of Colonel and passes away in 1971 at age 71.

Col. John Wofford, the Chamberlin student fated to ride the sometimes-erratic Babe Wartham in the *Prix des Nations* of 1932, goes on to become the first military attaché to Ireland. He retires with the rank of Colonel. He becomes the first president and a founding member of the United States Equestrian Team. Col. Wofford's efforts prove vital to transition from the Army Equestrian Team to the civilian US Equestrian Team. He passes away in 1955. His son John E.B. Wofford wins an Olympic Individual Bronze Medal in 1952. His son Warren remains the only US Equestrian Team member to qualify in both Show Jumping and Eventing. His son James wins one Olympic Individual Silver Medal and two Olympic Team Silver Medals in Eventing, five National Championships, two wins at the Rolex Kentucky Three-Day Event, and a Gold Medal at the Pan Am Games. As of this writing, he has trained at least one member of every US Olympic Equestrian Eventing Team, Pan Am Team, and World Championship Team since 1978.

General Lucien Truscott, Chamberlin's friend, subordinate, and teammate on the national championship 8th Cavalry polo team, goes on to found the Army Rangers. He then rises to the rank of Lieutenant General leading troops in Sicily, Italy, and Southern France during World War II. In Sicily, Italy, and southern France, he vindicates Harry Chamberlin's belief that horsemen and pack-horses remain useful in modern war in areas where terrain makes the deployment of vehicles and tanks difficult or impossible. Many view Truscott as the greatest Allied combat commander serving in Europe during World War II. After World War II, he retires to write two books, one his memoirs and the other a history of the last days of the US Cavalry. In the 1950s, President Eisenhower appoints Truscott as his "spy" to spy on the spies of the CIA. As President Eisenhower's trusted representative, Truscott foils more than one unwise effort initiated by CIA Director Allen Dulles.

Truscott passes away with the rank of four-star General in 1965 at age 70.

Major General Innis Palmer Swift, Chamberlin's Cavalry School polo teammate and long-time friend, goes on to command, as a Major General, the horse mounted 1st Cavalry Division. Horse-mounted, he reviews his troops at a full gallop. In the opinion of General of the Army Douglas MacArthur, Swift makes the 1st Cavalry Division the finest Army division fighting in the Pacific Theater. Swift later commands a Corps in MacArthur's 6th Army reporting to Lieutenant General Walter Krueger on the islands of Leyte and Luzon in the Philippines. Swift passes away in 1953 at age 71.

General George Patton, who knew Chamberlin from their days together at West Point and who often wrote Chamberlin asking for advice, goes on to command the Second Corps in North Africa and Sicily; and then the 3rd Army in France and Germany. He achieves the rank of four-star General as the finest commander of mechanized forces in World War II. He insists that had horse cavalry been available to him in Tunisia and in Sicily, "not a German would have escaped." [184] Patton dies in an auto accident in 1945 at age 60.

Major General Guy V. Henry, Jr. After his tour of duty as Chief of Cavalry ends in 1934, Henry becomes Commandant of the Cavalry School at Fort Riley and later he commands a mechanized unit. He retires from the Army in 1939. The Army recalls him to active duty in 1941 for service during World War II. He finally retires in 1948. After he retires from the Army, he remains devoted to horsemanship and Olympic sport. He remains active with the Army's Olympic Equestrian efforts of 1948. Later, he helps found the United States Equestrian Team, and he lives until the year 1967—two months short of his 93rd birthday.

Lt. Baron Takeichi Nishi, who wins the Gold Medal in the *Prix des Nations* in the Olympics of 1932 and to whom Chamberlin presents a chrome plated M-1911 semi-automatic pistol as a gift, rises to the rank of Colonel and commits ritual suicide at age 42 on Iwo Jima rather than surrender to American forces in 1945. The chrome plated pistol takes on significance in the film *Letters from Iwo Jima* directed by Clint Eastwood.

The US Army currently refers to the Fort Ord headquarters building as "The Chamberlin Building" and the library therein "The Chamberlin Library" which contains 60,000 volumes. Most of Harry Chamberlin's cavalrymen friends continue to agree that horse mounted cavalry has a place, though limited, in a modern army. The planners for the invasion of Japan include horse mounted formations to penetrate the mountainous regions of the Japanese home islands. Thankfully, the invasion proves unnecessary. The

184 See Herr and Wallace, *The Story of the US Cavalry*, Little Brown, 1953.

Army abandons all horse transport in 1950 (with the exception of a Constabulary operating in occupied Germany) and all mule transport in 1953. As of this writing, in light of experience in Afghanistan, select units of the Army's Special Forces and of the Marines now study elementary horsemanship and receive a rudimentary introduction to pack horses and mules. They do not achieve the levels of training and skill, however, that Chamberlin, Patton, and Truscott advocate.

Chamberlin as teacher and trainer: Chamberlin recognizes talent in both riders and horses. He proves a superb teacher and trainer of both. One also may judge the quality of the teacher by the accomplishments of his students. Thomson, Wofford, Cole, and so many other cavalrymen trained in his system perform well in Olympic competitions of 1936 and 1948 and then coach others behind the scenes many years beyond.

Chamberlin questioned: Occasionally, one reads criticism of some of Chamberlin's concepts. For example, Robert Dover, the American dressage rider and trainer, finds fault with Chamberlin's admonition that a rider must not make the "fleshy parts of the buttocks" a part of the rider's seat and that the "fleshy parts" should be "pushed to the rear." The concept and the admonition to Mr. Dover "make no sense." (His words.) [185] Perhaps the concept makes "no sense" to Mr. Dover because Dover is not aware of the historical context of the concept and the reasons for the admonition.

First, the concept does not originate only with Harry Chamberlin. The US Cavalry Board develops the admonition in 1929. Among others the Cavalry Board consists of:

General Walter Short, a graduate of Saumur;
Captain W. B. Bradford, a graduate of Riley and of Saumur;
Major H.D. Chamberlin, a graduate of Riley, Saumur, and Tor di Quinto;
Col. Guy V. Henry, a graduate of Saumur;
Col. William W. West, a graduate of Riley, Saumur and, Tor di Quinto;
Col. Benjamin Lear, a graduate of Saumur.

The following photos might make the concept "make sense." The photos depict the way cavalry troopers were taught to ride in the early twentieth century. As Harry Chamberlin writes:

185 Robert Dover, blog comments http://ushorsemanship.com/equestrian-news/

"Unfortunately...our officers and troopers were taught to ride with the buttocks pushed under them so that they were seated on the ends of their spines..." [186]

Figure 127 *The rider pushes his buttocks under him sits on the end of his spine just as all American military riders trained in the French school were taught in the late nineteenth and the first twenty or so years of the twentieth century. Photo from the author's collection.*

Figure 128 *This rider sits on his spine and with his buttocks pushed under him as Chamberlin describes. Photo from Horses, Saddles, and Bridles by Carter.*

186 See Chamberlin, *Riding and Schooling Horses*, Derrydale Press 1934.

Figure 129 *Captain George S. Patton, Jr. displays the close seat of Saumur: stirrups forward, buttocks tucked under the rider and pressed against the saddle's cantle. Patton sits on his spine. The seat Chamberlin and eventually the whole cavalry abandons. US Army photo.*

① Wrong seat at halt.

Rider's back and loin "humped."
Reins too long, as indicated by rearward position of elbow.
Weight concentrated to the rear near cantle.
Buttocks under rider so that he sits on the end of his spine.
Knees too high and so far forward that they are off saddle skirt.
Foot not far enough in stirrup and heels too high.
A heavy, unmilitary, and insecure seat.

FIGURE 1.—Positions of the soldier, mounted.

Figure 130 *From FM 25-5 Horsemanship and Horsemastership 1939 edition.*

In addition, many early twentieth-century cavalry recruits ride in the "old western style" well suited to working cattle—with buttocks pressed against the saddle's cantle and the legs well in front of the vertical "riding the dash board" so to speak. The Cavalry Board wants all military riders to abandon that style as well as the style of riding shown in the photos above. Hopefully, this helps make sense of the concept.

The following three photos display the seat that Chamberlin wants riders to attain.

Figure 131 *This trooper displays the proper seat circa 1942. US Army photo.*

Figure 132 *Riding in a Phillips Saddle, Chamberlin demonstrates the proper seat with normal stirrup length for hacking and general riding. Reprinted with permission of the US Cavalry and Armor Association.*

Figure 133 *Riding in his Pariani saddle, Chamberlin displays the proper seat with stirrups shortened for jumping. US Army photo.*

Lady Sylvia Loch in her book *Dressage, The Art of Classical Riding* also criticizes Chamberlin in one respect. She wonders how a man of such wide international influence like Chamberlin could say that, in the past, *high school* horses in France were "coarse" and "poorly bred." [187] The answer is simple: Chamberlin merely restates the opinions of Count d'Aure and General L'Hotte, each an *Ecuyer* of Saumur and each a leader of a French society to "improve" the breeding of French horses. Both men label then existing French stock as "coarse." Both men argue for refined Thoroughbred blood lines to improve French stock.

Chamberlin the theorist: A question sometimes arises as to whether Chamberlin merits the lavish credit that he garners for the theories of horsemanship espoused by the US Cavalry. In the introductions to his books, he attributes much of his knowledge to those who came before him. He derives much from French, Italian, and other Europeans such as the Poles, the Swedes, and the Germans—as do all of the others who contribute to the manual *Horsemanship and Horsemastership.* Innis Swift, Harry Disston, the members of the Cavalry Board most of whom graduated from Saumur—all contribute thoughts and refinements to the Army's theory of horsemanship.

Chamberlin, however, contributes several original ideas neither completely Italian nor French. He modifies the theories of the Italian Caprilli and melds his results with the theories of the Frenchman L'Hotte. Many of these French principles guide the riding theory of Fort Riley even before Chamberlin's time. Chamberlin adds, however, refinements that take those principles to a new level. He recommends that the army reject the Italian principles of horse *training* in favor of French training principles already adopted by Fort Riley but which Chamberlin modifies. For the rider, he maintains French "lightness" for the aids and adopts Italian "balance" for seat. Yet, he modifies other aspects of the Italian seat to such an extent that that ultimately the Army calls it "the Chamberlin Seat Military Seat." [188] He admires German precision but rejects the German's heavy use of the legs and the seat. He reasons that hot, American Thoroughbreds will not tolerate such practice. Finally, along with the French theorist *de la Guérinière,* he rejects the German emphasis on collection for the campaign horse.

Finally, from at least 1928 forward, Chamberlin makes major contributions to the various editions of *Horsemanship and Horsemastership.* The 1942 edition, however, shows an even stronger stamp. It displays photos of

187 See Lady Sylvia Loch, *Dressage, The Art of Classical Riding* Trafalgar Square 1990.

188 See *Historical and Pictorial Review, 1st Training Regiment, Cavalry Replacement Training Center, Fort Riley, Kansas of The United States Army,* The Army and Navy Publishing Company 1941.

Chamberlin mounted to depict fundamental concepts. Its language regarding the rider's "Military Seat" and the training of horses, in part, comes from Chamberlin's *Training Hunters, Jumpers, and Hacks* and from his book *Riding and Schooling Horses.* Col. Rodney Dorsey of the Cavalry School assumes primary responsibility for the re-write and production of the manual with Chamberlin exercising significant editorial supervision.

Vladimir Littauer states the essential point about Chamberlin:

> "In the prefaces to his books, he modestly says that: 'for the Seat advocated, the writer is principally indebted to the Italian Cavalry School,' while the 'credit for the system of training enunciated herein is due to the French Cavalry School.' He modified both seat and schooling, however, and his second book in particular represents neither the French nor the Italian school in its purity, but is his sound, original contribution to the cause of educated riding." [189]

In summation: Two key differences separate Chamberlin from the other Americans. Through his *writings*, he becomes the theory's greatest expositor. Through his *riding*, he provides its greatest example.

Chamberlin the horseman: Without question, Harry Dwight Chamberlin remains the US Cavalry's greatest horseman and one of the greatest in the world. In the opinion of many who consider all aspects of his career, he stands as the twentieth-century's greatest combined horsemen, theorist, teacher, and equestrian writer. Certainly, when one considers all of those roles together, he remains the best America has ever produced. And of course, Chamberlin implements theory with the style and grace of an athletic genius, something few theorists accomplish. This seems well recognized by his contemporaries:

> Recall the opinion of Vladimir Littauer, a great teacher and rider himself: "...to come right down to it, don't bother to try to go over obstacles the way Major Harry Chamberlin does, because you will never be able to do it anyway..."
>
> Recall the opinion of the Commandant of Tor di Quinto, Lt. Colonel Starita: "The pupil has surpassed his master."

---

189 Vladimir S. Littauer, *The Development of Modern Riding: The Story of Modern Riding From Renaissance Times to The Present.* Howell, 1991.

More than seventy years after his passing, Chamberlin garners high praise and respect from the most capable Olympic equestrians and coaches in the United States:

> George Morris, who wins an Olympic Team Silver Medal in 1960, serves as president of the of the United States Show Jumping Hall of Fame, and whose students win medals in the 1984, 1992, 1996, and the 2004 Olympic Games;
>
> James Wofford who wins two Team Silver Olympic Medals and one Individual Silver Olympic Medal in Eventing and, as a coach, has had at least one student on every US Olympic, World Championship, and Pan American team since 1978; and
>
> William Steinkraus who achieves one of the most decorated equestrian careers in US history as a five-time Olympian, four-time Olympic medal winner who wins the Individual Gold Medal in the *Prix des Nations* at the Olympics of 1968.

Each of these highly accomplished equestrians hold Chamberlin in the highest esteem and hope that the man and his methods will not fade from contemporary equestrian sport.

In a response to a survey from me, Mr. George Morris ranks Chamberlin the greatest combined theorist, teacher, trainer, writer, and rider of the twentieth-century and points out that many Olympic Eventing and *Grand Prix* riders "ride Chamberlin" even if they do not know his name.[190]

In the same survey, Mr. James Wofford maintains that "Chamberlin is to horsemanship as Mozart is to music." [191]

William Steinkraus writes to me in 2008: "So often, I think I have come up with an idea of my own, only to find it clearly stated in one of his books." [192]

Chamberlin, the soldier: His qualities of leadership along with the other attributes of the soldier become apparent from the beginning of his career forward.

Recall that Chamberlin's peers at West Point back in 1910 write in the *Howitzer,* "May West Point have more like him."

Army Chief of Staff, General George C. Marshal, who fires more officers than any other Chief of Staff in US history, writes of Chamberlin: "He was one of the ablest and most popular men in the Regular establishment... one

190 George Morris response to survey question submitted by the author.
191 James Wofford, response to author June 2008.
192 William Steinkraus, email to author June 2008.

of those rare individuals who excelled at everything he tried..."[193] Consider also, that Marshall does not retire the terminally ill Chamberlin. He keeps Chamberlin on active duty until the very end. Chamberlin, at least, never endures the "retirement" that he loathes so much.

Recall that the great commander General Lucien Truscott, Jr. writes of Chamberlin with admiration, affection, and respect: "He was tall, handsome, a magnetic personality—the very beau ideal of a cavalryman." Truscott relates a story that takes place in the late 1920s or early 30's. To give a presentation of effective horsemanship, Chamberlin arrives at the cavalry post where Truscott serves. Chamberlin requests that the location of his presentation be changed to accommodate the larger than expected crowd that arrives. The sponsor finds a larger room. The Colonel in command of the unit, however, must search for the new location. Once the Colonel arrives at the new location, he expresses his displeasure at the change. When informed that Major Chamberlin requested the change, the Colonel's demeanor softens and he says: "Oh, if Major Chamberlin asked for the change, well, that that is perfectly all right." [194] Such is the respect that Chamberlin earns in the officer corps of the US Cavalry.

Recall that the officer known only as "B.P." writes of Chamberlin in 1944: "He has been my brother officer, commanding officer, commanding General, and above all, my devoted friend. My association with him, in each of the aforementioned capacities has been an inspiration and has enriched my life. His loss, to me, can never be replaced." [195]

One may wonder what Chamberlin might have achieved as a soldier had cancer not robbed him of his future. General Marshall provides his assessment: "if his overseas service had not been terminated so prematurely by his health, I am confident he would have accomplished great things in combat." [196]

Evidence of genius: All of these appraisals of the man and of his accomplishments as horseman, theorist, teacher, trainer, soldier, and above all, as a leader—appraisals generated over a span of more than a century—reveal a rare and talented individual, a personable genius, the likes of which one seldom encounters.

---

193 See Association of West Point Graduates https://www.westpointaog.org/memorial-article?id=f3efb07e-1306-45c3-86dd-780dd099a6a0

194 General Lucian K. Truscott, Jr. *The Twilight of the U. S. Cavalry. Life in the Old Army 1917-1942,* University Press of Kansas, 1989.

195 See B.P. Association of West Point Graduates https://www.westpointaog.org/memorial-article?id=f3efb07e-1306-45c3-86dd-780dd099a6a0

196 Ibid.

There exist many definitions of genius. Some write that "in its broadest sense, genius encompasses curiosity, courage and creativity." [197] The genius asks questions and never stops learning. The genius keeps an open mind while manipulating a concept in search of something that transcends that which has come before. The genius learns a craft over many years of intense effort, but sees that effort not as work but as a personal voyage to a greater truth. The genius takes great pleasure in connecting many concepts, which at first sight, appear to have nothing in common. Vladimir Nabokov, the Russian novelist, writes: "*Genius is finding the invisible link between things.*"

Chamberlin displays all of these traits. He finds "the invisible link between things." And Chamberlin writes: "Nothing, aside from the dearest human relationships, can give the pleasure found in working and playing with a horse." Persons of genius often look upon their work as "play." As Harry Chamberlin "plays," he creates.

And so, as Saumur ignores and denigrates Tor di Quinto, as Tor di Quinto ignores and denigrates Saumur, and as the Germans of Hanover denigrate the French, Italians, Americans, and everyone else equally, the genius of Chamberlin integrates a little of each with the perspective of Fort Riley and transcends them all.

Harry Chamberlin's achievements in the field of horsemanship were many. In the words of his student General John Tupper Cole, Chamberlin achieves, through his theories "...a delightful blend of French lightness, Italian balance, and German accuracy." [198] In the opinion of the renowned Eventer and coach James Wofford, Chamberlin achieves international influence "second only to Caprilli." [199] And in the opinion of the founding father of hunt seat equitation George H. Morris: "...this one man is the founding father of equestrian sport in the United States." [200]

Of all those achievements and accolades, Harry Chamberlin and his descendants may be proud, and rightfully so. Still, one more achievement remains—an achievement rooted in late nineteenth-century Elgin, Illinois. When Dwight and Cora Chamberlin walk with him down the Avenue of Flags every Memorial Day; when his father Dwight speaks so often with pride about General Ulysses S. Grant who saved the Union; when the veterans of the Civil War and the Spanish American War show their respect for country

197 Curtiss DeMars-Johnson, *Igniting Your Genius: The Startling Fusion of Creativity, Curiosity, Intellect, Passion, and Awe,* The Scarecrow Press, Inc. 2002.

198 See General John Tupper Cole, Introduction to *Training Hunters, Jumpers, and Hacks,* Arco Publishing, 1973.

199 James Wofford in response to questionnaire from author.

200 George H. Morris, Forward to this biography.

and honor those who gave all; when General Howard of Gettysburg and Colonel Roosevelt of San Juan Hill speak in Elgin of duty, sacrifice, and valor, all of these messages resonate with him: Harry Chamberlin wants to be a soldier, a cavalryman—and a fine soldier and cavalryman he becomes. Recall that during World War II, Army Chief of Staff, General George C. Marshall wrote that Harry Chamberlin was "one of the ablest and most popular men" in the Regular Army. With the perspective of 75 years, the twenty-first century military historian and soldier, Lieutenant Colonel Louis DiMarco, (*ret*) PhD writes:

> "Beyond his horsemanship, in an era that produced the greatest crop of outstanding soldiers in America's history, Harry Chamberlin was a soldier's soldier. His peers—men whose names will forever be associated with the great American military that won World War II—Marshall, MacArthur, Eisenhower, Bradley, Patton and Truscott among many others, respected him, admired him, and valued him as a colleague and friend... He represents the model military professional: a caring leader who set the example in all things for his subordinates; a soldier who put duty first and made the sacrifices and bore the burdens of a life of service to his country; and finally, the expert professional whose tactical and technical knowledge, whose expert horsemanship and training methods, had the primary purpose of contributing to the ability of the US military to support and defend the interests of the citizens of his country. In this regard, Harry Chamberlin was an outstanding professional, perhaps the greatest American equestrian, and finally, a great American." [201]

201 Lt. Col. Louis DiMarco, USA Ret. PhD. Introduction to this biography.

Select Bibliography of Books, Articles, Blogs.

Alft, E.C., *Elgin, Days Gone By* and *Elgin: An American History.* Internet website, 2001. www.elginhistory.com.

Ashton, John. "A Visit to Saumur", *The Cavalry Journal, November-December 1925.*

Augur, Lt. Col. Wayland and Jones, Jr. Lt. William P., "C.R.T.C at End of First Cycle", *The Cavalry Journal, p. 42-47, July-August, 1941.*

B.P. "Memorial to Brig. General Harry D. Chamberlin" Association of West Point Graduates https://www.westpointaog.org/memorial-article?id=f3efb07e-1306-45c3-86dd-780dd099a6a0.

Beudant, Captain Etienne, *Horse Training Out-Door and High School.* Translated by Lt. Col. John A. Barry, US Cavalry, Xenophon Press, 2014.

Burnett, Lt. Col. E. M. and Zeller, Major M. "Horsemanship Training at our CRTC", *The Cavalry Journal, p.53, January-February, 1942.*

Carter, William H., General, United States Army, *Horses Saddles and Bridles,* The Lord Baltimore Press, The Friedenwald Company, 1906.

Cassini, Oleg, *In My Own Fashion, An Autobiography,* Simon and Schuster, 1987.

Cavalry Drill Regulations, United States Army, Adopted Oct. 3, 1891, D. Appleton and Company, New York, 1892.

Chamberlin, Brig. General Harry D., "Horsemastership, Four Exercises to Train Remounts and Reclaim Spoiled Horses", *The Cavalry Journal, November-December, 1941.*

Chamberlin, Brig. General Harry D., *Breaking, Training, and Reclaiming Cavalry Horses,* monograph, Headquarters, 2d Cavalry Division, Camp Funston, Kansas 12 November 1941.

Chamberlin, Colonel Harry D., "Cavalry Training", *The Cavalry Journal, September–October 1940.*

Chamberlin, Colonel Harry D., "Crossing Rivers" *The Cavalry Journal, January-February 1941.*

Chamberlin, Harry D. Lt. Col., *Riding and Schooling Horses,* Derrydale Press, 1934.

Chamberlin, Harry D., Lt. Col. *Training Hunters, Jumpers, and Hacks,* Derrydale Press, 1937.

Chamberlin, Lt. Colonel Harry D., "The Conformation of Three-Day Horses," *The Cavalry Journal, May-June 1937.*

Chamberlin, Major Harry D., "The Modern Seat," *The Cavalry Journal, May-June, 1934.*

Chamberlin, Major Harry D., "The Italian Cavalry School at Tor di Quinto" *The Cavalry Journal, 1924.*

Chamberlin, Major Harry D., "Observations on Riding and Training Jumpers", *The Rasp,* The Cavalry School, The Army of the United States, Ft. Riley, Kansas.1922.

Chenevix-Trench, Charles, *A History of Horsemanship, Doubleday & Company, 1970.*

Cole, General John Tupper, Introduction to Chamberlin's *Training Hunters, Jumpers, and Hacks,* Arco, Second Edition, 1973.

Cottingham, Henry, "Polo Here and There," *New York Times, November 1925.*

Cullum, Brevet-Major General, George W., *Biographical Register of the Officers and Graduates of the US Military Academy at West Point, New York Since its Establishment in 1802 Supplement, Volume IX 1940-1950,* Edited by Col. Charles N. Branham, USA Retired.

D'Este, Carlo, *Patton: A Genius For War,* Harper Perennial, 1995.

De Kerbrech, General Francois Faverot, *Methodical Dressage of the Riding Horse, From The last teachings of Francois Baucher as recalled by one of his students: General Francois Faverot de Kerbrech.* Translation by Michael L. M. Fletcher, Edited by Richard and Frances Williams, Xenophon Press LLC 2010.

Decarpentry, General Albert, *Academic Equitation,* Crowood Press, 2012.

Decarpentry, General Albert, *Baucher and His School,* Xenophon Press, 2011.

DeMars-Johnson, Curtis, *Igniting Your Genius: The Startling Fusion of Creativity, Curiosity, Intellect, Passion, and Awe,* The Scarecrow Press, Inc. 2002.

Dembo, Jonathan, Editor, *A Life of Duty, The Autobiography of George Willcox McIver 1858-1947,* The History Press, Charleston, South Carolina 2006.

DiMarco, Louis A., Major USA, *Brigadier General Harry D. Chamberlin, The Cavalry's Greatest Horseman 1887-1944,* unpublished manuscript.

Dover, Robert, blog comments at *US Horsemanship,* http://ushorsemanship.com/equestrian-news/

Drill Regulations, Cavalry 1891, United States War Department adopted October 3, 1891

Durand, Pierre, *L'Équitation français: Mon choix de coeur et de raison,* Actes Sud; edition June 23, 2008

Ellis, John, *Cavalry: The History of Mounted Warfare,* G.P. Putnam's Sons, 1978.

Fillis, James, *Breaking and Riding with Military Commentaries.* Aka *Principles of Dressage and Equitation,* Xenophon Press, 2017.

FM-25-5, Basic Field Manual, Animal Transport, War Department, United States Army, 1939.

George C. Marshall Research Library, Lexington, Virginia *George C. Marshall Papers, Pentagon Office Collection, Selected Materials*

Henry, Jr. Guy V., *A Brief Narrative of the Life of Guy V. Henry, Jr.*, Military History Research Collection, Carlisle Barracks Pennsylvania. 1974.

Henry, Jr., Major General Guy V., President of the FEI 1932, *Official Report of the International Olympic Committee Xth Olympiad, 1932.*

Herman, Arthur, *MacArthur: American Warrior,* Random House, 2016.

Herr, General John K and Wallace, Lew, *The Story of The US Cavalry,* Little Brown, 1953.

Historical and Pictorial Review, 1st Training Regiment, Cavalry Replacement Training Center, Fort Riley, Kansas of The United States Army, The Army and Navy Publishing Company 1941.

Horsemanship and Horsemastership, Volume 1 Education of the Rider, Education of the Horse, The Cavalry School, Academic Division, Fort Riley, Kansas 1942 (FM-25-5).

Howitzer, Yearbook of the United States Military Academy 1907.

Howitzer, Yearbook of the United States Military Academy 1908.

Howitzer, Yearbook of the United States Military Academy 1909.

Howitzer, Yearbook of the United States Military Academy 1910.

Hunt, Elvin, *History of Fort Leavenworth 1827–1937,* Second Edition, Command and General Staff School Press, 1937.

International Olympic Committee, *The Official Report of the Games of the Xth Olympiad Los Angeles 1932.*

Keegan, John, *The First World War,* Alfred A. Knopf, 1998.

Kendall, Captain Paul, "Horseman's Primer", *Horse and Horseman Magazine, November 1938.*

Leckie, Shirley A., *Elizabeth Bacon Custer and The Making of a Myth,* University of Oklahoma Press, 1998.

Littauer, Vladimir S., *Common Sense Horsemanship,* Second Edition, D. Van Nostrand Company, 1963.

Littauer, Vladimir S., *The Development of Modern Riding: The Story of Modern Riding From Renaissance Times to The Present.* Howell, 1991.

Loch, Lady Sylvia, *Dressage, The Art of Classical Riding* Trafalgar Square 1990.

Manuel of Equitation of the French Army, 1912 translated by Lt. A. Chaffee, Jr., US Cavalry, Mounted Service School, Ft. Riley. 1913.

Marshall, F.C., *Elements of Hippology,* US Military Press at West Point, 1906.

Mason, Jr. Herbert, *The Great Pursuit,* Random House, 1970.

Matloff, Maurice, Gen. Editor, "Hyper-War Strategic Planning for Coalition Warfare" *American Military History,* (Center of Military History: 1973) http://www.ibiblio.org/hyperwar/

Moncure, Lt. Col. John. *The Cowpens Staff Ride and Battlefield Tour,* Combat Studies Institute, US Army Command and General Staff College, Ft. Leavenworth, Kansas, 1996.

Morris, George H., *Four Show Jumping Masters—Part 4: Gordon Wright* https://www.horsemagazine.com/thm/2010/07/four-showjumping-masters-part-4-gordon-wright/ Mott, Lt. Co. T. Bentley, Second Field Artillery, "Mounted Service School Rejects Caprilli," *The Rasp 1912.* The Mounted Service School, Army of the United States, Fort Riley, Kansas 1912.

Nelson, Hilda, *Alexis-Francois L'Hotte: The Quest for Lightness in Equitation,* J.A. Allen, 1998.

Notes on Equitation and Horse Training, translated from the French by Major George H. Cameron, Fourteenth US Cavalry, Assistant Commandant, The Mounted Service School, Army of the United States, Ft. Riley, Kansas 1910.

Official Register of the Officers and Cadets of the United States Military Academy West Point, New York, June 1905.

Official Register of the Officers and Cadets of the United States Military Academy, West Point, New York, June 1906.

Official Register of the Officers and Cadets of the United States Military Academy, West Point, New York, June 1907.

Official Register of the Officers and Cadets of the United States Military Academy, West Point, New York, June 1908.

Official Register of the Officers and Cadets of the United States Military Academy, West Point, New York, June 1909.

Official Register of the Officers and Cadets of the United States Military Academy, West Point, New York, June 1910.

Olympic Games 1920 Official Report, International Olympic Committee, 1920. https://digital.la84.org/digital/collection/p17103coll8/id/9586/
Olympic Summer Games, Fonds List, Historical Archives, Olympic Studies Center, International Olympic Committee, April 2011.
Ottevaere, James A., *American Military Horsemanship, The Military Riding Seat of the United States Cavalry,* Author House 2005.
Peters, Ralph, *Fighting for The Future,* Stackpole Books, 1999.
Perret, Geoffrey *Old Soldiers Never Die, The Life of Douglas MacArthur,* Random House, 1996.
Phillips, Col. Albert E. "The Phillips Cross Country Saddle", *The Cavalry Journal, May-June, 1935.*
Phillips, Col. Albert E. "The Phillips Military Saddle", *The Cavalry Journal, March-April, 1939.*
Racinet, Jean-Claude, *Another Horsemanship: A Manual of Riding in the French Classical Tradition.* Xenophon Press, 1994.
Racinet, Jean-Claude, *Racinet Explains Baucher,* Xenophon Press, 1997.
Randolph, Captain Thomas J., "The Cavalry School Library", *The Cavalry Journal, November-December, 1936.*
"Report of the Cavalry Board on the Adoption of the Military Seat" The *Cavalry Journal, 1929.*
Report of the Games Committee compiled under the direction of Major George Wythe, Infantry, United States Army, 1919.
Robinson, Brig. General Donald A., "The Cavalry Replacement Training Center", *The Cavalry Journal, March-April 1942.*
Santini, Captain Piero, *Riding Reflections,* Huntington Press, 1933.
Santini, Captain Piero, *The Forward Impulse,* Huntington Press, 1936.
Saumur Notes, Notes on Equitation and Horse Training, In Answer to the Examination Questions at the School of Application for Cavalry at Saumur, France, Translated from the French by Captain George H. Cameron, Assistant Commandant, The Mounted Service School, Army of the United States, Ft. Riley, Kansas 1909.
The Games of the Xth Olympiad, Los Angeles 1932, Official Report, Xth Olympiade Committee of the Games of Los Angeles, U. S.S. 1932, LTD, 1933.
The World's Best Rider Demonstrates Correct Technique I, *The Chicago Tribune, May 11,1936.*
The World's Best Rider Demonstrates Correct Technique II, *The Chicago Tribune, June 7, 1936.*
The Rasp 1912, The Mounted Service School, Army of the United States, Fort Riley, Kansas 1912.

The Rasp 1922, The Cavalry School, Army of the United States, Fort Riley, Kansas, 1922.

The Rasp 1923, The Cavalry School, Army of the United States, Fort Riley, Kansas 1923.

Thompson, Robert D., *U.S. Army Olympic Equestrian Competitions 1912-1948,* Schiffer Military History, 2008.

Tompkins, Major Frank, Chasing Villa: *The Last Campaign of the Old Cavalry,* Military Service Publishing Company, 1934.

Truscott, Jr. Lucian K. *The Twilight of the U.S. Cavalry,* University Press of Kansas, 1989.

"U.S. Equestrian Team for Olympic Games," The Field Artillery Journal, July–August 1928.

Vogel, Victor, *Soldiers of the Old Army,* Texas A&M University, College Station, 1990.

Vuksic and Grbasic, *Cavalry: History of a Fighting Elite 650 BC–AD 1914,* Cassell, 1993.

Woods, Sergeant David F. "The C.R.T.C. in World War II," *The Cavalry Journal, October–November, 1945.*

Wythe, Major George, *The Inter-Allied Games,* The Games Committee, July, 1919.

https://ia800201.us.archive.org/18/items/cu31924014114353/cu31924014114353.pdf.

Yale, Major Wesley W., "Cavalry Instructional Methods," *The Cavalry Journal, November–December, 1930.*

Xenophon Press Library

www.XenophonPress.com
Xenophon Press is dedicated to the preservation
of classical equestrian literature.
We bring both new and old works to English-speaking riders.

30 Years with Master Nuno Oliveira, Henriquet 2011
A Rider's Survival from Tyranny, de Kunffy 2012
Another Horsemanship, Racinet 1994
Austrian Art of Riding, Poscharnigg 2015
Broken or Beautiful: The Struggle of Modern Dressage, Barbier 2020
Classic Show Jumping: the de Nemethy Method, de Nemethy 2016
Divide and Conquer Book 1, Lemaire de Ruffieu 2016
Divide and Conquer Book 2, Lemaire de Ruffieu 2017
Dressage for the 21st Century, Belasik 2001
Dressage in the French Tradition, Diogo de Bragança 2011
Dressage Principles and Techniques: A Blueprint for the Serious Rider, Tavora 2018
Dressage Principles Illuminated, Expanded Edition, de Kunffy 2020
Dressage Sabbatical: A Year of Riding with Classical Master Paul Belasik, Caslar 2016
École de Cavalerie Part II, Robichon de la Guérinière 1992, 2015
Equine Osteopathy: What the Horses Have Told Me, Giniaux 2014
Fragments from the Writings of Max Ritter von Weyrother, Fane 2017
François Baucher: The Man and His Method, Baucher/Nelson 2013
General Chamberlin: America's Equestrian Genius, Matha 2020
Great Horsewomen of the 19th Century in the Circus, Nelson 2015
Gymnastic Exercises for Horses Volume II, Eleanor Russell 2013
H. Dv. 12 German Cavalry Manual of Horsemanship, Reinhold 2014
Handbook of Jumping Essentials, Lemaire de Ruffieu 2015
Handbook of Riding Essentials, Lemaire de Ruffieu 2015

Healing Hands, Giniaux, DVM 1998
Horse Training: Outdoors and High School, Beudant 2014
I, Siglavy, Asay 2018
Learning to Ride, Santini 2016
Legacy of Master Nuno Oliveira, Millham 2013
Lessons in Lightness: Expanded Edition, Mark Russell 2019
Methodical Dressage of the Riding Horse, Faverot de Kerbrech 2010
Military Equitation or, A Method of Breaking Horses, and Teaching Soldiers to Ride, Pembroke, and *A Treatise on Military Equitation,* Tyndale 2018
Principles of Dressage and Equitation, a.k.a. Breaking and Riding, Fillis 2017
Racinet Explains Baucher, Racinet 1997
Riding and Schooling Horses, Chamberlin 2020
Riding by Torchlight, Cord 2019
Science and Art of Riding in Lightness, Stodulka 2015
The Art of Riding a Horse, D'Eisenberg 2015
The Art of Traditional Dressage, Volume I DVD, de Kunffy 2013
The Chamberlin Reader, Chamberlin/Matha, 2020
The de Nemethy Method: A training seminar, 8 DVD set, de Nemethy 2019
The Ethics and Passions of Dressage Expanded Edition, de Kunffy 2013
The Forward Impulse, Santini 2016
The Gymnasium of the Horse, Steinbrecht 2018
The Horses, a novel, Elaine Walker 2015
The Italian Tradition of Equestrian Art, Tomassini 2014
The Maneige Royal, de Pluvinel 2010, 2015
The New Method of Dressing Horses, Cavendish 2020
The Portuguese School of Equestrian Art, de Oliveira/da Costa 2012
The Spanish Riding School & Piaffe and Passage, Decarpentry 2013
To Amaze the People with Pleasure and Delight, Walker 2015
Total Horsemanship, Racinet 1999
Training Hunters, Jumpers, and Hacks, Chamberlin 2019
Training with Master Nuno Oliveira, 2 DVD set, Eleanor Russell 2016
Truth in the Teaching of Master Nuno Oliveira, Eleanor Russell 2015
Wisdom of Master Nuno Oliveira, de Coux 2012

Printed in the USA
CPSIA information can be obtained
at www.ICGtesting.com
LVHW070842100124
768548LV00012B/517

9 781948 717236